FEB   2012

PAGE
50

ON THE
ROAD

YOUR COMPLETE DESTINATION GUIDE
In-depth reviews, detailed listings
and insider tips

D0026867

**Mediterranean Coast
& the Rif**
p234

**Atlantic
Coast**
p164

**Imperial Cities,
Middle Atlas & the East**
p298

**Marrakesh
& Central Morocco**
p52

**Southern Morocco
& Western Sahara**
p360

*916.4
Morocco
2011*

PAGE
487

SURVIVAL
GUIDE

VITAL PRACTICAL INFORMATION TO
HELP YOU HAVE A SMOOTH TRIP

Health

THIS EDITION WRITTEN AND RESEARCHED BY

James Bainbridge,
Alison Bing, Paul Clammer, Helen Ranger

welcome to Morocco

Mountains & Desert

From Saharan dunes to the peaks of the High Atlas, Morocco could have been tailor-made for travellers. Lyrical landscapes carpet this sublime slice of North Africa like the richly coloured and patterned rugs you'll lust after in local cooperatives. The mountains – not just the famous High Atlas but also the Rif and suntanned ranges leading to Saharan oases – offer simple, breathtaking pleasures: night skies glistening in the thin air; views over a fluffy cloudbank from the Tizi n'Test pass. On lower ground, there are rugged coastlines, waterfalls and caves in forested hills, and the mighty desert.

Traditional Life

The varied terrain may inform your dreams, but it shapes the very lives of Morocco's Berbers, Arabs and Saharawis. Despite encroaching modernity, with motorways joining mosques and kasbahs as manmade features of the landscape, Moroccan people remain closely connected to the environment. The nomadic southern 'blue men' brave the desert's burning expanses in robes and turbans, with mobile phones in hand. Likewise, traditional life continues – with tweaks – in the techniques of Berber carpet makers; in date cooperatives; in medina spice trading; and in the lifestyles in ports like Essaouira and mountain hamlets.

Morocco is an exotic gateway to Africa; its mountains, desert and coast are populated by Berbers and nomads, and its ancient medina lanes lead to souqs and riads.

(left) The kasbah of Aït Benhaddou, south of Marrakesh
(below) Spice souq, Marrakesh

Moroccan Activities

Meeting the Moroccan people involves nothing more than sitting in a cafe and waiting for your mint tea to brew. The trick is to leave enough time to watch the world go by with the locals when there's so much else to fit in: hiking up North Africa's highest peak, learning to roll couscous, camel trekking, shopping in the souqs, getting lost in the medina, and sweating in the hammam. Between the activities, you can sleep in the famous riads, relax on panoramic terraces and grand squares, and mop up tajines flavoured with saffron and argan.

Ancient Medinas

Often exotic, sometimes overwhelming and always unexpected, these ancient centres are bursting with Maghrebi mystique and madness: the perfect complement to the serene countryside. When you hit town and join the crowds, you follow a fine tradition of nomads and traders stretching back centuries. Unesco has bestowed World Heritage status on medinas including Fez, the world's largest living medieval Islamic city, and the carnivalesque Djemaa el-Fna in Marrakesh. The terrorist bomb on the square in April 2011 was a tragic episode in its history, but travellers should not be discouraged from visiting this welcoming, tolerant country.

›Morocco

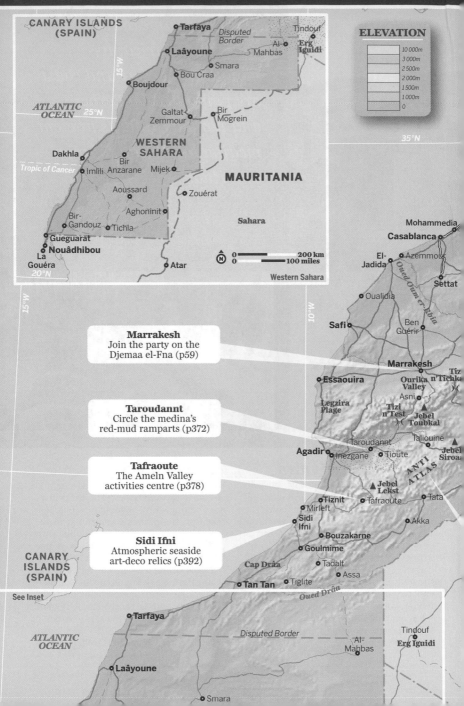

ELEVATION

	10 000m
	3 000m
	2 500m
	2 000m
	1 500m
	1 000m
	0

Marrakesh
Join the party on the
Djemaa el-Fna (p59)

Taroudannt
Circle the medina's
red-mud ramparts (p372)

Tafraoute
The Ameln Valley
activities centre (p378)

Sidi Ifni
Atmospheric seaside
art-deco relics (p392)

Western Sahara

SPAIN

Málaga

Cádiz

Algeciras

Gibraltar

Jebel Musa ▲ Ceuta

Tangier

Tetouan

Martil

Assilah

Larache

Chefchaouen

Ketama

Souk el-Arba
du Rharb

Al-
Hoceima

Melilla

Nador

Targuist

Jebel
Tidiquin

Berkane

Saïdia

Ahfir

Moulay
Bousselham

Ouezzane

Sidi
Kacem

Taourirt

Oujda

Kenitra

Volubilis

Salé

Moulay Idriss

Moulay
Yacoub

Fez

Taza

Guercif

Rabat

Khémisset

Meknès

Séfrou

Jebel
Tazzeka

Ben
Slimane

Ifrane

Azrou

Missour

Tendrara

Aïn
Sefra

Khouribga

Oued-Zem

Khenifra

Midelt

Bouarfa

ALGERIA

Beni
Mellal

Kasba-
Tadla

Jebel
Ayachi

Beni
Ounif

Figuig

Afourer

Imilchil

Azilal

Bin el-
Ouidane

Béchar

Demnate

Tinerhir

Erfoud

HIGH ATLAS

Oued Ziz

Irhill
M'Goun

Boulmalne
du Dadès

Tafilalt

Merzouga

Erg Chebbi

Taghith

Vallée
des Roses

Rissani

enhaddou

Skoura

Taouz

Grand Erg Occidental

Ouarzazate

Tazzarine

Tazenakht

Agdz

Dráa
Valley

Zagora

Beni
Abbès

Timimoun

Erg
Chigaga

M'Hamid

Gourara

Hamada du Dráa

Tinfouchy

Adrar

Mediterranean
Sea

Mers
el-Kebir

Mostaganem

Mascara

Assilah
Murals colour the
seaside medina (p207)

Chefchaouen
A blue medina in the
Rif Mountains (p267)

Volubilis
Roman mosaics, arches
and olive presses (p337)

Fez
Explore the medina
and tanneries (p300)

Moulay Idriss
The whitewashed hilltop
pilgrimage site (p340)

Figuig
An oasis town with
mudbrick kasbahs (p358)

Erg Chebbi
Ride a dromedary
into the dunes (p158)

High Atlas
Sublime peaks and
Berber villages (p109)

Dráa Valley
Hop between kasbahs
and oases (p128)

Erg Chigaga
Saharan dune hikes
by moonlight (p136)

Anti Atlas
Trek in the granite
mountain range (p378)

N

0 ————— 200 km
0 ————— 100 miles

18 TOP EXPERIENCES

Djemaa el-Fna Street Theatre

1 Circuses can't compare to the madcap, Unesco-acclaimed *halqa* (street theatre) in Marrakesh's main square (p59). By day, 'La Place' draws crowds with astrologers, snake-charmers, acrobats and dentists with jars of pulled teeth. Around sunset, 100 restaurant stalls kick off the world's most raucous grilling competition. 'I teach Jamie Oliver everything he knows!' brags a chef. 'We're number one...literally!' jokes the cook at stall number one. After dinner, Djemaa music jam sessions get underway – audience participation is always encouraged, and spare change ensures encores.

Fez Medina

2 The Fez medina (p301) is the maze to end all mazes. Don't be surprised if you get so lost you end up paying a small boy to take you back to familiar ground. But don't be afraid, because getting lost is half the point: blindly follow alleys into hidden squares and souqs, with the constant thrill of discovery. Treat it as an adventure, follow the flow of people to take you back to main thoroughfares, and experience the excitement of never quite knowing what's around the next corner.

High Tea in the High Atlas

3 Thirsty? Hot? Cold? Carpetless? In Morocco, mint tea is the solution to every critical condition. In Berber villages hewn from High Atlas mountainsides, vertiginous valley views and wild mountain herbs add extra thrills to Morocco's hallowed teatime traditions. Trekkers bound for North Africa's highest peak, Jebel Toubkal, should factor in time to accept friendly offers of tea starting at Armoud. This hilltop village is a couple of hours from Marrakesh and a 30-minute hike from Imlil, but all that seems centuries away inside a traditional *ighrem* (stone and earth house), sipping tea with wild absinthe while the family goat bleats in the courtyard.

Camel Trek in the Sahara

4 When you pictured dashing into the sunset on your trusty steed, you probably didn't imagine there'd be quite so much lurching involved. Don't worry: no one is exactly graceful clambering onto a saddled hump, and the side-to-side sway of a dromedary in motion only comes naturally to Saharawis, belly dancers and genies. The rest of us novices cling on comically, knock-kneed and white-knuckled, until safely over the first dune. But as rose-gold sands of Erg Chebbi rise to meet fading violet-blue Saharan skies, grips on the reins go slack with wonder – and by moonrise, Timbuktu seems totally doable.

Drâa Valley Kasbah Trail

5 Roads now allow safe, speedy passage through the final stretches of ancient caravan routes from Mali to Marrakesh, but beyond the rocky gorges glimpsed through car windows lies the Drâa Valley of desert-traders' dreams. The palms and cool mud-brick castles of Tamegroute, Zagora, Timidarte and Agdz must once have seemed like mirages after two months in the Sahara. Fortifications that housed gold-laden caravans are now open to overnight guests, who wake to fresh boufeggou dates, bread baked in rooftop ovens, and this realisation: speed is overrated.

Tafraoute

6 The Anti Atlas' main town, Tafraoute (p378) has a jumble of pink houses and market streets with extraordinary surroundings. The Ameln Valley is dotted with *palmeraies* (palm groves) and Berber villages, and the looming mountains stage a twice-daily, ochre-and-amber light show. With a relatively undeveloped tourist industry despite the region's many charms, it's a wonderful base for activities including mountain biking and seeking out prehistoric rock carvings. As if the granite cliffs and oases weren't scenic enough, a Belgian artist applied his paint brush to some local boulders – with surreal results.

Surfing

7 You can surf all along Morocco's Atlantic Coast, but the best place to catch waves is Taghazout (p371). It's clear what floats the village's board as soon as you arrive: the usual cafes and tèlèboutiques are joined by surf shops, where locals and incomers wax boards and wax lyrical about the nearby beaches. Taghazout's happy mix of villagers and surfers is more refreshing than a dip in the ocean. On the same stretch of coast between Agadir and Essaouira, Tamraght and Sidi Kaouki are also set up for surfing.

Anti Atlas Trekking

8 A sunburned granite range leading to the Sahara, the Anti Atlas remains unexplored compared with the High Atlas. The star attraction for trekkers is the quartz massif of Jebel L'Kest, the 'amethyst mountain', which you can walk to through the lush Ameln Valley. More farming villages and crumbling kasbahs are found around Jebel Aklim, another of the excellent trekking possibilities in this area of blue skies and Berber shepherds. The landscape has enough variety, from palm-filled gorges to brooding, volcanic Jebel Siroua, to justify multiple treks.

Sidi Ifni

9 Shhh! Don't tell your travelling friends, but this formerly Spanish seaside town (p392), a camel ride from the Sahara, is every bit as dilapidated, breezy and magical as well-trodden Essaouira. You can walk to the stone arches at Legzira Plage, or just explore the blue-and-white backstreets of one of southern Morocco's most alluring hang-outs. The best time to appreciate the art-deco relics – more reminiscent of Cuba than Casa – is sunset, when the Atlantic winds bend the palms and fill the air with a cooling sea mist.

Assilah Medina Art

10 In a refreshing take on graffiti, large expanses of walls in Assilah medina are adorned with colourful murals. In July every year, artists both local and foreign are invited to contribute to the Assilah Festival (p210) by painting the walls. Some murals, like those near the El-Khamra Tower or the lookout at the Koubba of Sidi Mansur, are huge. But you might turn a corner of the medina and spot a small corner down an alleyway that's been brightly decorated.

Fès Festival of World Sacred Music

11 From humble beginnings this festival (p312), held every June, has become a major player on the world-music festival scene. It's easy to understand why – the organisers work hard to bring in big names, and the city buzzes with visitors, and spin-off events and happenings. Many of the highlights are the unexpected – free public concerts and musical gatherings of Sufi brotherhoods that take you deep into the night. Mali's Tarti Womens Ensemble perform at the festival.

Moulay Idriss

DOUG MCKINLAY / LONELY PLANET IMAGES ®

12 This holy town (p340) cresting two hills is a whitewashed gem. For years, foreigners were barred from spending the night here, but recently there's been a mini-boom in local families opening their homes up as guesthouses, allowing you to get away from the nearby cities and drop your pace a gear. Tour groups only ever stop here for an hour during the day, so catching the sunset over the town and watching the locals promenade from the cafes on the main square are real treats.

Volubilis

13 The long grasp of Roman North Africa stretches back to grab you at Volubilis (p337), with its triumphal arches and dazzling array of mosaics. The setting, in the rolling countryside just north of the Middle Atlas, is superb. History continues to play out in the landscape here as well – turn your head from the Roman olive press to nearby Moulay Idriss, where presses still continue to produce some of the finest olive oil in the country.

Figuig

14 At the end of a long road and hard against a closed Algerian border, Figuig (p358) isn't really on anyone's route to anywhere. But in many ways, that's the point. Make the effort to get here and you're surprised by one of Morocco's truly secret corners, one of its most charming oasis towns, with mudbrick kasbahs and swathes of palm trees as far as you can see. There's little to do but chill out and explore, and feel like you're discovering somewhere new and special.

Chefchaouen Medina

15 Tear yourself away from the laid-back joints on the square to explore one of the best little medinas in Morocco (see p268). Climb up cobbled streets to discover tiny blue-washed lanes, massive studded doors and all the trappings of medina life: women in Riffian pompom hats selling vegetables on street corners; the hammam; the communal oven; and the mosque. Emerge at the top at Ras el-Maa to watch the sunset over the medina from a cafe. Best of all, this medina is small enough that you won't get horribly lost.

JOHN ELK III / LONELY PLANET IMAGES ©

Taroudannt

16 With views of both the High Atlas and Anti Atlas, this Souss Valley trading centre (p372) is known as Little Marrakesh, offering a medina and souqs without the big-city hustlers. Day trippers from Agadir will certainly find it charming. The town's red-mud ramparts are unique, changing colour according to the time of day. Circle the 7.5km perimeter by foot, bike or horse-drawn calèche, then return to the medina through one of the gates. After the sunset glow fades from the walls, the town is a relaxing, everyday place with some good restaurants.

Moonlight Dune Hikes in Erg Chigaga

SARA-JANE CLELAND / LONELY PLANET IMAGES ©

17 Even if you've never been to Erg Chigaga (p136) before, you'll instinctively find your way to the summit of the dunes at nightfall. Sun-dazzled eyes gladly adjust to the clear moonlight, and bare feet soon find their footing along the rippled ridges. Soft sand catches any stumble, and as you reach the crest, you can hear the Sahara singing in the night winds. Stars have never seemed clearer, and with good reason: at Erg Chigaga, you're not only off the grid, but two and a half hours by 4WD or a couple of days by camel from the nearest streetlight.

Casablanca's Architectural Heritage

AUT / IMAGEBROKER

18 If anyone tells you there's nothing to see in Casablanca (p166) except the Hassan II Mosque, they haven't looked up. Dating from the early 20th century when Casa was the jewel of the French colonies, a wealth of Mauresque and art-deco buildings can be found in the downtown areas, with rounded corners, tumbling friezes of flowers and curved wrought-iron balconies. Some buildings have been cared for while others are shamefully neglected. The Casablanca walking tour (p172) showcases most of them.

need to know

Currency
» Dirham (Dh)

Language
» Moroccan Arabic (Darija)
» Berber
» French

When to Go

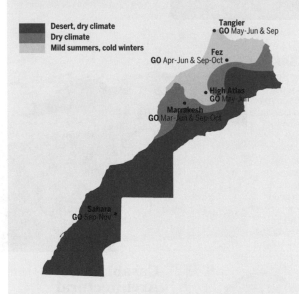

Desert, dry climate
Dry climate
Mild summers, cold winters

Tangier
• GO May-Jun & Sep

Fez
GO Apr-Jun & Sep-Oct •

• High Atlas
GO May-Jun

Marrakesh •
GO Mar-Jun & Sep-Oct

Sahara •
GO Sep-Nov

High Season
(Nov–Mar)

» Spring and autumn are the most popular times to visit.

» Accommodation prices are highest.

» Marrakesh and the south are popular at Christmas and New Year.

Shoulder
(Apr & Oct)

» Spring sandstorms in the Sahara and rain persists in the north.

» Popular elsewhere.

» Accommodation prices and demand jump around Easter.

Low Season
(May–Sep)

» Discounts in accommodation and souqs.

» Domestic tourism keeps prices high on the coast.

Your Daily Budget

Budget less than
Dh350

» Basic double (shared bathroom) from Dh50

» Soup or sandwich Dh4–30

» Food souqs plentiful for self-catering

» Buses cheaper than grands taxis and trains

Midrange
Dh550-1000

» Admission to sights Dh10–50

» Small riads offer minimal single-occupancy discounts

» Accommodation and tours will be your greatest expenses

» Dinner main Dh70–150

Top end over
Dh1400

» Hire a car (Dh300) to cover ground quicker

» Day tour Dh300

» Double in a city riad more than Dh1200

Money

» ATMs widely available. Major credit cards widely accepted in main tourist centres.

Visas

» Generally not required for stays of up to 90 days. Passports must be valid for six months beyond date of entry.

Mobile Phones

» Phones work on roaming or, if unlocked, with a local prepaid mobile SIM card (about Dh20).

Transport

» Trains connect Tangier, Fez and Marrakesh. Buses are plentiful and cheap.

Websites

» **The View from Fez** (http://riadzany. blogspot.com) News and opinions.

» **Visit Morocco** (www. visitmorocco.com) Moroccan National Tourist Office website.

» **BBC** (www.bbc. co.uk) Morocco page.

» **The Guardian** (www.guardian.co.uk) Travel and world news Morocco pages.

» **Maroc Blogs** (http:// maroc-blogs.com) Blog aggregator.

» **Al-Bab** (www.al-bab. com/maroc) Handy links.

» **Lonely Planet** (www. lonelyplanet.com/ morocco) Information, bookings and forums.

Exchange Rates

Australia	A$1	Dh8.17
Canada	C$1	Dh8.26
Europe	€1	Dh11.24
Japan	Y100	Dh9.95
Mauritania	UM100	Dh2.98
New Zealand	NZ$1	Dh6.25
UK	UK$1	Dh13.13
USA	US$1	Dh8.22

For currency exchange rates see www.xe.com.

Important Numbers

Dial the local four-digit area code even if you are dialling from the same town or code area.

Ambulance	☏15
Fire	☏15
Police (city)	☏19
Police (countryside)	☏177

Arriving in Morocco

» **Mohammed V International Airport, Casablanca**

Train – Dh40, 35 minutes, hourly from 6am to midnight

Taxi – Dh300-Dh350, 45 minutes

» **Tanger Med ferry terminal, Tangier**

Shuttle bus – free, 40 minutes, every hour on the hour

» **Menara airport, Marrakesh**

Bus – Dh20, every 20 minutes

Petit taxi – Dh70/100 day/night

Hotel transfer – city Dh150–200, Palmeraie Dh150–250

Guides

Morocco has a long-standing reputation for its *faux guides* (unofficial guides). In fact, tourist-friendly initiatives have improved the situation in most cities, but street hustlers are still part of the landscape. If you want to be left alone, be polite but firm, pretend you know exactly where you are going, or just play dumb. These unofficial ushers can be useful for navigating the disorientating medinas, but try to find out the going rate (normally about Dh50 to Dh100 per day) from an impartial source, and establish the fee before setting off. If you don't want to finish the tour at his brother/uncle/ friend's carpet shop, make it clear; if you do wind up there, remember you're under no obligation to buy anything. Official guides, engaged through tourist offices and hotels, are considerably more expensive.

if you like...

Medinas

If you pause for a moment in the medina, stepping out of the stream of shoppers, you can watch Morocco's very essence flash by. These ancient, crowded quarters – with winding lanes, dead ends, riad hotels, piles of spices, traders, tea drinkers, and a sensory assault around every corner – offer a strong dose of Morocco's famous Maghrebi mystique.

Fez The planet's largest living Islamic medieval city and its biggest car-free urban environment, with donkeys trekking to tanneries in the leather district (p301)

Marrakesh Exuberant Marrakshis course between souqs, palaces and the Djemaa el-Fna within the medina's 19km of ramparts (p59)

Tangier Hop off the ferry for a fitting introduction to North Africa in this gem of a medina, contained by the walls of a 15th-century Portuguese fortress (p243)

Mellow mazes Medinas aren't always like diving from the top board; smaller, stylish examples include Andalusian-blue Chefchaouen (p270)

Craft & Culture

Whether you want to catch some Gnaoua (bluesy music developed by freed slaves), see the Maghreb's hottest contemporary art or forever transform your mantel with quality craftwork, Morocco will inundate you with options.

Taroudannt Pick up Chleuh silver jewellery, influenced by Saharan tribes and Jewish silversmiths, in the souqs (p376)

Fès Festival of World Sacred Music In June, Morocco's premier music festival features international names and intimate concerts by *tariqas* (Sufi orders; p312)

Marrakesh Shop beyond the souqs, alongside design fanatics in Quartier Industriel Sidi Ghanem, and collectors including the king in Guèliz' hip art galleries (p69)

Carpets Compared with the cities, towns like Ouarzazate and Tafraoute have cooperatives, ensembles and shops that are low-pressure spots to bag a tasselled souvenir (p380)

Tangier The American Legation Museum contains the 'Moroccan Mona Lisa' and a wing devoted to Paul Bowles, Burroughs and the Beat writers' associate in Tangier (p243)

Towns & Villages

Morocco's small towns and picturesque villages are ideal for unwinding and meeting the locals over mint tea.

Afella-Ighir The road to these oasis villages is barely covered; in Tiwadou, stay in an auberge with a local museum (p382)

Agdz Watch the rest hurry along the Drâa Valley, and relax as only villagers with a resident *palmeraie* (palm grove) and mudbrick kasbahs can (p128)

Imilchil The Middle Atlas village is famous for its marriage *moussem* (festival), but the journey there is stunning year-round (p152)

Midelt Between the Middle and High Atlas, visit the surrounding villages and kasbahs, enjoy the mountain views and leave with a carpet (p347)

Tarfaya Clear up in a tented pool hall near a shipwrecked ferry, and watch the Saharawi world go by (p400)

Around Essaouira Leave the crowds in the medina and follow the surf trail south to Sidi Kaouki and Taghazout (p233)

CHRISTIAN ASLUND / LONELY PLANET IMAGES ©

» Skiing in Oukaïmeden (p33)

Activities

Apart from the coast, Morocco is not well developed for adventure sports, instead offering virgin territory to discover.

Mountain biking Bikes can be hired in Tafraoute, near Anti Atlas spots such as a valley of blue-painted boulders (p379)

Climbing The sheer rock faces of the Dadès and Todra Gorges are prime climbing territory (p32)

Skiing Oukaïmeden has North Africa's highest ski lift, and the Aït Bougomez Valley has Morocco's best ski-trek routes (p33)

Trekking With its mesas, gorges and volcanic pinnacles, Jebel Sarhro's proximity to the Sahara means its trails are passable year-round (p143)

Water and wind Essaouira and nearby Sidi Kaouki are good for surfing, windsurfing and kitesurfing; not far south, Taghazout is Morocco's top surf spot (p233)

Riding Diabat is a hub for horse rides along the Atlantic Coast; to ride a dromedary somewhere more ambitious than the beach, head to Erg Chebbi's Saharan dunes (p32)

Indulgence

A growing number of places allow you to experience the best of the country's culture and countryside in the lap of Moroccan luxury.

Marrakesh riads The city has more restored beauties than any other; at the best, as well as a courtyard garden, you'll find tradition and style, luxury and sustainability (p74)

Hammams There's no better way to invigorate medina-weary bones than a soak in the hammam, and Fez medina's plush riads have on-site spas (p308)

Seaside style El-Jadida, Essaouira, Mirleft and Sidi Ifni are our favourite Atlantic spots to crash by the surf; expect medina hideaways and infinity pools (p213)

Kasbah du Toubkal Why rough it in the mountains when you can sleep like a sultan in Imlil's kingly kasbah, with a hammam at 1800m (p111)?

Ksar Sania Likewise, experiencing the Sahara doesn't mean sandy sheets – or compromising the desert environment – at Merzouga's mudbrick eco-retreat (p160)

Food Adventures

Morocco offers culinary adventures from couscous rolling to eating camel tajine.

Fez On a culinary course or walking tour, pack your *tangia* (slow-cooked stew) at the butchers and spice shop, then leave it in the hammam woodfire oven (p309)

Desert food Learn Saharawi recipes or the secrets of elaborate traditional couscous at M'Hamid's Saharan retreats (p138)

Marrakesh Buy your ingredients at the souq, learn to cook like a *dada* (chef) and feast on the results in the comfort of a riad (p72)

Seafood Buy your dinner fresh off the boat in Al-Hoceima port, then try Atlantic catches al Essaouira's fish souq and outdoor fish grills (p279)

Taliouine Tour saffron and argan producers and learn how to make a saffron-tinted tajine (p378)

Demnate Try local almonds, olive oil and wildflower honey, and choose between 40 restaurants in this Berber foodie hub near Marrakesh (p91)

» Medersa Bou Inania, Fez (p302)

Architecture

Morocco's buildings, whether being reinvented as a boutique medina retreat or crumbling into a hillside, reflect the country's long history as a cultural melting pot.

Ali ben Youssef Medersa, Marrakesh Inside the splendid 14th-century theological seminary are five-colour *zellij* (tilework) walls and stucco archways (p59)

Art deco The Atlantic Coast has some wonderful art deco architecture, mostly in Casablanca, where it influenced the local Mauresque style, and white-and-blue Sidi Ifni (p172)

Kairaouine Mosque and University, Fez One of Africa's largest mosques and the world's oldest universities, the 1150-year-old complex has a green pyramidal roof (p301)

Essaouira The town's name means 'well designed', and it still suits the whitewashed medina behind seafront ramparts (p222)

Rissani On a 21km loop, you can see a *zawiya* (shrine), a ruined Saharan trading post, multiple *ksour* and a museum about life in the fortified strongholds (p162)

Berber Culture

Morocco's proud indigenous people are a memorable part of many travellers' journeys here. Their Amazigh colour and character are a big part of special spots such as Marrakesh and the Atlas.

Regional costumes Women display their local allegiances; from black shawls and colourful dresses around Tata to Riffian hats and candy-striped skirts (p383)

Demnate Just 1½ hours from Marrakesh, immersion in indigenous culture and cuisine awaits, with Morocco's best olive oil and a Berber Romeo and Juliet (p91)

Imilchil marriage moussem Berbers look for marriage material in the Middle Atlas village (p152)

Ameln Valley The Berbers have always been excellent hosts: in the traditional houses-turned-museums around Tafraoute, the best room was reserved for guests (p381)

Maison Tiskiwin Understand how the Berbers tie into the rest of North Africa in Marrakesh's museum of trans-Saharan culture (p68)

Al-Hoceima The seaside town is an unofficial capital for Morocco's northern Berbers (p278)

History

At the meeting of Europe, Africa and the Muslim world, Morocco's historical tapestry weaves in Arabs and Berbers, traders and invaders, and others who crossed the Med and the Sahara.

Volubilis One of the Roman Empire's most remote outposts is now Morocco's best preserved archaeological site, with many beautiful mosaics (p337)

Medinas In ancient medinas such as Fez, Meknès and Marrakesh, life continues as it has for centuries with donkeys winding down narrow lanes (p329)

Aït Benhaddou Hollywood does history at this 11th-century Almoravid caravanserai, which has been touched up for films such as *Gladiator* (p123)

Colonial echoes European visitors left their mark on Morocco, from the fine patisseries to Hispano-Moorish spots like Tetouan and Larache (p260)

Jewish Jews have been in Morocco for over two millennia, with historic *mellahs* (Jewish quarters) in the imperial cities and a dedicated museum in Casablanca (p169)

If you like... Islamic architecture, 650-year-old Medersa Bou Inania, the finest of Fez medina's theological seminaries, is a good place to see Fassi *zellij* (ceramic tilework; p303)

Beaches

Its coastline stretching from the Mediterranean to the Sahara, Morocco packs in beaches for every taste between its coves, cliffs, boardwalks and ports. Some are fit for family fun, others wait and will development to happen, and many are untrodden apart from the odd surfer and migratory bird.

Marabout's Beach With its eponymous saint's tomb and savage rocks, this is the most dramatic of Mirleft's half-dozen Atlantic beaches (p391)

Agadir The city is a concrete grid, but its long, curving beach, clean and well-lit at night, will have families scrambling for buckets and spades (p392)

Yellich Facing a small Mediterranean island you can walk to; visit Yellich and Cala Iris' other beaches before the fishing village becomes a resort (p282)

Tangier Escape the city on a day trip to Plage Robinson, at the northwestern extremity of Africa's Atlantic Coast, or Ksar es-Seghir on the Strait of Gibraltar (p252)

Deserts

Morocco's Saharan expanses are some of Africa's safest and most evocative places to experience the great desert. Not only can you see curvy dunes and harsher *hammada* (stony desert), you can also meet blue-robed Berbers and try the nomadic lifestyle.

Erg Chebbi This classic Saharan sandscape, its dunes rising to 160m, can be explored by camel, 4WD or sandboard, followed by a night in a Berber tent (p158)

Figuig It's worth trekking east to Morocco's oasis par excellence, with *palmeraies*, *ksour* and views of Algeria (p358)

Erg Chigaga Enlist a 'Blue Man' in M'Hamid, where dunes nuzzle against the guesthouses, to find this 40km stretch of sand mountains reaching 300m (p136)

Drâa Valley Timbuktu-bound caravans once passed through this desolate valley; now you can board a 'ship of the desert' (read: camel) to palm-shaded oases (p128)

Mountains

With Berber villages nestling beneath snowy peaks, the High Atlas is one of the world's most awe-inspiring mountain ranges. Whether you want to climb, trek, experience rural life or just escape the rat race far below, Morocco's other mountains are also worth exploring.

Jebel Toubkal Trek to the top of North Africa for thin air and views across the High Atlas (p112)

Ameln Valley Stay in a traditional village house among *palmeraies* and the gold-pink Anti Atlas (p383)

Middle Atlas Around towns like Azrou and Midelt, the mellower northern Atlas range is ideal for day hikes though hills and forests (p345)

Jebel el-Kelaâ There's more to the Rif than kif crops – as you'll see from this peak, walkable in a day from the idyllic mountain town of Chefchaouen (p273)

Eastern Atlas Barren, Martianred mountains overlook the Ziz Gorges and Imilchil's turquoise lakes (p153)

month by month

Top Events

1 Fès Festival of World Sacred Music, June

2 Festival of Popular Arts, July

3 Marriage Moussem, September

4 Marathon des Sables, March

5 Riffian Trekking, April

January

Moroccan winter: the north is wet and snow makes many mountains impassable for trekkers and even motorists. Marrakesh and the south receive the most tourists, especially around New Year.

Marrakesh Marathon

The year-round Djemaa el-Fna carnival acquires a sporty dimension in the annual road race, when 5000 marathoners cross the finish line on the grand square. The route follows the city ramparts and alleys of palms, orange and olive trees (p73).

February

Winter continues: the weather is generally poor, although drier, balmier spots such as Marrakesh and Agadir are bearable. Outside overlanders and city-breakers, few visitors are spotted.

Moussem of Sidi ben Aïssa

One of Morocco's largest *moussems* (festivals) takes place at the Sufi saint's mausoleum, outside Meknès medina walls. Public displays of glass-eating, snake bites and ritual body piercing are no longer allowed, but *fantasias* (musket-firing cavalry charges), fairs and the usual singing and dancing are (p332).

March

The country wakes up with the beginning of spring, when the mountains thaw and wildflowers and almond and cherry trees blossom. Winds begin to disturb the desert and Souss Valley, continuing through April.

Almond Blossom Festival

A very pretty festival held in the Anti Atlas in spring, when the Tafraoute area is awash with blossoms. Traditionally celebrating the harvest in Morocco's almond capital, the festival is now also about local folklore, with singing, dancing, theatre and storytelling (p378).

Marathon des Sables

Starting and finishing in Morocco's movie town, Ouarzazate, the Saharan ultramarathon is as epic as films made in 'Ouallywood'. The gruelling six-day challenge, held in March or April, crosses 243km of desert. Water is provided (p125).

April

Spring continues: the country is lush and green and temperatures are now reliably hot nationwide. Tourist numbers are high, particularly around Easter, when prices jump.

Festival of Sufi Culture

Fez' four-year-old festival hosts events including films and lectures, and concerts with Sufi musicians from around the world. The setting is the Andalusian-style garden of the Batha Museum, which is housed in a 19th-century summer palace (p312).

Jardin'Art

Marrakesh celebrates its spring bloom with temporary gardens, garden-inspired art shows and botanical talks. In addition to the usual picnicking families, canoodling couples and stately 19th-century pavilion, you'll see special displays in the Menara Gardens (p73).

🏃 Riffian Trekking

Between the wet northern winter and fierce summer, spring is perfect for trekking trails in the Rif Mountains. The best scenery is found in Talassemtane National Park, including the God's Bridge rock formation, and, closer to the Mediterranean, the National Park of Al-Hoceima (p283).

May

Prices drop in hotels and souqs as the tourist season ends, although the heaviest summer heat is yet to come; the average temperature in Marrakesh is about 28°C. Ideal for mountain trekking.

★ Rural Festivals

During the Festival du Desert, Er-Rachidia hosts performers from across the Sahara, including local Gnaoua band Les Pigeons du Sable. Down the Dadès Valley, garlands come out for Kelaâ M'Gouna's festival to celebrate the rose harvest (p141).

June

Summer's hotting up, although High Atlas peaks are still snowy. Northern Morocco and the coast are good places to be. During the Fès Festival of World Sacred Music, there is major demand for local accommodation.

★ Gnaoua & World Music Festival

A passionate celebration held in Essaouira on the third weekend of June, with concerts featuring international, national and local performers, and art exhibitions. A great chance to hear some bluesy Gnaoua, developed here by freed slaves (p225).

★ Cherry Festival

Sleepy Sefrou awakes for Morocco's longest-running town festival, held in early June. Folk music, artists' displays, parades, *fantasias* and sports events celebrate the cherry harvest – culminating in the picturesque crowning of the Cherry Queen (p326).

★ Fès Festival of World Sacred Music

Organise tickets well in advance for Fez' successful world-music festival, which has hosted the likes of Ravi Shankar and Youssou N'Dour. Equally impressive are the concerts by Moroccan *tariqas* (Sufi orders); fringe events include exhibitions, films and talks (p312).

July

Snow melts from the mountains and even the High Atlas are scorching. Temperatures in the main cities average around 30°C. The beaches are breeziest, but busy with domestic and European tourists in the north.

★ Festival of Popular Arts

Unesco praised this street-theatre festival, a typically colourful Marrakshi event,

as a 'masterpiece of cultural patrimony'. Djemaa el-Fna is even more anarchic than usual during the opening-night parade, featuring 500-plus performers (p73).

★ Assilah Festival

Assilah confirms its arty leanings with this cultural jamboree, which attracts some 200,000 spectators to three weeks of public art demonstrations, workshops, concerts and exhibitions. A concurrent three-day horse festival features a *fantasia* (p210).

August

Ramadan adds intensity to the uncomfortable temperatures – which average 40°C in Marrakesh, and can easily exceed that in the interior. Head to southern Atlantic beaches to avoid the crowds.

★ Moussems

During Morocco's largest *moussem*, picturesque whitewashed Moulay Idriss fills with *fantasias*, markets and music. Five pilgrimages to this *moussem* are said to equal one to Mecca. *Moussems* also take place in Setti Fatma, southeast of Marrakesh, and Ouarzazate (p341).

September

With autumn, Morocco is once again prime travelling territory. Accommodation prices rise, but everyone's in high spirits after Ramadan. The beaches empty and even the desert is pleasant with dates and gentle breezes.

Marriage Moussem

At this famous three-day festival in the Middle Atlas village of Imilchil, local Berbers search for a partner. Everyone looks their best, sporting woollen cloaks, white *jellabas* (flowing garments) and elaborate jewellery (p152).

Religious Moussems

Hamdouchi Moussem is a dance-off between religious fraternities outside Demnate's two *zawiyas* (shrines); Fez' Moussem of Moulay Idriss sees a musical, rosewater-showered procession through the medina; thousands of pilgrims head east to the *moussem* at Sidi Yahia Oasis, which includes a *fantasia* (p312).

October

Another popular month to visit, although, north of the Middle Atlas, rain is beginning to set in. Eid al-Adha interrupts transport and life in general for a few days in late October/ early November.

Rallye Saint-Exupéry

In late September/early October, Tarfaya remembers the colonial French airmail service that stopped here, and its most famous pilot, the writer Antoine de Saint-Exupéry. Planes pass through en route from Toulouse, France to Saint Louis, Senegal (p401).

November

A busy time in Marrakesh and further south, with more people heading to the desert or trekking nearby. Birdwatchers stalk out wetlands and Mauritania-bound overlanders roll through.

Harvests

Around the Immouzzer des Ida Outanane waterfalls in the High Atlas foothills, villagers climb into the trees to shake olives from the branches. In Taliouine, a festival celebrates the saffron harvest, and you can see locals picking the flowers (p371).

December

The country is busy at the end of the month with Christmas holidaymakers. Snow closes High Atlas passes, but the white blanket is good news for skiers.

International Film Festival

The Marrakesh event lives up to its name, with stars from Hollywood to Bollywood jetting in to walk the red carpet. The week culminates in wildly eclectic awards shows – recent honourees include Ben Kingsley and Harvey Keitel (p73).

itineraries

Whether you've got six days or 60, these itineraries provide a starting point for the trip of a lifetime. Want more inspiration? Head online to lonelyplanet.com /thorntree to chat with other travellers.

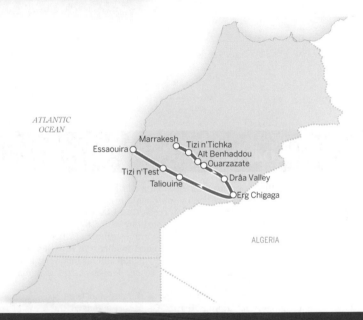

Two Weeks
Kasbah Crawl

Start with an all-singing, all-snake-charming bang on **Marrakesh's** Djemaa el-Fna, where acrobats, Gnawa musicians, meat grillers, dentists and storytellers converge at sunset. Toast the madness with a freshly squeezed juice from a stall piled with oranges. You could easily spend a week here, getting lost in the medina, buying a carpet, soaking in the hammam and getting lost again. But tear yourself away after a few days and take the **Tizi n'Tichka** pass (2260m), surrounded by the High Atlas mountains, to **Aït Benhaddou's** mudbrick kasbah.

Unless you're making a film, only hang around in **Ouarzazate** long enough to watch the crowds disappear up the Dadès Valley, then head down the kasbah-dotted **Drâa Valley**. At the far end is one of Morocco's open seas of Saharan dunes, **Erg Chigaga**, where you can appreciate the desert's silent majesty on a moonlight hike.

If time allows, take a different route back to Marrakesh via **Taliouine**, the saffron centre beneath the Anti Atlas mountains. Cross the High Atlas on the **Tizi n'Test** before ending your trip on **Essaouira's** Atlantic-facing ramparts, a few hours from Marrakesh and Agadir.

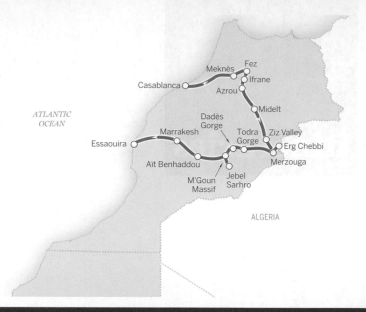

One Month
Moroccan Odyssey

With a month at your disposal and taking a little time to rest, you can get a taste of the best Morocco has to offer, by journeying from the sea to the Sahara and back again. Touch down in northern Morocco at **Casablanca**, the commercial capital, and if you get caught overnight, start the next day with a tour of Hassan II Mosque, the world's third-largest mosque. Head to the easternmost imperial cities and plunge into the more romantic, historic Morocco in their medieval medinas. In **Meknès**, wander between the buildings and squares left by Sultan Moulay Ismail and his followers; in **Fez**, venerable heart of Moroccan religious and cultural life, seeing donkeys carrying animal skins to the tanneries is like looking back in time.

Next, leave behind the noise and hassles of the city and head south to the relatively under-visited Middle Atlas around **Ifrane**. The resort stands at the heart of some stunning mountain and woodland scenery, offering enticing possibilities for hiking. Further south, the Barbary apes in the forests and hills around **Azrou** are one of Moroccan wildlife's most mischievous sights, and the landscape is even more scenic around **Midelt**. The road through the delightful palm-and-*ksar* (fortified stronghold) terrain of the **Ziz Valley** is one of the country's most beautiful journeys, crossing the eastern High Atlas to **Merzouga**, southeastern Morocco's gateway to the Sahara. Lorded over by towering dunes, the village is an ideal spot to saddle up a camel or strap on a sandboard, and sleep under the stars amid Morocco's largest sand sea, the perfectly sculpted **Erg Chebbi**.

Shadowing the High Atlas as you head west brings you to the sharp cleft of the **Todra Gorge**. From here, you can travel through dramatic boulder-strewn valleys, full of nomad camps in springtime, into the **Dadès Gorge**. If time allows, strike out from Boumalne du Dadès for some spectacular trekking around the **M'Goun Massif** or **Jebel Sarhro**, before heading past Ouarzazate to **Aït Benhaddou**, with its fairytale-like 11th-century kasbah.

En route to the Atlantic, check into a luxurious riad in **Marrakesh**, spend as many sunsets as possible on the theatrical Djemaa el-Fna, and then don't stop until you reach **Essaouira's** artsy seaside medina.

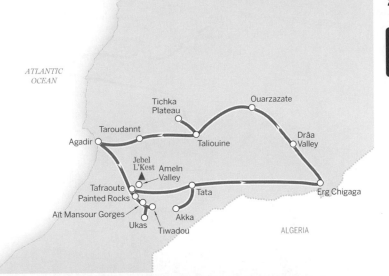

Three Weeks
Circling the South

> Morocco is far more than trendy riads and tourist hordes shuttling between hotel, souq and sun lounger. This itinerary takes you deep into the south for wild mountain and desert landscapes, far from clicking cameras, with plenty of activities to stimulate the mind and body.

Agadir is a handy entry point, but adventurers will want to leave quickly. Head to tiny but vibey **Tafraoute**, surrounded by beautiful Anti Atlas scenery such as the **Ameln Valley**, with its lush *palmeraies* (palm groves) and pink-hued houses. Spend a few days trekking through the valley and up **Jebel L'Kest**, bike past rock formations and engravings to the surreal **Painted Rocks**, and continue south through the **Aït Mansour Gorges**. At the far end of the gorges, where the beautiful scenery belies the ancient slave routes that passed this way, stay in the Afella-Ighir oasis. Use **Tiwadou** as a base for more trekking or discovering the rock carvings at **Ukas**.

By now you've developed a taste for Morocco's secluded southern corners. Once back in Tafraoute, wind east through the Anti Atlas and descend to the equally silent and epic Sahara. The last stop before Jebel Bani and a whole lot of *hammada* (stony desert), **Tata** makes a convenient base for exploring the oases, kasbahs, *agadirs* (fortified granaries) and magnificent rock engravings in spots such as **Akka**. A dusty journey to the east, **Erg Chigaga's** yellow-gold dunes are more remote and less visited than Merzouga. In nearby M'Hamid, find yourself a camel to lead you north into the kasbah-littered **Drâa Valley**.

At the top of valley, head back towards the mountains (this time, Jebel Sarhro and the High Atlas). Commandeer a bike (mountain or motor), horse, mule or dromedary in film favourite **Ouarzazate**, where the stony desert landscape has been a celluloid stand-in for Tibet, Rome, Somalia and Egypt. Return to the coast via **Taliouine**, where you can buy the world's most expensive spice in Africa's saffron capital. Pause here or in **Taroudannt** for a trekking reprise in a mountainous area such as the **Tichka Plateau**. With its red walls and backdrop of snowcapped peaks, Taroudannt has hassle-free echoes of Marrakesh. Its souqs and squares are pleasant places to enjoy some well-deserved chillaxation, and it's handy for Agadir's Al-Massira Airport.

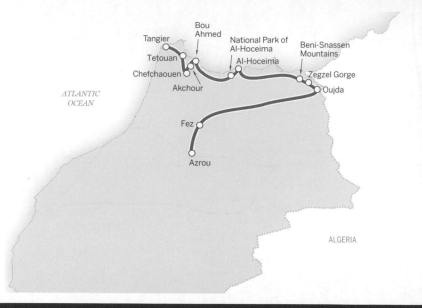

Three Weeks
The Med & The Mountains

While the previous itinerary suggested heading south to escape the crowds, a northern alternative is Morocco's Mediterranean littoral and Rif Mountains. The region has seen huge investment from the government and there are plans to push tourism in the area. If you get in now, you'll be ahead of the pack.

Start in **Tangier**, ideally arriving by ferry across the Strait of Gibraltar to feel the thrill of crossing from Europe to Africa. In the mid-20th century, characters from gunrunners to Beatnik literati mixed in this legendary port city. After a few days taking in the history, nightlife and restaurants, skip inland to **Tetouan**, the old capital of Spanish Morocco, with its charming blend of Arab medina and Andalusian architecture. The Spanish left a lighter imprint on nearby **Chefchaouen**, nestled in the Rif Mountains with its gorgeous blue-painted medina. It's tempting to spend a string of sunsets listening to the minarets chorus each other's call to prayer, but this is a good trekking spot. You can head deep into the mountains on a five-day trek via riverside **Akchour** to **Bou Ahmed**, a fishing village in the Oued Bouchia valley.

Continue east along the coast to the proud, modern seaside resort **Al-Hoceima**, gateway to the **National Park of Al-Hoceima's** dry canyons and limestone cliffs. You can walk to the park along the coast, or book a memorable tour including hiking or mountain biking and a homestay with a Berber family. En route to the Algerian border, there's more fine scenery in the **Beni-Snassen Mountains**, which you can enjoy in a swimming pool with mountain views, or a 300-year-old rural lodge. With its gorges, caves, mesa and Barbary sheep, this verdant area is far removed from classic images of Morocco. In the **Zegzel Gorge**, pluck a cumquat and see why the Romans remarked on this small citrus fruit.

From here, head to **Oujda** to refresh yourself with some city comforts, before taking the train to that grandest of imperial cities, **Fez**. Dive into the medina and relax in a riad, but if you find yourself missing the countryside, you can make an easy day (or several-day) trip into the cedar-clad Middle Atlas around the Berber market town of **Azrou**.

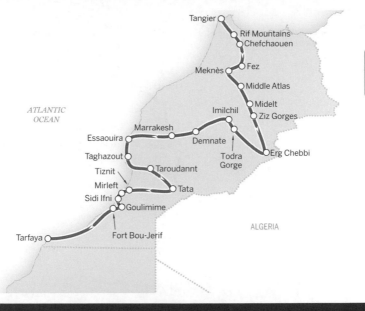

Highlights & Hidden Gems

> Climb off a ferry in famously decadent **Tangier**, with its Europe-facing medina, and head into the **Rif Mountains**. The influence of that continent across the Med continues in **Chefchaouen**, with its bright blue, Andalucian-tinted medina. Further south, the imperial cities **Meknès** and **Fez** are more quintessentially Moroccan in their ancient medinas.

After a few days of labyrinthine lanes and dye pits, you'll be ready for some more mountains. Wind through the **Middle Atlas** to the Berber village of **Midelt**, then on through the Martian landscape of the **Ziz Gorges**. It's now just a few dusty hours to **Erg Chebbi**, the achingly beautiful expanse of rolling dunes, which you can explore on a camel or sandboard.

Brush off the Sahara and return to the High Atlas at **Todra Gorge**. Hike between the enclosing rock walls, then jump in a market-bound truck through villages where the main activity is sipping mint tea. High in the mountains, **Imilchil**, surrounded by red rock and turquoise lakes, is the site of a wedding *moussem* (festival) in September.

Descend through the Middle Atlas and turn southwest, pausing to refuel in Berber foodie and cultural hub **Demnate**. The next stop, **Marrakesh**, needs no introduction with its famous riad hotels, medina shopping and Djemaa el-Fna. Hit the Wild West coast at hippie-turned-boutique hang-out **Essaouira**, then head south to vibrant **Taghazout**, Morocco's premier surf spot. Leave the waves for a second time and take the N10 to **Taroudannt**, the Souss Valley's prettiest market town with its mud-walled medina and kasbah.

The mountains get more barren as you travel the empty roads to **Tata**, a Saharan gateway where blue-robed guides can show you the desert. The road from here back to the Atlantic passes oases, *palmeraies*, kasbahs, *agadirs* and rock carvings. Near the coast, detour north to **Tiznit's** jewellery souq, particularly if it's a Thursday (market day).

Arcing west and south, you come to **Mirleft**, with its pink-and-blue arches, and **Sidi Ifni**, a jumble of wind-whipped art-deco relics surrounded by coastal walks. Try to pass through **Goulimime** on a Saturday morning, when the camel market takes place, and stay at **Fort Bou-Jerif**, near a ruined French Foreign Legion fort. End your journey on the edge of the Western Sahara in sandy, gloriously isolated **Tarfaya**.

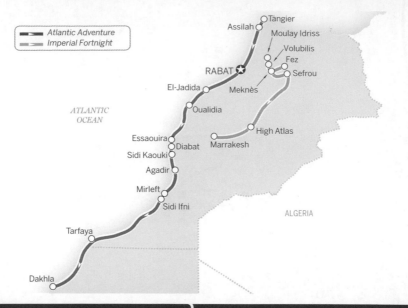

Atlantic Adventure
Imperial Fortnight

Tangier
Assilah
Moulay Idriss
Volubilis
Fez
RABAT
Sefrou
El-Jadida
Meknès
ATLANTIC
OCEAN
Oualidia
Essaouira
Diabat
High Atlas
Sidi Kaouki
Marrakesh
Agadir
Mirleft
Sidi Ifni
ALGERIA
Tarfaya
Dakhla

Three Weeks
Atlantic Adventure

❯ Morocco's Atlantic seaboard takes you from the clamour of the north to the deserted coastline of the south.

Take the ferry from Spain to **Tangier**, at once a quintessentially Moroccan mosaic and a decadent outpost of Europe. Catch the train south, first to artsy **Assilah**, which is loaded with whitewashed charms, and then to **Rabat**, with its colonial architecture and palm-lined boulevards. Follow Casa's suburbanites to the sleepy 'Cité Portugaise', **El-Jadida**, then take the spectacular ocean road to **Oualidia**, the St Tropez lookalike with a perfect crescent lagoon.

Further south, the hippies once gravitated to **Essaouira**, and its white-walled ramparts, bohemian beat and renovated riads still make travellers linger. When you've eaten your fill at the outdoor fish grills, follow Jimi Hendrix and today's surfers to the peaceful beaches at **Diabat** and **Sidi Kaouki**.

Past more surf spots, **Agadir** is a family-friendly seaside resort, but **Mirleft's** beaches and boutique accommodation are more appealing, as is art-deco **Sidi Ifni**. If you're overlanding south to Mauritania, break your journey at **Tarfaya**, like the early-20th-century French airmail pilots, and breezy **Dakhla**.

Two Weeks
Imperial Fortnight

❯ This trip begins in two cities once ruled by enlightened dynasties, which crossed the Strait of Gibraltar and pulled Europe out of its Dark Ages. Throw back a shot of Maghrebi exoticism in **Fez**, where modern Morocco and its rich past crowd for space in the extraordinary medina. Next, catch your breath in nearby **Meknès**, bypassed by many travellers despite its echoes of Sultan Moulay Ismail's glory days.

A detour north takes you to **Volubilis**, Morocco's best-preserved ancient city, and testament to the Roman Empire's astonishing breadth. Nearby **Moulay Idriss**, with the mausoleum of the founder of Morocco's first imperial dynasty, is another wonderful antidote to urban clamour.

Unless you're a completist and want to visit all four Moroccan imperial cities, skip Rabat and head into the Middle Atlas. We've suggested a few stops in our Moroccan Odyssey itinerary; another is the Berber town **Sefrou**, its medina pierced by the Oued Aggaï, 30km south of Fez. The route now follows the N8 beneath the **High Atlas**, where there are numerous side trips if you have time, to the icon of contemporary Morocco, **Marrakesh**. The city's souqs, street performers and imperial architecture form an intoxicating mix.

Activities in Morocco

Mountains

Hoist yourself up here for rock climbing from bouldering to mountaineering; downhill skiing and ski trekking; spotting wildlife including apes, sheep and leopards, all of the Barbary variety; trekking, mountain biking and white-water rafting.

Desert

Hotfoot it to the Sahara for camel treks, moonlight dune hikes, sleeping in a Berber tent, sandboarding and wildlife-watching including desert warblers and the bat-eared fennec fox.

Coast

Hit the beach for surfing, windsurfing, kitesurfing, kayaking and canoeing; and for marine mammals and bird life such as the endangered bald ibis.

Hammams

Every self-respecting town has a hammam, where you can get a good scrub.

Morocco is arguably Africa's top trekking destination: walking between Berber villages in the High Atlas is a classic travel experience, the kind you will rave about for years to come. However, with the country's diverse terrain, numerous other activities are on offer. Birdwatching enthusiasts, golfers, cyclists, climbers, riders and spa devotees will all find options to challenge, excite and relax. Another bonus: whether you're skiing, surfing or camel trekking, between activities you can enjoy the wonderful Moroccan culture and hospitality.

Birdwatching

Morocco is a birdwatcher's paradise. A startling array of species inhabits the country's diverse ecosystems and environments, especially the coastal wetlands.

Around 460 species have been recorded in the country, many of them migrants passing through in spring and autumn, when Morocco becomes a way station between sub-Saharan Africa and breeding grounds in Scandinavia, Greenland and northern Russia. Other birds fly to Morocco to avoid the harsh northern-European winters.

A pleasant time for birdwatching is March through May, when the weather is comfortable and a wide variety of species is usually present. The winter is also a particularly active time in the wetlands and lagoons.

For more information on Morocco's bird life, see p482.

Guides & Tours

In addition to local birdwatching guides, the following UK-based companies offer Moroccan tours:

Birdfinders (www.birdfinders.co.uk)

Birdwatching Breaks (www.birdwatching breaks.com)

Naturetrek (www.naturetrek.co.uk)

Wild Insights (www.wildinsights.co.uk)

Camel Treks

Exploring the Sahara by camel – whether on an overnight excursion or a longer desert safari – is one of Morocco's signature activities and most rewarding wilderness experiences.

Morocco's most evocative stretches of Saharan sand are Erg Chebbi (p158), near Merzouga, and Erg Chigaga (p136), near M'Hamid and Zagora, and past the more accessible Tinfou Dunes (p134).

Only consider doing your camel trek in autumn (September and October) or winter (November to early March). Outside these months, the desert experiences gruelling extremes of heat, plus sand storms in the spring.

Prices start at around Dh300 per person per day, but vary depending on the number of people, the length of the trek and your negotiating skills.

The agency will organise the bivouac (temporary camp), which may be a permanent camp for shorter trips, and may offer Berber music and *mechoui* (barbecued lamb).

Organising a Camel Trek

Travellers with lots of time can organise a guide and provisions in situ. This benefits the local community and counters the trend towards young guides leaving home to look for work in the more popular tourist centres.

M'Hamid is probably the most hassle-free of the main desert gateways, although the choice is wider at Zagora and Merzouga. Try to get recommendations from other travellers.

It's quicker and easier, involving less negotiations and waiting, to organise a trip in advance – either through an international tour operator or a company based in Ouarzazate or Marrakesh.

Horse Riding

Southern Morocco is popular for horse riding, from beaches such as Diabat to hills, mountains, valleys, gorges and the desert.

Specialist travel companies offer guided horse-riding tours:

Club Farah (www.clubfarah.com) Meknès-based Swiss-Moroccan company running trips throughout Morocco, from the imperial cities to the southern Atlantic coast.

Unicorn Trails (www.unicorntrails.com) UK-based operator offering four expeditions in the High Atlas, Sahara and Essaouira area.

Mountain Biking

Ordinary cycling is possible in Morocco, but mountain biking opens up the options considerably.

For the very fit, the vast networks of *pistes* (dirt tracks) and footpaths in the High Atlas offer the most rewarding biking. The Anti Atlas, Jebel Sarhro plateau and the Drâa Valley also offer excellent trails.

Travel agencies, hotels and shops hire out mountain bikes, for example in Tafraoute, but the quality isn't really high enough for an extended trip. Adventure tour companies cater to serious cyclists.

Rock Climbing

There is a growing climbing scene in Morocco, with some sublime routes. Anyone contemplating climbing should have plenty of experience and be prepared to bring all their own equipment.

The Anti Atlas and High Atlas offer everything from bouldering to very severe mountaineering routes that shouldn't be attempted unless you have a great deal of experience.

The Dadès and Todra Gorges are prime climbing territory.

Des Clark's new guidebook *Mountaineering in the Moroccan High Atlas* (published by Cicerone), subtitled 'walks, climbs and scrambles over 3000m', is destined to become a classic. It covers some 50 routes and 30 peaks in handy pocket-sized, plastic-covered form, with plenty of maps, photos and practical information.

The following are useful for information and hooking up with other climbers:

Visiting a hammam (traditional bathhouse) is infinitely preferable to cursing under a cold shower in a cheap hotel. They're busy, social places, where you'll find gallons of hot water, and staff available to scrub you clean. They're also good places to meet the locals and, especially for women, somewhere to escape street hassle.

Every town has at least one hammam, often a modern, white-tiled and spacious affair. Often there are separate hammams for men and women; others open to either sex at different hours or on alternate days.

Some hammams are unmarked and others simply have a picture of a man or woman stencilled on the wall outside; locals will happily direct you. Most hammams are welcoming, but a few (often those close to a mosque) are unwilling to accept foreign visitors.

Bring your own towels (in a waterproof bag), a plastic mat or something to sit on, and flip-flops (thongs). Some hammams sell toiletries; look out for *ghassoul* (handfuls of clay mixed with herbs, dried roses and lavender), *el-kis* (coarse glove), black soap made from the resin of olives (which stings if you get it in your eyes), and henna (used by women).

You'll be given a bucket and scoop; remember to use the communal bucket when filling yours with water. Most hammams have showers.

Hammam admission is typically around Dh10, plus the optional extras of *gommage* (scrub) and massage.

A few midrange and top-end hotels have more expensive hammams, which normally require advance notice to heat up, and a minimum of four or five people.

Nicolò Berzi (nicolobe@tiscalinet.it) Italian climbing guide organising trips to Todra Gorge.

PlanetMountain.com (www.planetmountain.com/english/rock/morocco) Has a section on Morocco.

Royal Moroccan Ski & Mountaineering Federation (www.frmsm.ma, in French) Has a list of routes.

Serac Outdoors Sports (http://tinyurl.com/4neemp6) UK operator offering climbing trips in Morocco.

Skiing

Skiing is viable from November to April, although Morocco's ski stations are somewhat ramshackle.

Downhill Skiing

Popular resort Oukaïmeden, about 70km south of Marrakesh, has North Africa's highest ski lift, and equipment for hire. There are other spots dotted around the Middle Atlas, including Mischliffen, although some seasons the snow is thin on the ground.

Ski Trekking

Ski randonné is increasingly popular, especially from late December to February, when the Aït Bougomez Valley has prime routes.

Surfing, Windsurfing & Kitesurfing

With thousands of kilometres of coastline, the Moroccan Atlantic is a fine, if underrated, destination for surfing, windsurfing and kitesurfing. Lessons, equipment hire and surf holidays are available.

Northern & Central Morocco

North of Rabat, Mehdiya Plage (p202) has strong currents but reliable year-round breaks. Moving south, Plage des Nations and Temara Plage, both within 20km of the city, are also good for surfing. Sidi Bouzid (p214) and the beaches around El-Jadida also attract surfers.

Oualidia is known for surfing, windsurfing and kitesurfing. En route to Safi, the Lalla Fatna area (p221) has some of Morocco's best breaks: one of the world's longest tubular right-handers has drawn some of the biggest names in surfing.

Southern Morocco

Essaouira has been singled out by some surfers, although the 'Windy City of Africa' is a better windsurfing and kitesurfing destination year-round. Nearby Sidi Kaouki is an upcoming destination for all three sports.

Near Agadir, the Taghazout area has some of Morocco's best surfing beaches and numerous businesses catering to surfers.

Other destinations to consider in southern Morocco are Agadir, Aglou Plage, Mirleft, Sidi Ifni and Dakhla.

Tours

Hiring a guide or going on a tour is a good idea if you want to gear your trip towards enjoying a certain activity. Not only will a local expert help you sniff out the best spots, which might be deep in the mountains or desert for some activities, but they will help organise gear, accommodation and transport, practical details that could take days to arrange in remote areas.

An important fringe benefit is that the guide will give you a greater understanding of Morocco and its people. Two areas where joining a tour is recommended, as it can be tricky to get around and enjoy activities independently, are the Sahara and higher sections of the Atlas. In addition to the specialist operators listed in this chapter, tour companies offering activity holidays are listed on p513 and p519.

Trekking

Morocco is a magnificent trekking destination offering an array of landscapes and treks to suit all abilities. The snow-capped High Atlas are justifiably famous, especially North Africa's highest peak, Jebel Toubkal (4167m), which can be tackled as a straight ascent or as part of a circuit. Heading towards the Sahara, the Anti Atlas and Jebel Sarhro ranges also offer top trekking. In the north, there are easier routes in the forests and hills of the Middle Atlas; and superb trails through the Rif Mountains – notably in Talassemtane National Park near Chefchaouen. For more details, see the Trekking in Morocco chapter.

White-Water Rafting & Kayaking

Although white-water rafting and kayaking are underdeveloped in Morocco, the rivers in the High Atlas near Bin el-Ouidane have stunning scenery.

Water by Nature (www.waterbynature.com) The specialist UK- and USA-based adventure company offers rafting and kayaking trips, including family rafting trips, and caters to all levels of experience.

Trekking in Morocco

High Atlas

Tackle North Africa's highest peak, Jebel Toubkal, and meet the Berbers on the longer Toubkal Circuit (p112).
Escape the crowds and be inspired by the remote M'Goun Massif's spectacular valleys and beautiful villages (p99).

Jebel Sarhro

Head southeast to some of Morocco's most rugged and stunning scenery, perfect for winter walking (p143).

The Rif

Take a gentler path through little-visited cedar forests in the Talassemtane National Park, near Chefchaouen (p283).

Anti Atlas

Visit a few of the Ameln Valley's 26 villages, en route to an ascent of the 'amethyst mountain', Jebel L'Kest (p386).
Enjoy serious trekking and stark beauty among the remote villages and tremendous gorges beneath volcanic Jebel Siroua (p386).

Trekking in Morocco was once the preserve of dedicated climbers, and a few intrepid amateurs, en route to the top of North Africa's highest peak, Jebel Toubkal (4167m). Things have changed: there are now treks for all times of year and levels of fitness; treks to test the fittest athletes and those where you can have your bags carried, arrive to find your lunch laid out for you and sleep in luxury.

Morocco is blessed with some of the world's most dramatic and beautiful mountains, many of which see few travellers while others remain unexplored by foreigners. The broad range of climates is also a blessing for trekkers. When December snows make Jebel Toubkal impossible to trek, Jebel Sarhro, closer to the Sahara on the southern side of the Atlas, is passable. When the summer sun makes the Rif too hot to trek, it also melts the snow off Toubkal, enticing crowds to the summit.

As trekking in Morocco has grown in popularity, so have the options available. You could buy a package, including flights and transfers, guides and food; or turn up at the trailhead, hire a guide and mules, and head off into the Berber heartland. Whichever you choose, trekking is often the highlight of visits to Morocco.

TREKKING GUIDEBOOKS

» *Great Atlas Traverse* by Michael Peyron. The two-volume work by the Morocco-based British writer is the definitive text for the great traverse. Less useful for the casual trekker.

» *The Atlas Mountains: A Walking and Trekking Guide* by Karl Smith. Published by the walking specialist Cicerone, this has route descriptions and information on subjects such as ski-touring, although it gets mixed reviews.

» *Mountaineering in the Moroccan High Atlas* by Des Clark. Also published by Cicerone, this new guide, subtitled 'walks, climbs and scrambles over 3000m', is destined to become a classic. It covers some 50 routes and 30 peaks in handy pocket-sized, plastic-covered form, with plenty of maps, photos and practical information.

» *Trekking in the Moroccan Atlas* by Richard Knight. Has 43 maps and information from green hiking tips to language advice, although it also has both fans and detractors. Likely to be the most useful for inexperienced trekkers, but also the bulkiest.

Getting Started

Maps

Morocco is covered by a 1:100,000 and also a 1:50,000 topographical map series.

Some of the 1:50,000 series are unavailable to the public; travellers exploring wide areas are advised to stick to the 1:100,000 series.

Although marked in Cyrillic script, 1:100,000 maps of Morocco made by the Soviet military are as topographically accurate as any available.

The best place in Morocco to buy maps is Direction de la Cartographie in Rabat (see the boxed text on p231), which lists the maps it sells online.

Maps and photocopies are also available at other bookshops around Morocco, listed in the destination chapters, as well as at stalls around the Djemaa el-Fna in Marrakesh and, as a last resort, on the approaches to the Atlas trekking routes.

The Foyle Reading Room of the **Royal Geographical Society** (www.rgs.org; cnr Exhibition Rd & Kensington Gore, Kensington, London, UK; admission per day £10) has one of the world's largest private collections of maps, and you can view its catalogue online.

In addition to the international shops listed in the boxed text, websites including **Amazon** (www.amazon.co.uk) sell maps such as West Col Productions maps of the Toubkal and M'Goun Massifs.

Books

The booklet *Morocco: Mountain and Desert Tourism* (2005), published by Office National Marocain du Tourisme (ONMT), the Moroccan tourist office, has a good introduction to trekking in Morocco; plus lists of car-hire companies, *bureaux des guides* (guide offices), tourist offices, *gîtes d'étape* (trekkers' hostels), huts, *refuges* (huts), camp sites, souq (market) days and other information.

You should be able to pick it up in ONMT offices overseas and in Marrakesh and other major cities, or at Imlil's *bureau des guides*.

Edisud/Belvisi publishes *Gravures Rupestres du Haut Atlas,* which looks at the rock art of Plateau du Yagour, northeast of Setti Fatma, and *Randonnées Pédestres Dans le Massif du Mgoun*. These are available online, and sporadically at tourist offices, in bookshops in Rabat and Marrakesh, from the Club Alpin Français (CAF) and in the CAF's Oukaïmeden *refuge.*

The Mountains Look on Marrakech is Hamish Brown's atmospheric account of a 96-day trek across the mountains.

Clubs, Information & Tours

For details of foreign and Moroccan operators offering trekking tours in Morocco, see p513.

Atlas Mountains Information Services

(AMIS; http://tinyurl.com/48efeva; Fife, Scotland) A trusted source of information as well as trekking tours. Organiser Hamish Brown, a specialist author, lecturer, photographer and guide for the Atlas, has been travelling in Morocco for 50 years. He's often away leading treks, so you are advised to contact him well in advance.

Club Alpin Français (CAF; www.caf-maroc. com, in French; Casablanca) Operates *refuges* in the Toubkal area. Its website is a good source of information.

La Fédération Royale Marocaine de Ski et Montagne (Royal Moroccan Ski & Mountaineering Federation; FRMSM; www.frmsm. ma, in French; Casablanca) Has basic information on its website.

Clothing & Equipment

Tents

In addition to the essentials listed in the boxed text, the key decision, when planning a route, is whether or not to sleep in a tent. A good tent opens up endless trekking possibilities and will get you away from the crowds.

You can hire tents from tour operators and guides, and at trailheads.

If you would rather not carry a tent, in most regions you can stay in the villages (see p39).

Sleeping Bags

Whether you are camping or staying in houses, a four-season sleeping bag is essential for the High Atlas and Jebel Sarhro from September to early April, when temperatures as low as -10°C are not unknown.

In lower ranges, even in high summer, a bag comfortable at 0°C is recommended. A thick sleeping mat or thin foam mattress is a good idea since the ground is extremely rocky. Guides can usually supply these.

Stoves

Many *gîtes* have cooking facilities, but you may want to bring a stove if you are camping. Multifuel stoves that burn anything from aviation fuel to diesel are ideal.

Methylated spirits is hard to get hold of, but kerosene is available. Pierce-type butane gas canisters are also available, but not recommended for environmental reasons.

Your guide will be able to advise you on this.

Other Equipment

Bring a basic medical kit as well as water-purification tablets or iodine drops or a mechanical purifier. All water should be treated unless you take it directly from the source.

To go above 3000m between November and May, as well as having experience in winter mountaineering, you will need essentials including crampons, ice axes and snow shovels. Again, this equipment is available for hire.

If you are combining trekking with visits to urban areas, consider storing extra luggage before your trek rather than lugging around unwanted gear. Most hotels will let you leave luggage, sometimes for a small fee. Train stations in larger cities have secure left-luggage facilities (see p521).

Guides

However much trekking and map-reading experience you have, we strongly recommend that you hire a qualified guide – if for no other reason than to be your translator (how is your Tashelhit?), chaperone (*faux guides* won't come near you if you are with a guide), deal-getter and vocal guidebook.

A good guide will also enhance your cultural experience. They will know local people, which will undoubtedly result in invitations for tea and food, and richer experiences of Berber life.

If something goes wrong, a local guide will be the quickest route to getting help. Every year foreigners die in the Moroccan mountains. Whatever the cause – a freak storm, an unlucky slip, a rock slide – the presence of a guide would invariably have increased their

---

ESSENTIAL CLOTHING

Year-Round

» Strong, well-broken-in walking boots (see the boxed text, p40).

» A waterproof and windproof outer layer; it's amazing how quickly the weather can change.

» Sunhat, sunglasses and high-factor sunscreen.

Summer (June to August)

» Light, baggy, cotton trousers and long-sleeved shirts.

» Even at 1800m, nights are cold enough to require a fleece or jumper.

Winter (November to March)

» Prepare for very cold weather wherever you trek in the country.

» Pack warm clothing, including a woollen hat and gloves for High Atlas trekking.

Australia
Melbourne Map Centre (www.melbmap.com.au; Malvern East, Victoria) Australia's largest map shop stocks half-a-dozen Morocco maps.

France
Au Vieux Campeur (www.au-vieux-campeur.fr, in French)

UK
Stanfords (www.stanfords.co.uk; London & Bristol) The world's largest travel map and bookshop, it sells maps including Editorial Piolet's 1:40,000 map of the Jebel Toubkal area; and West Col's series of 1:160,000 maps of the Atlas, based on the Soviet military survey maps.
The Map Shop (www.themapshop.co.uk; Upton upon Severn, Worcestershire)

USA
East View Map Link (http://store.maplink.com) Has a list of other map shops in the United States and elsewhere.
Omnimap (www.omnimap.com; Burlington, North Carolina) Sells an excellent range of maps, including the West Col and Soviet military survey maps, some available digitally.
Rand McNally (http://store.randmcnally.com)

chances of survival. So however confident you feel, we recommend that you never walk into the mountains unguided.

Choosing a Guide

A flash-looking, English-speaking *faux guide* (unofficial guide) from Marrakesh is no substitute for a gnarled, old, local mountain guide who knows the area like the back of his hand.

Official guides carry photo-identity cards. Guides should be authorised by the Fédération Royale Marocaine de Ski et Montagne or l'Association Nationale des Guides et Accompagnateurs en Montagne du Maroc. They should be credited as *guides de montagne* (mountain guides), which requires study for at least six months at the Centre de Formation aux Métiers de Montagne, a school for mountain guides at Tabant in the Aït Bougomez valley.

Accompagnateurs (escorts) will have had only one week's training, and will not be insured to lead mountain trips; *guides de tourisme* (tourist guides) are not qualified to lead treks.

Official mountain guides, who can always show an identity card as proof of their status, have been trained in mountain craft, including first aid. In times of uncertain weather or in an emergency, they will be infinitely more efficient than a cheaper guide lacking

proper training. If a guide is reluctant to show a photo card, it probably means he/she either doesn't have one or it has expired (they should be renewed every three years).

Some *guides de montagne* have additional training in rock climbing, canyoning and mountaineering. All guides speak French, and some also speak English, Spanish or German. Several young Moroccan female guides, who have succeeded in breaking into the previously all-male world of mountain guiding, are in high demand.

Hiring a Guide

There are more than 400 accredited mountain guides in Morocco, and many can be found through the *bureaux des guides* in Imlil, Setti Fatma, Chefchaouen, and Maroc Profond in Tabant (Aït Bougomez Valley).

At the time of writing, the minimum rate for official guides was Dh300 per day (per group, not per person). This rate can vary according to season and location. The rates do not include food and accommodation expenses.

Guides generally get free accommodation in *refuges* and *gîtes,* but you may be asked to cover their meals. If you walk a linear route you'll also be expected to pay for their return journey.

Negotiate all fees before departure and count on giving at least a 10% tip at the end, unless you have been unhappy with the service.

If your guide is organising your trip (rather than a tour operator), be sure to go through all aspects of the trek ahead of time. Discuss where each day will start and end; whether tents will be shared (most guides have a tent and/or sleeping bag); how many mules will be hired; who will be cooking (if there are enough of you, the guide may insist on hiring a cook, usually for about Dh100 a day); food preferences, water provision, and the division of food and equipment among the group.

Mules

Mules (and the odd donkey) are widely used in Morocco for transporting goods through the mountains, and you can easily hire one to carry your gear.

If you are relying on heavy local supplies, or are in a large group, hiring a mule makes especially good sense. As a rough guide, mules can carry up to 120kg – or up to four sets of gear. If the route is very steep or demanding, the muleteer may insist upon carrying less. He will have the wellbeing of his meal ticket in mind, although Moroccans are unsentimental about their pack animals.

Some trekking routes are not suitable for mules, although detours (for the mule) are often possible. If high passes are covered in snow, porters may have to be used instead of mules (one porter can carry up to 18kg).

There is usually a standard charge for a mule and muleteer of about Dh100 per day. As with guides, if you trek a linear route you'll also be expected to pay for the muleteer's return journey.

On the Trek

Accommodation

If you would rather not carry a tent, you can often stay in *refuges* and in villages at either *gîtes d'étape* (basic homestays or hostels) or *chez l'habitant* (in someone's home). Especially in remote areas, village rooms may not even have a mattress on the floor, although in places such as Imlil they often come with the luxury of a bed.

The bulk of trekking accommodation options in the High and Middle Atlas are *gîtes*. In the Rif and Anti Atlas, *gîtes* are uncommon, and accommodation is more often in local homes or in tents.

For more information, see destination chapters and p489.

Gîtes d'Étape

Gîtes provide basic accommodation, often offering little more than a foam mattress in an empty room, or on a roof terrace or balcony. They have basic bathrooms and toilets, although the better ones have hot showers. Given notice, the proprietor can rustle up a tajine.

At the time of writing, the standard rate was Dh50 per person per night, although

---

WORDS TO TREK BY

Even just a few words in a foreign language can make a big difference to your experience. The following words may be helpful on these treks. '(A)' indicates Arabic, '(B)' indicates Berber; other useful Arabic and Berber words can be found in the Glossary (p533).

adfel (B) – snow

adrar (B) – mountain (plural *idraren*)

afella (B) – summit

agdal (B) – pasture (also *aougdal*)

aghbalu (B) – water spring

ain (A) – water spring

aman (B) – water

anzar (B) – rain

argaz (B) – man

asserdoun (B) – mule

assif (B) – watercourse, river

azaghar (B) – plane, plateau (also *izwghar*)

azib (B) – seasonal shelter for shepherds

brhel (A) – mule

châba (B) – ravine

iferd (B) – lake

ifri (B) – cave

jebel (A) – mountain or hill

kerkour (B) – cairn

taddart (B) – house

talat (B) – dried-up ravine or watercourse

tamada (B) – lake

tigm (B) – house

tizi (B) – mountain pass

HAPPY FEET

Mountain Berbers manage to walk and, often, even run up and down mountains in sandals. They have had a lifetime to hone this skill, and you are not advised to copy them if you want to carry on walking. The most common difficulty that visitors experience on a trek is blisters from ill-fitting boots or ill-chosen footwear. If you want to do more than stroll across a valley, you will greatly enhance your outing by buying a pair of properly fitted, waterproof (preferably Gore-Tex) boots, and giving yourself time to break them in. Even then you may get blisters. Many trekkers carry 'second skin', a plastic layer that can be put over blisters and usually stops them hurting. Happy feet make for a happy walker.

prices can vary according to season and location. Meals are extra (usually Dh30 to Dh50 per person), as are hot showers (usually Dh10 to Dh15 per shower).

The more upscale, privately owned *gîtes* typically charge up to Dh200 per person for half-board, while rooms at one luxury kasbah in Imlil cost up to Dh2780 (see p111).

Refuges

CAF operates *refuges* in Imlil, Oukaïmeden, Tazaghart, Tacheddirt and on Toubkal. Officially, bookings should be made in advance through the Oukaïmeden *refuge* (see p111). However, in practice you can usually find out if space is available at the other *refuges* in the Toubkal region by asking in Oukaïmeden or Imlil. *Refuges* are often packed in July and August.

CAF members and HI members get the cheapest price for a bed. Members of affiliated and recognised alpine organisations (eg the UK's Alpine Club) and children aged under 16 years are also eligible for discounts.

Food

The choice of dry rations is limited in rural Morocco. You cannot be sure of finding much beyond powdered milk, a range of dried fruit and sachets of soup, biscuits, some tinned fish and dates. Supermarkets in larger towns and cities are a much better op-

tion, and if you take a mule, you will be able to plan a more varied diet.

Bread, eggs, vegetables and some basic supplies (eg tea and tinned tuna) may be available in some mountain villages, but you cannot count on it. Meals can also be arranged in some villages (Dh30 to Dh50 per person is standard), especially at *gîtes* and *refuges,* although they usually need to be ordered in advance. Again, do not rely on local suppliers as your only source of food unless you have made previous arrangements.

Change money in the nearest major town and ensure that you have plenty of small notes. If you do get stuck, euro notes may be accepted.

Responsible Trekking

Morocco is being developed as a walking destination, but many regions remain remote – and susceptible to the cultural and environmental impact of tourism. Many travellers return home warmed and heartened by Berber hospitality, but as visitor numbers increase so too does the pressure on locals. In response, travellers should adopt an appropriate code of behaviour.

Cross-Cultural Considerations

For advice on alcohol, photography and giving gifts to children see the boxed text, p42.

Dress

The way you dress is important, especially among remote mountain people, who remain conservative. In villages, wear buttoned shirts or T-shirts and not sleeveless vests, which villagers use as underwear. Above all, trousers should be worn rather than shorts. This applies equally to men and women.

The importance of dress in the villages cannot be overemphasised (as many a frustrated and embarrassed trekking tour leader will affirm). However much you might disagree with this conservatism, respecting local traditions will bring greater rewards, not least by way of contact, hospitality and assistance.

Hospitality

Invitations for tea and offers of food are common in the mountains. By taking a guide, who may have friends in many villages, you'll open yourself to even more offers of genuine hospitality.

While these offers are unconditional, it is worth bearing in mind that the mountain economy is one of basic subsistence farming. No one has large supplies, and in outlying villages there may be no surplus food. Offering your hosts some Chinese gunpowder tea and some sugar (preferably in cones) is a very welcome gesture. Dried fruits are also appreciated, as is a taste of any imported food you may have.

For this reason, it is important to be generous when buying provisions for yourself and guides.

Medicine

In remote areas, people along the way will often ask for medicine, from disinfectant and bandages to painkillers or cream for dry skin (which many children have). Always make sure the guide explains what to do

with what you offer – how often to take it and so on.

Environmental Considerations
Rubbish

Carry out all your rubbish; never bury it or burn it (Western-style packaging never burns well). Your guide may be happy to bag up all your rubbish and hurl it over a cliff, but that approach is unsustainable, especially given that more and more people are now trekking in Morocco. So if you have carried it in, then you should carry it out.

Minimise the waste you'll carry out by taking minimal packaging, and by repackaging provisions into reusable containers when appropriate. If you want to make a gesture, consider carrying out some of the rubbish left by others.

Don't rely on bought water in plastic bottles, as disposal of these bottles is creating

Trekking Areas

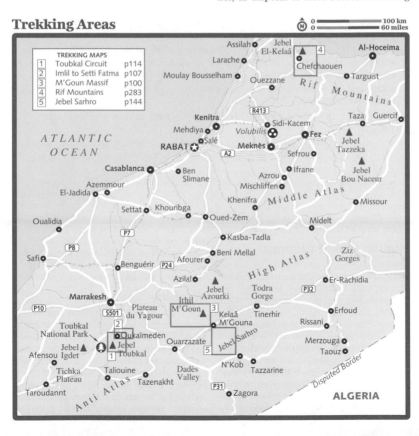

TREKKING THE WAY ALLAH INTENDED

Morocco, beloved for its casual, God-willing, now-pass-another-cup-of-tea charm, does not provide trekkers with many resources for safe and responsible exploration, or for protecting the environment. The following tips should help, and this chapter gives more detail on many of them.

» Dress appropriately according to local custom.

» Use current topographical maps.

» Run maps by a local if you can: someone who lives in the area can verify water sources and indicate rivers that are now dry.

» Camp only in designated camp sites; fields are a private source of business for local families.

» Buy or collect firewood (do not chop) and use it sparingly to respect its scarcity.

» Carry out rubbish to the nearest town or city.

» Hitchhike at your own risk.

» If you flag down a grand taxi you're no longer hitchhiking; expect to pay the fare to the next town.

» Scorpions hide under rocks – and potentially in shoes and sleeping bags, so shake them out occasionally. Scorpions will not sting unless provoked.

» Laundering or bathing in rivers and streams pollutes a village's primary water source.

» Some villages consider photography blasphemous, while in others a camera makes you the Pied Piper. It is always inappropriate to photograph someone without permission, and cameras can cause particular offence when pointed at women.

» Refrain from feeding or handling animals – even Barbary macaques, who will tease you with their charisma!

» Consider the impact of 4WDs before embarking on off-*piste* adventures (see the boxed text, p483).

» Give a warm smile and some kind words to the friendly children who live in rural areas.

» Handing out money, candy and other gifts teaches kids to beg and harass tourists. If you wish to give something, it's better to give a donation to a local charity or school.

» Don't drink alcohol in remote villages where the practice is considered offensive.

a major problem in Morocco. Instead purify locally sourced water.

Human Waste Disposal

Contamination of water sources by human faeces can lead to the transmission of hepatitis, typhoid and intestinal parasites. This is a particular problem in more populated trekking areas.

Where there is a toilet, it is a good idea to use it; where there is none, bury your waste. Dig a small hole 15cm (6in) deep and at least 100m from any watercourse – an important point to remember, given how many trekking routes follow rivers and streams. Consider carrying a lightweight trowel: in the arid Atlas Mountains, digging without one can be difficult. In snow, dig down to the soil; otherwise, your waste will be exposed when the snow melts.

Use toilet paper sparingly, burn it when possible or bury it with the waste. Cover the waste with soil and a rock.

Washing

Don't use detergents or toothpaste in or near watercourses, even if they are biodegradable. For personal washing use biodegradable soap and wash at least 50m away from any watercourse. Disperse the waste water widely to allow the soil to filter it fully before it makes its way back to the watercourse. Use a scourer, sand or snow to wash cooking utensils rather than detergent.

Again, make sure you're at least 50m from any watercourse.

Erosion

Hillsides and mountain slopes, especially at high altitudes, are prone to erosion. Stick to existing tracks and avoid short cuts that bypass a switchback. If you blaze a new trail straight down a slope, it will turn into a watercourse with the next heavy rainfall, eventually causing soil loss and deep scarring.

Low-Impact Cooking

Don't depend on open fires for cooking. As you will see, cutting wood for fires has caused widespread deforestation in Morocco. Ideally, cook on a lightweight multifuel or kerosene stove and avoid those powered by disposable butane gas canisters. If you do make a fire, ensure it is fully extinguished after use by spreading the embers and dousing them with water. A fire is only truly safe to leave when you can comfortably place your hand in it.

Camping

Vegetation at high altitude is highly sensitive. When camping, minimise your impact on the environment by not removing or disturbing the vegetation around your camp site. In order to avoid aggravating the persistent and serious problem of overgrazing in many of the regions, sufficient fodder (barley) for all baggage mules and donkeys should be brought in. Enquire about this before setting off.

Travel with Children

Best Regions for Kids

Marrakesh

With so much culture and shopping, there's always something to amuse children in Marrakesh. The Djemaa el-Fna is Morocco's carnival capital, and all generations can retire to pool, park, horse-drawn calèche or camel back.

Coast

Beaches are an obvious hit – the Atlantic Coast offers plenty of water and wind sports. Agadir's long, sandy beach is popular; mix it with somewhere more colourful like Essaouira.

Drâa Valley

Tour Ouarzazate's film studios and kasbah, then head down the valley for dunes and dromedary rides.

Rabat

With its souqs, ruins and gardens, this is a relatively mellow, manageable slice of urban Morocco. Attractions include a zoo, amusement park and pony rides.

Middle Atlas

For mountain scenery, waterfalls, forest walks and less hair-raising passes than the High Atlas. Easily visited from spots like Azrou and accommodation on the outskirts of Marrakesh.

There's plenty to capture children's imaginations in Morocco. In cities such as Fez and Marrakesh, the sensory explosion and chaos of the medinas and souqs are endlessly fascinating, and supply many exciting (and possibly exasperating) moments. Marrakesh has the most to offer families in urban Morocco. A night around a campfire or a camel ride on the beach will be memorable, but be sure to factor in some time by the hotel pool at the end of a hot day.

Morocco for Kids

Morocco is ideal for parents who once travelled to intrepid destinations, and don't necessarily fancy a Western poolside now they have knee-high travelling companions. Compared with Asia, it's easily accessible from Europe and North America; Marrakesh is less than four hours from London. And when you touch down, you'll find that children open numerous doors, getting you closer to the heart of this family-orientated country.

Meeting the Locals

Moroccans love children so much that you may even want to bring a backpack to carry smaller kids, in case they grow tired of the kissing, hugging, gifts and general adulation. Locals have grown up in large families and children break the ice and encourage contact with Moroccans, who are generally

If you look hard enough, you can buy just about anything you need for young children in Morocco. Before leaving home, think about what you can take with you to Morocco's various environments; wet-weather gear is vital in the mountains in case the weather turns bad.

Lonely Planet's *Travel with Children* has more information and tips.

Accommodation

Some hotels are more family-friendly than others, so check your children will be well catered for before booking.

Like the airlines, many hotels will not charge children under two years of age. For those between two and 12 years sharing a room with their parents, it's often 50% off the adult rate. If you want reasonable toilet and bathroom facilities, you'll need to stay in midrange hotels.

Transport

Northern Morocco has a great rail infrastructure and travel by train may be the easiest, most enjoyable option: children can stretch their legs and fold-out tables are useful for drawing and games. Travellers and children are eligible for reductions and discount cards (see p520).

Grands taxis and buses can be a real squeeze with young children, who count not as passengers in their own right but as wriggling luggage, and have to sit on your lap. The safety record of buses and shared taxis is poor, and many roads are potholed.

Hiring a vehicle – a taxi in Marrakesh or a 4WD to the mountains – is well worth the extra expense. Bring a child seat! They allow children to see out of the window and hire-car companies normally don't have them; seats generally cost more in Morocco than in Europe.

Health & Hygiene

Alcohol gel is essential, as children tend to touch everything. Disposable nappies are a practical solution when travelling despite the environmental drawbacks; international brands are readily available. All travellers with children should know how to treat minor ailments and when to seek medical treatment.

Make sure the children are up to date with routine vaccinations, and discuss possible travel vaccines well before departure, as some are not suitable for children aged under a year.

Upset stomachs are always a risk for children when travelling, so take particular care with diet. If your child is vomiting or experiencing diarrhoea, lost fluid and salts must be replaced. It may be helpful to take rehydration powders for reconstituting with sterile water; ask your doctor.

In Morocco's often-searing heat, sunburn, heat exhaustion and dehydration should all be guarded against, even on cloudy days. Bring high-factor sunscreen with you, and avoid travelling in the interior during midsummer, when temperatures rise to 40°C plus.

Encourage children to avoid dogs and other mammals because of the risk of rabies and other diseases – although there isn't likely to be a risk on camel rides in the desert, or with donkeys and mules working in places like Fez medina.

See p523 for more information on health.

very friendly, helpful and protective towards families.

As you travel the countryside, women may pick up their own child and wave from their doorway. Such moments emphasise your children's great benefit: having yet to acquire any stereotypes about Africa and the Middle East, their enduring impression of Morocco is likely to be its people's warmth and friendliness.

Of course, this certainly doesn't mean parents receive special treatment from the salesmen in the country's souqs. However, even the grizzliest shopkeeper generally welcomes Western women and children, as it gives their store the image of having a broad, family-friendly appeal. Letting your kids run amok in carpet shops can also be an excellent bargaining technique!

Adapting to Morocco

Morocco is a foreign environment and children will likely take a day or so to adapt, but it has plenty of familiar and fun aspects that kids can relate to. British traveller Emma Catling says of her five-year-old son Finlay's first impressions of Marrakesh: 'It was hectic at first: with bikes and horses coming past you in narrow alleyways and different smells, it was beyond his normal experience – but the snakes on the Djemaa el-Fan turned him around.' In the countryside, simple things like beehives and plants endlessly fascinate children.

Taking your Time

A key to successful family travel in Morocco is to factor in lots of time: to acclimatise at the beginning, and just relax and muck about at the end. Trying to cram everything in, as you might if you were by yourself, will lead to tired, cranky kids. Distances are deceptive due to factors such as bad roads, and you need to build in contingency plans in case children get ill. However, having to slow your pace to your kids – for example, having to stay put in the hottest hours between noon and 4pm – is another way children draw you closer to the Moroccan landscape, people and pace of life.

Eating Out

Tajines contain many familiar elements, such as potatoes and carrots. Although you may want to encourage your child to try Moroccan food, you may struggle if they don't like potatoes or bread; in which case Western foods, such as pasta, pizza and fries, are available.

Be careful about choosing restaurants; steer clear of salads and stick to piping-hot tajines, couscous, omelettes and soups such as *harira* (lentil soup). Markets sell delicious fruit and vegies, but be sure to wash or peel them.

To avoid stomach upsets, stick to purified or bottled water. Milk is widely available – UHT, pasteurised and powdered – but baked beans are not, and you should bring any special foods.

Children's Highlights

Sights and activities appropriate for children are covered throughout this book, with dedicated boxed texts under Marrakesh, Tangier, Casablanca and Rabat.

Animal Encounters

» Travelling by road to a High Atlas trailhead such as Imlil, then taking a day walk in the mountains with a guide and mule.

» Camel or horse rides along the beaches around Essaouira or in the Sahara, with accessible dunes in the Drâa Valley and Merzouga.

» Calèche (horse-drawn carriage) rides around the ramparts of places like Marrakesh and Taroudannt.

Splashing Around

» Wind and water sports around Essaouira or Agadir's beach for young children.

» Oualidia lagoon, with safe, calm waters and a wide, sandy beach.

» Ceuta's creative Parque Marítimo del Mediterráneo, its pools surrounded by restaurants and cafes.

Fun & Games

» Jardin Majorelle and Djemaa el-Fna, Marrakesh; on the latter, children enjoy amusements such as the 'fishing for a bottle' game.

» Atlas Film Corporation Studios, Ouarzazate, featuring sets and props from famous films made hereabouts.

regions at a glance

Marrakesh & Central Morocco

Adventure ✓✓✓
Architecture ✓✓✓
Food ✓✓

Adventure

With its dunes, mountains, souqs, caravanserai, extreme conditions and the sheer unpredictability of its landscapes, Central Morocco piles on the adventures. Before you even leave Marrakesh, you have to brave the traffic and rise to the moment on the Djemaa el-Fna. The square's peculiar magic – like a circus, jam session, giant barbecuing competition, and a wonky satellite TV feed where every channel is on – soon sweeps travellers into a jubilant, up-for-anything party mood.

Architecture

The region has a stunning variety of traditional architecture in site-appropriate, sustainable materials. Marrakesh has more riads than any other city, kasbahs dot the Drâa Valley and *ksour* (fortified strongholds) line the Rissani road. White window frames and blue doors distinguish mimetic stone, mud and thatch villages from their High Atlas settings. Inspired adaptations are being made to Marrakesh interior architecture.

Food

Fantastic street food, lavish riad dining, fresh, local, organic ingredients...and that's just in Marrakesh. Slow Food is taking off in the Sahara: traditional organic dry-farming practices turn oasis-grown products into taste explosions, and farmers are working local heritage varietals into inspired recipes – date syrup, date energy bars, honey from Berber medicinal herbs. Try some local wines, particularly rose, gris and white, which preserve better in the heat.

p52

Atlantic Coast

Beaches ✓✓✓
Architecture ✓✓
Birdwatching ✓✓

Beaches

This stretch encompasses the aptly named Paradise Beach, a carriage-ride from Assilah, and Sidi Kaouki, a top surfing and windsurfing spot. In between, Tamara and Haouzia beaches are near Rabat and Casablanca, and chic Oualidia has a sand-fringed lagoon.

Architecture

Gems include Essaouira and El-Jadida, fortified seaside towns with wave-lashed ramparts. Hispano-Moorish Larache recalls its two spells under Spanish rule and murals decorate nearby Assilah's medina. Mauresque beauties are found in Casablanca, along with the world's third-largest mosque, and Rabat.

Birdwatching

Beaches and coastal wetlands offer excellent birdwatching, particularly around Moulay Bousselham: Merja Zerga (Blue Lagoon) attracts thousands of birds. Lac de Sidi Bourhaba is one of the last places to see large numbers of marbled ducks.

p164

Mediterranean Coast & the Rif

Beaches ✓✓✓
National Parks ✓✓
Trekking ✓✓

Imperial Cities, Middle Atlas & the East

Souqs ✓✓✓
History ✓✓✓
Food ✓✓

Southern Morocco & Western Sahara

Coastal Hideaways ✓✓✓
Oases ✓✓✓
Activities ✓✓

Beaches

From beaches near Tangier – such as bracing Plage Robinson, where you might feel like its shipwrecked namesake – the Mediterranean coast ripples east. Top beaches include Oued Laou, Cala Iris, Al-Hoceima and Saídia, all unruffled in comparison with Europe's Mediterranean beaches.

National Parks

Two stunning national parks offer the best of the region's coastline and mountains. Talassemtane National Park encompasses green mountains, tiny villages, an eco-museum and the God's Bridge rock formation; and the National Park of Al-Hoceima's great mesas, dry canyons and thuya forests lead to limestone sea cliffs.

Trekking

Trekking through the Rif Mountains in Talassemtane National Park is superb, and largely undiscovered compared with High Atlas routes. From Chefchaouen, multiday trails lead through forests of cedar, cork oak and fir.

p234

Souqs

Fez medina includes the henna souq (actually best for blue pottery) and the Carpenters' Souq, with thrones built for weddings. Meknès has souqs devoted to textiles, jewellery, carpets and embroidery, and Middle Atlas souqs are piled with Berber carpets.

History

Fez medina is the world's largest living medieval Islamic city, and the Fès Festival of World Sacred Music showcases Sufi musical traditions. Memories of Meknès' past glories remain in its imperial city; Volubilis was a Roman outpost; Moulay Idriss is dedicated to its 8th-century namesake; and an 11th-century minaret overlooks oasis town Figuig.

Food

Fez' nationally renowned dishes include wild thistle/artichoke stew, and the medina has a snail stand. The Middle Atlas has home-grown delights, such as the red goodies at Sefrou's Cherry Festival.

p298

Coastal Hideaways

En route to the Sahara, remote seaside escapes offer empty beaches and dilapidated charm. Mirleft is a favourite hang-out with its cafes and boutique accommodation; art-deco Sidi Ifni is as perfectly faded as a sepia photo; and Tarfaya's colonial Spanish relics peel between the eddying sands.

Oases

Beneath ochre cliffs, palms worthy of *Lawrence of Arabia* nestle in the Aït Mansour Gorges and Ameln Valley. *Palmeraies* (palm groves) also line the winding road through Paradise Valley, and refresh Saharan travellers around Tata and Tighmert.

Activities

Taghazout is Morocco's premier surf spot, the sun-and-sand fun continues year-round in Agadir, and Mirleft and Sidi Ifni offer wind and water sports. Inland, the Anti Atlas is a trekking and mountain-biking playground, and Tata is an emerging destination for desert excursions.

p360

» (above) Handmade wooden crafts in a medina souq
» (left) European brass canons line the Skala de la Ville (p223) on the medina rampart of Essaouira

Look out for these icons:

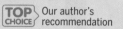 Our author's recommendation

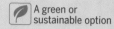 A green or sustainable option

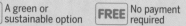 No payment required

On the Road

Marrakesh & Central Morocco
مراكش وسط المغرب

Includes »

Best Places to Eat

» Mechoui Alley (p80)
» Le Relais Saint Exupéry (p126)
» Café-Restaurant Al Jazeera (p93)
» Djemaa el-Fna (p80)
» Al-Fassia (p82)

Best Places to Stay

» Erg Chigaga dunes (p136)
» Riad Al Massarah (p74)
» Chez Pauline (p154)
» Dar Raha (p133)
» Ksar Sania (p160)

Why Go?

Through no fault of their own, maps can't do central Morocco justice. Even the best satellite technology can't capture the meanderings of covered souqs and back-flipping Gnawa musicians in the legendary Djemaa el-Fna. Topographic maps duly note Jebel Toubkal, but fail to convey how its snowcapped summit cools the brain on a hot day.

Somehow, all this vibrant life exists on the edge of the desert. You'll never guess from remote GPS coordinates that a burbling river interrupts stony-faced Todra Gorge, or rocks melt like wax candles into the green carpet of the Dadès Gorge. Just when the rocky Ziz and Drâa Valleys seem utterly barren, water seeps through fissures and bursts into exuberant palm oases. Mileage suggests you can return from the Sahara to Marrakesh in one day, but central Morocco is the place to put down the map, get lost, and live a little.

When to Go
Marrakesh

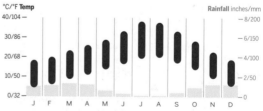

March–April
Mountains thaw; desert blooms. Fresh fruit. Skip Easter holidays when prices jump.

May–June
Ideal High Atlas hiking: hot, not scorching. Accommodation and souq bargains.

September–October
Prime time in the desert; gentle breezes, dates galore.

History

Imagine our world minus the outsized contributions of Central Morocco over the past millennium. How would the world look, taste, and sound?

Without the ambitious Almoravids expanding their empire from Marrakesh into Europe, Moorish arches may not have uplifted buildings from Spain to California. Without Saadian sugar dealers and Jewish salt traders moving product into Europe and beyond, meals might've remained medievally bland – and insatiable sugar cravings might not have driven colonial traders as far as the Dominican Republic. Without trade routes through desert oases, bluesy Gnawa inflections may not have echoed from the Sahara into musical traditions worldwide, from slave spirituals to Led Zeppelin's rock anthems.

True, you might not miss certain movies filmed locally with the help of Ouarzazate movie studios (though *Sex and the City II, Prince of Persia, Alexander* and *Ishtar* do have their defenders) or the alarming resurgence of harem pants abetted by Marrakesh fashion merchants. But to witness cultural developments in the making, Central Morocco remains a must.

Even in the snowy High Atlas at Oukaïmeden, climbers may stub their toes on petroglyphs from 1500 years ago. Since then, Marrakesh has served as the capital to three separate dynasties – more than the imperial cities of Fez and Meknès. Watchtowers of mudbrick *ksour* (castles) dotting desert oases were the satellite radio towers of the Middle Ages, spreading news from Mauretania to Spain via Skoura, Zagora and Rissani. Glaoui mountain strongholds played pivotal roles in French colonialism in Africa, and also in independence movements. Today Central Morocco is Morocco's main draw for visitors, building its future while remaining true to its history as a cultural crossroads.

Climate

Spring and autumn are the best times to explore, with temperatures averaging 20°C to 25°C. Cold High Atlas winters may start in September and last through April, while sweltering deserts will leave you panting for water by May. April is sandstorm season in the desert, when wind speeds of only 10km/h kick up fine sand and dust; allow a few extra days for dune visits to ensure visibility.

Language

In the High Atlas the main language is the Berber dialect of Tashelhit, with some pockets of Tamazight. Elsewhere Darija (Moroccan Arabic) and French are widely spoken. You'll hear some Spanish and English, and possibly German and Italian – especially when there's a carpet deal at stake.

ℹ Getting There & Away

Marrakesh is the transport hub of the region, with train, bus and air links. Direct flights from London to Marrakesh's Menara airport are offered by low-cost airlines such as easyJet, Ryanair and Thompson Air plus British Airways, and frequent flight and train services from Casablanca expand travel options. Royal Air Maroc (RAM) also offers flights to Marrakesh and Ouarzazate, though delays and lost luggage in transit are worryingly common.

A direct three-hour rail service to/from Casablanca links Marrakesh to major northern cities. Supratours buses link Marrakesh to the southern Atlantic coast, from Essaouira and Agadir to Laâyoune and Dakhla, plus key Saharan oases and gorges, including Ouarzazate, Zagora, Boumalne du Dadès, Kelaâ M'Gouna and Merzouga. Similar services are offered by CTM and local bus companies, though these tend to be more crowded and less comfortable.

ℹ Getting Around

Except for the line from Casablanca to Marrakesh, there are no rail links in Central Morocco. Buses are the cheapest way to get around Central Morocco, but they're becoming more expensive to operate as the price of petrol soars. According to bus company officials, current prices may be expected to rise, so pad your budget if your plans include bus travel.

CTM provides adequate service, but Supratours and other private companies are now offering more frequent departures, air-conditioned coaches and reserved seating to tourist destinations. Shared grands taxis are an alternative, since there are good sealed roads to most destinations in this chapter. Mountain regions are best traversed on foot, mountain bike, mule or 4WD (around Dh1000 to Dh1500 per day). Desert travellers will want either 4WDs or camels (Dh350 to Dh400 per person per day) for that ultimate experience at the sand dunes of Erg Chigaga and Erg Chebbi.

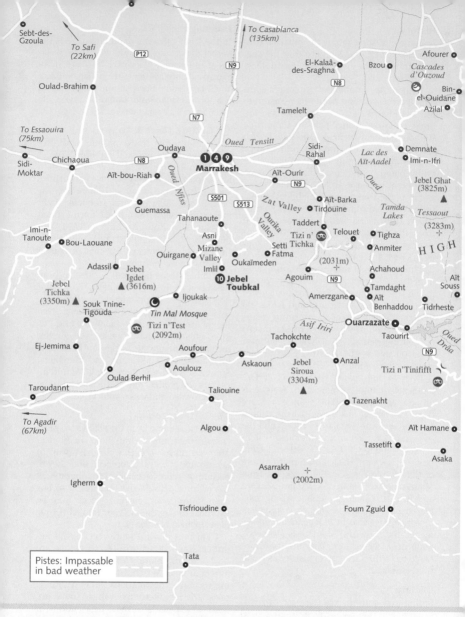

Marrakesh & Central Morocco Highlights

1 Catch the show that's played nightly for 1000 years: street theatre in the **Djemaa el-Fna** (p59)

2 Walk through Morocco's Shangri-la, the stunning and secluded **Aït Bougomez Valley** (p95)

3 Follow desert caravan routes from kasbah to kasbah through the **Drâa Valley** (p128)

4 Rediscover long-lost social graces behind austere pink walls at an authentic Marrakshi **riad** (p74)

5 Stargaze in the rolling dunes at **Erg Chigaga** (p136)

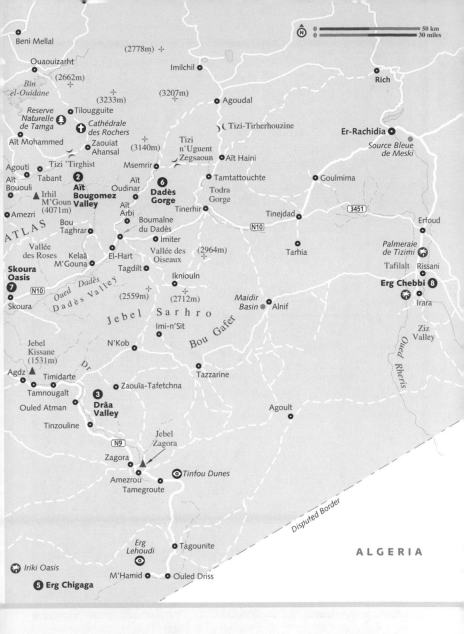

Beni Mellal

Ouaouizarht

(2778m) +

Imilchil

Rich

(2662m)

Bin el-Ouidane

(3233m) +

(3207m)

Agoudal

Er-Rachidia

Tilougguite

Reserve Naturelle de Tamga ❷ ⊕ *Cathédrale des Rochers*

Tizi-Tirherhouzine

Source Bleue de Meski

Aït Mohammed

Zaouiat Ahansal

(3140m) +

Tizi n'Uguent Zegsaoun

Aït Haini

Msemrir

Agouti

Tizi 'Tirghist

Aït Oudinar ❻

Tamtattouchte

Goulmima

Aït Bououli

Tabant

❷ **Aït Bougomez Valley**

Dadès Gorge

Todra Gorge

▲ Irhil M'Goun (4071m)

Aït Arbi

Tinerhir

Tinejdad

3451

Erfoud

Amezri

Bou Taghrar

Boumalne du Dadès

N10

ATLAS

Vallée des Roses

Kelaâ M'Gouna

El-Hart

Imiter

Tarhia

Palmeraie de Tizimi

Vallée des Oiseaux

(2964m) +

Tafilalt

Rissani

Skoura Oasis ❼

N10

Tagdilt

Ikniouln

Maidir Basin

Erg Chebbi ❽

Skoura

Oued Dadès

Dadès Valley

(2559m) +

(2712m) +

Alnif

Irara

J e b e l   S a r h r o

Ziz Valley

Imi-n'Sit

B o u   G a f e r

Jebel Kissane (1531m)

N'Kob

Oued Rheris

Agdz ▲

Timidarte

Zaouïa-Tafetchna

Tazzarine

Dr

Tamnougalt

❸ **Drâa Valley**

Agoult

Ouled Atman

Tinzouline

Jebel Zagora

N9

Zagora ▲

Amezrou

◎ *Tinfou Dunes*

Tamegroute

Disputed Border

A L G E R I A

Erg Lehoudi ◎

Tagounite

❺ *Iriki Oasis*

M'Hamid

Ouled Driss

❺ **Erg Chigaga**

---

❻ Spot crag-top villages and extreme geological formations in the **Dadès Gorge** (p146)

❼ Slow down and stroll amid swaying palm trees in Unesco-protected **Skoura Oasis** (p140)

❽ Hear the shifting sands sing in the magnificent rose-pink dunes of **Erg Chebbi** (p158) near Merzouga

❾ Witness troubled history and impeccable artistry at

Telouet's **Glaoui kasbah** (p121) now, before it collapses

❿ Summit North Africa's highest peak, the **Jebel Toubkal** (p112)

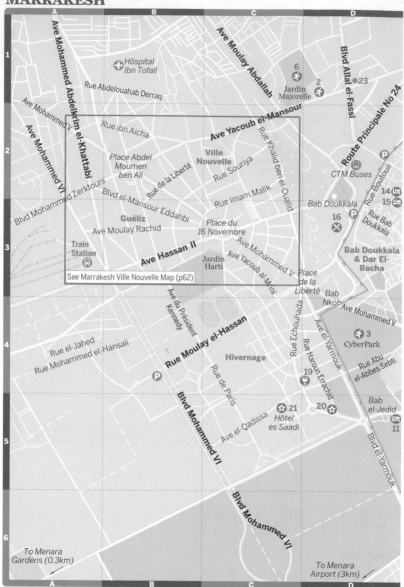

MARRAKESH

مراكش

POP 1,608,100

From the moment you arrive in Marrakesh, you'll get the distinct feeling you've left something behind – a toothbrush or socks, maybe? But no, what you'll be missing in Marrakesh is predictability and all sense of direction. Never mind: you're better off without them here. Marrakesh is too packed with mind-boggling distractions and labyrinthine alleyways to adhere to

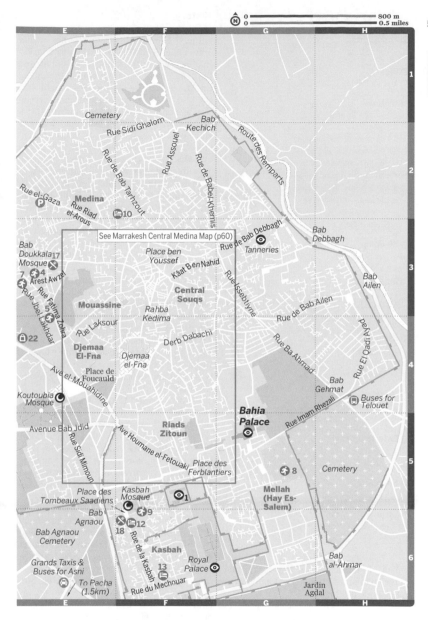

boring linear logic. If you did have a destination, you'd only be waylaid by snake charmers, careening donkey carts, trendy silver leather poufs and ancient Berber cures for everything from relationships to rent.

Start at action-packed Djemaa el-Fna, and if you can tear yourself away from the castanet-clanging water-sellers and turbaned potion-sellers, head into Marrakesh's maze of covered market streets. Dive in headfirst at any street headed north off the

MARRAKESH

Djemaa el-Fna, and with any luck you'll emerge exhilarated and triumphant some hours later, carpet in tow.

Marrakesh's medina is an ideal place to explore palaces, stay in a palatial riad guesthouse, and sample a dish of piping-hot snails. But it's worth leaving the old city occasionally for dinner, drinks, art galleries and fixed-price boutiques in the ville nouvelle (new town). Go with the flow, and become an honorary Marrakshi *bahja* (joyous one).

History

Many desert caravans passed through this outpost before Almoravid Berber leader Youssef ben Tachfine and his savvy wife Zeinab recognised its strategic potential, and built ramparts around the encampment in AD 1062. The Almoravids established the city's *khettara* (underground irrigation system) and signature pink mudbrick architecture. But when Almohad warriors stormed the city like a marauding construction crew, they left only the plumbing and the Koubba Ba'adiyn intact. Almohad Yacoub el-Mansour remodelled Marrakesh with a fortified kasbah, glorious gardens, *qissaria* (covered markets), rebuilt Koutoubia and Kasbah Mosques, and a triumphal gate (Bab Agnaou). But the Almohads soon lost their showpiece to the Merenids, who turned royal attention to Meknès and Fez.

Life became sweet again in the 16th century, when the Saadians made Marrakesh the crux of lucrative sugar-trade routes. With the proceeds, Sultan Moulay Abdullah rebuilt Almoravid Ali ben Youssef Mosque and Medersa, established a trading centre for Christians and a protected *mellah* (Jewish quarter) in 1558. His glitz-loving successor, Ahmed al-Mansour ed-Dahbi (the Victorious and Golden), paved the Badi Palace with gold and took opulence to the grave in the gilded Saadian Tombs.

Alawite leader Moulay Ismail preferred docile Meknès to unruly Marrakesh, and moved his headquarters there – though not before looting the Badi Palace. Marrakesh entered its Wild West period, with big guns vying for control. Those who prevailed built extravagant riads, but medina walls were left to crumble, and much of the population lived hand to mouth in crowded *funduqs* (rooming houses). In 1912 the French protectorate granted Pasha Glaoui the run of southern Morocco and several medina palaces, while French and Spanish colonists built themselves a ville nouvelle. After the independence movement reduced the pasha to snivelling before King Mohammed V, independent Morocco got organised. Rabat became the nation's capital, Fez remained the spiritual centre, and Casablanca was business as usual – but what would become of Marrakesh?

Without a clear role, Marrakesh resumed its fall-back career as a caravanserai – and became the nation's breakaway success. Roving hippies and spiritual seekers built the city's mystique in the 1960s and '70s, and visits by the Rolling Stones, Beatles and Led Zeppelin gave the city star power. Fashion arrived in fierce force with Yves Saint Laurent, Jean-Paul Gaultier, sundry *Vogue* editors and gaggles of supermodels, all demanding chic digs. In the 1990s private medina mansions were converted into B&Bs, just as low-cost airlines delivered weekenders to brass-studded riad doors.

The city has doubled in size, and now eagerly awaits your arrival. After a thousand years of trading-post hospitality, a 2011 bomb blast in the Djemaa el-Fna left the city in shock (for more see www.lonely planet.com/marrakesh). But after surviving historic tragedies and triumphs, Marrakesh knew what to do: it dried its tears, gathered its wits, and put on another pot of mint tea.

◉ Sights
MEDINA
Most monuments are inside the medina ramparts (a 19km circuit). If you wander off-course exploring souqs and palaces, ask someone to point you towards Djemaa el-Fna (preferably a shopkeeper – kids sometimes mislead tourists) or head towards the Koutoubia minaret, the tallest in town.

Small budget hotels cluster along narrow streets heading south from the Djemaa el-Fna. West of Djemaa el-Fna is the Koutoubia minaret. Marrakesh's main souqs, mosques and *zawiyas* (saints' shrines) are north of Djemaa el-Fna, while most of the palaces are south along Rue Riad Zitoun el-Jedid toward the *mellah* (Jewish quarter). Turning west at the covered Mellah Market and south along the ramparts, you'll reach Bab Agnaou, triumphal gateway to the royal kasbah. Inside are gilded tombs of Saadian princes, the royal palace (closed to visitors), and 16 acres of royal gardens dating from AD 1166.

During Ramadan, official sites may close an hour or two early; souqs are generally open 9am to 7pm, though many shops are closed on Friday afternoon.

TOP CHOICE **Djemaa el-Fna** LANDMARK
(Map p60; ☉9am-1am) Think of it as live-action channel-surfing: everywhere you look in the Djemaa el-Fna, Marrakesh's main square and open-air theatre, you'll discover drama already in progress. The hoopla and *halqa* (street theatre) has been non-stop here ever since this plaza was the site of public executions around AD 1050 – hence its name, which means 'assembly of the dead'.

By 10am, the daily performance is underway. Snake charmers blast oboes to calm cobras hissing at careening Vespas; henna tattoo artists beckon to passersby; water-sellers in fringed hats clang brass cups together, hoping to drive people to drink.

The show doesn't peak until shadows fall and 100 chefs arrive with grills in tow, cueing musicians to tune up their instruments. This is a show you don't want to miss – but stay alert to horse-drawn-carriage traffic, pickpockets and rogue gropers. Arrive early in the evening to nab prime seats on makeshift stools (women and elders get dibs). By 7.30pm, families are rocking out at electric-lute jam sessions; even toddlers bounce to the beat and yell *Helwa!* (Sweet!)

Applause and a few dirhams ensure an encore. A bargain show, and critically acclaimed too: for bringing urban legends and oral history to life nightly, Unesco declared the Djemaa el-Fna a 'Masterpiece of World Heritage' in 2001. While a 2011 cafe bombing on the square left the country stunned, the legendary performers quickly regrouped. After 1000 years of performances no matter the weather or political climate, the show goes heroically on in the Djemaa el-Fna.

TOP CHOICE **Ali ben Youssef Medersa** MEDERSA
(Map p60; ☎0524 44 18 93; Pl Ben Youssef; admission Dh50, with Musée & Koubba Dh60; ☉9am-6pm; ☻) 'You who enter my door, may your highest hopes be exceeded' reads the inscription over the entryway to the Ali ben Youssef Medersa, and after almost six centuries, the blessing still works its charms on visitors. Founded in the 14th century under the Merenids, this Quranic learning centre was once the largest in North Africa, and remains among the most splendid.

Entry & Courtyard
Sight lines and spirits are lifted in the entry with carved Atlas cedar cupolas and *mashrabiyya* (wooden-lattice screen) balconies. The *medersa's* courtyard is a mind-boggling profusion of Hispano-Moresque ornament: five-colour *zellij* (mosaic) walls; stucco archways, with Iraqi-style Kufic letters ending in leaves; cedar windows with weather-worn carved vines; and a curved mihrab (eastern-facing niche) of prized, milky-white Italian Carrara marble.

Student Quarters
The medersa is affiliated with nearby **Ali ben Youssef Mosque** (Map p60; closed to non-Muslims), and once 900 students in 132

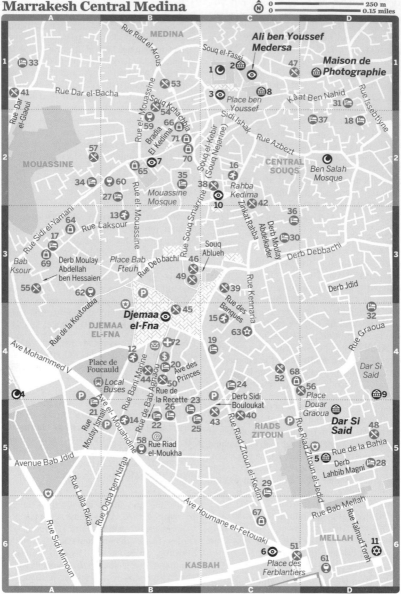

dorms studied religious and legal texts here. Despite upgrades with its 19th-century renovation, the Ali ben Youssef Medersa gradually lost students to its collegiate rival, the Medera Bou Inania in Fez, but the medersa still exudes magnificent, studious calm.

Koutoubia Mosque
MOSQUE

(Map p60; cnr Rue el-Koutoubia & Ave Mohammed V; ☺mosque & minaret closed to non-Muslims, gardens 8am-8pm) Five times a day, one voice rises above the Djemaa din in the *adhan* (call to prayer): that's the muezzin calling the faithful from atop the Koutoubia Mosque minaret. After a few days in Marrakesh, even non-Muslim visitors unconsciously respond to the *adhan* throughout the day: a flutter of eyelashes at the dawn call, a surge of sudden purpose with the afternoon call, a calming breath when the evening call arises.

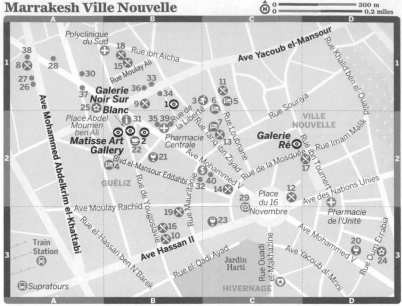

Minaret

The Koutoubia serves a spiritual purpose, but its minaret is also a point of reference for international architecture. The 12th-century 70m-high minaret is the prototype for Seville's La Giralda and Rabat's Le Tour Hassan, and it's a monumental cheat sheet of Moorish ornament: scalloped keystone arches, jagged *merlons* (crenellations), and mathematically pleasing proportions. The minaret was sheathed in Marrakshi pink plaster, but experts opted to preserve its exposed stone in its 1990s restoration.

Mosque & Gardens

The mosque is off-limits to non-Muslims, but the recently refurbished gardens are fair game. Excavations confirm a longstanding Marrakshi legend: the original mosque built by lax Almoravid architects wasn't properly aligned with Mecca, so the pious Almohads levelled it to build a realigned one. When the present mosque and its minaret were finished by Almohad Sultan Yacoub el-Mansour in the 12th century, 100 booksellers were clustered around its base – hence the name, from *kutubiyyin,* or booksellers.

Bahia Palace MUSEUM

(Map 57; ☎0524 38 95 64; Rue Riad Zitoun el-Jedid; admission Dh10; ☺9am-4.30pm) Imagine what you could build with Morocco's top artisans at your service for 14 years, and here you have it: *La Bahia* (the Beautiful) has floor-to-ceiling decoration begun by Grand Vizier Si Moussa in the 1860s and embellished from 1894 to 1900 by slave-turned-vizier Abu 'Bou' Ahmed.

Grand & Petit Courts

Painted, gilded, inlaid woodwork ceilings in the Grand Court still have the intended effect of subduing crowds, while sunburst *zellij* in the Petit Court dazzled dignitaries. But the Bahia proved too beguiling: in 1908, warlord Pasha Glaoui claimed the palace as a suitable venue to entertain French guests, who were so impressed that they booted out their host in 1911, and installed the protectorate's *résident-généraux* here.

Harem

Though only a portion of the palace's 8 hectares and 150 rooms is open to the public, you can see the unfurnished, opulently ornamented harem that once housed Bou Ahmed's four wives and 24 concubines. The quarters of his favourite, Lalla Zineb, are the most spectacular, with original woven-silk panels, stained-glass windows, intricate marquetry and ceilings painted with rose bouquets.

Marrakesh Ville Nouvelle

Top Sights
- Galerie Noir Sur Blanc ... B2
- Galerie Ré ... C2
- Matisse Art Gallery ... B2

Sights
- 1 David Bloch Gallery ... B1
- 2 Gallery 127 ... B2

Activities, Courses & Tours
- 3 Les Secrets de Marrakesh ... C1

Sleeping
- 4 Bab Hotel ... B2
- 5 Caspien ... C1
- 6 Hôtel du Pacha ... C1
- 7 Hôtel Toulousain ... C2

Eating
- 8 ACIMA Supermarket ... A1
- 9 Al-Fassia ... B1
- 10 Azar ... B3
- 11 Beyrouth ... C1
- 12 Café 16 ... C2
- Café du Livre ... (see 7)
- 13 Catanzaro ... C2
- 14 Grand Café de la Poste ... C2
- 15 L'Annexe ... B1
- 16 Le Chat Qui Rit ... B3
- 17 Marcheé Ibn Toumert ... D2
- 18 Plats Haj Boujemaa ... B1
- 19 Samak al-Bahriya ... B3

Drinking
- Bab Hotel Pool Lounge & SkyBab. (see 4)
- 20 Coffee Marrak'chic ... D3
- 21 Kechmara ... B2
- 22 Le Melting Pot ... B2
- 23 Yellow Sub ... C3

Entertainment
- 24 Diamant Noir ... D3
- 25 Le Colisée ... A1

Shopping
- Marcheé Ibn Toumert ... (see 17)

Information
- Café du Livre ... (see 7)
- 26 DHL ... A1
- 27 FedEx ... A1
- 28 Instituto Cervantes ... A1
- 29 Main Post Office ... C3
- 30 Mountain Voyage ... A1
- 31 Office National Marocain du Tourisme (ONMT) ... B2
- 32 Voyages Schwartz (AmEx) ... B2

Transport
- 33 Budget ... B1
- 34 Europcar ... B1
- 35 Hertz ... B2
- 36 KAT ... B1
- 37 La Plaza Car ... A1
- 38 Marrakesh Motos ... A1
- 39 National ... B2
- 40 Royal Air Maroc ... C2

Courtyards

Through the harem is a flowering garden attached to the stark, sternly official Court of Honour, where people waited in the sun for hours to beg for Bou Ahmed's mercy. Apparently they cased the joint too: before the despot's body was cold, enemies and wives of Bou Ahmed stripped the palace bare.

Saadian Tombs HISTORIC SITE

(Map p56; Rue de la Kasbah; admission Dh10; 9am-4.45pm) Anyone who says you can't take it with you hasn't seen the Saadian Tombs, near the Kasbah Mosque. Saadian Sultan Ahmed al-Mansour ed-Dahbi spared no expense on his tomb, importing Italian Carrara marble and gilding honeycomb *muqarnas* (stalactite plasterwork) with pure gold to make the Chamber of the 12 Pillars a suitably glorious mausoleum.

Hidden Passages

Al-Mansour died in splendour in 1603, but a few decades later, Alawite Sultan Moulay Ismail walled up the Saadian Tombs to keep his predecessors out of sight and mind. Accessible only through a small passage in the Kasbah Mosque, the tombs were neglected by all except the storks until aerial photography exposed them in 1917. You can wander around the compound solo, or engage a guide at the entryway to explain what you're seeing (customary tip Dh15to Dh20).

Courtyard Tombs

Al-Mansour played favourites even in death, keeping alpha-male princes handy in the Chamber of the Three Niches, and relegating to garden plots some 170 chancellors and wives – though some trusted Jewish advisors earned pride of place, literally closer

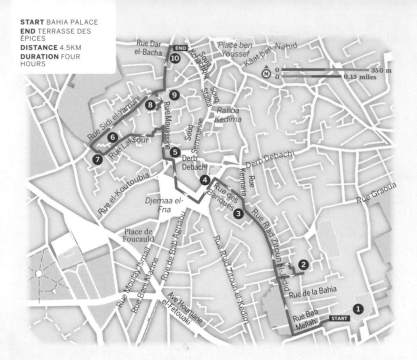

START BAHIA PALACE
END TERRASSE DES
ÉPICES
DISTANCE 4.5KM
DURATION FOUR
HOURS

Walking Tour
Medina Souqs & Funduqs

❯ To discover the medina's hidden hot
spots, you don't need to get hopelessly
lost in the souqs (though it's highly recommended) or hit the *derbs* (alleys) running
at dawn. After lazing around the riad or
sunning on your hotel terrace, begin your
leisurely afternoon stroll at the **1 Bahia
Palace**. After ogling the Bahia's intricately
painted ceilings, head up Rue Riad Zitoun el-
Jedid and follow the signs to the right under
an archway for **2 Dar Si Said** where the
painted dome of the wedding chamber will
blow what's left of your Bahia-addled mind.

Head back to Rue Riad Zitoun el-Jedid
and follow the road north past the broken-
tile-paved entrance and Bollywood posters
of the **3 Cinéma Eden** on your left to the
4 Djemaa el-Fna. You'll need to look
sharp to dodge scooters, horse carriages,
slithery snake charmers and henna tattoo-
ists who consider your hands blank canvas-
es begging for art. Head for the mint sellers
in the northwest corner, swing right towards
Pl Bab Fteuh, and cross the plaza towards

the covered entrance of Rue el-Mouassine.
On your right is the **5 Bab Fteuh Funduq**
where you can glimpse jewellery and trays
being hammered out in crammed artisans'
studios.

Follow Rue el-Mouassine north until you
reach an intersection with Rue el-Ksour,
which heads left under an arch. Here you
can take a shopping detour loop west along
Rue el-Ksour to **6 Al-Kawtar** and
7 Kif-Kif and back to Rue el-Mouassine
via Rue Sidi el-Yamani. Otherwise, continue
north past the Mouassine mosque entrance
on your right and look for a sign for **8 Dar
Cherifa** at your next left. Signs will point
you left, then right under an archway to this
15th-century showplace, where you can enjoy mint tea in Saadian-stuccoed splendour.
Head back to Rue el-Mouassine and follow
your rumbling stomach north past the
9 Mouassine Fountain to **10 Terrasse
des Épices**. Go right to the top floor, flop
on a couch, and watch the sun set on your
glorious afternoon in Marrakesh.

DJEMAA EL-FNA DINNER THEATRE

Arrive just before sunset to watch chefs set up shop right in the heart of the action in the Djemaa el-Fna. Djemaa stalls have a better turnover of ingredients than most fancy restaurants, where you can't typically check the meat and cooking oil before you sit down to dinner. Despite alarmist warnings, your stomach should be fine if you clean your hands before eating, use your bread instead of rinsed utensils and stick to your own bottled water.

Pull up a bench and enjoy the show: the action continues in 'La Place' until after midnight. Storytellers recite ancient tales near dentists' booths displaying jars of teeth, not far from a performance involving clowns and worryingly amateur boxers. Some of the Djemaa's evening entertainments haven't changed much in a millennium, including astrologers, potion-sellers and cross-dressing belly dancers.

to the king's heart than his wives or sons. All tombs are overshadowed by his mother's mausoleum in the courtyard, carved with poetic, weathered blessings and vigilantly guarded by stray cats.

Dar Si Said   MUSEUM
(Map p60; ☑0524 38 95 64; admission Dh30; ⊗9am-4.30pm Wed-Mon) A monument to Moroccan *mâalems* (master artisans), Dar Si Said showcases Marrakesh's graceful riad architecture and regional craftsmanship – though artisans from Fez are credited for the spectacular painted wedding-chamber dome upstairs. Grand Vizier Bou Ahmed had the power, but his brother Si Said apparently had the *mâalems* (master artisans) to make his home a model of quiet elegance. It's signposted from Riad Zitoun el-Jedid.

It now houses the **Museum of Moroccan Arts**, starting with the oldest object in Marrakesh: an AD 1002–1007 chest that belonged to a chamberlain of Spain's Umayyad Caliphate. Arrows direct visitors past antique yet fashion-forward Marrakshi man-bags; 20th-century High Atlas carpets in striking shades of purple; heavy silver headdresses worn by Berber Jewish women; and doors carved with talismans, warding off the evil eye.

Upstairs, flower-painted musicians' balconies flank the domed wedding-reception chamber. At the far end of the room, a small bedroom features uninvitingly narrow wooden beds and special-occasion caftans, including one enviable red, silk-velvet number with gold braid.

The rear staircase leads upstairs to a musical instruments display, or downstairs to the exit via the most delightful artefact of all: a Ferris wheel for babies, with pint-sized palanquins on a hand-cranked axis.

Badi Palace   HISTORIC SITE
(Map p56; admission palace/palace plus Koutoubia minbar Dh10/20; ⊗9am-4.30pm) As 16th-century Sultan Ahmed el-Mansour was paving the Badi Palace, near Pl des Ferblantiers, with gold, turquoise and crystal, his court jester wisecracked, 'It'll make a beautiful ruin'. That jester was no fool: 75 years later the place was looted. Today it's hard to guess the glories of *el-Badi* (the Incomparable) from the stark courtyard.

Check out the view of Marrakesh atop the pisé ramparts, and keep an eye out for upcoming events here. The king occasionally entertains royal visitors here, and the stately setting adds instant atmosphere to the Festival of Popular Arts in July. To reach the entrance, head through Pl des Ferblantiers and turn right along the ramparts.

Minbar
El-Badi's main attraction (well worth the additional Dh10 ticket) is the Koutoubia *minbar* (prayer pulpit), its cedar-wood steps intricately inlaid with marquetry and gold and silver calligraphy by 12th-century Cordoban artisans under a *mâalem* named Aziz – the Metropolitan Museum of Art restoration surfaced his signature.

Maison de la Photographie   ART GALLERY
(Map p60; ☑0524 38 57 21; www.maison-dela photographie.com, in French; 46 Rue Fassi; adult/ child Dh40/free; ⊗9.30am-7pm) When art collectors seek the same works, bidding wars ensue – but when Parisian Patrick Menac'h and Marrakshi Hamid Mergani realised they were both collecting vintage Moroccan photography, they decided to open a Marrakesh gallery to show their collections in their original context.

Together the collectors 'repatriated' 4500 photos, 2000 glass negatives and

LOCAL KNOWLEDGE

AHMAD NMEIS: KOUTOUBIA MOSQUE MUEZZIN

Job requirements

The basic job of a muezzin is not difficult. The essential thing is to give the *adhan* (call to prayer) on time, five times a day. The first time I gave the *adhan* was before there were megaphones, and it took a lot of strength. The Koutoubia muezzin was getting older, and one day when he was too tired to climb the minaret stairs and give the *adhan*, he asked me to do it for him. I became a regular volunteer, and when the muezzin retired the Koutoubia asked me to replace him.

Live Poetry

Today we have sound systems to amplify the call, but most mosques in Morocco don't use recordings. The muezzin should fill the words with their full meaning, every time. At first my job performance was fine – I was on time, I said the words correctly, I gave the *adhan* facing the four cardinal directions – but I had to learn to convey the spirit of the *adhan*. Each word should be pronounced in such a way that it captures its poetry.

The Message

The *adhan* begins: *Allahuakbar*, God is great. The words are simple, but each one is meaningful. All of Islam flows from that one phrase. If we can keep that in mind, we are naturally more mindful of our actions towards one other. For people who are not Muslim and don't understand Arabic, my hope is that they sense the intention of the words, and it fills them with beauty, with comfort, with understanding.

80 documents dating from 1870 to 1950; select works on view here fill three floors, organised by region and theme. Fascinating, well-documented works include a 1907 Djemaa el-Fna vista, a 1920 photo of Ali ben Youssef Medersa with students, and a rare, full-colour 1957 documentary shot in Morocco. Most works are editioned prints from original negatives, and available for sale.

Don't miss the panoramic terrace for coffee or one of Marrakesh's best lunch deals: a fragrant chicken tajine with preserved lemon for Dh35. If you're heading to Ourika Valley, save your ticket for free admission to the Ecomusée Berbere (p105).

Musée de Marrakech   MUSEUM
(Map p60; ☑0524 44 18 93; www.museedemarrakech.ma, in French; Pl ben Youssef; admission Dh40, with Ali ben Youssef Medersa & Koubba Dh60; ◷9am-6.30pm) Maybe the rumours are true of a curse on the Mnebhi Palace, now home to Musée de Marrakech. Its low walls and light-filled inner courtyard left no place to hide for Mehdi Mnebhi, defence minister during Sultan Moulay Abdelaziz's troubled 1894–1908 reign. While Minister Mnebhi was away receiving a medal from Queen Victoria, sneaky England conspired with France and Spain to colonise North Africa. In Mnebhi's absence, autocrat Pasha Glaoui

filched his palace – but after independence, it was seized by the state. The palace became Marrakesh's first girls' school in 1965, but upkeep proved a problem.

The palace's fortunes turned around in 1997 with restoration by the Omar Benjelloun Foundation. Traditional arts displays include Rabati embroidery, inlaid daggers and Fassi pottery, plus displays of historic photos in the original hammam and variable contemporary art in the former kitchen. Outside, there's a courtyard cafe serving powerful espresso, and a small bookshop.

Koubba Ba'adiyn   HISTORIC BUILDING
(Map p60; admission with Medersa Dh60; ◷9am-6pm) The Almohads destroyed everything else their Almoravid predecessors built in Marrakesh, but overlooked this small, graceful 12th-century *koubba* (shrine) across from Ali ben Youssef Mosque, which was probably used for ablutions. This architectural relic reveals what Hispano-Moresque architecture owes to the Almoravids: keyhole arches, ribbed vaulting, interlaced arabesques and domed cupolas on crenellated bases.

FREE **Dar Bellarj**   ART GALLERY
(Map p60; ☑0524 44 45 55; Ali ben Youssef Medersa; ◷exhibitions 9.30am-12.30pm & 2-5.30pm Mon-Sat) Flights of fancy come with the territory at Dar Bellarj, a stork

hospital (*bellarj* is Arabic for stork) turned into Marrakesh's premier arts centre. Each year the nonprofit Dar Bellarj Foundation adopts a program theme, recently ranging from film to women's textiles and storytelling. Calligraphy demonstrations, art openings, crafts exhibits and arts workshops are regular draws, and admission is usually free (there's a charge for some events) – though a Dh20 coffee in the art library makes a blissful break from the souqs.

Mellah   HISTORIC SITE
(Map p56) South of Bahia Palace is the historic home of Marrakesh's Jewish community.

Most Jewish families moved away in the 1960s, but the *mellah* remains notable for tall mudbrick homes along single-file streets and cross-alley gossip through wrought-iron *mellah* balconies. Local guides may usher you into the local **synagogue** (Map p60; Rue Talmud Torah; donation per person Dh20-30), and the **miaâra** (Map p56), or Jewish cemetery, where the gatekeeper admits visitors paying respects to whitewashed tombs topped with rocks for remembrance (Dh10 tip expected).

In this extremely impoverished neighbourhood, you can also be a support to the living: a new **Mellah cultural complex** near Pl des

---

TOP THREE WAYS TO REPAY MARRAKSHI HOSPITALITY

Urban Marrakesh may surprise you with small-town social graces. Offers of mint tea, assistance for the elderly, treats for children and invitations to share meals are common courtesies in Marrakesh. Offering money for generous gestures creates an awkward situation – only *faux guides* and naughty children expect to be paid for pointing you towards the Djemaa el-Fna. Your sincere *shukran* (thanks) is reward enough, but if you're feeling overwhelmed by kindness, you can always make a generous gesture in return.

Give Your Blessing

To acknowledge or graciously refuse a kind gesture, all you need to know is one phrase: *Barakllafik*, literally, 'blessings with you'. More than a pleasantry, this is considered a potent blessing, especially when uttered with one hand on the heart and looking directly in the eye of the intended recipient. Your blessing may or may not have magical properties – only the magic dealers in the Djemaa el-Fna can say for sure – but it's heartwarming for everyone involved, and establishes instant friendships.

Do Something for the Kids

Marrakshis are known across Morocco as the *bahja* (the joyous ones), and while Marrakshis do specialise in good times, they're also justifiably concerned for the welfare of future generations. Illiteracy remains a serious problem, especially for girls from impoverished families. A Marrakesh-based NGO, **Education for All** (www.efamorocco .org) has already built three school dormitories outside Marrakesh, so that girls who show early promise in school are able to continue to attend. Visitors can volunteer onsite or attend a fundraising event, such as High Atlas bike rides or school open houses (see the website for a calendar).

Take It to the Streets

In addition to the jokes and small kindnesses you'll encounter in Marrakesh streets, you'll also notice homeless kids with nothing much to do and nowhere to go. **Atfalouna** (www.atfalouna-marrakech.com; donation requested; ☺5-7pm Mon-Thu & Sat) provides a home, meals, education and a future to 320 Marrakesh children under age 15 who otherwise have no shelter, no food and scant prospects. Travellers are welcome to visit Atfalouna's centre near Bab Doukkala – two-day advance notice is required. Small groups (three to six) can organise volunteer efforts to enhance the centre. Travellers have already established a library, painted a mural on the terrace, set up a computer training lab, and even payed the centre's rent for a year; sliding-scale donations of Dh400 to Dh800 supply a student's food for a month, or allow a child who's never had a summer holiday to see the ocean for the first time. Warm, clean clothing is also appreciated, and can be dropped off on pre-scheduled visits. The response to your generosity is a sincere *barakllafik*.

Ferblantiers is underway (for info, contact Riad Ifoulki, see p75), with proceeds from the centre's restaurant and shop supporting community initiatives – look for donated silk cravats fashioned into adorable toy doves, with proceeds aiding a local girls' school. To get here, go east on Rue Riad Zitoun el-Jedid.

Maison Tiskiwin MUSEUM
(Map p60; ☑0524 38 91 92; 8 Rue de la Bahia; www.tiskiwin.com; adult/child Dh20/10; ☺9.30am-12.30pm & 2.30-6pm) Travel to Timbuktu and back again via Dutch anthropologist Bert Flint's art collection, displayed at Maison Tiskiwin. Each room represents a caravan stop from the Sahara to Marrakesh with indigenous crafts, from Tuareg camel saddles to High Atlas carpets. The accompanying text is often more eccentric than explanatory (an example: 'By modifying his pristine nakedness Man seeks to reveal his image of himself') but Tiskiwin's well-travelled artefacts offer tantalising glimpses of Marrakesh's trading-post past.

Mouassine Fountain HISTORIC SITE
(Map p60; Rue Sidi el-Yamani) The medina had 80 fountains at the start of the 20th century, and each neighbourhood had its own for water for cooking, public baths, orchards and gardens. The Mouassine Fountain, near Rue el-Mouassine, is a prime example, with carved wood details and continued use as a neighbourhood wool-drying area and gossip source.

VILLE NOUVELLE
If the medina starts to wear down your nerves and shoe leather, escape to Guéliz

---

JARDIN MAJORELLE HIGHLIGHTS

» **Majorelle Museum** Villa displays cover Jacques Majorelle artworks and rotating exhibits, such as vintage Morocco travel posters and YSL fashion sketches.

» **Rare flora** Lording it over the garden is a tree-sized African *Tirucalli euphorbia*, with appendages that seem determined to elbow visitors off the pathway.

» **Yves Saint Laurent memorial** The designer's memorial is a simple stone pillar in the back of the garden, where rare African songbirds flock.

---

for art galleries around Rue Yougoslavie, fixed-price boutiques along Rue de la Liberté, and perennially fashion-forward Jardin Majorelle, while most budget hotels, restaurants, cafes, galleries and boutiques cluster around Ave Mohammed V. Along Ave el-Qadissia, you can make an evening of it at Hivernage clubs. For a quick getaway 20 minutes from the city, try a cooking class, hammam, pool day or overnight stay in the Palmeraie.

Count on a 30-minute walk from downtown ville nouvelle to Djemaa el-Fna. Since the blocks are long and boring until you enter the medina, you might take a bus or taxi.

TOP CHOICE Jardin Majorelle HISTORIC PARK
(Map p56; ☑0524 30 18 52; www.jardinma jorelle.com; cnr Aves Yacoub el-Mansour & Moulay Abdullah; garden Dh30, museum Dh15; ☺8am-6pm summer, 8am-5.30pm winter; ☻) Other guests bring flowers, but Yves Saint Laurent gifted the entire Jardin Majorelle to Marrakesh, the city that adopted him in 1964 after a sequence of events that included, in rather unfortunate order: launching hippie fashion; fame as a ground-breaking gay icon; and an obligatory stint in the French military. Saint Laurent and his partner Pierre Bergé bought the electric-blue villa and its garden to preserve the vision of its original owner, landscape painter Jacques Majorelle, and keep it open to the public. Per his instructions, Yves Saint Laurent's ashes were scattered over Jardin Majorelle upon his June 2008 passing.

Garden
Thanks to Marrakshi ethnobotanist Abderrazak Benchaâbane and director Touriya Abd, the garden Majorelle began cultivating in 1924 is now a psychedelic desert mirage of 300 plant species from five continents. Fuchsia bougainvillea explode from lemon-yellow terracotta planters; skinny cacti slouch against cobalt-blue plaster walls; colourful African songbirds flit through dense green bamboo.

Museum & Facilities
Majorelle's art-deco villa houses Saint Laurent's collection of Moroccan decorative arts and rotating exhibitions, plus Majorelle's elegant southern Morocco landscapes. A boutique features pricey souvenirs: Majorelle blue slippers, perfume, and pillows embroidered with YSL Marrakesh New Year's card designs. The cafe offers drinks at high-

TOP FIVE ART GALLERIES

While the tourist market still trades in harem girls, men with muskets and other Orientalist clichés, these Guéliz galleries offer fresh takes and original talent you won't find elsewhere.

Galerie Rê   ART GALLERY
(Map p62; ☑0524 43 22 58; www.galeriere.com; Résidence Al Andalous III, cnr Rues de la Mosquée & Ibn Toumert; ⊙10am-1pm & 3-8pm Mon-Sat) A showcase for next-generation Moroccan art stars: Khadija Kabbaj's mummified Barbies, Hicham Benohoud's pop portraits of heroes with faces erased, M'barek Bouhchichi's dynamic colour-blocks that resemble exploding Rothkos. Don't miss gallery opening soirées – always packed, always fabulous.

Galerie Noir sur Blanc   ART GALLERY
(Map p62; ☑0524 42 24 16; 1st fl, 48 Rue Yougoslavie; ⊙3-7pm Mon-Fri, 10am-1pm & 3-7pm Sat) Major Moroccan talent covers the walls and spills onto the courtyard patio, from Hassan's Bourkia's smouldering abstracts in chalk and ash to Hassan Echair's delicately wrought iron installations.

Matisse Art Gallery   ART GALLERY
(Map p62; ☑0524 44 83 26; www.matisseartgallery.com; 43 Passage Ghandouri; ⊙9.30am-noon & 3-7.30pm Mon-Sat) This polished black-marble storefront off Rue Yougoslavie, showcases ethereal figures in beeswax by Morocco's Venice Biennale representative, Marrakesh native Mahi Binebine, and abstract henna paintings evoking Berber *baraka* (blessings) by Farid Belkahia.

David Bloch Gallery   ART GALLERY
(Map p62; ☑0524 45 75 95; 8 bis Rue des Vieux Marrakchis; www.davidblochgallery.com; ⊙10.30am-1.30pm & 3.30-7.30pm Tue-Sat, 3.30-7.30pm Mon) Artists from both sides of the Mediterranean strike fine lines between traditional calligraphy and urban graffiti, from Marrakshi Larbi Cherkaoui's abstract calligraphic flourishes on goatskin to Parisian graffiti artist Tanc's 1980s wild-style, Zen circle paintings.

Gallery 127   ART GALLERY
(Map p62; ☑0524 43 26 67; 2nd fl, 127 Blvd Mohammed V; www.galerienathalielocatelli.com; ⊙11am-7pm Tue-Sat) A scuffed entry, dimly lit stairway, and exposed brick walls set the scene for new and vintage works by international photographers at reasonable prices. Morocco's first photography showcase cultivates emerging collectors – including King Mohammed VI, who's bought dozens of works here.

fashion prices (Dh60 for a grapefruit juice) but you can't argue with the view.

CyberPark   GARDEN
(Map p56; Ave Mohammed V, near Bab Nkob; ⊙9am-7pm; @奈) Stop and smell the roses while checking email at this 8-hectare royal garden, dating from the 18th century but now offering free wi-fi. Wait your turn for free outdoor kiosk access alongside teenagers and secretive internet daters, or pay to use the swanky air-conditioned cybercafe (Dh10 per hour).

Menara Gardens   GARDEN
(off Map p56; Ave de la Menara, Hivernage; garden free, picnic pavilion Dh20; ⊙9am-5pm) Local lore tells of a sultan who seduced guests over dinner, then lovingly chucked them in the Menara's reflecting pools to drown. Nowadays dunking seems the furthest thing from the minds of couples canoodling amid these royal olive groves, or families picnicking in the stately 19th-century pavilion. On clear days, come for dromedary rides and photo ops against the Atlas Mountain backdrop but if you stay for sunset, stick to paths to leave couples their privacy.

🏃 Activities

Cycling

Rent bikes from budget hotels around Djemaa el-Fna, and at hotels along Ave

Mohammed Abdelkrim el-Khattabi in the ville nouvelle for Dh70 to Dh120 per day. To escape city traffic, head 5km northwest to the Palmeraie, where you'll spot celebrity villas amid the palms.

Marrakech Roues
CYCLING
(Map p60; ☑0663 06 18 92; Imm Roux, 3 Rue Bani Marine; www.marrakech-roues.com; per hr/half-day/full-day Dh50/80/120) Bike rental in the medina.

Actions Sports Loisirs
CYCLING
(Map p56; ☑0661 24 01 45; www.marrakechbike action.com; Apt 4, 2nd fl, Blvd Yacoub el-Mansour, Guéliz; 2hr Dh160, half-day Dh260-350, full-day Dh620-925) Organises circuits of the Palmeraie and Marrakesh gardens (Dh260 per half-day, minimum four people).

D&O
CYCLING
(☑0524 42 19 96) Full day excursions to Ouirgane from Marrakesh from Dh1250, including lunch and lounging poolside.

CycleActive
CYCLING
(☑44 1768 840 400; www.cycleactive.co.uk) UK-based company offering weeklong Atlas mountain-biking trips from £945, not including airfare.

Public Hammams
For authentic Moroccan spa experiences at bargain prices, head to your local neighbourhood hammam, where entry costs about Dh10, *gommage* (scrub) Dh15 to Dh30 and massage Dh50 to Dh100. Bring your community hammam kit: towel, flip-flops, plastic mat and a change of knickers (you'll be expected to wear yours). Public hammams are a greener option than private ones, since less water and fuel is required per person to get squeaky clean.

Hammam Dar el-Bacha
HAMMAM
(Map p56; 20 Rue Fatima Zohra; admission Dh10; ☺men 7am-1pm, women 1-9pm) The city's largest traditional hammam, with star-shaped

TOP FIVE MARRAKESH ACTIVITIES FOR KIDS

» **Magic-supply shopping in Rahba Kedima** Ringed with apothecaries selling mysterious roots, vats of rosebuds and jars of eerie coloured liquids, this square is where Harry and the Hogwarts crew would surely shop for school supplies in Marrakesh. Few scooters pass through here, so kids can stop, gawk and bargain at will, or just take in the view with orange juice at Café des Épices (p81).

» **Calèche rides** When kids' legs and parents' backs start to give out, do what Marrakshi parents do: hire a horse carriage in the Djemaa el-Fna (p90). Go for a short ride up Derb Debachi, or take a grand tour past Bab Agnaou to the Saadian Tombs and back.

» **Playtime at Flower Power Café** Getting here is a game of hide-and-seek: head out of town, turn onto the driveway through an olive grove and head inside an organic plant nursery, and at last you'll find this organic juice bar-cafe and toddler wonderland of **Flower Power Café** (☑0524 48 40 87; Pépinière Casa Botanica, Rte de Sidi Abdellah Ghiat; www.flower-power-cafe.com; ☺10am-5.30pm Wed-Sun), 3.5km past Royal Golf. Squeals of delight will direct you to the rabbit run, pony and donkey paddock, and a playhouse and play-*hanout* (neighbourhood grocery) where kids can pretend-haggle.

» **Palmeraie dromedary rides** Calèche circuits of the Palmeraie usually stop at **Café le Palmier d'Or** (Circuit de la Palmeraie), which has a small playground, Dh10 orange juice, and dromedaries in the parking lot. With some gentle bargaining, Dh100 should cover a 15- to 30-minute guided ride, which is usually enough time to get the hang of the dromedary's rocking motion and take the obligatory holiday-card photo.

» **Take a dare at Terres d'Amanar** For active kids not easily impressed (or worn out) by pools, a day trip to the High Atlas nature activity park **Terres d'Amanar** (☑0524 43 81 03; www.terresdamanar.com), 2km past Tahanaoute and 37km from Marrakesh, should do the trick: adventurous types can learn to master zip-lines, river-rafting, BMX cycling and donkey polo, while creative prodigies take hands-on courses in *zellij* mosaic, baking, glass-painting, and leather craft. Overnight accommodation is available in a mudbrick lodge or tented bungalow (double including breakfast from Dh1000, kids under 11 free).

vents in the vast domed ceiling. Clean, with cheerful bath attendants and a chatty atmosphere during women's hours. It's the public hammam of choice for women, who get prime afternoon/evening hours here.

Hammam Bab Doukkala
HAMMAM

(Map p56; Rue Bab Doukkala; admission Dh10; ☺women noon-7pm, men from 8pm) A historic hammam in the southeast corner of Bab Doukkala Mosque, dating from the 17th century. It has heated *tadelakt* (polished plaster) floors in good repair and a mellow atmosphere during men's hours.

Private Hammams

Many riads and hotels have their own hammams in-house, as do Marrakesh spas; some accommodate couples. Book private hammams in advance, as they can take a couple of hours to heat.

TOP CHOICE Le Bain Bleu
HAMMAM

(Map p60; ☎0524 42 69 99; www.lebain bleu.com; 32 Derb Chorfa Lakbir; ☺by appointment 10am-9pm) This new riad spa-hammam delivers top-notch style and value in a top-secret location. Follow signs for Dar Cherifa off Rue el-Mouassine onto Derb Chorfa, where this double riad features secluded patios, sleek subterranean steam rooms and professional services (massages Dh350 per hour, hammam/*gommage* Dh150, couples hammam/massage Dh600 per person, manicure or pedicure Dh280).

Sultana Spa
HAMMAM

(Map p56; ☎0524 38 80 08; www.lasultanamar rakech.com; Rue de la Kasbah; P☒) An opulent, all-marble spa near the Saadian Tombs offering services from hammam (Dh200, cinnamon *gommage* Dh350) to three-hour-plus 'absolute pleasure' treatments for couples: hammam/*gommage*, mineral-enriched tub soak, mani/pedi, sauna and Jacuzzi (Dh3500).

Les Secrets de Marrakesh
HAMMAM

(Map p62; ☎0524 43 48 48; 62 Rue de la Liberté; ☺10am-8pm Mon-Sat) Upscale treatments inside an art-deco villa, with hammam/*gommage* treatments (Dh200) in a sleek graphite-*tadelakt* hammam, argan-oil and Atlas cedar body wraps (Dh100) and rose-petal massages (Dh500 for 45 minutes).

La Maison Arabe
HAMMAM

(Map p56; ☎0524 38 70 10; www.lamaisonarabe .com; 1 Derb Assehbe, Bab Doukkala) Marinate in local herbs and minerals in this double

hammam, followed by *gommage* and masque of *ghassoul* (clay), crushed rose petals and spices – all for Dh300, plus optional 30-minute massage (Dh350). This is the place to try threading, traditional epilation done with thread and fast hands (Dh100 to Dh150 per half-leg).

Medina Spa
HAMMAM

(Map p60; ☎0524 38 50 59; www.medina-spa -marrakech.com; 27 Derb Zaari; ☺9.30am-9pm) Steps from the dusty Djemaa, off Rue des Banques, enjoy a brisk scrubbing and rejuvenating massage at the right price (30-minute hammam/*gommage* Dh100, massage Dh330 per hour). This is a busy riad-spa, so expect some noise, line-dry-damp (though clean) robes, and waits for walk-ins.

Swimming

Medina riads are restricted to plunge pools, since leakage from larger pools endangers mudbrick foundations. There are Olympic-sized pools and water parks outside of Marrakesh in parched central and southern Morocco. Swimmers who are concerned about their 'wet footprint' can make donations to a local charitable organisation (see p67). The following are some attractive day-use pool options near Marrakesh.

Jnane Tamsna
SWIMMING POOL

(☎0524 32 84 84; www.jnanetamsna.com; Douar Abiad, Palmeraie; admission Dh400; P) To swim laps with a clean conscience, go for lunch (an organic three-course lunch with wine is included in the admission price) and a dip in a pool that's oxygen-filtered and shaded by aromatic organic gardens, a short 20-minute drive from the medina.

Mamounia
SWIMMING POOL

(Map p56; ☎0524 38 86 00; www.mamounia.com; Ave Bab Jedid; day pass weekday/2-day weekend Dh500/1200; P) Definite value when you consider the €650 rack rate, a Mamounia day pass provides access to Mamounia's ozone-treated pool, historic gardens, fitness centre, three swanky bars and *zellij*-paved spa (basic treatment hammam/*gommage*/ honey scrub Dh900), a 10-minute walk from the Djemaa el-Fna.

Ferme Berbère
SWIMMING POOL

(☎0524 38 56 85; www.lafermeberbere.net; 9km Route d'Ourika; incl lunch & hammam per person from Dh350) Getaway packages to this family-friendly rustic retreat in an olive grove include hammam, *gommage,* massage,

WORTH A TRIP

MARRAKESH'S SECRET GETAWAY: OUIRGANE

Framed by High Atlas foothills and the Ouirgane reservoir, mellow Ouirgane is just 60km south of Marrakesh and accessible by grand taxi (Dh30) from Bab er-Rob. In summer, trekkers storm Imlil and picnickers swamp Ourika, not realising that mountain hikes and outdoor dining are available in Ouirgane without the crowds – and you can hit Ouirgane's **Thursday souq** before lunch.

Afternoon escapes

Enjoy lunch in an olive grove with a glass of wine by the pool at **L'Oliveraie de Marigha** (☑0661 31 04 82; www.oliveraie-de-marigha.com; ✿). Linger over espresso, admire High Atlas mountain views floating in the pool, and let them drive (transfers to/from Marrakesh Dh200). It's at 59km on the Route de Taroudannt, 100m right off the main road in Ouirgane town centre.

Romantic overnights

Country living comes with Marrakesh style and comfort at **Chez Momo** (☑0524 48 57 04; www.aubergemomo.com, in French; d with half-board Dh680-890, ste Dh1110-1390; ✿🛜). The restaurant offers Berber couscous (Dh120 to Dh180) and wi-fi, but the garden pool and organised nature walks make you forget Facebook. Garden bungalows have *tadelakt* baths, pine-beam ceilings, *kilim*-upholstered armchairs, and panoramic patios; suites have fireplaces and extra beds for kids (Dh320 half-board). It's at 61km on the Route de Taroudannt, 150m off main road in Ouirgane town centre.

Eco-safaris

Nature lovers flock like Barbary sheep to **Dar Tassa** (☑0524 48 43 12; www.dartassa.com; Douar Tassa, Ouirgane; d with half-board Dh605, with private bathroom Dh775-990; @✿), in the mountain hamlet of Tassa Ouirgane (1300m) at the edge of the Takherkhort nature preserve. Follow a mountain road from Ouirgane to find tea in the library, cooking lessons in the kitchen, and a hammam on the terrace. Ask about excursions to see Barbary sheep, Amaseen gazelles, and other endangered species. Eco-travellers can rest easily knowing that a percentage of rates helps the High Atlas Foundation plant trees.

Family outings

A former French Legionnaire's retreat, **Au Sanglier Qui Fume** (☑0524 48 57 07; www.ausanglierquifume.com; d incl half-board Dh605-700, ste Dh860; ✿) has 14 simple rooms and 10 suites surrounding a courtyard restaurant, bar, and pool. Rooms vary in appeal, from cramped garden doubles to a split-level Marrakshi-pink suite for four, with a fireplace and *tadelakt* bathtub. Active kids start tournaments of table tennis, billiards and darts, and take horse-riding and mountain-bike trips. It's at 61km on the Route de Taroudannt.

lunch and access to a small pool starting at Dh350. Families get the best deal: hammam and *gommage* for two adults, donkey rides for two kids, lunch and pool access costs Dh600.

Riad Bledna　　SWIMMING POOL
(☑0661 18 20 90; www.riadbledna.com; 2km Route de Ouarzazate; incl lunch & transfer per person Dh250) The top-value, eco-friendliest option: day rates cover lounging by an oxygen-filtered pool, tasty homemade lunches and transfers to/from the Djemaa el-Fna at

this family-friendly, 4-acre organic garden retreat in a quiet Marrakesh suburb.

Other venues offering pool day use within an hour's drive of Marrakesh include Les Deux Tours (p79), La Pause (p79) and L'Oliveraie de Marigha (p72).

🍴 Courses

Many riads in the medina organise sessions with their cook, but hands-on cookery workshops open to nonguests are available at a number of venues.

Souk Cuisine COOKING
(Map p60; ☎0673 80 49 55; www.soukcuisine. com; Zniquat Rahba, 5 Derb Tahtah, Medina; per day incl meal & wine Dh400) Learn to cook as the *dadas* (chefs) do: shop in the souq for ingredients with English-speaking Dutch hostess Gemma van de Burgt, work alongside two Moroccan women wedding-feast *dadas*, then enjoy the four-course lunch you helped cook. Courses are two-person minimum, 12 participants maximum; vegetarian courses possible.

Jnane Tamsna COOKING
(☎0524 32 84 84; www.jnanetamsna.com; Douar Abiad, Palmeraie; course incl meal Dh600) Whip up a healthy Moroccan lunch of salad, pastry, tajine and light dessert with instruction from chef Bahija and just-picked produce from Tamsna's organic gardens – and loll by the pool afterwards.

Bled Al-Fassia COOKING
(☎0524 32 96 60; www.bledalfassia.com; Rte de Fez, Douar Sidi Mbarek) Learn the secrets of the chefs behind Al-Fassia restaurant (p82) in the spotless stainless-steel kitchen of a luxury villa on the outskirts of Marrakesh. Rates available on request.

Institut Français LANGUAGE
(Map p60; ☎0524 44 69 30; www.ifm.ma, in French; Rte de Targa, Guéliz; ⊙10am-noon & 3-6pm Mon-Sat) Offers private classes in Arabic and French (Dh250 per hour), plus courses in Moroccan dialect (Dh1800) and French (Dh1000). Also hosts worthwhile concerts, films and dance performances.

Study Arabic in Marrakech LANGUAGE
(www.arabicmarrakech.com) Private teachers here cover the basics of polite Arabic conversation in five lessons.

☞ Tours

Having a guide in the medina undermines its adventure, but you may want one to cover specific landmarks in an hour or two. Just don't expect sweet souq deals: guides get commissions on whatever you buy, which inflates prices. Hotels, riads and travel agencies can arrange guides, or you can book official guides directly via the tourist office (p89) for Dh250/400 for a half/full day. Many travel agencies have offices in Guéliz. For a good, safe time had by all, request licensed, insured guides and specify English-speaking guides as needed.

Inside Morocco Travel EXCURSIONS
(☎0661 18 20 90; Riad Bledna; ⊙9am-noon & 3-7pm Mon-Sat) Get to know Morocco inside-out on bespoke adventures designed for you by ecotourism expert Mohamed Nour and his multilingual team – sunset tea for two in the Sahara, hikes and home cooking in pristine Berber mountain villages and Moroccan crafts workshops with visits to inspiring women's cooperatives. It's at 2km on Rte de Ouarzazate.

Mountain Voyage EXCURSIONS
(Map p62; ☎0524 42 19 96; www.mountain-voyage.com; 2nd fl, Immeuble El Batoul, 5 Ave Mohammed V, Guéliz; ⊙9am-12.30pm & 3.30-7pm Mon-Sat) This British-owned company based in Marrakesh provides licensed, English-speaking guides for tailor-made Marrakesh tours, sustainable tourism excursions in the Middle Atlas, and High Atlas excursions with stays at its own property, the Kasbah du Toubkal (p111).

Tawada Trekking EXCURSIONS
(☎0524 44 65 72; www.tawadatrekking.com, in French) Trekking tours and cultural immersion experiences are the speciality of Hafida H'doubane – among the first Moroccan women to be licensed as mountain guides – while river-guide Pascal Perron specialises in literal immersion experiences, including rafting, kayaking and stream hikes.

Desir du Maroc EXCURSIONS
(☎0661 16 35 85; www.desirdumaroc.com) Marrakshi Abdelhay Sadouk has 30 years' experience introducing visitors to Moroccan culture, leading history and culture tours from Marrakesh to the coast, desert and mountains. Yoga and tai-chi workshops and English-language guides available.

★☆ Festivals & Events

Marrakesh Marathon RACE
(www.marathon-marrakech.com; half-marathon fee €30, full €50) Run like there's a carpet salesman after you: 5000 marathoners cross the finish line at Djemaa el-Fna at this annual road race in January.

Jardin'Art GARDEN
(www.jardinsdumaroc.com, in French) Celebrate Marrakesh in bloom mid-April, with temporary gardens, garden-inspired art shows, botanical talks and displays.

Festival of Popular Arts STREET THEATRE
(www.marrakechfestival.com) Unesco declared Marrakesh's July street-theatre festival

a 'masterpiece of cultural patrimony' for highlighting Morocco's dance, music and storytelling traditions. The opening-night parade is musical mayhem, with 500-plus performers thronging the Djemaa el-Fna.

Marrakesh International Art Fair   FAIR (www.marrakechartfair.com/en) Forty art openings are rolled into one at this October showcase of contemporary art talent from across Morocco and the Mediterranean.

International Film Festival   FESTIVAL (☑0524 42 02 00; http://en.festivalmarrakech. info) Stars from Hollywood to Bollywood strut the Berber red carpet at this week-long December festival, culminating in wildly unpredictable awards shows – recent honourees include Bosnian director Emir Kusturica, Ben Kingsley, Michelle Yeoh, and Harvey Keitel.

🛏 Sleeping

Marrakesh has it all: you can sleep anywhere from the funkiest fleapit to palaces straight out of some Orientalist Hollywood fantasy. Take your pick: authentic riads hidden in the heart of the souqs; budget-friendly inns right off the Djemaa; ville-nouvelle hotels, ranging from budget to business class; or Palmeraie villas, with pools amid swaying palms. Luxury resorts are closing ranks around Marrakesh, offering suburb-sized rooms at rates from €600 (Mamounia) to €6000-plus (Royal Mansour) – but for personal attention and trendsetting Marrakshi style, they can't compete with medina riads and Palmeraie villa guesthouses.

Wherever you go, know that the rates for Marrakesh accommodation are more expensive than anywhere else in Morocco. Prices are continuing to rise, as the value of the dirham fluctuates against the euro, petrol prices make supplies dearer, and the state levies additional taxes on guesthouses. Even so, more travellers are coming back for their second, third and seventh helpings of Marrakshi hospitality.

MEDINA

TOP **CHOICE** / **Riad Al Massarah**   RIAD €€€ (Map p56; ☑0524 38 32 06; www.riadal massarah.com; 26 Derb Jedid; d incl breakfast Dh1200-2000; ❋@🛜🏊) The ultimate feel-good getaway: British-French owners Michel and Michael redesigned this ancient riad to maximise comfort and sunlight, and

minimise electrical and water use. Offers excellent tradition-with-a-twist Marrakesh cuisine, in-house hammam and massages, cooking lessons and spot-on shopping tips – all while donating to a Marrakesh shelter for street children, providing full benefits to a staff of five, and earning environmental distinction as Morocco's first Green Key–certified riad.

TOP **CHOICE** **Tchaikana**   RIAD €€ (Map p60; ☑0524 38 51 50; www.tchai kana.com; 25 Derb el Ferrane, Azbest; d incl breakfast Dh1000-1800; 🛜) With a Tuareg tent-post bed in one room and a boat suspended from the ceiling in another, Tchaikana has the adventurous spirit of a true Marrakesh caravanserai. Travellers plot souq forays over lavish breakfasts hosted by witty English-speaking Belgian owner Jean-Francois, and return at happy hour to compare bargains and plan Sahara eco-adventures. Navigating the winding *derb* is a challenge, but staff can walk you at night, arrange bicycle rentals and make reservations at nearby restaurants.

TOP **CHOICE** **Riad Akka**   RIAD €€€ (Map p60; ☑0524 37 57 67; www.riad-akka.com; 65 Derb Lahbib Magni; d incl breakfast Dh1200-1500; ❋🛜🏊) Arabic sayings about cross-cultural understanding painted around the patio ring true at Akka, where heartfelt hospitality meets worldly chic. Fresh flowers grace graphite-*tadelakt* guest rooms, homemade tarts appear at teatime, and French and Moroccan hosts mingle easily with guests from Australia to Argentina. Luxury amenities include a plunge pool, rooftop lounge, in-house hammam, and in-room wi-fi; proceeds support a local staff of five and a Moroccan women's microcredit association. It's near Rue Riad Zitoun el-Jedid.

Noir d'Ivoire   RIAD €€€ (Map 56; ☑0524 38 09 75; www.noir-d-ivoire. com; 31-33 Derb Jedid, Bab Doukkala; d incl breakfast Dh2000, ste Dh3290-5140; ❋@🛜🏊) Gobsmacking, over-the-top opulence, from its 4.5m foyer chandelier to the grand piano in the courtyard cocktail bar. Silk-draped suites are just the beginning – enjoy Shiatsu and chocolates by the spa fireplace, shop for hand-tailored eveningwear in the boutique and unwind by the water-conserving filtered pool. Don't bother packing: owner/tastemaker Jill Fechtmann supplies every-

R&R WITH B&B: MARRAKESH RIADS

Marrakesh's medina has 200 authentic riads (mudbrick courtyard mansions) converted into guesthouses, more than any other city in North Africa. Step from clamorous souqs through a riad's ancient wooden doors and you'll find yourself listening to songbirds, ice clinking in drinks and your own thoughts – suddenly, Marrakesh's balance of extremes makes perfect sense.

The licensed riads in this chapter have been selected not on looks alone, but for convenient locations, gracious staff, home-cooked meals and prime opportunities for relaxation and cultural immersion. Lonely Planet recommends riads that promote environmentally sustainable practices, fair compensation, time off, community engagement, cultural exchange and genuine Moroccan hospitality. You can help – send your candid riad feedback to talk2us@lonelyplanet.com.

thing you need, from organic beauty products to guest mobile phones.

Riad L'Orangeraie
RIAD $$$

(Map p60; ☏0661 23 87 89; www.riadorangeraie.com; 61 Rue Sidi el-Yamani; d incl breakfast Dh1450-1890; @ 🛜 ☎) Smooth and suave, with perfectly buffed *tadelakt* walls, massaging showers (the best in town), sprawling rooms, and a generous chlorine-free pool (recycled water is used for the garden). This place has all the right moves, with five employees looking after seven rooms, a car and driver on call, excellent breakfasts, soothing hammam treatments, ecofriendly body-care products and a pioneering recycling program.

Riad Ifoulki
RIAD $$

(Map p60; ☏0524 38 56 56; www.riadifoulki.com; 11 Derb Maqadem, Rue Arset Loghzail, Debbachi; d Dh1100-1780, ste Dh1670-3680; ☎) Guests become instant locals at this 300-year-old triple riad in an un-touristy neighbourhood east of Djemaa el-Fna. Rooms here are suites elsewhere, and 74m suites accommodate entire families. Perks include in-house hammam, candlelit massages, workshops on Marrakesh traditions from Sufism to belly-dancing and impromptu concerts from Metropolitan opera-star regulars. Multilingual owner Peter Bergmann moved to Marrakesh 35 years ago, and he's a passionate community advocate – ask about his latest initiative, a *mellah* cultural complex.

Maison Mnabha
DAR $$

(Map p56; ☏0524 38 13 25; www.maisonmnabha.com; 32-33 Derb Mnabha, Kasbah; d incl breakfast Dh830-1150, tr Dh1800; ☀ @) Treasure-hunters will seek out this 17th-century kasbah mansion for adventure, authenticity and fascinating company. Rose petals and candles mark the way to chandelier-lit salons and roof terraces, where celebrity chefs, noted authors and fellow travellers chat over seasonal cocktails and creative canapés. Brothers Peter and Lawrence and manager Aziz offer valuable antiques advice and cultural insights (Peter holds a PhD in kasbah history), and arrange restorative massages, traditional beauty treatments and eco-adventures.

Riad el Borj
RIAD $$

(Map p60; ☏0524 39 12 23; www.riadelborj.com; 63 Derb Moulay Abdelkader; d/ste Dh950/1560; ☀@🛜☎) Once this was Grand Vizier Madani Glaoui's lookout, but now you can lord it over the neighbours in the suite with original *zellij,* double-height ceilings and sky-lit tub, or the tower hideaway with a private terrace. Loaf by the pool in the 'Berber annex', let off steam in the hammam, watch DVDs in the salon or take advantage of mountain excursions. A babysitting service is available, and Djemaa el-Fna is just around the corner.

Dar Attajmil
RIAD $$

(Map p60; ☏0524 42 69 66; www.darattajmil.com; 23 Rue Laksour; d incl breakfast Dh880-1100; ☀🛜) This riad is rosy and relaxed, and you will be too after a few days within these Marrakshi pink *tadelakt* walls near the heart of the souqs. Lucrezia and her attentive staff offer a warm welcome and an even warmer rooftop hammam, plus Moroccan-Italian dinners, cooking classes, *tadelakt* workshops, music concerts, Arabic calligraphy lessons and Essaouira escapes.

Riad Eden
RIAD $

(Map p60; ☏0672 04 69 10; www.riadeden-marrakech.com; 25 Derb Jdid; d incl breakfast Dh500-1000; ☀@🛜) Generous cooks, a homey living room and energetic young French family owners make the Eden, off Rue Riad Zitoun el-Kedim, a magnetic, sociable spot. Pull up

TOP TIPS FOR RIAD BARGAINS

» **Avoid major European holidays** Especially avoid Christmas to New Year, Easter/Passover, and the end of April/first week of May. Low season is summer (mid-June to August) and winter (mid-January to mid-March). Mid-season rates cover most of spring and autumn, and are indicated in this chapter.

» **Make them an offer** Off-season or last-minute, you've got a bargaining advantage: most riads have fewer than 10 guest rooms, and they need to fill rooms to cover operating costs.

» **Stay longer** If you're staying a week or more you might get rates of up to 30% off; those are often posted on riad websites.

» **Bring friends and family** Renting out an entire riad in exclusivity with friends or family is a good deal for everyone; rates usually start around Dh5000/8000 per night in low/high season for up to six rooms and 15 people. Browse riad and villa rentals at www.terremaroc.com, www.riads morocco.com, www.habibihomes.com and www.ilove-marrakech.com.

a chair in the air-conditioned kitchen and watch culinary magic happen. Families prefer the spacious Cannelle room, while couples snag the snug, rooftop Orange room; all rooms are air-conditioned except the naturally cool, ground-floor Berber room.

Riad Magellan
RIAD $$

(Map p60; ☎0661 08 20 42; www.riadmagel lan.com; 62 Derb el Hammam, Mouassine; d incl breakfast Dh770-990) The long and winding *derb* leads to your door at this hip hideaway behind the Mouassine Fountain. English-speaking French owner Philippe has anticipated every world explorer's needs: *tadelakt* hot tub on the terrace, multilingual library stocked with Tintin adventures in the fireplace salon, and deep-tissue massages to soothe away economy-airfare kinks. Antique globes, steamer trunks and rocking chairs add retro flair to sleek *tadelakt* guest rooms strewn with rose petals.

Dar Soukaina
RIAD $$

(Map p56; ☎0661 24 52 38; www.darsoukaina. com; 19 Derb el-Ferrane, Riad Laârouss; s incl breakfast Dh770-970, d Dh970-1300, tr Dh1115-1400; ❋❅) Fraternal twin riads: the first (Dar I) is all soaring ceilings, cosy nooks and graceful archways, while the spacious double-riad extension (Dar II and III) across the *derb* offers sprawling beds, grand patios, a plunge pool and handsome woodwork. Omar keeps both houses running like clockwork and can give you insider tips on Marrakesh. A 20-minute walk from the Djemaa and nearest gate, but near parking on Riad Laarous.

Hotel du Trésor
RIAD $

(Map p60; ☎0524 37 51 13; www.hotel-du-tresor. com; 77 Derb Sidi Bouloukat; s incl breakfast Dh425, d Dh390-525, ste Dh840; ❋❅❅) Not since the Rolling Stones tumbled down these *derbs* has Marrakesh seen such rock-n-roll style. Fourteen rooms flank a cool whitewashed courtyard with chequered tile, a towering orange tree and mod Panton chairs perfect for posing by the large plunge pool. Behind painted doors are walls of vintage mirrors reclaimed from the Mamounia, crystal chandeliers over a red-velvet-padded bed, and in the terrace Blue Suite, a soaking tub and gold-mosaic fireplace. The proprietor is, obviously, Italian; French, Italian, and Spanish are spoken here.

Riad Hanane
RIAD $$

(Map p60; ☎0524 37 77 37; www.dar-hanane.com; 9 Derb Lalla Azzouna, Kaat ben Nahid; d incl breakfast Dh1115-1785; ❋❅) Lounging comes naturally at this chic retreat. Sunny guest rooms have architect-designed details – skylights, book niches, domed bathrooms – and mod cons: iPod docks, safes, hairdryers, Sens de Marrakesh toiletries, free coffee and mineral water. Guests are drawn to the panoramic terrace, honour bar and English- and French-speaking concierge, who arranges car hire, guides and dinners. Located near Ali ben Youssef Medersa, it's a hike to the Djemaa, but worth it.

Les Jardins de Mouassine
RIAD $

(Map p60; ☎0672 58 10 78; www.lesjardinsde mouassine.com; 20 Derb Chorfa el-Kebir; d incl breakfast Dh500-990; ❅❋❅) Hidden behind the souqs off Rue el-Mouassine, a couple of blocks from the Djemaa el-Fna, this double riad offers 20 snug guest rooms and top-notch communal facilities: lounges, library, bar, plunge pool, hammam and a barbecue grill on the vast terrace. Themed rooms highlight Marrakshi artisan specialities – drums, camel bags, children's slippers – and a few have a private terrace. New parents will appreciate that baby beds are free, and massages and mani-pedis are available.

Dar Tayib
RIAD $

(Map p60; ☎0524 38 30 10; www.riad-dartayib. com; 19 Derb Lalla Azzouna; d Dh500-850, ste Dh600-950; ✲) Marrakshi owner Latifa and French architect husband Vincent bring on the Berber charm, from good-luck-symbol carpets to winking tinwork lamps on rustic palm-beamed ceilings. The Yasmina room beats love potions with its canopy bed, tub and mood lighting, while the Aïcha room lifts spirits with windows on the sunny *derb* and a cushy platform bed.

Riad Magi
RIAD $$

(Map p60; ☎053 634230; www.riad-magi.com; 79 Derb Moulay Abdelkader, Derb Debbachi; s/d incl breakfast Dh650/980; ✲☁) Six refreshing rooms in shades of citrus and sky-blue, with *tadelakt* tubs and a well-stocked library. Souqs are just around the corner, but the world seems miles away under orange trees in this serene courtyard. Ask English-speaking manager Abderrazak about onsite cooking classes and restaurants.

Hôtel Sherazade
INN $

(Map p60; ☎0524 42 93 05; www.hotelsherazade. com; 3 Derb Djemaa; s/d Dh180/230, s/d with bathroom Dh220-500, ste 690; ✲) Conversation comes easily in this inn off Riad Zitoun el-Kedim, run by a Moroccan-German family, with 23 rooms, sunny terraces, and a mellow-yellow courtyard with a trickling fountain. Ten rooms have air-con and a couple have slinky *tadelakt* tubs. Terrace rooms are bargains, but you'll want earplugs to sleep through the muezzin's call and the breakfast rush (Dh50 extra). Light sleepers should ask for rooms in the ivy-covered rear courtyard.

Hotel Belleville
DAR $

(Map p60; ☎0524 42 64 81; 194 Riad Zitoun el-Kedim; www.hotelbelleville.ma; s/d/tr/q incl breakfast Dh250/350/500/600; ✲☁) Tucked right behind the Djemaa el-Fna, but with nicer digs and more attentive service than higher-end hotels. What the nine rooms lack in size they make up for in personality: canopy beds, bathrooms with *zellij* fixtures, and roof gardens. Ground-floor rooms have fans, not air-con; request rooms facing the quiet courtyard.

Le Gallia
INN $

(Map p60; ☎0524 44 59 13; fax 0524 44 48 53; www.ilove-marrakesh.com/hotelgallia; 30 Rue de la Recette; s/d/tr Dh320/500/765; ✲) Madcap Djemaa el-Fna is around the corner, but the Gallia maintains the calm and graces of another era with 19 comfortable, air-con/heated rooms with gleaming brass lamps and marble sinks. Get tanned over rooftop breakfasts (Dh40), and chat in stuccoed salons around bougainvillea-bedecked courtyards. Run by the French Galland family since 1929, the Gallia is often packed with repeat visitors; book ahead by fax.

Jnane Mogador
RIAD $

(Map p60; ☎0524 42 63 24; www.jnanemogador.com; 116 Derb Sidi Bouloukat; s/d/tr/q Dh360/480/580/660; ◉) A 19th-century riad with 21st-century amenities: a prime location off Rue Riad Zitoun el-Kedim, in-house hammam, tea salon, double-decker roof terraces and owner Mohammed's laid-back hospitality. A favourite with visiting diplomats and artists; book well ahead and enjoy fascinating conversation over breakfast (Dh40). Ask for quieter, airier upper-floor rooms.

Riad Julia
RIAD $

(Map p60; ☎0524 37 60 22; www.riadjulia.com; 14 Derb Halfaoui; d incl breakfast Dh600-800, tr Dh800; ✲☁☀) Each room pays tribute to a Marrakesh handicraft, from mother-of-pearl inlay to chip-carved cedar wood. Five of seven comfy rooms have air-con; all have soft bathrobes and bright Berber wedding blankets. There's a small plunge pool and TV in the salon, and English-speaking Ziad arranges excursions, babysitting services, henna tattooing, and candlelit dinners.

Hotel Essaouira
INN $

(Map p60; ☎0524 44 38 05; www.jnanemogador.com/hotelessaouira-marrakech.htm; 3 Derb Sidi Bouloukat; s/d with shared bathroom Dh50/100, r with private bathroom Dh400, mattress on roof Dh30) Quite the colourful character, this family home was converted to a 28-room hotel back in the 1960s, and psychedelic painted-wood ceilings and polychrome stucco may induce flashbacks. A tiny spiral staircase leads to a sociable roof terrace, where breakfast (Dh22 to Dh40) comes with glimpses of the Koutoubia.

Hôtel Central Palace
HOTEL $

(Map p60; ☎0524 44 02 35; www.lecentralpalace.com; 59 Derb Sidi Bouloukat; d with shared bathroom Dh155, with private bathroom Dh255-

305, ste Dh405; ❋) Surprisingly stately, with 40 clean rooms climbing four floors around a courtyard fountain, and breakfasts (Dh25) on the roof terrace. Wrought-iron beds and stained-glass windows cheer somewhat dim rooms; 1st-floor rooms are cooler, while suites are slightly bigger air-conditioned rooms.

Hôtel de Foucauld
HOTEL $

(Map p60; ☑024 440806; Ave el-Mouahidine; s/d Dh215/280; ❋) One block from the Djemaa el-Fna, Foucauld offers tiled, backpack-scuffed rooms with teensy private bathrooms and a reliable restaurant at the right price. Consult trekkers and bikers converging on the buffet breakfast (Dh30) about High Atlas conditions, request rooms with balconies overlooking Pl Foucauld, and bring earplugs for 5am calls to prayer from the Koutoubia next door.

VILLE NOUVELLE

Many medina riads offer 'only in Marrakesh' experiences at reasonable rates, unlike most generic, overpriced ville-nouvelle hotels. That said, ville-nouvelle hotels are handier if you're passing through town quickly, seeking disabled-accessible accommodation, or visiting in high season.

Several ville-nouvelle budget hotels are neon-signed in Guéliz; best options are listed below. Search online for deals, since midrange hotels can be bargains when booked as part of a holiday package.

To taste some Marrakesh luxury without the bitter aftertaste of multi-digit guest-room bills, go for drinks, dinner or a day pass at the Mamounia hotel (p71), the grande dame of North African hotels that has just undergone a multimillion-euro facelift.

Bab Hotel
BOUTIQUE HOTEL $$$

(Map p62; ☑0524 43 52 50; www.babhotelmar rakech.com; cnr Rue Mohammed el-Beqal & Blvd Mohamed ed-Dahbi; d incl breakfast Dh1115-1450, ste from Dh2010; ❋☎☒) Upscale boutique hotels are new to Marrakesh, but the Bab Hotel may set a trend. Marrakesh's first boutique hotel is like sleeping in an iPod, with minimalist all-white rooms and a giant white apple at the entry. Deluxe rooms have tubs, Nespresso machines, and movie channels on flat-screen TVs; suites echo. Of the many amenities – spa, library, parking, bicycles, cars with drivers – the chill-out lounges are the coolest (p84).

Hôtel Toulousain
INN $

(Map p62; ☑0524 43 00 33; http://hoteltoulou sain.com; 44 Rue Tariq ibn Ziyad; s/d with shared bathroom incl breakfast Dh140/190, d Dh230-280; ☎) An easygoing budget hotel run by a kindly Moroccan-American family in a prime Guéliz location, with tasty restaurants, boutiques, laundry, local travel agency and a literary cafe right at your doorstep. Book ahead for private bathrooms, or spacious, cheerful 1st-floor guest rooms with classic blue *beldi* (country-style) tile. When upstairs rooms get stuffy, guests hang out on patios under banana trees.

Hôtel du Pacha
HOTEL $

(Map p62; ☑0524 43 13 27; www.hotelpacha. net; 33 Rue de la Liberté; s/d Dh320/400; ❋) Novels beg to be set in this period-piece colonial hotel, with tall French windows to catch breezes and neighbourhood gossip. Ground-floor rooms are smartly renovated with marble sinks and dark woodwork, but upstairs rooms have art-deco tile and turquoise bathtubs. The shadowy stuccoed entry, hidden courtyard, and salon club chairs add *noir*-novel intrigue.

Caspien
HOTEL $

(Map p62; ☑0524 42 22 82; www.lecaspien-hotel. com; 12 Rue Loubnane; s/d Dh460/580; ❋☎☒) In a quiet Guéliz location near boutiques, spas and restaurants, the Caspien is cosy and personable. Pointed archways, *zellij* floors, pierced-brass lamps and balconies add Marrakesh atmosphere. For maximum quiet, choose upper-floor rooms overlooking the pool, well above the restaurant and piano bar.

PALMERAIE & OUTSKIRTS

When the medina seems a bit much, villas in the Palmeraie let you chill out in a palm oasis. Once your blood pressure dips and you begin to miss the madness of Marrakesh, you're within a 30-minute drive from the heart of the action. A taxi into town is the easiest way, but is rather costly (Dh150 to DH250) since you often have to pay for the driver's round-trip to fetch you.

TOP CHOICE Jnane Tamsna
RESORT $$$

(☑0524 32 94 23; www.jnanetamsna. com; Douar Abiad, Palmeraie; d incl breakfast from Dh2730, ste from Dh3700; ❋@☒) A-list celebrities (Brad Pitt, Giorgio Armani, David Bowie) flock to this North African nirvana with cloistered patios, reading nooks and sunny terraces amid 9 hectares of

WHERE TO STAY WITH KIDS

Fair warning: riad plunge pools and steep stairs aren't exactly child-proof, and sound reverberates through riad courtyards. Most riad owners and staff dote on babies, but the same can't always be said of sleep-deprived fellow guests giving you the evil eye over breakfast. But bringing the kids doesn't mean you have to settle for a generic hotel. Standout accommodation for families in Marrakesh include the following.

» **Les Jardins de Mouassine** (p76) Central Medina location, plunge pool, free baby beds.

» **Riad Bledna** (p79) Toys, board games, pool, walled garden estate outside Marrakesh.

» **Hôtel Toulousain** (p78) Strollers, kids in residence, convenient locale – pizza, cafes, laundry, pharmacy and hammam within one block.

» **Riad Eden** (p75) Family rooms, central medina location, board games, kids' meals on request.

» **Riad Julia** (p77) Babysitting, plunge pool, extra beds, located in medina near taxi stop.

» **Les Deux Tours** (p79) Pool, hammam, suites with separate rooms for parents and independent-minded kids in a plush Palmeraie resort.

organic gardens. Sustainability meets style at Meryanne Loum-Martin's oasis of water-conserving plants, filtered pools, all-organic cuisine, fair-trade design gallery and cultural immersion **Diversity Excursions** (www.diversity-excursions.co.uk) organised by her English ethnobotanist husband, Gary Martin, founder of the Global Diversity Foundation. Book ahead for excursions, cooking classes, yoga retreats and literary salons with Booker Prize winners.

TOP CHOICE **La Pause** RESORT $$
(☎0661 30 64 94; www.lapause-marrakech.com; Douar Lmih Laroussiéne, Agafay Desert; d half-board from Dh1100; ☎) Skip off the grid to a desert getaway 45 minutes from Marrakesh (chauffeured transport to/from Marrakesh provided). Days are spent playing turf-free golf or disc golf using available

clubs or Frisbees, or hanging out in hammocks under olive trees by the filtered pool. Ride off into the sunset on mountain bikes, Arabian stallions, donkeys or dromedaries, and return to candlelit organic feasts. Sleep in generous Berber tents with foam mattresses, thick carpets and open-air showers, or read by firelight in your own minimalist-chic, solar-powered abode.

Les Deux Tours RESORT $$$
(☎0524 32 95 25; www.les-deuxtours.com; Douar Abiad, Circuit de la Palmeraie; d incl breakfast from Dh1800, ste from Dh2320; ☀@☎☎) Tunisian architect Charles Boccara's deliciously decadent oasis resort started the Palmeraie villa trend – but few of its cookie-cutter neighbours can match its amenities, distinctive modern style, and attentive new management. Hidden passageways lead to cushy guest rooms with four-poster beds, fireplaces and French doors that open onto private terraces and plunge pools. Cocooning guests emerge for candlelit Mediterranean meals, deluxe hammam treatments (Dh1450 for four hours) and poolside cocktails.

Riad Bledna MAISON D'HÔTE $
(☎0661 18 20 90; www.riadbledna.com; 2km on Rte de Ouarzazate; d incl breakfast Dh600-800; ☎) Welcome home to the garden villa of the Moroccan-British Nour family, who pamper visitors like favourite house guests, urging them to relax by the filtered pool, enjoy more quail and apricot tajine, and sip more fresh-squeezed juice (made with organic fruit from their 4-acre gardens). Airport transfers and daily transit to/from the medina are included in the rates, and your hosts can arrange babysitting, desert trips, mountain eco-excursions, and hands-on Moroccan crafts workshops for adults and kids alike.

Eating

Slow-roasted lamb cooked in a hammam, roasted-eggplant caviar, hearty white bean soup...Marrakesh's traditional specialities are mouth-watering. The least thrilling part of the Marrakesh dining experience is the arrival of the bill. Marrakshis don't eat out often, and with Dh65-80 for a scrawny chicken tajine on the Djemaa and set-price restaurant menus starting at Dh300-plus, you can see why.

Good-value restaurants can be found, especially in the ville nouvelle, but if you're staying at a riad, home cooking is an attractive option. Many riad chefs are *dadas* who once cooked for Marrakesh's high society, so the meals you enjoy on your riad terrace may be truly royal.

MEDINA

TOP Mechoui Alley   LOCAL $
CHOICE (Map p60; east side of Souq Ablueh; 0.25kg lamb with bread Dh30-50; ☺11am-2pm) Just before noon, the vendors at this row of stalls start carving up steaming sides of *mechoui* (slow-roasted lamb), as though expecting King Henry VIII for lunch. Point to the best-looking cut of meat, and ask for a *nuss* (half) or *rubb* (quarter) kilo. The cook will hack off falling-off-the-bone lamb and hand it to you with fresh-baked bread, cumin, salt and olives in a takeaway baggie, or serve it to you on paper in a nearby stall – no linens necessary to make this a proper feast.

TOP Mama Tilee   FUSION $$
CHOICE (Map p60; ☏0524 38 17 52; www.mama tilee.blogspot.com; 13 Derb Laarsa; 3-course prix fixe Dh220; ☺7.30-11pm Mon-Sat) The restaurant every chef dreams of opening is tucked around the corner from Dar Si Said, off Riad Zitoun el-Jedid, in Marrakesh. Chef Cecile's intimate riad restaurant seats 22 on three floors artfully arranged with red cushions, custom leather carpets and bistro tables. Each course features local, organic ingredients and offers one choice: mango gazpacho or foie gras with fig? Sole roulade with kaffir lime or steak rubbed with High Atlas herbs? Passionfruit crème brûlée or Moroccan mint and chocolate macaroons? Reserve by phone in the afternoon; cash only, alcohol licence pending.

TOP Villa Flore   MEDITERRANEAN $$
CHOICE (Map p60; ☏0524 39 17 00; www.villa -flore.com; 4 Derb Azzouz, Mouassine; mains Dh80-150; ☺12.30-3pm & 7.30-11pm Wed-Mon) Dine in an art-deco-fabulous, black-and-white riad on reinvented Moroccan salads and aromatic, meltingly tender lamb and duck, all presented with flair by stylishly suited waiters. Pull up a sofa near the French doors or sit in the sunny courtyard and unwind with a glass of wine, right in the heart of the souqs.

Souk Kafé   LOCAL $
(Map p60; ☏0662 61 02 29; 11 Derb Souk Jedid, near Rue Riad Laaroussa; mains Dh65-80; ☺9am-9pm; ✷☛) Pull up a hand-hewn stool under terrace sun umbrellas and stay awhile: this is authentic local food worth savouring. The Moroccan *mezze* of six savoury, cooked veg-

etable dishes qualifies as lunch for two, and the vegetarian Berber couscous is surprisingly hearty – but wait until you get a whiff of the aromatic Marrakshi *tanjia*, beef that flakes apart after slow-cooking in a hammam across the street.

Dar Moha   LOCAL, FUSION $$$
(Map p60; ☏0524 38 64 00; www.darmoha.ma; 81 Rue Dar el-Bacha; prix-fixe lunch Dh220, dinner Dh550; noon-3pm & 7.30pm-midnight Tue-Sun) Mohamed Fedal is Morocco's foremost celebrity chef, giving tastebuds a tweak with updated Moroccan classics: quail in a flaky *warqa* pastry nest, foie-gras and arganoil couscous, melon 'couscous' with thyme honey. Lately you're as likely to catch Chef Moha in action on YouTube as in the kitchen – but lunch by the pool is a worthy feast, with orange-flower-scented cucumbers and spice-rubbed grilled lamb chops (wine is additional).

Un Dejeuner á Marrakesh
   MEDITERRANEAN, SANDWICH SHOP $
(Map p60; ☏0524 37 83 87; 2-4 Rue Kennaria, cnr Rue Riad Zitoun el-Jedid; mains from Dh60; ☺9am-5pm; ☛) Come early, or forfeit just-baked quiche of the day with asparagus to ravenous vegetarians. Omnivores practically pig out on decadent *croque monsieur* made with turkey ham, served with a tangy side salad. Ground-floor booths are comfy and quick; the tented terrace has pillows, Koutoubia views and leisurely service.

Terrasse des Épices   LOCAL, MEDITERRANEAN $$
(Map p60; ☏0524 37 59 04; 15 Souq Cherifia; www.terrassedesepices.com; mains from Dh75; ☺noon-11pm) Follow the basket bubble-lamps to lunch on top of the souqs in a mudbrick *bhou* (booth) off Rue Dar el-Bacha. Check the chalkboard for daily à la carte specials, such as dinner-sized Caesar salads, traditional pigeon *pastilla*, and vegetarian aubergine pasta with thyme. Save room for house-specialty chocolate *pastilla*: layers of *warqa* pastry, apricots, prunes and almonds smothered in chocolate. Reserve ahead in high season; cards accepted; no alcohol.

Marrakech Korner   LOCAL $
(Map 56; ☏0524 38 99 27; 93 Arset Aouzal; www. marrakechkorner.over-blog.com; mains from Dh55; ☺11am-10.30pm; ☎) Finally, an à la carte menu that's easy on the wallet and kind to the tastebuds. Head to the rooftop for a *merguez* sausage sandwich or garlicky courgette salad, or hang out in the primary-coloured salon for restorative vervain tea

infusions and free wi-fi. Unless you have a Moroccan grandma, this is the place to go for Friday couscous, properly fluffy and infused with fragrant *smen* (seasoned butter). It's near Rue Dar el-Bacha.

Tobsil
LOCAL $$$

(Map p60; ☑0524 44 40 52; 22 Derb Abdellah ben Hessaien; 5-course menu incl wine Dh600; ☺7.30-11pm Wed-Mon) In this intimate riad near Bab Ksour, 50 guests max indulge in button-popping, five-course Moroccan menus with aperitifs and wine pairings, as Gnawa musicians strum quietly in the courtyard. No excess glitz or belly dancers distract from noble attempts to finish 11 salads, *pastilla*, tajines (yes, that's plural) and couscous, capped with mint tea, fresh fruit and Moroccan pastries. Booking required.

Dar Mimoun
LOCAL $$

(Map p60; ☑0524 44 33 48; 1 Derb ben Amrane, cnr Rue Riad Zitoun el-Kedim; mains from Dh80; ☺noon-11pm) Stagger in from the souqs and feel instantly revived in an arcaded courtyard restaurant that's all soothing greenery, blue and white *zellij*, and tantalising aromas of classic chicken, prune and almond tajine. Get yours à la carte or as part of a Dh130 set menu with salads, tea and sweets, served in the garden or cupola-capped dining alcoves.

Chegrouni
LOCAL $

(Map p60; Djemaa el-Fna; tajine Dh60-70, omelette Dh25-35; ☺8am 11pm; ☑) You're expected to write down your own order, but your server could probably guess it anyway: you're either a foodie here for the classic Dh60 tajine with chicken, preserved lemons and olives; a vegetarian in for flavourful vegetable-broth-only, seven-vegetable couscous; or a tajine-weary traveller in dire need of a decent omelette with superior chips. It's near Rue des Banques.

Haj Mustapha
LOCAL $

(Map p60; east side, Souq Ablueh; tanjia with bread & olives Dh35-50; ☺6-10pm) As dusk approaches, several stalls set out paper-sealed crockpots of *tanjia*. This 'bachelor's stew' makes for messy eating, but Haj Mustapha offers the cleanest seating inside a well-scuffed stall. Use bread as your utensil to scoop up *tanjia*, sprinkle with cumin and salt, and chase with olives.

Café des Épices
CAFE, SANDWICH SHOP $

(Map p60; ☑0254 39 17 70; Pl Rahba Kedima; breakfast Dh25, sandwich or salad Dh25-50; ☺8am-9pm) Watch the magic happen as you sip freshly squeezed OJ overlooking the Rahba Kedima potion dealers. Salads and sandwiches are fresh and made to order – try the tangy chicken spiked with herbs, nutmeg and olives – and service is surprisingly efficient, given the steep stairs.

Le Foundouk
FUSION $$$

(Map p60; ☑0524 37 81 90; www.foundouk. com; 55 Souq el-Fassi; mains Dh90-160; ☺noon-midnight Tue-Sun) Like a prop from a Tim Burton movie, a spidery iron chandelier lit with candles sets the mood for offbeat à la carte choices, including beef with wild artichoke and orange-carrot soup. When the food lives up to the decor, it's fabulous, and when not, well, at least you got your money's worth for atmosphere. Terrace seating is scenic but sometimes windy; book ahead for downstairs *bhous* (seating nooks), or take walk-in seating in the plush, fully stocked bar. It's near Ali ben Youssef Medersa.

Ryad Jama
LOCAL $

(Map p60; ☑0524 42 98 72; 149 Toualat Kennaria; mains Dh40-70; ☺11am-9.30pm) À la carte meals at realistic prices served in a family-run riad restaurant. Fragrant preserved lemon and lamb tajines with crusty French bread are graciously presented in the leafy, candlelit garden for only slightly more than you'd pay for a skimpy version shoved your way in a dusty Djemaa cafe.

Dar TimTam
LOCAL $$

(Map p60; ☑024 391446; Zinkat Rahba; meals Dh95-250; ☺11.30am-4pm; ☑) Head through the rug shop under the sign and hang a right into this 18th-century riad's innermost courtyard, where you can take your pick of cushioned nooks and the à la carte menu (you may have to request it). Some menu items are inexplicably overpriced (Dh200 *tanjia* for example), but a rejuvenating mint tea and a generous assortment of eight Moroccan salads (Dh95) makes a fine light lunch amid the songbirds near the Rahba Kedima.

Earth Café
FUSION, VEGETARIAN $

(Map p60; ☑0661 28 94 02; 2 Derb Zouak; mains Dh60-80; ☺11am-11pm; ☑) Now for something completely different: a vegetarian spring roll stuffed with organic spinach, pumpkin, blue cheese and grated carrot with a sesame dressing, right in the heart of the souqs off Rue Riad Zitoun el-Kedim. The Earth Café's sunshine-yellow courtyard is small, but its veggie culinary ambitions are great – the warm beet salad with goat cheese may make believers out of carnivores. The name may sound familiar, because Earth Café's advertisements were recently scrawled on geological formations across the High Atlas – but since customers pointed out this wasn't the most earth-friendly move, management has begun removing the grafitti ads.

Nid'Cigogne
LOCAL/SANDWICH SHOP $

(Map p56; ☎0524 38 20 92; 60 Place des Tombeaux Saadiens; meals Dh45-85; ☺9am-9pm) Get up close and personal with the storks across the way at the Saadian Tombs in this rooftop eatery. The grilled *kefta* (meatball) sandwiches, light salads and tajines are passable, but the view is memorable and service pleasant.

Pâtisserie des Princes
PATISSERIE $

(Map p60; ☎0524 44 30 33; 32 Rue Bab Agnaou; ☺9am-9pm; ✦) This is one of the city's most famous patisseries, with enough pain-au-chocolat, petit fours, almond cookies and ice cream to keep Djemaa el-Fna dentists in business. The small cafe at the back is a welcome respite for women, or anyone in search of a quiet coffee; tea for two with sweets runs to Dh50.

Restaurant Place Ferblantiers
LOCAL $

(Map p60; west entrance Pl des Ferblantiers; tajines Dh45-65; ☺lunch) Plop down on a plastic chair in the courtyard, and have whatever's bubbling away and well-caramelised on the burner. The meat and produce are fresh from the Mellah Market across the street, and the chef whips up dishes in front of you.

Fast Food Alahbab
SANDWICH SHOP, FAST FOOD $

(Map p60; Rue de Bab Agnaou; salads Dh15-25, sandwiches Dh20-30; ☺7am-11pm) The awning boasting 'recommended by Lonely Planet' must be decades old now, and still we stand by our initial assessment of the Dh35 *shwarma* accompanied by four sauces and just-right French fries, with great people-watching at communal sidewalk tables.

VILLE NOUVELLE

TOP CHOICE **Al-Fassia**
LOCAL $$

Guéliz (Map p62; ☎024 434060; 55 Blvd Mohammed Zerktouni, mains Dh120-180; ☺noon-10.30pm Wed-Sun; ✦); Zone Touristique de l'Aguedal (Al Fassia Aguedal; ☎024 383839; www.alfassia-aguedal.com; MH 9 Bis, Route de l'Ourika) Glassy-eyed diners valiantly grip morsels of bread, scraping the last savoury caramelised onion from what was once a Berber pumpkin and lamb tajine. The *mezze* of nine

starters alone is a proper feast, but there's no resisting the classic mains perfected over a decade by the Marrakshi sisters who own the place – especially when each dish is presented with a heartfelt *B'saha!* (to your health). Book ahead for the Guéliz location, which is cosier and more convenient.

TOP CHOICE **Plats Haj Boujemaa**
LOCAL $

(Map p62; ☎25 Rue ibn Aicha; Dh35-75; ☺noon-10pm Tue-Sun) Grab a tidy booth or hold out for courtyard seating in back, and try to save some spicy olives and warm bread for the parade of grilled meats that's coming. If you're feeling adventurous, this is the place to try offal, correctly cleaned and prepared – though even when properly cooked until golden, sheep's testicles have a floury texture, not to mention stringy bits that stick in your teeth. That said, the chips are fantastic, and steak well-marinated.

Le Chat Qui Rit
ITALIAN $$

(Map p62; ☎0524 43 43 11; 92 Rue de Yougoslavie; pizzas Dh50-80, set menu Dh150; ☺7.30-11pm Tue-Sun; ✦) Come here for proper pasta: al dente, tossed with fresh produce and herbs, and drizzled with fruity olive oil. Corsican chef/owner Bernard comes out to ask about everyone's pasta with the delight of a chef who already knows the answer. Seasonal seafood options are a good bet, with fixings just in from the coast daily.

L'Annexe
FRENCH $$

(Map p62; ☎0524 43 40 10; www.lannexemarrakech.com; 14 Rue Moulay Ali; mains Dh100-140; ☺noon-3.30pm Sun-Fri, 7-11pm Mon-Sat; ☎) French lunches in a mirrored cafe-bistro setting, handy to all the ville-nouvelle boutique action. A welcome switch to light, clean flavours after the umpteenth tajine: Provencale fish soup, *duck confit* (duck slowly cooked in its own fat) atop salad, and a mean crème brûlée.

Samak al-Bahriya
LOCAL $

(Map p62; 75 Ave Moulay Rachid, cnr Rue Mauritanie; seafood with chips Dh30-80; ☺10am-midnight) The best option along this stretch of sidewalk stalls, al-Bahriya serves fresh fish and perfectly tender fried calamari with generous chunks of lemon, plus salt, cumin, and hot sauce.

Azar
MIDDLE EASTERN $$

(Map p62; ☎0524 43 09 20; www.azarmarrakech.com; cnr Ave Hassan II & Rue de Yougoslavie; mains Dh120-170; ☺noon-3pm & 7pm-midnight; ✦♪) Imagine a Beirut lounge teleported to Marrakesh via Mars, and here you have it. With space-captain chairs and star-patterned stucco walls, the decor is out of this world – and the Lebanese-inspired fare isn't far behind. Authenticity sticklers will appreciate the shish *taouk* (plump marinated chicken cubes), and though they may want more lemon in the hummus, shared *mezze* with Dh50 glasses of wine keep vegetarians happy and bills in this stratosphere.

Grand Café de la Poste   MEDITERRANEAN **$$$**
(Map p62; ☎0524 43 30 38; www.grandcafe delaposte.com; Blvd Mohamed ed-Dahbi, cnr Ave Imam Malik; starters Dh75-120, mains Dh120-190; ☺8am-1am; ✱) Recently restored to its flapper-era, potted-palm glory, this landmark bistro delivers swanky comfort and a seared beef tartare to write home about just behind the main post office. Prices run high for dinner, and service can be agonisingly slow – but during the 6pm to 8pm happy hour, a parade of appetisers are offered with drinks, and the wine list is the best in town.

Beyrouth   MIDDLE EASTERN **$**
(Map p62; ☎0524 42 35 25; 9 Rue Loubnane; mains Dh80-160; ☺noon-3pm & 7-11pm; ✱🍴) Bright, lemony Lebanese flavours, with a mix-and-match *mezze* that's a feast for two with tabouli, spinach pies and felafel for Dh160 – and a welcome switch from seven-vegetable couscous for vegetarians. The smoky, silky *baba ghanoush* (eggplant dip) here gives Moroccan eggplant caviar serious competition for the best Middle Eastern spread.

Café du Livre   CAFE **$**
(Map p62; ☎0524 43 21 49; 44 Rue Tariq ibn Ziyad; www.cafedulivre.com; dishes Dh55-90; ☺9.30am-9pm Mon-Sat; ✱🛜🍴) A bookish beauty, with walls of used books in English and French to browse, board games, cushy seating, quiz nights and poetry readings, plus free wi-fi and tasty salads.

Café 16   PATISSERIE **$**
(Map p62; ☎0524 33 96 70; 18 Pl du 16 Novembre; desserts Dh20-50; ☺9am-12am) The blonde-wood decor and the prices may seem European, but the welcome is Marrakshi and so are intriguing ice-cream flavours like mint tea and *kaab el-gazelle* (almond cookie). Light lunches and salads are available, if only to justify homemade, gold-leafed chocolate-coffee cream cake and raspberry-mousse cake afterwards.

Catanzaro   ITALIAN **$**
(Map p62; ☎0524 43 37 31; 42 Rue Tariq ibn Ziyad; pizzas or pasta Dh60-80, mains Dh80-120; ☺noon-2.30pm & 7.15-11pm Mon-Sat; ✱) Where are we, exactly? The thin-crust, wood-fired pizza says Italy, the wooden balcony and powerful air-con suggest the Alps, but the spicy condiments and spicier clientele are definitely mid-town Marrakesh. Grilled meat dishes are juicy and generous, but the Neapolitan pizza with capers, local olives and Atlantic anchovies steals the show.

Self-Catering

For a solid selection of fresh produce, dried fruits and nuts, try the **Marché Municipale ibn Toumert** (Map p62; Rue ibn Toumert), off Ave Mohammed V. The souqs are also filled with food stalls selling olives, dates and sweets, and carts loaded with fruit and vegetables; prices are better in the Bab Doukkala food souq than right off the Djemaa.

For staples such as cheese, cereal and alcohol (often difficult to find elsewhere) plus speciality items, a few supermarkets in the ville nouvelle are useful.

ACIMA supermarket   FOOD & DRINK
Guéliz (Map p62; cnr Aves Mohammed V & Mohammed Abdelkrim el-Khattabi); Jardin Majorelle (Ave Yacoub el-Mansour)

Aswak Assalam   FOOD & DRINK
(Map p56; Ave du 11 Janvier, Bab Doukkala)

Carrefour   FOOD & DRINK
(Al-Mazar Mall, Route d'Ourika, Aguedal)

Marjane   FOOD & DRINK
(Km4, Casablanca road, Palmeraie)

🍷 Drinking

As with elsewhere in Morocco, traditional bars in Marrakesh are mostly frequented by men, with a few shady types (men and women alike) in tight, revealing clothing trolling for trade at the bar. Trendy lounge bars are more accommodating and appealing for women, as are restaurant-bars that turn into party places later at night, such as Le Foundouk and Grand Café de la Poste. Most cafes are strictly for coffee, tea and sweets; for alcohol, try bars, restaurants or clubs.

TOP CHOICE **Dar Cherifa**   CAFE
(Map p60; ☎0524 42 64 63; 8 Derb Chorfa Lakbir; tea & coffee Dh20-25; ☺noon-7pm) Revive souq-sore eyes at this serene late-15th-century Saadian riad near Rue el-Mouassine, where tea and saffron coffee are

MARRAKESH & CENTRAL MOROCCO MARRAKESH

Cocktails: Get Creative

Since Morocco is a Muslim country, mixology remains an emerging art. James Bond and other cocktail sticklers head to Piano Bar Les Jardins de la Koutoubia for properly powerful gin drinks, garnished with a rose for your lapel. Marrakesh specialises in classics with twists – mojitos with bourbon and champagne at Mamounia's Churchill Bar – and creative breakthroughs like the Jack Is Back, made with gin or vodka, kaffir lime, fresh ginger and fig puree at the Bab Hotel Pool Lounge & SkyBab.

Beer: No Bargains

Flag and Casablanca are the two local brands: 'Casa' is crisply innocuous, while Flag has a herbal aftertaste. Heineken may cost about the same as Casa or Flag – around Dh25 to Dh60, with the cheapest at Bar du Grand Tazi. Beer almost always comes bottled, not on tap.

Wine: Drink Locally

Volubilis and Meknès are key growing regions for Moroccan reds, but due to heat stability issues in transit, coastal gris, rosé and crisp whites from nearby Essaouira are safer bets. Many Marrakesh bars feature wine by the glass for Dh50 to Dh80, as well as bottles of the well-priced Ferme Rouge line from coastal vineyards. You'll also find lower-end French and Spanish wines – possibly the same brand imbibed on the airline flight here, at a considerable mark-up. For imported and Moroccan wines at realistic prices, head to **L'Atelier du Vin** ([🖉0524 45 71 12; 87 Rue Mohamed el-Beqal; ⊗9.30am-1pm & 3.30-8pm Tue-Thu & Sat, 2.30-8pm Mon, 9.30am-12.30pm & 3.30-8pm Fri); check the store's Facebook page for wine-tasting events.

---

served with contemporary art and literature downstairs, or terrace views upstairs.

⌜TOP⌐ **Bab Hotel Pool Lounge &**
⌞CHOICE⌟ **SkyBab** BAR
(Map p62; 🖉0524 43 52 50; www.babhotelmar rakech.com; Rue Mohammed el-Beqal, cnr Blvd Mohamed ed-Dahbi) Up or down? Either way, you can't go wrong for creative cocktails in splashy settings. SkyBab offers rooftop sunsets, red carpets and Red City (vodka, lemon and pomegranate); the Pool Lounge showcases the refreshing Jack Is Back, original art, Marrakshi lady DJs rocking chillout sets and rainbow poufs crafted from recycled plastic bags.

Churchill Bar BAR
(Map p56; 🖉0524 38 86 00; www.mamounia.com; Ave Bab Jedid; ⊗6pm-1am; ❋) Opinion remains divided over the Mamounia's recent restoration and its estimated €120 million price tag, but critics agree: such weighty matters are best discussed over drinks in the Churchill Bar. The bar named for the Mamounia regular and sometime head of state retains its speakeasy appeal, with padded fuchsia leather walls, wood panelling, and splashy

leopard print. Call ahead to book, dress to impress strict doormen, and go retro with 20-year-old Scotch or flapper-favourite Mamoune Lady: gin, lemon, and orange-flower water. At about €20 per cocktail, let heads of state buy the first round.

Kosybar BAR
(Map p60; 🖉0524 38 03 24; http://kozibar.tripod. com; 47 Pl des Ferblantiers; ⊗noon-1am; ❋) The Marrakesh-meets-Kyoto interiors are full of plush, private nooks, but keep heading upstairs to low-slung canvas sofas and Dh40 to Dh60 wine by the glass on the rooftop terrace. At the aptly named Kosybar you can enjoy drinks with a side of samba as storks give you the once-over from nearby nests; skip the cardboard-tasting sushi and stick with bar snacks.

Piano Bar Les Jardins de la
Koutoubia BAR
(Map p60; 🖉024 388800; www.lesjardinsdelakou toubia.com; Les Jardins de la Koutoubia Hotel, 26 Rue de la Koutoubia; entry with drink free; ⊗5pm-1am) Step from the red Berber carpet into the classiest gin joint in Marrakesh, with powerful long drinks (Dh70 to Dh90) de-

livered to leather club chairs as jazz classics soar to carved cedar ceilings. A second plush seating area behind the reflecting pool makes a serene escape for nonsmokers and jazz-avoiders, and the terrace restaurant serves a decent Indian curry quite late.

Café Arabe
CAFE/BAR

(Map p60; ☎0524 42 97 28; www.cafearabe.com; 184 Rue el-Mouassine; ☺10am-midnight; ✸) Gloat over souq purchases with cocktails on rooftop sofas at sunset, or a glass of wine next to the Zen-*zellij* courtyard fountain. The pasta is bland, but *merguez* tajines are tasty and Caesar salads loaded with anchovies and real Parmesan, and wine prices are down to earth for such a stylish perch.

Le Melting Pot
CAFE

(Map p62; ☎0524 45 77 73; Rue de Yougoslavie; ☺9am-9pm; ✸☏) With rotating local art shows, a strong wi-fi signal, hand-chiselled sunburst stucco walls, and espresso to revive the dead, Le Melting Pot is a smart, modern, and thoroughly Marrakshi cafe. Service is attentive but not intrusive, and quite correct in boasting about their Nutella crepes. It's near the tourist office.

Kechmara
CAFE, BAR

(Map p62; ☎0524 42 25 32; 3 Rue de La Liberté; ☺8am-midnight; ✸) Pull up a Saarinen tulip chair and stay awhile with a hip Marrakshi crowd, local art, groovy music and a low-key cocktail bar on the silvery *tadelakt* terrace. Come after trawling local boutiques for a fashionably late lunch, and stick around for sunsets, Dh65 to Dh90 cocktails and DJs or live music.

Coffee Marrak'chic
CAFE, BAR

(Map p62; ☎0644 49 79 91; Residence al-Morad, Ave Mohammed V; ☺noon-midnight; ✸) Stay cool and look cooler under canvas canopies ideal for people-watching along downtown sidewalks. Brunches here are straight out of *Sex in the City,* with bagels, bacon, pancakes and champagne cocktails, but nights here are pure Marrakesh, thanks to house-special Morocco martinis (vodka, mint and green tea extract) and rosy backlighting.

Bar du Grand Tazi
PUB

(Map p60; ☎0524 44 27 87; cnr Ave el-Mouahidine & Rue de Bab Agnaou; ☺7pm-1am) Raucous but not sleazy, serving Dh25 local beer to throngs of travellers and Marrakshis just off work in the souqs. Grab a wooden chair in the scuffed hotel lobby bar for football matches on a large flat-screen TV, and tales that grow increasingly outrageous as the night wears on.

Yellow Submarine
BAR

(Map p62; ☎0672 56 98 64; www.yellowsub-mara kech.com; 82 Ave Hassan II; ☺7pm-1am) Back in Marrakesh's hippie heyday, the streets were positively littered with Rolling Stones and Beatles – and this lounge-bar intends to revive those glory days with wall-to-wall psychedelic murals, aglow with submarine-shaped lights. Some anachronisms boggle the mind – such as the portrait of Al Pacino as Scarface near the slogan 'All You Need Is Love' – but have another Cuba Libre and go along for the ride.

☆ Entertainment

Nightclubs

Sleeping is overrated in a city where the nightlife begins around midnight. Most of the hottest clubs are in the Hivernage, or in the fast-expanding city suburb along Blvd Mohammed VI known as Zone Aguedal. Admissions range from Dh150 to Dh350 including the first drink, but those who arrive early and dressed smartly midweek may get in free (especially women). Taxis back from out-of-town clubs like Pacha are expensive – taxi drivers know they've got you stranded.

TOP CHOICE Comptoir
NIGHTCLUB, BAR

(Map p56; ☎0524 43 77 02; Rue Echou-hada; www.comptoirdarna.com; ☺4pm-2am; ✸) Never mind the restaurant downstairs; the flash lounge upstairs is the place for dashing diplomats, visiting fashion designers and married Casa playboys to mingle over cocktails or bottles of wine. There's no avoiding the belly dancers, who descend en masse every other hour like scantily clad chaperones to break up all that flirting.

Jad Mahal/Silver
NIGHTCLUB, BAR

(Map p56; ☎0524 43 69 84; 10 Rue Haroun Er-rachid, Hivernage; www.jad-mahal.com; admission with drink/dinner free; ☺7.30pm-2am) Through the restaurant at the far end of the courtyard, the Jad Mahal's bar is where locals linger over cocktails until staff crank up a catchy song, the house cover band arrives or diners break into spontaneous dance moves over an '80s tune, whichever comes first. After midnight, take the free back-door entry to Silver, the next-door nightclub with not one, but 100 disco balls – a subtle hint to dance.

Pacha
NIGHTCLUB/BAR

(off Map p56; ☎0524 38 84 00; www.pachamarrakech.com; Complexe Pacha Marrakech, Blvd Mohammed VI, Zone Aguedal, Hivernage; Mon-Wed before/after 10pm free/Dh150, Thu men/women Dh150/free, Sat & Sun Dh200-300; ⏰8pm-1am Mon-Thu, 8pm-2am Fri & Sat; ⌘) Pacha Ibiza was the prototype for this clubbing complex that's now Africa's biggest, with DJs mashing up international and Magrebi hits for weekend influxes of Casa hipsters and raging Rabatis. Pacha doesn't come close to hitting its 3000-people occupancy during the week, so bring your own entourage and you might get in free. Ladies arrive en masse Thursdays to drink gratis at Rose Bar; come early to lounge by the pool until the party starts.

Diamant Noir
NIGHTCLUB

(Map p62; ☎0524 44 63 91; Hôtel Marrakech, cnr Ave Mohammed V & Rue Oum Errabia; admission with drink from Dh150; ⏰10pm-4am) For its rare gay-friendly clientele on weeknights and seedy charm complete with go-go dancers on weekends, the gravitational pull of 'Le Dia' remains undeniable. The dark dance floor thumps with hip hop and gleams with mirrors and bronzer-enhanced skin, while professionals lurk at the upstairs bar. Cash only.

Cinema

For a good selection of French and sometimes Moroccan films, check out the program at the Institut Français (see p73), where films are usually in French or subtitled in French.

Le Colisée
CINEMA

(Map p62; ☎0524 44 88 93; Blvd Mohammed Zerktouni; orchestra/balcony Mon Dh25/35, Tue-Sun Dh25/35; ⏰3pm, 5pm, 7pm & 9.30pm) The plushest cinema in town, Le Colisée, near Rue Mohammed el-Beqal, is plenty comfortable, with Dolby sound and a mixed male-female, Moroccan and expat crowd. Films are sometimes in the original language (including English) and subtitled in French.

Cinéma Eden
CINEMA

(Map p60; Derb Debachi; tickets Dh15; 3pm, 6pm & 9pm) Broken-plate tilework on mudbrick walls spells out the name of this classic single-screen cinema near Rue des Banques. The crowd here is rowdy, local and all-male, and Bollywood singalongs reign supreme. Films are usually dubbed into Darija, except for the songs.

Shopping
MEDINA

Marrakesh will leave you cursing carry-on restrictions, especially in the medina. Be selective, chat before you begin bargaining for items you're sure you want and buy only from shopkeepers who are pleasant in return – that way, you'll have a great story to accompany your scores, and won't wind up hot and bothered in the souqs.

WORTH A TRIP

QUARTIER INDUSTRIAL SIDI GHANEM

Modern Moroccan design fanatics hire taxis in the morning or late afternoon to scour the local designer factory outlets in this warehouse district, 4km outside Marrakesh on the Rte de Safi. Most of the original designs you'll see in Sidi Ghanem are made for export, with prices to match – but sharp-eyed shoppers will notice that some items made here are sold in ville-nouvelle boutiques at a considerable mark-up.

Negotiate a set rate of Dh150 to Dh250 for the roundtrip ride from the medina, and score a map of the quarter at an open showroom. Hours are erratic, but many storefronts open 9am to 6pm Monday to Friday and 9am to noon Saturday. Standout design outlets include:

» **Le Magasin General/Le Manufacture** Retro-styled, luxury handmade housewares.

» **ZidZid Kids** Hand-embroidered toy dromedaries from an award-winning Moroccan-American design team.

» **Sens de Marrakesh** Botanical beauty products.

» **Atelier Nihal** Hand-woven leather bags and floor mats.

» **16bis** Design collective with designer goods ranging from boudoir candles to blown glass.

No matter how you're faring elsewhere in the souqs, you can count on retail highs from boutiques selling items made by local cooperatives and with recycled materials, supporting fair trade and local nonprofits – and prices at these stores are fair and fixed. All the places listed in this section are great sustainable shopping options.

TOP CHOICE Cooperative Artisanale des Femmes de Marrakesh   ART & CRAFT
(Map p60; [☎]0524 37 83 08; 67 Souq Kchachbia; [⊙]10am-1pm & 3.30-7pm Sat-Thu) A showcase for Marrakesh's women *mâalems* (master artisans), the cooperative is eye-opening and a total bargain. Original, handcrafted designs include handbags made from water-bottle caps wrapped in wool, hand-knit *kissa* (hammam gloves), and black-and-white caftans edged with red silk embroidery – ask cooperative director Souad Boudeiry about getting tunics and dresses tailor-made.

TOP CHOICE Al-Kawtar   ART & CRAFT
(Map p60; [☎]0524 37 82 93; www.alkawtar.org; 57 Rue Laksour; [⊙]10am-6pm) A smart non-profit boutique where you can find luxe household linens minutely embroidered along the edges for less than you'd pay for plain cotton back home. You can also get fabulous hand-stitched Marrakesh-mod tunics, dresses and shirts for men, women and kids, and there's no extra charge for alterations. All items here are made by disabled local women, and purchases pay for their salaries, training programs and a childcare centre.

TOP CHOICE Michi   ART & CRAFT
(Map p60; [☎]0661 86 44 07; http://michi -morocco.com, in Japanese; 21 Souq Kchachbia) When an intrepid Japanese traveller met a hip Marrakshi designer, they discovered a shared love for craft, reclaimed materials and *wabi-sabi* (organic forms). Hicham and Michiko now have a family and this highly original boutique, featuring *babouches* (slippers) made from flour sacks, mirrors made of Libya oil drums, and hammam tote bags made with recycled feed bags.

L'Art du Bain Savonnerie Artisanale   ACCESSORIES
(Map p60; [☎]0668 44 59 42; www.lartdubain.net; Souq Lebbadine; [⊙]10am-7pm Mon-Sat) Do your skin and the planet a favour with biodegradable, pure plant-oil soaps made in Marrakesh with fragrant blends of local herbs, flowers and spices. As Khadija will explain, some ingredients in these soaps aren't easy to come by, especially prickly-pear cactus extract and donkey's milk. It's near Souq Sebbaghine.

Kif-Kif   ART & CRAFT
(Map p60; [☎]0661 08 20 41; www.kifkifbys tef.com; 8 Rue Laksour; [⊙]10am-8pm) A hip boutique near Bab Ksour that engages the city's most inventive artisans to come up with clever designs: handbags woven from recycled T-shirts, rings with interchangeable felt baubles and adorable children's nightgowns embroidered with 'good night' in Arabic. Fifteen percent of the price on all kids' items goes to a local nonprofit children's organisation.

Assouss Cooperative d'Argane   ACCESSORIES/FOOD & DRINK
(Map p60; [☎]0524 38 01 25; 94 Rue el-Mouassine; [⊙]9am-1pm & 3-7pm Sat-Thu, 9am-noon Fri) For pampering and foodie finds, this is the Marrakesh retail outlet of a women's argan cooperative outside Essaouira. The all-women staff will ply you with free samples of *amlou* (argan-nut butter) and proudly explain how their ultra-emollient cosmetic oil and gourmet dipping oils are made. You'll find it near Mouassine Fountain.

Jamade   ART & CRAFT
(Map p60; [☎]0524 42 90 42; 1 Pl Douar Graoua, cnr Rue Riad Zitoun el-Jedid; [⊙]10am-noon & 3-7.30pm) A standout collection of locally designed items at fixed prices. Recent scores include graphite ceramic olive-oil cruets, breezy ice-blue linen tunics, citrus seed-bead necklaces with a clever antique-coin closure, and hip, hand-sewn coasters from Tigmi women's cooperative (p120).

Creations Pneumatiques   ART & CRAFT
(Map p60; [☎]066 091746; 110 Rue Riad Zitoun el-Kedim; [⊙]10am-/pm) To buy crafts directly from Marrakesh's recycling artisans, head over to Riad Zitoun el-Kedim and check out lanterns, bowls and bells cleverly fashioned from tin cans and tyres. There are several to choose from, but this place has a good selection of Michelin mirrors, inner-tube jewellery boxes, and man-bags with street cred (look for the framed Bob Marley poster).

VILLE NOUVELLE

Upscale fixed-price boutiques worth checking out in the ville nouvelle for gifts, fashion and household linens line Rue de la Liberté and intersecting Rue Vieux Marrakshis in Guéliz. While you're in the neighbourhood, don't miss galleries showcasing contemporary Moroccan artists (p69). To give your home a complete fashion-forward Marrakshi makeover, hop a cab from downtown to the design outlets of Quartier Sidi Ghanem.

Good bargainers can get better deals on traditional Marrakshi crafts in the medina, but for a wide selection, it's worth checking out two ville-nouvelle crafts hot spots.

Ensemble Artisanal ART & CRAFT
(Map p56; Ave Mohammed V; ☺9.30am-12.30pm & 3-7pm Mon-Sat) To get a jump start on the souqs, come to this government-sponsored showcase, across from Cyber Park, to glimpse master artisans at work and see the range of crafts and prices Marrakesh has to offer. The set prices are higher than in the souqs, but it's hassle-free shopping and the producer gets paid directly.

Marcheé Ibn Toumert ART & CRAFT, FOOD & DRINK
(Map p62; Rue ibn Toumert; ☺8am-7pm) Past the butcher and behind the florists off Ave Mohammed V, you'll spot stalls selling silver jewellery, hand-painted ceramics, preserved lemons and other food products at reasonable prices – if you're prepared to bargain a little.

 Information

Emergency
Ambulance (☏0524 43 30 30)

Brigade Touristique (Map p56; ☏0524 38 46 01; Rue Sidi Mimoun; ☺24hr)

Fire (☏15)

Police (Map p62; ☏19; Rue Ouadi el-Makhazine)

Polyclinique du Sud (Map p62; ☏0524 44 79 99; cnr Rues de Yougoslavie & ibn Aicha; ☺24hr) Private hospital for serious cases and emergency dental care.

Internet Access
Many hotels and riads offer free internet access or wi-fi, and wi-fi is free with purchase at Café du Livre (p83) and Le Melting Pot (p85). Cyber-cafes ringing the Djemaa el-Fna charge Dh8 to Dh12 per hour; just follow signs reading 'c@fe'. Most open by 10am and close around 10pm.

Cyber Café in CyberPark (Map p56; Ave Mohammed V; www.arsatmoulayabdeslam.ma; per hr Dh10; ☺9am-6pm) Surprise: 15 terminals with fast connections amid the olive trees in the CyberPark, near the entry across from Ensemble Artisanal.

Hassan Internet (Map p60; ☏0524 44 19 89; Immeuble Tazi, 12 Rue Riad el-Moukha; per hr Dh8; ☺7am-midnight) A bustling place near the Tazi Hotel with 12 terminals.

Money
Most banks change cash or travellers cheques and there's no shortage of ATMs. On Sundays, ATMs on Rue Bab Agnaou (near Djemaa el-Fna) and in Rahba Kedima often run out of funds; try ATMs on Rue Fatima Zohra near Bab Ksour, or in the ville nouvelle. Private *bureaux de change* (exchange bureaus) offer official exchange rates but may charge commission.

Crédit du Maroc Ville Nouvelle (Map p62; 215 Ave Mohammed V); Medina (Map p60; Rue de Bab Agnaou) ATMs and exchange facilities.

Voyages Schwartz (Map p62; ☏0524 43 74 69; 22 Rue Moulay Ali Cherif; ☺8.30am-noon & 2.30-6.30pm Mon-Fri, 8.30am-noon Sat) Represents American Express.

Pharmacies
Pharmacie Centrale (Map p62; ☏0524 43 01 58; 166 Blvd Mohammed V; ☺9am-7pm) Conveniently located near Rue de la Liberté to fill prescriptions, personal care and women's needs.

Pharmacie de l'Unité (Map p62; ☏0524 43 59 82; Ave des Nations Unies; ☺8.30am-11pm) Open late for all your imported drugs, homeopathic remedies and aromatherapy needs; off Pl de la Liberté.

Pharmacy, Night Depot (Map p60; ☏0524 39 02 38; Djemaa el-Fna; ☺9am-midnight) Central location; open late and covers all the basics.

Post & Telephone
Public card phones are widely available, especially near Rue de Bab Agnaou in the medina and Ave Mohammed V in Guéliz, and cards can be bought from news vendors and *téléboutiques* (private phone offices).

DHL (Map p62; ☏0524 43 76 47; www.dhl.com; 113 Ave Mohammed Abdelkrim el-Khattabi; ☺8am-6pm Mon-Fri, 8.30am-12.20pm Sat) International courier service; insurance subject to surcharge.

FedEx (Map p62; ☏0524 44 82 57; 113 Ave Abdelkrim el-Khattabi; ☺8am-6pm Mon-Fri, to 12.15pm Sat) International courier service.

Main Post Office (Barid al-Maghrib; Map p62; ☏024 431963; Pl du 16 Novembre; ☺8.30am-2pm Mon-Sat) Poste restante is at window 3 and the parcel office is around the corner on Ave Hassan II.

Post Office (Map p60; Rue de Bab Agnaou) Branch office facing the Djemaa el-Fna.

Toilets
When nature calls in the medina, brave the toilets in cafes ringing the Djemaa or make an OJ pit stop at the Café des Épices (p81). Along Ave

Mohammed V in Guéliz there are dozens of spiffy cafes where you can nip to the loo.

Tourist Information

Office National Marocain du Tourisme (ONMT; Map p62; ☏0524 43 61 79; Pl Abdel Moumen ben Ali) Offers boosterish pamphlets and numbers of licensed guides.

Websites

Head to **Lonely Planet** (www.lonelyplanet. com/morocco/marrakesh) for planning advice, author recommendations, traveller reviews and insider tips.

🛈 Getting There & Away

Air

Six kilometres southwest of town is the recently expanded **Menara Airport** (☏0524 44 78 65; ☺information desk 8am-6pm). The airport has an information desk in the check-in hall and banks to exchange currency.

Several low-cost European airlines service Marrakesh – **easyJet** (www.easyjet.com) flies to Marrakesh directly from London/Gatwick, Manchester, Paris/Charles de Gaulle, Milan and Geneva. **Ryanair** (www.ryanair.com) offers flights to Marrakesh from London Luton/Stansted, Bristol, Edinburgh and East Midlands airports in the UK, plus Rome, Brussels, Barcelona, Frankfurt, Marseille and Madrid. **British Airways** (www.ba.com) offers low-cost London/Gatwick–Marrakesh flights.

Last-minute deals are often available on **Air France** (www.airfrance.com), which flies Paris–Marrakesh at least once a day, and **Iberia Air** (www.iberia.com), which offers direct Madrid–Marrakesh flights.

Royal Air Maroc (RAM; Map p62; ☏call centre 090 000800, 024 436205; www.royalairmaroc. com; 197 Ave Mohammed V; ☺8.30am-12.20pm & 2.30 7pm) has several flights daily to and from Casablanca (round trip from Dh525, 40 minutes), where you can pick up domestic and international connections. Reconfirm your flight with their 24-hour call centre, and leave extra time for connections in Casa – even if you make your connecting flight, your luggage may not. RAM operates direct international flights to/from London and Brussels (3½ hours each), Madrid (2½ hours) and Geneva and Milan (three hours each), plus daily flights to Paris (3¼ hours). Flights from New York connect to Marrakesh via Casa.

Bus

Most CTM buses arrive and depart from the new **CTM main bus station** (Map p56; ☏0524 43 44 02; Rue Abu Bakr Seddik; ☺6am-10pm), southwest of the train station (about 15 minutes on foot), a block south of Ave Mohammed VI.

Get tickets for early-morning departures the day before (especially for Essaouira), as morning buses fill quickly on holidays and weekends. There's not much at the station in the way of facilities, beyond a smoky 24-hour cafe with stuttering wi-fi.

CTM operates the following services:

Agadir Dh95, four hours, nine daily

Casablanca Dh85, four hours, three daily

Er-Rachidia Dh155, eight hours, one daily

Essaouira Dh70, three hours

Fez Dh150, 8½ hours, one daily

Laâyoune Dh310, 14 hours, four daily

Ouarzazate Dh80, four hours, one daily

Tan Tan Dh200, six hours, one daily

Tiznit Dh125, five hours, one daily

Supratours (Map p62; ☏0524 43 55 25; Ave Hassan II) is located west of the new Marrakesh train station, in the old train station building.

Supratours buses depart to the following places.

Agadir Dh100, four hours, 12

Dakhla Dh440, 25 hours, one daily

Essaouira Dh70, 2½ hours, six daily

Laâyoune Dh300, 15 hours, three daily

Tan Tan D 180, 10 hours, three daily

Supratours also offers connecting buses to trains. The Supratours bus station has a room where you can check baggage (per day Dh10, open 6am to 10pm).

The parking lot in front of the Supratours office is the arrival and departure point for most international buses, including CTM buses to/from Paris (from Dh1040, 48 hours) and Madrid (from Dh1090, 36 hours), on Tuesday, Wednesday and Saturday.

Some CTM buses also stop outside the city walls at Bab Doukkala, a 15-minute walk northeast of Pl du 16 Novembre or a 20-minute walk from Djemaa el-Fna. A number of local transport companies offer services from Bab Doukkala to Fez (from Dh130, 8½ hours, six daily) and Meknès (from Dh120, six hours, three daily). There's at least one local bus a day to Telouet (Dh50, four hours) that leaves in the afternoon from Bab Gehmat in the medina's southwest wall.

Car

Local car-rental companies often offer more competitive deals than international operators, with quoted rates starting at around Dh450 per day with unlimited mileage, possibly cheaper if you take a car for a minimum of three days. For 4WD rentals, count on Dh700 to Dh1000 per day with minimal insurance. However, you should be able to negotiate a 10% to 20% discount, and even more in the low season (late October to mid-December and mid-January to the end of February). If you'd rather look at the scenery than the road in the mountains or desert, a driver through a local car-rental agency (see p73) starts at Dh1250 plus tip per day all-inclusive for a 4WD or a small minibus.

INTERNATIONAL AGENCIES The following international agencies operate in Marrakesh.

Avis (☎0524 43 31 69; www.avis.com; airport)

Budget (www.budget.com) Blvd Mohammed Zerktouni (Map p62; ☎0524 43 11 80; 80 Blvd Mohammed Zerktouni); airport (☎0524 37 02 37)

Europcar (www.europcar.com) Blvd Mohammed Zerktouni (Map p62; ☎0524 43 12 28; 63 Blvd Mohammed Zerktouni); airport (☎0524 43 77 18)

Hertz (Map p62; ☎0524 43 99 84; www.hertz.com; 154 Blvd Mohammed V)

National (Map p62; www.nationalcar.com) Operates through Marrakesh Europcar offices.

LOCAL AGENCIES There are also some local agencies.

KAT (Map p62; ☎0524 43 35 81; http://membres.lycos.fr/katcar; 68 Blvd Mohammed Zerktouni)

La Plaza Car (Map p62; ☎0524 42 18 01; www.laplazacar.com; Immeuble 141, 23 Rue Mohammed el-Beqal)

Lhasnaoui Rent (Map 56; ☎0524 31 24 15; www.lhasnaouirent.com; cnr Blvd Allal el-Fassi & Yacoub el-Mansour, 15 Immeuble el-Omairi)

Taxi

Departing from outside Bab er-Rob near the royal palace are grands taxis to destinations in the High Atlas, including Asni (Dh30), Ouirgane (Dh40) and Setti Fatma (Dh40). Those serving destinations further afield gather on a dirt lot near Bab Doukkala, including grands taxis bound for Agadir (Dh120), Azilal (Dh75), Beni Mellal (Dh110), Demnate (Dh60), Essaouira (Dh130), Ouarzazate (Dh90) and Taroudannt (Dh110).

Train

Marrakesh's new **train station** (gare; Map p62; ☎0524 44 77 68, information only 0890 20 30 40; www.oncf.ma; cnr Ave Hassan II & Blvd Mohammed VI), next door to the Supratours station, is big, clean and convenient, with ATMs, cafes, fast food and Supratours down the platform in the old station. From the train station you can take a taxi or city buses 3, 8 or 10 (Dh3) into the centre.

Casablanca 2nd/1st class Dh90/140, three hours, nine daily

Fez Dh295/195, seven hours, eight daily

Meknès Dh265/174, 6½ hours

Rabat Dh120/185, four hours, nine daily

Safi Dh62 (2nd class), three hours, one daily

Tangier Dh310/205, 10½ hours, one daily

The Tangier train travels overnight. For sleeping berths to Tangier the ticket costs Dh350 each for a sleeping-car compartment; book at least two days in advance.

Getting Around

To/From the Airport

A petit taxi to Marrakesh from the airport (6km) should be no more than Dh70 by day or Dh100 by night, but you may have difficulty convincing the driver of this. Airport transfers to the Palmeraie or arranged through hotels or riad guesthouses in the medina or ville nouvelle cost Dh150-250, including luggage transport by handcart to your riad's front door. Alternatively, airport bus 19 runs every 20 minutes from outside the airport carpark to near the Djemaa el-Fna (Dh20), and local bus 11 runs irregularly to Djemaa el-Fna (Dh3.50).

Bus

Local buses (Map p60; all fares Dh3.50) leave for the ville nouvelle at seemingly random intervals from Pl Foucauld near the Djemaa el-Fna.

Key bus lines include the following:

NO 1 medina-Guéliz (along Ave Mohammed V)

NO 3 & 10 medina-train station

NO 11 & 18 medina-Menara Gardens

NO 4 & 12 Jardin Majorelle-medina

Calèches

These are the horse-drawn green carriages you'll see at Place Foucauld next to the Djemaa el-Fna. They're a pleasant way to get around, if you avoid the rush hours (8am, midday and 5.30pm to 7.30pm). One-way trips on set medina routes down Rue Debachi officially cost Dh20 per person; otherwise, state-fixed rates of Dh100 per hour apply (rates are posted inside the carriage). Expect a tour of the ramparts to take 1½ hours, and allow three hours for the Palmeraie. In Hivernage, calèches linger outside major hotels along Ave el-Qadissia and Rue Echouhada.

Car & Motorcycle

Your feet are the best way to get around the medina, which is mostly closed to car traffic. Driving in Marrakesh is an extreme sport, with scooters zooming from all sides and traffic roundabouts the meek may never escape – best to leave the driving to unfazed taxi drivers whenever possible. Cars present an additional problem of parking, so rent them only when strictly necessary for trips out of the city.

If you're feeling brave and/or foolhardy, you might join the fray on a scooter or motorcycle. Rentals are available from Action Sports Loisirs (p70) and **Marrakesh Motos** (Map p62; ☑0524 44 83 59, 061 316413; 31 Ave Mohammed Abdelkrim el-Khattabi; scooter & 125cc rental from Dh300 per day; ☺9am-8pm), located about 2km out of the town centre on the Casablanca road just beyond the Goodyear garage.

If you do rent a car or motorcycle, there are public parking lots near the Koutoubia Mosque and just south of Pl de Foucauld on Ave el-Mouahidine; expect to pay Dh20/40 during the day/24 hours. If you find street parking, a guardian will expect a Dh10 tip for keeping an eye on your car; look for the guy in the blue coat, and pay your tip afterwards.

Taxi

The creamy-beige petits taxis around town charge Dh8 to Dh20 per journey, with a Dh10 surcharge at night. They're all supposed to use their meters, but you may need to insist, especially coming from the airport – but if the meter is mysteriously broken, just know that no trip within town should cost more than Dh20 by day, or Dh30 at night. If your party numbers more than three you must take a grand taxi, which requires negotiation.

EAST OF MARRAKESH

After a few especially hot days, Marrakesh can leave you feeling as cooked as a kebab left on a Djemaa el-Fna grill. For a dramatic, restorative change of scenery, head for Berber villages tucked into the striped hills of Aït Bougomez Valley, or the rainbow-raising waterfalls of Cascades d'Ouzoud.

Demnate   دمنات

Who knew that an authentic immersion experience in Berber culture and cuisine could be found less than 1½ hours from Marrakesh? A cultural hub for centuries, Demnate is often overlooked by bus-tour hordes rushing to the Cascades d'Ouzoud – conveniently leaving intrepid travellers room to see, hear and taste Demnate's rich Berber culture.

The once-grand Glaoui kasbah and mudbrick ramparts have been left to crumble, yet Demnate's fascinating interfaith heritage has survived. At the heart of town is a **mellah**, with an entry about 150m on the right after the town's main gate. Hundreds of Jewish families from Morocco, France,

Israel, Canada and the United States arrive each July for the **Jewish moussem** (festival), a weeklong mystical event said to offer miracle cures. Demnate also has two *zawiyas*, making the annual **Hamdouchi Moussem** in September twice as raucous. Each *zawiya* dances to a different rhythm in an all-day music festival in the town centre before going their separate ways in three-hour parades to the *zawiyas*. Sometimes the *moussem* peaks in blood purification, with dancers cutting themselves on the scalp in dramatic acts of ritual cleansing.

The 100-year-old olive groves dotting hillsides around Demnate produce Morocco's best olive oil, with trace mineral salts, a golden colour, and subtle woodsy flavours that compare favourably to prized Tuscan oils. Almonds are another renowned local product, and the flowering of the local orchards makes March a lovely time to visit. Meals at Restaurant Al Jazira, Kasbah Illy and Kasbah Timdaf are prime opportunities to sample Demnati olive oil and almonds.

⊙ Sights & Activities

TOP CHOICE\ **Association Attadamoun Pour les Handicapés**   CULTURAL CENTRE (☑0668 90 98 01; handicadem1@yahoo.fr; Demnate) Afternoon *mellah* tours and evening musical concerts are arranged through this nonprofit organisation providing schooling, job training and essential life skills to disabled youth. The association's director, Mr Hassan Khallaf, speaks fluent English and French and is extremely knowledgeable about Demnate's mixed Muslim/Jewish heritage (he's currently finishing his PhD in sustainable cultural tourism). By prior arrangement (one week in advance, with confirmation the day before arrival) he gives wonderful historical tours of Demnate's *mellah*, passing through souqs and *funduqs* and ending at the Attadamoun centre and school. Given at least one week's advance notice and small groups of five to 10 visitors, Mr Khallaf can also arrange a concert of local Hamadcha-style music with a local musicians' union.

Proceeds for *mellah* walking tours and benefit concerts support the association's efforts to extend essential support services and educational opportunities to all. Donations are on a sliding scale: Dh500 provides one week's petrol for the school bus; Dh800 offers breakfast to 46 disabled students for

AÏT BLEL TO AÏT BOUGOMEZ

With a 4WD and dry weather April to November, exploration of this spectacular valley portal to Aït Bougomez is the next best thing to time travel. On this meandering drive through High Atlas foothills, you'll pass centuries-old **mountain oaks** dotting vertically striped sedimentary **rock formations** from the Triassic period, some 230 million years ago. You won't encounter many cars, but you will spot rare birds including kestrel, a type of falcon. Villagers often wave as you pass, and if you stop, you may get invited for tea.

The road sometimes narrows to one lane, but it's paved or graded the entire way (though bridges can wash out in winter). The cliff-edge villages you'll pass make it worth the additional two hours you're taking to reach Aït Bougomez over the Tizin-Oubadou, instead of going the faster route via Aït Mohammed. If you're heading through Aït Blel, gas up before you go: the biggest town is Khemis Aït Blel, with a Tuesday souq and stalls selling sundries and occasionally petrol.

Near the pass, **Gîte Tizi-n-Oubadou** (☑0661 44 36 02; per person incl breakfast/half-board Dh50/120) is a cheerful, lilac-painted house at the top of the village, overlooking meticulously trimmed terraces with carob and almond groves. If you call as you leave Demnate in the morning, they may be able to provide lunch (Dh60 to Dh80).

two days; or for philanthropists moved by what they see at the centre, Dh3000 sends a student to consult a medical specialist in Casablanca about available treatments. Donations may be left in the front office at the Attadamoun centre, and a receipt is provided. Donations have already helped fund a school bus, and is helping Attadamoun graduates open a boutique selling items made by disabled artisans; look for the 'Handishop' sign along the main road.

TOP CHOICE Imi-n-Ifri
NATURAL SCENERY

Just 6km east of Demnate is Imi-n-Ifri ('Grotto's Mouth' in Berber), a natural bridge over a gorge that looks like a monster's yawn. You can clamber down into the gorge and pass through this toothy maw by yourself – the paths are clearly marked and recently levelled – but you might pay a small tip (Dh20 to Dh30) to a local guide to help you over some tricky boulders and explain local lore associated with this travertine bridge formed some 1.8 million years ago.

The two sides of the bridge are said to represent two local lovers whose families kept them apart, so this Romeo and Juliet held hands and turned to stone. On the south side of the gorge is a spring with water rich in natural mineral salts, where brides come for pre-wedding rites; in summer you may hear women singing and playing drums and tambourines at Berber bachelorette parties. On the other side of the gorge is a freshwater spring said to cure acne, which explains the number of teens hanging out here. Pass under the bridge, and suddenly you're in a *Lord of the Rings* setting, with flocks of crows swooping down from dramatic stalactites overhead.

Aït Blel
NATURAL SCENERY

Follow the road that forks to the left at Imin-Ifri into the breathtaking Aït Blel Valley, which connects to Aït Bougomez Valley via Aït Bououli Valley. In spring, Aït Blel is like an animated Impressionist painting, with golden wheat fields rippling in the breeze, dotted with red poppies. Women in pinafores and polka-dotted kerchiefs harvesting these fields often look up as cars pass, and wave with their scythes.

The road here is fairly new, so the entire valley seems untouched by time. Mountains are striped gold, orange and purple, with green crops sprouting from stone-walled terraces. Follow the road 6km from Imi-n-Ifri to the village of **Iouaridene**, and you're in prehistoric territory. Signs point you towards what geologists claim are **dinosaur footprints** dating from the mid-Jurassic period, about 170 million years ago. Quadruped and carnivorous dinosaurs once roamed this area, and local kids do a mean impersonation of a T-rex.

🛏 Sleeping

TOP CHOICE Kasbah Timdaf
MAISON D'HÔTE $$

(☑0523 50 71 78; GPS coordinates N 31°46,50 W 007°01,13; www.kasbah-timdaf.com;

s/d Dh495/660-880, extra adult/child Dh220/110) A cosy eco-castle 15 minutes from Demnate on the road to Azila, with vast rooms warmed by fireplaces and snazzy *tadelakt* bathrooms. It may seem palatial, but this stone and mudbrick kasbah is a working farm surrounded by almond and olive groves, providing inspired Mediterranean-Berber meals. Owners Jacqueline and Yannick are active in **Assaphar** (www.assaphar.com), a Demnate medical association providing pre- and post-natal care to those in need. When they're not making olive oil, cooking feasts or helping new mums, they organise transfers to/from Marrakesh by car (Dh500) and bicycle, trekking and fishing trips.

Eating

TOP CHOICE Café-Restaurant
Al Jazeera   BERBER $$

(☑0524 45 82 39; near Gare Routiére, Demnate; 3-course menus from Dh130; ⊗8am-8pm; ☀) Call ahead to reserve a table for savoury seasonal salads that are a prelude to Demnate's signature fine-grain couscous, decadently laced with local olive oil and sprinkled with toasted Demnati almonds. Enjoy a leisurely dining experience with a refreshing dip in the courtyard pool (open in summer) and excellent espresso in the garden.

Kasbah Illy   BERBER $$
(☑0523 50 89 53; set lunch menu Dh130; ❄☀) This splashy kasbah-hotel, 5km from Demnate on road to Imi-n-Ifri, offers lunch by a dolphin-tiled pool overlooking the valley. Reserve ahead, and request their speciality tajine: free-range *beldi* (country-style) chicken smothered in caramelised onions.

Also recommended:

Snak Itrane   LOCAL $
(¼/whole chicken with chips or bread Dh20/65) Some 300m after the city gate on the left, this sidewalk restaurant serves a mean rotisserie chicken.

Kasbah Timdaf   LOCAL $$
(☑0523 50 71 78; GPS coordinates N 31°46,50 W 007°01,13; www.kasbah-timdaf.com; guest/nonguest Dh140/160) Offers fixed-price lunches and dinners to guests and nonguests by prior reservation.

Shopping

The Sunday weekly **souq** 10 minutes south of town is an opportunity to taste-test local olives, olive oils and almonds, and browse Demnate's local woodwork, wool outerwear and yellow-glazed pottery painted in henna with Berber good-luck symbols. The **potteries** are located 2km outside town in the village of Boughlou; turn right at the mosque and head 4km off-road.

Honey that's considered rare elsewhere abounds in the hills around Demnate. You'll notice a sign with a bee on it at the **hanout** (grocer) on the main road on your right about 500m before reaching the eastern edge of town: approach the counter and ask the grocer to let you sample local honey (Dh100 per 500g). The mountain herb and wildflower honey is a standout with a peppery, thyme flavour; the juniper honey is a classic caramel with woodsy notes; the *zriga* (a local blue wildflower) honey tastes fruity, almost like guava; and carob honey tastes like maple syrup.

❶ Getting There & Away

Grands taxis to Marrakesh (Dh55) and Azilal (Dh35) leave from the main gate in Demnate. Buses leave for Marrakesh (Dh35, two hours) from 6am to 9pm and to Azilal (Dh20, one hour) from 7am to noon from the bus station (take the road to the right before the town gate).

Cascades d'Ouzoud
شلالات أزوض

Some 167km northeast of Marrakesh and a world away from the city heat are the Cascades d'Ouzoud, one of the most popular day trips from Marrakesh for tourists and Moroccans alike. The Oued Ouzoud drops 110m into the canyon of Oued el-Abid in three-tiered waterfalls, and the view only gets better as you descend into the cool of the canyon, past the late-afternoon rainbow mists to the pools at its base. The falls are most dramatic from March to June when there's more water, but young Moroccans often camp here in summer on terraces facing the falls. To reach the falls, walk past the signs for Riad Cascades d'Ouzoud towards the precipice, where converging paths wind down towards the falls.

The Cascades are so universally beloved that the scenery around the mouth of the falls has become touristy. The path leading from the left side of the town square to the base of the falls is lined with souvenir stalls, cafes and camp sites, and no one paddling the pools below the falls really wants to think about what happens with runoff from hole-in-the-ground toilets built into the hillside.

Most cafes on the banks flanking the falls offer meals for Dh60 to Dh80, and several offer camp sites for Dh15 – but until serious steps are taken to keep garbage and outhouses in check, the environmental cost of these establishments is too high to recommend them to nature lovers.

Two local environmental organisations are working on solutions. Two portable toilets are now installed along the main path, and a garbage collector has been hired to keep trash in check. You can help keep the falls beautiful by packing out trash and using the portable toilets.

◉ Sights & Activities

Locals might lead you into the gorge for a few dirham, but you can follow well-trodden paths. At the bottom, you can hike along the riverbed to pools where you can swim, or cross the river to another path where **Barbary apes** clamour for attention – though a signpost advises not to feed them. To see the picturesque Berber village of **Tanaghmelt**, follow the path by the lower pools past a farmhouse and up the slopes about 1.5km. For longer treks, follow the course of the river to caves (two hours) and the **Gorges of Oued el-Abid** (another two hours).

⏢ Sleeping & Eating

TOP CHOICE Riad Cascades d'Ouzoud

MAISON D'HÔTE **$**

(☎0662 14 38 04; www.ouzoud.com; s incl breakfast Dh510-610, d Dh710-810, tr Dh950, ste Dh1050-1150; ❖) At this stylish mudbrick guesthouse located 30m from the top of the Cascades, the gentle rushing sound of the falls has been known to lull guests to sleep while dining on the terrace or reading in the library. Solar-heated showers, ceilings painted with Berber talismans, and family-style welcomes from local staff make you feel part of the scenery. The riad arranges kayaking, river-sliding, visits to rural souqs and tea with local families.

Hotel Chellal INN **$**

(☎0523 42 91 80; http://hotelchellal.weebly.com; s/d incl breakfast Dh220/350) On the hilltop a few steps down the path leading left from the town square is this chipper inn, featuring simple rooms in pastel colours with en-suite bathrooms, post-hike hang-out spots, and a terrace restaurant; cash only.

ⓘ Getting There & Away

From Marrakesh, it's easiest to get transport direct to Azilal, from where grands taxis run when full to Ouzoud (per person/taxi Dh25/250 return). Head back to Azilal before 4pm, when taxis become scarce and drive hard bargains.

Azilal أزيلال

This flag-waving centre for regional development is mainly of interest to travellers as a handy transport hub between Demnate, the Cascades d'Ouzoud and the Aït Bougomez Valley, and for inventing a new car game: how many flags can you count driving down the main street? At last count, the answer was 456, which must be a record for a town not celebrating a king's visit or state holiday. There's a **Thursday souq**, and the town's **Complexe Artisanal** (☉Mon-Sat), on the right across from the town hall, occasionally hosts regional arts-and-crafts showcases.

⏢ Sleeping & Eating

Hôtel Souss HOTEL **$**

(☎0672 32 84 95; s/d with shared bathroom Dh40/80, hot showers Dh10) Diagonally across from Ibnou Ziad Restaurant, this laid-back hotel offers a friendly welcome, pink rooms, thick blankets and oddly endearing child-sized desks; a video-game arcade is next door.

Ibnou Ziad Restaurant LOCAL **$**

(Ave Hassan II) A good pit stop for Dh40 lunches of salad, tasty rotisserie chicken and chips, though football fans might be delayed by matches shown on TV here.

ⓘ Information

Attijariwafa ATM (Ave Hassan II) ATMs and credit-card machines are scarce inside Aït Bougomez, so use this one next to the police station.

Cyber Espace Bleu (Ave Hassan II; per hr Dh8; ☉9am-10pm Mon-Sat) One of the last internet outposts before heading into Aït Bougomez is next to Hôtel Assounfou.

ⓘ Getting There & Away

Buses run between Azilal and Marrakesh (Dh50, three daily) and Azilal and Demnate (Dh20, three daily). Plenty of grands taxis run from the taxi lot behind Marrakesh's bus station to Azilal (Dh70 to Dh100) and, less frequently, from Azilal to Demnate (Dh35).

Aït Bougomez Valley

وادي عيت بو غومز

The best-kept secret in Morocco is the region known as the 'happy valley', which until 2001 was snowbound four months a year and was largely inaccessible except on foot. Though some roads are still accessible only by mule or 4WD, paved roads have given unprecedented entry to High Atlas foothills faceted with mudbrick towers and reddish *ighremt* (stone-reinforced houses) with windows outlined in white stone. Here you can escape the reach of mobile phones, bosses and the other minor irritants of modern living, and spend days happily absorbed by orchards in bloom, mysterious petroglyphs and golden eagles soaring up toward snowcapped M'Goun Massif.

Beyond natural beauty, Aït Bougomez has a remarkable resourcefulness that never ceases to impress. Cliffsides are dotted with tiny plots of wheat inside stone-walled terraces. Villages are built from rock and clay quarried on the spot, blending mimetically with their spectacular backdrops. High in the hills, you'll spot villagers collecting mountain plants to make wild-crafted herbal remedies and natural dyes for carpets.

Aït Bougomez is stunning but remote, and people here have to work hard to put food on the table and send their children to school. To ensure the happiness of future generations, locals have undertaken ambitious initiatives to end illiteracy, food insecurity and poverty – including girls' schools, organic farming cooperatives, woodworkers' collectives and ecotourism ventures – and they would be very happy indeed if you stopped by and showed your support – try the Happy Valley Goodwill Tour.

AÏT BOUOULI VALLEY

From Azilal you'll arrive at Aït Mohammed, where the road leads southwest, through hills marking geologic time in red-, purple- and white-striped mineral deposits. Before you reach Agouti, adventurers equipped with 4WD and steely nerves can detour south through a steep red-clay gorge to the Aït Bououli Valley, which until a couple of years ago was inaccessible even by mule for months at a time.

Sebt Aït Bououli
NATURAL SCENERY

In the remote outpost of Sebt Aït Bououli, 14km off the main road, trekkers stock up on food for their M'Goun traverse at the Saturday souq.

Some 2.5km beyond Sebt Aït Bououli you'll have to squint to make out a picturesque trio of villages built right into a two-toned purple and ochre bluff. Like chameleons, these villages blend into the geologic formations immediately behind them. On green terraces are gambolling lambs that are the valley's claim to fame: Bououli means 'Those who keep sheep'.

Petroglyphs
NATURAL SCENERY

About 7km west of this triplet village, you'll see **Jebel Ghat** (3797m) and the pass called **Tizi n'Tirghist**. Around this area are petroglyphs some geologists estimate are 4000 years old; ask a local guide to point out the enigmatic symbols, which local lore links to ancient rain-making ceremonies.

TOP CHOICE Cooperative Feminin de Tissage Aït Bououli
ART & CRAFT, CULTURAL CENTRE

(☎0671 41 91 06; ⊗8am-noon) Immediately below Aït Bououli's trio of mimetic villages is a stone-walled community association with a sign pointing visitors toward the Aït Bououli women's carpet-weaving cooperative. This 30-member cooperative take every aspect of carpet-making into their own hands, tending and shearing sheep, carding and spinning fluffy lambswool into yarn; and collecting plants to dye yarn fascinating tertiary hues. The members also take turns minding the shop, so you'll be buying carpets from the woman who made it, her sister or her neighbour – no middlemen involved.

If you find the door to the co-op closed, just call Fatima, the dynamic director of the cooperative, and she'll come down from the village to open the co-op's small storeroom, packed with surprisingly soft, modern-art carpets. As Fatima explains, pinkish purple is from madder root, henna yields golden yellow, chocolate brown comes from pomegranate and acid green is from dyers' rocket. Designs range from simple stripes and checkerboard patterns to enigmatic geometry and Berber talismans, all at great fixed prices. If you buy multiple carpets, you may get a slight discount, and a tea invitation into the bargain.

Driving Tour
Happy Valley Goodwill Tour

Take in spectacular scenery and bring the happiness home with you after supporting 11 worthy local causes on this five-day adventure.

Day 1

Depart Marrakesh for **Demnate**. Head east through Demnate for a walk under a natural bridge formed 1.8 million years ago at **Imi-n-Ifri**, returning to Demnate for a lavish local lunch at **Restaurant Al Jazeera**.

By prior arrangement, take an afternoon tour of Demnate's ancient **mellah** and visit **Association Attadamoun Pour les Handicapés**, a pioneering life-skills training centre for disabled students aged five to 18. Families and small groups of five to 10 might reserve ahead for a benefit dinner concert organised by Association Attadamoun Pour les Handicapés.

Dine on garden-fresh dishes and enjoy a comfortable overnight at **Kasbah Timdaf**, which supports a local initiative to extend prenatal and postnatal care to those in need.

Day 2

Depart Demnate; lunch at **Ibnou Ziad Restaurant** in Azilal. Visit the **Cooperative Feminin des Tissages Aït Bououli** carpet cooperative to admire Berber carpets made of local wool dyed with mountain plants, and meet the women *mâalems* (master artisans) who made them.

Watch wood-carvers at work at **Association Ighrem Atelier du Sculpture**, where free-form spoons and bowls are whittled from fallen wood, and sales support valley reforestation.

Sample cows-milk cheese, walnut butters and mountain honey made by an enterprising local women's cooperative: **Cooperative Tikniouine**.

Experience authentic Berber hospitality over dinner or overnight in a historic family home at **High Atlas Home**, where a generous portion of proceeds support a village women's association focusing on organic farming and local crafts.

Day 3

In the morning, hike to **Zawiya Sidi Moussa**, for Happy Valley views and good *baraka* (blessings) from the local patron saint. Lunch at **Café des Amis** in Tabant.

Drop off English- or French-language books for beginners at **Tabant girls' boarding school**, or by prior arrangement, teach an after-school English class.

Off-road to **Zaouiat Ahansal**; visit the women's weaving collective and training program at **Atelier du Tissages de l'Association du Zaouiat Ahsal**.

Eat dinner and spend the night at *gîte* **Sidi Ahmed Amahdar**, where rates include a Dh10 donation to support the local medical dispensary.

Day 4

Drive to **Reserve Naturelle de Tamga** for wildflower hikes, birdwatching, and rock-climbing around **Le Cathédrale du Rocher**. Lunch at **Gîte le Cathédrale**.

Drive around lake Ben Ouidane to Azilal and onward to **Cascades d'Ouzoud**, where you can dine on the terrace and nod off to the sound of the rushing waterfall at ecofriendly **Riad Cascades d'Ouzoud**.

Day 5

Follow the rainbows and Cascades' well-trodden paths to the base of the **waterfall** and onward to Berber villages along the river, and support local environmental organisations' efforts by picking up any stray plastic water bottles you spot along the way.

Return to **Marrakesh** in time for a pre-arranged afternoon visit to **Atfalouna**, a shelter meeting the needs of 320 homeless kids in Marrakesh.

Reward yourself for a holiday well spent with a dinner of local delicacies and a luxurious stay in **Riad al-Massarah**, a green-certified riad that also supports Atfalouna.

AGOUTI

Beloved by trekkers for scenic M'Goun views and down-to-earth Berber hospitality at several *gîtes d'étape* (rustic hotels), Agouti is also home to a ground-breaking woodworkers' cooperative.

◉ Sights

TOP CHOICE **Association Ighrem Atelier du Sculpture**   ART & CRAFT, CULTURAL CENTRE
(☑0673753163; www.etsy.com/shop/Association Ighrem; ⊙8am-6pm) Visitors can watch artisans carve free-form spoons and bowls from fragrant walnut, juniper and boxwood salvaged from fallen trees at this centre, 500m from Flilou, on the left. With proceeds from sales, the association is reforesting the valley with fast-growing boxwood and planting vetiver to harvest for basket-weaving. For every piece visitors buy, they plant an apple tree to help feed local families; add a Dh200 to Dh400 donation, and they'll plant seven to 15 more saplings in your honour.

⨂ Sleeping & Eating

Flilou   GÎTE $
(☑0524 34 37 98; tamsilt@menara.ma; s/d incl half-board Dh120/150) The first *gîte* on your left offers clean dorm rooms, doubles with hand-painted beds around the rear courtyard, savoury meals and clean, updated bathrooms with blessedly hot water. Climb the ladder to the roof terrace, where Berber tents beckon and mirrored wedding blankets reflect sunsets.

Chez ben Ali   GÎTE $
(☑0523 45 87 26; s/d/tr/q with shared bathroom Dh70/120/170/210) A large pinkish retreat at the northeast end of Agouti with welcome amenities. Cheerfully painted rooms share clean bathrooms, washing machine, terrace, three kitchens for guest use, and a computer with a slow internet connection. Ask for rooms with garden views; if you're sensitive to hard beds, opt for softer foam mattresses on the floor. Breakfast is Dh20 and lunch or dinner Dh60, plus drinks.

TIKNIOUINE

Some 5km along the main road from Agouti is the village of Tikniouine, a key stop for gourmet treats and cultural immersion.

◉ Sights

TOP CHOICE **Cooperative Tikniouine**
   FOOD & DRINK, CULTURAL CENTRE
(☑0523 45 97 36; ⊙9am-4pm Mon-Thu & Sat) Follow the signs from the road 50m down-

hill to this gourmet centre formed in 2005 by plucky young women who secured EU funding to start cultivating organic walnuts, collecting mountain wildflower honey, and making their own mild, aged cows-milk cheese, which tastes like a cross between gouda and emmental. At the co-operative's centre, you can sample and purchase their products.

'Food-packaging companies are capitalising on our local produce, and we wanted to prove we could make better products for a fair price by producing them artisanally', explains the collective's precocious president, Malika el-Ouarkhoumi, who cofounded the collective at age 19. 'At first some people didn't want their daughters involved, but now there are 12 of us involved full-time, and since we've won an award from Morocco as a model collective, every family wants to be involved.'

⨂ Sleeping & Eating

High Atlas Home   HOMESTAY $
(☑0642 34 56 67; www.highatlashome.com; dm Dh80, adult/child incl half-board Dh180/150) In a valley dotted with generic *gîtes*, this historic Berber home is a breath of fresh mountain air with family-friendly dorms and cosy, comfortable doubles clustered around three sunny courtyards. Your host family lives in the rear courtyard, and can arrange birdwatching excursions, treks to hidden petroglyphs and Berber botanical hikes. Meals are served family-style on cushions in the living room, under a lovingly preserved ceiling painted 50 years ago. High Atlas Home extends Berber hospitality to guests and neighbours, too: 20% of proceeds from every stay support a Tikniouine women's microcredit association, helping local women launch organic farming cooperatives and crafts collectives.

TABANT

The heart of the valley in more ways than one, Tabant attracts locals and visitors alike with its official mountain guide school and bustling regional **Sunday souq**, with a fresh produce market along the main street next to the used-donkey sales lot.

The local association runs **Tabant girls' boarding school**, a trailblazing school for children from local mountain villages, broadening the horizons and prospects of their entire families. Postcards written in English or French are awarded to students for outstanding effort, and travellers are

DON'T MISS

HIGH ATLAS WILDLIFE

» Mouflons An endangered mountain sheep with big horns, these shaggy, nimble creatures were brought back from the brink of extinction in this area, and now have a dedicated reserve in the Toubkal National Park.

» Moorish geckos These skittish, spotted little creatures with big eyes and splayed toes might be drawn to lamplight at night or glimpsed dashing across mountain paths, along with tiny striped Iberian wall lizards.

» Raptors Look up, and you may spot some magnificent golden eagles, lammergeyers (bearded vultures), Egyptian vultures and golden eagles coasting on a mountain breeze.

» Wild boars Rare finds; small, bristly bundles of energy making snuffling sounds in the underbrush.

» Gazelles The sight of corkscrew-horned gazelles gracefully scampering up rocky High Atlas terrain inspires awe, and possibly a twinge of envy.

» Endangered snakes Most High Atlas snake species are small and non-threatening, and have more to fear from intruders than vice versa – larger snakes are trapped by snake-charmers for performances in the Djemaa el-Fna.

» Painted frogs Brownish spots camouflage them in High Atlas terrain, but you might hear them croaking, or spot them mating for two hours at a stretch between January and November.

invited to participate: postcards in simple English can be written to 'Dear Student' and sent to the school, care of the English teacher, Merzouk Farami, at Al Hay Al Idari, Tabant, Aït Bougomez, Morocco.

Travellers who wish to donate beginner-level books for students learning English can arrange visits to the school Thursday to Sunday afternoons (one or two weeks' advance notice required) with **Mr Farami** (📞0672 18 09 37; farami1982@hotmail.com; ⏰3-6pm Thu-Sun). Visitors with previous teaching experience may also volunteer to teach an after-school English lesson to the students, who are eager to practise with native speakers. Lesson plans must be sent to Mr Farami two weeks in advance for approval by the school; bring any printed materials.

◉ Sights & Activities

TOP CHOICE **Sidi Moussa**
MONUMENT & NATURAL SCENERY

For a spectacular sunset, take the road west out of Tabant, and you'll find the trailhead leading up a cone-shaped hill to the *zawiya* of local *marabout* (saint) Sidi Moussa. It's a straightforward 20-minute uphill hike (15 minutes downhill), and you won't need a guide. The round structure served as a collective granary and has been restored through a community effort, with fitted-stone walls and weather-beaten wooden doors making a worthy photo backdrop. The *zawiya* may or may not help women get pregnant as promised, but it certainly delivers stirring, romantic views over the valley.

Maroc Profond TREKKING
(📞0523 45 93 46; marocprofond@wanadoo.fr) Hikes through the valley and into the mountains can be arranged with officially licenced mountain guides at this Tabant-based agency. Suggested treks range from two- to three-hour valley strolls to geological formations, to four-day trans-mountain treks following ancient nomad routes.

🛏 Sleeping & Eating

TOP CHOICE **Ecolodge Dar Itrane** INN $$
(📞010 086930; www.origins-lodge.com; Imelghas; per person incl half-board Dh500) Just outside Tabant in Imelghas village, seemingly opposing ideas happily coexist at this inn: ecological and comfortable, rural and hip, internationally owned and locally engaged. Eighteen whitewashed guest rooms are kitted out with handmade Berber-style furnishings, plus en-suite bathrooms in *tadelakt* and hammered brass with solar-powered hot showers. The open organic kitchen invites the curious, a hydroelectric-powered hammam soothes the weary, and downtime is whiled away in the library of books and videos on Berber culture or browsing the boutique of locally made goods.

Tisami N'Ouayour GÎTE $
(📞0523 45 93 27; dm incl half-board Dh120) Of the three *gîtes* in the nearby village of Ikhf-

n-Ighir, this has the sunniest disposition, with light streaming into the salon through picture windows, clean rooms strewn with locally made rugs, and views of geological formations from living-room sofas. Request rooms with outside windows for light and village views; you can check email on the computer with a sputtering internet connection. It's past Dar Itrane on the left as you head north; look for the yellow door painted with a red rose.

Café des Amis
CAFE

Across from the Tabant post office, 50m down main street, this cafe whips up a scrumptious tajine in 30 minutes from garden-fresh vegetables, free-range meat and wildly aromatic mountain herbs for just Dh20.

ℹ Getting There & Away

Minibuses occasionally run from Azilal to Tabant (Dh35, three hours) in the morning when full, from near the central mosque. You might share a grand taxi (Dh65 per person) or ride in trucks headed to Azilal on Thursday for its market.

TREKKING THE M'GOUN MASSIF
جبل المكون

While crowds flock to Jebel Toubkal, nature lovers are increasingly heading to the other High Atlas range within striking distance of Marrakesh: the M'Goun Massif, with pristine, prehistoric landscapes that make rewarding challenges for trekkers.

If you're going in spring, be prepared to get your boots wet and dress warmly: walking river gorges is one of the great pleasures of M'Goun. The M'Goun Traverse outlined here follows one river up to its mountain source, crosses the mountain range, and then follows another river down into its valley.

The M'Goun Massif has an intimidating name and reputation, with some of Morocco's highest peaks and toughest trekking. But this walk will suit all grades of trekkers, including families, since children will enjoy riding mules on the steeper sections and through rivers. The landscape is incredibly varied, ranging from lush valleys to rocky gorges within a day.

The Berber architecture you'll see along the way includes *ighremt*, houses hand-built from stone and clay in a distinctive High Atlas style that has more in common

with architecture from Yemen and Afghanistan than decorative Moroccan styles. These stone houses blend in so well with the landscape that they may only be identifiable by contrasting white-stone window frames, painted blue doors, and thatching poking out from flat roofs.

Arrival Day

To stretch your legs and camp overnight, you could stroll down the valley to Agerssif to a riverside camping spot shaded by walnut trees near the bridge. Alternatively, you might make the hour-long walk down the road from Agouti to Tabant for supplies and bubbling hot tajines at Café des Amis. There is accommodation around Tabant and right near the trailhead in Agouti.

Day 1: Agouti to Rougoult
6-7 HRS/17KM/326M ASCENT & DESCENT

After a leisurely 1½ hour walk south along the road from Agouti, a tarmac road forks to the left, down from the main road. Continue on this road, or take a steeper, shorter path that zigzags down into the valley, rejoining the tarmac road at the village of **Agerssif** (1469m), which you should reach less than three hours from Agouti. Agerssif sits at the confluence of the Lakhdar and Bougomez Rivers, and there's a good resting/camping spot by the bridge.

The Lakhdar Valley narrows as the road climbs its south side. A half-hour upstream is the picturesque village of **Taghoulit** (1519m), surrounded by juniper trees, and with a simple **gîte** (per person Dh45). The road scales the gorge, then enters the broad, fertile upper valley, until it reaches **Sebt Aït Bououili**, where you'll find **Gîte Hassan Benkoum** (per person Dh40) – but we advise continuing to Rougoult for a head start tomorrow. Several valleys meet at Sebt Aït Bououili, and looking up past the village of Abachkou you'll notice **Jebel Rat** (3781m).

A graded *piste* road heads left to the south, through a valley of waving wheat and barley fields interrupted by juniper, wild fig and almond trees. The village of **Tazouggart**, on the opposite side of the valley, marks a more-than-halfway point between Sebt Aït Bououili and the day's end at Rougoult. The landscape becomes ever more Shangri-la-like until, after two to 2½ hours, you reach **Rougoult** (1850m). Here you'll find a Tifra River camp site and

Trekking the M'Goun Massif

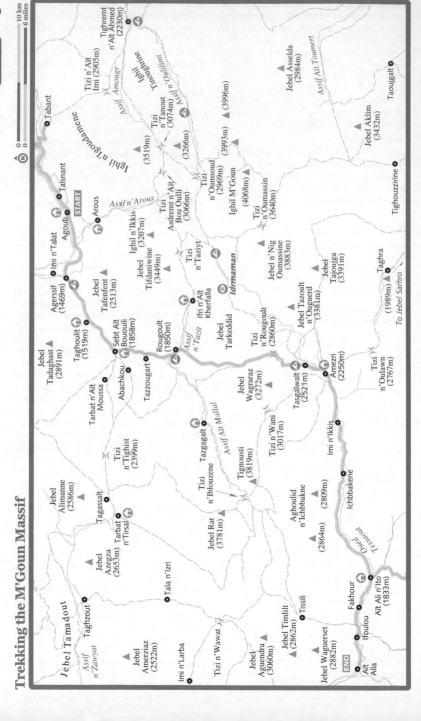

possible homestays (per person Dh30) – ask around to see who has space.

Day 2: Rougoult to Amezri
6-7 HRS/14KM/600M DESCENT/970M ASCENT

For two hours, the morning walk follows the Tifra along a stony path criss-crossing the river. As the well-trodden mule path climbs, the landscape becomes more barren, occasionally leading above rocky gorges – but the path always follows the course of the river south.

The source of the Tifra River is no more than a trickle at the best of times, as you'll discover just below the pass of **Tizi n'Rougoult** (2860m). From the broad saddle beneath the pass, a path leads left (east) to a ridge that climbs to over 3500m. The well-worn Rougoult pass is straight ahead, and the summit of **Ighil M'Goun** (4068m), only 100m lower than Jebel Toubkal – due east. In the near distance across the **Tessaout River**, exposed mountain slopes reveal great gashes of rust, green and grey rock.

From the Rougoult pass, the mule path is clearly marked, winding gradually downhill for two hours before reaching the village of **Tasgaïwalt**. Curious village children may keep you company on the easy 40-minute walk along the track, keeping the river to your left, to the village of **Amezri** (2250m). The **Gîte d'Etape Agnid Mohamed** (per person Dh40, breakfast Dh20, meals Dh50) has large sleeping rooms, some overlooking the valley, with a rudimentary shower and toilets, and convenient camping (Dh20).

Day 3: Amezri to Aït Ali n'Ito
6HR/18KM/427M DESCENT/150M ASCENT

Your path follows the Tessaout River, shelving gently from 2250m to 1833m. The valley is flanked by impressive cliffs, particularly the sheer Ichbbakene escarpment, which rises 600m above the river

The river has few fish since floods flushed them out years ago, but it does irrigate exceptionally lovely terraces cultivated by Aafan Berbers. In spring, the area is covered with wildflowers and blooming fruit and nut trees. Here the Tessaout flows west, fed by streams of melted mountain snow.

Where the path crosses the river, you can often hop across on stones. In spring, you may have to wade across the river, as at the village of **Imi-n-Ikkis**, 5km from Amezri. The village has a shop (no sign) that sometimes stocks water, soft drinks, tinned food and plastic shoes to ford rivers.

Duration four days

Distance 57km

Standard medium

Start Agouti

Finish Aït Alla

Highest point Tizi n'Rougoult (2860m)

Accommodation camping and *gîtes*

Public transport yes

Summary This walk through the heart of the M'Goun will suit most trekkers, even younger ones. There is one long day of walking, but this varied trek crosses stunning mountain landscapes, and travels through river gorges, up one river and down another into remote valleys.

An hour and a half downstream, the path passes beneath the larger village of **Ichbbakene**, backed by a sheer escarpment. The path becomes a *piste* (unsealed road), and keeping the river on your left for another 2½ hours, the *piste* squeezes between the stone and mud houses of **Aït Hamza**. At the bottom of the village is a working **water mill**, used to grind wheat. Another hour leads to the village of **Aït Ali n'Ito**, where you'll find great views at the **Gîte d'Etape Assounfou** (☎066 075060, 024 385747; fax 024 385744; per person Dh50, breakfast Dh25), plus electricity, hot showers (Dh10), a boutique and even a hammam.

Day 4: Aït Ali n'Ito to Aït Alla
2½-3 HRS/8KM/150M DESCENT

A dirt road leads alongside the river with gentle climbs to the lovely village of **Fakhour**, where houses scale the hillside. Fakhour is noted for its *agadir* (fortified granary), which can be visited (a Dh10 tip for the guardian is customary).

Less than an hour beyond Fakhour, the village of **Ifoulou** sits on a bend of the river and road, drawing villagers from miles around for its Monday souq. From here, a tarmac road leads to the main Demnate–Skoura road by the bridge over the Tessaout River, below the village of **Aït Alla**. Here it's possible to find transport, although you may need to wait awhile – but after your M'Goun Traverse, you've earned the rest.

BEFORE YOU GO: M'GOUN TRAVERSE TREKKING CHECKLIST

» Maps & Books The 1:100,000 survey sheets *Azilal*, *Zawyat Ahannsal*, *Qalat M'Gouna* and *Skoura* cover all of the major trekking areas. West Col Productions' 1:100,000 *Mgoun Massif* is occasionally available in Morocco, and often stocked by **Stanfords** (www.stanfords.co.uk) and **Omnimap** (www.omnimap.com). Although devoid of contours, this map is a good trail reference. The German-produced *Kultur Trekking im Zentralen Hohen Atlas* shows the trek from Aït Bougomez to Kelaâ M'Gouna, and usefully marks and grades *gîtes* throughout the range. *Randonnées Pédestres Dans le Massif du M'Goun* is a French trekking guidebook available in major Moroccan cities.

» Guide Since Morocco's main mountain-guide school is in Tabant, there are many licensed local guides with M'Goun expertise. Guides with High Atlas training from the Imlil, Marrakesh, and Dadès and Sarhro regions usually have the know-how and contacts to lead M'Goun trips.

» Food Basic food supplies are available in Tabant and sometimes in Abachkou.

» Water Bottled water is widely available, but purifying locally sourced water is a more responsible alternative (see p40).

» Fuel For gas canisters, the hypermarket in Marrakesh is the best bet. Petrol, diesel and kerosene can be bought in Azilal.

» Gear When walking in spring or after heavy rain or snowfall, a stick or trekking pole will help you vault over streams. When water is high, you may want plastic or waterproof sandals to wade through rocky riverbeds.

» Tent Optional, but looking for lodging makes hiking days longer. There is no *gîte* in Rougoult, but there is excellent camping beside the river. Your guide should be able to arrange tents. If you don't have a tent and don't want to sleep under the stars, you'll need to spend the night in Sebt Aït Bououili, making the second-day walk longer.

» Mule Guides can sort out local muleteers and mules.

Zaouiat Ahansal   زاوية أحنصال

You'll need a 4WD for 40km of *piste* over the 2629m Tizi n'Tirghist to Zaouiat Ahansal. At the northern end of Imelghas, there's a *piste* that leads left towards Zaouiat Ahansal, and about 15km along atop a rocky hill, there's another fork in the road and a sign pointing right towards Zaouiat Ahansal. Stretches of this road are paved, but it's narrow and slow going along twisting mountain roads, especially when locals converge on Zaouiat Ahansal's Monday souq.

Arriving in Zaouiat Ahansal, cross the bridge towards the magnificent mudbrick *douar* (village) atop a steep hill; this structure once housed the entire 300-person community. You can stay here or bunk at *gîtes* in the surrounding villages of Agoudim, Amezrai and Taghia, the latter being two hours' walk upstream. North of town is Ouaouizarht (wah-ri-zat), which has a hotel and Wednesday souq.

⊙ Sights

Atelier du Tissages de l'Association du Zaouiat Ahsal

ART & CRAFT, CULTURAL CENTRE

(☺1-6pm Tue-Sun) Just past the ancient *douar* is this women's weaving centre and after-school vocational training program, where you can watch carpets woven with pronged antique carpet tools that could easily put an eye out in lesser hands. To give everyone a laugh, ask to give it a try yourself – just don't be offended if they take out your knot. The carpets are for sale, and part of the proceeds support the weaving training program and the village association's medical dispensary; the rest goes directly to the woman who made it, no middlemen involved.

🛏 Sleeping

Sidi Ahmed Amahdar   GÎTE **$**

(☏0678 53 88 82; dm with/without breakfast Dh30/50, half-board Dh120) Bunk here for hot showers, clean shared bathrooms and a clamorous welcome from the women who manage the place. For every night's stay, Dh10 is donated to the village medical dispensary and women's weaving school.

ℹ️ Getting There & Away

Your only reliable bet is 4WD, though trucks head from Tabant to Zaouiat Ahansal on Sunday, and minivans run between Zaouiat Ahansal and Aït Mohammed (Dh40) and less frequently to Ouaouizarht via Tilougguite.

Cathédrale des Rochers & Reserve Naturelle de Tamga

Continuing north along the main road from Zaouiat Ahansal leads to La Cathédrale des Rochers, the 'rock cathedral' with sheer stone faces that are a climber's challenge and delight, and the Reserve Naturelle de Tamga, a vast national reserve with eight separate parks. Birdwatchers will have a field day (or several) observing 107 species of birds, including rare and endangered species. A **botanical garden** 3km from the sign marking the park's entry highlights the park's diverse flora, including medicinal herbs said to cure rheumatism.

Overnight stays and meals are available at **Gîte le Cathédrale** (📞0523 44 20 23; dm incl half-board Dh150; lunch/dinner Dh50/60), 2km after the sign for the cathédrale.

Bin el-Ouidane

Once you've reached the cathédrale, you can loop back to Azilal via a paved road to Bin el-Ouidane. Confusingly, a lake, the dam that created the lake and a town on the shores of the lake all share the same name. The dam provides the majority of the electricity in the region, and though there isn't much of a beach scene on these jagged shores, the lake is still a sight for dry eyes. The best stretch of shoreline is southwest of the dam, mostly occupied by private villas.

🛏️ Sleeping & Eating

Dar Samy   HOMESTAY $$
(s/d incl half-board Dh500/800) A Casa family getaway that doubles as a guesthouse, with gardens and lake access downstairs and ping-pong table, barbecue grill and caidal tent on the panoramic roof terrace. Twelve themed guest rooms are inspired by Moroccan cities: Zagora has a Tuareg four-poster

bed; Volubilis has Greco-Roman murals; Ourika has *beldi* wooden furnishings. One room is wheelchair-accessible; all have ensuite bathrooms. It's on the west side of road to Ben el-Ouidane.

SOUTH OF MARRAKESH

For a quick getaway from Marrakesh, you're headed in the right direction. Popular destinations are the waterfalls of Setti Fatma; the terraced town of Imlil, wedged into a crevice below Jebel Toubkal; and the ski resort of Oukaïmeden, especially during the peak December–February snow season. But there's more to this region than meets the eye: off the Ourika Valley road, you'll find archaeological sites, healing footpaths, medicinal plant gardens, and ancient petroglyphs. Around the Lalla Takerkoust (see p110) and Ouirgane reservoirs (see p72), mountain retreats and organic farmsteads attract escapees from the heat and hubbub of Marrakesh. Further afield, this High Atlas hinterland has hidden valleys, cliffside villages, moonscape plateaux and *marabout* shrines that offer good luck to passers-by.

Ourika Valley   وادة اوريكة

This blooming valley 45 minutes by car or grand taxi from Marrakesh is the city's escape hatch. Temperatures are cooler in the shadow of snowcapped High Atlas peaks, and a patchwork of fields unrolls towards Marrakesh like a green carpet, providing places to picnic, loll and listen to your blood pressure drop. The valley is especially mood-altering from February to April, when almond and cherry orchards bloom manically and wildflowers run riot.

ℹ️ Getting There & Away

Grands taxis to Setti Fatma leave frequently from Bab er-Rob in Marrakesh (Dh35) and you may also find less-frequent minibuses to Ourika Valley destinations (Dh15 to Dh25). Most grands taxis will drop you anywhere along the Route d'Ourika, but return taxis and minibuses are easiest to find in Setti Fatma, Tnine and Aghbalou. Transport returns when full.

AGHMAT

Drivers speeding past Aghmat (aka Rhmat, Ghmat or Jemaa Rhmat) 31km from Marrakesh en route to Setti Fatma are missing a key turning point in Moroccan history – and

SOUQ DAYS

In the Ourika Valley, around Jebel Toubkal, and towards the Tizi n'Tichka pass, local market days featuring local crafts, fresh produce and donkeys include the following.

» **Monday** Tnine

» **Tuesday** Tahanaoute, Aït Ourir

» **Wednesday** Tighdouine

» **Thursday** El-Khemis

» **Friday** Aghmat

» **Saturday** Asni

» **Sunday** Setti Fatma

naturally, there was a woman involved. This town was an Idrissid dynastic capitol from AD 828 to 1058, when it was conquered by Almoravids. One of Aghmat's leading citizens was killed in the fray, leaving his brilliant, wealthy widow Zeinab en-Nafzawiyyat free to marry Almoravid leader Abu Bakr. When Abu Bakr was recalled to the Sahara to settle disputes, he divorced Zeinab so that she could remarry his cousin, Yusuf bin Tachfin. With Zeinab's financing and counsel, Yusuf bin Tachfin proved unstoppable, founding Marrakesh and expanding the Almoravid empire to the doorstep of Barcelona.

Once Almoravids moved to Marrakesh, Aghmat became a place of exile for political dissidents, including Andalusian poet-king Al-Mutamid ibn Abbad. Poetry outweighed politics in the end, and Al-Mutamid was allowed an honourable burial with his wife and children. Arts continue to prevail in Aghmat: in June the town hosts performers from Belgium to Burkina Faso for **Awaln'art** (www.awalnart.com), an international festival of street artists.

⊙ Sights & Activities

Visitors can glimpse Aghmat's former glories just behind the town's main marketplace, where Aghmat's **Friday souq** is held.

Urban Foundations   HISTORIC SITE

Excavations about 200m to the left off the main road began in 2010, co-financed by the state and (oddly enough) McDonald's, revealing ancient urban foundations, including a hammam, mosque, marketplace and irrigation. As long as the dog sleeping on the ruins remains uninterested in watchdog duty, history buffs can look around archaeological areas that aren't roped off for safety.

Mausoleum   HISTORIC SITE

Al-Mutamid's tomb is marked with an Almoravid-style domed mausoleum, signed right off the main road after the commune building, inside a garden enclosure 200m along on the left. The dissident's tomb was the site of a 1950 protest against French occupation that was violently suppressed by Pasha Glaoui – an inciting incident in Morocco's independence movement. As Al-Mutamid famously wrote in his poem 'Death' (with Dulcie Smith's 1931 translation):

Dead are the princes and the potentates
And none shall wake them.
Tell them who triumph at my death
that Death
Shall overtake them.

TNINE

Beyond the turn-off for Aghmat and 33km from Marrakesh along Rte d'Ourika is the town of Tnine (aka Tnin l'Ourika), where you may run into donkey traffic at the Monday souq – but the remarkable gardens and eco-museums in and around Tnine make the area a must-see for nature and Berber culture.

⊙ Sights & Activities

TOP CHOICE **Dar Taliba**   GARDEN, CULTURAL CENTRE

(☏0524 48 26 90; www.globaldiversity. org.uk/north-africa-community-and-conservation; El Hanchane) The Berber botany experts aren't professionals: they're students at this ground-breaking girls' secondary school about 7km west of Tnine. Through their school science program, the girls compiled an encyclopaedia of indigenous herbs with University of Marrakesh ethnobotanists. Now they're completing their second book on Berber oral histories of medical uses for mountain herbs.

'Dar Taliba students come from remote High Atlas villages, and didn't have the option of school before', explains Rachida Mouch, advisor to the school's botany club and director for the Association for Ourika Basin Well-being and Development, the local NGO running the school. 'But there's so much we can learn from these mountains. The closer you look at them, the more it broadens your horizons.'

Guests are greeted with refreshing tisanes of eight wild herbs successfully propagated on-site: verbena, mint, rosemary, marjoram, geranium, sage, thyme and absinthe. BBC's *Ground Forces* helped the girls expand their school gardens in 2004, and visits to the thriving garden can be arranged with a few days' notice and a sliding-scale donation of Dh250 to Dh500, which allows the school to provide breakfast or lunch to 84 students from impoverished backgrounds. Visiting is possible from 3pm to 5pm Monday to Thursday and Saturday.

✍ Ecomusée Berbere   MUSEUM

(☑0524 38 57 21; km37 Rte de l'Ourika, Tafza; www.ecomuseeberbere.com; admission Dh40; ☉10am-5pm) A discreet sign points from the road 4km after Tnine up a dirt path well trodden by free-range chickens into the Berber village of Tafza: here, the three-storey mudbrick *ksar* that once housed the local *caid* (chief) is now a museum. Enthusiastic guided visits cover every detail of household life, from symbols carved in door frames to silver dowry jewellery. Call ahead to reserve meals on the terrace, organise a village homestay, or arrange to visit Tafza pottery workshops to try your hand at the wheel. Before you leave, ask your host to point you towards **Tafza's marabout shrine** – unlike most whitewashed, cupola-topped shrines, it's built from local red stone and is thatched. Admission is free with a ticket stub from Marrakesh's Maison de la Photographie.

Safranerie   GARDEN

(☑0522 48 44 76; www.safran-ourika.com; km34 Rte de l'Ourika, Tnine; garden tours Dh10; ☉7.30am-5.30pm) Almost anything thrives in Ourika's rich soil, including saffron (*Crocus sativus*), organically grown here from bulbs that are cultivated near Talouine. Saffron is a high-maintenance plant, with flowers harvested before dawn for maximum potency. Guided tours are given by rather bored staff who reiterate key points on explanatory placards before trudging out to the truly fascinating garden. Tours end with a soft-sell of Safranerie saffron, but the real bargains are estate-grown herbal tisanes (Dh20 to Dh40). The place gets busy during saffron harvest (end of October to mid-November); otherwise you can relax on the patio with complimentary tea.

Nectarôme   GARDEN

(☑0524 31 38 00; www.nectarome.com; km34 Rte de l'Ourika, Tnine; garden visits Dh10; ☉10am-5pm) In the town centre of Tnine, signs off the main road point west towards the organic botanical gardens of a Franco-Moroccan natural bath-product company combining Berber herbal remedies with modern aromatherapy. The garden certainly smells great, and a footbath and foot massage with organic essential oils (Dh100 to Dh200) is just the thing after a trek.

La Clédes Huiles   MUSEUM

(☑0524 48 20 30; km35 Rte de l'Ourika; www.lacledeshuiles.com; admission with tasting Dh25; ☉8am-5pm) A couple of kilometres past Tnine is this farmhouse eco-museum housing a traditional Moroccan olive-oil press. The French wall text covers some interesting facts – olive trees can reach 2000 years of age, and 80% to 90% of Moroccan olive trees yield Picholine olives – plus enough industry-insider minutiae to satisfy olive obsessives. Tastings of estate-grown oils, jam and bread are offered in an adjoining room; a restaurant was under construction at the time of our visit. A stone villa guesthouse and bungalows (doubles/quads Dh880/1100) offer comfortable quarters in 10-hectare gardens, plus a pool right in the olive grove.

🛏 Sleeping & Eating

🏅TOP CHOICE Jardin de Timalizene   DAR $

(incl half-board per adult Dh440, child 12-18yr Dh330) Follow the garden path to the Café des Arts' sister property: a mudbrick country house with five cosy bedrooms available to guests with en-suite bathrooms, wood-beamed ceilings, garden views, and reading nooks (ask for the double with the sleeping loft). Your hosts Mustapha and Rémi have called this *dar* home since 1996 – trust them to organise botanical treks, excursions by dromedary or donkey, and walks to local spots where High Atlas rock salt is found. Discounts are offered online

Café des Arts   FUSION $

(☑0524 48 40 59; www.timalizene.com, in French; km41 Rte de l'Ourika, Timalizene) Lunch, hammocks, sculpture and bunnies await your arrival at this garden getaway approximately 8km after Tnine – look for red banners to the east across the bridge. Call ahead for creative meals (Dh150) that make the most of wild herbs and garden-grown organic produce, including seasonal specialities like local turkey in Oaxaca-style molé sauce and fennel braised in mountain honey. Afterwards, wander organic gardens to meet resident rabbits, and check out shows by Moroccan contemporary artists in the gallery.

ℹ Information

Centre d'Informations Touristique Ourika
(☑0668 46 55 45; ⊘8.30am-7pm Mon-Sat, 8.30am-1pm Sun) Just outside Tnine, this local NGO-operated information office provides maps of valley vista points and updates on trekking conditions. December to March, flash floods can make hiking dangerous and render parts of Ourika Valley inaccessible – in 1995, winter floods nearly wiped out the village of Oulmes.

AGHBALOU

A **red stone mosque** and **minaret** are the signature landmarks of Aghbalou, a village some 47km along the Rte de l'Ourika from Marrakesh. Around town are prime spots to dine along the rushing river, and rural retreats to sleep in peace away from Setti Fatma crowds.

⊨ Sleeping

Auberge le Maquis   HOTEL $
(☑0524 48 45 31; www.le-maquis.com, in French; km45 Rte de l'Ourika; s/d half-board Dh450/840) A warm welcome awaits at this eight-room, family-style getaway and launching pad/ finish line for bikers and trekkers. The local management makes meals feel like dinners among friends, and there's a play-yard where kids cut loose. Nonguests can use the pool for Dh80, and the *auberge* arranges treks to Yaggour plateau petroglyphs and mule treks for little ones.

Ourika Garden   HOTEL $$
(☑0524 48 44 41; www.ourika-garden.com; km49.5 Rte de l'Ourika, outside Aghbalou; s incl breakfast Dh660-880, d Dh760-1280; ❉☀☲) A gardener's dream, with flagstone paths through aromatic herbs and vegetables leading over footbridges to a stone-walled lodge. Guest rooms have fireplaces, seating nooks, hewn-wood furnishings, and en-suite bathrooms with variable hot water (shower early). Breakfasts on the terrace feature High Atlas views, local honey and olive oil, and there's wi-fi by the patio bar.

✘ Eating

There are cafes dotting the riverbanks from Aghbalou through Oulmes serving kebabs and salad (Dh50) or tajines big enough for two (Dh60), with carpets spread out under shady trees in good weather.

Auberge Le Maquis   RESTAURANT $$
(☑0524 48 45 31; www.le-maquis.com, in French; km45 Rte de l'Ourika; meals Dh70-120) If you're just passing through Aghbalou, you might call ahead for reasonably priced and reliably tasty Berber meals on linen-topped tables here.

Ikalimo Ourika   RESTAURANT $$
(☑0524 38 54 46; km46 Rte de l'Ourika; lunch Dh90-150) Lunch comes with a side of adventure just outside of Aghbalou at this *auberge*-restaurant, located across the river via a wobbly swing bridge and following arrows along an uphill path through a hillside village. Call a couple hours ahead to secure Berber tajines and a spot by the fireplace, or enjoy brochettes and salad on the sunny terrace with spectacular valley views.

TREKKING IMLIL TO SETTI FATIMA

Day trippers glimpse the High Atlas through car windows, but with a day or two more, you can walk from Imlil to Setti Fatma through impressive scenery that can't be seen by car. A scenic and relatively leisurely three-day walking route leads over one rocky high pass, followed by a long descent into the upper Ourika Valley, where green terraces and shady walnut groves cascade down steep mountainsides. The route passes through a dozen Berber villages, some of which have yet to be connected with electricity – hard to believe the Imlil trailhead is only two hours from Marrakesh, and easily accessible by public transport.

Day 1: Imlil to Ouaneskra
3HR/7KM/560M ASCENT
This trek begins with almost the same route as the Toubkal Circuit, heading from the trailhead into the mountains. Once you reach **Tizi n'Tamatert** (2279m), it's an easy 45-minute walk to the village of **Ouaneskra** with lovely views across the valley.

Ouaneskra has three well-run **gîtes** (per person Dh50, meals Dh20-50, hot shower Dh10). The first one is reliably clean, and you'll reach it just before you cross the river outside the village. The other two are five minutes away at either end of the village.

If you walked to Ouaneskra in the morning, you could spend the afternoon in the Imenane Valley, which stretches from Ouaneskra and Tacheddirt northwest towards Asni. The land is meticulously cultivated, and you could explore the seven remote Berber villages lining the valley.

Alternatively, you could get a head start on the next day's walk by continuing another half-hour (2km) to **Tacheddirt** (2300m), following the paved road as it veers to the right before Ouaneskra and crossing the Amagdoul plateau, which in summer is a popular camp site. In Tacheddirt you can stay at the **CAF refuge** (dm CAF/HI members/nonmembers Dh30/45/60) or in the house of one of the *refuge* operators (Dh40), but the best option is **Tigmmi n' Tacheddirt** (☑0662 10 51 69; per person from Dh50), with memorable views and good facilities.

Day 2: Ouaneskra to Timichi
6-7 HRS/12KM/900M ASCENT/1300M DESCENT

Follow the well-used mule path out of Ouaneskra to Tacheddirt, which is surrounded by beautifully terraced fields. On the far side of the village, the track begins to climb steadily 870m to **Tizi n'Tacheddirt** (3230m), with the pass ahead of you visible the entire way.

The rocky path keeps to the left-hand side of the riverbed, zigzagging steeply up towards the south face of Jebel Angour (3616m) for the last half-hour. The pass is exposed and windy but offers stunning views, followed by an exhilarating and very long descent (at least three hours) to Timichi. There's a sheltered spot for lunch 30 minutes' walk beyond Tizi n'Tacheddirt.

The path heads down past ancient, gnarled juniper trees and around the sloping eastern flank of Jebel Angour, where sheep and goats are brought to graze from early spring. Though fairly well defined, this part of the trail is very rocky and at times clings precariously to the mountain-side. Proceed with caution if there's any precipitation, as it gets dangerously slippery when wet.

The landscape gradually changes from a pale coffee colour to red and green. Finally, the cascading terraces of Iabassene village come into view. Head for the huge old walnut tree standing guard outside the village, then follow the path that leads past the houses. The path veers northeast from here, and Timichi is another 2km further.

There are two *gîtes* at this point of the trail: **Chez Ali Ouhya** (dm Dh30, hot shower Dh10) in Iabassene, and **Chez Oussalem Brahim** (dm with hot shower Dh40) in Timichi. The latter is outside the village proper, on the south side of the river, and has a great terrace overlooking the bustling village. Basic meals are usually available at both places.

BEFORE YOU GO: IMLIL TO SETTI FATIMA CHECKLIST

» **Map** Get the 1:100,000 *Oukaïmeden-Toubkal* government survey sheet.

» **Guide** Setti Fatma has a **bureaux des guides** (☑/fax 0524 42 61 13).

» **Transport** Buses and grands taxis (Dh30) travel between Setti Fatma and Bab er-Rob in Marrakesh (67km).

» **Weather check** The Tizi n'Tacheddirt mountain pass closes December through February, and in November and March; check to ensure it's open before you begin your trek.

THE TREK AT A GLANCE

Duration three days (possibly two days by very fit walkers)

Distance 30km

Standard easy to medium

Start Imlil village

Finish Setti Fatma

Highest point Tizi n'Tacheddirt (3230m)

Accommodation Camping and *gîtes*

Public transport yes

Summary A superb and relatively leisurely three-day walk through some of the most spectacular country in the High Atlas. The route leads over only one rocky high pass, which is followed by a long descent into the upper Ourika Valley.

Day 3: Timichi to Setti Fatma
3½-4 HRS/12KM/370M DESCENT

Cross the river bed and turn right to follow the long, easy trail that runs east above cornfields and walnut groves, passing through Tiourdiou and a string of other small villages: Tiwediwe, Anfli and Tadrart. Along the way are bird's-eye views onto intricate irrigation channels and village terraces. In late May and early June, many of these terraces are crammed with golden barley, ready for summer harvest. As the valley gradually opens, the path starts to climb higher, clinging to bare mountainsides.

Since the path becomes increasingly rocky at Tadrart, you might prefer to follow the dirt road, which brings you into Setti Fatma in 1½ hours. To extend your vacation from road traffic a little longer, pick your way along the river's course from Tiwediwe to the trail's end in Setti Fatma, where piping-hot tajines await at riverside cafes.

SETTI FATMA ستي فتما

A little village that's seen a whole lot of tourist action in the past decade, Setti Fatma is a scenic stop for lunch by the river and hikes to seven waterfalls. The village is neatly nestled in a canyon beneath the High Atlas mountains at the southern end of the Ourika Valley road, 24km south of the Oukaïmeden turn-off at Aghbalou. Waterfall hikes range from an easy 20-minute stroll to arduous stream hikes; ignore the

faux guides and follow the paths, or find a licensed guide to lead the way on foot or mule at the bureau des guides (p127).

Prime times to visit are in early March where the cherry and almond trees are in bloom, or in August for the four-day *moussem*, with its fair and market at the *koubba* of Setti Fatma. During the summer the place is clogged with visitors from Marrakesh gasping for air; to cool down without the crowds, head instead to the splendidly untrammelled Zat Valley (p120).

🛏 Sleeping & Eating

TOP CHOICE **Hôtel Restaurant La Perle D'Ourika**　　　　CAFE, GUESTHOUSE **$**
(📱0666 34 95 99; d incl breakfast Dh200-450; set meals Dh100-120) Kitted out colourfully as a Marrakshi water-seller, this cliff-edge cafe is smartly run by motherly Ammaria, who will ply you with her legendary seasonal couscous dishes, including wild mushroom. Simple, sunny whitewashed guest rooms with colourful wedding bedspreads and shared bathrooms are downstairs.

Hôtel Asgaour　　　　CAFE, GUESTHOUSE **$**
(📱0666 41 64 19; 3-person tr shared/private bathroom Dh150/100) Basic but airy, clean rooms with lumpy pillows and hot showers (Dh5) upstairs, plus a restaurant downstairs serving bubbling, well-caramelised tajines (Dh50 to Dh60).

From Oulmes to Setti Fatima, both sides of the river are dotted with rustic cafe-restaurants offering tajines priced to move, though some on the east riverbank are accessed by dodgy rope-and-plank bridges. Two of the better choices in Setti Fatma proper are **Café-Restaurant Imlil** (on left side near the parking at the end of town), and **Café-Restaurant Azrrabzou** (opposite the river) over a plank bridge in a patch of almond trees. Both offer set meals with salad, tajine/kebabs and bottled water for Dh50 to Dh60, or large Dh50 tajines to satisfy two famished trekkers.

ⓘ Information

Bureau des Guides (📱/fax 0524 42 61 13) Located 200m beyond the Hôtel Asgaour. Offers advice on treks to Imlil (p106), east to Tourcht, north to Imi-n-Taddert, to Anammer and Tiz n'Oucheg in the Aït Oucheg Valley, and from the Yaggour Plateau into the Zat Valley.

Pharmacy Asgaour (🕙10am-8pm) A helpful pharmacist with a good selection of first aid, medicine and women's products.

OUKAÏMEDEN

اوكيمدين

Best known as Morocco's ski resort, Oukaïmeden (elevation 2650m, 75km from Marrakesh) is also a High Atlas trekking destination, with outer-space landscapes, ancient petroglyphs, and **alpine wildflowers** in spring; Club Alpin Français (CAF) can point you towards trailheads.

In snow season, skiers will find **seven ski runs** from nursery to black, six tows, and the highest ski lift in Africa (3243m). Gear, passes and lessons are available in town at prices that will delight skiers used to European and American rates. Peak season has historically been late January to March, but in recent years snow has been scarce by March. When snow is low on the slopes, skiers can **cross-country ski** here or 'snowboard' the dunes in Merzouga (p158).

Long before snow bunnies arrived, there was a high-altitude civilisation in Oukaïmeden. A sign points toward **petroglyphs** on the right side of road as you enter town. For a modest tip (Dh10) a local guide can help you locate six different enigmatic symbols carved into the rock face: a hunter, bull, dagger, human, a mysterious circle thought to represent feminine power, and an animal that looks like a deer but is believed to be an elephant.

🛏 Sleeping & Eating

CAF refuge HOSTEL €
(📞0524 31 90 36; www.caf-maroc.com; dm CAF or HI members/nonmembers Dh69/110, hot showers Dh5; 🛜) Offers heated dormitories (four to eight beds per room), a bar-restaurant (breakfast/dish/meal Dh22/60/80, beer Dh15 to Dh32, wine Dh65 to Dh120), a well-equipped kitchen, a library and wi-fi, but you'll need your own sleeping bag. They can arrange group pick-ups from Marrakesh (Dh400 for one to four by grand taxi or Dh700 to Dh900 for nine to 12 by minibus or 4WD), and they sell French trekking guidebooks. Bathrooms are on the 1st floor, but the nicest bunk beds are in pine-ceilinged rooms upstairs. Kids under age 16 are eligible for discounts on meals and stays.

Hôtel Chez Juju HOTEL €€€
(📞0524 31 90 05; www.hotelchezjuju.com; d incl half-board Dh1330-1580) Reliable restaurant with a bar (whiskey and wine Dh60 to Dh120), plus simple alpine-style rooms with en-suite bathrooms. Nicer renovated doubles have mountain views, pine panelling, cotton quilts and flowered drapes;

grimmer rooms in back have frayed carpet and bathrooms curtained off in the corner.

Hotel Club Louka HOTEL €€€
(📞0524 31 90 41; www.clublouka.com; s/d Dh850/1100, chalet Dh3900; ❄🛜) Sticking out amid snowcapped mountains like a fake tan in winter is this apricot-tinted high-rise, with 101 bland rooms and generic international restaurant-lounge (breakfast/dinner Dh110/240). On the plus side, there's a big indoor swimming pool and hammam on the premises, and new wooden alpine chalets to house four friends or a family in style – picture windows and fireplaces downstairs, sleeping lofts and Finnish saunas upstairs. Call ahead; off-season, the hotel often closes for maintenance.

❶ Getting There & Away

If you're not travelling by rental car, your best bet is transport through CAF. Otherwise, you can charter a grand taxi from Marrakesh's Bab er-Rob (Dh400 to Dh600).

Toubkal & High Atlas

Welcome to North Africa's highest mountain range, known by local Berbers as 'Idraren Draren' (Mountains of Mountains), and a trekker's paradise from spring through to autumn. The High Atlas runs diagonally across Morocco for almost 1000km, but the Toubkal region contains all the highest peaks – and since these mountains are 2½ hours from Marrakesh, it's the most frequently visited High Atlas region.

The first road was cut through this remote region in the early 20th century, over the Tizi n'Test pass. Before that, the only way to travel was via mountain mule trails, leading from the Sahara to northern plains. You can still walk these ancient tracks, following the footsteps of dauntless pilgrims and desert traders under brilliant blue African skies.

For pure mountain air that cuts through the heat and leaves you giddy, don't miss the highest mountain in North Africa: snow-capped Jebel Toubkal. Mountain trails crisscrossing the High Atlas (p113) start from base camps at Imlil. On the way to Imlil, you could make a pit stop 47km south of Marrakesh at **Asni** for roadside tajines and the **Saturday souq**, where you may spot Berber rugs and silver jewellery amid fruit stalls and donkey auctions. You could walk the rest of the way in about six hours; an

WORTH A TRIP

GREAT ESCAPES FROM MARRAKESH: LALLA TAKERKOUST COUNTRY RETREATS

Involving as Marrakesh is, it's surprisingly easy to put it behind you an hour down the Rte d'Amizmiz, near the reservoir of Lalla Takerkoust. The artificial lake is a sight for dry eyes, but better still are new country retreats in nearby farmsteads, olive groves and Berber villages.

Jnane Tihihit
FARM, RESORT $$

(☎0668 46 55 45; Douar Makhfamane; www.riad-t.com/jnane-tihihit; d Dh500-720; ☒) Relax the way nature intended, on an organic farmstead with solar-heated, whitewashed pisé (rammed-earth) bungalows amid pomegranate trees. Foodies can tend saffron gardens and learn to make couscous, while kids help feed donkeys and chickens in the barnyard. Lounge by the chemical-free basin pool, head to the lakefront beach, get steam-cleaned in the hammam or hole up by the library fireplace. It's to the right 500m off km40 on the Rte d'Amizmiz, in Douar Makhfamane.

Tigmi
RESORT $$$

(☎0524 48 40 20; km24 Route d'Amizmiz, Douar Tagadert; www.tigmi.com; s/d incl half-board Dh1750/2250, ste Dh2100; ☒☒) Poolside deck chairs overlook a palm oasis, un-rolled like a green carpet at the foot of this Berber village. Tunisian architect Charles Boccara designed this village resort from local materials without sacrificing modern comfort: guest rooms have mudbrick fireplaces, sabra coverlets over thick duvets, high palm-beam ceilings overhead and thick red Chichaoua carpets underfoot. Stroll through the oasis, but return for sunset aperitifs, a hammam and argan-oil massage.

Dar Zitoune
RESORT $$

(☎0662 40 83 80; Douar Zii; www.dar-zitoune.com; s incl breakfast Dh480-530, d Dh660-810) Escape the urban hustle in this stone-walled country house, with a pool in the garden, spacious guest rooms with hand-carved Berber furnishings, and lazy breakfasts on the patio overlooking a patchwork of farmland. Your host Anouar organises on-site hammams and massages, plus eco-excursions from canoeing to dromedary-riding. Pets are welcome, and pet-sitting services are available. It's off Rte d'Amizmiz.

---

old mule track outside Asni leads through the **Mizane Valley** past tiny Berber villages to Imlil.

❶ Getting There & Away
Frequent local buses (Dh15, 1½ hours) and grands taxis (Dh30, one hour) leave south of Bab er-Rob in Marrakesh for Asni. Local mini-buses and occasional taxis travel the final 17km between Asni and Imlil (Dh15 to Dh20, one hour). Expect a car journey from Marrakesh to Imlil to take at least 2½ hours.

IMLIL
إمليل

A favourite hitching post for mountain trekkers and overheated Marrakesh escap-ees, Imlil (elevation 1740m) is just a five-hour hike from the base of Jebel Toubkal. Day trippers from Marrakesh can hike from Imlil to neighbouring Armoud, but in spring, you won't want to miss waking up in these flowering High Atlas foothills.

🛏 Sleeping & Eating
Prices at local *gîtes* increase by at least 15% in high season between April and October; some places close in the cold off-season be-tween November and February. Additional options are nearby in Armoud.

TOP CHOICE **Douar Samra**
DAR $$

(☎0524 37 86 05; www.douar-samra. com; Tamartet village; per person incl half-board Dh480-645; ☎) At the east end of the val-ley facing Imlil, a trail zigzags among low-slung houses made of pisé; the triple-decker one is Douar Samra guesthouse. A sheep parked on a nearby rooftop bleats a neigh-bourly hello, and hewn stone steps lead to candlelit, wood-beamed guest rooms. Don-keys deliver luggage, but there's wi-fi in the organic garden and aperitifs with terrace sunsets. Garden rooms accommodate fami-lies, and for romance, there's an alpine wood cabin.

Kasbah du Toubkal KASBAH $$$

(☎0524 48 56 11, 33 0549 050135; www.
kasbahdutoubkal.com; dm incl breakfast Dh1440-
1780, d Dh1780-2780, ste Dh3440-4890; ☎)
This converted historic kasbah (1800m)
lords it over Imlil with views of snowy
peaks and verdant valleys. The 11 bed-
rooms range from quaintly cute to kasbah
cool, and 'Berber salons' allow families and
groups to bunk communally. At guests'
disposal are a traditional hammam, moun-
tain guides, board games, wi-fi and tasty
meals (Dh160 to Dh390). Two nights mini-
mum; a 5% community tariff on stays has
helped build a local girls' school and buy an
ambulance.

Dar Zaratoustra INN $

(Chez Jean Habib, Atlas Gîte Imlil; ☎0524 48 56
01; http://toubkal-maroc.voila.net; Imlil; d incl
half-board Dh350-550; ☺Mar-Oct; ☎) Enter
through the green tunnel of a grape arbour
to this mountain retreat with unexpected
amenities: a garden shaded by a chestnut
tree, terrace sunbeds, communal library,
wi-fi in the lobby and a domed hammam
with starry tiles (Dh60). Carpet-strewn
guest rooms have communal bathrooms,
and some doubles have views; downstairs is
Imlil's best-stocked bar, and Moroccan food
with a hint of Burgundy.

Dar Ouassaggou DAR $

(☎0667 49 13 52; www.guesthouseouassaggou.
com; Douar Aït Soukka; d incl breakfast Dh320-
400; ✱▣@) A walnut orchard shades the
valley path east of Imlil to this eight-room
guesthouse, where visitors are received like
long-lost relatives by Houssein, an English-
speaking mountain guide, and his family.
Cosy, comfortable bedrooms have en-suite
bathrooms, one with a *tadelakt* tub. The
sunny terrace is ideal after a morning trek,
internet and washing machines are avail-
able (Dh10), and homemade meals include
soup, tajine and dessert (Dh100).

Hôtel Etoile de Toubkal HOTEL $

(☎0524 48 56 18; s/d incl breakfast Dh120/180,
d with bathroom Dh250-300) Not exactly a
scenic view of the parking at the village
entrance, but the 10 rooms have balconies,
carved doors and wood-beamed ceilings,
and some have bathrooms with *tadelakt*
showers. Tiled tables in the garden offer
a quiet retreat, though a mosque is under
construction next door; laundry is available
and credit cards accepted.

Riad Imlil MAISON D'HÔTE $$

(☎0524 48 54 85; www.riadimlil.com; s/d incl
breakfast Dh500/770; ✱☎) Marrakesh style
heads for the mountains in Imlil's new 20-
room stone guesthouse. Bedrooms are comfortable and climate-controlled with hewn
wood furnishings, wrought-iron windows
and modern en-suite bathrooms, though
keeping dust at the doorstep is a challenge.
Rooms facing the courtyard are quieter but
darker; there's in-room wi-fi, and dining by
the salon fireplace.

Hôtel el-Aïne INN $

(☎0524 48 56 25; d incl breakfast without/with
bathroom Dh300/350; ☎) Get the light, pleasant upstairs rooms around a tranquil courtyard with an old walnut tree. Expect hot
showers, solid meals (Dh70 to Dh90) and
shared toilets.

Café-Hotel Soleil HOTEL $

(☎0524 48 56 22; www.hotelsoleil.com; d incl
breakfast without/with bathroom Dh300/350;
☎) A sociable spot that offer five basic
dorm-style rooms with shared bathrooms,
eight renovated rooms with en-suite bathrooms, and meals (Dh70 to Dh90) in the
riverside restaurant. Through the downtown parking lot, opposite the *bureau de
guides*.

CAF Refuge HOSTEL $

(☎0524 48 56 12; www.caf-maroc.com; dm CAF
& HI members/nonmembers Dh45/60, camping
incl shower per person/tent Dh30/20) A climbers' hostel offers dorm-style bunks, camping, cooking facilities, hot showers, picnics
(Dh50), hot meals (Dh80), and baggage
storage (Dh10 per day).

ℹ Information

Imlil has a highly informative **bureau des guides**
(☎/fax 0524 48 56 26), though travel agencies
in Marrakesh can also arrange Toubkal treks
with English-speaking guides.

ARMOUD

For Berber hospitality above the trekker
fray in Imlil, head 3km up to the hilltop
village of Armoud (aka Armed or Aroumd),
at 1960m. You could take the drivable *piste*
from Imlil instead – but the walking path
passes a burbling stream, stone houses
and shady orchards. Follow the path uphill
(southwest) through Armoud to **number
106** (look for the ochre door), where the
women of the house will invite trekkers for

tea among sheep and carpets woven from shredded T-shirts, with views over the orchards and mountains (Dh20 tip gratefully received).

🛏 Sleeping & Eating

TOP CHOICE Les Roches Armed/Chez Lahcen
DAR $

(📞067 644915; dm Dh40, d per person incl half-board Dh150) Atop Armoud, guests enjoy 360-degree mountain views, admire courtyard gardens, and chat by the living room fireplace before retreating to private rooms with *tataoui* (woven palm) ceilings or clean dorms. Shared bathrooms are clean and spiffy, with hot showers; hearty cooking made with High Atlas produce is served on local crockery emblazoned with Berber power symbols.

Dar Warawt/Chez Omar Jellah
DAR $

(📞0667 41 46 23; omarjellah@yahoo.co.uk; per person Dh50) Ideal for families trekking together, this guesthouse is a new, fully equipped apartment downstairs from the family home of English-speaking guide Omar Jellah. Through arched doorways is a salon with Jebel Toubkal views, stucco-edged bedrooms, and an enviable kitchen with new appliances. You can cook here, or arrange meals (Dh100).

Dar Adrar
DAR $

(📞070 726809; www.daradrar.com; s/d incl breakfast Dh130/200, with bathroom from Dh250/300,) Sitting on top of the world across from Armoud, Dar Adrar has simple rooms that don't distract from the mountaintop views, an in-house hammam (Dh40) and an excellent resource in owner and mountain guide Mohamed Aztat.

Hôtel Armed
HOTEL $

(📞0524 48 57 45; s/d incl breakfast Dh150/300) Across the valley from Armoud, this hotel-restaurant offers straightforward rooms with stiff beds, hot showers, help arranging treks, a panoramic terrace and solid Berber cooking – even local guides eat here.

Camping-Auberge Atlas Toubkal/Chez Omar le Rouge
CAMPING, INN $

(📞0524 48 57 50; s/d Dh50/100, camping per person Dh15; 🅿) Hillside camp site with parking (Dh10) or basic rooms with hard mattresses and communal facilities, including hot showers (Dh10) and meals (breakfast/tajine Dh20/40).

JEBEL TOUBKAL ASCENT
تساق جبل توبقال

North Africa's tallest peak, Jebel Toubkal (4167m), doesn't require climbing experience. In summer, anyone in good physical condition can reach the summit. In early October runners of the **Toubkal Marathon** (www.toubkaltrail.com) scamper 42km up and down Jebel Toubkal, with current record times of 7:23 hours set by an Italian woman and 5:39 hours by a local hero from Imlil. For extreme ultramarathoners, the organisers tacked a 106km High Atlas trail onto the marathon, calling it the **Toubkal Trail**.

Although the 3313m ascent from Imlil isn't technically difficult, challenges include Toubkal's notoriously extreme, fast-changing climate, steep slopes of volcanic scree, and altitude sickness. Hikers should factor in sufficient time to ascend slowly and steadily; for a more leisurely ascent, camp en route at Sidi Chamharouch. An ascent of Toubkal can be combined with satellite peaks, and very fit trekkers ascend Ouanoukrim (4088m) as well.

Day 1: Imlil to Toubkal Refuge
5-6 HRS/10KM/1467M ASCENT

Toubkal looms above the trailhead at **Imlil** heading towards the Toubkal *refuge;* ideally head off early morning – it's uphill all the way, with little shade past Armoud. Follow the dirt track leading to **Armoud** (Armed) past the **Kasbah du Toubkal**. Beyond the kasbah, the path zigzags steeply upwards to

---

THE TREK AT A GLANCE

Duration two days

Distance 22km

Standard medium to hard

Start/Finish Imlil village

Highest Point Jebel Toubkal (4167m)

Accommodation camping and mountain *refuges*

Public Transport yes

Summary The most popular walk in the High Atlas, with magnificent views. The route is straightforward, but the trek up the scree slope is hard, and trekkers can be struck with altitude sickness. The trek is best in summer and autumn, but check conditions before departure – there can be snow even in June.

» **Maps** The same maps are recommended as for the Toubkal Circuit (p116).

» **Water** Purifying locally sourced water is a more responsible alternative than bottled water (see p40), but don't count on finding available water sources. Pack plenty of water from June to October.

» **Guide** Although the route is marked, a guide is recommended for the ascent, especially for inexperienced mountaineers and in variable conditions from October to June. Experienced, licensed guides are listed at Imlil's **bureau des guides** (✆/fax 0524 48 56 26).

» **Food** Meals and snacks are available at Toubkal Refuge and Refuge Mouflon, but you can also find lunch supplies in Imlil and a wide selection of portable snacks in Marrakesh supermarkets.

» **Mule** For this two-day trek with limited gear requirements, most experienced trekkers won't require a mule. If you would prefer one, guides can organise mules and muleteers for you.

» **Gear** Bring a sleeping bag. You won't need a tent, unless you'd rather camp than stay at *refuges* – just ask your guide to arrange tents in advance.

rejoin the road at Armoud, where towering slopes begin to close around you.

Past Armoud, cross the stony valley floor and follow the well-defined mule trail uphill towards a very large rock above the eastern side of the Assif Reraya, which leads to the hamlet and *marabout* of **Sidi Chamharouch** (2310m). Legend has it that Sidi Chamharouch is king of the *djinn* (genies), which might help explain why there's no body in his mausoleum (open to Muslims only).

The number of pilgrims and peak-baggers has given birth to a cluster of stalls almost halfway between Imlil and the Toubkal *refuge* selling soft drinks, food and souvenirs. Beyond the *marabout* to the left of the track are cascades, pools and a prime picnic spot in the shady overhang of the rocks.

After crossing the river by the bridge at Sidi Chamharouch, the rocky path veers away from the river for a couple of kilometres and zigzags above the valley floor. It then levels off, before rejoining the course of the river. The **Toubkal refuge** is visible for an hour before you reach it, immediately below the western flank of Jebel Toubkal.

Day 2: The Ascent
9HR/12KM/960M ASCENT & DESCENT
Set off as early as possible to avoid climbing in the sun – there is no shade, only rocks – and be sure to dress warmly and pack extra water and snacks. If you've trekked here directly from Imlil you may not be acclimatised, so walk at a steady, slow pace to avoid

altitude sickness. If you experience severe headache or vomiting, descend immediately. However tempting, do not lie down to sleep on the slope.

Two cwms (valleys formed by glacial activity) run down the western flank of Toubkal, divided by the west-northwest ridge, which leads down from the summit. The southern cwm is the more usual route, and starts immediately below the *refuge* to the left, where you cross the river and head eastwards to the scree slope.

Start to climb the well-defined path to the left of the slope, cross the field of boulders, then follow the path that zigzags up to **Tizi n'Toubkal** (3940m), straight ahead on the skyline. From there the path turns left (northeast) and follows the ridge to the summit (4167m). Allow up to four hours to reach the top, depending on your fitness and weather conditions.

Stick to the same route coming down, bearing left when the *refuge* comes into view. The descent to the *refuge* should only take 2½ hours, after which you can return to Armoud or Imlil. If you are planning on spending a second night at the *refuge,* you could come down the longer route via the Ihibi sud, or south circuit. It's a straightforward four-hour walk down to the *refuge* for well-earned congratulations and celebratory chocolate.

TOUBKAL CIRCUIT   جولة جبل توبقال

Beyond the majestic peaks and fabulous views of Jebel Toubkal, this circuit offers

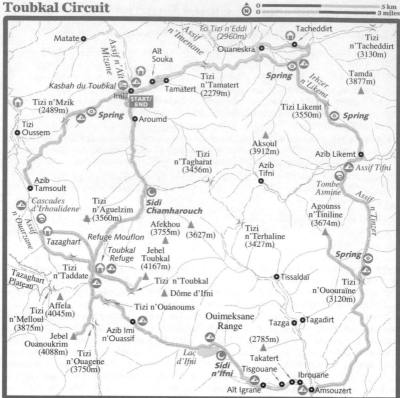

fascinating glimpses into Berber life in remote High Atlas villages. You will need camping gear for this route, though with short detours you could use basic village accommodation and mountain *refuges*.

Challenge Level

Since this trek is fairly strenuous, you might want an extra rest day. The ascent of Jebel Toubkal takes place on the sixth day, allowing five days of acclimatisation to altitude. Most of the route is above 2000m, with several passes over 3000m.

When to Go

Late April to late June is ideal: alpine flowers bloom April–May and by June, when Marrakesh is melting, daytime temperatures are pleasantly warm. Temperatures often drop below freezing November–May, and snow covers higher peaks and passes. Only lower-valley walking is possible dur-

ing this season, unless you're prepared to bring ropes and crampons.

Midsummer guarantees long daylight hours and snow-free passes (though not always a snow-free Toubkal), but in the lower valleys temperatures can be extremely hot and water nonexistent. July and August are the busiest months in the High Atlas, but trekking is best done early morning and later in the afternoon, leaving plenty of time for a shady lunch and rest.

Before you set off on your trek, check the weather forecast. Flash flooding can occur in summer after thunderstorms – something to bear in mind when deciding where to camp. Rivers have maximum flow in autumn (November) and late spring (April or May).

Day 1: Imlil to Tacheddirt

3½-4½ HRS/9.5KM/560M ASCENT

Much of today's relatively gentle route follows the 4WD track linking **Imlil** (1740m) to the village of **Ouaneskra**, 2km west of Tacheddirt (2300m). Follow the track through Imlil and take the left-hand fork over the river, **Assif n'Aït Mizane**. The road climbs gently eastwards through fields of barley and orchards of walnuts, apple and cherries before zigzagging up to **Aït Souka**.

After an hour, just past a stream known as Talat n'Aït Souka, you can either take the road north directly to the pass at **Tizi n'Tamatert** (2279m), or follow a fairly well defined but rocky path east, skirting **Tamatert** village. The rocky path continues eastwards for 15 minutes, passing through a small pine grove and crossing the road, before climbing steeply northeast to reach Tizi n'Tamatert. The walk up takes 30 to 45 minutes.

At the pass is **Bivi Thé**, a weather-beaten shack selling soft drinks and mint tea only when there is enough business. To the northeast are great views of **Tizi n'Eddi** (2960m), the pass leading to Oukaïmeden, and **Tizi n'Tacheddirt** (3130m), northeast of which is the beautiful **Ourika Valley**.

The path and tarmac meet at Tizi n'Tamatert, where it's an easy 45-minute walk to Ouaneskra. Along this stretch you'll be treated to views across the valley to neat Berber houses and lush terraces in Talate n'Chaoute, Tamguist and Ouaneskra.

Shortly before Ouaneskra, the path divides. The mule track to the right traverses the southern side of the valley to an ideal camping place near the track, close to the **Irhzer n'Likemt** stream and the starting place for tomorrow's climb.

The longer route via **Ouaneskra** and **Tacheddirt** takes the northern side of the valley after crossing Tizi n'Tamatert. There are three *gîtes* in Ouaneskra and a pleasant little restaurant – but tomorrow's walk is long, so it's best to have lunch and carry on. The village of **Tacheddirt** is 2km further along the well-defined mule trail or the tarmac road that runs along the north side of the slope. In Tacheddirt, 50 people can sleep at **Tigmmi n Tacheddirt** (☑0662 10 51 69; per person incl half-board & shared/private bathroom Dh130/200), a new *gîte* that's the nicest for miles around. You may be able to stay at the CAF Refuge or *chez l'habitant* (Dh30 to Dh50). From Tacheddirt, the hiking track loops south, up to the camp site near Irhzer n'Likemt.

Day 2: Tacheddirt to Azib Likemt

5-6 HRS/9KM/1200M ASCENT/900M DESCENT

Leave Tacheddirt early to make the two- to three-hour walk up to **Tizi Likemt** (3550m), winding around the head of the valley on a more gentle ascent instead of heading straight down and across the **Assif n'Imenane** and up past the camp site. Though the walk is mostly shaded by mountain shadows in the morning, it's a hard climb, especially a very steep scree slope towards the top.

Close to the camp site, a well-defined rocky path heads up the centre of the gully on the east side of the riverbed (though it crosses over twice). It climbs for about 50 minutes before bearing left (southeast) up to the col (pass). Atop Tizi Likemt are views of verdant valleys and jagged peaks, including Oukaïmeden and Jebel Toubkal on clear days.

The rocky path leading down the other side (southeast) passes a semipermanent water source on the left after 30 minutes, and irrigated pastures above **Azib Likemt** after another hour. An *azib* is a summer settlement, and Azib Likemt (2650m) is occupied from May through October by local people growing crops on irrigated terraces and fattening cattle in lush pastures.

You may be offered shelter or a place to pitch your tent in Azib Likemt. Otherwise, walk through terraces down to the **Assif Tifni**, cross the river, turn right and walk upstream to a group of large boulders, where you'll find a flat camp site close to the river.

THE TREK AT A GLANCE

Duration seven to 10 days

Distance 60.2km

Standard medium to hard

Start/Finish Imlil village

Highest Point Jebel Toubkal (4167m)

Accommodation camping, village *gîtes* and mountain *refuges*

Public Transport yes

Summary Easily accessible from Marrakesh, this circuit around (and up) Jebel Toubkal passes through landscapes ranging from lush, cultivated valleys and Berber villages to forbidding peaks and bleak passes. This is a demanding trek, with long, gruelling climbs over rocky terrain. A guide is highly recommended, fitness essential.

BEFORE YOU GO: TOUBKAL CIRCUIT CHECKLIST

» Maps The 1:50,000 sheet map *Jebel Toubkal* covers the whole Toubkal Circuit and is sometimes available through the **bureau des guides** (☑/fax 0524 48 56 26) in Imlil. Occasionally you'll find the 1994 edition, which is clearer and more accurate. Four-sheet, 1:100,000 topographical *Toubkal Massif Walking Map* also covers the circuit, produced by the Division de la Cartographie (Moroccan Survey) and obtainable from their office in Rabat, at **Stanfords**, in London (at **Stanfords** (www.stanfords.co.uk), or in Marrakesh on the Djemaa el-Fna at Hotel Ali (Dh150). Government-produced 1:100,000 *Cartes des Randonnées dans le Massif du Toubkal* marks trekking routes but includes less topographical detail. Orientazion's 1:50,000 *Toubkal and Marrakech* is clear and water-resistant, but does not show all gullies and cliffs.

» Guide The best place to engage an experienced, licensed guide is at Imlil's *bureau des guides*. Allow at least a day to hire a guide and make trekking arrangements – though if you have specific needs, it may take more time. Of the 60 official guides based in the Toubkal area, only 10 or so may be in Imlil at any one time. In high season, you might need to hire an experienced Toubkal guide through a reputable Marrakesh agency (p73).

» Mule Mountain guides can organise mules and muleteers for you. Trekkers should be aware that mules have problems crossing Tizi n'Ouanoums, east of Lac d'Ifni, and from November to May, some areas may be impassable by mule. If mules have to take lengthy detours, you may need to carry one day's kit and food. Talk this through with your guide and muleteer.

» Food Basic food supplies (meat, fruit, vegetables and bread) are available in Imlil, and trail mixes, packaged soups and other light, portable food is stocked by Marrakesh supermarkets.

» Water Purifying locally sourced water is a responsible alternative to bottled water (see p40), but don't count on finding available water sources – pack plenty of water.

» Gear When walking after rain or snowfall, a stick or trekking pole is useful. Petrol, diesel and kerosene can be bought in Marrakesh or Asni.

» Tent Your guide can arrange tents. The circuit outlined here requires some camping, but you could add detours to seek out lodging, or possibly do without tents in summer.

Day 3: Azib Likemt to Amsouzert
6-6½ HRS/15.2KM/470M ASCENT/1380M DESCENT

This direct route south to Amsouzert is less demanding than yesterday's walk, but offers some good ridge walking. From **Azib Likemt**, the well-worn trail leads behind the camp site south, up the mountainside and into the tremendous gorge formed by **Assif n'Tinzer**. Above the river's eastern bank, the trail snakes above the **Tombe Asmine waterfall** before descending close to the river. Follow the river for about two hours past stunning cliffs and through wide pastures, until an obvious track leads up the valley to **Tizi n'Ououraïne** (3120m; also known as Tizi n'Ouaraï) and brilliant views of the eastern face of Toubkal, **Dôme d'Ifni** (3876m) and the rest of the jagged Toubkal massif. By way of contrast is **Agounss n'Tiniline** (3674m), 90 minutes away to the northwest, and other softer, rounded peaks to the east.

Continue over the col, where the trail traverses the head of the valley to a spur and trail crossroads. Heading southwest, a trail leads down the ridge to **Tagadirt** (after 50m there's a fantastic viewpoint south to **Jebel Siroua**), but turn left (southeast) and follow the mule track south. Traverse the head of another valley and along the side of a spur to reach the ridge after 90 minutes; **Lac d'Ifni** is visible to the west. After a further 15 minutes, just before two pointed outcrops, the path forks. Turn right and continue descending slowly southwards to a large cairn. Descend southwest, then west down the end of the spur to **Amsouzert** (1797m) in 30 minutes.

Amsouzert is a prosperous village (one mosque and several satellite dishes at last count) spread on both sides of the river. If you're planning a rest day, this is an excellent place to take it. Next to the school is an outdoor tearoom shaded by an enormous walnut tree where you may able to **camp** (per tent Dh20). Otherwise, you can stay at **Gîte Himmi Omar** (dm Dh40, tajine Dh30).

In Amsouzert are small shops, a couple of cafes west of the river and early morning transport to the N10 highway connecting Marrakesh and Ouarzazate. About 3km south of Amsouzert is another village called Imlil (not to be confused with the Imlil trailhead on the northern side of the range), which hosts a wildly popular **Wednesday souq** featuring wild herbs, timeworn tools, a whole lot of mules and local gossip.

Day 4: Amsouzert to Azib Imi n'Ouassif
5½-6 HOURS/10.5KM/1100M ASCENT

Between November and June, mules will not make it much beyond Lac d'Ifni, the largest lake in the High Atlas. Muleteers have to take mules to the Toubkal Refuge via Sidi Chamharouch, which means you'll have to carry your kit to **Azib Imi n'Ouassif** over **Tizi n'Ouanoums** (3600m) to Toubkal Refuge.

From **Amsouzert** follow the level, well-used 4WD track that continues northwest towards Lac d'Ifni above the north side of the river. The path takes you through the villages of **Ibrouane**, **Takatert** and **Tisgouane** before reaching **Aït Igrane**, where there are a couple of cafes and **Gîte Belaïde** (dm Dh40). There is also a shady **camp site** (Dh30) on a flat, stony site just beyond the Café Toubkal, with a cold shower and toilet.

Follow the 4WD track along the riverbed northwest out of Aït Igrane, picking up the narrow rocky mule path where the 4WD track crosses the river then turns sharp left. The mule path leads around the north side of **Lac d'Ifni** (2295m), across sharp, rocky, barren, inhospitable terrain. The climb is steep at first, but it descends to the northeastern corner of Lac d'Ifni, an inviting expanse of green water where anglers fish for trout. The walk to the lake should take three hours. Before you reach the shore, you will pass a **shack** marked 'café'. There's no coffee here, but if it's attended you may able to buy water, soft drinks and, with any luck, a tajine.

On the small beach on the northern shore are shady (if occasionally fly-filled) **stone shelters**. The ground is rocky without vegetation, but the lake offers safe, refreshing swims. If it's rainy, camping nearer the next pass is treacherous, and you're better off finding a camp site above the lake.

Every October, villagers from the surrounding area gather at Lac d'Ifni for a three-day *moussem* in honour of a local *marabout*, whose **tomb** sits high above the southeastern corner of the lake. A track leads from the northeast shore up to the tomb.

From the northwestern side of the lake, the track crosses the wide, dry part of Lac d'Ifni before the long, snaking trudge towards **Tizi n'Ouanoums** (3600m). The path climbs through a rocky gorge, keeping to the south side of the river. About 3.5km from the lake, you'll reach **Azib Imi n'Ouassif** (2841m), situated at a crossing of dramatic gorges. Beyond this point the path climbs steeply to Tizi n'Ouanoums, with winds near the summit and small, frigid waterfalls. You'll find flat, rocky areas for pitching tents and shelters in surrounding cliffs long used by local shepherds.

Day 5: Azib Imi n'Ouassif to Toubkal Refuge
4HR/4KM/759M ASCENT/393M DESCENT

The path to Tizi n'Ouanoums is immediately northwest of the camp site, leading up into a particularly rocky, rugged landscape. It's a steep, demanding climb, but the views are spectacular from the top over **Assif n'Moursaïne**, hemmed in by jagged ridges of **Adrar bou Ouzzal** and **Ouimeksane**. The path crosses the river several times after leaving the camp, reaching a stone shelter and water source after an hour and the col another hour further. Even in midsummer it's cold and blustery at the top, with snow in shady crevices.

Coming down the other side, there's treacherous loose rock and snow until July. From here you can see Jebel Toubkal and, to the west, the path to **Tizi n'Melloul** (3875m). After the descent, the track levels out and heads due north to Toubkal Refuge (3207m), about two hours from Tizi n'Ouanoums.

CAF's **Toubkal Refuge** (☎064 071838; dm CAF members/HI members/nonmembers Dh46/69/92), formerly known as Neltner, was completely rebuilt in the 1990s but suffers from overcrowding, damp, and a lack of facilities. Queues for showers (Dh10) and toilets are interminable in busy periods. Meals are available and there's a shop selling chocolate, cola, biscuits and limited

BERBER BOTANY IN THE HIGH ATLAS

Despite icy winters and scalding summers, the High Atlas Mountains are extremely fertile. Overgrazing, agriculture and wood collection for fuel has impacted the High Atlas; much of its indigenous vegetation has disappeared. But through painstaking reforestation and resourceful mountainside terrace farming using *targa* (channel) irrigation, the hills are alive with a diversity of flora. For a fascinating introduction to Berber botany, stop by Dar Taliba (p104) for botanical garden visits and tea with eight High Atlas herbs.

Here's what you'll spot on High Atlas walks:

» **Valleys** Riots of flowers erupt in spring, when valley almond, cherry and apricot orchards bloom. In summer, you'll enjoy the shade of carob, quince, pomegranate, apple and fig trees. Terraces scale High Atlas valley walls to surprising heights, and resourceful farmers manage to eke multiple crops from tiny plots: barley October through to May, and potatoes, carrots, turnips, onions, lentils and beans spring through to autumn. Walnuts are a major crop in higher villages, with harvest in late September.

» **Subalpine zone** (2400m to 3200m) Thickets of gnarled Spanish juniper (*Juniperus thurifer*) are blasted into extraordinary shapes by the wind, and exposed roots cling like fingers to the rock. Cedar is being planted to prevent erosion, and replace fragrant Atlas cedar used for woodworking.

» **High elevations** The easiest to spot are 'hedgehog plants', spiny, domed bushes that briefly burst into flower in spring. Even when you don't spot plants on the trail, you'll get a whiff of lavender, rosemary and wild thyme underfoot, perfuming your boots as you walk.

supplies. The new **Refuge Mouflon** (☑061 213345; afoud@wanadoo.net.ma; dm Dh75), next to Toubkal Refuge, provides a welcome choice, with more facilities (shower Dh10), a better-stocked shop and good meals (Dh50) in the chilly lounge. You can also camp downstream from the *refuge* or 20 minutes south of the *refuge* on flat pasture.

Assuming you reach the *refuge* before lunch, there are trekking options to occupy the afternoon – including the three- or four-hour descent directly north back to the starting point, **Imlil** (see p112), if you don't want to climb Jebel Toubkal. You could ascend the second-highest mountain in the region, **Jebel Ouanoukrim** (4088m, five to six hours return). The best option is to rest all afternoon to prepare for the climb up Jebel Toubkal the following morning.

Day 6: Toubkal Refuge to Azib Tamsoult

5HR/8KM/493M ASCENT/1300M DESCENT

From the **Toubkal Refuge** pick up the mule track that heads northwest then gently climbs north across the slope for about 15 minutes. You will come to a fork near a small rounded wall, used as a sheepfold. Turn left, westwards, up the zigzagging mule path,

which will bring you to **Tizi n'Aguelzim** (3560m) after two hours. It's a slower trail but less treacherous than the southern route at Tizi n'Taddert, which is often abruptly closed due to dangerous conditions.

Panoramic views await at Tizi n'Aguelzim pass: east to the Toubkal summit, northeast to the Imlil valley, northwest to Azzadene and west to the Tazaghart plateau. From here, the track twists in some 92 hairpin bends downhill for almost an hour. At the bottom, it crosses a stream. Twenty minutes further on, at a fork, take the left-hand track, and take another left 15 minutes later. Here the track leads uphill for 10 minutes to cosy **CAF Tazaghart Refuge** (☑067 852754, Oukaïmeden 024 319036; dm CAF/HI members/ nonmembers Dh42/63/83), which sits beside a stunning waterfall. There are mattresses for 22 people, gaslights and a basic kitchen.

You'll probably find the place closed unless you've made a reservation, and the *gardien* (attendant) is based in Tizi Oussem. Phone ahead, or else try passing a message to him via muleteers or shepherds, who may run all the way to Tizi Oussem to fetch him. Campers can pitch tents beside the *refuge,* or on flat ground above the falls.

Tizi n'Melloul (3875m), southeast of Tazaghart *refuge*, offers a harder route to and from the Toubkal Refuge, but provides access to Afella (4045m) southeast of the pass and to the jagged ridge leading north to Biginoussem.

The route down to Azib Tamsoult (2400m) passes the impressive Cascades d'Irhoulidene, where vegetation and tree coverage increases. A five-minute walk from the falls brings you to a pleasant wooded area for camping. To reach the village, walk north for 10 to 15 minutes.

Day 7: Azib Tamsoult to Imlil
4-5 HRS/7KM/89M ASCENT/749M DESCENT

If you have made good time and you have the legs, you could continue down to Imlil at the end of day six. From the vegetable patches of Azib Tamsoult, with the Assif n'Ouarzane down to the left, a mule track traversing the forested valley is visible to the north. Head towards it past the village and over the stream, and stay on it, avoiding left forks into the valley.

Climbing slightly and heading steadily northeast, towards the juniper forest with Tizi Oussem due west, you arrive at Tizi n'Mzik (2489m), where a sheep shed might serve as shelter. Imlil is a 90-minute descent along a well-worn mule track; there's a spring to the right of the trail after 40 minutes. Comfortable beds and hot tajines await in Imlil – after a full week on the highest trail in the High Atlas, you've earned them.

To Tizi n'Test

Even with white knuckles and gritted teeth, you'll have to admire the route to Taroudannt as it winds through the High Atlas, careens over the Tizi n'Test pass at 2092m, then swoops down onto the Souss plain. As if the single-lane road weren't enough of an adventure, the weather is subject to sudden changes. Heavy clouds and mist often cut visibility to near zero at the top of the pass and you might find your way blocked by snow in winter, so check weather conditions before leaving.

⊙ Sights & Activities

TOP CHOICE Tin Mal mosque   MOSQUE
Heading south towards Tizi n'Test from Marrakesh, you'll notice Tin Mal village on the right of the road, just past a kasbah perched on a rocky outcrop to your left. The village's Almohad-era mosque was built in 1156 in honour of the dynasty's strict spiritual leader, Mohammed ibn Tumart, and it remains an architectural wonder. The mosque is still used for Friday prayers, but on other days the guardian will usher you through its massive doors and rose-coloured archways into the serene prayer hall (Dh10 to Dh20 tip expected). The intricate geometry of the carved cedar ceilings has been preserved through painstaking restoration, and the soaring keyhole archways give a sense of solidity and grace.

Café Dar Issouga   TREKKING
(☏0670 10 65 21) On the north side of the pass, you'll spot a reserve for mouflons, endangered long-horned Barbary sheep. As you approach the pass, you may suddenly break through fog into clear blue sky, and catch breathtaking airplane-window views over cloudbanks. On the south side of the pass, the van ominously embedded into the hillside is your cue for a pit stop at this cafe. The balcony offers stunning valley views of green terraces and cypress forests cascading down the hillside – a prime spot for a Berber beef or goat tajine (Dh70 to Dh90). Afterwards, owner Larbi can organise half- to three-hour walks or donkey rides down the valley for tea in a mountainside village.

To Tizi n'Tichka

Higher than Tizi n'Test to the west but an easier drive, the Tizi n'Tichka connects Marrakesh with pre-Saharan oases. In winter, check with the Gendarmerie of the Col du Tichka (☏0524 89 06 15) whether the pass is open; in 2005, several tourists stranded on the pass died in their car.

On your way to the pass, there are a couple of worthy detours: Aït Ourir and the Zat Valley. If you have a date with the desert, you can make it over Tizi n'Tichka from Marrakesh within three hours. As you pass Aït Ourir, the road ascends and takes a turn for the scenic amid oak trees, walnut groves and oleander bushes. Past the village of Taddert, the road gets steeper and the landscape is stripped of colour, except for hardy wildflowers and kids along the road selling geodes dyed shocking red.

Atop the Tizi n'Tichka, reward yourself with bracing espresso, cool air and dizzying views at the Assanfou cafe (☏061 132130; ⊙9am-7pm). Once over the pass, you gradually descend into the lunar landscape

WORTH A TRIP

COOPERATIVE TIGMI

With a needle and thread, 30 women *mâalems* (master artisans) are setting trends from Morocco to Milan and improving prospects for their rural community at **Cooperative Tigmi** (☑0524 48 08 19; http://cooperative-tigmi.spaces.live.com; km37 Rte de Ouarzazate, No. 110, Lotissement Tafoukt Hay el-Massira, Aït Ourir; ⊘2.30-5.30pm Mon-Fri), 35km from Marrakesh. Tigmi's distinctive (and much-imitated) designs are simple and striking: asterisks, Berber talismans, and architectural outlines embroidered on heavyweight cotton in rich, contrasting colours.

Proceeds from sales at Tigmi support literacy programs and maternal-child health programs, and visitors are spoiled for choice at the cooperative workshop (signed 250m to the right off the main road, before Aït Ourir's mosque). Periwinkle starbursts grace chocolate-brown pillowcases, and kasbah motifs are embroidered in saffron on aubergine table runners. But what's that tangerine pouch with the powder-blue Berber power symbol?

'It's like a tea cosy, only for mobile phones or iPods,' explains a hip young Cooperative Tigmi member. The cooperative has secured backing from Oxfam and Spanish NGOs to diversify, producing phone covers, hand-painted glassware, and embroidered duvet covers. These bed linens are a comfort in more ways than one: they introduce a style the women here call 'Berber Zen' into any home, and furnish this enterprising rural community with an ever brighter outlook.

of the Anti Atlas and the desert beyond. But if you speed along the highway to Ouarzazate, you'll miss some of the most fascinating destinations in Morocco: the splendid, near-ruined **Glaoui Kasbah** in **Telouet**, and ancient mudbrick *douar* (villages) lining **Oued Ounilla**, including **Anmiter** and **Tamdaght**. The tarmac road from the highway to Telouet is pockmarked, but the historic *piste* linking Telouet to Aït Benhaddou via Oued Ounilla has recently been graded, and makes a fascinating and relatively smooth 36km ride by 4WD or mountain bike to **Aït Benhaddou**. Hotels in Telouet can arrange guides and mules to walk the route to Aït Benhaddou for around Dh300 per day.

Zat Valley

For decades trekkers have jealously guarded the secret of one of the most pristine hidden valleys in the High Atlas. When Marrakesh is sweating it out 50km to the northwest, breezes are rippling through barley and swaying poplar trees along this charmed river valley.

To reach Zat Valley, take the N9 towards Ouarzazate until it crosses the Oued Zat at Aït Ourir, then head south towards the transport town of **Tighdouine** at the near end of the valley. Tighdouine offers tasty

roadside tajines before entering Zat's land of make-believe: gardens built right into cliff faces, stone houses with bright-blue doors, white-framed windows with families leaning out to say hello. This is all best appreciated on foot or mule. There's a *piste* winding above the valley floor, but only physicist drivers should attempt it.

Time seems to have forgotten the Zat Valley, which is a mixed blessing: some small villages here are without running water or medical supplies, and children walk upwards of 8km to reach the nearest school. But without spoiling the landscape, local self-help associations are coming up with home remedies. One- to five-day walking tours are organised by Inside Morocco Tours (p73), with proceeds shared by local Association Ajlal to underwrite Zat schooling and medical initiatives.

When villagers who eke out a living from tiny terrace plots invite you home for their best homemade bread, butter, walnuts and wild-sage tea, the hardest hearts melt like snow on the High Atlas mountains framing the Zat Valley. In terms of etiquette, it's fine to offer a small monetary token of appreciation, but don't press the issue if it's refused. Save larger donations for local associations, who will use it wisely on bridges, reforestation, literacy programs and a medical dispensary.

Sights & Activities

TOP CHOICE **Isafarne Honey Collective**
FOOD & DRINK

(☑077 787548) On the left about 13km after the turn-off from the Ouarzazate road at Aït Ourir (about 2km before Tighdouine), you'll spot an eye-catching pink building with the sign of a bee. This initiative involves 120 Zat locals in labour-intensive production of a rare and truly exceptional dark, spicy honey from wild Berber medicinal plants that thrive in the Zat Valley. The president of the collective, Mr Ahmed Zaki, will gladly treat you to a taste of the collective's honey (250/500g Dh80/150) with local bread. Mr Zaki can help you identify the complex flavours you're tasting, which depending on the time of year, may include verbena, wild sage, lavender, carob flower, wild mint, walnut and mountain thyme. He's here on weekdays, though you might spot him on weekends here or walking the road from Zat, his pack laden with fresh honeycomb.

L'Association des Amis du Zat TREKKING
(☑0670 21 92 51) For groups of six or more, this local NGO can arrange mule treks and stays at *gîtes* built by Zat villagers with donations from the many trekkers besotted with this valley.

Telouet تلوات

Before 1928, anyone passing through Tizi n'Tichka paid tolls to local warlords for the privilege. But Telouet's privileged position ended in 1953, when native son and French collaborator Pasha Glaoui was ousted by the Moroccan independence movement. Legend has it that when the imposing doors of Telouet's Glaoui kasbah were thrown open at last, locals who had mysteriously disappeared from their villages years before stumbled dazed onto Telouet streets, after years locked in the pasha's basement.

Telouet also once had a thriving Jewish community, entrusted by the Glaoui with managing the all-important salt trade. **Salt mines** are still active in the area, and prized pink salt found along the nearby **Oued Mellah** (Salt River) was once accepted as currency. Near the Glaoui Kasbah is what remains of an ancient **slave village**, another important piece of local and global trade history in need of preservation. But Morocco's government remains ambivalent about the Glaoui clan's home town, and with little outside investment and a highway bypassing the town entirely, Telouet seems arrested in time half a century ago.

Narrow river valley oases beyond Telouet are lined with crumbling Glaoui kasbahs, gorges riddled with caves, and ancient fortified villages such as **Anmiter** (11km from Telouet), which has two well-preserved red kasbahs and a historic **mellah**. Walking tours, spelunking, salt-mine visits and teas in the Anmiter kasbah can be arranged through Homestays Morocco (see p122).

Sights & Activities

TOP CHOICE **Glaoui Kasbah** HISTORIC SITE
(suggested donation Dh20) The once-glorious stronghold has been left to crumble, and the best indication of Telouet's former position as the centre of a trans-Saharan trading empire is the 2nd-floor **receiving court**. No less than 300 artisans were recruited (if that's the word) to complete salons faceted with stucco, *zellij* and painted cedar ceilings that make Marrakesh's royal Bahia Palace seem like a freshman artisan effort. But the Telouet kasbah was not destined to be the Pasha's ultimate pleasure palace. After independence, Pasha Glaoui was ousted from the Bahia Palace and died shortly thereafter of cancer in exile in Telouet.

Glaoui family descendents have recently reclaimed ownership of this architecturally splendid and politically charged landmark, but without state funding underwriting considerable costs for structural reinforcement and restoration, the family may be obliged to consider offers to turn it into a restaurant or resort, merely to prevent the kasbah from collapsing. See this masterpiece of Moroccan craftsmanship while you can – ceilings have already collapsed in rooms marked with a red X. Local associations are doing their part to help preserve the fort, but you can also help by not touching the *zellij* (the ceramic chips easily), not leaning on window sills, door frames or other structural supports, and collecting any trash you see.

Baraka Community Partnerships CULTURAL CENTRE
(www.barakacommunity.com) Volunteers build schools, plant trees and supply basic medical care through this locally run NGO. Baraka Partnerships offers one-day

WORTH A TRIP

OFF-ROAD IN OUNILLA VALLEY

Travellers equipped with 4WD, mountain bikes or good walking shoes and a guide from Homestays Morocco can follow the ancient desert caravan routes from Telouet to Aït Benhaddou through the splendid **Ounilla Valley**. With a freshly graded *piste*, this off-road route follows the course of the Oued Mellah and passes Anmiter, Assaka, Tizgui and other picturesque villages dotting the **Gorge Assaka**. For a pit stop and gorge photo-ops in Tizgui village, **Chez Abdellah Nbarda** (☑0676 52 73 42; Tizgui; meals Dh90-120) offers tea on the sunny terrace (Dh10), a traditional hammam (Dh20) and home-style cooking. Exiting the Ounilla Valley to the south, you'll spot **lime-stone threshing terraces** notched into an east-facing hillside. In harvest season, you'll see villagers threshing grain on these stone platforms, just as they've done for centuries.

'*baraka* vacations' in the remote village of Tighza, where visitors can spend an afternoon restoring ancient stone terraces on the hillside or painting a child's room in a local mudbrick home with nontoxic paint in bright *beldi* (country-style) colours. These cultural exchanges are organised for sliding-scale donations that extend *baraka* (blessings): Dh250 equips a Tighza family with a first-aid kit, Dh500 covers a Tighza child's school books and fees for a year, and Dh700 provides medical care to an entire Tighza family for a year.

✖ Eating

Local guesthouses offer half-board, and restaurants around Telouet's central square serve simple Dh40 tajines and Dh30 Berber omelettes (with tomato, olives and herbs).

Café Restaurant Palace/Chez Mohamed
FUSION, BERBER **$$**

(☑0524 88 57 30; www.palacedetelouet.com; Telouet centre; mains Dh85-160) Chicken with almonds and peaches, lamb with dates, rabbit with thyme and fresh ginger are among the gourmet tajine options you'll find here.

🛏 Sleeping

TOP CHOICE **Homestays Morocco**   HOMESTAY **$**

(☑0677 84 04 87; www.homestays morocco.net; Tighza) Overnight stays with local families in the village of Tighza provide much-needed income to this remote subsistence farming community, 21km from Telouet by *piste*. The family welcome received by guests is that of a minor football hero, meals are farm-fresh and embarrassingly generous, and the stars seem within reach at night. Homestays with half-board are offered for sliding-scale donations (Dh300to Dh500 per person), which helps purchase essential medical supplies. Tighza native Mohamed El Qasemy and his British wife Caroline Logan Taylor (yes, they met on vacation) run this program, and are also launching a new solar- and wind-powered guesthouse, **Kasbah Tighza** (☑0668 44 30 40).

TOP CHOICE **I Rocha**   MAISON D'HÔTES **$$**

(☑0667 73 70 02; www.irocha.com; Tisseldi, Ighrem N'Oudal; d per person incl half-board Dh450-550; ☀) Halfway between the turn-off for Telouet and Aït Benhaddou along the Marrakesh–Ouarzazate road is this cliffside stone guesthouse, lifting travel-worn spirits above the green river valley. Ten sunny, cream-coloured rooms have easygoing Berber charm, with wood-beamed ceilings, plush local carpets, and *beldi*-tiled bathrooms. The split-level room by the pool is an ideal family retreat, with a sleeping loft and a tub. Owners Ahmed and Katherine make terrific French-Moroccan dishes with herbs fresh from the terrace garden; guests can learn how to cook them for Dh350. To unwind after a guided hike out to the Fint Oasis and natural springs, go for a hammam (Dh90), a Tazzarine henna treatment, or a dip in the small pool.

Dar Aissa
GÎTE D'ETAPE **$**

(☑0670 22 22 47; www.maisondhotesdaraissate louet.com; Telouet; per person incl breakfast/half-board Dh120/200) In downtown Telouet near the Glaoui Kasbah, this new guesthouse offers clean, cheerful mattress-on-floor accommodation in pink and yellow rooms with modern shared bathrooms.

❶ Getting There & Away

From the N9 Marrakesh–Ouarzazate Rd, the turn-off to Telouet is signed a few kilometres beyond the pass. There's a daily bus from Bab Gehmat in Marrakesh (Dh55), which returns to

Marrakesh at 7am. A bus leaves Ouarzazate for Telouet at noon, returning at 7am (Dh40-50). Grands taxis are Dh50-70 per seat, but you might get stuck renting out all six seats.

Aït Benhaddou آيت بنحدو

Like certain Botoxed stars, this Unesco-protected kasbah seems suspiciously frozen in time: with Hollywood touch-ups, it still resembles its days in the 11th century as an Almoravid caravanserai. Movie buffs recognise this red mudbrick kasbah 32km from Ouarzazate from *Lawrence of Arabia*, *Jesus of Nazareth* (for which much of Aït Benhaddou was rebuilt), *Jewel of the Nile* (note the Egyptian towers) and *Gladiator*.

If you're headed to the desert, Aït Benhaddou is a worthy detour for a tasty lunch and kasbah stroll. From the Hôtel la Kasbah, head down past the souvenir stalls to the kasbah across the parched Oued Ounilla riverbed. But where are all the people? The few remaining residents make a few dirham providing access through their family homes to the **kasbah** (customary tip Dh10). Climb the kasbah to a ruined **agadir** with magnificent views of surrounding *palmeraie* and unforgiving *hammada* (stony desert).

A less retouched kasbah can be found 7km north along the tarmac from Aït Benhaddou: the **Tamdaght kasbah** (tip to caretaker Dh10), a crumbling Glaoui fortification topped with storks' nests. To see what Aït Benhaddou may have looked like in its original state, follow the Telouet-bound *piste* north of Tamdaght to the red-tower kasbah of Anmiter.

🛏 Sleeping

TOP CHOICE **Kasbah Ellouze**   KASBAH **$$$**
(✆0524 89 04 59; www.kasbahellouze. com; Tamdaght; incl half-board s Dh528-755, d Dh704-1054, ste Dh1054; ❉❅🛜@🏊) This pisé guesthouse blends in with the adjacent kasbah, overlooking almond orchards (*luz* means almonds). The best rooms have orchard views, especially stylish doubles by the heated pool. Guests gather in the kitchen to learn to make local bread, for aperitifs and wi-fi in the jazz salon, and for watercolour-painting excursions into the Ouinilla and Drâa Valleys – but whenever resident camels Ella and Maryline poke their heads curiously into the courtyard, all activities are abandoned in favour of camel rides.

Fibule d'Or   KASBAH **$**
(✆0524 88 76 82; www.lafibule-dor.com; d incl breakfast Dh360, per person half-board Dh250) An all-natural pisé guesthouse that threatens to steal scenes from the glammed-up movie-star kasbah directly across the valley. In this nine-room guesthouse, rooms numbered 6, 5 and 7 are high-ceilinged and bright, but number 8 has the best view of the historic kasbah. Prices are reasonable for rooms with en-suite bathrooms, and thick mudbrick walls keep rooms naturally cool without air-con.

Etoile Filante d'Or   GUESTHOUSE **$$**
(✆024 890322; www.etoilefilantedor.com; d incl breakfast/half-board Dh385/550; ❉🛜@) Moonlit desert nights on the Etoile's roof terrace lure guests out of 19 spacious, newly renovated rooms for movie-script-inspiring kasbah views. Guest rooms are a savvy combination of traditional (*tataoui* ceilings, Berber blankets) and modern (en-suite bathrooms, air-con), and there's wi-fi and à la carte lunches (meals Dh60 to Dh90). Trust Moroccan-French hosts Hind and Aurélien to organise dromedary rides and bike tours.

🍴 Eating

Hotel-Restaurant Baraka   BERBER, LOCAL **$$**
(✆0524 89 03 05; www.hotel-labaraka.com; meals Dh70-90) The à la carte couscous with chicken, vegetables and trade-route spices is bountiful, but you'll be scraping the tajine for traces of local-specialty *kalia*, with meat slowly simmered in *smen* (seasoned butter) and caramelised onions, and an egg poached on top. If you need a nap afterwards, there are scuffed, basic rooms upstairs (doubles with/without air-con Dh200/150).

Auberge La Goulade
   MEDITERRANEAN/BERBER **$$**
(✆0524 88 48 72; www.lagoulade.net; meals Dh70-100) The eclectic, cosy little restaurant run by Moroccan-French couple Sami and Michel features fresh salads with flavourful local produce, pizza with Berber herbs, decadent *kefta* tajines and a well-stocked bar.

Chez Brahim   LOCAL **$**
(✆0671 81 63 12; meals Dh70) Sure, there are other tajines in town, but only Brahim's improve international relations: the chef/owner has a letter from Hilary Rodham Clinton thanking him for a meal in her First Lady days. The set menu includes salads, tajine and dessert in a pisé-walled salon with Kasbah views.

Auberge Cafe-Restaurant Bilal   LOCAL $
(②0668 24 83 70) For lunch with a view, pull up a patio chair and gaze at Aït Benhaddou across the way. À la carte options include omelettes (Dh35), couscous (Dh50), and kebabs (Dh60).

① Getting There & Away

To get here from Ouarzazate, take the main road towards Marrakesh to the signposted turn-off (22km); Aït Benhaddou is another 9km down a bitumen road. Cycling from Ouarzazate takes three hours.

Grands taxis run from outside Ouarzazate bus station when full (Dh20 per person) and from the turn-off (Dh120 one-way or Dh250 to Dh350 half-day with return). Minibuses run from Tamdaght to Ouarzazate in the morning when full.

Ouarzazate   ورزازت

POP 79,000

Strategically located Ouarzazate (war-zazat) has gotten by largely on its wits instead of its looks. For centuries, people from the Atlas, Drâa and Dadès Valleys converged to do business at Ouarzazate's sprawling Taourirt Kasbah, and a modern garrison town was established here in the 1920s to oversee France's colonial interests. The movie business gradually took off in Ouarzazate after the French protectorate left in the 1950s, and 'Ouallywood' movie studios have built quite a résumé providing convincingly exotic backdrops for movies supposedly set in Tibet, ancient Rome, Somalia and Egypt.

Since King Mohammed VI started visiting here and fixing up the roads, Ouarzazate has been developing quickly, with new condo-hotel complexes and a spacious pedestrian plaza in the town centre. Ouarzazate is always ready for action, with well-stocked supermarkets where you can pick up essential desert supplies from wet wipes to whisky. With scores of agencies offering bikes, motorbikes and camels, this is an ideal launching pad for mountains, desert and gorges. But from November to March, be prepared for icy winds that can come whipping down from the High Atlas.

◉ Sights

Taourirt Kasbah   KASBAH
(admission Dh20; ◷8am-6.30pm) Unlike other Glaoui kasbahs, Taourirt escaped ruin by moonlighting as a Hollywood backdrop (*Sheltering Sky*, *Gladiator*, *Prince of Persia*) and attracting the attention of Unesco, which has carefully restored small sections of the Glaoui inner sanctum. You could tour the restored Glaoui kasbah with a guide (Dh50 per group), but photographers will want to explore at their leisure to capture the light through arched doorways and palm-oasis views through slit windows. Follow the maze of salons and stairwells to the top floor, where you'll find a prayer room through keyhole archways, traces of polychrome stucco and an original *tataoui* ceiling. Wander through the village inside the kasbah walls, and you might find deals on local crafts in backstreet shops.

Atlas Film Corporation Studios

NOTABLE BUILDING

(②0524 88 22 12/23; www.atlasstudios.com; adult/child Dh50/35; ◷8.30am-5.15pm) The first 'Ouallywood' studio displays sets and props from movies filmed here, including *Jewel of the Nile*, *Kingdom of Heaven* and *Kundun*. Who knows, you may even get discovered by a talent scout – though as locals point out, the Dh40 to Dh100 day rates for extras aren't exactly Screen Actors Guild pay. The studio is 5km west of town on the Marrakesh road and easily accessible on the yellow STUDID bus (see p128). There are guided tours every 20 to 40 minutes.

✗ Activities

Though many agencies and hotels still offer them, quad bikes cause considerable damage to the fragile desert ecosystem and are not recommended. On motorbikes and bicycles, riders are advised to stay on well-marked trails to minimise their air-quality impact as well as displacement of native species.

Saïd Mountain Bike   CYCLING
(②062 869324; www.saidmountainbike.com; cnr Ave Moulay Rachid & Rue de la Poste; per day/week Dh220/990) In addition to 43 rental mountain bikes, this local tour company offers guided walking tours and desert expeditions via mountain bike, mule and dromedary.

Wilderness Wheels   ADVENTURE SPORTS
(②0524 88 81 28, in Marrakesh 024 330443; www.wildernesswheels.com; 61 Hay al-Qods; 3-day/2-night excursions from Dh8470) Professionally guided motorbike tours are organised by this British-run company based off Ave Mohammed V. Prices include overnight stays, complete riding gear and a support car for up to 20 bikes.

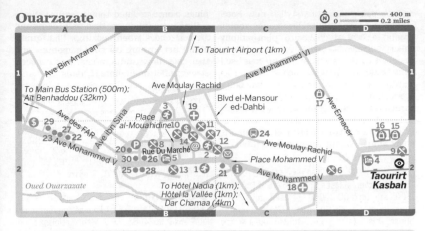

Ouarzazate

◎ **Top Sights**
Taourirt Kasbah D2

Activities, Courses & Tours
1 Daya Travels B2
2 Saïd Mountain Bike B2
3 Wilderness Wheels B1

🛏 **Sleeping**
4 Dar Kamar D2
5 Hôtel Royal B2

🍴 **Eating**
6 Akabar D2
7 Aux Delices B2
8 Central Souq B2
9 Douyria D2
10 Patisserie-Glacier des Habouss B2
11 Pizzeria Veneziano B2
12 Restaurant 3 Thés C2
13 Supermarché B2
14 Supermarket B2

🛍 **Shopping**
15 Coopérative de Tissage D2
16 Ensemble Artisanal D2
17 Horizon Artisanat D1

Information
18 Hôspital Bougafer C2
19 Kabinet Kabir B1
Ksour Voyages .... (see 29)
20 Lavanderie B2
21 Night Pharmacy C2

Transport
22 Avis A2
23 Budget A2
24 CTM Bus Station C2
25 Desert Evasion B2
26 Dune Car B2
27 Europcar/InterRent A2
28 Hertz B2
29 National Car Rental A2
30 Royal Air Maroc B2

Daya Travels   CYCLING
(☑0524 88 77 07; www.dayatravels.com; Ave Mohammed V) The English-speaking Dutch-Moroccan owners organise desert excursions, rent mountain bikes and provide free bike-trail maps.

🎊 Festivals & Events

The **moussem of Sidi Daoud** is held in Ouarzazate each August. **Marathon des Sables** (www.saharamarathon.co.uk) is a gruelling six-day, 243km desert ultramarathon each March/April where you take only what you can carry on your back – though race organisers thoughtfully provide water, 3200 diarrhoea tablets and about 1.8km of bandages. The course is revealed when runners converge in Ouarzazate.

🛌 Sleeping

Dar Chamaa   BOUTIQUE HOTEL $$$
(☑0524 85 49 54; www.darchamaa.com; Tajdar, Ouarzazate Palmeraie; s/d incl half-board Dh633/955; 🅿❄📶🏊) At the fringe of Ouar-

zazate's palm oasis, this stylish new hotel offers Moroccan-minimalist guest rooms around a central courtyard photography gallery. Spacious rooms are architect-designed to the last detail, from fossilised stone sinks to *tadelakt* niches serving as wardrobes. Ask for rooms with balconies overlooking the pool in the palm-shaded garden, and take advantage of wi-fi and a well-stocked bar. Follow signs for Dar Da-iff left off the Zagora road; Dar Chamaa is about 3km along the *piste* on the left.

Dar Kamar KASBAH $$$

(☑0524 88 87 33; www.darkamar.com; 45 Kasbah Taourirt; incl breakfast s Dh1020-1275, d Dh1200-1500, ste Dh2400-3000; ☉closed Jul; ❋☎) Once a stern 17th-century Glaoui courthouse, this cosy pisé guesthouse has a sense of humour: upturned tajines serve as sinks and sewing-machine tables are repurposed as desks. Local iron-workers went wild decorating en-suite bathrooms, though showers are poorly ventilated – a fine excuse to use the in-house hammam and massage room. Ask for upstairs doubles – as nice as suites at half the price, only smaller.

◢ Dar Daïf KASBAH $$$

(☑0524 85 42 32; www.dardaif.ma, in French; Douar Talmasla; s/d incl half-board Dh710/1143; ❋☎) On the edge of the *palmeraie,* this solar-powered, pisé family home is a maze of courtyards, hideaway guest rooms, private terraces and a courtyard pool. Dar Daïf has a quirky shoes-off policy, compulsory dinners and small bathrooms – but it's well staffed, offers free hammam use, and organises desert tours and village visits on foot, donkey and camel. To get here, take a left after Hotel la Vallée and follow signs along the 5km *piste.*

Hôtel La Vallée HOTEL $

(☑0524 85 40 34; www.hotellavaleemaroc.com; per person incl half-board Dh200; ❋☎) Trekkers, bikers and families fill these 41 rooms, and live musical accompaniment makes the mealtime race to poolside buffets even more madcap (breakfast Dh20). Guest rooms feature stuccoed ceilings, hard beds, desert murals and reliably hot showers. It's 2km down the Rte de Zagora.

Hôtel Royal HOTEL $

(☑0524 88 22 58; 24 Ave Mohammed V; s/d/tr Dh70/130/175, with bathroom Dh115/170/235; ❋) Central and far more pleasant than you'd expect for the price, though bring ear-

plugs. Some updated rooms feature stucco ceilings, carved doors, tiled bathrooms and air-con (check when booking). The terrace and courtyard are traveller hang-outs, and the cafe downstairs offers fresh juices, strong coffee and tajines (Dh40).

Hôtel Nadia HOTEL $

(☑0524 85 49 40; www.hotelnadiaozt.com; s/d/tr incl breakfast Dh200/305/385; ❋@☎) Shiny new tiled bathrooms and guest rooms, stucco ceilings, hand-painted doors, chipper staff and a modest courtyard pool make a welcome switch from dusty budget hotels. It's 1km down the Rte de Zagora.

✕ Eating

TOP CHOICE Le Relais Saint Exupéry FUSION $$$

(☑0524 88 77 79; www.relaissaintexupery.com; 13 Blvd Moulay Abdallah; set menu Dh90-260, dinner mains Dh99-336; ☉lunch & dinner, closed lunch Wed & Jul) Creative dishes featuring local ingredients such as Talouine saffron and Saharan salt that made a splash at Slow Food's Terra Madre conference. Try flaky *pastilla* of fish, or dromedary meat in a Mali-inspired sauce of garlic, cumin, ginger, and paprika. It may seem odd to find adventurous gastronomy near the Ouarzazate airport, but this airport was inspiration to *Little Prince* author and pilot Antoine de Saint-Exupéry.

Douyria LOCAL $$

(☑0524 88 42 62; 72 Ave Mohammed V; mains Dh70-90; ☉breakfast, lunch & dinner) Romantic candlelit dinners served in cushion-lined nooks on a terrace overlooking the Taourirt Kasbah. Dare to dine on speciality dromedary tajine with raisins and figs, try unexpectedly tasty rabbit tajine with preserved lemon and olives, or stick to well-marinated beef skewers with wild thyme.

Aux Delices PATISSERIE, CAFE $

(☑0524 88 28 29; Ave Moulay Rachid; ☉6am-midnight) Legendary for its *chnek* (custard cinnamon-raisin twirl), this patisserie also rivals the best in Marrakesh for not-too-sweet *pain au chocolat,* elephant ears (flat sugar cookies), and flaky croissants that stay moist even in the desert.

Restaurant 3 Thés SANDWICH SHOP, LOCAL $

(☑0524 88 63 63; cnr Ave Moulay Rachid & Rue de la Poste; mains Dh25-55; ☉lunch & dinner) The wrought-iron sidewalk seating and get-cosy interiors say Paris cafe, but the menu says tasty vegetarian tajines (Dh30), cheeseburgers (Dh35) and meaty tajines with figs, prunes and almonds (Dh55).

Pizzeria Veneziano
ITALIAN $

(✆0524 88 76 76; Ave Moulay Rachid; pizzas Dh39-43,☺noon-9.30pm) Friendly, central, and reasonably priced, Veneziano serves thin-crust pizzas with local toppings like desert herbs, anchovies and goat cheese, plus real Italian espresso.

Patisserie-Glacier des Habouss
PATISSERIE, CAFE $

(Rue du Marché; ☺6am-9pm) On balmy evenings, all strolls lead here for French éclairs (Dh7), Moroccan pastries and ice cream in summer. In the mornings, trekkers and locals line up for fresh baguettes (Dh10), croissants (Dh2.5) and coffee.

Akabar
CAFE $

(✆0524 88 66 44; www.restaurant-akabar.com; Ave Mohammed V; mains Dh40-80,☺9am-10pm; 🛜) A splashy modern sidewalk cafe bang on Ave Mohammed V en route to the Taourirt Kasbah, this wi-fi hot spot stays open morning to night to satisfy hanger pangs and coffee cravings. Pastas and pizzas are bland; stick to sandwiches or tajines of *beldi* chicken with peas.

Self-catering

The **Supermarché** (Ave Mohammed V) carries all the desert essentials: water, toothpaste, lip balm, packaged soups, cookies, film, vodka and argan anti-cellulite lotion. There's another larger **supermarket** (Ave Moulay Rachid) with imported European foods. Fresh cheese, meat and vegetables can be found at the daily **central souq** (Rue du Marché).

🛍 Shopping

Coopérative de Tissage
ART & CRAFT

(Weaving Cooperative; ✆0662 61 05 83; Ave Mohammed V) Opposite the kasbah, glimpse women artisans at work on *hanbels* (locally woven carpets) and embroidered straw mats, and take one home at posted fixed prices of Dh550 to Dh1100 per sq metre.

 Horizon Artisanat
ART & CRAFT

(✆0524 88 69 38; 181 Ave Ennacer; ☺9am-6pm Mon-Fri) Henna-painted pottery, hand-painted tea glasses, and silver filigree rings produced by the local Horizon Association are sold at reasonable fixed prices, supporting Horizon's programs to provide vocational training for handicapped adults and integrate disabled children and adults into the community.

Ensemble Artisanal
ART & CRAFT

(☺9am-12.30pm & 1.30-6pm) State-run showrooms feature local stone carvings, inlaid daggers and embroidered linens.

Information

Emergency
Police (✆19; Ave Mohammed V)

Internet Access
Cyber Ouarzazate (Ave Mohammed V; per hr Dh10; ☺9am-10pm) Centrally located, family-friendly and relatively clean.

Laundry
Lavanderie (Rue du Marché; ☺9am-noon & 2-8pm) Modern appliances (per load wash/dry Dh30/18) and wash-and-fold services (per item wash/dry/press Dh4/2/3).

Medical Services
Hôpital Bougafer (✆0524 88 24 44; Ave Mohammed V) Public hospital east of the tourist office.

Kabinet Kabir (✆0524 88 52 76) Reliable private clinic.

Night Pharmacy (✆0524 88 24 90; Ave Mohammed V; ☺8am-1pm & 3.30-11pm)

Money
Banks with ATMs line the northern end of Ave Mohammed V.

Banque Populaire (Ave Moulay Rachid; ☺8.30-11.30am & 2.30-4.30pm Mon-Fri, 3-6pm Sat, 9am-1pm Sun)

Crédit du Maroc (cnr Ave Mohammed V & Ave Bir Anzaran)

Post & Telephone
There are numerous *téléboutiques* in the centre.

Main post office (Ave Mohammed V; ☺8.30am-4.30pm Mon-Fri)

Tourist Information
Délégation Régionale du Tourisme (ONMT; ✆0524 88 24 85; Ave Mohammed V; ☺8.30am-4.30pm) Unusually sharp, helpful tourist office.

Travel Agencies
Désert et Montagne (✆0524 85 49 49; www.desert-montagne.ma) Morocco's first female mountain guide and her company organise trips to meet Berber families in the mountains, walking and 4WD trips in the desert and High Atlas, and longer trips following caravan routes. Operates from Dar Daïf (see p126).

Desert Dream (☑0524 88 53 43; www.sahara -desert-dream.com; 4 Blvd Al-Mansour ed-Dahbi) Budget-minded, friendly agency offers fixed-rate, all-inclusive excursions to deserts or gorges by camel, 4WD or on foot.

Ksour Voyages (☑0524 88 28 40; www.ksour -voyages.com; 11 Place du 3 Mars) Books flights and organises trips from mountain hikes to 4WD desert excursions with English-speaking drivers; also rents mountain bikes.

ⓘ Getting There & Away

AIR Two kilometres north of town is **Taourirt airport** (☑0524 88 23 83). **Royal Air Maroc** (RAM; ☑0524 88 51 02; 1 Ave Mohammed V) has daily flights to Casablanca (direct or via Marrakesh) and on to London or Paris, plus charter flights from Belgium, France and Germany.

BUS The most convenient way to arrive is with **CTM** (☑0524 88 24 27; Ave Moulay Rachid; ⊙7am-10pm), with buses to Marrakesh (Dh80 to Dh100, 4½ hours, four daily), Casablanca (Dh160, 7½ hours, three daily), Agadir (Dh130, 6½ hours, two daily), Er-Rachidia (Dh90, 4½ hours, one daily), M'Hamid (Dh60, five hours, one daily) and Zagora (Dh40, two hours, two daily).

From the main local bus station, 1.5km northwest of the town centre, buses head to Marrakesh (Dh65, four to five hours, six daily), Er-Rachidia (Dh75, six hours), Agadir (Dh115, four to five hours, six daily), Boumalne du Dadès (Dh25, five daily), Taroudannt (Dh75, five hours, five daily), Tazenakht (Dh20), Foum Zguid (Dh45, four hours), Tata (Dh60, five hours) and M'Hamid (Dh70, seven hours, four daily) via Zagora (Dh45, four hours).

CAR For desert detours at splendid *ksour* along the Drâa Valley, you might want to rent a car (from Dh350 per day). Car hire with a driver runs Dh900 (car) to Dh1250 (4WD).

Avis (☑0524 88 80 00; www.avis.com; cnr Ave Mohammed V & Place du 3 Mars, plus airport)

Budget (☑0524 88 42 02; www.budget.com; Ave Mohammed V & airport)

Desert Evasion (☑0524 88 86 82; www.desert -evasion.net; Imm El Ghifari, Ave Mohamed V) Payment due upon receipt of keys.

Dune Car (☑0524 88 73 91; fax 024 884901; Ave Mohammed V) Reliable and much cheaper than the international agencies; also has 4WDs.

Europcar/InterRent (☑0524 88 20 35; www. europcar.com; Place du 3 Mars)

Hertz (☑024 882084; www.hertz.com; 33 Blvd Mohammed V & airport) Child seats available.

National Car Rental (☑024 882035; www. nationalcar.com; Place du 3 Mars & airport)

TAXI Taxis leave from outside the main bus station to Agdz (Dh40), Aït Benhaddou (Dh30), Boumalne du Dadès (Dh40), Marrakesh (Dh90

to Dh110), Skoura (Dh25), Tinerhir (Dh60) and Zagora (Dh70).

ⓘ Getting Around

Petits taxis run up and down Ave Mohammed V for flat rates of Dh5 per person (based on three people sharing). The yellow STUDID bus (Dh5) runs half-hourly services up and down Ave Mohammed V. Taxis into town from the airport cost Dh35 to Dh60.

DRÂA VALLEY

Until you see the desolate Drâa Valley, you can't fully appreciate the amazing feat of Morocco's existence. Before the Almoravids could conquer territory all the way up to Barcelona, and Saadians could monopolise the sugar trade, first they had to get past unassailable gorges, mudbrick watchtowers and fiercely autonomous oases. Today a well-paved road and cushy hotels make the going considerably less rough, yet this desert landscape still seems wildly adventurous.

From Ouarzazate the N9 plunges southeast into the Drâa Valley, formed by a narrow ribbon of water from the High Atlas that occasionally emerges triumphantly in a lush oasis. The lushest and most fascinating section of the valley lies between Agdz and Zagora, a stretch of about 95km. The drive from Agdz to Zagora takes three to four hours, though the more scenic route is the *piste* through the oasis (see Circuits Touristiques, p131). Beyond that, a road takes you 96km further south to M'Hamid, a town 40km short of the Algerian border that recently opened as a desert tourism destination and still has a no-man's-land feel.

Agdz اكدز

POP 9400

Travellers who zoom from Ouarzazate to Zagora are missing out on Agdz (ag-daz), a classic caravanserai oasis with a still-pristine *palmeraie*, ancient mudbrick kasbahs, ground-breaking community garden, and a secret desert prison.

As you approach Agdz, you'll see tajine-shaped Jebel Kissane on the horizon, and spot mountain bikers heading off from Agdz to 1660m Tizi n'Tinififft, some 20km away. The mountains glisten with what looks like snow, but that's a mirage: it's sunlight bouncing off deposits of reflective

THE IDEAL DATE

Had enough disappointing dates for one lifetime? The Drâa Valley is out to change all that. In the October–November date season, you'll spot even elderly gentlemen shimmying up tall palms with a strap, bag, and knife to collect local-speciality boufeggou dates. This is a date to remember: nicely caramelised outside by the desert sun, and tender and savoury-sweet inside. The skin shouldn't be too hard or leathery, so that the fruit slides right off the pit.

For prime date selection, head to **Tinzouline**, about 36km north of Zagora. You're getting close when you spot vendors with dates overflowing from palm-frond baskets along the Zagora road. You may run into traffic for the Monday souq, where you'll be elbow to elbow with local grandmothers vying for the hottest dates around. Naturally the grandmothers win every time, but you can always ask them to help you pick a good one.

If you're not visiting the valley in autumn, you still have a standing dessert date in **Timidarte**, where local dates become Slow Food sensations at **Timarine Tijara** (☑0664 93 22 42; Timidarte; ⊘by appointment) – 1km east of Rte de Zagora, 15km south of Agdz. Head past historic mudbrick kasbahs, through the garden of a traditional family home, and into a spotless white-tiled kitchen with a single industrial cauldron bubbling merrily away. Along one counter are a few dozen jars of Timarine Tijara's signature date jam and *tahalout* (date syrup) – all that's left after a recent run on the products at Slow Food's Terra Madre conference in Turin, Italy.

'Of course they're both good on *beghrir* [Moroccan pancakes], but people especially like the syrup with savoury foods,' says owner and date gourmet innovator Abderrahim Ouagarane. 'Try drizzling some on warm goat cheese or seared foie gras – it brings out the nutty, fruity flavours in our dates.' Though it's not how you imagined your ideal date might turn out, this could definitely be The One.

---

mica. Agdz crafts traditions include carving, pottery and basket-weaving, and you might spot a few prime examples outside shops downtown or at the **Thursday souq** (October and November).

That said, none of Agdz' key attractions are apparent from the main road. The historic centre of Agdz is east of the N9 about 1.5km along a dusty *piste*, so the old town has been largely bypassed by mass-tourism development schemes. For that very reason, an unusual number of authentic mudbrick kasbahs have been preserved, instead of being demolished to build faux-kasbah hotels.

Life goes on in Agdz – in fact, it's flourishing as never before in the Hart Chaou community garden. Overnight visitors might take a morning stroll through the vast **Agdz palm oasis**, and spend the rest of the day oasis-hopping from Hart Chaou to Zagora.

◉ Sights

Caïd's Kasbah   KASBAH
(adult/child Dh40/20) The 170-year-old kasbah that once belonged to the *caïd* (leader) of Agdz is next door to Casbah Caïd Ali and owned by descendents of the *caïd*. Stop at Casbah Caïd Ali's reception for admission to the mudbrick structure, and explore a maze of rooms spread over three stories. The play of light and shade in the ancient kasbah could obsess photographers for hours, and occasional displays give glimpses of 19th-century kasbah life – but best of all are rooftop views over the neighbouring oasis.

Glaoui Kasbah   HISTORIC SITE
Long-time residents of Agdz report their shock at discovering that the walled Glaoui kasbah in Agdz (marked 307 on the gate, located on the south side of the *piste* near Rose du Sable guesthouse) was used as a secret desert detention centre. Hassan II's purges to suppress political dissidents led to the establishment of such secret detention centres, details of which emerged recently through Morocco's Equity and Reconciliation Commission. The government is said to be considering plans to turn the now-crumbling Glaoui kasbah into a memorial of Morocco's 'Years of Lead' under Hassan II, as a monumental end to this chapter of Morocco's history.

In the meantime, if you see the next-door neighbour who keeps an eye on the place,

DON'T MISS

HART CHAOU COMMUNITY GARDEN

Desert tourism has boomed in the past decade, but until recently, you wouldn't know it from the agricultural village of Hart Chaou, 1km immediately south of Agdz. Droughts left several families with no arable land or water, and teachers noticed children falling asleep in class for want of food – so the village rallied, and turned a vacant lot near a functioning well into a community garden. Villagers took turns using the water and communal compost pile, and two years later, this **organic community garden** (☏0662 84 04 55; khalah10@yahoo.fr; Hart Chaou; by sliding-scale donation Dh200-800; ⊗by appointment 3.30-6pm Mon-Fri) was providing three harvests a year and as much as 80% of the nutritional needs of the village's 114 families.

To see this amazing oasis run by the village development association, call at least a couple of hours ahead, so there's someone to meet you by the main road and lead you to the garden. Try garden-ripe fava beans or tomatoes, exchange gardening tips, have some tea at the village school and leave a sliding-scale donation to help buy next year's seeds (tip: Dh200 plants an entire plot of fava beans or onions, and Dh800 plants delicious dry-farmed tomatoes). The association reports that since travellers' generous donations helped introduce more fresh vegetables into village children's diets, schoolteachers have observed marked improvement in students' attention spans.

'We never imagined people from so many countries would be interested in our garden,' says the project's director, Lahcen Khallouki. 'Our mission was to make sure village children had enough healthy food to thrive, and that remains our objective. But visitors from the United States, Bangladesh, Germany and Great Britain have helped us realise that there are gardeners all over the world who share the same idea: to turn unused land into organic gardens that can feed our communities. Now we're striving to be a model community garden, so that we can say to our children and anyone else thinking about starting a garden, "Look, this is what a small piece of land and many hands can do."'

you can ask him to let you in the door to look around (Dh20 tip customary). The upstairs rooms are unstable, but if you pass through the sun-beaten courtyard and turn right, you'll find dark, windowless cells. In recent years, they have been used for community grain storage – but if a museum could finally shine a light on these secret cells, similar chapters in many nations' histories might also be illuminated.

🛏 Sleeping

TOP CHOICE **Dar Qamar** DAR **$$**
(☏0524 84 37 84; www.locsudmaroc. com; s Dh610, d Dh720-1100, tr Dh1055-1280; ⊛) Red-stained pisé walls, Tamegroute-tiled walkways, and fish in the fountain to eat the mosquitoes: eco-savvy chic has arrived at Agdz. Rooms with original ceilings and port-hole windows keep the cool, authentic character of this converted family home. Rent bikes to tour kasbahs, pick up maps at reception for *palmeraie* strolls, hit the in-house hammam, and unwind by the chlorine-free pool with local Larroque white wine.

Kasbah Azul MAISON D'HÔTES **$$**
(☏0524 84 39 31; www.kasbahazul; Agdz; d incl breakfast Dh833-1000, tr Dh1165, q Dh1387-1997, ste 1330; ℗⊛❄⊠) Hiding in a garden at the eastern end of the historic centre like an arty recluse, this seven-room kasbah has rooms with en-suite *tadelakt* bathrooms in contrasting hues: acid green and plum, terracotta and powder blue. The owner contributed her own collaged lamps and paintings to the striking decor – but this artist's retreat has a keyhole pool and copious breakfasts (no starving artists here).

Casbah Caïd Ali KASBAH **$**
(☏0524 84 36 40; www.casbah-caidali.net; Rue Hassan II; d with/without breakfast Dh220/190, mattress on roof Dh35, tent Dh10-25; ⊛) Descendants of the local *caïd* welcome guests to their partially restored kasbah, in courtyard guest rooms with original painted Berber motifs, simple wood and wrought-iron furnishings and shared bathrooms. Your multilingual (German/English/Darija/French) hosts arrange meals (half-board Dh170) in Berber tents by the spring-water

pool. Camp sites are available in the garden under the palms.

Rose du Sable MAISON D'HÔTES **$$**
(☑0524 88 64 52; www.rosedusable.com; s/d/tr incl breakfast Dh466/633/800; [P][❄][♨]) Like a rock star in the desert, this eight-room guesthouse keeps a low profile but can't help standing out, with psychedelic stained-glass windows, Flintstone-esque granite walls, and two wheelchair-accessible guest rooms. The Jolie-Pitts recommend this guesthouse, and who are we to argue with Shiloh?

✖ Eating

At the entry to town on the left, there's a gas station with a convenience store and cafe, the **Kasbah Total** (⊙8am-9pm), where you can fuel up on good espresso and packaged snacks galore, though it's sometimes closed in summer and winter. Cafes ring Pl Marché Vert in downtown Agdz, including **Sable d'Or**, which serves sensational saffron-scented rotisserie chicken with chips (Dh35).

ℹ Getting There & Away

CTM and other buses stop here between Ouarzazate and Zagora, and occasional grands taxis go to Ouarzazate (Dh25) and Zagora (Dh28).

Agdz to Zagora

TAMNOUGALT
Just down the road from Agdz is a star attraction of the Drâa Valley: a 16th-century fortified village that's among the oldest mudbrick *ksour* still standing and an essential stop on any Moroccan architecture pilgrimage.

⊙ Sights

TOP CHOICE **Tamnougalt Ksar** KSAR
(admission Dh 10, compulsory guide Dh50) The maze of rooms at Tamnougalt *ksar* leads through a sizable *mellah*, dips underground with strategically placed skylights and candle nooks, and emerges into sunny courtyard stables lined with horseshoe arches. See if you can distinguish between the Arab, Andalusian and Berber Jewish motifs that blend so seamlessly here – or at least recognise scenes shot here from Oscar-winning movies *Babel* and *The English Patient*. As you emerge into the courtyard stable at the back of the complex, blinded by the sunlight, try not to stumble

over architecture students from Spain and Belgium sketching key details.

🛏 Sleeping & Eating

TOP CHOICE **Bab el Oued** MAISON D'HÔTES **$$**
(☑0524 88 53 95; www.babeloued-maroc.com; d Dh660-825, tr Dh990, ste Dh935; [❄][♨]) Shaded by date palms in a walled organic garden, these charming guest bungalows fairly beam with local pride thanks to wooden doors carved in town, carpets from nearby Tazenakht, palm-beamed ceilings, and glossy *tadelakt* bathrooms. By keeping the pool small and toilets low-flow, the French- and English-speaking owners conserve enough water to grow 60 types of plants, including herbs and vegetables for Moroccan-Mediterranean meals and treats for resident rabbits. Nonguests can call ahead for organic lunches, and nap in hammocks by goldfish ponds afterwards. It's 1km east of Rte de Zagora, 5km south of Agdz.

Chez Yacob KASBAH **$$**
(☑0524 84 33 94; www.lavalleedudraa.com; half-board per person Dh300; [❄]) Next door to Tamnougalt's ancient *mellah* are eight unfussy, snug rooms with en-suite bathrooms ringing a torch-lit courtyard, capped by a scenic terrace overlooking the *palmeraie*. Set menus are Dh80-90, and bountiful enough to count as lunch and dinner. It's 2km from Route de Zagora, the turn-off is 4km south of Agdz.

ℹ Getting There & Away

Turn left off the main road 4km past Agdz, then 2km east up a *piste*.

CIRCUITS TOURISTIQUES

Those with 4WD shouldn't miss the slower, scenic *piste* that runs from Tamnougalt to just north of Zagora, parallel to highway N9. The dirt road winds along the north side of the valley through palm oases, villages, patchwork fields and river vistas all the way to Zagora. For shorter 4WD excursions along the scenic north side of the Drâa, follow signposts for 'circuits touristiques' off N9 that lead past **Kasbah Said Arabi** at Ouled Atman and the **Tinzouline kasbah**. At Tansikht, about 30km before Zagora, look out for the old **watchtower** guarding the *palmeraie*, signposted 'Oasis Du Drâa'.

TIMIDARTE

If you want to (all together now) rock the kasbahs, turn west off N9 to check out prime specimens in Timidarte village. The finest example dates from the 17th century, recently converted by Timidarte's responsible tourism association into an authentic kasbah guesthouse, Kasbah Timidarte.

🛏 Sleeping & Eating

Kasbah Timidarte　　　　　　　KASBAH $

(☎0668 68 00 47; www.kasbahtimidarte.com; d with shared bathroom incl breakfast/half-board Dh200/350, d with private bathroom incl breakfast/half-board Dh300/540) For a night, you can live much as kasbah inhabitants have for centuries: in seven mudbrick rooms arranged around a central light well, with palm-frond mats and mattresses on floors. Instead of TV, there's socialising under the stars on the roof terrace, next to a Berber bread oven. Some improvements have been made since the 17th century – there's electric light for reading, and a couple of rooms have en-suite bathrooms – but it's impressive how cool and calm thick pisé walls keep these rooms, without air-conditioning or street noise. Association members have taken to the task of cooking for guests with gusto, and home-style Berber meals are a point of pride at Kasbah Timidarte. Passersby can call ahead for a tajine (Dh75) and a peek at the roof terrace. It's 1km east of Route de Zagora, 15km south of Agdz.

TOP CHOICE Timarine Tijara　　　　　　LOCAL

(☎0664 93 22 42; Timidarte; ⊙by appointment) Timidarte is becoming a magnet for foodies with this artisan producer of date jam and syrup – call ahead for tastings and bargain Dh15 to Dh40 purchases.

Zagora　　　　　　زاكورة

POP 35,000

The original, iconic 'Tombouctou, 52 jours' (Timbuktu, 52 days) sign featuring a nomad with a smirking camel was recently taken down in an inexplicable government beautification scheme, only to be replaced by a new, equally shoddily painted sign – but Zagora's fame as a desert outpost remains indelible. The Saadians launched their expedition to conquer Timbuktu from Zagora in 1591, and desert caravans passing through Zagora gave this isolated spot cosmopolitan character.

Zagora remains a trading post at heart, hosting a **regional souq** on Wednesdays and Sundays selling fruit, vegetables, herbs, hardware, handicrafts, sheep, goats and donkeys. The **moussem of Sufi Moulay**

Zagora

Activities, Courses & Tours

1	Caravane Desert et Montagne A2
2	Caravane Hamada Drâa.....................A2
	Irahalen................................. (see 6)

🛏 Sleeping

3	Auberge Restaurant Chez Ali A3
4	Camping les Jardins de Zagora.........B2
5	Hotel la Fibule du Draa B3
6	Hotel Zagour B3
7	Les Jardins du Drâa..........................B3
8	Riad Lamane B3
9	Villa Zagora B3

🍴 Eating

10	Hôtel-Restaurant la Rose des Sables.................................... B1
11	Supermarket.................................. B1

Transport

12	Bus Station.....................................A1
13	CTM Bus Station............................A3
	Grands Taxis ....(see 12)

Abdelkader Jilali takes place at the same time as Moulid an-Nabi (see p497), and it brings the town to life. Members of the Sufi Jilala brotherhood make a pilgrimage to Zagora to pay their respects, and you may hear their hypnotic music of praise and celebration with the *bendir* (hand-held drum).

As you head into downtown Zagora, the palmeraie forms a dramatic green backdrop to drab administration buildings dating from Zagora's tenure as a French colonial outpost.

◎ Sights

TOP CHOICE **Musée des Arts et Traditions de la Valleé du Drâa** MUSEUM

(☏0661 34 83 88; Kasbah de Tissergat; admission Dh20) From the parking lot, follow 'Musée' signs out of the desert sun, through cool, dark corridors of the ancient *ksar* (fortified village), and into the triple-storey mudbrick home that houses this fascinating desert-culture museum, 8km north of Zagora. Artifacts are tagged with insightful explanations of their origins and purpose in French and English – very helpful for otherwise mysterious tattooing implements, and markedly different wedding garments from five local tribes.

In the tea salon, you'll find key equipment for desert entertaining c 1930: a vintage ham radio, gramophone, and tea glasses believed to shatter on contact with poison. Still more intriguing is the birthing room, with a single rope dangling rather ominously from the ceiling. A woman in labour was expected to use the rope to hoist herself into sitting or squatting position as she bore down, while the midwife massaged her stomach and whispered soothing blessings – not an epidural, exactly, but certainly a comfort. The tour ends in the traditional kitchen on the breezy roof, where it comes as something of a shock to glimpse satellite dishes on the horizon.

Jebel Zagora NATURAL SCENERY

This spectacular mountain rises over the Oued Drâa – worth climbing for the views, provided you have stamina, water and sunblock and set off in the early morning. The round trip to Jebel Zagora takes about three hours on foot, or 45 minutes by car along the *piste* to the right beyond Camping de la Montagne. Halfway up are the faint ruins of an 11th-century **Almoravid fortress**, but the military installation at the summit is off-limits.

Amezrou NEIGHBOURHOOD

Zagora's desert-crossroads culture can be glimpsed in the adjacent village (about 1.5km south of downtown Zagora, across the Oued Drâa), where artisans in the historic **mellah** work good-luck charms from African, Berber, Jewish and Muslim traditions into their designs – when crossing the desert for 52 days, you need all the luck you can get. In the 1930s, Amezrou had some 400 Jewish households, but almost all had left town by the 1960s. In Amezrou, ask an elderly resident to point you towards a tiny **ancient synagogue**, currently being restored by the village. The family next door will let you into the prayer room (Dh20 tip customary), where you'll notice that the archways and Torah niche were blackened by the room's use as a kitchen after its abandonment. Yet the arch supports have held up well, and the palm-beam ceiling is being restored with help from neighbours and Dar Raha.

🏃 Activities

Dromedary rides are not only possible in Zagora, but practically obligatory. Cost-compare at local agencies, ask about water, bedding, toilets and how many other people will be sharing your camp site. Prices start at about Dh300 per person per day.

Caravane Desert et Montagne (☏0524 84 68 98; www.caravanedesertetmontagne. com; 112 Blvd Mohammed V) Partners with local nomads to create adventures off the beaten camel track for individuals and small groups.

Caravane Hamada Drâa (☏0524 84 69 30; www.hamadadraa.com, in French; Blvd Mohammed V) English-speaking guides; treks to nomadic camps by licensed guide and native nomad Youssef M'hidi.

Discovering South Morocco (☏0524 84 61 15; www.discoveringsouthmorocco.com) Run by English- and French-speaking, Zagora-born Mohamad Sirlrou.

Excursions Kasbah Tifawte (☏0524 84 88 43; www.tifawte.com) The kohl-eyed owner was one of the first official guides in the south.

Irahalen (☏0524 84 86 27; www.irahalen. com; Hotel Zagour, Rte de M'Hamid) Organises two- to 14-day desert and oasis excursions; English-speaking guides by prior arrangement.

🛏 Sleeping

TOP CHOICE **Dar Raha** DAR $$

(☏0524 84 69 93; www.darraha.com; Amezrou; per person incl breakfast/half-board Dh235/310) 'How thoughtful!' bears repeat-

QUICK GETAWAY: TINFOU DUNES

The great inland sea of dunes in Merzouga or Erg Chebbi can make this small patch of two to three big dunes seem like a kiddie sand box by comparison – but when you'd rather spend your time relaxing than driving, the Tinfou Dunes offer a sneak preview of Sahara sand just south of Zagora. Around 8km south of Tamegroute, you'll spot them on your left. On busy days it can feel like a playground here, but it's still fun to climb and run down the big dunes. Better still, you can get here and back in a day the time-honoured, eco-savvy way: by dromedary from Zagora or Tamegroute.

ing here, from welcoming gifts of dates to oasis-appropriate details like local palm mats, baskets made of recycled plastic bags and thick pisé walls eliminating the need for aircon. Comfortable, exposed-mudbrick rooms come with *ghandouras* (robes) for lounging, but no en-suite bathrooms. Enjoy home-cooked meals, admire local folk art in the courtyard gallery, and check the website for literary evenings showcasing Mid-Eastern authors. Your host Antoine gladly arranges visits to Amezrou's ancient synagogue, 18th-century *ksar* and village self-help organisations.

Villa Zagora
MAISON D'HÔTES **$$**
(☎0524 84 60 93; www.mavillaausahara.com; d incl half-board with shared/private bathroom Dh860/1030, ste Dh1322; ✿✿) Light, breezy, and naturally charming, this converted country home makes desert living look easy. French doors reveal plush Moroccan carpets, soaring ceilings, and an eclectic art collection, including Zagora-inspired abstracts. Staff fuss over you like Moroccan relations you never knew you had, and marathon meals feature oasis-fresh ingredients. Pool water is wisely reused on aromatic herb gardens; forget dromedaries and read your days away on the verandah.

Riad Lamane
RESORT **$$$**
(☎0524 84 83 88; www.riadlamane.com; d incl breakfast Dh900-1200, incl half-board Dh1200-1800; ✿✿✿) Two-storey round bungalows and buffed-*tadelakt* 'tents' (rooms with gossamer textiles draped from the ceiling), set in a wi-fi-enabled garden with an African-style bar. Tuareg style prevails in lodge rooms, from tent-post bedsteads to leather-covered light switches.

Les Jardins du Drâa
MAISON D'HÔTES **$$$**
(☎0524 84 67 66; www.riad-zagora.com; d incl breakfast/half-board Dh880/1100, ste Dh945/1220; ✿✿) A converted home inside the Amezrou palm oasis that's a cheerful cacophony of stucco, cushions and tile downstairs, with soothing, contemporary guest rooms featuring canopy beds and sand-hued walls. Families appreciate standards big enough for three, but romantics upgrade to the Sahara room, with a private balcony. Follow light-blue markers about 300m from Fibule du Drâa.

Auberge Restaurant Chez Ali
INN **$**
(☎0524 84 62 58; www.chez-ali.com; Ave de l'Atlas Zaouiate El Baraka; garden tents per person Dh40, d incl half-board Dh360-400, showers Dh10) The peacocks stalking the garden can't be bothered, but otherwise the welcome here is enthusiastic. Sky-lit standard rooms upstairs have simple pine furnishings, bathrooms and air-con; tents with pisé walls in the garden sleep four to five and share bathrooms; and 'traditional' rooms have wood-beamed ceilings, mattresses on carpets and shared bathrooms (room 14 has a private terrace). Enjoy Berber meals and overnight trips run by friendly English-speaking guides Mohamed and Yusuf.

Hotel la Fibule du Draa
HOTEL **$**
(☎0524 84 73 18; s/d/tr incl breakfast Dh480/550/700; ✿) Unexpected calm at the Amezrou crossroads, with a palm-shaded pool, garden bar, in-house hammam (from Dh100) and on-site massages (from Dh330). The 24 basic rooms have pisé walls, en-suite bathrooms, fridges and climate control of varying reliability. Choose garden-view rooms, and take full advantage of buffet breakfasts. It's 50m to the right off the Rte de M'Hamid in Amezrou.

Hotel Zagour
HOTEL **$**
(☎0524 84 61 78; www.zagour.com; Rte de M'Hamid; d incl breakfast/half-board Dh250/400; ✿✿) A sharp local team of 11, terrace pool, and air-conditioned rooms with local decor make stays here a comfortable bargain. Camel reins serving as towel racks and stained-glass caravan lanterns set a desert mood, and the stuccoed restaurant spe-

cialises in Zagora's namesake tajine: beef heaped with apricots, plums, raisins, onions, and toasted almonds. It's 600m before the bridge.

Camping les Jardins de Zagora CAMP SITE $ (☑0524 84 69 71; Berber tent Dh40, camping per person Dh20, per tent Dh10, per car Dh10, r with shared bathroom per person Dh50) Unwind in this flowered camp site next door to hotel Ksar Tinzouline, overlooking Jebel Zagora. Beds in walled Berber tents have electricity, and tajines are cooked to order (set menu Dh80).

✖ Eating & Drinking

Hotels provide Dh100 to Dh150 set meals to guests and nonguests by prior reservation. Moroccan fare with less flair can be had at cheap, popular restaurants along Blvd Mohammed V. Picnic makings can be found at market stalls, the supermarket at the northern end of town (no alcohol) and a bakery. For a stiff drink, head to La Fibule du Draa's garden bar, or the African bar at Riad Lamane.

Hôtel-Restaurant la Rose des Sables LOCAL $ (☑0524 84 72 74; Ave Allal Ben Abdallah; meals Dh40-60) Join off-duty desert guides unwinding over tasty beef and chicken tajines.

ℹ Information

Banque Populaire & BMCE (Blvd Mohammed V) Stock up on cash at two of the last ATMs you'll find before you hit the Sahara – M'Hamid has no functioning ATMs.

Pharmacy Zagora (☑0524 84 71 95; Blvd Mohammed V; ⊙8.30am-1pm & 3-8pm Mon-Fri, 8.30am-1pm Sat)

Placenet Cyber Center (95 Blvd Mohammed V; per hr Dh10) Internet access.

ℹ Getting There & Away

AIR Plans are in the works to open the new Zagora airport to domestic and international flights, but fuel prices and commercial viability currently restrict the airport to charter usage.

BUS The **CTM bus station** (☑0524 84 73 27; Blvd Mohammed V) is at the southwestern end of Mohammed V, and the bus station and grand taxi lot is at the northern end. **Supratours** (☑0524 84 76 88; Blvd Mohamed V) offers a daily 6am bus to Marrakesh (Dh180, eight hours) via Agdz (Dh40) and Ouarzazate (Dh40). There's also a daily CTM bus to Ouarzazate (Dh50, four hours), which continues to Marrakesh (Dh120, 9½ hours) and Casablanca (Dh190, 12½ hours).

Other companies have at least one run a day to Boumalne du Dadès (Dh75), Tinerhir (Dh70), Er-Rachidia (Dh125), Marrakesh (Dh100) and Ouarzazate (Dh50). There are buses to Rissani (Dh80) via N'Kob (Dh 20) and Tazzarine (Dh30) three times a week. A bus passes through Zagora to M'Hamid (Dh20, two hours) in the morning. More frequent minibuses run to M'Hamid (Dh25) throughout the day when full.

TAXI Grands taxis are more regular early in the morning. Destinations include Tamegroute (Dh7, 15 minutes), Agdz (Dh30, 1½ hours), Ouarzazate (Dh65, three hours), M'Hamid (Dh25, 1½ hours), Tazzarine (Dh50, 2½ hours) and N'Kob (Dh40, 1½ hours).

South of Zagora

TAMEGROUTE تامكروت

Stressed out? You've come to the right place: Tamegroute's Zawiya Nassiriyya is said to cure anxiety and high blood pressure, thanks to the post-mortem calming influence of Sidi Mohammed ben Nassir – founder of the influential and very studious Nassiri brotherhood in the 17th century. Bibliophiles should plan desert trips around visits to the *zawiya's* library of ancient illuminated texts.

Besides relieving tension, Tamegroute is known for its labyrinth of *ksour* connected by dark passageways, which you can explore with a local guide or by yourself to test your internal compass. Tamegroute also has a Saturday souq.

⊙ Sights

Zawiya Nassiriyya MEDERSA [TOP CHOICE] (suggested donation Dh20; ⊙morning & late afternoon Sat-Thu) While non-Muslims can't visit Sidi ben Nassir's green-roofed mausoleum, anyone can visit the library inside the adjacent *medersa* for Quranic scholars. Among the 4000 books on these glassed-in shelves are ancient medical, mathematics, algebra and law texts, in addition to splendid 13th-century Qurans written on gazelle hide.

Cooperative des Potiers ART GALLERY [TOP CHOICE] (⊙8am-6pm Mon-Fri) Oxidised copper yields the distinctive 'Tamegroute green' glaze used on the local pottery collective's rustic bowls, stamped tiles, and elegant platters.

☞ Tours

Travel Tamegroute DESERT (☑0662 20 09 75; www.traveltamegroute.com) For quick dromedary jaunts to nearby Tinfou dunes (or longer trips oasis-hopping to dunes, this agency offers reliable service and good deals (Dh500 per day with lunch, Dh550 overnight).

🛏 Sleeping & Eating

Auberge-Restaurant-Camping-Jnane Dar Diafa   GUESTHOUSE $
(⌖0524 84 06 22; www.jnanedar.ch; s/d with shared bathroom Dh125/170; s/d/tr/ste with bathroom from Dh200/300/400/600) In this breezy garden-gazebo restaurant, enjoy leisurely lunches made with vegetables grown on the premises. Scuffed but winsome pisé-walled guest rooms overlook the garden, some featuring air-con, mosquito nets over beds and star-patterned walls.

TAMEGROUTE TO M'HAMID

If a taste of dunes at Tinfou leaves you craving more, you could head east to the mighty pink dunes of Merzouga, Erg Chebbi (see p158) or into open desert at Erg Chigaga via M'Hamid. The road south disappears into the sand at M'Hamid, 96km south of Zagora and some 40km from Algeria (the southern border remains a contentious issue). The journey to M'Hamid takes you through a dauntingly bleak landscape of sun-scorched rubble, until the road ascends up and over **Tizi Beni Selmane** pass. The village of **Tagounite** has petrol and several cafes, and a worthwhile pit stop before the final 5km run into M'Hamid is the **ksar of Ouled Driss**, including a small **ethnographic museum** (admission Dh20) displaying traditional household objects in a lovely mudbrick courtyard.

M'Hamid   المحاميد

POP 3000

Once it was a lonesome oasis, but these days M'Hamid is a wallflower no more. Border tensions between Algeria, Morocco and the Polisario had isolated this caravan stop until the 1990s, when accords allowed M'Hamid to start hosting visitors again. M'Hamid's main attractions begin where the buildings end and relentless desert takes over, despite woven-palm barriers to keep it at bay.

From here, it doesn't take long to reach the dunes – some nuzzle right up against guesthouses on the west side of town – but to be enveloped by large dunes, you'll have to trek across the *reg*, hard-packed rocky desert. The star attraction is **Erg Chigaga**, a mind-boggling 40km stretch of golden Saharan dunes up to 300m high some 56km from M'Hamid that can take 2½ to three hours to reach by 4WD in good conditions on the *reg*. In poor conditions, any experienced guide will suggest you wait until tomorrow, and you'll be wise to listen. As the metallic light of sandstorms settles over M'Hamid, roads disappear into nowhere.

Many overnight camel treks (from Dh300 per person) from M'Hamid go 10km north of town to **Erg Lehoudi** (Dunes of the Jews), which has 100m-high dunes dotted with semipermanent bivouacs in need of attention from M'Hamid's recently established rubbish collection service. With a 4WD, you can drive there by *piste* off the main road 18km before M'Hamid, but a guide is advisable. Other nearby desert destinations include **Erg Ezahar**, a tall 'screaming dune' that wails eerily when the wind kicks up; the **Iriki oasis** mirage (see p138); and smaller dunes at **Mesouria**, 8km from M'Hamid.

M'Hamid itself encompasses two towns and five different ethnic groups: the Harratine, Berber, Chorfa, Beni M'Hamid and the fabled nomadic 'Blue Men'. M'Hamid Jdid, the prematurely aged 'new' town, has a mosque, roadside cafe-restaurants, small, mostly grim hotels, a few hodge-podge craft shops and a **Monday souq**. There's a frontier-town feel here, with tough guys in *shesh* (turban) and sunglasses hanging around M'Hamid Jdid at dusty cafes, swapping stories about the tourist who got lost in the desert only to turn up years later, married with children.

The old town of M'Hamid Bali, 3km away across the Oued Drâa, has a well-preserved kasbah. After a devastating bout of Bayoud disease in the region, palm trees are making a comeback in the oasis on the edge of town, forming a green line of resistance against the advances of the Sahara.

🏃 Activities

The best way to reach Erg Chigaga is in classic movie style: by camel, which takes five days or a week (from Dh400 per day) round trip. Once you've got the hang of camel-riding, consider an epic 12-day camel trip to Foum Zguid via Erg Chigaga. Shorter camel rides to smaller Saharan dunes are also recommended, though Erg Chigaga has the biggest ones this side of Merzouga.

» Don't show up in M'Hamid expecting a bargain Once you're here, you don't have a lot of room to negotiate: guides know if you've come this far, you're not likely to turn back without seeing the dunes, and price trips accordingly. Since top tour operators are often booked in advance through Marrakesh agencies (p73), you may have to settle for less experienced guides with sputtering vehicles – and car trouble in the desert isn't fun. In larger, longer-established Zagora, you'll find more options for worthwhile, budget-minded, last-minute desert excursions (p133).

» First time? Keep it short As any Sufi mystic will attest, being alone with your thoughts in the desert can be an illuminating, uplifting experience – but those not accustomed to such profound isolation may get bored quickly. Some visitors experience 'desert panic', a state of distress that makes every aspect of the Sahara's alien landscape seem threatening, from whistling dunes to harmless sand beetles. Local tour operators report that some visitors ask to turn back even before they reach the dunes. On the other hand, many visitors claim that the Sahara helped them put personal difficulties – tragedy, divorce, job loss – behind them. Try an overnight trip, so you can see what the desert brings to mind.

» Before you commit to a longer trip, get names The guide can make or break your experience, especially for multiday trips. Even at recommended tour agencies with licensed guides, ask for the name of the individual guide with whom you'll be travelling, do an internet search for reviews, and solicit feedback on **Lonely Planet's Thorn Tree** (www.lonelyplanet.com/thorntree). Personal experiences vary, but language skills are important. Conversation naturally trails off in the desert, but in a sandstorm, you'll want a guide who can put your mind at ease in a language you understand.

To reach Erg Chigaga in a few hours, you'll need to shell out for a 4WD, which costs Dh1000 to Dh1300 with insurance, plus another Dh250 for the camp. Many agencies offer guides *and* drivers, which is a good idea – even local drivers familiar with desert conditions can stray off-course or get stuck in sand.

Have you heard the one about the tourists who declined a local guide's services, and were lost to a sandstorm just 2km from town? Stick around, and you will – sales ploys come with the territory here, but don't be reeled in by *faux guide* scare tactics. Treks on foot, camel or 4WD to Erg Chigaga with reliable, licensed guides can be arranged in Marrakesh, Zagora or in M'Hamid. Bear in mind that many desert tour operators only accept payment in cash, and since there are no banks in M'Hamid, you'll need to hit ATMs in Zagora before you hit the dunes.

Sahara Services TREKKING
(☎061 776766; www.saharaservices.info; Kasbah Sahara Services, M'Hamid) All-inclusive desert trips via camel and 4WD, including overnights to an encampment of walled Berber tents in Erg Chigaga with

amenities: dinner and music by firelight in the dunes, dromedary rides from base camp, plus toilets, hot meals, even hot showers. It's 300m on the right after you enter M'Hamid.

Zbar Travel TREKKING
(☎068 517280; www.zbartravel.com) Offers overnights at an Erg Chigaga encampment, sleep-outs under the stars, sandboarding, dromedary and walking treks, and insights on Saharawi culture and botany.

Dar Azawad TREKKING
(☎0524 84 87 30; www.darazawad.com; Douar Ouled Driss) For a decadent desert honeymoon, this M'Hamid guesthouse teamed up with Marrakesh's Mamounia to offer a luxury Sahara 'camping' experience: champagne at sunset, king-size beds, a barber, masseur, and henna-tattoo artist upon request, and most impressive of all, en-suite composting toilets.

🛏 Sleeping & Eating

TOP CHOICE **Dar Sidi Bounou** DAR $
(☎0524 84 63 30; www.darsidibounou.com; per person incl full board in tent/hut/r Dh330/420/540) A desert dream: dunes in

the backyard, sand hammams, Saharawi music jam sessions, *mechoui* (whole roast lamb) feasts on starry-tiled terraces. Retreat to Berber tents and mudbrick huts that sleep six to eight, sleep on the roof under meteor showers, or curl up between crisp cotton sheets in main-house guestrooms. Instead of the usual sandy pool, Dar Sidi Bounou offers desert immersion experiences: landscape-painting expeditions by dromedary, belly-dancing classes, even authentic Saharan weddings. Reserve ahead; cash or travellers cheques only. It's 4km beyond Ouled Driss.

Dar Azawad RESORT $$$
(☑0524 84 87 30; www.darazawad.com; Douar Ouled Driss; d incl half-board Dh1600-1800, ste Dh2200-2500; ✿✾⊛) Adventurous souls craving creature comforts, look no further. Designer bungalows set in organic gardens feature sleek *tadelakt* walls, lofty palm-beam ceilings and en-suite bathrooms with local, organic skincare products. Suites have bonus amenities: fireplaces, king-sized beds, Nespresso machines, iPod docks, hidden flat-screen TVs and Jacuzzi tubs. Go luxury 'glamping' in the dunes (from Dh1350 per person) or enjoy a hammam, manicure-pedicure and exfoliating scrub with Sahara sand and argan oil. Meals range from tasty herb-marinated turkey kebabs to elaborate traditional couscous – learn how it's done in on-site cooking classes – and there's a well-stocked bar, boutique, and filtered swimming pool.

Kasbah Sahara Services INN $$
(☑0524 84 80 33; www.hotelmhamid. com; per person incl half-board tent/d/ste Dh200/300/350) When siroccos blow through town, retreat to air-conditioned, candy-coloured rooms with en-suite bathrooms, Berber tent with sinks and shared bathroom, or a family suite with *tataoui* ceilings and *tadelakt* bathroom. Menus include oasis-fresh salad, kebabs and chips (Dh80); learn a few Saharawi recipes at on-site cooking classes. It's 300m on the right after you enter M'Hamid.

ℹ Getting There & Away

Daily Supratours buses head to Marrakesh (Dh180, eight hours) via Zagora (Dh20), Agdz (Dh40) and Ouarzazate (Dh60). Daily afternoon CTM bus runs to Zagora (Dh25, two hours), Ouarzazate (Dh60, six hours), Marrakesh (Dh155, six hours) and Casablanca (Dh220, 15 hours).

Erg Chigaga to Tizi n'Tichka

Exiting Erg Chigaga by 4WD, head north to Marrakesh via Foum Zguid. En route through the *sahel* and *reg*, you'll pass **Iriki oasis** under an imposing plateau on your right, with a lonesome cafe offering cool drinks under sun umbrellas. From here, you'll spot thirsty birds and gazelles drinking from a vast lake. But look again: 'Lake Iriki' is actually a mirage, with deceptive silhouettes of poisonous calitropis bushes.

Another 30km or so from Cafe Iriki you'll turn north, and as you near a blocky plateau you'll swear is a hotel (another desert illusion), you'll approach the guardhouse for **Foum Zguid**, where you'll be asked to show your passport. Foum Zguid is a strategic military base, and the town is a crossroads with all the necessities: water, petrol, a public phone, and coffee.

Follow the *piste* 2.5km east of Maison d'Hôtes Hiba, and you'll come to Co-operative Ahilal des Tapis (see p139). Admire the carpets woven on clean, well-equipped premises, tajine-shaped baskets and *lugnâa*, a local-style black wrap with graphic flower patterns in vivid colours. Your next stop en route to Tizi n'Tichka is **Tazenakht**, a handy stop for a quick bite, coffee, petrol and yes, carpets.

More heirloom-quality carpets await discovery 26km up the N10 at Jemaite Tifawin (see p139). This women's carpet-weaver's association hosts Sunday open-houses, where visitors can learn to weave a bookmark or spin raw wool into yarn under expert tutelage (sliding-scale donation Dh200 to Dh500). Donations go directly to the democratically run association to pay for rent, loom, and wool purchases, and charismatic director Khadija Ighilnasaf provides donation receipts with a heartfelt *Barakllafik* (blessings go with you). Look for the roadside sign in the village of Anzal, 30 minutes along the N10 north of Tazenakht.

🛏 Sleeping & Eating

Maison d'Hôtes Hiba GUESTHOUSE $
(☑0615 72 72 82; 8km Foum Zguid; per person incl half-board Dh220; ✿) A rock-studded guesthouse and restaurant serving restorative meals of tajine, salad, and fruit (Dh80) on the scenic terrace or on sofas in the air-conditioned salon. Comfy grotto-style rooms with new en-suite bathrooms make this a

DON'T MISS

MAGIC CARPET RIDE: FOUM ZGUID TO ANZAL

On this two-hour drive, you'll find carpets to delight feet, enchant guests, and remind you of sipping tea with Morocco's talented women weavers. By buying directly from these weavers, you'll score carpet deals and immediately improve life for families eking out a living in this rocky terrain.

Cooperative Ahilal des Tapis   CARPETS

In this sunny studio, you'll spot tightly knotted carpets in some surprising non-traditional styles and colours. One plush aubergine carpet fairly begs for a fireplace, and there's a rock-star red carpet with alternating stripes of scarlet wool and shaggy, glossy black goat hair. Still on the loom on a recent visit was a free-form 'Berber Picasso', with jagged indigo mountain ranges and saffron polygons. 'That one's my house,' explains the weaver, pointing to a square.

Prices are set, with a small percentage going to the association for equipment, training and childcare, and the rest directly to the women who made the items – income that's often the sole support for families in this semidesert location. It's 8km from Foum Zguid, 2.5km along a graded *piste*.

Tazenakht Ensemble Artisanal   CARPETS

The crossroads town of Tazenakht has several carpet shops that mostly sell to trade, but you can skip the middlemen and browse high-quality carpets at fixed prices inside this government-run showroom. The tricky part is finding the Ensemble Artisanal in downtown Taznakht, where few streets are labelled. Entering the town from the south, turn right, then left towards the post office. Nearing the post office parking lot, turn right, and at the next T junction, turn left: this is the Ensemble Artisanal, which you should find open 10am to 5pm.

Jemaite Tifawin Carpet Cooperative   ART & CRAFT

(Association of Light; ☑0674 74 48 30; Anzal village, ☺carpet showroom 9am-noon & 2-6pm Mon-Thu, studio open house 9am-5pm Sun) The women of Anzal village are impressive multitaskers – in addition to farming, household management, and foraging for mountain herbs, 88 local women weave carpets. They're also daringly creative. While other local weavers stick to traditional tufted yellow Glaoui carpets with classic diamond patterns, these women are making wildly original pieces, experimenting with dyes from Anti Atlas plants and finding new design inspirations.

In the sale showroom, one arresting crimson kilim is edged with graphic black-and-white zigzags – 'like a traffic sign, you know?' says Fatima, the weaver who made it. A madder-root-dyed deep purple carpet with a henna-yellow wriggle was inspired by Kufic calligraphy, conveying *baraka* (blessings). All are marked with fixed prices and proceeds go directly to the carpet maker, with a small percentage underwriting shared weaving supplies. No need to worry about baggage limits here: table runners, throw pillows, and Mac-sized laptop bags are available. Of all the women's carpet cooperatives in southern Morocco, this is surely the hippest. It's 26km on N10 from Tazenakht.

---

welcome overnight stop after roughing it in the desert. Head 8km north of Foum Zguid towards Marrakesh; look for the right-hand turn-off onto the *piste* to Zagora/Amezrou.

Restaurant La Liberté   RESTAURANT $$
(Foum Ziguid; meals Dh70-80; ☺7am-10pm) Hot breakfasts and serviceable kebabs on the west side of the town square, on your right after the major/only intersection.

DADÈS VALLEY & THE GORGES سهول داداس والمضايق

Nomad crossings, rose valleys and two-tone kasbahs: even on paper, the Dadès Valley stretches the imagination. From the daunting High Atlas to the north to the rugged Jebel Sarhro range south, the valley is dotted with oases and mudbrick palaces that give the region its fairytale nickname – Valley of a Thousand Kasbahs. Some of the best views are only glimpsed on foot, on hidden passageways between the Dadès and Todra Gorges and nomad routes across the Sarhro.

Skoura سكورة

POP 2800

By the time caravans laden with gold and spice reached Skoura, the camels must've been gasping. After a two-month journey across the Sahara, blue-robed Tuareg desert traders offloaded cargo from caravans in Skoura, where Middle Atlas mountaineers packed it onto mules headed to Fez. Ouarzazate is now the region's commercial centre 39km west, but Skoura's historic mudbrick castles remain, and desert traders throng Monday and Thursday souqs brimming with intensely flavourful desert produce. When market days are done and palm-tree shadows stretch across the road, no one seems in a hurry to leave. Elsewhere, life goes on as usual – but in Skoura, it remains a wonder.

◉ Sights & Activities

TOP CHOICE **Palm Groves**   NATURAL SCENERY
Skoura's defining features remain its mudbrick kasbahs and vast Unesco-protected palm groves, earning the moniker 'Oasis of 1000 Palms'. Under this green canopy, a 15-mile patchwork of carefully tended garden plots are watered by an ingenious, centuries-old *khattara* system of locks, levers and canals. Plump birds twitter away in the trees; more than 100 bird species flourish here. To experience Skoura's splendours from the inside out, stay overnight in a pisé' guesthouse and explore the *palmeraie* on foot or bicycle (most guesthouses arrange rentals).

Kasbah Amridil   KASBAH
(unguided/guided visit Dh10/50) Morocco's most coveted kasbah is this 17th-century wonder, which appears on Morocco's 50-dirham note. Signposted just a few hundred metres from the main road, this living museum shows that traditional kasbah life hasn't changed much over the centuries, with hand-carved door locks, an olive-oil press, still-functioning bread ovens, and goats bleating in the courtyard.

Skoura Cultural Centre   CULTURAL CENTRE
(☑0524 85 23 92; N10; ⊗9am-noon & 2.30-5.30pm Sun-Thu) An enterprising NGO, show-casing local ingenuity at its crafts showcase on weekdays and offering Sunday tours by bicycle or on foot (five-day advance booking required) for a sliding-scale donation (Dh200 to Dh500 per person). Proceeds support the centre's water-conservation, literacy and palm-preservation programs (see p141). It's 300m on the left after the Skoura crossroads.

🛏 Sleeping & Eating

Note that there is no ATM in Skoura, and since most local guesthouses don't accept credit cards, you'll need to stop for cash in Ouarzazate.

TOP CHOICE **Sawadi**   MAISON D'HÔTES $$
(☑0524 85 23 41; www.sawadi.ma; Palmeraie de Skoura; s/d incl breakfast Dh615/725, s/d ste Dh715/860, 6-10-person villa Dh2570; ❋ ☒) An oasis within an oasis, 9 acres of walled organic gardens make a bucolic setting for pisé bungalows – and they also yield sumptuous, three-course organic feasts. Unwind after visits to local artisans or kasbah architecture tours by bicycle with a steamy hammam, or chilled white wine by the salt-filtered, chlorine-free pool. Follow green triangle markers from the road into the north end of the oasis; cash only.

Jardins de Skoura   MAISON D'HÔTES $$
(☑0524 85 23 24; www.lesjardinsdeskoura. com; Palmeraie de Skoura; r/ste incl breakfast Dh770/1120; ❋ ☒) Low-key, high-romance Skoura style: intimate nooks carved from pisé walls, lined with custom-designed rugs. In the organic garden are a small chlorinated pool, a boutique of local crafts, and dinners (Dh130 to Dh180) featuring Moroccan mains and French desserts with Skoura-grown produce. If you can't finish, pudgy pet donkeys will be happy to help – they're the resident composters. Follow orange triangle markers from the main road; cash only.

Chez Talout   INN $$
(☑0662 49 82 83; www.talout.com; per person incl half-board Dh370-420; ❋ ☒) On a desert rise with a scenic overlook of the Skoura oasis are fraternal-twin mudbrick guesthouses: one with simple, sunny rooms, the other with a chlorinated pool and air-conditioning. Follow oasis outings by foot, horse or mountain bike with decadent roof-terrace lunches featuring *tannour* (flatbread) and seasoned local butter. It's signposted 7km northwest of Skoura.

Walking the Skoura Oasis, feet naturally fall into rhythm with the bossa-nova sway of stately palms. But they're not here for looks: palms have work to do in the oasis, providing dates, shade and fronds to be woven into roofing material, floor coverings and fencing to contain grumpy donkeys.

Palms are plentiful in this 'Oasis of 1000 Palms', but not one of them can be taken for granted. One concern is Bayoud disease, a fungus that passes from palm to palm. Unesco is taking steps to protect palm oases from Aït Benhaddou to Figuig, declaring the oases a biosphere reserve, and the Moroccan government is planting palms believed to be Bayoud-resistant.

But Skoura's majestic palms face another danger, reports Mohamed Elkasbaoui, director of the Skoura Cultural Centre's palm preservation initiative. 'The biggest threat to our palms isn't actually Bayoud: it's poverty,' he says. 'When crops fail, to support their families, some people illegally sell palms to decorate big-city resorts.'

To address this problem, the centre recently opened an oasis arts showcase on the eastern edge of town. Here Skoura residents sell items made with palm fronds, sustainably harvested without harming the trees. For travellers who've admired Morocco's majestic palm groves, these sun hats, breadbaskets, mats and glass-lined lanterns make meaningful mementos – and purchases support the centre's palm preservation efforts.

'The showcase provides income to people between crop harvests, when there is the greatest need,' Elkasbaoui explains. 'It's a small showcase, but it represents a big idea: if we take care of these trees, they'll provide for us, our children, and our children's children.'

Kasbah Aït ben Moro   KASBAH **$$$**
(☑0524 85 21 16; www.aitbenmoro.com; s/d with shared bathroom & half-board Dh450, d with private bathroom Dh1000-1200; ✸) An 18th-century kasbah given a stylish 2000 makeover remains true to its desert roots with original palm-beam ceilings, moody low-lit passageways, and water-conserving cactus gardens (hence no pool). The three tower rooms are the sweetest deals, with shared bathrooms and oasis views; ask for the one with a fireplace. It's 2km from downtown Skoura.

Espace Kasbah Amridil   KASBAH **$$**
(☑0524 85 22 79; www.espaceamridil.com; s Dh200, d Dh400-500, half-board Dh650) Wake up overlooking the kasbah next door in mudbrick tower rooms (much nicer than the dim ones downstairs). The salon's plasma TV detracts from the romance, but lures sports fans. It's next to Kasbah Amridil; cash only.

Kasbah Aït Abou   KASBAH **$**
(☑0524 85 22 34; www.chez.com/kasbahaitabou; Palmeraie de Skoura; per person incl half-board Dh180) Sleep like a dignitary in this 1825 kasbah built by the local caïd, with a 25m mudbrick tower that's an engineering marvel. Ground-floor rooms are big and

naturally cool, with wonky but serviceable en-suite bathrooms, or opt for new tented rooms in the garden. Follow red arrows from the main road; cash only.

ℹ Getting There & Away

There are regular but infrequent buses from Ouarzazate and Tinerhir (Dh40), but a grand taxi from Ouarzazate (Dh25) is a better option.

Kelaâ M'Gouna   قلعة مكونة

Although it takes its name from the nearby M'Goun mountain, the small town of Kelaâ M'Gouna is famous for roses and daggers. Some 50km from Skoura, pink roses start peeking through dense roadside hedgerows, and you can't miss the bottles of local rosewater for sale in town. During the May rose harvest you'll see rose garlands everywhere, especially during the town's signature **rose festival** (first weekend of May). At **Wednesday souqs**, you can load up on dried edible roses.

To stop and smell the roses with a nature walk, call the **bureau des guides** (☑0661 79 61 01, 0662 13 21 92) or book official guides through local hotels. At Kelaâ's downtown crossroads are some handy facilities before hitting the trail: an ATM, pharmacies and internet cafes.

Sleeping & Eating

Kasbah Itran   KASBAH $
(☏0524 83 71 03; www.kasbahitran.com; d incl half-board with shared/private bathroom Dh350/ 500; ❋) A maze of private terraces, fireplaces and rooms, most with en-suite bathrooms, stiff beds, and views over the M'Goun River. Trekking excursions are available, but for a cushier experience, try sunset calèche rides and air-conditioned doubles. It's 2km northwest of Kelaâ M'Gouna; minivans from town run past Kasbah Itran en route to the village of Torbis (Dh5).

Kasbah Assafar   KASBAH $
(☏0524 83 65 77; www.kasbahassafar.com; d incl half-board with shared/private bathroom Dh350/ 500) Other guesthouses call themselves kasbahs, but this is the real deal: a converted family home where you'll duck through doorways into pisé-walled rooms with views over mountain gorges. Snug rooms have portable heaters and shared bathrooms. Count on host and licensed mountain guide Abdelaziz Boullouz for reliable trekking advice and Berber home-cooking. It's 4km northwest of Kelaâ M'Gouna; follow the Kelaâ road northwest past Kasbah Itran, and follow signs 1km through the village.

Café Restaurant Rendez-Vous des Amis   RESTAURANT $
(☏0661 87 14 43; http://rendezvousdesamis.webobo.biz; Ave Mohammed V) Cinnamony à la carte tajines (Dh35 to Dh50) and restorative herbal tisanes with wild absinthe make this the go-to cafe-restaurant in the centre of town.

🛍 Shopping

Unité de Distillation de Rose   SOUVENIRS
(☏0661 34 81 77; ⊗8am-5.30pm) A collective of five farms with an immaculate shared rosewater distillery, located 500m before you reach downtown on your right. The adjoining showroom offers a full range of bath products, including uncoloured, untreated rosewater used locally as aftershave and to bring down fever – perfect for all those feverish shaving sessions.

Cooperative Artisan du Poignards Azlag   ART & CRAFT
(⊗9am-5pm) Life in Kelaâ M'Gouna must not always have been so rosy, because the region also has a tradition of making daggers. At this set-price showroom on the main road at the eastern edge of town, ceremonial daggers range from Dh250-1200. On the wall is a collection of local styles, ranging from Tuareg (leather-handled, straight blade) to Aït Aitta (inlaid hilt, curved blade). It's sometimes closed for lunch.

❶ Getting There & Away

Buses run between Ouarzazate and Tinerhir via Kelaâ, but are often full. You can catch a grand taxi to Ouarzazate (Dh30), Skoura (Dh10), Boumalne du Dadès (Dh7) and Tinerhir (Dh6).

Boumalne du Dadès
بوملنه داده

POP 11,200

At the Dadès Gorge crossroads, Boumalne has river valley views and handy amenities for gorge-bound trekkers. Head 24km northeast of Kelaâ M'Gouna until you reach a fork: the main road continues over the river to the hillside town of Boumalne du Dadès, while the left-hand road leads into stunning Dadès Gorge. Market day is Wednesday.

If you think this place is for the birds, you're right: the *hammada* and grassy plains south of Boumalne du Dadès offer rewarding birdwatching opportunities. Take the *piste* leading off the main road beyond town south towards the village of Tagdilt and Vallée des Oiseaux (Valley of the Birds) to look for larks, wheat-ears, sand grouse, buzzards and eagle owls.

🏃 Activities

Hamou Aït Lhou   TOURS & BIKING
(☏0667 59 32 92; hamou57@voila.fr; Ave Mohammed V) Knowledgeable official guide who leads trips on foot or bicycle and rents mountain bikes (Dh120 per day).

Hammam Warda   HAMMAM
(admission Dh8, plus tip; ⊗8am-8pm) Through the gate to the souq and across the plaza, this public hammam serves men and women separately.

🛏 Sleeping

Xaluca Dadès   HOTEL $$$
(☏0635 57 84 50; s/d/ste half-board Dh1056/ 1533/2033; ▣❋🌐@✉) A neo-Saharan makeover transformed this 1970s convention-centre into a destination hotel. The 106 guest rooms have balconies with Tuareg chairs, plush beds with thick duvets

and mud-cloth bedspreads, and en-suite bathrooms with gleaming beaten-copper sinks. Since Boumalne is a mining region, there's an underlying mining decor theme: rock walls, lobby grotto, torch-lit mine-shaft corridors. Expect all the mod cons, plus hammam (Dh100), massage (Dh250 per half-hour), swanky bar, billiards, panoramic terrace swimming pool, Jacuzzi, and a noisy gym. It's signposted at the top of the hill on Ave Mohammed V.

Hôtel Almanader INN $
(☏0524 83 01 72; Ave Mohammed V; s/d/tr incl half-board Dh250/400/500; ❈) High above the river valley, Almanader makes a splash with colourful murals and 12 tidy, quirky rooms with balconies, hat posts and candy-coloured stucco ceilings; four have air-conditioning. Easygoing staff are quick with hellos, espresso, and homestyle Berber cooking (meals Dh70 to Dh100).

✕ Eating

Restaurant Oussikis LOCAL $
(☏0666 64 14 21; Pl de Souk; dishes Dh50-90) Inside the souq plaza on your left, you'll spot chef Fadil Faska in his spotless open kitchen transforming fresh, local ingredients into savoury tajines. Get today's special, call ahead for float-away-flaky *pastilla*, or opt for quick, satisfying salads (Dh10) and roast chicken (Dh30).

Hôtel-Restaurant Adrar LOCAL $
(☏024 830765; Ave Mohammed V; meals Dh35-Dh70; ❈) Handy to the bus station yet clean, with popular, filling meals of salads and brochettes or the local speciality: *gallia* (game hen) tajine.

❶ Information

On Ave Mohammed V, there's an **Attijariwafa ATM**, four pharmacies, and internet access at **Taziri Net** (per hr Dh10; ☺9am-10pm).

❶ Getting There & Away

BUS Buses leave daily to Ouarzazate (Dh40), Zagora (Dh60), Tinerhir (Dh25), Fez (Dh135 or Dh160), Casablanca (Dh120 to Dh160) and Rabat (Dh140 or Dh195), and multiple times daily to Er-Rachidia (Dh40), Erfoud (Dh60) and Marrakesh (Dh70 to Dh104).

TAXI, TRUCK & MINIBUS You may have to wait awhile for a grand taxi or minibus to fill up; fares are Dh35 to Ouarzazate, Dh20 to Tinerhir and Dh15 to Aït Oudinar (inside the Dadès Gorge).

Trekking Jebel Sarhro

The starkly beautiful Jebel Sarhro (aka Jebel Saghro or Djebel Sahro) range shrugs its mighty shoulders between the High Atlas and Dadès Valley. Few tourists venture here: most of the flat-topped mesas, volcanic pinnacles and deep gorges dotted with palm groves are only accessible on foot. This arid, isolated territory is home turf to the seminomadic Aït Atta, legendary warriors famous for their 1933 stand against the French here, on Jebel Bou Gafer.

Jebel Sarhro is accessed from three trekking hubs: Kelaâ M'Gouna and Boumalne du Dadès on the north side of the range, and the southern village of N'Kob (p161). The most scenic routes head through the heart of the range, between Igli and Bab n'Ali.

This circuit has one big advantage over the classic Sarhro north–south traverse: it begins and ends on the north side of the mountains, so you can easily resume journeys to Dadès gorges, Merzouga and the dunes. Tents could be used, but staying in *gîtes* or *chez l'habitant* is preferable in winter, when you may wake to find a metre of snow has fallen overnight.

When to Go

While many High Atlas trails are impassable between November and February, Sarhro is a prime winter trekking destination. Sarhro winter temperatures can dip below freezing, and snow may fall as low as 1400m – but even when it does snow, it is usually possible to trek. In autumn and spring, night-time temperatures rarely fall below zero. When summer temperatures get scorching hot (above 40°C), water sources disappear, and even scorpions hunker under rocks for shade.

❶ Getting There & Away

Minibuses run from Boumalne du Dadès to Ikniouln (Dh25), at the northern edge of the range, departing around noon and returning to Boumalne early the next morning. There may be extra buses on Wednesdays, when Ikniouln has its weekly souq.

Day 1: Tagdilt to the Assif Ouarg Valley

4HR/17KM/200M ASCENT

Tagdilt is an uninspiring village but a useful trailhead, with three *gîtes* and a daily

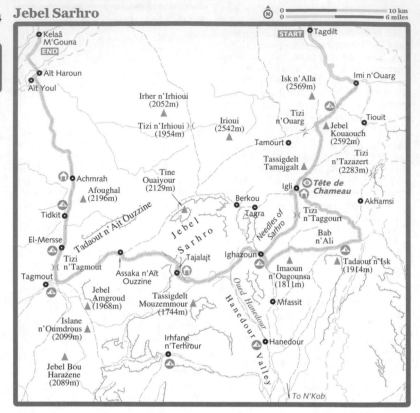

camionette (pick-up truck) from Boum-alne. For 2½ hours, you could follow the *piste* used by vans crossing the mountain to N'Kob, or veer onto the track that occasionally strays to the side, rejoining the *piste* further up the slope.

At **Imi n'Ouarg**, the third village above Tagdilt, the path leaves the road (which continues to mines at Tiouit). The path turns right (southwest) beside the village school, marked by a Moroccan flag. There's a nice lunch stop to the right, just beyond the village.

The path follows the right-hand side of the winding Assif Ouarg valley, beneath the summit of **Jebel Kouaouch** (2592m). After an hour (about 3km), there's a farm above terraced fields where you can stay **chez l'habitant** (☑0661 08 23 21; per person Dh30-50). The host's sons can be hired as muleteers and hot meals may be available.

Day 2: Assif Ouarg Valley to Igli
6-7 HR/19KM/620M ASCENT/860M DESCENT

The most memorable walk on this trek is also the most difficult, starting with a 35-minute climb towards the head of the valley, with a scattering of stone houses and rocks ahead. The path leads left (south) and **Jebel Kouaouch** is the highest of a row of peaks straight ahead. The path zigzags over a stream, up towards Kouaouch and a lone juniper tree – a good place for a breather. Depending on fitness and weather, it could take another hour to reach the pass. As you climb, there are good views back towards Tagdilt, and once over the ridge, the High Atlas and Jebel Sarhro come into view.

The path drops steeply down ahead, but our track veers right (southwest) across the valley's shoulder and over another ridge, with views south to the palms and kasbahs of **N'Kob**. **Igli** is due south over a series of slopes, with the famous **Tête de Chameau**

(Camel's Head) cliffs appearing as you walk down towards the settlement. Three low buildings form a *gîte* (per person Dh30) with a toilet and wood-fired hot showers (Dh10). There's no electricity or sleeping mats here, but the friendly *gardien* runs a shop selling trekkers' necessities, including mule shoes, and if you bring flour he'll have it baked into bread.

For breathtaking mountain sunsets, you've come to the right place. You might add a round trip to **Bab n'Ali**, one of the most spectacular rock formations in the Sarhro, returning to Igli for another night or continuing to the **Irhazzoun n'Imlas** *gîte* (per person Dh30).

Day 3: Igli to Tajalajt
7-7½ HR/24KM/350M ASCENT/400M DESCENT

Looming on the right-hand side as you walk is the peak of **Jebel Amlal**, sacred to the Aït Atta and the site of August pilgrimages. The morning's walk is gentler than the previous day's, leading through wide, rocky valleys. After 1½ hours, beneath the village of **Taouginte**, the path curves around an **Aït Atta cemetery**, where graves are marked with piles of stone. The path leads then below the **Needles of Sarhro**, a long, dramatic cliff that slopes down after another 1½ hours to the Amguis River. Several valleys meet at a beautiful camping spot, amid palms and oleander. Half an hour southwards down the valley is **Ighazoun**, a village above well-tended fields with a riverside lunch spot.

At Ighazoun the path joins a *piste* that runs left to N'Kob and right towards the Dadès. Take the right track (northwest) towards a sheer cliff on the left, with the rocky path leading beneath it and up to a broadening valley. The *piste* loops around the north side of **Jebel Tassigdelt Si el-Haj** (1722m) and then south again towards **Tiguiza**, where there is a basic **gîte** (☑0671 72 80 06; Dh 30). Before Tiguiza, another *piste* leads right (west) to **Akerkour village**, into a narrowing valley dotted with palms, and up an incline to **Tajalajt**, where you can stay **chez l'habitant** (per person Dh30) and maybe obtain basic meals.

Day 4: Tajalajt to Achmrah
8-8½ HR/26KM/200M ASCENT/300M DESCENT

Take the valley *piste* from Tajalajt, above splendid terraced cornfields and palm and almond groves. Less than 1½ hours brings

you to **Assaka n'Aït Ouzzine** (1584m), its ruined kasbah teetering above the beautiful valley. Next, the *piste* leads out of the valley into a different landscape: a rocky, windy steppe that might have been lifted from Central Asia.

After 1½ hours from Assaka spent wedged between 2000m ridges, you'll arrive at **Tagmout** (also called Amgroud after one of the mountains overlooking the village) and a well-kept **gîte** (per person Dh30, breakfast Dh25) with electricity, mattresses, blankets, and possibly lunch (Dh25 to Dh30).

From Tagmout the *piste* leads northwest to Kelaâ M'Gouna and south to N'Kob, with transport headed to N'Kob's **Sunday souq**. The trek heads due north, climbing over an hour to **Tizi n'Tagmout** (1754m) for stunning views to the M'Goun Massif. Another hour leads to **El-Mersse**, where shade and a year-round spring facilitate camping.

The track continues due north, mostly in gentle descent, but with occasional climbs. Under 1½ hours after El-Mersse, there's a riverside camp site at **Tidkit** under shade trees and it may be possible to sleep *chez l'habitant* here or in **Achmrah**, another hour down the track. However, the Berbers on this side of Jebel Sarhro are seminomadic and may be absent April–May. If the houses are empty, the animal shelters will be too – a less glamorous but practical place to sleep.

THE TREK AT A GLANCE

Duration five to six days

Distance 56km

Standard medium

Start Tagdilt

Finish Kelaâ M'Gouna

Highest Point Tizi n'Ouarg (approximately 2300m)

Accommodation camping and *gîtes/chez l'habitant*

Public Transport yes

Summary A great alternative to the classic Sarhro traverse, showcasing the staggering and varied beauty of the range. Given demanding climbs and long days of walking, you might add another night to the route.

BEFORE YOU GO: JEBEL SARHRO CHECKLIST

» **Maps** The 1:100,000 *Boumalne* and *Tazzarine* maps cover the region, but a more detailed trekking map with history and information on the back is 1:100,000 *Randonnée culturelle dans le Djebel Sarhro* by Mohamed Aït Hamza and Herbert Popp, published in Germany, written in French and available in Morocco, including hotels in Boumalne and N'Kob (Dh150).

» **Guide** Several foreign tour operators (including Explore, Exodus and Walks Worldwide) run good-value trips here, but many of them subcontract to local guides. You can find a licensed local guide directly through a **bureau des guides** (☑Kelaâ 0661 79 61 01, 0662 13 21 92, Boumalne 0667 59 32 92, N'Kob 0667 48 75 09) in any of the three Sarhro trekking centres. Expect to pay Dh300 a day for a guide and Dh100 for a mule.

» **Water** Dehydration is common any time of the year, so pack extra water.

» **Food** Stock up in Ouarzazate or Marrakesh. There's tea, tinned fish, biscuits and bread in the three Sarhro departure towns, and you may find eggs, dates, almonds, bread and tinned fish in some villages.

» **Mule** Given the amount of water you must carry in this arid environment, mules are a worthwhile investment. Your guide can organise mules and muleteers.

» **Gear** Bring a sleeping bag. You won't need a tent, unless you'd rather camp than stay at *refuges*.

Day 5: Achmrah to the Kelaâ M'Gouna

4 HRS/14KM/150M ASCENT/450M DESCENT

The best parts of this morning walk are the beginning and end. The track north of Achmrah makes a short climb, suddenly revealing M'Goun and Siroua vistas. Less than half an hour later, it crosses a *piste* that leads to an anthracite mine and should not be followed. Instead continue north, occasionally northwest, on a well-worn track that leads down a gully towards the Dadès Valley. As you get closer, you will see the villages of **Aït Youl** on your left, **Aït Haroun** on the right, and a valley studded with old kasbahs. Head for Aït Haroun, where there is a bridge over the Dadès River. The Boumalne–Kelaâ M'Gouna road is nearby, but long after you return to the modern world, Sarhro's semi-nomadic spirit stays with you.

Dadès Gorge

مخنف ا مفيق ا دادس

Those art-deco tourism posters you'll see all over Morocco showing a red-and-white kasbah in a rocky oasis aren't exaggerating: just 6.5km into the gorge at **Aït Youl**, almond and fig trees provide a lush green backdrop for two-tone kasbahs and *ksour*.

A couple of kilometres past Aït Youl, the road crosses an *oued*; this river valley offers a sneaky back way to Kelaâ M'Gouna on foot. After another 5km and over a small pass, the hidden **Gorge de Miguirne** (Sidi Boubar Gorge) joins from the right, with springs and rock pools for a good half-day stream hike.

Another 4km brings you to extraordinary **red rock formations** that look like wax, melting right into the green carpet of the *palmeraie* below **Aït Arbi**. Further on where the gorge suddenly narrows, you'll find the village of **Aït Oudinar**, with a women's carpet cooperative, shops and a Sunday souq.

About 2km beyond Aït Oudinar the road takes a turn for the harrowing, with hairpin bends. When the road flattens out again, you might take that as your cue to turn around: you've covered the best gorge scenery you can see without 4WD or good hiking shoes. There's a good **trekking trail** heading northwest, beginning just across the river, 28km from Boumalne du Dadès.

The road is sealed all the way to Msemrir (63km), but you'll need a 4WD beyond that – especially for the *piste* that leads southeast into Todra Gorge. If you're up for a challenge, you could travel north from Msemrir over the High Atlas to Imilchil. Market day in Msemrir is Saturday.

Sights

Aït Oudinar Women's Weaving Cooperative
ART & CRAFT

(☎0666 39 69 49, 0677909670; 24km Aït Oudinar; ⊗9am-noon Mon-Thu, to 3pm Sat & Sun) Tufted carpets are made at this village association-run cooperative, but soft kilim blankets made with undyed, extra-fluffy lambswool are signature pieces. The women are introducing non-chemical dyes made from local walnuts shells (brown), onion skins (yellow) and poppies (black). Items are sold at fixed prices and the weaver is paid directly, with a small percentage to fund cooperative initiatives – including renovating an abandoned mosque to house the growing cooperative. To support their efforts, visitors are welcome to make sliding-scale donations (Dh100 to Dh300). From the roadside sign, follow arrows to the western bank to find the converted stable currently housing the cooperative.

Activities

Most hotels in the gorge and Boumalne du Dadès can arrange **hiking** guides (Dh180 to Dh250 per day), **4WD trips** to the Todra Gorge and **bicycle hire** (Dh75 to Dh100).

Sleeping

Most accommodation listed below is within 28km of Boumalne du Dadès, and the kilometre markings refer to the distance from Boumalne. Most will let you sleep in the salon or on the terrace (even in summer you may need a sleeping bag) for around Dh30, or camp by the river for Dh10 to Dh30.

TOP CHOICE **Kasbah de Mimi** MAISON D'HÔTES $$
(☎0524 83 05 05; mimi.kasbah@laposte. net; 12km, Aït Ibrine; per person incl half-board Dh500; ❉☎) Save yourself the trouble of cultivating friends with fabulous country houses, and book a weekend at one of four rooms in Kasbah de Mimi. At this painstakingly restored cliffside getaway, everything is in excellent taste: Berber *baraka* painted on living-room walls, pâté hors d'ouevres, water-conserving terrace gardens and a grand piano in the fully stocked library. The cliffhanger of a driveway is harrowing, but village kids will cheer your arrival.

Riad des Vielles Charrues MAISON D'HÔTES $$
(☎0524 83 06 52; http://riadv.ifrance.com; km24, Aït Oudinar; per person incl half-board Dh250) Sunlight streams into this converted pisé family home through a central

lightwell, illuminating large guest rooms and lightening the mood of weary travellers. Owner Said Naïm outfitted the place with clever Berber style – baskets become lampshades and couscous platters serve as sinks. The welcome here is warm, literally: rooms have fireplaces and electric heating for chilly nights.

Les 5 Lunes MAISON D'HÔTES $
(☎0524 83 07 23; 23km, Aït Oudinar; d & tr per person incl half-board Dh200) Get ready to rock: this stone guesthouse teeters on a cliff above valley treetops, with six cave-like rooms (five have en-suite bathrooms). Owner Daoud is an accomplished jazz/Berber/flamenco musician, and with fair warning or friendly cajoling, he arranges concerts and Berber music workshops. Book ahead for picnics with organic garden-grown produce or dinner beside the fireplace.

Auberge des Gorges du Dadès INN $
(☎0524 83 02 21; www.aubergeaitoudinar.com; 24km; camping per person Dh15, r per person incl breakfast/half-board Dh120/200) A bubbly personality overlooking the river, the Auberge has 15 rooms that cover the waterfront with Moroccan motifs: pisé Amazigh designs and fossil sinks in one wing, ornate stucco and *beldi* tile in another. All have en-suite bathrooms, half have air-con, and 10 have private balconies.

Auberge Tissadrine INN $
(☎0524 83 17 45; 27km; per person incl half-board Dh200, mattress on roof Dh40) Squeezed into a rock cleft at a river bend, this pisé guesthouse has 14 simple, Berber-style rooms with *tataoui* ceilings, Middle Atlas carpets, and small en-suite bathrooms. In summer, sleep on the terrace under astonishing stars, near tarps spread with drying figs.

Hôtel le Vieux Chateau du Dadès HOTEL $
(☎0524 83 12 61; 25km; per person half-board d Dh200-300, ste Dh350) River views, a terrace restaurant amid chirping songbirds, and 30 rooms. Ground-floor standard rooms with auspicious Amazigh symbols carved into pisé walls out-charm new terrace suites with tubs.

Chez Pierre INN $
(☎0524 83 02 67; http://chezpierre.ifrance.com; 27km, Aït Ouffi; s/d incl breakfast Dh470/615, tr & q Dh895; ⊗Apr-Oct; ☎) Eight airy rooms and one apartment are notched right into the gorge wall, with simple decor, flowering terraces and poolside sun decks.

Hôtel El-Ouarda HOTEL $
(☎0524 83 16 09; r per person Dh70) At Msemrir, you can bunk at this basic but cheerful place.

✗ Eating

Restaurant Riad Bleu Afriqua BERBER $
(☎0666 39 69 49; 29km; menu Dh50-100) Your reward for reaching the far end of the gorge is a generous local-speciality lunch: salads with mountain herbs, meaty Berber tajines with locally grown walnuts and figs, and platters of valley-grown fruit.

Le Jardin de Source LOCAL $
(☎0524 83 04 83; 11km, Aït Ibrirne; mains Dh55-60) Quick lunches at this garden restaurant near the mouth of the gorge include flavourful vegetarian options, omelettes (Dh30) and marinated turkey kebabs; menus include salads and tea (Dh70).

Restaurant Isabelle LOCAL $
(15km; menu Dh70) Hearty omelettes or tajines with salad and drink are served on the terrace with a side of wonder at the melting rocks across the valley.

❶ Getting There & Away

Grands taxis and minibuses run up the gorge from Boumalne and charge Dh15 per person to the cluster of hotels in the middle of the gorge (near Vieux Chateau) and Dh30 to Msemrir. To return, flag down a passing vehicle. Hiring a taxi for a half-day trip into the gorge costs around Dh200. Minibuses run up to Msemrir often; the last one back to Boumalne leaves around 4pm.

The energetic could cover the distance from Dadès and Todra Gorges on foot (a two- to three-day walk); otherwise you'll need a 4WD.

Tinerhir تنرهير

POP 36,000

Charm falls a distant third to dust and hustle in this mining-town transit hub, but intrepid travellers can discover attractions in Tinerhir (aka Tinghir). The Todra Gorge beckons just 12km away, but if you need a break after the 51km drive from Boumalne du Dadès, head to the eastern edge of town, where a palm oasis unfolds like a green umbrella. Under the canopy, you'll discover crumbling kasbahs, the abandoned 19th-century **Medersa Ikelane** (look for the whitewashed mudbrick cupola) and to the north of town, the ruins of **Ksar Asfalou**, where Muslim and Jewish students once studied under the same roof. An enormous

> ### GORGE YOURSELF: TODRA TO DADÉS
>
> The 42km from Tamtattouchte to the Dadès Gorge is a tough five-hour journey that might threaten to shake teeth loose – but with twisting hills and the boulder-strewn valley of Tizgui n'Ouadda, it's certainly easy on the eyes.
>
> The *piste* begins just after Tamtattouchte, below the *auberge* on top of the hill. The crossing is prone to flash floods, so seek up-to-date advice on the state of the *piste* before setting off. About midway on this route, you'll crest the 2639m-high **Tizi n'Uguent Zegsaoun** before a bone-rattling descent to Msemrir.
>
> The trip should only be attempted by 4WD during the summer months (May to September), and a local guide is recommended. In May, many nomadic Berbers with homes in Aït Haini head to this valley to pitch tents and graze large herds of sheep. If you stop, you may be invited into tents to sip tea and swap stories.

souq is held 2.5km west of the centre on Monday, and there's a Saturday livestock souq in town.

⭐ Activities

Bicycles and oasis guides are available at Hôtel Tomboctou.

Hôtel de l'Avenir HORSE RIDING
(☎0672 52 13 89; www.avenir.tineghir.net; 27 Rue Zaid Ouhmed) Arranges horseback-riding excursions into the oasis and gorge.

🛏 Sleeping

Retour au Calme DAR $
(☎0524 83 49 24; www.retouraucalme.com; Palmeraie de Tinerhir; d Dh70-120, with private bathroom Dh150-180, tr/q Dh200-250) Local colour goes wild at this *dar*, so vividly painted it might make Matisse blush. Owners Mohamed and Alexandra preserved the pisé architecture, but added unexpected touches: Dalmatian-spotted bedspreads in an all-blue room, World Cup memorabilia in a girly hot-pink double, and ping-pong on the terrace overlooking Tinerhrir's oasis. Meals (Dh50) and ping-pong are also available to

nonguests. Turn south off Ave Mohammed V at the eastern end of town, and follow signs 150m down the *piste*.

Hôtel Tomboctou
KASBAH **$$$**
(☎0524 83 51 91; www.hoteltomboctou.com; 126 Ave Bir Anzarane; s incl breakfast Dh480-680, d Dh560-760; ✳🌊) Quirky, cosy rooms with en-suite bathrooms in a renovated kasbah built in 1944 for the local *caïd*. For more space, upgrade to the converted kitchen guest room with high, palm-beam ceilings. Traditional kasbah windows are porthole-sized, but sunshine surrounds the courtyard pool and bar. Oasis walking tours and bicycle trips are organised on-site.

✖ Eating

Hôtel l'Oasis
LOCAL **$$**
(☎024 833670; Ave Mohammed V; meals Dh80-100) A cut above, with marinated turkey brochettes, local-speciality *gallia* (game hen), a breezy roof terrace and clean bathrooms.

Chez Michelle Supermarket
SUPERMARKET **$**
(☎0524 83 46 68; Ave Mohammed V; ☺9am-9pm Sat-Thu) Excellent range of trekking provisions, snacks and homemade jam.

Grill restaurants line Ave Mohammed V and Ave Hassan II, including **Café des Amis** (Ave Hassan II), **Café Central** (Ave Hassan II) and **Restaurant Essaada** (Ave Hassan II).

❶ Information

Banks with ATMs flank Ave Mohammed V, including BMCE and Crédit du Maroc.

Tichka Internet (Rue Zaid Ouhmed; per hr Dh6; ☺7am-9.30pm) Next to Hôtel de l'Avenir.

❶ Getting There & Away

BUS Buses leave from Pl Principale, off Ave Mohammed V. Supratours stops through Tinerhir en route to Marrakesh (Dh120), Ouarzazate (Dh50), Casablanca (Dh210), Erfoud (Dh55), Er-Rachidia (Dh30), Merzouga (Dh80) and Boumalne du Dadès (Dh25). On other lines, there's frequent bus service from Tinerhir to Marrakesh (Dh100 to Dh110) via Ouarzazate (Dh40), and to Casablanca (Dh175), Erfoud (Dh30 to Dh45, four daily), Meknès (Dh110), and Zagora (Dh70) and Boumalne du Dadès (Dh15).

TAXI & MINIVAN Grands taxis to Ouarzazate (Dh50) and Er-Rachidia (Dh50) leave from the eastern end of the town gardens, where you may also find taxis, trucks or pick-up trucks into Todra Gorge (Dh7) and beyond to Tamtattouchte (Dh7 to Dh15). An 8am minivan runs

to Tamtattouchte (Dh15), Aït Haini (Dh20) and Imilchil (Dh40).

Todra Gorge
مخنف ا مفيق ا تودرغة

Being stuck between a rock and a hard place is a sublime experience in the Todra Gorge, where the massive fault dividing the High Atlas from the Jebel Sarhro is at some points just wide enough for a crystal-clear river and single-file trekkers to squeeze through. The road from Tinerhir passes green *palmeraies* and Berber villages until, 15km along, high walls of pink and grey rock close in around the road. The approach is thrilling and somehow urgent, as though the doors of heaven were about to close before you.

Besides day hikes in and around the gorge (see the boxed text, p150), the gorge is lined with palm oases and ruined kasbahs that are a photographer's dream. If you want to push on, you could walk back to Tinerhir through *palmeraies* in three or four hours. With a 4WD or a couple of days walking, you can cover the rough *piste* west of Todra to Dadès Gorge.

Arrivals at the Todra are best timed in the morning, when the sun briefly illuminates the gorge in a golden moment of welcome.

Todra Gorge Walk

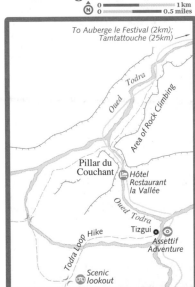

TODRA LOOP HIKE

For a vigorous morning hike, try a three-hour loop from north of the gorge to Tizgui, south of the gorge (Map p149). A 30-minute walk beyond the main gorge is the **Petite Gorge**, where you'll find a trailhead near Auberge le Festival. Take the track leading uphill to the left (southwest)regular donkey and mule traffic keep this path well defined. Head to the pass, and from there, ascend southeast to the next pass. This would be a good place to stray from the main route to look over the rim of the gorge – but be careful, as the winds get mighty powerful up here. From the second pass, descend to the Berber village of **Tizgui**, where you can stroll through the *palmeraies* back to the gorge.

Souvenir vendors and tour buses clog the throat of the gorge in afternoons, until it suddenly turns dark and bitterly cold. Through the gorge and 18km up the road is the Berber village of Tamtattouchte, with Imilchil some 95km beyond.

🏃 Activities

The vertical rock face of the gorge offers sublime rock-climbing routes (French grade 5), some of them bolted. **Pillar du Couchant**, near the entrance to the gorge, offers classic long climbs; the **Petite Gorge** is better for novice climbers, with good short routes. Most hotels can provide further information.

Assettif Aventure TREKKING, ADVENTURE SPORTS
(☏0668 35 77 92; www.assettif.org; km14) Arranges treks and horse riding (per hour/day Dh150/500) and hires out bikes (per day Dh100) and mountaineering equipment. Advance booking is recommended for overnight horse treks with guide and food (Dh800).

🛏 Sleeping & Eating

Auberge Le Festival INN **$$**
(☏0661 26 72 51; www.auberge-lefestival.com; main house with half-board s/d Dh300/460, d/tr cave r Dh700/900) Get back to nature in cave guest rooms with fossil-fixture bathrooms dug right into the hillside, or rock-walled, solar-powered lodge rooms surveying the Petit Gorge. After treks and climbs

arranged by the multilingual owner, relax in the hillside hot tub or dig in the organic garden, helping harvest vegetables for dinner.

Dar Ayour MAISON D'HÔTES **$$**
(☏0524 89 52 71; www.darayour.com; 13km Gorges du Todra; per person incl half-board with shared/private bathroom Dh150/250) Riads have arrived in Todra with this warm, artsy five-storey guesthouse that's all Middle Atlas rugs, winking mirrorwork pillows, and colourful Berber-inspired abstract paintings. Most guest rooms have en-suite bathrooms, and breakfasts with valley views are served on the roof terrace.

Auberge Les Amis INN, CAMPING **$**
(☏0670 23 43 74; www.amistamtt.wg.vu; km34, Tamtattouchte; per person s incl half-board Dh130, d & tr Dh200, camping per person/car Dh30/30) Your reward for venturing beyond tour-trammelled lower Todra Gorge is this kasbah-style guesthouse that goes the extra mile for guests, with generous home cooking, vast bathrooms (most en-suite), and hand-made *tataoui* ceilings, local rugs and jugs repurposed as sink basins. There's camping out back with electrical hook-ups (Dh10) and laundry (Dh15 per load).

Hôtel Amazir HOTEL **$**
(☏0524 89 51 09; km16, Todra; s/d/tr incl breakfast Dh300/400/600, incl half-board Dh500/600/800; ❄❄) Beyond that stern, stony exterior are relaxed, unfussy rooms with en-suite bathrooms, a pool terrace surrounded by palms, and lulling sounds of the rushing river.

Auberge Baddou INN, CAMPING **$**
(☏0672 52 13 89; www.aubergebaddou.com; km36, Tamtattouchte; d with private bathroom incl breakfast Dh200, camping per person Dh30) Pass gorge-gawking crowds and head to Tamtattouchte for Berber tents or bungalows with candy-coloured walls and a dominant Flintstones aesthetic, plus heating, hot showers and comfortable beds.

Hôtel Restaurant la Vallée HOTEL **$**
(☏0524 89 51 26; Todra; d with shared bathroom incl breakfast Dh120, d with private bathroom incl breakfast/half-board Dh150/300) Overlooking the river on one side and facing the gorge on the other, this down-to-earth hotel is all about the views from 2nd-floor rooms. Nine of 12 rooms have private bathrooms with showers right over toilets, but plenty of sunlight.

Camping

Along the road to the gorge, about 9km from Tinerhir, is a line of camp sites in a gorgeous *palmeraie* setting.

Camping le Soleil   CAMP SITE $
(☑0524 89 51 11; www.hotelcampinglesoleil.
com; camping per person Dh15, plus per tent/car/
campervan/electricity Dh18/18/28/25, d Dh240)
The first site you reach is among the best, with a good restaurant, clean hot showers, shady sites and a washing machine (per load Dh29). Basic rooms with en-suite bathrooms are also available.

Camping Poisson Sacrée   CAMP SITE $
(☑0613 68 38 74; per person Dh25-35) A surreal camping experience, in a garden where namesake freshwater 'sacred fish' miraculously survive in a saltwater spring. Camp in Berber tents (Dh30 per person) near the garden restaurant (meals Dh60 to Dh90), or crash on salon sofas (Dh70 per room) or mattresses on the terrace (Dh25 per person).

Hôtel-Camping Atlas   CAMP SITE $
(☑0524 89 50 46; per person/tent/car Dh15/
20/30) Camp sites surrounded by palms, hot meals (breakfast Dh25, dinner Dh60 to Dh70) and showers with new showerheads, plus laundry (Dh30 per load).

ⓘ Getting There & Away

For transport to the gorge, see p149. Transit minivans head northwards from Tinerhir to Aït Haini (market day Thursday) and onward to Imilchil.

Tinejdad

POP 7500

Back when caravans arrived loaded with gold and dazed after months of Sahara sun, they were understandably skittish – but Tinejdad ('nomad' in Tamazight) put them at ease. Five Berber and Saharan tribes crossed paths at this hitching post, quenching thirsts at the **Sources de Lalla Mimouna** natural springs, sleeping peacefully in well-fortified *ksour* in the **Ferkla oasis** and conducting business at 1000-year-old **Ksar Asir**, a medieval commercial centre that housed an Almoravid mosque and a sizeable Jewish community. Water, shelter, business and *baraka* (blessings): what more could a nomad need?

Zooming through Tinejdad, this crossroads culture remains remarkably intact just off the N10. The springs are signposted on the left (north) 3km before town, and the green line of the Ferkla oasis begins on the southwest edge of town, where you'll spot towering Ksar Asir.

Inside restored Ksar el-Khorbat is **Musée de Oasis** (admission Dh20), a fascinating museum that traces movements of tribes through artefacts of seminomadic life: saddles worn shiny; contracts inscribed on wooden tablets in Arabic and Hebrew; Tinejdad jars for water and preserved butter; heavy silver jewellery; and to protect it all from would-be thieves, inlaid muskets and handcuffs. To see what treasures you can find from desert traders, hit the **Sunday and Wednesday souq** on the west side of town.

✖ Sleeping & Eating

Ksar el-Khorbat   KSAR €
(☑0535 88 03 55; www.elkhorbat.com; Ferkla Oasis, Tinejdad; s/d incl half-board Dh600/800; ▣)
Seasonal meals of garden-grown pumpkin soup and Saharan beef tajines with dates (Dh80 to Dh100) are served in the walled garden of the *ksar*, a regular stop for 19th-century Aït Merghad nomads. The *ksar* is still inhabited, and you too can spend the night in this living museum. Ten rooms are big enough to house a small, seminomadic tribe of your own, with en-suite bathrooms, air-con, mosquito nets over the beds and Tinejdad clay pots as lampshades.

🛍 Shopping

Galerie d'Art Chez Zaid   ART & CRAFT
(☑0661 35 16 74; ⊙9am-1pm & 3.30-6pm) Snoop around this converted home of a local calligrapher and you might find Tinejdad-made crockery in the courtyard, sand-worn bracelets in the salon, and wonderful, well-patched nickel silver teapots in the kitchen. Located in downtown Tinejdad, 200m after the Shell station on the right.

ⓘ Information

There's an Attijariwafa ATM on the left side of the street across from the Tinejdad commune.

ⓘ Getting There & Away

Grands taxis run from town when full to Goulmima and Tinerhir.

Goulmima   غولميما

POP 16,600

An ancient hub of Berber culture, with towering **ksour** lining the palm oasis that runs north–south through town, a **pre-Islamic**

WORTH A TRIP

IMILCHIL: MOROCCO'S MEET MARKET

Just another striking Middle Atlas Berber village most of the year, Imilchil is flooded with visitors during its three-day September **marriage moussem**. At this huge festival, local Berbers stock up for long months of isolation in winter, and scope the scene for marriage material. Women strut their stuff in striped woollen cloaks and elaborate jewellery, and boys preen in flowing white jellabas.

The festival usually runs Friday to Sunday in the third or fourth week of September; dates are posted at tourist offices throughout the country. Organised tours to the event are available from cities throughout Morocco, and newly paved roads from Rich and Aït Haini to Imilchil have brought busloads of tourists to see romance blossom. With hustlers, *faux guides* and souvenir stalls eyeing the tourists, onlookers are beginning to outnumber the young lovers – but there's no denying the voyeuristic fascination of the event.

Accommodation

During the festival, the area is covered in tented accommodation. Otherwise, there are three basic hotels in town, in order of relative amenities:

Chez Bassou   HOTEL €

(☎0523 44 24 02; www.chezbassou.com; s/d incl half-board Dh260/400) Fifteen rooms with en-suite bathrooms.

Hotel Izlane   HOTEL €

(www.hotelizlane.com; s/d incl half-board Dh195/360) Fourteen rooms, four with en-suite bathrooms.

Aït Yaselmane Hotel-Restaurant   HOTEL €

(☎0523 42 66 88; d per person incl half-board Dh150) Four rooms and hot meals (Dh60).

Getting There & Away

To get to Imilchil from Marrakesh, head northeast by bus or grand taxi to Kasba Tadla, and onward by grand taxi to El-Ksiba. At El-Ksiba there is a daily bus to Aghbala. The turn-off for Imilchil is near Tizi n'Isly, about 10km before Aghbala. From the turn-off, 61km of paved road leads south to Imilchil. You may also find local grands taxis or trucks Imilchil-bound for Friday and Sunday souqs.

With more time, it's possible to reach Imilchil (a breathtaking 160km by 4WD or souq-bound lorry) from Boumalne du Dadès or Tinerhir. Minivans leave Imilchil for Tinerhir (Dh50 to Dh55) on Saturday.

---

necropolis northeast of town (signposted from N10), and three **souqs** per week (Tuesday, Thursday and Saturday) where you can score locally made couscous platters. Lining the main street are ATMs, internet cafes, and as of late, huge billboards of the king in snappy traditional attire.

The main attraction is the labyrinthine **Ksar Aït Goulmima**, a walled village on the southeast end of Goulmima's oasis that's home to several hundred. A guide can lead you through the *palmeraie* and ksar to the 500-year-old mosque and historic Jewish **mellah**. To get to there, head through downtown, turn right at the Er-Rachidia roundabout; the *ksar* is signed straight on.

🛏 Sleeping & Eating

Head northeast of town to the village of Tadighoust for overnight stays on a wildly imaginative organic farmstead – Chez Pauline (p154).

Maison d'Hôtes les Palmiers   HOTEL €€
(☎/fax 0535 78 40 04; www.palmiersgoulmima.com; Palmeraie de Goulmima; s/d/tr/q Dh220/350/450/524; ℗) Many houses have lawns, but this oasis home of a French-Moroccan couple has palms, a Berber sleeping tent and an impressive collection of ancient water jars. Guest rooms are spacious and spotless, with tiled bathrooms; all are heated in winter, and one has air-con. The

garden-fresh, mostly Berber menu is fabulous (dinner Dh95); trekking information and *ksar* guides are available.

Chez Michéle CAMP SITE €
(📞0535 88 54 13; Ave Hassan II; camping d Dh60, additional person Dh15, electricity Dh20; 🛜🖭) Camping with all the mod-cons, including hot showers, laundry (Dh50 per load), a garden cafe and a chlorinated pool.

ℹ Getting There & Away
Grands taxis run when full to Er-Rachidia and Tinerhir via Tinejdad.

ZIZ VALLEY & THE TAFILALT وادة زيز و تافلالت

The Oued Ziz brings life to this barren landscape, carving out a valley that continues south beyond Merzouga. The tough Tafilalt was one of the last areas to succumb to French control under the protectorate, with tribes putting up sporadic resistance until 1932. Two years later Morocco was officially considered 'pacified', but just to be on the safe side, Erfoud was built as a garrison town to keep a watchful eye on Tafilalt tribes.

Today the road to Er-Rachidia reveals the spectacular Jurassic geography of the Ziz Gorges, beginning 20km south of the town of Rich at the French-built Tunnel du Légionnaire. Beyond Er-Rachidia, the road zooms past oases into rolling dunes at Merzouga.

Er-Rachidia الراشيدية
POP 76,800

Garrison towns aren't generally known for their hospitality or culture, but Er-Rachidia is trying to change that. Every May, its enormous theatre hosts performers from throughout the Sahara at the **Festival du Desert** (www.festivaldudesert.ma). **Market days** are Sunday, Tuesday and Thursday.

🛏 Sleeping
Hotel le Riad HOTEL $$
(📞0535 79 10 06; www.hotelleriad.com; Rte de Goulmima, Er-Rachidia; s Dh600, d & tr Dh700; 🟦@🛜🖭) A true business-class hotel has landed in Er-Rachidia, with 30 sprawling suite guest rooms with marble bathtubs, a new spa, a huge pool and business conferences. Exceedingly cushy and reasonably priced, given the high standard of service.

Hôtel Errachidia HOTEL $
(📞0535 57 04 53; 31 Rue Ibn Battuta; s/d/tr Dh250/320/410; 🖭) Don't be fooled by the setting behind the bus station (handy for early or late arrivals): inside are 26 comfortable, quiet rooms (half with air-con) with en-suite bathrooms, plus a cafe downstairs.

🍽 Eating
Restaurant Imilchil RESTAURANT $
(📞0535 57 21 23; Ave Moulay Ali Cherif; set meal Dh70) Good tajines served on a big terrace and sports matches on a giant flat screen.

Café Restaurant Snak Fiesta CAFÉ $
(Rue el-Mesjia; ⏰lunch & dinner) Fresh Moroccan salads (Dh15) and sandwiches (Dh20).

ℹ Information
Banque Populaire and Attajariwafa ATM are on Ave Mohamed V.

ℹ Getting There & Away
AIR Royal Air Maroc offers international flights to Er-Rachidia from Barcelona, Madrid, Paris and Lyon, and domestic flights to/from Casablanca.

EDEN IN AFRICA: CHEZ PAULINE

No, this organic oasis/African art gallery/farmyard petting zoo/gourmet retreat outside a small Berber village is not a figment of your imagination, though you'll probably wish you'd thought of it first. **Chez Pauline** (☑0535 88 54 25; www.gitechezpauline.com; Tadighoust; GPS coordinates N31°48.954, W004°584.064; s & d Dh350, 1-5 person ste Dh550, d camping with car Dh60; ☎) is a highly unusual farmstead named after a pet donkey that's open to wild ideas and visitors, too.

Franco-Catalan owners André and Chantal Boyer were hoteliers for a decade in Guinea and Sierra Leone, where they amassed a collection of rare ceremonial masks and statuary that might make museum curators weep. Guest rooms at Chez Pauline double as galleries, with masks covering walls above plush four-poster beds. For those not accustomed to so many new faces at bedtime, one room has no masks in the bedroom – though there are some in the bathroom facing the toilet, revealing your host-curators' sly humour.

But they're serious about cooking here, and sustainability too. Recipe ingredients are strictly local and organic, given the Boyers' commitment to organic farming since 1983. Where other hoteliers would plunk a pool, here there's a wildflower meadow and four palm-shaded camp sites.

It's off Rte de Rich, 18km north of Goulmima. The road is paved, with the splendid Aït Yahia *ksar* on the right and palm groves on the left heading north from the Goulmima roundabout. Ahead is a formidable stretch of *hammada* (rocky desert) backed by the High Atlas, with the oasis village of Tadighoust (aka Tadirhoust) curled at its feet. Follow signs leading you left into the village, down a *piste* that curves northwest, past whitewashed mudbrick houses.

When you're beginning to think this drive is a wild goose chase, you arrive at a mudbrick-walled garden, where ducks waddle under apricot trees. Sheep bleat hello from the olive grove's edge, where they're doing their job as lawn mowers. Gideon the hog is a layabout, but he'll lumber over in his enclosure for a scratch behind the ears. If you ever wonder what pigs do in a Muslim country, here's your answer: Gideon weighs 280kg and wears a massive grin. Chez Pauline has that effect on pigs, and people too.

BUS Buses operate from the central **bus station** (Rue M'Daghra). **CTM** (☑0535 57 20 24) departs to Rabat/Casablanca (Dh155/150, 10/11 hours), Fez (Dh130, 8½ hours) and Meknès (Dh110, seven hours).

Private buses run to Fez (Dh85, five daily), Marrakesh (Dh125, 11 hours, three daily), Ouarzazate (Dh65, six hours, three daily), and Rissani (Dh25, two hours, nine daily) via Erfoud (Dh20).

TAXI Grands taxis depart three blocks northeast of the main bus station. Destinations include Azrou (Dh90, five hours), Erfoud (Dh20, one hour), Fez (Dh120, five hours), Meknès (Dh110, five hours), Tinerhir (Dh40, 1½ hours), Rissani (Dh25, 1½ hours) and Merzouga via Rissani (Dh50, 1½ hours).

Around Er-Rachidia

Diving south to Erfoud you come to the Source Bleue de Meski, then the road turns onto a desert plateau just north of Aufous, revealing a green gorge below. About 15km after the scenic overlook, you'll reach the town of **Aufous**, which offers useful services – coffee, petrol, phone, CTM buses and a Supratours office – and has some stunning pisé buildings and an impressive kasbah ruin above.

⊙ Sights

Source Bleue de Meski NATURAL SCENERY

This spring-fed swimming pool, the Source Bleue de Meski 17km southeast of Er-Rachidia, is a weekend draw for heat-struck locals. During the week, it's not a bad place for a quick dip (Dh5) and a hike to deserted **Ksar Meski** on the far side of the *oued*. The spring is signposted about 1km west of the main road.

Cooperative Al Ouaha CULTURAL CENTRE

(☑0662 22 58 33; ⊙10am-4pm daily Oct-Nov, Tue, Thu & Sat year-round) Visitors who come through Aufous looking for a date are in luck: there are seven kinds grown in the Aufous oasis, and you can sample them all here. In the October-to-November date season, the women of the cooperative will walk you through a date tasting (Dh20), and in the off-season on Tuesday, Thursday and Sunday souq days, they'll offer you tastes (Dh20) of nutty *tahalout* (date syrup) and natural energy bars made with dates – 'for athletes, like Luna bars,' a cooperative member explains. Product sales and tasting fees help the cooperative extend microcredit to women to develop new date specialities. The cooperative is signed on the main road past the village mosque on the left, next to the village commune.

🛏 Sleeping & Eating

TOP CHOICE Maison d'Hôtes Zouala
MAISON D'HÔTES $

(📱0555 57 81 82; http://labrisenet.free.fr/maison_zouala, in French; per person incl half-board Dh250) A peaceful pisé hideaway with private and shared bathrooms, home cooking (they bake their own bread) and local touches like embroidered shawls for curtains and jugs as lamps. Ask about bike rental (half/full day Dh50/80), treks to hidden springs and visits to local homes during date and olive harvests. A portion of proceeds supports the village association's literacy program. It's 30km along the Er-Rachidia–Erfoud road, in the centre of Douar Irgroum.

Camping Tissirt
MAISON D'HÔTES $

(📱0662 14 13 78; tissirtziz@yahoo.fr; per person/car/car-camping/caravan Dh15/15/20/30, d incl half-board Dh150) At the edge of the *palmeraie* before Aufous is this palm-shaded camp with two appealing pisé bungalows and meals of local *kalia* (spiced, minced mutton).

ℹ Getting there & Away

Public buses travel from Er-Rachidia to a terminal above the spring from 7am to 9pm (Dh3.5). Any bus or grand taxi to Erfoud or Aufous can drop you at the turn-off. When leaving, flag down a grand taxi from the main road.

Erfoud
ارفود

POP 24,000

Fossilised bathtubs and moist, sweet dates are Erfoud's current claims to fame, though it was once the end of the road. Now that the tarmac reaches the dunes, you can sit at Erfoud sidewalk cafes and hear 4WDs gunning past to Merzouga hotels with dune views. Savvy travellers brake for wood-fired *madfouna* (Berber calzone), fossils, and a

look at ancient **Ksar M'Aadid** (5km north of Erfoud).

In September or October Erfoud has an increasingly well-attended **date festival**, with dancing and music. The souq at the southern end of town sells local dates alongside fresh produce.

🛏 Sleeping

Riad Nour
INN $

(📱0535 57 77 48; http://riad-nour.ifrance.com; s/d/tr Dh310/380/460; ❋ ❋) Peace and quiet is the aim here, with 12 whitewashed garden guest rooms with blue tiled floors, wrought-iron beds and framed calligraphy. There's a palm-shaded pool, well-stocked bar, and songbirds in the garden courtyard. It's 5km before Erfoud on the right.

Kasbah Xaluca Maadid
RESORT $$$

(📱0535 57 84 50; www.xaluca.com; s/d Dh700/900, junior/royal ste Dh1200/2900; ❋ ❋) A flashy pool-party scene straight out of music videos (Moroccan MTV films here), only with more kids. Junior suites are the rock stars here, with fossilised marble bedsteads and mineral lamps; suites are frilly, with chintz dust ruffles on four-poster beds. Desert travellers appreciate the full-service spa, but kids head for the pool and minigolf course. It's 5km before Erfoud on the right.

🍴 Eating

TOP CHOICE Pizzeria-Restaurant des Dunes
BERBER, ITALIAN $

(📱0535 57 67 93; www.restaurantdesdunes.com; Ave Moulay Ismail; pizza Dh40, set menu Dh80-100) Do not adjust your GPS: there's authentic wood-fired pizza here, including a pizza margherita with local anchovies, olives and oregano. If you can wait 15 minutes longer, order the stellar *madfouna:* a dough pocket stuffed with minced onions and herb-spiked lamb, baked until puffy and golden.

Hotel-Restaurant Benhama
CAFE, SANDWICHES $

(📱0661 82 64 57; Ave Moulay Ismail; sandwiches Dh20-25) Roast chicken or cheese sandwiches, hamburgers, fruit smoothies and espresso served at spiffy sidewalk tables on the main road or inside the glam, air-conditioned lobby-restaurant.

🛍 Shopping

Museum of Fossils & Minerals SOUVENIRS
(📱0535 57 68 74; brahimtahiri@hotmail.com; ◷8am-7pm) Prize fossils in museum display cases aren't for sale, but in the boutique you

can buy tiny fish frozen in a final flip and ingenious espresso cups studded with ammonite fossils. It's 5km along the Rissani road.

Manar Marbre SOUVENIRS
(☏0535 57 81 26; www.manarmarble.com; Rte de Jorf; ☺8am-6pm) Watch fossilised marble being cut into prehistoric sinks at this showroom selling some portable items, including prehistoric bookends and trilobite earrings.

ℹ Information

Banque Populaire (Ave Moulay Ismail) and **BMCE** (Ave Moulay Ismail) have ATMs. Internet access is available at **Internet Moulay el Hassane** (Ave Moulay el-Hassan; per hr Dh8; ☺10am-11pm).

ℹ Getting There & Away

BUS The **CTM station** (☏0535 57 68 86; Ave Mohammed V) runs buses twice daily to Fez (Dh135, seven hours) via Er-Rachidia (Dh25, 1¼ hours), Marrakesh (Dh175, 1½ hours), Meknès (Dh125, 6½ hours) and Rissani (Dh20, 20 minutes).

Supratours and other buses leave from Pl des FAR (Dh55, twice daily), Ouarzazate (Dh105, three daily) and Fez (Dh135, three daily).

TAXI Grands taxis and taxi minivans depart Pl des FAR and opposite the post office for Merzouga (Dh30, one hour), Rissani (Dh7, 20 minutes), Er-Rachidia (Dh20, one hour) and Tinerhir (Dh60, five hours).

Association Tamounte (☏0535 57 75 23; 5 Ave Moulay Ismail) rents a car and driver for Dh450 to Dh550 a day, plus the cost of diesel.

Rissani الريصاني

POP 20,500

Dune-bound visitors may be tempted to zoom through Rissani, but photographers, history buffs and architecture aficionados could spend days exploring decrepit *ksour*,

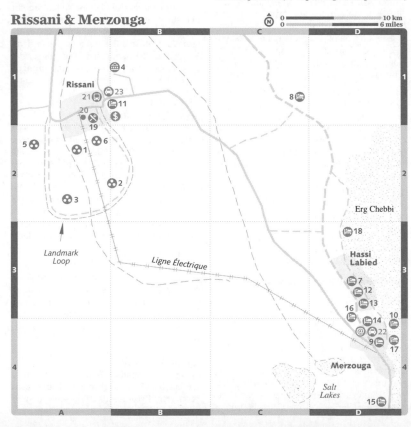

Rissani & Merzouga

an important *zawiya,* artfully crumbling kasbahs and the ruins of the fabled desert city of Sijilmassa on the landmark loop. More mudbrick *ksour* flank the road to Merzouga, including Ksar al-Beidha and Ksar Haroun; look for signposts on your left leaving town.

Rissani is where Oued Ziz quietly ebbs away, but it was once a desert capitol where fortunes flowed from caravans crossing the *sahel.* Rissani was so strategic that the Filali (ancestors of the ruling Alawite dynasty) staged their epic battle here to supplant the Saadians. Today, you'll hear epic haggling over birds, sheep, and trinkets at Sunday, Tuesday and Thursday souqs.

◉ Sights

Discover Rissani's ancient architectural splendours on this 21km circuit – the 'Landmark Loop' – just south of Rissani. From Rissani, head north from the souq and follow the main road west to these landmarks.

FREE **Zawiya Moulay Ali ash-Sharif** MONUMENT
(admission free; ◔8am-6pm) About 2km to the southeast of Rissani is this cheering yellow shrine, open to non-Muslims, and built to honour the Alawite dynasty's founder.

Ksar Aber HISTORIC SITE
Behind the *zawiya* along a dirt track you'll see the fantastic crumbling towers of this 19th-century stronghold, which formerly housed the dynasty's disgraced or unwanted members and – like those black sheep – has been abandoned to its ruination.

Ksar Oulad Abdelhalim KSAR
About 1km or so past the *zawiya* on your right, this glorious ruin once called the 'Alhambra of the Tafilalt' was built around 1900 for Sultan Moulay Hassan's elder brother. Walk through the wooden door into the walled compound, then veer right, left and right again to admire the palace's few intact painted ceiling beams and carved stucco windows.

Ksar Tinheras KSAR
Back on the road, you'll continue past another group of *ksour,* some of which are still inhabited by the Filali. This one's a standout for views.

Sijilmassa HISTORIC SITE
Just before you reach Rissani are the ruins of the capital of a virtually independent Islamic principality adhering to the Shiite 'heresy' in the early days of the Arab conquest of North Africa. Sijilmassa's foundation is lost in myth – some speculate it was AD 757 – but by the end of the 8th century it was a staging post for trans-Saharan trade. Caravans of up to 20,000 camels departed Sijilmassa for the remote desert salt mines of Taodeni and Tagahaza (in modern-day Mali), then continued to Niger and Ghana, where a pound of Saharan salt was traded for an ounce of African gold.

But as Berbers say, where there's gold, there's trouble. Internal feuding led to the collapse of fabled Sijilmassa in the 14th century. Alawite Sultan Moulay Ismail rebuilt Sijilmassa in the 18th century, only for it to be conquered and destroyed by Aït Atta nomadic warriors. Sijilmassa has remained a ruin, with only two decorated gateways and other partially standing structures. With

Rissani & Merzouga

all this glorious decay, album-cover photo shoots fairly beg to be set here.

Musee Ksar El Fida
MUSEUM
(☎0661 84 78 17; Rissani; entry with guide Dh10) Just 2.5km south of town you'll see signs for this enormous restored Alawaite kasbah (1854–72) displaying key artefacts of kasbah life, from elaborate costumes to a 19th-century toolbox.

Sleeping & Eating

Auberge Kasbah Derkaoua
RESTAURANT, INN $$$
(☎/fax 0535 57 71 40; www.aubergederkaoua. com, in French; meals Dh150-300; ⊙closed Jan, some of Jun-Aug; ❉☒) Signposted off the main road south of Rissani, this former Sufi centre makes a welcome retreat from society, with lavish Moroccan-French fusion lunches and dips in the garden pool.

Hôtel Sijilmassa
HOTEL $
(☎/fax 0535 57 50 42; Pl al-Massira al-Khadra; s Dh80, d Dh140-160; ❉) Located near the bus and grand-taxi station for late/early arrivals, with clean, air-conditioned rooms and cramped en-suite bathrooms, plus a downstairs restaurant featuring a hearty *kalia*.

Chez M'Barek
LOCAL $
(☎0667 50 16 58; 7 Rue Moulay Ali Chrif, Rissani; breakfast Dh15, set menu Dh40) If you're passing through at lunch, you might call ahead and reserve *kalia* or well-spiced *madfouna* big enough for three (Dh80) to enjoy in the cool basement or breezy terrace.

ⓘ Information

There's a post and phone office at the northern end of the medina walls, and a Banque Populaire with an ATM opposite the souq.

ⓘ Getting There & Away

Buses leave from the *gare routière* 400m from the square on the road to Erfoud. There are services to Fez (Dh130, 13 hours, two daily) via Meknès (Dh140, nine hours) and Marrakesh (Dh180, 10 hours, one daily), plus an evening run to Casablanca (Dh200, 15 hours, one daily). Buses run occasionally to Zagora (Dh90, five hours) and Tinerhir (Dh50, six hours); check station for departures. There are six buses a day to Er-Rachidia (Dh20, three hours) via Erfoud.

CTM (☎0666 36 70 06; Pl de la Marche Verte) has an office in the centre of town, and runs one bus a day at 8pm to Fez/Meknès (Dh145, eight to nine hours) via Er-Rachidia (Dh30, 1½ hours).

Grands taxis run frequently from opposite the Hôtel Sijilmassa to Erfoud (Dh7), Er-Rachidia (Dh25), Tinerhir (Dh70), Merzouga (Dh12) and occasionally Taouz (Dh30).

You can also reach Merzouga by *camionette* (minivan; Dh10), which leaves hourly from outside Chez M'Barek.

Merzouga

When a wealthy local family didn't offer hospitality to a poor woman and her son, God was offended, and buried them under the mounds of sand 50km south of Erfoud called **Erg Chebbi**. So goes the legend of the dunes rising majestically above the twin towns of **Merzouga** and **Hassi Labied** – but reality is even more unbelievable. Shapeshifting to reach heights of 160m, Erg Chebbi glows a stunning shade of rose gold, until afternoon sunlight tints the dunes orange, pink and purple.

This is perhaps the best area in Morocco for spotting many **desert bird species**, including desert sparrows, Egyptian nightjars, desert warblers, fulvous babblers and blue-cheeked bee-eaters – all worth seeking, if only to put a face to those eccentric names. Sometimes in spring a shallow lake appears northwest of Merzouga, attracting flocks of **flamingos** and other waterbirds.

Purists lament the encroachment of hotels flanking the western side of Erg Chebbi from the village of Merzouga north past the oasis village of Hassi Labied – but there's no denying the spectacular dune views from rooms and terraces. Sand toys (snowboard, skis etc) and bicycles are free to use at many hotels.

⚐ Activities

Most hotels offer excursions into the dunes, ranging from Dh80 to Dh250 for two-hour sunrise or sunset camel treks. Overnight trips usually include a bed in a Berber tent, dinner and breakfast, and range from Dh300 to Dh650 per person. Outings in a 4WD are more expensive: up to Dh1200 per day for a car taking up to five passengers. Camels are recommended over 4WDs for dune exploration – though they might growl occasionally, they're ecofriendly.

The same cannot be said for noisy, invasive quads (dune buggies). The constant pounding of quads especially has been levelling dunes, and their reverberating vibrations disturb wildlife, travellers and local residents. The town has begun to rally, posting signs prohibiting quad use in the dunes. Better yet, the demand for quads seems to be dropping as travellers become more attuned to the issues (and dust) they raise.

If you show up in town unaccompanied by a guide or a dromedary, you can anticipate repeated offers of both. Try to keep it in perspective: since getting by in the desert is notoriously tough, you might get a little pushy sometimes too. If you feel pressured, step away from the interaction.

🛏 Sleeping & Eating

Many hotels are reached by *pistes* that run 1km or more east off the tarmac road. Since they're not all close together – Hassi Labied is 5km from Merzouga – it's worth calling ahead to make sure hotels have space. Most hotels offer half-board options, and you can sleep on a terrace mattress or in a Berber tent for Dh30 to Dh50 per person.

In May 2006, heavy rains caused a freak flash flood in Merzouga that took six lives, 300 homes and a dozen hotels. All but one of the hotels (Riad Maria) is now rebuilt. Sometimes a taxi driver may insist that the hotel where you want to stay was lost in the flood, but if it's in this guidebook, that's clearly not the case. There's an easy way to resolve this with a mobile phone: call and ask hotel staff to explain to the driver where you want to go.

HASSI LABIED

Dar el Janoub RESORT **$$$**
(☎0535 57 78 52; www.dareljanoub.com; d standard/large/ste per person Dh580/725/800; ❄☀) Neighbouring hotels take the *1001 Nights* approach to hospitality, but Dar el Janoub is an Amazigh haiku, with little adornment beyond the Berber alphabet on the lobby wall. Rooms are all clean lines and cool colours, because when you're facing the dunes, why compete? Rates are on the high end, and dune-view rooms cost extra – but for the price you're getting half-board, a chlorinated pool, and pure poetry.

Maison Merzouga MAISON D'HÔTES **$$**
(☎0535 57 72 99; www.merzouga-guesthouse.com; per person incl half-board Dh350-450; ❄☀) Unlike places nearer the dunes, this 14-room local family-run guesthouse focuses on Berber hospitality instead of desert-themed decor. Besides lounging poolside and enjoying the in-house hammam, you're

Before you agree to a dromedary trek, ask the guide the following questions.

» How big is your camp, and how many people are headed there tonight? Overnight treks often congregate in the same spot, so if you have a romantic notion of being alone in the dunes under the stars, find an outfit with a separate camp.

» How far is it to the camp site? Not everyone is cut out for dromedary-riding – it makes some seasick, and others chafe. For long treks, bring motion-sickness pills and cornstarch or talcum powder.

» Does the trek guide speak English, or another language I know? This is important in the unlikely case of emergency in the desert, and to avoid awkward hand-gesture explanations when you need to use the bathroom.

» Is that camel mad at me? Don't take it personally – but do make sure your camel is well rested. Cranky, overtired camels are notorious for sudden shifts, dead stops and throat-rattling spitting. Well-rested camels are sweeter and slow-moving, and gamely pose for photos.

invited to join local holiday celebrations, bake bread in the kitchen, and explore the *palmeraie*. The best room is the cheapest tower room, with dune views.

Ryad Amazir INN **$$**
(☎0535 57 72 03; http://amazir.merzouga.free.fr; per person incl half-board Dh200-300; ❄) Where crowds thin out and dunes take over, you'll find this naturally pleasing 18-room inn. The walls are pisé, the garden organic, and dune views from seven terrace rooms phenomenal. Since the location is isolated, there's no light or traffic to interrupt stargazing. There's no pool – with an ocean of sand out front to explore, you won't miss it.

Kasbah Mohayut RESORT **$$$**
(☎0666 03 91 85; www.mohayut.com; d/ste per person half-board Dh350/450; ☀) Find your niche in sculpted-*tadelakt* guest rooms, in the shade by a small pool, or on the roof overlooking the dunes. Canopied beds,

WHICH DESERT?

Watching the sunset over rolling Sahara dunes is a once-in-a-lifetime experience that can actually be found two places in Morocco: Erg Chebbi (next to Merzouga) and Erg Chigaga (near M'Hamid). Here's how the two destinations match up on Lonely Planet–visitor criteria.

» **Natural beauty** Both. Merzouga's rose-gold dunes are framed by sun-blackened *reg* (hard-packed desert), while Erg Chigaga's dunes are yellow-gold, surrounded by sun-bleached *reg* and *sahel* (a mix of soft and hard sand) dotted with pretty, poisonous calitropis trees.

» **Dromedary trips** Merzouga. Within half an hour's dromedary ride from downtown Merzouga, you can be inside rolling dunes, while it takes a two-hour 4WD drive to reach dunes in M'Hamid.

» **Calm** Erg Chigaga is more remote and further from city noise. Merzouga is finally limiting the use of quad bikes on the dunes, after noise and dune deterioration got locals riled and turned off tourists. But both regions need to work on restricting 4WD access to the dunes, since dromedary rides lose a certain magic when cars are roaring past, and late 4WD arrivals rudely interrupt stargazing.

» **Romance** Erg Chigaga has the edge here, with fires and candles setting the mood without hindering night-time visibility in the desert. In longer-established Merzouga, some long-standing encampments have streetlights that affect stargazing and romantic prospects with their brash fluorescent glow.

» **Convenience** In Merzouga, you can stay at a comfy hotel with a fabulous view onto the dunes, and take in the scenery on a two-hour dromedary ride. Erg Chigaga is faster to reach from Marrakesh, but it involves a guided 4WD trek from M'Hamid that takes at least 2½ hours.

» **Ecotourism** Neither. M'Hamid has recently begun rubbish collection and water-bottle recycling efforts, which is a promising start. Agencies must also do their part at desert encampments to curtail waste – flush toilets are especially worrying, since water treatment plants are far from here. Morocco is instituting a ban on non-biodegradable plastic bags, but if every visitor who loves these dunes packed out their litter and picked up stray plastic bottles, the sunsets and environmental outlook in the Sahara would be rosier.

» **Child-friendliness** Both. Since sound travels in the desert, you'll need to switch off electronic games and anything else that bleeps to preserve the dunes' tranquil timelessness. But no matter: this is nature's own playground, where kids really cut loose and frolic. With any luck, they'll sleep the whole ride back to Marrakesh.

Berber rugs and *tataoui* ceilings add charm; angle for one with a fireplace. Four suites have windows on the dunes, including a family room with sleeping loft and private deck.

Auberge Camping Sahara INN, CAMPING $
(☎ 0535 57 70 39; www.aubergesahara.com; d per person incl half-board Dh200-300, terrace camping per person Dh25; [P][❄][▣]) Twenty basic, spotless rooms with en-suite bathrooms in a friendly Tuareg-run place with a pool, backing right onto the dunes at the southernmost end of the village. Four rooms feature dune views and air-con.

Kasbah Sable d'Or INN $
(Chez Isabelle & Rachid; ☎ 0535 57 78 59; http://kasbah-sable-dor.com; per person with shared/private bathroom incl half-board Dh150/180) When the goat bleats welcome, you're in the right place. Rachid and Isabelle offer four rooms with hand-painted murals, fans instead of air-con and home-cooked dinners. On starry nights, opt for Bedouin tents by the dunes (per person with/without half-board Dh40/120).

MERZOUGA

TOP CHOICE **Ksar Sania** RESORT $$
(☎ 0535 57 74 14; www.ksarsaniahotelmerzouga.com; s/d/tr incl half-board Dh500/600/810,

s/d hut incl half-board Dh300/460, camping per person Dh25; **P**) When this oasis destination below a 150m dune washed out in devastating 2006 floods, owner Françoise built a new eco-retreat even better matched to its environment: hexagonal bungalows built of mudbrick and sand with en-suite bathrooms, naturally air-conditioned with cool air rising from well-water under flagstone floors. Whitewashed A-frame mud-huts reinforced with palm beams shield against sand and heat, with solar-heated water in shared baths – and like the bungalows, this time they're on higher ground. After starlit dinners in the courtyard restaurant and drifting off to the whistling dunes, you might find your higher ground too. It's 1km southeast of Merzouga centre.

Chez Julia MAISON D'HÔTES **$**
(☏0535 57 31 82; Merzouga centre; s/d/tr/q Dh160/400/600/800) Pure charm in the heart of Merzouga, behind the mosque: nine simply furnished rooms in sunwashed colours with straw-textured pisé walls, antique mantelpieces, and white-tiled shared bathrooms, plus a furnished family apartment (Dh400 to Dh800). Book ahead for à la carte Moroccan specialities like *kalia* and *madfouna*, vegetarian meals and Austrian apfelstrudel (meals Dh60 to Dh120, breakfast Dh36 to Dh50). Ask about birdwatching tours, Saharan music concerts and geology expeditions seeking fossils and *roses des sables*, desert-sand crystals.

Riad Totmaroc MAISON D'HÔTES **$$**
(☏0670 62 41 36; www.totmarroc.com; per person incl half-board Dh330; **P**❋) A mod kasbah provides instant relief from the white-hot desert with five guest rooms in bold blue and green, shady patios facing the dunes, an open kitchen turning out solid meals, and dromedary overnights with an experienced, local official tour leader.

❶ Information

Merzouga has *téléboutiques*, supply kiosks, a mechanic, a couple of carpet shops and **Cyber Shop Le Amis** (per hr Dh5; ⏱9am-10pm).

❶ Getting There & Away

Desert *pistes* can be rough, so if you're driving, bring water and a mobile phone in case you get stuck in sand.

Grands taxis leave from Merzouga centre, opposite Dakar Restaurant, heading north to

Rissani (Dh12), and minibuses head south to Taouz (Dh15).

Minibuses will pick up or drop off in Hassi Labied – your hotel can make arrangements. Minivans run from Merzouga between 7.30am and 9.30am in high season.

Supratours offers a daily 8am service from Merzouga to Marrakesh (Dh185) and a 7pm bus to Fez (Dh165).

Taouz تاوز

Come to Taouz to spot mineral formations and possibly dinosaur bones where the desert swallows the road. Between Merzouga and Taouz is the village of **Khamlia**, whose inhabitants are believed to be descended from escaped slaves. This frontier town is home to notable Gnawa musicians, including Les Pigeons du Sable (Sand Pigeons). Their music is available on CD in Europe, and they occasionally perform locally and at Er-Rachidia's Festival du Desert (see p153). Ask at their house (marked by a banner) for details.

A house beyond Taouz village, **Casa Taouz**, offers tea and occasionally food. If you have a 4WD, several places to stay in the desert are signposted from the road with GPS locations.

RISSANI TO ZAGORA

Desert travellers often return to Marrakesh via the N10, but the more scenic Rissani–Zagora route heads west through fossil-rich Alnif, Tazzarine oasis and castle-filled N'Kob before turning north through Zagora 98km towards Ouarzazate.

N'Kob, Tazzarine & Alnif نيكوب تزارين و النيف

One of Morocco's best-kept secrets is the Berber oasis of N'Kob, where 45 **mudbrick ksour** make you stop and stare – and a couple of castles are converted to guesthouses (see p162). On the main square at the eastern edge of town, you might also spot a member of the legendary local Aït Atta warrior tribe striding into the N'Kob post office wearing a scimitar, which must certainly make letter-opening simple.

Across the street from the post office is **Aït Atta Chassures**, a cobbler banging out traditional walking sandals with leather,

Instead of turning back at Taouz, you could take the *piste* by 4WD about one hour/30km southwest towards the 2km stretch of dunes at **Ouzina**, a desert destination known only to Sahara savants and seldom visited by casual tourists. Here you'll find **Kasbah Ouzina** (☎0668 98 65 00; per person incl half-board Dh250), a small, tidy *auberge* with mercifully sand-free beds. At Ouzina the *piste* turns west toward the Drâa Valley, heading 45km to **Mhaje village**, where you can turn north onto a well-graded *piste* to **Alnif**, where it intersects with the tarmac road to Zagora. Otherwise, you could follow a bumpy *piste* from Taouz west towards the Drâa Valley south of Zagora. Either way, the Taouz–Zagora journey takes at least seven hours, equipped with plenty of water, petrol, food, a spare tyre, mobile phone and Sahara-savvy guide – if you take a wrong turn too far south, you could end up in Algeria, and that's a whole other guidebook.

rope, and used tyre treads – more comfortable than they sound and quite stylish, with Berber Pride symbols embroidered where logos might be (Dh80 to DH120). Wander 500m down the sidestreet with signs for Kasbah Baha Baha and through a doorway bedecked with dented pots to find N'Kob's teapot mender, whose services are in high demand on Sunday souq days.

To reach N'Kob, head out of Rissani 100km across the *hammada* towards Alnif and one of Morocco's richest seams of fossils: the Maidir basin. The next pit stop before N'Kob is Tazzarine, a scruffy crossroads town 150km from Rissani where the roads from Zagora and Agdz meet, and drivers brake for internet cafes, lunch, petrol and a Tuesday souq.

⊙ Sights & Activities

N'Kob Bureau des Guides   TREKKING
(☎0667 48 75 09; N'Kob) On the main road, this bureau organises Jebel Sarhro treks (see p143) and hikes to explore N'Kob's castles, vast palm oasis, and rock formations.

Ihmadi Trilobites Centre   TREKKING, SHOP
(☎066 22 15 93; trilobites@caramail.com; Alnif) Genuine fossils are sold here at fixed prices, and the geologist owner leads short trips to local fossil sites (Dh180 for the afternoon).

⌂ Sleeping

TOP CHOICE **Kasbah Baha Baha**   KASBAH $$
(☎0524 83 97 63; N'Kob; Berber tents s/d/tr Dh80/150/210, with private bathroom Dh200/300/400) A gorgeously restored kasbah with a vast Berber botany garden, wood-fired bread oven, gourmet poolside meals (breakfast/dinner Dh30/100), on-site

ethnographic museum, and 360-degree oasis views. Guests are greeted like neighbours, and are even invited to local marriages hosted at the kasbah in summer.

Kasbah Imdoukal   KASBAH $$
(☎0524 83 97 98; www.kasbahimdoukal.com; N'Kob; d/tr/ste Dh700/900/1000; ✳✳⊠) Berber pride meets Marrakesh chic: chip-carved beds with luxurious pillows, Amazigh friezes atop *tadelakt* walls, oasis mule treks with poolside lounging after, and dinners of *madfouna* (Dh120 to Dh190) by the restaurant fireplace with private concerts. Guest rooms have big, splashy en-suite bathrooms; 16 of 20 rooms have air-con.

Auberge Restaurant Ennakhil   MAISON D'HÔTES $$
(☎0524 83 97 19; N'Kob; d incl half-board shared/private bathroom Dh160/300) A warm Berber-country welcome, with tea and Jebel Sarhro views from palm-stump terrace seating. Downstairs rooms have wedding blankets, palm-beam ceilings, and shared bathrooms with sinks that are upturned water jars. Snazzy upstairs 'kasbah' rooms have en-suite bathrooms, sculpted pisé walls and stone floors; three have oasis views.

Ksar Jenna   MAISON D'HÔTES $$$
(☎0524 83 97 90; www.ksarjenna.com; d incl half-board Dh1100; ✳⊠) Holding its own with Marrakesh riads, this place 2km before N'Kob has seven sprawling rooms with designer-fabulous, en-suite bathrooms (albeit with erratic hot water). Dinner is served under the painted dining-room ceiling, breakfasts amid palms in the garden, and aperitifs or espresso in the patio bar (it's a Moroccan-Italian venture).

Ouadjou CAMPING, INN **$**

(☎0524 83 93 14; www.ouadjou.com; tent without/with half-board Dh50/150, r Dh225; [P][🗷]) Welcome comforts for desert-dazed travellers: cool pisé-clad courtyard rooms with hot showers in en-suite bathrooms, or Berber tents in the garden with end tables, reading lamps, linens and blankets. Guests can use the pool free, as can visitors ordering lunch (Dh90 to Dh120). It's 2km before N'kob.

Camp Amasstou CAMPING **$**

(☎0524 83 90 78; Tazzarine; per person incl half-board Dh150; [P][🗷]) Follow signs pointing south into Tazzarine's oasis to find this gorgeous walled garden featuring four large Berber tents and a small pool. Pull up a goatskin bench and swap life stories with fellow travellers, or call it a night on your narrow tent bed with clean linens.

✖ Eating

Kasbah Riad Du Sud BERBER **$$**

(☎024 886453; www.hotelriaddusud.com; Tamsahlte via Tazzarine; set lunch Dh100) Call ahead for millet couscous or goat or dromedary tajine at this gastronomical oasis. Reservations essential.

Kasbah Meteorites LOCAL **$**

(☎0535 78 38 09; www.kasbahmeteorites.com; Alnif; meals Dh70-80; [🗷]) A pleasant pit stop for filling set lunches and dips in an oversized chlorinated pool.

❶ Getting There & Away

Grands taxis run between Rissani and Alnif (Dh30), Alnif and Tazzarine (Dh30), and Tazzarine and Ouarzazate (Dh70), so you can cobble together transport. A bus runs between Rissani and Zagora via Alnif, Tazzarine and N'Kob on Tuesday, Friday and Sunday.

Atlantic Coast
شاطىء الأطلنطي

Best Places to Eat

» Outdoor fish grills (p228)

» Restaurant du Port de Pêche (p177)

» Le Petit Beur – Dar Tajine (p194)

Best Places to Stay

» Dar el-Manar (p214)

» La Sultana (p217)

» Riad Oudaya (p193)

Why Go?

Miles of glorious sands peppered with small fishing villages, historic ports and fortified towns weave along Morocco's blustery coast. The French called it 'Maroc Utile' (useful Morocco): this is one of Morocco's most prosperous regions, home to the nation's capital Rabat and the economic hub of Casablanca. Their Mauresque architecture, excellent restaurants, stylish cafes and liberal attitudes are a far cry from traditional Morocco.

Throughout history, control of this coast was imperative for both invading forces and local tribes hoping to expand their empires. The Phoenicians, Romans, Portuguese, Spanish and French all fought for control, leaving a legacy in the beautiful walled towns, wide boulevards and relaxed attitude.

Outside the towns, farmland rolls gently down to the sea and wetland reserves showcase rich birdlife. But developers are arriving with plans for mega-resorts that may transform a region that already has more than enough attractions.

When to Go
Casablanca

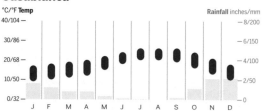

May & June
Rabat's world-music Mawazine fest in May, Essaouira's Gnaoua Festival in June

September
Hit the beaches after the Moroccan tourists leave, while the weather's still good.

December–March
Huge flocks of bird species descend on wetlands and lagoons

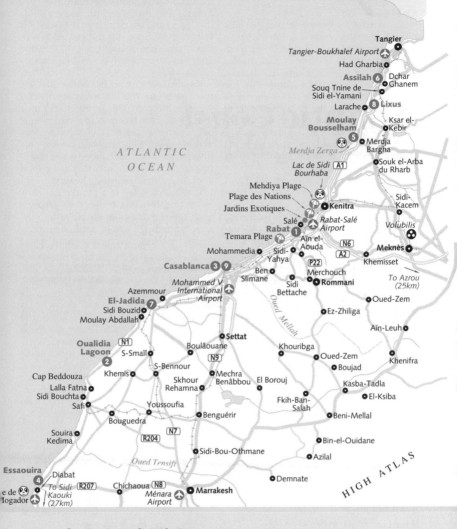

Atlantic Coast Highlights

❶ Sip tea at the Andalusian Gardens in the **Kasbah Les Oudaias** (p192) in Rabat

❷ Swim in the warm waters of the **Oualidia lagoon** (p216), before gorging on local oysters for lunch

❸ Hang out with trendy locals in Casablanca's smart pavement **cafes** (p180)

❹ Kitesurf the day away on Essaouira's blustery **beach** (p224)

❺ Twitch in **Moulay Bousselham** (p202)

❻ Gaze at the murals in Assilah's **medina** (p209)

❼ Marvel at the water cistern in El-Jadida's **Cité Portugaise** (p214)

❽ Imagine yourself as a Roman at the ancient site of **Lixus** (p206)

❾ Look up in Casablanca at the glorious **Mauresque buildings** (p172)

CASABLANCA (DAR AL-BAÏDA) الدار البيضاء

POP 4 MILLION

Many travellers stay in Casablanca just long enough to change planes or catch a train, but the sprawling metropolis deserves more time. It may not be as exotic as other Moroccan cities, but it is the country's economic capital, and it represents Morocco on the move: Casablanca is where the money is being made, where the industry is, where art galleries show the best contemporary art and where fashion designers have a window on the world. The old pirate lair is looking towards the future, showing off its wealth and achievements.

The first French resident-general, Louis Hubert Gonzalve Lyautey hired French architect Henri Prost to redesign Casablanca in the early 20th century as the economic centre of the new protectorate and, indeed, as the jewel of the French colonies. His wide boulevards and modern urban planning still survive, and mark the city as more European than Moroccan. However, Lyautey underestimated the success of his own plans and the city grew far beyond his elaborate schemes. By the end of WWII, Casablanca had a population of 700,000 and was surrounded by heaving shanty towns.

Casablancais are cosmopolitan, and are more open to Western ways than other places in Morocco. This is reflected in their dress, and in the way men and women hang out together in restaurants, bars, beaches and hip clubs. But Europe is not the only inspiration. More and more young Casablancais are realising that they come from a country with a fascinating history.

Casablanca is full of contradictions. It is home to suffocating traffic jams (at least until the new tramway system is in operation towards the end of 2012), simmering social problems and huge shanty towns

Casablanca

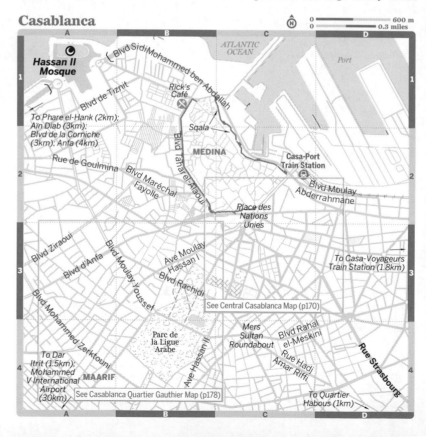

as well as wide boulevards, well-kept public parks, fountains and striking colonial architecture.

The bleak facades of the suburbs stand in sharp contrast to the Mauresque, art-deco and modernist gems of the city centre, and to Casablanca's exceptional landmark, the enormous and incredibly ornate Hassan II Mosque.

The medina – the oldest part of town – is tiny and sits in the north of the city close to the port. To the south of the medina is Pl des Nations Unies, a large traffic junction that marks the heart of the city. The city's main streets branch out from here: Ave des Forces Armées Royales (Ave des FAR), Ave Moulay Hassan I, Blvd Mohammed V and Blvd Houphouët Boigny.

Ave Hassan II leads to Place Mohammed V, easily recognised by its grand art-deco administrative buildings. Quartiers Gauthier and Maarif, west and southwest of the Parc de la Ligue Arabe, are where most of the action is, with shops, bars and restaurants.

To the southeast is the Quartier Habous (also known as the nouvelle medina) and to the west is Aïn Diab, the beachfront suburb home to upmarket hotels and nightclubs.

Development in Casablanca today is so exciting that you'd think the ghosts of General Lyautey and Henri Prost were working on a new plan for the city, though this time with Moroccan pride rather than French colonial might. Along the coastal road in Anfa, huge new projects are being built. About to open at the time of research is the environmentally friendly, award-winning 200,000-sq-m Morocco Mall, the biggest 'destination mall' in North Africa, housing shops and offices as well as a large aquarium and a 400-seater Imax theatre. On the coast east of the Hassan II Mosque the Casablanca Marina is a few years from being completed.

History

The Phoenicians established a small trading post in the now-upmarket suburb of Anfa from the 6th century BC onwards. In the 7th century AD, Anfa became a regional capital under the Barghawata, a confederation of Berber tribes. The Almohads destroyed it in 1188, and 70 years later, the Merenids took over.

In the early 15th century, the port became a safe haven for pirates and racketeers. Anfa pirates became such a serious threat later in the century that the Portuguese sent 50 ships and 10,000 men to subdue them. They left Anfa in a state of ruins. The local tribes, however, continued to terrorise the trade routes, provoking a second attack by the Portuguese in 1515. Sixty years later the Portuguese arrived to stay, erecting fortifications and renaming the port Casa Branca (White House).

The Portuguese abandoned the colony in 1755 after a devastating earthquake destroyed Lisbon and severely damaged the walls of Casa Branca. Sultan Sidi Mohammed ben Abdullah subsequently resettled and fortified the town, but it never regained

Casablanca

its former importance. By 1830 it had only around 600 inhabitants.

By the mid-1800s Europe was booming and turned to Morocco for increased supplies of grain and wool. The fertile plains around Casablanca were soon supplying European markets, and agents and traders flocked back to the city. Spanish merchants renamed the city Casablanca and by the beginning of the 20th century the French had secured permission to build an artificial harbour.

Increased trade brought prosperity to the region, but the activities and influence of the Europeans also caused resentment. Violence erupted in 1907 when Europeans desecrated a Muslim cemetery. The pro-colonialist French jumped at the chance to send troops to quell the dispute; a French warship and a company of marines soon arrived and bombarded the town. By 1912 it was part of the new French protectorate.

◉ Sights

Casablanca is Morocco's commercial hub and locals are far more interested in big international business than in tourism. Tourists are few in town and it's very much a workaday place with remarkably few traditional tourist attractions. Apart from the grand Hassan II Mosque, the city's main appeal is in strolling around its neighbourhoods: the wonderful Mauresque architecture of the city centre, the peaceful Parc de la Ligue Arabe, the gentrified market district of the Quartier Habous and the beachfront views of the Corniche. Join the Casablancais in enjoying the cosmopolitan pleasures of their city, go out for dinner, visit an art gallery, shop till you drop in the Morocco Mall in Anfa, try out the funky nightlife or go roller skating outside the Hassan II Mosque.

DOWNTOWN CASA

It is often said that Casablanca has no sights apart from the Hassan II Mosque, but the French-built city centre is packed with grand colonial buildings, some of which are being restored. The best way to take it all in is by strolling in the area around the Marché Central, or by doing the walking tour (see p172). The rundown Marché Central quarter is slowly being revived, particularly around the pedestrian street of Rue Prince Moulay Abdallah.

Place Mohammed V   NEIGHBOURHOOD
(Map p170) This is where the architect Henri Prost really went to town. The grand square is surrounded by public buildings whose designs were later copied in buildings throughout Morocco, including the law courts, the splendid *wilaya* (old police headquarters, now the Governor's office), the Bank al-Maghrib, the post office and the Ministry of Defence building. Many grand boulevards lined with wonderful architecture go off this square. To the south is the Parc de la Ligue Arabe, designed in 1918 with a majestic palm tree–lined promenade.

CASABLANCA IN...

One Day

Start your day with a hearty breakfast at **Frédéric Cassel Haute Pâtisserie** in Anfa. As no visit to Casablanca is complete without marvelling at the seaside mosque, hop in a taxi to the **Hassan II Mosque** and take in a tour. Then head to **Sqala Restaurant** in the ramparts for lunch in the garden. Browse the artisan shops in the **Quartier Habous** for Moroccan souvenirs, stopping for tea and cakes at **Pâtisserie Bennis Habous**. Treat yourself to stunning views over the ocean by dining at one of the **cliff-top restaurants** by el-Hank lighthouse before joining the city's pretty young things in the bars and clubs along **Blvd de la Corniche**.

Two Days

With another day to enjoy the city, start with breakfast at **Paul** in the beautiful Zevaco building. Work it off by following the **walking tour** in this guide, taking in the best of Casa's Mauresque heritage. After lunch, check out the trendy boutiques or take in an Imax movie at **Morocco Mall** before a hammam and massage at **Gauthier Bain Turc**. **Restaurant Port de Pêche** is just the place for local fish before a nightcap at **La Bodega**.

FREE **Villa des Arts** ART GALLERY
(Map p178; ☎0522 29 50 87; 30 Blvd Brahim Roudani; ☻10am-7pm Tue-Sat) Located in a converted art-deco building near the Parc de la Ligue Arabe, this gorgeous 1930s gallery holds exhibitions of contemporary Moroccan and international art.

ANCIENNE MÉDINA
Casablanca's small and dilapidated medina (Map p170) gives an idea of just how petite the city was before the French embarked on their massive expansion program. Most of the buildings date from the 19th century, so it lacks the medieval character of other medinas. Plans are afoot to restore many buildings.

Enter the medina from the northeast corner of the Pl des Nations Unies near the restored **clock tower** (Map p170), and note the dilapidated **Excelsior Hotel** opposite it. The narrow lanes to the east are piled high with cheap shoes, high-sheen underwear and household goods. The rest of the medina remains largely residential. The old city's main Friday mosque is the **Jemaa ash-Chleuh** along Rue Jemaa ash-Chleuh Arsalane.

On the north side of the medina, facing the port, you'll see the last remains of Casablanca's 18th-century fortifications. Known as the **sqala** (Map p166), the bastion offers panoramic views over the sea.

MAARIF
Southwest of the Parc de la Ligue Arabe is the city's business centre and the place to head for international designer brands.

Twin Center CLOTHING
(Map p178; cnr Blvd Mohammed Zerktouni & Al-Massira al-Khadra) Twin Center marks the high-end of the chic shopping area and contains a shopping mall, luxury hotel and office space. Smaller boutiques on the side streets and around the covered Maarif market are more atmospheric and good for bargains.

Jewish Museum MUSEUM
(☎0522 99 49 40; 81 Rue Chasseur Jules Gros, Quartier Oasis; admission Dh20, with guide Dh30) South of Maarif in the suburb of Oasis is Casablanca's only museum. Rarely open since the 2003 bombings that targeted Jewish interests in the city, it's important to phone ahead to check. If you're lucky enough to see this beautiful villa surrounded by lush gardens, you'll be setting

Casablanca's French street names are slowly being replaced with Moroccan names. Be very specific when asking for directions, as many people, including taxi drivers (and some local street directories) have yet to make the transition. You'll often see several different names for one street.

foot in the only Jewish museum in the Islamic world. It relates the history of the once-thriving Jewish community and its influence on modern Moroccan society, with more than 1500 historical artefacts including documents, traditional clothing, ceremonial items and a vast collection of photographs. Oasis is a 15-minute taxi ride (Dh30) from the city centre.

QUARTIER HABOUS (NOUVELLE MEDINA)
The Quartier Habous, or nouvelle medina, is Morocco-lite – an idealised, almost Disney version of a traditional medina, with neat rows of streets and shop stalls. Built by the French in the 1930s, it was a unique experiment: a medina built to Western standards to accommodate the first rural exodus in the 1920s. As such, it blends Moroccan architecture with French ideals, epitomised by a mosque and a strip of grassy lawn, reminiscent of European village churches.

However sanitised it may feel, if you have some last-minute souvenir shopping to do, Habous is more peaceful than most souqs and has a decent selection of bazaars, craft shops, bakeries and cafes.

The **Royal Palace** (closed to the public) is to the north of the district, while to the south is the old **Mahakma du Pasha** (courts & reception hall; admission free; ☻8am-noon & 2-6pm Mon-Sat), which has more than 60 rooms decorated with sculpted wooden ceilings, stuccowork, wrought-iron railings and earthenware floors. It's not always open to visitors.

The Quartier Habous is located about 1km southeast of town. Take bus 81 from Blvd de Paris, across from the main post office.

AÏN DIAB & ANFA
These affluent suburbs on the Atlantic beachfront, west of the centre, are home to

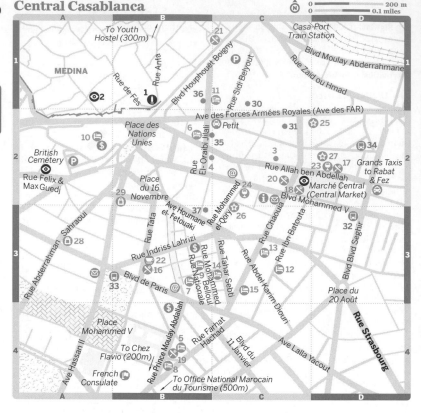

the happening **Blvd de la Corniche**. Lined with beach clubs, upmarket hotels, restaurants, bars and clubs, it is the city's entertainment hub and *the* place for young, chic professionals to see and be seen.

However, in between the busy beach clubs along the promenade, the view is spoiled by abandoned pleasure grounds and concrete swimming pools filled with construction rubbish. Nevertheless, the beach remains extremely popular. The easiest way to find space on the sand is to visit one of the beach clubs. Two of the better ones, **Miami Plage** (per day Dh80-150) and **Tahiti** (per day Dh80-150) have beach umbrellas, a pool, restaurant and bar.

Bus 9 goes to Aïn Diab from Pl Oued al-Makhazine. A taxi from the centre costs around Dh30 (Dh70 at night).

The new **Morocco Mall** in Anfa is some 4km west of the city centre. Due to open at the time of research, the mall will sport a large **aquarium**.

🏃 Activities

Hammams

Hammam Ziani   HAMMAM
(☏0522 31 96 95; 59 Rue Abou Rakrak; admission Dh45; ☺7am-10pm) Sparkling clean and decidedly modern, this is an upmarket hammam offering the traditional steam room and *gommage* (scrub) for Dh50, and massage, as well as a Jacuzzi and gym. It's off Rue Verdin. As is the case when visiting any public place, it may be better to leave your valuables at your hotel.

Gauthier Bain Turc   HAMMAM
(Map p178; ☏0661 14 59 26; 25 Rue Jean Jaures; Mon-Fri Dh50, Sat & Sun Dh60; ☺7am-10pm) You'll find similar facilities at this ultramodern hammam, where a scrub costs Dh15 and a 30-minute massage Dh100.

Spa 5 Mondes HAMMAM
(✆0522 99 66 08; 18 Rue Ibrahim En-Nakhai, Maarif; ◑10am-8pm) For a traditional hammam, a Japanese bath, a Balinese massage or an ayurvedic treatment, head for this trendy spa.

🍴 Courses

Casablanca has a multitude of language schools, almost all of which have French classes.

Institut Français FRENCH
(Map p178; ✆0522 77 98 70; www.ambafrance-ma.org, in French; 121-123 Blvd Mohammed Zerktouni; ◑9am-2.30pm Tue-Sat) Only runs semester-long courses. Also offers a good library, films, lectures, exhibitions and other events.

École Assimil-Formation ARABIC
(Map p170; ✆0522 31 25 67; 71 Rue Allah ben Abdellah) Offers private tuition in Arabic.

👉 Tours

Both tourist offices (p182) offer a three-hour walking tour of the city (Dh450 for up to

three people) that can be customised to suit the client's interests.

Olive Branch Tours TOURS
(Map p170; ✆0522 22 03 54; www.olivebranch tours.com; 35 Rue el-Oraïbi Jilali) This outfit offers a Grand Tour of Casablanca, which takes in the main squares in the city centre, the medina and Quartier Habous, as well as a stroll along the Corniche.

⭐ Festivals

L'Boulevard Festival of Casablanca LIVE MUSIC
(www.boulevard.ma) This three-day urban-music festival takes places every year in June, with hip-hop, electro, rock, metal and fusion music, featuring bands from Morocco, France, the USA and the UK.

🛏 Sleeping

Most of Casablanca's hotels are in the centre of town with the exception of the youth hostel, which is in the medina, and the upmarket hotels along the Blvd de la Corniche. Hotels fill up fast during the summer months,

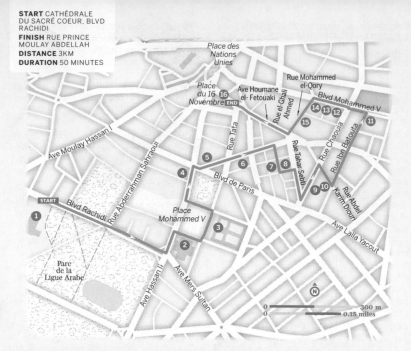

START CATHÉDRALE
DU SACRÉ COEUR, BLVD
RACHIDI
FINISH RUE PRINCE
MOULAY ABDELLAH
DISTANCE 3KM
DURATION 50 MINUTES

Place des
Nations
Unies

Place
du 16　16
Novembre END

Ave Houmane
el- Fetouaki

Rue Mohammed
el-Qory

Blvd Mohammed V

14　13　12

11

Rue el-Ghali
Ahmed

15

Rue Chaouia

Rue Ibn Batouta

Rue Moulay Hassan I

Rue Abderrahman Sahraoui

Rue Tata

5

6

7　8

Rue Tahar Sebti

9　10

Rue Abdel
Karim Diouri

Blvd de Paris

4

START

Blvd Rachidi

1

Place
Mohammed V

3

2

Ave Lalla Yacout

Ave Hassani

Ave Mers Sultan

Parc
de la
Ligue Arabe

N

0 ──────── 300 m
0 ──────── 0.15 miles

Walking Tour
Central Casablanca

❯ Central Casablanca has a rich architectural heritage. The style of colonial
architecture found here in abundance is
known as Mauresque and came into being
during General Lyautey's term of office as
resident governor of Morocco between 1912
and 1924.

The style blended aspects of traditional
Moroccan design such as Islamic arches,
columns, scrollwork and tilework with
the more liberal influences of early-20th-
century Europe. By the 1930s, Mauresque
architecture began to reflect the Parisian
art-deco style, characterised by ornate
wrought-iron balconies, staircases, and
windows; carved facades and friezes; and
rounded exterior corners. Some of these
buildings have been restored or are kept in
good condition, and are a visual reminder
of Casa's early protectorate history. Some,
however, are in a sorry state.

It was General Lyautey, as Governor, who
decided to make Casablanca the economic
hub of Morocco. He hired French architect

and town planner Henri Prost (1874–1959)
to design a model new town. Prost had
already proved his worth in Antwerp, and
went on to work on plans for Meknès, Fez
and Rabat in Morocco, as well as Paris
and Istanbul. Delighted at the prospect of
building a city from scratch, Prost designed
Casablanca from the air, the first city in
history to be laid out by aeroplane. The city
was considered the pinnacle of French colonial achievement.

Wherever you go in downtown Casa,
look up! The humblest block of apartments
could sport decorative details such as
carved friezes of tumbling flowers, ornate
tilework and rounded balconies, even if the
building itself is shamefully neglected.

This walking tour takes in the best Mauresque buildings, and some other Casa
treasures.

Start on the northwest edge of the Parc
de la Ligue Arabe, where you can't miss the
imposing white ❶ **Cathédrale du Sacré
Coeur**, a graceful cathedral designed by

Paul Tornon and built in 1930. This is a good example of the style, with some neo-Gothic influence. The church was deconsecrated in 1956 and is occasionally used as a cultural centre, but inside it's quite dilapidated.

From here, walk two blocks east to Pl Mohammed V, which is the grand centre-piece of the French building scheme. The vast square, much beloved by Casablancais who congregate here in the evenings and on weekends, is surrounded by an impressive array of august administrative buildings, most designed by Robert Marrast and Henri Prost. The ❷ **wilaya** (old police headquarters, now the governor's office), dating from 1930, dominates the south side of the square and is topped by a modernist clock tower.

The nearby ❸ **palais de justice** (law courts) was built in 1925. The huge main door and entrance were inspired by the Persian *iwan*, a vaulted hall that usually opens into the central court of the *medersa* (theological college) of a mosque.

Stroll across the grand square and admire the 1918 ❹ **main post office**, a wonderful building fronted by arches and stone columns and decorated with bold mosaics. More in the style of traditional Moroccan architecture is the ❺ **Banque al-Maghrib**, on Blvd de Paris. Fronted with decorative stonework, it was the last building constructed on the square.

From here, walk east on Rue Indriss Lahrizi, where impressive facades line both sides of the street, the best being ❻ **La Princière Salon de Thé**, easily recognised by the huge stone crown on the roofline. Turn right into Rue Mohammed Belloul to see ❼ **Hôtel Guynemer** with its carefully restored art-deco panelling, and almost opposite, the slightly less impressive ❽ **Hotel Oued Dahab**. Then walk one block east and turn right down Rue Tahar Sebti, which is lined with colonial buildings that now serve as apartments and offices.

Turn left into Rue Chaouia and look out for ❾ **Hôtel Transatlantique**, which dates from 1922 and has been beautifully restored. Just around the corner, another restored gem, the ❿ **Hotel Volubilis**, has a great facade.

Turn left up Rue Ibn Batouta and continue to the corner of Blvd Mohammed V. On your right is the enormous derelict shell of the ⓫ **Hôtel Lincoln**, a Mauresque masterpiece built in 1916. Its restoration is in limbo while the owner cannot afford to carry out the work and the authorities will not allow such an important building to be torn down.

Turn left into Blvd Mohammed V and look out for an array of wonderful facades along the south side of the street. The Central Market ⓬ **post office**, with its delicate, carved motifs, and the ⓭ **Le Matin/Maroc Soir** building, with its classic style, are two of the most impressive. There are plans in place to restore this entire area.

At the end of this block, on the corner of Rue Mohammed el-Qory, is ⓮ **Petit Poucet** bar and pavement cafe, where such characters as Antoine de Saint-Exupéry whiled away his time in the 1920s between flights to the Sahara. Edith Piaf and Albert Camus were also customers. It's worth looking inside at the original bar counter. Turn left here into Rue Mohammed el-Qory to find the ⓯ **Cinéma Rialto**, a classic art-deco building with some wonderful touches, including a pretty paint job. Continue south to the junction with Ave Houmane el-Fetouaki and turn right to reach ⓰ **Place 16 Novembre**, which is home to an array of art-deco buildings.

For information on Casablanca's architectural heritage, look out for *Casablanca: Colonial Myths and Architectural Ventures* by Jean-Louis Cohen and Monique Eleb and *Casablanca – Portrait d'une Ville* by JM Zurfluh (in French).

DON'T MISS

HASSAN II MOSQUE

Built by the late King Hassan II to commemorate his 60th birthday, this enormous **mosque** (Map p166; ☑0522 22 25 63; guided tours adult/child/student Dh120/30/60; ◑9am, 10am, 11am & 2pm Sat-Thu, 9am, 10am & 2pm Fri) was funded by public subscription. It was completed in 1993 and provides Casablanca with an important landmark. A new **Islamic media centre and library** (admission free; ◑8am-6pm Mon-Fri) can be found in the grounds.

Designed by French architect Michel Pinseau the mosque rises above the ocean on a rocky outcrop reclaimed from the sea, echoing the verse from the Quran that states that God's throne was built upon the water. The 210m-high minaret, the tallest building in the country, is topped by a spectacular laser beam that shines towards Mecca. It is the world's third-largest mosque, accommodating 25,000 worshippers inside, and a further 80,000 in the courtyards and squares around it. Believers can enjoy praying on a centrally heated floor, seeing the Atlantic washing the rocks underneath the glass floor in the basement and feel the sunlight through the retractable roof.

Above all, the vast size and elaborate decoration of the **prayer hall** is most striking. Large enough to house Paris' Notre Dame or Rome's St Peter's, it is blanketed in astonishing woodcarving, *zellij* (tilework) and stucco moulding. A team of over 6000 master craftsmen was assembled to work on the mosque, delicately carving intricate patterns and designs in cedar from the Middle Atlas, marble from Agadir and granite from Tafraoute.

To see the interior visitors must be 'decently and respectfully dressed' and, once inside, will be asked to remove their shoes. Hour-long tours are conducted in French, English, German and Spanish, and take in the prayer hall, the ablutions rooms and the hammam.

---

particularly in August, so it's a good idea to make reservations in advance.

Casablanca's budget hotels are pretty basic. The medina hotels are invariably grotty and overpriced and don't offer good value compared with their ville-nouvelle counterparts. Casablanca has a good selection of midrange accommodation scattered around the city centre. You'll also find some nice alternatives with ocean views and easy access to the beach along Blvd de la Corniche. Casablanca has a glut of top-end hotels, with all the major international chains represented in town. Most are along Ave des FAR, with a few others along the Blvd de la Corniche. For something less generic try one of the following.

TOP CHOICE **Hôtel Guynemer** HOTEL €
(Map p170; ☑0522 27 57 64; www.guynemerhotel.com; 2 Rue Mohammed Belloul; s/d/tr Dh372/538/626; ❋☞) Readers recommend the friendly and super-efficient, family-run Guynemer, in a gorgeous Mauresque building. The 29 well-appointed and regularly updated rooms are tastefully decked out in cheerful colours. Flat-screen TVs, wi-fi access and firm, comfortable beds make them a steal at these rates and the service

is way above average: staff will happily run out to get anything you need. There's an airport pick-up service (Dh400) and city tours. There is also an interactive info post in the lobby, a dedicated PC for guest use and a phone to call the USA and Canada free, though these services don't always work. The hotel also rents out two contemporary, fully equipped flats on the same street, which are ideal for longer stays and for families.

Hôtel Astrid HOTEL €
(Map p170; ☑0522 27 78 03; hotelastrid@hotmail.com; 12 Rue 6 Novembre; s/d/tr Dh324/386/486; ☞) Tucked away on a quiet street south of the centre, the Astrid offers the most elusive element of Casa's budget hotels – a good night's sleep. There's little traffic noise here and the spacious, well-kept rooms are all en suite, with TV, telephone and frilly decor. There's a friendly cafe downstairs and wi-fi in the lobby.

Hôtel de Paris HOTEL €
(Map p170; ☑0522 27 42 75; fax 0522 29 80 69; cnr Rues Ech-Cherif Amziane & Prince Moulay Abdallah; s/d/tr Dh350/450/550; ☞) Newly renovated, this small hotel has spacious rooms

that are clean and relatively quiet. Rooms are decorated with dark wood and equipped with good mattresses, satellite TV and direct phone line. There's a swish cafe downstairs on the pleasant pedestrian street, and the hotel is in a good central location.

Hôtel les Saisons
HOTEL €€€

(Map p170; ☑0522 49 09 01; www.hotelles saisonsmaroc.ma; 19 Rue el Oraïbi Jilali; s/d Dh1100/1400; ✷❄☎) This small hotel offers extremely comfortable, well-appointed and quiet rooms with all the usual facilities: a safe, minibar, satellite TV and direct-dial phone. It's a more personal place than the larger international hotels and offers good value for money and an excellent location. The staff speak English.

Youth Hostel
HOSTEL €

(off Map p170; ☑0522 22 05 51; lesauberges@ menara.ma; 6 Pl Ahmed el-Bidaoui; ⊙8-10am & noon-midnight; s/d/tr Dh60/135/190, tr with bathroom Dh200; @) Clustered around a bright central lounge area, the rooms are basic but well kept and quiet, with high ceilings and a lingering smell of damp in winter. The staff are friendly and the hostel is on a leafy square. There are good hot showers. No IYHF or YHA cards are required.

Hôtel Maamoura
HOTEL €

(Map p170; ☑0522 45 29 67; www.hotel maamoura.com; 59 Rue Ibn Batouta; s/d/ste Dh430/570/800; ✷❄☎) Another favourite with readers, this modern hotel offers excellent value for money. The spotless and spacious rooms may lack period detail, but they are very quiet for this central location, tastefully decorated in muted colours and have neat bathrooms. The staff are friendly and helpful.

East-West Hotel
HOTEL €€

(Map p178; ☑0522 20 02 10; www.eastwest-hotel. com; 10 Ave Hassan Souktani, cnr Rue Washington, Quartier Gauthier; s/d incl breakfast Dh450/600; ❄) Readers recommend this bright and cheerful three-star hotel. All rooms have clean bathrooms with modern fittings, free internet and a safe, and the hotel boasts a good restaurant and an Irish pub. Located in the residential but upcoming Quartier Gauthier, this choice is very quiet.

Hôtel du Palais
HOTEL €

(Map p170; ☑0522 27 61 91; 68 Rue Farhat Hachad; s/d Dh90/130, d/tr with bathroom Dh140/240) At the lower end of the price range, this basic hotel is a good choice, offering clean, spacious rooms with large windows. Though recently upgraded, it's still fairly spartan and can be noisy. A hot shower costs Dh10.

Hotel de Foucauld
HOTEL €

(Map p170; ☑0522 22 26 66; 52 Rue el-Oraïbi Jilali; s/d Dh100/150, s/d/tr with bathroom Dh150/180/220) Rooms in this simple hotel

THE SHANTY TOWNS

In May 2003, 13 suicide bombers blew themselves up at public places in Casablanca, killing themselves and 32 other people. They belonged to Salafia Jihadia, a radical Islamic group whose founding members trained in Afghanistan. The bombers were all young Moroccan men living in Casablanca's worst slums, less than half an hour from the city centre.

In 2007, 24 Islamists were arrested for plotting another wave of bombings after their leader blew himself up at an internet cafe. Many came from the same slums.

Most Casablancais openly condemn the killings, and claim their city is the most tolerant in the country. But a quarter – perhaps even a third – of the city's population lives in shanty towns, where living conditions are harsh: makeshift houses are made of cardboard and plastic, there is no running water, sewage system or electricity, no schools, no work and no hope. Many youngsters feel they have nothing to lose.

After the bombings, many charities were set up to improve the conditions, and the government has become more aware of the problems. The Housing Ministry has a plan to abolish all slums in Casablanca by 2012 and several slums have already been destroyed, with residents moved to new housing. Tens of thousands of houses are under construction, but slum residents complain that the new housing is too expensive and too small for extended families. There has been a serious improvement, but many feel it's not enough, and unless the government addresses the underlying problems there will be no improvement in conditions. It is hoped this will happen before anger and frustration boil over into support for violent alternatives.

in the centre of town don't live up to the plasterwork decoration in reception, but they're much bigger than average and have a certain faded charm. Some rooms have en-suite bathrooms. Streetside rooms can be noisy.

Hôtel Mon Rêve HOTEL €

(Map p170; ✆0522 41 14 39; 7 Rue Chaouia; s/d/tr Dh90/130/170, s/d/tr with bathroom Dh150/200/250) This charming old-style hotel has been a favourite with budget travellers for years. It is conveniently located near the Central Market but can be quite noisy, and the rooms painted in blue are spartan but clean. Choose a higher room to avoid the noise. Note that Rue Chaouia is sometimes referred to by its old name, Rue Colbert.

Hôtel Transatlantique HOTEL €€

(Map p170; ✆0522 29 45 51; www.transatcasa. com; 79 Rue Chaouia; s/d/tr Dh770/925/1025; ❋ 🛜) Set in one of Casa's architectural gems, the decor at this 1922 hotel is all a bit over the top. Popular with tour groups, it has a snack bar, a shady outdoor seating area and comfortable, but fairly plain, bedrooms. Avoid the 1st floor, as it gets the brunt of noise from the popular and very rowdy piano bar and nightclub. There are several newly decorated suites. Staff are keen to tell you that Edith Piaf was a resident and Telly Savalas of *Kojak* fame sucked his lollipop here.

Hôtel Riad Salam HOTEL €€€

(✆0522 39 13 13; fax 0522 39 13 45; Blvd de la Corniche, Aïn Diab; d incl breakfast Dh2700; ❍❋🛜🏊) Riad Salam is the top spot along the waterfront. The nonsmoking rooms with low couches, woven rugs and decorative tiling are centred on the hotel's three swimming pools and landscaped terrace. It has a thalassotherapy centre, a health club and tennis courts, and substantial discounts in the off-season. It's located on the Corniche 3km south of central Casablanca.

Hôtel Bellerive HOTEL €€

(✆0522 79 75 04; www.belleriv.com; 38 Blvd de La Corniche, Aïn Diab; s/d/tr incl breakfast Dh550/750/1050; ❋🏊) The lovely terrace, pool and garden make up for the dated, standard rooms at this small, family-run hotel. Many rooms have ocean views though, and it's cheaper than most along this waterfront strip. There's plenty of space and a playground, which makes it a good bet if you're travelling with children.

Hôtel le Littoral HOTEL €€€

(✆0522 79 73 73; fax 0522 79 73 74; Blvd de l'Océan Atlantique, Aïn Diab; s/d incl breakfast Dh990/1380;❋🛜🏊) This cavernous, well-kept hotel is rather dark, with rooms that were being upgraded at the time we visited. The large balconies have wonderful views over the beach. The hotel has two restaurants, a discotheque and beach umbrellas for hire.

Dar Itrit B&B €€

(✆0522 36 02 58; www.daritrit.ma; 9 Rue Restinga; s/d Dh870/980; 🛜) There are only three double rooms in this charming B&B, each decorated in a different Moroccan style – Marrakesh, Berber and Mogador. A delicious breakfast is served in a bright living room or on the terrace, in this slightly out-of-the-centre location.

Hôtel Oued-Dahab HOTEL €

(Map p170; ✆0522 22 38 66; 17 Rue Mohamed Belloul; s/d/tr Dh120/160/220; s/d/tr with bathroom Dh150/220/295) Run by the same family as the Guynemer, this hotel with spacious rooms is cheap and clean and offers rooms either sharing communal facilities or with private bathrooms. Rooms facing inwards are quieter but a bit darker. Good value.

Hôtel Hyatt Regency HOTEL €€€

(Map p170; ✆0522 43 12 34; www.casablanca. hyatt.com; Pl des Nations Unis; r Dh1900; 🅿❋🛜🏊) The best and the most central of all the five-star hotels, the Hyatt is a favourite meeting place for Casablancais for a meal in one of the many restaurants, or a drink at the bar. The spacious rooms are equipped with modern amenities and decorated in an elegant contemporary style, and have magnificent views of Casablanca, the old medina, the ocean and the Hassan II Mosque. The hotel also has a discotheque and spa.

✖ Eating

Casablanca has a great selection of restaurants, and you can eat anything from excellent tajine to French pâté and Thai dumplings. However, as elsewhere along the ocean, fresh fish and seafood are the local speciality and it's worth checking out the restaurants at the port or on the way to Aïn Diab for a culinary treat.

Rue Chaouia, located opposite the Marché Central is the best place for a quick eat, with a line of rotisseries, stalls and res-

LOCAL KNOWLEDGE

TAHIR SHAH, WRITER & CASABLANCA RESIDENT

I love the wild vibrancy of Casablanca. It's the hotchpotch melting pot of Morocco. I've lived here for seven years and it just keeps on getting better and better – it's always enthralling. There are so few tourists that you do a double-take if you see one.

My favourite places? It depends on my mood. The old art-deco downtown around Pl Mohammed V is one. What a jewel, a treasure! It's grimy and grubby, but the faded grandeur is a jaw-dropping travel experience. Most Casablancais wouldn't be seen dead down there!

Another art-deco building is the Stade Velodrome where they have greyhound racing every week. Going to the dogs in Casablanca – it's very seedy and I love it.

I think the Casablanca medina is one of the most genuine in Morocco. There's absolutely nothing for tourists; it's totally for the local people.

And my very secret place is the Socco de Moina souq in the middle-class area of Hay Hassani. It's a great secret. You'll find all the antiques left by the French, great architectural stuff, immense chandeliers, grand pianos, roll-top baths and gramophones. I've furnished my home with treasures discovered here.

taurants serving roast chicken, brochettes and sandwiches (Dh20 to Dh30). It's open until about 2am.

DOWNTOWN CASA

TOP CHOICE **Restaurant du Port de Pêche** SEAFOOD €€
(✆0522 31 85 61; Le Port de Pêche; mains Dh140; ☺lunch & dinner) This authentic and rustic seafood restaurant in the middle of the fishing harbour is packed to the gills at lunch and dinner as happy diners tuck into fish freshly whipped from the sea and cooked to perfection. The fish and tangy paella are some of the best in town. The decor is very 1970s with paper tablecloths. Service is professional and swift. Book ahead as this place is very popular with Casablancais from all walks of life.

TOP CHOICE **Le Rouget de l'Isle** FRENCH €€€
(Map p178; ✆0522 29 47 40; 16 Rue Rouget de l'Isle, off Blvd Moulay Hassan I; mains Dh160; ☺lunch Mon-Fri, dinner Mon-Sat) One of Casa's top eateries, Le Rouget is set in a glorious 1930s villa and has a wonderful garden redolent with night-blooming jasmine. Sleek, stylish and charming, it's renowned for its simple but delicious and light French food. The owner's contemporary artworks grace the walls. The impeccable food is reasonably priced though. Book in advance.

Rick's Cafe MEDITERRANEAN €€
(Map p166; ✆0522 27 42 07; www.rickscafe.ma; 248 Blvd Sour Jdid; mains Dh160; ☺lunch & dinner) This restaurant scores top marks for ambience and decor. Cashing in on the

Hollywood hit *Casablanca*, the beautiful bar, lounge and restaurant is run by a former American diplomat, with furniture and fittings inspired by the film. The menu features excellent French and Moroccan specialities, concentrating on fresh fish. At lunchtime, the Obama family's chilli con carne is on offer. The pianist, Issam, will play *As time goes by*, and there's a Sunday jam session, wi-fi access and, inevitably, souvenir T-shirts. You can watch the film again and again on the 1st floor. The upstairs bar, The Blue Parrot (p180) – of course! – is a good place for late-night drinks. Here's looking at you kid!

Sqala Restaurant LOCAL €€
(✆0522 26 09 60; Blvd des Almohades; mains Dh90-160; ☺lunch & dinner Tue-Sun, daily summer) Nestled in the ochre walls of the *sqala*, an 18th-century fortified bastion north of the centre, this lovely restaurant is a tranquil escape from the city. The cafe has a rustic interior and a delightful garden surrounded by flower-draped trellises. No alcohol is served, but there's a good selection of teas and fresh juices. It's a lovely spot for a Moroccan breakfast or a selection of salads for lunch. Tajines are a speciality and the menu features plenty of fish, as well as a selection of meat brochettes.

Taverne du Dauphin SEAFOOD €€
(Map p170; ✆0522 22 12 00; 115 Blvd Houphouët Boigny; mains Dh140; ☺lunch & dinner Mon-Sat) A Casablanca institution, this traditional Provençal restaurant and bar has been serving up local *fruits de mer* (seafood) since it

ATLANTIC COAST CASABLANCA (DAR AL-BAÏDA)

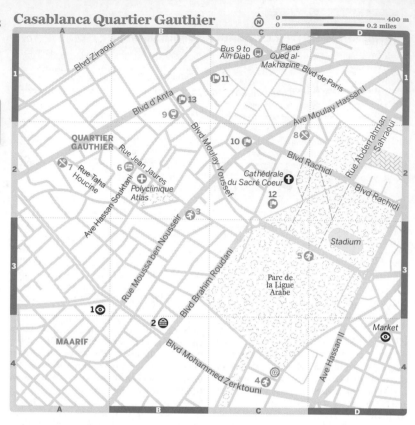

Casablanca Quartier Gauthier

0 — 400 m
0 — 0.2 miles

Blvd Ziraoui

Bus 9 to Aïn Diab 🚌

Place Oued al-Makhazine

Blvd de Paris

11

Blvd d'Anfa

13

9

Ave Moulay Hassan I

QUARTIER GAUTHIER

Rue Jean Jaures

Blvd Moulay Youssef

10

8

Rue Abderrahman Sahraoui

7

Rue Taha Houcine

6

Polyclinique Atlas

Ave Hassan Souktani

Blvd Rachidi

Cathédrale du Sacré Coeur ✝

12

Blvd Rachidi

Rue Moussa ben Nousseir

3

Stadium

Parc de la Ligue Arabe

5

Blvd Brahim Roudani

1

2

Market

MAARIF

Blvd Mohammed Zerktouni

Ave Hassan II

@

4

---

opened in 1958. This is an old-fashioned, family-run place, and one taste of the succulent grilled fish, fried calamari and *crevettes royales* (king prawns) will leave you smitten.

Ostréa SEAFOOD €€
(☎0522 44 13 90; Le Port de Pêche; mains Dh150; ⊙lunch & dinner) Across the road from Restaurant du Port de Pêche inside the port is this more upmarket seafood restaurant specialising in Oualidia oysters and fresh lobster.

Restaurant al-Mounia LOCAL €€
(Map p170; ☎0522 22 26 69; 95 Rue Prince Moulay Abdallah; mains Dh150; ⊙dinner) Eat the best Moroccan food in the centre of Casablanca at this delightful traditional restaurant where you can choose to sit in the Moroccan salon elegantly decorated with *zellij* (tilework) and sculpted wood, or under the pepper tree in the cool, leafy garden. There's a

selection of salads worthy of any vegetarian restaurant and an array of exotic delicacies such as pigeon *pastilla* (rich, savoury pie) and sweet tomato tajine.

La Brasserie la Bavaroise FRENCH €€€
(Map p170; ☎0522 31 17 60; 129 Rue Allah ben Abdellah; mains Dh150-200; ⊙dinner) Locals and expats like to hang out in this upmarket brasserie behind the Marché Central, partly for the French cuisine, partly to see and be seen. It offers a good selection of fish as well as French classics such as veal, steak and pheasant cooked to perfection. Meat is grilled on a wood fire. It has a pleasant atmosphere and a friendly welcome. Every month the menu features specialities from a different region of France. The same owners also run La Bodéga (p180) next door, a great tapas bar.

La Maison du Gourmet FRENCH, LOCAL €€€
(Map p178; ☎0522 48 48 46; Rue Taha Houcine, Maarif; meals Dh400-500; ⊙lunch Mon-Fri,

dinner Mon-Sat) This upmarket gourmet restaurant serves an inventive menu of the finest of French and Moroccan cuisine, run by a couple, he French, she Moroccan, both trained by Paul Bocuse. Specialities include a heavenly *pastilla* with confit of duck and foie gras. The elegant surroundings, excellent service and exceptional food make this the perfect address for a special occasion. Book ahead.

Paul   MEDITERRANEAN €€
(Map p178; cnr Blvd d'Anfa & Blvd Moulay Rachid; ⊘7am-9pm) The French chain of bakery and patisserie has arrived in Casa, in the gorgeous art-deco Villa Zevaco once occupied by Edith Piaf. There is a constant flow of people here, coming as much for the food and decor as for the pleasure of being seen in this trendy hang-out. Excellent breakfast is served, and there is also a menu of salads, snacks and other Mediterranean delights.

Patisserie Bennis Habous   PATISSERIE €
(2 Rue Fkih el-Gabbas) One of the city's most famous and traditional patisseries, this place in the Quartier Habous is Casa's best spot for traditional Moroccan treats, including some of the best *cornes de gazelle* (gazelle horns; almond paste) pastries in town, as well as made-to-order *pastillas*.

Ifrane   LOCAL €
(Map p170; cnr Rues Tata & Mouftakar; mains Dh40-65) Almost always crowded and spilling customers onto the streetside seating, this friendly cafe serves a choice of grills and brochettes at bargain prices. It's a relaxed place with a mixed clientele and offers hassle-free eating for women.

Chez Flavio   ITALIAN €€
(☑0522 29 45 29; 3 Blvd Mohamed Abdou; pizzas Dh80, mains Dh120; ⊘lunch & dinner) One of the most popular Italian restaurants, Chez Flavio makes for a welcome break from tajine if you've been in Morocco for some time. These are definitely some of the best pizzas in town.

Snack Amine Adam   SEAFOOD €
(Map p170; Rue Chaouia; mains Dh70) Tucked between the chicken rotisseries by the Marché Central, Snack Amine Adam serves up big plates of simple but tasty fried fish, and platters of the freshest seafood.

AÏN DIAB & ANFA
The best of this neighbourhood's restaurants are clustered together on a cliff top overlooking the crashing Atlantic waves near el-Hank Lighthouse.

La Fibule   LOCAL, MEDITERRANEAN €€€
(☑0522 36 06 41; Blvd de la Corniche, Phare el-Hank; meals Dh300-500; ⊘lunch & dinner) The subtle lighting, warm colours and elegant decor give La Fibule an inviting atmosphere. The food here is a mixture of well-prepared Moroccan and Lebanese, served at low tables overlooking the ocean through large windows.

La Mer   SEAFOOD €€€
(☑0522 36 33 15; Blvd de la Corniche, Phare el-Hank; meals Dh400; ⊘lunch & dinner) Right next door to La Fibule, and under the same management, this seafood restaurant is a more refined place with white linen and bone china replacing the ethnic vibe. The menu and service is very French, bordering on stuffy, but the food is divine.

CASABLANCA FOR CHILDREN

Casablanca is a big, grimy city and your best bet when travelling with children is to retreat from the noise and traffic of the city centre. The beaches and beach clubs in **Aïn Diab** are the places to go. Along with swimming pools, slides and playgrounds, they have various sports courts and countless facilities. Staying at a hotel along the Blvd de la Corniche means you'll probably have your own swimming pool and won't have too far to walk for entertainment.

Continuing west from Aïn Diab, the upmarket suburb of **Anfa** is home to the enormous **Morocco Mall**, which has an aquarium and an Imax theatre in addition to its shops.

Back in town, Casa's biggest open space is the **Parc de la Ligue Arabe**. It's a good place for games and walks, and has a choice of small cafes and the **Yasmina amusement park** (Map p178; admission Dh150; ☉10am-7pm), with plenty of small-scale rides and fun-fair atmosphere.

A Ma Bretagne SEAFOOD, FRENCH €€€
(☎0522 36 21 12; Sidi Abderrahman, Blvd de la Corniche; meals Dh500; ☉dinner) Locally promoted as the best restaurant in Africa, this self-consciously cool establishment is all modern lines and superb food. Although seafood tops the bill here, you can opt for some other French delicacies, cooked by the *maître cuisinier* (master chef) André Halbert. It's 5km out of town.

Frédéric Cassel Haute Patisserie PATISSERIE €€
(8 Blvd Moulay Rachid, Anfa) Be seen at the latest trendy cafe in upmarket Anfa serving mouth-watering breakfasts and light meals, along with ice cream and cakes that display mind-boggling artistry.

Hediard PATISSERIE €€
(Résidence Jardin d'Anfa, Blvd Lido Route Côterie, Aïn Diab) Very slick, and popular with the young and beautiful, this cafe in Aïn Diab serves a range of sumptuous cakes as well as light meals and deli-style sandwiches (Dh50 to Dh90).

SELF-CATERING

Marché Central MARKET €
(Map p170) If you're planning a picnic on the beach, head for the central market, located between Blvd Mohammed V and Rue Allah ben Abdellah. It's a fascinating place to just stroll and has a great selection of fresh produce and a couple of good delis.

 Drinking

Although there are plenty of classic French-style drinking dens in the centre of town, they are pretty much a male preserve and are usually intimidating for women. Casablanca's bars can be pretty rough around the edges and generally attract a male-only clientele (plus prostitutes). In general, the bars in the larger hotels are more refined places to drink, especially for women.

Café Alba CAFE €
(Map p170; 59-61 Rue Indriss Lahrizi) High ceilings, swish, modern furniture, subtle lighting and a hint of elegant colonial times mark this cafe out from the more traditional smoky joints around town. It's hassle-free downtime for women and a great place for watching Casa's up-and-coming.

Sqala Café Maure CAFE €
(Blvd des Almohades) Another exception to the men-only rule, this lovely cafe is set behind the *sqala* in the medina wall. The flower-filled garden is quiet all afternoon and makes a great place for coffee or delicious juices.

Blue Parrot BAR
(248 Blvd Sour Jdid) Upstairs at Rick's Cafe (p177), this Caribbean-style bar is partially open-air with wonderful views over the port. It's a great place for a drink (and comfortable for women) and also serves a simple menu of barbecued fish and grills (mains Dh75 to Dh160).

La Bodéga TAPAS BAR
(Map p170; 129 Rue Allah ben Abdellah) Hip, happening and loved by a mixed-aged group of Casablanca's finest, La Bodega is essentially a tapas bar where the music (everything from salsa to Arabic pop) is loud and the *rioja* (Spanish wine) flows freely. It's a fun place with a lively atmosphere and a packed dance floor after 10pm.

Petit Poucet BAR
(Map p170; cnr Blvd Mohammed V & Rue Mohammed el-Qory) A die-hard relic of 1920s France, this strictly male-only bar was where Saint-Exupéry, the French author and aviator, used to spend time between mail flights across the Sahara. Today, the bar is low-key but is an authentic slice of long-ago Casa life. Look out for the old-time advertising signs.

Le Trica BAR
(Map p178; 5 Rue el-Moutanabi, Quartier Gauthier; ⊙closed lunch Sat & Sun) This bar-lounge, set over two levels with brick walls and 1960s furniture, is the place to feel the beat of the new Morocco. The atmosphere is hot and trendy at night, stirred by the techno beat and a flow of beer and *mojitos* (rum cocktails), but things are a lot calmer at lunch.

☆ Entertainment

Nightclubs
The beachfront suburb of Aïn Diab is the place for late-night drinking and dancing in Casa. However, hanging out with Casablanca's beautiful people for a night on the town doesn't come cheap. Expect to pay at least Dh150 to get in and as much again for drinks. Heavy-set bouncers guard the doors and practise tough crowd control – if you don't look the part, you won't get in. Many of these clubs cater for well-heeled Middle-Easterners (a Saudi prince has a palace on the Corniche), with Egyptian or Lebanese performers.

Balcon 33 CLUB
(33 Blvd de la Corniche) A Fellini-esque, cabaret-style bar-cum-restaurant.

Le Carré Rouge CLUB
(Hotel Villa Blanca, Blvd de la Corniche; ⊙11.30pm-4am) An ultramodern pop sensation.

VIP club CLUB
(Rue des Dunes) Gay-friendly.

Le Village CLUB
(11 Blvd de la Corniche) Also has a slightly gay-friendly atmosphere.

Armstrong Legend CLUB
(41 Blvd de la Corniche) Incredibly packed and one of the few places with funky live music.

Other than Aïn Diab, the only real options are clubs at the large international hotels, including those listed here. Prostitutes work all of the clubs, men are always expected to pay for drinks and women shouldn't expect hassle-free drinking anywhere.

Hôtel Transatlantique HOTEL CLUB
(Map p170; www.transatcasa.com; 79 Rue Chaouia) The seedy nightclub here is good for late-night *couleur locale* as the belly dancers and singers provoke the mostly male locals into throwing money at them.

Sky 28 HOTEL CLUB
(Kenzi Tower Hotel, Twin Centre, Maarif) Serves cocktails to more middle-of-the-road live music.

Caesar HOTEL CLUB
(Map p170; Hôtel Sheraton, 100 Ave des FAR)

Black House HOTEL CLUB
(Map p170; Hôtel Hyatt Regency, Place des Nations Unies)

Theatres
Complex Culturel Sidi Belyout THEATRE
(Map p170; 28 Rue Léon L'Africain; ⊙performances 9pm) This 200-seat theatre hosts plays (usually in Arabic) and the occasional music recital or dance performance.

Les Abattoirs de Casablanca CULTURAL CENTRE
(☎0537 73 26 50; www.abattoirs-casablanca.net; Quartier Hay Mohammadi) The old city abattoirs built in 1922 have been transformed into an impressive cultural centre dubbed the Culture Factory. Near Casa Voyageurs railway station, the centre hosts exhibitions and performances, plays, concerts and workshops in anything from maskmaking to rollerblading, including some for children. See www.casa-pocket.com for the latest events.

Cinemas
Most English-language films are dubbed in French, unless it specifically mentions 'version originale'.

Megarama CINEMA
(☎0522 79 88 88; www.megarama.info, in French; Blvd de la Corniche; afternoon/evening shows Dh40/50) The plushest cinema in town, this huge complex in Aïn Diab has four comfortable theatres that are usually packed.

Cinéma Lynx CINEMA
(150 Ave Mers Sultan; screen/balcony/club Dh30/40/50) A good option if you don't want to trek out to Aïn Diab, this spacious and comfortable cinema has an excellent sound system.

Cinéma Rialto CINEMA
(Map p170; ☑0522 26 26 32; Rue Mohammed el-Qory; screen/balcony/club Dh30/40/50) A classic, cavernous, single-screen, art-deco cinema.

Imax Theatre CINEMA
(Morocco Mall, Rte Azemmour, Anfa) Nearing completion at the time of research, this cinema will seat 400 people.

 Shopping

Although not an artisan centre, Casablanca has a good choice of traditional crafts from around Morocco. The most pleasant place to shop is Quartier Habous, south of the centre. Merchants here are pretty laid-back, but the quality of crafts can vary and hard bargaining is the order of the day.

Exposition Nationale
d'Artisanat ART & CRAFT
(Map p170; ☑0522 26 70 64; 3 Ave Hassan II; ☺8.30am-12.30pm & 2.30-8pm) If you'd rather avoid haggling altogether, head here where you'll find three floors of fixed-price crafts.

Disques GAM MUSIC
(Map p170; ☑0522 26 89 54; 99 Rue Abderrahman Sehraoui) A good selection of traditional Arab and Berber music.

 Information

Head to **Lonely Planet** (www.lonelyplanet.com/morocco/the-atlantic-coast/casablanca) for planning advice, author recommendations, traveller reviews and insider tips.

Emergency
Fire/ambulance (☑15; ☺24hr)
Police (☑19; ☺24hr)
Service d'Aide Médicale Urgente (SAMU; ☑0522 25 25 25; ☺24hr) Private ambulance service.
SOS Médecins (☑0522 44 44 44, 0522 25 30 49; house call Dh400; ☺24hr) Private doctors who make house calls.

Internet Access
EuroNet (51 Rue Tata; per hr Dh10; ☺8.30am-11pm)
G@.net (29 Rue Abdelkader al-Moftaker; per hr Dh8; ☺9am-midnight) Very clean and modern, with fast connection.
Gig@net (140 Blvd Mohammed Zerktouni; per hr Dh10; ☺24hr)
LGnet (81 Blvd Mohammed V; per hr Dh8; ☺9am-midnight)

Medical Services
Polyclinique Atlas (Map p178; ☑0522 27 40 39; 27 Rue Mohammed ben Ali, Quartier Gauthier; ☺24hr) Off Rue Jean Jaures.

Money
There are banks – most with ATMs and foreign-exchange offices – on almost every street corner in the centre of Casablanca.
BMCE (Hôtel Hyatt Regency, Pl des Nations Unis; ☺9am-9pm) Good for after-hours and weekend services.
Crédit du Maroc (48 Blvd Mohammed V) Separate *bureau de change* that is very central; American Express (Amex) travellers cheques cashed for free.
Voyages Schwartz (Rue Prince Moulay Abdallah) Amex representative; does not cash or sell travellers cheques.
Wafa Cash (15 Rue Indriss Lahrizi; ☺8am-8pm Mon-Sat) Open longer hours; has an ATM and cashes travellers cheques.

Post
Central Market post office (cnr Blvd Mohammed V & Rue Chaouia)
FedEx (☑0522 54 12 12; 313 Blvd Mohammed V)
Main post office (cnr Blvd de Paris & Ave Hassan II)
Medina post office (Pl Ahmed el-Bidaoui) Near the youth hostel.

Tourist Information
Although the staff are polite, tourist offices in Casablanca are of very little practical use. Try **Visit Casablanca** (www.visitcasablanca.ma) for information before you travel or ask the receptionist at your hotel for help.
The ever-helpful **Casa Pocket** (www.casapocket.com) lists events.
Office National Marocain du Tourisme (ONMT; off Map p170; ☑0522 27 95 33; 55 Rue Omar Slaoui)
Syndicat d'Initiative (Map p170; ☑0522 22 15 24; 98 Blvd Mohammed V)

Travel Agencies
Carlson Wagonlit (☑0522 20 30 51; www.carlsonwagonlit.com/en/countries/ma; 60-62 Rue Araibi Jilali) A respected international chain of travel agencies.
Supratours (☑0522 24 81 72; www.supratourstravel.com; Casa Voyageurs train station) Organises rail and bus connections.
Voyages Wasteels (☑0522 54 10 10; www.wasteels.fr, in French; 26 Rue Léon L'Africain) A good place for cheap intercontinental rail tickets.

Getting There & Away

Air

Casablanca's **Mohammed V International Airport** (✆0522 53 90 40; www.onda.ma) is 30km southeast of the city on the Marrakesh road. Regular flights leave here for most countries in western Europe, as well as to West Africa, Algeria, Tunisia, Egypt, the Middle East and North America. For a list of airlines with flights in and out of Casablanca see p507.

Internally, the vast majority of Royal Air Maroc's (RAM) flights go via Casablanca, so you can get to any destination in Morocco directly from the city. Regional Air Lines flies to over a dozen Moroccan destinations, mostly south along the coast.

Bus

The modern **CTM bus station** (Map p170; ✆0522 54 10 10; www.ctm.ma; 23 Rue Léon L'Africain) is close to Ave des FAR. It's a pretty efficient place with a cafe. There are daily CTM bus departures. Night buses include the following:

DESTINATION	COST (DH)	DURATION (HR)
Al-Hoceima	200	11
Dakhla	530	28
Er-Rachidia, via Tinerhir	190	14
Nador	190	13
Ouarzazate	170	7½
Oujda	190	11
Taroudannt	190	10

CTM also operates international buses to Belgium, France, Germany, Italy and Spain from Casablanca (see p509).

The modern Gare Routière Ouled Ziane, 4km southeast of the centre, is the bus station for almost all non-CTM services. The main reason to trek out here is for destinations not covered by CTM. A taxi to the bus station will cost about Dh20, alternatively take bus No 10 or 36 from Blvd Mohammed V near the market.

Also on Route Ouled Ziane, but more than 1km closer to town, is the SAT bus station. SAT runs national and international buses of a similar standard to CTM, though to fewer destinations. Fares are slightly cheaper.

Car

Casablanca is well endowed with car-rental agencies, many with offices around Ave des FAR, Blvd Mohammed V and at the airport.

Avis Casablanca (Map p170; ✆0522 31 24 24; 19 Ave des FAR); Mohammed V International Airport (✆0522 53 90 72)

Budget Casablanca (Map p170; ✆0522 31 31 24; Tours des Habous, Ave des FAR); Mohammed V International Airport (✆0522 33 91 57)

Hertz Casablanca (Map p170; ✆0522 48 47 10; 25 Rue el-Oraïbi Jilali); Mohammed V International Airport (✆0522 53 91 81)

National Casablanca (Map p170; ✆0522 27 71 41; 12 Rue el-Oraïbi Jilali); Mohammed V International Airport (✆0522 53 97 16)

President Car (Map p170; ✆0522 26 07 90, 0661 21 03 94; presidentcar@menara.ma; 27 Rue el-Ghali Ahmed) A reliable local agency

DAY BUSES FROM CASABLANCA

DESTINATION	COST (DH)	DURATION (HR)	DAILY FREQUENCY
Agadir	200	6½	6
Chefchaouen	125	7	1
El-Jadida	40	2	6
Essaouira	145	6	2 with CTM; hourly with private companies
Fez	100	4	8
Laâyoune	410	20	2
Marrakesh	90	3½	8
Meknès	90	3½	6
Ouezzane	80	4	1
Tangier	145	5½	5 with CTM; regularly with private companies
Taza	155	7	4
Tetouan	145	6	5

that has a well-maintained fleet of cars, very competitive rates, and comes much recommended by the local expat community. The Bouayad brothers will do their utmost to help, and can deliver a car to the airport or Marrakesh if requested. It's off Blvd Mohammed V.

Casablanca has parking meters (Dh2 per hour, two hours maximum), operating from 8am to noon, and 2pm to 7pm daily, except on Sunday and public holidays. If you don't pay, you may be fined or have your wheels clamped. There is a guarded car park next to the British cemetery (per day/night Dh20) and another just off of Rue Tata (Dh5 per hour). Anywhere else a guard will ask for a tip for watching your car; it is common practice to pay Dh5.

Taxi

Shared grands taxis to Rabat (Dh30) and to Fez (Dh120) leave from Blvd Mohammed V opposite the old Hotel Lincoln. However, the train is more convenient and comfortable.

Train

If your destination is on a train line, it's generally the best way to travel. Casablanca has five train stations, but only two of interest to travellers.

All long-distance trains as well as trains to Mohammed V International Airport depart from Casa Voyageurs train station, 4km east of the city centre. Catch bus 30 (Dh4), which runs along Blvd Mohammed V, or hop in a taxi and pay about Dh15 to get there.

The **Casa Port train station** (Map p170) is a few hundred metres northeast of Place des Nations Unies. Although more convenient, trains from here only run to Rabat (Dh35, one hour, every 30 minutes) and Kenitra (Dh48, 1½ hours, every 30 minutes).

Destinations include the following:

Azemmour Dh31, seven daily

El-Jadida DH35, 1½ hours, seven daily

Fez Dh110, 3½ to 4½ hours, 18 daily

Marrakesh Dh90, three hours, nine daily

Meknès Dh90, 3½ hours, 18 daily

Nador Dh185, 11 hours, five daily

Oujda Dh205, 10 hours, three daily

Tangier Dh125, five hours, eight daily

ℹ Getting Around
To/From the Airport

The easiest way to get from Mohammed V International Airport to Casablanca is by train (2nd class Dh40, 35 minutes). The trains are comfortable and reliable, and leave every hour from 6am to 10pm and at midnight. You can also continue to Rabat (Dh75) or Kenitra (Dh88), though you'll have a change of train at Casa Voyageurs or Aïn

Sebaa. The trains leave from below the ground floor of the airport Terminal 1 building.

From Casa Voyageurs train station to the airport, the first train leaves at 4.40am and then every hour from 6.07am to 10.07pm. Additional trains go from Casa Port, with a change at Aïn Sebaa.

A grand taxi between the airport and the city centre costs Dh300, though you may be asked for Dh350 at unsocial hours. Some taxi drivers receive commissions if they bring clients to particular hotels.

Bus

The local bus system has been revamped, but unless you're travelling alone and on a very limited budget a petit taxi is generally much easier. Buses cost Dh4 and stop at designated bus stops. The following bus routes are useful, but numbers and routes may change in the re-structure for the tramway.

BUS 2 Blvd Mohammed V to Casa Voyageurs train station.

BUS 4 Along Blvd de Paris and down Ave Lalla Yacout to Nouvelle Medina.

BUS 9 From Blvd d'Anfa to Aïn Diab and the beaches.

BUS 10 From Place de la Concorde, along Blvd Mohammed V to Gare Routière Ouled Ziane.

BUS 11 From Ave des FAR to Gare Routière.

BUS 15 Northbound from Pl Oued al-Makhazine to the Hassan II Mosque.

Taxi

Casa's red petits taxis are excellent value and can generally get you to your destination far faster than any bus. You can hail one anywhere, or there's a petit-taxi stand on Ave des FAR. The minimum fare is Dh7, but expect to pay Dh15 in or near the city centre. Most drivers use the meter without question, but if they refuse to, just get out of the cab. Prices rise by 50% after 8pm. Have plenty of small coins to hand, and check your change.

Tram

Casablanca's tramway system should be operational by the end of 2012.

RABAT الرباط

POP 2.5 MILLION

While Rabat, Morocco's political and administrative capital since independence in 1956, has not established itself as a tourist destination, visitors who do go find a gem of a city. The colonial architecture is stunning, the palm-lined boulevards are well kept and relatively free of traffic, and the atmosphere is as cosmopolitan as its economic big brother down the coast. All in all, life here is pleasant and civilised. Casablancais say that, with all the bureaucrats, Rabat is dull, and they have a point. Yet the city is more laid-back, pleasant and more provincial than Casablanca, and far less grimy and frantic.

The quiet medina has an authentic feel to it, some good shops and fascinating architecture. You'll be blissfully ignored on the streets and souqs, so it's easy to discover the city's monuments and hidden corners at your own pace. The picturesque kasbah, with its narrow alleys, art galleries and magnificent ocean views, is also worth exploring.

Rabat has a long and rich history, and plenty of monuments to show for it from the Phoenician, Roman, Almohad and Merenid times. The power shifted at times between Rabat and Salé, the whitewashed town across the Bou Regreg river, where time appears to have stood still.

Rabat is also a good place to eat; there are plenty of wonderful restaurants around town. The nightlife is not what it is in Casablanca, but an early afternoon stroll along the main avenues of the happening suburb of Agdal, where local hipsters flaunt their skinny jeans, is entertaining enough. And if city life gets you down, you can escape to the beaches further north.

The mega project to link the cities of Rabat and Salé by developing the waterfront on both sides of the river and building a tramway between them was about to open at the time of research.

History

The fertile plains inland from Rabat drew settlers to the area as far back as the 8th century BC. Both the Phoenicians and the Romans set up trading posts in the estuary of the Oued Bou Regreg river in Sala, today's Chellah. The Roman settlement, Sala Colonia, lasted long after the empire's fall and eventually became the seat of an independent Berber kingdom. The Zenata Berbers built a *ribat,* a fortress-monastery after which the city takes its name, on the present site of Rabat's kasbah. As the new town of Salé (created in the 10th century) began to prosper on the north bank of the river, the city of Chellah fell into decline.

The arrival of the Almohads in the 12th century saw the *ribat* rebuilt as a kasbah, a strategic jumping-off point for campaigns

in Spain, where the dynasty successfully brought Andalusia back under Muslim rule. Under Yacoub al-Mansour (the Victorious), Rabat enjoyed a brief heyday as an imperial capital, Ribat al-Fatah (Victory Fortress). Al-Mansour had extensive walls built, added the enormous Bab Oudaïa to the kasbah and began work on the Hassan Mosque, intended to be the greatest mosque in all of the Islamic West, if not in all of the Islamic world.

Al-Mansour's death in 1199 brought an end to these grandiose schemes, leaving the great Hassan Mosque incomplete. The city soon lost all significance and it wasn't until the 17th century that Rabat's fortunes began to change.

As Muslim refugees arrived from Christian Spain, so did a band of Christian renegades, Moorish pirates, freebooters and multinational adventurers. Rabat and Salé became safe havens for corsairs – merciless pirates whom English chroniclers called the Sallee Rovers. At one point they even created their own pirate state, the Republic of Bou Regreg. These corsairs roved as far as the coast of North America seeking Spanish gold, and to Cornwall in southern England to capture Christian slave labour. The first Alawite sultans attempted to curtail their looting sprees, but no sultan ever really exercised control over them. Corsairs continued attacking European shipping until well into the 19th century.

Meanwhile, Sultan Mohammed ben Abdallah briefly made Rabat his capital at the end of the 18th century, but the city soon fell back into obscurity. In 1912 France strategically abandoned the hornet's nest of political intrigue and unrest in the traditional capitals of Fez and Marrakesh and instead shifted power to coastal Rabat, where supply and defence were more easily achieved. Since then, the city has remained the seat of government and official home of the king.

◉ Sights

MEDINA

Rabat's walled medina (Map p190), all there was of the city when the French arrived in the early 20th century, is a rich mixture of spices, carpets, crafts, cheap shoes and bootlegged DVDs. Built on an orderly grid in the 17th century, it may lack the more intriguing atmosphere of the older medinas of the interior, but it's a great place to roam, with no aggressive selling.

Rabat

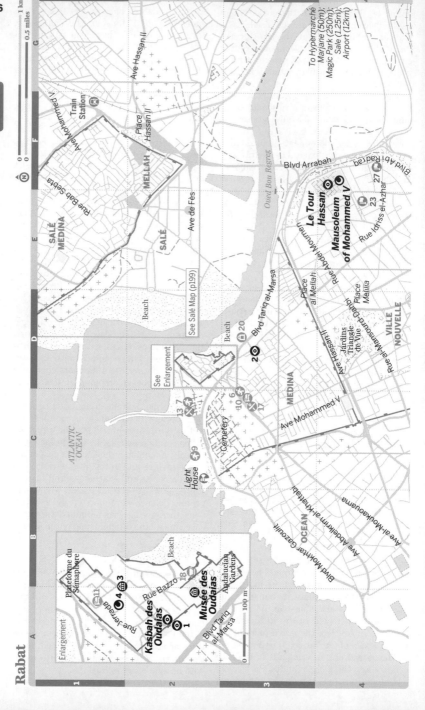

Enlargement

Plateforme du Sémaphore

Rue Jeraida

11

4 3

Kasbah des Oudaias

1

Rue Bazzo

Musée des Oudaias

18

Beach

Andalucian Gardens

Blvd Tariq al-Marsa

0   100 m

ATLANTIC OCEAN

Light House

9

13 7

Cemetery

6

10

17

20

2

MEDINA

Ave Mohammed V

Blvd Tariq al-Marsa

See Enlargement

See Salé Map (p199)

Beach

SALÉ MEDINA

SALÉ

Rue Bab Sebta

Ave de Fès

Ave Hassan II

MELLAH

Place Hassan II

Train Station

Ave Mohammed V

Oued Bou Regreg

To Hypermarché Marjane (50m); Magic Park (250m); Salé (1.25km); Airport (12km)

Blvd Arrabah

Le Tour Hassan

Mausoleum of Mohammed V

3

Rue Idriss el-Azhar

23

27

Blvd Abi Rad'rad

Place al Mellah

Rue Abdel Moumen

Rue Hassan II

Jardins Triangle de Vue

Place Melilia

VILLE NOUVELLE

Ave al-Mansour

Rue Oqba

OCEAN

Blvd Mokhtar Gazouli

Ave Abdelkrim al-Khattabi

Ave al-Mohaouama

0   0.5 miles

0   1 km

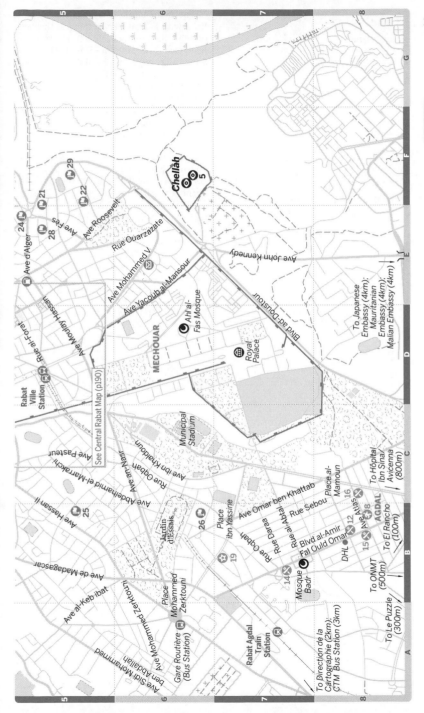

Chellah

5

29

21

22

24

28

Ave Fès

Ave Roosevelt

Ave d'Alger

Rue Ouarzazate

Ave Mohammed V

Ave Yacoub al-Mansour

Ave Moulay Hassan

Rue el-Forcat

Rabat Ville Station

See Central Rabat Map (p190)

Ahl al-Fès Mosque

MECHOUAR

Royal Palace

Blvd ad-Doustour

Ave John Kennedy

To Japanese Embassy (4km); Mauritanian Embassy (4km); Malian Embassy (4km)

Ave Pasteur

Ave ibn Khaldoun

Rue Oqbah

Ave ibn-Nasr

Ave Abdelhamid el-Marrakchi

Municipal Stadium

To Hôpital Ibn Sina/ Avicenna (800m)

Place al-Mamoun

Ave Omar ben Khattab

Rue Sebou

Rue al-Abtal

Place ibn Yassine

26

19

Rue Daraa

Rue Oqbah

16

12

15

8

Ave Atlas

DHL

Blvd al-Amir Fal Ould Omar

AGDAL

To El Rancho (100m)

14

Mosque Badr

To ONMT (500m)

To Le Puzzle (300m)

Ave Hassan II

25

Jardin d'Essais

Place Mohammed Zerktouni

Ave de Madagascar

Ave al-Keb ibat

Ave Mohammed Zerktouni

Ave Sidi Mohammed ben Abdallah

Gare Routière (Bus Station)

Rabat Agdal Train Station

To Direction de la Cartographie (2km); CTM Bus Station (3km)

Rabat

The main market street is Rue Souika, lined with food and spice shops at the western end, then textiles and silverware as you head east. The **Souq as-Sebbat** (Jewellery Souq; Map p190) specialises in gaudy gold and begins roughly at Rue Bab Chellah. The **Grande Mosquée** (Map p190), a 14th-century Merenid original that has been rebuilt in the intervening years, is just down this road to the right.

If you continue past the Rue des Consuls (so called because diplomats lived here until 1912), you'll come to the *mellah* (Jewish quarter) with an interesting **flea market** going down to Bab el-Bahr and the river. Turning north along Rue des Consuls is one of the more interesting areas of the medina, with craft shops and some of the grand diplomatic residencies. After the **carpet souq** (Map p186) the street ends in an open area lined with craft shops, which was once the setting for the slave auctions in the days of the Sallee Rovers. From here you can make your way up the hill to the kasbah.

EAST OF THE CENTRE
Le Tour Hassan   HISTORIC SITE
(Hassan Tower; Map p186) Towering above Oued Bou Regreg, and surrounded by well-tended gardens, is Rabat's most famous landmark. The Almohads' most ambitious project would have been the second-largest mosque of its time, after Samarra in Iraq, but Sultan Yacoub al-Mansour died before it was finished. He intended a 60m-tall minaret, but the tower was abandoned at 44m. The mosque was destroyed by an earthquake in 1755, and today only a forest of shattered pillars testifies to the grandiosity of Al-Mansour's plans. The tower is built to the same design as the Giralda in Seville, and the Koutoubia in Marrakesh.

Mausoleum of Mohammed V   LANDMARK
(Map p186; admission free; ☺sunrise-sunset) Near the tower stands this marble mausoleum, built in traditional Moroccan style. The present king's father (the late Hassan II) and grandfather have been laid to rest here. The decoration, despite the patterned *zellij* and carved plaster, gives off an air of tranquillity. Visitors to the mausoleum must be respectfully dressed, and can look down into the tomb from a gallery.

Chellah   HISTORIC SITE
(Map p186; cnr Ave Yacoub al-Mansour & Blvd Moussa ibn Nassair; admission Dh10; ☺9am-

One day

Start with a delicious breakfast at the **Pâtisserie Majestic** before browsing the **bookshops** on Ave Mohammed V. A stroll through the **medina** will bring you to a superb lunch at **Riad Oudaya**. Cross Blvd Tariq al-Marsa and enter the **Kasbah des Oudaias** through the spectacular gate, Bab Oudaia. Climb to the top for magnificent views, then head to **Galerle d'Art Nouiga**. Stop for tea at **Café Maure** overlooking the Bou Regreg river. Take a taxi to the **Archaeology Museum** to see the famous Volubilis bronzes. By this time, you'll have earned a beer on the terrace at the **Hôtel Balima**, before dinner at the swish **Le Grand Comptoir**.

Two days

Take the tram to **Salé** for a Moroccan-style breakfast at a cafe on **Place Bab Khebaz**. Head into the medina to view the beautiful **Grand Mosque and zawiyas** (shrines). Wander down to the river and be rowed across to Rabat, have fish for lunch at **Borj Eddar** overlooking the ocean, then take a taxi to the **Tour Hassan** and **Mausoleum of Mohammed V**. Another short taxi ride gets you to the **Chellah**, perfect for an afternoon stroll. For dinner, **L'Entrecôte** in trendy Agdal hits the spot, before dancing the night away at **Amnesia**.

5.30pm) Abandoned, crumbling and overgrown, the old Roman city of Sala Colonia and the Merenid necropolis of Chellah is one of Rabat's most evocative sights. The Phoenicians were the first to settle on the grassy slopes above the river, but the town grew when the Romans took control in about AD 40. The city was abandoned in 1154 in favour of Salé, but in the 14th century the Merenid sultan Abou al-Hassan Ali built a necropolis on top of the Roman site and surrounded it with the towers and defensive wall that stand today.

Overgrown by fruit trees and wild flowers, it is an atmospheric place to roam around. From the main gate, a path heads down through fragrant fig, olive and orange trees to a **viewing platform** that overlooks the ruins of the Roman city. Making out the structures takes a bit of imagination, but the mystery is part of the magic of this place. A path leads through the ruins of the triple-arched entrance known as the Arc de Triomphe, past the Jupiter Temple (to the left) and to the forum (at the end of the main road), while another goes to the octagonal Pool of the Nymph, part of the Roman system of water distribution.

Far easier to discern are the remains of the **Islamic complex**, with its elegant minaret now topped by a stork's nest. An incredible colony of storks has taken over the ruins, lording over the site from their tree-top nests. If you visit in spring, the clacking bills of mating pairs is a wonderful soundtrack to a visit.

Near the ruined minaret is the **tomb of Abou al-Hassan Ali** and his wife, complete with ornate *zellij* ornamentation. A small *medersa* is nearby, where the remains of pillars, students' cells and scalloped pools – as well as the blocked-off mihrab (prayer niche) – are still discernable. On leaving the mosque, the path passes the **tombs** of several saints on the far right. To the left, the murky waters of a walled pool (marked *'bassin aux anguilles'*) still attract women who believe that feeding boiled eggs to the eels here brings fertility and easy childbirth.

CENTRAL RABAT

Archaeology Museum   MUSEUM
(Map p190; ☑0537 70 19 19; 23 Rue al-Brihi Parent; admission Dh10; ☺9am-4.30pm Wed-Mon) The interesting (even if the labels are only in Arabic and French) Archaeology Museum gives a good account of Morocco's history. Prehistoric finds include a beautiful Neolithic rock carving of a man surrounded by concentric circles. The highlight of the collection is the **Salle des Bronzes**, which displays ceramics, statuary and artefacts from the Roman settlements at Volubilis, Lixus and Chellah. Look out for the beautiful head of Juba II and don't miss the tiny acrobats – all found at Volubilis. The fate of the artefacts here is unsure, as a new ethnographical museum is planned as well as a museum at Volubilis itself.

ATLANTIC COAST RABAT

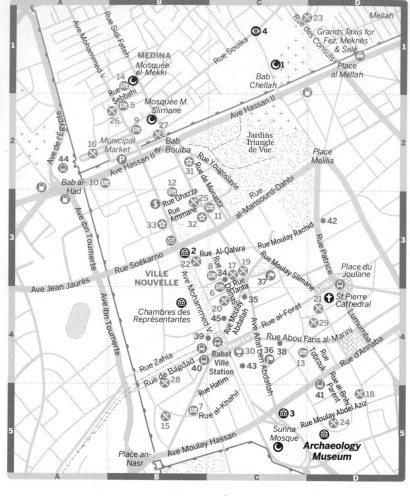

FREE **Money Museum** MUSEUM

(Map p190; www.bkam.ma; cnr Ave Mohammed V & Rue Al-Qahira) Housed in the historic Mauresque building of the Bank al-Maghrib, this quirky museum and art gallery will tell you everything you want to know about the history of coinage.

Museum of Contemporary Art
MUSEUM, GALLERY

(Map p190; Ave Moulay Hassan) Under construction at the time of research, this will be the first public gallery of contemporary art in Morocco.

🏃 Activities

Oudayas Surf Club
WATER SPORTS

(Map p186; ☎0537 26 06 83; Plage des Oudaias; 90min surfboard/bodyboard lesson Dh250/180) King Mohammed VI was a founding member of this club.

Club Nautique de la Plage de Rabat
WATER SPORTS

(Map p186; ☎0537 26 16 09; www.cnpr@menara.ma; Plage des Oudaias) Below the kasbah, this club offers similar services and equipment rental.

📷 Courses

Rabat has many language schools offering year-long courses, but the following offer short-term classes:

Center for Cross-Cultural Learning   LANGUAGES
(CCCL; Map p186; ☎ 0537 20 23 65; www.cccl -ma.com; Ave Laalou, 11 Zankat Hassani) Intensive short courses in Modern Standard and Moroccan Arabic.

Institute for Language & Communication Studies   LANGUAGES
(Map p186; ☎ 0537 67 59 68; www.ilcs.ac.ma; 29 Rue Oukaimeden, Agdal) Offers intensive courses and private tuition in Modern Standard and Moroccan Arabic, as well as Amazigh.

✨ Festivals & Events

Rabat hosts a number of festivals and events each year.

Festival Mawazine   LIVE MUSIC
(www.mawazine.ma) Held in May, this festival draws big names from the world-music scene.

Festival International de Rabat   LIVE MUSIC, FILM
(www.rabatfilmfestival.org, in French) The biggest drawcard, attracting hoards of music lovers and film buffs to the capital for two weeks in late June and early July.

🛏 Sleeping

Most of Rabat's better accommodation is in the new city between Ave Mohammed V and Ave Abderrahman, while the old medina has a host of low-budget dives and a couple

DON'T MISS

KASBAH LES OUDAIAS

The **kasbah** (Map p186) occupies the oldest part of the city, the site of the original *ribat*, and commands magnificent views over the river and ocean from its cliff-top perch. Predominately residential, with tranquil alleys and whitewashed houses mostly built by Muslim refugees from Spain, this is a picturesque place to wander. Many foreigners are buying up the houses here, and it's easy to see the appeal. Some 'guides' offer their services but there is no need.

The 12th-century Almohad **Bab Oudaia** (Map p186), the most dramatic kasbah gate, is elaborately decorated with a series of carved arches. Inside the gateway, the main street, Rue Jamaa, runs straight through the kasbah. About 200m ahead on the left is the **Mosque el-Atiqa** (Map p186), the oldest mosque in Rabat, built in the 12th century and restored in the 18th century. You'll also find a number of low-key tourist shops and a couple of art galleries, such as the **Galerie d'Art Nouiga** (Map p186), along this street.

At the end of the street is the **Plateforme du Sémaphore** (Signal Platform) with sweeping views over the estuary and across to Salé. The elevated position provided an excellent defence against sea-going attackers negotiating the sandbanks below.

Returning from the Plateforme, turn left down Rue Bazzo, a narrow winding street that leads down to the popular **Café Maure** (p196) and a side entrance to the formal **Andalusian Gardens** (☼sunrise-sunset). The gardens, laid out by the French during the colonial period, occupy the palace grounds and make a wonderful shady retreat.

The palace itself is a grand 17th-century affair built by Moulay Ismail. The building now houses the **Musée des Oudaias** (Map p186; admission Dh10), the national jewellery museum with a fascinating collection of prehistoric, Roman and Islamic jewellery found in the different regions of Morocco.

of upmarket riads (townhouses set around an internal garden). Rabat caters mainly for business travellers and has a disproportionate number of top-end hotels.

The medina and kasbah are full of budget hotels that are pretty basic and many lack any kind of creature comforts, including showers. However, there are some good options, too, listed here. Rabat has a limited choice of midrange accommodation, most of it located on or just off Ave Mohammed V. The city offers all the usual top international chain hotels, but for something with a little more local flavour the medina options offer ultrachic style and service.

VILLE NOUVELLE

Le Piétri Urban Hotel   HOTEL €€
(Map p190; ☎0537 70 78 20; www.lepi etri.com; 4 Rue Tobrouk; s/d Dh720/790; ❄☎) Awarded the La Cle Verte for sustainable practices, this good-value boutique hotel in a quiet street in a central, but more residential, part of town, is modern and chic. The 36 spacious bright rooms with wooden floors are comfortable, well equipped and decorated in warm colours in a contemporary style. Fifth-floor rooms have huge

balconies. The hotel has an excellent restaurant, Les Sessions du Piétri (see p195).

Hôtel Balima   HOTEL €€
(Map p190; ☎0537 70 77 55; www.hotel-bali ma.net; Ave Mohammed V; s/d incl breakfast Dh543/716; ❄) The grand dame of Rabat hotels is showing its age a bit, but still offers newly decorated and comfortable en-suite rooms, all immaculately kept and with great views over the city. The hotel has a decent restaurant and nightclub. The glorious shady terrace facing Ave Mohammed V is still the place to meet in Rabat.

Hôtel Royal   HOTEL €€
(Map p190; ☎0537 72 11 71; www.mtds.com/roy alhotel; 1 Rue Ammane; s/d Dh528/748) In a very central location, the Royal has tastefully renovated rooms that are very comfortable, with polished wooden furniture, new mattresses and sparkling clean bathrooms. The rooms on the 4th floor have the best views over the park and city, are quieter and come with a large terrace. An adequate breakfast is served in the downstairs restaurant.

Hotel Central   HOTEL €
(Map p190; ☎0537 70 73 56; 2 Rue Al-Basra; s/d Dh100/150, s/d with bathroom Dh150/200, hot

shower Dh10) Opposite the imposing Balima and right in the heart of town, the Hotel Central has a good-value range of simple rooms. It's a little past its best, but remains a friendly place handy to everything in town.

Hôtel Majestic
HOTEL €

(Map p190; ☑0537 72 29 97; www.hotelmajestic. ma; 121 Ave Hassan II; s/d Dh284/348) Another excellent option, though not as palatial as it sounds. Readers recommend this modern place with smallish rooms and sleek new furniture and fittings – if not a lot of character. Despite the double glazing the rooms can be noisy, so it's best to forgo the medina view for a room at the back.

Hôtel Bélère
HOTEL €€

(Map p190; ☑0537 20 33 01/2; www.belerehotels. com; 33 Ave Moulay Youssef; s/d Dh677/888; ☺✳☏) This four-star hotel is a step up from the other options in this price range and offers small but extremely comfortable nonsmoking rooms with tasteful (albeit very 1970s) modern decor, now back in fashion. It has a bar and restaurant and it's handy to the train station.

MEDINA & KASBAH

TOP CHOICE Riad Oudaya
RIAD €€€

(Map p190; ☑0537 70 23 92; www.riadra bat.com; 46 Rue Sidi Fateh; d/ste Dh1300/1650) Tucked away down an alleyway in the medina, this gorgeous guesthouse is a real hidden gem. The rooms around a spectacular courtyard are tastefully decorated with a blend of Moroccan style and Western comfort. Subtle lighting, open fireplaces, balconies and the gentle gurgling of the

fountain in the tiled courtyard below complete the romantic appeal. Meals here are sublime but need to be ordered in advance (see p195).

Hôtel Dorhmi
HOTEL €

(Map p190; ☑0537 72 38 98; 313 Ave Mohammed V; s/d/tr Dh80/130/195, hot shower Dh10) Immaculately kept, very friendly and keenly priced, this family-run hotel is the best of the medina cheapies. The simple rooms are bright and tidy and surround a central courtyard on the 1st floor above the Banque Populaire. Despite being in the hub of things, the Dorhmi (also spelt Doghmi) offers quiet rooms.

Hôtel al-Maghrib al-Jadid
HOTEL €

(Map p190; ☑0537 73 22 07; 2 Rue Sebbahi; s/d Dh80/120, hot shower Dh10) Although the rooms at this hotel are fairly small and spartan, they are pristinely clean, and have shuttered windows that let in lots of light. You'll either love or hate the shocking pink walls but it's all part of the rather quirky character of this place.

Hôtel Splendid
HOTEL €

(Map p190; ☑0537 72 32 83; 8 Rue Ghazza; s/d Dh125/160, with bathroom Dh190/230) Slapbang in the heart of the medina, the spacious, bright rooms with high ceilings, big windows, cheerful colours and simple wooden furniture are set around a pleasant courtyard. Bathrooms are modern and rooms without bathrooms have a hot-water washbasin.

Dar Al Batoul
RIAD €€€

(Map p186; ☑0537 72 72 50, 0661 40 11 81; www. riadbatoul.com; 7 Derb Jirari; d/ste Dh870/1400;

RABAT FOR CHILDREN

Hassle-free shopping in the souqs and the impressive **kasbah** make Rabat a pleasant place to visit with children. The **Chellah** offers a wide open space. However, there are few specific attractions in the city for younger visitors. The best bet is to head out of town to the beach, or the **Jardins Exotiques**.

The 52-hectare **Jardin Zoologique de Rabat** (zoological gardens) northwest of Temara was being upgraded at the time of research. Long a neglected place with concrete pens for the animals, the new zoo, due to open at the end of 2011, is partially funded by the Emirates and will offer an aquarium, night safaris and children's activities in large, park-like surroundings.

The **Poney Club de Rabat** (☑0537 66 63 63; www.poneyclubderabat.ifrance.com; 45min private lesson Dh150), to the west of town, offers riding lessons and events for children and has English-speaking staff.

Across the river in Salé is the **Magic Park** (off Map p199; ☑0535 88 59 90; Rte N6; admission Dh10; ☺12.30-11pm Mon-Fri, 4.30-11pm Sat & Sun) with rides and cafes, providing just about enough entertainment to while away an afternoon.

☎) This grand 18th-century merchant's house has been transformed into a sumptuous hotel with just eight rooms in traditional Moroccan style. Centred on a graceful columned courtyard, each room is different, with stunning combinations of fabrics, stained glass and intricate tilework.

Riad Kasbah RIAD €€
(Map p186; ☑0537 70 52 47; www.riadrabat.com; 49 Rue Zirara; s/d Dh700/770) Set in the heart of the kasbah away from the hubbub of the city, this sublimely peaceful guesthouse is a sister property to the Riad Oudaya. Although the decor is much plainer, this pretty house has five rooms arranged around the garden.

✖ Eating

Rabat has a wonderful choice of restaurants from cheap and cheerful holes-in-the-wall to upmarket gourmet pads feeding the city's legions of politicians and diplomats.

The best place for quick, cheap food in Rabat is on Ave Mohammed V just inside the medina gate. Here you'll find a slew of small joints dishing out tajines, brochettes, salads and chips for cheap and cheaper. You'll know the best ones by the queue of locals waiting patiently to be served.

Another good spot is around Rue Tanta in the ville nouvelle, where you'll find a selection of fast-food joints serving everything from burgers and brochettes to pizza and panini.

VILLE NOUVELLE

TOP CHOICE **Le Petit Beur – Dar Tajine** LOCAL €€
(Map p190; ☑0537 73 13 22; 8 Rue Damas; mains Dh100; ⊙lunch & dinner Mon-Sat; ☻) A modest little place renowned for its excellent Moroccan food, from succulent tajines and heavenly couscous to one of the best *pastillas* in town, and it's licensed. It's quieter at lunchtime but livens up at night when the waiters double as musicians and play oud (lute) music to accompany your meal. Book ahead or get there early as it fills up quickly.

La Veranda MEDITERRANEAN €€
(Map p190; ☑0674 84 12 44; Institut Français, 1 Rue Abou Inane; mains Dh80-130; ⊙lunch & dinner Mon-Sat) Run by the same owner as Le Grand Comptoir, this loft-style restaurant, in a modernist villa with a pleasant garden under majestic palm trees, is the place to be at lunchtime. It serves good contemporary French-Mediterranean bistro food from a changing menu written on a blackboard.

The staff are young and trendy. It's just behind the church at the French Institute.

Le Grand Comptoir FRENCH €€€
(Map p190; ☑0537 20 15 14; www.legrandcomptoir.ma; 279 Ave Mohammed V; mains Dh100-160; ⊙lunch & dinner; ☎) Sleek, stylish and oozing the charms of an old-world Parisienne brasserie, this suave restaurant and lounge bar woos customers with its chic surroundings and classic French menu. Candelabras, giant palms and contemporary art adorn the grand salon while a pianist tinkles in the background. Go for the fresh fish or be brave and try the *andouillette* (tripe sausage) or veal kidneys. A good place to have breakfast or coffee, or an aperitif.

Tajine wa Tanja LOCAL €€
(Map p190; ☑0537 72 97 97; 9 Rue de Baghdad; mains Dh80; ⊙lunch & dinner Mon-Sat; ☎) Down-to-earth Moroccan dishes are the speciality at this small, friendly restaurant near the train station. Choose from a range of wood-fired grills or tajines prepared to traditional recipes, or make a special outing for the magnificent Friday couscous. It's a fairly quiet spot, and not so intimidating for women travelling alone.

Pâtisserie Majestic PATISSERIE €
(Map p190; cnr Rue Ammane & Ave Allal ben Abdallah) An excellent and extremely popular patisserie, perfect for breakfast or an afternoon cake with superb coffee, and right in the centre of town.

Ty Potes MEDITERRANEAN €€
(Map p190; ☑0537 70 79 65; 11 Rue Ghafsa; set menu Dh100; ⊙lunch Tue-Sun, dinner Thu-Sun) A pleasant and welcoming lunch spot and teahouse, serving sweet and savoury crepes, healthy salads and sandwiches. It's popular with well-heeled locals. The atmosphere is more European, with a little garden at the back, and the Sunday brunch is particularly well attended.

La Mamma ITALIAN €€
(Map p190; ☑0537 70 73 29; 6 Rue Tanta; mains from Dh80; ⊙lunch & dinner) It looks pretty dark from the outside, but this Italian-owned old favourite serves some of the best pizza and pasta in town. The beamed ceilings and candlelit tables add a touch of 1970s romantic atmosphere, and the wood-fired pizzas and grilled meats will leave you planning a return visit. There's a good wine list, and women will feel comfortable here.

Cafe Weimar
CAFE €

(Map p190; 7 Rue Sana'a; pizzas Dh80) This hip cafe in the Goethe Institut is where the young and beautiful hang out for cake and coffee or lunch. It also does a simple Mediterranean menu and is a good spot for Sunday brunch. Book ahead, but there are no reservations on Friday and Saturday.

La Koutoubia
LOCAL €€

(Map p190; ☑0537 70 10 75; 10 Pierre Parent; mains Dh80; ☺lunch & dinner) Old-fashioned Moroccan restaurant with plenty of traditional *zellij* and colourful painted panels. All the classic Moroccan dishes are on the menu here, including tajines and couscous, but labour-intensive specialities like pigeon *pastilla* or *mechoui* (roast lamb) need to be ordered in advance. Good wine list.

L'R du Gout
FRENCH €€

(Map p190; ☑0537 76 06 10; 8 Rue Moulay Abd el-Aziz; set lunch menu Dh160; ☺lunch & dinner) This large restaurant with a colourful interior – a blend of French bistro and Moroccan flair – is run by young Frenchmen. The menu serves traditional French brasserie food such as foie gras, veal kidneys, and steak with a pepper sauce.

La Dolce Vita
ICE CREAM €

(Map p190; 8 Rue Tanta) Delicious homemade Italian gelato comes in a dozen flavours. It's next to the Italian La Mamma restaurant.

MEDINA & KASBAH

Riad Oudaya
LOCAL €€€

(Map p190; ☑0537 70 23 92; 46 Rue Sidi Fateh; lunch/dinner set menu Dh220/330) This lovely restaurant squirreled away behind a wooden door in the depths of the medina is reason enough to come to Rabat. Set in a gorgeous riad, it dishes up gourmet five-course dinners featuring anything from juicy tajines or *pastilla* to stuffed calamari.

Restaurant el-Bahia
LOCAL €

(Map p190; Ave Hassan II; mains Dh60; ☺lunch & dinner) Built into the outside of the medina walls and a good spot for people-watching, this laid-back restaurant has the locals lapping up hearty Moroccan fare. Sit on the pavement terrace, in the shaded courtyard or upstairs in the traditional salon.

Restaurant Dinarjat
LOCAL €€€

(Map p186; ☑0537 72 42 39; 6 Rue Belgnaoui; meals Dh300-400; ☺lunch & dinner) Stylish and elegant, Dinarjat is a favourite with well-heeled locals and visitors alike. It's set in a superb 17th-century, Andalusian-style house at the heart of the medina, and has been carefully restored and decorated in a contemporary style but in keeping with tradition. The restaurant is an ode to the Arab-Andalusian art of living with its sumptuous architecture, refined traditional food and peaceful oud music. The tajines, couscous and salads are prepared with the freshest ingredients, using little fat, and are surprisingly light. Book in advance.

Les Sessions du Piétri
FUSION €€

(Map p190; ☑0537 70 91 30; Hotel Le Piétri, 4 Rue Tobrouk; mains from Dh80; ☺lunch & dinner) This newly refurbished restaurant is where the bright young things come for a drink after work, and stay on for dinner. There are live concerts on Tuesday, Friday and Saturday. An eclectic menu features everything from Asian chicken to steaks, Atlas trout to mussels, and a chocolate fondue for dessert.

Le Ziryab
LOCAL €€€

(Map p190; ☑0537 73 36 36; 10 Zankat Ennajar; set menus from Dh400; ☺lunch & dinner) This chic Moroccan restaurant is in a magnificent building just off Rue des Consuls. The blend of old-world character and stylish contemporary design is reflected in the excellent menu of interesting variations on tajine, couscous, *pastilla*, and grilled meat and fish.

Restaurant de la Libération
LOCAL €

(Map p190; 256 Ave Mohammed V; mains Dh60; ☺lunch & dinner) Cheap, cheerful and marginally more classy than the string of other eateries along this road (it's got plastic menus and tablecloths), this basic restaurant does a steady line in traditional favourites. Friday is couscous day when giant platters of the stuff are delivered to the eager masses.

Borj Eddar
SEAFOOD €€

(Map p186; ☑0537 70 15 00; mains Dh120; ☺lunch & dinner) Just outside the kasbah down at the beach, this restaurant overlooking the sea has a menu of excellent fresh fish and seafood dishes. The next door **Restaurant de la Plage** has a similar menu and the same views, if the Borj Eddar is full. There's little to choose between them: both have glass-fronted terraces overlooking the ocean.

AGDAL

Bert's
CAFE €€

(Map p186; ☑0802 00 07 07; cnr Ave de France & Rue Melouya) This very stylish cafe in smart Agdal dishes up a seasonal menu of vitamin-packed salads and sandwiches, very special desserts and fresh fruit juices, and they deliver from 8am to 10pm Monday to Saturday.

L'Entrecôte
FRENCH €€€

(Map p186; ☑0537 67 11 08; 74 Blvd al-Amir Fal Ould Omar; mains Dh180; ⊙lunch & dinner) The menu and attitude at this upmarket, old-style restaurant in Agdal are very French but the dark woods and rough plaster are more reminiscent of Bavaria than Bordeaux. Steak, fish and game specialities dominate the classic French menu, and to further confuse the ambience there's jazz or traditional Spanish music at night.

Paul
MEDITERRANEAN €€

(Map p186; 2 Ave al-Oumam al-Muttahida) This French bakery and patisserie is the place to hang out in Rabat, serving the best croissants in town for breakfast, good sandwiches, somewhat tired salads and a light menu throughout the day. Sit in the elegant interior or on the pleasant, if noisy, streetside terrace.

Galapagos Café
CAFE €

(Map p186; 14 Blvd al-Amir Fal Ould Omar) Slick cafe-terrace with dark-wood panelling, contemporary furniture and floor-to-ceiling windows. It's popular with young professionals for its ice cream, pizzas, panini and people-watching.

SELF-CATERING

The medina is the best place to go for self-catering supplies.

Fruit & Vegetable Market
MARKET

(Map p190; Ave Hassan II) The indoor market has a fantastic choice of fresh produce, dried fruits and nuts. You should be able to find everything else you need (including booze) at the surrounding stalls or along Rue Souika and near Bab el-Bouiba.

Hypermarché Marjane
SUPERMARKET

(off Map p186; ⊙7am-7pm) You'll find Western food at this vast place on the road to Salé.

Drinking

Most Rabat bars are pretty intimidating for women. The more modern, popular joints are a safer bet.

Café Maure
CAFE

(Map p184; Kasbah des Oudaias) Sit back, relax and just gaze out over the estuary to Salé from this chilled, open-air cafe spread over several terraces in the Andalusian Gardens. Mint tea is the thing here, accompanied by little almond biscuits delivered on silver trays. It's an easy place to pass time writing postcards, and a relaxed venue for women.

Cafetéria du 7ème Art
CAFE

(Map p190; Ave Allal ben Abdallah) Set in the shady grounds of a cinema, this popular outdoor cafe attracts a mixed clientele of students and professionals. It's a relaxed place serving snacks such as pizza and panini.

El Rancho
BAR

(off Map p186; ☑0667 33 00 30; 30 Rue Mischliffen, Agdal) Tex-Mex restaurant and bar where Rabat's well-heeled go for a bite and a drink before clubbing. The atmosphere on weekends is electric, when the world-music beat gets turned up a few notches.

Le Puzzle
BAR

(off Map p186; ☑0537 67 00 30; 79 Ave ibn Sina, Agdal; ⊙closed lunch Sun) A happening bar-restaurant in Agdal, favoured by suburban sophisticates. It has a strange mix of traditional style and modern design but pulls in the punters with half-price beer and daily live gigs (except for Wednesday and Sunday karaoke nights).

Hôtel Balima
BAR

(Map p190; ☑0537 70 77 55; Ave Mohammed V) Less self-conscious than the chic town bars and an excellent place to watch Rabat go by, the leafy terrace in front of the Balima is a great place to just see and be seen. It's a relaxed place for women and pleasantly cool on summer nights. There's beer only on the terrace.

Henry's Bar
BAR

(Map p190; Place des Alaouites) If you're in search of old-time local haunts rather than squeaky-clean trendsetters, there are some dingy bars around Pl des Alaouites. Henry's is an old favourite, a staunchly male-only preserve where the smoke is thick and the alcohol neat. It's open all day but closes by about 10pm.

☆ Entertainment

Rabat has a large international community and plenty of young, well-heeled and well-educated locals looking for entertainment so there's usually a good choice of events on offer. Check the French-language newspapers for listings.

Nightclubs

Rabat's nightlife is a lot more limited – and subdued – than Casablanca's but there's still a fairly good range of clubs to choose from. All the large hotels have their own discos, usually fairly standard fare, and there's a few try-hard theme clubs where you need plenty of booze to numb the decor. Expect to pay about Dh150 to Dh200 to get in and the same for drinks, and dress up or you won't even make it past the door.

Amnesia   NIGHTCLUB
(Map p190; 18 Rue de Monastir) The hippest club in downtown Rabat, this USA-themed place (complete with a diner-style backroom) buzzes most nights of the week. The music is pretty standard chart pop but the young socialites who come here just lap it up.

5th Avenue   NIGHTCLUB
(Map p186; 5 Rue Bin al-Widane, Agdal) Another US-themed bar, this one styled on a Moroccan impression of New York, it plays a better range of music than the others and features everything from hip hop to techno to Middle Eastern.

Cinema

Most films are dubbed in French, unless marked as *'version originale'*.

Cinéma Renaissance   CINEMA
(Map p190; 360 Ave Mohammed V; orchestra/balcony Dh40/50) This large cinema complex on the main drag shows mainstream Hollywood flicks.

Cinéma du 7ème Art   CINEMA
(Map p190; Ave Allal ben Abdallah; admission Dh35) A good bet for more local offerings and art-house films, this cinema shows mainly Moroccan, Middle Eastern and European films.

🛍 Shopping

Rabat's great shopping secret is its laid-back merchants. There's little pressure to buy, so you can stroll the stalls in relative peace, but there is also less room to bargain. The souqs still have a fair bit of good handicrafts, particularly in and around the Rue des Consuls in the medina and Blvd Tariq al-Marsa towards the kasbah. You'll find everything in this area from jewellery, silks and pottery to *zellij* and carved wooden furniture.

Weaving is one of the most important traditional crafts in Rabat, and the more formal, Islamic style (see p460) is still favoured. On Tuesday and Thursday mornings women descend from the villages to auction their carpets to local salesmen at the carpet souq off Rue des Consuls, a great sight even though tourists are not allowed in on the action.

For fixed prices head for the **Ensemble Artisanal** (Map p186; Blvd Tariq al-Marsa), which sells a good selection of crafts. For ceramics, your best bet is to head across to Salé to the Complexe des Potiers (p201).

ⓘ Information

Emergency
SAMU (☑0537 73 73 73) Private ambulance service.

SOS Médecins (☑0537 20 21 23; house call Dh400; ☺24hr) Doctors on call.

Internet Access
Internet (Rue Tanta; per hr Dh8; ☺9am-7.30pm) Next to La Mamma.

Medical Services
Town pharmacies open nights and weekends on a rotational basis; check the rota posted in French and Arabic in all pharmacy windows.

Hôpital Ibn Sina/Avicennes (off Map p186; ☑0537 67 28 71, emergencies 0537 67 44 50; Pl Ibn Sina, Agdal)

Money
Numerous banks (with ATMs) are concentrated along Ave Mohammed V and the parallel Ave Al-lal ben Abdallah, including Banque Populaire.

BMCE (Ave Mohammed V)

Post
DHL (☑0537 77 99 34; Ave de France, Agdal)
Main post office (cnr Rue Soékarno & Ave Mohammed V)

Tourist Information
Office National Marocain du Tourisme (ONMT; off Map p186; ☑0537 67 40 13; visit-morocco@onmt.org.ma; cnr Rues Oued el-Makhazine & Zalaka, Agdal) Smiles and vacant faces await at this bureaucratic office. To get here, take bus 3 from the train station or take a taxi.

Travel Agencies
CAP Tours (Map p190; ☑0537 73 35 71; www.captours.ma; 7 Rue Damas) A good place for cheap flights to African destinations; also makes ferry reservations.

MAPS

Rabat is one of the few places in Morocco where you can get a range of topographical Moroccan maps and town plans. The **Direction de la Cartographie** (off Map p186; ☑0537 23 08 30; www.ancfcc.gov.ma, in French; Ave Hassan II km4; ⊗9am-3.30pm) sells topography maps, but staff can be sensitive about selling some maps. Take your passport. Most maps need to be ordered and can be picked up 48 hours later.

Carlson Wagonlit (Map p190; ☑0537 70 96 25; www.carlsonwagonlit.com; 1 Ave Moulay Abdallah)

ℹ Getting There & Away

AIR Tiny Rabat-Salé Airport, 10km northeast of town, only has direct flights to Paris with **Royal Air Maroc** (RAM; Map p190; ☑0537 70 97 66; www.royalairmaroc.com; Ave Mohammed V) and **Jet4You** (www.jet4you.com). A grand taxi to the airport will cost about Dh250. There are no buses.

BUS Rabat has two bus stations – the main **gare routière** (Map p186; Place Mohammed Zerktouni) where most buses depart and arrive, and the less chaotic **CTM station** (off Map p186), situated about 3km southwest of the city centre on the road to Casablanca. The main station has a **left-luggage service** (per item per day Dh5; ⊗6am-11pm). To get to the town centre from either station, take bus 30 (Dh5), the tram or a petit taxi (Dh30).

Arriving by bus from the north, you may pass through central Rabat, so it's worth asking if you can be dropped off in town. Otherwise, you could save some time by alighting at Salé and taking the tram into central Rabat. Buses include:

Agadir Dh220, 10 hours, three daily

Casablanca Dh35, 1½ hours, every hour

Er-Rachidia Dh155, 10 hours, one daily

Fez Dh70, 3½ hours, nine daily

Laâyoune Dh420, 22½ hours, one daily

Marrakesh Dh130, five hours, 10 daily

Nador Dh155, 9½ hours, one daily

Oujda Dh155, 9½ hours, one daily

Tangier Dh100, 4½ hours, five daily

Tetouan Dh100, five hours, one daily

There are also international services to Barcelona (Dh1220), Madrid (Dh940) and Paris (Dh1380).

CAR Rabat has no shortage of local car-rental agencies – most of which offer cheaper rates than these international agencies.

Avis (Map p190; ☑0537 72 18 18; 7 Rue Abou Faris al-Marini)

Budget (Map p190; ☑0530 20 05 20; Rabat Ville train station, Ave Mohammed V)

Europcar (Map p190; ☑0537 72 23 28; 25 Rue Patrice Lumumba)

Hertz (Map p190; ☑0537 70 73 66; 467 Ave Mohammed V).

City-centre parking restrictions apply from 8am to noon and 2pm to 7pm Monday to Saturday; meters cost Dh3 per hour. There's a convenient car park near the junction of Ave Hassan II and Ave Mohammed V.

TAXI Grands taxis leave for Casablanca (Dh40) from just outside the intercity bus station. Other grands taxis leave for Fez (Dh60), Meknès (Dh45) and Salé (Dh5) from a lot off Ave Hassan II behind the Hôtel Bou Regreg.

TRAIN Train is the most convenient way to arrive in Rabat, as the sparkly new **Rabat Ville train station** (Map p190) is right in the centre of town (not to be confused with Rabat Agdal train station to the west of the city). The station has a food court and wi-fi, as well as Budget car-rental and Supratours offices.

Trains run every 30 minutes from 6am to 10.30pm between Rabat Ville and Casa-Port train stations (Dh35) and Kenitra (Dh15, 30 minutes). Taking the train to Mohammed V Airport (Dh75, 1½ hours) in Casablanca requires a change at Casa Voyageurs or at Aïn Sebaa.

On all long-distance routes there's always one late-night *ordinaire* train among the rapide services (see p520 for information on train classes). Second-class *rapide* services include Fez (Dh80, three hours, hourly), Marrakesh (Dh120, 4½ hours, nine daily), Meknès (Dh 65, two hours), Oujda (Dh180, nine hours, three daily), Tangier (Dh95, four hours, eight daily) and Taza (Dh111, five hours).

ℹ Getting Around

BUS Some useful bus routes (Dh4) are listed below:

Buses 2 & 4 Ave Moulay Hassan to Bab Zaer, for the Chellah.

Bus 3 Rabat Ville train station to Agdal.

Buses 12 & 13 Place Melilla to Salé.

Buses 17 & 30 From near Bab al-Had to Rabat's gare routière via the map office; 17 goes on past the zoo to Temara Beach.

Bus 33 From Bab al-Had to Temara Beach.

 TAXI Rabat's blue petits taxis are plentiful, cheap and quick. A ride around the centre of town will cost about Dh15 to Dh20. There's a petit-taxi rank near the entrance of the medina on Ave Hassan II and at the train station.

TRAM The tramway system links Rabat with Salé and serves stations across the city. The fare is DH7.

NORTH OF RABAT

Salé سلا

POP 500,000

Still a long way from its lively counterpart and old rival on the other bank of the Oued Bou Regreg, Salé is a quiet and traditional kind of place, where time seems to have stood still. But all that is about to change with the massive project to bring the city into the 21st century that was about to be completed at the time of research: the new tramway, new bridge and a new development with apartments and shopping malls.

The centre of Salé feels more like a typical Moroccan village with its narrow alleys, old medina houses and beautiful monuments, but beyond it lies a sprawling town with characterless apartment buildings, mostly home to Rabat commuters. People are noticeably more conservative here, and the dress code is a lot tighter.

People began to settle in Salé in the 10th century and the town grew in importance as inhabitants of the older settlement at Sala Colonia began to move across the river to the new town. Warring among local tribes was still rampant at this stage and it was the Almohads who took control of the area in the 12th century, establishing neighbouring Rabat as a base for expeditions to Spain.

Spanish freebooters attacked in 1260; in response the Merenids fortified the town, building defensive walls and a canal to Bab Mrisa to allow safe access for shipping. The

Salé

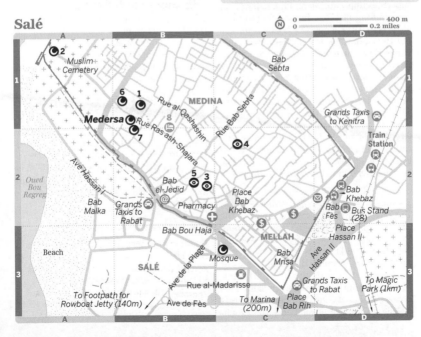

town began to flourish and established valuable trade links with Venice, Genoa, London and the Netherlands.

As trade thrived so too did piracy, and by the 16th century the twin towns prospered from the activities of the infamous Sallee Rovers pirates. It was here that Robinson Crusoe was brought into the town in Daniel Defoe's novel.

By the 19th century the pirates had been brought under control, Rabat had been made capital and Salé sank into obscurity.

☉ Sights

Salé is worth a day trip from Rabat. The main entrance to the medina is Bab Bou Haja, on the southwestern wall, which opens onto Pl Bab Khebaz. From here walk north to the souqs, and find the Grande Mosquée 500m further northwest along Rue Ras ash-Shajara (also known as Rue de la Grande Mosquée). Alternatively walk along the road that runs inside the city walls past Bab Bou Haja and Bab Malka for a more straightforward approach.

Grande Mosquée & Medersa   MOSQUE, MEDERSA

Central to life in pious Salé and one of the oldest religious establishments in the country, the Grand Mosquée and *medersa* are superb examples of Merenid artistry. They were built in 1333 by Almohad Sultan Abou al-Hassan Ali. The mosque is closed to non-Muslims, but the splendid **medersa** (admission Dh10) is open as a museum. Similar to those in Fez or Meknès, it takes the form of a small courtyard surrounded by a gallery. The walls are blanketed in intricate decoration from the *zellij* base to the carved stucco and elegant cedar woodwork.

Small student cells surround the gallery on the upper floor, from where you can climb to the flat roof, which has excellent views of Salé and across to Rabat. The guardian who shows you around will expect a small tip.

Shrines   NOTABLE BUILDINGS

To the rear of the Grande Mosquée is the **Zawiya of Sidi Abdallah ibn Hassoun,** the patron saint of Salé. This respected Sufi died in 1604 and is revered by Moroccan travellers in much the same way as St Christopher is revered among Christians. An annual pilgrimage and procession in his honour makes its way through the streets of Salé on the eve of Mouloud (the Proph-

et's birthday). On this day, local fishermen dress in elaborate corsair costumes, while others carry decorated wax sculptures and parade through the streets, ending up at the shrine of the *marabout* (saint).

There are two more shrines in Salé: the **Zawiya of Sidi Ahmed Tijani,** on the lane between the mosque and *medersa,* and the white **Koubba of Sidi ben Ashir at-Taleb** in the cemetery northwest of the mosque.

Souqs   SOUQS

From the Grande Mosquée, head back to the souqs via the Rue Ras ash-Shajara which becomes Rue Mellah el Kadim, a street lined with houses built by wealthy merchants. Shaded by trees and unchanged for centuries, the atmospheric **Souq el-Ghezel** (Wool Market), makes an interesting stop. Here, men and women haggle over the price and quality of rough white wool as it hangs from ancient scales suspended from a large tripod.

In the nearby **Souq el-Merzouk,** textiles, basketwork and jewellery are crafted and sold. Also on sale are the woven grass mats used in mosques, for which Salé is famous. The least interesting souq for travellers is the **Souq el-Kebir,** featuring second-hand clothing and household items.

⏝ Sleeping & Eating

Now that the tram has made Salé more accessible, guesthouses are opening in the medina. There are plenty of hole-in-the-wall cafes in the souqs and surrounding streets, as well as in the area just south of Pl Bab Khebaz.

⬛ The Repose   RIAD €€

(☏0537 88 29 58; www.therepose.com; 17 Zankat Talaa, Ras Chejra; ste Dh650-850; ☏⬛) This traditional medina house has been carefully renovated to provide four delightfully different rooms. The leafy roof terrace is a haven of peace and very private. The knowledgeable owners will help with tours and cooking classes, and only vegetarian food is served.

ⓘ Information

There are a few banks along Rue Fondouk Abd el-Handi.

Perfect Computer (Bab al-Jedid; per hr Dh4; ⏱9am-10pm) Internet access.

Pharmacy (Pl Bab Khebaz).

Getting There & Away

BUS Salé's main bus station is 1km east of the medina, but buses from Rabat also stop outside Bab Mrisa. From Rabat take bus 12, 13, 14, 16 or 34 (Dh5) from Place al-Mellah just off Ave Hassan II, and get off at Bab Khebaz. This is also the place to take the bus back.

TAXI Pick up a taxi in Rabat close to the Hôtel Bou Regreg, on Ave Hassan II; ask for the Bab Bou Haja or Bab Mrisa. From Salé there are departures from Bab el-Jedid and Bab Mrisa (Dh4 one way). Note that petits taxis are not permitted to travel between Rabat and Salé. Grands taxis for Kenitra leave from just north of the train station (Dh15).

TRAIN Trains run to/from Rabat, but the tram or grands taxis are probably the simplest options. Trains north to Kenitra run every 30 minutes (Dh15).

TRAM The easiest way to travel between Rabat and Salé is by tram (Dh7).

Around Rabat & Salé

Complexe des Potiers   ART & CRAFT

(Pottery Cooperative; ☉sunrise-sunset) The village of Oulja, 3km southeast of Salé, is home to the Complexe des Potiers, which produces a huge range of ceramics. The potters work at the back of the complex, bringing in clay from a rich seam in the surrounding hills (you'll see it on the left as you drive in), throwing and turning it on kick wheels, then glazing and firing the finished pieces in enormous kilns. A firing takes 15 hours and reaches 900°C. Fine domestic pottery is fired in gas kilns designed to reduce environmental degradation and air pollution, but more rustic pieces are still fired in kilns fuelled by twigs and leaves from nearby eucalyptus forests.

The centre has a cafe and some workshops used by basket weavers and blacksmiths. To get here, take a petit taxi from Salé (about Dh18) or catch bus 35 or 53 (Dh4) from Bab Khebaz.

Jardins Exotiques   GARDEN

(www.jardinsexotiques, in French; adult/child Dh10/5; ☉9am-5pm winter, to 7pm summer) Created by French horticulturist Marcel François in 1951, these gardens were declared a Natural Heritage site in 2003 and reopened in 2005 after several years of restoration. They are divided into the **Jardin Nature**, plantations that evoke the exotic vegetation the horticulturalist encountered on his many travels; the **Jardin Culture**,

referring more to the philosophy of the garden in different cultures; and the **Jardin Didactique**, with birdcages, an aquarium and a vuivarium. Colour-coded paths lead through overgrown Brazilian rainforest, Polynesian jungle, Japanese pleasure grounds and an Andalusian garden. Jardins Exotiques is managed by the Mohammed VI Foundation for the Protection of the Environment.

The gardens are tranquil on weekends, and are a great place to bring children. It's also a popular spot for courting couples.

The gardens are 13km north of Rabat on the road to Kenitra. Take bus 28 from Ave Moulay Hassan in Rabat, or Bab Fès, the main gate at Salé medina.

Musée Belghazi   MUSEUM

(☎0537 82 21 78; www.museebelghazi.com, in French; main collection Dh50, private rooms by reservation Dh100; ☉9am-7.30pm) The first museum in Morocco has a vast collection of traditional Andalusian, Jewish Moroccan and Islamic arts and crafts amassed by the Belghazi family.

Displays include measuring instruments, (one of the first Belghazis was an astrologist at the Qarawiyin court in Fez), 17th-century carpets, exquisitely carved wooden *minbars* (pulpits from a mosque), doors and ceilings dating from the 10th century, intricate gold and silver jewellery, exceptional pottery and embroidery from Fez, and miniature copies of the Quran. There is a boutique with souvenirs and a restaurant.

The museum is 17km from Salé on the road to Kenitra. Take bus 28 from Ave Moulay Hassan in Rabat or from the main gate of the Salé medina.

Temara Plage   BEACH

There are beautiful beaches close to Rabat, such as the wild and sandy Temara Plage, 13km southwest of the city, popular with surfers and sunbathers alike. It can be reached on bus 17 from Bab al-Had in Rabat.

Plage des Nations   BEACH

The clean, sandy strip of beach at Plage des Nations, 17km north of Rabat, is a popular spot with Rabat locals. It gets some serious wave action, good for surfers, but the currents can be dangerous for swimming.

Above the beach, the **Hôtel Firdaous** (☎0537 82 21 31; www.hotelfird.com; r Dh600; ☒) is remarkable for its original '70s decor. The peeling paint, rusty radiators and threadbare carpets are only just mitigated by rooms with ocean views and new bathrooms. Book in advance to have any chance of a room in summer.

To get to the beach, drive north as far as the Musée Belghazi and turn left down a road known as Sidi Bouknadel. Bus 9 or 48 from Rabat or Salé will drop you at the turn off, from where it's a 2km walk to the beach past huge developments of holiday apartments.

Mehdiya Plage   BEACH
Further north along the coast, 50km from Rabat, is another strip of beach lined with holiday homes and beach bars, but here again the currents are dangerous for swimmers. It gets busy with day trippers in summer but is deserted for the rest of the year. There are regular trains from Rabat to Kenitra, from where you take bus 9 or 15 to Mehdiya. Both of these buses (Dh6) and grands taxis (Dh10) leave from the corner of Rue du Souk el-Baladia and Ave Mohammed Diouri in Kenitra.

Lac de Sidi Bourhaba   NATURE RESERVE
Inland from Mehdiya is the beautiful freshwater Lac de Sidi Bourhaba, part of a larger protected wetland reserve. As a refuelling stop for thousands of birds migrating between Europe and sub-Saharan Africa, the lake provides some of the best birdwatching in the country, especially between October and March. It's also a great place for gentle hiking, with well-appointed walking trails in the forested hills around the lake.

More than 200 species of birds have been spotted here and many choose to winter or nest here – among them a number of rare or endangered species. This is one of the last places on earth where you can still see large numbers of marbled ducks, distinguished by the dark patch around their eyes. Other birds to look out for include the beautiful marsh owl (seen most often at dusk), the crested coot, black-shouldered kite and greater flamingo.

The **information centre** (☎0537 74 72 09; ☺noon-4pm Sat & Sun) on the northern side of the lake is useful but has limited opening hours.

To get to the lake follow the signposts from the beach road to Mehdiya Plage, 300m past the Cafe Restaurant Belle Vue. If you're on foot, the lake is a 3.3km walk from the turn-off.

Moulay Bousselham   مولاي بوسلهام

The idyllic fishing village of Moulay Bousselham is a tranquil place, protected by the shrines of two local saints. The village is slowly expanding, as retired Europeans are starting to buy homes here. There is a sweeping beach (empty for most of the year), friendly people, good fish restaurants and an impressive, internationally important wildfowl reserve. Except for the summer months, this is a great place to spend a few days, with little more to do than birdwatching, fishing or strolling along the beach. Surfers come here for the crashing waves, but the strong currents are dangerous for swimmers. In summer the pace changes dramatically as the village becomes a low-key resort for Moroccans, and the inhabitants swell from around 1000 to 65,000.

Moulay Bousselham is named after a 10th-century Egyptian saint who is commemorated in one of the *koubbas* (shrines) that line the slope down to the sea, and guards the mouth of the river. Moroccans seeking a cure for psychological problems are locked into the tomb for 24 hours. Across the river is another shrine of Sidi Abd el-Galil, believed to cure sterile women. You'll find everything you need along the one main street, including a bank, post office, pharmacy and a couple of internet cafes (Dh8 per hour), but there is no alcohol in town.

⊙ Sights & Activities

Merja Zerga National Park   NATIONAL PARK
One of the great pleasures in Moulay Bousselham, even for the most unconvinced of twitchers, is to take a boat out on Merja Zerga (the Blue Lagoon), preferably with a bird guide who will bring the place to life. The 73-sq-km Merja Zerga National Park (4 sq km of water and the rest marshland) is protected by the Ramsar Convention and attracts thousands of migrant birds, including wildfowl, waders and flamingos in huge numbers, making it one of Morocco's prime birdwatching habitats. The lagoon is between 50cm and 4m deep depending on the tide. Ninety percent of the water comes from the sea, 10% is sweet water from the Oued Dredr, south of the lagoon. At the time of research, the new tourist office was not yet open.

Although the largest flocks are present in December and January, you'll find herons, flamingos, ibises, spoonbills, plovers and egrets here as late as March or April, and there are about 100 species all year round. The calm lagoon is also a good place to see slender-billed and Audouin's gulls, and the African marsh owl. Shelducks, teals, and numerous terns are frequently seen, as are marsh harriers and peregrine falcons.

There are six villages around the lake, four of which depend on agriculture, two on fishing – the men fish the lagoon and the ocean while the women gather shellfish.

Most of the fishermen take tourists around the lake as a sideline. Boat trips with the local boatmen, who have had some guide training, are easily arranged if you wander down to the small beach where the boats are moored. Expect to pay about Dh100 per hour for the boat. The only officially recognised (and by far the best) guide is **Hassan Dalil** (☎0668 43 41 10; guide half-day Dh200, plus motorboat per hr Dh100), who can also be contacted at the Café Milano (on the main road into town), where the bird log is kept. Call him rather than ask for him as several people have been known to pretend to be him in order to take his business. Otherwise ask the waiters at the Café Milano to call him. Trips can also be arranged through Villanora. The boatmen can also arrange fishing trips (Dh100 per hour, including equipment).

Hard-core birdwatchers may also want to explore **Merja Khaloufa**, an attractive lake about 8km east of Moulay Bousselham and part of the park, which offers good viewing of a variety of wintering wildfowl.

🛏 Sleeping & Eating

The friendly owner of Restaurant l'Ocean can help to arrange a **house rental** (Sep-May Dh500, Jun-Aug Dh700-1000), which sleeps up to six people. During the summer months they fill up quickly, so it's best to call and reserve in advance.

Villanora   B&B €€
(☎0537 43 20 71, 0664 87 20 08; http://villanoramorocco.ifrance.com; s/d incl breakfast Dh300/400, with sea view Dh400/500; ⊛) This B&B, the holiday home of an English family who fell in love with this quiet corner of Morocco, sits on top of a high dune with glorious ocean views. It's run by the Anglophile Mohammed, a family friend. There are just a few homey rooms (some with shared bathroom) where you can fall asleep to the sound of crashing waves, and breakfast is served on the terrace. It is possible to order dinner in advance – ask for the fish. Villanora is at the far northern end of town, about 2km from the main street and it's essential to book in advance. Mohammed can also organise boat trips on the lake. The family has also just opened **Farm Nora** (☎0537 43 20 71, 0664 87 20 08; http://villanoramorocco.ifrance.com; s/d Dh300/400), the only accommodation on the nearby lake Merja Bargha. It's perfect for birdwatching.

Hôtel Le Lagon   HOTEL €
(☎0537 43 26 50; fax 0537 43 26 49; d Dh300; ⊛) The saving grace of this faded '70s hotel is its stunning location overlooking the lagoon below. The rooms are big, bright and clean, but in dire need of updating in spite of the fresh paint. The large terrace makes up for that. The restaurant is mediocre, and the swimming pool and nightclub are only open in July and August.

La Maison des Oiseaux   B&B €€
(☎0537 43 25 43, 061 301067; http://moulay.bousselham.free.fr; half board per person Dh350) Another friendly guesthouse set in a lovely garden with nine simple but beautifully styled traditional rooms. There's a seminar room upstairs for visiting school groups and birdwatching excursions can be arranged for Dh200 to Dh300 for 2½ hours. The guesthouse is hidden down a maze of sandy lanes to the left as you drive into town. Ask around or call for directions.

Camping Caravaning International   CAMP SITE €
(☎0537 43 24 77; www.atlantisgatemb@yahoo.fr; 2-person tent/camping/car Dh60/70/30, extra person Dh13; ⊛) An excellent site in a superb location, open all year.

Restaurant l'Ocean   RESTAURANT
(☎0678 31 09 54, 0669 43 42 45; mains Dh50; ⊙lunch & dinner) The road down to the seafront is lined with cafes and restaurants serving platters of grilled fish and tajines. One of the best is this small place, with a terrace and an indoor seating area, serving excellent fish, couscous, tajines and paella.

ℹ Getting There & Away

Moulay Bousselham is about 40km due south of Larache. To get here by public transport you'll need to make your way to the little town of Souk el-Arba du Rharb, from where there are frequent grands taxis (Dh20, 45 minutes) and a few buses

(Dh12, 45 minutes) to Moulay Bousselham. You can get to Souk el-Arba du Rharb by grand taxi from Kenitra or Larache (Dh35, one hour) and Rabat (Dh40, 1½ hours). Souk el-Arba du Rharb also has a train station with daily trains in either direction. Villanora can arrange a private taxi from Larache to Moulay Bousselham (Dh150, one hour).

Larache العرائش

Larache, like the other towns on this stretch of coast, is sleepy and laid-back for most of the year, bursting into life in summer when Moroccan tourists come to the beach. The charming town otherwise sees few visitors. The new town has some grand Spanish-era architecture, particularly around the central Pl de la Libération (the former Plaza de España), while the tiny crumbling medina is worth a stroll. North of the river Loukos, on the edge of town sit the overgrown ruins of ancient Lixus, the legendary site of the Gardens of Hesperides.

Larache was occupied by the Spanish for most of the 17th century. The port activities were limited because of some dangerous sandbars offshore, but the locals made ships for the corsairs further south. It became the main port of the Spanish protectorate in 1911. Today the whitewashed houses with blue doors, the church, the market, the hotels and bars still reveal the strength of the Spanish influence. The town may be as picturesque as Assilah, but it gets far fewer visitors and has none of the hustle.

All Larachians seem to come out for the *paseo* (evening stroll) in the centre of town. The cafes and few restaurants fill up as the locals drink coffee, play cards and chew over the day's events, and by 10pm the streets are again deserted.

The French writer Jean Genet loved the bay of Larache and although he died in France, he was buried here.

◎ Sights

Old Town HISTORICAL SITE
Perched on a cliff top overlooking the ocean are the ruins of the **kasbah** (Qebibat), a 16th-century fortress built by the Portuguese and closed to visitors as it is now in a state of serious disrepair. Head south from here to the old cobbled **medina**, through **Bab al-Khemis**, a large, unmistakable Hispano-Moorish arch on Place de la Libération. You come immediately into a colonnaded market square, the bustling **Zoco de la Alcaice-**

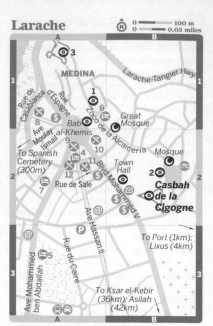

Larache

ria, which was built by the Spaniards during their first occupation of Larache in the 17th century. The Archaeological Museum was closed at the time of research.

Casbah de la Cigogne LANDMARK
(Fortress of the Storks) South of the square, through the medina, is this 17th-century

fortification was built by the Spaniards under Philip III. Unfortunately, the building is not open to visitors.

Jean Genet's Grave
LANDMARK

To the west of town, the old Spanish cemetery is the final resting place of French writer Jean Genet (1910–86). If the gate is not open, ring the bell on the right and the caretaker will let you in. A small tip is expected for showing you to the grave.

Galerie Afnar
ART GALLERY

(58 Assadr Alaadam; www.lafnargalerie.blogspot. com ⊙10am-2pm & 4-9pm) This gallery shows some interesting local art. The building itself is an old wheat *fondouq*. A plaque on the outside identifies it as the house of Abuel Ualid Mohammed ben Ahmed Ben Rox (also known as Averroes), the famous Andalusian philosopher who lived from 1120 to 1198.

Music Conservatory
NOTABLE BUILDING

On the square northeast of the Casbah de la Cigogne and opposite the closed Archaeological Museum, you'll come across a large, remarkably ornate building with its own minaret. This is now the music conservatory and is worth a peek.

Beaches
BEACH

Larache has a small strip of sand below the town but the best beach is 7km north across the Loukos Estuary. This beach also houses a huge holiday resort, Port Lixus, with a golf course, several resort hotels, villas and a luxury marina. To get there take the hourly bus 4 (Dh5, June to August). Out of season, bus 5 will drop you at the turnoff just before Lixus (Dh5), from where it's a 3km walk to the beach. Both buses leave from opposite the Casbah de la Cigogne.

🛏 Sleeping

Larache has a small but decent selection of accommodation, most of which is clustered along the streets just south of the Pl de la Libération.

TOP CHOICE La Maison Haute
RIAD €€

(☎0665 34 48 88; www.lamaisonhaute. com; 6 Derb ben Thami; r Dh440-550, apt Dh700-924) The most atmospheric accommodation in Larache, this wonderfully restored Hispano-Moorish house in the medina has a choice of six charming rooms with modern bathrooms. Eclectic decor, bright colours, stained-glass windows and Spanish-tiled floors give this place a feeling of simplicity, warmth and tradition, while the roof terrace boasts incredible views of the ocean and market square, and offers a nice corner to read a book or sunbathe. There's dinner on request.

Hôtel España
HOTEL €

(☎0539 91 31 95; hotelespana2@yahoo.fr; 6 Ave Hassan II; s/d/tr Dh260/300/380; ❄🕸) A relic of colonial times, this hotel is a great place to stay. The decor is still old-style with dark wood furnishings, but the beds are comfortable, the rooms spotless, and the bathrooms modernised. Ask for rooms higher up as the noise from the square can be a problem. The service is friendly. There's no breakfast, but there are lots of cafes nearby.

Pension Amal
HOTEL €

(☎0539 91 27 88; 10 Rue Abdallah ben Yassine; s/d/tr Dh50/100/150, hot shower Dh10) Dirt cheap, immaculately kept and extremely friendly, this little pension has tiled rooms with shared facilities. The mattresses are renewed every year and the beds are very comfortable. The owner's son, who likes to exchange ideas more than make money, is always happy to meet new people. If you like music, he will jump at the chance to get out his guitar for an impromptu performance.

Hôtel Riad
HOTEL €€€

(☎0539 91 26 26; Ave Mohammed ben Abdallah; 🕸) This grand old 19th-century mansion, which belonged to the Duchesse de Guise when she was exiled from France, is set in landscaped gardens just south of the centre. Undergoing renovation at the time of research, it opens at the end of 2011, transformed into a boutique all-suite hotel and spa.

🍴 Eating

Eating out in Larache is cheap and cheerful with plenty of little places around Place de la Libération and the Zoco de la Alcaiceria serving simple but substantial meals. The Spanish influence lingers on in the paella served in most restaurants, and the *churros* (a kind of doughnut) stall on the main square.

Restaurant Commercial
LOCAL €

(Pl de la Libération; mains Dh40; ⊙lunch & dinner) The locals' favourite, this basic place on the main square does a roaring trade in simple soup, brochettes and fried fish. It's ultra cheap, has friendly service, is packed with happy diners every night and is a great place for people-watching.

Restaurant du Port SEAFOOD €€
(☎0539 41 74 63; Larache Port; ⊙summer) Out of town by the port, but worth the trip, this slightly upmarket place specialises in fresh seafood cooked simply but to perfection. Open only in summer; phone ahead to check.

Restaurant Puerta Del Sol LOCAL €
(5 Rue Ahmed Chaouki; mains Dh40; ⊙lunch & dinner) For more seafood and a choice of Moroccan dishes, this no-nonsense place is a good bet. It's popular but a little quieter than the Restaurant Commercial.

Balcón Atlantico CAFE €
(cnr Rue de Casablanca & Rue Tarik Ibnou Ziad) Overlooking the beach, and the nicest spot in town for a relaxed breakfast or simple lunch, this bright, bustling cafe has plenty of outdoor seating and passable pizzas, though service is very slow.

For a quick breakfast or ice cream your best options are the **Salon de Thé Triana** (Ave Mohammed ben Abdallah), which also serves decent pizza (from Dh40) in summer, or, just off the square, **Le Sourire Salon de Thé** (Ave Hassan II).

ℹ Information

The banks cluster at the northern end of Blvd Mohammed V; most accept cash and travellers cheques and have ATMs.

Cyber Space (Rue 2 Mars; per hr Dh6; ⊙10am-midnight) Internet access.

Marnet (Ave Mohammed ben Abdallah; per hr Dh6; ⊙10.30am-midnight Sat-Thu, 3pm-midnight Fri) Internet access.

ℹ Getting There & Away

The bus station is south of the town centre on Rue du Caire. Destinations covered by CTM buses include Agadir (Dh260, 12 hours), Casablanca (Dh100, four hours, three daily), Fez (Dh80, four hours, three daily), Marrakesh (Dh190, eight hours), Meknès (Dh65, three hours, three daily), Rabat (Dh70, three hours, three daily) and Tangier (Dh40, 2½ hours, three daily).

Cheaper non-CTM buses are generally more frequent. They cover the same destinations as CTM buses, as well as Ouezzane (Dh30), Tetouan (Dh25) and Kenitra (Dh35).

Grands taxis run from outside the bus station to Ksar el-Kebir (Dh13) and occasionally to Assilah (Dh15), Souk el-Arba (Dh25) and Tangier (Dh30).

Lixus الاوكوس

Set on a hill overlooking the Loukos Estuary are the Carthaginian and Roman ruins of Lixus (admission free), a rather mysterious and neglected site that is one of the oldest inhabited places in the country. Only about a quarter of the ancient city has been excavated but the visible ruins, though badly damaged and overgrown, are impressive. Although not as extensive or as well excavated as Volubilis, the location, size and serenity of Lixus give it a lingering sense of gravitas and with a little imagination you can picture just how grand and important this city once was.

At the time of research, the site was not enclosed, but an information centre was being built. Few visitors make it here outside the summer months, and in winter your only companions will be the wind and the odd goat quietly grazing. The knowledgeable custodian, El Mokhtar el Hannach, will show you round for around Dh50 per person.

History

Megalithic stones found in the vicinity of Lixus suggest that the site was originally inhabited by a sun-worshipping people with knowledge of astronomy and mathematics. However, little more is known about the area's prehistory until the Phoenicians set up the colony Liks here in about 1000 BC. According to Pliny the Elder, it was here that Hercules picked the golden apples of the Garden of Hesperides, thus completing the penultimate of his 12 labours. The golden apples may well have been the famous Moroccan tangerines.

In the 6th century BC the Phoenician Atlantic colonies fell to the Carthaginians. Lixus remained a trading post, principally in gold, ivory and slaves and, by AD 42, had entered the Roman Empire. Its primary exports soon changed to salt, olives, wine and *garum* (an aromatic fish paste) and its merchants also grew rich from the export of wild animals for use in the empire's amphitheatres.

The colony at Lixus rapidly declined as the Romans withdrew from North Africa, and was abandoned completely in the 5th century, after the collapse of the Roman Empire. Later, the site became known to Muslims as Tuchummus.

LOCAL KNOWLEDGE

EL MOKHTAR EL HANNACH, LIXUS GUIDE

I was born here at Lixus. The family house was over there, where they're building an information centre; my father planted those fig trees. Now I live in the countryside and take a bus to work. My father was the first guide here, starting in 1923. I learned from him and took over; I've been here 40 years.

In those early times when the ancient people lived here, the sea came right up to Lixus; now it's 4km away. That's what made it such an important place. You can see the Carthaginian building remains – they're the large stone blocks of the lower sections of the walls, the amphitheatre and the temples. The Romans were neater and used smaller blocks. But the Romans abandoned the rainwater collection pits that the Carthaginians built, which wasn't very sensible. Apart from the fish *garum*, the main export from Lixus was olives. Now the olives are wild up here, and only for the birds.

If I had a choice, I'd rather have been a Carthaginian than a Roman.

⊙ Sights

Ruins
HISTORIC SITE

The main gate to Lixus is in the green railings that border the Larache–Tangier road. Inside the railings to the left are the remains of the *garum* factories, where fish was salted and the prized paste produced, beloved in Rome. A gravel path leads up the hill from the gate past a number of minor ruins to the **public baths** and **amphitheatre**. The amphitheatre provides impressive views of the surrounding countryside and makes a wonderful place just to sit and relax.

Most mosaics from the site were removed and are now on display at the archaeology museum in Tetouan. The Grand Temple mosaics depicting Helios, Mars and Rhea, the three Graces, and Venus with Adonis are all there. The only remaining mosaic at Lixus is that of **Oceanus** (the Greek Sea God). Unfortunately, it's been exposed both to the elements and to local vandalism, so is in rough shape.

Continue up the path to the main assembly of buildings, which straddle the crest of the hill. From here there are incredible views down over the Loukos Estuary and salt fields below.

The civic buildings, additional public baths and original city ramparts are here, while to the south is the striking citadel, a flurry of closely packed ruins standing stark against the sky. Although most of the antiquities are in an advanced state of decay, you should be able to make out the main temple and associated sanctuaries, an oratory, more public baths and the remains of the city walls.

ⓘ Getting There & Away

Lixus is approximately 4.5km north of Larache on the road to Tangier. To get there take bus 9 from outside the Casbah de la Cigogne (Dh5). A petit taxi costs about Dh25 one way.

Assilah
أصيلا

The gorgeous whitewashed resort town of Assilah feels like somewhere on a Greek island, but the tapas and paella on the Spanish menus in the restaurants and the wrought-iron windows on the white houses are but a few reminders that the town was Spanish territory for a long time. Assilah is an easy and hassle-free introduction to Morocco and, with a good selection of budget hotels and restaurants, and a burgeoning art scene, the town has become a favourite stop on the traveller's trail of the North Atlantic coast.

The town's mayor lives in the picturesque medina and has vowed to make it as clean as Switzerland. The old medina has been seriously gentrified in the last few years as more and more houses have been bought by affluent Moroccans and Europeans, mainly Spanish. The town is sleepy for most of the year, but in the summer months the population grows from 12,000 to 110,000, when Moroccan families descend here, as elsewhere along the coast. The small town is then completely overrun, the beaches are packed and the touts come out in force. The best time to visit is in spring or autumn when the weather is still pleasant but the crowds are gone.

Assilah has had a turbulent history as a small, but strategic port since it began life as the Carthaginian settlement of Zilis.

ATLANTIC COAST NORTH OF RABAT

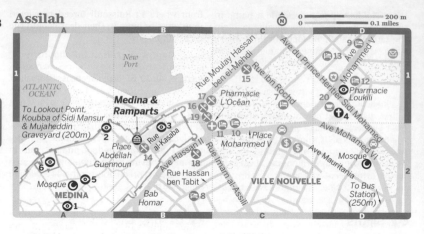

Assilah

During the Punic Wars the people backed Carthage, and when the region fell to the Romans, the locals were shipped to Spain and replaced with Iberians. From then on, Assilah was inexorably linked with the Spanish and with their numerous battles for territory.

As Christianity conquered the forces of Islam on the Iberian Peninsula in the 14th and 15th centuries, Assilah felt the knock-on effects. In 1471 the Portuguese sent 477 ships with 30,000 men, captured the port and then built the walls that still surround the medina, a trading post on their famous gold route across Africa. In 1578, King Dom Sebastian of Portugal embarked on an ill-fated crusade from Assilah. He was killed, and Portugal (and its Moroccan possessions) passed into the hands of the Spanish, who remained for a very long time.

Assilah was recaptured by Moulay Ismail in 1691. In the 19th century, continuing piracy prompted Austria and then Spain to send their navies to bombard the town. Its most famous renegade was Er-Raissouli (see p210), one of the most colourful bandits ever raised in the wild Rif Mountains. Early in the 20th century, Er-Raissouli used Assilah as his base, becoming the bane of the European powers. Spain made Assilah part of its protectorate from 1911 until 1956.

◎ Sights & Activities

With more than 50 resident artists, five galleries and several artist studios and exhibition spaces, Assilah is renowned as a city of arts. It all started in 1978 when several Moroccan artists were invited to hold workshops for local children and to paint some walls in the medina as part of the town's *moussem* (saint's day celebrations). Several Zaïlachi artists and some of these children have now made a name in the contemporary-art world, among them the late Abdelilah Bououd, Brahim Jbari, Elina Atencio, Mohamed Lhaloui and several members of the Mesnani family.

Ramparts & Medina
HISTORICAL BUILDING, MEDINA

Assilah's largely residential medina is surrounded by the sturdy stone fortifications built by the Portuguese in the 15th century and it is these walls, flanked by palms, that have become the town's landmark.

The medina and ramparts have been restored in recent years and the tranquil narrow streets lined by whitewashed houses are well worth a wander. Although the restoration work has left the medina much sanitised, the ornate wrought-iron window guards, pale green *jalousies* (wooden, trellis-like window shutters) and colourful murals (painted each year during the Assilah Festival) give it a very photogenic quality. Craftsmen and artists have opened workshops along the main streets and invite passers-by in to see them work.

Access to the ramparts is limited. The southwestern bastion is the best spot for views over the ocean and is a popular spot at sunset. It also offers a peek into the nearby **Koubba of Sidi Mansur** (which is otherwise closed to non-Muslims) and the **Mujaheddin Graveyard**.

The southern entrance to the medina, **Bab Homar** (Ave Hassan II), is topped by the much-eroded Portuguese royal coat of arms. There are a few **old cannons** just inside the medina's seaward wall, but they are cut off from the walkway below and can only be seen from a distance. The **Bab al-Kasaba** leads to the **Croat Mosque** (closed to non-Muslims) and the Centre Hassan II des Rencontres Internationales. The medina is busiest on Thursdays, Assilah's main market day.

Palais de Raissouli
HISTORIC BUILDING

Also known as the Palais de Culture (Palace of Culture) on the seaside of the medina, the palace was built in 1909 by Er-Raissouli and still stands as a testament to the sumptuous life he led at the height of his power. It has been beautifully restored, but is only open during the Assilah Festival or for temporary exhibitions, although if you can find the caretaker you may be able to persuade him to let you in. The striking building includes a main reception room with a glass-fronted terrace overlooking the sea,

from where Er-Raissouli forced convicted murderers to jump to their deaths onto the rocks 30m below.

[FREE] Centre de Hassan II Rencontres Internationales
ART GALLERY

(📞0539 41 70 65; foundationdassilah@yahoo.fr; ⊙8.30am-12.30pm & 2.30-5pm, to 8pm summer) The main exhibition space in town is just inside the medina walls. It's in a beautiful medina house and displays a revolving exhibition of international painting and sculpture in its gallery, and at times, in the nearby **El-Khamra Tower**, a renovated Portuguese fortification on Pl Abdellah Guennoun.

Aplanos Gallery
ART GALLERY

(📞0661 99 80 30; Rue Tijara) Belgian painter Anne-Judith Van Loock created this gallery with her Moroccan husband Ahmed Benraadiya, where foreign and local artists can exhibit.

Galerie Hakim
ART GALLERY

(📞0539 41 88 96, 061 799535; hakimghailan@yahoo.fr; 14 Place Sidi ben Issa) Zaïlachi artist Hakim Ghaïlan started this space and exhibits mainly young Moroccan artists.

New Town
LANDMARK

The centre of the small new town is Pl Mohammed V. Northwest of the square is the **Church of San Bartolome**, built by Spanish Franciscans in a typical colonial Moorish style. It is one of the few churches in Morocco allowed to ring the bells for Sunday Mass. Nearby is the **marché central** (central market).

Beaches
BEACH

Assilah's main beach, flanked by camp sites and hotels, stretches north from town. It's a wide sweep of golden sand and although pleasant in low season, the crowds and noise from the nearby road make it much less appealing in summer. For more peace and quiet head 3km south to **Paradise Beach**, a gorgeous spot that really does live up to its name, though it's not cleaned much out of season. It's a pleasant walk along the coast or, alternatively, hop on one of the horse-drawn carriages that ply this route in summer.

Asilah Marina Golf, an entirely new resort, lies south of the town, but like many such developments, its completion is delayed. It will have a marina, golf course, a luxury hotel and apartments. Further north, 23km south of Tangier, yet another resort,

RASCALLY ER-RAISSOULI

Feared bandit, kidnapper and general troublemaker, Moulay Ahmed ben Mohammed er-Raissouli (or Raisuni) was one of Assilah's most legendary inhabitants. He started life as a petty crook in the Rif Mountains but saw no problem in bumping off unwilling victims and was soon renowned as a merciless murderer, and feared right across the region.

Internationally, Er-Raissouli was best known for kidnapping Westerners. He and his band held various luminaries to ransom, including Greek-American billionaire Ion Perdicaris, who was ransomed in 1904 for US$70,000.

In an attempt to control the unruly outlaw, consecutive sultans appointed him to various political positions, including governor of Assilah and later Tangier. However, Er-Raissouli continued with his wicked ways, amassing great wealth in whatever way he could. He held considerable sway over the Rif tribes and the Spanish funded his arms in the hope of keeping order in the mountains, but Er-Raissouli often used them against his benefactors.

The Spaniards eventually forced Er-Raissouli to flee Assilah after WWI, but he continued to wreak havoc in the Rif hinterland until 1925, when the Rif rebel Abd al-Krim arrested him and accused him of being too closely linked with the Spanish.

Al Houara, is being built along this fabulous stretch of coast. But again, construction has been stopped for the time being.

★★ Festivals & Events

Assilah Festival　　　　　　CULTURAL FESTIVAL
(www.c-assilah.com) The Centre Hassan II des Rencontres Internationales is the main focus for this annual festival, held over three weeks in July, when artists, musicians, performers and about 200,000 spectators descend upon the town. More than 30 years old, the cultural festival features numerous workshops and public art demonstrations, concerts, exhibitions and events with participants from all over the world. A three-day horse festival, including a Moroccan *fantasia* (musket-firing cavalry charge) takes place towards the end of the festival. Download the iPhone app from the Apple App Store.

🛏 Sleeping

Assilah has a choice of decent but uninspiring accommodation options in the new part of town; a more interesting option is to rent a medina house. A host of properties in Assilah's medina have been bought by foreigners and wealthy Moroccans and renovated as holiday homes. At any time of the year it is possible to rent a house in the medina or near the beach through the agency **House in Asilah** (www.housein asilah.com). There are some wonderful two-, three- and four-bedroom houses available with stunning decor and all the comforts you are likely to want. Prices range from about Dh600 to Dh3000 per night. Per week, a house rents for Dh4000 in low season to about Dh15,000 in high season.

During high season (Easter week and July to September), the town is flooded with visitors so it's advisable to book well in advance. Assilah has a limited choice of budget hotels.

Hôtel Patio de la Luna　　　　HOTEL €€
(☑0539 41 60 74; 12 Pl Zellaka; s/d Dh350/450; ⊛) The only accommodation option in Assilah with any local character is this intimate, Spanish-run place secluded behind an unassuming door on the main drag. The somewhat spartan, rustic rooms have wooden furniture, woven blankets and tiled bathrooms and are set around a lovely leafy patio. The staff are friendly and it's very popular, so book ahead.

Hôtel Belle Vue　　　　　　HOTEL €
(☑0539 41 77 47; Rue Hassan ben Tabit; d Dh200, low season Dh100) A friendly, small hotel in a quiet side street, run by young Moroccans who are very welcoming and up to date on what's happening in town. Some of the rooms have been decorated by local artists. The mattresses are good and everything is immaculately kept, including the shared facilities. A few rooms have their own bathroom (Dh50 extra) and balconies, and there are four pleasant apartments (Dh100 per person), with two double rooms and a sitting area. The rooftop terrace is a great place for an evening drink or to re-

lax. It's particularly popular with Spanish travellers.

Hôtel Azayla
HOTEL €€

(☑0539 41 67 17; www.hotel-azayla.com; 20 Rue ibn Rochd; s/d Dh326/386, Jul & Aug Dh350/486) Big, bright, comfy and well equipped, the rooms here are a good deal. The bathrooms are modern, the decor is tasteful with great photographs of Morocco and Moroccans by the owner, and the giant windows bathe the rooms in light. The larger rooms include a spacious seating area where up to three people could easily sleep. The place may lack local character, but the staff are friendly, helpful and reliable.

Hôtel Sahara
HOTEL €

(☑0539 41 71 85; 9 Rue de Tarfaya; s/d/tr Dh98/150/240, hot showers Dh5) By far the best budget option, this small, immaculately kept hotel offers simple rooms set around an open courtyard, with a very Moroccan atmosphere. Patterned tiles and potted plants adorn the entrance, and the compact rooms, though fairly spartan, are comfortable and well maintained. Some have tiny windows, so it may be worth checking more than one. The sparkling shared toilets and showers are all new and scrubbed till they gleam.

Hôtel Marhaba
HOTEL €

(☑0539 41 71 44; Rue Zellaka; s/d Dh100/200, hot shower Dh5) This place has a good central location, next to the Pl Zellaka, and gives a friendly welcome. The rooms have seen better days, though all of them are spotless. Go for the rooms in the front which are larger and brighter, if a bit noisier. The shared facilities are ancient but there's a nice roof terrace that overlooks the medina.

Hôtel Mansour
HOTEL €€

(☑0539 41 73 90; www.hotelmansour.cabanova.fr; 56 Ave Mohammed V; s/d incl breakfast Dh350/420) You'll get a hint of traditional character in the tiled public areas at this small hotel, northeast of the centre, but the bedrooms are fairly bland with faded decor and tiny bathrooms. It's still a good deal for the price that includes breakfast, but it's worth asking for a larger room with balcony and sea view.

Hôtel Zelis
HOTEL €€

(☑0539 41 70 69; fax 0539 41 70 98; 10 Ave Mansour Eddahabi; s/d/tr Dh300/400/550, Jul & Aug Dh400/550/650; ❇@≋) Packed out in summer and deserted the rest of the year, this big holiday hotel has 65 comfortable, modern rooms with funky blue-and-white textiles, TV and fridge. You can eat in the traditional Moroccan restaurant with low seating and tables, or the characterless cafeteria-style alternative. The pool is fine and there's a games room for children and a cyber cafe (Dh10 per hour).

Eating & Drinking

Assilah has a string of restaurants clustered around Bab Kasaba and along the medina walls on Ave Hassan II. There are a few other cheap options on Rue Ahmed M'dem near the banks on Pl Mohammed V.

Casa García
SEAFOOD €€

(☑0539 41 74 65; 51 Rue Moulay Hassan ben el-Mehdi; mains from Dh80; ⊘lunch & dinner) Spanish-style fish dishes and fishy tapas are the speciality at this small restaurant opposite the beach. Go for succulent grilled fish or a more adventurous menu of octopus, eels, shrimp and barnacles, served with a glass of crisp Moroccan gris wine on the large and breezy terrace. The paella is delicious too.

Restaurante Oceano Casa Pepe
SEAFOOD €€

(☑0539 41 73 95; 8 Place Zellaka; mains Dh80-120; ⊘lunch & dinner) Black-tied waiters lure in the punters from the street at this slightly more formal dining option, where fresh seafood tops the bill. Spanish and Moroccan wine,

---

ⓘ BEWARE THE TOUTS

Accommodation Touts meeting the buses or trains offer basic accommodation in the medina for about Dh75. It's usually a large room sleeping up to seven people on thin mattresses on the floor. Some also offer rooms in unofficial B&Bs at much higher prices. Be careful however when renting through touts: there are many scams.

Drugs As tourism and kif (dope) use have increased in recent years, so too has the number of touts operating in Assilah. Assilah has a large young population, and unemployment is high. Kif plays a big role in Assilah: increasingly, tourists are being offered it, often as part of an elaborate scam to fleece them (see p497).

WORTH A TRIP

MONOLITHS OF M'SOURA

The mysterious Monoliths of M'Soura make an interesting half-day trip from Assilah. This prehistoric site consists of a large stone circle (actually an ellipse) of about 175 stones, thought to have originally surrounded a burial mound. Although many of the stones have fallen or been broken, the circle is still impressive, its strange presence heightened by the desolation of its location. The tallest stone reaches about 5.5m in height and is known as El-Uted (The Pointer).

The stone circle is about 25km (by road) southeast of Assilah. To get there you'll need a sturdy vehicle. Head for the village of Souq Tnine de Sidi el-Yamani, off highway R417, which branches east off the main Tangier to Rabat road. Veer left in the village and follow a poorly maintained, unsealed track 6km north to the site. It can be difficult to find so you may want to ask for directions or hire a guide in the village.

Another interesting trip from Assilah is a visit to the lively Sunday market in the village of **Had Gharbia**, 16km north of town off the road to Tangier.

low lighting and soft music make it a more refined atmosphere.

Restaurant la Place　LOCAL, SEAFOOD €€
(☎0539 41 73 26; 7 Ave Moulay Hassan ben el-Mehdi; mains Dh75; ☺lunch & dinner) Friendly, less formal and more varied than its neighbours, this restaurant offers a choice of traditional Moroccan dishes as well as the ubiquitous fish and seafood. The delicious fish tajine provides the best of both worlds.

Restaurant Yali　LOCAL €
(Ave Hassan II; mains Dh50; ☺lunch & dinner) Although there's little to choose between them, this is one of the most popular of the string of restaurants along the medina walls. It serves up a good selection of fish, seafood, pizza and traditional Moroccan staples.

La Symphonie II des Douceurs　CAFE €
(26 Pl Zellaka) This cafe is the best place for breakfast or an afternoon sugar fix. Devour pastries and ice cream (in summer only) in very civilised surroundings.

Al-Madina　CAFE €
(Pl Abdellah Guennoun) The main attraction of this simple little cafe in the medina is its sunny seating area in the square in front of El-Khamra Tower. It's a great place to sip a coffee and watch the world go by.

Café Tanger　CAFE €
(52 Ave Mohammed V) For a more authentic experience, head for this cafe north of the square, where the predominantly male clientele sip coffee, suck their teeth and watch over the world.

ⓘ Information

Pl Mohammed V is crowded with banks, including BMCE and Banque Populaire, both of which will change cash and travellers cheques and have ATMs.

Cyber Haytam (197 Ave Hassan II; per hr Dh6; ☺9am-midnight) Internet access.

Pharmacie l'Océan (Pl Zellaka)

Pharmacie Loukili (Ave Mohammed V).

ⓘ Getting There & Away

BUS Assilah is 46km south of Tangier and has good bus connections to most towns. The tiny bus station is on the corner of Ave Mohamed VI and the Tangier–Rabat Rd. Since the highway was built, CTM doesn't stop in Assilah anymore. Several private bus companies offer various services to destinations including Casablanca (Dh80, 4½ hours, eight daily), Fez (Dh60, 4½ hours, four daily), Marrakesh (Dh120, nine hours, three daily), Rabat (Dh60, 3½ hours, eight daily) and Tangier (Dh15, one hour).

It's a good idea to book long-distance buses in advance as they tend to fill up in Tangier. Buses to Tangier and Casablanca leave roughly every half-hour, from 6.30am to 8pm. Just wait until a bus pulls in and hope there's a seat available.

CAR There is guarded parking (Dh10 per 24 hours) outside Bab al-Baha (Sea Gate), near the port.

TAXI Grands taxis to Tangier (Dh20) and Larache (Dh15) depart when full from Rue 2 Mars, off Ave Mohammed VI, across from the mosque. Tangier's airport is only 26km north of here, so taking a taxi from Assilah (Dh250) may save you spending a lot of time and energy in Tangier. The petit-taxi stand is at Pl Mohammed V.

TRAIN The train station is 2km north of Assilah, but a bus (Dh6) generally meets trains and drops passengers at Pl Mohammed V and

Bab Homar. Destinations include Casablanca (Dh109, four hours), Fez (Dh87, four hours, five daily), Meknés (Dh70, three hours, five daily), Rabat (Dh83, three hours, nine daily) and Tangier (Dh16, 45 minutes, 10 daily). One overnight train goes direct to Marrakesh (Dh186, 9½ hours), but this train originates (and fills up) in Tangier, so you may want to buy your ticket in advance.

SOUTH OF CASABLANCA

El-Jadida الجديدة

POP 148,000

In 1506 the Portuguese built a fortress here to protect their ships and baptised it Mazagan, which soon developed into the country's most important trading post. Sultan Sidi Mohammed ben Abdallah seized Mazagan from the Portuguese following a siege in 1769, but the Portuguese blew up most of the

fort before leaving. Most of the new settlers preferred to live in the new town and the citadel remained a ruin until the early 19th century when Sultan Abd er-Rahman resettled some of the Jews of Azemmour in old Mazagan, and renamed the town El-Jadida, 'the New One' in Arabic.

The large and influential Jewish community soon grew rich on trade with the interior, and unlike most other Moroccan cities, there was no *mellah* (Jewish quarter); the Jews mixed with the general populace and an attitude of easy tolerance was established in the city. During the French protectorate, the town became an administrative centre and a beach resort, but its port gradually lost out to Safi and Casablanca.

The old Portuguese town, now known as the Cité Portugaise, is a sleepy but atmospheric medina, which was granted World Heritage status by Unesco in 2004. A lack of investment has helped maintain the integrity of the picturesque Portuguese town's rambling alleys and ramparts. For much of the year El-Jadida is a quiet backwater, disturbed only by the crowds of Moroccans flocking to its beautiful beaches and strolling its boulevards in July and August.

But all of this looks set to change. Over the last few years, both Moroccans and

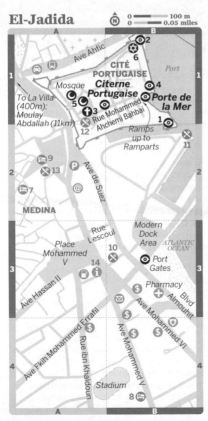

El-Jadida

foreigners have started buying up property in the old walled town, including the old colonial church. This is bringing about a regeneration, as the crumbling houses are being given a facelift. Just north of the town, on a gorgeous stretch of beach, is the recently-opened tourist resort of **Mazagan**, which includes a golf course, casino, spa and large resort hotel. The old town of El-Jadida in the next few years will be given a new, if very different, lease of life.

◉ Sights & Activities

Cité Portugaise   HISTORICAL SITE
El-Jadida's main sight, the Cité Portugaise (Portuguese city), is a compact maze of twisting streets, surrounded by ochre ramparts. The main entrance is just off Pl Mohammed ben Abdallah and leads into Rue Mohammed Ahchemi Bahbai. Immediately on the left is the Portuguese-built **Church of the Assumption**, which was being restored at the time of research and will open as an upmarket hotel. Almost next door is the **Grande Mosquée**, which has a unique pentagonal-shaped minaret; it originally acted as a lighthouse.

Citerne Portugaise   HISTORIC BUILDING
(Portuguese Cistern; Rue Mohammed Ahchemi Bahbai; admission incl entry to ramparts Dh10; ◉9am-1pm & 3-6.30pm) On the main street past the souvenir shops is a vast, vaulted cistern lit by a single shaft of light. The spectacularly tranquil spot, with a thin film of water on the floor reflecting a mirror image of the vaulted ceiling and elegant columns, was originally used to collect water. It is famous as the eerie location for the dramatic riot scene in Orson Welles' 1954 *Othello*.

Porte de la Mer   LANDMARK
(◉ramparts 9am-6pm) Further down the street are the ramparts with the Porte de la Mer, the original sea gate where ships unloaded their cargo and from where the Portuguese finally departed. To the left of the gate, through the archway, is one of the town's **communal bakeries**, where local women bring their bread to be baked.

To the right of the sea gate, a ramp leads up to the windy ramparts and **Bastion de L'Ange** (southeast corner), an excellent vantage point with views out to sea and over the new town and port. Walk along the ramparts to the left to reach **Bastion de St Sebastian** (northeast corner), from where you can see the old Jewish cemetery. Next to the

bastion is the abandoned **synagogue** (originally the old prison) with its Star of David.

Beaches   BEACH
The beaches to the north and south of town are fairly clean and safe, enjoyable out of season, but packed in July and August. The beach at **Haouzia**, northeast of town, is lovely. The Mazagan resort is situated on this beach. **Sidi Bouzid**, 5km southwest of El-Jadida, is a popular spot with sunbathers and surfers. **Le Requin Blue** (◻0523 34 80 67; mains around Dh80; ◉lunch & dinner) overlooking the beach in Sidi Bouzid serves excellent fish.

Local bus 2 runs from El-Jadida to Sidi Bouzid (Dh3.50) every hour.

🛏 Sleeping

A few hotels near the Cité Portugaise make El-Jadida a nice option to spend a couple of days. The hotels in the new town are more modern and comfortable but have less character.

TOP\ CHOICE Dar el-Manar   B&B €€
(◻0523 23 35 16 45, 061 495411; www.dar-al-manar.com; r Dh800-1000; ❋ @) Fatima fell in love with this wheat field overlooking the ocean and town while out cycling, and decided to build a lovely house with a vast garden, where it would be good to live and receive guests. Everything is done to make guests feel at ease, in the five simple but stylish and spacious rooms, decorated in a contemporary Moroccan style. Guests can use the garden and the bright dining room. Dinner can be ordered in advance, and is cooked with vegetables from the organic garden. You'll get a warm welcome from Fatima and her French husband Pascal, a professional masseur (massage Dh300). Call for directions; it is near the Phare Sidi Mesbah, a lighthouse, and is signposted on the road from El-Jadida north to Azemmour.

Riad Le Mazagao   RIAD €€
(◻0523 35 01 37; 6 Derb el-Hajjar; www.lemazagao.com; d Dh550-825; ❋) The rooms are set around the courtyard and on the roof terrace of this welcoming, atmospheric 19th-century guesthouse located in the medina. The large rooms are decorated in a warm Moroccan style with lots of tiling and local textiles, and feel very homey. Half board is obligatory if you stay more than a week. The communal bathrooms are spotless.

La Villa
RIAD €€€

(☎0523 34 44 23, 0661 41 86 81; www.la-villa-david.com; 4 Ave Moulay Abdelhafid; r/ste Dh1100/1540; ❋ 🛜 ❄) This is a charming contemporary-style hotel in an old villa, built using local materials and vegetation, just outside the old city and run by two Frenchmen. The rooms are set around a white courtyard. Stylish neon lights lead you upstairs, and rooms have plasma screens, wi-fi and *tadelakt* (lime plaster) bathrooms and floors. The effect is very Zen rather than high tech. There is a little bar on the roof by the pool and the top terrace has a solarium with spectacular views over the old city. La Villa has the best restaurant in town serving inventive French-Moroccan cuisine (dinner Dh350).

Hôtel de Bordeaux
HOTEL €

(☎0523 37 39 21; 47 Rue Moulay Ahmed Tahiri; s/d Dh80/130, with bathroom Dh150/180) The best of the cheapies, this friendly, good-value hotel in a traditional house in the medina has comfortable but compact rooms around a covered courtyard. Only the rooms on the 1st floor have en-suite bathrooms. Rooms get cheaper the higher up you go. You'll have to use the communal shower downstairs for hot showers. The hotel is well signposted from Rue ben Tachfine.

Hôtel Royal
HOTEL €

(☎0523 34 11 00; 108 Ave Mohammed V; s/d Dh125/140, with bathroom Dh198/245) This large hotel has big, bright rooms with cheap furnishings and retro-fitted showers separated from your bed by a sheet of glass panelling. Quality and comfort varies, so check first. The public areas have colourful tiling and a lovely courtyard that becomes a lively bar at night.

✕ Eating

El-Jadida has a handful of reasonable restaurants and a thriving cafe culture.

Restaurante La Portugaise
LOCAL €

(Rue Mohammed Ahchemi Bahbai; mains from Dh40; ⊙lunch & dinner) Just inside the walls of the old city, this characterful little place with red-checked tablecloths and a friendly welcome serves up a decent menu of good-value fish, chicken and tajine dishes.

Restaurant du Port
SEAFOOD €€

(☎0523 34 25 79; Port du Jadida; mains Dh80; ⊙lunch & dinner Mon-Sat, lunch Sun) Head upstairs for excellent views over the port and ramparts from one of El-Jadida's best

restaurants, naturally focused on fish and seafood, cooked simply but well. The atmosphere is pretty mellow, which maes it a comfortable spot for women and – joy of joys – it's licensed.

Restaurant Tchikito
SEAFOOD €

(4 Rue Mohammed Smiha; mixed fish platter Dh40) This hole-in-the-wall, just off Pl Hansali, is popular with readers for its delicious and cheap fried fish served with a fiery chilli sauce.

Patisserie Royale
PATISSERIE €

(Pl Mohammed V) Readers compliment the coffee here. The Royale is an old-style kind of joint where you can blend into the woodwork or chat to the locals without feeling under any pressure.

❶ Information

There are numerous banks located in the centre of town which have ATMs. There are several internet cafes on Ave Mohammed VI.

@Kiltec (1st fl, 62 Place Hansali; per hr Dh6; ⊙9am-11pm, closed lunch Fri)

Clinique Les Palmiers (☎0523 39 39 39; Rte de Casablanca) With 24-hour emergency service.

Main post office (Pl Mohammed V)

Syndicat d'Initiative (Pl Mohammed V; ⊙closed Wed) This tourist office is a rarity in Morocco – it's actually knowledgeable and helpful.

❶ Getting There & Away

BUS The **bus station** (Ave Mohammed V) is a 10-minute walk from the centre. Destinations include Casablanca (Dh27, 1½ hours, four daily), Essaouira (Dh80, 4½ hours, one daily), Oualidia (Dh30, 1½ hours, three daily) and Safi (Dh60, 2½ hours, six daily). Cheaper local buses go to all the same destinations as well as Azemmour (Dh5), Rabat (Dh40, four hours, 12 daily) and Marrakesh (Dh40, four hours, hourly). In summer, buses to Casablanca (Dh23) and Marrakesh should be booked at least one day ahead. Bus 2 for Sidi Bouzid (Dh3.5) and bus 6 for Moulay Abdallah (Dh4.5) leave from just north of the Cité Portugaise.

TAXI Grands taxis for Azemmour (Dh6) and Casablanca (Dh35) leave from the side street next to the long-distance bus station. Taxis to Oualidia (Dh25) and Safi (Dh55) depart from a junction on the road to Sidi Bouzid. You'll need to take a petit taxi (Dh5) to get there. The grand-taxi rank for Sidi Bouzid (Dh5) and Moulay Abdallah (Dh6) is beside the local bus station north of the Cité Portugaise.

TRAIN El-Jadida train station is located 4km south of town. There are five services a day to and from Casablanca (Dh30, one hour). A petit taxi to the centre costs around Dh10. For timetable details ask at the tourist office or see www.oncf.ma.

Azemmour

El-Amine, one of Azemmour's most successful painters, got it right describing his favourite view of town from his roof terrace, which he has painted numerous times: the old walled medina squeezed in between the Oum er-Rbia (Mother of Spring) river and the ocean, with the fields spread beyond.

The picturesque town has inspired many artists, who have come to live here. Although it is close to the art market of Casablanca, life is still simple, with the farmers and fishermen going door-to-door with their produce. It's a sleepy backwater with a languid charm, a sturdy Portuguese medina and some wonderful accommodation options – a great place to while away a few days overlooking the river.

The Portuguese built the town in 1513 as one of a string of trading posts along the coast. The town's most famous inhabitant was Estevanico the Black. Captured and made a slave, he later became one of the first four explorers to cross the entire mainland of North America from Florida to the Pacific.

◉ Sights

The main sight is the medina, an ochre-walled town of narrow winding streets and whitewashed houses. Unlike Assilah, to the north, it is completely unadorned and still gives an authentic glimpse of life in modern Morocco. You can get up onto the **ramparts** near Pl du Souk or via steps at the northeastern corner of the medina. Walk along the walls to see **Dar el Baroud** (the Powder House), a Portuguese gunpowder store of which only the tower remains. To the north of the medina is the *mellah* and further on you'll get wonderful views over the river. All over the medina are walls painted by local artists, artists' studios including **Ahmed el-Amine** (🖉0523 35 89 02; 6 Derb el-Hantati) and a few places selling the typical Azemmour embroidery.

🛏 Sleeping & Eating

There are lots of small restaurants outside the city walls in the new town.

L'Oum Errebia HOTEL €€€
(🖉0523 34 7071; www.azemmour-hotel.com; 25 Impasse Chtouka; s/d/tr incl breakfast Dh750/900/1250, with river view Dh900/1200/1650; 🛜) This place blends traditional Moroccan style with chic contemporary design. The simple rooms are delightful and the large lounge, complete with open fireplace and grand piano, acts as a modern art gallery. There's an in-house hammam (*gommage* Dh150) and treatments available (massage Dh250). The large terrace overlooks the river and communal meals (Dh250) are served at the big dining-room table.

Riad Azama RIAD €€
(🖉0523 34 75 16, 0648 24 14 85; www.riadazama.com; 17 Impasse Ben Tahar; s/d incl breakfast Dh500/800) A grand 19th-century house complete with original carved woodwork and rather dark rooms surrounding a leafy courtyard. The carved, painted ceilings here are some of the finest and the rooftop terrace has great views of the medina. Dinner is available on request (Dh200), but can be disappointing.

Mazagan Beach Resort RESORT €€€
(🖉0523 38 80 00; www.mazaganbeachresort.com; r from Dh2900; ❋🛜🏊) Three kilometres south of Azemmour is this resort, set on a lagoon and 7km of beautiful Haouzia beach. The resort boasts several restaurants and bars, a nightclub, casino, golf course, spa and horse riding. There are a couple of upmarket golf resorts between El-Jadida and Azemmour.

ℹ Information

Azemmour has several banks, a pharmacy and internet access at **Capsys** (off Pl du Souk; per hr Dh7).

ℹ Getting There & Away

Trains now stop at Azemmour Halte, linking the town to El-Jadida (Dh15, 20 minutes, seven daily) and Casablanca (Dh31, 1¼ hours, seven daily).

A grand taxi to/from El-Jadida costs Dh10, a bus trip costs Dh5.

Oualidia الوالدية
POP 4200

The drive from El-Jadida to Oualidia along the coastal road, where the fields come down to the wild shore of the ocean, is spectacular enough, but the view upon arrival is more than pleasing. The delightful small-scale resort of Oualidia spreads around a gorgeous crescent-shaped lagoon fringed with golden sands and protected from the wild surf of the ocean by a rocky breakwater. A quiet backwater for many years, with a good selection of accommodation and great fish restaurants, Oualidia is becoming increasingly chic as a weekend resort for Marrakchis and Casablancais.

Out of season it is still quiet, with little more to do than relax, surf, swim and eat well, but avoid the crowds in summer. A lot of building work is threatening to destroy the tranquil charm of this stunning location.

◎ Sights & Activities

The town is named after the Saadian Sultan el-Oualid, who built the atmospherically crumbling kasbah on the bluff overlooking the lagoon in 1634. The lagoon also attracted Morocco's royalty and the grand villa on the water's edge was Mohammed V's summer palace. Most hotels and restaurants are along the road to the beach (1km) – follow signs down beside the post office. There are no taxis on this route, but hotels will arrange transport.

Lagoon   LAGOON
The safe, calm waters of the lagoon are perfect for **swimming**, **sailing** and **fishing**, while the wide, sandy beach on either side of the breakwater is good for **windsurfing** and **surfing**.

Surfland   WATER SPORTS
(☎0523 36 61 10; ☺Apr–mid-Nov) Signposted left off the road to the beach is a well-organised surfing school run by Moroccan surf champion Noureddine Joubir. Tuition costs Dh250/200 per adult/child for 1½ hours.

Dream Surf Oualidia   WATER SPORTS
(☎0661 81 78 17; ☺year-round) On the beach in town, this outfit also offers surfing and kitesurfing lessons, as well as equipment rental, fishing trips and quad-bike hire. Scooters cost Dh400 per half-day.

Maison de l'Ostréa II   LANDMARK
(☎0523 36 63 24; www.ilove-casablanca.com/ostrea) Oualidia is famous for its oyster beds, which produce about 200 tonnes of oysters annually. You can visit oyster farm No 7 at Maison de l'Ostréa II to see how it all works. Oysters (per dozen Dh180) and other seafood are available at the excellent restaurant attached. If you can't tear yourself away, there are double rooms for Dh700. It's at the entrance of Oualidia on the Casablanca road.

🛏 Sleeping & Eating

All hotels listed have their own restaurants. There are some slightly cheaper places lining the road down to the beach, and other apartments and villas can be rented through numerous agencies in town. For bargain meals there is a selection of cheap eateries on the main road up in the village.

TOP CHOICE **Hôtel-Restaurant L'Initiale** B&B **€€**
(☎0523 36 62 46; initialhotel@menara.ma; r with breakfast Dh500) This little white villa, with a warm orange interior and just six pleasant and comfortable rooms, is well equipped with new fittings, spotless bathrooms and tiny balconies. The popular licensed restaurant (mains from Dh80) is one of the best in town and serves a wide selection of fish dishes and pizzas.

Motel A l'Araignée Gourmande   HOTEL **€**
(☎0523 36 64 47; fax 0523 36 61 44; s/d Dh250/300; 🖘) A friendly hotel with spacious, comfortable rooms that could do with some modernising. The ones over the restaurant have balconies overlooking the lagoon, while rooms in the new building next door don't, and are not quite as pleasant. The restaurant serves up a feast of well-prepared seafood (mains from Dh80).

L'Hippocampe   HOTEL **€€€**
(☎0523 36 61 08; d with demi pension Dh1600, low season Dh1200, ste with sea view Dh3200, low season Dh2600) A friendly hotel with immaculate rooms off a magnificent garden filled with flowers, looking over the lagoon. There's an excellent fish restaurant (mains around Dh120), and steps down to the beach. It's family friendly.

La Sultana   HOTEL **€€€**
(☎0524 38 80 08; www.lasultanaoualidia.com; Parc à Huîtres No 3; r from Dh4100; 🌸🖘🏊) Spectacularly luxurious, this gorgeous hotel has just 11 rooms with fireplace, private Jacuzzi and terrace overlooking the lagoon. There's a choice of three restaurants, an indoor pool, and an infinity pool and spa – all set in beautiful landscaped gardens. It was designed to have minimal impact on the surrounding environment; local materials were used in the building and innovative technology reduces water use.

Villa La Diouana
RENTAL HOUSE €€€

(☑0666 55 16 46, in UK 00 44 7810 54 39 51; www.ladiouana.com; Quartier Moulay Abdelsalam; up to 10 people per week from £1650, cottage/apt for 2 per night from £80; @☎) All you can hear at night from this stunning 1930s villa is the crash of the ocean and the wind. High on a cliff with panoramic ocean views, the chic villa is simply but luxuriously decorated in a mixture of traditional and contemporary Moroccan design. There is a three bed-roomed villa, a lovely one-bedroom garden cottage and a studio flat with roof terrace, all surrounded by a 2323-sq-m garden with palm trees. The accommodation is rented out for the week and prices include a maid and breakfast.

Hotel Thalassa
HOTEL €

(☑0523 36 60 50; s/d Dh150/200, low season Dh100/150) The only hotel on the main drag up in the town, this slightly dated place is better than you might expect, with bright, airy whitewashed rooms that have old-fashioned, spick-and-span bathrooms. It's good value but far from the beach.

ⓘ Information

You'll find a bank, CTM office and **internet cafe** (per hr Dh10) here, and a Saturday souq when people from surrounding villages come to town to sell their wares.

ⓘ Getting There & Away

Local buses and grands taxis run at irregular times to El-Jadida (bus/taxi Dh25/25) and Safi (bus/taxi Dh25/25). They leave from near the post office on the main road. CTM has an office here and has a daily bus (Dh34) in either direction.

Safi
آسفي

POP 285,000

An industrial centre and a thriving port for the export of phosphates, Safi is a lot less picturesque than the neighbouring coastal towns, but it offers an insight into the day-to-day life of a Moroccan city. Most tourists stop here en route to or from Essaouira to visit the giant pottery works that take over a whole city quarter and produce the typical brightly coloured Safi pottery.

The new town is pleasant enough with tree-lined boulevards and whitewashed villas, but the alleys of the walled and fortified medina are more atmospheric to stroll through, and you often have the sites to yourself. The beaches are famous for their impressive surf. The immaculate sands north of town were the location for the 2006 Billabong Challenge and are said to have some of the finest waves in the world. Just south of town the landscape is largely industrial and of no interest to visitors.

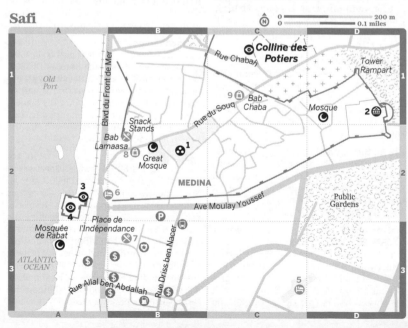

Safi's natural harbour was known to the Phoenicians and the Romans, but in the 11th century it was known as a port for the trans-Saharan trade between Marrakesh and Guinea, where gold, slaves and ivory were sold. In the 14th century the town became an important religious and cultural centre, when the Merenids built a *ribat* (fortified monastery) here. The Portuguese took the city for a brief spell from 1508 until 1541, when the Saadians took it back. They built the monumental Qasr al-Bahr fortress, a cathedral and generally expanded the town, but destroyed most monuments upon their departure.

In the 16th century, Safi grew wealthy from the trade in copper and sugar, and European merchants and agents flocked to the city, but when the port at Essaouira was rebuilt in the 18th century and all external trade was diverted, Safi was largely forgotten.

Safi's real revival came in the 20th century when its fishing fleet expanded and huge industrial complexes were built to process the 30,000 tonnes of sardines caught annually. A major phosphate-processing complex was established south of the town and the city began to expand rapidly. Today, Safi is one of Morocco's largest ports.

◉ Sights

Colline des Potiers   LANDMARK
Outside Bab Chaba, on the hill opposite the medina gate, you can't miss the earthen kilns and chimneys of the Colline des Potiers (Potters' Hill). The skills used here are predominantly traditional and you can wander around the cooperatives and see the potters at work. If a potter invites you in to watch him at work, you'll be expected to give a small tip or buy an item or two from the shop.

Qasr al-Bahr   HISTORICAL BUILDING
(Castle on the Sea; admission Dh10) The impressive castle dominates the crashing waves of the Atlantic on the rocky waterfront. The fortress was built to enforce Portuguese authority, house the town governor and protect the port. The ramp in the courtyard leads to the southwest bastion with great views. Prisoners were kept in the basement of the **prison tower**, right of the entrance, before being killed or shipped as slaves. You can climb to the top for views across the medina.

Medina   MEDINA
Across the street from the Qasr al-Bahr stands the walled medina. The main street, Rue du Souq, runs northeast from Bab Lamaasa, and you'll find most of the souqs, stalls, jewellery, clothing and food in this area. To the right of this street, down a twisting alley, are the remains of the so-called **Cathédrale Portugaise** (admission Dh10), which was never finished by the Portuguese who started it.

Musée National de Céramique   MUSEUM
(admission Dh10) The **Kechla**, a massive defensive structure with ramps, gunnery platforms and living quarters, has been restored and opened as this museum. Exhibits here include pottery from Safi, Fez and Meknès, and some contemporary pieces by local artists.

🛏 Sleeping & Eating

There is not much reason to spend the night in Safi, but if you do decide to stay, go for a better place than an average budget hotel (which can be pretty grim). The cheapest places are around the port end of Rue du Souq and along Rue de R'bat, though neither of these are great choices for women.

Hôtel Assif   HOTEL €
(☑0524 62 29 40; www.hotel-assif.ma; Rue de la Liberté; s/d Dh276/342; ❋) Comfortable, slightly faded rooms with clean en-suite bathrooms and small balconies are available at this reliable, three-star hotel. The set menu in the restaurant is Dh140. It's close

to Pl Mohammed V in the centre of the new town.

Hôtel Farah
HOTEL €€€

(☎0524 46 42 99; www.goldentulipfarahsafi.com; Ave Zerktouni; s/d/ste Dh615/880/1828; ❋❄🛜🏊) The best hotel and the best value in Safi, the renovated Farah is a bargain with large and stylish rooms in pale neutrals, sparkling bathrooms, anti-allergy duvets and a mini-bar. There are good views from the pool terrace, a fitness room, hammam, a restaurant and nightclub.

Hôtel Majestic
HOTEL €

(☎0524 46 40 11; Pl de l'Indépendance; s/d/tr Dh50/100/150, hot shower Dh10) This is the best of the medina options, with large, good-value rooms, although it can be noisy. The rooms are basic and have shared bathrooms, but everything is clean and well kept, and half the rooms have ocean views.

Restaurant Gégène
LOCAL €€

(☎0524 46 33 69; 11 Rue de la Marne; mains Dh80; ☺Mon-Sat) Old-fashioned service, tasteful decor and a surprisingly fine menu, with a wide choice of Moroccan and Mediterranean dishes from lamb tajine and pizza to Oualidia oysters, all served with a glass of wine.

Restaurant La Trattoria
ITALIAN €€

(☎0524 62 09 59; 2 Rue l'Aouinate; meals Dh200; ☺Mon-Sat) Run by the same management as Gégène, but more upmarket, La Trattoria is a pleasant place with a relaxed ambience and passable Italian food. The menu has a full range of pizzas and pasta, and a good choice of fish and seafood. It's located on Blvd du Front de Mer, 400m north of the medina.

Open-air Fish Restaurants
LOCAL

Fish and seafood, particularly sardines, are a speciality in Safi, and the best place to sample them is at the restaurants on the hill at the *rond-point de Sidi Bouzid* (the Sidi Bouzid roundabout). Establish the price before ordering, as fish is charged by weight, or order the fish special – a plate of fish served with bread and a spicy tomato sauce for about Dh35. A petit taxi to get there costs around Dh10.

🛍 Shopping

Safi is an excellent place to buy pottery of all types. To get a feel for prices visit the **fixed-price pottery shop** (☺9am-8pm) on the right-hand side of Rue du Souq as your enter

the medina from Bab Lamaasa. To the left, towards the eastern end of the same street, you'll find the colourful **pottery souq**.

Information

There are plenty of banks and ATMs clustered around Pl de l'Indépendance and Pl Driss Ben Nacer. Visit www.safi-ville.com for tourist information.

Cyber Club Lascala (Ave Sidi Mohammed Abdallah; per hr Dh5; ☺8am-midnight) Fantastic games den, with pool tables (Dh5 per game) and heaving with students.

Main post office (Ave Sidi Mohammed Abdallah)

Syndicat d'Initiative (Rue de la Liberté; ☺9am-noon & 3-7pm) Tourist information centre, but not very helpful.

Getting There & Away

BUS Most of the CTM buses stopping in Safi originate elsewhere, so consider booking at least a day in advance. Destinations include Agadit (Dh110, five hours, one daily), Casablanca (Dh85, four hours, 15 daily), El-Jadida (Dh50, two hours, four daily) and Essaouira (Dh50, two hours, nine daily). Other operators run daily departures to the same destinations as well as to Oualidia (Dh25, one hour, one daily) and Tiznit (Dh90, six hours, one daily).

TAXI There are grands taxis to Marrakesh (Dh65) and Essaouira (Dh50), among other destinations, which leave from the parking lot beside the bus station. The rank for Oualidia (Dh27) and El-Jadida (Dh45) is a good kilometre north of town on the El-Jadida road.

TRAIN From Safi **train station** (Rue de R'bat) there are two services per day at 5.50am and 3.50pm involving a change at Benguérir and calling at Casablanca (Dh84, 4½ hours), Rabat (Dh110, 5½ hours) and Fez (Dh185, eight hours).

Getting Around

Both the **bus station** (Ave Président Kennedy) and the **train station** (Rue de R'bat) are quite a distance south from the centre of town. A metered petit taxi from either will cost around Dh12. Local buses operate from just north of Pl Driss ben Nacer.

Around Safi

The wonderfully wild coastline north of Safi, with its dramatic cliffs sheltering gorgeous sandy coves, makes a great drive. The first stop is the headland of **Sidi Bouzid**, where you'll get a great view back over town. It's a good spot for lunch at the popular fish restaurant **Le Refuge** (⌀0524 46 43 54; Rte Sidi Bouzid; mains Dh100; ⊗Tue-Sun).

Driving further on, you'll hit some undeveloped beaches that are up-and-coming surf spots and home to one of the longest tubular right-handers in the world. Professionals such as Gary Elkerton, Tom Carroll and Jeff Hackman come here to train and in 2006 the Billabong Challenge was held here. At 12km from Safi, sheltered **Lalla Fatna** is one of the nicest spots on this stretch. Take a left by the Lalla Fatna cafe down a series of hairpin bends to the sands beneath the cliffs. Further on you'll reach the headland and lighthouse at **Cap Beddouza** (23km), where there's a wide, sandy beach.

In summer (May to September) bus 15 runs along this route from Rue Driss ben Nacer in Safi.

ESSAOUIRA الصويرة

POP 70,000

Essaouira (pronounced 'essa-weera', or 'es-Sweera' in Arabic) is at once familiar and exotic with its fortified walls, fishing harbour and seagulls soaring and screaming over the town. At first it seems as though this could be a town in Brittany, France – not such a strange thought given that Essaouira was designed by the same Frenchman who designed Brittany's most famous port town, Saint-Malo. And yet once you enter the walls, it is also infinitely Moroccan: narrow alleyways, the wind that reputedly drives people crazy, the smells of fish guts and damp sea air mixed with the aroma of spices and thuya wood, women in white *haiks* (veils), the midday shadow reflection of the palm trees on the red city walls, and the sound of drums and Gnawa singing that reverberates from shops and houses.

It is the wind – the beautifully named *alizee*, or *taros* in Berber, that, despite the crowds, ensures Essaouira retains its character. It blows too hard to attract sun, sand and sea tourists: for much of the year, you can't sit on the beach at all as the sand blows horizontally in your face. No surprise then that Essaouira has been dubbed 'Wind City of Africa' and attracts so many windsurfers. Sun-seekers head further south to the temperate clime of Agadir. The charm of the town is that it hasn't been entirely taken over by tourism. The fishing harbour is just as busy as it always was, the wood-

workers are still amazing at their craft and the medina is just as important for locals as it is popular with tourists.

Essaouira lies on the crossroads between two tribes: the Arab Chiadma to the north and the Haha Berbers in the south. Add to that the Gnawa, who came originally from further south in Africa, and the Europeans and you get a rich cultural mix. The light and beauty have forever attracted artists to Essaouira, and the town has a flourishing art scene. The sculptor Boujemaa Lakhdar started the local museum in the 1950s and, in the process, inspired a generation of artists. Since then, the autodidactic naïf painters, who paint their dreams in a colourful palette, have earned international renown, mainly thanks to the efforts of the Galerie Frederic Damgaard.

Winter is the time to get closer to the real Essaouira, when the wind howls at its strongest and the waves smash against the city's defences. In summer the town is invaded by throngs of Moroccan tourists, the beach is crowded and it is hard to find accommodation.

History

Most of the old city and fortifications in Essaouira today date from the 18th century, but the town has a much older history that started with the Phoenicians. For centuries, foreigners had a firm grip over the town, and although Moroccans eventually reclaimed it, the foreign influence lingers on in the way the town looks and feels today.

In 1764 Sultan Sidi Mohammed ben Abdallah installed himself in Essaouira, from where his corsairs could go and attack the people of Agadir who rebelled against him. He hired a French architect, Théodore Cornut, to create a city in the middle of sand and wind, where nothing existed. The combination of Moroccan and European styles pleased the Sultan, who renamed the town Essaouira, meaning 'well designed'. The port soon became a vital link for trade between Timbuktu and Europe. It was a place where the trade in gold, salt, ivory, and ostrich feathers was carefully monitored, taxed and controlled by a garrison of 2000 imperial soldiers.

By 1912 the French had established their protectorate, changed the town's name back to Mogador and diverted trade to Casablanca, Tangier and Agadir. It was only with independence in 1956 that the sleepy backwater again became Essaouira. After Orson

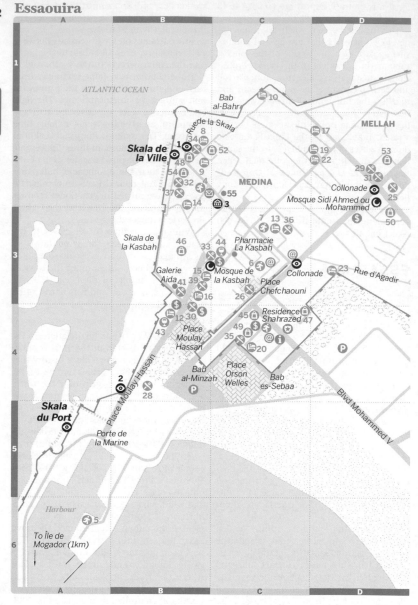

Welles filmed *Othello* here, and since Jimi Hendrix paid a fleeting visit and the hippies chose Essaouira as a hang out, the town has seen a steady flow of visitors, from artists, surfers and writers to European tourists escaping the crowds of Marrakesh.

⊙ Sights

Although there aren't so many formal sights in Essaouira, it's a wonderful place for rambling. The medina, souqs, ramparts, port and beach are perfect for leisurely dis-

layout is a prime example of European military architecture in North Africa. For the visitor, the mellow atmosphere, narrow winding streets lined with colourful shops, whitewashed houses and heavy old wooden doors make it a wonderful place to stroll.

The dramatic, wave-lashed ramparts that surround the medina are a great place to get an overview of the labyrinth of streets. The ramparts were famously used in the opening scene of Orson Welles' *Othello* for a panoramic shot where Iago is suspended in a cage above the rocks and sea. The easiest place to access the ramparts is at **Skala de la Ville**, the impressive sea bastion built along the cliffs. A collection of European brass cannons from the 18th and 19th centuries lines the walkway here and you'll also get great views out to sea and gorgeous sunsets.

Skala du Port   HISTORIC BUILDING
(adult/child Dh10/3; ⊘9am-5.30pm) Down by the harbour, the Skala offers more cannons and picturesque views over the fishing port and the Île de Mogador. Looking back at the walled medina from here, through a curtain of swirling seagulls, you'll get the same evocative picture that is used on nearly all official literature.

The large working port is a bustling place with plenty of activity throughout the day. Along with the flurry of boats, nets being repaired and the day's catch being landed you can see traditional wooden boats being made. The boat-builders supply fishing boats for the entire Moroccan coast and even as far away as France, as the design is particularly seaworthy. It's also worth visiting the **fish auction** (⊘3-5pm Mon-Sat), which takes place in the market hall just outside the port gates.

Île de Mogador   LANDMARK
Used in Phoenician and Roman times for the production of Tyrian purple dye from local molluscs, and once known as the Îles Purpuraires (Purple Isles), the Île de Mogador is actually two islands and several tiny islets. A massive fortification, a mosque and a disused prison are all that is left of what was once a thriving settlement, and today the uninhabited islands are a sanctuary for **Eleonora's falcons** (*falca eleonorae*). The islands are strictly off limits.

The elegant birds of prey come to breed from April to October before making their incredible return journey south to Madagascar. The falcons can be seen through binoculars from Essaouira beach, with the

covery interspersed with relaxed lunches and unhurried coffee or fresh orange juice.

Medina   MEDINA
Essaouira's walled medina was added to Unesco's World Heritage list in 2001. Its well-preserved, late-18th-century fortified

best viewing in the early evening. Another viewing place (not recommended in the evening if you're alone) is south of town, about 1km or so beyond the lighthouse, on the shore by the mouth of the river.

Sidi Mohammed ben Abdallah Museum   MUSEUM
(☑0524 47 53 00; Rue Laâlouj; adult/child Dh10/3) Essaouira's beautifully refurbished museum in an old riad, has a small but interesting collection of jewellery, costumes,

weapons, amazing musical instruments and carpets of the region. There's a section explaining the signs and symbols used by local craftspeople and some interesting photographs of Essaouira at the turn of the century. Note also the Roman and Phoenician objects found in the bay.

Activities
There are several opportunities to ride horses or camels in the countryside around Essaouira (see p232).

Beach
BEACH

Essaouira's wide, sandy beach is a great place for walking, but the strong winds and currents mean it's not so good for sunbathing or swimming. Footballers, windsurfers and kitesurfers take over the town end of the beach, while fiercely competitive horse and camel owners ply the sands further on. They can be quite insistent, so be firm and make it clear if you don't want to take a ride – and bargain hard if you do.

If you're walking, head south across the Ksob River (impassable at high tide) to see the ruins of the **Borj el-Berod**, an old fortress and pavilion that's partially covered in sand. Local legend has it that this was the original inspiration for the Jimi Hendrix classic 'Castles Made of Sand'; however, the song was actually released a year before he visited. From here you can walk inland to the village of Diabat (p232) or continue along the sands to the sand dunes of Cap Sim.

Union Nationale des Centres Sportifs de Plein Air
WATER SPORTS

(UCPA; ☎0661 24 98 01; ucpam_essaouira@yahoo.fr) UCPA rents surfboards (three days Dh420) and bodyboards (three days Dh220). Rental of windsurfing equipment is available (half-day/three days Dh350/1450). A two-hour lesson costs Dh440. A kitesurfing course of three two-hour lessons is Dh1600. It also has surfing lessons for children (two hours Dh250).

Océan Vagabond
WATER SPORTS

(☎0524 78 39 34; www.oceanvagabond.com; ☺9am-6pm) This outfit rents surfboards (three days Dh750) and gives two-hour surfing lessons (adult/child Dh440/340). It also offers kitesurfing lessons (six hours Dh2310) and rental (three days Dh1600), and windsurfing lessons (two/six hours Dh825/1750) as well as rental (two hours Dh440). It has a cool cafe-restaurant on the beach, with a laid-back terrace.

Hammam Lalla Mira
HAMMAM

(☎0524 47 59 07; www.lallamira.ma; 14 Rue d'Algerie; hammam with gommage Dh75; ☺women 9.30am-7pm, men 7-10pm) One of the oldest, this restored hammam is heated by solar energy and, although aimed at tourists, has a wonderful traditional interior. Good-value massages with argan oil. If you're not staying at this guesthouse, you'll need to make a reservation for the hammam.

Hammam de la Kasbah
HAMMAM

(7 Rue de Marrakesh; admission Dh10) For a more traditional, local experience. Women only.

Hammam Riad el-Madina
HAMMAM

(☎0524 47 59 07; 9 Rue el-Attarine; admission Dh70, massage from Dh300; ☺women 9-10am & 3-4pm, mixed 10am-12.30pm & 4-7pm) Another good place to break a first sweat.

Sofitel Mogador
HAMMAM, SPA

(☎0524 47 90 00; Blvd Mohammed V; from Dh200; ☺mixed 8.30am-2pm & 6.30-10.30pm, women 2.30-6pm) A traditional hammam, also offering hydrotherapy, aquagym and massages. Excellent service.

➤ Courses

L'Atelier Madada
COOKERY

(☎0524 47 55 12; 5 bis Rue Youssef el-Fassi; www.lateliermadada.com; ☺10.30am-2.30pm & 3-5pm) A former warehouse is the setting for this beautifully presented cookery school with places for eight people per session. Learn the secrets of tajines and couscous in the morning (Dh450, including lunch), or Moroccan patisserie in the afternoons (Dh200). The courses are presented in English and French.

Alliance Franco-Marocaine
LANGUAGE

(☎0524 47 61 97; www.ambafrance-ma.org/institut/afm-essaouira/index.cfm; Derb Lâalaouj, 9 Rue Mohammed Diouri; ☺9am-12.30pm & 2.30-6.30pm Mon-Fri) Offers semester-long French classes and eight-week Arabic classes as well as regular films, exhibitions and cultural events.

☞ Tours

Essaouira Sailing Tour
SAILING

(☎0661 62 63 13; www.essaouira-resort.com; port) This company offers two-hour sailboat trips (per adult/child Dh250/125, 10am and 2.30pm) out into the bay and around the Mogador islands. In the summer they also have a sunset sailing trip (adult/child Dh300/150, 1½ hours).

★ Festivals

Essaouira has two major festivals that draw hoards of performers and spectators to town.

Gnaoua and World Music Festival
LIVE MUSIC

(www.festival-gnaoua.net) A four-day musical extravaganza in the third weekend in June featuring international, national and local performers as well as a series of art exhibitions.

JIMI HENDRIX: CASTLES OF SAND OR PIE IN THE SKY?

There are a few stories that you might hear in Essaouira: that Jimi Hendrix lived here on and off for a few years in the 1960s. That he owned a riad that you can now stay in, or maybe it's a restaurant you can eat at. He stayed in quite a few other riads. He stayed in a campervan, or perhaps a tent. He tried to buy Île de Mogador. He composed *Castles Made of Sand* here. He signed a photo of himself that now graces the walls of a local restaurant. He wanted to adopt a Moroccan boy. He sired various children. He shared a room with Timothy Leary.

You can hear all of these stories in Essaouira – but they're all bunkum. Hendrix did visit Morocco for about a week, once only, in July 1969, with his then girlfriend, Colette Mimram, and spent two or three days in Essaouira. But he didn't even bring a guitar. This was 18 months after the album containing the song *Castles Made of Sand* was released.

And that photo, signed *'A mon ami Sam, 63'* is quite simply a forgery!

Festival des Andalousies Atlantiques　　　　LIVE MUSIC
(www.festivaldesandalousiesatlantiques.com)
An eclectic mix of Andalusian music, art and dance by local and international performers held in late October.

🛏 Sleeping

Accommodation in Essaouira isn't cheap but there's now a seemingly endless selection of properties to choose from at all price levels. Most hotels and riads are within the walls of the medina, so everything you need is within walking distance. In summer book ahead or at least arrive early in the day to find a room. As the medina gets increasingly crowded, hotels are being built along the coast further south and on the seafront.

The choice of budget accommodation in Essaouira is well above the usual Moroccan standard. Not only will you find a place where the bathrooms won't scare you, you'll probably get a character-laden room and terrace as well. In the midrange you'll be spoilt for choice in Essaouira. Each place is more charming than the next.

Essaouira has a great selection of apartments and riads to rent, most done up in impeccable style. If you're travelling as a family or in a group, they can be an affordable and flexible option. Prices range from about Dh600 per night for a one-bed apartment up to Dh3000 per night for the grand three-bedroom former British consulate.

TOP CHOICE　**Dar Adul**　　　GUESTHOUSE €€
(📞0524 47 39 10; www.dar-adul.com; 63 Rue Touahen; d Dh600-880; 📶) This lovingly restored house has just a few comfy rooms with subtle lighting, beautiful furniture, restrained muted colours and little touches that make it feel like a home rather than a hotel. The owner has hung the walls with his colourful paintings. The staff are incredibly friendly – you'll feel more like family than a paying guest by the time you leave. Dinner (Dh165) is available here on request.

Hôtel Beau Rivage　　　HOTEL €
(📞0524 47 59 25; www.essaouiranet.com/beaurivage; 14 Pl Moulay Hassan; s/d/tr incl breakfast Dh270/390/510; 📶) Readers recommend this friendly hotel in a perfect spot, overlooking the main square. The Beau Rivage has bright, cheerful rooms with modern fittings and spotless bathrooms. The rooms are a bit noisy but offer the greatest spectacle in town, while breakfast is served on the charming and quiet roof terrace with views over the port and town. There's a restaurant, too.

Lalla Mira　　　GUESTHOUSE €€
(📞0524 47 50 46; 14 Rue d'Algerie; www.lallamira.net; s/d/tr incl breakfast & hammam Dh436/692/860; 📶♨) This gorgeous little place, the town's first eco-hotel, has simple rooms with ochre *tadelakt* walls, wrought-iron furniture, natural fabrics and solar-powered underfloor heating. The hotel also has anti-allergy beds, a great hammam and a good restaurant serving interesting organic dishes such as rabbit with peaches and nuts, or goat with argan oil, as well as a good selection of vegetarian food.

Riad Nakhla　　　RIAD €
(📞/fax 0524 47 49 40; www.essaouiranet.com/riad-nakhla; 2 Rue d'Agadir; s/d/ste incl breakfast Dh230/360/500; 📶) Riad Nakhla comes as a

bit of a shock. It looks like any other budget place from the outside, but inside the weary traveller is met with a friendly reception in a beautiful courtyard, with elegant stone columns and a fountain trickling, more what you'd expect from a hotel in a higher price bracket. The well-appointed bedrooms are simple but comfortable and immaculately kept, full of local flavour with shuttered windows, colourful bedspreads and great *tadelakt*-clad bathrooms. All have a TV. Breakfast on the roof terrace with views over the ocean and town is another treat. It's an incredible bargain at this price.

Dar Afram
B&B €€

(☑0524 78 56 57; www.dar-afram.com; 10 Rue Sidi Magdoul; s Dh250, d Dh400-600) This extremely friendly guesthouse has simple, spotless rooms with shared bathrooms and a funky vibe. The Aussie-Moroccan owners are musicians and an impromptu session often follows the evening meals shared around a communal table.

Hôtel Les Matins Bleus
RIAD €€

(☑0524 78 53 63; www.les-matins-bleus.com; 22 Rue de Drâa; s/d/tr incl breakfast Dh310/470/940) Hidden down a dead-end street, this charming hotel has bright, traditionally styled rooms surrounding a central courtyard painted in cheerful colours. The rooms all have plain white walls, lovely local fabrics and spotless bathrooms. Breakfast is served on the sheltered terrace from where you'll get good views over the medina.

Riad Etoile d'Essaouira
GUESTHOUSE €€

(☑0524 47 20 07; www.riadetoiledessaouira.com; 2 Rue Kadissiya, Av Sidi Mohammed ben Abdellah; s/d/tr/ste Dh385/495/660/990; 🕸) Here's a newly opened guesthouse that's comfortably appointed and brightly decorated with local fabrics. It's in the *mellah* quarter of the medina. All rooms have televisions. Some rooms are designed for families.

Le Grand Large
GUESTHOUSE €€

(☑0524 47 28 66; www.riadlegrandlarge.com; 2 Rue Oum-Rabia; s/d/tr incl breakfast Dh440/550/660) After the simple whitewash and muted colours of many riads in town, Le Grand Large is much more colourful with pink, green and blue walls, bright throws on cast-iron beds and buckets of character. It's a friendly, cheerful place.

Dar Al-Bahar
GUESTHOUSE €€

(☑0524 47 68 31; www.daralbahar.com; 1 Rue Touahen; d without/with sea view Dh550/660,

ste Dh880) Readers have recommended this lovely medina guesthouse. The rooms at the Al-Bahar are elegantly simple, with plain white walls, wrought-iron furniture and a contrasting touch of blue, pink, green or yellow in the traditional bedspreads and curtains. Local art adorns the walls and the views from the terrace overlooking the ocean are magnificent.

La Casa del Mar
GUESTHOUSE €€

(☑0524 47 50 91; www.lacasa-delmar.com; 35 Rue D'Oujda; d incl breakfast Dh825) Delightful guesthouse that seamlessly blends contemporary design with traditional style and creates a stunning yet simple atmosphere where you can sit back and relax. Retire to your room, join the other guests for a communal Moroccan meal or Spanish paella (by reservation), arrange a home visit from a masseur or henna artist, or just watch the sunset from the seafront terrace.

Madada
GUESTHOUSE €€€

(☑0524 47 55 12; www.madada.com; 5 Rue Youssef el-Fassi; d Dh1265-1700, ste Dh1870; 🕸🛜) Sleek, stylish and very, very slick, Madada offers luxurious, contemporary rooms in a traditional house. Ivory and sand *tadelakt*, pared-back minimalism, designer furniture, neutral colours and a profound sense of Zen-like calm run throughout. The spacious, bright rooms have subtle decor, brass hand basins, private terraces and rosewood furniture. The upstairs rooms have a large terrace with sweeping views of the bay. The cooking school L'Atelier Madada (p227) and After 5 (p228) cocktail lounge and restaurant are both part of this guesthouse.

Hôtel Smara
HOTEL €

(☑0524 47 56 55; 26 Rue de la Skala; s/d/tr Dh76/104/174, d/tr with view Dh196/236) All whitewashed, the Smara has just four rooms overlooking the sea, the best ones on the roof terrace where breakfast is served. The other rooms open onto an internal room, but can be damp in winter. The communal bathrooms are tiled and clean. It's popular because it's good value, especially the quadruple rooms, so book ahead or arrive early.

Palais Heure Bleue
RIAD €€€

(☑0524 47 42 22; www.heure-bleue.com; 2 Rue Ibn Batouta; d/ste Dh3300/5830; 🕸🛜🛝) A decided hush falls as you walk through the doors of the Heure Bleue, Essaouira's top hotel. This swish riad has everything you could ever want, from a rooftop swimming pool to its own private cinema and billiard room. Chic European style and colonial charm meet in the lounge, where a grand piano sits beneath trophy heads from a long-forgotten hunting trip, and in the bedrooms where zebra prints, dark woods and marble counter tops vie for attention.

Dar Beida   RENTAL HOUSE €€€
(☑0667 96 53 86, in UK 00 44 07768 35 21 90; www.castlesinthesand.com; per week per person from Dh3300) A stunning 18th-century traditional Moroccan house, the 'White House' right in the centre of Essaouira, was lovingly restored by London interior decorator Emma Wilson and her husband with iconic 1950s and '60s furniture found in local junk markets. The house has several bedrooms, the best one on the upper roof terrace, and two living rooms with lots of books and CDs, and a large terrace. Rental includes cleaning, firewood and a pair of *babouches* (leather slippers) each. This is definitely the place to be in Essaouira. Dar Emma is Emma's other house for rent, more traditional but equally comfortable and funky.

Jack's Apartments (☑0524 47 55 38; www.essaouira.com/apartments; 1 Pl Moulay Hassan) and **Karimo** (☑0524 47 45 00; www.karimo.net; Pl Moulay Hassan) both have a good selection of rental properties. Book well in advance during the high season.

✗ Eating

TOP / CHOICE **Riad Al-Baraka**   LOCAL €€
(☑0524 47 35 61; 113 Rue Mohammed el-Qory; mains Dh110; ۞lunch & dinner) Set in a former Jewish school, this hip place has several dining rooms and a bar set around a large courtyard shaded by a huge fig tree. The food is mainly Moroccan with some Middle Eastern and Jewish influences, the decor cool, and there's live music by local bands at weekends.

Taros   MEDITERRANEAN €€
(☑0524 47 64 07; 2 Rue du Skala; mains Dh120; ۞lunch & dinner) One of the most atmospheric terraces in town, you can dine by candlelight inside or out. With great views over the square and port, and an interesting menu specialising in fish, it's a great place to be. There's often live music, too, and the magician will have you mesmerised. It's also good for afternoon tea, or a drink at the bar.

Outdoor Fish Grills   LOCAL
Essaouira is packed with cafes and restaurants so there's no difficulty finding somewhere to eat. However, the standards vary substantially. One of Essaouira's best food experiences is the outdoor fish grills that line the port end of Place Moulay Hassan. Just choose what you want to eat from the colourful displays of fresh fish and seafood at each grill, agree on a price (expect to pay about Dh60 for lunch) and wait for it to be cooked on the spot.

Restaurant El-Minzah   LOCAL, SEAFOOD €€
(☑0524 47 53 08; 3 Ave Oqba ben Nafii; mains Dh85-130, set menus from Dh95; ۞lunch & dinner) Sit on the outside terrace or in the elegant dining room inside at this popular place facing the ramparts. The menu features a good selection of international dishes with specialities such as blue shark and fresh fish, and there's lively Gnawa music here on Saturday nights.

Restaurant d'Orient et d'Ailleurs   FRENCH, LOCAL €€
(☑0524 45 59 77; 67bis Rue Touahen; set menus Dh90-130; mains Dh90-160; ۞lunch & dinner; ☑) A restaurant with romantic lighting and an eclectic decor, the d'Orient et d'Ailleurs serves up a wide variety of local fish, Moroccan and French dishes, and a good selection of vegetarian options.

After 5   MEDITERRANEAN €€€
(☑0524 78 47 26; 5 Rue Youssef el-Fassi; mains Dh200; ۞7-11pm Wed-Mon, noon-3pm Sat & Sun) Deep-purple seating, warm stone arches and giant lampshades dominate this trendy restaurant that serves well-cooked and original Mediterranean and Moroccan dishes. One of the favourite places to head for dinner.

Restaurant Ferdaous   LOCAL €€
(☑0524 47 36 55; 27 Rue Abdesslam Lebadi; mains Dh60-80, set menu Dh105; ۞lunch & dinner Tue-Sun) A delightful Moroccan restaurant, and one of the few places in town that serves real, home-cooked, traditional Moroccan food. The seasonal menu offers an innovative take on traditional recipes, the service is very friendly and the low tables and padded seating make it feel like the real McCoy.

Restaurante Les Alizés   LOCAL €€
(☑0524 47 68 19; 26bis Rue de la Skala; mains Dh120; ۞lunch & dinner) This popular place, run by a charming Moroccan couple in a

19th-century house, has delicious Moroccan dishes, particularly the couscous with fish and the tajine of *boulettes de sardines* (sardine balls). You'll get a very friendly welcome, and it's a good idea to book ahead. It's above Hôtel Smara.

La Licorne
LOCAL €€
(☏ 0524 47 36 26; 26 Rue de la Skala; menu Dh160; ☺ dinner) This is a cosy place with a most un-Essaouiran feel – wooden beams and heavy chairs give it the ambience of a hunting lodge. A no-nonsense, standard Moroccan menu of tajines is served up by friendly staff.

Café d'Horloge
CAFE €
(Pl Chefchaouni) Set on the attractive square beneath the clocktower, this popular cafe is an excellent choice for a breakfast of *amlou* (a spread made of local argan oil, almond and honey) and crepes or bread (Dh25). It's away from the hoards of people on the main cafe drag and a good choice for a quiet coffee or snack.

Gelateria Dolce Freddo
ICE CREAM €
(Pl Moulay Hassan) With more than 20 varieties of authentic Italian ice cream on offer, you'll find it hard to resist temptation at this little place on the main square. It's just Dh10 a scoop and the best you'll find in town.

Au Bonheur des Dames
CAFE €
(Pl du Marché au Grains) An elegant terrace on this picturesque square, purported to be the old slave market, that serves a good selection of teas, coffee, fresh juices and an excellent breakfast (Dh35).

Ocean Vagabond
CAFE €
(off Blvd Mohammed V; mains Dh60-90; ☺ lunch & dinner) Although a good walk from town, this simple little cafe is the best of the beachfront offerings. It serves a decent but limited range of sandwiches, pizza, pasta and salads and has plenty of comfy seats in the sand from where the kids can run free.

Côté Plage
MEDITERRANEAN €€
(Blvd Mohammed V; mains Dh150; ☺ lunch & dinner) Part of the looming Sofitel across the road, this beachfront cafe has a nice and elegant decked area where you can sit beneath the shade of giant white umbrellas. You can nibble on tapas (Dh35) as you look out over the ocean for the afternoon or arrive on Sunday for the all-day barbecue.

Fish Souq
LOCAL
(just off Ave de l'Istiqlal) Alternatively, you can visit the fish souq to buy some of the day's catch and take it to one of the grill stands in the southern corner. It'll come back cooked and served with bread and salad for Dh30.

For morning croissants or an afternoon pastry the best places to go are **Pâtisserie Driss**, which has a hidden seating area at the back, and **Café Faid**, both near Pl Moulay Hassan. There are plenty of **snack stands** and hole-in-the-wall type places along Ave Sidi Mohammed ben Abdallah, Ave Zerktouni and just inside Bab Doukkala.

Drinking
Despite its popularity as a tourist destination, Essaouira isn't the hottest place for nightlife. To warm up for an evening out,

---

DON'T MISS

ESSAOUIRA ART NAÏF

Wherever you go in Essaouira, you'll see artists at work, and their paintings for sale in almost every shop. The local artists were influenced by the influx of Westerners in the 1970s and developed their own style of naive paintings, mostly using acrylics. It's a mixture of naive and modern art, often influenced by the Gnawa movement, and the artists are self-taught. The paintings are brightly coloured and often feature musicians or groups of singers.

Latifa Boumazzourh is one such painter. Born into an artistic family, she was encouraged to paint by her late husband, himself an artist. She first exhibited at the Marrakech Palais de Congres in 1996, and has since shown in Germany, Switzerland and France. Latifa is president of the Association of Women Artists and Painters. She shows her work at the Galerie Sadiqi and at Riad al-Khansaa.

Latifa's work mostly depicts women musicians. Members of her family have always belonged to the Hamadcha Sufi brotherhood. The paintings show women in trance in this Sufi tradition (*hadra*) and prices for her work start at around Dh2000.

you could visit the **alcohol shops** (⊗9am-12.30pm & 3-6pm) just outside the medina near Bab Doukkala and take your drinks to your hotel terrace to watch the sun go down. Alternatively, try one of the following.

Le Patio   BAR
(28 Rue Moulay Rachid; ⊗dinner Tue-Sun) For something sultry, this hip bar and restaurant is a candlelit den with blood-red furnishings and a black mirror ball. You'll need to buy some tapas (Dh35) to just sit and drink or you might even be tempted by the whiff of grilled fish coming from the canopied restaurant (mains from Dh90).

Taros   BAR
(2 Rue du Skala) The terrace is a great place for a sundowner.

Café Restaurant Bab Laachour   CAFE
(Pl Moulay Hassan) Try the terrace. Beer is served in the evenings only.

🛍 Shopping
Riad al-Khansaa   ART & CRAFT
(60-62 Rue Touahen; 🛜) The ground floor of this remarkable house is packed with treasures from quirky clothing to beautiful lamps, paintings, sculptures and objets d'art. If you can't tear yourself away, there are rooms available upstairs (Dh400).

Woodcarving Workshops   ART & CRAFT
Essaouira is well known for its woodwork and you can visit a string of shops near the Skala de la Ville. The exquisite marquetry work on sale is made from local fragrant thuya wood, which is now an endangered species. Although the products are beautiful and sold at excellent prices, buying anything made from thuya threatens the last remaining stands of trees by increasing demand and therefore encouraging illegal logging. For a guilt-free conscience look for crafts made from other woods instead.

Coopérative Artisanal des Marqueteurs   ART & CRAFT
(6 Rue Khalid ibn Oualid) Come here for fixed-price shopping.

Rafia Craft   ART & CRAFT
(82 Rue d'Agadir) Essaouira's other great product is its raffia work, made from the fibres of the doum palm. Much of its line is sold to European outlets.

Spice Souq   FOOD & DRINK
This is the place to go for herbal Viagra, Berber lipstick, cures for baldness and exotic spices. You can also buy argan-oil products here, as well as the traditional *amlou* (about Dh40 per bottle).

Jewellery souq   JEWELLERY
A small area of jewellery shops with everything from heavy Berber beads to gaudy gold.

Essaouira also has a reputation as an artists' hub, and several galleries around town sell works by local painters. It's a mixed bag of talent and you may need to look in all of them before finding something you like.

Galeries Frederic Damgaard   ART & CRAFT
(www.galeriedamgaard.com; Rue Oqba ben Nafi) This gallery is the best and oldest in town and features the work of local artists.

Association Tilal des Arts Plastiques   ART & CRAFT
(4 Rue de Caire) Up-and-coming artists.

Espace Othello   ART & CRAFT
(9 Rue Mohammed Layachi; ⊗9am-1pm & 3-8pm) Up-and-coming artists.

Galerie Sadiqi   ART & CRAFT
(cnr Rue Laalouj & Rue Touahen) Latifa Boumazzourh shows her naive paintings at this small gallery.

Galerie Aida   BOOKS
(2 Rue de la Skala) Run by a former New Yorker, this place stocks a small but good selection of English-language books and some funky junk.

ℹ Information
For planning advice, author tips and traveller reviews, head to **Lonely Planet** (www.lonelyplanet.com/morocco/the-atlantic-coast/essaouira).

Dangers & Annoyances
Essaouira is still mostly a safe, relaxed tourist town but you should be on your guard in the backstreets of the *mellah* after dark. Although the town, and particularly the *mellah,* have been much cleaned up in recent years, there are still problems with drugs and drinking. Drug dealers and junkies hang out in the backstreets in an area north of Ave Zerktouni and east of Ave Sidi Mohammed en Abdallah, making this the least salubrious part of town.

Emergencies
Medical emergencies (☎0524 47 57 16)
Police (☎19, 0524 78 48 80; Rue du Caire) Opposite the tourist office.

Internet Access

There are internet cafes all over town. Most open from 9am to 11pm and charge Dh8 to Dh10 per hour.

Cyber Les Remparts (12 Rue du Rif)

Espace Internet (8 bis, Rue du Caire)

Mogador Informatique (5 Ave de l'Istiqlal)

Maps

The tourist office sells a useful map of town (Dh25) and an interesting guidebook called *Essaouira – La Séductrice* (Essaouira – the Enchantress, in French, Dh40), which has information on everything from local history and arts to traditional music, festivals and architecture. Another good buy (though not always available locally) is *Essaouira de Bab en Bab: Promenades* (in French) by Hammad Berrada, a wonderful book of walking tours. It provides details of eight different walks, accompanied by descriptive text, photographs and comprehensive maps of the medina.

Medical Services

Hôpital Sidi Mohammed ben Abdallah (0524 47 57 16; Blvd de l'Hôpital) For emergencies.

Pharmacie la Kasbah (0524 47 51 51; 12-14 Rue Allal ben Abdellah)

Money

There are several banks with ATMs around Pl Moulay Hassan and along the main road leading northeast to Bab Doukkala. Most are good for foreign exchange and credit-card cash advances.

Post

Main post office (Ave el-Mouqawama; ⊙8.30am-4.15pm Mon-Fri, 8am-noon Sat)

Post office (Rue Laâlouj; ⊙Mon-Fri)

Tourist Information

Délégation du Tourisme (0524 78 35 32; www.essaouira.com; 10 Rue du Caire) This helpful tourist office has lots of information and advice for travellers, as well as noticeboards with information on events and activities around town.

Getting There & Away

AIR Two dairly direct flights to Casablanca leave from **Aéroport de Mogador** (Route d'Agadir), 15km south of town. There are flights to Paris in summer, though the schedule is unreliable.

BUS The bus station is about 400m northeast of the medina, an easy walk during the day but better in a petit taxi (Dh10) if you're arriving/leaving late at night. The **left-luggage office** (Dh7 per item) is open 24 hours.

CTM has several buses daily to the following destinations:

DESTINATION	COST (DH)	DURATION (HR)
Agadir	60	3
Casablanca	135	6
El-Jadida	95	4
Inezgane	60	3½
Marrakesh	75	2½
Safi	50	2½

It's best to book a day in advance for long-distance services.

Other companies run cheaper and more frequent buses to the same destinations as well as Taroudannt (Dh70, six hours), Tan Tan (Dh130, six hours) and Rabat (Dh90, six hours).

Supratours, the ONCF subsidiary, runs buses to Marrakesh train station (Dh70, 2½ hours, five daily) to connect with trains to Casablanca from the station near Bab Marrakesh. You should book several days in advance for this service, particularly in summer.

Local bus 5 to Diabat (Dh5) and Sidi Kaouki (Dh6) leaves from Blvd Moulay Youssef outside Bab Doukkala. There are about eight services a day.

TAXI The grand-taxi rank lies immediately west of the bus station. The fare to Agadir (or Inezgane) is Dh75.

Getting Around

To get to the airport take bus 5 (Dh10, 15 minutes) or a grand taxi (Dh200). The blue petits taxis are a good idea for getting to and from the bus station (Dh10) but they can't enter the medina. If you're happy to walk but don't want to carry your bags, there are plenty of enterprising men with luggage carts who will wheel your bags directly to your hotel (about Dh20).

You can hire bikes from **Résidence Shahrazed** (0524 47 29 77; 1 Rue Youssef el-Fassi; per day Dh100) and **Résidence Hôtel Al-Arboussas** (0524 47 26 10; 24 Impasse Rue Laâlouj; per day Dh100).

Cars can be hired from **Wind Car** (/fax 0524 47 28 04; Rue Princesse Lalla Amina) for around Dh450 per day. **Avis** (0524 47 49 26) also has an office at the airport.

Around Essaouira

If you have your own transport, it's worth taking a trip to one of the small women's co-operatives around Essaouira that sell argan products, natural cosmetics and foodstuffs. Try **Assafar Imitaghant** (0661 55 35 86) 8km from town on the road to Marrakesh or the **Coóperative Tiguemine** (0524

ARGAN OIL

Organic argan oil is 'the new olive oil', increasingly used in hip restaurants around the world to season salads with its nutty flavour. The wrinkled argan tree is unique to this part of the world and, as a result, the argan forests of the Souss Valley and the Haha Coast south of Essaouira have recently been designated by Unesco as a biosphere reserve.

The tree, *Argania spinosa*, is resistant to heat and survives temperatures up to 50°C, so is an essential tool in the fight against desertification in southern Morocco. It has become vital to the local economy, providing firewood, fodder for the goats – you can see them actually climb into the branches – and oil for humans. Berber women harvest the fruits in spring. They then feed them to goats, whose digestive juices dissolve the tough elastic coating on the shell. The nuts are then recovered from the goats' dung, and the kernels are split, lightly toasted, pulped and pressed.

To produce just one litre of oil takes 30kg of nuts and 15 hours of manual labour, solely done by women. In a recent change to this tradition, some cooperatives have decided to cut the goats out of the process and are hand-picking fruits from the trees to produce a more subtle-tasting oil. You can see this whole process in a guided tour at the **Coopérative Amal** (☎0524 78 81 41; www.targanine.com, in French; Tamanar; admission free; ☺8am-7pm Mon-Fri), 80km north of Agadir, whose organic oil won the 2001 Slow Food Award.

The Berbers have long used argan oil to heal, but modern research suggests that the oil may help reduce cholesterol and prevent arteriosclerosis. In the kitchen its rich and sweet nutty flavour works wonders as a salad dressing, or added to grilled vegetables or tajine. Berbers mix it with ground almonds and honey to make *amlou*, a delicacy believed to have aphrodisiac properties.

Cold-pressed oil from untoasted nuts is increasingly recognised as a prized cosmetic, particularly for the hair. The oil has a high vitamin E content, which makes it a great addition to anti-wrinkle creams.

79 0110) 7km further on. The tourist office has a full list of places to visit. Best of all, travel south to the village of Tamanar to see the whole argan process at the Coopérative Amal (p232).

DIABAT الديابات

The sleepy Berber village of Diabat, just south of Essaouira, was once a dope-smoking colony popular with hippies. Today it is the site of a major new tourist development, Golf Mogador, not fully completed at the time of research. Comprising three luxury hotels and villas, the resort has a golf course designed by Gary Player. Fortunately the grey water from the complex will be used to water the golf course.

🏃 Activities

To try something more serious than the horse and camel rides on the beach, several companies offer cross-country trekking and multiday rides in the countryside around Essaouira. Tailor-made horse trips can be arranged through the following outfits.

Zouina Cheval   RIDING
(☎0669 80 71 01; www.zouina-cheval.com; 1hr ride Dh155, day incl picnic Dh600, treks 2/5 days Dh1760/6600) Recommended by several readers, this outfit is owned and run by Najib and Sophie, highly qualified and experienced instructors who cater for all levels, including children and beginners.

Maison du Chameau   CAMEL RIDING
(☎0661 34 71 08; maisonduchameau@yahoo.fr; Douar Al Arab; per hr Dh 160, per day incl lunch Dh400) This remote guesthouse is home to eight *meharis* (white Sudanese racing camels). The guesthouse offers weeklong camel-riding courses, shorter excursions and a selection of peaceful rooms decked out in vibrant fuchsia pink and electric blue. It's 7km along Route de Marrakech.

Ranch de Diabat   RIDING
(☎0662 29 72 03; www.ranchdediabat.com; 1hr lesson Dh165, 7-day trek incl accommodation Dh7700) Riding lessons for adults and children, as well as day-rides and longer treks.

Abouda Safar RIDING
(☑0528 31 45 70, 0662 74 34 97; www.abouda
-safar.com; 8-day trek Dh9000) Offers eight-
day treks in various parts of southern
Morocco.

🛏 Sleeping

Auberge Tangaro GUESTHOUSE €€
(☑0524 78 47 84; www.aubergetangaro.com; s/d
incl breakfast Dh500/770, ste Dh880-1100; 🔊) If
you want to stay in Diabat, your best bet is
this rustic and remote old house in a serene
location, close to the new golf course. The
rooms here are chic and all recently decorated, each has its own open fireplace and
the whole house is romantically lit by candlelight (there's electricity for charging batteries only). Dinner is available, and there's
a hammam.

❶ Getting There & Away
To get to Diabat drive south on the coast road to
Agadir and turn right just after the bridge about
7km out of town. Alternatively, local bus 5 leaves
from outside Bab Marrakech (Dh5, every two
hours).

SIDI KAOUKI سيدي كاوكي
The constant blustery winds, wild beach
and decent accommodation at Sidi Kaouki
are fast turning it into one of Morocco's top
windsurfing and surfing spots. There's a
wind farm just north of the village to prove
it. It's not for the faint-hearted and the
waters here can be dangerous for inexperienced surfers.

The large building on the rocks, washed
by the sea, is the final resting place of Sufi
saint Sidi Kaouki who was known for his
healing abilities. People still visit the shrine.
You can rent a horse (Dh70/120 per half-
hour/hour) or a camel (Dh100 per hour)
and ride along the long stretch of beautiful
beach. For water sports, the quintessential
surfers' hang-out on the beach is **Station**

Sidi Kaouki (☑0672 04 40 16; www.sidi-kaouki.
com), a brightly decorated cafe and restaurant with a cool vibe. Here you can hire a
surfboard (Dh275/660 per one/three days)
or kitesurfing and windsurfing equipment
(Dh1430 per three days) as well as arrange
excursions to remote beaches.

A clutch of guesthouses are set back from
the beachfront. They all serve dinner.

🛏 Sleeping

Auberge de la Plage GUESTHOUSE €€
(☑0524 47 66 00, 0661 10 26 64; www.kaouki.
com; s/d/tr incl breakfast Dh350/550/650) This
is a delightfully rustic house with comfortable rooms with sea views. There are cheaper rooms with shared bathrooms. Dinner
can be ordered in advance and is excellent.
The menu depends on what the local fishermen have caught. The garden is a shady haven, while there's nowhere better than the
roof terrace to watch the sunset. The owner
is very knowledgeable about the area.

Hotel Le Kaouki GUESTHOUSE €€
(☑0524 78 32 06; www.sidikaouki.com; s/d/
tr incl demi pension Dh330/550/730) Decorated in bright blue with local fabrics, this
is also a good choice. The staff are friendly
and welcoming. There's electricity on the
ground floor only.

Windy Kaouki APARTMENT €€€
(☑0524 47 22 79; www.windy-kaouki.com;
apt Dh750-1100; 🔊) These spacious apartments are ideal for families. They are fully
equipped, nicely decorated and have fireplaces. The balconies have wonderful sea
views. Staff can arrange windsurfing, quad
bikes and horse riding.

❶ Getting There & Away
Sidi Kaouki is about 27km south of Essaouira.
Bus 2 or 5 (Dh6) leaves from outside Bab Marrakech every two hours. A grand taxi will cost
around Dh150 and takes an hour.

Mediterranean Coast & the Rif شاطىء البحر المتوسط والريف البحري

Best Places to Eat

» Populaire Saveur de Poisson (p246)

» Blanco Riad (p262)

» Auberge Dardara (p272)

Best Places to Stay

» Dar Nour (p243)

» Dar Ech-Chaouen (p271)

» Gîte Tagma (p297)

Why Go?

Northern Morocco offers a beautiful coastline, a mountainous hinterland rarely explored by visitors and just one major city. The beguiling gateway to Africa, Tangier has emerged from its shady past to become a tantalising experience. Eastward lies one of the last stretches of undeveloped Mediterranean coast with high cliffs and sandy coves.

Tetouan and Al-Hoceima reflect former Spanish protectorate days in architecture and food. More still can be found in the Spanish enclaves of Ceuta and Melilla with their medieval fortifications and spectacular architectural treasures. Ranging over the mountains inland are magnificent national parks, from the coastal Al-Hoceima to the remote Beni-Snassen, that beg to be discovered.

Go soon: a highway along the coast nears completion, and resorts are blooming in Martil, M'Diq and Saïdia. Progress has been slowed by the recession, but these developments will change the coastline irrevocably.

When to Go?

Tangier

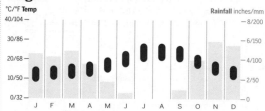

April
Spring is perfect for trekking in the Rif or exploring national parks.

July
Head to Chefchaouen for the annual arts festival.

September
Mediterranean beaches await, without the crowds.

S P A I N

Cap Spartel
Strait of Gibraltar
Tarifa
Tangier
Jebel Musa (842m)
Ceuta (Spain)
Grottes d'Hercule
Ksar es-Seghir
Fnideq
Cabo Negro
M'Diq
Martil
Tetouan

MEDITERRANEAN SEA

Oued Laou
Targa
Bou-Ahmed/Steha
El-Jebha

Cala Iris
Torres de Alcala
Al-Hoceima
Al-Hoceima National Park
Ajdir
Imtzouren

Isla de Mar & Isla de Tierra (Spain)
El Peñón de Velez de la Gomera (Spain)
El Peñón de Alhucemas (Spain)

Cap Des Trois Fourches
Islas Chafarinas (Spain)
Melilla (Spain)
Beni Ansar
Kariat Arkmane
Selouane
Nador

Ras el-Maa
Moulouya Estuary
Saïda
ALGERIA
Oujda
Ahfir
Zegzel Gorge
Beni-Snassen Mountains
Berkane
Taforalt
Zaïo
Oued Moulouya

Midar
Driouch

R i f   M o u n t a i n s

Targuist
Jebel Tidiquin (2448m)
Issaguen (Ketama)
Bab Berret
Bab Taza
Chefchaouen
Dardara
Ackoubaa
Dar
Souk el-Arba-des-Beni-Hassan
Talassemtane National Park
Jebel Bouhachem Nature Reserve
Ouezzane

N16

50 km
30 miles

Mediterranean Coast & the Rif Highlights

❶ Dream the day away at a pavement cafe beneath the kasbah in Chefchaouen's **Plaza Uta el-Hammam** (p270)

❷ Browse the treasure-filled shops of **Tangier's medina** (p243) and stop for coffee at the Petit Socco, haunt of the Beat poets

❸ Marvel at the dragons launching from the roof of a palace in **Ceuta** (p255)

❹ Wander the streets of **Melilla** (p288) and gaze at the Modernist buildings, before tapas for lunch

❺ Discover Roman mosaics from Lixus in the Archaeology Museum in **Tetouan** (p261)

❻ Soak up the sun on the remote beaches of the **National Park of Al-Hoceima** (p281)

❼ Take in remarkable views as you trek to Berber villages in the **Talassemtane National Park** (p283) in the Rif Mountains

❽ Enjoy a fish platter at **Club Nautique** (p281) in Al-Hoceima

Tangier

طنجة

POP 700,000

Always of huge strategic importance at the entrance to the Mediterranean, Tangier is the enthralling gateway to Africa, a tantalising introduction to a culture vastly different from that across the Strait of Gibraltar.

After WWII, Tangier became an International Zone that attracted eccentric foreigners, artists, spies and hippies. The city fell into neglect and dissolution, gaining a dismal reputation thanks to the sleaze and hustles that beset every arrival. But now the white city has turned over a new leaf, and is looking to the future with renewed vigour.

With the arrival of the new monarch in 1999 and his forward-thinking ideas about commerce and tourism, suddenly the community woke up to the potential of this great city. There's a spanking new port of enormous proportions, a new business district and a revamped airport. Buildings have been renovated, beaches cleaned up, hustlers chivvied off the streets, there's an explosion of cultural activities and now some great places to stay and excellent restaurants.

Tangier is divided into an old walled city, or medina, a nest of medieval alleyways, and a new, modern city, the ville nouvelle. The medina contains a kasbah, the walled fortress of the sultan, which forms its western corner; the Petit Socco (also known as Socco Chico, and officially as Pl Souq ad-Dakhil), an historic plaza in the centre; and of course, the souqs, or markets. The much more impressive Grand Socco (officially renamed Pl du 9 Avril 1947), a pleasant square with a central fountain, is the

Tangier

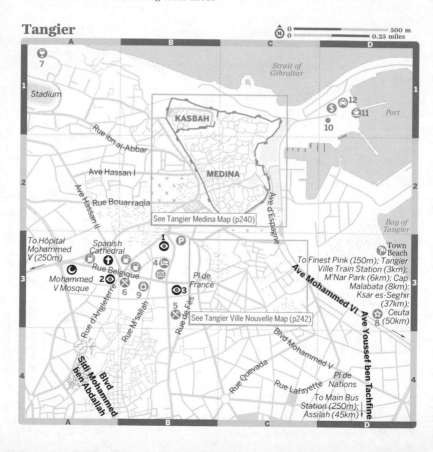

hinge between the two sides of town, and the postcard entrance to the medina.

History

Tangier's history is a raucous tale of foreign invasion, much of it driven by the city's strategic location at the entrance to the Mediterranean. The area was first settled as a trading base by the ancient Greeks and Phoenicians (who brought the traditional Moroccan hooded robe, the jellaba, with them), and named for the goddess Tinge, the lover of Hercules, whose Herculean effort separated Europe from Africa to form the Strait of Gibraltar. Under Roman rule, it was the capital of the province of Mauretania Tingitana. The Vandals attacked from Spain in AD 429, followed by the Byzantines, and then the Arabs, who invaded in 705 and quelled the Berber tribes. Tangier passed between various Arab factions before finally coming under Almohad rule in 1149. Then the Portuguese arrived, capturing the city on their second attempt in 1471, only to hand it to the British 200 years later as a wedding gift for Charles II. Its value is difficult to assess: the English diarist Samuel Pepys called it 'the excrescence of the earth'. Moroccans regained control of the city under Sultan Moulay Ismail in 1679,

destroying much of the city in the process. They remained in power until the mid-19th century, when North Africa once again piqued the interest of the European powers.

The modern history of Tangier begins here. While the rest of Morocco was divided between France and Spain, strategic Tangier was turned into an 'International Zone' of various sectors, similar to West Berlin in the Cold War. France, Spain, Britain, Portugal, Sweden, Holland, Belgium, Italy and the USA all had a piece of the pie, which was managed by the sultan, at least on paper. This situation lasted from 1912 until shortly after Moroccan independence, in 1956, when the city was returned to the rest of the country. During this famous Interzone period, expats flooded in, forming half the population, and a wild, anything-goes culture broke out, attracting all sorts of people, for reasons both high and low. Socialites, artists, currency speculators, drug addicts, spies, sexual deviants, exiles, eccentrics – the marginalia of mankind all arrived, giving the city a particularly sordid reputation.

When the Interzone period ended, Tangier entered a long period of decline. As the economic base moved on, so did the cultural scene. The city became a dreary port, while retaining its criminality. Having taken a dislike to it, successive monarchs cut off access to key funds. Street hustlers multiplied, turning off tourists. The numbers of expats dwindled, until there were only a few thousand left.

Since 1999, Tangier has been the site of major development with its new port, Tanger Med, and a drive towards increasing tourism across the region with Tangier the central hub.

◉ Sights

Grand Socco LANDMARK
(Map p240) The Grand Socco is the romantic entrance to the medina, a large, sloping, palm-ringed plaza with a central fountain that stands before the keyhole gate Bab Fass. Once a major market, its cobblestone circle is now the end of the line for taxis, the point at which the modern streets narrow into the past. For the best ground-floor view, climb the steps at the highest point on the circle, across from the large tan building (the police station), to what locals simply call La Terrasse. This is what you came

One Day

After breakfast at **Le Salon Bleu** in the kasbah, take a wander through the **sultan's palace**, and a meander down the **medina** streets. Don't miss **Majid's** treasure-trove of a shop before lunch at **Le Nabab**. The **Grand Socco** is the perfect place for mint tea. Wander up to **St Andrew's Church** for a spot of gravestone reading, then take in the latest art exhibition at **Ibn Khaldoun Gallery** before heading to **El-Minzah Spa** for a hammam. A drink in the **Caid's Bar** is followed by dinner at **Les Passagers de Tangier**, before heading to the **Tangier Inn** just like a Beat poet.

Two Days

Discover the vibe of the new city with breakfast at the plush **La Giralda** where you can check the views over to Spain from **La Terrasse des Paresseux**. Head to **DARNA** and browse the craft shop before a fishy lunch at **Populaire Saveur du Poisson**. A post-prandial stroll through the **Mendoubia Gardens** is perfect, followed by a photo-opportunity visit to the **fresh produce market**. Just around the corner is the **American Legation Museum** where you can seek out Morocco's Mona Lisa. After dinner at **Casa de España**, dance the night away at **Beach Club 555**.

for, one of those dreamy moments when you think you've entered a movie set.

The Grand Socco is also the hub of several other sights, all visible from within it. First is the Cinema Rif, which stands on the circle. The brightest light on Tangier's cultural scene, it is a combination art-house cinema, cafe and archive, and is the local focal point for anything to do with film. Young Tangaouis come to soak up the ambience and use the free wi-fi.

DARNA, the Women's Association of Tangier   ART & CRAFT

(Map p240) The yellow building opposite La Terrasse is a small complex offering an inexpensive restaurant, a boutique shop with crafts and clothing, and a sunny courtyard, making it a popular stop for lunch or just a place to relax. Since 2002, DARNA has served as a community house to help local women in need, such as those suffering the after-effects of divorce.

Mendoubia Gardens   PARK

(Map p240) Across the Grand Socco from the Cinema Rif is this large park full of strolling couples and children playing football. The Mendoubia Gardens are flanked by an elegant line of colonial buildings, perhaps the most attractive of its kind in the city. At the top of the central hill is a monument flanked by cannons that contains the speech given by Mohammed V asking for independence.

St Andrew's Church   CHURCH

(Map p240; ☺services 8.30am, 11am Sun) A short walk down Rue d'Angleterre brings you to one of the more charming oddities of Tangier. Built from 1894 to 1905, on land granted by Queen Victoria, the interior of this Anglican church is in Moorish style, with no graven images, and the Lord's Prayer in Arabic. Behind the altar is a cleft that indicates the direction of Mecca; carved quotes are from the Quran. A real interfaith experience!

Outside in the church graveyard, there are some fascinating wartime headstones, including the fighter pilot shot while escaping (which reads 'Good Hunting, Tim') and the moving sight of entire downed aircrews, their headstones attached shoulder to shoulder. Caretakers Ali and his son Yassine are always on-site and will let you in.

Medina   MEDINA

The medina is the top attraction of Tangier, a labyrinth of alleyways both commercial and residential, contained by the walls of a 15th-century Portuguese fortress. Clean and well lit, as medinas go, the place is full of traveller's treasures, from fleeting glimpses of ancient ways of living, to the more material rewards of the souqs. The thing to do is to get lost and wander for a few hours, although there are a few sites you don't want to miss. Get as close to your destination as possible, then ask if you run into problems. Young people will be happy to take you anywhere (for a few dirhams).

From the Grand Socco, enter the medina opposite the Mendoubia Gardens, on Rue as-Siaghin, and follow the road downhill until it widens at Café Central, on the left. This is the **Petit Socco** (Map p240) once the most notorious crossroads of Tangier, the site of drug deals and all forms of prostitution. Today the facades are freshly painted, tourists abound and it's a wonderful square for people-watching while you drink your mint tea.

From the Petit Socco, Rue Jemaa el-Kebir (formerly Rue de la Marine) leads east past the **Grande Mosquée** (Map p240), which at one time housed a Portuguese church. A little further on you reach a **scenic lookout** (Map p240) over the port.

Now to avoid getting lost, head out of the medina a moment, and circle down to its southernmost corner, where you will re-enter via the steps to Rue D'Amerique/Zankat America. A dog-leg brings you to a door in a covered passageway on your left. Here you will find another great local oddity, and must-visit, the **Tangier American Legation Museum** (Map p240; ☑0539 93 53 17; www.legation.org; 8 Rue D'Amerique; admission free, but donations appreciated; ⊙10am-1pm & 3-5pm Mon-Fri, weekends by appointment). Morocco was one of the first countries to recognise the fledgling United States, and this was the first piece of American real estate abroad (look for the letter of thanks from George Washington to Sultan Moulay Suleyman). It is also the only US National Historic Landmark on foreign soil. The elegant five-storey mansion holds an impressive display of paintings that give a view of the Tangerine past through the eyes of its artists, most notably the Scotsman James McBey, whose hypnotic painting of his servant girl, Zohra, has been called the Moroccan Mona Lisa. The new director of the Legation, Gerald Loftus (see the boxed text, p245), has introduced a well-stocked bookshop and a wing dedicated to Paul Bowles. The romantic map room upstairs contains walls lined with ancient parchments and diplomatic mementoes, including a hilarious letter from the US consul recounting his gift of a lion from the sultan in 1839. It is at this point you realise that you have entered the plot of an exotic historical novel.

Just off the Petit Socco is the **Musée de la Fondation Lorin** (Map p240; fondationlorin@gmail.com; 44 Rue Touahine; admission free, donations appreciated; ⊙11am-1pm & 3.30-7.30pm Sun-Fri), which is another eclectic stop. Here

in this former synagogue, you will find an open two-storey room with an engaging collection of black-and-white photographs of 19th- and 20th-century Tangier on the walls. Meanwhile there is likely a children's theatre going on in the centre, as the museum doubles as a workshop for disadvantaged kids, bringing life to the static display.

Now continue along Rue Touahine to Rue as-Siaghin, and exit the medina from where you started. Follow the perimeter all the way to the western end, to the highest part of the city, enter the Porte de la Kasbah, and follow the road to the **Kasbah Museum** (Map p240; Pl de la Kasbah; adult/child Dh10/3; ⊙9-11.30am & 1.30-4pm Wed-Mon). The museum is perfectly sited in Dar el-Makhzen, the former sultan's palace (where Portuguese and British governors also lived) and has recently been completely renovated. The new focus is on the history of the area from prehistoric times to the 19th century, most of it presented in seven rooms around a central courtyard. Placards are in French and Arabic. Some highlights are pre-Roman tools; a sculpture with scenes of a bacchanalian feast; some 16th-century jewellery; an extraordinary floor mosaic from Volubilis; and a fascinating wall map of trade routes past and present. Before you leave, don't miss the exotic Sultan's Garden off the main courtyard, opposite the entrance, which was being restored at the time of research.

VILLE NOUVELLE
With its Riviera architecture and colonial ambience, the area around Pl de France and

ART GALLERIES

Mohamed Drissi Gallery of Contemporary Art

(Map p236; 52 Rue d'Angleterre) Housed in the former British Consulate.

Galerie Delacroix

(Map p242; 86 Rue de la Liberté; ⊙Tue-Sun) Exhibition space of the Institut Français.

Centre Culturel Ibn Khaldoun

(Map p242; Rue de la Liberté) Exhibits contemporary art.

Instituto Cervantes Gallery

(Map p236; Rue Belgique) Contemporary exhibitions.

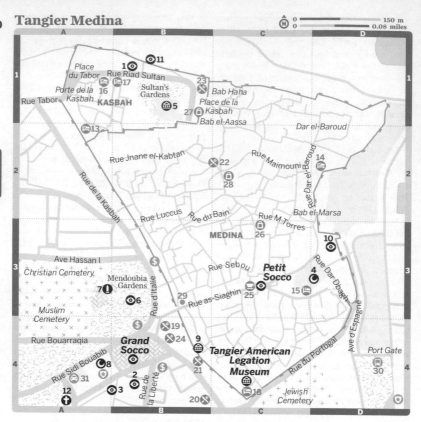

Blvd Pasteur still hints at the glamour of the 1930s. It's a popular place for an early evening promenade, or a few hours sipping mint tea in one of the many streetside cafes – particularly the landmark Gran Café de Paris, whose retro facade is screaming to be captured on canvas. Where is that Tangier expat Matisse when we need him?

Next door is the aptly named **Terrasse des Paresseux** (Idlers' Terrace; Map p242), which provides sweeping views of the port and, on a clear day, Gibraltar and Spain. A set of ancient cannons faces the bay, symbolically warding off usurpers.

Nearby you'll find **Librairie des Colonnes** (Map p242; 54 Blvd Pasteur; ⊘9.30am-1pm & 4-7pm Mon-Sat). This bookshop, an absolute institution in Tangier, was once the haunt of Paul Bowles, Jean Genet, Samuel Becket and William Burroughs. It has recently reopened after renovation, and to-

day you might bump into Tahar Ben Jelloun or Bernard Henri-Levy.

Town Beach   BEACH
The wide **town beach** (Map p236) has been improved – it's actually cleanest in the bustling summer. In any case, locals advise that it is still not clean enough for swimming, particularly the section closest to the port. It works well for a seaside stroll, however, and the new corniche makes walking easy. It's not a great place late in the day, when muggings aren't unknown. There are plenty of attractive beaches down the nearby Atlantic Coast.

🏃 Activities
Spas & Hammams
El-Minzah Wellness   HAMMAM
(Map p242; ☑0539 93 58 85; www.elminzah.com; 85 Rue de la Liberté; fitness room Dh200) Pamper yourself at the luxury spa, where there's a fully equipped gym (with superb views to

sea), sauna and Jacuzzi, as well as a range of both massage and therapeutic treatments.

Serenity Day Spa HAMMAM
(☏0539 37 28 28; serenity@serenityspa.ma; Rue Adolfo Fessere, in Quartier California; hammam & gommage Dh400) Here is a chance for women to escape the all-too-male world of Morocco, at least for a few hours, and indulge the body in luxurious surroundings. This female-only hammam gets high marks from local customers. It's west of Pl de Koweit, on the road to the golf course; take a cab.

Juan Guilleri BARBER
(Map p242; near Casa Pepe, Rue Ibn Rochd) Recommended by Jean-Olivier and Philippe at Dar Nour, this barber will lather and scrape for a mere Dh25. Appointments are not necessary.

Horse Riding

Royal Club Equestre HORSE RIDING
(☏0539 93 43 84; Rte de Boubana; 30min Dh75, 1hr Dh150; ☺8am-noon & 2-6pm, Tue-Sun) Along the road to Cap Spartel, the stables are set in the midst of forested hills, a pleasant place to explore on horseback. All riders must be accompanied by a guide, which is included in the price of the horse hire.

 Tours

To find a reputable guide, inquire at any hotel or the tourism information office. Alternatively, an excellent choice is **Said Nacir** (☏0671 04 57 06; www.d-destination.com). An English-speaking national guide with over 20 years experience, he specialises in private tours of Tangier for small parties, from individuals to families, at Dh350 per day including transport and entry fees. For Dh800, he offers a day trip from Spain including ferry tickets, pick-up, entry fees, lunch and guide services – a bargain. Itineraries can be customised to your taste.

Festivals & Events

The place to go for listings of events and local info is *Tanger Pocket,* a brochure (in

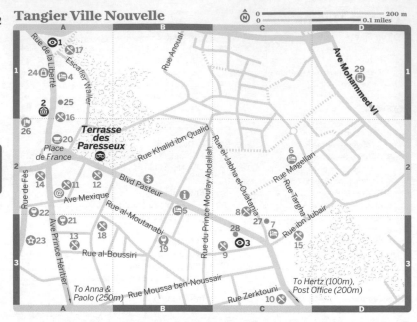

Tangier Ville Nouvelle

◎ Top Sights
Terrasse des Paresseux........................ A2

◎ Sights
1 Centre Culturel Ibn Khaldoun............... A1
2 Galerie Delacroix A1
Gran Café de Paris........................(see 20)

Activities, Courses & Tours
El-Minzah Wellness ....(see 4)
3 Juan Guilleri Barber............................... C3

🛏 Sleeping
4 El-Minzah... A1
5 Hotel de Paris.. B2
6 Hôtel el-Muniria C2
7 Hôtel Rembrandt C3

🍴 Eating
8 Casa de España C2
9 Casa Pepé C3
10 Champs Élysées C3
11 Fast Food Brahim A2
12 La Giralda A2
13 Le Pagode A3
14 Mix Max A2
15 Number One.. C3

16 Pâtisserie La Española........................... A1
17 Populaire Saveur de Poisson A1
Restaurant el-Korsan....................(see 4)
18 San Remo A3

🍸 Drinking
19 Americain's Pub B3
Caid's Bar..................................... (see 4)
20 Gran Café de Paris A2
21 Hole in the Wall Bar................................ A3
22 Pilo A2
Tanger Inn .... (see 6)

✪ Entertainment
23 Cinéma Paris A3

🛍 Shopping
24 Bazar Tindouf A1

Information
25 Carlson Wagonlit A1
26 French Consulate A2
27 Hispamaroc C3

Transport
28 Avis C3
29 Local Buses for Train Station............... D1

MEDITERRANEAN COAST & THE RIF WEST MEDITERRANEAN COAST

French) available at most hotels and online (www.tangerpocket.com).

Salon International de Tanger des Livres et des Arts BOOKS
(☑0539 94 10 54; Institut Français, 41 Rue Hassan ibn Ouazzane; www.amba-france-ma.org) Annual weeklong book festival with varying themes, held in April.

Le Festival International de Théâtre Amateur THEATRE
(☑0539 93 03 06; Fondation Lorin, 44 Rue Touahine) A week of Arabic- and French-speaking theatre, traditionally held every May, run by Fondation Lorin.

TANJAzz LIVE MUSIC
(www.tanjazz.org) Held in September, this ever-popular festival hosts concerts by local and international jazz musicians, including some leading names.

Festival du Court Métrage Méditerranéen SHORT FILMS
(International Mediterranean Short Film Festival; www.ccm.ma) Weeklong festival of short films from around the Mediterranean, held in October.

Tanja Latina LIVE MUSIC
(☑0539 93 03 06; Fondation Lorin) Held in November, this is Tangier's growing attempt to follow in Rio's footsteps.

🛏 Sleeping

Tangier's sleeping options cater to all budgets and styles, spanning the spectrum from the ultra-cheap *pensiónes* (guesthouses) near the port to the chic hotels along the oceanfront. Most budget accommodation options are clustered around the medina and close to the port gate. They're cheap but only occasionally cheerful, so it can pay to hunt around. In addition to those listed here, you can find plenty of choice in the streets around Ave Mokhtar Ahardan and the Rue Magellan. Low-season travellers might get a reduced rate. Before accepting your room, however, make sure that it has not grown musty from the sea.

MEDINA

TOP CHOICE **Dar Nour** GUESTHOUSE €€
(Map p240; ☑0662 11 27 24; www.darnour.com; 20 Rue Gourna, Kasbah; d/ste incl breakfast from Dh720/1300; 🛜). With no central courtyard, rooms here branch off two winding staircases, creating a maze of rooms and salons, each more romantic than the last. Rooms are stylishly decorated with

For kids, **M'Nar Park** (☑0539 34 38 29; www.mnarparktanger.com; Cap Malabata; aquapark adult/child Dh100/50; ☺8am-6pm, pool 15 Jun-15 Sep) is heaven, and the only game in town. Located south of Cap Malabata, with great views across the Bay of Tangier, this cliffside resort offers a water park, an electronic game park, karting, a small train, a mini-football field, restaurants, a cafe and 38 residential bungalows for families.

In town and close to the Grand Socco, the **Mendoubia Gardens** is a park with grass for playing football and swings for letting off steam.

objets d'art and packed with books creating a relaxed and homely atmosphere, while bathrooms are *tadelakt* (polished plaster). Some rooms have a private terrace. Once you get to the top of the house, there is an impressive view over the roofs of the medina. Breakfasts are huge and are usually served on the terrace.

La Tangerina GUESTHOUSE €€
(Map p240; ☑0539 94 77 31 19; www.latangerina.com; Rue Sultan, Kasbah; d incl breakfast Dh600-1620; 🛜) This is a perfectly renovated riad at the very top of the kasbah, with 10 rooms of different personalities, easily accessible by car (a rarity), with highly attentive hosts. Bathed in light and lined with rope banisters, it feels like an elegant, Berber-carpeted steamship cresting the medina. The roof terrace overlooks the ancient crenellated walls of the kasbah, while below, neighbourhood washing hangs from abandoned coastal cannons, proclaiming the passage of history. Reserve early. Dinner is available on request.

Nord Pinus Tanger GUESTHOUSE €€€
(Map p240; ☑0661 22 81 40; www.nord-pinus-tanger.com; Rue Sultan, Kasbah; d/junior ste/deluxe incl breakfast €220/310/340; ❄🛜) This very grand house with somewhat Gothic stone columns and staircase is sister to the Nord Pinus in Arles, France. Rooms are a delight with an eclectic decor and every comfort. Excellent meals are served on request (lunch/dinner Dh240/300) in the superbly opulent dining room or on the roof terrace. The bar on the terrace overlooking the sea is a favourite for an aperitif.

The Beat Generation was a post-WWII American counterculture movement that combined visceral engagement in worldly experiences with a quest for deeper understanding. It reached its apotheosis in Tangier. Many Beat artists – writer Jack Kerouac, and poets Allen Ginsberg and Gregory Curso – were just passing through, while writers William Burroughs and Paul Bowles, and the multitalented Brion Gysin, spent significant parts of their lives here, further inspiring a coterie of local artists. The result was a mixed bag, from the heights of artistic creativity to the lows of moral depravity. Today Beat history can still be found throughout the city:

» **Hotel el-Muniria** William Burroughs wrote *The Naked Lunch,* his biting satire of the modern American mind, here. Originally titled 'Interzone', the book was written in the cut-up technique developed by Brion Gysin. Ginsberg and Kerouac also shacked up here in 1957.

» **Tanger Inn** Photos of Beat customers abound on the walls of this bar below the el-Muniria.

» **Café Central** Burroughs' principal hang-out on the Petit Socco, where he sized up his louche opportunities.

» **1001 Nights** A legendary cafe in the kasbah established by Brion Gysin, also known for his Dreamachine, a kinetic work of art that induces a trance-like condition. The cafe was famous for its house band of trance musicians, the Master Musicians of Jajouka, who released a record produced by the Rolling Stones' Brian Jones. It has been 'closed for renovations' for years.

» **Tangier American Legation Museum** Houses a wing dedicated to Paul Bowles.

» **Hotel Continental** Scenes from the movie version of Paul Bowles' *The Sheltering Sky* were filmed here.

» **Café Hafa** Paul Bowles and the Rolling Stones came here to smoke hashish.

» **Gran Café De Paris** The main literary salon during the Interzone, it also drew Tennessee Williams and Truman Capote.

Hotel Continental HOTEL €€
(Map p240; ☑0539 93 10 24; www.continental -tanger.com; 36 Rue Dar el-Baroud; s/d incl breakfast Dh595/735; ❋🖭) Nothing appears to have been touched here for decades, making this piece of faded grandeur a fascinating bit of archaeology. The rooms are spartan, although some have been renovated. The huge terrace overlooking the port and the sea is superb. Manager Jimmy also dabbles in retail, as a dated sign on the way in reveals: 'Jimmy's World Famous Perfumerie, patronised by film stars and the international jet set'. The hotel has a large craft shop.

Hotel Mamora HOTEL €
(Map p240; ☑0539 93 41 05; 19 Mokhtar Ahardan; s/d with shower Dh60/120, d with toilet Dh200-260) Readers enjoy this hotel in a good location near the Petit Socco with its variety of rooms at different rates. It's a bit institutional, like an old school, but clean, well run, and strong value for the money. The rooms overlooking the green-tiled roof of the Grande Mosquée (such as room 39, from D200) are the most picturesque, if you don't mind the muezzin's call. Prices are always negotiable. The street is sometimes known by its old name of Rue des Postes.

Riad Tanja GUESTHOUSE €€
(Map p240; ☑0539 33 35 38; www.riadtanja.com; Rue du Portugal, Escalier Américain; d Dh800-1000; ❋🖭) Near the American Legation, the Tanja is a stylishly decorated rendition of a traditional house. Rooms are exceedingly comfortable, with TV, large bathrooms, brick floors and decorations drawn from Tangier's artistic heritage. The dining room, with probably the best restaurant in Tangier, has a small terrace overlooking the medina. However, an apparent lack of hands-on management makes it all rather impersonal.

VILLE NOUVELLE
Many of the unrated hotels and *pensiónes* along Rue Salah Eddine el-Ayoubi and Ave d'Espagne are little better than the cheapies in the medina. This Salah/Espagne area can be dodgy at night, and questionable

for women travelling alone. Following are some alternatives. Nicer hotels line the Ave Mohammed VI, offering spectacular views over the Bay of Tangier and close proximity to the attractions of the city, with a couple of options right in the centre.

Hotel de Paris
HOTEL €

(Map p242; ☎0539 93 18 77; 42 Blvd Pasteur; s/d incl breakfast high season Dh350/450) This reliable choice in the heart of the ville nouvelle has a classy, old-world aura in its lobby, although the breakfast area is dim. There is a variety of room types and prices depending on bathroom arrangements and balconies. All are clean and modern, but those overlooking Blvd Pasteur can get noisy. The helpful front desk makes up for the lack of service across the road at the tourist office.

Marco Polo
HOTEL €

(☎0539 94 11 24; www.marco-polo.ma; 2 Rue al-Antaki; s/d Dh462/616, breakfast Dh40) Readers have recommended this bright hotel with lots of light, sparkling marble floors and pastel walls. An excellent, central location across from the beach provides easy access to both the ville nouvelle and the medina, and its popular restaurant is also convenient. All 35 rooms are freshly painted, there's a large fitness centre and hammam, and a bar.

Hotel El-Muniria
HOTEL €€

(Map p242; ☎0539 93 53 37; 1 Rue Magellan; s/d Dh200/250, on terrace Dh250/300; 🖤) This is your best low-end option in the ville nouvelle, and an important cut above the gloomy and often dirty competition, not to mention chock-full of Beat Generation history (see the boxed text, p244). French windows and bright, flowery fabrics set it apart, revealing the careful touch of a hands-on family operation. Room 4 is a great hideaway, a quiet corner double with lots of light, as is Room 8 on the terrace, a quiet double with a harbour view. Noise from the Tangier Inn below is the only drawback.

Hotel El Djenina
HOTEL €

(☎0539 92 22 44; eldjenina@menara.ma; 8 Rue al-Antaki; s/d Dh351/451; 🖤) This hotel is just up the hill from the Marco Polo, but it's just below it in quality. The rooms here are still bright and modern, albeit smaller, and the facilities are less impressive, although the cosy bar/restaurant with patio views to the sea is pleasant. Don't expect to receive any service if there's football on the television.

Pension Hollande
HOTEL €

(Map p236; ☎0539 93 78 38; 139 Rue de Hollande; s/d Dh200/350) Tucked away in a quiet street a short walk from Place de France, this former hospital has sparkling whitewashed rooms and high ceilings, though the bathrooms can be claustrophobic. All rooms have sinks; doubles come with a shower. Hot water is available on demand. Of the main rooms, Room 11 and Room 8 are your best bets, but for a budget steal, don't miss the loft rooms up the hidden

---

LOCAL KNOWLEDGE

GERALD LOFTUS, DIRECTOR, AMERICAN LEGATION MUSEUM

After a career in the foreign service, I'd retired to Brussels. But then this job came along and I so enjoy the cultural aspects of living in North Africa that I couldn't resist it. I particularly love the old part of the Legation house as it represents the essence of a medina home.

I'm busy changing the context of the museum to give it a better sense of history. In the James McBey room there's the famous painting of Zohra. She's still alive – she was only 15 when the painting was done in 1952. Her sons live in the US now and her daughter works at the US Embassy in Rabat.

We have a whole wing for Paul Bowles now at the museum, and a comprehensive bookshop. Bowles was not only a writer, but spent many years recording indigenous music in Morocco, which was very important work. The recordings were always pretty much unobtainable, but for the Paul Bowles Centenary in 2010, I asked the Library of Congress to digitalise the music, and it's now available.

Our library is open to writers and researchers, and we continue to teach literacy, cooking, sewing, art and foreign languages to medina women. One of our students became an artist and earned enough money to electrify her home. Our oldest student is 81.

SPOT THE CELEB

Sashay past the doorman at El-Minzah Hotel and glide down the stairs to the beautiful Andalusian courtyard where there are dozens of photographs of celebrity visitors around the walls. Most of the photos date from the 1950s and '60s. A suave Rock Hudson, Aristotle Onassis in a white car, Jackie O too, Winston Churchill with his cigar, glitzy Rita Hayworth and even Errol Flynn are just some that we spotted. Then head for the Caid's Bar for a cocktail while you decide where they'll hang your photo.

spiral staircase (single/double Dh100/150, with shared bathroom).

Hotel Rembrandt   HOTEL €€
(Map p242; ☏0539 33 33 14; www.hotel-rem brandt.com; Ave Mohammed V; s/d Dh650/790, sea view add Dh100, breakfast Dh80; ❋ � ☎) Rooms here are pretty standard and are in marked contrast to the elegant downstairs lobby, with its classic elevator and curving staircase. However, the glassed-in restaurant (set menu Dh150, alcohol served) is a welcome addition, the green garden cafe is a tranquil spot to relax, and the swank Blue Pub with its oddly purple velvet couches is a popular night spot (beer from Dh20, wine from Dh80).

El-Minzah   HOTEL €€€
(Map p242; ☏0539 93 58 85; www.elminzah.com; 85 Rue de la Liberté; d/ste from Dh1725/2450; ❋ � ☎) The classiest five-star hotel in Tangier proper, and a local landmark, this beautifully maintained 1930s period piece offers three excellent restaurants, three equally good bars, a fitness centre, a spa, pleasant gardens and even a babysitting service. It's shaped like an enormous hollow square, with a tremendous Spanish–Moorish courtyard, and has history oozing from its walls. Portside rooms offer beautiful views, but can be noisy when the wind is blowing. The owner is currently restoring its sister ship, the Grand Hotel Villa de France.

🍴 Eating

Tangier's 800-plus cafes are a study in local culture, and can be characterised many ways, beginning with old versus new. The former are almost exclusively male, and often shabby, while the latter (such as those listed here) are bright, modern and design-conscious, with light food, high ceilings and lots of light. Coffee purists should see Drinking (p248).

In the medina there's a host of cheap eating possibilities around the Petit Socco and the adjacent Ave Mokhtar Ahardan, with rotisserie chicken, sandwiches and brochettes all on offer. In the ville nouvelle, try the streets immediately south of Pl de France, which are flush with fast-food outlets, sandwich bars and fish counters.

MEDINA

TOP CHOICE Populaire Saveur de Poisson   SEAFOOD €€
(Map p242; ☏0539 33 63 26; 2 Escalier Waller; prix fixe Dh150; ☉lunch & dinner, closed Fri; 👶) This charming little seafood restaurant offers excellent, filling set menus in rustic surroundings. The owner serves a four-course meal of fish soup followed by inventive plates of fresh catch and fresh vegetables, all of it washed down with a homemade juice cocktail made from 15 kinds of fruit (have a look at the vat in back). Not just a meal, a whole experience.

Riad Tanja Restaurant   LOCAL €€€
(Map p240; ☏0539 33 35 38; www.riadtanja.com; Rue du Portugal; menus Dh250-450; ☉dinner) With a justified reputation for some of the best food in the city, and a romantic view of the ville nouvelle climbing up the opposite hill, this is a great place to splurge, particularly with that special someone. The bi-level dining area feels more like a well-designed living room, with a dozen tables, high ceilings, discrete staff and a superb take on Moroccan cuisine.

Les Passagers de Tanger MEDITERRANEAN €€€
(Map p240; Grand Socco; mains from Dh80; ☉lunch & dinner) In just the right spot overlooking the Grand Socco, this smart restaurant has a chic, eclectic decor. The menu is chalked on a blackboard and ranges from fresh fish to duck breast. There's a good wine list, too. The outside terrace is perfect for balmy summer evenings.

Le Nabab   LOCAL €€
(Map p240; ☏0661 44 22 20; 2 Rue al Kadiria; mains Dh80, menu Dh170; ☉lunch & dinner) This is a beautifully restored old *fondouq* (rooming house), all grey *tadelakt*, comfortable seating and swathes of airy pink fab-

ric. Dine around the huge fireplace or in a private alcove. The menu is Moroccan, the welcome friendly and it's licensed.

Le Salon Bleu LOCAL €€
(Map p240; Pl de la Kasbah, entrance 71 Rue Amrah; menu Dh100; ☻lunch & dinner) The owners of guesthouse Dar Nour have recently opened this pretty seaside house as a tearoom and restaurant. The roof terrace has magnificent views.

VILLE NOUVELLE

Anna e Paolo ITALIAN €€
(Map p242; ☏0539 94 46 17; 77 Rue de Prince Heretier; mains from Dh80; ☻lunch & dinner, closed Sun) This is the top Italian bistro in the city, a family-run restaurant with Venetian owners that feels like you have been invited for Sunday dinner. Expect a highly international crowd, lots of cross-table conversations about the events of the day, and wholesome food including excellent charcuterie and pizzas. Watch your head on the way upstairs.

La Fabrique FRENCH €€€
(Map p242; ☏0539 37 40 57; Residence Salima, 7 Rue d'Angleterre; meals Dh200-350; ☻lunch & dinner, closed Mon) This new restaurant is housed in what looks like a hangar. It's very trendy and serves good French cuisine.

Casa de España SPANISH, SEAFOOD €€
(Map p242; ☏0539 94 73 59; 11 Rue el-Jabha el-Ouatania) An old favourite, this Spanish bar-restaurant was being renovated at the time of research. Expect more of the signature classic Spanish dishes, with some wonderful specials like lamb with summer fruits, and free tapas with drinks.

Number One LOCAL, FRENCH €€
(Map p242; ☏0539 94 16 74; 1 Ave Mohammed V; mains from Dh75; ☻lunch & dinner) The rose walls and white windows in this renovated apartment provide the feel of a holiday cottage, while the red lighting, background jazz and exotic mementoes lend it an intimate, sultry allure. The Moroccan-French cuisine gets high marks from locals, who have been coming here for almost 50 years.

Restaurant el-Korsan LOCAL €€€
(Map p242; ☏0539 93 58 85; El-Minzah Hotel, 85 Rue de la Liberté; mains around Dh160; ☻lunch & dinner) One of Tangier's top restaurants, this chic and classy place inside the El-Minzah offers a smaller, more intimate version of the palace restaurant theme but without the bus tours. Well-presented Moroccan classics are served to soft live music, and often traditional dancing. Reservations are necessary, including one day prior notice for lunch. Dress well.

San Remo ITALIAN, LOCAL €€
(Map p242; ☏0539 93 84 51; 15 Rue Ahmed Chaouki; pizzas around Dh50, mains from Dh150; ☻lunch & dinner) An international menu, long on Italian and with a slant towards fish, tables with bright cloths facing the street, Moroccan background music and a mix of clientele – expats, tourists, local businesspeople – make this a lively spot with a great cultural-crossroads feel.

Le Pagode CHINESE €€
(Map p242; ☏0539 93 80 86; Rue al-Boussiri; mains from Dh80; ☻Tue-Sun) If you're tired of tajines and pasta, this realistic bit of Asia is the answer. An intimate and classy dining area, with lacquered furniture, white tablecloths and low lighting is mated with a classic Chinese menu.

Eric Kayser PATISSERIE, FRENCH €€
(cnr Rue des Amoureux & Rue Granada; mains Dh140, dish of the day Dh100; ☻7am-10.30pm) This renowned French *boulanger* has recently opened a bakery and restaurant in Tangier. Trendy and stylish, it's very popular for its good French cuisine.

Patisserie La Española PATISSERIE €
(Map p242; 97 Rue de la Liberté; ☻7am-10.30pm winter, 7am-12.30am summer) A heavily mirrored tearoom, this cafe tempts people off the street with its pretty arrangements of cakes and pastries. Everyone seems to come here – locals and foreigners, businessmen and courting couples.

La Giralda CAFE €
(Map p242; 1st fl, 5 Blvd Pasteur; breakfast from Dh20; ☻7am-midnight; ✽) The young and beautiful adore this grand cafe overlooking the Terrasse des Paresseux, with its sumptuous furniture and intricately carved ceiling. Huge windows give great sea views. A light menu of crepes and paninis make it a good lunch stop, too.

Champs Élysées CAFE €
(Map p242; 6 Ave Mohammed V; breakfast from Dh25; ☻6am-10pm) This enormous cafe-in-the-round is high on opulence, with a huge central chandelier and red velour upholstery. Great sticky pastries.

Fast Food Brahim FAST FOOD €

(Map p242; 16 Ave Mexique; sandwiches Dh18-25; ⊘11am-midnight) Great made-to-order sandwiches. You can't go wrong here with half a baguette filled with *kefta* (spicy lamb meatballs) and salad to eat on the hoof.

Mix Max FAST FOOD €

(Map p242; 6 Ave du Prince Héritier; meals Dh25-45; ⊘noon-2am) A trendy and popular fast-food joint, Mix Max serves up great paninis, *shwarma* and other creative fast fare.

SELF-CATERING

The covered markets (Map p240) near the Grand Socco are the best places for fresh produce, particularly on Thursday and Sunday, when Riffian women descend on the city in traditional hats and candy-striped skirts to sell their agricultural products. **Fès market** (Map p236), to the west of the city centre, is good for imported cheese and other treats.

Casa Pepé GROCERY STORE

(Map p242; 39 Rue ibn Rochd; ⊘9am-10.30pm) One of several general stores in this area. You can stock up at the deli here, and buy imported foods, dry goods and liquor.

🍷 Drinking

For pastries or more, see those listed under Eating. Given its hedonistic past, it's no surprise that the drinking scene is firmly entrenched in Tangerine culture. It's equally unsurprising that bars are principally the domain of men, although there are a few more-Westernised places where women can take a drink. Many only get going after midnight. For coffee purists, there are three legends.

Gran Café de Paris CAFE

(Map p242; Pl de France; ⊘6am-10.30pm) Gravity weighs upon the grand letters of the Gran Café de Paris, reminding us of its age at the crossroads of Tangier. Facing the Place de France since 1927, this is the most famous of the coffee establishments along Blvd Pasteur, most recently as a setting in *The Bourne Ultimatum*. In the past it was a prime gathering spot for literati.

Café Hafa CAFE

(Map p236; Ave Hadi Mohammed Tazi; ⊘8.30am-11pm Mon-Fri, 8.30am-2am Sat & Sun) With its stadium seating overlooking the strait, you could easily lose an afternoon lazing in this open-air cafe, but you need good weather. Locals hang out here to enjoy a game of backgammon. There's no menu, but scrambled eggs, *b'sara* and olives are on offer.

Café Central CAFE

(Map p240; Petit Socco; ⊘6am-11.30pm) The premier people-watching site in the medina, with tables on the pavement. See the local Mafiosi arrive in his new Benz, watch odd specimens of humanity drift past, hear the strange shouts echo down the alleys, and wonder what is going on upstairs. It's the perfect place to sip your coffee.

Tanger Inn BAR

(Map p240; Hotel El-Muniria, 1 Rue Magellan; ⊘10pm-2am) This small, dark place with a grand piano in the corner is hugely atmospheric and well worth a visit. Photos of the Beat poet crowd, signed by Jack Kerouac, adorn the walls. A Flag beer will set you back Dh25.

Nord Pinus Tanger BAR

(Map p240; Rue Sultan, Kasbah) On the top floor of this kasbah guesthouse is a bar and terrace, with fabulous views across to Spain. Sip a cocktail in the retro-chic lounge full of quirky chairs, Moroccan cushions and contemporary photography.

Caid's Bar BAR

(Map p242; El-Minzah, 85 Rue de la Liberté; wine from Dh50; ⊘10am-midnight) Long the establishment's drinking hole of choice, this el-Minzah landmark is a classy relic of the grand days of international Tangier. There's a pianist tinkling away; when he takes a break, it's likely the Bee Gees will croon instead. Women are more than welcome, and the adjacent restaurant-wine bar is equally good.

Pilo BAR

(Map p242; cnr Ave Mexique & Rue de Fès) A party atmosphere pervades these two floors of local colour, underscored by some high-energy music and festive lighting. Recently redecorated, it sports red walls and year-round Christmas decorations. Women can feel comfortable here, though the working girls are upstairs.

Americain's Pub BAR

(Map p242; Rue al-Moutanabi; ⊘noon-2am) Don't be fooled by the name: this pub is outfitted as an authentic part of the London underground, with white tiled walls, ubiquitous red trim and signage far more authentic than the Bobbies would appreciate. It's the perfect place to hide: there's no street number, and the phone is out of order.

Hole in the Wall Bar BAR

(Map p242; Rue du Prince Heretier; beer from Dh18; ⊙11am-midnight) For chuckles only, walk up Rue du Prince Heretier from the Terrasse des Paresseux one-and-a-half blocks and you will see a pair of swinging black doors, Old West style. Welcome to the smallest bar in Tangier, if not the world. Beer only.

☆ **Entertainment**

Nightclubs

Tangier's clubbing scene picks up in the summer, when Europeans arrive on the ferries. Discos cluster near Pl de France and line the beach, appealing to a wide range of clientele, from grey-haired couples to sex tourists. Cover charges vary and may be rolled into drink prices. If leaving late, have the doorman call a taxi.

Loft NIGHTCLUB

(⎆0673280927; www.loftclub-tanger.com; Rte de Boubana; ⊙10pm-4am, Thu & Sat) Easily Tangier's premier nightspot, this world-class, state-of-the-art club holds 2000 people and feels like an enormous silver cruise ship, with upper-storey balconies, sparkling metal railings, billowing sail-like curtains, spot lights cutting through the artificial fog – and no cover. DJ Spicy spins house and R&B. Go after midnight.

Beach Club 555 NIGHTCLUB

(Map p236; Ave Mohammed VI; ☞▣) A beach club by day with pool, pizzeria and bar with a sports screen (admission Dh60), at night the Triple 5 morphs into one of the best discos in the city. Dance up a storm with the resident and visiting DJs.

Regine Club NIGHTCLUB

(8 Rue al-Mansour Dahabi; ⊙10pm-3am Mon-Sat) Welcome to the 1980s. This disco has stayed the same so long it is a museum piece, replete with glass-reflecting ball and purple velour couches. It has a great atmosphere from 1.30am, especially on weekends.

Finest Pink NIGHTCLUB

(off Map p236; Ave Mohammed VI; ⊙11pm-late) This gay-friendly lounge, restaurant and tapas bar opposite the Hotel Shahrazad sports a popular disco with, of course, the finest bright pink walls.

Cinemas

Films are either in Arabic or dubbed in French.

PAUL BOWLES IN TANGIER

Perhaps the best-known foreign writer in Tangier was the American author Paul Bowles, who died in 1999, aged 88. Bowles made a brief but life-changing trip to Tangier in 1910, on Gertrude Stein's advice, then devoted the next 15 years to music composition and criticism back home. In 1938 he married Jane Sydney Auer, but they were never a conventional couple – he was an ambivalent bisexual and she was an active lesbian. After WWII Bowles took her to Tangier, where he remained the rest of his life. Here he turned to writing amid a lively creative circle, including the likes of Allen Ginsberg and William Burroughs.

During the 1950s Bowles began taping, transcribing and translating stories by Moroccan authors, in particular Driss ben Hamed Charhadi (also known by the pseudonym Larbi Layachi) and Mohammed Mrabet. He was also an important early recorder of Moroccan folk music. This has, until very recently, been held exclusively, on 78rpm records, at the Library of Congress in the US.

Thanks partly to Bernardo Bertolucci's 1990 film, Bowles' best-known book is *The Sheltering Sky* (1949), a bleak and powerful story of an innocent American couple slowly dismantled by a trip through Morocco. His other works include *Let It Come Down* (1952), a thriller set in Tangier; *The Spider's House*, set in 1950s Fez; and two excellent collections of travel tales: *Their Heads Are Green* (1963) and *Points in Time* (1982). *A Distant Episode: the Selected Stories* is a good compilation of Bowles' short stories.

There is a dark and nihilistic undercurrent to the Bowles' writing as fellow writer Norman Mailer describes, 'Paul Bowles opened the world of Hip. He let in the murder, the drugs, the death of the Square...the call of the orgy, the end of civilization'. Other commentators have tried to link aspects of Bowles' life to his writing. Bowles autobiography *Without Stopping* (1972; nicknamed 'Without Telling') sheds little light on these matters.

The official Paul Bowles website is at www.paulbowles.org.

Cinema Rif   CINEMA
(Cinematheque de Tanger; Map p240; Grand Socco) In this fine art-deco building that's been well restored, you'll find both indie and mainstream films, mostly American, Moroccan, Spanish or French (with Spanish and American films typically dubbed into Arabic).

Cinema Paris   CINEMA
(Map p242; Rue de Fès; downstairs Dh15, balcony Dh25) Shows French, American and Bollywood films, the latter two dubbed into French or Arabic.

🛍 Shopping

VILLE NOUVELLE

Bazar Tindouf   ANTIQUES, LOCAL
(Map p242; 72 Rue de la Liberté) This shop opposite El-Minzah Hotel is bursting to the seams with antiques, glassware, brassware, ceramics, lamps, jewellery, clothing and more besides. It's definitely worth a browse.

El Tapisero   CARPETS
(www.eltapisero.com; 31 Rue el Hassan el Youssi Aziz Bou Charf) Make like Madonna and order a handmade carpet at El Tapisero. The team at this carpet-weaving enterprise is very creative and works with some of the big European decorators. Expect to pay about €50 to €250 per square metre.

La Casa Barata   FLEA MARKET
(Ave Abou Kacem Sebti at Ave Fayçal Ben Abdel Aziz, ◌9am-8pm Thu & Sun) Literally 'the cheap house', this large flea market carries everything you can imagine, from vegetables to electronics to carpets. The best opportunity to find real treasure, and an experience unto itself.

Ensemble Artisanal   SOUVENIRS
(Map p236; cnr Rue Belgique & Rue M'sallah; ◌9am-1pm & 3-7pm Sat-Thu) This government-backed arts-and-crafts centre is a good place to see the range of local crafts and watch the artisans at work. There's no haggling, as prices are fixed, but they are also much higher than in the souqs.

MEDINA

The souqs of the medina are a wonderful place to spend hours shopping. Following are some unusual places you might want to see.

Boutique Majid   ANTIQUES, JEWELLERY
(Map p240; Rue Les Almohades) You can get lost for hours in this exotic antique shop, but the real gem is Majid himself. Straight out of central casting (including his red fez) he will regale you with stories of the Rolling Stones and other luminaries while showing you his amazing collection of Moroccan doors, jewellery and artefacts, clothing, fabrics and carpets.

Laura Wefling   ART & CRAFT, CLOTHING
(Map p240; Pl de la Kasbah) Next to the Kasbah Museum, this is a beautiful shop with some stunning one-off pieces of clothing, bags, decor items and ceramics. Look out for the chandelier in the shape of a sailing ship.

Bazaar of Silver Jewelry   JEWELLERY
(13 Rue Jamaa Jadida) The name says it all: two floors of glass cases full of silver jewellery from throughout Morocco, both new and antique, and great staff, too. Located in an obscure alley near the Café Central, Petit Socco.

No 5 Rue Ben Raissoull   CLOTHING
(Map p240) This nameless hole-in-the-wall garment factory is noted for its fascinating combinations of traditional Moroccan dress and Western women's wear. Watch them winding threads in the street using a modified fishing line motor.

ℹ Information

Dangers & Annoyances

As it any big city, it's best to stick to the beaten path at all times, and to take cabs point to point at night. Solo women may be subject to being hassled after about 10pm, and should avoid the port area after dark. If you have a serious problem and need help of the authorities, contact the **Brigade Touristique** (Tourist Police; Map p240; ☑177; Ave Mohammed VI, Tangier Port).

Emergency
Emergency Service (☑177; ◌24hr)

Internet Access
There are several internet cafes in the Blvd Pasteur area:

Espace Net (Map p242; 16 Ave Mexique; per hr Dh5; ◌9.30am-1am)

Medical Services
Clinique du Croissant Rouge (Red Cross Clinic; Map p242; ☑0539 94 25 17, 0539 94 69 76; 6 Rue al-Mansour Dahabi)

Hopital Mohammed V (☑0539 93 08 56; Rue Val Fleurie) On the road to the airport.

Pharmacy Anegay (Map p240; Rue as-Siaghin)

Money

Blvds Pasteur and Mohammed V are lined with numerous banks with ATMs and *bureau de change* counters. Outside of working hours, try the exchange bureaus in the big hotels.

BMCE (Banque Marocaine du Commerce Extérieur; Map p242; Blvd Pasteur) One of several in this area.

Post

Main post office (off Map p242; cnr Rue Quevada & Ave Mohammed V) Post restante is at the counter furthest to the right; parcel post is on the south side of the building.

Tourist Information

ONMT (Délégation Régionale du Tourisme; Map p242; ☏0539 94 80 50; 29 Blvd Pasteur; ⊙closed Sat & Sun) The recent investment in tourism infrastructure hasn't made it here. Verbal help, but hardly any printed material. The Hotel de Paris across the road has lots of brochures and staff are willing to help.

Travel Agencies

The following both sell ferry, as well as flight, tickets.

Carlson Wagonlit (Map p242; ☏0539 33 10 24; 91 Rue de la Liberté)

Hispamaroc (Map p242; ☏0539 93 21 78; hispamaroc@mamnet.net.ma; 2 Rue el-Jabha el-Ouatania)

Websites

Head to **Lonely Planet** (www.lonelyplanet.com/morocco/the-mediterranean-coast-and-the-rif/tangier) for planning advice, author recommendations, traveller reviews and insider tips.

Getting There & Away

Tackling anywhere unfamiliar after dark is always more traumatic, so try to arrive early in the day. Remember to change money to pay the cab fare.

Air

The Ibn Batouta International Airport (TNG) is 15km southwest of the city centre. It attracts a number of budget airlines (including easyJet from Madrid and Paris, Jet4you from Barcelona and Brussels and Ryanair from Paris, Brussels, Madrid and Milan) as well as Iberia and Royal Air Maroc. Check the internet for the latest service providers and schedules, as these are constantly changing.

Boat

You have two options for crossing the Strait of Gibraltar: the fast catamaran ferries owned by FRS and Balearia (to Tarifa Dh350, 35 minutes) or the slower ones (Dh350 to Algeciras). The former are more susceptible to weather delays, which can close the port for days, but they're lifesavers for those prone to seasickness.

Ferries to and from Tarifa currently leave from Tanger Port (Map p236); all other destinations are served by Tanger Med, the new terminal north of the city. A free shuttle bus leaves Tanger Med every hour on the hour for the CTM bus station at Tanger Port.

Tickets are available from the company ticket booths outside the ferry terminal building at Tanger Port, in the terminal itself, or from virtually any travel agency around town; be sure to pick up an exit form so you can avoid hassles later. The main destination is the Spanish port of Algeciras, with less frequent services to Tarifa and Málaga (Spain), Gibraltar and Sète (France; advance reservation required). The Tarifa service includes a free bus transfer to Algeciras (50 minutes) on presentation of your ferry ticket. Book in advance during peak periods (particularly Easter, the last week in August and the last week in October), allow 90 minutes before departure to get tickets and navigate passport control, and remember the time difference with Spain (Morocco is one hour behind or two hours during Spanish daylight saving (summer; see p501).

Remember to get your passport stamped on the ferry before arrival in Morocco.

Bus

The **CTM station** (Map p240) is conveniently beside the port gate. CTM buses also call at the main bus station on their way out of town. Destinations include the following:

DESTINATION	COST (DH)	DURATION (HR)
Agadir	320	14
Casablanca	130	6
Chefchaouen	40	3
Fez	110	6
Marrakesh	230	10
Meknès	90	5
Rabat	100	4½
Tetouan	20	1

Baggage is Dh5 (4kg to 10kg).

Cheaper bus companies operate from the **main bus station** (*gare routière*; Pl Jamaa el-Arabia), about 2km to the south of the city centre by the Syrian mosque – the distinctly un-Moroccan-looking minarets are a useful nearby landmark. There are regular departures for all the destinations mentioned above, plus services to Al-Hoceima (Dh97, 10 hours) and Fnideq (Dh19, 1½ hours) – a small town 3km from the Ceuta border. The main bus station can be busy, but pretty hassle-free, thanks to the police office in the centre. It has a **left-luggage facility** (per item per 24hr Dh5-7; ☺5am-1am). A metered petit taxi to/from the town centre is around Dh8.

Car

The major car rental agencies are at the airport. The following have in-town locations:

Avis (Map p242; ☑0539 93 46 46; fax 0539 33 06 24; 54 Blvd Pasteur; ☺8am-noon & 2-7pm Mon-Sat, 9am-noon Sun)

Budget (Map p242; ☑0531 06 09 50; Tanger Ville station; ☺8.30am-noon & 4.30-8.30pm Mon-Fri, 9am-noon & 3-6pm Sat, 9am-noon Sun)

Hertz (off Map p242; ☑0539 32 22 10; fax 0539 32 21 65; 36 Ave Mohammed V; ☺8am-noon & 2.30-6.30pm Mon-Fri, 9am-noon & 3-6pm Sat, 9am-noon Sun)

A reasonably secure and convenient **car park** (Map p236; 42 Rue Hollande; per hr Dh2, per night Dh15, per 24hr Dh25) is next to the Dawliz complex.

Taxi

The grand-taxi rank for places outside Tangier is across from the main bus station. The most common destinations are Tetouan (Dh30, one hour), Assilah (Dh20, 30 minutes) and Larache (Dh30, 1½ hours). For Ceuta, travel to Fnideq (Dh40, one hour), 3km from the border. There are no direct taxis to the border (Bab Sebta). Grands taxis to Tetouan also frequently wait for arriving trains at Tanger Ville train station. For destinations on the outskirts of Tangier, such as the Caves of Hercules or Cap Malabata, use the grand-taxi rank on the Grand Socco.

Train

Tanger Ville, the recently renovated train station, is hassle-free. Five trains depart daily for Sidi Kacem, Meknès, Fez, Rabat (Ville), Casablanca (Casa Voyageurs) and Marrakesh, including a night service with couchettes, and the famed *Marrakesh Express*, which should be reserved a day in advance (Dh310/205 for 1st/2nd class, Dh350 with couchette). From Sidi Kacem you can get connections south to Marrakesh or east to Oujda. Schedules are best checked at www.oncf.ma. Note that the **left luggage office** (per item Dh10; ☺7am-1pm & 2-9.30pm) only accepts locked bags. A petit taxi to/from Tangier centre should cost around Dh10.

ℹ Getting Around

To/From the Airport

From the port to the airport, a grand taxi takes 30 to 40 minutes and costs Dh200 for the entire car, but if you find the cab beyond the port, the price falls to Dh150. If you want to pick up a local bus from the airport, bus 17 and bus 70 run to the Grand Socco, but you'll need to walk 2km to the main road.

To/From Tanger Med

A rail link is planned from Tanger Med to the city of Tangier, but was not yet operational at the time of research. A free shuttle bus runs every hour from Tanger Med to the CTM bus station near Tanger Port (40 minutes). The driver will drop you off near the train station if you ask.

Bus

Buses aren't really necessary for getting around Tangier, but two potentially useful services are bus 13, which runs from the train station via Ave Mohammed VI to the port gate, and bus 17, which links the train station and the main bus station. Tickets cost Dh6.

Taxi

Distinguishable by their ultramarine colour with a yellow stripe down the side, petits taxis do standard journeys around town for Dh7 to Dh10; they charge 50% more at night.

Around Tangier

CAP SPARTEL   رأس سبارطيل

Just 14km west of Tangier lies Cap Spartel, the northwestern extremity of Africa's Atlantic Coast. It is a popular day trip with locals and tourists alike. A dramatic drive takes you through La Montagne, an exclusive suburb of royal palaces and villas, and over the pine-covered headland to the **Cap Spartel Lighthouse**. This is normally closed, but the caretaker might be convinced to let you in for a few dirhams. The beaches to the south are clean and quiet outside the summer season, so you can find your own private cove.

Below Cap Spartel, the beach **Plage Robinson** stretches off to the south – a great place for a bracing walk. Five kilometres further you reach the **Grottes d'Hercule** (admission Dh5; ☺8am till dark), next to Le Mirage hotel, the mythical dwelling place of Hercules. Since the 1920s these caves have been quarried for millstones, worked by prostitutes and used as a venue for private parties by rich celebrities from Tangier. A much-photographed view of the Atlantic from within resembles a map of Africa. Camel rides are available here, just before the entrance to the caves on the right. A beach ride is a special treat.

Sleeping & Eating

Camping Achakkar   CAMP SITE €

(☎0612 24 97 27; camping per person Dh20, plus per tent/car/campervan Dh20/20/45, bungalows Dh500; hot shower Dh20) Inland from the grotto and opposite Le Mirage, this shady site has clean facilities and hot water (electricity Dh30). It has a shop that stocks essentials and a cafe with simple meals, though a new restaurant was being built at the time of research.

Le Mirage   HOTEL €€€

(☎0539 33 33 32; www.lemirage-tanger.com; d from Dh2400; ❉⊛❂) This is one of the finest hotels in the Tangier area, with a dramatic location perched on the cliff beside the grotto, offering a view of miles of broad Atlantic beach. The bungalows are exquisite, as the price suggests, and there's a spa and golf course. Nonguests can get a taste of the opulence in the immaculate restaurant (meals from Dh300), or just stop by for a drink beneath the pergola. From the sunny terrace you can see the Roman ruins of Cotta, where fish oil was processed.

Restaurant Cap Spartel   SEAFOOD €€

(Cap Spartel Rd; salads Dh50-70, mains from Dh80) This average seafood restaurant next to the lighthouse is popular on weekends.

❶ Getting There & Away

Grands taxis from Tangier are the best way of getting to Cap Spartel. A one-way charter should cost around Dh60, and slightly more than double for a round trip including waiting time. Taxis leave from the rank in front of St Andrew's Church in Tangier. Petits taxis are reluctant to make the trip one way only – the price isn't much different from a grand taxi.

Road to Ceuta

The scenic road from Tangier to Ceuta is worth taking: green patchwork fields, alluring mountain roads, rolling hills, rocky headlands and good sandy beaches reveal a different side to Morocco, now under siege by development. A complete grand taxi to Fnideq, the town before the border, will cost Dh220.

The road begins at **Cap Malabata**, the headland opposite Tangier and some 8km from the city. Here you'll find the large **M'nar Park** (☎0539 34 38 29; www.mnar parktanger.com; family apt from Dh1400; ❂), a

MOVING ON?

For tips, recommendations and reviews, head to shop.lonelyplanet. com to purchase a downloadable PDF of the Cádiz Province & Gibraltar Province chapter from Lonely Planet's *Andalucía* guide.

great place for children. It has everything from waterslides to boating, and there's a restaurant with superb views back towards Tangier.

Ksar es-Seghir, 25km further around the coast, is a small fishing port dominated by the remains of a Portuguese fort. The beach is popular with locals in summer, and will become even more so once the new corniche is completed. Among the decent seafood restaurants here is **Laachiri** (☎0539 39 00 06; fish platter Dh90; ⊙lunch & dinner) looking across the Strait to Gibraltar. Just beyond you'll spot **Tanger Med**, the massive new container facility and ferry port, 45km from Tangier.

The best view along the way is the great crag of **Jebel Musa**, one of the ancient Pillars of Hercules (the Rock of Gibraltar being the other), which rises up 10km or so further on.

Ceuta (Sebta)   سبتة

POP 78,700

Ceuta is one of a handful of Spanish possessions on the coastline of Morocco (see the boxed text, p258), and a real gem. Located on a peninsula jutting out into the Mediterranean, it offers a compact dose of fantastic architecture, interesting museums, excellent food, a relaxing maritime park and bracing nature walks, with A-plus traveller support at every turn. The city is particularly beautiful at night, a skyline of artfully lit buildings and bursting palms.

Ceuta served as one of the Roman Empire's coastal bases (its Arabic name, Sebta, stems from the Latin *Septem*). After a brief stint under the control of the Byzantine Empire, the city was taken in AD 931 by the Arab rulers of Muslim Spain – the basis for Spain's claim of historical rights to the land. For the next 500 years, however, this city at the tip of Africa was like a prized possession, fought over and ruled successively by Spanish princes, Moroccan sultans and

Portuguese kings. Things began to settle down when Portugal and Spain united under one crown in 1580, and Ceuta passed to Spain by default. When the two countries split in 1640, Ceuta remained Spanish, and has been ever since.

If entering from Morocco, Ceuta is also an eye-opener. Like the former West Berlin, it comes across as a grand social experiment concocted by rival political systems. Leaving the beggars and street hustlers behind, you cross over a grim border zone, a 100m no-man's-land of haphazardly placed barricades, part of a €30 million fence erected by the EU to prevent illegal immigration, to find yourself blinking in the light of Spanish culture, a relaxed world of well-kept plazas, beautiful buildings and tapas bars bubbling over until the wee hours. This experience alone is worth the trip and lingers thereafter.

This cultural-island phenomenon is the essence of Ceuta. It explains the heavy Spanish military presence, the Moroccan immigrants, the duty-free shopping, the shady cross-border commerce, the tourism and the local caution towards foreigners. Many people simply pass through here to avoid the hassles of Tangier, but this small piece of Spain has more than enough charms of its own, and is the perfect weekend getaway.

Sights & Activities

Ceuta's history is outlined by the *ruta monumenta*, a series of excellent information boards in English and Spanish outside key buildings and monuments.

Plaza de Africa LANDMARK
This is the charming heart of Ceuta, with manicured tropical plantings, a square of cobblestone streets and some of the city's finest architecture. Moving clockwise from the oblong **Commandancia General**, a military headquarters closed to visitors, you encounter the striking yellow **Santuario de Nuestra Señora de Africa** (9am-1pm & 5-9pm Mon-Sat, 9am-1pm & 6.30-9pm Sun & holidays), an 18th-century Andalucian-style church; the 19th-century **Palacio de la Asamblea** with its elegant dome and clock, a combination palace and city hall; and finally the 17th-century, twin-spired **Cathedral Santa Maria de la Asuncion** (9am-1pm & 6-8pm Tue-Sun) with its **museum** (10am-1pm Tue-Sat). The centre of the plaza contains a memorial to soldiers lost in the Spanish–Moroccan War of 1860, a conflict over the borders of Ceuta.

Ceuta

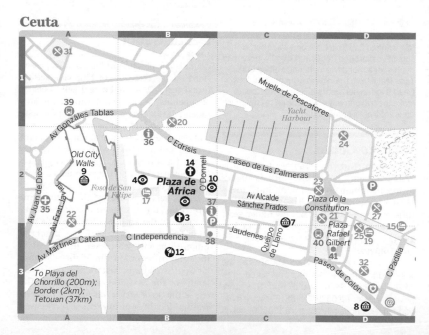

FREE **Royal Walls** HISTORIC BUILDING
The most impressive sight in Ceuta is the medieval **Royal Walls** (Av González Tablas; ☺10am-2pm & 5-9pm), dating back to the 5th century. These extensive fortifications, of great strategic complexity, have been beautifully restored, with information boards in English. The beautifully designed **Museo de los Muralles Reales**, a gallery that houses temporary art exhibitions, lies within the walls themselves. It's a most atmospheric space, worth visiting regardless of what's on show – although if you're lucky enough to catch local artist Diego Canca, don't miss his work.

Beaches BEACH
Easily overlooked, the two town beaches, **Playa del Chorillo** and **Playa de la Ribera**, lie to the south of the isthmus, beneath Av Martinez Catena. They are well kept and conveniently located, although the sand is a bland grey.

Museo de la Legión MUSEUM
(Paseo de Colón; admission free, donations appreciated; ☺10am-1.30pm Mon-Sat) This intriguing museum is dedicated to and run by the Spanish Legion, an army unit set up in 1920 that played a pivotal role in Franco's republican army. Loaded to the gills with memorabilia, weaponry and uniforms, not to mention glory, pomp and circumstance, it is a fascinating glimpse into the military culture that shaped the north, from the imperious statue of Franco, to the explanation of how the legion's intrepid founder, Millan Astray, lost his right eye, to the history of the legion in cinema. They even check your passport at the door. Alternatively, you can enlist at http://lalegion.es. There are guided tours in English.

Museo de Ceuta MUSEUM
(30 Paseo del Revellín; admission free; ☺10am-2pm & 5-8pm Mon-Sat, 10am-2pm Sun & holidays) This ageing municipal museum has a small collection showing the peninsula's pre-Spanish history, with all labels in Spanish. The temporary exhibitions are of more interest.

Plaza de los Reyes LANDMARK
With its green triumphal arch (inscribed 'a monument to coexistence') and fountain, this plaza borders the twin-towered yellow **Iglesia de San Francisco**. But the real treasure lies across the street: the **Casa de los Dragones** (House of Dragons), a fantastic dream that has entered the real world. Perfectly restored, this former home is an extraordinary example of eclectic architecture, with Moorish arches, polished brick facades, Mansard roofs, fabulous balconies, and the pièce de résistance: four enormous dark dragons springing from the roof. The intricate anagram of the Cerni Gonzalez Brothers, the builders, is emblazoned on the corner. Tip your hat.

Museo de la Basilica Tardorromana
MUSEUM
(☺10am-1.30pm & 5-7.30pm Mon-Sat, 10am-1.30pm Sun) This superbly executed underground museum is integrated into the architectural remains of an ancient basilica discovered during street work in the 1980s, including a bridge over open tombs, skeletons included. The artefacts become a means of branching out into various elements of local history. In Spanish, but definitely worth a lap through. Enter via Calle Queipo de Llano.

Parque Marítimo del Mediterráneo PARK
(admission €1; ☺10am-7pm, pool Apr-Sep, closed Thu) This creative maritime park is one of several versions developed by the brilliant artist and architect Cesar Manrique of the Canary Islands. The architect borrowed the city-walls theme to construct a huge pool deck on the sea,

MEDITERRANEAN COAST & THE RIF CEUTA (SEBTA)

Ceuta

including a grand lagoon and two other saltwater pools, surrounded by 10 bars, pubs, restaurants and cafes. A central island holds a fortress **casino** (⊙from 10pm). A pictorial display of Manrique's work lies just inside the entrance, 50m to the right. This is a real hit in the summer, and perfect for families. A disco was being added at the time of research.

Baños Arabes   HISTORIC BUILDING
(Calle Arrabal 16; ⊙11.30am-1.30pm & 6.30-8.30pm) Accidentally discovered during street work, these ancient Arab baths sit on a main road, an incongruous sight. There are two of them, with barrel-vaulted roofs originally covered with marble – the high-tech spa of its time.

Monte Hacho   NATURAL SCENERY
A walk around Monte Hacho is an option on a nice day; maps are available at the

tourist office or you can wing it and follow the coast. Since it's an uphill slog from town, a good option is to start by taking a cab (€10) to the **Mirador de San Antonio** two-thirds of the way up, which offers magnificent views over Ceuta and north to Gibraltar. The summit of the peninsula is crowned by the massive Fortaleza de Hacho, a fort first built by the Byzantines, and still an active military installation. No visitors are allowed.

Back down at the main road, you keep going clockwise until you reach the **Castillo del Desnarigado** (admission free; ⊙11am-2pm Sat & Sun), a small fort on the southeastern tip of the peninsula, which houses a small military museum. There is a lighthouse above, and a secluded beach, **Playa Torrecilla**, below.

García Aldave
NATURAL SCENERY

If you've done everything else, the García Aldave can be crossed from coast to coast along the N354, either by car or on foot (a hiking map from the tourist office will help). The route contains a series of circular neomedieval watchtowers, closed to visitors. Several of these are visible from the excellent **Mirador de Isabel II**, which offers great views across the isthmus to Monte Hacho. On 1 November, the Day of the Dead, there is a mass pilgrimage here to remember the deceased.

The road ends at Benzú, a small town on the northern coast, which faces the grand sight of Jebel Musa rising across the border. The mountain is known here as the Dead Woman, as it resembles one, lying on her back. Contemplate mortality here over a cup of mint tea.

🛏 Sleeping

Ceuta isn't overrun with sleeping options, so if you're arriving late in the day an advance reservation is a good idea. Most cheap places are *pensiónes*, some of which are identifiable only by the large blue-and-white 'CH' plaque.

TOP CHOICE Hostal Central
HOTEL €€

(📞956 51 67 16; www.hostalesceuta.com; Paseo del Revellín; s/d/tr €45/66/76; 🌣🛜) This good-value, two-star hotel in an excellent location has ultra-modern decor and is very welcoming. Bright rooms are small but spotless, and all come with bathroom and fridge. Low-season discounts are available.

Parador Hotel La Muralla
HOTEL €€€

(📞956 51 49 40; ceuta@parador.es; 15 Plaza de Africa; s/d from €80/100; 🌣🛜🚗) Ceuta's top address is this spacious four-star hotel perfectly situated on the Plaza de Africa. Rooms are comfortable, but not luxurious, with simple wooden doors and plain ceramic tiles. Balconies overlook a pleasant garden overflowing with palm trees. A bar-cafe adds value, but the best asset is the value-for-money price.

Hostal Plaza Ruiz
HOTEL €€

(📞956 51 67 33; www.hostalesceuta.com; 3 Plaza Ruiz; s/d/tr €45/66/76; 🌣🛜) Sister hotel to the Central, this place has a similar, welcoming style and a charming location. Rooms are airy, with nice pine furniture; the best have wrought-iron balconies overlooking the cafes of the plaza. Bathrooms and fridges are standard.

Pensión La Bohemia
HOTEL €

(📞956 51 06 15; 16 Paseo del Revellín; s/d €25/35) This well-run operation, one flight above a shopping arcade, offers a bright and spotless set of rooms arranged around a central court, with potted plants and shiny tile floors. Bathrooms are shared, with plenty of hot water and communal showers. Rooms have small TVs and fans.

Pensión Charito
HOSTEL €

(📞956 51 39 82; pcharito@terra.es; 1st fl, 5 Calle Arrabal; s/d €15/20) This place is not signed apart from a worn CH sign that's easy to miss – look for the green and cream building above the bar-cafe Limité. Though a bit aged, the inside is clean and homey with hot showers and a small, well-equipped kitchen. If rooms are full the staff may not be present.

SURVIVAL SPANISH

Hello/Goodbye	¡Hola!/¡Adiós!
Yes/No	Sí/No
Please/Thankyou	Por favor/Gracias
Where is...?	¿Dónde está...?
hotel	hotel
guesthouse	pensión
camping	camping
Do you have any rooms available?	¿Tiene habitaciones libres?
a single room	una habitación individual
a double room	una habitación doble
How much is it?	¿Cuánto cuesta?
What time does the next...leave?	¿A qué hora sale/llega el próximo...?
boat	barca
bus	autobús
I'd like a...	Quisiera un...
one-way ticket	billete sencillo
return ticket	billete de ida y vuelta
beer	cerveza
sandwich	bocadillo

THE LAST PIECES OF EMPIRE

Some of the most fascinating places in northern Morocco are not Moroccan at all, they are Spanish. When Spain recognised Moroccan independence in 1956, it retained a collection of historical oddities that had predated the Spanish protectorate. Known by the euphemism *plazas de soberanía* (places of sovereignty), they have a population of 145,000, and are divided into two groups.

The *plazas mayores* (greater places) contain virtually all the people, and include the coastal cities of Ceuta and Melilla. Politically these are 'autonomous cities', with governmental powers placing them somewhere between a city and a region of Spain.

The *plazas menores* (lesser places) are only inhabited by a handful of Spanish legionnaires, if that. These include three islands in the Bay of Al-Hoceima: Isla de Mar, Isla de Tierra (both deserted, apart from Spanish flags) and El Peñón de Alhucemas, a striking white fortress home to some 60 soldiers. El Peñón de Velez de la Gomera, at the end of a long canyon in the National Park of Al-Hoceima, is another ancient rock fortress, connected to the mainland by a narrow spit of sand – and a guardhouse, one of the oddest national borders you'll ever see. The Islas Chafarinas, 3km from Ras el-Mar, have three small islands: Isla del Congreso, Isla del Rey and Isla Isabel II, the last with a garrison of 190 troops. Spain also owns the tiny Isla Perejil, near Ceuta, which was the cause of one of the world's smallest conflicts, when Spanish troops evicted a handful of Moroccan soldiers in 2002; and the Isla de Alborán, about 75km north of Melilla, which has a small navy garrison.

While the two fortress *peñones* (rocky outcrops) are must-sees, none of the *plazas menores* can be entered, as they are military sites. Morocco claims them all, making their defence necessary. Otherwise, their strategic importance is more elusive than the Mediterranean monk seal, the last of which disappeared from the Islas Chafarinas in the 1990s.

Recent history has been focused on problems with Spain over immigration and political sovereignty. In 2002 there was a bizarre conflict over the tiny nearby isle of Perejil, after half a dozen Moroccan soldiers tried to reclaim it from Spain. In 2006 youths set fire to several mosques in Ceuta, after a number of local Muslims were arrested on the Spanish mainland in connection with the Madrid bombings. In 2007 the king of Spain visited the city for the first time in 80 years, sparking protests from the Moroccan government. So far none of this has closed a single tapas bar. In late 2010 Moroccan youths rioted in both Ceuta and Melilla over sovereignty of the cities, sparked by a lack of jobs.

✖ Eating & Drinking

In addition to the places listed here, the Pablado Marinero (Seamen's Village) beside the yacht harbour is home to a variety of decent restaurants, of which one of the best is **El Refectorio** (☑956 51 38 84; mains from €15; ⊙lunch & dinner). The best place to look for tapas bars is in the streets behind the post office and around Calle Millán Astray to the north of Calle Camoens. In addition to tapas, they all serve more substantial *raciones* (a larger helping of tapas) and *bocadillos* (sandwiches).

Mucha Kaña
TAPAS BAR €

(7 Sargento Mena; tapas from €0.85, mains from €6; ⊙lunch & dinner) Styled as a *cervecería* but also serving Spanish wines, this is a great place for all ages. There are bar stools around barrels and well as tables, and good music. In addition to tapas and *raciones*, there are pastas and meat dishes.

Mesón el Bache
TAPAS BAR €

(Sargento Mena Algeciras; tapas €1.50, raciones from €7.50; ⊙9am-3pm & 8.30pm-midnight, closed Sun) Have your tapas in a rustic hunting lodge. The locals love it, especially as you get one free tapa with every drink. Just downhill from Plaza Real, looking towards the port.

El Angulo
LOCAL €€

(1 Muralles Reales; mains from €15; ⊙lunch & dinner, closed Sun) Here's your chance to eat inside the Royal Walls. The local meats and seafood are just as good as the unique atmosphere. The white tablecloths and stone

fortifications work well, or you can sit outside by the moat.

Cala Carlota
LOCAL €€

(Calle Edrisis; set menu from €7; ☺lunch & dinner) This simple restaurant has a prime location in the Club Nautico overlooking the yacht harbour, with outdoor seating in season. The three-course *menú del diá* (daily set menu) is a popular choice, while the luscious fish dishes will set you back the same amount on their own.

Mesón el Cortijo
TAPAS BAR €

(14 Calle Cervantes; tapas from €1.50; ☺lunch & dinner, closed Sun) A classic neighbourhood gathering place heavy on tapas, *cerveza* (beer) and friendliness. Catch up on football, gossip and practise your Español.

La Marina
SEAFOOD, LOCAL €€

(☎956 51 40 07; 1 Alférez Bayton; ☺lunch & dinner, closed Sun, closed Feb) This old favourite was closed for renovations at the time of research. No doubt it will continue to specialise in fish dishes, and do a great-value three-course set menu of the chicken/fish and chips variety.

Gran Muralla
CHINESE €

(Plaza de la Constitución; mains from €5; ☺lunch & dinner) If you've had enough local food, you'll find hearty portions of Chinese standards here. Window tables have views over the plaza and out to sea.

Café Central
CAFE, BAR €

(3 Calle Millán Astray; ☺3.30pm-4am) Conviviality reigns in this sophisticated bar-coffee lounge, with subdued music and an art-deco entrance. The bronze statue of an arm lifting a tankard over the bar – a working beer pull – is an eccentric touch. An excellent place for coffee, brandy or ice cream (or all three) at any time.

La Jota
PATISSERIE, ICE CREAM €

(6 Calle Méndez Nuñez; breakfast €2, ice creams from €2) Offers a delightful array of cakes and ice cream in a variety of flavours. A good place to start – or end – a day of exploring the city.

El Puente Cafeteria
CAFE €

(Plaza de la Constitution; sandwiches from €3.50) Opening out onto a plaza made for people-watching, El Puente is a trendy and modern cafe-bar with great sandwiches. It gets busy, so work hard to catch the eyes of the staff.

Dublin
PUB €

(Delgado Serrano; pints €3.50; ☺3.30pm-3am Mon-Sat) It's like every other Irish pub you've ever been in, but if you need that Guinness fix, this is the place, even if the ambrosial brew does taste a bit watery here. If the volume gets to you, you can escape to the tables outside. Go down the steps where Calle Delgado Serrano takes a 90-degree bend.

SELF-CATERING

The **Supersol supermarket** (Av Muelle Cañonero Dato) is the best place to stock up on essentials and treats alike; there's a smaller branch in the city centre on Dean Navarro Acuña.

The cavernous **Central Market** (☺8am-3pm Mon-Sat) is the local spot for fresh meat and produce, and a vibrant experience as well.

Information

To phone Ceuta from outside Spain, dial ☎0034. Remember that Ceuta is one hour ahead of Morocco, and two hours ahead during Spanish daylight saving (see p501), and that most businesses will be closed on Sunday.

Internet Access

Cyber Ceuta (Paseo de Colón; per hr €2.50; ☺11am-2pm & 5-10pm Mon-Sat, 5-10pm Sun)

Medical Services

Instituto Gestión Sanitaria (Ingesa; ☎956 52 84 00; ☺24hr) Two locations, one next to the Royal Walls, another east of the fishing port.

Money

Euros are used for all transactions in Ceuta. ATMs are plentiful; outside banking hours you can change money at the more expensive hotels. There are informal moneychangers on both sides of the border, although it's technically illegal to take dirhams out of Morocco.

Post

Correos (Post Office; 59 Calle Real; ☺8.30am-8.30pm Mon-Fri, 9.30am-2pm Sat)

Tourist Information

Main tourist office (☎856 20 05 60; www.ceuta.es, in Spanish; Baluarte de los Mallorquines; ☺8.30am-8.30pm) Very friendly and efficient, with good maps and brochures.

Plaza de Africa Kiosk (☎956 52 81 46; ☺10am-1pm & 5-8pm 15 Sep-31 May, 10.30am-1.30pm & 6-9pm 1 Jun-14 Sep) A smaller satellite office.

Estacion Marítima Kiosk (☎956 50 62 75; ☺9am-9pm) Another satellite office.

Travel Agencies

Av Muelle Cañonero Dato and the approach to the *estación marítima* are lined with agencies selling ferry tickets to Algeciras.

Viajes Flandria (✆956 51 20 74; fax 956 51 45 59; ventas@viajesflandria.com; 1 Ave Independencia)

❶ Getting There & Away

Morocco

Buses and grands taxis to Ceuta often terminate at Fnideq, rather than at the border (Bab Sebta). If so, the border is a further 1km walk, or Dh5 by taxi. Although the border is open 24 hours, public transport is sparse from 7pm to 5am.

On the Moroccan side, you'll either fill out a departure form at the passport window, if on foot, or at the vehicle registration window (ignore any hustlers trying to sell you these free forms). If you're driving a hire car, you will be required to show proof of authorisation to take the vehicle out of the country. The 100m crossing is surprisingly disorganised, with multiple people asking for your passport. Pedestrians must frequently walk in the car lanes.

Coming the other way, there is a large grand taxi lot next to Moroccan border control. Departures are plentiful to Tetouan (Dh30, 40 minutes), from where you can pick up onward transport. Taxis to Chefchaouen or Tangier are rare, and you'll most likely have to bargain hard to hire a vehicle yourself (Chefchaouen Dh300, 90 minutes; Tangier Dh200, one hour). A good alternative is to take a grand taxi to Fnideq (Dh5, 10 minutes), just south of the border, from where transport to Tangier is more frequent (Dh30, one hour).

Mainland Spain

The unmissable **Estación Marítima** (ferry terminal; Calle Muelle Cañonero Dato) is west of the town centre. There are several daily high-speed ferries to Algeciras (p511). Ticket offices are around the corner. Much flashier (and far more expensive) is to take the helicopter service **Inaer** (www.inaer.com) from Ceuta to Algeciras (seven minutes) or Málaga airport (30 minutes).

You can purchase train tickets to European destinations at the **Renfe office** (✆956 51 13 17; 17 Plaza Rafael Gilbert; ☺9.30am-1pm, 4.30-8.30pm Mon-Fri, 9.30am-1pm Sat) or at a travel agency. Several agencies in the ferry terminal also sell Enatcar (the main Spanish coach company) bus tickets.

❶ Getting Around

Bus 7 runs up to the border (*frontera*) every 10 minutes or so from Plaza de la Constitución (€0.70). If you arrive by ferry and want to head straight for the border, there's a bus stop on Av

González Tablas opposite the entrance to the ramparts. There's also a taxi rank outside the terminal building.

If you have your own vehicle, street parking is restricted to a maximum of two hours (€1) during the day. If you are staying longer, use the car park (per hour €0.50, per 12 hours €4) on Calle O'Donnell or near the Poblado Marinero.

THE RIF MOUNTAINS

جبل اريف

Tetouan

تطوان

POP 330,000

Tetouan is a jewel of a town in a striking location at the foot of the Rif Mountains, and just a few kilometres from the sea. It's unlike Tangier or the imperial cities in that it has not yet been discovered by foreign tourists. There is an air of authenticity here that adds great value to a visit. The ancient medina, a Unesco World Heritage site, looks like it has not changed in several centuries. There have been some recent upgrades – a modern bus station, restorations to the medina wall, some public gardens – but nothing like the towns along the coast. The city is poised on the edge of discovery and in the words of one hotelier, is about to 'explode'. To the savvy traveller, this spells opportunity.

From 1912 until 1956 Tetouan was the capital of the Spanish protectorate, which encompassed much of northern Morocco. This and the town's long relationship with Andalucia have left it with a Hispano-Moorish character that is unique in Morocco, as physically reflected in the Spanish part of the city, known as the Ensanche (extension), whose white buildings and broad boulevards have been restored to their original condition.

The Ensanche is centred on Pl Moulay el-Mehdi and the pedestrian stretch of Ave Mohammed V, which runs east to Plaza Al-Jala. Here you'll find hotels, banks and places to eat. The entrance to the medina is off the grand Pl Hassan II, which faces the Royal Palace. The rest of the sprawling town has little to offer the visitor.

History

From the 8th century onwards, the city served as the main point of contact between Morocco and Andalucia. In the 14th century the Merenids established the town as a base from which to control rebellious Rif tribes, and to attack Ceuta, but it was destroyed by Henry III of Castille in 1399. After the Reconquista (the reconquest of Spain, completed in 1492), the town was rebuilt by Andalucian refugees. It prospered due in part to their skills, and to thriving pirate activity.

Moulay Ismail built Tetouan's defensive walls in the 17th century, and the town's trade links with Spain developed. In 1860, the Spanish took the town under Leopoldo O'Donnell, who extensively Europeanised it, but upon recapture two years later the Moors removed all the signs of European influence.

At the turn of the 20th century, Spanish forces occupied Tetouan for three years, claiming it was protecting Ceuta from Rif tribes. In 1913 the Spanish made Tetouan the capital of their protectorate, which was abandoned in 1956 when Morocco regained independence. Lately the Andalucian government has provided a great cultural boost to the city by financing various restoration projects.

◉ Sights

MEDINA

The whitewashed medina of Tetouan is an authentic time machine, and very traveller-friendly, with moped-free lanes, few street hustlers, amiable residents and a general lack of congestion, particularly in the large residential areas. In the commercial spaces, the sights and sounds of traditional life are everywhere: craftsmen pound brass, silk merchants offer thousands of spools of multicoloured thread and bakers tend the public ovens. There are some 35 mosques as well, of which the **Grande Mosquée** and **Saïda Mosque** both northeast of Place Hassan II, are the most impressive, although non-Muslims are not allowed to enter. If you get lost, a few dirhams in local hands will get you to any doorstep.

The medina is bordered to the south by the pretty **Lovers Park**, a pleasant escape. At the time of research the old train station just south of here had been transformed into the **Contemporary Art Museum** but was not quite ready to open.

Ethnographic Museum   MUSEUM
(admission Dh10; ☺9am-4pm Mon-Sat) Just inside the picture-perfect eastern gate, Bab el-Okla, is the Ethnographic Museum

which is worth a visit for the terrace views of the Rif (ask the caretaker to open it for you, if necessary), its pleasant garden with old cannons and the display of silk wedding gowns.

Artisanal School   NOTABLE BUILDING
(admission Dh10; ☺8.30am-2.30pm Sat-Thu, 8.30-11.30am Fri) Just outside Bab el-Okla is the best artisan centre in northern Morocco. This is a fascinating opportunity to see masters teaching apprentices traditional arts, including ornamental woodwork, silk costumes, carved plaster, intricate mosaics and decorative rifles. A fantastic central treasury holds the best of the best – don't miss the ceiling. Staff will open it upon request. The building itself is of interest, set around a large courtyard, with fine doors upstairs.

Place Hassan II   LANDMARK
The broad and empty Place Hassan II, which is mostly roped off for security reasons, links the medina to the Ensanche. It looks like it houses the Wizard of Oz with guards standing in front of the long flat facade of the royal palace, and four fountains with central columns towering all around. These are not minarets, as one might suppose, but art-nouveau light towers designed by a student of Gaudí. The large decorations on the opposite wall are abstract Hands of Fatima, a common symbol used to ward off the evil eye. There are a few nondescript cafes which are good for a rest, particularly on the 2nd floor, which allows a grander view.

THE ENSANCHE

Take in the Ensanche by walking along Ave Mohammed V from **Place Al-Jala** to **Place Moulay el-Mehdi**. The broad boulevard is lined by bright white Spanish colonial architecture, with a few art deco elements, reminiscent of styles found elsewhere (eg Casablanca, Larache) with restoration funded by the Andalucian government.

Archaeology Museum   MUSEUM
(Ave al-Jazaer; admission Dh10; ☺10am-6pm Mon-Sat) A few blocks from the Place al-Jala there is an extensive museum with an excellent collection of artefacts from the Roman ruins at Lixus, displayed both inside and in the gardens. Labelling is in French, Spanish and Arabic.

Tetouan

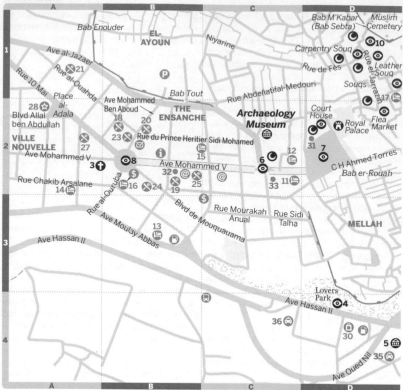

Iglesia de Bacturia   CHURCH
(Place Moulay el-Mehdi; ☉Sunday mass 11am, daily mass 7pm) This Roman Catholic church was built in 1926 and is still active.

🛏 Sleeping

Due to the rapid development of the nearby coast, the first question one must now answer is whether to stay in town or not. Tetouan's port, Martil, is only an inexpensive 15-minute cab ride away; M'Diq, the classiest option, is twice that. The contrast could not be greater between the ancient medina and these modern resorts with their snazzy corniches, and can be either jarring or a relief. The beachfronts are very quiet outside the holiday season of July and August.

If you choose the city, your next decision is whether to stay in the medina or not. A night or two within the ancient walls is an unforgettable adventure and an opportunity to see typical Tetouan architecture and furniture, usually studded with mother-of-pearl inlay.

TOP **Blanco Riad**   RIAD €€€
CHOICE (📞0539 70 42 02; www.blancoriad.com; 25 Rue Zawiya Kadiria; d incl breakfast Dh880, ste from Dh1320; 🕸🛜) This beautiful medina house with its typical Tetouan architecture has been carefully restored and furnished with a blend of modern and antique pieces. It offers large, comfortable rooms and a Zen-like garden. One of the salons contains an enormous hammam, and another, an excellent restaurant open to non-guests. The welcome is friendly and help is available to discover the medina.

El Reducto   RIAD €€€
(📞0539 96 81 20; www.riadtetouan.com; 38 Zanqat Zawiya; incl breakfast s Dh400-600, d Dh550-850) This superb house is worth a visit just to see the traditional mosaic tiles with their coppery sheen. The spot-

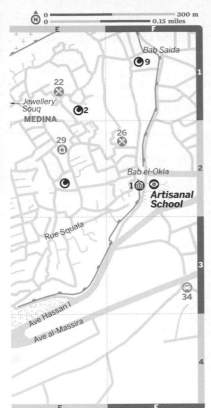

Hotel Regina
HOTEL €

(☑0539 96 21 13; 8 Rue Sidi Mandri; s/d/tr Dh90/123/160) One of the larger budget choices, the Regina initially feels a bit tired, but the whitewashed walls and bright Riffian fabrics manage to wake you up. While the bathrooms are sometimes worn, everything is sparklingly clean which makes it decent value for money. There's a cafe on the ground floor for breakfast.

Hotel Paris
HOTEL €

(☑0539 96 67 50; 31 Rue Chakib Arsalane; s/d Dh257/309, breakfast Dh40) Not your honeymoon suite, but performs the basic functions. The simple, uninspiring rooms are clean, but the bathrooms are small. Institutional hallways accelerate you outdoors.

Riad Dalia
RIAD €€

(☑0539 96 43 18; www.riad-dalia.com; 25 Rue Ouessaa; s without bathroom Dh150, d incl breakfast Dh400, ste Dh600) The first riad hotel in the medina, this funky, family-run option desperately needs an overhaul. The 300-year-old former Dutch consul's house has been transformed into a hotel without much renovation, so it feels like the consul may turn up at any moment. In fact, the proprietor has his ancient letters in a scrapbook at the front desk, not to mention his stamp collection. The master suite is immense but it all smells a bit musty.

Hotel Panorama Vista
HOTEL €€

(☑0539 96 49 70; www.panoramavista.com; Ave Moulay Abbas; s/d incl breakfast Dh307/404; ✴🛜) This is the best bet outside the medina. The rooms are chain-hotel style, without any local ambience, but clean and with dramatic views over the Rif. The popular cafe on the 1st floor, with its wall of glass, offers a strong Moroccan continental breakfast. Management would prefer you to shower, but you can insist on a bath plug.

✕ Eating

Tetouan has not been known for its restaurants in the past, but things are looking up as tourism is encouraged. There are a couple of palace options (popular with tour groups, so reserve ahead) but the best restaurants are those in medina guesthouses. Otherwise, you are restricted to grilled food and sandwiches.

Restaurant Blanco Riad
LOCAL €€€

(☑0539 70 42 02; 25 Rue Zawiya Kadiria; meals Dh400) Located in the guesthouse of the same name, the chef here has taken

less, palatial rooms are truly fantastic with big bathrooms (one has a Jacuzzi for two), the highest quality antique furniture and beautiful silk bedspreads. There's also a good, licensed restaurant with a Spanish touch to the menu.

Pension Iberia
HOTEL €

(☑0539 96 36 79; 5 Pl Moulay el-Mehdi; s/d/tr Dh60/100/150) This is the best budget option, with classic high-ceilinged rooms and shuttered balconies that open out to the Pl Moulay el-Mehdi – book Room 11 if possible. Views of the white city flowing over the hills and the fountain in the Place – better observed from here than from the street – add a dash of romance. Bathrooms are shared and hot showers an extra Dh10. Located on the 3rd floor above a bank, it has convenient public parking (Parking Hammadi; Ave al-Jazaer) 100m away.

Tetouan

Moroccan cuisine and modernised it with flair. A traditional *pastilla* might contain foie gras along with the pigeon, the stuffed calamari tubes come with a saffron sabayon, and the desserts are sinfully good. Decor is pared down and there are chairs and tables as well as Moroccan banquette seating. Book ahead.

Snack Taouss   FAST FOOD €
(3 Rue 10 Mai; mains from Dh25; ☺lunch & dinner) Known for its burgers and chips, this little snack bar has a Syrian influence and does good felafel and delicious *shwarma* as well as inexpensive pizzas, salads, *harira* (tomato and chickpea soup), tajines and more. There's a small seating area upstairs (handy if you're waiting for a pizza), or you can eat on the move. If it's full, there's a similar place, 10 Mai, next door.

Restaurant Restinga   LOCAL €
(21 Ave Mohammed V; mains from Dh50, beer Dh15; ☺lunch & dinner) The open-air courtyard shaded by a huge ficus tree is this charming restaurant's primary attraction –

along with the rare alcohol licence. A great place to duck out of the crowded boulevard for a rest and a beer, as well as some seafood from the coast.

Restaurant Albahr   FAST FOOD €
(21 Rue Almoukawama; mains from Dh30; ☺lunch & dinner) Nothing fancy here – fried foods, burgers and good fish and chips – but they do it well and the price is right. Salads are a plus, and there's couscous on Fridays (Dh50).

Riad Saada   LOCAL €€
(☏0661 46 71 29; 18 Rue Jenoui; set menu Dh100; ☺lunch & dinner) This is a classic Moroccan experience, from the endless plates of food (soup, couscous, tajines, salads, kebabs) to the entertainment (belly dancing, traditional musicians) to the superb setting in a 16th-century caliph's house. There are even two golden throne chairs for weddings and beautiful carved plaster walls. Enter via Bab el-Okla, turn right immediately, take second left at Optique Seffar, and you will see the entrance, a very long tiled corridor.

Palace Bouhlal
LOCAL €€
(☎0670 85 95 63; 48 Jamaa Kebir; set menu Dh100; ☺lunch) Another sumptuous palace option with plush couches, wall rugs, intimate dining spaces (especially upstairs), gurgling fountains and a grand Moorish arch complementing the usual four-course meal. Follow the lane north around the Grande Mosquée and look for signs directing you down a tiny alley. Be sure to duck into Les Secrets des Plantes first, on the right just before the entrance, where 670 spices line the walls.

Cafeteria Emirates
CAFE €
(5 Ave Ouahda; ☺6am-10pm) This large place with its shiny black and chrome decor is the trendiest place to be seen in town, and is a good option for women. The coffee is good and they make great juices (Dh15).

Oahda
CAFE €
(16 Rue al-Ouahda; ☺7am-9pm, closed Fri afternoon) Another female-friendly cafe, not as nicely appointed as Emirates, but just as popular with locals. Sticky cakes are a speciality. A bit claustrophobic on the upper floor.

Dallas
PATISSERIE €
(11 Rue Youssef ben Tachfine; ☺6am-10pm) Yes, named after the TV show, but otherwise the name has no bearing on this place, a patisserie stacked to the rafters with plates of pastries. This is where local families come to load up on sweets. One block off Ave Mohammed V.

Pannini
FAST FOOD €
(5-6 Ave Mohammed Ben Aboud; panini from Dh20; ☺noon-11pm) Made-to-order sandwiches make this a standout option. Choose from a smorgasbord of ingredients both normal and exotic.

SELF-CATERING
There's loads of fresh fruit and veg for sale in the medina on the road leading east to Bab el-Okla. The central market (closed Friday) around the corner from Lovers Park puts on a good display, with fish brought in from the coast. Epicerie Restinga (cnr Rue du Prince Héritier Sidi Mohamed & Rue Ben Aboud; ☺9am-10pm) sells alcohol.

Drinking
As is the Moroccan norm, Tetouan's drinking establishments are firmly in the male sphere. The more welcoming cafes are listed under Eating; for a drop of the hard stuff, head for the dark and smoky bars along Rue 10 Mai, northwest of Pl Moulay el-Mehdi. If you just want a beer, Restaurant Restinga is the place.

Entertainment
Apart from a palace meal, Cinéma Avenida (Pl al-Adala; admission Dh20-35; ☺film times 3.30pm, 6.30pm & 9.30pm) is the only game in town. Films are usually in French or Arabic, with some Spanish.

Shopping
Wood and leatherwork are the local specialities; for the latter go straight to the source at the small tannery (Bab M'Kabar) in the north of the medina.

Dar Lebadi
ART & CRAFT, CARPETS
(Jenoui section) The shopping palace of the medina, this 200-year-old building, a former governor's house, has been meticulously restored, and is a clearing house for Berber artisans and Rabati carpets, with friendly staff. Worth a stop just to see the building, but be careful: you may be there for hours.

Ensemble Artisanal
ART & CRAFTS
(Ave Hassan II; ☺8am-8pm Mon-Sat) This government-sponsored emporium is a hive of activity, with carpet weavers, leatherworkers, jewellers and woodworkers all plying their trades. Prices are fixed.

Information
Internet Access
Imex Media (19 Ave Mohammed V; per hr Dh5)
Remote Studios (13 Ave Mohammed V; per hr Dh9; ☺9am-midnight)

Medical Services
Clinique du Croissant Rouge (Red Cross Clinic; ☎0539 96 20 20; Pl al-Hammama, Quartier Scolaire)
Main hospital (☎0539 97 24 30; Martil Rd) About 2km out of town.
Pharmacie El-Feddan (☎0539 96 80 51; Pl Hassan II; ☺9am-1pm, 3.30-8pm) Pharmacy in medina.

Money
There are plenty of banks with ATMs along Ave Mohammed V.
BMCE (Pl Moulay el-Mehdi) Change cash and travellers cheques outside regular banking hours.

Post
Post office (Pl Moulay el-Mehdi)

Tourist Information

ONMT (Délégation Régionale du Tourisme; ☑0539 96 19 15; fax 0539 96 19 14; 30 Ave Mohammed V) The staff here are helpful and have lots of brochures and maps available. The 1951 murals of northern Morocco here are worth a visit, too.

Travel Agencies

Voyages Travelmar (☑0539 71 42 37; 5 Ave Mohammed V; ☺9am-noon & 2.30-6.30pm Mon-Sat)

Voyages Hispamaroc (☑/fax 0539 71 33 38; 23 Ave Mohammed V; ☺8.30am-12.30pm & 3-7pm Mon-Fri, 9am-12.30pm Sat)

Getting There & Away

Air

The Tetouan airport opens for occasional charter flights from Paris and Brussels but has no scheduled service. Persistent rumours that a full-fledged airport is coming may be inspired by efforts to sell foreigners real estate.

Bus

Tetouan is now blessed with a modern bus station. There is an electronic timetable but bus touts are still in place – just walk past them and read the departure times on your own. You can get to any town in the north from here. There's a left-luggage office (medium/large bag Dh6/10).

CTM has its own station a five minute taxi ride away from the main bus station. It is a better bet for quality reasons and for any long-haul destinations.

Fez Dh90, five hours

Rabat Dh100, four to five hours

Marrakesh Dh235, 11 hours

Local destinations include:

Martil Dh4, 25 minutes

M'Diq Dh8, one hour

Fnideq Dh10, 1¼ hours

Left luggage is Dh5 per kilogram per day.

Taxi

Grands taxis to Fnideq (for Ceuta; Dh15, 30 minutes) and Martil (Dh5, 15 minutes) leave from Ave Hassan II, near Lovers Park. Occasional grands taxis to Al-Hoceima (Dh150, eight hours) wait on a dusty lot 100m further east behind the new Modern Art Museum.

The taxi rank on Place al-Hammama, 2km west of central Tetouan, is the place to pick up grands taxis to Chefchaouen (Dh30, one hour) and Tangier (Dh25, 1¼ hours). If you are arriving from either of these places, the taxi driver may drop you closer to the town centre.

Grands taxis to Oued Laou are located underneath the Ave al-Massira overpass – which is easily missed.

ⓘ Getting Around

Petits taxis are canary yellow but don't have meters; a ride around town should be around Dh10. If you have your own vehicle, you can keep your car at the guarded **Parking Hammadi** (Ave Al Jazaer; per 4hr daytime Dh10, per night Dh10).

Around Tetouan

While Tetouan itself sees few foreigners, in summer both local and Europe-based Moroccans flock to the golden beaches so close to the town. Huge developments are under way, from Fnideq near Ceuta southwards to M'Diq, Cabo Negro and Martil. There will be large golf resorts and swathes of holiday apartments along new corniches (beachfront roads). Most of these projects lie half-completed; building has largely been halted due to lack of investment during the credit crunch.

MARTIL   مارتيل

Tetouan's port of Martil is a rapidly growing, modern beach town with a broad mountain view and a long corniche paralleled by streets full of cafes, ice-cream shops and restaurants. It has year-round weekend visitors, and heaves in the summer, but is deserted the rest of the time. It's a viable base if you don't mind the 8km, 10-minute cab ride to Tetouan.

🛏 Sleeping & Eating

Hotel Etoile de la Mer   HOTEL €

(☑0539 97 90 58; Ave Hassan II; s/d incl breakfast Dh177/231; ☎) With its funky design – a central, plant-filled atrium criss-crossed by stairways – and good location one block from the beach, this is Martil's top sleeping option at the moment. Riffian textiles and green paint brighten things up. The best rooms have balconies overlooking the sea, and the restaurant serves alcohol.

Camping al-Boustane   CAMP SITE €

(☑/fax 0539 68 88 22; Corniche; camping per person Dh20, per tent/car/campervan Dh30/20/35, electricity Dh30; ☺office 7.30am-noon, 7-11pm; ☎☒) This secure camp site is one block from the beach, set in a pretty garden. Facilities are showing their age, but it does have a reasonable restaurant (mains from

Dh55) and a pool in summer. There are serious drainage problems when it rains. Turn off corniche at fountain.

Ras Tarf Restaurant   LOCAL €€
(☎0539 68 83 00; Corniche; pizza from Dh70; ☺lunch & dinner) One of a number of beachfront restaurants, this one is pleasant and serves a decent array of pizzas, burgers and *shwarma*. During the week out of season, you'll be the only customer.

ⓘ Getting There & Away
Local buses to Tetouan (Dh5, 15 minutes) leave from the bus station near the water tower at the southern end of the beach. You'll find grands taxis to Tetouan (Dh5, 10 minutes) near the big mosque.

CABO NEGRO & M'DIQ   الرأس الاسود و مضيق
About 5km up the coast from Martil, the headland of Cabo Negro juts out into the Mediterranean and is clearly visible from Martil. Tucked into the lee of its north side is the surprising town of M'Diq. Once a small fishing village, it has rapidly grown into the classiest resort on the coast, with a grand entrance, excellent hotels and restaurants, a fine beach and a yacht club. There is really little to separate this place from Florida, but if you are suffering from medina fatigue, it's the perfect stop, and only 20 minutes from Tetouan.

🛏 Sleeping & Eating
M'Diq's sleeping options tend to cater to the summer tourist trade and ignore the lower end of the price bracket. Ask for discounts outside the summer months. Given the number of new apartments, it is worth inquiring about rentals on site. There's a string of cafes and cheap eateries along the seafront.

Golden Beach Hotel   HOTEL €€
(☎0539 97 50 77; www.goldenbeachhotel.com; 84 Rte de Sebta; s/d incl breakfast Dh478/709; ☜❄⊛) This four-star, aptly named hotel right on the beach is worth the splurge – short on charm, but well run, well maintained and with great facilities, including a restaurant, disco, pool by the corniche and a piano bar with a most clever bar top: piano keys in marble.

Hotel Narijiss   HOTEL €
(☎0539 66 37 70; Ave Lalla Nezha; s/d Dh150/250; ❄) This decent hotel is 200m up the hill rising from the seafront to the Tetouan road. It's a bit nondescript, but rooms have bathrooms and satellite TV, and there's a cafe tucked outside.

Las Olas Restaurant and Cafe   LOCAL €
(☎0539 66 44 33; Corniche; mains from Dh50; ☺lunch & dinner; ☜) You can't miss this waterfront landmark dressed up as a lighthouse, with a hopping downstairs cafe and an upstairs seafood restaurant. The decor is snappy, the rooftop views superb, and they don't have to go far to get fresh catch. Located directly on the corniche car park.

Royal Yachting Club de M'Diq   RESTAURANT
(M'Diq port) The entire port was being rebuilt at the time of research, and a marina added. No doubt the private yacht club will reopen its classy seafood restaurant once the development is complete.

ⓘ Getting There & Away
Grands taxis and buses travelling between Tetouan and Fnideq (3km short of the border with Ceuta) pass through M'Diq. Grands taxis to Tetouan (Dh5, 15 minutes) depart from a stand near the Narijiss Hotel. Those for the border (Dh10) gather on the north side of town beside the Banque Populaire.

Chefchaouen   شفشاون
POP 45,000

Beautifully sited beneath the raw peaks of the Rif, Chefchaouen is one of the prettiest towns in Morocco, an artsy, blue-washed mountain village that feels like its own world. While tourism has definitely taken hold, the balance between ease and authenticity is just right. The old medina is a delight of Moroccan and Andalucian influence with red-tiled roofs, bright-blue buildings and narrow lanes converging on busy Plaza Uta el-Hammam and its restored kasbah. Long known to backpackers for the easy availability of kif (marijuana), the town has rapidly gentrified and offers a range of quality accommodation, good food, lots to do and no hassles to speak of, making it a strong alternative to a hectic multi-city tour. This is a great place to relax, explore and take day trips in the cool green hills. Families take note.

Chefchaouen is split into an eastern half (the medina), and a western half (the *ciudad nueva,* or new city). The heart of the medina is Plaza Uta el-Hammam, with its unmistakeable kasbah. The medina walls have recently been repaired, with Spanish funding. The principal route of the new city

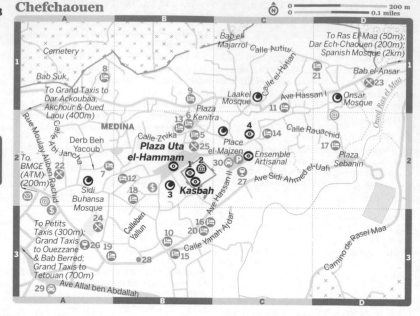

is Ave Hassan II, which stretches from Plaza Mohammed V, a leafy square designed by artist Juan Miró, past the western gate of Bab el-Ain, around the southern medina wall, and into the medina itself. Here it dead-ends at Place el-Majzen, the main drop-off point. The bus station is a steep 1.5km hike southwest of the town centre. The falls of Ras-el-Maa lie just beyond the medina walls to the northeast.

History

Chefchaouen was originally known as Chaouen, meaning 'peaks'. Under Spanish occupation the spelling changed to Xaouen, and in 1975 the town was renamed Chefchaouen (Look at the Peaks). These days, the names are used interchangeably.

Moulay Ali ben Rachid founded Chaouen in 1471 as a base for Riffian Berber tribes to launch attacks on the Portuguese in Ceuta. The town expanded with the arrival of Muslim and Jewish refugees from Granada in 1494, who built the whitewashed houses, with tiny balconies, tiled roofs and patios (often with a citrus tree in the centre), that give the town its distinctive Spanish flavour. The pale-blue wash prevalent today was introduced in the 1930s – previously windows and doors had been painted a traditional Muslim green.

The town remained isolated and xenophobic – Christians were forbidden to enter on pain of death – until occupied by Spanish troops in 1920. When the Spanish arrived they were surprised to hear the Jewish inhabitants still speaking a variant of medieval Castilian. The Spanish were briefly thrown out by Abd al-Krim during the Rif War in the 1920s, but they soon returned and remained until independence in 1956.

◎ Sights

Medina   MEDINA

Chefchaouen's medina is one of the loveliest in Morocco. Small and uncrowded, it's easy to explore, with enough winding paths to keep you diverted, but compact enough that you'll never get too lost. Most of the buildings are painted a blinding blue-white, giving them a clean, fresh look, while terracotta tiles add an Andalucian flavour.

The heart of the medina is the shady, cobbled **Plaza Uta el-Hammam** which is lined with cafes and restaurants, all serving similar fare. This is a peaceful place to relax and watch the world go by, particularly after a long day of exploration. The plaza is dominated by the red-hued walls of the **kasbah** and the adjacent **Grande Mosquée**. Noteworthy for its unusual octagonal tower and recently restored, the Grande Mosquée was built in the 15th century by the son of the town's founder, Ali ben Rachid, and is closed to non-Muslims. The **kasbah** (admission incl museum & gallery Dh10; ⊙9am-1pm & 3-6.30pm Wed-Mon, 9-noon & 3-6.30pm Fri) is a heavily restored walled fortress that now contains a lovely garden, a small **Ethnographic Museum**, and an even smaller **art gallery**. The ethnographic museum contains some fascinating views of old Chefchaouen, including the plaza and the kasbah; the gallery promotes the work of talented local artists.

🏃 Activities
Spas & Hammams

Centre Viva Form   SPA
(☎0539 98 61 65; Atlas Chaouen Hotel; ⊙noon-9pm) A sophisticated, full-service spa located at the Atlas Chaouen Hotel. Prices range from reflexology (Dh100) to the 50-minute slimming massage, which will trim your wallet of Dh500.

Douches Barakat   HAMMAM
(hammam Dh10; ⊙men 8am-noon, women noon-8pm) A traditional, and far less expensive, option is the local hammam.

Trekking

There are numerous trekking opportunities of various durations in the vast 580-sq-km **Talassemtane National Park**, which begins just outside town. The name means 'cold spring' in Berber. Some popular destinations include the small villages of Kalaa and Akchour, and God's Bridge, a natural formation that looks like a stone arch. The duration of these excursions depends on how much you wish to drive versus walk.

The **Eco-Museum** (near Camping Azilane) at the entrance to the Talassemtane National Park is well worth a visit. It has info on the park, maps of treks and an extensive display of the flora and fauna found in the park. Register here if you intend to camp during your trek.

Le Caiat (☎0666 28 87 15; www.caiat.com; per person from Dh160-300; meals Dh100) is a wonderful mountain *refuge* 12km from Chefchaouen on the road to Oued Laou. It offers various guided treks of two hours to two days and has a range of accommodation and a restaurant with stunning views across the valleys.

DON'T MISS

SPANISH MOSQUE

Looking west, you'll easily spot the so-called Spanish mosque on a hilltop not far from the medina. It's a pleasant walk along clear paths and well worth the effort. Start at the waterfall **Ras el-Maa**, just beyond the far northeastern gate of the medina. It's here, where the water comes gushing out of the mountain, that local women come to do their washing. The sound of the water and the verdant hills just beyond the medina wall provide a sudden, strong dose of nature.

Continuing over the bridge, you can walk to the Spanish mosque following the hillside path. The mosque was built by the Spanish for the local population in the 1920s, but was never used. It fell into disrepair, but has been newly restored (by the Spanish, again) and at the time of research, was about to open as a cultural centre. From the hilltop minaret, you'll have a grand view of the entire town sprawling over the green hills below. The mosque is a popular destination, but women may not feel comfortable there by themselves.

☞ Tours

The Association des Guides du Tourisme de Chefchaouen TREKKING
(✆0662 11 39 17; mouddenabdeslam@yahoo.fr; half-day city tour Dh120, mountain treks half/full day Dh250/400) The association is an NGO set up to provide trekking information and to train and register guides. Association President, Abdeslam Mouden, speaks fluent English and has a wealth of local knowledge and guide experience.

⚜ Festivals & Events

The active cultural association **Rif el-Andalus** (✆0539 98 68 00) organises two events in July. One is a large open-air art exhibition, and the other is the Alegria, an international music festival.

🛏 Sleeping

Chefchaouen has a large number of accommodation options. As the medina is what you'll come to Chefchaouen for, it's best to stay here, though there are some good options outside the walls. Few hotels have heating. You will be sleeping beneath plenty of blankets during cold winter nights.

MEDINA

TOP CHOICE **Hostal Guernika** GUESTHOUSE €
(✆0539 98 74 34; hostalguernika@hotmail.com; 49 Onssar; d/tr Dh200/300; ☎) This is a warm and charming place, with a very caring and attentive owner, not far from the Plaza Uta el-Hammam. There are several great streetside rooms – large and bright, facing the mountains – but others can be dark. All have showers. The terrace has

spectacular views. Reserve in summer, Easter and December.

Dar Terrae GUESTHOUSE €€
(✆0539 98 75 98; www.darterrae.com; Ave Hassan I; s/d/tr incl breakfast Dh290/390/600; ☎) These funky, cheerfully painted rooms are individually decorated with their own bathroom and fireplace, and hidden up and down a tumble of stairs and odd corners. The Italian owners prepare a fantastic breakfast spread every day, and other meals on request. It's poorly signed – if in doubt ask for the 'Hotel Italiano'.

Dar Baraka GUESTHOUSE €
(✆0614 68 24 80; www.riad-baraka.com; Derb Ben Yacoub; d with shared bathroom incl breakfast Dh240, q per person Dh120 d with private bathroom Dh280; ☎) Another brand new guesthouse with English owners, Dar Baraka is sunny and bright. The rooms are comfortable and share spotless facilities. The terrace is particularly good, with some sun and some shade/warmth. There's dinner on request – it could be a barbecue, or if it's Sunday, Mum whips up a good roast.

John's House RENTAL HOUSE €€
(17 Calle Autiui; www.johndirkwilkinson@gmail.com; for 3 per night/week Dh715/3850; ✼ @) This cosiest of medina houses has just two bedrooms, a heated bathroom and a fabulous terrace with a fountain large enough to dip your toes in. Owned by the British Consular warden of Chefchaouen, the Union Jack flies proud alongside the Moroccan flag. In winter, have a sing-song round the piano in front of a blazing fire.

Dar Meziana   GUESTHOUSE €€
(☎0539 98 78 06; www.darmezianahotel.com; Rue Zagdud; s/d/tr from Dh475/650/950; ❄🤚🌐) Beautifully decorated, this boutique hotel is an artful creation, with a unique angular courtyard, lush plantings, lots of light, the highest quality furniture and extraordinary ceilings. On the edge of the medina and not signposted, but otherwise perfect.

Hotel Mouritania   GUESTHOUSE €
(☎0539 98 61 84; 15 Rue Qadi Alami; s/d Dh60/120; 🌐) Rooms are simple here, but staff are helpful, there's a comfy courtyard lounge ideal for meeting other travellers, and the breakfasts (Dh20) are great.

Hostal Yasmina   GUESTHOUSE €
(☎0539 88 31 18; yasmina45@hotmail.com; 12 Zaida Al-Horra; r per person Dh75) For the price bracket, this place sparkles. Rooms are bright and clean, the location is a stone's throw from Plaza Uta el-Hammam, and the roof terrace is very welcoming. This bargain doesn't have many rooms, though, so it can fill up quickly.

Hotel Koutoubia   GUESTHOUSE €
(☎0668 11 53 58; Calle Andalouse; s/d Dh150/200) This hotel does budget accommodation perfectly, with friendly and attentive management, a central location, traditional decor, spotless rooms and a closed-in roof terrace for those cold mornings where you can have breakfast (Dh15).

Dar Baiboo   GUESTHOUSE €€€
(☎0539 98 61 53; www.casahassan.com; Rue Targhi; ❄) Across the street from Casa Hassan and under the same management, this newly opened guesthouse is light and airy. Rooms open off the central courtyard and are large and comfortable.

Casa Hassan   GUESTHOUSE €€€
(☎0539 98 61 53; www.casahassan.com; 22 Rue Targhi; s/d with half-board from Dh850/1000; ❄) A large guesthouse on the 2nd floor above its restaurant, this long-established upmarket choice is showing its age a bit, but has sizable rooms with creative layouts, including beds tucked into alcoves, fireplaces and an in-house hammam. The terrace provides an elegant lounge, and the cosy Restaurant Tissemlal a warm hearth.

Hotel Barcelona   GUESTHOUSE €
(☎0539 98 85 06; 12 Rue Targhi; r per person with shared bathroom Dh70, s/d with private bathroom Dh300) A friendly budget option in bright Chefchaouen blue. The fixtures and fittings are pretty basic, but the hotel has recently been repainted, and the rooftop terrace is wonderful.

🏆 **Hotel Molino**   GUESTHOUSE €€
(☎0539 98 74 23; Plaza Seloannine; www.hotelchefchaouen.com; s/d with shared bathroom incl breakfast Dh250/350, d/q with bathroom Dh550/750; 🌐) Another newly opened guesthouse, Hotel Molino offers a range of rooms with funky design and local fabrics. Unusually, there's a wonderful garden where local children learn about planting their own vegetables. The American owner has plans for a spa and Lebanese restaurant. There's dinner on request, or you can cook your own in the kitchen.

OUTSIDE THE MEDINA
Most other accommodation options are clustered along Ave Hassan II, which runs south of the medina alongside the old city walls.

TOP CHOICE **Dar Ech-Chaouen**   GUESTHOUSE €€€
(☎0539 98 78 24; www.darechchaouen.ma; 18 Rte Ras el-Mar; s/d incl breakfast Dh490/690, ste s/d Dh600/890; ❄🌐♨) This recently opened guesthouse provides excellent high-end accommodation in Chaouen and is close to Ras el-Maa, just outside the medina walls. It's well designed with even staircases, spacious, comfortable rooms and a shady garden terrace. There's a pool with great views, and a restaurant. Five family-

---

MOSTAPHA EL-HABTI: MOUNTAIN GUIDE

As long as you're fit, people of any age can trek in the Rif. We do half-day walks as well as longer treks of a few days. I'm passionate about preserving the environment so I always tell everyone at the beginning, no throwing! Take your rubbish home with you.

» **Best trek:** Akchour to Oued Laou on the coast over two days

» **What to see:** herbs like juniper, lavender, rosemary and *fliou* (pennyroyal) that are used by local people as medicines; trees like cedar, thuya and conifers; Barbary apes, foxes, lizards, vipers; golden eagles and other birds of prey

» **Best experiences:** having tea with local families; visiting weaving or cheese-making cooperatives

sized cottages around the pool were being built at the time of research.

Dar Zman GUESTHOUSE €€
(☎0539 98 93 46; darzmanguesthouse@gmail. com; Bab el Hammar, Ave Hassan II; s/d incl breakfast Dh450/600; ☏) A lovely, finely restored guesthouse with eight brightly painted rooms and a wonderful rooftop breakfast area, created by some ambitious young hoteliers. The faux artefacts revealed in the walls are a clever touch.

Hotel Salam HOTEL $
(☎0539 98 62 39; 39 Ave Hassan II; s/d/tr Dh60/120/180) Another out-of-medina experience, the freshly painted Salam has perked up its bright courtyard rooms. Shared facilities are adequate, but sinks in all rooms are a bonus. In peak season, there's an espresso machine in the ground-floor salon.

Hotel Marrakesh HOTEL €
(☎0539 98 77 74; Hotel.Marrakech1@hot mail.com; 41 Ave Hassan II; s/d incl breakfast Dh150/240, d/tr with shower Dh300/360; ☏) Set downhill from the action, the Marrakesh is a hotel with a bit of soul. Bright pastel rooms invite the fresh air in, bathrooms have powerful showers, the common room attracts with its central fireplace and carved-plaster ceiling, and the roof terrace offers fine views over the valley.

Hotel Rif HOTEL €
(☎0539 98 69 82; hotelrif@hotmail.com; 29 Ave Hassan II; s/d incl breakfast Dh150/180, with bathroom & breakfast Dh180/240; ✳) Just below the medina walls, it has some good rooms with great views, and adequate rooms without. Suffering from dark and jumbled aesthetics, it's nevertheless popular with tour groups, so advance booking is a good idea. There's a restaurant too. Mountains treks can be arranged.

Hotel Madrid HOTEL €€
(☎0539 98 74 97; www.moroccanhouse hotels.com; Ave Hassan II; s/d/tr incl breakfast Dh327/428/605; ☏) The old-world lobby here is cheery, and the cosy rooms a pleasant surprise, with wrought-iron beds and frilly canopies and well-appointed bathrooms. Watch your step on the loose stair carpet.

Camping Azilane CAMP SITE €
(☎0539 98 69 79; Hay Ouatman; camping per adult Dh25, plus per tent/car/campervan Dh20/20/35, electricity Dh15; ☏) A shady setting with great views makes this site popular, even if it is a stiff 20-minute walk from the medina. There's a small restaurant and a shop that sells some essentials, but otherwise facilities are pretty basic (hot showers Dh10).

Chaouen Youth Hostel HOSTEL €
(☎0666 90 84 42; Hay Ouatman; per person incl breakfast Dh40, per person in groups Dh30) Next to the camp site, this hostel is bright and clean. Hot showers cost Dh20, and there's a washing machine. In season, you must produce a membership card.

Atlas Chaouen HOTEL €€€
(☎0539 98 60 02; www.hotelsatlas.com; s/d/ tr incl breakfast Dh612/774/1161; ✳☏≋) Unmistakeably perched on the hills overlooking the town, this hotel doubles as a decent art museum, with some fantastic works by local artist Zaidi Mohammed, including a wall-length painting of the medina. All the amenities of a European four-star are present, including a huge lobby, a full-service spa, a pool with gorgeous mountain views, the only nightclub in the area, an average restaurant and a bar. Nonguests can use the pool (adult/child Dh100/70).

Auberge Dardara INN €€
(☎0539 70 70 07, 0661 15 05 03; www.dardara. ma; Rte Nationale 2; d/tr/q incl half-board Dh790/1200/1500; ✳≋) This is an authentic French *auberge* in the Moroccan countryside offering large rustic suites with TVs and fireplaces. The 10-hectare complex includes an active farm and gardens, pool, craft shop, hammam, fitness centre, horses and the most sophisticated kitchen in the Chefchaouen area. Guest programs include crafts, gardening and more. It's a 10-minute taxi ride (Dh5) to Bab Taza.

🍴 Eating

It's hard to get past the cafes on Plaza Uta el-Hammam for a long juice or a relaxing mint tea. From mid-afternoon, hawkers do the rounds of the cafes carrying trays laden with sticky pastries for sale. In the back rooms, local men play cards and smoke kif – worth a look, although women won't feel particularly welcome.

TOP CHOICE **Auberge Dardara Restaurant** LOCAL €€
(☎0539 70 70 07, 0661 15 05 03; Rte Nationale 2; meals around Dh90; ☉lunch & dinner) This is the best kitchen in the area, and worth the 10-minute drive from town (to Bab Taza,

Looming over Chefchaouen at 1616m, Jebel el-Kelaâ might initially appear a daunting peak, but with an early start and a packed lunch, it can easily be climbed in a day if you're in reasonably good shape.

The hike starts from behind Camping Azilane, following the 4WD track that takes you to the hamlet of Aïn Tissimlane. Rocks painted with a yellow and white stripe indicate that you're on the right path. The initial hour is relatively steep as you climb above the trees to get your first views over Chefchaouen, before cutting into the mountains along the steady *piste*. You should reach Aïn Tissimlane within a couple of hours of setting out, after which the path climbs and zigzags steeply through great boulders for nearly an hour to a pass. Turn west along the track, which leads to the saddle of the mountain, from where you can make the final push to the summit. There's a rough path, although you'll need to scramble in places. The peak is attained relatively quickly, and your exertions are rewarded with the most sublime views over this part of the Rif.

It's straightforward and quick to descend by the same route. Alternatively, you can head north from the saddle on a path that takes you to a cluster of villages on the other side of the mountain. One of these villages, El-Kelaâ, has 16th-century grain stores and a mosque with a leaning minaret. From here, a number of simple tracks will take you back to Chefchaouen in a couple of hours.

Dh5). The Tangerine owner uses only the freshest ingredients from the garden, bakes his own bread and makes his own goats cheese. Try the superb venison cooked with dried figs or the succulent rabbit with quince.

Plaza Cafe-Restaurants   LOCAL €
(Plaza Uta el-Hamman; breakfast from Dh20, mains from Dh30) A popular eating option in Chefchaouen is to choose one of about a dozen on the main square. Menus are virtually identical – continental breakfasts, soups and salads, tajines and seafood – but the food is generally pretty good and the ambience lively.

Lala Mesouda   LOCAL €€
(Calle Znika; menu Dh120; ⊘lunch & dinner) This new restaurant is a welcome addition as there are dishes on offer not found elsewhere in the town. Both the steak with Roquefort sauce and the chicken with cream and mushrooms are recommended, and fish is also available. The interior is comfortable and intimate and the welcome warm.

La Lampe Magique   LOCAL €
(Rue Targhi; mains from Dh45, set menu Dh75; ⊘lunch & dinner) This magical place overlooking Plaza Uta el-Hammam serves delicious Moroccan staples in a grand setting. Three bright-blue floors include a laid-back lounge, a more formal dining area and a

rooftop terrace. The menu – featuring favourites like lamb tajine with prunes and some great cooked salads – is much better than average, and the ambience relaxed.

Chez Hicham   LOCAL €€
(Rue Targhi; mains around Dh80; ⊘lunch & dinner) Another new restaurant next to La Lampe Magique, Chez Hicham has a lovely warm interior, comfortable seating and views over the kasbah from the terrace. The usual suspects are on the menu.

Assaada   LOCAL €
(Bab el-Ain; set menu Dh40; ⊘lunch & dinner) This reliable cheapie tries hard to please. Located on both sides of the alley just prior to Bab el-Ain, it offers the usual menu *complet,* and recommends its no-cholesterol goat *kefta*. There's a funky graffiti rooftop terrace that exudes an urban charm but the staircase is not for the faint-hearted.

Bab el-Ansar Café   CAFE €
(Bab el-Ansar) Set into the outside wall of the medina, this cafe has a great location overlooking the falls of Ras el Maa, with three terraces tumbling down the hill. Views are particularly nice in the late afternoon, with the sun catching the mountains opposite.

Chez Aziz   PATISSERIE €
(Ave Hassan II) For a great selection of pastries, make your way here. Pizzas and paninis are also on the menu. They squeeze a

MEDITERRANEAN COAST & THE RIF CHEFCHAOUEN

mean juice and make good coffee too, for a quick breakfast on the run.

SELF-CATERING

The market off Ave Hassan II is excellent for fresh fish, meat, fruit and vegetables, and gets particularly busy on Monday and Thursday, when people come from outside Chefchaouen to sell produce.

Several local specialities are worth checking out, particularly the fragrant mountain honey and soft ewe's cheese – both served up at breakfast. Add fresh *dial makla* (a type of bread) and you have your picnic.

Drinking

While it's easy to find kif in Chefchaouen, it's hard to find a beer.

Bar Oum-Rabiá BAR
(Ave Hassan II; ⊗10am-10pm) A very masculine option.

Hotel Parador BAR
(Pl el-Majzen; beer Dh23; ⊗2-11pm) The soulless bar here is better but wine is only available if you eat in the somewhat dubious restaurant.

Atlas Chaouen BAR
(beer Dh20; ⊗2pm-late) The jazzy bar here is the nicest but further away.

Entertainment

Atlas Chaouen NIGHTCLUB
(⊗11pm-3am) The disco here is the only nightclub in the area. Hotel guests are the clientele during the week, joined by locals on weekends.

Shopping

Chefchaouen remains an artisan centre and, as such, an excellent place to shop – especially for Riffian woven rugs and blankets in bright primary colours. Many shops have looms in situ, so you can see the blankets being made. Previously silk was the material of choice: the mulberry trees in Plaza Uta el-Hammam are a legacy of these times. Most of the weaving nowadays is with wool, one of the area's biggest products.

The largest concentration of tourist shops is around the Uta el-Hammam and Pl el-Majzen.

Well worth a visit is the **Ensemble Artisanal** (Place el-Majzen; ⊗10am-2pm & 4-6pm) across from the Parador Hotel. It's one of the best we've seen in Morocco, although information boards are in Arabic and Spanish only. There are weavers at their looms, cobblers, artists, knitters and wireworkers.

Information

Internet Access
Cyber-Net (Zanqat Sbâa; per hr Dh5; ⊗10am-midnight)
IRIC (Institut Raouachid pour l'Information et le Commerce; Ave Hassan II; per hr Dh5; ⊗8am-midnight) Next to Librairie Al-Nahj.

Medical Services
Hospital Mohammed V (☎0539 98 62 28; Ave al-Massira al-Khadra)
Pharmacie Chefchaouen (☎0539 98 61 58; Ave Moulay Driss)

Money
Banque Populaire Medina (Plaza Uta el-Hammam); New City (Ave Hassan II) There's an ATM at the medina.
BMCE (Ave Hassan II) ATM.

Post
Post office (Ave Hassan II)

Travel Agencies
Preference Voyages Agency (☎0539 98 79 13; www.preferencevoyages.com; 39 Ave Hassan II; ⊗9am-12.30pm & 3-6.30pm Mon-Fri, 9am-12.30pm Sat) This extremely helpful travel agency – the first in Chefchaouen – has tourist information and organises mountain treks with registered guides. English-speaking.

Getting There & Away

Bus
Many bus services from Chefchaouen originate elsewhere, so are often full on arrival. Buy the ticket for your onward journey on arrival in Chefchaouen to secure a seat. The bus station is 1.5km southwest of the town centre at the far end of Ave Mohammed V (Dh10 in a petit taxi from Place el-Majzen). CTM and all other buses use the same station.

CTM (☎0539 98 76 69) serves the following destinations:

DESTINATION	COST (DH)	DURATION (HR)
Al Hoceima	80	6
Casablanca	115	8
Fez	70	4½
Nador	135	9
Ouezzane	20	1½
Rabat	85	5
Tangier	40	3
Tetouan	20	1½

Other companies run a number of cheaper services to the same destinations, including a daily departure for Oued Laou (Dh30, 1½ hours).

Taxi

The fixed price for a grand taxi from Tangier airport to Chefchaouen is Dh600, and from Tanger Med Dh500. Unless you can find several people to split the fare with you, it is far cheaper to go to Tangier first, then hop to Chefchaouen via Tetouan. Even if you buy two places, you will save over Dh500 and add less than an hour.

Grands taxis north leave Chefchaouen from just below Plaza Mohammed V. Most just run to Tetouan (Dh30, one hour), where you must change for Tangier or Ceuta – direct taxis are rare. From Ave Allal ben Abdallah you can catch a grand taxi to Dar Ackoubaa (Dh6, 20 minutes) from Ave Moulay Abdesalam, the junction for Oued Laou.

Grands taxis headed south gather below the central market. Catch one to Ouezzane (Dh30, one hour), where you can pick up onward transport to Fez and Meknès. There is very little transport heading east to the coast. The best option is to take a grand taxi to Dardara junction (Dh8, 15 minutes) or Bab Taza (Dh15, 30 minutes) and hope for the best from there.

ⓘ Getting Around

Chefchaouen's 37 blue petits taxis congregate on Pl el-Majzen and near the market. They're unmetered; most fares shouldn't top Dh10. The safe and convenient Hotel Parador **car park** (Pl el-Majzen; per night Dh10) can be used by nonguests.

Chaouen Car (ⓓ0539 98 62 04; Ave Hassan II) A couple of doors away from Preference Voyages, this agency rents cars and also organises 4WD trips and quad bikes.

Ouezzane   وزان

POP 53,000

Ouezzane is a scruffy industrial town with little to offer the traveller, although the medina is being ungraded. It might be unappealing, but Ouezzane is the home of the popular Ouazzaniyya Sufi order, as well as being the centre for Riffian jellabas, the thick woollen, striped, sleeveless garments with colourful pompoms on the shoulders.

The centre of town is a large triangle known as Pl de L'Independence. There are a few restaurants and rough hotels across the street, and behind them, the medina. Uphill there are several streets that form a commercial area, with numerous stalls,

which are worth a walk around. The green mosque here has an interesting octagonal minaret.

There is no reason to stay here unless you run out of petrol. Police checkpoints are common both entering and leaving the town. There's no alcohol available in the town.

🛏 Sleeping & Eating

If you do suffer a thrown piston, you have two acceptable choices for sleeping.

Hotel Bouhlal   HOTEL €
(ⓓ0537 90 71 54; Rue 1, Hay el-Haddadine Echaouen; s/d/tr Dh80/120/150, air-con per 2hr an extra Dh40; ▣) This is your best budget option, although located in a nondescript industrial side street with nothing nearby. Inside, the rooms are clean, and the roof terrace a welcome oasis. The shared bathrooms have hot water and a choice of squat or Western toilets. Friendly staff can rustle up breakfast on request, but otherwise head to the Motel Rif for a meal.

Motel Rif   RESORT €
(ⓓ0537 90 71 72; www.motel-rif.ma; r Dh250, 5-person apt Dh700; ▣) This odd, sprawling blue-and-white complex on the outskirts of town – on the way to Chefchaouen, and 3km before the road to Fez – fancies itself as a drive-in resort, with sun umbrellas by the pool, campervan parking (Dh70 for two) with electricity and hot showers, a cavernous restaurant (set menu Dh100) and a 35-hectare farm to provide it with produce. The large proportions of the concrete block buildings makes it feel like a factory converted to hotel use.

There are several other budget hotels across from the Pl de L'Independence, all of which seem to be competing for the bottom rung of a short ladder. **Restaurant des Négociants** (Place de l'Indépendence) is the most popular eatery, but given the flies, you may end up staying in Ouezzane longer than you wish.

ⓘ Getting There & Away

Bus

Two dusty car parks on Rue de la Marche Verte, 50m northwest of the main square, function as the bus station and grand-taxi stand. Get an early start when trying to leave Ouezzane, as there are virtually no buses after 5pm.

ISSAGUEN & KETAMA

Issaguen and Ketama have a notorious reputation. This is an area beyond the law. People will wonder what you are doing here, and naturally assume you are buying hashish. There is nowhere to turn if you get into trouble, and little to hold anyone back who wants some. Travellers are strongly advised to pass through and not spend the night here.

CTM has buses to Fez (Dh50, two hours, two daily) and Tetouan (Dh40, two hours, one daily) via Chefchaouen (Dh20, 1½ hours).

There are frequent non-CTM buses before 5pm, including:

Casablanca Dh65, five hours

Chefchaouen Dh20

Fez Dh40

Kenitra Dh25, 2½ hours

Meknès Dh40

Tangier Dh50, four hours

Tetouan Dh35

Most non-CTM buses for Chefchaouen actually stop at Dardara junction, on the main road, from where you can pick up a grand taxi (Dh10) for the final 10km into town.

Taxi

There are grands taxis to Chefchaouen (Dh30, 75 minutes) and Fez (Dh60, two hours). For longer-distance destinations (such as Rabat or Tangier) you may have to take a taxi to Souk el-Arba-du-Rharb (Dh20, 45 minutes) or Ksar el-Kebir (Dh25, one hour) and change.

East of Chefchaouen

ISSAGUEN
POP 5000

Heading southeast out of Chefchaouen, the road N2 plunges into the heart of the Rif, running about 150km along the backbone of the mountains. The roads are rough, and the endless twists and turns make the going slow. There are few petrol stations.

The small, rough town of Bab Berret marks the unofficial entry point to kif country, which is the largest hashish production area in the world. Marijuana fields are all around, but out of sight from the road. Huge stacks of chemical fertiliser are on sale in the markets.

Issaguen appears unexpectedly from the middle of the cedar forests. A scruffy frontier town, it is one of the commercial centres of kif cultivation and smuggling (Ketama, 20km away, being the other. The

two towns are sometimes marked on maps as being the same place). Traffic moves haphazardly down its pitted dirt main street, where gutted sheep hang by the roadside and hooded men walk furtively about.

To the southeast, Jebel Tidiquin (2448m), the highest peak in the Rif Mountains, dominates the skyline.

The Coast North & East of Chefchaouen

OUED LAOU واد لاو
With its dusty main street lined with slapdash construction, small but growing Oued Laou looks like a Wild West town on the sea. Waterfront budget rooms, cheap beer and food, internet cafes and a very long, empty beach make it a backpacker paradise, especially in summer. There's nothing to do aside from watching the fishermen haul their boats in the morning.

The road from Chefchaouen to Oued Laou has recently been upgraded and the journey is now reduced to one hour.

🛏 Sleeping & Eating
Hotel Oued Laou   GUESTHOUSE €
(☎0655 21 37 89/0650 18 43 38; Blvd Massira; s/d from Dh150/200) There are several new budget hotels to choose from, but this is the best. Located on the beach, it has a pool room, one of the better cafe-restaurants and an energetic young manager. Get a room with views to the sea.

Mare Nostrum   HOTEL €€€
(☎0664 37 60 57; www.marenostrumhotel.net; family bungalow incl breakfast Dh1500; ▨) In a glorious position on the cliffside, this is the perfect getaway. Located 4km from town on the road to Tetouan, the small, self-contained resort consists of a series of bungalows, with a pool, a restaurant (mains Dh150), a charming lounge and its own private cul-de-sac beach far below. The bungalows are large and have recently been

refurbished. They offer magnificent views towards the rocky headland. Reserve ahead in summer.

La Plage Restaurant SEAFOOD €
(Corniche; mains from Dh20) Facing the fishing boats, this place has great sardines fresh from the boat, and filling meals of chicken and chips and tajines.

❶ Information
Cyber Costa (per hr Dh5; ⊘9am-midnight) Opposite La Plage Restaurant but unlikely to be open out of season.

❶ Getting There & Away
If you're driving from Chefchaouen turn off the main Tetouan road at Dar Ackoubaa, 11km north of Chefchaouen. It's a wonderful drive past the large hydroelectric dam and through rolling hills and the stunning Laou Gorge. Coming from Tetouan, the upgraded N16 hugs the dramatic coastline for 140km all the way to El-Jebha.

Three buses a day connect Tetouan and Oued Laou (Dh25, two hours). There's also one bus from Chefchaouen (Dh20, 90 minutes), which continues along the coast to El-Jebha (Dh35, five hours); the return service leaves El-Jebha early in the morning. However, at Oued Laou it dumps you out by the souq, leaving you a 45-minute walk or Dh5 grand-taxi ride to town.

Grands taxis run from beside the mosque in Oued Laou to Tetouan (Dh30, one hour) via Dar Ackoubaa (Dh15, 20 minutes), where you can pick up a passing taxi for Chefchaouen.

TARGA TO EL-JEBHA من ترگ إلى الجبهة
This stretch of the coast is very dramatic, and still remote. Pine-clad hills are interspersed with valleys of cultivated fields that roll down to the sea and beaches of grey pebbles. However, the coastal road linking Tetouan to El-Jebha was under construction at the time of research, and is likely to be completed in 2012. Already there are massive development projects underway such as the Golf Paradise Resort and the Marina Playa Vista. These will contain luxury hotels and apartments.

Seventeen kilometres southeast of Oued Laou, **Targa** is a little village with a history of piracy. High atop an outcrop of black rock, a stone fort overlooks the village, built during the Spanish protectorate. The 13th-century mosque is associated with a local saint.

About 18km southeast of Targa, in the wide valley of Oued Bouchia, are the twin

---

THE CANNABIS INDUSTRY

The Rif is home to the largest acreage of cannabis cultivation in the world, an estimated 1340 sq km, or 42% of global production. Cultivation has expanded rapidly since the 1980s, in part due to increasing European demand. The cannabis trade is now the region's main economic activity, involving an estimated 800,000 people, and probably Morocco's main source of foreign currency, although rural farmers reap little from it.

Cannabis cultivation started around Ketama in the 15th century. In 1912 the right to cultivate cannabis was granted to a few Rif tribes by Spain. In 1956, when Morocco gained independence, cannabis was prohibited, but Mohammed V later condoned cultivation in the Rif after the prohibition led to conflict there.

Most large shipments of Moroccan hashish (a concentrated form of marijuana) are smuggled into Europe by boat, including small speedboats that can make a round trip to Spain in an hour. The primary departure points are Martil, Oued Laou and Bou Ahmed, although the bigger ports of Nador, Tetouan, Tangier and Larache are also used. Traffickers also export hashish concealed in trucks and cars embarked on ferries leaving from the Spanish enclaves of Ceuta and Melilla or from Tangier. Not surprisingly, of all hashish seizures worldwide, half are made in Spain. It is now thought that terrorist groups are entering the market in order to fund operations. Traffickers have also branched out into human smuggling, to include smuggling hashish and migrants into Europe together.

To counter this illegal trade, the government, encouraged by the European Union, is actively promoting rural tourism by supporting the establishment of *gîtes* and training programs for guides. This is beginning to provide an alternative source of income for local people.

villages of **Steha** (an administrative centre) and **Bou-Ahmed**. Set back from the coast, the latter is the end point for a long-distance trek from Chefchaouen (see p286). There's an interesting souq every Tuesday, and a basic camping area in summer.

From here the road follows the coast on a splendid roller-coaster ride to the blue and white town of **El-Jebha**, 52km to the southeast. The rugged coastline forms a number of breathtaking and secluded bays – worth exploring if you have your own transport. While the road is under construction, there are no buses plying this route and few taxis will undertake it. Each Tuesday, the local souq draws Rif farmers from the surrounding villages. At El-Jebha you can turn south into the Rif to Issaguen, or continue on the new coastal road to Al-Hoceima.

Al-Hoceima الحسيمة

POP 103,000

Al-Hoceima is a great place to spend a few days. Quiet, safe, relaxing and hassle-free, this modern seaside resort is full of proud and genial Berbers with a surprisingly independent, Western outlook, far more than any other town in the north. In fact, if the northern Berbers had their own country, this would be its capital. There is far more

of the Berber tongue, Tarifit, spoken than Spanish.

Founded by the Spanish as Villa Sanjuro, the town was built as a garrison after the Rif Wars in the early 20th century; rebel Abd al-Krim operated nearby. Independence brought the name change to Al-Hoceima, but Spanish influence remains strong in language, architecture and business.

In recent years many of Al-Hoceima's émigrés have returned and have ploughed money into the town, particularly into its booming tourism industry. The town is being revamped with the wide **Place Mohammed VI** given new fountains, a sweeping corniche built along the coast and new hotels opening. The pretty **Place du Rif** with its Mauresque buildings, is slated to be turned into a pedestrian zone. Best of all, the wonderful **National Park of Al-Hoceima** has

Al Hoceima

Al Hoceima

been carefully opened to rural tourism – an opportunity not to be missed.

The town sits atop high cliffs overlooking two coves, one a beach (**Plage Quemado**) and the other a commercial port. Blvd Mohammed V parallels the edge from the Spanish College at one end to Place du Rif at the other. Most of the banks, hotels and restaurants are along or close to here, with budget options clustered around Place du Rif. The flat grid of wide streets is easy to walk and navigate. The three other town beaches lie further south, along with El Peñón de Alhucemas, one of the last bits of the Spanish protectorate.

◉ Sights & Activities

BEACHES

Plage Quemado   BEACH
A pretty steep-sided bay protects the town beach. The beach is clean enough, but the seaside resort atmosphere is marred by the port to the north and the construction of a new hotel.

Cala Bonita, Plage Isly and Plage Asfiha   BEACHES
In the summer, a better option is one of the three white sandy beaches that begin 5km south of town. During the low season they tend to be strewn with rubbish. Plage Asfiha has several ramshackle restaurants right on the beach serving sardines and chips, and feels the most remote. The best way to reach these beaches is by grand taxi. For the entire taxi, reckon on about Dh50 to Cala Bonita and Dh75 to Plage Asfiha. Local buses to Ajdir and Imzouren, which pass the turn-offs for these beaches (Dh4 to Dh5), leave from beside the Mobil petrol station at the south end of Blvd Mohammed V.

EL PEÑÓN DE ALHUCEMAS

One of the *plazas de soberanía* (see the boxed text, p258), this extraordinary white island fortress can be seen a few hundred metres off Playa Asfiha, along with the uninhabited islets Isla de Mar and Isla de Tierra, which fly the Spanish flag. Spanish rule dates back to 1559, when the Saadi dynasty gave it to Spain in exchange for military assistance. In 1673, the Spanish military established a garrison there, and never left. Today, the fort hosts 60 soldiers, and cannot be visited. Spanish sovereignty has been contested by Morocco since independence in 1956.

THE PORT

The port is mainly used for a large commercial fishing operation. It is a great place to watch the catch being unloaded, and to find dinner: take your selected fish to the Club Nautique for cooking.

🛏 Sleeping

The streets between the Place du Rif and the souq are packed with ultracheap hotels. Some are pretty dingy, so look around before committing.

TOP CHOICE **Hotel Villa Florido**   HOTEL €€
(☑0539 84 08 47; http://florido.alhoceima.com; Place du Rif; s/d/tr Dh386/492/638; 🕸) This curvaceous art-deco hotel dating from 1920, an island in the Place du Rif, has been completely revamped in great style. Spotless rooms have bathrooms and satellite TV, and most have a balcony too. There's a smart cafe downstairs (breakfast Dh10), and the hotel could hardly be better placed for taxis. No need to look elsewhere.

Hotel al-Khouzama   HOTEL €€
(☑/fax 0539 98 56 69; Calle al-Andalous; s/d/tr Dh286/372/468; 🕸) Just off Blvd Mohammed V, this two-star hotel is a long-time favourite for business travellers, and is suitably comfortable, with spacious rooms (though those facing away from the street are a bit dark). All come with bathroom and satellite TV, and the guys at reception are friendly and helpful.

Hotel al-Hana   HOTEL €
(☑0666 90 32 00; 17 Calle Imzouren; s/d/tr Dh50/80/120) With rock-bottom prices, this simple hotel is tucked into the tiny streets east of Place du Rif. All facilities are shared, including the clean squat toilets (hot showers cost Dh10). It's well kept, and the cafe on the ground floor is full of men throwing dice.

Hotel Maghreb Jadid   HOTEL €
(☑0539 98 25 04; fax 0539 98 25 05; 56 Blvd Mohammed V; s/d/tr Dh280/360/474) This is a reliable standby if the other hotels in this price range are booked. Rooms are spacious, and most have enclosed balconies and TVs. There's a licensed restaurant and a cafe.

Suites Hotel Mohammed V   HOTEL €€€
(☑0539 98 22 33; fax 039 983314; Pl Mohammed VI; ste Dh2200-5000; ❋🕸🌊) Al-Hoceima's top option, this hotel has undergone a complete overhaul. Ultramodern and pretty

SURVIVAL TARAFIT

Hello/Goodbye	salam/beslama
Yes/No	naam/alla
Please/ Thank you	minfadlak/ shoukran
Where is...?	fin...?
hotel	hotel
camping	el moukhayam
Do you have any rooms available?	wash kayan shi bit khawi?
a single room	bit dyal wahad
a double room	bit dyad jouje danass
How much is it?	beshhal?
What time does the next...leave?	foukash yam shi...?
boat	en babour
bus	el car
I'd like a...	bghit
one-way ticket	warga aller
return ticket	warga aller retour
beer	bira
sandwich	cascrout

characterless, it occupies a prime position perched above Plage Quemado. Rooms are spacious and comfortable and come with balconies giving lovely views over the bay. There's a restaurant, bar and gym to complete the picture.

La Perla
HOTEL €€

(☑0539 98 45 13; hotel.perla@gmail.com; Ave Tariq ibn Zaid; s/d Dh650/750;❷❇❄) This modern mirrored-glass high-rise business hotel has comfortable, if bland, rooms with satellite TV and large bathrooms. The tiled floors, thin walls and location on a busy corner make it quite noisy. There's a cafe on the ground floor and a restaurant upstairs.

Hotel Rif
HOTEL €

(☑0539 98 22 68; 13 Calle Sultan Moulay Youssef; s/d/tr Dh97/170/225, hot shower Dh10) If your budget is really maxed-out, you'll end up in this long hallway lined with simple rooms. Bathrooms with squat toilets are shared,

but you do get your own sink. Keep your door locked: the staff sleeps during the day.

✖ Eating

Cheap restaurants cluster around Place du Rif, serving up filling tajines, brochettes and a bit of seafood to the bus-station crowd from about Dh25 per head. There are also many snack shops around town.

TOP CHOICE Club Nautique
SEAFOOD €€

(Gate 2, Port d'Al-Hoceima; mains Dh60-120; ☾lunch & dinner) This is the main restaurant at the port, and a good one. After 6pm, buy your fish fresh off the boat and have them grill it for you. The 2nd floor overlooks the whole port and is a great place to relax and a have a beer.

Espace Miramar
FAST FOOD €

(Rue Moulay Ismail; mains from Dh35; ☾lunch & dinner) It's hard to go wrong at this 5000-sq-m complex with a pizzeria, two cafes, a grill and restaurant as well as a children's playground, all of it perched on the cliffs overlooking the sea, and with occasional live music as well. The nice view is marred by the strip-mined hill and the port opposite, but this is the place to start.

La Dolce Pizza
FAST FOOD €

(Place du Rif; pizza from Dh30; ☾lunch & dinner) Also signed as DP, this cute Italian bistro thrust out into the chaos of Place du Rif has just four tables inside and some on the pavement, but lots of charm. Service is appallingly slow, and the cook is a microwave, but the ambience makes it a pleasant place to people-watch and have some pizza, hamburgers or salads.

Café La Belle Vue
CAFE €

(131 Blvd Mohammed V; breakfast Dh12) This cafe gets its name from the terrace at the back overlooking the bay. There are several similar cafes on this stretch of Mohammed V with great views.

Boulangerie Patisserie Azir
PATISSERIE €

(14 Rue Youseff Beni Tachafine; ☾5am-8.30pm) This patisserie is the town favourite, with great home-baked bread and tons of different sweets.

SELF-CATERING

Many small general food stores are dotted around town, including **Épicerie Hassouni** (Blvd Mohammed V) and **Supermarché el-Bouayadi** (Calle Abdelkrim Khattabi).

For alcohol try **Bougamar** (near cnr of Rue Micra), the local liquor store, where bottles are dispensed from behind the counter pharmacy-style.

Drinking

Club Nautique BAR
(Gate 2, Port d'Al-Hoceima; beer Dh18) An atmospheric option, and the bar here usually attracts quite a crowd.

Suites Hotel Mohammed V BAR
(Pl Mohammed VI) This has an inviting bar, particularly as the terrace has some excellent views over Plage Quemado.

☆ Entertainment

Calypso NIGHTCLUB
(Plage Tala Youssef; admission Dh100; ☺midnight-4am) This nightclub at Chafarina Beach Resort is the only option if you're carrying your dancing shoes; a lively place in the summer months, partly due to the professional female company.

Shopping

There is a weekly market Monday and Tuesday in the **souq**.

ℹ Information

Internet Access
Cyber Bades (Calle Al Amir Moulay Abdallah; per hr Dh5; ☺8am-9.30pm)

Medical Services
Pharmacie Nouvelle (Calle Moulay Idriss Alkbar; ☺8.30am-12.30pm & 3-7.30pm Mon-Thu, 8.30am-noon Fri, 8am-12.30pm Sat)

Money
Blvd Mohammed V has several banks with ATMs, including branches of BMCE, BMCI and Banque Populaire.

Post
Post office (Calle Moulay Idriss Alkbar)

Tourist Information
Tourist Bureau (Délégation du Ministère de Tourisme; ☏0539 98 11 85; Zanqat Al Hamra, Cala Bonita)

Travel Agencies
All sell ferry tickets from Al-Hoceima in season, and from Nador year-round.
Chafarinas Tours (☏0539 84 13 23; www.charafinas@menara.ma; 109 Blvd Mohammed V)
Ketama Voyages (☏0539 98 51 20; www.ktmahu@menara.ma; 146 Blvd Mohammed V)

ℹ Getting There & Away

Air
From June to September, Royal Air Maroc flies from Amsterdam and Brussels to the small local airport located 12km (Dh120 by taxi) from town. Royal Air Maroc offers sporadic service from Paris and various parts of Spain, as well as Casablanca. Otherwise the best option is a flight to Nador, 150km east.

Boat
At the time of research, there were no ferry services to Spain.

Bus
All the bus companies have offices around Place du Rif and at the smart new bus station. CTM runs the following services:
Chefchaouen (Dh75, six hours, three daily)
Oujda via Nador (Dh60, 3½ hours, one daily)
Nador direct (Dh55, three hours, two daily)
Tetouan (Dh80, seven hours, three daily) via Chefchaouen (Dh65, six hours)
Casablanca (Dh170, 11½ hours, one daily) via Taza (Dh60, four hours)
Fez (Dh90, six hours)
Meknès (Dh105, 7½ hours)
Rabat (Dh140, 10 hours) This bus is timed to arrive in Taza in time to connect with the night train headed for Marrakesh.

Several small companies also serve the aforementioned destinations. There are at least three buses a day to Tetouan and Tangier (Dh80 to Dh90, nine hours). These stop in Chefchaouen only if there's enough demand. Otherwise, they'll drop you on the main road at Dardara, from where you can share a grand taxi into Chefchaouen (Dh10, 15 minutes). Heading east, there are also a couple of buses a day to Nador (Dh35, two hours) and Oujda (Dh120, six hours).

Taxi
Grands taxis line up on the road at the southern end of Blvd Mohammed V and at Place du Rif. The most popular destinations are Taza (Dh70, 2½ hours) and Nador (Dh55, 2½ hours), although occasional taxis do go to Fez (Dh120). Taxis go through Nador to Melilla, not direct.

Around Al-Hoceima

NATIONAL PARK OF AL-HOCEIMA
المنتزه الوطني للحسيمة

The undiscovered National Park of Al-Hoceima is the hidden jewel of this region. Its great mesas and dry canyons are reminiscent of the American southwest, except that they border the sea, where the limestone cliffs resemble Mallorca. Its isolation has helped preserve several at-risk species, from its thuya forests to an important colony of fish eagle. The park extends to 485 sq km (including 190 sq km at sea). The area is dotted with Berber settlements and criss-crossed by dirt roads, making it an ideal trekking and mountain-bike territory. While a 4WD opens up your options, a 2x4 will get you through the main tracks. The park offers two regions: the central Rif bordered by the N16 in the south and west, and the coast.

Central Rif region: Of the 15,000 people living in the park, most are of the Bokkoya tribe and live in rural communities and villages centred around fresh water supplies. The women have good knowledge of the medicinal use of local herbs such as the abundant lavender and thyme.

A number of rare trees can be found here, such as wild carob (mostly disappeared throughout Morocco) and the endangered thuya, highly prized for its wood. Other plants include wild olive, ilex, pomegranate, ericas, bulbs and orchids. Animals include jackals, wild boar, rabbits and hares.

Coastal region: This area of the park extends out to sea and is rich in biodiversity. There are 86 species of fish and three types of dolphin (Pandion haliaetus). Many species represented here are rare elsewhere in the Mediterranean, such as red coral, various molluscs and algae. Among the birds, there is a considerable population of osprey.

There are several remote and scenic beaches, of which the highlight is the fantastic sight of El Peñón de Velez de la Gomera, one of the *plazas de soberanía* (see the boxed text, p258). After a long trek through a canyon, the fortress looms on the edge of a striking scythe of beach below high walls of rock. Attached by a spit of sand that ends at a guardhouse, this tiny piece of Spain is one of the world's strangest national borders. A few stone walls nearby are all that is left of Bades, a city wiped out by a flood in ancient times.

At the time of research, there was no office at the park, but information brochures including a map are available from the tourist bureau in Al-Hoceima, and guides are being trained. However, an excellent way to experience the park is to go through **RODPAL** (Rif Association for the Development of Rural Tourism; ☎0539 98 18 33; www.rodpal.

org/www.parquenacionalalhucemas.com; riftourisme@yahoo.fr; 19 Calle Ajdir), a network of local NGOs with Spanish backing that is developing the park's rural tourism potential. So far they manage 30km of paths and three bird hides. This energetic and helpful group will lay out an itinerary that will involve inexpensive stays in one of the four *gîtes*, which each sleep between two and 12 people and have a kitchen and hot water, or with a local family. Mules are available to carry luggage. Prices vary from Dh242 to Dh308 including half-board per person depending on size of party and length of stay. Visits to local artisans are encouraged – women make pottery and basketware, cosmetics and essential oils, honey and jam and other products from the prickly pear.

You can also walk to El Peñón de Velez de la Gomera along the coast from Cala Iris in 1½ hours. Without your own transport, you'll need to hire a grand taxi to get there. In summer there may be enough people to share one, otherwise expect to pay Dh130 one way.

CALA IRIS & TORRES DE ALCALA

كالا إيريس و نهر الكالا

Cala Iris is a small fishing village that is about to be changed forever. At the time of research the construction of a huge resort with apartments, a hotel, a marina and a golf course had not quite started. It was due to be completed in 2012, but like so many others, has been delayed. The previous camp ground has been closed. The scruffy port remains, and is full of sardine boats that fish at night with lamps. There is also a rough-looking, nameless restaurant behind the Cooperative des Marins Pecheurs that serves typical Berber food. The port is flanked by attractive beaches: Yellich (to the east) faces an island that you can walk out to; Oued Sahfa lies to the west; and an hour's hike over the hill lies Mestaza.

There are a couple of very basic shops at Torres de Alcala, 5km east. Three semi-ruined Spanish towers stand sentinel over this village, set back from a shingle beach caught between two rocky headlands. Torres now lies inside the National Park of Al-Hoceima. Look out for the **Café Mediterreanée** (☎0660 35 75 01), which makes a pleasant stop and also has an apartment to rent.

TREKKING IN THE RIF MOUNTAINS: TALASSEMTANE NATIONAL PARK

Chefchaouen to Bab Taza

شفشاون إلى باب تازة

This is the best introductory walk to the Rif Mountains. Within the **Talassemtane National Park** (www.talassemtane.com) and starting from Chefchaouen, it takes in some spectacular scenery, including the geologically improbable God's Bridge, a natural stone arc spanning the Oued Farda. You are also likely to meet troupes of Barbary apes.

The full trek takes five days, but there are plenty of ways to shorten the distance or duration. One option would be to arrange transport from Akchour back to Chefchaouen at the end of day two. Transport isn't too hard to find in Akchour, or you can arrange for a grand taxi from Chefchaouen to pick you up at a specified time. Alternatively, you may be able to hike back along an alternate route.

The Rif Mountains

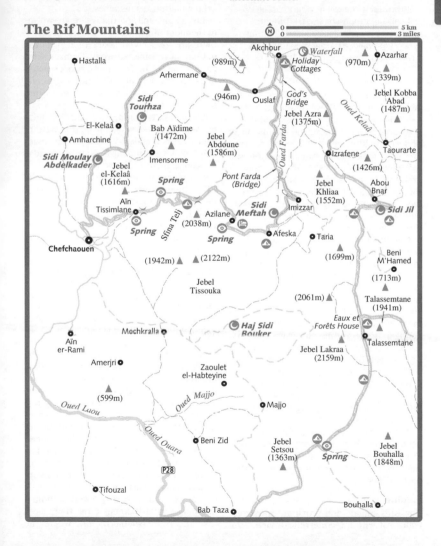

TREK AT A GLANCE

Duration four to five days

Distance 56km

Standard medium

Start Chefchaouen

Finish Bab Taza

Highest Point Sfiha Telj Pass (approximately 1700m)

Accommodation *gîtes* and camping

Public Transport yes

Summary The walking here is relatively undemanding but the mountain scenery is spectacular, the tiny Riffian villages worth a detour, and the gorges and weird geology fascinating.

The Talassemtane National Park is one of two parks in the Rif Mountains (the other being Bouhachem). It's a largely undiscovered area and yet these mountains make perfect trekking country, blessed as they are with magnificent ranges, gorges and valleys, clothed in forests of cedar, cork oak and fir. Being close to the Mediterranean, the Rif are also the greenest of Morocco's mountains and springtime, with its riot of wildflowers, is one of the most delightful times to walk here.

One thing that does deter trekkers is the region's reputation as an area of drug production. But although kif production takes up over three quarters of cultivatable land east of Chefchaouen, trekkers have little reason to feel threatened, especially if travelling with a guide – villagers will be genuinely interested and welcoming. The trek detailed here, setting out from Chefchaouen, is well trodden and unproblematic in this respect. In a concerted effort to reduce reliance on the cannabis industry, local organisations, backed by the government, are setting up rural tourism facilities such as *gîtes* and homestays, managing routes and training guides.

The Rif Mountains rarely top more than 2500m in height, with most treks only occasionally venturing over 2000m, so altitude sickness isn't the worry it can be in other parts of Morocco.

Wildlife

The Rif's climate and proximity to Europe endows it with a Mediterranean vibe – the area closely resembles the sierras of southern Spain. Cedars make up the majority of tree species, including a rare endemic species *Abies maroccana,* a variant of the Spanish cedar that is only found above 1200m. It's a relic of an older, cooler period in Morocco's history. In addition, cork oak, holm pine, wild olive, juniper and the rare carob are some that dot the limestone mountains. The stony land is hard to cultivate and thin in nutrients; deforestation is an issue here as in other parts of Morocco. Various herbs such as lavender and thyme grow in abundance and are used by the local population as medicines.

Locals may tell you that there are wolves in the mountains, but it's a mistranslation – there are foxes. Wild boar are also native, but have a retiring nature that makes them hard to spot. The Rif's most famous mammals are the Barbary apes (known locally as *mgou*), whose range extends south into the Middle Atlas.

You'll have better luck with birdlife. Raptors easily spotted wheeling on thermals include black-shouldered kites, golden eagles and long-legged buzzards. Ravens can also be seen against the limestone cliffs.

Scorpions present a small risk in the Rif, although less so than further south. Be wary of the red scorpion; stings are extremely painful. The venomous *fer à cheval* viper (named for the horseshoe-like mark on its head) is more likely to flee from you than vice versa.

Day 1: Chefchaouen to Afeska

5½-6½ HRS/14.5KM/1200M ASCENT/600M DESCENT

An early morning start is recommended for the first day, which starts on the 4WD track behind Camping Azilane (see Map p268), with an initially steep ascent climbing through the trees to give great views over Chefchaouen's medina. Skirting the southern slopes of **Jebel el-Kelaâ** (1616m), the track evens out to follow the stream passing through the hamlet of **Aïn Tissimlane**, before once again rising in an arc to a high pass by the jagged limestone crags of **Sfiha Telj**. The views here are astounding in both directions, and on a clear day you can see the Mediterranean in the distance. The climb is a killer with a full pack – the hardest of the trek – which explains the necessity for a cool early morning start.

The track turns east before descending. Stopping regularly to enjoy the fine views, take the right (southern) fork where the track splits – this takes you down in an hour or so to the village of **Azilane**, where there's a *gîte*. If you don't want to stop here, continue for another hour along a mostly level path to **Afeska** where there's another *gîte*.

Day 2: Afeska to Akchour
3½-4½ HRS/10KM/860M DESCENT

From Afeska, the wide *piste* you've been following deteriorates to a smaller track. Heading north, you pass through more oak and pine woods to **Sidi Meftah**, where there's a *marabout* and spring, before leaving the woods and descending the switchbacks to **Imizzar** on the **Oued Farda**. Once beside the river, turn left (away from the village, northwest), then cross the river below some impressive overhanging cliffs and continue heading northwest. You'll join a well-worn mule track that eventually leads down to **Pont Farda**, an ancient bridge over Oued Farda.

Cross to the west bank of the river and continue north, dwarfed by the surrounding scenery. After an hour, the trail bears left away from the river towards **Ouslaf**, which is overshadowed by a giant rock buttress, but keep on the same path while it bears right, descending to rejoin the river on the outskirts of **Akchour** (398m), which sits on the **Oued Kelaâ**.

PLAN YOUR TREK

Weather

Trekking is possible year-round, though it can be bitterly cold between November and March, with snow. There's frequent rain between late September and June. It's fiercely hot in summer, when some water sources dry up.

Guides

Organise trekking guides through Abdeslam Moudden, the president of the **Association des Guides du Tourisme de Chaouen** (☑0662 11 39 17; mouddenabdeslam@ yahoo.fr; day tour Dh400) in Chefchaouen. No office; call directly. Guides charge Dh350 per day.

An excellent guide is **Mustapha El-Habti** (☑0671 25 31 55; aventure_akchor@hot mail.com), secretary of Association Akchour pour le Développement et pour Préserver l'Environnement.

Accommodation

Many villages have simple *gîtes* that cost from Dh200 per person including dinner and breakfast. It's also possible to arrange *gîtes* in person during the trek, though there is a risk that the *gardien* may not be around and the *gîte* may be closed – not uncommon.

Camping is not encouraged as local people don't benefit. But in some areas there are no *gîtes*, so it's the only alternative. There's one official camping site at the village of Talassemtane. Permission to camp (free) must be obtained from the Eco-Museum in Chefchaouen in advance. Staying with local families is not yet authorised, but it is possible to stop for tea with them and to visit weaving and cheese-making cooperatives.

Maps

From the government 1:50,000 topographical series, survey sheets *Chaouen* and *Bab Taza* cover the Chefchaouen to Bab Taza trek.

The Eco-Museum at the entrance to the park has maps of the routes.

Equipment

Where there are no *gîtes*, a tent is necessary. A decent sleeping bag is essential, and a light waterproof jacket – rain showers are common. Food and fuel supplies can be bought in Chefchaouen.

Mules to carry your luggage cost from Dh250 per day including muleteer. From August to October, mules can be hard to organise as they're used for the kif harvest, and prices increase accordingly.

Akchour is strung out along the river. As you approach it, you first come to a small cafe with very welcome river-cooled soft drinks, and a dam with a deep pool that seems made for swimming, although the water temperature means short dips only!

Akchour has a brand new *gîte* that's very comfortable and provides excellent meals.

From Akchour, it's usually possible to get transport back to Chefchaouen – most likely one of the rugged vans or 4WDs that battle it out on the *piste*. If there's nothing going from Akchour, try **Talembote**, 2km further north, which has a market on Tuesdays with regular transport to Chefchaouen (Dh15). Most passing vehicles will stop to pick you up if they have space – a case of paid hitchhiking. They may drop you at Dar Ackoubaa, the junction town 10km north of Chefchaouen on the N2 highway.

Side Trip: God's Bridge

With an early start from Afeska, you can reach Akchour by lunchtime, giving time for the short hike (1½ hours, 3km return) to **God's Bridge** – an unlikely geological structure that shouldn't be missed.

The path south from Akchour's dam up the Oued Farda is rough in places, but well worth any scrambling. You'll also have to cross the river twice but this is quite easy where it's not deep – if you don't mind the occasional splash. (However, if you're trekking in spring, check in Afeska that snow melt hasn't made the river impassable.) God's Bridge is about 45 minutes from Akchour. A huge red stone arch towers 25m above the river and it almost beggars belief that it was carved by nature and not by human hand. Over countless millennia, the river flowed as an underground watercourse, eroding the rock and carving a path deeper and deeper, leaving the bridge high and dry.

Day 3: Akchour to Pastures above Abou Bnar

4½-SIX HRS/12KM/977M ASCENT

An early morning start (with full water bottles, since there are no springs on the route until you reach Izrafene) sees you leaving Akchour by heading to the north, crossing the bridge over the Oued Kelaâ and then cutting right (southeast) along the track to Izrafene. It's a particularly picturesque walk as you climb up and around **Jebel Azra** (1375m). Your eyes lift from the steep gorges you've trekked through and out over the sweep of open mountains. If you're up for some scrambling, add half an hour to attain the peak, from where you can drink in further gorgeous views.

Having cut around the mountain, the countryside becomes gentler – rolling even – as the trail heads south. The village of **Izrafene** marks the halfway point of the day's trek. Just before the village, a track bears east at a col, tempting the adventurous to abandon the Bab Taza hike and walk to Taourarte (where there's a *gîte*) and on to **Bou-Ahmed** on the coast, a further two to three days' walk.

From Izrafene, the track turns into a 4WD *piste* – the first since Afeska. It follows a narrow valley, gradually turning east up onto a ridge with gentle views. Where it forks, turn left, and then, just 25m later, turn right onto a trail that heads southeast to **Abou Bnar** through a pretty stretch of oak wood. There's little to detain you here, so continue alongside the river (not the 4WD track) through the open, grassy country to the *marabout* of **Sidi Jil**. This is a pretty area for camping, but if you continue for another 30 minutes, you'll come to an even more beautiful spot, set in wide pasture near the El-Ma Souka spring – an idyllic place for a night's rest.

Alternative Route: Return to Chefchaouen

It's possible to trek back to Chefchaouen from Akchour in a day by an alternate route. The route goes via the villages of **Ouslaf, Arhermane** and **El-Kelaâ**. El-Kelaâ is the site of fascinating **Mosquée Srifiyenne**, with its strange leaning tower. This route takes a quick six hours and avoids any major climbs or descents.

Day 4: Pastures Above Abou Bnar to Talassemtane Village

2-2½ HRS/6KM/352M ASCENT

From the camp site southwest of Abou Bnar, walk back to the 4WD track. Turn left and cross the river, and walk south into the pine woodland. You will quickly come to a T-junction, where you should keep on the right (the left goes downhill to Beni M'Hamed) where the path starts to ascend again.

Keep on the main track, ignoring further side tracks and junctions. As you rise and go through several mini-passes, the views return. To the west, the huge mass of **Jebel Lakraa** (2159m) dominates the countryside.

By late morning you'll reach **Talassemtane** village. A small sign indicates that you should turn left off the 4WD track to the house of the park's Eaux et Forêts *guardien*. There's an official camping site here.

Side Trips

The short walking day allows plenty of time to explore the area and watch wildlife, particularly Barbary apes.

Head north, back along the 4WD track above the *guardien's* house to a clearing and junction. Here you turn right and follow the track east into *mgou* country. Troupes are relatively common here, although they quickly retreat into the safety of the trees if you get too close. The track bends south, giving great views out across the valley to the long ridge of **Jebel Taloussisse** (2005m), before turning briefly east again. Here a trail on the right leads south over the spur of **Talassemtane** (1941m) to a football pitch – strange, but true! – on an area of flat land. From here it's possible to make a rocky traverse west, back to the camp site.

Climbing **Jebel Lakraa** is another alternative for gung-ho trekkers. The best approach is from the north of the mountain, trekking along the ridge to descend one of the stream gullies southeast of the summit. However, there's no fixed path and it's a scramble in places. Allow around 3½ hours return.

Day 5: Talassemtane Village to Bab Taza

2½-3½ HRS/13.5KM/825M DESCENT

The final day is a quick descent along the 4WD track to Bab Taza, where local kif cultivation is much in evidence. The trail swings through a wide pasture and on through the cork woodland of **Jebel Setsou** (1363m) before revealing the sprawl of **Bab Taza** (or so it seems after a few days in the mountains) below.

In Bab Taza, there are quite a few cafes and a couple of grotty-looking hotels strung along the main road. The main business seems to be in huge sacks of fertiliser used for growing kif. Grands taxis leave regularly throughout the day for Chefchaouen (Dh12, 30 minutes) from the western end of town.

Melilla

مليلية

POP 75,000

Who would expect to find 900 Modernist buildings, the second largest such collection outside Barcelona, in North Africa? Yet here they are, along with one perfectly preserved medieval fortress, several fascinating museums and nearly 50 tapas bars. The result is Melilla, a nirvana for architecture and history buffs, as well as a great place to spend the weekend.

Along with Ceuta, Melilla is one of two autonomous Spanish cities on the Moroccan coast, known as the *plazas majores* (see the boxed text, p258). These cultural islands have much in common: their economies are rooted in cross-border commerce, their societies are strongly multicultural and there is a significant military presence, the result of strained relations. Melilla is nearly equally divided between Christian and Muslim, with the latter being predominantly Berber. Various forces such as immigrants trying to get in and Moroccan claims to sovereignty, and more – have caused headaches in the past, and at the time of research, there were riots over local employment issues. A result of sub-Saharan immigrants trying to get in was the construction of a €33 million fence that stretches from one side of the enclave to the other. The visit of the king and queen of Spain in 2007, the first royal visit in 80 years, met with great local acclaim but was strongly reviled by the Moroccans.

Melilla is very easy on the traveller, and tourist infrastructure is excellent. While ferry-loads of visitors pour in during summer, in the low season you'll have plenty of breathing room.

Melilla oozes with history, but it is neither as broad nor as deep as you might expect. While the area has been inhabited for more than 2000 years, the old city wasn't begun until after Spanish conquest in 1496, then built up in four stages. Up until the end of the 19th century, virtually all of Melilla was contained within a single impregnable fortress. Current borders were fixed by several treaties with Morocco between 1859 and 1894, the last following an unsuccessful siege by rebellious Rif Berbers. The method involved shooting a cannonball and seeing how far it went. More fighting with

Melilla

Melilla

◉ Top Sights

◉ Sights

◉ Sleeping

◉ Eating

Information

Transport

rebel Berbers broke out several times in the ensuing years, until the Spanish protectorate consolidated its grip in 1927. In 1936, Franco flew here from the Canary Islands to launch the Spanish Civil War. Local politics still tip to the right.

Melilla is a semicircle of 12 sq km carved out of the Moroccan coastline. The old town, Melilla la Vieja, is a highly complex, multilevel fortress that juts out into the sea. It contains numerous museums, as well as some small residential areas. The port and major beaches lie to the south, with the ferry terminal directly east.

The 'new town' is a broken grid of streets with an attractive commercial centre full of Modernist buildings. The heart is the long triangular Parque Hernandez, which ends at the circular Plaza de España. Most of the hotels, banks and restaurants are located to the north. Like neighbouring Morocco, 4km to the south, you'll find few locals wearing shorts in the city, even when it is hot.

◉ Sights & Activities

MELILLA LA VIEJA (OLD MELILLA)

The fortress of Old Melilla has been restored to perfection. The main entrance is

Puerta de la Marina, fronted by a statue of Franco, from where you ascend to the summit, passing several small museums. There is a lift, too, though it was not working at the time of research. Signage, in Spanish, French and English, is very good.

Museo de Arqueología e Historia MUSEUM
(Plaza Pedro de Estopiñán) This museum was closed for renovation at the time of research. Expect it to open again with its nifty little collection of architectural drawings, ancient ceramics and coins, and numerous models and archaeological finds.

FREE **Aljibes de las Peñuelas**
HISTORIC BUILDING
(☺10am-2pm & 5-9.30pm Tue-Sat, 10am-2pm Sun Apr-Sep) The small door across the courtyard leads into the cave-like, otherworldly cistern that is still flowing.

Iglesia de la Purísima Concepción CHURCH
(Parish of the Immaculate Conception; ☺10am-3pm & 4-9pm Tue-Sat, 10am-12.30pm Sun) This 17th-century is worth a stop for its resplendent nave.

Cuevas del Conventico HISTORIC BUILDING
(Caves of the Convent; admission €1.20; ☺10.30am-1.30pm & 4.30-8pm Tue-Sat, 10.30am-2pm Sun) These extensive and well-restored caves were used as a refuge during sieges, and pop out at a small beach below the cliffs. The guided tour (in Spanish) is excellent.

FREE **Museo Militar** MUSEUM
(☺10am-2pm Tue-Sun) Finally you reach the summit of the fort, with its panoramic views. The history of the Spanish protectorate is dominated by military history, and this museum is the one place where you can feel the grand sweep of that violent drama, with martial music playing in the background. Don't miss the antique photographs room, where biplanes, legionnaires and Berber horsemen all fuse into a dreamy adventure novel, or the 'do not touch the cannonballs' sign, which is straight from *Dr Strangelove*.

NEW TOWN
At the turn of the 20th century, Melilla was the only centre of trade between Tetouan and the Algerian border. As the city grew, it expressed itself in the architectural style of Modernisme, the Catalan version of art nouveau (not to be confused with the cultural movement of modern-

ism), which was then in vogue. Inspired by the Catalan architect Enrique Nieto, a disciple of Gaudí who made Melilla his home, this trend continued locally even after it went out of fashion elsewhere. The result is a living museum of some 900 Modernist and art-deco buildings. Unlike Ceuta, many of these treasures have yet to be dusted off, but the overall architectural wealth is greater.

The best way to appreciate this heritage is to stroll through the area to the north of Parque Hernandez; it's known as 'the golden triangle'.

Plaza de España LANDMARK
Several fine examples are on the Plaza de España, including Nieto's art-deco **Palacio de Asamblea**, whose floor plan depicts a ducal crown; his **Casino Militar**, whose facade still depicts a republican coat of arms; and the **Banco de España**. Architecture fans seeking more detailed information should see the resources listed under Tourist Information, p292.

While the Palacio is an operating town hall, the staff at the entrance are willing to show tourists around upon request. Worth seeing are two rooms on the upper floor: Salon Dorado, which contains a large painting of the arrival of Spaniards in Melilla in 1497, and the Sala de Plenos, where the local congress meets.

With its central fountain, the Plaza is a pleasant place to sit. At the centre is an art deco military monument to campaigns in Morocco. In the distance you can see Melilla's most striking contemporary building, the new courthouse, which looks like a flying saucer has landed on the roof. This observation deck is closed to visitors.

Parque Hernández PARK
From the Plaza you can usually take a pleasant stroll down the long, palm-lined Parque Hernández, but it was closed for renovation at the time of our visit. At the end, turn left down Calle Sotomayor. The **Plaza De Toros** the only operating bull ring in Africa, lies straight ahead.

FREE **Gaselec Museum** MUSEUM
(☺6-9pm Mon-Fri, 11.30am-1.30pm & 6-9pm Sat & Sun) On the other side of the park is this intriguing oddity, the passion of the president of the local gas and electric company. It houses a museum of Ancient Egypt completely composed of reproductions, including King Tut's mask and sarcophagus.

MODERNISME & MELILLA

Like many of the movements from which it drew its inspiration (eg the English Arts & Crafts Movement) Modernisme was a broad reaction to the material values of an industrial age, which suffused culture with a machinelike spirit. Centred in Barcelona, it was the Catalan version of art nouveau. Modernist architecture is characterised by the use of curves over straight lines, the frequent use of natural motifs (especially plants), lively decoration and rich detail, asymmetrical forms, a refined aesthetic and dynamism. Its chief proponent was Antoni Gaudí, the architect of Barcelona's famous Sagrada Familia cathedral. But in Melilla, Modernism is synonymous with Enrique Nieto.

Nieto was a student of Gaudí, who worked on his Casa Milá in Barcelona. Wanting to escape his master's shadow, however, he left for booming Melilla in 1909, in his late twenties, and stayed the rest of his life. He became the city architect in 1931, retired in 1949, and died four years later. During his long career he took part in over 1000 projects and finished 457, forever changing the face of his city. His work drew on many styles, including art deco. He also helped found one, known as Sgraffito Architecture, a blend of art deco and aerodynamic forms. His work included Melilla's main synagogue, the main mosque and several buildings for the Catholic Church, representing the diversity of the city's culture. Perhaps due to the distant location of his canvas, however, this great painter in concrete is not well-known outside of Melilla.

Future plans include faux exhibitions on entirely different subjects. While many of the artefacts look fake, the unusual concept works in its own way, and could well be – ahem – reproduced elsewhere.

BEACHES

The one distressing sight in Melilla is the state of its coastline, which is everywhere strewn with plastic bottles and bags. While efforts are made to clean certain beaches, it is hard to escape this problem, particularly out of season, making you fear for the future of the Mediterranean.

There is one large beach south of the port, divided into four sections. During research there was a plastic bag visible in the water on average every 10m. The foul Rio de Oro empties into this area as well. Needless to say, stick to sunbathing.

An intriguing alternative is the secluded **Playa de la Ensanada de los Galápagos**, which is reached by taking a tunnel under the fort. It is open May to September.

Sleeping

There aren't many hotels in Melilla, so they tend to fill up even in the low season.

Hotel Nacional HOTEL **€€**
(☎956 68 45 40; fax 956 68 45 41; 10 Calle Primo de Rivera; s/d €35/55; ❄📶) This hotel has mostly compact rooms, with minibar, quaint iron furniture and modern bathrooms. Those facing inside are a bit dark, so get one looking to the street. Management is friendly, and there's a lift. Corner room 104 is a strong choice, and room 103 is enormous.

Hotel Anfora HOTEL **€€**
(☎956 68 33 40; fax 956 68 33 44; 8 Calle Pablo Vallescá; s/d incl breakfast €46/73; ❄📶) This rather industrial-feeling three-star hotel is in an excellent location and offers standard-fare rooms with TV, fridges and balconies. The highlight is the roof terrace with its cafe and restaurant, offering vistas of Melilla La Vieja and out to the sea beyond.

Hotel Rusadir HOTEL **€€€**
(☎956 68 12 40; 5 Calle Pablo Vallescá; s/d incl breakfast €91/102; ❄📶) This four-star hotel has been completely renovated to excellent effect, including an impressive lobby and design-conscious rooms with TV, minibars and balconies. The restaurant puts out an impressive breakfast buffet.

Hostal La Rosa Blanca HOTEL **€**
(☎952 68 27 38; 7 Calle Gran Capitán; s €20-24, d €30-35, tr €45) A very basic option; the rooms are clean but vary in quality, so make sure to look before you buy. Rooms have sinks and shared bathrooms.

Residencia de Estudiantes y Deportistas
HOSTEL €

(Residence of Students & Athletes; ☎952 67 00 08; Calle Alfonso X; per person incl breakfast €20, half-board €26, full-board €32; 🖭) This is the best budget choice if you don't mind being away from the town centre. Imagine a well-run college dormitory and you'll get the picture: there are 87 sparkling rooms, internet access, cafeteria, library and TV lounge. Rooms above the 2nd-floor have balconies. Take local bus 3, which stops near Plaza España on Calle Marina every 10 minutes, though there are fewer services on weekends. The trip takes 10 to 15 minutes.

Hostal Residencia Cazaza
HOTEL €

(☎956 68 46 48; 6 Calle Primo de Rivera; s/d €26/36) While the rooms here are beat up, this old building with its high ceilings and small balconies manages to be charming, and has a central location in the golden triangle. Management is friendly.

Parador de Melilla
HOTEL €€€

(☎956 68 49 40; www.parador.es; Av Cándido Lobera; s/d €99/121; ❄🖭🖭🖭) You'll need a vehicle to get to this very classy choice with large, grand rooms, warm use of wood throughout, a high level of quality furnishings and balconies with great views to sea. The circular dining room overlooking the city is an elegant touch. The adjacent Parque Lobera is great for kids.

✖ Eating

Many of Melilla's restaurants are associated with hotels (like the Rusadir or the Parador), but there are plenty of others around Av de Juan Carlos I Rey.

La Pérgola
SEAFOOD €€

(☎952 68 56 28; Calle General Marcías; menu €10; ⊙lunch & dinner) A waterfront terrace, white tablecloths and cafe music make this classy spot a very pleasant place for a meal, or just a late afternoon drink. The speciality is seafood, and at €10 the prix-fixe menu cannot be beaten.

La Vinacoteca
CAFE, TAPAS BAR €

(Plaza de la Culturas; tapas from €1.20, raciones €5) This lively place spills out onto the wide Plaza de la Culturas and attracts all ages. Watch the football over a beer or coffee while the kids rollerskate on the square.

Casa Marta
TAPAS BAR €

(Calle Justo Sancho Miñano; ⊙lunch & dinner) This is a rockin' tapas bar that brims with people of all ages both inside and out: outdoor seating is under a tent in the street. Each beer comes with free tapas, so three beers gets you a free dinner. Don't miss the *filetillo,* thin strips of beef with gravy.

Los Salazones
LOCAL €€

(☎952 67 36 52; 15 Calle Conde de Alcaudete; mains from €12; ⊙lunch & dinner) Another local favourite, this meat and seafood restaurant is located a block from the beach, and is the perfect place to end a day in the sun. Sit at the marble-topped barrels and enjoy the grilled fish.

Café Rossy
CAFE €

(5 Calle General Prim; sandwiches from €2; ⊙lunch & dinner) Another reliable place to grab a quick eat or while away an hour with a book and a coffee. The *bocadillos* are a perfect lunchtime snack.

La Cervecería
TAPAS BAR €

(23 Calle de General O'Donnell; tapas from €1.50; ⊙lunch & dinner) High on decoration, this one-room bar is a green explosion of decorative tile on all surfaces, including the furniture.

Antony Pizza Factory
ITALIAN €

(Av de la Democracia; pizza from €5, pasta from €6; ⊙dinner) Less factory than cosy brasserie, its staff still works hard to dish out heavily loaded pizzas and some rich pasta sauces. Popular with Melilla's young, it has a sunken snug area for quiet dining.

Real Club Marítimo
CAFE €

(Yacht Harbour) This is a private yacht club but travellers are welcome to come and sample a croissant and coffee by the sea.

SELF-CATERING

There are plenty of small grocery shops in the streets around Parque Hernández. For the complete supermarket experience, go to **Supersol** (Calle General Polavieja; ⊙10am-10pm, closed Sun) on the road to the frontier.

🍷 Drinking

Puerto Deportivo Noray
BAR

Look no further, this is Melilla's bar zone, with 12 different options grouped side by side on the waterfront. Enter through the car park next to the courthouse.

ℹ Information

To phone Melilla from outside Spain, dial 🖉0034. Melilla is one hour ahead of Morocco, and two hours ahead during Spanish daylight saving (see p501). Most shops and businesses are closed on Sunday.

Internet Access

There are numerous internet cafes downtown.

Locutoria Dosmil (14-25 Calle Ejercito España; per hr €2; ☺9am-2pm & 4-9pm)

Medical Services

Hospital Comarcal (🖉956 67 00 00) South side of Río de Oro.

Urgencias Sanitarias (🖉956 67 44 00; 40 Alvaro de Bazan; ☺5pm-9am Mon-Sat, 24hr Sun & public holidays) Night pharmacy.

Money

Euros are used for all transactions in Melilla. You'll find several banks (with ATMs) around Av de Juan Carlos I Rey. Most will buy or sell dirham at an inferior rate to the Moroccan dealers hanging around the ferry port or the border.

On the Moroccan side of the border you can change cash at the Crédit du Maroc. There's also a Banque Populaire with an ATM 200m further into Morocco; walk straight ahead to the crossroads and it's on your left on the road to the port.

Post

Main post office (Correos y telégrafos; Calle Pablo Vallescá; ☺8.30am-8.30pm Mon-Fri, 9.30am-1pm Sat)

Tourist Information

Fundación Melilla Ciudad Monumental (🖉952 97 62 01; www.melillamonumental. org, in English; C/Miguel Acosta, 13) In-depth information on local architecture.

Oficina del Turismo (main) (🖉952 97 61 89; www.melillaturismo.com, in English; Plaza de la Culturas; ☺10am-2pm & 4.30-8.30pm Mon-Sat, 10am-2pm Sun) Lots of maps and brochures and friendly, English-speaking staff. Offers special tours of religious sites. Website contains a comprehensive history and architectural tour.

Oficina del Turismo (kiosk) (🖉952 97 61 51; www.melillaturismo.com, in English; Plaza de España; ☺10am-2pm & 4-8pm Mon-Fri) Faces the Palacio de Asamblea.

Travel Agencies

Viajes Melilla (🖉952 679352; 1 Ave Duquesa de la Victoria)

ℹ Getting There & Away

Air

Air Nostrum (Iberia) (www.airnostrum.com; Melilla Airport) offers 12 daily flights between Melilla and Málaga, as well as two daily flights to Almeria, Valencia and Madrid, and one daily flight to Granada. The airport is a 10-minute (€5) taxi ride, and has no ATM.

Car

Melilla is a duty-free zone, so if you're driving it's worth filling up here. Petrol is Dh10 per litre, about one-third cheaper than in Morocco or Spain.

Ferry

Melisur (🖉956 68 66 13; 8 Calle de General Marina; ☺9am-1pm & 5-7pm Mon-Fri, 9am-noon Sat) sells Acciona (Transmediterraneo) ferry tickets to Málaga and Almeria. Tickets are also available for purchase at the **estación marítima** (ferry port; 🖉956 68 16 33). Ferry services to Malaga:

Monday noon arriving at 7.35pm, and midnight arriving at 8am on Tuesday

Tuesday to Saturday midnight

Ferries from Malaga to Melilla leave on Monday (11pm, arriving at 8am on Tuesday) and Tuesday to Saturday (2pm arriving at 9.30pm). Prices begin at €30.70.

Ferry services to Almeria leave on Monday (9am) and Sunday (2.30pm).

Ferries from Almeria to Melilla lave on Monday (4.30pm) and Tuesday to Sunday at midnight.

Border Crossing

To get to the border, you'll need to either take a taxi (€6) or catch local bus 2 (marked 'Aforos'), which runs between Plaza de España and the Beni Enzar border post (€0.60, every 30 minutes from 7.30am to 11pm). From where the buses stop, it's about 50m to Spanish customs and another 200m to Moroccan customs.

Before entering Morocco, fill in a white form and get your passport stamped at the booth. Touts may approach trying to charge you for these forms, or ask a fee to fill them out for you. If you're driving into Morocco, remember to retain the green customs slip, which you must present when you (and your vehicle) leave the country. Large queues of vehicles entering Morocco are frequent and time-consuming; procedures for foot passengers are quick and easy.

On the Moroccan side of the border, bus 19 (usually unmarked) runs hourly to Nador (Dh25, 25 minutes). Frequent grands taxis (Dh5, 15 minutes) to Nador are tucked away in a car park to the right of this crossroad.

When entering Melilla from Morocco, fill in a yellow form and get your passport stamped. Some nationalities require visas to enter Spain: if they don't stop you here, they will when you try to move on to the mainland. Bus 43 goes to Plaza España (€0.60).

ⓘ Getting Around

The centre of Melilla is compact and easy to walk around. Buses ply the route between Plaza de España and the border. The local **taxi service** (⏱956 68 36 21) is also useful.

Nador
الناظور

POP 180,000

There is a new road from Al-Hoceima to Nador (130km) that is a delight to travel, even when squashed into a grand taxi. It passes through red cliffs, verdant gorges and, midway, an enormous sculpture of deeply eroded hills. A new resort, Atalayoun Golf, was being constructed at the time of research.

Within 60km of Nador there are several ramshackle, clifftop cafes that are perfect for a mint tea as you gaze out over the sea. Don't look too closely at the deserted beaches, though, as they're knee-deep in litter.

Unfortunately Nador itself offers little when you arrive, regardless of its size. Apart from Marchika, its pretty lagoon, there are no sights or attractions in this endless sprawl of concrete blocks. The city serves more as a transport link, with a major airport, active ferry port and sleek new train station with a service to Fez. Like the rest of the coast, this situation is changing, with the requisite corniche and palm-lined boulevards now complete. The accompanying development of hotels, restaurants and marina has stalled, as it has everywhere on the coast. It's best not to linger in Nador.

🛏 Sleeping

There's no shortage of hotels of all classes in Nador but be warned, many prefer to sell their rooms by the hour. The cheaper places are near the bus and grand-taxi stations.

Hotel Annakhil HOTEL €€
(⏱0536 33 58 67; 185 Blvd de Tanger; s/d/ste Dh420/520/800; ❄) The Annakhil might be overkill on decor with its orange corridors, plastic plants and bright blue bedrooms,

but it's the best midrange option. There's good linen, comfortable beds, TVs and fridges in the rooms. The cafe next door serves breakfast. The bar rocks at night – only a very brave woman would venture alone into this den.

Hotel Mediterranée HOTEL €
(⏱0536 60 64 95; hotel.mediterranee@gmail. com; 2-4 Ave Youssef ibn Tachfine; s/d Dh252/326; ❄⏱) Views from this hotel have been annihilated by the new Hotel Rif being constructed at the time of research. But it's still only one block back from the corniche and lagoon. The corner rooms have plenty of light, and all have TVs. Air-conditioning is an extra Dh50. There's a dull restaurant (dishes from Dh60) on the ground floor serving breakfast, omelettes and fish.

Hotel Geranio HOTEL €
(⏱0536 60 28 28; 16 Rue No 20; s/d Dh160/188) Just away from the chaos of the bus station, streetside rooms here can be noisy, but the low prices make this the top budget option. Clean rooms come with tiny bathrooms. There's a ground-floor cafeteria as well.

Hotel Ryad HOTEL €€€
(⏱0536 60 77 17; hotelryad@hotmail.com; Ave Mohammed V; s/d incl breakfast Dh700/950; ❄) Once plush but now showing its age and somewhat overpriced, the Ryad is a large hotel with two bars and a disco that make rooms on the 2nd and 4th floors unbearably noisy until midnight. The rooms have standard features and those on the top floor have views over the lagoon.

🍴 Eating & Drinking

There are numerous cheap eats around the CTM bus station, serving up quick brochettes, sandwiches and tajines. Ave Mohammed V is the place for a lazy coffee – street cafes line the road under shady orange trees.

Restaurant Marhaba SEAFOOD €€
(⏱0536 60 33 11; Calle Ibn Rochd; mains from Dh60; ⏱lunch & dinner) The smartest restaurant in town, the Marhaba specialises in fish and does it very well. The main room is very large, but there's a cosier terrace at the back with fishing nets and plastic lobsters. There's no alcohol.

Café Club CAFE, LOCAL €
(Ave Mohammed Zerktouni) Jutting into the lagoon at the far end of Mohammed V, this island cafe comes as a surprise and a welcome bit of maritime focus in an otherwise

concrete forest. Great for coffee, it also serves a tajine of the day (around Dh40).

Café Antalya
CAFE €

(Bld Prince Héritier Sidi Mohammed; pizzas from Dh50) All glass and chrome and spilling out onto the pavement, this smart cafe shows a new face of Nador. The pizzeria upstairs is popular with young trendies.

ⓘ Information

Credit Maroc (64 Ave Mohammed V) One of several banks on Mohammed V with foreign-exchange services and ATM.

Cyber Milano (Bld el Massira; per hr Dh5; ☺8am-8pm) Internet cafe.

Ketama Voyages (☎0536 60 61 91; ketama-voyage@hotmail.fr; 55 Ave Mohammed) Sells ferry tickets to Almería.

Pharmacy al-Farabi (☎0536 60 60 11; Ave Mohammed V)

Post office Next to Grande Mosquée.

Royal Air Maroc (Ave Mohammed V; ☺8.30am-12.15pm & 2.30-7pm Mon-Fri, 9am-noon & 3-6pm Sat)

ⓘ Getting There & Away

Air

The airport is 23km south of Nador. Atlas Blue and Ryanair operate numerous flights to Europe. Iberia connects Nador with Spain, and Air Berlin flies to Cologne.

Boat

Acciona has started a new fast ferry service to Almeria. It leaves Almeria Sunday to Tuesday, Thursday and Friday at 10am and arrives in Nador at 3pm, then turns around and leaves at 10pm, arriving the next day in Almeria at 6am. Comanav offers a service to Sète, France on Monday.

The port of Beni Enzar is 7km from the city but traffic makes it feel much further. The quickest way to get there is by grand taxi (Dh8, 15 minutes).

Bus

From the **CTM office** (Rue Genéral Meziane) there are departures to all the usual suspects: Casablanca, Rabat, Meknès, Fez, Tangier, Larache, Sidi Kacem, Al-Hoceima, Chefcha-ouen and more. In the evening, several slightly cheaper Casablanca-bound coaches run by other companies leave from the same area. CTM also has a small office in the main bus station in addition to its main office.

The main bus station is southeast of the centre. There are frequent departures:

Tetouan (Dh110, nine hours), some via Chef-chaouen (Dh100, six hours)

Oujda (Dh25, 2½ hours) via Berkane (Dh15, 1½ hours)

Al-Hoceima (Dh30, three hours)

Fez (Dh60, 5½ hours)

Ras el-Maa (Dh10, one hour)

Beni Enzar (Melilla border; Dh3, 25 minutes)

Taxi

The huge grand-taxi lot next to the main bus station serves plenty of destinations.

DESTINATION	COST (DH)	DURATION (HR)
Al-Hoceima	56	3
Beni Enzar (the Melilla border)	5	¼
Berkane	40	1
Fez	110	5
Oujda	50	3
Taza	60	

Train

Nador's new train station (Nador Ville) serves the following destinations:

Beni Enzar/Melilla border (Dh10, 12 minutes)

Beni Enzar port (Dh10, 25 minutes)

Fez (Dh98, six hours, four daily).

Two of these trains go via Taourirt where you can change for Casablanca.

East of Nador

East of Nador, on the opposite side of the lagoon, the coast is a mix of salt marsh and sand dunes, which attract a wide-variety of birdlife, including the greater flamingo. Two scruffy towns, **Kariat Arekmane** and **Ras el-Maa**, lie on the new road (N16) east-wards to Saïdia, which affords good views of the Islas Chafarinas, the last bit of Spain on the northern coast (see the boxed text, p258). Arekmane is being developed: the corniche has been built and apartments will follow. But the pretty beach, with its fishing boats, is full of rubbish, and the wet-lands inland of the corniche are in danger of disappearing.

Ras el-Maa, also known as Cap de l'Eau, is faring better. The pedestrianised cor-niche has a few small restaurants and a beautiful beach. The wetlands around the mouth of the Moulouya west of the small town are Ramsar protected, making them a prime birdwatching area. Migrant birds from Europe include Moussier's Redstart

(Phoenicurus moussieri), the Marbled Teal (Marmaronetta angustirostris) and Audouin's Gull (Larus audouinii). Some endemic and rare fish are also found in the wetlands here.

From the eastern side of the Moulouya River estuary, the much-vaunted Station Balnéaire (seaside resort) begins and runs for 5km to Saídia along a truly magnificent beach. But it's all a sorry sight. So far, there are hundreds upon hundreds of blocks of apartments; those on the seafront corniche have been completed and a few sold, while those stretching back from the coast for at least a kilometre lie unoccupied or incomplete. Even if they have been sold, the apartments are only occupied during the season (July and August) which gives the entire development a ghostly air.

Morocco has largely escaped the recent world financial crisis, but it's here and in similar developments all along the coast, that the crunch can definitely be felt. There are the beginnings of two golf courses, with more to come. The best area of beach along this 5km stretch is at **Mediterreanéa Saídia**, where the marina is unfinished but the shopping centre complete. At the time of research, there was just one hotel in operation here, the **Barceló Mediterranéa Saídia** (☑ in Spain 00 34 9021 01 10 01; www.barcelo.com; r from €160; ✽⚡☎⚞), which offers a spa, sporting facilities and several restaurants and bars.

Saídia
السعيدية
POP 18,000

At time of research Saídia was still the sleepy little seaside town it has always been but is holding its breath in anticipation of developments along the coast. The financial crisis has prevented the Station Balnéaire from taking off as was hoped.

Saídia has a fine beach and a new corniche with restaurants and clubs along it. Those that have been completed, though, are closed out of season. One block back from the beach, Blvd Hassan II has some pre-existing hotels, banks, cafes and internet facilities.

The adjacent border with Algeria remains closed. While Morocco would like to reopen it, Algeria has so far refused to agree. However, there is no active conflict.

Berkane
بركان
POP 80,000

Berkane is a dusty modern town about 80km southeast of Nador on the road to Oujda. While the name means 'black' in the local Berber language, Berkane is famous for its oranges and everything in the town is, well, orange. The taxis, the buildings and the wonderful statue of an orange as you enter the town. It's most useful to travellers as a transit point, including the gas smugglers who blow through town like bats out of hell on their nightly runs to Algeria. And it's not olive oil being sold in plastic bottles at the side of the roads around town, but pirated petrol from Algeria, which it's better not to use as it's probably adulterated. Berkane can serve as a base for exploring the Beni-Snassen Mountains.

The town is easy to navigate as it's stretched along Blvd Mohammed V, which leads from the orange Grande Mosquée in the west (don't miss the many stork nests in the trees) to the large roundabout at the other end, dominated by a large orange municipal building. You'll find the post office and plenty of ATMs here. Halfway between is the main square, with the CTM station on the south side and a petrol station opposite.

◉ Sights & Activities

French Church   CHURCH
(◔8.30am-noon & 2.30-6pm Mon-Sat, closed Wed afternoon) The only site of interest in Berkane is the French Church. Built in 1909, it was the life project of a single priest with a very broad view of religion. The interior contains a strange amalgamation of alchemy, signs of the zodiac and biblical scenes transplanted to Morocco, all painted by the priest himself. From the Grand Mosquée, head down Blvd Mohammed V and turn left at Maroc Telecom. The church is straight ahead.

The church is now home to the **Association Homme et Environment** (Man & Environment Association; www.hee.ouvaton.org)

MOVING ON?

For further information, head to shop. lonelyplanet.com to purchase a downloadable PDF of the Algeria chapter from Lonely Planet's *Africa* guide.

a dedicated, and rare, local environmental group. Ask for its president, Najib Bachiri (☑0661 10 53 73), who speaks fluent English and enjoys giving tours. Entrance is free, but donations to the association are most welcome.

🍴 Sleeping & Eating

The main options for sleeping and eating in Berkane are strung along or near Blvd Mohammed V.

Hotel Rosalina   HOTEL €€
(☑0536 61 89 92; 82 Blvd Mohammed V; rosalina_hotel@hotmail.fr; s/d/ste Dh400/460/1000; ❄️🛜) This new hotel is pleasant, with lots of polished wood and friendly staff. It offers clean, comfortable rooms with TVs.

Hotel Zaki   HOTEL €€
(☑0536 61 37 43; 27 Rte d'Oujda; s/d incl breakfast Dh360/420; ❄️🛜) This three-star hotel is 400m east of the main roundabout next to a Chinese restaurant. The 2nd floor is like a designer showroom, with each room tastefully decorated in its own style, but be careful of dangerous carpets jumbled on the stairs, which have been there for years.

Café du Jardin   CAFE €
(Blvd Mohammed V) Located in a garden opposite the main square, this place has the closest thing to atmosphere in Berkane, although the clientele is decidedly masculine.

Café Royal   FAST FOOD €
(Blvd Mohammed V) Near the square, this is the local place for pizza.

ℹ️ Getting There & Away

Berkane's bus and taxi stands are scattered all over town. The **CTM office** is next to Café Laetizia on the west side of the main square. There is just one early evening departure for Fez (Dh110, six hours), Meknès (Dh125, 7½ hours), Rabat (Dh160, 10 hours) and Casablanca (Dh185, 11 hours). Long-hauls to Spain also leave from here.

Most other long-distance buses gather in the streets behind the CMH petrol station, and serve the above destinations. The buses to Nador (Dh20, one hour) stop immediately behind the petrol station, and run hourly until mid-afternoon.

Local buses for Taforalt (Dh9, 30 minutes) depart from Blvd Mohammed V twice a day, while grands taxis for Taforalt (Dh10, 25 minutes) and Nador (Dh25, one hour) use the car park on the opposite side of the road, between the Shell petrol station and the bridge.

Grands taxis for Oujda (Dh18, one hour) leave from near the bus station; for Saídia (Dh8, 15 minutes) or Ras el-Mar (Dh10, 15 minutes) from the square in front of the municipal building at the end of Blvd Mohammed V; and for Nador from the car park opposite the Great Mosque.

Beni-Snassen Mountains

جبال بني سناسن

Far more alluring than Berkane are the beautiful Beni-Snassen Mountains that border it to the south. While technically termed a 'site of biological and ecological interest', they are for all intents and purposes a national park. This is a verdant area of scenic gorges that few imagine when they think of Morocco, and even fewer visit.

From Berkane, take the national road to **Taforalt** (Tafoughalt) which passes through beautiful mountain scenery. Taforalt is a somewhat haphazard settlement that arose around a former French military installation, but the northern end, which you come upon first, contains a charming strip of cafes and restaurants. One of these is the **Rotana Club Touristique** (☑0648 91 92 22/0673 58 97 40; http://taforaltclub.com; ⏰Apr-Oct; ❄️) with a simple restaurant and swimming pool (admission Dh50) in a pretty garden.

Soon after you enter Taforalt from Berkane, turn left at the post office, then immediately turn left again and follow signs to the Infokiosk, which has a small but well-done display on the natural history of the park, and an observation platform with heavenly views of a distant mesa. If you're lucky you will catch sight of a big-horned Barbary sheep from the adjacent reserve. They generally arrive around 4pm, when it is cooler.

About 2km back down the national road is a right turn signposted for two *grottes* (caves). The **Grottes des Pigeons** (1km) is the site of an active excavation by Oxford University that has revealed human remains from the Pleistocene era, including some of the earliest human jewellery (80,000 years old).

Another 5km brings you to the **Grottes de Chameau**, a multistorey cave complex with three entrances that has been closed for years due to flooding damage. Three kilometres more brings you to the pretty **Zegzel Gorge** and a beautiful serpentine drive. Don't miss the chance to sample the kumquats, a local industry. Even the Romans remarked upon them.

The source of the **Charaâ River** provides a worthwhile detour. Follow signs to the tiny hamlet of Zegzel, 2km up a side road. At the end there's a popular picnic spot near where the river gushes out of the cliff. Not far from here, a spectacular ridge road cuts east to Oujda. You'll need a 4WD vehicle, a good map and an early start.

A delightful place to stay is **Gîte Tagma** (🕿0666 79 29 49; www.gitetagma.com; r per person incl full-board Dh300; @), about half an hour's drive beyond Taforalt. It doesn't get any more authentic, or tranquil, than this remote, 300-year-old rural lodge midway up the mountains, with its small working farm. The five simple bedrooms surround a common compound, with wonderful views of pine-dotted canyons. From here you can easily trek out to the postcard-pretty Sidi Ali Oussaidi Mosque, which stands against the mountains like a Bavarian chapel, and the romantic town of Tagma, which sits in the valley below like a small Berber fortress. Or you can just kick back with a book and

dream. The *gîte* ('sjeet' in French) is a joint project between the owner and Association Homme et Environment (p295), and the model for rural tourism development in this region. It is signposted about 15km on the national road from Berkane to Taforalt. Only 4WD vehicles can reach the house, but phone ahead and you will be met in the village and escorted down the mountainside. Be aware that mobile phone coverage is not always perfect in the mountains.

If you don't have your own vehicle, the easiest way to access the park is to take a shared taxi from Berkane (Dh10). Alternatively hire your own taxi; the minimum fare will be in the region of Dh200 for two hours, although not all drivers will be willing to take their vehicles along the poor roads near the hamlet of Zegzel. A cheaper alternative is to take a bus or grand taxi to Taforalt and walk down. Two buses each morning make the journey from Berkane (Dh10, 30 minutes), with return services in the afternoons. Grands taxis cost Dh10, and are most frequent on market days (Wednesday and Sunday).

Imperial Cities, Middle Atlas & the East

الامبراطوري المدن و الأطلس المتوسط و الشرق

Best Places to Stay

» Ziyarates Fes (p313)
» Dar Bensouda (p314)
» Ryad Bahia (p333)
» Walila (p340)
» Dar Zerhoune (p341)
» Auberge Oasis (p359)

Best Places to Eat

» Fès et Gestes (p318)
» Tours Around Fez (p312)
» Marhaba Restaurant (p335)
» B'sara Stalls (p318)
» Bou Jeloud Restaurants (p318)
» Maison Blanche (p320)

Why Go?

If you're looking for Morocco in microcosm, this region takes the title, running the whole spectrum from imperial cities and ancient ruins to grand mountain vistas and desert oases.

The fertile plains of the north have acted as Morocco's breadbasket for centuries. The Romans left the remains at Volubilis, followed in turn by the Muslim dynasties who birthed Morocco's grandest imperial city: Fez.

The narrow streets of Fez' medina are a true assault on the senses. Meknès, another old imperial capital, offers a slightly more pocket-sized experience.

The Middle Atlas, home to the Barbary ape, rise to the south and the area is made for hiking.

Across the mountains the distinctive kasbahs of the south begin to make an appearance. The desert isn't far away, and by the time you reach the oasis of Figuig, the olive tree has long given way to the date palm.

When to Go

Fez

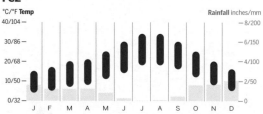

June
Hit Fez for the Festival of World Sacred Music.

September
Summer's heat has burned off and Ramadan is finished: perfect sightseeing conditions.

December & January
Cold in Fez and Meknès, but perfect for a desert trip to Figuig.

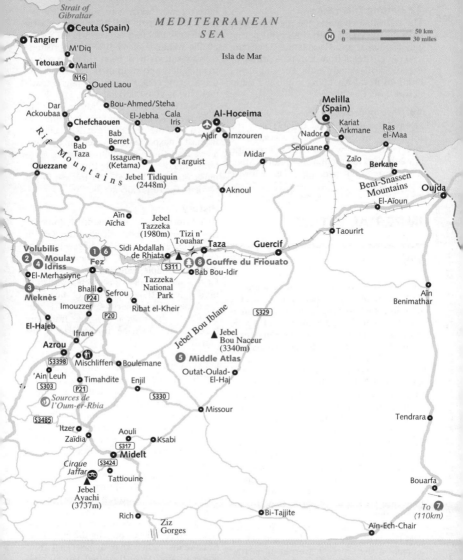

Imperial Cities, Middle Atlas & the East Highlights

❶ Dive into the warren of the **medina** (p301) looking for souqs and souvenirs in ancient Fez

❷ Time travel amid the mosaic-strewn **Roman ruins** (p337) of Volubilis

❸ Explore the outsized **imperial architecture** (p329) of Meknès

❹ Spend a day and night on pilgrimage in the holy town of **Moulay Idriss** (p340)

❺ Hike into the wooded slopes of the **Middle Atlas** (p345) around Azrou

❻ Enjoy the sound of the sublime at the **Festival of World Sacred Music** (p312) in Fez

❼ Get away from everything amid the palms and kasbahs of the oasis town of **Figuig** (p358)

❽ Make like a troglodyte in the weird **caverns** (p353) of Gouffre du Friouato

ℹ Getting There & Away

The train line connects the region's major cities to the coast, with direct links from Tangier, Rabat and Casablanca. There are also direct flights from Europe – primarily France – to Fez and Oujda. Fez and Oujda link into Royal Air Maroc's internal flight network, via Casablanca.

ℹ Getting Around

From Marrakesh and Casablanca, the train line runs east through Meknès, Fez and Taza all the way to Oujda. Travelling around the mountainous Middle Atlas, however, requires catching a bus or hiring a grand taxi.

IMPERIAL CITIES

Fez فاس

POP 1 MILLION

In recent years Fez has boomed as a tourist destination. Money has poured into the city, from foreigners buying riads in the medina to new parks and fountains in the ville nouvelle. If you believe the travel and style pages of the Western media, Fez has become the new Marrakesh.

Tell a Fassi that however, and they'll laugh in your face. This is an old and supremely self-confident city that has nothing to prove to anyone. Dynasties and booms have all come and gone in the city's 1200-year existence, and Fez will be around long after the next fashion has burned itself out.

The city's allegiance, or at least submission, has always been essential to whoever held Morocco's throne. Morocco's independence movement was born here, and when there are strikes or protests, they are always at their most vociferous in Fez.

For visitors, the medina of Fès el-Bali (Old Fez) is the city's great drawcard. It's an assault on the senses, a warren of narrow lanes and covered bazaars fit to bursting with aromatic food stands, craft workshops, mosques and an endless parade of people. Old and new constantly collide – the man driving the donkeys and mules that remain the main form of transport is likely to be chatting on his mobile phone, while the ancient skyline is punctuated equally with satellite dishes and minarets.

Years of neglect have taken their toll on the medina, however. The authorities have recently taken note, and much is being done to repair buildings and replaster facades. Scaffolding is everywhere. Yet for all the romance of medina life to visitors, many residents have been happy to sell up to foreigners and swap their sometimes medieval living conditions for a modern apartment in the ville nouvelle.

The trick is to dive straight in. It is initially overwhelming, but once you adjust to the pace of the city, Fez reveals its charms in most unexpected ways. Seemingly blind alleys lead to squares with exquisite fountains, filled with the rhythmic hammer-music of copper beaters. Getting lost in Fez is where the fun really starts.

History

In AD 789, Idriss I – who founded Morocco's first imperial dynasty – decided that Oualili (Volubilis) was too small and drew up plans for a grand new capital. He died before the plans were implemented, however, so credit for the founding of Fez is often awarded to his son, Idriss II, who carried out the will of his father. The memory of Idriss II is perpetuated in his *zawiya* (religious fraternity based around a shrine) in the heart of Fez el-Bali.

The city started as a modest Berber town, but then 8000 families fleeing Al-Andalus settled the east bank of the Oued Fez. They were later joined by Arab families from Kairouan (Qayrawan) in modern-day Tunisia, who took over the west bank, creating the Kairaouine quarter. The heritages of these two peoples formed a solid foundation for future religious, cultural and architectural richness. Idriss II's heirs split the kingdom, but Fez continued to enjoy peace and prosperity until the 10th century.

Over the next centuries, the fortunes of Fez rose and fell with the dynasties. Civil war and famine – incited by Berber invasions – were relieved only by the rise of the Almoravids. When that dynasty fell from power around 1154, they fled Fez and destroyed the city walls as they went. Only when the succeeding Almohad dynasty was assured of the Fassis' loyalty were the walls replaced – large sections still date from this period.

Fez continued to be a crucial crossroads, wielding intellectual rather than political influence. With the Kairaouine Mosque and University already well established, it was *the* centre of learning and culture in an empire stretching from Spain to Senegal. It recovered its political status only much later, with the arrival of the Merenid dynasty around 1250.

During the 19th century, as central power crumbled and European interference increased, the distinction between Marrakesh and Fez diminished, with both effectively serving as capitals of a fragmented country. Fez retained its status as the 'moral' capital. It was here, on 30 March 1912, that the treaty introducing the French and Spanish protectorates over Morocco was signed. Less than three weeks later, rioting and virtual revolt against the new masters served as a reminder of the city's volatility.

The French may have moved the political capital to Rabat, but Fez remains a constituency to be reckoned with.

As one of Morocco's most traditional cities, Fez is generally regarded with a certain amount of awe, perhaps tinged with jealousy, by the rest of the country. Indeed, a disproportionate share of Morocco's intellectual and economic elite hail from here and it's a widely held belief (especially among Fassis) that anyone born in Fez medina is more religious, cultured, artistic and refined; that the king's wife, Princess Lalla Salma is from Fez, and the royal family spend much time here is a source of great pride for the city.

◎ Sights

THE MEDINA (FÈS EL-BALI)

Travelling from the ville nouvelle to Fès el-Bali is like stepping back in time. The essential footprint of the medina hasn't changed in nearly a millennium, as the surrounding hills have constrained expansion – the last big growth of the traditional medina was in the 13th century with the construction of Fès el-Jdid. Today, around 150,000 Fassis still call this maze of twisting alleys, blind turns and hidden souqs home, while tourists call it one of the most mind-boggling places they'll visit in Morocco.

Bab Bou Jeloud in the west is the main entrance to the old city, with two main streets descending into the medina's heart. On your left as you enter is Talaa Kebira (Big Slope), with Talaa Seghira (Little Slope) on your right. Both converge near Place an-Nejjarine, continuing to the Kairaouine Mosque and Zawiya Moulay Idriss II – the heart of the city. From here, it's uphill to reach the northern gates of Bab Guissa and Bab Jamaï, or head south towards Bab R'cif –

one of the few places where vehicular traffic penetrates the old city. The R'cif area was undergoing a big facelift (including refurbishing its square) when we most recently visited, and is likely to provide an alternate focus for the medina.

While we've listed the major sights below, they're really only a small part of the charm of the medina. It pays to give yourself a little random exploration, and simply follow your nose or ears to discover the most unexpected charms of Fez' nature. Following your nose will lead you to women with bundles of freshly cut herbs, children carrying trays of loaves to be baked in the local bakery or a cafe selling glasses of spiced Berber coffee. Around the next corner you might find a beautifully tiled fountain, a workshop making wooden hammam buckets, a camel's head announcing a specialist butcher, or just a gang of kids turning their alley into a football pitch. Everywhere, listen out for the call to prayer or the mule driver's cry *balak!* (look out!) to warn of the approach of a heavily laden pack animal.

Navigation can be confusing and getting lost at some stage is a certainty, but look at this as part of the adventure. A handy tip is to note the 'main' streets that eventually lead to a gate or landmark – just follow the general flow of people. Ask shopkeepers for directions, or you can fall back on the eager kids happy to rescue confused foreigners for a dirham or two.

Kairaouine Mosque & University MOSQUE

(Map p304) One of Africa's largest mosques and possibly the oldest university in the world, this mosque complex is the spiritual heart of Fez and Morocco itself. Established in 859 by Tunisian refugees and expanded by the Almoravids in the 12th century, it can accommodate up to 20,000 people at prayer. It's so large that it can be difficult to actually see: over the centuries the streets and houses of the Kairaouine quarter have encroached on the building so much they disguise its true shape. The mosque has recently been restored, but non-Muslims are forbidden to enter and will have to be content with glimpses of its seemingly endless columns from the gates on Talaa Kebira and Place as-Seffarine. Better still, take the view from any vantage point over the medina: the huge green pyramidal roof and minaret immediately announce their presence.

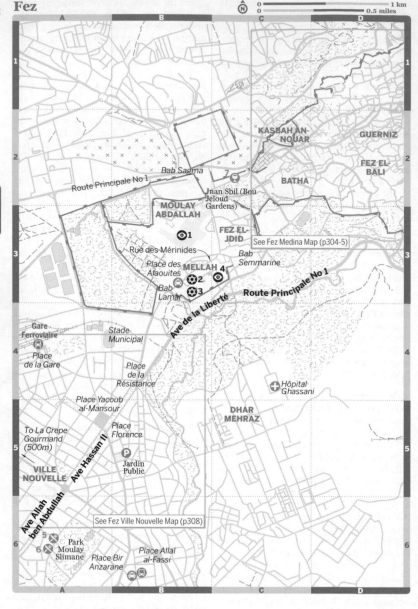

Fez

0   1 km
0   0.5 miles

A   B   C   D

KASBAH AN-NOUAR   GUERNIZ

FEZ EL BALI

Bab Sagma   BATHA

Route Principale No 1

Jnan Sbil (Bou Jeloud Gardens)

MOULAY ABDALLAH

FEZ EL-JDID

See Fez Medina Map (p304-5)

①1

Rue des Mérinides

Place des Alaouites   MELLAH   4

②2   Bab Semmarine

Bab Lamar   ③3

Route Principale No 1

Ave de la Liberté

Gare Ferroviaire   Stade Municipal

Place de la Gare

Place de la Résistance

Hôpital Ghassani

Place Yacoub al-Mansour

DHAR MEHRAZ

To La Crepe Gourmand (500m)

Place Florence

VILLE NOUVELLE

Ave Hassan II

Jardin Public

See Fez Ville Nouvelle Map (p308)

Ave Allah ben Abdullah

5   Park Moulay Slimane

6   Place Bir Anzarane

Place Allal al-Fassi

Medersa el-Attarine   ISLAMIC COLLEGE
(Map p304; admission Dh10; ⊙9am-6pm, closed
during prayers) Founded by Abu Said in 1325
in the heart of the medina, the Medersa
el-Attarine was designed as a separate annexe to the Kairaouine Mosque. Halls for
teaching and a modest masjid flank the
central courtyard. Displaying the traditional patterns of Merenid artisanship, the
zellij (tilework) base, stuccowork and cedar
wood at the top of the walls and on the ceil-

Fez

ing are every bit as elegant as the artistry of the Medersa Bou Inania.

Medersa Bou Inania   ISLAMIC COLLEGE
(Map p304; admission Dh10; ☺9am-6pm, closed during prayers) A short walk down Talaa Kebira from Bab Bou Jeloud, the Medersa Bou Inania is the finest of Fez' theological colleges. It was built by the Merenid sultan Bou Inan between 1350 and 1357. The *medersa* underwent extensive restoration a few years ago, and the results are amazing: elaborate *zellij* and carved plaster, beautiful cedar *mashrabiyyas* (lattice screens) and massive brass doors.

Whereas most *medersas* just have a simple prayer hall, the Bou Inania is unusual in that it hosts a complete mosque, complete with a beautiful green-tiled minaret. The mihrab (niche facing Mecca) has a particularly fine ceiling and onyx marble columns. It's thought that the *medersa* required a larger-scale mosque because there was none other nearby at the time.

Nejjarine Museum of Wooden Arts & Crafts   MUSEUM
(Map p304; ☎0535 74 05 80; Place an-Nejjarine; admission Dh20; ☺10am-7pm) Opened in 1998, this museum is in a wonderfully restored *funduq* – a caravanserai for travelling merchants who stored and sold their goods below and took lodgings on the floors above. Centred on a courtyard, the rooms are given over to displays of traditional artefacts from craftsmen's tools, chunky prayer beads and Berber locks, chests and musical instruments (compare the traditional wedding furniture with the modern glitzy chairs outside in Place an-Nejjarine). Ev-

erything is beautifully presented, although the stunning building gives the exhibits a run for their money. The rooftop cafe has great views over the medina. Photography is forbidden.

Batha Museum   MUSEUM
(Map p304; ☎0535 63 41 16; Rue de la Musée, Batha; admission Dh10; ☺8.30am-noon & 2.30-6pm Wed-Mon) Housed in a wonderful 19th-century summer palace, converted to a museum in 1916, the Batha Museum houses an excellent collection of traditional Moroccan arts and crafts. Historical and artistic artefacts include fine woodcarving, *zellij* and sculpted plaster, much of it from the city's ruined or decaying *medersas*. It also has some fine Fassi embroidery, colourful Berber carpets and antique instruments.

The highlight of the museum is the superb ceramic collection dating from the 14th century to the present. These are some fantastic examples of the famous blue pottery of Fez. The cobalt glaze responsible for the colour is developed from a special process discovered in the 10th century.

The museum's Andalucian-style garden offers temporary respite from the bustle and noise of the medina, and the spreading holm oaks provide a backdrop for the open-air concerts the museum hosts during the Sacred Music and Sufi Culture festivals.

Chaouwara Tanneries   CRAFTS
(Map p304; Derb Chouwara, Blida) The Chouwara tanneries are one of the city's most iconic sights (and smells). Head east or northeast from Place as-Seffarine and take the left fork after about 50m; you'll soon pick up the unmistakeable waft of skin and dye that will guide you into the heart of the leather district (the touts offering to show you the way make it even harder to miss).

It's not possible to get in among the tanning pits themselves, but there are plenty of vantage points from the streets that line them, all occupied (with typical Fassi ingenuity) by leather shops. Each shop has a terrace that allows you to look over the action. Try to get here in the morning when the pits are awash with coloured dye. Salesmen will happily give an explanation of the processes involved and will expect a small tip in return or, even better, a sale. While this might feel a little commercialised, you probably won't find a better selection of leather in Morocco, and prices are as good as you'll get.

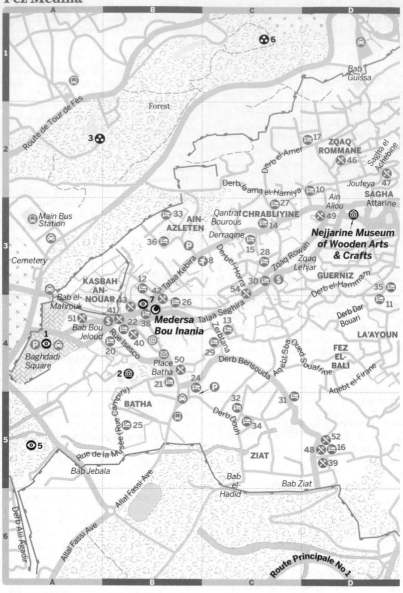

In recent years, there have been plans mooted to move the tannery out of the medina altogether and redevelop the site as a green area. However, with both the economic and cultural impact of the plans for this district of the medina remaining uncertain, it's unsure whether these plans will ever leave the drawing board.

FEZ EL-JDID (NEW FEZ)

Only in a city as old as Fez could you find a district dubbed 'New' because it's only 700

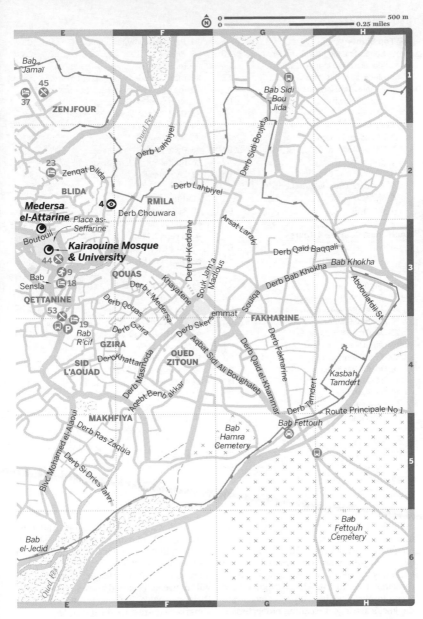

years old. The paranoid Merenid sultan Abu Yusuf Yacoub (1258–86) purpose-built the quarter, packing it with his Syrian mercenary guards and seeking to isolate himself from his subjects. Even today almost half of the area is given over to the grounds of the Royal Palace, still popular with Mohammed VI. Its other main legacy is the architectural evidence of its early Jewish inhabitants.

Dar el-Makhzen   PALACE
(Royal Palace; Map p302; Place des Alaouites) The entrance to Dar el-Makhzen is a stunning

example of modern restoration, but the 80 hectares of palace grounds are not open to the public. Visitors must suffice with viewing its imposing brass doors, surrounded by fine *zellij* and carved cedar wood. Note the lemon trees to one side – tour guides are prone to plucking the fruit to demonstrate the juice's astringent cleaning properties on the palace gates.

Mellah   JEWISH QUARTER
(Map p302) In the 14th century Fez el-Jdid became a refuge for Jews, thus creating a *mellah* (Jewish quarter). The records suggest that the move was orchestrated to of-

fer the Jews greater protection. And they certainly did enjoy the favour of the sultan, repaying him with their loyalty during conflict. Around 200 Jews remain in Fez, but all have now left the Mellah in favour of the ville nouvelle. Their old houses remain, with their open balconies looking onto the streets a marked contrast to Muslim styles.

Jewish Cemetery & Habarim Synagogue   CEMETERY
(Map p302; donations welcome; ◷7am-7pm) The southwest corner of the *mellah* is home to the sea of blindingly white tombs that stretch down the hill; those in dedicated

enclosures are tombs of rabbis. One of the oldest, high up against the north wall, is that of Rabbi Vidal Hasserfaty, who died in 1600. On the slope below, the large tomb with green trimming is that of the martyr Solica. In 1834 this 14-year-old girl refused to convert to Islam or accept the advances of the governor of Tangier and subsequently had her throat slit.

The Habarim Synagogue, at the far end of the cemetery, now houses a museum with a whole mishmash of articles, including some poignant photos and postcards, left behind after the Jewish exodus. If the museum is locked, the gatekeeper will open it for you.

Ibn Danan Synagogue SYNAGOGUE
(Map p302; donations welcomed) Near the cemetery, this synagogue was restored with the aid of Unesco in 1999. There are no set opening times as such, but someone will usually let you in and point out the main features, including a *mikva* (ritual bath) in the basement.

Jnan Sbil (Bou Jeloud Gardens) GARDENS
(Map p304; Ave Moulay Hassan) These gardens have been providing welcome green space for well over a century. They're a good halfway break between the *mellah* and Bab Bou Jeloud, and have recently undergone extensive renovation and replanting.

Rue des Mérinides NOTABLE BUILDINGS
(Map p302) This street is lined with houses which are distinguished by their wooden and wrought-iron balconies, as well as by their stuccowork.

Baghdadi Square MARKET
(Map p304) An open-air market on the edge of the medina.

NORTH OF THE MEDINA
Viewed from the surrounding hills, Fez' jumbled buildings merge into a palette of white-flecked sandstone. Only here and there do the green-tiled roofs of the mosques and *medersas* provide a hint of colour.

Borj Nord VIEWPOINT
(Map p304) Head up here for one of the best panoramas of the city. Like its counterpart on the southern hills (Borj Sud), Borj Nord was built by Sultan Ahmed al-Mansour in the late 16th century to monitor the potentially disloyal populace of Fez.

Merenid Tombs RUINS
(Map p304) Further up, these tombs are dramatic in their advanced state of ruin, although little remains of their fine original decoration. The views over Fez are spectacular and well worth the climb. Look for the black smoke in the southern part of the city, marking the potteries. It's best at dusk as the lights come on and the muezzins' prayer

LIFE IN THE LEATHER DISTRICT

Tanneries provide perhaps the greatest illustration of how resolutely some parts of Morocco have clung to practices developed in medieval times. Moroccan leather, and more particularly the Fassi leather produced in Fez, has for centuries been highly prized as among the finest in the world. One type of leather, a soft goatskin used mainly in bookbinding, is simply known as 'morocco'.

It's claimed that tanning leather in Morocco goes back several millennia, and little has changed since medieval times. Donkeys still labour through the narrow street carrying skins to dye pits, which are still constructed to traditional designs (with the addition of modern ceramic tiles). Tanners are organised according to ancient guild principles, with workers typically born into the job. Unfortunately, health and safety principles are similarly old-fashioned, and health problems among the workers, who are knee-deep in chemicals all day, are not uncommon.

Rank odours abound at the tanneries, and the delicate tourists who come to view the work will often be offered a sprig of mint to hold to their noses to take the edge off the pong (rain also dampens the smell). Major components in processing the skins are pigeon poo and cow urine (for potassium) with ash; more delicate ingredients such as indigo, saffron and poppy are added later for colour.

Modern Fassi tanneries – amazingly there are over 50 tanneries in Fez – tend to use synthetic chemicals, washing pollutants into the Oued Sebour river, although the city's chrome removal plant is removing much, if not all, of the worst pollutants.

calls echo around the valley, although you shouldn't go on your own; we've received more than one account of travellers being mugged here after dark. A taxi from Bab Bou Jeloud should cost around Dh7; it's a 10-minute walk back downhill to the medina.

🏃 Activities

HAMMAMS

For a luxury blow-out, several guesthouses offer opulent hammam experiences. Riad Laaroussa (p316), Riad Maison Bleue (p315) and Riad Zitouna (p314) have excellent private spas, with treatments starting at around Dh300.

Ain Azleten Hammam   HAMMAM
(Map p304; Talaa Kebira, Ain Azleten; ⊘men 6am-noon & 8.30-11pm, women noon-8.30pm) Convenient and used to foreigners, this is a good option if you want to try a public hammam.

A session will cost you around Dh40, with attendants on hand to help you slough away the dirt.

Seffarine Hammam   HAMMAM
(Map p304; Place as-Seffarine; ⊘men 6am-midnight, women 8am-10pm) A beautiful example of traditional bathhouse architecture, restored with the help of the Venice Institute for Urban Sustainability. Sessions cost around Dh40.

Nausikaa   SPA
(www.nausikaaspa.com; Ave Bahnini, Rte Ain Smen; ⊘7am-9pm) In the ville nouvelle, Nausikaa offers one of the most complete packages in Fez, blending hammam traditions with a modern spa experience. A variety of sumptuous massages and therapies are on offer, along with gym and pool.

Fez Ville Nouvelle

📖 Courses

Clock Kitchen   COOKING
(Map p304; ☑0655 32 40 82; www.fez-food.com, Derb El Magana, Talaa Kebira; day course Dh600) Held in Café Clock (see p318) these classes are the place to perfect your tajine and couscous-making skills. After planning your menu, you shop for ingredients in the souq, spend the day honing your technique and finishing up with the feast you've prepared. Other options include bread-baking classes, patisserie workshops, making *tanjia* (slow-cooked stews) and hand-rolling couscous.

Subul Assalam   LANGUAGE
(☑0535 63 18 62; www.sacal-fez.com; 4-week courses Dh400, hourly lessons from Dh180) A new and active language school touting its services in cross-cultural understanding, Subul Assalam ('Pathways to Peace') can arrange homestays for its longer courses, which are offered in Darija (Moroccan Arabic), modern standard and classical Arabic, as well as Tamazight Berber.

DMG Arabophon   LANGUAGE
(☑0535 60 34 75; www.arabicstudy.com; courses from Dh2500) Runs intensive programs in Darija and modern standard Arabic, as well as shorter courses aimed at travellers: a half-day 'Curious Explorer' (Dh500) and a one-week 'Serious Explorer' (Dh1500). DMG also offers courses in Tamazight Berber. Lessons are offered in English, French, German and Spanish.

Arabic Language Institute   LANGUAGE
(Map p308; ☑0535 62 48 50; www.alif-fes.com; 2 Rue Ahmed Hiba; 3-/6-week courses Dh5600/9900) Offers longer courses aimed at foreigners, and can assist in finding accommodation for students, in apartments or with local families. Lessons are held at the American Language Center.

🚶 Tours

The Fassi authorities have woken to the difficulties tourists have in navigating the medina, and introduced a series of well-signed self-guided walks through the old city. Each highlights different aspects of traditional Fez:

Dark blue Monuments and souqs

Green Andalucian palaces and gardens

Orange Fès el-Jdid

Pale blue Andalucian quarter

Purple Artisanal crafts tour

The head-height signs are easy to follow, showing the direction of the next major landmark, and there are excellent English information boards at regular intervals, although some have been allowed to fall into disrepair. The *Fes Medina Tourist Circuits Guide* accompanies these self-guided walking tours marked throughout the medina, while the excellent *Fez from Bab to Bab: Walks in the Medina* by Hammad Berrada further details 11 different walks, allowing readers to discover otherwise unknown corners and courtyards amid this labyrinth.

An alternative is to hire a guide. As well as pointing out incredible architecture and clandestine corners, guides can answer cultural questions, help overcome language barriers, and – perhaps most importantly – ward off other would-be guides. A full-day tour with an official guide costs Dh250 – always ask to see identification.

The quality of guides can vary considerably, so communication is very important to ensure that you get the best out of the experience. If you're not interested in shopping, say so firmly at the outset, although be aware that the guide who won't take

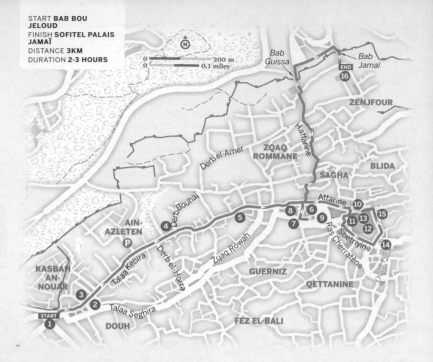

Walking Tour
Mazing Medina

❯ This route takes you from Bab Bou Jeloud to the Kairaouine Mosque, then north to the Sofitel Palais Jamaï. It could take a few hours or all day, depending on the number of distractions.

Unlike much of the rest of the city walls and gates, the main entry, **❶ Bab Bou Jeloud**, is a recent addition, built in 1913. Pass through it and you come upon a hive of activity. The touts and *faux guides* that used to pester visitors here have largely disappeared, but if you need to get your bearings, the street cafes where the street turns towards Talaa Seghira are excellent places for people-watching.

For the tour, take the first left and then right downhill along Talaa Kebira. This part of the street is a produce market – watch out for the camel butchers displaying the heads of their wares. Where the produce ends you're at the **❷ Medersa Bou Inania**, which represents the Merenid building style at its most perfect.

Opposite the entrance to the *medersa* (above eye-level) is a famous 14th-century **❸ water clock** designed by a clockmaker and part-time magician. Carved beams hold brass bowls with water flowing between them to mark the hours, but the secret of its mechanism apparently died with its creator.

Continuing downhill, take the time to slip off the main street to have a look at the many old *funduqs* (caravanserai) on the left hand side of Talaa Kebira. These once hosted merchants and their caravans, and have rooms on several levels around a wide courtyard big enough for both goods and pack animals. A particularly interesting one is **❹ Funduq Kaat Smen**, which specialises in selling more varieties of honey than you could imagine, and vats of *smen*, the rancid butter used in cooking. Try honey and *smen* smeared on bread – it's a singular (but tasty) experience.

About 400m from the Medersa Bou Inania, as you go around an unmistakeable dogleg, you'll catch sight of the pretty, green-tiled minaret of the **5 Chrabliyine Mosque** (named for the slipper-makers who can still be found working in this area) straight ahead.

Still heading downhill, past the shoe sellers and a group of leatherworkers, about 230m from the Gazleane mosque, look out for a right turn onto Derb Fkahrine and a sign indicating the entrance to a tiny tree-filled square known as the **6 henna souq** – if you reach the Dar Saada restaurant, you've gone too far. Nowadays there are more stalls here selling blue Fez pottery than henna, which Moroccan women use to decorate their hands and feet for events such as weddings.

Exiting the henna souq the same way you entered, head south with your back to Dar Saada. After roughly 50m a right turn brings you into **7 Place an-Nejjarine**, a larger square dominated by one of the city's most beautiful fountains and a most impressive *funduq* – now beautifully restored and transformed into the Nejjarine Museum of Wooden Arts & Crafts. The lanes immediately north of the museum form part of the **8 Souq an-Nejjarine** (Carpenters' Souq), where you'll see craftsmen putting finishing touches to glittering thrones used in wedding ceremonies.

From Place an-Nejjarine, continue south and turn left almost immediately down a lane, ducking under the bar that prevents the passage of mules and donkeys. The lane leads between stalls piled high with candles and other offerings, to the entrance of **9 Zawiya Moulay Idriss II**. You may peer into the bright, tiled interior, although non-Muslims may not enter. Moulay Idriss II is highly revered – to Fassis this is the heart of their city.

Afterwards, the simplest thing is to backtrack to Dar Saada on Talaa Kebira. Follow the lane east – over a slight hummock and past haberdashers' stalls – until it ends at a T-intersection about 100m later, where you'll find the **10 Medersa el-Attarine**.

On emerging from the *medersa*, turn left (south). After you've passed the **11 Pâtisserie Kortouba** – a handy stop – the shops come to a sudden end at the walls of the great **12 Kairaouine Mosque & University**. The university claims to be the world's oldest and is surpassed only by Al-Azhar in Cairo as a centre of Muslim learning. Among its many luminaries was

the pre-eminent historian Ibn Khaldun, and you may catch sight of his successors hurrying to lessons.

As you proceed along the university walls anticlockwise, the sound of metalworkers leads you into another small and attractive square, **13 Place as-Seffarine** (Brass-makers' Square). The air rings with the sound of metalwork. Look out for the huge pans and plates that are hired out for wedding parties. With the university walls (and the entrance to its library) still on your left, there is the small **14 Medersa as-Seffarine**, with a studded cedar door, on the square's east side. Built in 1280, it is the oldest *medersa* in Fez, but is in an advanced state of disrepair.

Still following the mosque walls anticlockwise (now heading north) keep a lookout on the right for the 14th-century **15 Funduq Tastawniyine**, with its rickety wooden galleries. Originally the preserve of businessmen from Tetouan, it served for centuries as a hotel and warehouse for travelling merchants.

If you continue around the Kairaouine, you'll pass its ornate north door before arriving back where you started beside the patisserie. From here you can retrace your steps uphill to Bab Bou Jeloud. If you prefer an alternate route, turn south off Talaa Kebira at Ain Allou – this street turns into Talaa Seghira, the medina's other main thoroughfare.

Otherwise, return only as far as Dar Saada, then turn north to reach Bab Guissa in the northern medina. Stick to the wider streets and you'll reach a little square with a disused cinema on its north side. Take the lane heading northwest and keep going up – you'll pass plenty of donkeys carrying sacks from the local cement merchant.

As you near Bab Guissa you can see the late-19th-century **16 Sofitel Palais Jamaï**. What is now a luxury hotel was built by Sidi Mohammed ben Arib al-Jamaï, the grand vizier to Moulay al-Hassan I. Set in well-watered gardens, the former palace is a wonderful place to rest and admire the view. You can catch an onward petit taxi from Bab Guissa.

Every June the **Fès Festival of World Sacred Music** (☑0535 74 06 91; www.fesfesti val.com) brings together music groups and artists from all corners of the globe, and it has become one of the most successful world music festivals around. Based on the pluralism of Moroccan Sufism, the festival has attracted big international stars such as Ravi Shankar, Youssou N'Dour and Salif Keita. Concerts are held in a variety of venues, including the Batha Museum and the square outside Bab Bou Jeloud. While the big names are a draw, equally fascinating are the more intimate concerts held by Morocco's various *tariqas* (Sufi orders). Fringe events include art exhibitions, films and talks at literary cafes. In 2001 the festival was praised by the UN as a major event promoting dialogue between civilisations. Tickets can go like hot cakes and accommodation books up far in advance (often attracting a festival premium) – so organise as far ahead as possible if you plan on attending.

a tourist to a single shop probably hasn't been born yet. It may be necessary to pay an extra Dh50 to Dh100 as a 'no shopping' supplement. If possible, get a recommendation for a guide from other travellers; alternatively, arrange one through the tourist office, Syndicat d'Initiative or the larger hotels. For an alternative take on the medina, **Fez Food** (www.fez-food.com) offers excellent culinary walking tours. **Tours Around Fez** (www.toursaroundfez. com) runs excellent tours in and outside the city, including walking around nearby Mount Zalagh, visiting Berber farms and villages and trying local produce.

The tourist office offers panoramic tours of Fez, taking in the best viewpoints of the city, including Borj Nord and Borj Sud, and the potteries. A 45-minute tour costs Dh200.

TOP CHOICE **Tours Around Fez** PICNICS €€ (☑0649 422951; www.toursaroundfez. com; mountain dinner tour Dh495, min 2 people) Here's your opportunity look down on Fez from afar while dining. Your vehicle whisks you out of the city to the slopes of Mt Zalagh, which offers views over rolling countryside, olive groves and the city itself. Meanwhile, your hosts spread out the carpets and prepare your three-course dinner – best served at sunset for a truly fabulous dining experience. The maximum group size is eight (at which point prices come to Dh350 per guest). Bookings by phone/web only.

✸✦ Festivals & Events

Fez has several festivals that are worth being aware of when you're planning your trip. The Fès Festival of World Sacred Music is the city's internationally famous drawcard, but there are two newer festivals that bear a

visit. Just outside Fez, Sefrou's Cherry Festival every July is worth a day trip (see p326).

Festival of Sufi Culture MUSIC (www.par-chemins.org) The festival debuted in 2007 and hosts a series of events every April including films and lectures, and some spectacular concerts held in the garden of the Batha Museum with Sufi musicians from across the world.

National Festival of Berber Culture MUSIC In July, the festival, run in association with the Institut Royal de la Culture Amazigh, aims to promote and protect Amazigh (Berber) culture. Its program includes musical performances as well as lectures and workshops.

Moussem of Moulay Idriss RELIGIOUS Fez' biggest religious festival is also one of the country's largest. It's currently in September but the date moves according to the Islamic calendar. The *moussem* (festival in honour of a saint) of the city's founder, Moulay Idriss, draws huge crowds. Local artisans create special tributes and there's a huge procession through the medina. Traditional music is played and followers dance and shower the musicians (and onlookers) with orange-blossom water or rosewater.

🛏 Sleeping

Fez doesn't lack for variety in its accommodation options, with everything from simple pensions to boutique riads. Your main choice is whether to stay in the colour and chaos of the medina, or a petit-taxi ride away in the ville nouvelle (where budgets tend to go further). Room rates in Fez are in the higher (city) bracket – see p488 for details. Booking in advance is advised during high season, and especially during the Festival of World Sacred Music in June, when supplements also often apply. Note that although prices here are listed in dirham, many riads actually list (and charge) rooms in euros, so be aware of currency exchange rates when booking.

The agency **Fez Riads** (☎0572 51 33 57; www.fez-riads.com) is a good place to find accommodation in the medina, and donates a percentage of profits to local restoration projects.

MEDINA

Most of the cheapest options are in touching distance of Bab Bou Jeloud, placing you right in the middle of the action. Unless noted, rooms have shared bathrooms at this price range – and don't expect hot water at the lower prices. Many midrange options in the medina, especially the riads and *dars,* edge close to the top-end price bracket. A few places offer simpler rooms at manageable prices. Rates here include breakfast unless mentioned.

TOP CHOICE **Ziyarates Fes** HOMESTAYS € (Map p304; ☎0535 63 46 67; www.ziyaratesfes.com, in French; 35 Sidi Kjih, Talaa Seghira; s/d from Dh200/300) If you really want to experience medina life up close, there might be no better way than through this innovative homestay scheme. Fassi families rent rooms in their homes to welcome foreign guests, while support from the regional tourism authorities ensures the quality of the places signed up. You might practise your Arabic, learn to cook or just help the kids with their homework in this unique cultural exchange. Exact prices vary, but all family homes are listed (with photos) on the organisation's website.

Pension Sekaya GUESTHOUSE € (Map p304; ☎0535 63 73 03; psekaya@hotmail.fr; 16 Sekayit Dymnati, Zqaq Roumane; d/tr Dh 300/400) Relatively deep in the medina (best accessed from Ain Azleten), this is a great budget option for those looking for a traditional medina house experience with a very homely welcome. It's compact, but a 1st-floor balcony running around the courtyard opens things up, and there's a nice roof terrace too.

Riad Verus GUESTHOUSE €€ (Map p304; ☎0535 57 49 41 www.riadverus.com; 1 Derb Arset Bennis, Batha; dm/d/q

Dh280/890/1100; ❂ ⏦) A relatively new player on the budget scene, rooms here seem to be configured to give the maximum flexibility for the best budget. Everything is open and airy inside, and the young owners play well to the backpacker crowd with regular live music and iPod docks in the rooms.

Hôtel Cascade HOTEL € (Map p304; ☎0535 63 84 42; 26 Rue Serrajine, Bab Bou Jeloud; dm Dh80, r Dh160, breakfast Dh20) One of the grand-daddies of the Morocco shoestring hotels, the Cascade still keeps drawing them in. Don't expect much for the price – it's all pretty basic – but if you need to stretch your budget and want to meet plenty of like-minded travellers then this might be the place for you.

Pension Kawtar GUESTHOUSE € (Map p304; ☎0535 74 01 72; pension_kaw@yahoo.fr; Derb Taryana, Talaa Seghira; s/d Dh150/250, d with bathroom Dh300; ⏦) A relatively new player, and well signed in an alley off Talaa Seghira, the Kawtar is a friendly, Moroccan, family-run concern, as much a home as a hostel. Amazingly, there are 10 rooms tucked into the place – those on the ground floor are a bit gloomy, but they get better the closer you get to the roof terrace. Great value for the price.

Pension Batha GUESTHOUSE € (Map p304; ☎0535 74 11 50; 8 Sidi L'Khayat, Batha; r Dh250) Slightly downhill from the main taxi rank in Batha, this is a very likeable place to stay. It's a tall, thin building with lots of stairs leading up to a nice terrace. Rooms are simple, but the place has a homely atmosphere. Not to be confused with the nearby Hôtel Batha.

Pension Campini HOTEL € (Map p304; ☎0535 63 73 42; pensioncampini@gmail.com; Rue Campini, Batha; s/d Dh200/300) A short walk away from the Batha Museum, this is a quieter location slightly outside the medina proper. Rooms are en suite and airy, and had just had a new lick of paint when we visited. There's a small terrace, with views just over the walls of Jnan Sbil (Bou Jeloud Gardens).

Dar Bouânania GUESTHOUSE € (Map p304; ☎0535 63 72 82; darbouanania@gmail.com; 21 Derb Bensalem, Talaa Kebira; s/d Dh200/300, with shower Dh300/400, q Dh600, breakfast Dh30) A popular choice with backpackers, this is a budget-style riad. A traditional house with courtyard, *zellij* tiles and painted woodwork, it has several well-sized rooms on several levels, although as all face inward they can be quite dark at times. Shared bathrooms are clean, and there's a roof terrace.

Dar Victoria
GUESTHOUSE €€
(Map p304; ☑0535 63 00 03; wwwdarvictoria. com; 31 Rue Makhfia, R'cif; r Dh890-1600; 🛜) Situated in a quiet street in up and coming R'cif, Dar Victoria is lovely old restored house. The seven rooms are named after precious stones, and are decorated in chic Moroccan style in soothing colours. The bathrooms are very good. The house itself has a lot of carved plaster, which is rich in Sufi symbolism. A sanctuary, from the moment the host welcomes you with homemade cordial made from an old family recipe.

Hôtel Batha
HOTEL €€
(Map p304; ☑0535 74 10 77; hotelbatha@men ara.ma; Place Batha; s/d Dh495/629; ❋🐾) The great location, room capacity and pool keep the Batha perennially busy. It's a reasonably modern set-up, with fair rooms and cool quiet areas to retreat from the hustle of the medina. Good value.

Hôtel Bab Boujloud
HOTEL €
(Map p304; ☑0535 63 31 18; www.hotelbabbou jloud.com; 49 Place Isesco, Bab Bou Jeloud; s/d Dh200/350; ❋) Fantastically located, this hotel sits just outside Bab Bou Jeloud with all the medina action right on your doorsteps. The rooms are as simple as the price tag suggests, but cosy enough and great value.

Dar el Menia
GUESTHOUSE €€
(Map p304; ☑0535 63 31 64; www.medinafes. com; 7 Derb el Menia, Talaa Kebira; r from Dh780, whole house from Dh1600; 🛜) Dar el Menia is compact townhouse with four rooms tucked off the main drag. It's had a sympathetic restoration job and is relatively restrained in its decor, giving an air of calm the moment you close the door. We liked the addition of the kitchen for guests' use – a great idea, especially if you fancy renting the whole house out.

Riad Zitouna
GUESTHOUSE €€
(Map p304; ☑0535 63 30 02; www.riadzitou nafes.com; 5 Derb Rami, Zqaq Labghal, Qettanine; r Dh880-990; ❋🛜🐾) A new and fresh addition to the Fez townhouse scene, Riad Zitouna ('house of olives') wants to do things its own way. Zellij tiling abounds, but the

owners have chosen bright non-Moroccan colours, and decorated rooms in a veritably pan-African style. The plunge pool and hammam finish things off nicely: expect good things here.

Dar Bensouda
GUESTHOUSE €€
(Map p304; ☑0535 63 89 39; www.riaddarben souda.com; 14 Zqaq Labghal, Qettanine; r Dh850-1700; 🛜) A converted palace, Dar Bensouda is the most impressive medina restoration project we've seen in a while. Enter into a large column-flanked courtyard and admire the attention to detail here and in the immaculate rooms. The scale here is grand without being overwhelming, and the service excellent. Make sure you check out the photo album and history of the building to get a full insight into the rebuilding project.

Palais Amani
PALACE HOTEL €€€
(Map p304; ☑0535 63 32 09; www.palaisamani. com; 12 Derb el Miter, Oued Zerhoune; r from Dh2000, ste from Dh3000; ❋🛜) On the eastern edge of the medina, this gorgeously converted palace is barely a century old, but has been turned into a truly luxurious retreat. Pad around the chic rooms in your complimentary Moroccan slippers and robe, have a drink in the terrace bar or dine in a courtyard garden big enough to host a small forest of trees.

Dar Fes Medina
GUESTHOUSE €€
(Map p304; ☑0535 63 83 92; www.darfesmedina. com; Derb Mokri, Ziat; s/d/tr Dh550/660/880; ❋) There's a very clever trick being played here: walk through the doors and you think you're finding yourself in a restored medina townhouse, but this *dar* is a brand new build. You get the best of both worlds – slightly more spacious and modern rooms, but the whole thing is brushed with a pleasingly traditional veneer. It's location near Bab Ziat gives another medina rarity: taxis can drop you right outside the front door.

Dar El Hana
GUESTHOUSE €€
(Map p304; ☑0535 63 58 54; www.moroccanget away.com; 22 Rue Ferrance Couicha, Chrabliyine; r from Dh800; 🛜) If there's a cosier and more intimate guesthouse in Fez than this *dar,* we'd like to know about it. There are just three rooms (sleeping a maximum of eight altogether), all charmingly finished and presented: we fell for the 'secret' windows allowing you to spy on the street, and the open-air shower on the terrace. This is a real home from home, and it's possible to

rent out the entire house so you can fully indulge your own fantasies of medina life.

Riad Lune et Soleil   GUESTHOUSE €€
(Map p304; ☑0535 63 45 23; www.riadluneet soleil.com; 3 Derb Skalia, Batha; r Dh800-1200; ❉🛜) Hospitality is all at this riad, where you'll be swept past the lemon trees in the courtyard and made to feel impossibly at home. Each room is a cornucopia, filled with the evidence of a lifetime of collecting everything from old postcards and embroidery to carvings and metalwork – and each item with a story behind it. It's not a museum though; there's plenty of comfort too, and some rooms have their own Jacuzzi. You might just make it downstairs for dinner – from one of the best kitchens in the medina.

Dar Seffarine   GUESTHOUSE €€
(Map p304; ☑0671 11 35 28; www.darseffarine. com; 14 Derb Sbaalouyat, R'cif; r from Dh780; ❉🛜) If you check into Dar Seffarine, ask to see the photo album of its restoration – it's the only way you'll believe that such a fabulous building was ever a complete wreck. The central courtyard is positively opulent, with pillars and painted plasterwork reaching skywards, while rooms are more understated with simple plain wood and fabrics to decorate them – only the suite with the painted domed ceiling makes a palatial exception. There's a pleasant terrace, and a more intimate side courtyard off the kitchen to relax in. The *dar* is a short walk from Bab R'cif.

Dar Dmana   GUESTHOUSE €€
(Map p304; ☑0535 74 09 17; www.riaddardmana. net; 21 Rue Sournas; r/ste Dh1200/1800; ❉) With 14 rooms, this *dar* successfully bridges the gap between traditional Moroccan house and hotel. The ground floor has decor that's stepped out of a palace restaurant, but the high covered courtyard (with fine carved cedar balustrade) keeps things airy. After all this, the rooms are more modern and restrained, but with enough Moroccan styling to remind you where you are.

Dar Attajali   GUESTHOUSE €€
(Map p304; ☑0535 63 77 28; www.attajalli.com; Derb Qettana, Zqaq Rommane; r Dh990-1430; ❉🛜) Dar Attajali is a magnificent testament to the art of patient and sympathetic restoration. Everything has been done to maintain the building's integrity, using a minimum of modern techniques and chemicals, while producing a supremely comfort-

able guesthouse. Decoration is set off with gently colour-themed Fassi fabrics – colours further reflected in the planting of the terrace roof garden, and all designed to get you instantly relaxing (as if the organic, locally sourced breakfasts didn't get your day off to a good enough start).

Dar Roumana   GUESTHOUSE €€
(Map p304; ☑0535 74 16 37; www.darroumana. com; 30 Derb el-Amer, Zqaq Roumane; r Dh950-1620; ❉🛜) One of those bigger-on-the-inside townhouses, Dar Roumana will always win fans by virtue of its beautiful restoration job and gorgeous roof terrace commanding one of the finest views across the Fez medina (perfect for taking breakfast or sampling the well-thought-out dinner menus). That's if you even leave the rooms, which are perfect romantic hideaways. There's a close attention to detail at play too: there are even personalised toiletries in the bathrooms.

Riad 9   GUESTHOUSE €€€
(Map p304; ☑0535 94 76 10; www.riad9.com; 9 Derb Lamsside, Zqaq el-Maa; r Dh1100-2200; 🛜) This is a tiny gem of a guesthouse, and when we learned that the owner is a designer and fashion historian, we weren't at all surprised. The decoration is idiosyncratic but lots of fun – witness the room with dentists' chairs and a wall full of antique luggage. At night, the many windows looking into the courtyard are lit with candles, turning the whole place into a glittering jewel box. We're looking forward to Riad 9's companion restaurant, opening around the corner sometime after this book goes to press.

Riad Maison Bleue   GUESTHOUSE €€€
(Map p304; ☑0535 74 18 73; www.maisonbleue. com; 33 Derb el Mitter, Ain-Azleten; s/d from Dh1700/1900; P❉🛜❉) You have to be careful not to get lost in this riad – it's four houses knocked together and even extended across the street. Start in the orange-tree-clad, Andalucian-style courtyard, then find your way to any of the 13 rooms, possibly stopping en route at the private spa, bar, dining salon and fashionably dark and plush 'Blue Lounge', where there is more eating and drinking on offer. If you don't want to crash in your room, chill on the terrace with its fine views to Borj Nord.

Riad Fès   GUESTHOUSE €€€
(Map p304; ☑0535 94 76 10; www.riadfes. com; Derb ibn Slimane, Zerbtana; r/ste from

THE FOUNTAINS OF FEZ

It seems like you can barely turn a corner in the Fez medina without coming across a *seqqâya* (public fountain) – Fassis have historically had something of an obsession for them. It was largely the Almoravid (1061–1147) and Almohad (1147–1248) dynasties that were the great water engineers. To supply water to their cities they diverted rivers, created lakes and constructed vast canal systems. While they did this across the country, fountain construction reached its zenith in imperial Fez.

There are well over 60 public fountains inside the medina. Along with the hammam, they are usually located near the neighbourhood mosque. Many were paid for by princes and wealthy merchants. Some of these fountains are simple basins against a wall. The majority are beautifully decorated structures of coloured tiles, often under a canopy of intricately carved wood. One of the finest is the Nejjarine fountain. Built in the 18th century, it features *zellij* (tilework) and stucco that form patterns as delicate as lacework.

Many fountains are still widely used for water collection and washing by their neighbourhoods. Those you see abandoned are likely to suffer from a broken mains pipe somewhere beneath the city (others are directly spring-fed). The booking agency **Fez Riads** (www.fez-riads.com) puts a percentage of its profits into restoring and maintaining many of the medina's most neglected fountains.

And if you think that a love of fountains is restricted to the medina, check out the ultramodern and sparkly fountains recently installed along Ave Hassan II in the ville nouvelle.

Dh1700/3000; ✹☎✉) This labyrinthine riad blends ancient and modern with impressive panache. The older section shows off the best of traditional decor, while the newer quarters wouldn't look out of place in a Parisian boutique hotel yet remain unmistakably Moroccan. It has a trendy courtyard bar, restaurant, hammam and a plethora of terraces.

Riad Laaroussa
GUESTHOUSE €€€
(Map p304; ☎0674 18 76 39; www.riad-laaroussa.com; 3 Derb Bechara, Talaa Seghira; r Dh1400-2800; ✹☎) Although a garden is meant to be the defining feature of a riad, it still comes as something of a surprise to pass through the dark entrance here to meet such a large green space, with its orange trees and softly playing fountain. Instantly relaxed, you continue to the fine rooms decorated with modern art and unusual furniture that make it clear the owners haven't just stolen ideas from this month's Moroccan style magazine. The new in-house hammam is open to nonguests.

Riad Les Oudayas
GUESTHOUSE €€€
(Map p304; ☎0535 63 63 03; www.lesoudayas.com; 4 Derb el Hamiya, Ziat; r from Dh1400; ✹☎✉) The Moroccan owner of this riad is a Paris-based designer, and it certainly shows in its careful blend of traditional styles and

modern design aesthetic in everything from the downstairs salons to the chic but comfortable bedrooms. Steps lead down from street level into the courtyard garden, with a plunge pool and the riad's own hammam leading off it. Up top there's a large terrace, but if you crave privacy, two of the five rooms have private terraces.

Ryad Mabrouka
GUESTHOUSE €€
(Map p304; ☎0535 63 63 45; www.ryadmabrouka.com; 25 Derb el-Mitter, Ain-Azleten; r Dh1150-1450, ste Dh1600-2000; ✹☎✉) An old favourite and early player on the Fez riad scene, Mabrouka is a meticulously restored Arab-Andalucian townhouse. The courtyard, with its stucco, mosaics, magnificent cedar doors and babbling fountain, opens onto a pleasant garden of flowers and trees. There are seven rooms, decked out with tiled floors and Berber fabrics. Enjoy a simple breakfast or an all-out Moroccan feast on the veranda overlooking the medina.

Sofitel Palais Jamaï
GUESTHOUSE €€€
(Map p304; ☎0535 63 43 31; www.sofitel.com; Bab Guissa; s/d from Dh1950/2600; ✹@✉) Once the pleasure dome of a late-19th-century vizier to the sultan, this grand hotel is set in Andalucian gardens overlooking the medina. Its rooms have had

a recent makeover to keep it in line with the trendy medina guesthouses, although some parts still suffer bland international decoration. Nonguests should still visit to enjoy a sunset drink on the terrace.

VILLE NOUVELLE

In the ville nouvelle, room rates drop considerably compared to the more popular medina, so much of the time you can get midrange service at budget prices. The ville-nouvelle hotel scene is currently undergoing a mini-boom, with several new hotels due to open between Place de la Resistance (Fiat) and the old city, including the five-star Atlas Fes (with a modern shopping complex attached) and four-star Barceló.

Hôtel Splendid
HOTEL €

(Map p308; ☑0535 62 21 48; splendid@iam.net.ma; 9 Rue Abdelkarim el-Khattabi; s/d Dh350/450; ✳ ☀) Although in the budget category, this hotel makes a good claim for three stars. It's all modern and tidy, with good bathrooms and comfy beds, plus a pool for the hot days and a bar for the evenings. There's a dining room, but breakfast isn't included in the price. Excellent value.

Hôtel Central
HOTEL €

(Map p308; ☑0535 62 23 33; 50 Rue Brahim Roudani; s/d Dh140/180) A bright and airy budget option just off busy Blvd Mohammed V. All rooms have external toilets, but even those without a shower have their own sinks. It's good value and popular so there's sometimes not enough rooms to go around.

Hôtel Olympic
HOTEL €

(Map p308; ☑0535 93 26 82; fax 055 932665; cnr Blvd Mohammed V & Rue 3; s/d incl breakfast Dh275/350; ✳) A handy choice near the central market. Rooms are nondescript but comfortable, and come equipped with bathroom, TV, phone and stylish brass bedsteads. Its central location means it's often heavily booked (it's popular with tour groups), so call in advance.

Hôtel de la Paix
HOTEL €

(Map p308; ☑0535 62 50 72; www.hotellapaixfes.com, in French; 44 Ave Hassan II; s/d Dh320/425; ✳) Cast from the bland tourist-class mould, this place is nevertheless good value for the money. Rooms are solidly comfortable, with TV and bathroom; there's also a bar and a reasonable restaurant.

Hôtel Mounia
HOTEL €

(Map p308; ☑0535 62 48 38; www.hotelmouniafes.ma, in French; 60 Blvd Zerktouni; s/d incl breakfast from Dh351/462; ✳) A *zellij* lobby guides you into this modern and classy hotel that's popular with tour groups. Rooms are bright and tidy, with satellite TV. The restaurant is fair, and there's a smoky bar with plenty of water pipes. Rooms on corridors near the bar can be noisy. Staff are helpful, and good discounts are often available.

Hôtel Royal
HOTEL €

(Map p308; ☑0535 62 46 56; 36 Ave Soudan; s/d with bathroom Dh 120/150, with shower only Dh100/140) Well-situated near Place Florence, this is one of the more reliable if old-fashioned budget options. A few of the bathrooms are a bit clunky (hot water in mornings only), but rooms are large and many come with balconies.

Youth Hostel
HOSTEL €

(Map p308; ☑0535 62 40 85; 18 Rue Abdeslam Serghini; dm Dh50; ☺gate open 8-10am, noon-3pm & 6-10pm) One of the better youth hostels in Morocco, the Fez branch is well looked after, and right in the centre of the ville nouvelle. Tidy rooms and facilities (including Western-style toilets) are superbly clean. If you're not a Hostelling International (HI) member, there's a Dh5 surcharge. Cold showers mean that you should look to hammams – particularly in winter.

Hôtel Menzeh Zalagh
HOTEL €€€

(Map p308; ☑0535 62 55 31; menzeh.zalagh@fesnet.net.ma; 10 Rue Mohammed Diouri; s/d incl breakfast Dh950/1300; ✳ ☀) This four-star hotel has a great location, stretched along a low ridge in a sinuous wave with amazing views across to Fès el-Bali, yet is convenient to the centre. Rooms are full of modern comforts with a splash of traditional Moroccan decor, and many come with balconies.

Hôtel Menzeh Fes
HOTEL €€€

(Map p308; ☑0535 94 38 49; menzeh.zalagh@fesnet.net.ma; 28 Rue Abdeslam Serghini; s/d incl breakfast Dh950/1300; ✳ ☀) Just up the road, Menzah Zalagh's sister offers virtually identical facilities, albeit with slightly smaller rooms.

✗ Eating

Dining in Fez is something to be taken seriously. Fassi cuisine is famed across Morocco, and there are plenty of places in the medina to choose from. Popular with tour groups and their guides are the so-called 'palace restaurants' – dinner and show in lavish surroundings, usually with plain set menus and hefty price tags. A more intimate experience can be had dining at a riad, many of which are open to nonguests and offer excellent fare. A good range of cheaper places can be found around Bab Bou Jeloud. The ville nouvelle has more options, including more non-Moroccan menus.

MEDINA

If it's just a snack you're after, you don't have to walk far in the medina to find someone selling food – tiny cell-like places grilling brochettes or cooking up cauldrons of soup, sandwich shops or just a guy with a pushcart selling peanut cookies. The top of Talaa Kebira has quite a cluster of options, otherwise follow your nose.

TOP CHOICE **Café Clock** CAFE €
(Map p304; ☑0535 63 78 55; www.cafe clock.com; Derb el-Mergana, Talaa Kebira; mains Dh55-80; ☺9am-10pm; ☺) Even we need a break from Moroccan food every now and then, and Café Clock remains love at first sight. In a restored townhouse, this funky place has a refreshing menu with offerings such as falafel, grilled sandwiches, some interesting vegetarian options, a monstrously large camel burger, and delicious cakes and tarts. Better still, the 'Clock Culture' program includes calligraphy and conversation classes, a lecture program and sunset concerts every Sunday (cover charge around Dh20), attracting a good mix of locals, expats and tourists.

Dar Touria MOROCCAN €€€
(Map p304; ☑0663 03 71 02; Derb el Kateb, Zqaq Roumane; set meal Dh200) Tucked right into the medina, this traditional house-turned-restaurant is worth hunting out. Go for the set menu and go on a very empty stomach: feast is a better description and we've rarely seen so much great food for the price. It's close to plenty of guesthouses, and staff are often happy to walk you home if you think you might get lost in the lanes.

Chameau Bleu MOROCCAN €€
(Map p304; ☑0535 63 89 91; 1 Derb Tariana; mains Dh55-130; ☺lunch & dinner) Well-signed just off Talaa Kebira, Chameau Bleu is a converted medina house on several levels, with tables all the way up to the roof terrace. There are tajines a plenty, although

we found the grilled meat and fish dishes to be particular winners; we've also had several good reports about the standard of the pasta on offer.

Bou Jeloud Restaurants LOCAL €
(Map p304; Rue Serrajine; mains Dh30-70; ☺8am-11pm) Walking in from Bab Bou Jeloud to the top of Talaa Seghira, you run the gauntlet of a host of restaurants touting for business. They're all pretty much of muchness, offering plenty of tajines, couscous, grilled meat and the like. They're also great places to sit and people-watch over a mint tea, so pick one you fancy and while away an hour or so. If you particularly want a view, try **Le Kasbah** for its roof terrace, but the cost of drinks is double if you're not eating.

B'sara Stalls LOCAL €
(Map p304; Talaa Kebira; soup Dh4) The Fassi speciality of *b'sara* (garlic and butter-bean soup) shouldn't be missed. Served from hole-in-the-wall places throughout the medina from huge cauldrons, our favourites are at the top of Talaa Kebira (there are good places in Acherbine too). Perfect fuel for exploring the city, the soup is ladled into rough pottery bowls and served with a hunk of bread and dash of olive oil.

Dar Anebar MOROCCAN €€€
(Map p304; ☑0535 63 57 87; 25 Derb el-Miter, Zqaq Roumane; mains from Dh120; ☺from 7.30pm) Another good riad for dining, where you'll eat in truly fine surroundings, in the splendid courtyard, or one of the cosy salons. The menu is strictly Moroccan, but of the highest standard, and you can accompany dinner with a bottle of wine.

Fès et Gestes CAFE €€
(Map p304; ☑0535 63 85 32; 39 Arsat el Hamoumi, Ziat; meals around Dh90; ☺noon-9.30pm, closed Wed) In a bustling medina, this converted French colonial house is a positive oasis: step through the gates into its pretty, richly planted garden with a trickling fountain, and the cares of the day melt away. Ideal for light lunches, full tajine-style dinners, or just a refreshing tea or juice to recharge the batteries in the cool green shade.

Dar Roumana MEDITERRANEAN €€€
(Map p304; ☑0535 74 16 37; 30 Derb el Amer, Zqaq Roumane; set menu Dh300; ☺7.30-9.30pm Tue-Sat) As reliably excellent as you'd expect from a guesthouse whose owner

is a cordon-bleu chef, the menu here is Mediterranean with a Moroccan slant, and frequently takes cues from the *dar's* name: house of pomegranates. Eat in the courtyard or on the wonderful terrace in fine weather. Alcohol is served, but walk-in diners can't be catered for, so call in advance for a reservation.

La Maison Bleue
MOROCCAN €€€
(Map p304; ☎0535 63 60 52; 2 Place de l'Istiqlal; set menu incl wine Dh550; ⊙dinner from 7.30pm) Reservations are necessary at this elegant riad restaurant. The setting is intimate and romantic, with diners serenaded by an oud player (replaced by livelier Gnawa song and dance at the end of the evening). You'll be treated to an array of cooked salads, tajines, couscous and *bastilla* (savoury pastries), plus filo-pastry desserts. Top marks for presentation and atmosphere.

Aji Chouf
PIZZA €
(Map p304; ☎0535 63 51 78; 17 Derb Mokri, Ziat; pizzas Dh35-65) A dial-out takeaway pizza place in the medina – can it be true? Yes it can, although we wouldn't discount actually walking to the restaurant in question. The pizzas are the closest we've come to proper Italian pizzas in Fez, but there are other interesting surprises in the good salads and terrines.

Snail Stand
LOCAL €
(Map p304; cnr Talaa Seghira & Derb el-Horra; snails Dh5) This permanent stand is a good place to fill up on a molluscan snack – the ultimate in pre-packaged fast food. Grab a pin to pluck the beasts out of their shells, then slurp down the aromatic broth. Delicious!

Najmat Souafine
MOROCCAN €€€
(Map p304; ☎0662 34 88 19; Oued Souafine, Ziat; lunch/dinner Dh120/150) The name means Souafine Star – a confident name but one that this stylish modern medina restaurant more than lives up to. Moroccan dishes are fresher and more inventive than you'd normally expect, blending traditional and contemporary palates and relying more on what's good in the souq that day than attempting a set menu. More than worth exploring.

Famille Restaurant Berrada
MOROCCAN €
(Map p304; ☎0662 34 88 19; 57 Sagha el Achebine; mains around Dh40; ⊙Sat-Thu) 'Famille restaurant' says it all here – a small medina place run with much hearty cheer. Every-thing is very traditional, but they're used to seeing tourists too, keeping dishes turned over quickly and inviting diners into the kitchen to taste the days selections before ordering.

Cremerie La Place
CAFE €
(Map p304; Place as-Seffarine; ⊙7.30am-8pm) Put a cafe in one of the most interesting spots in the medina, and you have a near perfect combination. Over juice, tea, coffee and pastries, the parade passes before you, accompanied by the tapping of the square's coppersmiths.

Fez Lounge
LOUNGE €€
(Map p302; ☎0535 63 30 97; www.fezlounge. com; 95 Zqaq Rowah, Chrabliyine; mains Dh50-80; ⊙11am-10pm) A funky lounge that fancies itself in London or Barcelona. Come here for two things: light meals of savoury tarts, *pastilla* and *briouates* (stuffed filo-pastry rolls), or to chill away the time slumped in the low seats gently puffing on a water pipe.

Mezzanine
TAPAS BAR €€
(Map p302; ☎0535 63 34 30; 17 Kasbah Chams; tapas selection from Dh100, per dish around Dh30; ⊙noon-1am) Opposite the entrance to the Jnane Sbil gardens slightly away from Bou Jeloud Sq, this tapas bar brings a bit of city chic to the medina. With modern Moroccan furniture and *tadelakt* (smooth lime plaster) walls, the setting is consciously cool. Order as you like from a good selection of Moroccan- and Mediterranean-styled tapas, and wrap things up with a sweet dessert on the lovely roof terrace. Alcohol is served.

Médina Café
MOROCCAN €€
(Map p304; ☎0535 63 34 30; 6 Derb Mernissi, Bab Bou Jeloud; mains Dh70-100; ⊙8am-10pm) Just outside Bab Bou Jeloud, this small restaurant is an oasis of serenity, decorated in *tadelakt*. During the day it's a decent place to visit for a quick bite or a fruit juice; in the evening, it has a more interesting range of tajines and couscous than most places offer.

Talaa Kebira Market
SELF-CATERING €
(Map p304) Tucked inside Bab Bou Jeloud, this is a good second choice, and ideally located.

R'cif Market
SELF-CATERING €
(Map p304; inside Bab R'cif; ⊙Sat-Thu) Those who shop for fresh produce in the medina know that R'cif is the best place to go – its

traders always have the freshest fruit, vegetables and meat.

VILLE NOUVELLE

For quick, filling meals, there are a few cheap eats on or just off Blvd Mohammed V, especially around the central market. You'll also find a good choice of sandwich places around Place Yacoub al-Mansour.

Chicken Mac   LOCAL €

(Map p308; Ave Lalla Meriem; mains around Dh30; ☺9am-11pm) Several eateries seem to run into each other along this strip in a continuously busy row of tables and chairs on the street. Chicken Mac is the last one away from Hassan II, and quickly serves up generous plates of rotisserie chicken, kebabs, fried fish, bowls of *harira* (lentil soup) and other cheap, filling meals.

Restaurant Marrakech   MOROCCAN €

(Map p308; ✆0535 93 08 76; 11 Rue Omar el-Mokhtar; mains from Dh55; ✳) A charming restaurant that goes from strength to strength behind thick wooden doors. Red *tadelakt* walls and dark furniture, with a cushion-strewn salon at the back, add ambience, while the menu's variety refreshes the palate, with dishes such as chicken tajine with apple and olive, or lamb with aubergine and peppers (there's also a set three-course menu).

Maison Blanche   FRENCH €€€

(Map p302; ✆0535 94 40 73; 12 Rue Ahmed Chaouki; mains Dh140-220) Making a strong bid for Fez' classiest restaurant, Maison Blanche is all about cool stylish minimalism: the modern furniture and rough-hewn stone tiling give it the air of a Bond villain's lair. Food has a strong French classical influence and service is excellent (as is the wine list). Retire to the upstairs bar at the end of the evening or swing by in the middle of the day for the Dh200 lunch menu.

Fez Café   FRENCH €

(✆0664 64 76 79; 13 Akbat Sbaa, Douh; mains around Dh80; ☺Tue-Sun) A charming new medina restaurant set in a wonderful garden. The set-up is relaxed bistro-style, and dishes are a delicious seasonal mix of French, Italian and Moroccan. Sunday night offers up great pizzas from a wood-fired oven.

Kaï Taï   JAPANESE, THAI €€

(Map p302; ✆0535 65 17 00; 12 Rue Ahmed Chaouki; sushi Dh50-105; maki rolls Dh20-25; ☺lunch & dinner; ✳) Come to Fez and eat sushi? Why not? With suitably minimalist surroundings, Kaï Taï carries off the challenge with aplomb. Choose individual sushi or tempura (battered seafood or vegetable) dishes from a wide selection or grab a mix through the set menus. An extensive Thai menu also adds a chilli-zing to palates jaded by one tajine too many.

Chez Vittorio   ITALIAN €€

(Map p308; ✆0535 62 47 30; 21 Rue Brahim Roudani; mains from Dh80, pizza or pasta from Dh56) This dependable favourite covers the rustic Italian restaurant angle well, right down to the candles and checked cloths. The food is good value, and while the initial service can be a bit creaky your meal tends to arrive in a trice. Go for the pizzas or steak, as the pasta often disappoints. You can also enjoy a glass of wine with your meal.

Restaurant Zagora

MOROCCAN, INTERNATIONAL €€

(Map p308; ✆0535 94 06 86; 5 Blvd Mohammed V; mains Dh80-100) Just off the southern end of Blvd Mohammed V, this perennial restaurant is popular with tour groups and locals alike. Both the wine list and menu are equally broad, although the pleasant setting (complete with oud player) means that both food and drink attract a sizeable surcharge.

Crémerie Skali   CAFE €

(Map p308; Blvd Mohammed V; breakfast around Dh20; ☺6am-10pm) With a good corner location, this is an ideal stop for breakfast – one that's popular with office workers and families alike. As well as pastries and juice, it can rustle up some mean scrambled eggs.

Central Market   SELF-CATERING €

(Map p308; Blvd Mohammed V; ☺8.30am-2.30pm) If you're in the ville nouvelle in need of fresh fruit and vegies, spices, nuts, olives or a parcel of delicious dates, you can't beat the ville nouvelle's central market. It also has a couple of good cheese stalls and there are alcohol shops around the corner.

🍸 Drinking

It can seem as if the main occupation in the ville nouvelle is sitting in cafes nursing a coffee and croissant. Blvd Mohammed V and Ave Hassan II have the greatest concentration, but you don't have to go far to grab a table, order a drink and watch the day unfold. In the medina, many of the res-

Want to learn how cook like a proper Moroccan chef? We caught up with Souad Maidja of Fez' Clock Kitchen (p309) to get the inside track.

What was the first thing you learnt to cook? Fried fish with a simple salad. I'm from Nador on the coast, so we eat a lot of fish. Fried fish and fish tajines.

Who taught you? My mother. When I got married, I moved to Fez and lived with my husband's family for six months. My mother-in-law taught me about Fassi cooking, which is to say, the best Moroccan cooking there is.

What were the first things she taught you? *Harira,* a traditional soup. It's such an important dish, I was embarrassed that I didn't know how to cook it already! And then *pastilla,* which is thin sheets of pastry around layers of pigeon or chicken. It's a mix of sweet and savoury. I was so happy to learn this as it's such an important dish.

The mix of sweet and savoury seems important in Moroccan food. Yes. We serve guests something sugary first for hospitality so that they come back! Then the main dish is savoury.

What's your favourite dish to cook? I really love a tajine of chicken with olives and preserved lemons.

When you teach tourists to cook Moroccan food, you start in the market first. I like to show our traditional produce, as there are lots of things they aren't familiar with, so I explain what everything is. Products like orange-blossom water, which we use a lot, and herbs that we use for cosmetics as well as in food. I also get to learn a lot from talking to the market sellers – it's like travelling all over Morocco just in the souq.

What do people particularly like cooking? Hand-rolled couscous is very popular. It's a long process, steaming the grains several times. It's totally different to the couscous they might have at home.

What surprises them most? People always ask why we don't cook tajines in a tajine [dish]. It takes such a long time and you need to cook over wood or charcoal. We're modern people – a pressure cooker is much better! The tajine dish is often just for serving.

Any problems? People can sometimes get a bit frustrated as I make them do everything in a totally Moroccan way. They have to chop and peel vegetables by hand like I do, not using a chopping board. Just a knife! But they laugh about it and all get there in the end.

Finally, when you're not teaching cookery, what do you love to eat yourself? It has to be couscous, because it's always a big family feast. But I prefer it when someone else cooks! At home I like light, easy food – a simple bowl of *harira* is wonderful.

taurants around Bab Bou Jeloud double as cafes, otherwise hole-in-the-wall places are often the order of the day.

Hôtel Batha   BAR
(Map p304; Place Batha) There are a couple of options for drinks in this handily located medina hotel. The bar by the pool catches the overspill from the Churchill Bar, which is inside the hotel and in winter even features a log fire to warm yourself. At the back of the hotel (side entrance), the outside Consul Bar is a more relaxed place for late-night drinks, and has its own disco until midnight (closed Monday).

Riad Fès   BAR
(Map p304; 5 Derb ibn Slimane) The classiest place for a drink in the whole city, the courtyard bar of Riad Fès is a delight. Stucco columns catch the light reflected off the central pool, and soft music plays while you sit at the glass bar or slump into the cushions. There's a good range of beer and spirits, plus wine available by the glass. Open to the elements, it's a little cold in winter, but fashionably cool in summer.

FASSI POTTERY

Ceramics seem to be everywhere in Fez – from the distinctive blue pottery to the intricate mosaics decorating fountains and riads. **Art Naji** (☎0535 66 91 66; www.artnaji. net; Ain Nokbi; ⊙8am-6pm) is the place to go to buy the real deal. You can see the entire production process, from pot-throwing to the painstaking hand painting and laying out of *zellij* (tilework) – it's a joy to behold. The potteries are about 500m east of Bab el-Ftouh, an easy trip in a petit taxi – look for the plumes of black smoke produced by olive pits, which burn at the right temperature for firing the clay. You can even commission a mosaic and arrange for it to be shipped home.

Maison Blanche BAR
(Map p302; 12 Rue Ahmed Chaouki) Dark leather, stylishly rough stone walls and a well-stocked bar make this place the perfect ville-nouvelle retreat for a classy drink or two.

Mezzanine BAR
(Map p302; 17 Kasbah Chams; ⊙noon-1am) Scoring highly on the fashion meter and for late opening, this bar is more Ibiza than Moulay Idriss, and popular with the hip young Fassi crowd. The terrace overlooking Jnan Sbil gardens is a good place to chill with a beer or cocktail, and there's tapas too if you want some finger food.

Sofitel Palais Jamaï BAR
(Map p304; Bab Guissa) A great place for a sundowner, the Palais Jamaï has a great terrace looking out across old Fez: an ideal way to finish up a day in the medina. Drinks are slightly more expensive before dinner, but you can help yourself to as many free bar snacks as you like.

☆ Entertainment

Live-music buffs know the best time to visit Fez is festival time. Café Clock (see p318) has regular Sunday sunset concerts worth checking out.

Institut Français (☎0535 62 39 21; www.institutfrancaisfes.com; 33 Rue Loukili) organises a packed program of films, concerts, exhibitions and plays.

🔒 Shopping

Fez is the artisanal capital of Morocco. The choice of crafts is wide, quality is high, and prices are competitive, so take your time to shop around. As usual, it's best to seek out the little shops off the main tourist routes (principally Talaa Kebira and Talaa Seghira in the medina).

For leather, the area around the tanneries, unsurprisingly, has the best selection of goods.

In the medina, there are many well-restored riads and *funduqs* that have been converted into carpet showrooms. While they certainly offer a great opportunity to sit with a mint tea in spectacular surroundings and look at some fabulous rugs, the hard sell is like no other place in Morocco. You can pick up some wonderful pieces, but also pay over the odds for factory-made rubbish.

Information

Dangers & Annoyances

Although Fez is safe in comparison to Western cities of the same size, it's not really safe to walk on your own in the medina late at night, especially for women. Knife-point robberies are not unknown. Hotels and many restaurants are usually happy to provide an escort on request if you're out late.

Fez has long been notorious for its *faux guides* (unofficial guides) and carpet-shop hustlers, all after their slice of the tourist dirham. *Faux guides* tend to congregate around Bab Bou Jeloud, the main western entrance to the medina, although crackdowns by the authorities have greatly reduced their numbers and hassle.

Even many official guides will suggest visitors turn their tour into a shopping trip, and the pressure to buy can be immense. Fez' carpet sellers are masters of their game. If you really don't want to buy, it might be best not to enter the shop at all: once the parade of beautiful rugs begins, even the hardest-minded of tourists can be convinced to buy something they didn't really want (honeyed words suggesting that you could always sell the carpet later on eBay at vast profit should be treated with extreme scepticism). It's also worth remembering that any time you enter a shop with a guide, the price of the goods immediately goes up to cover their commission. Shopping in Fez needn't be a battle – indeed it's best treated as a game – but it's worth being prepared.

The touts who used to hang about Fez train station to pick up custom have now taken to boarding trains to Fez, often at Sidi Kacem junction. Be particularly aware of overly friendly young men approaching you claiming to be students or teachers returning to Fez – they'll often have 'brothers' who have hotels, carpet shops or similar.

Internet Access
Wi-fi is common across most midrange accommodation and above.

Cyber Batha (Map p304; Derb Douh; per hr Dh10; ☺9am-10pm) Has English as well as French keyboards.

Cyber Club (Map p308; Blvd Mohammed V; per hr Dh6; ☺9am-10pm)

Teleboutique Cyber Club (Map p308; Blvd Mohammed V; per hr Dh7; ☺9am-11pm) Above téléboutique on corner.

Media
L'Agenda Free bimonthly listings magazine (in French) produced by the regional tourism board. Available at the tourist office and some riads and restaurants.

Medical Services
Hôpital Ghassani (Map p302; ☑0535 62 27 77) One of the city's biggest hospitals; located east of the ville nouvelle in the Dhar Mehraz district.

Night Pharmacy (Map p308; ☑0535 62 34 93; Ave Moulay Youssef; ☺9pm-6am) Located in the north of the ville nouvelle; staffed by a doctor and a pharmacist.

Money
There are plenty of banks (with ATMs) in the ville nouvelle along Blvd Mohammed V, virtually all offering foreign exchange. There's not much happening in the medina, with these useful exceptions:

Banque Populaire (Map p304; Bab Bou Jeloud; ☺8.45am-noon & 2.45-6pm Mon-Thu, 8.45am-noon Sat) ATM and foreign exchange.

Société Générale (Map p304; Talaa Seghira; ☺8.45am-noon & 2.45-6pm Mon-Thu, 8.45-11am Fri, 8.45am-noon Sat) ATM and foreign exchange.

Post
Main post office (Map p308; cnr Ave Hassan II & Blvd Mohammed V) Poste restante is at the far left; the parcels office is through a separate door.

Post office (Map p304; Place Batha) Located in the medina; also has an ATM.

Tourist Information
There is no tourist information situated in the medina.

Syndicat d'Initiative (Tourist Information Office; Map p308; ☑0535 62 34 60; Place Mohammed V) Not always open, and not always helpful when it is.

Travel Agencies
Carlson Wagonlit (Map p308; ☑0535 62 29 58; fax 035 624436) Behind Central Market; useful for flights and ferries.

Websites
Culture Vultures (http://culturevulturesfez.wordpress.com) Listings for arts and music events.

The View From Fez (http://riadzany.blogspot.com) Essential news and views blog for keeping up to date with what's happening in Fez.

 Getting There & Away

Air
Fez airport (☑0535 67 47 12) is 15km south of the city, at Saïss. **RAM** (Map p308; ☑0535 62 55 16; 54 Ave Hassan II) operates daily flights to Casablanca; for international connections (mainly to France) see p507.

Bus
The main bus station for **CTM buses** (☑0535 73 29 92) is near Place Atlas in the southern ville nouvelle (Map p302). In high season, buy tickets

---

WHAT'S ON IN THE VILLE NOUVELLE?

Compared to the sensory assault provided by the medina, the ville nouvelle can seem boring: very modern, but with little actually going on. But for most Fassis, the ville nouvelle is the place where it's at: far more interesting and progressive than crumbling Fès el-Bali. In the last few years, huge amounts of money have been poured into the area, which can best be seen along the long boulevard of Ave Hassan II, with its manicured lawns, palm trees, flower beds and fountains. A stroll here is a favourite evening pastime, when it's packed with families with kids, trendy teenagers and courting couples. Stop for an ice cream or just sit on a bench and people-watch: this is the 'real' Morocco as much as any donkey-packed lane in the old city.

in advance, particularly to Tangier, Marrakesh and Chefchaouen.

CTM runs seven buses a day to Casablanca (Dh105, five hours) via Rabat (Dh70, 3½ hours) between 6.30am and 4.30pm, and six buses to Meknès (Dh25, one hour) between 8.30am and 8.30pm. Buses for Marrakesh (Dh150, nine hours) run twice daily (morning and evening).

Heading north and east, there are three buses for Tangier (Dh115, six hours), three for Chefchaouen (Dh45, four hours), two for Tetouan (Dh100, five hours), one for Al-Hoceima (Dh90, six hours), two for Nador (Dh74, seven hours), and a daily service for Oujda (Dh110, six hours).

International services to Spain and France with Eurolines also depart from the CTM bus station.

Non-CTM buses depart from the **main bus station** (Map p304; ☑0535 63 60 32) outside Bab el-Mahrouk on the edge of the medina. Fares are slightly lower than CTM, and reservations can be made for popular routes. It has a **left-luggage facility** (per item Dh5, ⏱6am-midnight).

At least six buses run daily to Casablanca, Chefchaouen, Er-Rachidia, Marrakesh, Meknès, Midelt, Oujda, Rabat, Tangier and Tetouan. Less frequent buses go to Rissani (Dh120, 10 hours), Ouarzazate (Dh142, 14 hours) and Tinerhir (Dh108, 10 hours).

Locally, there are frequent departures to Azrou (Dh18, two hours), Ifrane (Dh16, 90 minutes), Moulay Yacoub (Dh8, 30 minutes), Sefrou (Dh8, 40 minutes), Taza (Dh34, three hours, hourly) and Ouezzane (Dh34, three hours, twice daily).

Car

There are several car parks near the medina: just south of Place l'Istiqal, on Ave des Français outside Bab Bou Jeloud, and inside the medina wall north of Talaa Kebira at Ain Azleen. In the ville nouvelle is a guarded car park in front of the central market. **Transport Touristique** (☑0615 450128; chriftrans@gmail.com) is a reliable transport and vehicle-hire company, offering services from airport pick-ups to day trips from Fez and longer hires.

Taxi

There are several grand-taxi ranks dotted around town. Taxis for Meknès (Dh18, one hour) and Rabat (Dh60) leave from in front of the main bus station (Map p304; outside Bab el-Mahrouk) and from near the train station (Map p308). Taxis for Taza (Dh50, 2½ hours) depart from near Bab Fettouh (Map p304), the medina's southeastern gate. Those going to Moulay Yacoub (Dh9, 20 minutes) leave from the open ground to the west of Bab Bou Jeloud (Map p304). The rank for Sefrou (Dh12, 30 minutes) is located just below Place de la Résistance in the ville nouvelle (Map p308). Azrou (Dh28, one hour) and Ifrane (Dh20, 45 minutes) taxis wait at a parking lot to the west of the CTM bus station in the south of the ville nouvelle (Map p302).

Train

The glorious new **train station** (Map p308; ☑0535 93 03 33; 📶) is in the ville nouvelle, a 10-minute walk northwest of Place Florence. To take advantage of the **left-luggage office** (per item Dh10; ⏱6am-8pm), bags must be locked or padlocked.

Trains depart every two hours between 7am and 5pm to Casablanca (Dh110, 4¼ hours), via Rabat (Dh80, 3½ hours) and Meknès (Dh20, 45 minutes). There are two additional overnight trains. Eight trains go to Marrakesh (Dh195, eight hours) and one goes to Tangier (Dh105, five hours) direct (four more via Sidi Kacem). Direct trains for Oujda (Dh108, six hours) via Taza (Dh40, two hours) leave three times daily.

ⓘ Getting Around

To/From the Airport

There is a regular bus service (bus 16) between the airport and the train station (Dh3, 25 minutes), with departures every half-hour or so. Grands taxis from any stand charge a set fare of Dh120.

Bus

Fez has a reliable local bus service. At certain times of day, however, the buses are like sardine cans and are notorious for pickpockets. The standard fare is Dh2.50. Some useful routes:

NO 9 Place Atlas via Blvd Abdallah Chefchaouni (both in the ville nouvelle) to near the Batha Museum (Fès el-Bali); the bus returns via Place de la Résistance, Ave Hassan II and Ave des FAR.

NO 10 Train station via Bab Guissa (northern Fès el-Bali) to Bab Sidi Bou Jida (northeastern Fès el-Bali).

NO 19 Train station via Ave Hassan II (both in ville nouvelle) and Bab el-Jdid (southern Fès el-Bali) to Place R'cif (central Fès el-Bali).

NO 47 Train station to Bab Bou Jeloud (Fès el-Bali).

Taxi

Drivers of the red petits taxis generally use their meters without any fuss. Expect to pay about Dh9 from the train or CTM station to Bab Bou Jeloud. As usual, there is a 50% surcharge after 8pm. You'll find taxi ranks outside all the gates of the medina. Only grands taxis go out to the airport.

Around Fez

SEFROU   صفرو

The small Berber town of Sefrou, just 30km southeast of Fez, is a picturesque

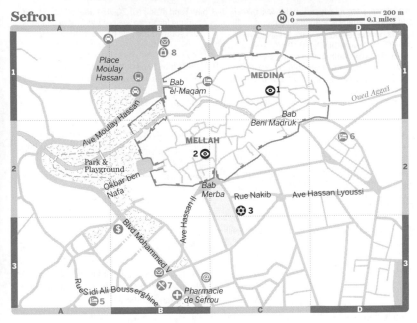

place situated on the edge of the Middle Atlas. It has a small but interesting medina, which once hosted one of Morocco's largest Jewish communities (as many as 8000 people, according to some accounts), and it was here that Moulay Idriss II lived while overseeing the building of Fez. It's an easy day trip from Fez, ideal if you need to escape the big city.

⊙ Sights & Activities

Medina　　　　　　　WALLED TOWN CENTRE
Sefrou's medina is a manageable place to get around, especially compared to Fez. The Oued Aggaï flows through its centre, opening the place up and giving it more of an airy feeling than many old medinas. The best point of entry is the northerly **Bab el-Maqam**. Follow the main flow of people downhill to the southeast and pass two mosques. Cross over the river and continue up the main shopping street to where the road splits: straight ahead takes you to Bab Merba, in the medina's southern wall, next to another mosque; the right fork brings you to the beginning of the mellah.

Mellah　　　　　　　NEIGHBOURHOOD
The *mellah* stretches from here northwest along the river. Although its Jewish population has gone, the district still retains a few distinctive wooden-galleried houses and lanes so narrow two people can only just pass. In its heyday, the *mellah* was so dark and crowded that street lamps had to be lit even in the middle of the day.

Synagogue　　　　　　　SYNAGOGUE
Just south of Bab Merba, this synagogue is now closed. When we visited, the king had just announced money to restore the city walls, although there were mixed feelings about a plan to pave over sections of the river in the medina.

THE CHERRY FESTIVAL

Sefrou is a sleepy place on the whole, except in early June when the annual **Cherry Festival** (Festival des Cerises; www.festival-cerises-sefrou.com) fills the streets for four days to celebrate the local cherry harvest. There's plenty of folk music, along with displays by local artists, parades, *fantasias* (cavalry charges) and sports events, as well as the crowning of the Cherry Queen. Sefrou lays claim to the longest running town festival in Morocco – it celebrated its 90th year in 2010.

Cascades
WATERFALL

A 1.5km walk west of town are the Cascades, a modest waterfall. Follow the signs from Ave Moulay Hassan around Al-Qala' (a semifortified village) and along the river's lush valley.

🛏 Sleeping

Dar Attamani GUESTHOUSE €

(☑0535 96 91 74; www.darattamani.com; 414 Bastna, Medina; s/d/tr from Dh150/280/390; 🛜) This lovely guesthouse is tucked right in the heart of the medina. For the budget, the owner has taken a great deal of attention to styling, and each room has a different look, giving the place an idiosyncratic style. Some rooms are en suite, others have shared bathrooms, and for shoestringers there are beds on the roof terrace (Dh100). For such a small town, it's a gem – if this were in Fez it would cost three times as much to stay here. Half-board is also available.

Hôtel Sidi Lahcen el-Youssi HOTEL €

(☑0535 68 34 28; Rue Sidi Ali Bousserghine; s/d Dh170/220; 🛏) Situated in a very quiet part of town, this complex has adequate rooms with attached bathrooms (and some with balcony), a restaurant and an ever-so-slightly tired air. Ask about discounts if you're visiting outside the spring and summer months.

🍴 Eating

There's a string of cafes and a bar along Blvd Mohammed V, all fairly masculine places to drink coffee. There are a few cheap eats with soup, kebabs, rotisserie chicken and the like in the medina.

Restaurant Café Oumnia MOROCCAN €

(☑0535 66 06 79; Ave Massira al-Khadka; set menu Dh65; ⏰8am-9pm) This is Sefrou's only formal restaurant, near the post office. Set on two levels, with clean and bright restaurant decor, its daily three-course set menu is good value at Dh65, and there's a licensed bar.

🛍 Shopping

You might snap up a bargain at the market held every Thursday.

Ensemble Artisanal HANDICRAFTS

(Rte de Fès) The usual selection of rugs, pots, clothes and leather at fixed prices.

ⓘ Information

BMCE (Blvd Mohammed V) Has an ATM.

Club Internet Ibn Battouta (off Blvd Mohammed V; per hr Dh7; ⏰9am-midnight)

Main post office (Blvd Mohammed V)

Pharmacie de Sefrou (Blvd Mohammed V)

Post office (Rte de Fès)

ⓘ Getting There & Away

Regular buses (Dh8, 40 minutes) and grands taxis (Dh12, 30 minutes) run between Sefrou and Place de la Résistance in Fez. For Azrou, take a grand taxi to Immouzzer (Dh12) and change.

BHALIL
بهاليل

This curious village is 5km from Sefrou, and worth a visit if you have your own transport. It contains a number of troglodyte houses (cave dwellings) built into the picturesque mountainside and picked out in pastel hues of pink, yellow and blue. Some go so far as to utilise caves for the primary room of the house. The result is a cool, spacious room, usually used as a salon, while bedrooms and private areas are built above.

Meknès
مكناس

POP 700,000

Of the four imperial cities, Meknès is the most modest by far – neither capital (Rabat), trendy tourist hub (Marrakesh) or home to a famed medina (Fez). In fact, Meknès, which receives fewer visitors than it really should, is rather overshadowed because of its proximity to Fez. Quieter and smaller than its grand neighbour, it's also more laid-back with less hassle, yet still has all the winding narrow medina streets and grand buildings that it warrants as a one-time home of the

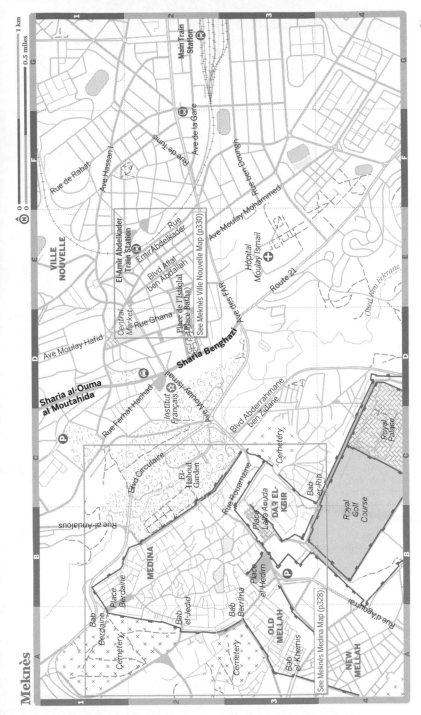

Meknès

1 km
0.5 miles

VILLE NOUVELLE

Main Train Station

Ave de la Gare

Rue de Tunis

Rue de Rabat

Ave Hassan I

Rue ben Dough

Rue Moulay Mohammed

El-Amir Abdelkader Train Station

Rue Emir Abdelkader

Blvd Allal ben Abdallah

Central Market

Place de l'Istiqlal (Place Batha)

Rue Ghana

See Meknès Ville Nouvelle Map (p330)

Ave Moulay Mohammed

Ave Moulay Hafid

Hôpital Moulay Ismail

Route 21

Oued Bou Fekrane

Sharia Benghazi

Ave des FAR

Sharia al-Ouma al Moutahida

Rue Ferhat Hachad

Institut Français

Ave Moulay Ismail

Blvd Abderrahmane ben Zidane

Blvd Circulaire

Rue al-Andalous

El-Habouli Garden

Rue Rouamzine

Cemetery

Royal Palace

MEDINA

Place Berdaine

Bab Berdaine

Cemetery

Bab el-Jedid

Bab Berrima

Place Lalla Aouda

DAR EL-KBIR

Bab er-Rih

Royal Golf Course

Place el-Hedim

OLD MELLAH

Bab el-Khemis

Cemetery

NEW MELLAH

Rue d'Agourrai

See Meknès Medina Map (p328)

Moroccan sultanate. Sultan Moulay Ismail, the architect of Meknès' glory days, might be a little disgruntled at the city's current modesty, but visitors will find much to be enchanted by.

Encircled by the rich plains below the Middle Atlas, Meknès is blessed with a hinterland abundant with cereals, olives, wine, citrus fruit and other agricultural products that remain the city's economic backbone. In the midst of this agricultural region sit the Roman ruins at Volubilis and the hilltop tomb of Moulay Idriss, two of the country's most significant historic sites. If you base yourself in Meknès you'll find plenty to keep you busy.

The valley of the (usually dry) Oued Bou Fekrane neatly divides the old medina in the west and the French-built ville nouvelle in the east. Moulay Ismail's tomb and imperial city are south of the medina.

History

The Berber tribe of the Meknassis (hence the name Meknès) first settled here in the 10th century. Under the Almohads and Merenids, Meknès' medina was expanded and some of the city's oldest remaining monuments were built.

It wasn't until the 17th century that Meknès really came into its own. The founder of the Alawite dynasty, Moulay ar-Rashid, died in 1672. His successor and brother, Moulay Ismail, made Meknès his capital, from where he would reign for 55 years.

Ismail endowed the city with 25km of imposing walls with monumental gates and an enormous palace complex that was never completed. That he could devote the time and resources to construction was partly due to his uncommon success in subduing all opposition in Morocco and keeping foreign meddlers at bay, mainly because of his notorious Black Guard (see p332).

Meknès Medina

Ismail's death in 1727 also struck the death knell for Meknès. The town resumed its role as a backwater, as his grandson Mohammed III (1757–90) moved to Marrakesh. The 1755 earthquake that devastated Lisbon also dealt Meknès a heavy blow. As so often happened in Morocco, its monuments were subsequently stripped in order to be added to buildings elsewhere. It's only been in the past few decades, as tourist potential has become obvious, that any serious restoration attempts have taken place.

In 1912 the arrival of the protectorate revived Meknès as the French made it their military headquarters. The army was accompanied by French farmers who settled on the fertile land nearby. After independence most properties were recovered by the Moroccan government and leased to local farmers.

◉ Sights

THE MEDINA

The heart of the Meknès medina is Place el-Hedim, the large square facing Bab el-Mansour. Built by Moulay Ismail and originally used for royal announcements and public executions, it's a good place to sit and watch the world go by – kids playing football, hawkers selling miracle cures, and promenading families. There's always something going on, and you get the sense that the city authorities would love for it to turn into the local equivalent of Marrakesh's Djemaa el Fna. One edge is lined with cafes and restaurants; behind these is an excellent, covered produce market.

To the south, the impressive monumental gateway of Bab el-Mansour leads into Moulay Ismail's imperial city. The narrow streets of the old *mellah* are in the west of the medina – look for the old balconied houses so distinctive of the Jewish quarter.

The easiest route into the souqs is through the arch to the left of the Dar Jamaï Museum on the north side of Place el-Hedim. Plunge in and head northwards, and you'll quickly find yourself amid souvenir stalls and carpet shops.

Markets MARKETS

(Map p328) There are many *qissariat* (covered markets). A couple of these are devoted to textiles and carpets, which are noisily auctioned off on Sunday mornings. **Okchen Market** specialises in fine embroidery. On Rue Najjarine, you'll pass stalls of *babouches* (leather slippers) in multicoloured rows and **Qissariat ad-Dahab**, the jewellery souq. Outside of the city wall, you'll find a colourful souq, selling spices, herbs and nuts, and a lively **flea market**.

Dar Jamaï Museum MUSEUM

(Map p328; ☎0555 53 08 63; Place el-Hedim; admission Dh10; ◈9am-noon & 3-6.30pm Wed-Mon) Overlooking Place el-Hedim is Dar Jamaï, a palace built in 1882 by the powerful Jamaï family, two of whom were viziers to Sultan Moulay al-Hassan I. When the sultan died in 1894, the family fell afoul of court politics and lost everything, including the palace, which was passed on to the powerful Al-Glaoui family. In 1912 the French commandeered the palace for a military hospital.

Since 1920 the palace has housed the Administration des Beaux Arts and one of Morocco's best museums. Exhibits include traditional ceramics, jewellery, rugs and some fantastic textiles and embroidery. Look out for the brocaded saddles, and some exquisite examples of Meknasi needlework (including some extravagant gold and silver kaftans). The *koubba* (domed sanctuary) upstairs is furnished as a traditional salon complete with luxurious rugs and cushions. The museum also has a fine collection of antique carpets, representing various styles from different regions of Morocco.

The exhibits are well constructed; explanations are in French, Arabic and sometimes English. The museum's Andalucian garden and courtyard are shady, peaceful spots amid overgrown orange trees.

Medersa Bou Inania   THEOLOGICAL COLLEGE
(Map p328; Rue Najjarine; admission Dh10; ☉9am-noon & 3-6pm) Opposite the Grande Mosquée, the Medersa Bou Inania is typical of the exquisite interior design that distinguishes Merenid monuments. It was completed in 1358 by Bou Inan, after whom a more lavish *medersa* in Fez is also named. This *medersa* is a good display of the classic Moroccan decorative styles – the *zellij* base, delicate stucco midriff and carved olivewood ceiling.

Students aged eight to 10 years once lived two to a cell on the ground floor, while older students and teachers lived on the 1st floor. Anyone can climb onto the roof for views of the green-tiled roof and minaret of the Grande Mosquée nearby, but the *medersa* is otherwise closed to non-Muslims.

Mausoleum of Sidi ben Aïssa   MAUSOLEUM
(Map p328) This mausoleum is newly restored (closed to non-Muslims). Sidi ben Aïssa gave rise to one of the more unusual religious fraternities in Morocco, known for their self-mutilation and imperviousness to snake bites. His followers gather here in April from all over Morocco and further afield.

IMPERIAL CITY

Bab el-Mansour   GATEWAY
(Map p328) The focus of Place el-Hedim is the huge gate of Bab el-Mansour, the grandest of all imperial Moroccan gateways. The gate is well preserved with lavish (if faded) *zellij*

Meknès Ville Nouvelle

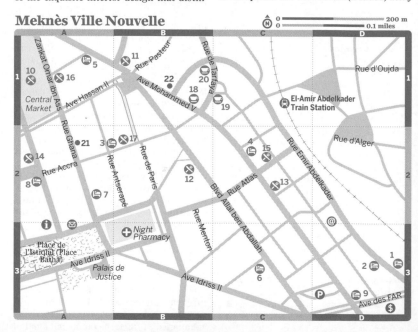

and inscriptions across the top. It was completed by Moulay Ismail's son, Moulay Abdallah, in 1732. You can't walk through the *bab* itself (although it's sometimes open to host exhibitions), but instead have to make do with a side gate to the left.

Mausoleum of Moulay Ismail MAUSOLEUM
(Map p328; donations welcome; ☺8.30am-noon & 2-6pm Sat-Thu) Diagonally opposite the Koubbat as-Sufara' is the resting place of the sultan who made Meknès his capital in the 17th century. Moulay Ismail's stature as one of Morocco's greatest rulers means that non-Muslim visitors are welcomed into the sanctuary. Entry is through a series of austere, peaceful courtyards meant to induce a quiet and humble attitude among visitors, an aim that's not always successful in the face of a busload of tourists. The tomb hall is a lavish contrast and showcase of the best of Moroccan craftsmanship. Photography is permitted, but non-Muslims may not approach the tomb itself.

Koubbat as-Sufara' MONUMENT
(Map p328; admission Dh10; ☺9am-noon & 3-6pm) South of Bab el-Mansour lies the *mechouar* (parade ground), now known as Place Lalla Aouda, where Moulay Ismail inspected his famed Black Guard. After bringing 16,000 slaves from sub-Saharan Africa, Moulay Ismail guaranteed the continued existence of his elite units by providing the soldiers with women and raising their offspring for service in the guard. By the time of his death, the Black Guard had expanded tenfold. Its successes were many, ranging from quelling internal rebellions, to chasing European powers out of northern Morocco, to disposing of the Ottoman Turk threat from Algeria.

Following the road around to the right, you'll find an expanse of grass and a small building, the Koubbat as-Sufara', once the reception hall for foreign ambassadors. Beside the entrance, you will notice the shafts that descend into a vast crypt. This dark and slightly spooky network of rooms was used for food storage, although tour guides will delight in recounting the (erroneous) story that it was used as a dungeon for the Christian slaves who provided labour for Moulay Ismail's building spree. Bring a torch.

Heri es-Souani RUINS
(admission Dh10; ☺9am-noon & 3-6.30pm) Nearly 2km southeast of the mausoleum, Moulay Ismail's immense granaries and stables, Heri es-Souani, were ingeniously designed. Tiny windows, massive walls and a system of underfloor water channels kept the temperatures cool and air circulating. The building provided stabling and food for an incredible 12,000 horses, and Moulay Ismail regarded it as one of his finest architectural projects.

The roof fell in long ago, but the first few vaults have been restored. They're impressive, but overly lit which robs them of much of their ambience – seek out the darker, more atmospheric corners. Those beyond stand in partial ruin, row upon row across a huge area.

In summer it's a long hot walk here from Moulay Ismail's mausoleum, so you might want to catch a taxi or calèche (horse-drawn carriage). If you do decide to walk, follow the road from the mausoleum south between the high walls, past the main entrance of the

Few men dominate the history of a country like the towering figure of Sultan Moulay Ismail (1672–1727). Originating from the sand-blown plains of the Tafilalt region, his family were sherifs (descendants of the Prophet Mohammed) – a pedigree that continues to underpin the current monarchy.

Ruthlessness as well as good breeding were essential characteristics for becoming sultan. On inheriting the throne from his brother Moulay ar-Rashid, Moulay Ismail set about diffusing the rival claims of his 83 brothers and half-brothers, celebrating his first day in power by murdering all those who refused to submit to his rule. His politics continued in this bloody vein with military campaigns in the south, the Rif Mountains and Algerian hinterland, bringing most of Morocco under his control. He even brought the Salé corsairs to heel, taxing their piracy handsomely to swell the imperial coffers.

The peace won, Moulay Ismail retired to his capital at Meknès and began building his grandiose imperial palace, plundering the country for the best materials, and building city walls, kasbahs and many new towns. This cultural flowering was Morocco's last great golden age.

Moulay Ismail also considered himself a lover. Although he sought (but failed to receive) the hand in marriage of Louis XIV of France's daughter, he still fathered literally hundreds of children. Rather foolishly, however, he did nothing to secure his succession. When he died the sultanate was rocked by a series of internecine power struggles, from which the Alawites never fully recovered.

Nevertheless, his legacy was to be the foundation of modern Morocco. He liberated Tangier from the British, subdued the Berber tribes and relieved the Spanish of much of their Moroccan territory. Moulay Ismail sowed the seeds of the current monarchy and beneath his strong-arm rule the coherent entity of modern Morocco was first glimpsed.

Royal Palace (no visitors) and a camp site, to find the entrance straight ahead.

Agdal Basin   LAKE

Immediately north of the granaries and stables lies an enormous stone-lined lake, the Agdal Basin. Fed by a complex system of irrigation channels some 25km long, it served as both a reservoir for the sultan's gardens and a pleasure lake. There are plenty of benches to break your stroll around the waters, and a giant Giacometti-like statue of a traditional water seller.

☞ Tours

Compared to Fez and Marrakesh, the Meknès medina is fairly easy to navigate. If you are short of time, or if you wish to gain some local insight, book an official guide through the tourist office for Dh250 for a day. Calèche rides of this imperial city with a guide are easy to pick up around the Mausoleum of Moulay Ismail – expect to pay around Dh150 for a couple of hours.

✯✯ Festivals & Events

One of the largest *moussems* in Morocco takes place on the eve of Moulid (around February during the lifetime of this edition of the guidebook) at the Mausoleum of Sidi ben Aïssa, outside the medina walls. Members of this Sufi brotherhood are renowned for trances that make them impervious to pain, but public displays of glass-eating, snake bites and ritual body piercing are no longer allowed (though you'll see pictures about town). It's a busy and popular festival with *fantasias* (musket-firing cavalry charges), fairs and the usual singing and dancing.

⌁ Sleeping

Most accommodation is located in the ville nouvelle, with the exception of a cluster of ultrabudget options and a few exquisite new riads.

MEDINA

Most of Meknès' cheapies cluster along Rue Dar Smen and Rue Rouamzine in the old city. In the high season and during festivals, they can fill up quickly. To be on the safe side, get here early in the day or reserve a room.

TOP CHOICE Ryad Bahia
RIAD €€

(Map p328; ☑0535 55 45 41; www. ryad-bahia.com; Derb Sekkaya, Tiberbarine; r incl breakfast Dh670, ste Dh950-1200; ✳☎) This charming little riad is just a stone's throw from Place el-Hedim. It's been in the same family since an ancestor came to work as a judge for Moulay Ismail in the 17th century, so you can even sleep in the room where the current owner was born, or the new Aladdin's Cave–like roof-terrace room. The main entrance opens onto a courtyard (also hosting a great restaurant), and the whole place has an open and airy layout compared to many riads. Rooms are pretty and carefully restored, and the owners (keen travellers themselves) are eager to swap travel stories as well as guide guests in the medina.

TOP CHOICE Riad Safir
GUESTHOUSE €€

(Map p328; ☑0535 53 47 85; www. riadsafir.com; 1 Derb Lalla Alamia; r Dh550-750, ste 770-1430; ✳☎) This delightful and intimate guesthouse comes in two halves: the original Safir is a homely confection that swaps the traditional *zellij* and plaster of some places for swathes of soft fabrics and carpets in creams and warm oranges, and plenty of wood. Recently expanded next door, the newer section is all ultramodern chic, with stylishly restrained colours and artful decoration. An unexpected, but winning, contrast.

Maroc Hôtel
HOTEL €

(Map p328; ☑0535 53 00 75; 7 Rue Rouamzine; s/d/tr Dh100/200/270) A perennially popular shoestring option, the Maroc has kept its standards up over the many years we've been visiting. Friendly and quiet, rooms (with sinks) are simple, and the shared bathrooms are clean. The terrace and courtyard filled with orange trees add to the ambience.

Riad Lahboul
GUESTHOUSE €€

(Map p328; ☑0535 55 98 78; www.riadlahboul.com; 6 Derb Ain Sefli, Rouamzine; s/d from Dh610/780; ✳☎) A family-friendly guesthouse run by a Moroccan-English couple. You enter into a salon in high-Moroccan style, but above this the seven rooms are positively cosy (although a couple felt a tad cramped). Dining in is a good option as the food is excellent, and the location puts you on the edge of the medina and across from the Jardin el Haboul if you need to escape from the city hustle.

Maison d'Hôtes Riad
RIAD €€

(Map p328; ☑0535 53 05 42; www.riadmeknes. com; 79 Ksar Chaacha, Dar el-Kabir; r incl breakfast Dh650-750; ✳☎⊠) This riad is located amid the ruins of the Palais Ksar Chaacha, the 17th-century imperial residence of Moulay Ismail. There are just six rooms, each tastefully decorated in traditional-meets-modern style, plus some unexpected touches like the collection of African masks and the wall of old clocks and radios. This place is noted for its food, and there are a couple of different salons where you can eat, or just relax by the chic plunge pool and cactus garden.

Riad d'Or
GUESTHOUSE €€

(Map p328; ☑0641 07 86 25; www.riaddor.com; 17 Derb el Anboub; r Dh550-900; ✳☎⊠) This converted townhouse is a warren of a place, with 14 rooms tumbling around unexpected courtyards and staircases. The variety on offer hides some good value: many rooms can sleep four or more people, so it's worth enquiring in advance of booking. The biggest surprise is hidden on one of the roof terraces: who expected to find a swimming pool there?

Hôtel Regina
HOTEL €

(Map p328; ☑0535 53 02 80; 19 Rue Dar Smen; s/d/tr Dh70/100/130, shower Dh5) This ultra-cheapie frankly feels a bit threadbare, but it's not entirely without merit. Rooms are completely no-frills, but the central courtyard opens the place up and wards off claustrophobia. Showers cost extra, and there's no guarantee of hot water.

VILLE NOUVELLE
The ville nouvelle also has some decent budget options, as well as more expensive establishments.

TOP CHOICE Hôtel Majestic
HOTEL €

(Map p330; ☑0535 52 20 35; 19 Ave Mohammed V; s/d Dh159/210, with shower Dh231/322) Open for business since 1937, the Majestic is one of the best deco buildings in Meknès. There's a good mix of rooms (all have sinks), and there's plenty of character to go around from the dark-wood dado to the original deco light fittings. A quiet courtyard, roof terrace and friendly management top things off, making this a hard budget option to beat.

Hôtel Palace
HOTEL €

(Map p330; ☑0535 40 04 68; fax 055 40 14 31; 11 Rue Ghana; s/d Dh180/230) Looking very dour from the street, this hotel turns out to be surprisingly good value: large airy rooms with attached bathrooms, many with balcony. The mezzanine sofas give an extra option for chilling out. It's frequently full, so call in advance.

Hôtel Ouislane   HOTEL €
(Map p330; ☎0535 52 48 28; 54 Rue Allal ben Abdallah; s/d Dh205/242) Another decent and clean option at the higher end of the budget bracket, the Ouislane has large airy rooms with attached bathrooms. It doesn't set the world alight, but for the prices it's reasonable value.

Hôtel Volubilis   HOTEL €
(Map p330; ☎0535 52 50 82; Ave des FAR; s/d Dh228/270) This is a reasonable option, with fair rooms and en-suite bathrooms. Try to avoid the rooms at the front above the main road, as they can stay pretty noisy throughout the night.

Hôtel Bab Mansour   HOTEL €
(Map p330; ☎0535 52 52 39; hotel_bab_mansour@menara/ma; 38 Rue Emir Abdelkader; s/d Dh397/521; ❀❂) It's a fine line between tasteful and characterless and, while comfortable enough, the Bab Mansour never quite seems to develop much of a personality – the famous *bab* is depicted in tiles in the bathrooms, but it's more DIY store than Moroccan *zellij*. That said, it's well run, with everything you'd expect in a tourist-class hotel.

Hôtel Akouas   HOTEL €
(Map p330; ☎0535 51 59 67; 27 Rue Emir Abdelkader; s/d Dh341/422; ❀❂) This friendly, family-run three-star has a little more local colour than its rivals. Rooms, while not huge, are modern, serviceable and very fairly priced. The place also has a decent restaurant and a nightclub.

Hôtel de Nice   HOTEL €
(Map p330; ☎0535 52 03 18; www.hoteldenice-meknes.com; cnr Rue Accra & Rue Antserapé; s/d Dh405/505, breakfast Dh48; ❀) This hotel continues to fly the flag for quality and service. Modern, efficient and ever-so-slightly shiny, it's a surprise that room rates aren't a good Dh100 more than they actually are. Rooms are nicely decorated and well sized, and there's a bar and restaurant too.

Hôtel Rif   HOTEL €€
(Map p330; ☎0535 52 25 91; hotel_rif@menara.ma; Rue Accra; s/d Dh650/750; ❀❂❂) The Rif

is a consistent performer in the midrange hotel stakes. The interior has a slightly funky modernist ambience, and we love the concrete-chocolate confection of the exterior. The courtyard pool is good for dipping toes in, but as it's overlooked by the bar, female bathers will feel enormously exposed.

Hôtel Malta   HOTEL €€
(Map p330; ☎0535 51 50 20; www.hotel-malta.ma; 3 Rue Charif Idrissi; s/d Dh650/850; ❀❂) The Malta sets its aim a little higher in its service than most of Meknès' midrange options, with pleasing results. The spacious rooms may never win any design awards, but they're comfy to relax in, and there's satellite TV and a plush piano bar.

🍴 Eating
MEDINA
Dar Sultana   MOROCCAN €€
(Map p328; ☎0535 53 57 20; Derb Sekkaya, Tiberbarine; mains from Dh70, 3-course set menu Dh150) Also going under the name Sweet Sultana, this is a small but charming restaurant in a converted medina house. The tent canopy over the courtyard gives an intimate, even romantic, atmosphere, set off by walls painted with henna designs and bright fabrics. The spread of cooked Moroccan salads is a highlight.

Sandwich Stands   FAST FOOD €
(Map p328; Place el-Hedim; sandwiches around Dh30; ⏱7am-10pm) Take your pick of any one of the stands lining Place el-Hedim, and sit at the canopied tables to watch the scene as you eat. There are larger meals like tajines, but the sandwiches are usually quick and excellent, while a few places nearer the medina walls do a good line in sardines.

Ryad Bahia   MOROCCAN €€
(Map p328; ☎0535 55 45 41; www.ryad-bahia.com; Derb Sekkaya, Tiberbarine; mains Dh80-100) Nonresidents are welcome to eat at the restaurant of this riad (book in advance), and it makes a pleasant evening dining spot with its tables around the courtyard. The menu is typically Moroccan, but all tasty and served and presented nicely.

Pavillon des Idrissides   CAFE €
(Map p328; 147 Dar Smen Lahdim; mains from Dh50) An ideal spot either for a quick coffee or a lazy meal, this new cafe-restaurant has scooped all the others in finding a great view overlooking Place Bab Mansour. The food is an unsurprising mix of grills, tajines

and couscous – perfectly decent, but the setting is really the thing here.

Restaurant Oumnia — MOROCCAN €€
(Map p328; ☑0535 53 39 38; 8 Ain Fouki Rouamzine; set menu Dh80) This is less a formal restaurant and more like a few rooms of a family home converted into dining salons, and the emphasis here is on warm service and hearty Moroccan fare. There's just a three-course set menu, with a real winner, with delicious *harira*, salads and a choice of several tajines of the day.

Restaurant Riad — MOROCCAN €€
(Map p328; ☑0535 53 05 42; 79 Ksar Chaacha; set menus Dh110-160) While all the riads in the Meknès medina have lovely restaurants, this is a great option for nonguests. Set around a lush green courtyard, it's a great place to relax, and while the menu of salads, tajines and couscous is simple, it's all delicious and served with care and attention.

Rue Rouamzine Eateries — FAST FOOD €
(Map p328; Rue Rouamzine; meals Dh30-50; ⏱11am-10pm) Particularly handy for the cheap hotels on the edge of the medina proper, this street has plenty of good eating places serving up sandwiches, kebabs, tajines, grilled chicken, fruit juices and ice cream.

Restaurant Mille et Une Nuits — MOROCCAN €
(Map p328; ☑0535 55 90 02; off Place el-Hedim; mains Dh45-85) Easily located off Place el-Hedim, this is another converted house, whose owners have leant towards the more showy 'palace' restaurant style of surroundings. You'll find all the Moroccan standards and classics on a reasonably priced menu.

Covered Market — SELF-CATERING €
(Map p328; Place el-Hedim) This is *the* place in Meknès to get fresh produce, and is virtually a tourist attraction in itself, with its beautifully arranged pyramids of sugary sweet delicacies, dates and nuts, olives and preserved lemons in glistening piles. There's also good-quality fruit and veg here, as well as meat – the faint-hearted may choose to avoid the automated chicken-plucking machines at the rear of the hall.

VILLE NOUVELLE

TOP CHOICE Marhaba Restaurant — MOROCCAN €
(Map p330; 23 Ave Mohammed V; tajines Dh25; ⏱noon-10pm) We adore this canteen-style place – the essence of cheap and cheerful – and so does everyone else, judging by how busy it is of an evening. While you can get tajines and the like, do as everyone else does and fill up on a bowl of *harira*, a plate of *makoda* (potato fritters) with bread and hard-boiled eggs – and walk out with change from Dh15. We defy you to eat better for cheaper.

Restaurant Gambrinus — MOROCCAN €
(Map p330; ☑0535 52 02 58; Zankat ibn Ass; mains around Dh50, set menu Dh70) A good place for Moroccan food in colourful surroundings in the ville nouvelle, which feels like something of a surprise when you discover that the original Gambrinus was a Czech immigrant in 1914. It's perennially popular with locals, who come for the good range of tajines.

Le Dauphin — EUROPEAN €€
(Map p330; ☑0535 52 34 23; 5 Ave Mohammed V; mains Dh75-120, set menu Dh150) It might have an uninspiring exterior, but the French dining room and lovely garden give this restaurant one of the nicest dining settings in town. The menu is continental, with some good meat and fish dishes. Alcohol is served.

Le Pub — FUSION €€
(Map p330; ☑0535 52 42 47; 20 Blvd Allal ben Abdallah; mains Dh75-150; ⏱11am-midnight) The dark mirrored windows and bouncers on the door make you wonder what you're letting yourself in for, but Le Pub is a welcome change if you're feeling tajine fatigue. The menu is split in two – half offering continental dishes, the other branching into a Moroccan take on Chinese and Thai dishes. We preferred the oriental dishes over the pasta, but there are some good steaks too. As befits the name, alcohol is served.

Palais de Poulet — FAST FOOD €
(Map p330; Rue Tetouan; mains from Dh25, salads Dh15) Looking down from the Hôtel Rif towards Ave Hassan II, this is one of several good and cheap rotisserie places where you can fill up quickly on chicken, chips, bread and salad. Although you order from the table, pay at the counter inside.

Restaurant Pizza Roma — PIZZA €
(Map p330; Rue Accra; mains from Dh20) Although the name suggests that pizzas are the speciality here, you could do far worse than load up on a filling plate of rotisserie chicken with rice and chips. An unassuming place, it's popular with female diners.

Pizzeria le Four
ITALIAN €

(Map p330; ☎0535 52 08 57; 1 Rue Atlas; pizzas Dh40-60, mains Dh65-85) This is as good a place as any in the ville nouvelle to load up on pizza, and the dark-wood and brick surroundings take you halfway out of Morocco towards Italy. Alcohol is served, so late at night you sometimes find local men getting sloshed among the clientele. Watch out for the steep service tax added to bills.

Central Market
SELF-CATERING €

(Map p330; Ave Hassan II) A good place to shop in the ville nouvelle, with a variety of fresh-food stalls, alcohol shops and various imported foodstuffs.

 ## Drinking

It's a popular adage that Meknès has more bars than any other Moroccan city, and if all you're after is a quick bottle of Flag beer, then you won't lack for options (in the ville nouvelle at least). Many are grouped around Blvd Allal ben Abdallah, but are generally pretty seedy affairs, designed for serious drinking and smoking, with women not at all welcomed.

The hotel bars listed in the sleeping section are more amenable, as well as the restaurants listed above as licensed. Le Pub is, appropriately, one of the nicer places to get a drink – slump in a comfy chair, drink at the bar itself, or head downstairs to smoke a sheesha and catch some live music on weekends.

When choosing sticky pastries in Meknès, don't overlook the *marakchia* – the local take on an éclair, full of cream and covered with gooey chocolate. The ville nouvelle is the place to go for relaxed cafe culture, especially on and around Ave Mohammed V and the pedestrianised area around Cinema Camera. Those following are female-friendly as far as Moroccan cafes go.

Les Palmiers d'Aziza
CAFE

(Map p330; 9 Rue de Tarfaya) With an exterior in bright Marrakesh pink, this popular cafe offers several options – sit in the sunny garden, hang at the tables near the mouth-watering cookie counter, or head upstairs to the covered terrace away from public view. The latter is a popular choice for boys and girls on dates. The ice cream and smoothies here are excellent.

Café Tulipe
CAFE

(Map p330; Rue de Tarfaya) Just off the main road, the Tulipe has a large shady terrace and modern interior; it's one of the most pleasant cafes in which to kill an hour or two.

Café Opera
CAFE

(Map p330; 7 Ave Mohammed V) Airy and old-fashioned, this grand cafe is a classic, and among the most popular for Moroccan men to sip their mint tea. Sitting outside and people-watching is a great breakfast pastime.

Entertainment

Institut Français (Map p327; ☎0535 51 58 51; inst.fr.mek@aim.net.ma; Rue Ferhat Hachad; ☺8.30am-noon & 2.30-6.30pm Mon-Sat) is the centre of Meknès' cultural life, with films, plays, concerts and exhibitions.

 ## Shopping

While the souqs of Meknès aren't as extensive as those of Fez or Marrakesh, the lack of hassle can make them a relaxed place to potter around looking for souvenirs. A particularly speciality of Meknès is silver damascene, where metalwork is intricately inlaid with silver wire.

Centre Artisanale
ART & CRAFT

(Map p328; Ave Zine el-Abidine Riad; ☺9am-1pm & 3-7pm Mon-Sat) This is the place to go if you want to get an idea of what to look for and how much to spend. Quality is high, but prices are fixed.

Pottery Stalls
ART & CRAFT

(Map p328) Set up on the western side of Place el-Hedim.

Pavillon des Idrissides
ART & CRAFT

(Map p328) The ground floor is set over for handicrafts, and is good for browsing.

ℹ Information

Internet Access

Cyber Bab Mansour (Map p328; Zankat Accra; per hr Dh6; ☺9am-midnight)

Quick Net (Map p330; 28 Rue Emir Abdelkader; per hr Dh6; ☺9am-10pm)

Medical Services

Hôpital Moulay Ismail (Map p327; ☎0535 52 28 05; off Ave des FAR)

Night Pharmacy (Map p330; Rue de Paris)

Pharmacy el-Fath (Map p328; Place el-Hedim)

Money

There are plenty of banks with ATMs both in the ville nouvelle (mainly on Ave Hassan II and Ave Mohammed V) and the medina (Rue Sekkakine).

BMCE (Map p330; 98 Ave des FAR; ☺10am-1pm & 4-7pm) An after-hours exchange office on the southeast side of the ville nouvelle.

Post

Main post office (Map p330; Place de l'Istiqlal) The parcel office is in the same building, around the corner on Rue Tetouan.

Post office (Map p328; Rue Dar Smen) In the medina.

Tourist Information

Délégation Régionale du Tourisme (Map p330; ☑0535 52 44 26; Place de l'Istiqlal; ☺8.30am-noon & 2.30-6.30pm Mon-Thu, 8-11.30am & 3-6.30pm Fri) Limited tourist information and pamphlets.

Travel Agencies

Carlson Wagonlit (Map p330; ☑0535 52 19 95; 1 Rue Ghana) A source for air, ferry and coach tickets.

RAM (Map p330; ☑0535 52 09 63; 7 Ave Mohammed V) Handles tickets for all major airlines.

❶ Getting There & Away

Bus

The **CTM bus station** (Map p327; ☑0535 52 25 85; Ave des FAR) is about 500m east of the junction with Ave Mohammed V. The main bus station (Map p328) lies just outside Bab el-Khemis, west of the medina. It has a left-luggage office and the usual snack stands.

CTM departures include Casablanca (Dh90, four hours, six daily) via Rabat (Dh55, 2½ hours), Fez and Marrakesh (Dh160, eight hours, daily), Tangier (Dh100, five hours, three daily), Oujda (Dh130, six hours, two daily) via Taza (Dh70, three hours), Er-Rachidia (Dh130, six hours, daily), and three buses to Nador (Dh125, six hours).

Slightly cheaper than CTM, other buses are available from the numbered windows in the main bus station:

NO 5 Rabat and Casablanca (hourly 6am to 3pm)

NO 6 Tangier (hourly 5am to 4pm), Tetouan (four daily), Chefchaouen (three daily), Ouezzane (five daily)

NO 7 Fez (hourly 5am to 6pm), Taza (four daily), Oujda (hourly 4am to 11.30pm), Nador (five daily)

NO 8 Moulay Idriss (hourly 8am to 6pm)

NO 9 Marrakesh (seven daily, mostly morning departures)

Taxi

The principal grand-taxi rank (Map p328) is a dirt lot next to the bus station at Bab el-Khemis. There are regular departures to Fez (Dh18, one hour), Ifrane (Dh24, one hour), Azrou (Dh33, one hour) and Rabat (Dh45, 90 minutes). Taxis leave less frequently for Taza (Dh70, 2½ hours). Grands taxis for Moulay Idriss (Dh10, 20 minutes) leave from opposite the Institut Français (Map p327) – this is also the place to organise round trips to Volubilis.

Train

Although Meknès has two train stations, head for the more convenient El-Amir Abdelkader (Map p330), two blocks east of Ave Mohammed V. There are a dozen daily trains to Fez (Dh20, 45 mins), three of which continue to Taza (Dh56, 3½ hours) and two to Oujda (Dh130, 6½ hours). Ten go to Casablanca (Dh90, 3½ hours) via Rabat (Dh65, 2¼ hours). There are seven direct services to Marrakesh (Dh174, seven hours). For Tangier, there are two direct trains (Dh80, four hours), or take a westbound train and change at Sidi Kacem.

❶ Getting Around

Bus

Overcrowded city buses ply the route between the medina and ville nouvelle. The most useful are bus 2 (Bab el-Mansour to Blvd Allal ben Abdallah, returning to the medina along Ave Mohammed V) and bus 7 (Bab el-Mansour to the CTM bus station). Tickets are Dh2.

Taxi

Urban grands taxis (silver-coloured Mercedes Benz with black roofs) link the ville nouvelle and the medina, charging Dh2.50 per seat or Dh15 for the whole taxi. Pale-blue petits taxis use the meter: from El-Amir Abdelkader train station to the Bab el-Mansour expect to pay around Dh8.

A more touristy way to get around the medina is by calèche, available for hire on Place el-Hedim and outside the Mausoleum of Moulay Ismail. They charge around Dh70 per hour.

Around Meknès

VOLUBILIS (OUALILI)   وليلي

The Roman ruins of Volubilis sit in the middle of a fertile plain about 33km north of Meknès. The city is the best preserved archaeological site in Morocco and was declared a Unesco World Heritage site in 1997. Its most amazing features are its many beautiful mosaics preserved in situ.

Volubilis can easily be combined with nearby Moulay Idriss to make a fantastic day trip from Meknès. The guides that hang

Volubilis

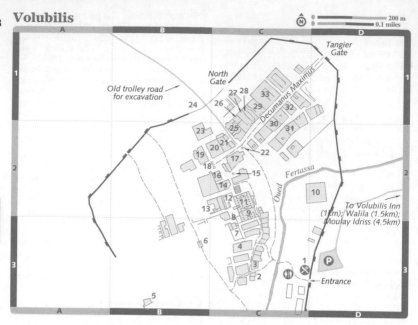

around the entrance conduct good one-hour tours for around Dh140. Most speak decent enough English to explain the site in detail. Many official guides in Fez and Meknès are also knowledgeable about the site.

In the heat of a summer day, the sun can be incredibly fierce at Volubilis, so bring a hat and plenty of water. Spring is the ideal season, when wildflowers blossom amid the abandoned stones, and the surrounding fields are at their greenest. The best time to visit is either first thing in the morning or late afternoon, when you're more likely to have the place to yourself, with just the guardian's donkey grazing among the ruins. At dusk, when the last rays of the sun light the ancient columns, Volubilis is at its most magical.

HISTORY

Excavations indicate that the site was originally settled by Carthaginian traders in the 3rd century BC. One of the Roman Empire's most remote outposts, Volubilis was annexed in about AD 40. According to some historians, Rome imposed strict controls on what could and could not be produced in its North African possessions, according to the needs of the empire. One result was massive deforestation and the large-scale

planting of wheat around Volubilis. At its peak, it is estimated that the city housed up to 20,000 people. The site's most impressive monuments were built in the 2nd and 3rd centuries, including the triumphal arch, capitol, baths and basilica.

As the neighbouring Berber tribes began to reassert themselves, so the Romans abandoned Volubilis around 280. Nevertheless, the city's population of Berbers, Greeks, Jews and Syrians continued to speak Latin right up until the arrival of Islam. Moulay Idriss found sanctuary here in the 8th century, before moving his capital to Fez. Volubilis continued to be inhabited until the 18th century, when its marble was plundered for Moulay Ismail's palaces in Meknès, and its buildings were finally felled by the Lisbon earthquake of 1755.

◎ Sights

Roman Ruins RUINS
(admission Dh20, parking Dh5; ☉8am-sunset)
Less than half of the 40-hectare site has been excavated. A major on-site museum displaying Volubilis' most celebrated finds has been in the works for several years. Despite repeated construction delays, it should open soon after this book goes to press. Until then, the prized discoveries

Volubilis

(including some fine bronzes) are to be found in the archaeology museum in Rabat (see p189).

Although parts of certain buildings are roped off, you are free to wander the site at will. Bar a couple of vague signboards, there's little in the way of signposting or information on what you're actually seeing. It's well worth considering taking a guide, especially if you're pressed for time. If you prefer to wander on your own, allow at least two hours to see the essentials, and up to a full day for the real enthusiast.

The better-known monuments are in the northern part of the site, although it's more convenient to start in the south. Once over the Oued Fertassa, the path leads onto the ridge and through the residential quarter.

Ancient Volubilis

Although the least remarkable part of the site, the **olive presses** here indicate the economic basis of ancient Volubilis, much as the plentiful olive groves in the surrounding area do today. Near the presses, the remains of a **female skeleton** (thought to be Muslim as she was buried facing Mecca) are entombed in one of the walls; she's now protected by an iron sheet.

Buildings

Next to the House of Orpheus are the remains of **Galen's Baths**. Although largely broken, they clearly show the highly developed underfloor heating in this Roman hammam. Opposite the steam room are the communal toilets – where citizens could go about their business and have a chat at the same time.

The capitol, basilica and 1300-sq-metre forum are, typically, built on a high point. The **capitol**, dedicated to the Triad of Jupiter, Juno and Minerva, dates back to AD 218; the **basilica** and **forum** lie immediately to its north. The reconstructed columns of the basilica are usually topped with storks' nests – an iconic Volubilis image if the birds are nesting at the time of your visit. Around the forum is a series of plinths carved with Latin inscriptions that would have supported statues of the great and good. Keep your eyes out for the carved stone drain-hole cover – an understated example of Roman civil engineering.

The marble **Triumphal Arch** was built in 217 in honour of Emperor Caracalla and his mother, Julia Domna. The arch, which was originally topped with a bronze chariot, was reconstructed in the 1930s, and the mistakes made then were rectified in the 1960s. The hillock to the east provides a splendid view over the entire site.

Houses with Mosaics

On the left just before the triumphal arch are a couple more roped-off mosaics. One, in the **House of the Acrobat**, depicts an athlete being presented with a trophy for winning a desultory race, a competition in which the rider had to dismount and jump back on his horse as it raced along.

From the arch, the ceremonial road, **Decumanus Maximus**, stretches up the slope to the northeast. The houses lining it on either side contain the best mosaics on the site. The first on the far side of the arch is known as the **House of the Ephebus** and contains a fine mosaic of Bacchus in a chariot drawn by panthers.

Next along, the **House of the Columns** is so named because of the columns around the interior court – note their differing styles, which include spirals. Adjacent to this is the **House of the Knight** with its incomplete mosaic of Bacchus and Ariadne. The naked Ariadne has suffered somewhat from the attentions of admirers – or Muslim iconoclasts.

The next couple of houses are named for their excellent mosaics: the **House of the Labours of Hercules** and the **House of the Nymphs Bathing**. The former is almost a circular comic strip, recounting the Twelve Labours. Several of Hercules' heroic feats were reputed to have occurred in Morocco, making him a popular figure at the time.

The best mosaics are saved until last. Cross the Decumanus Maximus and head for the lone cypress tree, which marks the **House of Venus**. There are two particularly fine mosaics here, appropriately with semi-romantic themes. The first is the **Abduction of Hylas by the Nymphs**, an erotic composition showing Hercules' lover Hylas being lured away from his duty by two beautiful nymphs. The second mosaic is **Diana Bathing**. The goddess was glimpsed in her bath by the hunter Acteon, whom she turned into a stag as punishment. Acteon can be seen sprouting horns, about to be chased by his own pack of hounds – the fate of mythical peeping toms everywhere. A third mosaic from this house, of **Venus in the waves**, can be seen in the Kasbah Museum in Tangier (p243).

🛏 Sleeping & Eating

Walila   FARMSTAY €
(TOP CHOICE)
(☎0662 52 81 05; www.walila.com; Ouali-li; half board Dh450; ℗🐾) A farmstay is something of a novelty in Morocco, but this place comfortably breaks new ground. There are just a handful of pleasant but simple rooms, but the real attractions are the wonderful surroundings: an organic farm with its own orchard, vegetables and animals. You can get your hands dirty helping out, ride horses into the hills and tuck into the home-grown food at dinnertime (cooking lessons are another option).

Volubilis Inn   HOTEL €€€
(☎0535 54 44 05; hotelvolubilisinn@gmail.com; Rte de Meknès; s/d from Dh856/996; ℗✳🐾) On a rise above the Roman site, this is a huge four-star hotel, with rooms all having views to the Volubilis ruins and countryside. There are several terraces with a couple of restaurants (mains from Dh70) and a noisy bar – the common parts are quite grand although rooms lapse into 'airport hotel' mood at times, and the atmosphere can be lacking.

ℹ Getting There & Away

The simplest and quickest way to get here from Meknès is to hire a grand taxi for the return trip. A half-day outing should cost Dh350, with a couple of hours at the site and a stop at Moulay Idriss (worth an overnight stay in itself).

A cheaper alternative is to take a shared grand taxi from near Meknès' Institut Français to Moulay Idriss (Dh10) and then hire a grand taxi to take you to Volubilis (Dh40 complete hire). If the weather isn't too hot, it's a lovely 45-minute walk between Moulay Idriss and Volubilis.

There are no buses to Volubilis.

MOULAY IDRISS   مولاي ادريس

The picturesque whitewashed town of Moulay Idriss sits astride two green hills in a cradle of mountains slightly less than 5km from Volubilis, and is one of the country's most important pilgrimage sites. It's named for Moulay Idriss, a great-grandson of the Prophet Mohammed, the founder of the country's first real dynasty, and Morocco's most revered saint. His tomb is at the heart of the town, and is the focus of the country's largest *moussem* every August.

Moulay Idriss fled Mecca in the late 8th century in the face of persecution at the hands of the recently installed Abbasid caliphate, which was based in Baghdad. Idriss settled at Volubilis, where he converted the locals to Islam, and made himself their leader, establishing the Idrissid dynasty.

Moulay Idriss' holy status kept it closed to non-Muslims until the mid-20th century, and its pious reputation continues to deter some travellers. However, the embargo on non-Muslims staying overnight in the town has long disappeared, and local family-run guesthouses have started to open to cater to visitors. Those who do stay are invariably charmed – it's a pretty and relaxed town with a centre free of carpet shops and traffic, and offers a chance to see Morocco as Moroccans experience it.

The main road leading from the bus/grands-taxis stand to the square (Place Mohammed VI) has a Banque Populaire ATM, and a couple of internet cafes.

◎ Sights

Mausoleum of Moulay Idriss   MAUSOLEUM

Although this twin-hill town is a veritable maze of narrow lanes and dead ends, it is not hard to find the few points of interest. The first is the Mausoleum of Moulay Idriss, the object of veneration and the reason for the country's greatest annual *moussem* in late August. An important pilgrimage for many, including the royals, it is accompanied by *fantasias,* markets and music. It's said locally that five pilgrimages to Moulay Idriss during the *moussem* equals one haj to Mecca.

From the main road (where buses and grands taxis arrive), head uphill and bear right where the road forks. You'll quickly find yourself on the wide square of Place Mohammed VI, lined with cafes and cheap food stands – a great place to sit and watch the pace of life. At the top of the square is the entrance to the mausoleum via a three-arched gateway at the top of some steps, surrounded by shops selling religious goods to pilgrims. Not far inside there's a barrier, beyond which non-Muslims cannot pass. Moulay Ismail created this pilgrimage site by building the mausoleum and moving the body of Moulay Idriss, in a successful attempt to rally the support of the faithful.

From here, head left up into the maze of streets to find your way to a couple of vantage points that give good panoramic views of the mausoleum, the town and the surrounding country. Plenty of guides will offer their services – you can get an informative, entertaining tour for as little as Dh30.

If you don't feel like being guided, head back to the fork and take the road heading uphill, signposted to the Municipalité. Near the top of the hill, just before the Agfa photo shop, take the cobbled street to the right. As you climb up you'll notice the only **cylindrical minaret** in Morocco, built in 1939. At the top of the hill ask a local for the **grande terrasse or petite terrasse**. These terraces provide vantage points high above the mausoleum and most of the town.

⌂ Sleeping & Eating

Rooms are at a premium during the *moussem,* so book in advance. The cheap food stands around the main square are all good for a quick snack. The grilled chicken with salad is something of a local speciality.

TOP CHOICE **Dar Zerhoune**   GUESTHOUSE €

(☎0535 54 43 71; www.buttonsinn.com; 42 Derb Zouak Tazgha; dm/s/d incl breakfast Dh200/300/500; ☎) To the right and uphill from the main mausoleum, this is a real gem of a guesthouse run with a welcoming family flavour. There are a variety of rooms and a couple of terraces (including a view to Volubilis), where you can take lazy breakfasts and opt in for a delicious home-cooked dinner. Tours, bike hire and cooking lessons are also offered.

Maison d'Hôte Slimani   MAISON D'HÔTE €

(☎0535 54 47 93; www.maisondhote-slimani.tk; 39 Rue Drazat; s/d Dh150/250, breakfast Dh30) Follow signs to the View Panoramique left from the main shrine to find this cheap and cheerful backpacker-style place. A handful of en-suite rooms on several levels cluster around a courtyard. Simple, but good value.

La Colombe Blanche   MAISON D'HÔTE €

(☎0535 54 45 96; www.maisondhote-zerhoune.ma; 21 Derb Zouak Tazgha; s/d incl breakfast Dh220/330) A traditional home turned guesthouse – the family occupies the ground floor while guests are up above. It also bills itself as a restaurant, with home-cooked meals available on request. In good weather eat on the terrace, with views to Volubilis. At the mausoleum, turn right uphill and follow the signs.

Hotel Diyar Timnay   HOTEL €

(☎0535 54 44 00; amzday@menara.ma; 7 Aïn Rjal; s/d/tr incl breakfast Dh160/240/300; ✳) Near the grands-taxis stands, this is the town's only formal hotel. It's unexpectedly large when you get inside, with plenty of rooms – good but unflashy. Most are en suite, although a few have separate (but still private) bathrooms. The restaurant (mains Dh50 to Dh60) does a roaring lunchtime trade with tour groups visiting Volubilis, and has great views to the archaeological site.

Dar Al Andaloussiya Diyafa   GUESTHOUSE €€

(☎0535 54 47 49; www.maisondhote-volubilis.com; Derb Zouak Tazgha; s/d incl breakfast Dh450/900; ✳) 'Dar Al Andalous' is Moulay Idriss' attempt at a bit of traditional Moroccan bling. For the most part it works, with good rooms and facilities and plenty of Moroccan fabrics. It's near Colombe Blanche, a big white corner building picked out in green.

ⓘ Getting There & Away

Grands taxis (Dh12, 20 minutes) to Moulay Idriss leave Meknès from outside the Institut Français, and buses (Dh6) leave from the Meknès bus station every hour from 8am to 6pm. Taxis leave Moulay Idriss from a stand at the bottom of town on the main road.

If you have your own transport, you might consider continuing to Fez via Nzala-des-Béni-Ammar, or to Meknès via the village of El-Merhasiyne. Both routes have wonderful views and eventually join back up with the main roads. As the road surfaces are very rough, these drives are really only possible in summer unless you have a 4WD.

MIDDLE ATLAS

Ifrane

As foreign tourists head to the medinas for a taste of the 'real' Morocco, Moroccan tourists find more favour with places like Ifrane. Tidy, ordered and modern, it feels more like Switzerland relocated to the Middle Atlas than North Africa.

The French built Ifrane in the 1930s, deliberately trying to recreate an alpine-style resort. It has neat red-roofed houses, blooming flower beds and lake-studded parks, all kept impeccably tidy. Many major employers (including the government) maintain apartment complexes here for their vacationing workers, and it's a popular summer day trip for picnickers. In the winter, the affluent flock here to ski, and the hoi polloi come for the pure fun of throwing snowballs at each other. Outside the holiday season, Ifrane's population is boosted by the rich, trendy students of the town's prestigious Al-Akhawayn University.

The main road from Meknès is called Blvd Mohammed V and it runs through Ifrane from west to east. This is where you will find the bus station, west of the centre, and the tourist office, at the intersection with Ave des Tilluels. Most of the cafes and hotels are clustered in the centre along two parallel roads a 10-minute walk to the south: Rue de la Cascade and Ave de la Poste.

◉ Sights

Al-Akhawayn University   UNIVERSITY

The campus of Al-Akhawayn University is at the northern end of town, and is a squeaky-clean showcase of Moroccan education. It was founded in 1995 by Morocco's King Hassan II and King Fahd of Saudi Arabia, and includes in its lofty aims the promotion of tolerance between faiths. For now, only the rich and beautiful need apply – the car parks are full of flash cars, and the air trills with the most fashionable of mobile-phone ring tones. Lessons in English are based on the American system and there are US staff and exchange students. You can wander into the well-kept grounds – weekday afternoons are the best, as there are plenty of students who are usually willing to show you around.

Stone Lion   MONUMENT

Ifrane's other landmark is the stone lion that sits on a patch of grass near the Hôtel Chamonix. It was carved by a German soldier during WWII, when Ifrane was used briefly as a prisoner-of-war camp, and commemorates the last wild Atlas lion, which was shot near here in the early 1920s. Having your picture taken with the lion is something of a ritual for day-trippers.

🛏 Sleeping

Hotel prices in Ifrane reflect the town's affluence, and its year-round popularity means demand for rooms runs high.

TOP CHOICE **Hôtel Mischliffen**   LUXURY HOTEL €€€
(✆0535 56 66 07; r from Dh2500; P✳🛜🏊) Overlooking Ifrane from the north, this oversized ski lodge has finally reopened after a renovation lasting several years, turning it into one of Morocco's most luxurious hotels. Local cedar is evident throughout in the refit, with rooms echoing a luxury chalet. The attention to detail goes as far as the carefully selected art decorating the walls. There are two pools: one on the terrace for summer, and another indoors for winter. Nonguests may use them for Dh450 (including buffet lunch).

Hotel les Tilleuls   HOTEL €
(✆0535 56 66 58; fax 0535 56 60 79; cnr Ave des Tilluels & Rue de la Cascade; s/d from Dh260/320) The cheapest hotel in Ifrane is this comfortable, old institution on the corner of the main square.

Hôtel Chamonix   HOTEL €€
(✆0535 56 60 28; Ave de la Marche Verte; s/d Dh360/410; ✳) This three-star place is well maintained and centrally located. Rooms are bright and clean, if a little bland, with attached bathrooms. There's a decent restaurant and bar (which turns into a night-

club on weekends), and the hotel can rent out ski equipment.

Hôtel Perce-Neige
HOTEL €€
(☎0535 56 64 04; fax 035 567116; Rue des Asphodelles; s/d Dh400/490) A pretty accommodation option situated about 200m southeast of the centre. The rooms could be a bit bigger, but they're very comfortable and come with satellite TV and bathrooms. The licensed restaurant is a good dining option (set menus Dh120). The shop in the lobby sells paintings by local artists.

Camp Site
CAMP SITE
(Blvd Mohammed V; camping per person Dh7, plus per car/tent/campervan Dh8/15/30; ☉closed winter) Leafy camp site just west of the bus station.

✖ Eating

Several cafes and cheap eats cluster around the bus station area, where you'll also find the market for fresh produce.

Café Restaurant la Rose
MOROCCAN €
(☎0555 56 62 15; 7 Rue de la Cascade; mains around Dh45, set menu Dh70) This small restaurant has always been popular in town for its Middle Atlas trout and traditional Moroccan fare. A recent renovation has lifted its spirits further.

Le Pain
MOROCCAN €
(Ave de la Marche Verte; mains around Dh60; ☉9am-10pm) Le Pain is situated just up from the Hôtel Chamonix. Among its features is a wide glass frontage, with different seating areas, including some for simple cafe drinkers and others for snacks. Another area again is set aside for full restaurant meals, including some decent pizzas.

Complexe Touristique Aguelman
CAFE, MOROCCAN €
(Ave Hassan II; meals Dh30-50; ☉9am-10pm) Overlooking the artificial lake on the main road, this is a huddle of options under one roof, aimed squarely at the local tourist market. There's a more formal dining room with Moroccan dishes for the evenings, a bar, and a simple diner with pizza, pasta, omelettes and sandwiches. In fine weather, eat at the tables outside overlooking the water.

Le Crouistillant
CAFE €
(Rue de la Cascade; ☉7am-10pm) On the corner facing the square, this is a good cafe for a drink and a sticky pastry.

❶ Information

BMCE (Ave de la Marche Verte) One of several banks with ATMs on this road.

Pharmacie Mischliffen (Rue de la Cascade)

Post office (Ave de la Poste)

Tourist office (☎0535 56 68 21; Ave Prince Moulay Abdallah; ☉8.30am-noon & 2.30-6.30pm Mon-Fri)

❶ Getting There & Away

The main bus and grand-taxi stations are next to the market, west of the town centre.

Each morning, CTM buses leave for Marrakesh (Dh140, eight hours) via Beni Mellal, and for Casablanca (Dh110, 4½ hours) via Meknès (Dh28, one hour) and Rabat (Dh70, 3½ hours).

Non-CTM buses are more frequent. There are hourly buses to Fez (Dh16, one hour) and Azrou (Dh7, 25 minutes). Less frequent are services to Beni Mellal (Dh55, four hours), Marrakesh (Dh110, eight hours) and Midelt (Dh42, 3½ hours).

There are plenty of grands taxis to Fez (Dh20), Meknès (Dh24) and Midelt (Dh55), as well as Azrou (Dh7).

Lake Circuit (Route des Lacs)

A pretty diversion north of Ifrane is the lake circuit around **Dayet Aoua**. Signposted off the main Fez road 17km north of Ifrane, the route winds for 60km through the lake country between the P24 and P20. If you don't have your own vehicle, hiring a grand taxi in Ifrane for a tour of a couple of hours should cost around Dh250. That said, the joy of the area is to get out and walk along the lake shore and enjoy the tranquillity of the scenery. This is an area made for hikers and mountain bikers. For longer treks and camping, see the boxed text Exploring the Azrou Area (p345).

Dayet Aoua is surrounded by woodlands, and the whole area is notably rich in bird life. Keep an eye out in particular for raptors, including booted eagles, black and red kites and harriers. The lake attracts significant numbers of ducks and waders, including crested coot, woodpeckers, tree creepers and nuthatches, which flit among the trees around the southeastern end of the lake.

The lake is a popular picnic destination for families at the weekend, but during the week you'll get the place largely to yourself. Beyond Dayet Aoua, the road loops east and then south, skirting past Dayet Ifrah and the even smaller lake of Dayet Hachlat. The road is decent, but is liable to be snowbound in winter. If you want to linger longer, there are two good sleeping options at Dayet Aoua.

Azrou

The Berber town of Azrou is an important market centre sitting at the junction of the roads to Fez, Meknès, Midelt and Khenifra. Deep in the Middle Atlas it sits amid stunning scenery, with sweeping views of cedar and pine forests, and high meadows that burst into flower every spring. Thoroughly unhurried, it's a relaxing spot to wind down if you've had too much of big cities.

Azrou (Great Rock) takes its name from the outcrop marking the town's western boundary. The big Ennour mosque, beautifully finished with local cedar, provides another handy landmark.

Azrou hosts one of the region's largest weekly souqs, and is particularly known for its Berber carpets, so timing your visit for market day (Tuesday) is a good idea. A museum of the Middle Atlas has been under construction for some years, yet its final opening seems permanently delayed.

It's probably better instead to just head out of town to enjoy the surrounding countryside; there are plenty of day walks that take in the mountain air and great views. You might even spot a few of the local Barbary apes.

🛏 Sleeping

For its size, Azrou has a surprising number of sleeping options, with more being added out of town along the Fez road (look out for the Disneyland-esque 'castle' being built to attract Gulf Arab tourists).

Hôtel Salame HOTEL €
(☑0535 56 25 62; salame_hotel@yahoo.fr; Place Moulay Hachem ben Salah; s/d Dh70/140) This small hotel is an exceedingly pleasant place to stay. Small, cute rooms are nicely present-

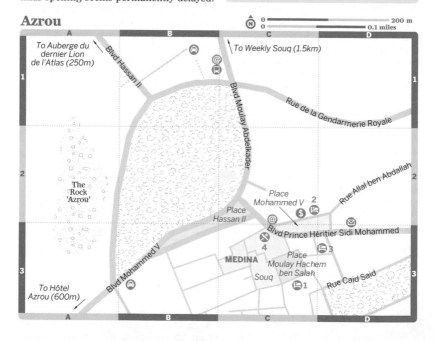

Azrou

Azrou sits on the edge of some of the prettiest parts of the Middle Atlas – ideal for throwing a few things in your day pack and setting out for a hike. The area is known for its Barbary apes, and you might be lucky enough to spot a troupe foraging in the woods. Although you can just head out of Azrou by foot and into the hills, some of the best walking spots require some wheels to get yourself started.

'**Ain Leuh** is a pretty village 25km southwest of Azrou. The drive here is through thick cedar forest, so you might just be tempted to stop your vehicle anywhere and hit the trail. Instead, take in the large Tuesday weekly souq (the best day to get public transport), which attracts market-goers from around the region, particularly from the Beni M'Guild Berbers. It's a pleasant climb through the rough streets of flat-roofed houses to a waterfall in the hills above.

Around 20km south of 'Ain Leuh, an even more picturesque walk leads to the waterfalls at the **Sources de l'Oum-er-Rbia**. Leave the road at Lac Ouiouane and follow the path down past a number of farmhouses to a small valley, where a bridge crosses the Rbia river. From here, it's about a 15-minute walk to the gorge where several dozen springs break out of the rocks to form a series of waterfalls. There are a couple of cafes where you can take a rest.

It's possible to incorporate these walks into a much longer circuit trek of up to six days from 'Ain Leuh. For more information, contact official local guide **Moulay Abdellah Lahrizi** (☑0663 77 26 87; www.tourisme-vert-ifrane.com) of the Association des Guides de Montagnes du Moyen Atlas.

IMPERIAL CITIES, MIDDLE ATLAS & THE EAST · AZROU

---

ed with a smattering of traditional Berber decoration, and you will be made welcome by the friendly staff. Shared bathrooms are kept constantly clean, with 24-hour hot showers (Dh10).

Auberge du Dernier Lion
de l'Atlas   GUESTHOUSE €
(☑0535 56 18 68; www.dernierlionatlas.ma; 16 Rte de Meknès; s/d Dh225/300, breakfast Dh25; ☞) A bit of a way from the centre of Azrou, this is nonetheless a great option, with pleasant rooms and a friendly atmosphere. If you're basing yourself in the Middle Atlas area, the owner is a mine of local information. Evening meals are also available.

Hôtel le Panorama   HOTEL €
(☑0535 56 20 10; www.hotelpanorama.ma; Hay Ajelabe; s/d/tr Dh274/330/435) Built in a grand alpine-chalet style, Azrou's most comfortable hotel is in a quiet wooded spot a short walk northeast of town, with a pleasant garden. Staff are friendly and efficient. Rooms are compact and modern, with balconies, and the restaurant is fair.

Hôtel Azrou   HOTEL €
(☑0535 56 21 16; Rte de Khenifra; s/d with shower Dh109/142, with shower & toilet Dh138/163) A decent midrange place on the south side of town, this is a fair choice. It has comfy

rooms – plus a bar, a restaurant and an ivy-covered terrace (although the atmosphere can be a little seedy at night). If you fancy a game, the staff are the local *petanque* champions.

Hôtel des Cèdres   HOTEL €
(☑0535 56 23 26; Place Mohammed V; s/d/tr Dh75/105/160) Built in 1925, this hotel still has plenty of interesting period features and a hint of deco styling in its fixtures. Rooms are good value – all have sinks, with separate showers and toilets.

Hôtel Beau-Séjour   HOTEL €
(☑0535 56 06 92; beau-sejour-hotel@yahoo. fr; 45 Place Moulay Hachem ben Salah; s/d/tr Dh70/100/180, cold/hot showers Dh5/10) Another decent budget option, rooms here are pretty simple and unaffected. The roof terrace has good views across Azrou.

✖ Eating
The best cheap eats are found in three main areas – strung along Blvd Moulay Abdelkader south of the bus station, and clustered around Place Hassan II and Place Moulay Hachem ben Salah. You can find all the trusty favourites here – rotisserie chicken, brochettes and steaming bowls of *harira*.

Café Boulangerie Bilal CAFE €
(Place Mohammed V; sandwiches Dh20) This is an always-busy cafe with upstairs seating, good sandwich and pastry options, plus fruit juices and the occasional ice cream for the hot weather.

Hôtel des Cèdres MOROCCAN €
(0535 56 23 26; Place Mohammed V; mains around Dh50) A hotel restaurant with a 1920s dining room and log fire, and our favourite eating place in Azrou. The local trout is always good, plus there are some more unusual dishes like rabbit tajine.

Hôtel le Panorama MOROCCAN, EUROPEAN €
(0535 56 20 10; set menu Dh130) Another hotel restaurant, the Panorama is better in the evenings, when you can also wash down your meal with a glass of wine or beer. Some decent tajines, and a handful of continental dishes in pleasant surrounds.

Shopping

The weekly souq is held on Tuesday about 1.5km northeast of town. Here you'll witness Berber women from the surrounding villages haggling with dealers over the flat-weave carpets, as well as fresh produce and other market goods. Take care if it's been raining though, as the souq area can easily turn into a muddy quagmire. At other times, you'll find carpets and handicrafts aplenty in the stores around Place Hassan II and in the medina.

❶ Information

BMCE (Place Mohammed V) *Bureau de change* and one of several ATMs on the square.

Cyber Abridnet (Place Mohammed V; per hr Dh6; ☺9am–midnight) Internet access.

Cyber Kawtar (Bus station; per hr Dh6; ☺9am–midnight) Internet access.

Post office (Blvd Prince Héritier Sidi Mohammed)

❶ Getting There & Away

Azrou is a crossroads, with one axis heading northwest to southeast from Meknès to Er-Rachidia, and the other northeast to Fez and southwest to Marrakesh.

Bus

CTM offers daily departures from the bus station on Blvd Moulay Abdelkader to Beni Mellal (Dh55, three hours), Casablanca (Dh110, six hours), Fez (Dh30, two hours), Marrakesh (Dh145, seven hours) and Meknès (Dh30, 1½ hours).

Other cheaper companies have frequent daily departures to Fez (Dh18), Meknès (Dh16), Ifrane (Dh7), Midelt (Dh30) and Er-Rachidia (Dh70).

Taxi

The grand-taxi lot is down a stepped path below the bus station. Regular taxis go to Fez (Dh28, one hour), Meknès (Dh30, one hour), Khenifra (Dh25, one hour) and Ifrane (Dh7, 10 minutes), and less frequently to Midelt (Dh50, 90 minutes). Those for 'Ain Leuh (Dh14, 20 minutes) wait beside the Shell petrol station on the main road out to the southwest.

Midelt   ميدلت

POP 35,000

Midelt sits in a no-man's land of north and the south, stuck between the Middle and the High Atlas. Coming from the north in particular, the landscape seems dry and barren but it offers some breathtaking views, especially of the eastern High Atlas which seem to rise out of nowhere.

CLIMBING JEBEL AYACHI

The highest mountain in the eastern High Atlas, Jebel Ayachi (3737m) is more a massif than a single peak, stretching along a 45km ridge southwest of Midelt. Its size offers a host of trekking opportunities, not least an ascent of Ichichi n'Boukhlib, the highest peak.

The best time to tackle Jebel Ayachi is April to May or September to November, although you should be aware that snow can persist above 3400m well into July. From Midelt, take a grand taxi to the village of Tattiouine, from where you start the climb. It's a tiring but nontechnical ascent achievable in a single day. There's a simple mountain bivouac at the summit, although you'll obviously need to bring your own supplies.

A guide is definitely a good idea. The best place to arrange one is through the Complexe Touristique Timnay Inter-Cultures (p348) north of Midelt. The daily rate is around Dh300. An alternative, if you're up to organising it, is to hire a mule and driver in Tattiouine.

Midelt is the sort of place people pass through, but it can make a handy break between Fez and the desert, and possibly for a spot of carpet shopping. It's also a good base for some off-piste exploring, most notably Jebel Ayachi (see boxed text, p347).

Midelt consists of little more than one main street (Ave Mohammed V in the north, which becomes Ave Hassan II to the south), a modest market (souq days are Sunday and Wednesday) and a number of oversized restaurants, which cater to the tourist buses whistling through on their way south.

⊙ Sights

Kasbah Myriem
WORKSHOP

(Atelier de Tissages et Borderie; ☎0535 58 24 43; ⊙8am-noon & 2-5.30pm Mon-Thu & Sat) If you're in the mood for carpets, this workshop, about 1.5km out of town, is worth a look. It assists Berber women develop their embroidery and weaving. The workshop provides looms and materials, as well as a simple place to work. Local girls – aged 15 or so – come here in order to learn these skills from more experienced women. Literacy lessons are also offered. Follow the signs from the main road, then enter behind the clinic.

While you are here, you may wish to peek into the **monastery** (⊙services at 7.15am daily &10am Sun), which is home to five Franciscan monks. The grounds and chapel are a peaceful place to collect your thoughts. Ring the bell at the gate to the right of the workshop.

Kasbah des Noyers
KASBAH

The village of Berrem, 6km west of Midelt, is also known as the Kasbah des Noyers for the ancient walnut trees shading its environs. There's not much going on here, but the quaint village, with its colourful mosque and ancient earthen walls, makes a good destination for a day hike from Midelt. Follow the main path through the kasbah to the scenic overlook of the **Gorges des Berrem**. Hiring a grand taxi from Midelt costs about Dh40.

🛏 Sleeping

Hôtel Taddart
HOTEL €€

(☎0535 58 02 28; www.hotel-taddart.com; Rte de Meknes; s/d half-board from Dh450/600; ❄🤫🛜🏊) This out-of-town brand-new hotel lifts Midelt's accommodation scene considerably. Rooms have balconies overlooking Jebel Ayachi, while a few even have fireplaces to ward off the Middle Atlas winter. Excursions can be arranged, or you can divert

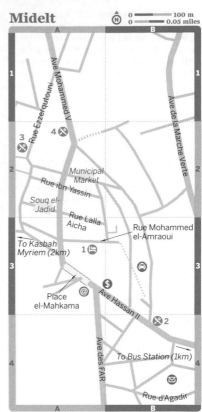

Midelt

🛏 **Sleeping**
1 Hôtel Atlas A3

🍴 **Eating**
2 Complexe Touristique Le Pin B4
3 Fast Food A2
4 Sandwich Atlas A2

yourself in the hotel's small museum (local crafts and fossils) or hammam.

Complexe Touristique Timnay Inter-Cultures
CAMP SITE €

(☎0535 36 01 88; http://timnay-tourisme.com; Rte de Zaïda; camping per person Dh20, plus per tent/car/campervan Dh15/15/25, bungalows from Dh200, Berber tents per person Dh25; 🏊) About 15km north of Midelt, this centre is a joint Moroccan-Belgian venture aimed at developing local tourism. Accommodation is simple – it works best with your own tent or campervan – but Camping Timnay (as it's known locally) is a good base for exploring the region, as you can organise treks and guides from here. For the evenings, there's a restaurant and bar. To get here, take a grand taxi headed for Zaïda (Dh10) and ask the driver to let you out at Timnay.

Auberge Jaafar HOTEL €
(☑0535 58 34 15; Berrem; r per person incl half-board Dh300; ⊛) This peaceful kasbah-style complex is about 6km west of Midelt, just past the village of Berrem. Rooms of all shapes and sizes are set up around terraces and blooming courtyards. All facilities are shared, but everything is clean (although the pool looked green and uninviting). Order during the day if you're going to eat in.

Hôtel Kasbah Asmaa HOTEL €
(☑0535 58 04 05; s/d half-board Dh300/600; ❋⊛) About 3km south of Midelt, this hotel is hard to miss – the kasbah-style exterior announces that you're on the road south. Another tour-group staple, it has fair rooms and an inviting pool at the bottom of the property, far away from the rooms so as not to be overlooked. The licensed restaurant, contained in several traditionally decorated salons, is worth eating at, even for nonguests – there's often live Gnaoua music.

Hôtel Atlas HOTEL €
(☑0535 58 29 38; 3 Rue Mohammed el-Amraoui; s/d Dh70/100) This tiny pension is a fair budget option, with home-cooked food on request. Rooms are predictably simple, but clean, as are the shared bathrooms with squat toilets (hot showers cost Dh10). Watch out for carpets though – we've had a couple of letters from travellers complaining of hard sell.

✗ Eating
As usual, cheap eats and snacks are plentiful in the area around the bus station. There's also a produce market here.

Complexe Touristique Le Pin MOROCCAN €€
(☑0535 58 35 50; Ave Hassan II; mains Dh50-60, buffet Dh70; ☺noon-5pm year-round, plus 7-10pm Apr-Aug) This large restaurant draws the coach groups (beware the lunchtime crush), but you can easily escape them in the garden, and the large turnover of covers ensures fresh meals, all served in generous portions. Alcohol is served.

Fast Food FAST FOOD €
(Rue Ezzerqutouni) Don't be fooled by the name, this is Midelt's best chicken: Dh25 gets you a quarter chicken with salad.

Sandwich Atlas FAST FOOD €
(Ave Mohammed V; sandwich Dh10, quarter chicken & chips Dh20) We enjoyed this place near the old bus station.

❶ Information
BMCI (Ave Hassan II) One of several banks with ATMs on this street.

Complexe Touristique Timnay Inter-Cultures (☑0535 36 01 88; http://timnay-tourisme. com; Rte de Zaidia) About 15km north of Midelt, this is the best source of information – including trekking guides and 4WD rental – in the eastern High Atlas, about 15km north of Midelt.

Cybernet (Ave Hassan II; per hr Dh6; ☺8am-midnight) Internet access.

Post office (off Ave Hassan II) South of the centre.

❶ Getting There & Away
Midelt's bus station is off Ave Mohammed V. CTM services mostly run at night. There's an evening departure to Casablanca (Dh145, seven hours) via Rabat (Dh110, 6½ hours), and to Rissani (Dh80, five hours) via Er-Rachidia (Dh45, 2½ hours) and Erfoud (Dh70, 4½ hours). There are also night-time services for Azrou (Dh55, 90 minutes), Meknès (Dh60, four hours) and Fez (Dh70, five hours).

Other buses cover the same routes at more sociable hours – Fez (Dh50, five hours) is serviced by six departures through the day.

Grands taxis run to Azrou (Dh40, two hours) and Er-Rachidia (Dh55, two hours).

Around Midelt
Midelt's location on the cusp of the eastern High Atlas makes it a great base for exploring. Off the main routes, roads are rough *piste*, with many only really negotiable between May and October and even then only by 4WD. It's heaven for mountain bikers, as well as ideal hiking country. Complexe Touristique Timnay Inter-Cultures and Safari Atlas in Midelt will rent you a 4WD (with driver) for around Dh1000 – good value if there's a group of you.

CIRQUE JAFFAR
The Cirque Jaffar winds through the foothills of Jebel Ayachi, 25km southwest of Midelt. It's a rough *piste*, and regular cars

will grumble on the route in all seasons but the height of summer. The scenery is wonderful though – the dramatic crests of the Atlas, carpeted in places with cedar forest, and studded with tiny Berber mountain villages.

From Midelt, take the Zaïdia road for about 10km and turn off at the signpost for the village of Aït Oum Gam. Then follow the signs to Matkan Tounfit. After that the route loops back through Tattiouine and on to Rte S3424 back to Midelt. Allow a day for the whole 80km circuit. The Complexe Touristique Timnay Inter-Cultures offers this day trip for Dh350 per person including meals.

If walking is more your thing, and you have a tent, it's possible to strike out from Timnay to the Cirque Jaffar on foot. A two-day round trip gives a good taste of the area. From Timnay you can walk to the village of Sidi Amar, which is surrounded by apple orchards and is particularly colourful during the souq each Wednesday. Camp further along at Jaffar, located in the valley in the centre of the spectacular circle. On day two, return to the Timnay complex via the impressive river gorges. A guide isn't strictly necessary, but can be organised via the Complexe Touristique Timnay Inter-Cultures. An equally good companion is the guidebook *Grand Atlas Traverse* by Michael Peyron.

GORGES D'AOULI

An interesting road trip takes you 25km northeast of Midelt along the S317 road to the Gorges d'Aouli. A series of cliffs carved by the Moulaya, they were until recently mined extensively for lead, copper and silver. The abandoned workings can be clearly seen – many halfway up the cliff face – although the mine entrances themselves are blocked off for safety reasons. Nevertheless, the place exudes a slightly creepy ghost-town feel, especially with the dipping sun at the end of the day. Further along the road, the small village of Aouli sits against the spectacular backdrop of the river gorge. This is a great stretch to explore by mountain bike – about two hours' ride from Midelt, if you're up to the gruelling uphill ride back; the road deteriorates to rough *piste* at some points. A round trip by grand taxi from Midelt should cost no more than Dh250.

Taza

At first glance, Taza seems to fulfil all the criteria of a sleepy provincial capital. The rush of activity common in Moroccan towns of comparable size seems entirely absent here, while its sprawling layout gives it a slightly abandoned air. But it makes an interesting break in a journey: climb the crumbling fortifications of Taza Haute, and the panoramic views of the Rif to the north and the Middle Atlas to the south are breathtaking. Taza also provides a handy base for exploring the eastern Middle Atlas, including Gouffre du Friouato (one of the most incredible open caverns in the world) and Tazzeka National Park.

Taza is divided neatly in two: the ville nouvelle (also called Taza Bas, or Lower Taza), centred on Place de l'Indépendance, and the walled medina (Taza Haute), occupying the hill 2km to the south. Local buses and sky-blue petits taxis (Dh6) run regularly between the two.

History

The fortified citadel of Taza is built on the edge of an escarpment overlooking the only

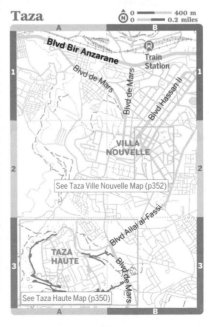

Taza

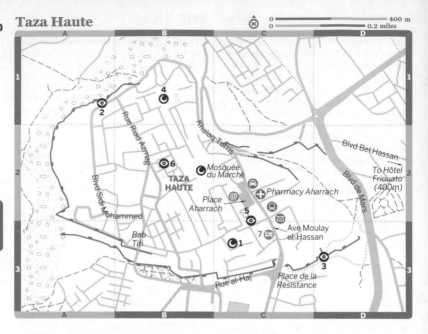

Taza Haute

feasible pass between the Rif Mountains and the Middle Atlas. It has been important throughout Morocco's history as a garrison town from which to exert control over the country's eastern extremities.

The Tizi n'Touahar, as the pass is known, was the traditional invasion route for armies moving west from Tunisia and Algeria. This is, in fact, where the Romans and the Arabs entered Morocco. The town itself was the base from which the Almohads, Merenids and Alawites swept to conquer lowland Morocco and establish their dynasties.

All Moroccan sultans had a hand in fortifying Taza. Nevertheless, their control over the area was always tenuous because the

fiercely independent and rebellious local tribes continually exploited any weakness in the central power in order to overrun the city. Never was this more so than in the first years of the 20th century, when 'El-Rogui' (Pretender to the Sultan's Throne) Bou Hamra, held sway over most of northeastern Morocco.

The French occupied Taza in 1914 and made it the main base from which they fought the prolonged rebellion by the tribes of the Rif Mountains and Middle Atlas.

◎ Sights & Activities

Medina Walls   RAMPARTS
(Map p350) The partially ruined medina walls, around 3km in circumference, are a legacy from when Taza served briefly as the Almohad capital in the 12th century. The **bastion** – where the walls jut out to the east of the medina – was added 400 years later by the Saadians. The most interesting section of wall is around **Bab er-Rih** (Gate of the Wind), from where there are superb views over the surrounding countryside. Look southwest to the wooded slopes of Jebel Tazzeka in the Middle Atlas, and then to the Rif in the north, and it's easy to see the strategic significance of Taza's location.

Grande Mosquée
MOSQUE

(Map p350) Not far from Bab er-Rih is the Grande Mosquée, which the Almohads began building in 1135; the Merenids added to it in the 13th century. Non-Muslims are not allowed to enter, and it's difficult to get much of an impression from the outside of the building. From here the main thoroughfare wriggles its way southeast to the far end of the medina. Keep your eye out for occasional examples of richly decorated doorways and windows high up in the walls, guarded by old, carved cedar screens.

Souqs
MARKETS

(Map p350) The **souqs** and **qissariat** start around the Mosquée du Marché, offering mats and carpets woven by the Beni Ouarain tribe in the surrounding mountains. It's a great chance to observe the workings of a Berber market.

Andalous Mosque
MOSQUE

(Map p350) At the end of the main street, close to the *mechouar,* is this mosque that was constructed in the 12th century.

Hammam
HAMMAM

(Map p349; Place Aharrach; Dh10; ☺men 5am-noon & 7pm-midnight, women noon-7pm) A good hammam to visit to scrub away the cares of the road.

🛏 Sleeping

Taza has only a handful of hotels, and the amount of business they do can be gauged by the general readiness to offer discounts of up to 25% if you stay more than a night.

Hôtel de l'Étoile
HOTEL €

(Map p350; ☑0535 27 01 79; 39 Ave Moulay el-Hassan; s/d Dh40/50) Spanish-owned, this cheapie next to Place Aharrach is easy to miss (the sign is hidden under the arcaded front), but inside, the strawberry-pink paint job is hard to escape. Friendly enough, it's as basic as the tariff suggests – rooms are fine for the money, with shared squat toilets. All have sinks but there's no shower: head for the nearby hammam to really clean up.

Hôtel Dauphiné
HOTEL €

(Map p352; ☑0535 67 35 67; Place de l'Indépendance; s/d Dh130/165) Ideally located on the main square, the Dauphiné is good value in the budget category. Rooms are hardly exciting, but most are generously sized, and those at the front have small balconies. There's a bar and restaurant on the ground floor.

Hôtel Friouato
HOTEL €

(Map p349; ☑0535 67 25 93; Blvd Bel Hassan; s/d Dh275/315; ℙ▨) Halfway between Taza Haute and Taza Bas, the Friouato is nevertheless a fair choice if you're after a bit of comfort and a pool to have a dip in, especially if you have your own transport. Some of the decor is a bit tired, but all the three-star amenities are there, including a bar and restaurant.

Hôtel Tour Eiffel
HOTEL €€

(Map p349; ☑0535 67 15 62; tourazhar@hotmail.com; Blvd Bir Anzarane; s/d Dh320/410; ❄) Stuck on the road out of town, the Tour Eiffel is named for its high aspirations. Past the cramped lobby, a lift swishes you up to well-sized and fairly comfy rooms, many with great views out towards the mountains. The house restaurant has good juices and is noted for its seafood.

🍴 Eating

There aren't really any restaurants in the medina, just snack stalls selling kebabs and the like, although there is plenty of fresh produce in the souqs. In the ville nouvelle, the street souq just off Place de l'Indépendance also has produce and lots of tasty snack stands that really come to life in the evening. Ave Mohammed V is well supplied for grocery stores. If you're waiting for onward transport and are in need of sustenance, there's a whole row of fast-food places where the buses stop on the Fez–Oujda road (Blvd Bir Anzarane).

Les Deux Rives
MOROCCAN, EUROPEAN €

(Map p352; ☑0535 67 12 27; 20 Ave d'Oujda; mains Dh30-60) This fresh and cosy little restaurant is a good option. The menu is a mix of Moroccan and continental – some tajines, couscous and a good *pastilla* (pie), with a smattering of pizzas and grilled meat thrown in.

Pizzeria du Jardin
PIZZA €

(Map p352; 44 Rue Sultan Abou el-Hassan; mains Dh35-40) This is a friendly place serving a few tajines, pizzas and fast-food options, with some huge salads, all overlooked by glossy photos of Bogart and Garbo. It's busy in the evenings but dead in the afternoon.

Hôtel Dauphiné
MOROCCAN €€

(Map p352; ☑0535 67 35 67; Place de l'Indépendance; meals Dh80) On the ground floor of the hotel, the Dauphiné serves up the usual range of Moroccan standards (with some good fish), plus a handful of con-

Taza Ville Nouvelle

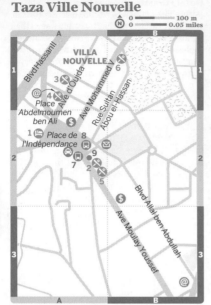

Taza Ville Nouvelle

tinental dishes thrown in. It's pretty tasty and efficiently served, but the big dining room could use a little atmosphere.

Mou Mou　　　　　　　　　FAST FOOD €
(Map p352; Ave Moulay Youssef; pizzas from Dh30, shwarma from Dh30) If you've been lulled into thinking that Taza is a sleepy place, hit this packed-out corner place, with happy customers spilling out of the door. Tasty fast-food is the order of the day

here: great shwarma, paninis, pizzas and juices.

Café Amsterdam　　　　　　BREAKFAST €
(Map p352; Ave Moulay Youssef; pastries from Dh8) This is a great breakfast stop with its own patisserie so you're never short of sticky pastry options. Sadly there's no outside seating, but the interior is crisply decorated.

Café la Joconda　　　　　　　　　CAFE €
(Map p352; Ave d'Oujda) Another good modern cafe with plenty of pavement seating, and one that's not threatened by the concept of female customers.

ⓘ Information
Attajariwafa Bank (Map p352; Ave Moulay Youseff) Has an ATM.

BMCI (Map p352; Place de l'Indépendance) Has an ATM.

Cyber Attoraya (Map p352; Rue Allal ben Abdallah; per hr Dh5; ⊘24hr) Internet access.

Cyber Friwato (Map p352; cnr Ave d'Oujda; per hr Dh4; ⊘8am-midnight) Internet access.

Cyber Taza Net (Map p350; Place Aharrach, Taza Haute; per hr Dh4; ⊘8am-11pm) Internet.

Main post office (Map p352; off Rue de Marché)

Pharmacy Aharrach (Map p350; Place Aharrach)

Post office (Map p350; Ave Moulay el-Hassan) Opposite the main square.

ⓘ Getting There & Away
Bus
Few buses actually originate in Taza, but plenty pass through on their way between Oujda and points west of Taza such as Fez, Tangier and Casablanca, as well as to the coast.

The **CTM office** (Map p352; Place de l'Indépendance) is located in the ville nouvelle. There's a morning departure for Casablanca (Dh150, eight hours), stopping at Fez (Dh55, two hours), Meknès (Dh75, 2½ hours) and Rabat (Dh120, 6½ hours). Two overnight buses leave for Tangier (Dh170, eight hours). There are also morning services for Oujda (Dh60, 3½ hours) and Nador (Dh55, 2½ hours).

Non-CTM buses servicing these same destinations stop on the Fez–Oujda road next to the grand-taxi lot. It's all a bit random, so ask around the day before as to what's expected – and jump in a grand taxi if the wait seems too long.

Taxi
Most grands taxis leave from the main Fez–Oujda road, near the train station. They depart fairly regularly for Fez (Dh50, 2½ hours).

Less frequently, taxis head for Oujda (Dh70, 3½ hours) and Al-Hoceima (Dh65, 2½ hours). Grands taxis to the Gouffre du Friouato (Dh14) leave from a lot to the south of the medina.

Train

Taza's location on the train line makes rail the best transport option. Three trains run to Fez (Dh40, two hours), continuing to Meknès (Dh56, three hours), Rabat (Dh111, six hours) and Casablanca (Dh136, seven hours). There are two connections to Tangier (Dh140, eight hours), changing at Sidi Kacem. In the opposite direction, two trains go to Oujda (Dh74, three hours).

Around Taza

JEBEL TAZZEKA CIRCUIT

It's possible to make an interesting day trip of a circuit around Jebel Tazzeka, south-west of Taza. This takes in the Cascades de Ras el-Oued at the edge of Tazzeka National Park, the cave systems of Gouffre du Friouato and the gorges of the Oued Zireg. The scenery is grand, although the road is very narrow and twisty in parts, with plenty of blind corners from which grands taxis can unexpectedly speed out.

The road is too quiet to hitch easily. If you don't have a vehicle, expect to pay around Dh500 for a grand taxi for the day from Taza, although a few direct grands taxis to the Gouffre du Friouato can sometimes be found near the medina.

The First Leg

The first stop is the **Cascades de Ras el-Oued**, 10km from Taza. A popular picnic site, they're at their grandest in the early spring, flushed with rain and snow melt – by the end of summer the flow is just a trickle. Just above the waterfalls is the village of **Ras el-Mar**, where there's a small cafe with great mountain views. The entry to **Tazzeka National Park** is also near here. With its stands of cork oak you could conceivably spend a day walking here.

Leaving the waterfalls, continue along the right fork onto the plateau and up to a small pass. On your left you'll see the strange depression of the **Daïa Chiker**, a dry lake bed. In early spring, however, a shallow lake often forms as a result of a geological curiosity associated with fault lines in the calciferous rock structure.

Gouffre du Friouato

Further along, 25km from Taza, the **Gouffre du Friouato** (☑0567 64 06 26; admission Dh3, guide Dh100, torch Dh100; ⊗8am-6pm) is well signposted and up a very steep road. The cavern is the main attraction of this circuit. At over 20m wide and 230m deep, it is said to be the deepest cavern in North Africa, and the cave system is possibly the most extensive. It was first investigated in 1935 and access is via 520 precipitous steps (with handrails) that lead you to the floor of the cavern (it's quite a strenuous climb back up). At the bottom, you can squeeze through a hole to start exploring the fascinating chambers that are found 200 more steps below. It's dark and dirty and eerily beautiful. The most spectacular chambers, full of extraordinary formations, are the **Salle de Lixus** and the **Salle de Draperies**. They do indeed resemble thin sheets of curtains, frozen and calcified. Allow at least three hours there and back. Speleologists have explored to a depth of 300m, but they believe there are more caves another 500m below.

The admission fee allows you to enter the cavern mouth. Beyond that, a guide is needed to go further underground to the grandest chambers. Bank on the occasional scramble, and squeezes through narrow sections; not recommended for claustrophobes. A torch (available at the entrance), good shoes and warm clothes are needed.

Back to Taza

Beyond the Gouffre du Friouato, the road climbs into coniferous forests past **Bab Bou-Idir**. Abandoned for much of the year, in summer holidaymakers fill its camp site and tiled alpine-style houses. This is a good base for day hikes in the area. A national park information office opens in summer, and marked trails starting in the village.

About 8km past Bab Bou-Idir, a rough track branches off to the right 9km up to **Jebel Tazzeka** (1980m). A piste goes to the summit, and it's a tough climb. At the top is a TV relay station, and great panoramic views out to the Rif and the Middle Atlas.

After 38km, main road joins the main Fez–Taza road at Sidi Abdallah de Rhiata. On the way you will wind around hairpin bends through some dense woodland and then down through the pretty gorges of the **Oued Zireg**. From the intersection at Sidi Abdallah de Rhiata, take the main highway back east to Taza, pausing at **Tizi n'Touahar** on the way for more views.

Oujda

POP 880,000

Oujda is the largest city in eastern Morocco, and its modern facade belies its millennium-old age. It's a relaxed place that seems surprised to see foreign travellers, but it wasn't always like this. A quick survey of the map and recent history gives the reason. The terminus of the train line, it has good links to the rest of the country, and was once near the busiest border crossing with Algeria, making it popular with traders and tourists alike. When the border closed in 1995 Oujda's economy took a major hit, from which it has yet to recover. It's hoped that the plans to develop tourism along the nearby Mediterranean coast will have a positive knock-on effect for the city. In the meantime Oujda's important university remains a mainstay of the economy and the city's intellectual life.

Despite few attractions, it's hassle-free so you can catch your breath, after heading down from the Rif Mountains or taking the long look to Figuig and the Sahara.

History

The site of Oujda lies on the main axis connecting Morocco with the rest of North Africa (the Romans built a road through here). Like Taza, it occupied a key position in controlling the east and was often seen as a vital stepping stone for armies aiming to seize control of the heartland around it.

The town was founded by the Meghraoua tribe in the 10th century and remained independent until the Almohads overran it in the 11th century. Later, under the Merenids, Algerian rulers based in Tlemcen took the town on several occasions, and in the 17th century it fell under the Ottoman in Algiers.

Moulay Ismail put an end to this in 1687, and Oujda remained in Moroccan hands until 1907, when French forces in Algeria crossed the frontier and occupied the town in one of a series of similar 'incidents'. The protectorate was still five years away, but the sultan was powerless to stop it.

The French soon expanded Oujda, which has since swelled in size as a provincial capital and in its role as the main gateway for commerce with Algeria.

☉ Sights

Medina   MEDINA

Oujda's medina isn't large but the walls and several surrounding squares have recently been renovated. Enter through the eastern gate, **Bab el-Ouahab**; its gruesome name is from the old habit of hanging heads of criminals here, which persisted until the French protectorate. It is chock-full of food stalls (Oujda olives are well regarded) and street cafes. Bustling without being overwhelming, it's a great slice of tradition and modernity. From Place el-Attarine, head north through the souqs past the 14th-century **Grande Mosquée** built by the Merenids, popping out near Place du 16 Août, the centre of the ville nouvelle. The square is marked by a 1930s clock tower and fine sandstone **mosque**.

Central Oujda   NOTABLE BUILDINGS

Although full of new buildings, the side streets in central Oujda are frequently rich in French protectorate and deco buildings (although often in poor condition). Walking south along Blvd Mohammed V, note the fine French neo-Moorish **Banque al-Maghrib**, before arriving at the **Cathedrale St Louis** (with nesting storks on its towers).

🛏 Sleeping

While the Algerian border remains closed, Oujda's hotels are filled to over-capacity, but at most hotels, rates fall on asking.

Hôtel Angad   HOTEL €

(☎0536 69 14 51; hotelangad@hotmail.fr; Rue Ramdane el-Gadhi; s/d Dh180/224, with air-con Dh232/274) The top pick of the budget hotels is this affordable two-star. Rooms are basic, with large bathroom and TV; get a room at the back as streetside can be noisy. The downstairs cafe does breakfast and pizza.

Hôtel Tlemcen   HOTEL €

(☎0536 70 03 84; 26 Rue Ramdane el-Gadhi; r per person Dh60) This friendly little place offers excellent value, and has an exceedingly grand-looking lobby. Quarters are small but bright, with bathrooms and TV.

Hôtel Atrah   HOTEL €

(☎0536 68 65 33; off Rue Ramdane el-Gadhi; s/d Dh113/178) The tiles and plasterwork in the lobby lend some traditional Moroccan flavour here. Self-contained rooms are a bit boxy, but otherwise this is a good budget choice.

Hôtel la Concorde   HOTEL €

(☎0536 68 23 28; 57 Blvd Mohammed V; s/d Dh177/206) The low-ceilinged reception – they've squeezed in a mezzanine bar – makes you feel cramped, but the rooms are better than you'd think. There's a slight impression of a good hotel fallen on hard times, but it's fine for the price and location.

Hôtel Oujda

HOTEL €

(☑0536 68 40 93; fax 036 685064; Blvd Mohammed V; s/d Dh278/352; ❇ ❦) According to the decor, this hotel's clock stopped in the early 1970s: there's a 'space age' lobby and funky bathroom tiles. Still, everything works, it's all comfy enough and the staff are eager to please. The restaurant offers lovely views of the nearby square and Cathedrale St Louis.

Hotel Al Manar

HOTEL €€

(☑0536 68 88 55; hotelalmanara@menara.ma; 50 Blvd Zerktouni; s/d Dh360/420; ❇) Centrally located, the Al Manar is suitably towering for its name. Functional and practical decor: rooms are fine value, although avoid the darker, small-windowed interior rooms.

Hotel Orient Oujda

HOTEL €€

(☑0536 70 06 06; www.hotelsatlas.com; Place Syrte, Ave Idriss el-Akbar; s/d Dh512/624, ste from Dh1200; ❘P❙❇❦) One of two Atlas hotels in Oujda, this is a swish and professionally run business-class outfit. Plush rooms look out to the medina or the lovely gardens; there are two restaurants, a nightclub and pool.

Hôtel Ibis Moussafir

HOTEL €€

(☑0536 68 82 02; www.ibishotel.com; Blvd Abdella Chefchaouni; r incl breakfast Dh555; ❇❦) Bang in front of you as you leave the train station, the Ibis has all the up-to-the-minute facilities and comfortable rooms you'd expect from this international hotel chain. Off the peg, you could be anywhere (or nowhere) in the world.

Atlas Terminus

HOTEL €€€

(☑0536 71 10 10; www.hotelsatlas.com; Place de la Gare; s/d from Dh800/1100; ❇❦❦) Sitting imperially, the Atlas Terminus must be the grandest hotel to have been built in this part of Morocco for years. Rooms and service are the best quality, with a fine restaurant, bar, pool and gym facilities.

✗ Eating

We asked a resident the best thing about the city. 'It has plenty of cafes,' was the reply. It's true; people-watching over coffee or mint tea is a major occupation for locals (well, the men). The most popular are along Blvd Mohammed V south of Place du 16 Août. Just wander and see what catches your eye.

In the ville nouvelle, Rue de Marrakesh and the pedestrianised area south of Place du 16 Août are good for kebabs, sandwiches, juice and quick snacks. In the medina, the stalls inside Bab el-Ouahab offer more traditional fare, including *kefta* (spiced meatballs), bowls of *harira* and boiled snails.

TOP CHOICE ▶ Restaurant Nacional

MOROCCAN €

(☑0536 70 32 57; 107 Blvd Allal ben Abdallah; meals from Dh25) This is a Oujda institution: people queue for tables at lunchtime (there's a big, packed salon upstairs). Salads are great, and waiters rush with plates of grilled meat, fried fish and tajines.

Restaurant Le Comme Chez Soi

FRENCH €€

(☑0536 68 60 79; 8 Rue Sijilmassa; mains from Dh85) This licensed restaurant is as close to fancy dining Oujda gets. The menu leans towards the French, with some good meat and fish dishes, plus a smattering of pastas.

Restaurant Le Dauphin

CONTINENTAL €€

(☑0535 68 61 45; 38 Rue de Berkane; mains Dh75-100) The Dauphin is well regarded for its fish dishes – a reminder of how close you are to the Mediterranean. Waiters pour the wine while you decide which catch of the day is to end up on your plate.

Restaurant Miami Inn

FAST FOOD €

(67 Blvd Mohammed V; meals around Dh30) Cheap, fast and popular, for rotisserie chicken, chips and large plates of salad.

Pizza Providence

PIZZA €

(Blvd Mohammed V; pizzas Dh30-60) Near the cathedral, the Providence serves good pizzas, paninis, burgers, salads and the like.

Café Pâtisserie Colombe

CAFE €

(Blvd Mohammed V) A popular and busy cafe, good for breakfast and people-watching.

Café la Défense

CAFE €

(Blvd Mohammed V) Another worthwhile cafe for wasting hours over a coffee.

ⓘ Information

Internet Access

K@ramoss Internet (Blvd Mohammed V; per hr Dh5; ☺24hr) Upstairs above a cafe.

Internet (Blvd Mohammed V; per hr Dh5; ☺9am-midnight) Above the téléboutique.

Medical Services

Hôpital el-Farabi (☑0536 68 27 05; Ave Idriss el-Akbar)

Pharmacie Mouslime (Blvd Mohammed V)

Money

Most banks with ATMs and *bureau de change* are located along Blvd Mohammed V in the medina and around Place du 16 Août near the town hall.

Western Union (Blvd Mohammed V; ☺8am-noon & 2-6pm Mon-Thu, 8-11.30am & 2.30-

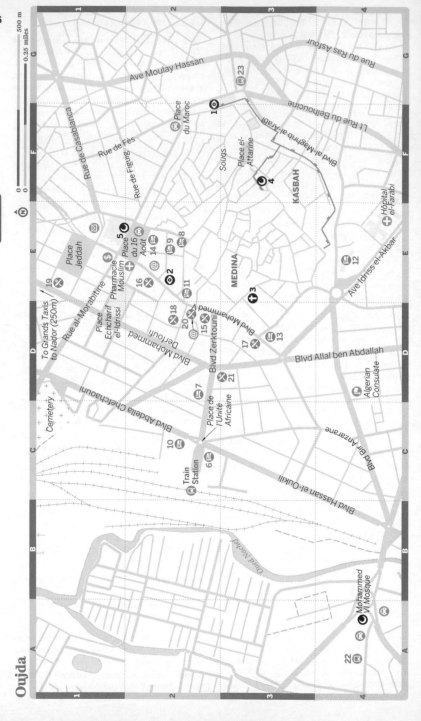

Oujda

500 m
0.25 miles

To Grands Taxis / to Nador (250m)

Cemetery

Rue de Casablanca

Rue de Fès

Rue de Figuig

Ave Moulay Hassan

Place du Maroc

1

Souqs

Place el-Attarine

4

KASBAH

Rue du Ras Astour

Lt Rue du Belhoucine

Blvd al-Maghrib el-Arabi

Hôpital el-Farabi

23

Place Jeddah

Place du 16 Août

5

Pharmacie Mouslim

Place Echcharif el-Idrissi

Rue al-Morabitine

8

9

14

16

2

11

MEDINA

Ave Idriss el-Akbar

12

3

Blvd Mohammed Derfouфi

18

20

15

17

13

Blvd Mohammed

Blvd Zerktouni

Blvd Allal ben Abdallah

Algerian Consulate

7

21

Blvd Abdella Chefchaouni

10

Place de l'Unité Africaine

6

Train Station

Blvd Bir Anzarane

Blvd Hassan el-Oukili

Oued Nacha

Mohammed VI Mosque

22

Oujda

6.30pm Fri, 9am-12.30pm Sat) Has a *bureau de change* to change cash outside banking hours.

Post
Main post office (Blvd Mohammed V)

Travel Agencies
Maroc Voyages (☏0536 68 39 93; 110 Blvd Allal ben Abdallah) For ferry and air tickets.

❶ Getting There & Away

Air
Oujda's **Angad Airport** (☏0536 68 32 61) is 15km north of the town off the road Saïdia. Grand-taxi fares are set at Dh120, but any bus to Nador, Berkane or Saïdia can drop you on the main road for a few dirham.

RAM (☏0536 68 39 09; 45 Blvd Mohammed V) has two (or three) daily flights to Casablanca. Also direct flights to France – see p508.

Border Crossing
Few anticipate the Algerian border reopening soon. Buses and grands taxis used to run constantly to the border, and on to Tlemcen.

Bus
The main bus station sits in the shadow of the huge new Mohammed VI Mosque. The **CTM office** (☏0536 68 20 47; Rue Sidi Brahim) has a suboffice just off Place du 16 Août selling tickets to Casablanca (Dh190, 11 hours) via Taza (Dh55, 3½ hours), Fez (Dh110, 4½ hours), Meknès (Dh120, five hours) and Rabat (Dh170, 9½ hours); and Tangier (Dh165, 12½ hours) also via Taza, Fez and Meknès. There is also a service every other day to Figuig (Dh95, seven hours).

Trans Ghazala runs several daily services to Casablanca via Fez, Meknès and Rabat. You also can buy tickets for these services at the **Trans Ghazala ticket office** (☏0536 68 53 87; Rue Sidi Brahim).

Numerous other companies with ticket offices in the bus station offer frequent departures for Taza, Fez and Meknès as well as Berkane (Dh12, one hour) and Nador (Dh30, three hours). There are two daily morning buses to Bouarfa (Dh55, five hours) and Figuig (Dh70, seven hours) with Champion Bus. There are also several buses a day to Saïdia (Dh15, 1½ hours) and Al-Hoceima (Dh58, five hours). There are also two daily buses to Tangier (Dh140, 14 hours) via Chefchaouen and Tetouan.

Taxi
Grands taxis to Taza (Dh70, 3½ hours) leave regularly outside the main bus station. Change here for onward connections. Grands taxis heading north to Nador (Dh55, three hours), Saïdia (Dh25, one hour) and Berkane (Dh18, one hour) congregate north of town near the junction of Rue ibn Abdelmalek and Blvd Mohammed Derfoufi.

Train
Oujda has a fine French neo-Moorish train station, at the west end of Blvd Zerktouni. Two daily direct trains leave for Casablanca (Dh205, 10 hours) and one for Tangier (via Sidi Kacem, Dh210, 11 hours). All stop at Taza (Dh74, three hours), Fez (Dh108, six hours) and Meknès (Dh130, 6½ hours).

Around Oujda

SIDI YAHIA OASIS
واحة سيدي يحيى

The oasis of Sidi Yahia, 6km south of Oujda, is venerated by Moroccan Muslims, Jews and Christians alike as being the last resting place of Sidi Yahia Ben Younes who, according to local tradition, is John the Baptist.

For most of the year it's a disappointingly scruffy place that's little more than a satellite town for Oujda. But every September (dates vary according to the lunar calendar), thousands of pilgrims flock here for a weeklong *moussem*. It is one of the bigger celebrations of this type in the country, complete with a *fantasia,* and is worth making a detour for. The trees around the shrine (closed to non-Muslims) are festooned with rags, tied to receive blessings – a throwback to pre-Islamic fertility beliefs.

To get to Sidi Yahia, take bus 1 (Dh4) from outside Bab el-Ouahab in Oujda. A petit taxi should cost around Dh20.

Bouarfa

Taking the long drive south to Bouarfa and on to Figuig can feel like a journey into limbo. The views of scrubby desert quickly fade to monotony, enlivened only by the occasional camel, and checkpoint staffed by bored gendarmes (the closer you get to Figuig, the closer you are to the sensitive Algerian border).

Bouarfa is an administrative and garrison town, a minor transport hub for this corner of Morocco, at the junction of the roads to Figuig and Er-Rachidia.

The **Hôtel Climat du Maroc** (☑0536 79 63 82; Blvd Hassan II; d/ste Dh380/500; ❉❊) is the best sleeping option, easily spotted with its domed entrance near the Figuig junction. Rooms are decent for this remote location, but order food far in advance of wanting dinner. The **Hôtel Tamlalt** (☑0536 79 87 99; Blvd Massira; d Dh60) south of the bus stand is spartan, but bearable for the price.

The area around the bus station has the usual assortment of places offering brochettes, rotisserie chicken and the like. **Restaurant Elwafa** (Blvd Hassan II; meals Dh30), near the Hôtel Climat du Maroc, is the best seated option, with tajines and couscous. **Café Amsterdam** (cnr Blvd Mohammed V & Blvd Hassan II) has pastries for breakfast.

A handful of buses leave daily to Oujda (Dh55, five hours), mostly in the morning. There are also several buses to Figuig (Dh25, two hours). There are two buses to Er-Rachidia, in the early morning and afternoon (Dh58, five hours). A grand taxi to Figuig costs around Dh300 to hire outright.

Figuig فجيج

POP 15,000

In the days of cross-border tourism, Figuig (fig-eeg) was popular with travellers. Few people make it here now, which is a tragedy because it is one of Morocco's best oasis towns: seven traditional desert villages amid 200,000 date palms fed by artesian wells. Once a historic way station for pilgrims travelling to Mecca, Figuig now sleeps, only waking for the autumn date harvest.

Figuig has an upper and lower town. The main road, Blvd Hassan II, runs through the upper (new) town, where there's ATMs, post office and pleasant municipal gardens.

Where the road passes the Figuig Hotel, it drops downhill towards the 'lower town' – the basin of palms and *ksour* (mudbrick castles) that make up the old part of Figuig. This ridge provides a handy landmark as well as views over the *palmeraie* (oasis-like area) and into Algeria: the best views are from Azrou, where the path leads towards Ksar Zenaga, or from the terrace of the Figuig Hotel.

SOLAR SAHARA

One thing the desert has in copious amounts (apart from sand) is sunshine, and in November 2009 Morocco revealed a US$9 billion investment plan to generate 20% of its energy from solar energy by the year 2020. Much of it will be produced in the Moroccan Orient, the region running along the Algerian border from the Mediterranean to Figuig. The upgrading of infrastructure on the highway south of Oujda (proclaimed from dozens of roadside billboards) point to the money pouring into the region.

At the same time the Desertec Industrial Initiative, a German-led consortium, has proposed an enormous pan-Sahara solar- and wind-generation project, stretching from Morocco to Egypt, with the aim of exporting electricity to Europe. Plans call for up to €400 billion to be invested by 2050. The first pilot projects are to be developed in Morocco, which currently has Africa's only European power cable link (to Spain). While the project hopes to provide 15% of Europe's electricity demands, some critics called it over-ambitious – a major stumbling block is likely to be cross-border cooperation between Morocco and Algeria: one reason Morocco's Orient has stagnated economically has been the forced closure of the border for over 15 years.

⊙ Sights

The Seven Ksour OLD TOWN

The landscape of Figuig is dotted with seven *ksour* that make up the town, all the same ochre colour as the earth. Each controls an area of *palmeraie* and its all-important supply of water. In the past, feuding families would divert these water channels to wash around the foundations of their enemy's kasbah, hoping the walls would collapse.

The largest and most rewarding of the *ksour* is **Ksar Zenaga**, south below the ridge splitting the oasis. Paths follow irrigation channels past palm trees and gardens, then suddenly you're among a warren of covered passages. As you tunnel between the houses, look out for some marvellous, ancient wooden doors; and watch out – you may find yourself in someone's backyard.

The crumbling state of many *ksour* lets you see their clever construction: palm-tree trunks plastered with pisé, and ceilings made of palm fronds. It's cool and dark and often eerily quiet. You may meet married women swathed in white robes, with the startling exception of one uncovered eye. It's easy to get lost. Village children will happily guide you for a few dirham, or arrange a half-day tour through Figuig Hotel.

Closer to the upper part of town, to the west of the main road, **Ksar el-Oudahir** is home to a lovely octagonal minaret built in the 11th century. It's known as the *sawmann al-hajaria* (tower of stone), and its design is quite unlike anything you see anywhere else in Morocco, instead echoing the minarets of Mauritania and the Sahel.

Near the minaret are two ancient cisterns, once covered but now open for children to swim: you may be tempted!

Ensemble Artisanal ART & CRAFT
(Blvd Hassan II; ☺4-8pm) Sells excellent local rugs and palm-frond basketwork.

🛏 Sleeping & Eating

The **Caid's House** (Blvd Hassan II), the old French governor's house is being restored into a guesthouse. Expect midrange prices.

Auberge Oasis GUESTHOUSE €
(✆0536 89 92 20; www.auberge-oasis.com; Rue Jamaa, Ksar Zenaga; s/d Dh100/170, incl full board Dh300/600; ⊛) A family home built of adobe in a *ksar*, this *auberge* is the best way to taste traditional Figuigi life. Rooms are traditionally decorated (and with en suite), and you can relax in the rooftop Berber tent. The home-cooked meals are excellent.

MOVING ON?

For tips, recommendations and reviews, head to shop.lonelyplanet.com to purchase a downloadable PDF of the Algeria chapter from Lonely Planet's *Africa* guide.

Figuig Hotel HOTEL €
(✆0536 89 93 09; Blvd Mohammed V; s Dh140-230, d Dh230-340, camping per person Dh15, tent Dh40, car Dh40; P❄☀) Figuig's main hotel, with reasonably comfy rooms. In the *palmeraie,* rooms have views towards Algeria: there's no mistaking this hotel is in the desert. There's a restaurant, but it's imperative to order in advance so staff can run to the market. Nonguests should visit to enjoy the terrace cafe, which has the best views in Figuig, especially at sunset.

Café des Palmeraie CAFE €
(Blvd Hassan II) Opposite the bus station. Staff can rustle up a basic omelette, brochettes and chips.

Tachraft Cafes CAFE €
(Tachraft Square, Zenaga) There are several cafes facing Tachraft Square – good spots for coffee, pastries and people-watching.

ℹ Information

Banque Populaire, (Blvd Hassan II) has an ATM and exchange facilities, while **Figuig Net** (per hr Dh10) plugs the town into the web. The post office sits opposite the Ensemble Artisanal.

ℹ Getting There & Away

Border Crossing

The border with Algeria is closed, but in the unlikely event of it reopening, it's 3km from Figuig to Moroccan customs, and a further 4km to the Algerian town of Beni Ounif.

Bus

Arriving in Figuig, buses stop at the 'bus station' – little more than a junction and three ticket offices – at the north end of town. They then continue on to the lower town, terminating at Tachraft Square in Zenaga; if you're staying at the Figuig Hotel, ask the driver to drop you off.

Always check out transport options the day before travelling. There are two buses a day with Champion Buses to Oujda (Dh70, seven hours), and one every other day with CTM (Dh95). All stop at Bouarfa, where you can change for connections to Er-Rachidia.

Southern Morocco & Western Sahara
جنوب المغرب والصحراء الغربية

Includes »

Best Places to Stay

» Dar Najmat (p391)
» Les 3 Chameaux (p391)
» Naturally Morocco Guest House (p374)
» Hôtel Salama (p380)
» Auberge Sahnoun (p382)
» Xanadu (p393)

Best Places to Eat

» Café-Restaurant Nomad (p397)
» L'Agence (p375)
» L'Arganier d'Ammelne (p383)
» Mezzo Mezzo (p366)

Why Go?

The Souss Valley, where goats climb argan trees beneath the sun-baked Anti Atlas, draws a line across Morocco. South of this fertile valley, the pace of life in mountain villages and Saharan gateways is seductively slow, free from the hassles of mass tourism and modern existence.

A sense of somewhere really fresh and undiscovered gusts through the region like the spring winds – and you'll want to savour it. On elegantly wrecked seafronts, sip a mint tea and gaze at the wild Atlantic coast. When trekking, mountain biking or driving through wrinkled Anti Atlas foothills, stop before the next oasis village. The silence is like cling film across your ears.

The locals, from Chleuh Berbers in the Souss to the Saharawi in the Western Sahara, seem determined to complement the landscapes. Their light robes flutter under desert skies, and their dark herds dot rocky hillsides.

Head south: you'll be surprised.

When to Go
Agadir

February
Trek the Anti Atlas and head to the southern Atlantic coast for winter sun.

March
See almond trees blossom, celebrated by Tafraoute's harvest festival.

November
Catch Taliouine's saffron festival and Immouzzer des Ida Outanane's olive harvest.

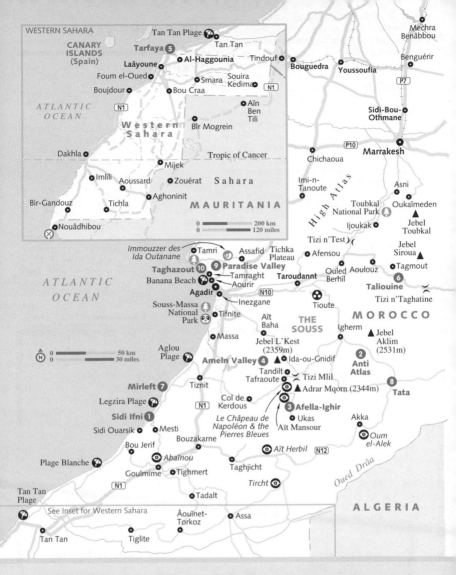

Southern Morocco & Western Sahara Highlights

1 Stroll past art-deco relics as a sea-spray sunset settles on **Sidi Ifni** (p392)

2 Trek, drive or cycle through the concertinaed granite foothills of the **Anti Atlas** (p378)

3 Explore green *palmeraies* beneath ochre cliffs in the **Afella-Ighir oasis** (p381)

4 Stay in a traditional **Ameln Valley** (p383) Berber house

5 Commune with Antoine de Saint-Exupery's *Little Prince* at **Tarfaya** (p400)

6 Taste saffron and argan oil in **Taliouine** (p377)

7 Hang loose in **Mirleft** (p390), the coolest spot in the

south with fabulous beaches and hotels

8 Find prehistoric rock carvings around **Tata** (p383)

9 Meander up **Paradise Valley** (p372), an accessible part of the High Atlas

10 Ride killer waves or just enjoy the mix of locals and surfers at **Taghazout** (p371)

Climate

The south divides into three distinct geographical areas, each with its own microclimate. The semitropical, verdant Souss Valley is hot and humid, with temperatures ranging between 22°C and a steamy 38°C, when water vapour rises like a mist from the huge citrus groves that fill the valley. The valley is also prone to heavy winds in spring. The climate of the barren Anti Atlas veers between freezing winters and hot, dry summers. The deep southern coast enjoys a more constant year-round sunny climate.

Language

Arabic remains the lingua franca of major cities in the south. The Chleuh tribes who dominate the Souss speak Tashelhit, a Berber dialect, most noticeable in the Anti Atlas. French is widely spoken and Spanish is still heard in some of Spain's former territories.

THE SOUSS VALLEY

Agadir

POP 679,000

اكادير

Agadir feels unlike anywhere else in Morocco. A busy port and beach resort sprawling beneath its kasbah, the city was completely rebuilt following a devastating earthquake in 1960. It is now the country's premier destination for sun, sand, televised soccer, pubs and pizza. Laid out as a large grid of downtown streets, surrounded by spacious residential suburbs, Agadir's concrete-covered inland quarters are ugly and sterile. However, the city hits its stride on the beachfront promenade, where Moroccan street life comes with a refreshing sense of space. Arching south of the shiny white marina, the sandy beach is more sheltered than many stretches of the Atlantic, offering clean water, safe swimming and 300 sunny days a year.

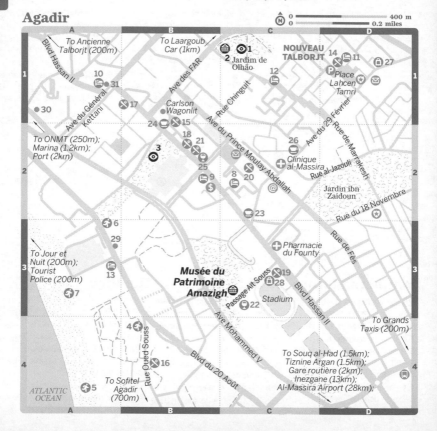

Agadir

Agadir caters mainly to package-tour holidaymakers, and will appeal less to independent travellers with an interest in Moroccan culture. Nonetheless, if you do pass through, relaxing on the beach and wandering around the handful of sights is a pleasant way to spend a day or two.

The city spreads over a large area, both along the coast and inland from the huge swathe of beach. From the northern end of the beach, near the marina and port, three parallel boulevards – 20 Août, nearest the ocean, Ave Mohammed V and Hassan II – run through the main tourist area. Many of the best hotels and resorts are found by the beach south of the centre. Inland, on the northeast side of town, Nouveau Talborjt (New Talborjt) has many budget hotels and restaurants.

History

Named after the *agadir* (fortified granary) of the Irir tribe, Agadir has a long history of boom and bust. It was founded in the 15th century by Portuguese merchants wanting to develop trade links with the Saharan caravans. From the mid-16th century, as the Saadian empire expanded, the port became prosperous from the export of local sugar, cotton and saltpetre, and products from Saharan trade, which the Moroccans then controlled. But this prosperity ended in the 1760s, when the Alawite Sultan Sidi Mohammed ben Abdallah diverted the trade north to Essaouira.

The French colonists went some way towards redeveloping Agadir in the 20th century, but the earthquake on 29 February 1960, which killed as many as 18,000 people, around half of the population, completely destroyed the city. The authorities, unable to cope with the apocalyptic aftermath of death and disease, sprayed the area with lime and DDT, and left the dead where they had been buried, in the collapsed city. The mound this created is now known as Ancienne Talborjt.

Since its reconstruction, Agadir has developed into an important port, with a large fishing fleet helping to make Morocco the world's largest exporter of tinned sardines. Agadir has also become Morocco's top

Agadir

SOUQ AL-HAD

Leave the seafront to shop with the locals at the **Souq al-Had** (Blvd Abderrahim Bouabid; ☺Tue-Sat), which slaps a big, messy dollop of Moroccan atmosphere onto concrete Agadir. On the left when you enter, among the lines of fresh fruit and veg, Berber apothecaries sell herbal incense, lipstick and potions that have all sorts of effects on the bowels. On the right, between stalls offering items from jellabas (a popular flowing garment) to fish, there are some good handicrafts including leatherwork and lanterns.

beach resort, and the new luxury marina complex signals plans to move the city upmarket.

☉ Sights

Musée du Patrimoine Amazigh　MUSEUM
(☏0528 82 16 32; Passage Aït Souss; adult/child Dh20/10; ☺9.30am-12.30pm & 2-5.30pm Mon-Sat) This small museum has an excellent display of Berber artefacts, especially strong on jewellery. Inspired by Marrakesh's Maison Tiskiwin (p68), it's a great place to learn about the traditional life and culture of the Berber people of the region.

Marina　AREA
(☏0661 21 57 46; off Ave Mohammed V) The city's newest attraction is a billion-dirham pleasure port between the beach and commercial port. As well as mooring for your floating palace, the complex of faux white kasbahs has holiday apartments, shops (mostly international brands), cafes, restaurants and boat trips for groups.

Mémoire d'Agadir　MUSEUM
(☏0528 82 16 32; cnr Ave du Président Kennedy & Ave des FAR; adult/child Dh20/10; ☺9.30am-12.30pm & 3-6pm Tue-Sat) This small museum in the southwest corner of Jardin de Olhão, entered from outside the park, is dedicated to the 1960 earthquake. Displays include interesting photos of Agadir since the 1920s, while others show the effects of the quake.

Jardin de Olhão　PARK
(Ave du Président Kennedy; ☺2.30-6.30pm Tue-Sun) A cool, relaxing garden created in 1992

to mark the twinning of Agadir with the Portuguese town of Olhão.

Vallée des Oiseaux　PARK
(Valley of the Birds; ☺11am-6pm) A leafy city-centre retreat in the dry riverbed running down from Blvd Hassan II to Blvd du 20 Août, with a shaded children's playground, aviary and small zoo.

Kasbah　KASBAH
(off Ave al-Moun) The hilltop kasbah, 7km northwest of the centre and visible from much of the city, is a rare survivor of the earthquake. The views from up here of the port, marina and Agadir are fantastic.

Built in 1541 by Saadian Sultan Mohammed ech-Cheikh, the kasbah was restored in the 1740s. The inscription over the entry arch in Dutch and Arabic ('Believe in God and respect the King') is a reminder of the beginning of trade with the Low Countries. Events took a turn for the worse in the 1750s when Agadir joined in a local revolt against the Alawite Sultan Moulay Abdallah. His revenge was to garrison the kasbah, move the Jewish community to Essaouira and forbid merchants to trade here. Later abandoned to the inhabitants of Agadir, the kasbah once provided housing for nearly 300 people. All that remains is the outer wall, though traces of the dwellings can still be made out.

The walk up to the kasbah is long, hot and uncomfortable: get a taxi (about Dh25) and walk back down.

Ancienne Talborjt　HISTORIC SITE
(off Ave al-Moun) The grassy area below the kasbah covers the remains of old Agadir town and constitutes a mass grave for all those who died in the 1960 earthquake.

Port　AREA
(off Ave Mohammed V) The commercial port is a good place to escape Agadir's tourist haunts and glimpse everyday Moroccan life, with boats being built and fish traded. Rather than walking around, drive or ask your taxi to detour en route from the kasbah to the centre. The police may want to see your passport or ID at the entrance.

⚡ Activities

BEACHES
Agadir's glory is its crescent beach, which usually remains unruffled when the Atlantic winds are blustering elsewhere. It's clean and well maintained, spotlit at night, and patrolled by lifeguards and police during

peak periods (mid-June to mid-September). There is a strong undertow.

The beach is mostly hassle-free, but single females or families will have a more relaxed time at one of the private beaches near the marina, or in front of the big hotels around **Sunset Beach** and **Palm Beach**. Facilities here include showers, toilets and kids' play areas; deckchairs and umbrellas can be hired.

The shops on the promenade just south of the marina sell bodyboards for about Dh130. Many beach hotels and surf clubs rent out windsurfing equipment, jet skis, bodyboards and surfboards.

If you prefer to stroll, the **promenade** runs for several kilometres from the marina to the royal palace.

OTHER

Petit Train d'Agadir   TOUR
(Blvd du 20 Août; adult/child Dh18/12; ⊘every 40 mins from 9.15am) This chain of buggies snakes around the city centre for 35 minutes.

Club Med   RESORT
(✆0528 82 95 00; Rue Oued Souss) Day passes for the all-inclusive resort, including lunch, dinner, drinks and a stage show, are available from Dh900 per person.

Tiznine Argan   HAMMAM, SPA
(✆0528 23 27 23; Lot 14, Immeuble 10, Amsernat) Near Souq al-Had, you can buy argan oil and cosmetics here, and enjoy massages (Dh300), a hammam (Dh150), manicures, pedicures and facials.

Several big hotels have spas offering hammam, massage and a range of treatments, with two of the best at the Royal Atlas and **Sofitel Agadir** (✆0528 82 00 88; Baie des Palmiers, Ben Sergao).

🛌 Sleeping

Agadir has set its sights on the midrange and top-end visitor, but if you move away from the beach, you will find a good selection of budget options (under Dh600 per night). High season in Agadir includes Easter, summer and the Christmas period, when European holidaymakers fly out on package tours. During these times, it's best to book ahead.

Midrange (Dh600 to Dh1200 per night) and top-end (over Dh1200 per night) hotels often offer discounts during low season; budget prices fluctuate less, but deals are available online. Many luxury hotels along the seafront are geared towards package tours, but discounts on their published rates are sometimes available to independent travellers.

Luxurious riads and kasbahs are found on the outskirts of Agadir – in the hills inland or to the south en route to Inezgane.

CENTRE & SEAFRONT

TOP\ CHOICE Hotel Atlantic   HOTEL €
(✆0528 84 36 61; www.atlantichotelagadir.com, in French; off Blvd Hassan II; s/d incl breakfast Dh298/393; 🛜🍴) The three-star Atlantic is one of the best deals in Agadir, offering comfortable rooms and, in the cool and breezy reception, professional service. There's a spa, a lovely little pool, and tours on offer.

Royal Atlas   HOTEL €€€
(✆0528 29 40 40; www.hotelsatlas.com; Blvd du 20 Août; s/d Dh1429/1658; ✳🛜@🍴) This beachfront colossus ticks all the five-star boxes with a Moroccan flourish. Carpets and antiques dot the tiled floors leading to the palm-fringed bar and pool area, and the 338 rooms and suites. Facilities include a nightclub, gym, Daniel Jouvance spa, Italian and Moroccan restaurants, and all the extras you would expect.

Hotel Riu Tikida Beach   RESORT €€€
(✆0528 84 54 00; www.agadirtikida.com; Chemin des Dunes; s/d Dh1266/1832; ✳🍴) Opposite the Atlantic Palace in the upmarket hotel area, the Riu Tikida Beach has a beachfront pool and golf course, restaurant and spa. Rooms are kitted out with two toilets and wardrobes, satellite TV and safe. For longer stays, it's cheaper to book through an agency such as First Choice or TUI.

Hôtel Kamal   HOTEL €
(✆0528 84 28 17; www.hotel-kamal.com; Blvd Hassan II; s/d/tr Dh404/465/569; 🛜🍴) A popular and well-run downtown hotel in a white block overlooking Place de L'Esperance, the Kamal manages to appeal to clients from package-tour groups to travelling Moroccans. Rooms are bright and clean, the staff are helpful and the pool is large enough to swim laps. Streetside rooms can be noisy, and breakfast (Dh36) is dull and overpriced. Discounts are offered online.

Hôtel La Petite Suède   HOTEL €
(✆0528 84 07 79; www.petitesuede.com; cnr Blvd Hassan II & Ave du Général Kettani; s/d/tr incl breakfast Dh215/350/465) Simple but

ⓘ TOP EATING SPOTS

» **Passage Aït Souss** Opposite the museum on this pedestrianised walkway, cafes serve Moroccan dishes and pizza.

» **Souq al-Had** At lunchtime, tajines bubble away outside the many cheap cafes.

» **Nouveau Talborjt** Cheap snack bars in and around this area are open after hours.

» **Port** At the entrance to the port, off Ave Mohammed V, you can pick up an ultrafresh, no-nonsense fish meal from around Dh50. The various types of seafood can differ greatly in price, so check costs before ordering. The stalls close in the early evening during the winter.

perfectly located hotel, five minutes' walk from the beach, with good service. It's one of Agadir's more Moroccan-styled hotels with an attractive, rug-scattered interior. The streetside rooms have large balconies, but the internal rooms are quieter.

NOUVEAU TALBORJT

The best area for budget options is away from the ocean in Nouveau Talborjt, where there are three budget hotels on Place Lahcen Tamri. The all-night bus activity and prostitution ensure that most hotel receptions here are open 24 hours.

Hotel Sindibad HOTEL €
(☎0528 82 34 77; sinhot@menara.ma; Place Lahcen Tamri; s/d Dh257/315; ❊❊) This blue-and-white building, overlooking the cafes on the square, has small en-suite rooms. The star attraction is the pint-sized rooftop pool.

Hotel Tamri HOTEL €
(☎0528 82 18 80; Ave du Président Kennedy; s/d Dh70/100) Recommended by readers, this modern riad hotel has turquoise balconies overlooking the palms in the tiled courtyard, and yellowed maps in reception for making plans. Rooms have basins, and the shared bathrooms have squat toilets.

✕ Eating

CENTRE & NOUVEAU TALBORJT

Mezzo Mezzo ITALIAN €€ [TOP CHOICE]
(☎0528 84 88 19; Blvd Hassan II; meals Dh200) A shining beacon among Agadir's

many stodgy pizzerias, Mezzo Mezzo offers unusual pizzas such as the spicy 'Bollywood'. The Italian chef also cooks up pasta and fish dishes, and there's a smooth European sophistication to the decor and service.

La Scala SEAFOOD €€
(☎0528 84 67 73; Rue Oued Souss; meals Dh150-250) Behind its unprepossessing brick exterior, La Scala is one of Agadir's best fish restaurants, with two pages of the menu devoted to seafood. Pasta and meat dishes are also available, and the food is generally elegant, fresh and beautifully presented. Free transport is offered if you book by telephone.

La Tour de Paris REGIONAL, SEAFOOD €
(☎0528 84 09 06; Blvd Hassan II; meals Dh110) One of the less pizza-orientated eateries in this area, La Tour de Paris has a pleasant terrace and art-nouveau stylings. Inside, the televised soccer and keyboard player are less impressive, but the menu features couscous, *pastilla* (pie), tajines, seafood, steaks and pasta.

1001 Nights REGIONAL, FAST FOOD €
(Place Lahcen Tamri; set menu Dh45) Recommended by readers, this Nouveau Talborjt institution with verandas on the square is one of Agadir's best budget eateries. Tajines (Dh35) and Western dishes are available.

Little Italy ITALIAN €
(☎0528 82 00 39; Blvd Hassan II; mains Dh50-75) One of the more attractive restaurants in the line of pizzerias between Uniprix and the Central Market, this cavernous joint is decorated with movie and mafia posters. 'Bingo' is a questionable pizza mixing prawns and turkey ham, but there's a good range of meat-free pizzas and pasta dishes.

SOS Poulet & Pizza FAST FOOD €
(☎0528 84 30 47; Ave du Prince Moulay Abdallah; half chicken Dh54, pizza Dh40-60) These adjoining snack bars are popular stalwarts for the tasty rotisserie chicken and pizzas.

MARINA

The upmarket Marina at the northern end of the seafront promenade has a concentration of midrange and top-end restaurants, where you can dine in style on international food.

Les Blancs SEAFOOD, SPANISH €€
(☎0528 82 83 68; meals Dh200-300) The city's best-located restaurant by a long way, occu-

pying a series of elegant white blocks by the beach at the entrance to the marina. Our grilled fish was rubbery, but it's worth giving the Andalucian and Moroccan dishes a try; paella, the house speciality, is available for two people minimum. In season, book ahead to score an outside table.

La Madrague   SEAFOOD, MEDITERRANEAN €€€
(✍0528 84 24 24; mains Dh120-250) This stylish restaurant occupies a quiet corner of the marina, with a view of the kasbah above the boats. It specialises in Mediterranean dishes such as tapas and risotto, plus fish and seafood including mussels and prawns.

Captain Tapas Bar   GERMAN, SEAFOOD €€
(✍0528 84 17 06; meals Dh175; ⊙breakfast, lunch & dinner) This typically mixed-up Agadiri affair is a German- and nautical-themed bar-restaurant serving everything but tapas: wiener schnitzel, Moroccan breakfast, fish and pizza.

Sud Ice   BREAKFAST, ICE CREAM €
(✍0528 84 07 75; sandwiches Dh45; ⊙breakfast, lunch & dinner; 🛜) This branch of the Venezia Ice chain is a popular spot to start the day.

SELF-CATERING

Souq al-Had   MARKET
(Blvd Abderrahim Bouabid; ⊙Tue-Sat) Pick up goodies including dates, olives, snails, chickpeas and chillies; plus fresh fruit, veg and eggs from the Souss Valley.

Uniprix   SUPERMARKET
(Blvd Hassan II) Stocks everything from cheese and biscuits to beer, wine and spirits.

Central Market   MARKET
(off Blvd Hassan II) Sells fresh food alongside the tourist tat.

🍷 Drinking

There's a great choice of cafes, where you can start the day with coffee and pastries or recover from the rigours of the beach. Many open midmorning, but the best time to hit the caffeine is late afternoon, when Agadiris return to consciousness after the hot afternoon and catch up with friends.

Blvd du 20 Août, inland from Sunset Beach, is good for bars and nightclubs, especially around the top of Rue Oued Souss. At the marina and along the promenade leading to it, there are also plenty of cafes and bars. The majority of bars have daily

happy hours between about 5pm and 8pm, and many offer the dubious pleasure of karaoke or crooning entertainers.

Restaurants in Agadir are generally licensed.

Uniprix Cafe   BAR, CAFE
(Blvd Hassan II) The outside tables at this bar are a prime spot for people-watching.

Jour et Nuit   CAFE
(promenade; ⊙24hr) A popular spot for a seafront sundowner. The newer of the two neighbouring branches is less male-dominated and has a panoramic terrace.

Patisserie Hassan   PATISSERIE, CAFE
(Blvd Hassan II) This patisserie diagonally opposite the Vallée des Oiseaux serves some of Agadir's best coffee and a good selection of sweet treats.

Yacout   PATISSERIE, CAFE
(Ave du 29 Février) With its shaded garden, screeching parrots and delicious Moroccan-European pastries, Yacout is a popular retreat from the concrete boulevards.

La Verandah   CAFE
(Immeuble Oumlil, Blvd Hassan II) Opposite the Royal Tennis Club, this meeting point offers strong coffee and a range of food, including sandwiches and omelettes, on its glassed-in veranda.

La Truite Irish Bar   PUB, CAFE
(Passage Aït Souss; 🛜) As its name suggests, this place is confused even by the standards of its genre, with more pictures of King Mohammed VI than shamrocks. Nonetheless, it offers outside tables, draught beer, English breakfasts and soccer broadcasts.

☆ Entertainment

There is a decent range of clubs, mostly scattered along Blvd du 20 Août and attached to the big hotels. Entry ranges from Dh50 to Dh250, including a drink. During the low season, tourists are sometimes allowed in free of charge and clubs close at around 2am.

So   NIGHTCLUB
(✍0528 82 00 88; Sofitel Agadir, Baie des Palmiers, Ben Sergao) The hippest club in Agadir and one of the most expensive, laid out on several levels with features including champagne and vodka bars, a live-music stage and a restaurant. Local players save this one for the climax of the evening's entertainment.

Papa Gayo NIGHTCLUB
(📞0661 99 97 68; Hotel Riu Tikida Beach, Chemins des Dunes) One of Agadir's most popular nightclubs, attracting international DJs. Dance the night away and chill on the beach.

Festival Timatar FESTIVAL
(http://festival-timitar-agadir.blogspot.com) The city's annual music festival attracts Moroccan and African musicians each July.

Club Med DINNER THEATRE
(📞0528 82 95 00; Rue Oued Souss) Evening passes (9pm to 2am) for the all-inclusive resort, including dinner, drinks and a stage show, cost Dh330 per person.

🛍 Shopping

Souvenirs are often trucked into Agadir from other parts of Morocco and tend to be of low quality, although Marrakshi vendors have started to outsource production here. The options in the centre are unatmospheric but low-pressure environments offering easy shopping.

TOP CHOICE Souq al-Had ART & CRAFT, FOOD & DRINK
(Blvd Abderrahim Bouabid; ⊗Tue-Sat) The most atmospheric and fun place to shop for craftwork.

Ensemble Artisanal ART & CRAFT
(Ave du 29 Février) Some of the best-quality craftwork found in Agadir.

Central Market ART & CRAFT
(off Blvd Hassan II) Pick up presents from chess boards to leatherwork in and around this concrete building.

Uniprix SUPERMARKET
(Blvd Hassan II) Sells swimwear, holiday essentials and some handicrafts.

Librairie Papetrie BOOKSHOP
(Passage Aït Souss) Has a decent selection of English and French paperback novels and guidebooks.

Al Mouggar Bookshop BOOKSHOP
(cnr Ave du Prince Moulay Abdallah & Ave du 29 Février) Has a wide selection of French books, and a small section of English paperback novels.

ℹ Information

Emergency
Most of the larger hotels are able to recommend reliable, English-speaking doctors.
Ambulance (📞15)

Police (📞19; Rue du 18 Novembre) There's also a Nouveau Talborjt office on Place Lahcen Tamri, and there's a Tourist Police post on the promenade.

Internet Access
There are dozens of internet cafes, charging Dh5 to Dh10 per hour.
Adrar Net (Ave du Prince Moulay Abdallah; per hr Dh5; ⊗9am-10pm)

Medical Services
Clinique al-Massira (📞0528 84 32 38; Ave du 29 Février; ⊗24hr) Medical clinic.
Pharmacie du Founty (📞0528 84 40 23; Immeuble Tigoremine, Blvd Hassan II) Pharmacy.

Money
Most banks have ATMs, and there are exchange booths and ATMs at the airport. Large hotels change cash and travellers cheques. There are banks all along Blvd Hassan II.
Banque Populaire (Blvd Hassan II) Has a bureau de change, one of two next to Hôtel Kamal.

Post
Main post office (Ave Sidi Mohammed)
Post office (Ave du 29 Février, Nouveau Talborjt)
Post office (Souq al-Had, Blvd Abderrahim Bouabid)

Tourist Information
Bureau du Port de Plaisance (📞0661 21 57 46; Marina) With an information board outside.
Information booth (Al-Massira Airport)
ONMT (Délégation Régionale du Tourisme; 📞0528 84 63 77; Immeuble Ignouan, Ave Mohammed V; ⊗8.30am-4.30pm Mon-Fri) In the blue building next to DHL; not particularly helpful.

Travel Agencies
There are many travel agencies around the junction of Blvd Hassan II and Ave des FAR.
Carlson Wagonlit (📞0528 84 15 28; 26 Ave des FAR) Represents major airlines.
Complete Tours (📞0528 82 34 01; Immeuble Oumlil 26, Blvd Hassan II; www.complete-tours.com) Runs trips to Taroudannt, Tafraoute and elsewhere in the region.

🚌 Getting There & Away

Air
Al-Massira Airport (📞0528 83 91 12; www.onda.ma; N10), mainly served by European charter flights and budget airlines, is 28km southeast of Agadir en route to Taroudannt. There are exchange facilities, ATMs, car-hire booths, a post office and a couple of cafes here.

Royal Air Maroc (RAM; ☎0528 82 91 20; www.royalairmaroc.com; Ave du Général Kettani) has daily flights to/from Casablanca and Paris, and to/from Dakhla on Wednesday.

Bus

Although a good number of buses serve Agadir, it is quite possible you'll end up in Inezgane, 13km south, the regional transport hub. Check before you buy your ticket. Plenty of grands taxis (Dh10) and local buses (Dh8) shuttle between there and Agadir.

All the major bus companies, and plenty of smaller companies, serve the massive circular **gare routière** (bus station; Blvd Abderrahim Bouabid), past Souq al-Had. If you want to travel on a specific bus, it is worth booking ahead.

CTM (☎0528 22 55 96; www.ctm.ma), which also has a Nouveau Talborjt office on Rue Yacoub el-Mansour, just off Place Lahcen Tamri, has regular departures to these destinations.

DESTINATION	COST (DH)	DURATION (HR)
Casablanca	200	6½
Dakhla	340	21
Essaouira	60	3
Laâyoune	220	10
Marrakesh	95	4
Rabat	220	10
Tangier	320	13
Taroudannt	28	1½
Tiznit	40	2

Supratours (☎0528 22 40 10; www.supratours.ma), which also has a city-centre office on the corner of Blvd Hassan II and Ave des FAR, offers similar, slightly more expensive services.

Car & Motorcycle

Car hire is never cheap in Morocco, but you can find some of the country's best deals in Agadir. The distances involved in touring the region, particularly further south, make it worthwhile considering car rental.

With the local agencies around the corner of Blvd Hassan II and Ave des FAR, prices start at around Dh300 per day for the smallest car, though there's usually room for haggling. The big companies (including Avis, Europcar and Hertz) and some smaller operators all have offices on Ave Mohammed V, near the bottom of Ave du Général Kettani. Scooters and motorbikes are also available, but check the state of the machines carefully.

Boutique Hotel Kenzi (☎0528 47 33 05; Blvd du 20 Août) Scooters available from Dh150 per half-day; no driving licence required.

TAXIS

You can catch a taxi straight from Al-Massira Airport to numerous destinations. Tariffs for private hire, which are displayed on a board at the airport:

Essaouira or Goulimime Dh800

Mirleft Dh600

Taghazout Dh300

Taroudannt or Tiznit Dh350/450 by day/night

Budget (☎airport 0528 83 91 01, office 0528 84 82 22; www.budget.ma; Immeuble Marhaba, Ave Mohammed V) The cheapest of the large companies in this area, charging Dh255 to Dh436 per day for the smallest car.

Laargoub Car (☎0661 57 59 72; www.laargoubcar.com; Ave des FAR) Recommended, with one-way rental available; charges Dh250 to Dh350 per day for the smallest car, depending on the length of time you hire for.

Taxi

The main grand-taxi rank is located at the south end of Rue de Fès. Destinations include Essaouira (Dh75), Inezgane (Dh5) and Taroudannt (Dh27).

Getting Around

To/From the Airport

There is no direct bus between the airport and Agadir.

BUS 37 Runs from outside the airport (about 500m straight out on the road) to Inezgane (Dh5) every 40 minutes or so until about 8.30pm.

GRAND TAXI Between the airport and Agadir costs Dh150/200 by day/night for up to six people. Expect to pay extra for luggage.

Bus

The main local bus station is next to the grand-taxi rank at the southern end of town. Journeys within Agadir cost Dh4 and you can buy tickets on the bus.

BUSES 6, 21 AND 23 Run along Ave Mohammed V every 10 minutes or so to/from Inezgane (Dh8), the latter two routes starting at Agadir port.

Taxi

Orange petits taxis run around town. Prices are worked out by meter, so ask for the meter to be switched on.

Around Agadir

INEZGANE إنزكان

One of the region's transport hubs, Inezgane, 13km south of Agadir, is not a tourist destination, but some travellers enjoy stopping here for that very reason. There's a vast fresh-produce market across Ave Mokhtar Soussi, the main street, from the combined bus station and grand-taxi lot. Tuesday is the main souq.

Hôtel-Restaurant La Pergola (☑0528 27 18 01; www.lapergola.ma; Km 8 Rte d'Agadir; s/d Dh223/264) is a relic of another, low-key Agadir, its bungalows set in a flowery garden. The traffic noise on the N1 outside is constant and the blandly comfortable rooms need a fresh coat of paint, but the pleasant bar-restaurant (breakfast Dh24, set menu Dh106) serves old-fashioned French cuisine with some Moroccan specialities, all very comforting after a long bus journey.

The best of the cheap hotels around the bus station, **Hôtel Hagounia** (☑0528 83 27 83; 9 Ave Mokhtar Soussi; s/d Dh143/190) is friendly and comfortable, if a little musty. Rooms at the front have balconies, but those at the back are quieter.

You'll find dozens of cheap cafes and restaurants around the main square and outside the market.

There are plenty of buses going in all possible directions. The bus station is just off the Agadir–Tiznit road. The CTM and Supratours offices are nearby, facing each other on Ave Mokhtar Soussi.

Loads of grands taxis to Essaouira (Dh80, three hours), Tiznit (Dh23, two hours) and Taroudannt (Dh23, 2½ hours) gather here, as well as less regular taxis for Goulimime (Dh60, 4½ hours) and Tan Tan (Dh80, six hours).

Adding to the organised chaos are regular local buses (Dh8) and grands taxis (Dh5) heading to Agadir, and to Al-Massira Airport (bus 37).

Souss-Massa National Park منتزه سو ماسه الوطني

Places like the Souss-Massa National Park are going to become ever more important in Morocco's future. The most significant of all the country's national parks stretches 70km south of Agadir, a block of over 330 sq km of protected land between the main north–south highway and the beach. It is a spectacular and wild place of cliffs, sand dunes, farmland, coastal steppes and forests.

The park was created in 1991 in recognition of its importance as a feeding ground for birds. Along with the Souss estuary near Inezgane, it has become popular with birdwatchers, although it is also a great place for walking. The best times to visit are March and April, as well as October and November.

During the winter, ospreys and large flocks of pochard and other ducks are commonly seen, as well as greater flamingos. But the biggest attraction is the population of bald ibises. These birds, revered in ancient Egypt and once widespread in central Europe, North Africa and the Middle East, are now an endangered species. A few small colonies or breeding pairs have been found around the eastern Mediterranean, but over half of the world's total population is found in the Souss-Massa. The greatest threat, now, comes from tourism development. For the moment, the breeding grounds remain off-limits, though you can spot the ibises around Oued Massa or at the mouth of the Tamri River.

Jackal, red fox, wild cat, genet and Eurasian wild boar are also found in the park, while a large fenced area in the north of the park contains species that have disappeared from the south, including Dorcas gazelles, addaxes, red-necked ostriches and scimitar horned oryxes. A new visitor centre, under construction at the park's main entrance near the village of Massa, will house the **Souss-Massa National Park headquarters** (☑0528 33 38 80). Some 58km south of Agadir, this is signposted from the N1.

Guides (Dh100 to Dh150) can be arranged in Massa, from where a track leads along the river to the estuary mouth (3km) and **Sidi R'bat**. This tiny village has two claims to fame. Supposedly it is where the biblical Jonah was vomited up by a whale, and also where Uqba bin Nafi, the 7th-century Arab conqueror of Morocco, rode his horse triumphantly into the sea and called on God to witness the fact that he could find no land left to conquer.

Ksar Massa (☑0661 28 03 19; www.ksarmassa.com; Sidi R'bat, Oued Massa; s/d/tr incl breakfast Dh1380/1900/2600, tent s/d Dh700/1100, lunch/dinner Dh170/300; ❄❄), spectacularly located in the middle of the park, is a fantastical destination in itself. The terracotta-and-blue contemporary kasbah on the beach is a wonderful place to unwind. Luxuriously spacious rooms and suites are painted in bright colours and the pool overlooks the ocean. Management can arrange guided trips into the park and throughout the region. To get there follow the signposts from Massa.

❶ Getting There & Away

From Agadir and Inezgane, Tiznit-bound local buses and grands taxis will drop you in Massa (about Dh20). From there, it is about an hour's walk to Oued Massa river mouth; 4WDs also head into the park, but both Oued Massa and Oued Souss are usually accessible by 2WD (or grand taxi).

North of Agadir

Despite the villas, fun parks, golf courses and development projects colonising the coast around Agadir, if you're looking for surf and less crowded beaches, head north. There are beautiful sandy coves every few kilometres.

❶ Getting There & Away

Bus 32 travels between Agadir port and Taghazout (Dh8) via Aourir and Tamraght; a grand taxi from the city costs the same.

TAMRAGHT & AOURIR
طمر ات و اوريد

Aourir and Tamraght are known collectively as Banana Village because of the banana groves alongside Oued Tamraght, which separates the villages. Respectively some 12km and 15km north of Agadir, they share Banana Beach, which can be good for beginner surfers. Aourir has a lively Wednesday souq on the ocean side of the N1.

At Rocher du Diable, round the headland to the north of Banana Beach, you can hire surf boards and bodyboards (from Dh100 per day) from **Surf Tours Maroc** (⌨0661 51 89 33; www.surftoursmaroc.co.uk) and **Imourane Surf Shop** (⌨0676 03 69 18).

Next to Banana Beach, **Villa Mandala** (⌨0528 20 03 68; www.surfmaroc.co.uk; Aourir; r per person incl breakfast Dh400-500; ☀) is run by Surf Maroc and geared towards surfers. The decor mixes traditional and contemporary; a swirl of pebbles greets you before you climb to the curvy pool and white, rug-scattered interior.

With a bar-restaurant, **Hotel Littoral** (⌨0528 31 47 26; www.hotellittoral.com; Aourir; s/d incl breakfast Dh200/300; ☀) is basic but

comfortable, offering better value than options in Agadir.

Tanit (⌨0528 31 48 75; Aourir; meals Dh50), a modern kasbah of a restaurant, has a cool, shady interior and a tower, where you can eat with views of the hills. Dishes include *pastilla* and all the classics, and there's entertainment on Friday and Saturday nights.

There is a basic cafe at the northern end of Banana Beach, but **Chez Brahim** (⌨0673 21 02 93; Rocher du Diable; meals Dh115) is better, offering hearty fish or meat platters on its seafront terrace.

TAGHAZOUT
تاغزوت

Six kilometres from Tamraght, the laid-back fishing village of Taghazout, which was once famous for calamari and hippies, is now considered Morocco's premier surfing destination. Surf breaks such as Killer Point, La Source and Anka Point continue to attract experienced surfers, while beginners try out the appropriately named Hash Point. The surf is most reliable from September to May.

Run by a group of British surfers, **Surf Maroc** (⌨0528 20 03 68, in UK 0044 208 123 0319; ☎) offers accommodation, guiding, lessons, equipment hire and yoga, appealing to beginners, pros and landlubbers who just want to hang out. Accommodation comes with splashes of surf cool at **L'Auberge** (r per person incl breakfast Dh250), the wonderful **Taghazout Villa** (r Dh350) at Hash Point, and Villa Mandala. Week, day and half-day packages are available.

There are apartments and rooms to rent in the village (Dh150 to Dh1000), including at **Riad Taghazout** (⌨0650 69 18 85; s/d Dh300/400; ☎), near Surf Maroc. Out of high season you can usually turn up and find somewhere to stay.

At the foot of the lanes leading from the town square to the beach, the cafe at **L'Auberge** (⌨0528 20 03 68; meals Dh50) is a funky hang-out serving Moroccan and international food.

There's internet at **Internet Cafe Amouage** (per hr Dh8; ◷8.30am-9pm).

Immouzzer des Ida Outanane
ايموزار ادو اوتنان

This thoroughly recommended detour takes you about 60km (two hours' drive) northeast of Agadir, into the High Atlas foothills. On the way you pass through the aptly named **Paradise Valley**, an oleander- and palm-lined gorge, and a popular picnic and swimming spot. Local producers have formed a **route du miel** (honey route), and stalls sell the sweet stuff as well as argan oil. Signs by the road point to a 3km walking trail.

Thirty kilometres beyond the hotels in Paradise Valley, the famous cascades of Immouzzer are one of North Africa's most beautiful waterfalls. They flow most strongly between February and August, although recent droughts have frequently reduced them to a trickle. Given the stream of tourist stalls and *faux guides* (unofficial guides) leading to the falls, you may prefer Paradise Valley.

When it's flowing, water falls off the edge of the plateau in several chutes, running down one cliff face known as the Bride's Veil. The path to the foot of the falls finishes at an iridescent blue plunge pool with overhanging rocks and foliage. If you can cross the river here, you can climb to a plateau and see the top plunge pool, and caves once inhabited by hippies. The steep, 4km road from Immouzzer village down to the path is one of many walks in the region.

The area turns white in spring when the almond trees blossom. There is a honey harvest and festival in July and August, and around late November you may be lucky enough to witness the olive harvest, when villagers climb into the trees to shake the olives from the branches. Thursday is souq day.

Sleeping & Eating

There are two cafes at the bottom of the path to the falls, and one on the way up.

Hôtel des Cascades　　　　HOTEL €€
(☎0528 21 88 08; www.cascades-hotel.net, in French; s/d Dh462/572; ☎) In a wonderful location on the edge of Immouzzer village, perched high above the valley, this hotel is set in a riotous garden with tennis courts. Flower baskets and artwork decorate the terrace and corridors; the 27 spacious rooms have small balconies, and there's a restaurant (set menu Dh180). A 4km path descends from the garden to the cascades.

Auberge Bab Immouzer　　　HOTEL €
(☎0670 13 10 06; Paradise Valley; r incl breakfast Dh300; ☎) The new kid in the valley has nine en-suite rooms with tiled floors, and a series of terraces overlooking the neighbouring *palmeraie* (palm grove) and valley. The res-

taurant's smoked-glass windows allow you to enjoy the views during the bright days.

Auberge le Panoramic　　　HOTEL €
(☎0528 21 67 09; Paradise Valley; s/d incl half-board Dh250/450; ☎) This *route du miel* stop has a gobsmacking view down the valley from its terrace, where you can eat a simple dinner of Moroccan salad and tajine, and breakfast on two homemade honeys. The basic rooms share a bathroom with sit-down toilet and cold shower. The same family runs nearby Hôtel Tifrit (single/double from Dh250/500).

ⓘ Getting There & Away

An unreliable local bus runs from Agadir bus station to Immouzzer (Dh30, three hours) – if there are enough passengers. You'll then have to wait until the following morning for the unreliable bus back. A better option Is a grand taxi (Dh35), easiest on Thursday, which is market day. Hotels and travel agencies in Agadir offer coach tours to Immouzzer.

Taroudannt　　　تارودانت

POP 70,000

Taroudannt (also spelled Taroudant) is sometimes called 'Little Marrakesh', but that description doesn't do the Souss Valley trading centre justice. Hidden by magnificent red-mud walls, and with the snow-capped peaks of the High Atlas beckoning beyond, Taroudannt's souqs and squares have a healthy sprinkling of Maghrebi mystique. Yet it is also a practical place, a market town where Berbers trade the produce of the rich and fertile Oued Souss basin.

There aren't any must-see sights. Instead, the medina is a place to stroll and linger. The two souqs are well worth a browse, more laid-back than Marrakesh, but with an atmosphere of activity that is missing in Agadir, 80km away. The town also makes an excellent base for trekking into the little-explored western High Atlas.

History

Taroudannt was one of the early bases of the Almoravids, who established themselves here in 1056 AD, at the beginning of their conquest of Morocco. In the 16th century the emerging Saadians made it their capital for about 20 years. By the time they moved on to Marrakesh, they had turned the Souss Valley, in which the city stands, into the country's most important producer of sugar cane, cotton, rice and indigo; all valuable trade items on the trans-Saharan trade routes the dynasty was keen to control. The Saadians constructed the old part of town and the kasbah, though most of it was destroyed and the inhabitants massacred in 1687 by Moulay Ismail, as punishment for opposing him. Only the ramparts survived. Most of what stands inside them dates from the 18th century.

Taroudannt continued to be a centre of intrigue and sedition against the central government well into the 20th century, and indeed played host to the Idrissid El-Hiba, a southern chief who opposed the Treaty of Fès, the 1912 agreement that created the French Protectorate.

⊙ Sights

Ramparts
HISTORIC SITE

The 7.5km of ramparts surrounding Taroudannt are among the best-preserved pisé walls in Morocco. Their colour changes from golden brown to deepest red depending on the time of day. They can easily be explored on foot (two hours), preferably in the late afternoon; or take a bike or calèche and see the walls by moonlight.

Gates
HISTORIC SITE

Built in the 16th and 17th century, a string of mighty defensive towers create the gates of the city. Considered the main gate, the triple-arched **Bab el-Kasbah** (also known as Bab Essalsla) is approached via an avenue of orange trees. Steps lead to the top of the tower, where you can walk along the

WORTH A TRIP

TIOUTE KASBAH

Southwest of Taroudannt, this **kasbah** is so picture-perfect that it was used as a location in the 1954 French production of *Ali Baba and the Forty Thieves*. The stone kasbah overlooks a *palmeraie* and a couple of restaurants, with the High and Anti Atlas in the distance. Visit early to ensure you find a grand taxi (Dh10, 30 minutes) there and back, and to beat the tour groups.

ramparts. Near Bab el-Kasbah, **Bab Sedra** (cyclists and pedestrians only) leads to the old kasbah quarter

Kasbah
KASBAH

The old kasbah quarter, was a fortress built by Moulay Ismail. Today it's a poor but safe residential area, where winding lanes and low archways lead to tiny squares and dead ends. The governor's palace, on the eastern side of the kasbah, now forms part of the Hôtel Palais Salam (p375).

🏃 Activities

Calèche
CARRIAGE TOUR

You can tour the ramparts in a calèche. The horse-drawn carriages gather just inside Bab el-Kasbah, on Place al-Alaouyine and at other prominent spots. A one-way trip across town should cost Dh7, the same as a petit taxi, but you may have trouble persuading the driver beneath Dh15. Likewise, a one-hour tour including the medina and

ARGAN COUNTRY

As you travel along the N10 east of Taroudannt you will see frizzy argan trees, beloved of local goats and international chefs (see p232), growing near the road.

In a restored 19th-century mansion on the edge of the Berber village of Ouled Berhil, some 45km northeast of Taroudannt, is **Hôtel Palais Riad Hida** (📞 0528 53 10 44; www.riadhida.com; s/d incl half-board Dh566/932; ✸). Accommodation is in nondescript bungalows, but it's a special environment from the moment you cross the tiled threshold and clap eyes on the central courtyard, with its towering palms and long pools.

Some 10km further on from Ouled Berhil, a signpost indicates the Tizi n'Test road (see p119), one of the most spectacular and perilous passes in the country, leading northeast over the High Atlas to Marrakesh.

Approaching the mountains, this secondary road leads through a lush state-run **argan preserve** – a dream destination for mountain goats accustomed to slim pickings in the High Atlas. Stop here to picnic in the shade among frolicking kids, or stake out the herds for the ultimate Anti Atlas postcard shot: a goat casually balanced on treetop, munching on sun-ripe argan nuts.

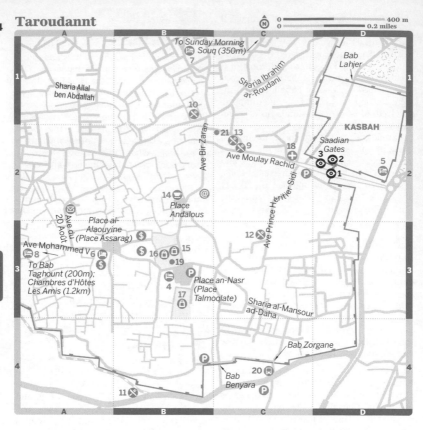

a circuit of the ramparts should cost Dh40, but the starting price will likely be closer to Dh80.

Trekking   TREKKING

Taroudannt is a great base for trekking in the western High Atlas region, including the secluded **Tichka Plateau**, a delightful area of highland meadows and hidden gorges. Agencies in town offer treks; insist on travelling only with a qualified guide. Based at Chambres d'Hotes Les Amis, recommended guide **Said Dayfollah** (☎0667 60 16 86; http://chambreslesamis.eu5.org; Sidi Belkas) organises homestays and oasis visits as well as walking trips. Charges are typically Dh350 per person per day, including transport and picnic (Dh250 if you have a vehicle).

🛏 Sleeping

Budget hotels on and around the two central squares offer basic accommodation and roof terraces, good for sunbathing and people-watching.

TOP CHOICE Naturally Morocco Guest House   GUESTHOUSE €

(☎bookings 0044 1239 710814, 0528 55 16 28, 0661 23 66 27; www.naturallymorocco.co.uk; 422 Derb Afferdou; s/d incl breakfast Dh350/550; ☎@). If only there were more places like this medina house, which gives a rare glimpse into Moroccan life and won a Responsible Tourism award. Run by locals in conjunction with UK-based Naturally Morocco, it offers delicious Moroccan meals and skilled guides. Activities include trekking, wildlife trips, coastal excursions and craft workshops, all with an emphasis on cultural contact. The eight-room house has a kitchen for self-catering, a roof terrace with views of the High and Anti Atlas, informative displays in the tiled corridors, and a small library. Packages and bike hire are available.

Taroudannt

Hôtel Palais Salam KASBAH €€
(☎0528 85 25 01; palsalam@menara.ma; kasbah; s/d/apt from Dh562/674/2412; 🛰🗐) This former pasha's residence, entered through the east wall of the kasbah, lives up to its palatial name, with gardens, pools and fountains (one inhabited by turtles) on various levels. Readers recommend the older, ground-floor rooms for their authenticity, but the newer rooms, behind pink walls and blue shutters, are spacious and pleasant. There's a bar and Moroccan and international restaurants.

Riad Maryam Résidence RIAD €€
(☎0666 12 72 85; Derb Maalem Mohammed 141; s/d incl breakfast Dh500/700; 🛰) Recommended by readers, this four-room riad is an

oasis of tranquillity in the medina, and its leafy courtyard could pass for a *palmeraie*. It's signposted from Ave Mohammed V and has been beautifully restored, with brightly painted doors, exposed wooden beams and rugs swathing the floors.

Chambres d'Hôtes Les Amis GUESTHOUSE €
(☎0667 60 16 86; http://chambreslesamis.eu5. org; Sidi Belkas; s/d incl breakfast Dh90/160) This good-value guesthouse has simple but sizeable rooms, basic bathrooms with intermittent hot water, a couple of salons, and a roof terrace for breakfast. It's a 10-minute walk west of Bab Taghount (on the west side of the ramparts) at the beginning of the open countryside – a peaceful retreat from the medina. The enthusiastic, helpful proprietor, Said Dayfollah, offers bike hire, pick-ups from Agadir Al-Massira Airport (Dh300) and meals on request (Dh70).

Hôtel Taroudannt HOTEL €
(☎0528 85 24 16; Ave Mohammed V & Place al-Alaouyine; s/d Dh160/200) This central option has the makings of the best budget hotel in town, with tiled corridors leading past a pleasant restaurant and jungly courtyard to rooms with simple bathrooms. The drawbacks are the insalubrious characters in the bar and hustlers hanging around outside.

Hôtel el-Warda HOTEL €
(☎0528 85 27 63; Place an-Nasr; s/d/tr Dh50/70/90) The best of the ultra-cheapies, with a funky *zellij* (tilework) terrace overlooking Place an-Nasr. The basic rooms, located on the 2nd floor, share toilets and showers. It is run by women, but solo female travellers might find the alley entrance and male-dominated 1st-floor cafe difficult.

✗ Eating
The hotel cafes and touristy eateries on Place al-Alaouyine are good for breakfast on the square, and serve tajines and simple grills later in the day (set menu Dh80). The best place to look for cheap eats is around Place an-Nasr and north along Ave Bir Zaran, where you find the usual tajines, *harira* (lentil soup) and salads.

TOP CHOICE L'Agence REGIONAL, FRENCH €
(☎0528 55 02 70; Ave Sidi Mohammed; set menu Dh95) Behind the Grand Mosquée, this delightful little restaurant serves dishes from the French-Moroccan proprietors' homelands, with mains such as chicken *pastilla* and sardine tajine on offer. The starters in-

clude delicious tasting plates, which you can enjoy among lanterns hanging from wooden beams and artworks in alcoves.

Chez Nada
REGIONAL €

(☎0528 85 17 26; Ave Moulay Rachid; set menu Dh80; ☀) West of Bab el-Kasbah, this 55-year-old restaurant is famous for its tajines, including one with pigeon and a rich one with chicken, egg and prunes. Above the male-dominated ground-floor cafe and elegant white 1st-floor dining room, the roof terrace has views over public gardens. Food is home-cooked and excellent. *Pastilla* and royal couscous (Dh60 to Dh95) should be ordered a couple of hours ahead.

Jnane Soussia
REGIONAL €€

(☎0528 85 49 80; mains Dh80; ☀☀) A delightful restaurant, a short walk from the grand-taxi station, with tented seating areas set around a large pool in a garden adjacent to the ramparts. The house specialities are *mechoui* (whole roast lamb) and pigeon *pastilla,* which have to be ordered in advance, but everything here is good.

Mehdi Snack
FAST FOOD €

(off Ave Moulay Rachid; set menu & pizza Dh30-60; ☺lunch & noon-6pm) Located at the back of Chez Nada, and run by the same family, this is a good snack bar with cheap burgers, salads and pizzas.

SELF-CATERING
Putting together a picnic is not a problem in Taroudannt. In addition to stalls in the souqs – fresh fruit and baskets are conveniently sold side by side at Souq Berbère – there's a **fruit and vegetable market** at the northern end of Ave Bir Zaran.

Drinking

Cafe Andalous
JUICE BAR

(Place Andalous; smoothie Dh10; ☺8am-1pm & 2-10pm) North of the Souq Arabe, this cheerful place on a small square adjoining Ave Bir Zaran is good for a mixed-fruit smoothie.

Shopping
Taroudannt is the central Chleuh city of the Souss, so it is a good place to look for the good-quality silver jewellery for which this tribe is renowned. The jewellery is influenced both by Saharan tribes and by Jewish silversmiths, who formed a significant part of the community until the late 1960s.

Souq Arabe
ART & CRAFT

CHOICE The main souq, also known as the *grand souq,* and east of Place al-Alaouyine, has antique and souvenir shops hidden in the quiet streets. The area just southwest of the mosque is good for present shopping, with a small square of jewellery shops.

Souq Berbère
ART & CRAFT, CARPETS

Also known as the *marché municipal,* this souq on the south side of Place an-Nasr sells carpets, jewellery, argan oil, musical instruments, lamps, leatherwork and ceramics – past the trainers and mobile phones on the central thoroughfare.

Argent du Sud
JEWELLERY

(☎0548 55 03 32; 60 Joutia, Souq Arabe) At this shop in the Souq Berbère, the low-pressure Abdul sells beautiful pieces (Dh50 to Dh400), mixing Berber and Western designs.

Sunday Morning Souq
FOOD & DRINK

This large market, held just outside Bab al-Khemis north of the kasbah, brings in people from the whole region.

❶ Information
Taroudannt has no 'European' quarter or ville nouvelle (new town). Most facilities are found on and around the two central squares, Place al-Alaouyine (formerly Place Assarag) and Place an-Nasr (formerly Place Talmoqlate).

Banks on Place al-Alaouyine have ATMs, money-changing facilities and visa services; Crédit du Maroc and BMCI provide the best service.

Hospital (Ave Moulay Rachid) By the kasbah.

Inezgane Voyages (☎0528 55 06 46; Place an-Nasr) Represents airlines including Royal Air Maroc.

Pharmacie du Sud (☎0528 85 22 59; Place an-Nasr)

Post office (Ave du 20 Août) Just northwest of Place al-Alaouyine.

Roudana Cyber Cafe (1st fl, Ave Bir Zaran; per hr Dh3; ☺8.30am-midnight) Has a slow connection (like the two 1st-floor internet cafes on Ave Mohammed V, west of Place al-Alaouyine) but entertains customers with rock music while pages are loading.

❶ Getting There & Away
Accommodation can organise pick-ups from Agadir Al-Massira Airport.

Bus
All buses leave from the main bus station outside Bab Zorgane.

» The flowers are harvested before sunrise, as sunlight depletes the saffron's taste and vitamin content.

» Only the flowers' three trumpet-shaped stigmas are used; these are extracted and placed in the dark to dry.

» During drying, the stigmas lose 80% of their weight; 1kg shrinks to 200g.

» It takes 140 flowers to produce 1g of saffron.

» High in vitamin B (especially B12) and pro-vitamin E, saffron has antiseptic, anti-spasmodic and antioxidant properties.

» Saffron is used in cooking, medicine (it's good for gums in particular), carpet-dying, calligraphy ink, soap and cosmetics.

» Beware 'counterfeit saffron'; the genuine article should stain your fingers yellow (rather than red), taste bitter (rather than sweet) and carry a spicy price tag.

CTM (Bab Zorgane) has the most reliable buses, with at least one daily service to each of the following.

DESTINATION	COST (DH)	DURATION (HR)
Agadir	28	1½
Casablanca	160	8
Marrakesh	80	6
Ouarzazate	70	5

Other companies serve Inezgane (Dh15, 1½ hours), Taliouine (Dh45, 1½ hours, three Salamaa buses per day) and Tata (Dh45, five hours, two Aoulouz buses per day).

Car
Tinghir Cars (☑0528 85 08 10; Ave Moulay Rachid Ferk Lahbab) This local agency hires out small cars for Dh500/400 per day for one/seven days.

Taxi
Grands taxis gather at the bus station outside Bab Zorgane.
Agad (Dh27) Infrequently.
Inezgane (Dh23) Change here for frequent services to Agadir.
Marrakesh (Dh100) To travel via the Tizi n'Test, you will need to hire the entire taxi (Dh700).

ⓘ Getting Around
Taroudannt is a good place to cycle; bikes can be rented at **Brahim Bikes** (Place al-Alaouyine; per hr/day Dh10/50), next to Hôtel Taroudannt. Petits taxis charge Dh7 per trip (Dh10 at night).

Taliouine
تالوين

The straggling village of Taliouine, halfway between Taroudannt and Ouarzazate, is dominated by hills and the impressive Glaoui kasbah.

Taliouine is the African centre of *l'or rouge* (red gold) – saffron, the world's most expensive spice. You can buy it here for about Dh40 per gram. The purple *crocus sativus* flower, from which the spice comes, grows only above 1200m. It flowers between mid-October and mid-November, when a festival is held to celebrate the harvest and you can see locals picking the flowers around villages 12km east of Taliouine.

A *maison safran* (saffron centre) is set to open here, with a market for the spice and a lab where you can check your purchase is the real deal.

⊙ Sights & Activities
Activities can be arranged through **Yallahtrek** (☑0667 39 80 78; www.yallah.ch), near Coopérative Souktana du Safran, as well as through the hotels. The Swiss-Moroccan company specialises in trekking activities, but it also offers saffron tours, programs for families, climbing, mountain biking, skiing, 4WD excursions, and dance and drumming workshops. Longer packages are available.

Coopérative Souktana du Safran MUSEUM
(☑0528 53 44 52; ☺8.30am-6pm) Founded in 1979, the oldest of Taliouine's 14 saffron co-operatives has 154 members (153 are men). The centre is well worth visiting for the small museum and informative employees. They can explain saffron production, give you a tasting and sell you the spice, plus related products including chocolates, bonbons and calligraphy ink.

TOP CHOICE Trekking

Taliouine is a popular trekking centre for nearby **Jebel Siroua** (see p386), which offers some of the finest walking in the Anti Atlas. The village is one of the best places in the region to find trekking guides.

Kasbah

Gazing at the brown hills, the kasbah is mostly disintegrating, but it makes a pleasant sunset stroll.

Souq

The village comes to life during the Monday souq, behind the kasbah.

🛏 Sleeping & Eating

Auberges le Safran and Souktana serve the best meals in the village (Dh75 to Dh100). At the other end of the main drag near the bus station, grills smoke away and you can get a tuna tajine (Dh50), made with saffron, at Auberge Siroua. Hotel Ibn Toumerte, the boxy 1970s monstrosity next to the kasbah, has Taliouine's only bar.

Auberge le Safran HOTEL €
(☑0528 53 40 46, 0668 39 42 23; www.auberge-safran.com, in French; r Dh150-220, ste Dh300; 🛜) The personable guide Mahfoud's *auberge* has attractive, brightly painted en-suite rooms, plus two basic options on the roof terrace and a spacious suite. The salon looks across the fields at the kasbah, and downstairs is a Berber tent on the patio. They harvest their own saffron, which they sell in the on-site shop-museum and use in the delicious meals. Mahfoud offers activities including trekking, hammam visits, saffron-based cookery courses, and a saffron and argan producers tour.

Auberge Souktana HOTEL €
(☑0528 53 40 75; souktana@menara.ma; room s/d/tr/q Dh180/220/300/360, bungalow s/d Dh100/160, tent 1/2 people Dh50/80; 🛜) The family-run Souktana is Taliouine's unofficial trekking centre and Jebel Siroua trailhead. Guests consult maps in the relaxing communal area, and advice is available from the multilingual Franco-Moroccan hosts, whose son Hassan runs Yallahtrek (see p377). It's east of the village, across the N10 from the kasbah with great views of the crumbling fort. Reservations are essential in trekking season and half-board is available.

Auberge Tobkal CAMP SITE €
(☑0528 53 43 43; www.maghrebtourism.com/aubergetoubkal, in French; half-board per person with bungalow accommodation Dh200, camping

Dh40; 🛜🅿) This tidy camp site, on the main road 500m east of the turn-off for the kasbah, also has comfortable bungalows with en-suite bathrooms.

ℹ Information

In the centre of the village on the main road are a post office and internet cafe.

ℹ Getting There & Away

The N10 east of Taliouine crosses a beautiful and immense landscape, before joining the N9 (the main Marrakesh–Ouarzazate road) near the turn-off to Aït Benhaddou.

Bus

Taliouine has a bus and grand-taxi station, although there are not always seats available on the buses passing through town. Buses go to Ouarzazate (Dh50) and Taroudannt (Dh30).

Taxi

Ouarzazate (Dh30) May need to change at Tazenakht, if direct grands taxis aren't available.

Taroudannt (Dh30) May need to change at Ouled Berhil, if direct grands taxis aren't available.

THE ANTI ATLAS
الأطلس الصغير

The Anti Atlas remains one of the least visited parts of Morocco's mountainscape, which is surprising, as it is beautiful and close to Agadir. The mountains are the stronghold of the Chleuh tribes, who live in a loose confederation of villages strung across the barren mountains, some of them still far beyond the reach of any central authority. The region was only finally pacified by the French relatively recently, in the 1930s.

Living in areas moulded by the demanding landscape of granite boulders and red-lava flows, the Chleuh have always been devoted to their farms in the lush oasis valleys, now some of the country's most beautiful *palmeraies*.

Tafraoute
تافراوت
POP 5000

Nestled in the gorgeous Ameln Valley, the village of Tafraoute is surrounded on all sides by red-granite mountains. Despite its unassuming appearance, the area is actually quite prosperous due to the hard-earned cash sent home by relatives working in the

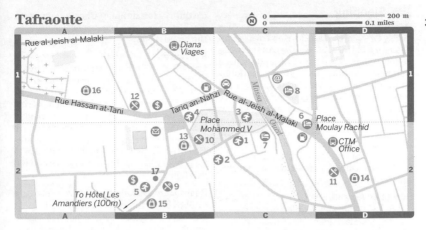

big cities or abroad. It is a pleasant and relaxed base for exploring the region.

🏃 Activities

The best way to see the beautiful surrounding countryside is by walking or cycling, and several companies and guides offer mountain-biking and trekking trips. Operators have booths west of Hôtel Salama. Tafraoute Aventure sells a basic colour map (Dh5) of the area; or you can pick up a free black and white photocopy elsewhere.

Cycling · MOUNTAIN BIKING

The palm-filled Aït Mansour gorges (see p382), leading towards the bald expanses of the southern Anti Atlas, are a great destination. **Au Coin des Nomades** (📞0661 62 79 21) and **Tafraoute Aventure** (📞0661 38 71 73; per day Dh100) are good for maps, information or to book a trip. They hire out mountain bikes and helmets, as does **Tafraoute Quadbikes** (📞0670 40 93 84; per day Dh50-80).

Trekking · TREKKING

Tafraoute and the Anti Atlas offer numerous possibilities for trekkers, though most of the walks are strenuous. As with cycling, Tafraoute Aventure and Au Coin des Nomades are good first ports of call; the latter is owned by Houssine Laroussi, a respected climber. See p385 for more information on trekking in the area.

Old Hammam · HAMMAM

Tafraoute is an excellent place for a completely authentic hammam experience as many houses here still lack water. There are three in town, but locals prefer the old hammam, just behind the market (Dh10).

Almond Blossom Festival · FESTIVAL

In February or March the Tafraoute area celebrates its almond harvest at the Almond Blossom Festival (see p22).

Souq · SOUQ

A lively souq takes place near Hôtel Salama from Monday evening through to Wednesday.

🛏 Sleeping

TOP CHOICE **Hôtel Salama** HOTEL €

(☎0528 80 00 26; www.hotelsalama.com; s/d/tr Dh178/256/314; ❄🛜) An exemplary hotel mixing local materials and modern standards, with an open fire in the lobby and Berber artefacts decorating the corridors. The staff, who speak some English, are one of Tafraoute's more impartial sources of information, and the wi-fi network is about the best in southern Morocco. The roof terrace has mountain views and the cafe-restaurant serves breakfast (Dh23) and full meals (Dh65) overlooking the market square.

Hôtel Les Amandiers HOTEL €€

(☎0528 80 00 88; www.hotel-lesamandiers.com; s/d incl breakfast from Dh400/546; ❄🛜🏊) This kasbah-like hilltop pile has 60 reasonably attractive rooms with small balconies, making the most of the incredible views of the rock formations ringing Tafraoute. The pool and restaurant share the views, but the bar is tucked away in a corner without any vistas. The furniture is rather tired and the hotel needs a renovation, but you may have the place to yourself. Les Amandiers is visible throughout Tafraoute. To get there, follow Route de Tazekka southwest past Maison Tuareg and turn left onto the road leading uphill.

Auberge Les Amis HOTEL €

(☎0527 54 30 93; dedroliko_24@hotmail.fr; s/d Dh100/150) This new hotel has 10 basic rooms on three floors, and a roof terrace. Rooms have external bathrooms and a pleasant Berber ambience courtesy of the carpet bed heads.

Hôtel Tanger HOTEL €

(☎0528 80 01 90; s/d Dh40/80) A small, friendly hotel with very basic rooms and reasonable shared bathrooms and toilets. Some English is spoken, there's a roof terrace, and the ground-floor cafe serves breakfast (Dh25), tajines (Dh35) and the usual dishes. The family also runs a guest house in Oumesnate.

🍴 Eating

Plenty of small food stores sell cheese and basic picnic supplies to supplement the fruit and veg available in the market.

Café Atlas CAFE €

(☎0667 12 02 93; meal Dh60; ⊙breakfast, lunch & dinner) Atlas' covered terrace is more of a local hang-out than the nearby L'Étoile d'Agadir restaurant. Cheese omelette, steak, tajines and sandwiches feature on the broad menu.

Restaurant La Kasbah REGIONAL €

(☎0672 30 39 09; set menu Dh100) This is aimed at tourists, with alcohol available, and the room is low on atmosphere, despite the kilims doing a brave job of covering the yellow walls. However, some thought has gone into the extensive menu, which includes a warming *harira*. The house speciality is *kalia* (minced mutton with tomato, peppers, egg, onion and 44 spices served in a tajine).

Restaurant L'Étoile du Sud REGIONAL €

(☎0528 80 00 38; set menu Dh90) L'Étoile du Sud serves a good set menu in a rather kitsch Bedouin-style tent, although you may have to share the place with tour groups, particularly at lunchtime. Still, the lamb tajine is commendable, the service professional and on warm nights it's one of the best places to eat.

🛍 Shopping

Tafraoute has several slipper shops around the market area selling the traditional leather slippers (yellow for men, red for women) for about Dh70, though expect to pay more for quality. Look out, too, for people selling local argan and olive oil.

Buying a carpet here is less pressure than in Marrakesh:

TOP CHOICE **Maison du Troc** CARPETS

A good range of Berber and Tuareg carpets and kilims.

Maison Tuareg CARPETS

The shop stocks Berber and Tuareg carpets and souvenirs from the Atlas and Sahara.

Souq CARPETS

Pick up Berber carpets from small dealers at the weekly market.

Artisanat du Coin JEWELLERY

Specialises in Berber jewellery and other portable knick-knacks.

ℹ Information

Banque Populaire (Place Mohammed V; ⊙8.15am-3.45pm Mon-Fri) Has an ATM and *bureau de change*.

BMCE (behind Restaurant L'Étoile d'Agadir) Has an ATM.

Internet Amelen (off Rue al-Jeish al-Malaki; per hr Dh5; ⊙8am-11pm)

Pharmacie al-Massira (☎0528 80 01 60; Place al-Massira; ⊗8am-8.30pm)

Post office (Place Mohammed V) Has pay phones outside.

❶ Getting There & Away

Bus

Buses depart from outside the various company offices, mostly on Rue al-Jeish al-Malaki.

CTM (Route Aguerd-Oudad) and **Diana Viages** (☎0671 74 99 19; Rue al-Jeish al-Malaki) have at least one daily departure for the following:

DESTINATION	COST (DH)	DURATION (HR)
Agadir (via Aït Baha or Tiznit)	40	6
Casablanca	140	14
Inezgane	40	6
Marrakesh	100	7
Tangier	250	18
Tiznit	25	4

Car

You can hire a 4WD with a driver from Tafraoute Aventure for around Dh700 per person per day. The driver can drop you at the Afella-Ighir oasis and pick you up at the other end.

Taxi

Station wagons and Land Rovers do the rounds of various villages in the area, mostly on market days. They hang around the post-office square, and on Rue al-Jeish al-Malaki near the Afriquia petrol station at the bottom of Tariq an-Nahzi. Grands taxis leave for Tiznit (Dh37.50) in the morning from the latter location.

Around Tafraoute

Renting a mountain bike is a great way of getting to most of the sights around Tafraoute. See p379 for information about maps and hiring bikes and 4WD vehicles.

TAZEKKA

The closest of the easily accessible examples of prehistoric rock engravings found in the Tafraoute area, the **Carved Gazelle** is on the edge of the village of Tazekka. It's a simple carving on the top face of a fallen block. The easiest way to find it is to walk along the Route de Tazekka, then make enquiries when you reach the village. It's not far from

Camping Tazka on Rte 104 to Tiznit, so you could, alternatively, ask for directions there.

The best option is to visit the carving as part of a tour of Tazekka's **Maison Berbere Traditionnelle** (☎0673 82 90 54; Maisonberbere30@yahoo.fr; adult Dh15; ⊗8am-6pm), in the largely uninhabited hilltop old village, where bulging boulders have been incorporated into the pisé walls of the centuries-old houses. It's possible to stay the night (Dh150 per person including breakfast) in the four-floor dwelling, where the knowledgeable proprietor Mahfoud's family lived until five years ago.

TIRNMATMAT

To find the **rock engravings** at Tirnmatmat, take Rte 104 towards Tiznit, then after 14km take Rte 7148 north from Tahala towards Aït Omar. Just before the village, an unmarked *piste* (track), opposite a well, leads to Tirnmatmat, where you will find the *gravures* (engravings) along the riverbed (the local kids will lead you there, or engage a guide from Tafraoute). The village sits in a lovely spot and there are excellent **walks** in all directions.

LE CHÂPEAU DE NAPOLÉON & THE PAINTED ROCKS

The village of Aguerd-Oudad, 3km south of Tafraoute, makes for a nice stroll or bike ride. From the roundabout by the Afriquia petrol station in Tafraoute, take the road to Tiznit via Izerbi. On the way you will see the unmistakable rock formation known as **Le Châpeau de Napoléon** (Napoleon's Hat).

Some 8km south of Tafraoute, just past the foot of the road to the Afella-Ighir oasis, a '*touritique piste*' leads uphill to the right – to the **Pierres Bleues** (Painted Rocks), the work of Belgian artist Jean Verame.

Verame spray-painted the smooth, rounded boulders in shades of blue, red, purple and black in 1984 and, although the rocks have a faded air, they remain strange and impressive against the landscape. Local lore has it that the villagers give these incongruous tourist attractions a fresh coat of paint every year.

The packed earth track is passable in a normal car, but this is prime mountain-biking territory. You can see the rocks after 3km on the track, then follow the yellow arrow to the left and ride right up to the rocks some 5km away.

SOUTHERN MOROCCO & WESTERN SAHARA AROUND TAFRAOUTE

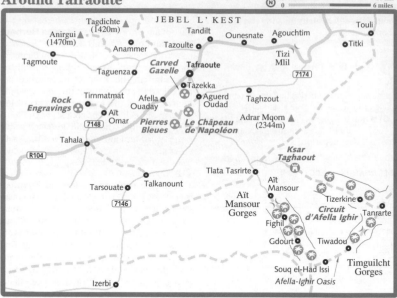

AFELLA-IGHIR

Southeast of Tafraoute is the pretty **oasis** of Afella-Ighir. Leave Tafraoute on the Aguerd Oudad road, turning left a few kilometres south of the village, and travel roughly 20km over a mountain pass through Tlata Tasrirte to the start of the dramatic **Aït Mansour Gorges**. You can see the Pierres Bleues from the road up to the pass, which is sometimes snowed over in winter.

You can drive through the gorges in a normal car if it hasn't rained, but walking or mountain biking is the best way to appreciate this atmospheric area, where red cliff faces tower above the palms. In the village of Aït Mansour at the beginning of the gorges, the water running across the road marks the start of the Afella-Ighir oasis. A little further on, the *gîte* (trekkers' hostel) **Chez Messaoud** (0528 21 83 38, 0670 79 35 67; r per person Dh60) serves tea and sells water and basic provisions. Breakfast (Dh45) and meals (Dh50) are available if you book ahead.

The road begins to disintegrate in the village, with sections of tarmac and *piste*. Keep right and follow the road through a string of villages perched above the oasis, until you reach the T-junction in Gdourt after about 8km. Turn right here for Izerbi, or left for Souq el-Had Issi, a rather depressing town that accommodates workers from the nearby gold mine, Mine de Akka. From the turn-off 1km beyond Souq el-Had Issi, you can loop round 25km through the **Timguilcht Gorges** and back up to Tlata Tasrite, mostly on rough *piste*, impassable in a normal vehicle. If you stay on the better road, following the sign to the mine, you can head 12km south to **Ukas** to see some impressive rock carvings, although you need a guide to find them.

Some 5km northeast on the *piste* is the village of Tiwadou, where the wonderful, family-run **Auberge Sahnoun** (0528 21 83 65, 0667 09 53 76; m_sahnoun@hotmail.com; r per person incl half-board Dh150) is on the edge of a *palmeraie*. The three basic but cosy rooms, with mattresses on the floor and a good shared bathroom with hot water, are gathered around a Berber tent. There's a roof terrace and a traditional hammam is being built. Owner Mohamed (see the boxed text p384), a guide who organises multi-day treks in the area, is passionate about preserving traditional local village life. He has created a small on-site museum: a room filled with objects from lanterns to scythes that were once part of everyday Afella-Ighir life.

A daily minibus runs through the villages to Tafraoute (Dh20), leaving Tiwadou at about 5am and returning at midday.

Ameln Valley & Jebel L'Kest جبل لكست و اميلن وادي

Tafraoute lies in a basin, largely surrounded by craggy brown cliffs and rocks. To the northwest lies one such ridge, on the other side of which runs the Ameln Valley. North of the valley is **Jebel L'Kest** (2359m). From Tafraoute you can make out a rock formation in this range that resembles a lion's face. Villagers will jokingly tell you that he is there to guard the women while their husbands are away working.

For trekking in the Ameln Valley and Jebel L'Kest, see p386.

From Tafraoute, the Agadir road takes you to the valley, dotted with picturesque Berber villages. Four kilometres out of Tafraoute, the road forks with the right branch turning east up the valley towards Agadir.

TANDILT

Shortly after the fork, this village stands on the left of the road, behind L'Arganier d'Ammelne.

🛏 Sleeping & Eating

Yamina GUESTHOUSE €
(☎0528 21 66 21, 0670 52 38 83; www.yamina-tafraout.com; r per person incl half-board Dh220; ✸) At the top of the village, Yamina is run by a Berber woman and her French husband, who have created a unique cross between a comfortable guesthouse and a *maison traditionnelle* (traditional house). The simple rooms are beautifully decorated and one has its own dinky courtyard; our favourite, saffron, is entered via a terrace, and has cheery yellow walls and pink beams.

L'Arganier d'Ammelne HOTEL €
(☎0528 80 00 69; argahotel@yahoo.fr; s/d incl breakfast Dh200/250; ✸) Promising a Berber atmosphere, this hotel and camp site's pleasant pink rooms open onto a flowery garden. The terrace restaurant (meals Dh50) is a knockout, serving delicious dishes including local specialities and the recommended beef tajine with apricots, almonds and prunes.

OUMESNATE

Another few kilometres on at Oumesnate, follow the signs through the village and the footpath to the **Maison Traditionnelle** (☎0666 91 77 68, 0668 32 28 66; admission Dh10; ☺8am-6pm). This three-storey granite, palm and argan house, some 400 years old, was inhabited by 20 family members – three generations – until 1982. Owner Abdesslam or one of his sons, who speak some English, will take you on a fascinating tour, telling tales of traditional life. Staying in the neighbouring **Maison d'Hôte** (www.maisontraditionnelle.com; s/d incl half-board Dh250/400), run by the same family, is a wonderful way to get an insight into Berber village life. If you don't have a pressing need for internet access and, ideally, you have a car, spending a night here would be more interesting than Tafraoute. The six rooms have en-suite bathrooms, and meals (Dh70) are available with some notice.

Tata طاطا

POP 40,000

Situated on the Saharan plain at the foot of Jebel Bani, Tata was an oasis settlement along the trade route from Zagora to Tan Tan. Close to the Algerian border, the small modern town has a garrison feel, with four types of police and military stationed here, and you may be questioned on your way into town. With new infrastructure and less hassle than other Saharan spots, Tata is poised to become more of a destination for travellers.

The **palmeraie** is well worth exploring. You can drive a 7km circuit of it, or catch a local bus (Dh5). Above the village at the far end of the *palmeraie* is a white hilltop *marabout* (saint's tomb), which you can see from Tata.

Tata is best as a base for off-the-beaten-track excursions, such as desert camping, Akka oasis, kasbah and *agadir*, and the rock engravings at Oum el-Alek, Tircht and Aït Herbil, among the finest in Morocco. Multilingual Berber guide Isam, based at the unimpressive souvenir shop **Maison du Patrimoine** (☎0613 24 13 12; issam3599@hotmail.com; Ave Mohammed V), charges about Dh350 per day for one or two people, including lunch and 4WD.

The basic hotels above the cafes on Ave Mohammed V typically charge Dh30 to Dh100 per room. The municipal camp site near Maison du Patrimoine, which was being renovated when we visited, charges Dh40 per person. **Dar Infiane** (☎0528 80

24 08, 0661 61 01 70; www.darinfiane.com, in French; r incl breakfast €63-103; ✳), Tata's old kasbah, perched above the *palmeraie,* has been turned into a Clef Verte guesthouse. Off a carpet-strewn central courtyard lie nine rooms, in which the original eccentricities such as low beams are intact, and an outdoor Jacuzzi with mountain views. The French owners arrange visits aimed at facilitating cultural contact between tourists and the local population, such as trekking in the *palmeraie* and *agadir* visits. Dinners (€19) are delicious, and evenings on the rooftop terrace are magical in the still of the Sahara night. Undergoing a renovation when we visited, central stalwart **Hôtel La Renaissance** (✆0528 80 22 25; larenaissance.tata@gmail.

LOCAL KNOWLEDGE

MOHAMED SAHNOUN OUHAMOU

Mohamed Sahnoun Ouhamou is a painter, teacher, guesthouse owner and tour guide.

How long have you lived in Tiwadou? I was born here, but I went to university in Agadir and worked near Beni Mellal as a photographer's assistant. I came back in 1987 when I heard they needed university graduates to work as teachers here.

Did others leave? Many people from this valley went to Casablanca in the 1950s, where they took over shops and businesses. Many of these families have become industrialists in Casa and many corner shops in Casa, Fez, Rabat and even Paris are owned by Berbers from this area.

The men usually leave their families behind and come home in their holidays to build big houses. The region is full of huge houses. But there is a problem: after a while many men take a new wife and start another family, and then they don't come back. Agriculture has come to a standstill, because there are no longer enough men to work the land. People move out of the old mud-brick villages, so the houses are disintegrating. We are losing our traditions, it's a big problem.

Why do you stay? I love this place; I wouldn't want to live elsewhere. There is still human exchange, and also something I value immensely: solidarity. If someone needs something, everyone helps. They have helped me build a house here and a small museum with objects from daily life as we used to know it.

How can tourism help? Tourism and education are the only solutions. That's why I built my guesthouse, and that's why I work with local women who got left behind. In some villages, 90% or more are women, the rest are children and old men. The day the husband stops sending money the hardship begins. So we started a women's cooperative and now have 86 women learning about weaving and embroidery, and how to read and write. Before the women were not really valued, now they have some income as they sell their work to tourists. I'm the only man allowed to go in because I teach them. We also teach their children, so they all now do at least three years' primary school and we've created an overflow for the local school. From 14 years onwards, boys often go into business, because local people value commerce and trade, while girls are the first to lose out when there are limited funds.

What else are you organising in the village? We've started organising a festival every year where the children collect rubbish; there are plastic bags everywhere, it's a big problem. The prize for collecting the most plastic bags went to a preschool boy, Abdullah. At first the teachers and other students didn't even notice him, then he was nervous on stage when we presented him with the award. Now he tells me he will always collect plastic bags, so it shows that messages can be communicated easily.

What is your favourite area? I am fascinated by the rock carvings – you can see engravings of elephants. I am a self-taught painter and I love what my ancestors did. The problem is there is no protection of the sites and some have been vandalised. The carvings in Ukas are famous but there are other sites and I organise treks of three or five days to go and see them. I love introducing foreigners to this area, going off to the mountains and finding total tranquillity.

com; Ave des FAR; s/d Dh170/210; 🛜) has restful rooms adorned with blue and maroon tiles. There are *palmeraie* views from the terrace and the helpful staff speak a little English. The only downsides are the cramped bathrooms, although there's plenty of hot water, and the occasional unsavoury character in the bar. **Hotel Les Relais des Sables** (📞0528 80 23 01; Ave des FAR; s/d/tr Dh219/268/389; ✦🛜🏊) is among the most comfortable accommodation options in town, and hence is popular with tour groups and overlanders. It has a large bar and restaurant, and rooms are arranged around flowery courtyards.

There are cafes on the main street near Maison du Patrimoine.

On Ave Mohammed V you'll find a post office, internet cafe, Banque Populaire and Attijariwafa Bank, which has money-changing facilities and ATMs, and the **Délégation de Tourisme** (Tourist Office; 📞0528 80 20 76, 0676 00 26 99; http://crt-guelmim.com/prevince-tata-en.html; ⏰9am-4.30pm Mon-Fri).

❶ Getting There & Away

Bus

Tata's new bus station is in the centre near Hotel Les Relais des Sables.

Agadir (Dh80, eight hours, three daily)

Goulimime (Dh60, six hours, two daily)

Marrakesh (Dh140, 11 hours, one daily)

Ouarzazate (Dh80, five hours, one daily)

Taroudannt (Dh60, five hours, four daily)

Tiznit (Dh60, 6½ hours, three daily)

Taxi

Grands taxis prices from Tata:

Agadir (Dh100)

Goulimime (Dh100)

Igherm (Dh40) Change here for Tafraoute or Taliouine

Taroudannt (Dh70)

Tiznit (Dh100)

TREKKING IN THE ANTI ATLAS

The last significant mountains before the Sahara, the arid, pink and ochre-coloured Anti Atlas are little visited by trekkers, and yet they offer some wonderful trekking opportunities. Taliouine (p377) is well set up for trekking, and Tafraoute

(p378) is the centre of the region. The quartzite massif of Jebel L'Kest (2359m, see p383), the 'amethyst mountain', lies about 10km north of Tafraoute, and the twin peaks of Adrar Mqorn (2344m) are 10km to the southeast. Beneath the jagged mass of these peaks lie lush irrigated valleys and a string of oases.

At the eastern end of the Anti Atlas near Taliouine, almost due south of Jebel Toubkal, Jebel Siroua (3305m) rises starkly above the landscape. This dramatic volcano makes an excellent centrepiece to varied long-distance treks.

Around Tafraoute

Morocco has such a wealth of trekking options that perhaps it is not surprising that an area with the potential of Tafraoute has not yet been fully exploited. The adventurous trekker will find here, as elsewhere in the Moroccan south, many challenging and rewarding treks.

This is a tougher area than the M'Goun or Tichka Plateau and trekkers will need to cope with a lack of facilities and the harsh climate. This close to the Sahara, the summers are blisteringly hot, and winter sees the occasional snowfall on the high passes and peaks, so the region is best walked at the end of winter. Late February is ideal. Daytime temperatures may be 20°C, but at night it can drop down to below freezing.

Other than the odd small store, you won't find many supplies in the area, so the great challenge is carrying enough food and water to keep you going. As with other remote Moroccan areas, it is often possible to stay in village houses, but you must still be prepared to camp and to carry food and water.

The best way of doing this is by hiring a guide and mules, which is most easily organised through Taliouine-based Yallahtrek (p377). A good contact in Taroudannt is guide Said Dayfollah (p374). Tafraoute is more focused on mountain biking, but there are trekking guides – and *faux guides* – in town. As ever, insist on seeing a guide's ID card before you start discussing possibilities. As a rule, trained mountain guides do not tout for business in the street. Mules are less commonly used around Tafraoute than on Jebel Siroua, but you may be able to arrange this through your guide.

Jebel L'Kest and the approaches from Tafraoute are covered by the 1:50,000 map sheets *Had Tahala* and *Tanalt,* while the whole area is covered by 1:100,000 sheets *Annzi, Tafrawt, Foum al-Hisn* and *Taghjijt.*

This part of the Atlas is not well developed for tourism, and transport is an issue throughout. *Camionettes* (pick-up trucks) provide a reliable though infrequent service to some villages and grands taxis run on souq days, but at other times you may need to hire one to get to trailheads.

JEBEL L'KEST

The area's star attraction is this massive ridge that stretches away northwest of Tafraoute. Despite the harshness of the landscape, the Berbers who live in villages such as Tagoudiche manage to grow the mountain staples of wheat, barley, olives, figs and almonds. The village of Tagdichte is the launching point for a day ascent of Jebel L'Kest.

AMELN VALLEY

There are some 26 villages neatly spaced out through the Ameln Valley, which runs along the south side of Jebel L'Kest, and they make for a great walk. You'd need weeks to do a full circuit, but a stunningly beautiful and suitably stretching five-day walk would start in Oumesnate, take in several villages, and head up to Tagdichte for an ascent of Jebel L'Kest. Alternatively, the ascent could be tackled as part of a gentle trek east through the valley from, say, Tirnmatmat to Oumesnate, both just off the road. This is an enchanting area to trek.

ADRAR MQORN & AROUND

Southeast of Tafraoute the possibilities are also exciting. The scramble up Adrar Mqorn is hard but worthwhile. Due south of its twin peaks are the palm-filled gorges of **Aït Mansour** and **Timguilcht**, which make up Afella-Ighir oasis. There is plenty to explore.

JEBEL AKLIM

Jebel Aklim (2531m) sits in an even remoter area than Jebel L'Kest, yet is still surrounded by Berber villages in valleys guarded by old kasbahs. From the top, there are great views over to the High Atlas and to Jebel Siroua. It makes a great focal point for a four- or five-day walk out of Igherm, which is roughly equidistant from Tafraoute (to the southwest), Taroudannt, Taliouine and Tata.

Jebel Siroua

Some way south of the High Atlas, at the eastern edge of the Anti Atlas, the isolated volcanic peak of Jebel Siroua offers unique trekking opportunities. Remote villages, tremendous gorges, a tricky final ascent and some dramatic scenery all make this an excellent place for trekkers in search of solitude, stark beauty and a serious walk.

The Jebel Siroua ascent is the most obvious walk, but, as ever in Morocco, lasting memories will be found elsewhere: in the beauty of lush valleys, in the hospitality shown in Berber homes, in the play of light on rock and the proximity of the Sahara. So if you don't fancy the climb to the summit, the mountain circuit still makes a wonderful trek.

Taliouine trekking agency Yallahtrek (p377) and, a couple of kilometres east of town on the main road, the affiliated Auberge Souktana are the best places to seek advice, and arrange guides, mules and gear. The *auberge* has become the trailhead.

Mules, as ever, can also be hired at short notice (often the next day) at villages around the mountain

The 1:100,000 *Taliwine* and 1:50,000 *Sirwa* maps cover the route. In winter it can be fiercely cold here, so the best times to trek are autumn, when the saffron harvest takes place, and spring.

If you need supplies, regional markets take place at Taliouine on Monday, Aoulouz on Wednesday and Saturday, Askaoun on Thursday, Tazenakht on Friday, and Igli on Sunday.

ROUTES

There's a challenging, weeklong trek that allows you to walk out of Taliouine along a gentle dirt trail, which heads eastward up the **Zagmouzen Valley** to **Tagmout**. The route then heads northeast through **Atougha**, from where it is a six-hour trek to the summit of Jebel Siroua. Walking at a regular pace, you'll ascend the summit on the morning of the fourth day.

After descending into the gorges for the night, you'll pass the extraordinary cliff village of **Tizgui** before reaching **Tagouyamt** on the fifth day. The village has limited supplies and, in case you can't find a room, a good place to camp in the amazing **Tislit Gorge**. From Tagouyamt, the valley continues to Ihoukarn, from where you can either head south to the Taliouine–Ouarzazate road at Tizi n'Taghatine (you'll be able to pick up passing transport here) or complete the circuit by walking west back to Taliouine.

An alternative circuit that is even less trekked starts at the village of Tamlakout, where there is a classified *gîte,* and takes in Aït Tigga, the Assif Mdist and the foot of Jebel Siroua. It then ascends the mountain, continues to Aziouane and exits via the Amassines. Some of the trek is strenuous but no one day should involve more than six hours' walking.

Taliouine and Anezale (for Tamlakout) are both on the main Taroudannt–Ouarzazate road, regularly served by grands taxis and buses.

SOUTHERN ATLANTIC COAST

Tiznit   تزنيت

POP 53,600

South of the Souss Valley and at the western end of the Anti Atlas, Tiznit is an old walled medina town surrounded by modern development. It was originally the site of a cluster of forts that were encircled in the 19th century by some 5km of pisé wall. It quickly became a trade centre and remains a provincial capital and centre for Berber jewellery, with a souq devoted to the silver stuff. You'll likely pass through en route between the Anti Atlas and Atlantic Coast; a few hours here would be enough to check out the medina and some silver craftsmanship.

History

In 1881 Sultan Moulay al-Hassan (1873–94) founded Tiznit as a base from which to assert his authority over the rebellious Berber tribes of the south. To do this, he built the town's perimeter walls. Jewish silversmiths were moved into the town and gave it a reputation for silver workmanship.

However, Tiznit remained embroiled in local sedition, and was a centre of dissent against the 1912 treaty that turned Morocco into a French and Spanish protectorate. This resistance movement was led by El-Hiba, the so-called 'Blue Sultan' from the Western Sahara, who earned his nickname for always wearing his Saharawi veil.

Following Sultan Moulay Hafid's capitulation to the French at the Treaty of Fès, El-Hiba proclaimed himself sultan here in 1912. The southern tribes rose to support him and El-Hiba marched north at the head of an army of men from the Tuareg and Anti Atlas tribes. They were welcomed as liberators in Marrakesh, but much of the army was slaughtered by the French as it moved towards Fez. El-Hiba retreated to Taroudannt, then Tiznit, then up into the Anti Atlas, where he pursued a campaign of resistance against the French until his death in 1919.

◉ Sights & Activities

Tiznit is a sleepy place with a medina where it is fun to wander around spots such as the jewellery souq and Rue Imzilne, a street of leather-sandal shops. The Berber traders here are tough salesmen, but it is still worth trying to strike a bargain. Things liven up considerably on Thursday, which is market day.

City Walls   HISTORIC SITE
It's possible to climb onto sections of the 5km-long city walls, which have some 30 towers and nine gates. From **Bab Targua**, for instance, you get a great view over the lush *palmeraie*, where there is a natural spring, used as a laundry by local women.

Grande Mosquée   MOSQUE
The minaret of the Grande Mosquée (closed to non-Muslims) is studded with jutting wooden sticks. Local legend suggests this is where the souls of the dead congregate. More likely, these were left in place by the masons who built the minaret to help them climb up and replaster. A similar arrangement is used on minarets across the Sahara in Mali and Niger.

Source Bleue   HISTORIC SITE
Near the Grande Mosquée, the original town spring is now a shallow, stagnant pool, green rather than blue. Legend has it that a woman of ill repute, Lalla Zninia, stopped to rest here at what was then plain desert. She spent the next three days repenting her wicked ways, and God was so impressed that he showed forgiveness by having a spring gush beneath her feet. Her name was thus given to the village that preceded Sultan Moulay al-Hassan's 19th-century fortress town.

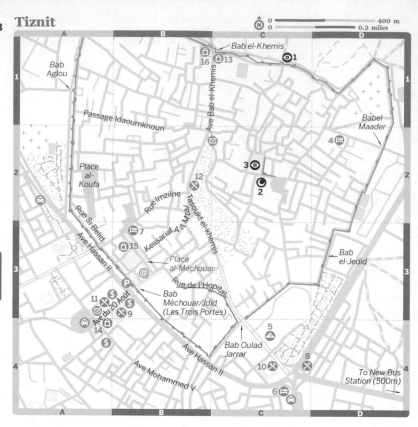

Sleeping

Midrange hotels are gathered around the large roundabout to the southeast of Bab Oulad Jarrar. There are budget hotels on Place al-Méchouar, although lone women may find the area off-putting late at night.

Bab el Maader   GUESTHOUSE €
(☑0528 86 42 52; www.bab-el-maader.com; 132 Rue El Haj Ali; r Dh265-315) Hotel Idou Tiznit is the most expensive in town, with a pool and vast marble lobby, but this is Tiznit's best address, a five-room guesthouse with a courtyard, plenty of great decorative touches and good use of Moroccan fabrics and materials. The owners will arrange trips in the region and meals are available on request (Dh100).

Hôtel des Touristes   HOTEL €
(☑0528 86 20 18; http://hoteltouristetiznit.voila. net; Place al-Méchouar; s/d Dh50/100; 🛜) Along with the nearby jewellery souq, this spot-less, welcoming hotel is one of the best reasons for budget travellers to pause in Tiznit. The attractive rooms are entered from a quiet, cheerful communal area with a book exchange; those overlooking the Place have small balconies.

Hôtel de Paris   HOTEL €
(☑0528 86 28 65; www.hoteldeparis.ma; Ave Hassan II; s/d Dh138/164; ✳) On a busy round-about a short walk from the old walls, this 19-room hotel does a good line in question-able colour schemes and faded tourist post-ers. It would be fine if you hit town feeling as tired as the en-suite rooms' decor and just wanted to crash between buses. There's a cafe-restaurant downstairs.

Camping Municipal   CAMP SITE €
(☑0528 60 13 54; Bab Oulad Jarrar; per person Dh36) This secure municipal camp site is next to the old walls.

Tiznit

✖ Eating

La Ville Nouvelle   CAFE, REGIONAL €
(☑0548 60 09 63; 1st fl, 17 Ave du 20 Août; mains Dh35-55; ☺breakfast & lunch) At this popular ville nouvelle lunch stop, brisk waiters serve the classic salads, brochettes and good *kefta* (spiced lamb or beef meatballs).

Complex Tiznit Essaada   FAST FOOD, SEAFOOD €
(☑0667 67 99 59; Rte d'Agadir; mains Dh35-55) With an adjoining juice bar and covered terrace, this snack bar does shwarma, paninis, pizza, spaghetti and fish dishes.

Snack Stands   FAST FOOD €
Along Ave Bab el-Khemis, the main road through the medina.

Food Market   MARKET
(Ave du 20 Août) Good option for picnic supplies.

Idou Tiznit Supermarket   SUPERMARKET
(Bab Oulad Jarrar) Behind the hotel of the same name, selling a range of local and imported food.

🛍 Shopping

TOP CHOICE **Jewellery Souq**   JEWELLERY
With its long history of silversmiths, the jewellery souq has some of the best work in southern Morocco. It's a pleasant place to wander, with blue-doored shops and windows full of silver wares. Some of the jewellery is made in Tiznit, and some bought from Saharan tribes to the south. You will need time to look around and bargain to get the best prices.

Trésor du Sud   JEWELLERY
(27 Ave Bab el-Khemis) Away from the souq, Trésor du Sud is not the cheapest, but the work is good and it deals in hallmarked solid silver.

Bijouterie Bab el-Khemis   JEWELLERY
(Ave Bab el-Khemis) A low-pressure boutique with Berber and Tuareg jewellery displayed on facing walls.

Ensemble Artisanal   JEWELLERY
(Ave du 20 Août) Craftsmen ply their wares in a hassle-free environment.

❶ Information

Banque Populaire (Ave du 20 Août) Has an ATM and changes money.

BMCE (Ave Mohammed V) Has an ATM and changes money.

BMCI (Ave du 20 Août) Has an ATM and changes money.

Cyber al-Méchouar (2nd fl, Place al-Méchouar; per hr Dh5; ☺8.30am-11pm) Internet access in the medina.

Main post office (Ave du 20 Août) In the ville nouvelle.

Post office (Ave Bab el-Khemis) In the medina.

❶ Getting There & Away

Bus

Buses leave from the new bus station just off the Tafraoute road, past the Thursday souq site. CTM has another office closer to the centre on the same road, and one on Place al-Méchouar. CTM, Supratours and other companies serve these destinations.

DESTINATION	COST (DH)	DURATION (HR)
Agadir	40	2
Dakhla	300	19
Goulimime	40	2
Laâyoune	190	9
Tafraoute	35	4
Tata	80	6½
Tan Tan	75	3½

Taxi

Unless mentioned otherwise, taxis leave from the main grand-taxi rank, opposite the post office in the western part of town. They serve the following destinations:

Berber jewellery serves a much wider purpose than simple adornment. The jewellery a woman wears identifies her as a member of a clan or tribe, it is a sign of her wealth, it reflects cultural traditions, and it has power beyond the visual – to protect her from the evil eye.

A woman will receive jewellery from her mother until she marries. For her marriage, her future husband will commission his mother or sister to provide jewellery for her. These pieces will be kept by her as a dowry and added to throughout her life; they will always be made of silver, as gold is considered evil.

Necklaces are important – the traditional assemblage in the southern oasis valleys sometimes features talismans of silver, pink coral, amazonite, amber, Czech glass and West African ebony beads. Women will also own bracelets, *fibulas* (elaborate brooches, often triangular, used for fastening garments), anklets, earrings and headdresses. Some jewellery will be worn every day, while the finest pieces will be saved for occasions such as festivals, pilgrimages and funerals.

Jewellery's protective, medicinal and magical properties are extremely important. The necklaces contain charms bought from magicians or holy men, offering protection against the evil eye, disease, accidents and difficulties in childbirth. Silver is believed to cure rheumatism; coral symbolises fertility and is thought to have curative powers; amber is worn as a symbol of wealth and to protect against sorcery (it's also considered an aphrodisiac and a cure for colds); amazonite and carnelian stones are used in divining fortunes; and shells traded from East Africa symbolise fertility.

Talismans feature stylised motifs of animals, sun, moon and stars, all of which are believed to have supernatural powers. A common symbol to ward off the evil eye is the hand of Fatima, the daughter of the Prophet Mohammed. Any depiction of the hand (which represents human creative power and dominance) or of the number five is believed to have the same effect as metaphorically poking your fingers into the evil eye with the words *khamsa fi ainek* (five in your eye).

Agadir (Dh27)

Aglou Plage (Dh5) From a stand on Ave Hassan II.

Goulimime (Dh32) From a stand just south of the Hotel Idou Tiznit roundabout, across Route de Goulimime from the petrol station.

Mirleft (Dh13)

Sidi Ifni (Dh23)

Tafraoute (Dh37.50)

Around Tiznit

AGLOU PLAGE   اكلو بلاج

Aglou Plage, 15km northwest of Tiznit, is a long beach with good surf, although the strong undertow makes it dangerous for swimming most of the time. When the Atlantic winds start blustering, it's a wild and woolly sort of place. Development is taking its toll, but the settlement has some of Mirleft and Sidi Ifni's charm, with a raised walkway for promenading between the seafront cafes.

At the south end of Aglou beach, French-Moroccan guesthouse **Le Chant du Cha-** meau (☑0667 90 49 91; www.chantduchameau. com, in French; tent/r per person incl breakfast Dh200/250) has accommodation in a rust-red house or nomad tents, all with a dramatic view of the beach and sea. Excursions in the area and a weeklong course in *tadelakt,* the local plaster-work, are offered.

Grands taxis come here from Tiznit (Dh5). If you're driving, this route from Tiznit to Mirleft takes you along a beautiful stretch of coastline once you've left the development around Aglou Plage.

Mirleft   ميرلفت

POP 6500

One of the region's most beautiful roads runs south of Aglou Plage, offering wonderful views of the ocean, rugged hills and the occasional empty cove. Then comes Mirleft, with beckoning cafes under the pink and blue arches on its main street. Historically popular with artists, musicians and overlanders recovering from Saharan crossings, the village is developing as fans of water and wind sports discover the area. Mirleft also has a healthy share of the best coastal accommodation south of Essaouira. The climate is gentle, the air clear, the views magnificent – and the fledgling tourism development has largely been the work of individuals, rather than corporations or chains.

◎ Sights & Activities

Walk along the short main street, where you can find arts and crafts, an argan product store, internet cafes, restaurants and a small vegetable market.

Beaches BEACHES
If at first the scruffy village seems uninspiring, the gentle bustle soon becomes contagious. A social morning coffee is followed by a trip to the beach – choose from Imin Tourga, Fish Beach, Camping Beach, Coquillage Beach, Aftas Beach, Plage Sauvage and Marabout's Beach; the last is the most dramatic with its *marabout*'s (saint's) tomb and savage-looking rocks.

Other Activities TOURS, PARAGLIDING
Out of the village there are plenty of activities to keep you busy. The beach is good for surf casting (fishing), and hotels and guides can organise trips from fishing to desert excursions. Recommended operators:

Mirleft Ride (✆0661 44 19 33; www.mirleftride.com) Runs surf schools and organises fishing trips and treks into the hills.

Paraglide Morocco (✆0676 31 86 55; www.paraglidemorocco.com) The English-run outfit is geared towards seasoned paragliders, but tandem flights (Dh400) are available.

Le Nid d'Aigle (✆0671 66 85 05; www.nidaigle.com) Also offers paragliding.

🛏 Sleeping

There are plenty of apartments in Mirleft, costing about Dh200 per night; ask in Hôtel Abertih or at the entrance to the village.

TOP CHOICE **Dar Najmat** BOUTIQUE HOTEL €€€
(✆0528 71 90 56; www.darnajmat.com; s/d incl half-board Dh1030/1390; ⊛ ☷) With its infinity pool seemingly melting into Marabout's Beach, Dar Najmat's view is up there with the best on the Moroccan coast. You'll want to start taking photos as soon as you pull of the road, 2km south of Mirleft. The decor in the five rooms has been perfectly judged, with Moroccan materials achieving a contemporary look and harmonious feel.

TOP CHOICE **Les 3 Chameaux** MAISON D'HÔTE €€€
(✆0528 71 91 87; www.3chameaux.com; s/d/ste incl half-board Dh1005/1260/1410; ☎ ☷) High on the hill, in a renovated 1930s military fort, is Mirleft's best address, a lovely guesthouse with fabulous views over the village to the sea beyond. It's worth extending your expenditure to one of the suites, which have balconies and low bathroom windows surveying the valley behind the property. Berber tents dot the walkways between the swimming pool (heated during the winter), hammam, restaurant and boutique. The only sound is the roar of the surf far below, and you'll feel yourself unwinding as soon as you arrive.

Sally's Bed & Breakfast GUESTHOUSE €€
(✆0528 71 94 02, 0661 46 98 88; www.sallymirleft.com; Les Amicales; r incl breakfast Dh600-800) Created by a horse-loving Englishwoman, Sally, this gorgeous cliff-top villa above Imin Tourga, one of Mirleft's largest and cleanest beaches, and has breathtaking views up the coast. With six en-suite rooms and antiques decorating the lounge, it's a stylish and comfortable hideaway.

Hôtel Abertih HOTEL €
(✆0528 71 93 04, 0672 22 58 72; www.abertih.com; r per person incl breakfast with/without bathroom Dh120/150; ☎) Looking like it popped out of a Cubist painting, blue-and-yellow Abertih is equally colourful inside, where open courtyards lead to five rooms on two levels. The ground-floor bar-restaurant (meals Dh100) is less vibrant following a change of ownership, but this remains a good option, popular with paragliding groups.

Hôtel Atlas HOTEL €
(✆0528 71 93 09; www.atlas-mirleft.com, in French; r per person incl breakfast without/with shower Dh120/150; ☎) Recommended by readers, Atlas has a 1st-floor balcony, palatial roof terrace and rooms entered from a corridor open to the elements. The blue-shuttered rooms are on the bare side of rustic and some bars of soap would be welcome in the bathrooms. Nonetheless, it's a relaxing hang-out with one of Mirleft's best restaurants.

✕ Eating

Apart from excellent restaurants at the above hotels, cafes on the main street serve up some of the tonnes of fresh fish that get caught here.

Restaurant Ayour   BERBER €

(☎0528 71 91 71; meals Dh85) Squeezed between the souq and Hôtel Atlas, cosy Ayour is one of Mirleft's best stand-alone restaurants. It's slightly overpriced but serves dishes including *pastilla*.

Restaurant Tigmi   REGIONAL €

(☎0670 70 60 43; meals Dh70) Readers recommend this friendly, family-run restaurant with a small terrace near Hôtel Abertih. Dishes include dromedary rib steak.

❶ Getting There & Away

Grands taxis run to Sidi Ifni (Dh10) and Tiznit (Dh13). For most destinations, including Goulimime, it's easiest to go to Tiznit and change there. There's a morning bus to Agadir (Dh30).

Sidi Ifni   سيدي إفني

POP 20,600

Returned to Morocco by the Spanish as late as 1969, Sidi Ifni adds a dash of Gabriel García Márquez to the usual Moroccan tajine. The slowly decaying art-deco buildings on the hilly streets are a haunting reminder of colonial ambitions. At the heart of what was the Spanish Sahara, Sidi Ifni was once a base for slave-trading operations and later a large exporter of fish to the Spanish mainland. When the sun sets on the esplanade and dilapidated *calles* (streets), and the Atlantic mist gives everything a soft focus, Ifni seems an eerie outpost.

The locals have painted the town blue and white, and continue the colour scheme in their turbans and robes. They support Spanish football teams, take siestas and are more likely to greet travellers with *hola* than *bonjour*. You might hear Bob Dylan blaring from a cafe or get into a philosophical conversation; it's an intellectual spot, where the expats and local cafe crowd are laid-back even by Moroccan standards.

Ifni is a unique place that, in the words of one European resident, keeps the spirit young.

History

Spain acquired the enclave of Sidi Ifni after defeating the Moroccan forces in the war of 1859. They christened their new possession Santa Cruz del Mar Pequeña, but seem to have been uncertain what to do with it as they did not take full possession until 1934. Most of Sidi Ifni dates from the 1930s and features an eclectic mix of art deco and traditional Moroccan styles.

On Moroccan independence in the late 1950s, Spain refused to withdraw, citing the fact that some 60% of the town's population was Spanish. The protracted dispute over territorial rights included the Ifni War, in which the town was sieged. It eventually ended in 1969, when the UN brokered an agreement for Spain to cede the enclave back to Morocco. Santa Cruz was renamed Sidi Ifni, after a holy man buried in the town in the early 1900s. Ifni still celebrates 'Independence Day' (30 June) with a festival on the abandoned airfield.

It might seem a contented place, but recent years have seen clashes between the police and townsfolk, sparked by high unemployment and the marginalisation of independently spirited Ifni.

◉ Sights & Activities

TOP CHOICE \ **Spanish Sidi Ifni**   HISTORIC BUILDINGS

The real draw of Sidi Ifni is its unique atmosphere, which has lured many a passing foreigner to settle. The small old Spanish part of town is one of the main attractions. At its heart is Place Hassan II (often still called Plaza de España), the colonial centrepiece. The large square with a small park in the middle is surrounded by the main administration buildings: **law courts (former church), royal palace, former Spanish consulate** and **town hall**, mostly in grand art-deco style.

Other interesting remnants of the colonial era include the **Hôtel Bellevue**, also on Place Hassan II, a nearby **lighthouse** and, next to Hôtel Suerte Loca, the cliff-top **ship house**, which served as the Spanish Naval Secretariat.

There's also some funky art-deco architecture in the streets east of Place Hassan II. The post office on Ave Mohammed V still has a **letterbox** outside marked 'Correos – Avion/Ordinario' (Post – Air Mail/ Ordinary).

Beach   BEACH

The beach is big and rarely busy, though not always clean. At the south end is the port: Ifni's economy is based on small-scale fishing, with most of the catch sold in Agadir. The odd construction just offshore is the remains of an old land-sea conveyor, which was used to take cargo from ships to the old Spanish port.

Surfing

There's some excellent **surfing** here, with three surf hire shops, including **Sahara Surf Shop** (☏0667 48 95 11), near Hôtel Suerte Loca – which is also a good place to pick up local knowledge.

🛏 Sleeping

Like the rest of Ifni, many of the hotels have seen better days. There are two camp sites at the north end of the beach down the steps from the boat-shaped house.

TOP CHOICE **Xanadu** MAISON D'HÔTES €€
(☏0528 87 67 18; www.maisonxanadu.com, in French; 5 Rue el Jadida; s/d incl breakfast Dh360/550; @) By far the town's best option, this restored house is tucked away on a lane off Ave Mohammed V. Soothing colours, elegance and subtlety pervade the five rooms, offering a contemporary take on the Ifni aesthetic. The charming French host, Patrick, speaks some English, and dinner is available on request (Dh165).

Hôtel Suerte Loca HOTEL €
(☏0528 87 53 50; suerteloca36@yahoo.com; Ave Moulay Youssef; s/d/tr without shower Dh80/125/170, with shower Dh150/200/250) This blue and white *auberge,* in a prime position next to the boat-shaped house, is Ifni's backpacker central. There's a roof terrace with beach views, plus table football and a pool table in the restaurant, which serves milkshakes and crepes for breakfast. It could use a renovation, but attractive bedspreads and balconies feature in the simple rooms.

Hôtel Bellevue HOTEL €
(☏0528 87 50 72; Place Hassan II; s Dh89-170, d Dh110-200) Historically the best address in Ifni, the art-deco charms of the Bellevue's exterior do not continue inside, where you will find little more than a few stylised lampshades and stained-glass windows. The rooms are uninspiring, but it's still a reasonable budget option, with a bar and restaurant.

Hôtel Ère Nouvelle HOTEL €
(☏0528 87 52 98; 5 Ave Sidi Mohammed ben Abdallah; s/d Dh30/50) Above a popular local restaurant, this central cheapie has spartan rooms with narrow beds. The shared bathrooms sport that classic shower/squat toilet combination. However, it's welcoming and secure, and the breakfast (Dh15) of bread, honey and snow-white butter is delicious.

🍴 Eating & Drinking

TOP CHOICE **Café-Restaurant Nomad** SEAFOOD, LOCAL €
(☏0662 17 33 08; 5 Ave Moulay Youssef; meals Dh100) The town's best restaurant is a great place to try local catches; dishes include the towering sardine and avocado salad and fish of the day, grilled on the outside terrace and served with fresh vegetables. The cosy dining room features an open kitchen and nautical paintings, and the multilingual proprietor is a good source

---

LOCAL KNOWLEDGE

LIVIN' LA SIDI LOCA

Jean-Pierre Esatoglu, originally from Switzerland, restored Auberge Figue de Barbarie (see p395) and his own house in Sidi Ifni.

What do you like about this part of Morocco? The gorgeous landscapes and the warm and friendly temperament of its inhabitants. There's a particular, genuine atmosphere to this place.

What were the biggest challenges involved in restoring the auberge? The state of the house, the complexity of the project, the remote place in the countryside where the hotel is located, and getting involved and being respected in the different cultural and social context of Sidi Ouarsik.

Best activities? This area offers you many tour options – hiking, biking, car or donkey tours – in between the seaside, countryside and desert. It's also the ideal place to relax out of the stress of modern life, and to practise surfing and fishing.

Favourite walk? Strolling on Sidi Ouarsik beach or walking in the countryside – with a guide of course.

Favourite restaurant? Café-Restaurant Nomad (see p397).

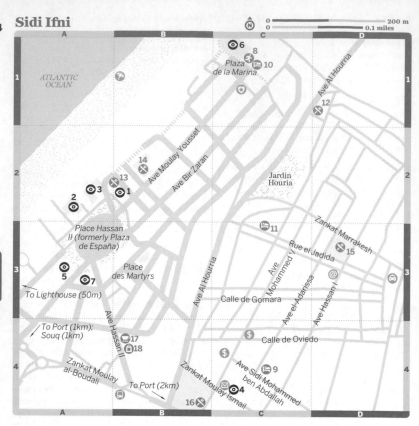

of local information. You can BYO wine. Order three hours in advance to try local specialities.

Café-Restaurant Mar
Pequeña   SEAFOOD, REGIONAL €

(☏0670 38 42 68; 2 Ave El Mowahidine; set menu Dh50-60; ☺breakfast, lunch & dinner) Less male-dominated than the neighbouring cafes, this good-value female-run restaurant is at the top of the seafront steps near Hôtel Bellevue. It offers set menus with fish, chicken or beef tajine; the fish option comes with prawns on the side.

Café-Restaurant
el-Hourria   REGIONAL, SEAFOOD €

(☏0668 16 45 06; Ave Al Hourria; mains Dh35-50; ☺breakfast, lunch & dinner) The Hourria serves a good selection of Moroccan favourites and Western snacks, with a calm dining room and a terrace on the edge of a public garden. There's plenty of fresh fish, including a commendable fish tajine.

Fish Market   SELF-CATERING
In the municipal market.

Fruit & Vegetable Market   SELF-CATERING
A covered market off Zankat Marrakesh.

Souq   SELF-CATERING
Takes place on Sundays, 1km out of town on the road to the port.

Snack Stands & Cafes   FAST FOOD
Set up around the municipal market at the southern end of Ave Mohammed V at dusk.

Cafes   CAFES
Along Ave Hassan II, with views of Place Hassan II and the airfield.

Hôtel Bellevue   BAR
On a terrace above the beach, the bar at Hôtel Bellevue is a pleasant spot for a beer.

Sidi Ifni

Shopping

Look out for *melhaf,* the very fine and colourful fabrics Saharan women use to cover themselves. The **Ensemble Artisanal** (Ave Hassan II) was being renovated when we visited.

⊕ Information

Good websites include www.ifniville.com and www.visit-sidiifni.blogspot.com.

Banque Populaire (Ave Mohammed V) Has currency exchange and ATMs.

BMCE (Ave Mohammed V) Has currency exchange and ATMs.

Hassan Cyber (Ave Hassan I; per hr Dh4; ⊗10am-1pm & 3pm-midnight) Internet access.

Post office (Ave Mohammed V)

⊕ Getting There & Away

The local bus to Tiznit via Legzira Plage (Dh5) leaves from the stop opposite the petrol station on Zankat Moulay al-Boudali.

The grand-taxi station is on the east side of town. They service Goulimime (Dh20), Legzira Plage (Dh10), Mirleft (Dh10) and Tiznit (Dh23).

Around Sidi Ifni

Hotels will advise on the many walks to be done in the countryside around Sidi Ifni.

LEGZIRA PLAGE

Ten kilometres north of Ifni, El Gzira, usually called Legzira Plage, is a superb secluded bay with excellent sand and two dramatic natural **stone arches** reaching over the sea. It's accessible from Rte 104 but better reached by walking along the beaches and cliffs. There's a new cliff-top development near Rte 104, but once you descend the access road it's mostly pristine and undeveloped.

The best of the three hotels at the foot of the access road are reached via a steep staircase. **Beach Club** (✆0670 52 28 00; www.legzirabeachclub.com; s/d incl breakfast Dh150/300) has the best rooms, with shared balconies. The remote location means that, like its neighbours, electricity is unavailable during the day.

Auberge Sables d'Or (✆0661 30 24 95; r Dh150-300) has small but comfortable rooms, opening onto terraces with glorious sea views. Its public areas were being renovated when we visited.

The hotels offer half-board options and you can get a simple lunch of grilled fish at the three nearby beach cafes for about Dh50.

The local bus between Tiznit and Sidi Ifni stops at Legzira Plage.

SIDI OUARSIK

The fishing village of Sidi Ouarsik, 18km south of Ifni along the coast, has a great beach. Overlooking it from the bare hillside, **Auberge Figue de Barbarie** (✆0619 38 59 95; www.aubergefiguedebarbarie.com; s/d Dh150/200), named after the surrounding prickly pears, occupies a beautifully restored farmhouse with green lizards painted on the walls. The four rooms are simple, traditional affairs with small salons and shared bathrooms, but certainly not lacking in style. Manager Daniel can organise activities, and hires out bicycles, surfboards and fishing rods. The *auberge* was previously a ruin and there are idiosyncrasies – high winds sometimes knock out the electricity – but it's a great place to savour the countryside. Half-/full board are an extra Dh100/150 per person.

A DESERT OF DREAMS & NIGHTMARES

The name is enough to make most of us dream. The Sahara, from the Arabic *sahra* ('desert') is the world's largest arid zone. It is also a place of nightmares, as only the well-attuned or well-prepared can survive in its 3 million sq miles of sand dunes, parched mountains and rock-strewn plains.

The Romans never managed to cross the desert, preferring instead to patrol its northern borders – with good reason: lucky travellers who survived the crossing described the trail of human and animal skeletons lining the Saharan caravan routes.

Late-18th- and early-19th-century European explorers struggled across the vast expanses, searching for answers to the geographical riddles of the Niger River, the legendary town of Timbuktu and the gold fields of West Africa. They were overwhelmed by the landscape as often as by raiders. The 18th-century British geographer James Rennell wrote in *Geographical Elucidations* (published 1790): 'Africa stands alone in a geographical view...its regions separated from each other by the least practicable of all boundaries, arid Desarts [sic] of such formidable extent, as to threaten those who traverse them, with the most horrible of all deaths, that arising from thirst!'

Even in the 20th century, the desert thwarted European colonisers and idle travellers, as Paul Bowles so elegantly captured in his novel *The Sheltering Sky*, in which a group of wealthy Americans run into increasing trouble, the further they move into the Sahara.

The dangers involved in Saharan travel give people who inhabit the wilderness a special place in society. Travel through southern towns such as Essaouira and Goulimime, both of which have depended on the desert and its trade, and you will meet some of them. Essaouira is musically linked to the Sahara by Gnaoua, developed by freed slaves from across the desert; see p446.

No group is more closely associated with the desert than the Tuareg, to whom the so-called blue men, found in places such as Goulimime, belong. Wrapped in their veils so only their eyes are exposed to the desert's withering conditions, and bound by strict tribal codes, they have long had a reputation for toughness and independence. The 14th-century Arab traveller Ibn Battuta wrote of them, 'They wear face-veils and there is little good to say about them. They are a rascally lot'. That opinion was echoed over the following centuries by many who plied the Saharan caravan routes, whose goods or lives were taken by Tuaregs. More recently, the Tuareg have battled in countries such as Mali and Niger for an independent homeland.

If the idea of survival in such an inhospitable place is part of what makes the Saharan dream so potent, so too is the mysticism associated with deserts' vast wastelands. Moses found guidance in a desert, Jesus went to the desert for 40 days to prove himself, and early Christian hermits headed there to draw themselves closer to divinity. The Prophet Mohammad brought his message of a new religion out of the desert. And in Morocco, many reformist movements came from the Sahara's fringes, most notably the zealous Almoravids and Almohads.

Yet for many visitors, the main attraction is nothing more complicated than the pure beauty of the landscapes. Morocco has few true sand dunes (Algeria and Libya have some of the best Saharan dunes), but it does have thousands of kilometres of arid land. You need only head south of Goulimime, or to the country's sandy southeast, to get a sense of the desert. After the cool beauty of the Saharan sunrise and the terrifying brilliance of the midday sun comes the extraordinary calm of dusk over a land that seems empty but is not – and that stretches not just as far as the eye can see but further than most visitors can even imagine.

MESTI

This Berber village is 25km southeast of Ifni on the road through the hills to Goulimime. At the Mesti turnoff, you can do a tasting at the shop of honey cooperative **Miel Afoulki** (☎0661 47 24 33). It sells some extraordinary local flavours, including orange and euphorbia. In the village, the **Tafyoucht Cooperative** (☎0528 21 84 16; ◷8am-noon & 2-6pm Mon-Fri) is a women's cooperative producing oil and cosmetic products (Dh40 to Dh150) from the versatile argan tree.

Goulimime

كلميم

POP 96,000

Once the 'Gateway of the Sahara', dusty Goulimime (or Guelmim) sprang up as a border town where farmers from the fertile Souss traded with nomads from the south.

In its heyday, Tuareg, the so-called 'blue men', came in from the desert to buy and sell camels at the weekly souq. In the evenings, women performed the mesmerising *guedra* dance to the sound of a drumbeat. Today, you might only get a taste of this during the weeklong *moussem* (festival) and camel fair held here in July or August (the dates change).

If you have come from the north, you will still recognise Goulimime as a border town. For the first time, you will see Saharawi in the majority. But there is little reason to stop, the only tourist sight being the unremarkable ruins of the early-20th-century Palace of Caid Dahman (admission free), in the street behind Hotel de la Jeunesse on Blvd Mohammed V. Turban-wrapped hustlers offer desert excursions, which we don't recommend.

The town is disturbed once a week by day-trippers from Agadir, who descend for the Saturday-morning souq, which includes a camel market. It's a few kilometres from town on the Tan Tan road.

Sleeping

You will only want to stay in Goulimime if necessary, as many hotels are basic and some may be tricky for women (full as they are of trans-Saharan tradesmen). If you have transport, there is better accommodation outside town.

Hôtel Adil Moussafir HOTEL €
(☑0528 77 29 30; HAM@menara.ma; off Route d'Agadir; s/d Dh310/370) Goulimime's grandest option, with one of its best restaurants, the Adil Moussafir has a friendly reception and spacious, good-value rooms with bright bedspreads.

Hôtel Hamza HOTEL €€
(☑0528 87 39 75; off Route d'Agadir; s/d Dh400/460; @) Behind the tourist office, this quiet caravanserai with efficient staff and expansive corridors is overpriced, but pleasant nonetheless.

Hôtel Ijdiguen HOTEL €
(☑0528 77 14 53; Blvd Ibnou Battouta; s/d Dh75/150) Situated across the road from the bus station, Hôtel Ijdiguen ('Ichdigen') is clean and welcoming, with tiled corridors, reasonable rooms and shared showers.

Eating

Around the bus station and north of Place Bir Anzarane are good areas for snack stands.

La Plage Blanche REGIONAL €
(☑0528 87 10 20; Ziz garage, Route d'Agadir; meals Dh70; ☺breakfast, lunch & dinner) Convenient from Place Bir Anzarane and the bus station, this is one of Goulimime's best restaurants, with well-stocked fish and patisserie counters. On Friday, join the locals and treat yourself to the seven-vegetable couscous, while the masses pray outside the mosque across the road.

Information

Place Bir Anazarane is the centre of town, and near here you'll find banks, internet cafes and the post office.

Cyber Negorich (Ave Hassan II; per hr Dh4; ☺9am-midnight) Internet access just northwest of Place Bir Anzarane.

Tourist office (☑0528 87 29 11; 3 Résidence Sahara, Route d'Agadir; ☺8.30am-4.30pm Mon-Fri) The helpful Hassan offers information on Goulimime and the region. Follow the sign for Hôtel Hamza and turn immediately left.

Getting There & Away

Bus

The bus station is off Ave Abaynou, a 10-minute walk northeast of Place Bir Anazarane.

CTM (off Ave Abaynou) and Supratours have at least one daily departure to the following places:

DESTINATION	COST (DH)	FREQUENCY (HR)
Agadir	85	4
Casablanca	260	12
Dakhla	305	15
Laâyoune	155	7
Marrakesh	165	7
Rabat	295	13½
Tan Tan	45	1½
Tiznit	40	2

Satas' daily buses are a cheaper option.

DESTINATION	COST (DH)
Agadir	50
Inezgane	50
Laâyoune	135
Tan Tan	35
Tiznit	35

Taxi

You can catch grands taxis from behind the bus station to Inezgane (Dh55), Laâyoune (Dh150), Sidi Ifni (Dh20), Tan Tan (Dh35) and Tiznit (Dh32).

For a grand taxi to Tighmert (Dh8), take a petit taxi (Dh7) to the central market, 300m south of Place Bir Anzarane on Blvd Mohammed V, and wait at the beginning of Rte d'Asrir.

Around Goulimime

TIGHMERT

There are a few basic guesthouses around this oasis, mostly located some 20km southeast of Goulimime off Rte d'Asrir.

Maison d'Hôtes Nomades   GUESTHOUSE €
(☎0667 90 96 42; www.darnomade.com, in French; off Rte d'Asrir; s/d/tr Dh150/200/250) This pisé house right in the oasis has camels in the stables, and argan and cactus products for sale. Rooms have en-suite bathrooms and the views from the roof terrace are magical. The proprietors offer oasis and desert tours, and meals on request (Dh80).

Domaine Khattab   CAMP SITE, HOMESTAY €
(☎0661 17 64 11; khattab2@menara.ma; Km 12 Rte d'Assa; caravan & camping Dh50; s/d Dh100/150; bungalow incl breakfast Dh150/200) This welcoming family farmstead has a tiny zoo featuring horses, rabbits and the like –

SAHARAN TRAVEL

As you head south of Goulimime, the desert quickly sets the tone of your journey. Given the long travel times from Goulimime and its neighbours to both the Western Sahara and central Morocco, night buses are the norm. You should also get used to police posts and answering uniformed officials' queries (see the boxed text, p406).

fun for children. There are spacious bungalows and sadder rooms in the so-called *maison d'hôte* (small hotel), plus camping and a restaurant serving simple set meals (Dh60).

FORT BOU-JERIF

This French **resort** (☎0672 13 00 17; www.fort boujerif.com; camping from Dh60, incl half-board s Dh470-580, d Dh760-960; khaïma per person incl half-board Dh300; ☒) offers a taste of the desert, 40km northwest of Goulimime via the Sidi Ifni and Plage Blanche roads (it's well signposted). The last 9km is rough *piste*, passable in a normal vehicle at glacial pace. Built near a ruined French Foreign Legion fort, the compound has a range of sleeping options, from hotel and motel rooms to *khaïmas* (nomad tents) and camping. There is also a bar-restaurant (set menu Dh180), where the speciality is dromedary tajine. Owner Pierre offer activities including 4WD trips to Plage Blanche, a little-visited and unspoiled stretch of beach 40km southwest of Bou-Jerif.

Tan Tan & Tan Tan Plage   طانطان

POP 50,000

South of Goulimime, across the dry Oued Drâa, you enter the cauldron of the Sahara proper. The 125km of desert highway to Tan Tan is impressive for its bleak emptiness and harsh *hammada* (flat, stony desert).

If you weren't stopped by security on the way in, you could probably drive along the N1 (known as Ave Hassan II within Tan Tan's boundaries) without realising you were in the middle of the town, which spreads south of the highway. The majority of the inhabitants are nomads who settled here, and blue robes are a big feature. The army and police presence is also noticeable, due to the proximity of the disputed Western Sahara. Look out for the middle-of-the-roundabout stop sign west of town; the police at the post beyond are not shy of issuing a ticket or pocketing a *petit cadeau* (little present) to overlook the infraction.

Tan Tan was founded in the 1940s during the Spanish Protectorate, but had its moment in 1975, when the area was the departure point for the Green March (see boxed text, p428). It's a rundown and occasionally hostile place, where the main attraction is the *moussem* in December, featuring camel racing and music. The Sunday souq is held 1.5km south of town.

Tan Tan Plage, also known as Al-Ouatia, 28km west of Tan Tan, is a large, windswept stretch of beach that first attracted a 19th-century Scottish trader, Donald Mackenzie, who built a trading post here. It's a derelict place with the feel of a perennially out-of-season seaside resort, but staying here is preferable to Tan Tan.

🛏 Sleeping & Eating

TAN TAN

There are cheap restaurants on Ave Hassan II, Ave Mohammed V and around the Place de la Marche Verte, although many close at lunchtime. To sip a mint tea or for breakfast (Dh30), head to Hôtel Sable d'Or.

Hôtel Sable d'Or HOTEL €
(☑0528 87 90 80; sablesorville@gmail.com; Ave Hassan II; s/d from Dh150/200) Next to the banks on the main road, this basic hotel is the best option in town, with comfortable en-suite rooms. The staff are friendlier than many Tan Tan townsfolk and there's a cafe-restaurant.

Hôtel Bir Azzarane HOTEL €
(☑0528 87 78 34; Ave Hassan II; s/d Dh50/80) A worn but friendly place, next to the royal palace (soldiers patronise the cafe here) on the west side of the river. The brown-carpeted upstairs corridor leads past a seemingly endless stream of boxy rooms.

TAN TAN PLAGE

A few hundred metres southwest of the centre on the port road, there are two camp sites opposite Hotel Hagounia. There are cafes and snack bars on the main square.

Hotel Hagounia HOTEL €
(☑0528 87 90 20; hotel-hagounia@menara.ma; s/d Dh150/250; 🖧) Run by the welcoming, English-speaking Abdul, the Hagounia is the best option, with all amenities. Rooms have small balconies with unbroken beach views and there's a restaurant (meals Dh85).

Hotel Belle Vue HOTEL €
(☑0528 87 91 33; s/d from Dh100/150) This appropriately named seafront hotel has cheery rooms, reached along corridors decorated by an obviously enthusiastic local artist. The cafe-restaurant (meals Dh110), popular with locals and overlanders, is one of Tan Tan Plage's best, serving dishes such as grilled sole and calamari.

ℹ Information

Tan Tan

Banks and internet cafes are clustered around the junction of Ave Hassan II and Ave Mohammed V.

Banque Populaire (Ave Mohammed V)

BMCE (Ave Hassan II) ATM and exchange, next to the Shell petrol station.

Club Internet (off Ave Hassan II; per hr Dh4; ⏰9am-midnight) Next to Samir Oil petrol station, it has a fairly fast connection.

Main post office (Ave Hassan II) To the east of town.

Tan Tan Plage

There's a Banque Populaire with an ATM opposite the post office, and a BMCE with an ATM and *bureau de change* one block inland. There's also an internet cafe, but Tan Tan has more reliable facilities.

ℹ Getting There & Away

Bus

CTM (Ave Hassan II) in Tan Tan has daily departures including the following:

DESTINATION	COST (DH)	DURATION (HR)
Agadir	100	4½
Dakhla	260	14
Goulimime	45	1½
Laâyoune	120	4½
Tiznit	75	3½

Supratours (☑0528 87 96 65; Ave Hassan II), which also stops at its office in Tan Tan Plage opposite the Dubai Hotel, operates similar services at slightly higher prices.

SOUTHERN MOROCCO & WESTERN SAHARA TAN TAN & TAN TAN PLAGE

Other, cheaper companies, all serving the same destinations, use Tan Tan **bus station** (Place de la Marche Verte), 500m south of the centre.

Taxi

From Tan Tan bus station, grands taxis head to Agadir (Dh120), Goulimime (Dh50), Inezgane (Dh120), Laâyoune (Dh120), Tarfaya (Dh90) and Tiznit (Dh80).

Grands taxis to Tan Tan Plage (Dh10) leave from the top of Blvd el-Amir Moulay Abdallah.

Tan Tan Plage to Tarfaya

The 200km drive from Tan Tan Plage to Tarfaya initially takes you along a monotonous stretch of desert highway. The road is good and the traffic relatively light.

Along the route you'll see anglers' huts perched on the cliff-tops (many of the anglers sell their catch by the roadside) and occasionally herds of camels wandering slowly through the *hammada*. Sidi Akhfennir, 95km southwest of Tan Tan Plage, is a good place to stop, either at one of the garages or at a cafe serving grilled fish straight from the sea.

Accommodation options include the family-run **Auberge Pêche et Loisirs** (☎0661 21 19 83; http://peche.sudmaroc.free.fr, in French; per person incl half-board Dh350), which has clean, restful rooms with a shared bathroom. The owner is passionate about fishing, and organises trips on the nearby Naïla Lagoon or the ocean.

South of Sidi Akhfennir the drive becomes extremely scenic, with wild, untouched Atlantic beaches and ochre dunes rolling away into the distance or lapping on to the road. The route passes through the **Khenifiss National Park**, where you can see flamingos on the Naïla Lagoon.

Tarfaya   طرفايه

POP 6000

The tiny fishing port of Tarfaya was the centre of the Spanish Protectorate of Cap Juby, now known as the Tarfaya Strip. A Scottish trader, Donald Mackenzie, created the original settlement in the late 19th century, building a small trading post on a rock just off-shore, which he called Port Victoria. When the Spanish took over, they appropriated the building, now known as Casa

Mar (house in the sea; see p401). The area gained independence from Spain in 1958.

The Moroccan government recently upgraded Tarfaya's municipal status, and the town is on the cusp of big developments. A new port is planned, with hopes for the relaunch of the ferry connection to the Canary Islands and greater tourist numbers. Tarfaya will likely retain its considerable charm; it's a friendly outpost with a seductively remote feel to the sand blowing between its crumbling colonial relics.

The town will forever be associated with the French pilot and writer Antoine de Saint-Exupéry. In 1926 he began flying in the mail service between France and Senegal, and Cap Juby was one of the stops. In 1927 he was appointed station manager for Cap Juby and he spent a couple of years here, writing his first novel *Courrier Sud* (*Southern Mail*), in which an airmail pilot dies south of Boujdour in the desert of Rio de Oro. He also picked up inspiration for his most famous story, *Le Petit Prince (The Little Prince),* which features a pilot lost in the desert. In the words of one local, 'The man was born in France but the writer was born in Tarfaya'.

◉ Sights & Activities

Historic Sites   HISTORIC SITES

There are some 22 historical sites in Tarfaya, mostly dilapidated buildings recalling the days when Saint-Exupéry and the chaps touched down here. The **Casa Mar** is abandoned but still standing, and can be easily reached at low tide. A **monument** was erected in Saint-Exupéry's memory at the north end of the beach: a dinky green Bréguet 14 biplane, the sort he used to fly. Behind the nearby museum is the 1930s **cinema** and next door is the **tower** built by Mackenzie; in the same area, swashbucklers swapped anecdotes between flights at **Bar des Pilotes**. By the airstrip on the northern edge of town is the **House of 100 soldiers**, where the Spanish stationed their Moroccan conscripts, and 2km south is the wrecked Armas ferry **Assalama**. It put paid to the short-lived connection between Tarfaya and Fuerteventura when it went down in 2008.

Musée Saint-Exupéry   MUSEUM

(☎0661 07 94 88; admission Dh10; ☺8.30am-4.30pm Mon-Fri, by appointment Sat & Sun) Tells the stories (in French) of Saint-Exupéry, the

Entering Tarfaya from the north, you might notice an incongruous site in the Sahara: a mangrove plantation. Near the beach, at the northern end of the sand-covered 900m airstrip, 2000 of the trees have been planted to help solve the local problem of desertification. The sand pile-ups here can get so chronic that cars are unable to drive the streets, and Tarfaya is cut off from the outside world for hours.

Building a greenbelt was an obvious solution. The big question was, what kind of plant could stand the Atlantic winds, grow in sand and survive on a salty diet of sea water. The Moroccan and international team decided on mangroves, and this is the tree's first appearance in Morocco.

The next issue was that sea water lacks three vital elements for plants: nitrogen, phosphate and iron. In the search for a solution, some of the fledgling trees are being watered with treated water; others with the good stuff straight from the Atlantic. The most experimental move, which proved successful, was to plant seeds alongside dead sardines; the fish contain the three important nutrients and certainly aren't in short supply here.

If the greenbelt flourishes, it could have wider resonations. Successfully treating sea water could allow oceans to be used for cultivation, or even deserts to be turned green.

airmail service's founder Pierre-Georges Latécoère, and the incredible service itself, which eventually became part of Air France.

Rallye Saint-Exupéry   FESTIVAL
(www.rallyetoulousesaintlouis.com) In late September or early October, the airmail service is remembered in the Rallye Saint-Exupéry, when planes fly from Toulouse, France to Saint Louis, Senegal and back. In October 2007, they landed at Tarfaya to commemorate the 80th anniversary of the writer taking up his post and the 25th year of the rally. In 2010 the last operational Bréguet 14 landed here.

🛏 Sleeping & Eating

There are a dozen self-catering apartments in Tarfaya, typically costing Dh200 per night. These are the best sleeping option; Les Amis de Tarfaya can help you find one.

On the port side of the public phone opposite the Supratours office, two unnamed eateries serve delicious, cheap fried fish, beans, chicken and tajines (meals Dh30).

**Residence Touristique
Addayouf**   APARTMENT €
(✆0665 43 58 92; alisalemtarfaya@gmail.com; apt Dh200) This blue-and-yellow building at the northern entrance to town, also known as Hotel Cap Juby, has two self-catering one-bedroom apartments with lounges. The more basic downstairs apartment has

a squat toilet. Meals are available and an adjoining booth sells basic provisions.

Casa Mar   HOTEL €
(✆0528 89 59 00; casamarhotel@gmail.com; s/d incl breakfast Dh120/150; 🛜) Casa Mar's tented pool hall, near the entrance to the port, is the town's hang-out of choice. It was a little dirty when we visited, the shared shower was disintegrating and the restaurant didn't extend beyond local interpretations of spaghetti bolognese. Nonetheless, when night falls on the Sahara, it has the wonderful air of a Wild West salon, as overlanders roll in and shoot the desert breeze.

ℹ Information

Tarfaya has a medical centre, internet cafe, laundrette and a Banque Populaire with an ATM. Attijariwafa Bank was set to open a branch here when we visited.

Les Amis de Tarfaya (✆0661 07 94 88; sadat@yours.com) Tourist information is available from the helpful, English-speaking Sadat at this local association, based at Musée Saint-Exupéry.

ℹ Getting There & Away

Bus companies including CTM stop in Tarfaya, but **Supratours** (✆0528 89 50 56; Rte du Port) has the only reliable office. It's the best option anyway, given the brutal journey times in the Western Sahara. Daily Supratours departures head for the following places.

DESTINATION	COST (DH)	DURATION (HR)
Agadir (via Inezgane)	180	8
Dakhla	220	11
Essaouira	245	11
Goulimime	130	3½
Laâyoune	40	2
Marrakesh	250	12
Tan Tan	80	3
Tiznit	150	5½

Grands taxis go to Laâyoune (Dh35) and Tan Tan (Dh70). Tarfaya has petrol stations and car-washing services.

WESTERN SAHARA

الصحراء الغربية

Ask any Moroccan about the status of the Western Sahara and they will insist it belongs to their country, yet the UN is clear that this is still under dispute. Local maps may show this region as a seamless continuation of the *hammada* around Tarfaya, but few outside Morocco will agree.

This area largely comprises the former colonies of Spanish Sahara and part of the Tarfaya Strip. Crossing the vast tracts of desert here, one does marvel at the dispute. The towns are merely administrative centres, and the terrain stretching away from the N1 is featureless, arid, inhospitable and uninviting. Despite this distinct lack of postcard prettiness, this environment has phosphate, oil and fishing potential – significant factors in the dispute.

It's one of the world's most sparsely populated territories, and, despite the 1991 ceasefire in the Polisario-led war, the Moroccan military sometimes seem to outnumber civilians. If you want to appreciate the Sahara and see oases and dunes, the likes of Merzouga, Figuig and Tata are better choices – more scenic, safer and reached via less gruelling journeys from central Morocco. For travellers who need to cross the Western Sahara to reach Mauritania, bear in mind that this is a disputed area and read our safety guidelines.

History

Despite its windswept desolation, the Western Sahara has a long and violent history. Islamic missionaries started to spread Islam among the Zenata and Sanhaja Berber tribes in the 7th century. A second wave of Arab settlers, the Maqil from Yemen, migrated to the desert in the 13th century, and the whole region became predominantly Arabic.

By the 19th century the desert had new overlords again: the Spanish, who grabbed the Western Sahara and renamed it Rio de Oro, even though it had neither water nor gold. In reality, until 1934 it was Sheikh Ma El-Ainin and his son El-Hiba who controlled the desert and the nomadic tribes. After that, an uneasy colonial peace prevailed until Moroccan independence in 1957, when new nationalist fervour contributed to the establishment of the Polisario Front and the guerrilla war against the Spanish.

When it was abandoned by Spain in 1975, Morocco and Mauritania both raised claims to the desert region, but Mauritania soon bailed out. In November 1975 King Hassan II orchestrated the Green March – 350,000 Moroccans marched south to stake Morocco's historical claims to the Western Sahara (see boxed text, p428).

In the following years 100,000 Moroccan troops were poured in to stamp out resistance, and Rabat gained the upper hand. The UN brokered a ceasefire in 1991, but the promised referendum, in which the indigenous Saharawi could choose between independence and integration with Morocco, has yet to materialise.

Ever since, Morocco has strengthened its hold on the territory, pouring money into infrastructure projects, particularly offshore oil exploration, and attracting Moroccans from the north to live here tax-free. Until late 2010, the troubled area seemed to be lying dormant, with the dispute largely forgotten by the world beyond this remote region. However, on 8 November 2010, Moroccan security forces stormed the Gadaym Izik camp near Laâyoune, in an attempt to break up the 15,000-strong protest camp. Both sides saw fatalities in the ensuing clashes, which turned to riots and engulfed the city, with 700-plus Saharawi injuries, and scenes of fire and destruction in the international media. The fighting jeopardised UN-mediated talks that opened in New York state the following day, although they began again in December 2010. Many now anticipate Polisario retaliations to Morocco's breach of the ceasefire, and Africa's longest-running territorial dispute continues.

For the most up-to-date information on the Western Sahara, or the Saharawi Arab Democratic Republic (as the separatist government calls the occupied territory), check these resources:

ARSO (www.arso.org)

BBC (http://tinyurl.com/37j6p8n)

CIA World Factbook (http://tinyurl.com/38nkck)

Global Voices (http://tinyurl.com/3a7hgqc)

UN (www.un.org)

Climate

Beyond the foothills of the Anti Atlas lies a parched hinterland starved of moisture. Here temperatures can exceed 45°C during the day and plunge to 0°C at night, while an annual rainfall of less than 125mm gives a suffocating aridity hovering between 5% and 30% – dry enough to mummify corpses. The desert wind, known locally as the *chergui, irifi* or *sirocco*, adds to the harsh conditions. From March to April, sandstorms also plague the desert, making driving inadvisable.

It is important to carry a good supply of water. In winter it is also essential to carry a warm sleeping bag and some warm clothing as desert nights can be bitterly cold.

Language

In the Western Sahara, Arabic and French are spoken almost universally. As a previous Spanish Protectorate, the more common second language was, until recently, Spanish, a habit that lingers on with the older generation. English is also spoken, due to the UN presence.

 Getting There & Away

There is no officially designated border between Morocco and the Western Sahara, and Morocco treats the region as an integrated part of the country.

Laâyoune and Dakhla are served by daily flights from Casablanca, and weekly flights from Gran Canaria. There's also a weekly flight from Agadir to Dakhla, and a new ferry line to Laâyoune from Gran Canaria.

Supratours and CTM both operate buses to Laâyoune and Dakhla, although Supratours provides the faster and more efficient service.

One of the benefits of the area's tax-free status is that petrol costs a couple of dirham less per litre than in the rest of Morocco. The first of the Atlas Sahara petrol stations is just south of Tarfaya.

For advice on travelling to/from Mauritania, see p510.

Laâyoune (Al-'uyun) العيون

POP 200,000

The Spanish created Laâyoune as an outpost from which to administer the nearby Bou Craa phosphate mines. The Moroccans had bigger ambitions and spent more than US$1 billion turning it into the principal city of the Western Sahara. Now neither Saharawi nor Spanish, its population is mostly Moroccans, lured from the north by the promise of healthy wages and tax-free goods.

A government centre and military garrison with UN Land Cruisers drifting along its drab avenues, Laâyoune is not worth a visit. Indeed, following the escalation of tensions in the Western Sahara, we recommend you avoid stopping here, as there's nothing to justify the risk of police hassle or getting caught in a riot. Whether you're heading north or south, distances are so great that you may have to pause here, but try to plan your trip so you rest up in Tarfaya or Dakhla, which are more pleasant and safer.

Due to the volatile situation in Laâyoune while this book was being researched, the information on the city has been updated remotely via phone and internet.

Dangers & Annoyances

See the boxed text, p406, for advice on staying safe in Laâyoune. Bored youths hang about at Place du Méchouar at night.

◎ Sights & Activities

Place du Méchouar　　NOTABLE BUILDINGS
The Moroccan government wants the grand Place du Méchouar to attract our attention, but the **Palais de Congrès** (Blvd de Mekka) and new **Grande Mosquée** (Moulay Abdel Aziz Mosque; Blvd Moulay Youssef) overlooking the place are unlikely to make you reach for your camera.

MOVING ON?

For tips, recommendations and reviews, head to shop.lonelyplanet.com to purchase a downloadable PDF of the Mauritania chapter from Lonely Planet's *West Africa* guide.

Laâyoune

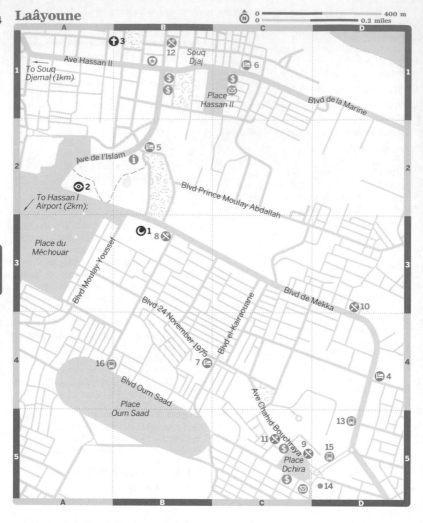

Spanish Cathedral
CATHEDRAL

(off Ave Hassan II; ⊙closed) The original Spanish town runs along the riverbed Saquia el-Hamra, over which presides the cathedral, its rounded white dome mimicking the local architecture.

Souq Djemal
SOUQ

(Ave Salem Bila) Southwest of the cathedral, this is the liveliest area of town.

Dunes
DUNES

There are kilometres of dunes north and west of town. To get among them, take a 4WD off the N1 north of the city.

Lagoons
BIRDWATCHING

Local travel agents can organise trips that cover the lagoons and the dunes.

🛏 Sleeping

The UN maintains a significant presence in Laâyoune and tends to fill the better hotels, so you would be wise to book ahead. Unsurprisingly, good accommodation in this desert outpost is expensive by Moroccan standards.

Sahara Line Hotel
HOTEL €€

(📞0528 99 54 54; Blvd el-Kairaouane; s/d/tr Dh430/537/644; ❄@) A UN favourite, the

Laâyoune

reliable Sahara Line has swish, carpeted, air-conditioned rooms with fridge, bathroom and TV. There's a restaurant on the top floor (breakfast Dh50), but no bar.

Hôtel Parador HOTEL €€€
(📞0528892814; Ave de l'Islam; s/d Dh1100/1400; ❄🏊) This survivor from Spanish days, built in hacienda style around gardens, has a faintly colonial bar and a good restaurant. The rooms are equipped with all the creature comforts you'd expect and each has a small terrace.

Hôtel Jodesa HOTEL €
(📞0528 99 20 64; 223 Blvd de Mekka; s/d without shower Dh100/155, with shower Dh144/215) Centrally located north of Place Dchira, this modern hotel is a good cheaper option. Rooms are basic, but reasonably spacious.

Hôtel Sidi Ifni HOTEL €
(📞0528 89 34 88; 12 Rue Sanhaja, Souq Djaj; s/d Dh40/60) By far the best of the real cheapies, this place in the old Spanish part of town is very local in flavour. The showers use cold, salty bore water, but there is a hammam nearby.

Eating

There are many cafes and simple restaurants around Place Dchira, where Dh20 should get you a filling meal. More lively food stalls can be found at the Souq Djemal.

The restaurants at the Sahara Line Hotel and the Parador offer more upmarket meals.

Le Poissonier SEAFOOD €
(📞0528 99 32 62; 183 Blvd de Mekka; meals Dh60-90) This friendly fish restaurant is one of Laâyoune's best eateries outside the hotels, serving dishes such as fish soup and lobster.

Pizzeria la Madone ITALIAN €
(📞0528 99 32 52; 141 Ave Chahid Bouchraya; pizzas Dh40-60) A cosy place to eat, although it also does a brisk takeaway trade. Dishes include thin-crust pizzas, *harira*, salads, omelettes and pasta marinara.

Au Palais des Glaces PATISSERIE €
(📞0528 98 04 76; Blvd de Mekka; breakfast Dh13-20) A modern, European-style tea-room, patisserie and ice-cream parlour, with the best ice creams in town. A good place to start the day, too.

Restaurant el-Bahja FAST FOOD €
(Blvd Mohammed V; set menu Dh25) Simple grilled meat – lamb certainly, camel perhaps – is served without ceremony here, but with plenty of grease and chips. Good for when you've had enough of fresh fish.

Information

The city's showpiece is the vast Place du Méchouar, but there is no obvious centre. The post office, banks and most hotels are along Ave Hassan II and Blvd de Mekka. There are several banks with ATMs and exchange facilities near the intersection of Ave Hassan II and Blvd Mohammed V, and internet cafes on Blvd de Mekka.

Attijariwafa Bank (cnr of Ave Hassan II & Blvd Mohammed V)

Banque Populaire (Place Dchira) Has another branch on Blvd Mohammed V.

BMCE (Place Hassan II) Has another branch at Place Dchira.

Délégation Régionale du Tourisme (📞0528 99 52 83; Ave de l'Islam; ⏰9am-noon & 2.30-6.30pm Mon-Fri)

Post office (Place Hassan II) There is a smaller branch on Place Dchira.

🚌 Getting There & Away
Air

Hassan I Airport (📞0528 89 37 91; www.onda.ma) Located 2km south of Laâyoune.

BinterCanarias (www.bintercanarias.com) Weekly flights to/from Gran Canaria.

Trouble flared in the Western Sahara in November 2010 (see p402) and travelling to the region has become inadvisable. It is recommended that you avoid Laâyoune in particular; the city was the focus of the violent clashes and remains in a volatile state. While there is the obvious danger of being caught in a riot or a confrontation between Moroccans and Saharawi, dealing with the Moroccan authorities at the numerous roadblocks actually poses more risks.

In engineering a media blackout, the Moroccans are determined to keep journalists from the region. Following the Gadaym Izik raid, reporters were prevented from boarding planes to Laâyoune, and Spanish journalists who reached the city were detained and deported. Spain has been most critical of Morocco's occupation and recent actions, so Spanish travellers are likely to field most questions from Moroccan officials.

However, everyone should treat the checkpoint stops seriously, tedious though they are, as there is a small risk of travellers being taken for a journalist or Polisario sympathiser. Even as you approach the Western Sahara, entering and travelling between towns such as Tarfaya, Tan Tan, Goulimime and Tata, foreigners are invariably asked about their profession, next destination and purpose in the region. Sometimes these questions will quickly dissolve into enquiries about your soccer allegiances, and you will be waved on. In the Western Sahara, your passport and visa details will be noted down, along with your vehicle details if you are driving. If you're on a bus, often you can stay in your seat while the police take your ID and write down your particulars; sometimes you will be summoned to speak to a head honcho in a hut.

Occupations that are likely to ring alarm bells at police posts are journalism or working in aid. If police confirm that you work in an occupation of that nature, you could be followed, detained, sent back to Morocco proper or even deported to a nearby location such as the Canary Islands. The authorities are generally more wary of travellers visiting Laâyoune than Dakhla or Tarfaya.

Once in both Laâyoune and Dakhla you will be aware of the military and police, both of whom are sensitive to photography around military installations. Similarly, they will not take too kindly to you photographing or trying to visit the depressing refugee camps around both cities, where many Saharawi still live. The busy red-light district in Dakhla, opposite the military headquarters and barracks, is also off-limits to visitors.

Royal Air Maroc (RAM; 0528 99 58 00; Immeuble Nagjir, Place Dchira) Daily afternoon or evening flights to/from Casablanca.

Boat

Armas (www.navieraarmas.com) was setting up a ferry line to/from Gran Canaria at the time of research; this weekly route takes seven hours.

Bus

Buses mostly leave from the offices towards the southern end of Blvd de Mekka. **CTM** (Blvd de Mekka) has daily departures to the following destinations.

DESTINATION	COST (DH)	DURATION (HR)
Agadir	220	10
Dakhla	175	8
Goulimime	155	7
Marrakesh	270	14
Tan Tan	120	4½
Tiznit	190	9

Supratours (Place Oum Essad) and **SATAS** (Blvd de Mekka) have similar daily services, respectively costing more and the same or marginally less.

Taxi

Red and white petits taxis charge about Dh5 to take you across town, including to the following grand-taxi stations, which are scattered around the city.

North Grands taxis leave from 'Place Tan Tan', about 1.5km east of Place Hassan II along Ave Hassan II, for Tan Tan (Dh120), Goulimime (Dh150) and Inezgane (for Agadir; Dh200).

South Grands taxis depart from 'Place Boujdour' in the southern suburbs to Boujdour (Dh75) and Dakhla (Dh175).

Dakhla (ad-Dakhla)   الداخلة

POP 40,000

Established by the Spanish in 1844 and formerly called Villa Cisneros, Dakhla lies just north of the Tropic of Cancer on a sandy peninsula, stretching out 40km from the main coastline. It's a very lonely 500km drive from Laâyoune (more than 1000km from Agadir) through endless *hammada*. After so many hours on the road, it is tempting to imagine that you are arriving at the end of the earth. It is certainly the end of Morocco, or at least the last major settlement, closer to Nouâdhibou (Mauritania) than Laâyoune.

And yet Dakhla feels less remote than many southern towns, and certainly more prosperous with a selection of good hotels and restaurants. The whitewashed, arcaded streets are a little soulless, but refreshing after some of the rundown backwaters to the north. Although Western Saharan tensions lurk under the carefree, sea-breeze surface – fishing rights are a touchpaper between the Saharawi and Moroccan settlers – Dakhla's inhabitants appear relatively modern and progressive. Men in overcoats and dapper, white-gloved policemen are as common as robes and *melhaf*.

Money continues to find its way along the peninsula, with investments made by the Moroccan government and developers, and workers tempted from the north. New apartment blocks stretch the town boundaries, the huge port is home to Morocco's largest fishing fleet, and the French campervan set is fond of wintering here.

Dakhla is reasonably easy to get around; hotels, cafes, bus offices and most of the main facilities are within walking distance of each other in the centre.

◉ Sights & Activities

There is a ruined 19th-century **Spanish fort** next to the black-and-white lighthouse east of the airport. Otherwise it's out into the desert for some four-wheel driving, or down to the beach to windsurf, kitesurf, paraglide or go fishing. Hotels can help arrange these activities, and operators include the following:

Kite Xperience (☑0642 52 82 79; www. kitexperience.com, in French; Bab al-Bahar, Ave Mohammed V) One-day kitesurfing class Dh900.

🛏 Sleeping

TOP CHOICE **Bab al-Bahar**   BOUTIQUE HOTEL €€€
(☑0528 93 14 40; www.bab-al-bahar. com, in French; Ave Mohammed V; r/ste from Dh1013/2013; 🛜@✳) This Best Western hotel is a relaxing destination in itself, from

the mini Zen garden on the reception desk to the 35 delightful rooms with window seats. Activities including kitesurfing and 4WD excursions in the dunes are offered. Next to the lapping water, the stylish French restaurant (set menu Dh120, snacks Dh70) is one of Dakhla's best, offering crayfish, tiger prawns, steaks and brochettes.

Sahara Regency   RESORT €€
(☑0528 93 15 55; www.sahararegency.com, in French; Ave al-Walae; s/d incl breakfast Dh600/800, ste Dh1000-2400; ✳🛜⛱) Entered through archways, the four-star Sahara Regency's rooms are mini-apartments, but the furniture and fittings are aged. Nonetheless, the overall package is good, with a rooftop pool and ground-floor tearoom and restaurant (set menu Dh120). A range of tours (Dh350) are available, including shell and oyster safaris and trips to the white dunes.

Hôtel Erraha   HOTEL €
(☑/fax 0528 89 88 11; Ave Beuchekroune; s/d/tr Dh250/300/500; 🛜) The Erraha's spacious rooms have hot water (you have to turn on the boiler yourself) and balconies overlooking the new Edderhem Mosque and its green square. The staff are a genial bunch and there's a cafe. The location, about 1km southwest of the centre, is a pain if you want to hang out in town, but convenient for grands taxis and the SAT and Supratours offices.

Hôtel Sahara   HOTEL €
(☑0528 89 77 73; Ave Sidi Ahmed Laaroussi; r Dh80-200) The friendly Sahara is the best of the three budget hotels overlooking the pedestrianised shopping lanes just southwest of the Supratours office. Rooms have little balconies. The basic options share showers and squat toilets; the better-value en-suite rooms have sit-down toilets and TVs.

Hotel Tafoudart   HOTEL €
(☑0668 72 27 39; Ave Beuchekroune; s without/ with shower & TV 60/120, d 170/80) Next to Hôtel Erraha, this friendly hotel is about 10 minutes' walk east of the grands-taxis station. Recommended if you want a comfortable, secure night with no frills.

Hôtel Aigue   HOTEL €
(☑0528 89 73 95; Ave Sidi Ahmed Laaroussi; s/d Dh80/120) In a tall, narrow building next to Hôtel Sahara, the Aigue has basic, pokey rooms with shared showers and squat toilets, but it's clean, secure and central.

SOUTHERN MOROCCO & WESTERN SAHARA DAKHLA (AD-DAKHLA)

Eating & Drinking

For an alcoholic drink with your meal before entering dry Mauritania, head to the restaurants at Bab al-Bahar and the Sahara Regency.

TOP CHOICE Café Restaurant Samarkand SEAFOOD, REGIONAL €
(☑0528 89 83 16; Ave Mohammed V; set menu Dh120) The best place to eat in Dakhla, with views of the white cliffs of Africa from the pergolas. The menu features a wide range of fish and other dishes; order in advance for couscous or fish *pastilla*. The three-course set menu is an excellent deal.

Café-Restaurant Bahia SEAFOOD €€
(☑0528 93 00 62; 16 Ave Mohammed V; meal Dh90) A good, unlicensed fish restaurant serving catches including calamari and octopus. The *pulpo alla gallega* is octopus cooked in water and covered with olive oil and paprika.

Hassan Fruits JUICE BAR
(Ave al-Walae) Across the pedestrian crossing from the Dakhla peninsula monument, this is popular for a slice of gateau and a mixed fruit cocktail (Dh15).

Shopping

A pedestrianised shopping lane runs north from Ave Sidi Ahmed Laaroussi between Hotels Sahara and Aigue. Vendors here sell goods from argan oil to bright *melhaf.*

Ensemble Artisinal JEWELLERY, SOUVENIRS
(Ave el-Moukouama) Marrakesh medina it ain't, but you can find last-minute gifts here, particularly Saharan jewellery.

ℹ Information

Dakhla has a number of banks with ATMs, in the centre of town and next to Hôtel Erraha. You'll also find internet cafes in these areas charging Dh10 per hour.

Pharmacie Oued Dahab (☑0528 89 81 25; Ave Mohammed V)

Post office (Ave el-Moukouama)

ℹ Getting There & Around

For advice on travelling to/from Mauritania, see p510.

Air

Aéroport Dakhla (☑0528 89 72 56; www.onda.ma) About 200m west of the Sahara Regency.

Canary Fly (www.canaryfly.es) Weekly flights to Gran Canaria.

Royal Air Maroc (RAM; ☑0528 89 70 49; www.royalairmaroc.com; Ave des PTT) Flies from Casablanca every afternoon apart from Tuesday and Saturday, returning in the evening, and from/to Agadir on Wednesday afternoon/evening.

Bus

CTM (☑0528 89 81 66; Blvd 4 Mars) and **Supratours** (Ave Mohammed V) have offices in the centre.

Companies including Supratours and SAT have offices on and around Ave Beuchekroune, between the grands-taxis station and the Edderhem Mosque.

Book in advance for daily services to these destinations:

DESTINATION	COST (DH)	DURATION (HR)
Agadir	340	21
Laâyoune	175	8
Tan Tan	260	14
Tarfaya	220	11

Car

There are plenty of mechanics, mostly in the newer part of town to the southwest, who can service vehicles before a trek south.

Laargoub Car (☑0528 93 04 47; www.laargoubcar.com; Ave Ahmed Bahnini) Recommended car hire, with one-way rental available within Morocco.

Taxi

White-and-turquoise petits taxis whiz around town (day/night Dh5/6). The grand-taxis station is in al-Messira, southwest of the centre. Sample destinations include Agadir (Dh350) and Laâyoune (Dh175).

Understand Morocco

Morocco Today

Renovations in Progress

Wherever you go in Morocco, you'll see work in progress. New roads are reviving ancient caravan routes across desolate stretches of desert; signs announce new women's artisans' associations in mountain hamlets; a mosaic *maalem* (master artisan) hunkers in a niche in a palace wall with a tiny chisel, tapping out a zigzag shape to match a gap in the *zellij* (tilework) mosaic. Development schemes, self-help organisations and a savvy young king are helping to repair damages from a colonial past, cycles of poverty and official repression of expression – or as Driss ben Hamed Charhadi described it in his 1964 book of the same name, 'a life full of holes'.

Social rifts are not easy to fill. While economic growth remains around 3% to 4%, unemployment hovers around 44% for youth, and a 2011 cafe bombing in Marrakesh's cosmopolitan Djemaa el-Fna tragically underlined economic and cultural tensions. Though the outlook is brighter and the public mood lighter since Mohammed VI took the throne, two popular magazines were forced to cease publication in 2010: *Nichane* after a mildly irreverent article about Moroccan humour, and *Le Journal Hebdomadaire* after publishing a poll citing only a 91% approval rating for the king.

Yet as you can tell from centuries-old stone minarets and remarkably intact mudbrick castle towers dotting its rugged landscape, Morocco has already weathered adverse conditions over the past millennium without crumbling. With all available means – vibrant local organisations, plucky media, resilient senses of humour, a tiny chisel if necessary – Moroccans are fashioning a modern society on the foundations of an ancient one.

Rise of the Tourism Economy

Your arrival is hotly anticipated in Morocco. The government's 'Vision 2010' of welcoming 10 million visitors by 2010 may have fallen shy of

» **Highest point** Jebel Toubkal (4167m)

» **Internet domain** .ma

» **Most popular Moroccan beverages**: Casa Flag Special beer (235 million bottles consumed per year); Sidi Ali mineral water (200 million bottles)

Top Books

» *The Sacred Night* Tahar Ben Jelloun's tale of a Marrakesh girl raised as a boy won France's Prix Goncourt.

» *Dreams of Trespass: Tales of a Harem Girlhood* Fatima Mernissi's memoirs of 1940s Fez blend with other women's stories.

Greeting People

» **Men** Handshake with right hand, then touch heart.

» **Women** Handshake plus one to four air kisses, depending on familiarity.

» **Men and women** Touch heart with right hand; optional handshake and air kisses.

Fashion

» **Jellaba** Unisex ankle-length robe with a pointy hood and knotted silk buttons.

» **Tunic** Thigh-grazing, open-necked tops for men and women.

ethnicity
(% of population)

60

Amazigh (Berber)

39

Arab/Other

1

European

if Morocco were 100 people

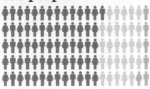

66 would be 15-64 years old
28 would be 0-14 years old
6 would be 65 years and older

---

achieving its goal, due to recession in Europe – but tourism has more than doubled since 2002, low-cost European airlines are servicing more Moroccan airports, and the new 'Plan Azur' to create six coastal resort magnets for tourism is well underway. In the past decade, tourism has handily overtaken agriculture and fishing as Morocco's main occupation, and services represent over half of Morocco's GDP, ahead of industry (mainly textile production) and phosphate mining (mostly in Western Sahara).

All this has changed everything and nothing about Morocco, which has been a crossroads culture for 1000 years. In the souqs, you'll still hear carpet salesmen delivering their best one-liners – but now they're in Arabic, Berber, French, Spanish, English, Italian, Portuguese, German and Russian. Many historic family homes in Moroccan medinas have been converted to guesthouses, where mint tea is ceremoniously poured for new arrivals in time-honoured hospitality.

Your visit couldn't be better timed: with tourism still in development, your choices shape Morocco's future. Tourism could mean more golf courses that strain local resources, or cultural tourism that rewards communities for conservation of local landmarks and traditions. Spending a day in Morocco's pristine countryside is even more helpful. The UN estimates that for every eight to 10 tourists who visit an urban area, one job is created locally, while in rural areas those tourists represent six or seven essential new job opportunities. Even short visits have an outsized impact, since the average traveller expenditure for a splashy Marrakesh weekend is equivalent to three or four months' salary for most Moroccans (about €900). For the 50% of Morocco's population that's under 25, opportunities to interact with visitors and practise foreign languages are key preparations to join Morocco's increasingly competitive and cosmopolitan workforce.

Myths

» **Caftan** Long, flowing women's gowns – sometimes with belts, but no hoods.

» **Smata** Pointy leather slippers worn indoors and outside.

» **Belly dancing** This is an Ottoman import, not a Moroccan custom.

» **Moroccan families** They may seem large, but they're actually smaller than the world average, at 2.4 children per family.

» **Head coverings and beards** These are far from universal in Morocco, and they may indicate cultural affiliations, practical choices or fashion statements rather than religious orthodoxy.

Morocco's Tangled Web

Royal rose gardens are lined with internet kiosks, cybercafe screens shield couples smooching via Skype, and commentators discuss breaking news in Libya via Twitter: welcome to Morocco, home of techie trend-setters.

Social-media adoption has accelerated across Morocco, often outpacing political controls. After limiting access to YouTube, Google Earth, LiveJournal and other sites, Morocco's 2010 ranking on Reporters without Borders' Press Freedom Index plummeted to 135 out of 178 countries.

Yet as Morocco's new National Press Syndicate reported in 2010, Moroccans' preferred information source is now the internet; some 8950 internet cafes were registered in 2009. To find the latest hot topics in the the Moroccan blogosphere visit http://maroc-blogs.com.

Moroccans are avid Facebook users, spending more time per visit (30 minutes) than Americans (23 minutes) or Japanese users (16 minutes).

Democratic Reforms

At the urging of human-rights advocates, the extreme measures of Hassan II's 'Years of Lead' have been curbed by Mohammed VI. Today Morocco has one of the cleaner recent human-rights records in the Middle East and Africa, with a commission to investigate political prisoners' mistreatment. But public demand for greater democratic participation, poverty alleviation and press freedoms has outpaced government liberalisation efforts, prompting nationwide demonstrations in 2011 demanding reforms..

While cautious official speeches promise democratic reforms, Amnesty International reports that measures to repress further protests have included fines, detention and abuse by police. But while Rabat takes two steps forward, one step back, Moroccans aren't waiting for permission for increased civic participation. In new village self-help initiatives, a burgeoning Moroccan blogosphere and the vibrant local arts scene, they are making their voices heard and staying true to their Berber roots as 'the free people'.

Do

» **Conserve water** Water is a scarce and valuable resource in this pre-Saharan country.

» **Cover knees and shoulders** Whether you're a man or woman; it shows your respect for your Moroccan hosts.

» **Learn basic greetings** Learn a few words in Darija or Berber to delight your hosts, who will also make an effort to speak your language.

Don't

» **Give money, sweets or pens to children** It encourages begging and shames families.

» **Eat in public during Ramadan** Or drink alcohol within view of a mosque.

» **Skip pleasantries** Say hello before asking for help or prices.

History

Before there were dunes, mosques, or even carpet dealers in Morocco, this region was under water. In the Atlas Mountains and Saharan steppes, strata mark the geologic time and place where tectonic plates shifted billions of years ago and civilisation surfaced from a rugged seabed. The earliest evidence of human settlement in Morocco dates from 75,000 to 125,000 BC, when most of North Africa was covered in lush semitropical forest, and the stone tools used locally were highly advanced technology for the time. But what the proto-Moroccan 'pebble people' really needed were radiators: the ice age wasn't kind to them, and left the country wide open for settlement when the weather finally began to warm around 5000 BC.

Live Free or Die Trying: The Berbers

The fertile land revealed after the great thaw was a magnet for near-eastern nomads, early ancestors of Morocco's Amazigh (plural Imazighen, loosely translated as 'free people') who may have been distant cousins of the ancient Egyptians. They were joined by Mediterranean anglers and Saharan horse-breeders around 2500 BC, with Phoenicians showing up fashionably late around 800 BC and East Africans around 500 BC.

When the Romans arrived in the 4th century, they didn't know quite what to make of this multicultural milieu. The Romans called the expanse of Morocco and Western Algeria 'Mauretania' and the indigenous people 'Berbers', meaning 'barbarians'. The term has recently been reclaimed and redeemed by the Berber Pride movement (see p421), but at the time it was taken as quite a slur.

The ensuing centuries were one long lesson for the Romans in minding their manners. First the Berbers backed Hannibal and the Carthaginians against Rome in a protracted spat over Sicily known as the Punic Wars (264–202 BC). Fed up with the persistently unruly Berbers, the new

Pre-Islamic Sites

» Carved Gazelle, Tafraoute

» Roman Diana mosaics at Volubilis

» Phoenician/Roman ruins at Lixus

» Prehistoric petroglyphs, Oukaïmeden

» Roman Sala Colonia, Chellah

TIMELINE	At the very start...	1-1½ million years ago	5000–2500 BC
	According to Amazigh folklore, the earth's first couple birthed 100 babies and left them to finish the job of populating the planet – no mention of who changed all those nappies.	The Steve Jobs and Bill Gates of their day, precocious 'pebble people' begin fashioning stone tools some 250,000 to 700,000 years ahead of the European Stone Age technology curve.	Once the ice age melts away, the Maghreb becomes a melting pot of Saharan, Mediterranean and indigenous people. They meet, mingle and merge into a diverse people: the Amazigh.

BERBERS

Roman Emperor Caligula finally declared the end of Berber autonomy in the Maghreb (North Africa) in AD 40.

Defying Orders under Roman Noses

True to his ruthless reputation, Caligula divided relatively egalitarian Berber clans into subservient classes of slaves, peasants, soldiers and Romanised aristocrats. This strategy worked with Vandals and Byzantines, but Berbers in the Rif and the Atlas drove out the Romans with a campaign of harassment and flagrant disregard for Roman rules. Many Berbers refused to worship Roman gods, and some practised the new renegade religion of Christianity in open defiance of Roman rule. Christianity took root across North Africa; St Augustine himself was a Berber convert.

Ultimately Rome was only able to gain a sure foothold in the region by crowning local favourite Juba II king of Mauretania. The enterprising young king married the daughter of Mark Antony and Cleopatra, supported scientific research and performing arts, and helped foster Moroccan industries still vital today: olive-oil production from the region of Volubilis (near Meknès), fishing along the coasts, and vineyards on the Atlantic plains.

The Roman foothold in Mauretania slipped in the centuries after Juba II died, due to increasingly organised Berber rebellions inland and attacks on the Atlantic and Mediterranean coasts by the Vandals, Byzantines and Visigoths. But this new crop of marauding Europeans couldn't manage Mauretania, and neither could Byzantine Emperor Justinian. Justinian's attempt to extend his Holy Roman Empire turned out to be an unholy mess of treaties with various Berber kingdoms, who played their imperial Byzantine connections like face cards in high-stakes games. The history of Morocco would be defined by such strategic gamesmanship among the Berbers, whose savvy, competing alliances helped make foreign dominion over Morocco a near-impossible enterprise for more than a millennium.

> The most comprehensive Berber history in English is *The Berbers* by Michael Brett and Elizabeth Fentress. The authors leave no stone carving unturned, providing archaeological evidence to back up their historical insights.

Islam Arrives in Morocco

By the early 7th century, the Berbers of Morocco were mostly worshipping their own indigenous deities, alongside Jewish Berbers and a smattering of local Christian converts. History might have continued thus, but for a middle-aged man thousands of miles away who'd had the good fortune to marry a wealthy widow, and yet found himself increasingly at odds with the elites of his Arabian Peninsula town of Mecca. Mohammed bin Abu Talib was his given name, but he would soon be recognised as the Prophet Mohammed for his revelation that there was only one God, and that believers shared a common duty to submit to God's will. The

1600 BC	950 BC	800–500 BC	4th–1st century BC
Bronze Age petroglyphs in the High Atlas depict fishing, hunting and horseback riding – a versatile combination of skills and cultures that would define the adaptable, resilient Amazigh.	Amazigh rebuff Rome and its calendar year, and start tracking Berber history on their own calendar on January 13; it's maintained for centuries after the Muslim Hejira calendar is introduced.	The Maghreb gets even more multiculti as Phoenicians and East Africans join the Berbers, making the local population make-up as complex as a *ras al hanout* spice blend.	Romans arrive to annex Mauretania and 250 years later, they're still trying, with limited success and some Punic Wars to show for their troubles.

polytheist ruling class of Mecca did not take kindly to this new religion that assigned them shared responsibilities and took away their minor-deity status, and kicked the Prophet out of town on 16 July AD 622.

This Hejira (exile) only served to spread the Prophet Mohammed's message more widely. By the Prophet's death in 632, Arab caliphs – religious leaders inspired and emboldened by his teachings – were carrying Islam east to Central Asia and west to North Africa. But infighting limited their reach in North Africa, and it took Umayyad Arab leader Uqba bin Nafi until 682 to reach the Atlantic shores of Morocco. According to legend, Uqba announced he would charge into the ocean, if God would only give him the signal. But the legendary Algerian Berber warrior Queen Al-Kahina would have none of Uqba's grandstanding, and with her warriors soon forced Uqba to retreat back to Tunisia.

Although an armed force failed to win the Berbers over to Islam, force of conviction gradually began to succeed. The egalitarian premise of Islam and its emphasis on duty, courage and the greater good were compatible with many Berber beliefs, including clan loyalty broadly defined to include almost anyone descended from the Berber equivalent of Adam and Eve. Many Berbers willingly converted to Islam – and not incidentally, reaped the benefits of Umayyad overland trading routes that brought business their way. So although Uqba was killed by his Berber foes before he was able to establish a solid base in Morocco, by the 8th century his successors were able to pull off this feat largely through diplomatic means.

Islam Stays, but Umayyads Must Go

The admiration between the Berbers and the Arab Umayyads was not always mutual, however. While the Umayyads respected Jews and Christians as fellow believers in the word of a singular God, they had no compunction about compelling polytheist Berbers to pay special taxes and serve as infantry (read: cannon fodder). The Umayyads greatly admired Berber women for their beauty, but this wasn't necessarily advantageous; many were conscripted into Umayyad harems.

Even the Berbers who converted to Islam were forced to pay tribute to their Arab overlords. A dissident school of Islamic thought called Kharijism critiqued the abuses of power of the Umayyads as a corruption of the faith, and called for a new moral leadership. In the mid-8th century, insurrections erupted across North Africa. Armed only with slings, a special force of Berbers defeated the elite Umayyad guard. The Umayyads were soon cut off from Spain and Morocco, and local leaders took over an increasingly lucrative trade in silver from the Western Sahara, gold from Ghana and slaves from West Africa.

Berber Languages in Morocco

» **Tashelhit** Central Morocco

» **Tamazight** Middle Atlas

» **Tarifit** Rif

» **Tuareg (Tamashek)** Sahara

Queen Al-Kahina had one distinct advantage over the Umayyads: second sight. The downside? She foretold her own death at the hands of her enemy.

---

49 BC	25 BC–AD 23
North African King Juba I supports renegade General Pompey's ill-fated power play against Julius Caesar. Rome is outraged – but senators pick up where Pompey left off, and assassinate Caesar.	Rome gets a toehold in Mauretania with farms, cities and art, thanks to Juba II. He expands Volubilis into a metropolis of 20,000 residents, including a sizeable Jewish Berber community.

JOHN ELK III / LONELY PLANET IMAGES ©

» Ruins at Volubilis (p337)

A Death-Defying Dynasty: The Idrissids

Looking back on early Berber kingdoms, the 14th-century historian Ibn Khuldun noted a pattern that would repeat throughout Moroccan dynastic history. A new leadership would arise determined to do right, make contributions to society as a whole and fill the royal coffers, too. When the pursuit of power and royal comforts began to eclipse loftier aspirations, the powers that be would forfeit their claim to moral authority. A new leadership would arise determined to do right, and the cycle would begin all over again.

So it was with the Idrissids, Morocco's first great dynasty. A descendant of the Prophet Mohammed's daughter Fatima, Idriss I fled Arabia for Morocco in AD 786 after discovering ambitious Caliph Haroun ar-Rashid's plan to murder his entire family. But Idriss didn't exactly keep a low profile. After being proclaimed an imam (religious leader) by the local Berbers, he unified much of northern Morocco in the name of Islam. Just a few days after he'd finally settled into his new capitol at Fez in 792, Haroun ar-Rashid's minions finally tracked down and poisoned Idriss I. Yet death only increased Idriss I's influence; his body was discovered to be miraculously intact five centuries later, and his tomb in the hillside town of Moulay Idriss remains one of the holiest pilgrimage sites in Morocco.

His son Idriss II escaped Haroun's assassins and extended Idrissid control across northern Morocco and well into Europe. In perhaps the first (but certainly not the last) approximation of democracy in Morocco, Idriss II's 13 sons shared power after their father's death. Together they expanded Idrissid principates into Spain and built the glorious mosques of Fez: the Kairaouine and the Andalous.

Warriors Unveiled: The Almoravids

With religious leaders and scholars to help regulate trade, northern Morocco began to take shape as an economic entity under the Idrissids. But the south was another story. A dissident prophet emerged near Salé brandishing a Berber version of the Quran, and established an apocryphal Islam called Barghawata that continued to be practised in the region for centuries. The military strongmen who were left in control of trading outposts in the Atlas Mountains and the Sahara demanded what they called 'alms' – bogus religious nomenclature that didn't fool anyone, and stirred up resentments among the faithful.

From this desert discontent arose the Sanhaja, the pious Saharan Berber tribe that founded the Almoravid dynasty. While the Idrissid princes were distracted by disputes over Spain and Mediterranean Morocco, the Sanhaja swept into the south of Morocco from what is today Senegal and

200–429	533	662–682	711
Vandals and Visigoths take turns forcing one another out of Spain and onto the shores of Morocco, until local Rif warriors convince them to bother the Algerians instead.	Justinian rousts the last Vandals from Morocco, but his grand plans to extend the Holy Roman Empire are soon reduced to a modest presence in Essaouira, Tangier and Salé.	Arabs invade the Maghreb under Umayyad Uqba bin Nafi, introducing Islam to the area. Berber warriors eventually boot out the Umayyads, but decide to keep the Quran.	Northern Morocco and most of Spain come under Umayyad control, and Berbers are strategically settled throughout Andalusia.

Mauritania. Tough doesn't do justice to the Sanhaja; they lived on camels' meat and milk instead of bread, wore wool in the scorching desert and abstained from wine, music and multiple wives. Their manly habit of wearing dark veils is still practised today by the few remaining Tuareg, the legendary 'blue men' of the desert (and the many tourists who imitate them in camel-riding photo-ops). When these intimidating shrouded men rode into Shiite and Barghawata outposts under the command of Yahya ibn Umar and his brother Abu Bakr, they demolished brothels and musical instruments as well as their opponents.

From Marrakesh to Barcelona, the Ultimate Power Couple

After Yahya was killed and Abu Bakr was recalled to the Sahara to settle Sanhaja disputes in 1061, their cousin Yusuf bin Tachfin was left to run military operations from a camp site that would become Marrakesh the magnificent. To spare his wife the hardships of life in the Sahara, Abu Bakr divorced brilliant Berber heiress Zeinab en-Nafzawiyyat and arranged her remarriage to his cousin. Though an odd romantic gesture by today's standards, it was an inspired match. It would be Zeinab's

WHEN PURPLE WAS PURE GOLD

The port that is today called Essaouira was hot property in ancient times, because it had one thing everyone wanted: the colour purple. Imperial purple couldn't be fabricated, and was the one colour strictly reserved for Roman royalty. This helps explain the exorbitant asking price, which according to Aristotle was 10 to 20 times its weight in gold. The natural dye came from the spiky murex marine snails that clung to the remote Purpuraire (Purple) Islands – as though that could save them from the clutches of determined Roman fashionistas.

Technically the Phoenicians were there first and discovered the stuff, but everyone wanted purple power. Savvy King Juba II established a coastal dye works in the 1st century BC to perform the tricky task of extracting murex dye from the vein of the mollusc, and kept his methods a closely guarded secret. The hue became wildly popular among royal celebrities of the day; Cleopatra loved the stuff so much that she dyed the sails of her royal barge purple to meet Mark Antony.

But violet soon turned to violence. Legend has it that Juba's son Ptolemy was murdered by Emperor Caligula for having the audacity to sport a purple robe, making trendy Ptolemy possibly the world's first fashion victim. The bright, nonfading dye was never successfully produced commercially, and the secret extraction methods were assumed lost in the siege of Constantinople in 1453. But in Essaouira the stuff is mysteriously still available, for a price. The mysteries of the colour purple are still passed down from one generation of murex collectors to the next, and jealously guarded.

788–829	8th century	1062	1069
Islam takes root in Morocco under Idriss I and Idriss II, who make Fez the epitome of Islamic art, architecture and scholarship and the capital of their Idrissid empire.	Through shared convictions and prudent alliances, Arab caliphates control an area that extends across the Mediterranean and well into Europe, just 320km shy of Paris.	With the savvy Zeinab as his wife and chief counsel, Berber leader Yusuf bin Tachfin founds Marrakesh as a launching pad for Almoravid conquests of North Africa and Europe.	The Almoravids take Fez by force and promptly begin remodelling the place, installing mills and lush gardens and cleaning up the city's act with running water and hammams.

third marriage: before marrying Abu Bakr, she was the widow of one of the leading citizens of Aghmat, and had considerable fortune and political experience at her command. Between bin Tachfin's initiative and Zeinab's financing and strategic counsel, the Almoravids were unstoppable.

The Almoravids took a while to warm up to their new capitol of Marrakesh – too many mountains and rival Berbers around, and too few palm trees. To make themselves more at home, the Almoravids built a mud wall around the city, 8m high and 19km long, and set up the ingenious *khettara* underground irrigation system that still supports the Palmeraie – a vast palm grove outside Marrakesh now dotted with luxury villas. The Jewish and Andalusian communities in Fez thrived under bin Tachfin, a soft-spoken diplomat and, like his wife, a brilliant military strategist. His Spanish Muslim allies urged him to intercede against Christian and Muslim princes in Spain, complaining bitterly of extortion, attacks and debauchery. At the age of almost 80, bin Tachfin launched successful campaigns securing Almoravid control of Andalusia right up to the Barcelona city limits.

Sticks & Stones: The Almohads

Yusuf bin Tachfin was a tough act to follow. Ali was his son by a Christian woman, and he shared his father's commitments to prayer and urban planning. But while the reclusive young idealist Ali was diligently working wonders with architecture and irrigation in Marrakesh, a new force beyond the city walls was gathering the strength of an Atlas thunderstorm: the Almohads.

Almohad historians would later fault Ali for two supposedly dangerous acts: leaving the women in charge and allowing Christians near drink. While the former was hardly a shortcoming – after all, his stepmother's counsel had proved instrumental to the Almoravids – there may be some merit in the latter. While Ali was in seclusion praying and fasting, court and military officials were left to carry on, and carry on they did. Apparently, Almoravid Christian troops were all too conveniently stationed near the wine merchants of Marrakesh.

The Hard Knocks of Ibn Tumart

None of this sat well with Mohammed ibn Tumart, the Almohad spiritual leader from the Atlas who'd earned a reputation in Meknès and Salé as a ninja-style religious vigilante, using his walking stick to shatter wine jars, smash musical instruments and smack men and women with the audacity to walk down the street together. Ibn Tumart finally got himself banished from Marrakesh in the 1120s for knocking Ali's royal sister off her horse with his stick.

1082

Almoravid control stretches south to Ghana and Timbuktu, east to Algiers, and north from Lisbon to Spain's Ebro River, near Barcelona.

1121–30

Almohad spiritual leader Ibn Tumart loudly condemns Almoravid indulgence in music and wine, but also champions scientific reasoning and political organisation based on a written constitution.

SARAH-JANE CLELAND / LONELY PLANET IMAGES ©

» A Berber nomad making a traditional mud oven

But though ibn Tumart died soon after, there was no keeping out the Almohads. They took over Fez after a nine-month siege in 1145, but reserved their righteous furore for Marrakesh two years later, razing the place to the ground and killing what was left of Ali's court (Ali died as he lived, quietly, in 1144). Their first projects included rebuilding the Koutoubia Mosque – which Almoravid architects, not up on their algebra, had misaligned with Mecca – and adding the soaring, sublime stone minaret that became the template for Andalusian Islamic architecture. The Tin Mal Mosque was constructed in the High Atlas to honour ibn Tumart in 1146, and it remains a wonder of austere graces and unshakable foundations.

Almohad Demolition & Construction Crews

A bloody power struggle ensued between the sons of ibn Tumart and the sons of his generals that wouldn't be settled definitively until 1185, when Abu Yusuf Yacoub, the young son of the Muslim governor of Seville and Valencia, rode south into Morocco and drove his foes into the desert. But he also kept and expanded his power base in Spain, winning so many victories against the princes of Spain that he earned the moniker Al-Mansour, 'the victorious'. He modelled Seville's famous La Giralda after Marrakesh's Koutoubia minaret, and reinvented Marrakesh as an Almohad capital and learning centre to rival Fez.

Yacoub el-Mansour's urban-planning prowess also made Fez arguably the most squeaky-clean city of medieval times, with 93 hammams, 47 soap factories and 785 mosques complete with ablutions facilities. Yacoub el-Mansour was also a patron of great thinkers, including Aristotle scholar Ibn Rashid – whose commentary would help spark a Renaissance among Italian philosophers – and Sufi master Sidi Bel-Abbes. However, Yacoub's enlightenment and admiration of architecture was apparently not all-encompassing; several synagogues were demolished under his rule.

Defeated by Bulls & Betrayal

Similar thinking (or lack thereof) prevailed in 12th-century Europe, where a hunt for heretics turned to officially sanctioned torture under papal bulls of the egregiously misnamed Pope Innocent IV. Bishop Bernard of Toledo, Spain, seized Toledo's mosque, and rallied Spain's Castilian Christian kings in a crusade against their Muslim rulers.

The Almohads were in no condition to fight back. When Yacoub's 16-year-old son was named caliph, he wasn't up to the religious responsibilities that came with the title. Instead, he was obsessed with bullfighting, and was soon gored to death.

Yacoub el-Mansour must've done pirouettes in his grave around 1230, when his next son tapped as caliph, Al-Mamun, allied with his

An incisive look at religious life on opposite ends of the Muslim world, anthropologist Clifford Geertz's groundbreaking *Islam Observed: Religious Development in Morocco and Indonesia* reveals complex variations within the vast mosaic of Islam.

Impress Moroccans with your knowledge of the latest developments in Moroccan society, Amazigh culture, and North African politics, all covered in English at www.magharebia. com/cocoon/awi/ xhtml1/en_GB/ homepage/ default

1147	1199	1276	1324–52
The Almohads finally defeat the Almoravids and destroy Marrakesh after a two-year siege, paving the way for Yacoub el-Mansour and his architects to outdo the Almoravids with an all-new Marrakesh.	A vast swath of prime Mediterranean commercial real estate from Tripoli to Spain is consolidated under Almohad control.	Winds of change blow in from the Atlas with the Zenata Berbers, who oust the Almohads and establish the Merenid dynasty with strategic military manoeuvres and even more strategic marriages.	Tangier-born adventurer Ibn Battuta picks up where Marco Polo left off, travelling from Mali to Sumatra and Mongolia and publishing *Rihla* – an inspired though not entirely reliable travel guide.

Christian persecutors and turned on his fellow Almohads in a desperate attempt to hang onto his father's empire. This short-lived caliph added the ultimate insult to Almohad injury when he climbed the Koutoubia *minbar* (pulpit) and announced that ibn Tumart wasn't a true Mahdi (leader) of the faithful. That title, he claimed, rightfully belonged to Jesus.

By Marriage or Murder: The Merenids

When Zenata Berbers from the Anti Atlas invaded the Almohad capital of Marrakesh in 1269, the Almohad defeat was complete. The Zenata had already ousted the Almohads in Meknès, Salé, Fez and most of the Atlantic Coast. To win over religious types, they promised moral leadership under their new Merenid dynasty. Making good on the promise, the Merenids undertook construction of a *medersa* (school of religious learning) in every major city they conquered, levying special taxes on Christian and Jewish communities for the purpose. In exchange, they allowed these communities to practise key trades, and hired Christian mercenaries and Jewish policy advisors to help conduct the business of the Merenid state.

But this time the new rulers faced a tough crowd not easily convinced by promises of piety. Fez revolted, and the Castilian Christians held sway in Salé. To shore up their Spanish interests, the Merenids allied with the Castilian princes against the Muslim rulers of Granada. Once again, this proved not to be a winning strategy. By the 14th century, Muslim Spain was lost to the Christians, and the Strait of Gibraltar was forfeited. The Merenids also didn't expect the Spanish Inquisition, when over one million Muslims and Jews would be terrorised and forcibly expelled from Spain.

Without military might or religious right to back their imperial claims, the Merenids chose another time-tested method: marriage. In the 14th century, Merenid leaders cleverly co-opted their foes by marrying princesses from Granada and Tunis, and claimed Algiers, Tripoli and the strategic Mediterranean port of Ceuta.

Death by Plague & Office Politics

But the bonds of royal marriage were not rat-proof, and the Merenid empire was devastated by plague. Abu Inan, son of the Merenid leader Abu Hassan, glimpsed opportunity in the Black Death, and proclaimed himself the new ruler despite one minor glitch: his father was still alive. Abu Hassan hurried back from Tripoli to wrest control from his treacherous son in Fez, but to no avail. Abu Inan buried his father in the royal Merenid necropolis outside Rabat in 1351, but he too was laid to rest nearby after he was strangled by one of his own advisors in 1358.

Key Moroccan Dynasties

» **Idrissid** 8th-10th century

» **Almoravid** 11th-12th century

» **Almohad** 12th-13th century

» **Merenid** 13th-15th century

» **Saadian** 16th-17th century

» **Alawite** 17th century-present

A Travellers History of North Africa by Barnaby Rogerson is a handy and accessible guide that puts Morocco into the wider currents of regional history.

1348	1377	1415	1480–92
Bubonic plague strikes Mediterranean North Africa; Merenid alliances and kingdoms crumble. Rule of law is left to survivors and opportunists to enforce, with disastrous consequences.	At Kairaouine University in Fez, Ibn Khaldun examines Middle Eastern history in his groundbreaking *Muqaddimah*, explaining how religious propaganda, taxation and revisionist history make and break states.	In search of gold and the fabled kingdom of Prester John – location of the Fountain of Youth – Portuguese Prince Henry the Navigator begins his conquests of Moroccan seaports.	Ferdinand and Isabella conquer Spain, and persecution of Muslims and Jews escalates.

The Merenids had an unfortunate knack for hiring homicidal bureaucrats. To cover his tracks, Abu Inan's killer went on a royal killing spree, until Merenid Abu Salim Ibrahim returned from Spain and terminated this rampaging employee. Abu Salim's advisor sucked up to his boss by offering his sister in marriage, only to lop off Abu Salim's head after the wedding. He replaced Abu Salim with a Merenid patsy before thinking better of it and strangling the new sultan, too. This slippery advisor was assassinated by another Merenid, who was deposed a scant few years later by yet another Merenid – and so it continued for 40 years, with new Merenid rulers and advisors offing the incumbents every few years. While the Merenids were preoccupied with murderous office politics in Meknès and Fez, the Portuguese seized control of coastal Morocco.

BERBER PRIDE & PREJUDICE

Despite a rich tradition of poetry, petroglyphs, music and art dating as far back as 5000 BC, the Amazigh were often misconstrued as uneducated by outsiders, because no standard written language had been consistently applied to their many distinct languages. The Romans tried for 250 years to take over Amazigh territory and institute Roman customs – and when that failed they bad-mouthed their adversaries, calling them 'Berbers', or Barbarians. The name stuck, and so did anti-Amazigh prejudice.

The protectorate established French as the official language of Morocco to make it easier to conduct (and hence control) business transactions and affairs of state. Complex Amazigh artistic symbolism and traditional medicine were dismissed as charming but irrelevant superstition by those not privy to the oral traditions accompanying them, and the educated classes were encouraged to distance themselves from their Berber roots. But Amazigh languages and traditions have persisted in Morocco, and the Berber Pride movement has recently reclaimed 'Berber' as a unifying term.

After independence (1955–56), Arabic was adopted as the official language, though French continues to be widely spoken among the elite, and Darija is the commonly understood Moroccan Arabic dialect. As recently as the 1980s, the use of Berber script was subject to censure in Morocco. But with the backing of King Mohammed VI – who is part Berber himself – the ancient written Tifinagh alphabet that first emerged around the time of Egyptian hieroglyphics was revived in 2003, and a modernised version is now being taught in some schools as a standardised written Berber.

More than 60% of Moroccans now call themselves Amazigh or Berber, and Berber languages are currently spoken by some 8.5 to 10 million Moroccans. Berber Pride is now mainstream in Morocco, with the introduction of the official Moroccan Chaîne Amazigh, offering TV and radio broadcasts in three Amazigh languages. Yet Human Rights Watch reported that in 2010, parents who gave their children Amazigh names were told the names were rejected by state bureaucrats as 'not recognizably Moroccan'. After a public outcry, the policy was reversed, so babies too can show Berber Pride in Morocco.

1497–1505	1498	1525	1578
Moroccan ports are occupied by English, Portuguese, and Spanish forces and sundry pirates, from Mediterranean Melilla to Agadir on the Atlantic coast.	Church Inquisitors present European Muslims and Jews with a choice: a) conversion and persecution; or b) torture and death. Many choose c) none of the above, and escape to Morocco.	Like a blast of scorching desert wind, the Beni Saad Berbers blow back European and Ottoman encroachment in Morocco, and establish a new Saadian dynasty in Marrakesh.	The Saadians fight both alongside and against Portugal at the Battle of Three Kings, ending with 8000 dead, a scant 100 survivors and the decimation of Portugal's ruling class.

Victory is Sweet: The Saadians

Much of Portugal (including Lisbon) had been under Muslim rule during the 12th century, and now the Portuguese were ready for payback – literally. The tiny, rugged kingdom needed steady supplies of food for its people and gold to fortify its growing empire, but Morocco stood in the way. No nation could wrest overland Saharan trade routes from the savvy Berber warriors who'd controlled key oases and mountain passes for centuries. Instead, the Portuguese went with tactics where they had clear technical advantages: naval warfare and advanced firearms. By systematically capturing Moroccan ports along the Mediterranean and Atlantic coasts, Portuguese gunships bypassed Berber middlemen inland, and headed directly to West Africa for gold and slaves.

Historic Moroccan Mellahs

» Tamnougalt
» Demnate
» Fez
» Zagora/Amezrou
» Essaouira
» Marrakesh

Sugar Caravans

Once trade in the Sahara began to dry up, something had to be done. Entire inland communities were decimated, and formerly flush Marrakesh was wracked with famine. The Beni Saad Berbers – now known to history as the Saadians – from the Drâa Valley took up the fight against the Portuguese. With successive wins against European, Berber and Ottoman rivals, the Saadians were able to reinstate inland trade. Soon the Saadians were in control of such sought-after commodities as gold, slaves, ivory, ostrich feathers and the must-have luxury for trendy European royals: sugar.

The Saadians satisfied European sugar cravings at prices that make today's oil and cocaine cartels look like rank amateurs. With threats of full-scale invasion, the Saadians had no problem scaring up customers and suppliers. The most dangerous sugar-dealer of all was Saadian Sultan Ahmed al-Mansour ed-Dahbi, who earned his names Al-Mansour (the Victorious) for defeating foes from Portugal to the Sudan, and Ed-Dahbi (the Golden) for his success in bilking them. This Marrakshi Midas used the proceeds to line the floor to ceiling of his Badi Palace in Marrakesh with gold and gems. But after the sultan died, his short-lived successor stripped the palace down to its mudbrick foundations, as it remains today. The Saadian legacy is most visible in the Saadian Tombs, decked out for a decadent afterlife with painted Carrara marble and gold leaf. The Saadians died as they lived: dazzling beyond belief and a touch too rich for most tastes.

Moulay Ismail was pen pals with England's James II and Louis XIV of France, and tried to convert the Sun King to Islam by mail.

The Rise of Mellahs

Under the Saadians, Jewish communities also took up crucial roles as dealers of the hottest Moroccan commodities of the time: salt and sugar. When European Jewish communities faced the Inquisition, forced conversions and summary executions, the comparatively tolerant Saadian

1591	1610–14	1659–66	1684
With 4000 European mercenaries, Ahmed al-Mansour ed-Dahbi crosses the Sahara and defeats a 40,000-strong army for control of the fabled desert caravan destination of Timbuktu.	Oxford graduate and erstwhile lawyer Henry Mainwaring founds the Masmouda Pirates Republic near Rabat, pillaging Canadian cod, French salt-fish and Portuguese wine. He is later elected to Britain's parliament.	The Alawites end years of civil war, and even strike an uneasy peace with the Barbary pirates controlling Rabati ports.	Barbary pirates take English captives and England seizes Tangier, leading to arguments over who stole what from whom. Prisoners are released when England relinquishes Tangier – after destroying its port.

dynasty provided Jewish communities with some security, setting aside a section of Marrakesh next to the royal kasbah as a Jewish quarter, or *mellah* – a name derived from the Arabic word for salt. This protection was repaid many times over in taxes levied on Jewish and Christian businesses, and the royally flush Saadians clearly got the sweet end of the deal. Yet several Jewish Moroccans rose to prominence as royal advisors, and in the Saadian Tombs of Marrakesh, trusted Jewish confidantes are buried closer to kings than royal wives.

By day, Jewish merchants traded alongside Christian and Muslim merchants, and were entrusted with precious salt, sugar and gold brought across the Sahara; by night they were under official guard in their quarters. Once the *mellahs* of Fez and Marrakesh became overcrowded with European arrivals, other notable *mellahs* were founded in Essaouira, Safi, Rabat and Meknès, and the traditions of skilled handicrafts that flourished there continue to this day. The influence of the *mellahs* spread throughout Morocco, especially in tangy dishes with the signature salted, pickled ingredients of Moroccan Jewish cuisine.

Pirates & Politics: The Early Alawites

The Saadian empire dissolved in the 17th century like a sugar cube in Moroccan mint tea, and civil war prevailed until the Alawites came along. With illustrious ancestors from the Prophet Mohammed's family and descendents extending to the current King Mohammed VI, the Alawites were quite a change from the free-wheeling Saadians and their anarchic legacy. But many Moroccans might have preferred anarchy to the second Alawite ruler, the dreaded Moulay Ismail (1672–1727).

A despot whose idea of a good time included public disembowelments and amateur dentistry on courtiers who peeved him, Moulay Ismail was also a scholar, dad to hundreds of children and Mr Popularity among his royal European peers. European nobles gushed about lavish dinner parties at Moulay Ismail's palace in Meknès, built by conscripted Christian labourers. Rumour has it that when these decidedly non-union construction workers finished the job, some were walled in alive. The European royal party tab wasn't cheap, either, but Moulay Ismail wasn't worried: piracy would cover it.

In Her Majesty's Not-So-Secret Service: Barbary Pirates

Queen Elizabeth I kicked off the Atlantic pirate trade, allying against her arch-nemesis King Phillip II of Spain with the Saadians and specially licensed pirates known as privateers. The most notoriously effective hires were the Barbary pirates, Moriscos (Spanish Muslims) who'd been forcibly converted and persecuted in Spain and hence had an added

Whatever happened to Barbary pirates? How did Islam mesh with Berber beliefs? And why was Morocco the exception to Ottoman rule? Jamil Abun-Nasr unravels these and other Moroccan mysteries in *A History of the Maghreb in the Islamic Period.*

18th century	1757–90
The Alawites rebuild the ancient desert trading outpost of Sijilmassa, only to lose control to Aït Atta Berber warriors, who raze the town. Only two not-so-triumphal arches remain.	Sidi Mohammed III makes a strategic move to the coast, to rebuild Essaouira and regain control over Atlantic ports. Inland imperial cities of Fez and Meknès slip into decline.

» Saadian Tombs (p63), Marrakesh

Historic Battle-grounds

» **Aghmat** Idrissids v Almoravids; Independence Movement v French protectorate

» **Sijilmassa** Almoravids v Almohads; Alawites v Aït Atta Amazigh

» **Chefchaouen** Rifians v Portuguese; Rifians v Spanish

» **Western Sahara** Spanish v Polisario; Polisario v Morocco

In *The Conquest of Morocco*, Douglas Porch describes a controversial colonial war promoted as a 'civilising mission' and supported by business interests – a chapter of Middle Eastern history since repeated, as Porch observes in the 2005 edition.

motivation to shake down Spaniards. James I outlawed English privateering in 1603, but didn't seem to mind when his buddy Moulay Ismail aided and abetted the many British and Barbary pirates who harboured in the royal ports at Rabat and Salé – for a price.

But pirate loyalties being notoriously fickle, Barbary pirates attacked Ireland, Wales, Iceland and even Newfoundland in the 17th century. Barbary pirates also took prisoners, who were usually held for ransom and freed after a period of servitude – including one-time English allies. Captives were generally better off with Barbary pirates than French profiteers, who typically forced prisoners to ply the oars of slave galleys until death. Nevertheless, after pressure from England secured their release in 1684, a number of English captives were quite put out about the whole experience, and burned the port of Tangier behind them. But other English saw upsides to piracy and kidnapping: when the Portuguese were forced out of Essaouira in the 17th century, a freed British prisoner who'd converted to Islam joined a French profiteer to rebuild the city for the sultan, using free labour provided by European captives.

Troubled Waters for Alwawites

After Moulay Ismail's death, his elite force of 50,000 to 70,000 Abid, or 'Black Guard', ran amok, and not one of his many children was able to succeed him. The Alawite dynasty would struggle on into the 20th century, but the country often lapsed into lawlessness when rulers overstepped their bounds. Piracy and politics became key ways to get ahead in the 18th and 19th centuries – and the two were by no means mutually exclusive. By controlling key Moroccan seaports and playing European powers against one another, officials and outlaws alike found they could demand a cut of whatever goods were shipped through the Strait of Gibraltar and along the Atlantic Coast.

In the late 18th century, when Sidi Mohammed ben Abdullah ended the officially condoned piracy of his predecessors and nixed shady side deals with foreign powers, the financial results were disastrous. With added troubles of plague and drought, Morocco's straits were truly dire.

With Friends Like These: European Encroachment

For all their successful European politicking, the early Alawites had apparently forgotten a cardinal rule of Moroccan diplomacy: never neglect Berber alliances. Sultan Moulay Hassan tried to rally support among the Berbers of the High Atlas in the late 19th century, but by then it was too late. France began to take an active interest in Morocco around 1830, and allied with Berbers across North Africa to fend off the Ottomans. After centuries of practise fighting Moroccans, Spain took control of areas of

1767–1836	1777	1830	1860
Cash-strapped Morocco makes extraordinary concessions to trading partners, granting Denmark trade monopolies in Agadir and Safi, and France and the US license to trade in Morocco for a nominal fee.	A century after the English leave Tangier a royal wreck, Morocco gets revenge and becomes the first country to recognise the breakaway British colony calling itself the United States of America.	France seizes the Algerian coast, increasing pressure on the Moroccan sultan to cede power in exchange for mafia-style protection along Morocco's coasts from the advancing Ottomans.	If at first you don't succeed, try for seven centuries: Spain takes control of a swath of northern Morocco reaching into the Rif.

northern Morocco in 1860 – and not incidentally, generated lasting resentment for desecrating graveyards, mosques and other sacred sites in Melilla and Tetouan. While wily Queen Victoria entertained Moroccan dignitaries and pressed for Moroccan legal reforms, her emissaries were busy brokering deals with France and Spain.

Footloose & Duty-Free in Tangier

Order became increasingly difficult to maintain in Moroccan cities and in Berber mountain strongholds, and Moulay Hassan employed powerful Berber leaders to regain control – but accurately predicting Moulay Hassan's demise, some Berbers cut deals of their own with the Europeans. By the time Moulay Hassan's teenage successor Sultan Moulay Abdelaziz pushed through historic antidiscrimination laws to impress Morocco's erstwhile allies, the Europeans had reached an understanding: while reforms were nice and all, what they really wanted were cheap goods.

2000 YEARS OF MOROCCAN JEWISH HISTORY

By the 1st century AD, Jewish Berber communities that were already well established in Morocco included farmers, metalworkers, dyers, glassblowers, bookbinders and cowboys. The Merenids established the first official Jewish quarter in Fez, where Jewish entrepreneurs excluded from trades and guilds in medieval Europe were able to conduct business. Jewish Moroccans were taxed when business boomed for the ruling dynasty and sometimes blamed when it didn't, yet they managed to flourish under the Merenids and Saadians, while European Jews faced the Inquisition and persecution.

Under Alawite rule in the 17th to 19th centuries, the official policy toward Jewish Moroccans was one of give and take: on the one hand they had opportunities as tradespeople, business leaders and ambassadors to England, Holland and Denmark in the 19th century; on the other they were subjected to taxes, surveillance and periodic scapegoating. But in good times and bad, Jewish Moroccans remained a continuous presence.

By 1948, some 300,000 Jewish Moroccans lived in Morocco. Many left after the founding of the states of Morocco and Israel, and today only an estimated 3000 to 8000 remain, mostly in Casablanca. A Jewish community centre in Casablanca was a bombing target in 2003, and though no one was harmed at the community centre, trade-centre blasts killed 33 and wounded 100. Yet the Casablanca community remains intact, and Casablanca is home to the recently expanded Museum of Moroccan Judaism.

Under the current king, Jewish schools now receive state funding, and a few Jewish expatriates have responded to a royal invitation to return, contributing to the revival of Essaouira's *mellah*. Yet the everyday champions of Jewish heritage in Morocco remain ordinary Moroccans, the one million people worldwide of Moroccan Jewish heritage, and culturally engaged travellers, who together ensure Moroccan Jewish customs, festivals, and landmarks get the attention they deserve.

1880	1906	1912	1921–26
France, Britain, Spain and the US meet in Madrid and agree that Morocco can retain nominal control over its territory – after granting themselves tax-free business licenses and duty-free shopping.	The controversial Act of Algeciras divvies up North Africa among European powers like a *bastilla* pigeon pie, but Germany isn't invited – a slight that exacerbated tensions among European powers.	The Treaty of Fez hands Morocco to the French protectorate, which mostly protects French business interests at Moroccan taxpayer expense with the ruthless assistance of Berber warlord Pasha el-Glaoui.	Under the command of Abd el-Krim, Berber leaders rebel against Spanish rule of the Rif, and Spain loses its foothold in the mountains.

By 1880, Europeans and Americans set up their own duty-free shop in Tangier, declaring it an 'international zone' where they were above the law and beyond tax collectors' reaches.

But the lure of prime North African real estate proved irresistible. By 1906, Britain had snapped up strategic waterfront property in Egypt and the Suez; France took the prize for sheer acreage from Algeria to West Africa; Italy landed Libya; Spain drew the short stick with the unruly Rif and a whole lot of desert. Germany was incensed at being left out of this arrangement and announced support for Morocco's independence, further inflaming tensions between Germany and other European powers in the years leading to WWI.

France Opens A Branch Office: The Protectorate

Whatever illusions of control Morocco's sultanate might've been clutching slipped away at the 1906 Conference of Algeciras, when control of Morocco's banks, customs and police force was handed over to France for 'protection'. The 1912 Treaty of Fez establishing Morocco as a French protectorate made colonisation official, and the French hand-picked a new sultan with all the backbone of a sock puppet. More than 100,000 French administrators, outcasts and opportunists arrived in cities across Morocco to take up residence in French villes nouvelles (new cities).

Résident-Général Louis Lyautey saw to it that these new French suburbs were kitted out with all the mod cons: electricity, trains, roads and running water. Villes nouvelles were designed to be worlds apart from adjacent Moroccan medinas (historic city centres), with French schools, churches, villas and grand boulevards named after French generals. No expense or effort was spared to make the new arrivals feel right at home – which made their presence all the more galling for Moroccans footing the bill through taxes, shouldering most of the labour and still living in crowded, poorly serviced medinas. Lyautey had already set up French colonial enterprises in Vietnam, Madagascar and Algeria, so he arrived in Morocco with the confidence of a CEO and a clear plan of action: break up the Berbers, ally with the Spanish when needed and keep business running by all available means.

Nationalist Resistance

Once French-backed Sultan Yusuf died and his French-educated 18-year-old son Mohammed V became sultan, Lyautey expected that French business in Morocco would carry on as usual. He hadn't counted on a fiery young nationalist as sultan, or the staunch independence of ordinary Moroccans. Mining strikes and union organising interfered with France's most profitable colonial businesses, and military attention was diverted

---

Read first-hand accounts of Morocco's independence movement from Moroccan women who rebelled against colonial control, rallied and fought alongside men in Alison Baker's *Voice of Resistance: Oral Histories of Moroccan Women*.

In Morocco's second parliamentary elections in 2007, 34 women were elected, representing 10.4% of all seats – that's just behind the US at 12.5% female representation after 110 elections.

1942	1943–45
In defiance of Vichy France, Casablanca hosts American forces staging the Allied North African campaign. This move yields US support for Moroccan independence and the classic Humphrey Bogart film *Casablanca*.	When the Allies struggle in Italy, US General Patton calls in the Goums, Morocco's elite force of mountain warriors. With daggers and night-time attacks, they advance the Allies in Tuscany.

CHRISTOPHER GROENHOUT / LONELY PLANET IMAGES ©

» Essaouira's walled medina (p222)

to force Moroccans back into the mines. Berbers had never accepted foreign dominion without a fight, and they were not about to make an exception for the French. By 1921 the Rif was up in arms against the Spanish and French under the leadership of Ibn Abd al-Krim al-Khattabi. It took five years, 300,000 Spanish and French forces and two budding Fascists (Francisco Franco and Marshal Pétain) to capture Ibn Abd al-Krim and force him into exile.

The French won a powerful ally when they named Berber warlord Thami el-Glaoui pasha of Marrakesh, but they also made a lot of enemies. The title gave the pasha implicit license to do as he pleased, which included mafia-style executions and extortion schemes, kidnapping women and children who struck his fancy, and friendly games of golf at his Royal Golf Club with Ike Eisenhower and Winston Churchill. The pasha forbade talk of independence under penalty of death, and conspired to exile Mohammed V from Morocco in 1953 – but Pasha Glaoui would end his days powerless, wracked with illness and grovelling on his knees for King Mohammed V's forgiveness.

Although the French protectorate of Morocco was nominally an ally of Vichy France and Germany in WWII, independent-minded Casablanca provided crucial ground support for the Allied North African campaign. When Morocco's Istiqlal (Independence) party demanded freedom from French rule in 1944, the US and Britain were finally inclined to agree. Under increasing pressure from Moroccans and the Allies, France allowed Mohammed V to return from exile in 1955. Morocco successfully negotiated its independence from France and Spain between 1956 and 1958.

A Rough Start: After Independence

When Mohammed V died suddenly of heart failure in 1961, King Hassan II became the leader of the new nation. Faced with a shaky power base, an unstable economy and elections that revealed divides even among nationalists, Hassan II consolidated power by cracking down on dissent and suspending parliament for a decade. With heavy borrowing to finance dam-building, urban development and an ever-expanding bureaucracy, Morocco was deep in debt by the 1970s. Attempts to assassinate the king underscored the need to do something, quickly, to turn things around – and then in 1973, the phosphate industry in the Spanish-controlled Western Sahara started to boom. Morocco staked its claim to the area and its lucrative phosphate reserves with the Green March (see the boxed text, p428), settling the area with Moroccans while greatly unsettling indigenous Saharawi people agitating for self-determination.

Global Voices Morocco provides a roundup of Moroccan news and opinion online, including English translations of bloggers' responses to Moroccan news at www.global voicesonline. org/-/world/ middle-east -north-africa/ morocco.

According to the 2010 Human Development Index, 28.5% of Moroccan households are poor, and another 11.4% at risk. Moroccan officials dispute the validity of these statistics, placing the poverty figure nearer 9%.

1944–53	1955–56	1961	1975
Moroccan nationalists demand independence from France with increasing impatience. Sultan Mohammed V is inclined to agree, and is exiled to Madagascar by the protectorate for the crime of independent thought.	Morocco successfully negotiates its independence from France, Spain cedes control over most of its colonial claims within Morocco, and exiled nationalist Mohammed V returns as king of independent Morocco.	When Mohammed V dies suddenly, Hassan II becomes king. He transforms Morocco into a constitutional monarchy in 1962, but the 'Years of Lead' deals heavy punishments for dissent.	The UN concludes that the Western Sahara is independent, but Hassan II concludes otherwise, ordering the Green March to enforce Morocco's claims to the region and its phosphate reserves.

MARCHING TO THE KING'S TUNE

Talk of 'Greater Morocco' began in the 1950s, but in the 1970s it became the official explanation for Morocco's annexation of phosphate-rich Spanish Sahara. There was a snag: the Popular Front for the Liberation of the Sahara and the Rio di Oro (Polisario – Saharawi pro-independence militia) declared the region independent. Putting his French legal training to work, Hassan II took up the matter with the International Court of Justice (ICJ) in The Hague in 1975, expecting the court would provide a resounding third-party endorsement for Morocco's claims. Instead the ICJ considered a counter-claim for independence from the Polisario, and dispatched a fact-finding mission to Spanish Sahara.

The ICJ concluded that ties to Morocco weren't strong enough to support Moroccan sovereignty over the region, and Western Sahara was entitled to self-determination. In a highly creative interpretation of this court judgment, Hassan II declared that Morocco had won its case and ordered a celebratory 'peace march' of more than 350,000 Moroccans from Marrakesh into Western Sahara in 1975 – some never to return. This unarmed 'Green March' was soon fortified by military personnel and land mines, and was vehemently resisted by armed Polisario fighters.

The Green March is no longer the symbol of national pride it once was; Green March murals that once defined desert-cafe decor have been painted over with apolitical dunescapes. Meanwhile, phosphate profits have dwindled, due to falling prices, mining sabotage and spiralling costs for Moroccan military operations, exceeding US$300 million annually by 1981.

A truce was finally established in 1991 between Morocco and the Polisario, but Morocco's 2010 raid of Gadaym Izik protest camp of 12,000 displaced Saharawi resulted in at least a dozen deaths and hundreds of injuries, according to the BBC, plus more than 100 detentions of activists, as reported by Human Rights Watch. The actions haven't altered Polisario's demand for a referendum, while Rabat maintains that it will grant Western Sahara autonomous status, but not a referendum. So the status of the Western Sahara remains unresolved – a rallying cry for many Saharawi, and an awkward conversation nonstarter for many deeply ambivalent Moroccan taxpayers.

Years of Lead

Along with the growing gap between the rich and the poor and a mounting tax bill to cover Morocco's military debt from the Western Sahara, King Hassan II's suppression of dissent fuelled further resentment among his subjects. By the 1980s, the critics of the king included journalists, trade unionists, women's-rights activists, Marxists, Islamists, Berbers advocating recognition of their culture and language, and the working poor – in other words, a broad cross-section of Moroccan society.

1981	1999	2002–07	2004–05
After the Casablanca Uprising, the military rounds up dissenters and unionists nationwide. But demands for political reforms increase, and many political prisoners are later exonerated.	Soon after initiating a commission to investigate abuses of power under his own rule, Hassan II dies. All hail Mohammed VI, and hopes for a constitutional monarchy.	Historic reforms initiated under Mohammed VI include regular parliamentary and municipal elections across Morocco, plus the Mudawanna legal code offering unprecedented protection for women.	Equity and Reconciliation Commission televises testimonies of the victims of Moroccan human-rights abuses during the 'Years of Lead'; it becomes the most watched in Moroccan TV history.

The last straw for many came in 1981, when official Moroccan newspapers casually announced that the government had conceded to the International Monetary Fund to hike prices for staple foods. For the many Moroccans subsisting on the minimum wage, these increases meant that two-thirds of their income would be spent on a meagre diet of sardines, bread and tea. When trade unions organised protests of the measure, government reprisals were swift and brutal. Tanks rolled down the streets of Casablanca and hundreds were killed, at least 1000 wounded, and an estimated 5000 protesters arrested in a nationwide *laraf,* or roundup.

Far from dissuading dissent, the Casablanca Uprising galvanised support for government reform. Sustained pressure from human-rights activists throughout the 1980s achieved unprecedented results in 1991, when Hassan II founded the Equity and Reconciliation Commission to investigate human-rights abuses that occurred during his own reign – a first for a king. In his very first public statement as king upon his father's death in 1999, Mohammed VI vowed to right the wrongs of the era known to Moroccans as the Years of Lead. The commission has since helped cement human-rights advances, awarding reparations to 9280 victims of the Years of Lead by 2006.

Talk Morocco offers frank, irreverent commentary about Moroccan identity, democracy, red tape, gender relations and more at www.talkmorocco.net.

New Regime, New Hopes

As Moroccans will surely tell you, there's still room for improvement in today's Morocco. The parliament elected in 2002 set aside 30 seats for women members of parliament, and implemented some promising reforms: Morocco's first-ever municipal elections, employment non-discrimination laws, the introduction of Berber languages in state schools, and the Mudawanna, a legal code protecting women's rights to divorce and custody. But tactics from the Years of Lead were revived after the 2003 Casablanca trade-centre bombings and a 2010 military raid of a Western Sahara protest camp, when suspects were rounded up – in 2010 Human Rights Watch reported that many of them had been subjected to abuse and detention without counsel. Civil society is outpacing state reforms, as Moroccans take the initiative to address poverty and illiteracy through enterprising village associations and non-governmental organisations.

2004	2006	2010	2011
Morocco signs free trade agreements with the EU and the US and gains status as a non-NATO ally.	Morocco proposes 'special autonomy' for the Western Sahara, and holds the first direct talks with Polisario in seven years – which end in a stalemate.	The state cracks down on Moroccan publication *Nichane* for a cover article called 'Jokes: How Moroccans Laugh at Religion, Sex and Politics,' arresting editors. *Nichane* ceases publication.	Pro-democracy revolutions in Tunisia and Egypt inspire Morocco's February 20 Movement; calls for curbs on government corruption, investments in public welfare and halting crackdowns on dissidents.

A Day in the Life of Morocco

Forget for a moment the glossy travel brochures about Marrakesh, movies filmed in the Moroccan Sahara, urban legends about decadent Tangier: as anyone who's been there knows, the best way to get to know Morocco is through Moroccans. So to introduce you to Morocco, meet Driss, Fatima, Rashid and Amina, four characters who are composites of people you might encounter during a day in Morocco. The way each of these characters spends the day illustrates the tremendous variation and some major recurring themes in Moroccan daily life.

More than 10% of the winners in Morocco's second parliamentary elections in 2007 were women, and women have been elected to municipal offices across the country: including lawyer Fatima Zahra Mansouri, elected mayor of Marrakesh in 2009 at age 33.

Morning: Meet Driss

Six days a week, Driss wakes at 6am to ride his scooter from his family's apartment in a Marrakesh suburb to the riad (courtyard house, converted into a guesthouse) where he works as assistant manager, dropping off his little sister at school on the way. He knows enough Spanish and English to explain the riad's breakfast menu to guests and speaks fluent Moroccan Arabic, French and classical Arabic (mostly from watching the news on Al-Jazeera) – though his native Berber language, Tashelhit, is getting a little rusty. Driss takes computer courses on his weekly morning off, and wants to take Spanish too. His father approves: he owns a small *hanout* (corner grocery) and doesn't read or write that well himself, but insisted that Driss and his four siblings attend school.

Driss knows his parents will start pressuring him to get married now that he's pushing 30, but he's in no rush and not especially interested in the village girls they have in mind. He'd rather have a girlfriend in the city first, and take things from there. He already has someone in mind, actually: she works at a cybercafe near the riad.

Noon: Meet Fatima

It's been a long, hot morning cracking argan nuts at a fair-trade women's cooperative near Agadir, and Fatima is ready for her lunch break. She's not really hungry – now that she has a steady hourly income through the cooperative, she doesn't go hungry anymore – but she could use a breather, and likes to chat. She speaks Tashelhit at home, can get by in Moroccan Arabic, and knows how to say 'hello' and 'welcome' in French and English to foreigners who sometimes visit the argan cooperative, but she doesn't read or write.

Moroccan girls account for almost two-thirds of the half-million Moroccan kids under 15 who work instead of getting an education.

Her five grandchildren do, though, and she's very proud of that fact. Fatima lives frugally, saving most of her income to cover their school fees. All her four children are married, and she always has stories and treats for her grandchildren when they visit. When she goes into town to visit her daughter, she's surprised how informal young people are towards

With an attractive climate and exchange rate, Morocco has 100,000 foreign residents – and counting. Moroccan emigrants from Europe and the US are increasingly returning to Morocco to live, retire or start businesses, creating a new upper-middle economic class. The carefree spending of returnees is a source of major revenue and a certain amount of resentment for Moroccans, who grumble openly about returnees driving up costs and importing a culture of conspicuous consumption that's unattainable and shallow.

An international vogue for riads (traditional courtyard houses) has spread from Marrakesh to medinas (old cities) across Morocco, with many Europeans buying and restoring historic structures – and pricing Moroccans out of the housing market in their hometowns. As Moroccans move to the peripheries, suburban sprawl and traffic has increased, and medina neighbourhoods can seem strangely empty and lifeless off-season. To many Moroccans who remember the hard-fought independence movement, European enclaves bring to mind colonial French-only villes nouvelles (see p426). In response to claims that their mere presence is changing the local culture, some expats point to the satellite dishes on their neighbours' houses, and claim that globalisation is inevitable.

Maybe, but travellers can make the exchange more equitable by venturing beyond riad walls to explore Moroccan culture, meet Moroccans on their own turf and ensure Moroccans benefit from tourism. Lonely Planet recommends licensed guesthouses that provide fair pay and working conditions to employees and promote positive cultural exchange; you can help by sharing your experience at talk2us@lonelyplanet.com.

their elders, though not offended – she thinks it's good for young people to think for themselves – and she's truly shocked by the prices.

As Fatima stands up, she feels a pang of arthritis. It's beginning to interfere with her work, and she worries about the family that has largely depended on her since her husband passed away a few years ago. She thanks God she can work, and is determined that in two years, she'll make the pilgrimage to Mecca, *inshallah* (God willing).

Afternoon: Meet Rashid

Looking for lizards, Rashid almost bumps into a trekker along the 4km mountain path from school. His sisters tease him that he's such a dreamer, he always lets the goats get away. They used to walk to school together, but last year's drought hit their Middle Atlas village hard. The family had to sell their donkey, and make tough choices about who they could spare this harvest season. Eleven-year-old Rashid is a better student and worse goatherd than his sisters, so he gets to go to school – for now, anyway.

He likes to surprise his sisters by bringing something home from school: a lazy lizard, beans from the school garden, and one time, a foreign trekker for tea. His family served their best bread and butter, and though no one understood a word the guy was saying, he wasn't bad at *koura* (football). The postcard the trekker sent through the village association is on the family-room shelf, and Rashid is sure that if he can go to the regional middle school, one day he'll write back in perfect English.

Evening: Meet Amina

It's 6.30pm, and though Amina just got back from her French literature class at university, she's ready to go out again. Not that there's anything special on the agenda: a stroll, maybe the library or an internet cafe so she can get some privacy from her pesky little brother, who always tries to read her IMs.

By now she should have Facebook responses from her cousins in France; her uncle in France is financing her education. Amina studies hard, and hopes to work in the Moroccan government like her dad –

Nineteenth-century Swiss adventurer Isabelle Eberhardt dressed as a Berber man, became a Sufi, smoked kif, operated as a triple agent, married an Algerian dissident and wrote her memoir *The Oblivion Seekers* – all before the age of 30.

maybe even the foreign service, though she's never been outside Morocco, and rarely gets a chance to leave their suburb of Rabat. But she's hooked on world news, keeping up in French, Arabic and English through the internet and watching satellite TV with her Rabati cousins.

Tonight she'll organise plans for the weekend, maybe going out to a restaurant with a big group of friends. Amina doesn't drink alcohol personally, but some people she knows do, and she doesn't judge them for it. As far as dating goes, she met a guy in an internet chat room a while back, but that was nothing serious. She's not ready to settle down yet – there's too much else to do first.

Social Norms
Family Values

As different as Driss, Fatima, Rashid and Amina may seem, they all show a profound attachment to family. While they each have ambitions and ideas of their own, their aspirations are tied in some way to family – a much-admired trait in Morocco.

HUMOUR

Catch Moroccan Arabic jokes you might otherwise miss with *Humour and Moroccan Culture*, a treasury of Moroccan wit in translation, collected by American expat Mathew Helmke.

Even major status symbols (like Driss' motor scooter and the satellite TV at Amina's house) are valued less as prized possessions than as commodities benefiting the family as a whole. This is beginning to change, as the emerging middle class Driss represents moves out of large family homes and into smaller apartments in the suburbs, where common property is not such a given. But family connections remain paramount in Morocco, and remittances from Moroccans living abroad to family back home represent as much as 20% of GDP.

Since family is a focal point for Moroccans, expect related questions to come up in the course of conversation: where is your family? Are you married, and do you have children? How are they doing? This might seem a little nosey, and a roundabout way of finding out who you are and what interests you. But to Moroccans, questions about where you work or what you do in your spare time are odd ice-breakers, since what you do for a living or a hobby says less about you than what you do for your family.

Education

Next to family, education is the most important indicator of social status in Morocco. Driss and Amina read and write, like 52.3% of Morocco's population. But even with her college degree, Amina may find her em-

MOROCCAN SOCIAL GRACES

Many visitors are surprised at how quickly friendships can be formed in Morocco, and often a little suspicious. True, carpet-sellers aren't necessarily after your friendship when they offer you tea, and an unexpected introduction to your new Moroccan friend's single cousin can be awkward. If you find yourself in these situations, just claim an obligation elsewhere, smile, and leave – no hard feelings.

But notice how Moroccans behave with one another, and you'll see that friendly overtures are more than a mere contrivance. People you meet in passing are likely to remember you and greet you warmly the next day, and it's considered polite to stop and ask how they're doing. Greetings among friends can last 10 minutes in Morocco, as each person enquires after the other's happiness, well-being and family.

Moroccans are generous with their time, and extend courtesies that might seem to you like impositions, from walking you to your next destination to inviting you home for lunch. (At the risk of stating the obvious, anyone who suddenly demands payment for services rendered is not your friend). To show your appreciation, stop by the next day to say hello, and be sure to compliment the cook.

Since they've had contact with Europeans for the last couple of millennia and satellite TV for a decade, Moroccans are not likely to be shocked by Western attire. In fact, you'll notice logo T-shirts and trainers widely worn by young urbanites – if copyright were enforced here, under-25 populations of major Moroccan cities would be half naked.

You are not expected to cover your head in Morocco – though it can be handy protection against desert sandstorms. As you'll notice, some Moroccan women do and some don't wear the *hijab* (headscarf). Some choose to wear it for religious, cultural, practical or personal reasons, try it for a while to see if it suits them, or alternate, wearing a head covering in the streets but taking it off at home and work. A full face-covering veil is unusual in cities, and even rarer among rural women working in the fields.

That said, your choice of attire still may be perceived as a sign of respect (or lack thereof) for yourself, your family and your hosts. For men and women alike, this means not wearing shorts, sleeveless tops or clingy clothing. If you do, some people will be embarrassed for you and the family that raised you, and avoid eye contact. So if you don't want to miss out on some excellent company – especially among older Moroccans – do make a point of dressing modestly.

A DAY IN THE LIFE OF MOROCCO

ployment options limited: 40% of Moroccan humanities graduates were unemployed in 2008.

Rashid's ability to read makes him an exception in rural Morocco – and if he does enrol in middle school, he will be among just 12% of rural boys to have that opportunity. Schooling to age 14 is now an official mandate, and local initiatives have dramatically improved opportunities for education in the Moroccan countryside. But for vulnerable rural families like Rashid's, just getting the children fed can be difficult, let alone getting them to school. According to the UN Food and Agriculture Organization (FAO), child malnourishment is on the rise in Morocco, doubling from 4% in the mid-1990s to 8% in 2006. Innovative school programs like Rashid's that provide food as well as literacy are much needed to build a healthier, brighter future for Morocco.

For a millennia-old civilisation, Morocco looks young. There's a reason for this, beyond rejuvenating hammams: half the population is under 25, almost a third is under 15, and less than 5% is over 65.

Shifting Gender Roles

A decade or two ago, you might not have met Fatima or Amina. Most of the people you'd see out and about, going to school, socialising and conducting business in Morocco would have been men. Women were occupied with less high-profile work, such as animal husbandry, farming, childcare, fetching water and firewood.

As of 2004, Morocco's Mudawanna legal code guarantees women crucial rights to custody, divorce, property ownership and child support, among other protections. Positive social pressure has greatly reduced the once-common practice of hiring girls under 14 years of age as domestic workers, and initiatives to eliminate female illiteracy are giving girls a better start in life. Women now represent nearly a third of Morocco's formal workforce, forming their own industrial unions, agricultural cooperatives and artisans' collectives.

The modern Moroccan woman's outlook extends far beyond her front door, and women visitors will meet Moroccan women eager to chat, compare life experiences and share perspectives on world events. Men visiting Morocco have less opportunity to befriend Moroccan women, since male–female interactions are still somewhat stilted by social convention – though you'll surely notice couples meeting in parks, at cafes and via webcam. Young Moroccan women are on the move, commuting to work on motor scooters, taking over sidewalks on arm-in-arm evening strolls, and running for key government positions.

Best-selling Moroccan author and academic Fatima Mernissi exposes telling differences and uncanny similarities in the ideals of women in Europe and the Middle East in *Scheherazade Goes West: Different Cultures, Different Harems*.

Social Behaviour

As you will probably notice in your travels through Morocco, behaviour that is considered unacceptable outdoors, in full public view – such as drinking alcohol, or making kissy faces at someone of the opposite sex – is often tolerated in the relative privacy of a restaurant terrace, riad, or internet cafe. In this context, Amina's views on drinking and internet dating are not so radical, and Driss may stand a chance with his cybercafe cutie. While there are still laws in Morocco restricting the consumption of alcohol in view of a mosque, sex outside of marriage and homosexuality, enforcement of these laws is very rare. With proper discretion, there is plenty of latitude when it comes to socially acceptable behaviour.

Keep tabs on the welfare of Morocco's street children and find out what you can do to help at http://gvnet.com/streetchildren/Morocco.htm, an information clearing house on at-risk youth.

Religion

Like nearly 99% of Moroccans today, Driss, Fatima, Amina and Rashid are Muslim. Christian and Jewish communities have been established in Morocco for 1700 years or more, but in recent years their numbers have dwindled (see p425).

The Five Pillars of Islam

Soaring minarets, shimmering mosaics, intricate calligraphy, the muezzin's mesmerising call to prayer: much of what thrills visitors in Morocco today is inspired by Moroccans' deep and abiding faith in Islam. Based on the teachings of the Old and New Testaments, Islam is built on five pillars: *shahada*, the affirmation of faith in God and God's word entrusted to the Prophet Mohammed; *salat*, or prayer, ideally performed five times daily; *zakat*, or charity, a moral obligation to give to those in need; *sawm*, the daytime fasting practised during the month of Ramadan; and *haj*, the pilgrimage to Mecca that is the culmination of lifelong faith for Muslims.

Shiites & Sunnis

To avoid conflict, French Général Lyautey banned non-Muslims from mosques in Morocco. Moroccans appreciated the privacy so much that they ousted the French from Morocco, and kept the ban.

While all Muslims agree on these basic tenets received by the Prophet Mohammed, some doctrinal disagreements ensued after his death. The Umayyads challenged his son-in-law Ali's claim to the title of caliph, or leader of the faithful. Some Muslims continued to recognise only successors of Ali; today they are known as Shiites. But in sheer numbers of followers, the Umayyad caliphate's Sunni Muslim practice is more mainstream today.

The Maliki School

Like many Muslim countries, Morocco is mostly Sunni. There are four main schools of thought among the Sunnis emphasising different aspects of doctrine, and today the one most commonly followed in Morocco is the Maliki school. Historically this school has been less strict, with Maliki *qaids* (judges) applying the sharia, or religious code, according to local custom instead of absolutist rule of law.

Marabouts & Zawiyas

Farida ben Lyzaid's film *A Door to the Sky* tells the story of an émigré's return to Morocco, and her delicate balancing act between activism and tradition.

One local tradition to emerge over centuries of Islamic practice in Morocco is the custom of venerating *marabouts,* or saints. *Marabouts* are devout Muslims whose acts of devotion and professions of faith were so profound, their very presence is considered to confer *baraka*, or grace, even after their death. Moroccans go out of their way to visit *marabouts'* mausoleums and *zawiyas* (shrines) – and many claim that for believers, the right *zawiya* can fix anything from a broken heart to arthritis.

This practice of honouring *marabout*s is more in line with ancient Berber beliefs and Sufi mysticism than orthodox Islam, which generally discourages anything resembling idol worship. Visits to *zawiyas* are side trips for the many devout Moroccans who – like Fatima – spend a lifetime preparing and planning for the *haj*. Moroccans do not necessarily see a conflict between *baraka* and belief, or local customs and universal understanding.

Prospects for the Future

Economic Mobility

Fatima, Driss and Amina would be considered very fortunate in Morocco, where steady income is a rarity and 35% of the average Moroccan income covers basic foodstuffs. Only 10% of Moroccans can afford imported foods at the supermarket, let alone eating at restaurants occasionally like Amina. While the gap between rich and poor is growing in Morocco, Driss and Fatima represent an emerging middle class – though on average, Moroccans make much less in a day than Europeans do in an hour.

Career Opportunities

Driss, Amina and Fatima's incomes come from foreign trade, tourism, farming, and remittances from relatives living abroad – broadly representative of the country as a whole. Social security is provided by the family in Morocco, not the government, so like Fatima, most Moroccans cannot afford to consider retirement. With fierce competition for limited employment opportunities and spots in state-sponsored universities, even star students like Amina must rely on family for help – and some take extreme risks to seek opportunities abroad.

Like many Moroccans born and raised in rural villages, 11-year-old Rashid probably won't be able to stay home much longer. Since 55% of rural Moroccan families struggle to meet subsistence-level needs, rural teens often must move to larger towns and cities to find work and educational opportunities.

Your visit to Morocco can have a positive impact on future prospects for Moroccans like Driss, Amina and Fatima, but especially Rashid – tourism in rural areas makes it possible for youth to remain with their families, and avoid an at-risk existence in the city. While Moroccans are working hard to extend their welcome to visitors, tourism can be a strain on local resources; your choice of sustainable alternatives can help reverse that pattern, and make tourism a net benefit for Morocco.

Morocco, 1980–2010

» Life expectancy increased by 14 years

» Expected years of schooling increased by five years

» GNI per capita increased by 86% (UNDP)

Médecins Sans Frontières (www.doctorswithoutborders.org) and Amnesty International (www.amnesty.org) provide essential aid to Moroccan migrants stranded between borders without family, funds or legal protection.

A DAY IN THE LIFE OF MOROCCO

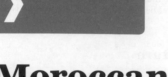

Moroccan Cuisine

Moroccan cuisine is the stuff of myth and legend – and sometimes sheer befuddlement, thanks to many seemingly indecipherable menus. Awkwardly phrased English and French menu descriptions often appear to require a special decoder ring, so visitors end up sticking to what they already know of Moroccan cuisine: couscous and tajines. Many other scrumptious Moroccan breakfast, lunch and dinner options are described in this chapter to take some of the mystery out of the menu, and help you explore your full range of dining options in Morocco.

Have no fear of the salad course, since these vegetable dishes are mostly cooked or peeled and among Morocco's finest culinary offerings. Entrées ominously described as 'spicy' on Moroccan menus are probably not overly hot or piquant – there could just be an extra pinch of delicate saffron or savoury-sweet cinnamon involved. Dessert is a temptation you won't want to resist, and includes flaky pastries rich with nuts and fragrant traces of orange-flower water. *B'saha* – here's to your health.

Eating reviews in this book are ordered by preference. Price ranges are based on the cost of an evening main course, excluding drinks and tips:
€ Up to Dh70
€€ Dh70 to Dh150; a set meal including wine would typically cost Dh250 to Dh400
€€€ More than Dh150; a set meal including wine would typically cost more than Dh400

Midrange and top-end restaurants are mostly found within the ville nouvelle of large cities, with a few notable exceptions in Fez and Marrakesh.

A service charge may automatically be added to your bill in better restaurants. A TVA tax (similar to value-added tax), usually around 10%, may also be charged, but generally this is built into the price of your meal.

Food

The food you find in Morocco is likely to be fresh, locally grown and homemade, rather than shipped in from Brazil, microwaved and served semi-thawed. Most Moroccan ingredients are cultivated in small quantities the old-fashioned way, without GMOs (genetically modified organisms), chemical fertilisers, pesticides or even mechanisation. These technologies are far too costly an investment for the average small-scale Moroccan farmer, as is organic certification and labelling – so though you may not see a label on it to this effect, much of the Moroccan produce you'll find in food markets is chemical- and GMO-free.

More than 186 reader-rated Moroccan recipes from foodie magazines *Gourmet* and *Bon Appétit* are online at www.epicurious.com, including quick and healthy options and suggested wine pairings.

For Moroccan recipes, a glossary of Arabic ingredients, and Moroccan cooking tips and anecdotes, surf Moroccan Gateway's foodie links at www.al-bab.com/maroc/food.htm.

During Ramadan, most Moroccans observe the fast during the day, eating only before sunup and after sundown. Dinner is eaten later than usual – around 11pm – and many wake up early for a filling breakfast before dawn. Another popular strategy is to stay up most of the night, sleep as late as possible, and stretch the afternoon nap into early evening. Adapt to the local schedule, and you may thoroughly enjoy the leisurely pace, late-night festivities and manic feasts of Ramadan.

Although you will not be expected to observe the fast, eating in public view is generally frowned upon. Hence many restaurants are closed during the day until *Iftour*, the evening meal when the fast is broken – though if you call ahead to restaurants in tourist areas, you may have luck. With a little planning, there are plenty of other workarounds: load up on snacks in the market to eat indoors, make arrangements for breakfast or lunch in the privacy of your guesthouse, and ask locals about a good place to enjoy *Iftour*.

Lftour comes with all the traditional Ramadan fixings: *harira* (a hearty soup), dates, milk, *shebbakia* (a sweet, coiled pastry that's guaranteed to shift your glucose levels into high gear), and *harsha* (buttery bread made of semolina and fried for maximum density). You may find that *harira* is offered free; even Moroccan McDonald's offers it as part of their special Ramadan Happy Meal.

Produce

The splendid appearance, fragrance and flavour of Moroccan market produce will leave you with a permanent grudge against those wan, shrivelled items trying to pass themselves off as food at the supermarket. There's a reason for this: Moroccan produce is usually harvested by hand when ripe, and bought directly from farmers in the souqs. Follow the crowds of Moroccan grandmothers and restaurant sous-chefs to the carts and stalls offering the freshest produce. Just be sure to peel, cook, or thoroughly wash produce before you eat it, since your stomach may not yet be accustomed to local microbes.

Meats

Carnivores and sustainability-minded eaters can finally put aside their differences and enjoy dinner together in Morocco. As you may guess, watching sheep and goats scamper over mountains and valleys in Morocco, herds live a charmed existence here – at least until dinnertime. Most of the meat you'll enjoy in Morocco is free-range, antibiotic-free, and raised on a steady diet of grass and wild herbs. If you wonder why lamb and mutton is so much more flavourful in Morocco than the stuff back home, you'll find your answer scampering around the High Atlas foothills.

Seasonal Variations

If there is one food you adore or a dish you detest, you might want to plan your visit to Morocco accordingly. Morocco offers an incredible bounty of produce, meats and fish, but these vary seasonally. The country's relative lack of infrastructure and hard currency can be advantageous to visitors – hence the picturesque mountain villages that seem untouched by time, and the jackpot of dirhams you get for your euros – but this also makes importing produce tricky. This means that if you're visiting in autumn, you may have to enjoy fresh figs instead of kiwi fruit (not exactly a hardship).

When you consider your menu options, you'll also want to consider geography. Oualidia oysters may not be so fresh by the time they cross

Hold the hot sauce: dousing your tajine with *harissa* (capsicum-pepper sauce) is generally done in Tunisia, Morocco's chief rival in the kitchen and on the football field.

Food Facts: Morocco's Farmers

» 47% of Morocco's population lives in rural areas

» 40% of the country is involved in food production, mostly small-scale

» 19% of Morocco's land is arable

mountain passes to Ouarzazate, and Sefrou cherries can be hard to come by in Tiznit. So if your vacation plans revolve around lavish seafood dinners, head for the coasts; vegetarians visiting desert regions in autumn should have a high tolerance for dates. For hints on where to find your favourite foods, see Local Treats (p439).

Quitting While You're Ahead

One final and important Moroccan dining tip: pace yourself. Moroccan meals can be lengthy and generous, and might seem a bit excessive to an unyielding waistband. Take your time and drink plenty of water throughout your meal, especially with wine and in dry climates, instead of pounding a drink at the end. There are better ways to end a meal than dehydration and bloating – namely, a dessert *bastilla* (multilayered pastry) with toasted almonds, cinnamon and cream. Your Moroccan hosts may urge you on like a cheerleading squad in a pie-eating contest, but obey your instincts and quit when you're full with a heartfelt '*alhamdulallah!*' (Thanks to God!).

Al-ftour (Breakfast)

Even if your days back home begin with just coffee, it would be a culinary crime to skip breakfast in Morocco. Whether you grab yours on the go in the souq or sit down to a leisurely repast, you are in for a treat. Breakfasts are rarely served before 9am in guesthouses and hotels, so early risers in immediate need of coffee will probably have to head to a cafe or hit the souqs.

Street Eats

Sidewalk cafes and kiosks put a local twist on Continental breakfast, with Moroccan pancakes and doughnuts, French pastries, coffee and mint tea. Follow your nose and rumbling stomach into the souqs, where you'll find tangy olives and local *jiben* (fresh goat's or cow's milk cheese) to be devoured with fresh *khoobz* (Moroccan-style pita bread baked in a wood-fire oven until it's crusty on the outside, yet fluffy and light on the inside). *Khoobz* can be found wrapped in paper at any *hanout* (cupboard-sized corner shops found in every neighbourhood).

> Foodies who equate Middle Eastern food with Lebanese cuisine stand corrected by Claudia Roden's *Arabesque: A Taste of Morocco, Turkey and Lebanon*, which showcases Moroccan cuisine and won the 2007 James Beard Award (the culinary Oscar).

BEEN THERE, EATEN THAT

Eat your way across Morocco, north to south, with these outstanding regional dishes:

» **Casablanca** *Seksu bedawi* (couscous with seven vegetables)

» **Chefchaouen** *Djaj bil berquq* (chicken with prunes)

» **Demnate** *Seksu Demnati* (couscous made with corn or barley instead of semolina)

» **Essaouira** *Hut Mqalli* (fish tajine with saffron, ginger and preserved lemons); *djej kadra toumiya* (chicken with almonds, onions and chickpeas in buttery saffron sauce)

» **Fez** *Kennaria* (stew with wild thistle or artichoke, with or without meat); *hut bu'etob* (baked shad filled with almond-stuffed dates)

» **High Atlas** *Mechoui* (slow-roasted stuffed lamb or beef)

» **Marrakesh** *Bessara* (fava beans with cumin, paprika, olive oil and salt); *tanjia* (crock-pot stew of seasoned lamb cooked for eight to 12 hours in a hammam)

» **Meknès** *Kamama* (lamb stewed with ginger, *smen,* saffron, cinnamon and sweet onions)

» **Southern Coast** *Amelou* (argan-nut paste with honey and argan oil)

» **Tangier** Local variations on tapas and paella

Agadir Oranges, lemons, argan oil
Casablanca Cactus fruit
Doukkala Melons
Erfoud Dates
Essaouira Fish, argan oil
Fez Wild artichokes, olive oil, oranges, orange-flower water, lemons
Kelaâ M'Gouna Edible rosebuds, rosewater
Marrakesh Pomegranates
Meknès Mint, olives, olive oil
Oualidia Oysters, lobster
Rif Walnuts, chestnuts, citrus, goat's cheese
Safi Shellfish
Sebou Shad, shad-roe caviar
Sefrou Cherries
Souss Almonds, lamb, dates

In the souqs, you can't miss vendors with their carts piled high with fresh fruit, singing their own praises. They're right: you'll never know how high oranges can be stacked or how delicious freshly squeezed *aseer limoon* (orange juice) can be until you pay a visit to a Moroccan juice-vendor's cart. Drink yours from a disposable cup or your own water bottle, because the vendor's glasses are rinsed and reused dozens of times daily.

One savoury southern breakfast just right for chilly mornings is *bessara* (a steaming-hot fava-bean puree with cumin, olive oil, and a dash of paprika), best when mopped up with *khoobz* still warm from the communal oven right down the street. For a twist on the usual French breakfast pastries, try *rghaif* (flaky, dense Moroccan pastries like flattened croissants), typically served with warm honey, apricot jam, or if you're lucky, nutty *tahalout* (date syrup). The truly adventurous can start their day with a rich stew of lamb's head or calves' feet, generously ladled into an enamel bowl from a huge vat precariously balanced on a makeshift Buddha gas burner.

Breakfast of Champions

As a guest in a Moroccan home, you'd be treated to the best of everything, and the best guesthouses scrupulously uphold this Moroccan tradition each morning. You'll carb-load like a Moroccan marathoner, with some combination of the following to jumpstart your day:

Ahwa (Coffee) *Ahwa* is one option, but also *café au lait*, *thé b'na na* (tea with mint) or *thé wa hleb* (tea with milk), *wa* (with) or *bla* (without) *sukur* (sugar).

Aseer limoon (Orange juice)

Bayd (Eggs) Cooked in omelettes, with a dash of *karnun* (freshly ground cumin) or *zataar* (cumin with toasted sesame seeds).

Beghrir Moroccan pancakes with an airy, spongy texture like crumpets, with honey or jam.

French pastries Croissants, *pain au chocolat* and others.

Khoobz Usually served with butter and jam or olive oil and *zataar*.

Rghaif Flat, buttery Moroccan pastries.

Sfenj Moroccan doughnuts.

El-Ghda (Lunch)

Lunch is traditionally the biggest meal of the day in Morocco, followed by a nice nap through the heat of the day. The lunch hour here is really a three- to four-hour stretch from noon to 3pm or 4pm, when most shops and facilities are closed, apart from a few stores catering to tourists.

What's in Season in Morocco?

» **Autumn** Figs, pomegranates, grapes.

» **Spring** Apricots, cherries, strawberries, peaches.

» **Summer** Watermelon, wild artichokes, tomatoes.

» **Winter** Oranges, mandarins, onions, beets, carrots, potatoes and other root vegetables.

» **Year-round** Almonds, walnuts, bananas, squash, pumpkin, fava beans, green beans, lentils, eggplant, peppers, lemons (fresh and preserved).

For speed eaters this may seem inconvenient, but especially in summer it's best to do as the locals do, and treat lunchtime as precious downtime. Tuck into a tajine, served à la carte with crusty bread, or upgrade to a *prix fixe,* three-course restaurant lunch. Afterwards, you'll have a whole new appreciation for mint tea and afternoon naps.

Snak Attack

If you're still digesting your lavish guesthouse breakfast come lunchtime, try one of the many *snak*s (kiosks) and small restaurants offering lighter fare – just look for people clustered around sidewalk kiosks, or a sign or awning with the word *snak*. Many hard-working locals do not take afternoon siestas, and instead eat sandwiches on the go. At the risk of stating the obvious, always join the queue at the one thronged with locals: Moroccans are picky about their *snak*s, preferring the cleanest establishments that use the freshest ingredients.

Here's what you'll find on offer at a *snak:*

Brochettes Kebabs rubbed with salt and spices, grilled on a skewer and served with *khoobz* and *harissa* (capsicum-pepper sauce), cumin and salt. Among the most popular varieties are lamb, chicken, *kefta* (spiced meatballs of ground lamb and/or beef), and the aggressively flavourful 'mixed meat' (usually lamb or beef plus heart, kidney and liver).

Merguez Hot, spicy, delicious homemade lamb sausage, not to be confused with *teyhan* (stuffed spleen; like liver, only less bitter and more tender) – *merguez* is usually reddish in colour, while *teyhan* is pale.

Pizza Now found at upscale *snak*s catering to the worldly Moroccan middle class. Look for *snak*s boasting wood-fired ovens, and try tasty local versions with olives, onions, tomatoes, Atlantic anchovies and wild thyme.

Shwarma Spiced lamb or chicken roasted on a spit and served with *tahina* (sesame sauce) or yoghurt, with optional onions, salad, *harissa* and a dash of *sumac* (a tart, pickle-flavoured purple spice; highly recommended).

Cooking at guesthouses is usually done by *dadas,* who are champions of Morocco's culinary traditions, cooking feasts with whatever's freshest in the market, usually without a recipe or a measuring cup. If a *dada*'s delights impress you, ask to thank her personally – it's good form, and good *baraka* (auspicious omen) besides.

TOP TIPS FOR ENJOYING STREET FOOD & STAYING HEALTHY

» **Make a beeline for busy stalls** Moroccans are sticklers for freshness, and know which places consistently deliver. *Snak* stalls have better turnover of fresh ingredients than most fancy restaurants, where you can't typically check the meat and cooking oil before you sit down to dinner.

» **Check out the cooking oil** Is it extremely smoky, pungent or murky? Hold out for fresher, cleaner cooking oil.

» **Always look over the ingredients** Check the food on display, especially if you'll be ordering meat or seafood. This is no time to get squeamish. Are the fish eyes still bright, the hearts bloody, and the snails alive? That's a good sign for adventurous foodies who want to try fried fish, skewered, grilled lamb hearts, and steaming snail soups.

» **Clean your hands right before eating** Much of what we call 'food poisoning' is actually illness caused by bacteria transferred from hand to mouth while eating.

» **Use your bread to scoop up food** This is how Moroccans eat, and it makes sense. If you're using utensils briefly rinsed in cold water, hygiene-wise, you're sharing a rather intimate moment with the stranger who used them before you.

» **Stick to your own purified or bottled water** It takes time adjusting to local water, so it's better to drink purified or bottled stuff – and never drink out of rinsed-and-reused stall glasses.

» **Wait until your second-to-last night** If your stomach is skittish, hold out for that street food adventure. If dinner goes down a treat – as it should – you'll be back tomorrow.

Berbers call it *seksu*, *New York Times* food critic Craig Claiborne called it one of the dozen best dishes in the world, and when you're in Morocco, you can call couscous lunch. You know that yellowish stuff that comes in a box, with directions on the side instructing you to add boiling water and let stand for three minutes? That doesn't count. What Moroccans call couscous is a fine, pale, grain-sized, hand-rolled pasta lightly steamed with aromatic broth until toothsome and fluffy, served with a selection of vegetables and/or meat or fish in a delicately flavoured reduction of stock and spices.

Since preparing and digesting a proper couscous takes awhile, Moroccans usually enjoy it on Fridays, when many have the day or the afternoon off after Friday prayers. Couscous isn't a simple side dish but rather the main event of a Moroccan Friday lunch, whether tricked out Casablanca-style with seven vegetables, heaped with lamb and vegetables in Fez, or served with tomatoes, fish and fresh herbs in Essaouira. Many delicious couscous dishes come without meat, including the pumpkin couscous of Marrakesh and a simple yet savoury High Atlas version with stewed onions, but scrupulous vegetarians will want to enquire in advance whether that hearty stock is indeed vegetarian. Sometimes a couscous dish can be ordered à la carte, but usually it's a centrepiece of a multicourse lunch or celebratory *diffa* – and when you get a mouthful of the stuff done properly, you'll see why.

MOROCCAN CUISINE FOOD

Tajines The famous Moroccan stews cooked in conical earthenware pots that keep the meat unusually moist and tender. The basic tajines served at a roadside *snak* are usually made with just a few ingredients, pulled right off a camping stove or *kanun* (earthenware brazier), and plonked down on a ramshackle folding table. Often you can pick your tajine; point to one that's been bubbling for an hour or two, with nicely caramelised onions and well-reduced sauce. Don't let appearances fool you: this could be one of the best tajines you'll eat in Morocco. Pull up a stool and dig in, using your *khoobz* as your utensil instead of rinsed-and-reused flatware.

The Moroccan Power Lunch

Some upscale Moroccan restaurants that serve an evening *diffa* (feast) to tourist hordes serve a scaled-down menu at lunch, when waitstaff are more relaxed and the meal is sometimes a fraction of the price you'd pay for dinner. You might miss the live music and inevitable belly dancing that would accompany a fancy supper – but then again, you might not. Three courses may seem a bit much for lunch, but don't be daunted: what this usually means is a delightful array of diminutive vegetable dishes, followed by a fluffy couscous and/or a small meat or chicken tajine, capped with the obligatory mint tea and biscuits or fruit.

Mezze (Salad course) This could be a meal in itself. Fresh bread and three to five small, usually cooked vegetable dishes that might include lemony beet salad with chives, herbed potatoes, cumin-spiked chickpeas, a relish of roasted tomatoes and caramelised onions, pumpkin puree with cinnamon and honey, and roasted, spiced eggplant dip so rich it's often called 'aubergine caviar'.

Main The main course is usually a tajine and/or couscous – a quasi-religious experience in Morocco not to be missed, especially on Fridays. The most common tajine choices are *dujaj mqalli bil hamd markd wa zeetoun* (chicken with preserved lemon and olives, zesty in flavour and velvety in texture); *kefta bil matisha wa bayd* (meatballs in a rich tomato sauce with a hint of heat from spices and topped with a sizzling egg); and *lehem bil berquq wa luz* (lamb with prunes and almonds served sliding off the bone into a saffron-onion sauce). If you're in Morocco for a while, you may tire of these classic tajine options – until you come across one regional variation that makes all your sampling of chicken tajine with lemon and olives

Moroccan Snacks

» fresh or dried fruit

» roasted almonds, chickpeas, and pumpkin and sunflower seeds

» hard-boiled eggs with fresh cumin

» roasted corn fresh off the brazier

» sandwiches of brochettes or *merguez* with cumin, salt and harissa

» escargot (snails) in hot, savoury broth

» ice cream

» patisseries (Moroccan or French)

» Breakfast Load up on Moroccan pastries, pancakes, fresh fruit and fresh-squeezed juice. Fresh goat's cheese and olives from the souq are solid savoury choices with fresh-baked *khoobz* (bread). *Bessara* is a delicious bean soup that's typically meat-free, but steer clear of bubbling roadside vats if you're squeamish – they may contain snails or sheep's-head soup.

» Lunch Try the *mezze* of salads, which come with fresh bread and may range from delicate cucumbers in orange-blossom water to substantial herbed beets laced with kaffir lime. Vegetarians can sometimes, but not always, order a Berber vegetable tajine or Casablanca-style couscous with seven vegetables. Ingredients are bought fresh daily in small quantities and the chef may not have factored vegetarians into the restaurant's purchases – so call ahead if you can. Pizza is another widely available and inexpensive menu option, best when spiked with local herbs and olives.

» Snacks Market stalls feature cascades of dried figs, dates and apricots alongside towering cones of roasted nuts with salt, honey, cinnamon, cane sugar or hot pepper. Chickpeas and other pulses are roasted, served hot in a paper cone with cumin and salt, and not to be missed. Tea-time menus at swanky restaurants may feature *brouiats,* cigar-shaped pastries stuffed with goat's cheese or egg and herbs, plus finger sandwiches, pastries and cakes. If that's not enough, there's always ice cream, and mint tea with cookies or nuts are hardly ever more than a carpet shop away.

» Dinner For a hearty change of pace from salads and couscous, try a vegetarian pasta (anything with eggplant is especially tasty) or omelette (usually served with thick-cut fries). If you're staying in a Moroccan guesthouse, before you leave in the morning you can usually request a vegetarian tajine made to order with market-fresh produce. Pity you can't do that at home, right?

---

worthwhile. That's when you cross over from casual diner to true tajine connoisseur, and fully appreciate the passionate debates among Moroccans about such minutiae as the appropriate thickness of the lemon rind and brininess of the olives. Variations on the classics are expected, but no self-respecting Moroccan restaurant should ever serve you a tajine that's stringy, tasteless, watery or overcooked.

Dessert At lunchtime, dessert is usually sweet mint tea served with almond cookies. You may not think you have room, but one bite of a dreamy *kaab al-ghazal* (crescent-shaped 'gazelle's horns' cookie stuffed with almond paste and laced with orange-flower water) will surely convince you otherwise. A light, refreshing option is the tart-sweet *orange á canelle* (orange slices with cinnamon and orange-flower water).

Moroccan Sauces

» Mhammar Paprika, cumin and butter

» Mqalli Saffron, oil and ginger

» Msharmal Saffron, ginger and a dash of pepper

» Qadra *Smen* (seasoned butter) with vegetable stock, chickpeas and/or almonds.

L'Asha (Dinner)

Dinner in Morocco doesn't usually start until around 8pm or 9pm, after work and possibly a sunset stroll. Most Moroccans eat dinner at home, but you may notice young professionals, students and bachelors making a beeline for the local *snak* or pizzeria. In the winter, you'll see vendors crack open steaming vats of *harira* (a hearty soup with a base of tomatoes, onions, saffron and cilantro, often with lentils, chickpeas and/or lamb). Dinner at home may often be *harira* and lunch leftovers, with the notable exception of Ramadan and other celebrations.

Diffa

With enough hard currency and room in your stomach, you might prefer restaurants to *snak* fare for dinner. Most upscale Moroccan restaurants cater to tourists, serving an elaborate *prix fixe* Moroccan *diffa* (feast) in a palatial setting. This is not a dine-and-dash meal, but an evening's entertainment that often includes live music or belly dancing and wine or beer.

Fair warning about palace restaurants: your meal may come with a side order of kitsch. Many palace restaurants appear to have been decorated by a genie, complete with winking brass lamps, mirrors, swagged tent fabric and tasselled cushions as far as the eye can see. Often it's the ambience you're paying for rather than the food, which can vary from exquisitely prepared regional specialities to mass-produced glop. Here's a rule of thumb: if the place is so cavernous that your voice echoes and there's a stage set up for a laser show, don't expect personalised service or authentic Moroccan fare.

Whether you're in for a *diffa* at a Moroccan home (lucky you) or a restaurant, your lavish dinner will include some combination of the following:

Mezze Up to five different small salads (though the most extravagant palace restaurants in Marrakesh and Fez boast seven to nine).

Briouat or brik Buttery cigar-shaped or triangular pastry stuffed with herbs and goat's cheese, savoury meats, or egg, then fried or baked.

Pastilla The justly famed savoury-sweet pie made of *warqa* (sheets of pastry even thinner than filo), painstakingly layered with pigeon or chicken cooked with caramelised onions, lemon, eggs and toasted sugared almonds, then dusted with cinnamon and powdered sugar.

Couscous Made according to local custom; couscous variations may be made of barley, wheat or corn.

Tajine Often your choice of one of a couple of varieties.

Mechoui Or some regional speciality.

Dessert This may be *orange á canelle,* a dessert *bastilla* (with fresh cream and toasted nuts), *briouat bil luz* (*briouat* filled with almond paste), *sfaa* (sweet cinnamon couscous with dried fruit and nuts, served with cream) or *kaab al-ghazal.*

Drinks

To wash your *diffa* down and stay hydrated, you'll need a good amount of liquid. Day and night, don't forget to drink plenty of bottled or purified water. Vying to quench your thirst are orange-juice vendors loudly singing their own praises, and water vendors in fringed tajine-shaped hats clanging brass bowls together. If you want to take up these appealing offers, ask the vendors to pour right into your water bottle or a disposable cup – the glass cups and brass bowls are often reused, and seldom thoroughly washed. Moroccan mint tea may be ubiquitous after meals, but you can find a mean cup of coffee in Morocco, too. Most of it is French-pressed, and delivers a caffeine wallop to propel you through the souqs and into the stratosphere.

Moroccan Beer, Wine & Spirits

Yes, you can drink alcohol in Morocco without offending local sensibilities, as long as you do it discreetly. Serving alcohol within many Moroccan medinas or within view of a mosque may be frowned upon, and liquor licences can cost an astronomical Dh20,000 – but many Moroccan

Top chefs consult Paula Wolfert's *Couscous and Other Good Food from Morocco,* which includes 20 tantalising recipes for the titular dish and won the 2008 James Beard Cookbook Hall of Fame Award.

Regional Moroccan Flavours with International Origins

» **Essaouira** Portuguese and Jewish

» **Fez** Andalucía (Spain) and Persia

» **Marrakesh** Senegal, France, Berber North Africa and Italy

» **Tetouan** Andalucía and Turkey

TASTY BEAST: MECHOUI

Special occasions call for Morocco's very best beast dish: *mechoui,* an entire slow-roasted lamb. The whole beast is basted with butter, garlic, cumin and paprika, and slow-roasted in a special covered pit until it's ready to melt into the fire or your mouth, whichever comes first. Local variations may include substituting a calf instead, or stuffing the lamb with some combination of almonds (or other nuts), prunes (or other dried fruit) or couscous. Sometimes *mechoui* is accompanied by kebabs or *kwa* (grilled liver kebabs with cumin, salt and paprika). Other than Moroccan weddings, the best place to have *mechoui* is right off Marrakesh's Djemaa el-Fna around lunchtime, served with olives and bread in Mechoui Alley (p80). Do not attempt to operate heavy machinery or begin a whirlwind museum tour post-*mechoui;* no amount of post-prandial mint tea will make such exertions feasible without a nap.

MINT TEA ETIQUETTE

When you're offered Moroccan mint tea, don't expect to bolt it and be on your way. Mint tea is the hallmark of Moroccan hospitality, and a sit-down affair that takes around half an hour. If you have the honour of pouring the tea, pour the first cup back in the teapot to help cool it and dissolve the sugar. Then starting from your right, pour each cup of tea from as high above the glass as you can without splashing. Your hosts will be most impressed.

guesthouses and restaurants get around these hurdles by offering booze in a low voice, and serving it out of sight indoors or on a terrace. So if you're in the mood for a beer and don't find it on the menu, you might want to ask the waiter in a low voice, speakeasy-style.

One note of caution: quality assurance is tricky in a Muslim country where mixologists, micro-brewers, and licensed sommeliers are in understandably short supply, and your server may not be able to make any personal recommendations from the wine menu. Since wines are subject to unpredictable heat exposure in transit and storage, be sure to taste your wine before the server leaves the table – red wines especially are subject to spoilage. Don't hesitate to send back a drink if something about it seems off; your server will likely take your word for it.

Before dinner, your host may appear with a pitcher and a deep tray. Hold out your hands, and your host will pour rosewater over them.

Beer

Casa A fine local pilsner beer

Flag A faintly herbal second-best

Flag Special Affordable and the most popular beverage in Morocco (25 million units consumed annually)

Wine

White Moroccan white wines are a solid bet, including the crisp, food-friendly Larroque; well-balanced, juicy Terre Blanche, a Chardonnay/Viognier/Sauvignon Blanc blend; citrusy, off-dry Cuveé de Président Sémillant; and Siroua S, a cool coastal Chardonnay.

Gris and Rosé These are refreshing alternatives, especially not-too-fruity Medaillon Rosé of Syrah; peachy-keen Eclipse Grenache/Cinsault blend; fresh, fragrant Domaine Rimal Vin Gris; and juicy, aptly named Rosé d'un Nuit d'Eté (Summer's Night Rosé) of Grenache/Syrah.

Red Reliable reds include the admirable Burgundian-style Terre Rouge from Rabati coastal vineyards; well-rounded Volubilia from Morocco's ancient Roman wine-growing region; and spicier Merlot-Syrah-Cabernet Sauvignon Coteaux Atlas

Vitamin-rich Moroccan argan oil is popular as a cosmetic, but also as a gourmet treat: the toasted-hazelnut flavour makes an intriguing dipping oil and exotic salad dressing.

Spirits

Moroccan tap water is often potable, though not always – so stick with treated water or local mineral water. Best bets are Sidi Ali and sparkling Oulmes; others have a chalky aftertaste.

Creative cocktails Mojitos, caipirinhas, and negronis are three imported cocktails that become local nightclub favourites when made with (respectively) Moroccan mint, local kaffir lime, and orange-blossom water. These Moroccan twists can make even low-end alcohol seem top-shelf...at least until tomorrow morning.

Local eau de vie Mahia is a Moroccan spirit distilled from figs that's around 80% proof, with a flavour somewhere between Italian grappa and Kentucky moonshine. You won't find it on most menus, because it's usually made in home distilleries for private consumption. If you're staying at a guesthouse, your hosts may know where you can get some, but they may try to warn you off the stuff – *mahia* hangovers are legendary.

Music

Any trip to Morocco comes with its own syncopated soundtrack: women tapping out a beat with tea glasses on brass trays, hawkers singing the praises of knock-off Armani right over the early evening *adhan* (call to prayer), and the ubiquitous donkey-cart-drivers' chants of *Balek!* – fair warning that since donkeys don't yield, you'd better, and quick. Adding to the musical mayhem are beats booming out of taxis, ham radios and roadside stalls, and live music performances at restaurants and weddings, on street-corners, and headlining at festivals year-round. For a memory bank of Maghrebi music any DJ would envy, sample these varieties.

Classical Arab-Andalusian Music

Leaving aside the thorny question of where exactly it originated (you don't want be the cause of the next centuries-long Spain–Morocco conflict, do you?) this music combines the flamenco-style strumming and heartstring-plucking drama of Spanish folk music with the finely calibrated stringed instruments, complex percussion and haunting halftones of classical Arab music. Add poetic lyrics and the right singer at dinner performances, and you may find that lump in your throat makes it hard to swallow your *bastilla* (pigeon pie).

You'll hear two major styles of Arab-Andalusian music in Morocco: Al-Aala (primarily in Fez, Tetouan and Salé) and Gharnati (mostly Oujda). The area of musical overlap is Rabat, where you can hear both styles. Keep an eye out for concerts, musical evenings at fine restaurants, and classical-music festivals in Casablanca and Fez, and look especially for performances by Gharnati vocalist Amina Alaoui, Fatiha El Hadri Badraï and her traditional all-female orchestras from Tetouan, and Fez Sacred Music Festival headliner Mohamed Amin el-Akrami and his orchestra.

> No, that's not a musical rugby scrum: the *haidous* is a complex circle dance with musicians in the middle, often performed in celebration of the harvest.

NOW HEAR THIS: MOROCCAN MUSIC FESTIVALS

Dates and locations may vary, so check www.maghrebarts.ma/musique.html for updates

March Rencontres Musicales de Marrakesh (Classical), Tremplin (Urban music)

April Festival of Sufi Culture (Fez; www.par-chemins.org), Jazzablanca (Casablanca)

May Jazz aux Oudayas (Rabat), L'Boulevard (www.boulevard.ma), Mawazine Festival of World Music (Rabat; www.festivalmawazine.ma)

June Festival of World Sacred Music (Fez; www.fesfestival.com), Gnaoua and World Music Festival (Essaouira; www.festival-gnaoua.net), Jazz au Chellah (Rabat)

July Marrakesh Popular Arts Festival (www.marrakechfestival.com), Voix des Femmes (Women's Voices; Tetouan), Festival Timitar (Amazigh Music; Agadir); Festival du Desert (www.festivaldudesert.ma)

September Marriage Festival (Imilchil), TANJAzz (Tangier; www.tanjazz.org)

October Atlantic Andalusian Music Fest (Essaouira), Jazz in Riad Festival (Fez)

FOR THOSE ABOUT TO MO'ROCK, WE SALUTE YOU

Not since Ozzy bit a live bat onstage has hard rock caused such an uproar. In 2003, police who didn't appreciate being rocked like a hurricane arrested 11 Moroccan metalheads for making their audiences 'listen, with bad intent, to songs which contravene good morals or incite debauchery'. Despite widespread protests that authorities were driving the crazy train, the rockers were ultimately sentenced to one year in jail for 'employing seductive methods with the aim of undermining the faith of a Muslim'.

But diehard Moroccan metalheads got organised, calling all rockers to the mosh-pit in Sidi Kacem, an inland agricultural centre near Meknès better known for braying donkeys than wailing guitars. The second SidiRock festival was held in February 2008, showcasing bands from the area with names sure to warm any true metalhead's heart, if not a mullah's, including Despotism from Casablanca and Sidi Kacem's own Damned Kreation (now Putrid Cadavers). Far from pleather-clad '80s hair bands, these Moroccan groups write their own rebellious lyrics, and rock hardcore in black jeans and torn T-shirts.

The metal scene has since outgrown its Sidi Kacem venue, storming the stage at L'Boulevard (www.boulevard.ma), Casablanca's May free festival of urban music held at the Casa stadium, and at L'Boulevard's March showcase for emerging artists, Tremplin (Trampoline), held at the coolest-ever rock venue: Casa's *anciens abbatoirs* (old slaughterhouses). Past editions of the festivals have focused on hip-hop and electronica, but there's a jittery excitement when the metal bands take the stage, and the police reinforcements brought in to monitor the mosh-pits look distinctly nervous.

With the 2010 editions of L'Boulevard and Tremplin featuring metal headliners and attracting 30,000 spectators over four days, the mainstreaming of Mo'rock raises another question: once metal goes legit, what's a Moroccan rebel to do? The answer seems obvious: go emo'rocco.

Gnawa

Joyously bluesy with a rhythm you can't refuse, this music may send you into a trance – and that's just what it's meant to do. The brotherhood of Gnawa began among freed slaves in Marrakesh and Essaouira as a ritual of deliverance from slavery and into God's graces. A true Gnawa *lila*, or spiritual jam session, may last all night, with musicians erupting into leaps of joy as they enter trance-like states of ecstasy that can send fez-tassels spinning and set spirits free.

To explore Amazigh music in a variety of styles, languages, and regions, check out samples, musician bios and CDs from basic bluesy Tartit to '70s-funky Tinariwen at www.azawan.com.

Join the crowds watching in Marrakesh's Djemaa el-Fna or at the annual Gnaoua and World Music Festival in Essaouira, and hear Gnawa on Peter Gabriel's Real World music label. Gnawa *mâalems* (master musicians) include perennial festival favourites Abdeslam Alikkane and his Tyour Gnaoua, crossover fusion superstar Hassan Hakmoun, rising star *mâalem* Saïd Boulhimas and his deeply funky Band of Gnawas, Indian-inflected Nass Marrakech and reggae-inspired Omar Hayat. Since Gnawa are historically a brotherhood, most renowned Gnawa musicians have been men – but the all-women Sufi group Haddarates plays Gnawa trances traditionally reserved for women, and family acts include Brahim Elbelkani and La Famille Backbou.

Berber Folk Music

There's plenty of other indigenous Moroccan music besides Gnawa, thanks to the ancient Berber tradition of passing along songs and poetry from one generation to the next. You can't miss Berber music at village *moussems* (festivals in honour of a local saint), Agadir's Timtar Festival of Amazigh music, the Marrakesh Popular Arts Festival and Imilchil's Marriage Festival, as well as weddings and other family celebrations.

The most renowned Berber folk group is the Master Musicians of Joujouka, who famously inspired the Rolling Stones, Led Zeppelin and

William S Burroughs, and collaborated with them on experimental fusion with lots of clanging and crashing involved. Lately the big names are women's, including the all-woman group B'net Marrakech and the bold Najat Aatabou, who sings protest songs in Berber against restrictive traditional roles. For more women vocalists, head to Tetouan for the Voix des Femmes (Women's Voices) festival.

From Marock to Hibhub

Like the rest of the Arab world, Moroccans listen to a lot of Egyptian music, but Moroccopop is gaining ground. A generation of local DJs with cheeky names like Ramadan Special and DJ Al Intifada have mastered the art of the unlikely mashup. And so have some of the more intriguing talents to emerge in recent years: Hobba Hobba Spirit, whose controversy-causing, pop-punk *Blad Skizo* (Schizophrenic Country) addresses the contradictions of modern Morocco head-on; Moroccan singer-songwriter Hindi Zahra, Morocco's answer to Tori Amos, with bluesy acoustic-guitar backing; Darga, a group that blends ska, Darija rap, and a horn section into Moroccan surf anthems; and the bluntly named Ganga Fusion and Kif Samba, who both pound out a danceable mix of funk, Berber folk music, reggae and jazz. For something completely different, check out the burgeoning Megadeth-inspired Moroccan metal scene at Casa's annual L'Boulevard festival (see p446).

But ask any guy on the street with baggy cargo shorts and a T-shirt with the slogan MJM (*Maroc Jusqu'al Mort*, Morocco 'til Death) about Moroccan pop, and you'll get a crash course in *hibhub* (Darija for hip hop). Meknès' H-Kayne rap gangsta-style, while Tangier's MC Muslim raps with a death-metal growl, and Fez City Clan features a talented but annoying kid rapper and an Arabic string section. The acts that consistently get festival crowds bouncing are Agadir's DJ Key, who remixes hip-hop standards with manic scratching and beat-boxing, and Marrakesh's Fnaire, mixing traditional Moroccan sounds with staccato vocal stylings. Rivalling *Blad Skizo* for youth anthem of the decade is Fnaire's *Ma Ktich Bladi* (Don't Touch My Country), an irresistibly catchy anthem against neocolonialism with a viral YouTube video.

Check out Morocco's latest top 10 hits and hear Darija DJ stylings on RealPlayer audio at Radio Casablanca online: www.maroc.net/newrc.

MUSIC

Marockumentaries

» *This Is Maroc* (2010) Hat Trick Brothers' road trip.

» *I Love HipHop in Morocco* (www.ilovehiphopinmorocco.com) H-Kayne, DJ Key, Bigg and other hip-hop groups struggle to get gigs.

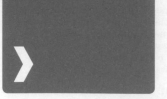

Literature & Cinema

Morocco has an ancient literary tradition that has only recently been recognised. Poetry and stories have traditionally been passed along by storytellers and singers, and in manuscripts circulated from one person to the next. Since the majority of the population couldn't read or afford books, Morocco's oral tradition has helped keep shared legends and histories alive. Watch the storytellers, singers and scribes in Marrakesh's Djemaa el-Fna in action and you'll understand how Morocco's literary tradition has remained so vital and irrepressible, despite ongoing press censorship.

Literature
A Different Beat

The international spotlight first turned on Morocco's literary scene in the 1950s and '60s, when Beat Generation authors Paul and Jane Bowles took up residence in Tangier and began recording the stories of Moroccans they knew. From these efforts came Larb Layachi's *A Life Full of Holes* (written under the pseudonym Driss ben Hamed Charhadi), Mohammed Mrabet's *Love with a Few Hairs,* and Mohammed Choukri's *For Bread Alone.* Like a lot of Beat literature, these books are packed with sex, drugs and unexpected poetry – but if anything, they're more streetwise, humorous and heartbreaking.

Coming up for Air

Encouraged by the outspoken 'Tangerine' authors, Moroccan poet Abdellatif Laâbi founded the free-form, free-thinking poetry magazine *Anfas/Souffles* (Breath) in 1966, not in the anything-goes international zone of Tangier, but in the royal capitol of Rabat. What began as a journal became a movement of writers, painters and filmmakers heeding Laâbi's outcry against censorship: 'A la poubelle poème/A la poubelle rythme/A la poubelle silence' ('In the trash, poetry/In the trash, rhythm/In the trash, silence'). *Anfas/Souffles* published 21 more daring issues, until the censors shut it down in 1972 and sent Laâbi to prison for eight years for 'crimes of opinion'. Government censorship notwithstanding, the complete French text of *Anfas/Souffles* is now available online at http://clic net.swarthmore.edu/souffles/sommaire.html.

The literary expression Laâbi equated to breathing has continued unabated. In 1975, *Anfas/Souffles* cofounder and self-proclaimed 'linguistic guerrilla' Mohammed Khaïr-Eddine published his confrontational *Ce Maroc!,* an anthology of revolutionary writings. A Souss Berber himself, Khaïr-Eddine called for the recognition of Berber identity and culture in

In *Moroccan Folk Tales*, Jilali El Koudia presents 31 classic legends ranging from a Berber version of Snow White to a tale of a woman who cross-dresses as a Muslim scholar.

his 1984 *Legend and Life of Agoun'chich,* which served as a rallying cry for today's Berber Pride movement (see p421).

Living to Tell

Still more daring and distinctive Moroccan voices have found their way into print over the past two decades, both at home and abroad. Among the most famous works to be published by a Moroccan author are *Dreams of Trespass: Tales of a Harem Girlhood* and *The Veil and the Male Elite: A Feminist Interpretation of Islam,* both by Fatima Mernissi, an outspoken feminist and professor at the University of Rabat. In Rabati author Leila Abouzeid's *The Year of the Elephant* and *The Director and Other Stories from Morocco,* tales of Moroccan women trying to reinvent life on their own terms become parables for Morocco's search for independence after colonialism.

The past few years have brought increased acclaim for Moroccan writers, who have continued to address highly charged topics despite repeated press crackdowns. Inspired by *Anfas/Souffles,* Fez-born expatriate author Tahar ben Jelloun combined poetic devices and his training as a psychotherapist in his celebrated novel *The Sand Child,* the story of a girl raised as a boy by her father in Marrakesh, and its sequel *The Sacred Night,* which won France's Prix Goncourt. In *The Polymath,* 2009 Naguib Mahfouz Prize–winner Bensalem Himmich reads between the lines of 14th-century scholar and political exile Ibn Khuldun, as he tries to stop wars and prevent his own isolation. Several recent Moroccan novels have explored the promise and trauma of emigration, notably Mahi Binebine's harrowing *Welcome to Paradise,* Tahar ben Jelloun's *Leaving Tangier,* and Laila Lalami's celebrated *Hope and Other Dangerous Pursuits.*

Cinema

On Location in Morocco

Until recently Morocco has been seen mostly as a stunning movie backdrop, easily stealing scenes in such dubious cinematic achievements as *Sex and the City II, Prince of Persia, Alexander, Ishtar, Troy* and *Sahara.* But while there's much to cringe about in Morocco's IMDB filmography, the country had golden moments on the silver screen in Hitchcock's *The Man Who Knew Too Much,* Orson Welles' *Othello* and David Lean's *Lawrence of Arabia.*

Morocco has certainly proved its versatility: it stunt-doubled for Somalia in Ridley Scott's *Black Hawk Down,* Tibet in Martin Scorsese's *Kundun,* and Lebanon in Stephen Gaghan's *Syriana,* and *Inception*'s Kenyan dreamscape was actually Tangier. Morocco also stole the show right out from under John Malkovich by playing itself in Bernardo Bertolucci's *The Sheltering Sky,* and untrained local actors Mohamed Akhzam and Boubker Ait El Caid held their own with Cate Blanchett and Brad Pitt in the 2006 Oscar-nominated *Babel.*

Morocco's Directorial Breakthrough

Historically, Morocco has imported its blockbusters from Bollywood, Hollywood and Egypt – but today, Moroccans are getting greater opportunity to see films shot in Morocco that are actually by Moroccans and about Morocco. The home-grown film industry produced 18 feature films and 80 shorts in 2010, compared with four features and six shorts in 2004.

Moroccan filmmakers are putting decades of Ouallywood filmmaking craft and centuries of local storytelling tradition to work telling epic modern tales, often with a *cinéma-vérité* edge. Morocco's 2010 Best Foreign Film Oscar contender was Nour-Eddine Lakhmari's *Casanegra,* about

---

LITERATURE & CINEMA

Author Tahir Shah moved his family from London to Casablanca to become a Moroccan storyteller groupie, collecting tales for his *In Arabian Nights: In Search of Morocco Through its Stories and Storytellers* – for more from Tahir Shah see p177.

In *Stolen Lives: Twenty Years in a Desert Jail,* Malika Oufkir describes her demotion from courtier to prisoner after her father's plot to assassinate Hassan II. After its success as an Oprah Book Club selection, the movie version is forthcoming.

None of the 1942 classic *Casablanca* was actually shot in Casablanca. It was filmed on a Hollywood back lot, and the Rick's Café Américain set was based on the historic El-Minzah hotel in Tangier.

Despite Morocco's creative boom, cinephiles have begun to fear for Morocco's movie palaces, since ticket prices can't compete with cheap pirated DVDs. In 2007, only 5% of Morocco's population went to the movies, while more than 400,000 pirated DVDs were symbolically seized from souq stalls in Rabat and Casablanca. Thirty years ago, there were 250 cinemas in Morocco; in 2010, only 30 were left.

Moroccan cinema buffs are rallying with Save Cinemas in Morocco (savecinemasin morocco.com), an initiative that is preserving and promoting Morocco's historic movie palaces as architectural wonders and key modern landmarks in Morocco's ancient storytelling tradition. Tangier's 1930s Cinema Rif reopened in 2006 as Tangier Cinematheque, a nonprofit cinema featuring international independent films and documentaries. Another endangered landmark currently undergoing restoration is Marrakesh's Cinema Eden, the mudbrick cinema right off the Djemaa el-Fna.

The Moroccan government is showing initiative, too: in 2008, the state launched Aflam, a new, free, national TV channel showcasing Moroccan-made movies, and films dubbed or subtitled in French, Darija and Tamazight. With the runaway success of the Marrakesh International Film Festival, state-sponsored movie festivals are springing up across Morocco; check www.maghrebarts.ma/cinema.html for schedules.

How big is Bollywood in Morocco? In 2005, more than a third of the movies shown in Morocco were Bollywood films, and a 2008 Casablanca screening of *Chalte Chalte* starring Shah Rukh Kahn with an in-person appearance by co-star Rani Mukherjee drew 50,000 devoted fans.

Casablanca youth thinking fast and growing up faster as they confront the darker aspects of life in the White City. Other recent hits include Latef Lahlou's 2010 *La Grand Villa,* tracking one couple's cultural and personal adjustments after relocating from Paris to Casablanca.

Euro-Moroccan films have already become mainstays of the international festival circuit, notably Faouzi Bensaïdi's family-history epic *A Thousand Months,* winner of the 2003 Cannes Film Festival Premier Regard, and Leila Marrakchi's *Marock,* about a Muslim girl and Jewish boy who fall in love, winning Un Certain Regard at Cannes in 2005. With their stylish handling of colliding personal crises in 2007's *Heaven's Doors*, 20-something Spanish-Moroccan directors Swel and Imad Noury are hitting the festival circuit with *The Man Who Sold the World,* a Dostoyevsist-existentialist fable set in Casablanca.

Thanks to critical acclaim and government support, new voices and new formats are emerging in Moroccan cinema. A 2009 film-festival favourite, Hakim Belabbes' feature-length documentary *Ashlaa* (In Pieces) collages 10 years of footage of the director's extended family into a compelling family portrait. Women directors have stepped into the spotlight, from Farida Benlyazid's 2005 hit *A Dog's Life of Juanita Narboni,* a Spanish expat's chronicle of Tangier from the 1930s through to the 1960s, to rising star Mahassine El Hachadi, who won the short-film prize at the 2010 Marrakesh International Film Festival while still in film school. Young directors are finding their voices through a new film school in Marrakesh and short-film showcases, including back-to-back short-film festivals in Rabat and Tangier in October.

Medina Life

Winding Lanes »
Shopping »
People »
Street Eats »

Checkers game in the medina, Tetouan

Winding Lanes

You could happily spend days in Morocco's best medinas – getting lost, drinking tea and getting lost again. Magical medinas are found from Taroudannt to Assilah – here are some of the most atmospheric.

Marrakesh Medina

1 Inside 19km of ramparts, the theatrical Djemaa el-Fna (p59) is the Marrakesh medina's beating, back-flipping heart. Follow crazy lanes – or thoroughfares if you forgot your compass – to sights such as Bahia Palace.

Chefchaouen Medina

2 High in the Rif Mountains, Chefchaouen medina is painted Andalucian blue, and terracotta tiles add to the effect. You won't get horribly lost in this mini-maze (p270).

Fès el-Bali

3 In Old Fez, every sense absorbs a millennium of history. Even old hands get lost in this maze of souqs and tanneries (p301) – you might chance upon a craft museum or a 14th-century *medersa* (theological seminary).

Tangier Medina

4 Europe's just across the Strait of Gibraltar, but it feels a world away among Tangier medina's kasbah and souqs (p238). Spots like Petit Socco have been given a fresh coat of paint as part of the city's makeover.

Meknès Medina

5 A descendant of the Prophet Mohammed built the medina (p329) in Fez' criminally underrated neighbour. Spot balconied houses in the *mellah* (Jewish quarter), and watch the world promenade on the local version of Marrakesh's Djemaa el-Fna.

Clockwise from top left
1. Alleyway, Marrakesh medina **2.** Street football, Chefchaouen medina **3.** Passage through Fez medina
4. Pastel hues in Tangier medina

3

Shopping

Three Weeks

Morocco's medinas have been commercial hubs for centuries, and they remain the best places to buy everything from craftwork to carrots. On this mammoth shopping trip, hit the lanes in search of medina goodies.

» Shop for Riffian woven rugs and blankets in **Chefchaouen** (p274).

» **Tangier** (p250) medina includes a silver jewellery bazaar and exotic antique shops.

» Pick up some contemporary art in the arty, mural-painted **Assilah** (p208) medina.

» **Rabat** (p197) medina salesmen are relatively relaxed, and you can pick up handicrafts including silks, pottery and carved wooden furniture.

» **Meknès** (p336) is another low-pressure medina, where the local speciality is silver damascene (metalwork with intricate silver thread).

» **Fès el-Bali** (Old Fez; p322) is Morocco's artisanal capital. Head to the tanneries for leather goods, and converted riads and *funduqs* (caravanserais) for carpets; ceramics are everywhere.

» Berber motifs meet Western styles in **Marrakesh** (p86) medina. The sustainable fashion includes *babouches* (slippers) made from flour sacks.

» **Essaouira** (p230) is well known for its palm-fibre raffia work and woodwork; both are sold throughout the medina.

» Silver jewellery is a speciality of the Souss Valley's Chleuh tribe; pick it up in the Souq Arabe in the **Taroudannt** (p376) walled medina.

» If you don't find a special silver something in Taroudannt, **Tiznit** (p389) has a dedicated jewellery souq.

Clockwise from top left

1. Scarves and crafts in Marrakesh **2.** Spices on display **3.** Traditional slippers for sale **4.** Tajines in the pottery souq

People

Morocco's population is more complicated than just Berbers, Arabs and a few French expats. There's the Saharawi in the Western Sahara, and the Berbers are composed of multiple tribes, their various dialects mostly beginning with the Berbers' beloved T. For example, the Berbers you'll see hauling Souss Valley produce in Taroudannt's souqs are Tashelhit-speaking Chleuh.

The country's medinas are great places to make the acquaintance of locals. Pretty much the whole of Morocco passes through to sell some argan nuts or buy a mosque alarm clock. Between the milling tourists, gawking at the pre-Facebook form of human interaction seen on medina lanes, you can watch Morocco going about its daily business. You'll see people engaged in all sorts of activities, contributing to the sensory layer cake: hawking fruit and veg; stuffing mattresses; hurrying to the *medersa;* turning a dripping spit; juggling a mobile-phone debate and a stall teetering with dates; selecting spices for a hammam-oven-bound *tanjia* (slow-cooked stew). Yes, a lot of what you'll notice will likely relate to food: navigating medinas like mighty Fez, inhabited by 150,000 Fassis and countless donkeys, is hungry work.

If your stomach's rumblings are drowning out the call to prayer, stop at one of the cafes found on every corner. Now you can join the locals in the most hallowed activity of all: drinking mint tea and watching the medina street theatre.

Clockwise from top left

1. Saharan camel herder, Er-Rachidia **2.** Street scene outside a Fez mosque **3.** Souq stallholder, Marrakesh

Street Eats

Two Weeks

From hearty mountain tajines to their delicate seaside counterparts, food reflects Morocco's many environments. On this street-food tour of Moroccan medinas, let your tastebuds appreciate the country's diversity.

» Head to the Petit Socco in **Tangier** (p246) medina for brochettes; look out for local variations on Spanish tapas and paella.

» In the heart of **Chefchaouen's** (p272) mountain medina, hawkers circulate the cafes on Plaza Uta el-Hammam bearing trays of sticky pastries.

» One Fassi speciality is *b'sara* (garlic and butter-bean soup), served in pottery bowls with a dash of olive oil at hole-in-the-wall eateries across **Fez** (p318) medina.

» **Meknès** (p334) is perfect for just sipping mint tea on Place el-Hedim – also good for sardines and sandwiches.

» Leave the restaurants to the politicos in **Rabat** (p194); around the medina, locals queue for quick eats and vegetable couscous.

» Hit the smoking grills and fresh orange-juice stands on the Djemaa el-Fna, **Marrakesh** (p80), and snack with the square coursing around you.

» Between **Essaouira** (p228) medina and port, the fish grillers will turn your pick into an outdoor feast.

» Escape the sanitised tourist eateries at Souq al-Had in **Agadir** (p364), where tajines bubble next to the fruit-and-veg stalls.

» Put together a picnic with Souss Valley produce in the **Taroudannt** (p376) souqs.

From top
1. Sweets souq, Marrakesh **2.** Ready-to-eat tajines

Art & Crafts

The usual arts and crafts hierarchy is reversed in Morocco, where the craft tradition (see p460) is ancient and revered, while visual art is a more recent development. Ornament is meant to be spiritually uplifting, while nonfunctional objects and representational images have traditionally been viewed as pointless – or worse, vanity verging on idolatry, as it is perceived in Orthodox Judaism and some (though not all) Muslim societies.

Visual Art

Perhaps because it has been relegated to a marginal position, Moroccan contemporary art has particular poignancy and a sense of urgency, expressing aspirations and frustrations that can be understood instinctively – while eluding media censorship.

The new artworks emerging from Morocco today are not kitschy paintings of eyelash-batting veiled women and scowling turbaned warriors, though you'll still find plenty of those in tourist showrooms. These form a 19th-century French Orientalist tradition made largely for export, and contemporary Moroccan artists like Hassan Hajjaj are cleverly tweaking it. Hajjaj's provocative full-colour photographs of veiled women are not what you'd expect: one tough lady flashing the peace sign wears a rapper-style Nike-logo veil, emblazoned with the slogan 'Just Do It' across her mouth.

Morocco's visual-art scene put down local roots in the 1950s and '60s, when folk artists in Essaouira and Tangier made painting and sculpture their own by incorporating Berber symbols and locally scavenged materials. Landscape painting became a popular way to express pride of place in Essaouira and Assilah, and abstract painting became an important means of poetic expression in Rabat and Casablanca.

Marrakesh's art scene combines elemental forms with organic, traditional materials (mud, henna, wax, goatskin), helping to ground abstract art in Morocco as an indigenous art form. The Marrakesh scene has taken off in the past decade, launching Morocco's first Biennale in 2005, the first School of Visual Arts MFA program in 2007, and Morocco's first International Art Fair in 2009. Morocco's 2010 representative to the Venice Biennale was Marrakshi Mahi BineBine, whose ghostly characters in wax and raw pigment constantly make and miss connections – tragicomic gestures recalling William Kentridge's animations about apartheid-era South Africa.

Calligraphy

Calligraphy remains Morocco's most esteemed visual art form, practised and perfected in Moroccan *medersas* (Quranic schools) over the last 1000 years. In Morocco, calligraphy isn't just in the Quran: it's on tiled walls, inside stucco arches, and literally coming out of the woodwork. Look carefully, and you'll notice that the same text can have an incredibly

---

**Moroccan
Art Stars**

» **Mahi Binebine**
Ethereal figures in beeswax, colliding, pulling apart, not seeing one another

» **Hassan Echair**
Objects hanging in tenuous balance: white fenceposts, charcoal, twigs wrapped in string

» **Larbi Cherkaoui**
Gestural and seemingly urgent calligraphic flourishes on goatskin

---

Artworks dubbed 'Orientalist' are trying too hard to fit the 'exotic Moroccan' mould – not exactly a compliment, as Edward Said explains in *Orientalism*, his breakthrough critique of Western distortions of Middle Eastern culture.

different effect in another calligraphic style. One calligrapher might take up a whole page with a single word, while another might turn it into a flower, or fold and twist the letters origami-style into graphic patterns.

The style most commonly used for Qurans is Naskh, a slanting cursive script introduced by the Umayyads. Cursive letters ingeniously interlaced to form a shape or dense design are hallmarks of the Thuluth style, while high-impact graphic lettering is the Kufic style from Iraq. You'll see three main kinds of Kufic calligraphy in Morocco: angular, geometric letters are square Kufic; ones bursting into bloom are foliate Kufic; and letters that look like they've been tied by sailors are knotted Kufic.

Lately, contemporary artists have reinvented calligraphy as a purely expressive art form, combining the elegant gestures of ancient scripts with the urgency of urban graffiti. Farid Belkahia's enigmatic symbols in henna and Larbi Cherkaoui's high-impact graphic swoops show that even freed of literal meanings, calligraphy can retain its poetry.

Crafts

For instant relief from sterile, predictable modernity, head to your nearest Moroccan souq to admire the inspired handiwork of local *mâalems* (master artisans). European designers may be known by their logos, but you can tell true *mâalems* by their hands. The most meticulous artisans work clean to avoid staining their work, but they may have calluses from specialised handiwork that don't come from, say, pointing and clicking a computer mouse. Most of Morocco's design wonders are created without computer models or even an electrical outlet, relying instead on imagination, an eye for colour and form, and steady hands you'd trust to take out a tonsil.

This takes experience, not just intuition. In Fez, the minimum training for a ceramic *mâalem* is 10 years, and it takes a *zellij* mosaic maker three to four months to master a single shape – and with 360 shapes to learn, mastery is a lifelong commitment. When you watch a *mâalem* at work, it's the confidence of the hand movements, not the speed, that indicates a masterwork is in the making. Techniques and tools are handed down from one generation to the next, and friendly competition among neighbours propels innovation.

Instead of sprawling factory showrooms, *mâalems* work wonders in cubby holes lining souqs specialised in a traditional trade – basketry, slippers, banjos. But artisans in rural areas are not to be outdone: many Moroccan villages are known not for their sports-team colours, but for a style of embroidery or signature rug design. Most of the artisans you'll see in the souqs are men, but you're likely to glimpse women *mâalems* working behind the scenes knotting carpets in Anti Atlas and Middle Atlas villages, weaving textiles along the Southern coast and painting ceramics in Fez, Salé and Safi.

Carpets

If you manage to return from Morocco without a carpet, you may well congratulate yourself on being one of few travellers to have outsmarted the wiliest salespeople on the planet. Huzzah! But then it sets in: they've got piles of plush, one-of-a-kind handmade carpet underfoot, and you're stuck with your faded acrylic bathmat. Hmmm.

Moroccan carpets hook travellers almost every time because there's a right carpet for almost everyone – and if that sounds like something your mother once said to you about soul mates, it's not entirely a coincidence. Women in rural Morocco traditionally created carpets as part of their dowries, expressing their own personalities in exuberant colours and patterns, and weaving in symbols of their hopes for health and married life. Now carpets are mostly made as a way to supplement household

Emerging Art Talents

» **Khadija Kabbaj** Basketry tables, mummified Barbies, and other subversively applied traditions

» **Hicham Benohoud** Self-portraits with face obliterated by shredded paper, sticky notes, corks

» **Hassan Hajjaj** Mock fashion photos of women in Louis Vuitton veils and Moroccan-flag jellabas

To find out more about where those splendid traditional designs originated and learn to trace a few yourself, check out *The Splendour of Islamic Calligraphy* by Mohammed Sijelmassi and Khatibi Abdelkebir.

You too can read Islamic calligraphy: vertical lines are usually consonants, smaller marks above and below are vowels, and that tall letter that looks like the letter 'l' is probably an *alif*, the first letter in Allah.

income, but in the hands of a true *mâalem*, a hand-woven carpet brings so much personality and *baraka* (good vibes) underfoot, it could never be mistaken for a mere doormat.

Carpets you see in the souqs may already have been bought and sold three or four times, with the final price representing a hefty mark-up over what the weaver was paid for her work. Consider buying directly from a village association instead: the producer is more likely to get her fair share of the proceeds, you'll get a better deal without extensive bargaining, and you may meet the artisan who created your new rug.

Textiles

Anything that isn't nailed down in Morocco is likely to be woven, sewn or embroidered – and even then, it might be upholstered. Moroccan women are the under-recognised *mâalem*s of Moroccan textiles, and the tradition they've established has recently helped attract emerging fashion enterprises and global brands to Morocco. One-third of Moroccan women are now employed in Morocco's industrial garment industry, but for meticulous handiwork with individual flair, check out these traditional textile handicrafts.

Embroidery

Moroccan stitchery ranges from simple Berber designs to minutely detailed *terz Fezzi*, the elaborate nature-inspired patterns stitched in blue upon white linen that women in Fez traditionally spent years mastering for their dowries. Rabati embroidery is a riot of colour, with bold, graphic flowers in one or two colours of silk thread that almost completely obscures the plain-cotton backing. But the ladies of Salé also deserve their due for their striking embroidery in one or two bold colours along the borders of crisp white linen. Though you might not be able to bring yourself to wipe your mouth or nose on anything this spectacular, it makes a lovely pillow case or table runner – and accident-prone dinner guests don't have to know why they're being served white wine with their steaks.

Fair-Trade Carpet Showrooms

» Jemaite Tifawin Carpet Cooperative, Anzal

» Cooperative Feminin de Tissage Aït Bououli, Aït Bououli

» Kasbah Myriem, Midelt

» Coopérative de Tissage, Ouarzazate

» Ensemble Artisanales in cities nationwide

CARPET CATEGORIES

Rabati carpets Plush pile carpets in deep jewel tones, featuring an ornate central motif balanced by fine detail along the borders. Many of the patterns may remind you of a formal garden, though you may see some newer animal motifs and splashy modern abstract designs. Rabati carpets are highly prized, and could run you Dh2000 per sq metre.

Chichaoua rugs Simple and striking, with spare zigzags, asterisks, and enigmatic symbols on a variegated red or purple background (about Dh700 to Dh1000 per sq metre).

Hanbels or kilims These flat-woven rugs with no pile make up for a lack of cushiness with character. Some *hanbels* include Berber letters and auspicious symbols such as the evil eye, Southern Cross and Berber *fibule* (brooch) in their weave. Ask the seller to explain them for you – whether it's folklore or fib, the carpet-seller's interpretation adds to the experience (about Dh700 to Dh900 per sq metre).

Zanafi or glaoua Kilims and shag carpeting, together at last. Opposites attract in these rugs, where sections of fluffy pile alternate with flat-woven stripes or borders. These are usually in the Dh1000 to Dh1750 per sq metre price bracket.

Shedwi Flat-woven rugs with bold patterns in black wool on off-white, so au naturel you can still feel the lanolin between your fingers when you rub it. At as little as Dh400 for a smaller rug, they're impressive yet inexpensive gifts.

MÂALEMS

Answers to your every 'how'd they do that?' are on display at state-run Ensemble Artisanals, where you can watch *mâalems* at work and purchase their handiwork at fixed (if somewhat stiff) prices.

Passimenterie

What's that guy doing with a blow-dryer and silk thread in front of a mosque? That would be a *passimenterie* (trims) *mâalem* at work, using a repurposed blow-dryer to spin thread from a nail stuck in the wall, until it's the perfect width and length to make into knotted buttons, silken tassels, and snappy jellaba trim. In a cupboard-sized Moroccan *passimenterie* shop, you'll find enough gold braid to decorate an army of generals and more tassels than a burlesque troupe could spin in a lifetime – but you'll also find a jackpot of small, portable gifts. Moroccan *mâalems* have made a stand-alone art of trimming, wrapping wire and washers with silk thread to create mod statement necklaces, napkin-ring holders, knotted keychains and curtain-pulls.

Felt

Handmade felt hats, slippers, coats, pillows bags or floor coverings really put wool through the wringer: it's dyed, boiled and literally beaten to a pulp. Instead of being woven or sewn, felt is usually pounded with *savon noir* (natural palm soap), formed into the intended shape on a mould and allowed to dry gradually to hold its shape. Felt makers are usually found in the wool souq in major cities, in case a bad hair day calls for a fez, or you need a shopping bag to haul your handicrafts.

Weaving

Beyond the sea of imported harem pants and splashy synthetic jellabas in the souqs, hand-woven Moroccan fabrics with exceptional sheen and texture may catch your eye: nubby organic cotton from the Rif, shiny 'cactus silk' (*soie végétale*) woven with cotton and rayon from the south, sleek Marrakesh table linens, and whisper-soft High Atlas woollen blankets. Some lesser quality knock-offs are industrially produced, but connoisseurs seek out the plusher nap, tighter weave, and elegant drape of hand-woven Moroccan fabrics.

TOP CARPET-BUYING TIPS

To avoid both carpet-buyer's remorse and non-carpet-buyer's remorse:

» Know your limits, namely how much blank wall and floor space you actually have, your airline's luggage weight limit, whether you're prepared to pay for shipping and duty (see Sending Parcels, p495, for details), and how much you want to spend on a wall hanging for Aunt Gladys.

» Tread cautiously with antique rugs. Prices are typically much higher for antique carpets. Genuine antiques can be hard to distinguish from rugs taken out back and stomped on awhile, so buyer beware.

» Inspect the knots. You'll be asked to pay more for carpets with a higher number of knots per sq cm, which you'll begin to discern by examining the back of carpets to look for gaps between knots. Some carpets are washed in hot water to bind the wool together more tightly, like that time you put your cashmere cardigan in the dryer – but you can often distinguish these shrunken rugs by their misshapen, irregular borders.

» Get plenty of vegetables. Prices are often higher for carpets whose wool is coloured using vegetable dyes (which tend to fade faster) instead of synthetics; you can usually tell these by their muted tones, and the carpet seller may be able to tell you what plant was used to make the dye.

» Enjoy the transaction. Be prepared to banter before you bargain, keep your sense of humour, come back tomorrow, and drink mint tea so sweet you'll want to brush your teeth twice. Besides fond memories, at the end of it all you should have a carpet that suits you.

In souqs, village cooperatives and Ensemble Artisanal showrooms, you might glimpse two to four women at a time on a loom, working on a single piece. Men work larger looms for jellaba fabric, pushing the shuttle with arms as they pound pedals with their feet – producing one yard of fabric this way is a workout equivalent to running several miles while dribbling a basketball. You can buy linens and clothing ready-made or get hand-woven fabric by the bolt or metre, and have Moroccan decor and couture custom-made to your specifications. Tailors can be found in every major city, but be sure to leave enough time for the initial consult plus two fittings for clothing.

Leatherwork

Now that there's not much call for camel saddles anymore, Moroccan leather artisans keep busy fashioning embossed leather book-covers and next season's must-have handbags with what looks like medieval dentistry tools. Down unpaved medieval *derbs*, you'll discover freshly tanned and dyed lime-green leather sculpted into fashion-forward square poufs (ottomans), yellow pompoms carefully stitched onto stylish fuchsia kidskin gloves, or shocking silver leather stretched and sewn into the ultimate glam-rock bedroom slippers. Along these leather souqs, you might spot artisans dabbing henna onto stretched goatskin to make 'tattooed' leather candle-holders, lampshades, or stand-alone artworks. If you're in town for a couple of days, you might even commission an artisan to make you a custom-made lambskin leather jacket, jodhpurs or whatever else you might imagine in leather (ahem).

If it's an authenticity trip you're after, for men you'll prefer the traditional yellow *babouche*s (slippers) or 'Berber Adidas', slippers with soles made from recycled rubber tyres. Women's *babouche*s come in a broader range of colours and designs, and you may see vats of vibrant dye used for them in tanneries in Fez. But as colourful as they may look from afar, the tanneries give off a putrid stench, and concerns about toxicity from chemical dyes have given rise to a proposal to turn the tanning pots of Fez into community gardens.

Ceramics

If Moroccan ceramics don't convince you to upgrade from Tupperware, nothing will. Blue-and-white pottery from Fez might even top your grandmother's china as the new family heirloom, and though the colour scheme might remind you of a Ming vase, you'll be pleased to hear that it's nowhere near as expensive – a decorative tajine may run you Dh150 to Dh400, depending on size and decoration. As usual, antiques have their own price range, and it can be hard to tell the real deal from a fake with a convincing patina.

Different regions have their own colour schemes: Meknès ceramics tend to be green and black, Safi offers black and white Berber patterns, and Tamegroute makes a distinctive green glaze from oxidised copper. Salé is strong on yellow and turquoise, geometric patterns and intricate dot-patterned dishes. Marrakesh specialises in monochrome ceramics in red, graphite or orange that emphasise geometric and whimsical forms instead of elaborate decoration. Many rural areas specialise in terracotta crockery, with plain, striking shapes and Berber good-luck symbols painted in henna.

Zellij

To make a Moroccan fountain, grab your hammer and screwdriver-sized chisel, and carefully chip a glazed tile into a geometrically correct shape. Good job – now only 6000 more to go to finish your water feature. Then again, you might leave it to the Moroccan mosaic masters to spiff up your

The most reliable resource in English on Moroccan carpets is the (aptly named) *Moroccan Carpets*, by Brooke Pickering, W Russell Pickering, and Ralph Yohe. Packed with photos to help pinpoint the origins and style of any carpet that mysteriously followed you home.

Top Moroccan Modern Textiles

» Cooperative Tigmi, Aït Oudinar

» Al-Kawtar, Marrakesh

» Cooperative Artisanale des Femmes de Marrakesh

» Cooperative Ahilal des Tapis, Foum Zguid

» Sidi Ghanem, Marrakesh

*Mâalem*s with saintly patience or a devilish sense of humour may invite you to try your hand at their craft, and you'll never know how many thumbs you have until you try to mimic the acute hand-eye coordination required to work that loom, leather awl or chisel. To learn how it's done, artisans' associations offer workshops, and many guesthouses can arrange sessions with local *mâalem*s.

foyer with glittering *zellij* end tables, entryway mirrors, and fountains of all sizes. Fez has a reputation for the most intricate, high-lustre *zellij*, and the historic fountains around town dating from the Middle Ages are convincing advertisements for Fassi masterworks. But compared to Meknès *mâalem*s, Fez *zellij*-makers are rookies: they've been making mosaics around Meknès since Romans walked the mosaic floors at nearby Volubilis.

Brass, Copper & Silver

Tea is something of a performance art in Morocco, and it requires just the right props. As though tea poured from over your head weren't dramatic enough, gleaming brass teapots and copper tea trays are hammered by hand to catch the light and engraved with calligraphy to convey *baraka* on all who partake. Pierced brass lamps and recycled tin lanterns add instant atmosphere – and if all else fails to impress, serve your guests a sliver of cake with an inlaid knife from Morocco's dagger capitol, Kelaâ M'Gouna.

Most 'silver' tea services are actually nickel silver, and should cost accordingly – about Dh50 to Dh250 for the teapot, and usually more for the tray (depending on size and design). But if you're having the motorcycle gang over to tea, you might prefer the studded rubber tea tray made from recycled tyres.

Jewellery

Not all that glitters is gold in Morocco, since Berbers traditionally believe gold to be the source of evil. You may see some jewellers with magnifying glasses working a tricky bit of gold filigree, but most gold you see in the souqs is imported from India and Bali. Sterling will be marked with 925, and is often sold by weight rather than design. Morocco's mining operations are more concerned with phosphates and fossils than with precious gems, but you will see folkloric dowry jewellery and headdresses with semiprecious stones, including coral, agate, carnelian and amber.

But Moroccan *mâalem*s don't need precious materials to create a thing of beauty. Ancient ammonite and trilobite fossils from Rissani make fascinating prehistoric amulets, and striking Berber *fibules* (brooches) in silver are Tiznit's speciality. Layered wood, nickel silver and brightly coloured enamel make groovy cocktail rings in Marrakesh, and desert Tuareg talismans in leather and silver are fitting gifts for a man of the world.

Woodwork

The most pleasingly aromatic area of the souq is the woodworkers' area, with scents of orangewood, cedar, lemonwood and pine rising from the curls of wood carpeting the floors of master carvers' workshops. These are the *mâalem*s responsible for those ancient carved, brass-studded cedar doors you've been obsessively photographing (don't worry, everyone does it), and those carved cedar *muqarnas* (honeycomb-carved) domes

Plain terracotta cooking tajines are oven safe, fine for stovetop cooking and cost less than Dh80. According to a recent *New York Times* review, new-fangled tajines made by major European brands cost 10 times that and don't cook as well.

The Art of the Islamic Tile, by Gerard Degeorge and Yves Porter, celebrates the splendours of ceramics across the Middle East, from Istanbul to Fez.

that cause wonderment and neck cramps in Moroccan palaces. Tetouan, Meknès and Fez have the best reputations for carved wood ornaments, but you'll see impressive woodwork in most Moroccan medinas.

You may not be able to take an entire building with you, but you might find carved wood architectural salvage at Bab el-Khemis in Marrakesh. For the gourmets on your gift list, hand-carved orangewood *harira* (lentil soup) spoons are small ladles with long handles that make ideal tasting spoons. Cedar is used for ornate jewellery boxes and hefty chip-carved chests sure to keep the moths at bay. The most prized wood is thuya wood, knotty burl from the roots of trees indigenous to the Essaouira region that is now endangered – buy from artisans' associations that practise responsible harvesting. Lutes, banjos and guitars are carved from woods chosen not for looks, but for their resilience in withstanding an all-night Gnawa *lila* (jam session).

Lots of the 'amber' you'll see in the souqs is plastic. The genuine article will have a faint incense smell when you light a match near it, and a slightly waxy feel.

ART & CRAFTS CRAFTS

Architecture

Stubbed toes come with the territory in Morocco: with so much intriguing architecture to gawp at, you can't always watch where you're going. Some buildings are more memorable than others – as in any developing country, there's a fair amount of makeshift housing and cheap concrete here – but it's the striking variation in architecture that keeps you wondering what could possibly be behind that wall, down the block and over the next mountain pass. Here is a brief catalogue of Moroccan landmarks most likely to leave your jaw on tiled floors, and your toes in constant jeopardy.

Deco Villas

When Morocco came under colonial control, villes nouvelles (new cities) were built outside the walls of the medina, with street grids and modern architecture imposing strict order. Neoclassical facades, mansard roofs and high-rises must have come as quite a shock when they were introduced by the French and Spanish – especially for the Moroccan taxpayers footing colonial construction bills.

Top Deco
» Villa des Arts, Casablanca
» Jardin Majorelle, Marrakesh
» Cinematheque, Tangier
» Plaza de España, Melilla
» El-Minzah Hotel, Tangier

But one style that seemed to bridge local Islamic geometry and streamlined European modernism was art deco. Painter Jacques Majorelle brought a Moroccan colour sensibility to deco in 1924, adding bursts of blue, green and acid yellow to his deco villa and Jardin Majorelle.

Author Tahir Shah's relocation to Casablanca and restoration of a historic home inspired *The Caliph's House,* including this observation: 'There can be no country on earth better suited to buying decorations than Morocco. Every corner of the kingdom has its own unique styles, each one perfected through centuries of craftsmanship.'

In its 1930s heyday, Casablanca cleverly grafted Moroccan geometric detail onto whitewashed European edifices, adding a signature Casablanca Mauresque deco look to villas, movie palaces and hotels, notably Marius Boyer's 1930 Rialto Cinema and the 1922 Hotel Transatlantique. Tangier rivalled Casablanca for Mauresque deco decadence, with its 1940s Cinematheque and 1930s El-Minzah Hotel – the architectural model for Rick's Café in the 1942 classic *Casablanca.* Today you'll see elements of Mauresque all over Morocco – in architecture and in everyday life, Morocco is making a remarkable effort to balance its indigenous traditions and global outlook.

Fondouqs

Since medieval times, these creative courtyard complexes featured ground-floor artisans' workshops and rented rooms upstairs – from the nonstop *fondouq* flux of artisans and adventurers emerged cosmopolitan ideas and new inventions. *Fondouqs* once dotted caravan routes, but as trading communities became more stable and affluent, most *fondouqs* were gradually replaced with private homes and storehouses. Happily, 140 *fondouqs* remain in Marrakesh, including historic *fondouqs* near

Place Bab Ftueh, several lining Rue Dar el-Bacha and one on Rue Mouassine featured in the film *Hideous Kinky*. In Fez, an exemplary *fondouq* dating from 1711 has undergone a six-year renovation to become the spiffy Nejjarine Museum of Wood Arts and Crafts. The state is investing Dh40 million to spruce up 98 more *fondouqs*, so now's the time to see them in all their well-travelled, shop-worn glory.

Hammams

Talk about neat freaks: the first thing the Almohads did after they seized power was raze unruly Marrakesh and its misaligned Koutoubia mosque, and start building 83 hammams (public bathhouses) in Fez. These domed buildings have been part of the Moroccan urban landscape ever since, and every village aspires to a hammam of its own. Traditionally they are built of mudbrick, lined with *tadelakt* (satiny hand-polished limestone plaster that traps moisture) and capped with a dome with star-shaped vents to let steam escape. The domed main room is the coolest area, with side rooms offering increasing levels of heat to serve the vaguely arthritic to the woefully hung-over.

The boldly elemental forms of traditional hammams may strike you as incredibly modern, but actually it's the other way around. The hammam is a recurring feature of landscapes by modernist masters Henri Matisse and Paul Klee, and Le Corbusier's International Style modernism was inspired by the interior volumes and filtered light of these iconic domed North African structures. *Tadelakt* has become a sought-after surface treatment for pools and walls in high-style homes, and pierced domes incorporated into the 'Moroccan Modern' style feature in umpteen coffee-table books. To see these architectural features in their original context, pay a visit to your friendly neighbourhood hammam – there's probably one near the local mosque, since hammams traditionally share a water source with ablutions fountains.

Historic Hammams

» Seffarine Hammam, Fez

» Hammam el-Bacha, Marrakesh

» Hammam Lalla Mira, Essaouira

» Douches Barakat, Chefchaouen

» Hammam Bab Doukkala, Marrakesh

» Archaeological excavations, Aghmat

Kasbahs

Wherever there were once commercial interests worth protecting in Morocco – salt, sugar, gold, slaves – you'll find a kasbah. These fortified quarters housed the ruling family, its royal guard, and all the necessities for living in case of a siege. The *mellah* (Jewish quarter) was often positioned within reach of the kasbah guard and the ruling power's watchful eye (for more on Moroccan *mellahs*, see p425). One of the largest remaining kasbahs is Marrakesh's 11th-century kasbah, which still houses a royal palace and acres of gardens, and flanks Marrakesh's *mellah*. Among the most photogenic northern kasbahs are the red kasbah overlooking all-blue Chefchaouen, and Rabat's whitewashed seaside kasbah with its elegantly carved gate, the Bab Oudaïa.

Unesco World Heritage designations saved Taourirt kasbah in Ouarzazate and the rose-coloured mudbrick Aït Benhaddou, both restored and

Why'd they build it that way? Eight of the world's leading Islamic architectural scholars give you their best explanations in *Architecture of the Islamic World: Its History and Social Meaning*, by Oleg Grabar et al.

ENDANGERED MONUMENTS: GLAOUI KASBAHS

The once-spectacular Glaoui kasbahs at Talouine, Tamdaght, Agdz, and especially Telouet have been largely abandoned to the elements – go and see them now, before they're gone. These are deeply ambivalent monuments: they represent the finest Moroccan artistry (no one dared displease the Glaoui despots) but also the betrayal of the Alawites by the Pasha Glaoui, who collaborated with French colonists to suppress his fellow Moroccans. But locals argue Glaoui kasbahs should be preserved, as visible reminders that even the grandest fortifications were no match for independent-minded Moroccans.

KSOUR

frequently used as film backdrops. To see living, still-inhabited kasbahs, head to Anmiter and Kasbah Amridil in Skoura Oasis.

Ksour

The location of *ksour* (mudbrick castles, plural of *ksar*) are spectacularly formidable: atop a rocky crag, against a rocky cliff, or rising above a palm oasis. Towers made of metres-thick, straw-reinforced mudbrick are elegantly tapered at the top to distribute the weight, and capped by zigzag *merlon* (crenellation). Like a desert mirage, a *ksar* will play tricks with your sense of scale and distance with its odd combination of grandeur and earthy intimacy. From these watchtowers, Timbuktu seems much closer than 52 days away by camel – and in fact, the elegant mudbrick architecture of Mali and Senegal is a near relative of Morocco's *ksour*.

To get the full effect of this architecture in splendid oasis settings, visit the *ksour*-packed Drâa and Dadès valleys, especially the fascinating ancient Jewish *ksar* at Tamnougalt and the 3 tonne pink/gold/white *ksar* of Aït Arbi, teetering on the edge of the Dadès Gorge. Between the Drâa Valley and Dadès Valley, you can stay overnight in an ancient *ksar* in the castle-filled oases of Skoura and N'Kob, or pause for lunch at Ksar el-Khorbat and snoop around 1000-year-old Ksar Asir in Tinejdad.

Caravan stops are packed with well-fortified *ksour*, where merchants brought fortunes in gold, sugar and spices for safekeeping after 52-day trans-Saharan journeys. In Rissani, a half-hour circuit will lead you past half a dozen splendid ancient *ksour*, some of which are slated for restoration. Along caravan routes heading north through the High Atlas toward Fez, you'll spot spectacular *ksour* rising between snowcapped mountain peaks, including a fine hilltop tower that once housed the entire 300-person community of Zaouiat Ahansal.

In 2009, Dh230 million were set aside to restore *ksour* and kasbahs, with top priorities in Er-Rachidia, Erfoud and Rissani.

Medersas

More than schools of rote religious instruction, Moroccan *medersas* have been vibrant centres of learning about law, philosophy and astronomy since the Merenid dynasty. For enough splendour to lift the soul and distract all but the most devoted students, visit the *zellij*-bedecked 14th-century Medersa el-Attarine in Fez and its rival for top students, the intricately carved and stuccoed Ali ben Youssef Medersa in Marrakesh. Now open as museums, these *medersas* give some idea of the austere lives students led in sublime surroundings, with long hours of study, several roommates, dinner on a hotplate, sleeping mats for comfort, and one bathroom for up to 900 students. While other functioning *medersas* are closed to non-Muslims, Muslim visitors can stay overnight in some Moroccan *medersas,* though arrangements should be made in advance and a modest donation is customary.

The only fully active mosque non-Muslims are allowed to visit in Morocco is Casablanca's Hassan II Mosque. It's the world's fifth-largest mosque, so you won't be cramping anyone's style.

Mosques

Even small villages may have more than one mosque, built on prime real estate in town centres with one wall facing Mecca. Mosques provide moments of sublime serenity in chaotic cities and busy village market days, and even non-Muslims can sense their calming influence. Towering minarets not only aid the acoustics of the call to prayer, but provide a visible reminder of God and community that puts everything else – minor spats, dirty dishes, office politics – back in perspective.

Mosques in Morocco are closed to non-Muslims, with two exceptions that couldn't be more different: Casablanca's sprawling Hassan II Mosque and austere Tin Mal Mosque nestled in the High Atlas. The Hassan II Mosque was completed in 1993 by French architect Michel Pinseau with great fanfare and considerable controversy: with room for

25,000 worshippers under a retractable roof and a 210m, laser-equipped minaret, the total cost has been estimated at €585 million, not including maintenance or restitution to low-income former residents moved to accommodate the structure (the cases are still apparently pending). At the other end of the aesthetic spectrum is the elegant simplicity of Tin Mal Mosque, built in 1156 to honour the Almohads' strict spiritual leader, Mohammed ibn Tumart, with cedar ceilings and soaring arches that lift the eye and the spirits ever upward.

Muslims assert that no Moroccan architecture surpasses buildings built for the glory of God, especially mosques in the ancient Islamic spiritual centre of Fez. With walls and ablutions fountains covered in lustrous green and white Fassi *zellij* (ceramic-tile mosaic) and mihrabs (niches indicating the direction of Mecca) swathed in stucco and marble, Fez mosques are purpose-built for spiritual glory. When vast portals are open between prayers, visitors can glimpse (no photos allowed) Fez' crowning glory: Kairaouine Mosque and Medersa, founded in the 8th century by a Fassi heiress. Non-Muslims can also see Morocco's most historic *minbar* (pulpit): the 12th-century Koutoubia *minbar,* inlaid with silver, ivory and marquetry by Cordoba's finest artisans, and housed in Marrakesh's Badi Palace.

In addition to ancient fortress walls, 3m- to 6m-high border barriers wrap the Mediterranean towns of Ceuta and Melilla. Spain and Morocco dispute their sovereignty, and local architecture does nothing to resolve the conflict: the Spanish point out Andalusian elements, which Moroccans will certainly remind you developed under Almohad rule.

Ramparts

Dramatic form follows defensive function in many of Morocco's trading posts and ports. The Almoravids took no chances with their trading capital, and wrapped Marrakesh in 16km of pink pisé (mudbrick reinforced with clay and chalk), 2m thick. Coastal towns like Essaouira and Assilah have witnessed centuries of piracy and fierce Portuguese–Moroccan trading rivalries – hence the heavy stone walls dotted by cannons, and crenellated ramparts that look like medieval European castle walls.

Riads

Near the palace in Morocco's major cities are grand riads, courtyard mansions where families of royal relatives, advisors and rich merchants whiled away idle hours gossiping in *bhous* (seating nooks) around arcaded courtyards paved with *zellij* and filled with songbirds twittering in fruit trees. Not a bad set-up, really, and one you can enjoy today as a guest in one of the many converted riad guesthouses in Marrakesh and Fez.

So many riads have become B&Bs over the past decade that riad has become a synonym for guesthouse – but technically, an authentic riad has a courtyard garden divided in four parts, with a fountain in the centre (for more on riads, see p431). A riad is also not to be confused with a *dar*, which is a simpler, smaller house constructed around a central light well – a more practical structure for hot desert locales and chilly coastal areas. With more than 1000 authentic riads, including extant examples from the 15th century, Marrakesh is the riad capital of North Africa.

From outside those austere, metre-thick mudbrick walls, you'd never guess what splendours await beyond brass-studded riad doors: painted cedar ceilings, ironwork balconies and archways dripping with stucco. Upkeep on these architectural gems isn't easy, and modernising mudbrick structures with plumbing and electricity without destabilising the foundations is especially tricky. But for all its challenges, this ancient material may be the building material of the future. Mudbrick insulates against street sound, keeps cool in summer and warm in winter, and wicks away humidity instead of trapping it like mouldy old concrete – no wonder green builders around the world are incorporating it into their construction methods.

LOST IN THE MEDINA MAZE? FOLLOW SOUQ LOGIC

In labyrinthine Moroccan medinas, winding souqs hardly seem linear, but they do adhere to a certain zoning logic. Centuries ago, market streets were organised by trade, so that medieval shoppers would know exactly where to head for pickles or camel saddles. More than other medinas, Fez souqs maintain their original medieval organisation: kiosks selling silver-braided trim are right off the caftan souq, just down the street from stalls selling hand-woven white cotton for men's jellabas. What about wool? That's in a different souq, near stalls selling hand-carved horn combs for carding wool. The smelliest, messiest trades were pushed to the peripheries, so you'll know you're near the edge of the medina when you arrive at tanneries, livestock markets and egg souqs. In Marrakesh, the saddle-making souq is at the northeast end of the souq, not far from the tanneries.

Souqs

As thrillingly chaotic as Morocco's ancient cities seem, there is a certain logic to their zoning that you can still discern today in Fez, Meknès and Marrakesh. At the centre of the medina (old city), you'll find labyrinthine souqs (covered market streets) beneath lofty minarets, twin symbols of the ruling power's worldly ambitions and higher aspirations. Souq means 'market', and the same word is used to describe weekly village farmers markets – but once you've gotten lost in the souqs of Marrakesh or Fez, you'll agree there's no comparison.

In Morocco, souqs are often covered with palm fronds for shade and shelter, and criss-crossed with smaller streets lined with food stalls, storerooms, and cubby-hole-sized artisans' studios carved into thick mudbrick walls. Unlike souqs, these smaller streets often do not have names, and are collectively known as *qissaria*. Most *qissaria* are through streets, so when (not if) you get lost in them, keep heading onward until you intersect the next souq or buy a carpet, whichever happens first.

Zawiyas

Don't be fooled by modest appearances or remote locations in Morocco: even a tiny village teetering off the edge of a cliff may be a major draw across Morocco because of its *zawiya* (shrine to a *marabout*). Just being in the vicinity of a *marabout* (saint) is said to confer *baraka* (a state of grace). Zawiya Nassiriyya in Tamegroute is reputed to cure the ill and eliminate stress, and the *zawiya* of Sidi Moussa in the Aït Bougomez Valley is said to increase the fertility of female visitors (consider yourself warned).

To boost your *baraka* you can visit the Tamegroute and Aït Bougomez *zawiyas* as well as the *zawiya* of Moulay Ali ash-Sharif in Rissani, which is now open to non-Muslims. Most *zawiyas* are closed to non-Muslims – including the famous Zawiya Moulay Idriss II in Fez, and all seven of Marrakesh's *zawiyas* – but you can often recognise a *zawiya* by its ceramic green-tiled roof and air of calm even outside its walls. In rural areas, a *marabout*'s shrine (often confusingly referred to as a *marabout* rather than *zawiya*) is typically a simple mudbrick base topped with a whitewashed dome – though in the Ourika Valley village of Tafza you can see a rare red-stone example.

Top Souqs

» Okchen Market, Meknès

» Souq Sebbaghine (Dyers' Souq), Marrakesh

» Souq an-Nejjarine (Woodworkers' Souq), Fez

» Souq el-Ghezel (Wool Souq), Rabat

» Marché Central, Casablanca

Medinas: Morocco's Hidden Cities explores the shadows of ancient Moroccan walled cities in painterly images by French photographer Jean-Marc Tingaud, with illuminating commentary by Tahar Ben Jelloun.

Natural Landscapes

Mountain Ranges »
Deserts & Oases »
Coastal Delights »
Moroccan Landmarks »

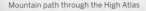
Mountain path through the High Atlas

Mountain Ranges

Visible from both the Mediterranean and the Sahara, Morocco's mountains are as iconic as medinas and tajines – and they've been around much longer than either. The High Atlas range rolls from snow-covered peaks such as Jebel Toubkal to the Dadès and Todra Gorges. Toubkal can be climbed by people in good physical condition, but if grands taxis are your preferred mode of transport, the High Atlas is still memorable. Roads pass crumbling kasbahs and Berber villages, and wind up the Tizi n'Test and Tizi n'Tichka passes.

The Middle Atlas and Rif are gentler landscapes, with forests carpeting slopes and valleys. In the Middle Atlas' alpine landscape, you might even think you're in the Alps among flower beds in the French-built resort of Ifrane. The Rif, Morocco's greenest range, is covered in wildflowers in spring.

Closer to the Sahara, the Anti Atlas is a land of jagged peaks such as quartzite Jebel L'Kest, with oasis villages in the valleys; and the wild, arid Jebel Sarhro is the home turf of the seminomadic Aït Atta.

TOP MOUNTAIN TREKS

» **The Rif** (p283) From Chefchaouen through Talassemtane National Park

» **The M'Goun Massif** (p99) Prehistoric rock forms, ridges, escarpments and river gorges

» **Jebel Toubkal** (p112) The two-day, 3313m ascent of North Africa's highest peak

» **Jebel Sarhro** (p143) Palm and almond groves beneath twisted volcanic pinnacles

» **The Anti Atlas** (p385) Unexplored trails among ochre cliffs and saffron fields

---

Clockwise from top left

1. Trekking in the High Atlas **2.** Kasbah Aït Arbi in the Dadès Gorge (p146) **3.** The Ourika River running through the Atlas mountains

Deserts & Oases

Head south from the snowy High Atlas to see mountains of a different kind, which will colonise just as much of your camera's memory card: the dunes at Erg Chebbi and Erg Chigaga, respectively rising to 160m and 300m. These are the places to disappear into the desert, accompanied by a camel and blue-robed guide, to see the sand sea by moonlight and sleep in a nomad camp.

Coming from Marrakesh, there are more accessible glimpses of the desert in the Drâa Valley, where a sign once advised desert caravans that Timbuktu was only 52 days away, and oases remain the region's lifeblood. In Ouarzazate, the desert stretches to the foot of the Atlas, and palms can be spotted through slit windows in the Taourirt kasbah.

It's all a long way – a day or so by bus – from the politically charged *hammada* (flat, stony desert) in the Western Sahara, en route to Mauritania.

TOP OASES

- » **Figuig** (p358) Seven traditional desert villages amid 200,000 date palms
- » **N'Kob** (p161) Mudbrick castles overlook the *palmeraie* (palm grove)
- » **Skoura** (p140) The Unesco-protected 'Oasis of 1000 Palms'
- » **Afella-Ighir** (p382) Rocky red gorges tower above the palms
- » **Ameln Valley** (p383) Village *palmeraies* beneath Jebel L'Kest
- » **Tata** (p383) Treetops are a welcome sight in this Saharan outpost
- » **Paradise Valley** (p372) *Palmeraies*, oleanders and beehives line the gorge

---

Clockwise from top left

1. The dunes of Erg Chebbi (p158) **2.** Date palms in the Drâa Valley (p128) **3.** Western Sahara dunes (p402)

2

Coastal Delights

Screeching seagulls, seafood tajines, Berber fishing villages, uncrowded beaches, salt-encrusted ramparts: the Moroccan coast is an unsung glory. Just as epic as the well-publicised mountains, it stretches from Mediterranean coves and cliffs to anglers' huts by the long, empty coastal highway through the Western Sahara.

Oued Laou

1 This sleepy fishing village (p276) recalls the era before developers discovered Mediterranean Morocco: blue boats on the beach, fishing nets spread out to dry, a few ramshackle hotels and empty golden sand.

Essaouira

2 At Essaouira fishing harbour (p223), gleaming bream and silvery sardines lie alongside wide, flat rays, inky-black lobsters, oysters by the dozen, browny-red crabs and prickly sea-urchins.

Al-Hoceima

3 The seaside town of Al-Hoceima (p278) sits high atop cliffs, while the 485-sq-km national park includes untouched beaches and limestone cliffs backed by great mesas and dry canyons.

Lagoons

4 Lagoons and lakes are the best places to spot migratory birds: from Merja Zerga (Blue Lagoon; p202) down to Naïla Lagoon in the Khenifiss National Park (p400), both sporting flamingos.

Assilah

5 Artists adorn the town's whitewashed medina walls with colourful murals during the annual Assilah Festival (p210). Some murals are huge, others are smaller and brighten alleyway corners.

Clockwise from top left
The ocean meets the desert in the Western Sahara (p402); Fishing boats in Essaouira (p219); Al-Hoceima's bay (p278)

Moroccan Landmarks

Three Weeks

This tour of pillars, peaks and other natural landmarks begins with an exciting first sight of Africa, then meanders through the mountains and along the fringes of the Sahara.

» Overlanders spy a landmark before they even step off the ferry from Europe: the **Mediterranean coast** (p236), backed by the Rif Mountains, is a first glimpse of Africa.

» On Moroccan soil, the great crag of **Jebel Musa** (p253) is one of the ancient Pillars of Hercules.

» Moving to the Atlantic, the **Monoliths of M'Soura** (p212), near Assilah, stand in a circle on a mysterious, prehistoric site.

» Heading south to the High Atlas, the route passes the landmark left by the Romans at hilltop **Lixus** (p206).

» Surrounded by mountains, **Jebel Toubkal** (p112) is North Africa's highest peak.

» There are plenty of icons and classic vistas to see without climbing Toubkal, including the rocky **Dadès Gorge** (p146) and **Todra Gorge** (149).

» Continuing south to the Sahara, **Erg Chigaga** (p136) is a landmark in this corner of the great desert, with 40km of dunes rising to 300m.

» The desert theme continues at **Afella-Ighir** (p382), a quintessential oasis occupying red-rock gorges.

» Nearby, a landscape artist created an Anti Atlas attraction when he daubed the **Pierres Bleues** (Painted Rocks; p381).

» Finish on the coast, where natural stone arches reach out to sea at **Legzira Plage** (p395).

From top

1. The Pierres Bleues (Painted Rocks) in the Anti Atlas
2. The sheer drop of Dadès Gorge

Natural Wonders

Morocco's Dramatic Changes of Scenery

Many people picture Morocco as one big oasis surrounded by sand, so the geographical variety of the country comes as a surprise. A day's journey can take you from breezy, silken-sand Atlantic beaches through a patchwork of rich farmland in the plains, past the snowy crags of the High Atlas Mountains, and into a barren, rocky stretch of desert. Everywhere, you'll spot people tending to this extraordinary land, harvesting barley on tiny stone-walled terraces hewn from cliffsides, tending to ancient argan trees and olive groves, or leading their flocks of sheep to faraway mountain pastures to avoid valley deforestation. Half of all Moroccans still live in rural areas, and their careful management of local resources brings life even to desolate stretches of terrain, making the scenery all the more remarkable.

Coastline

When the Umayyads arrived in Morocco, they rode their horses onto Atlantic beaches and dubbed the country *Al-Maghreb* (where the sun sets), knowing that the sea marked the westernmost limit of their conquests. The coast has played a central role in Moroccan history, from the Barbary pirates to the Allied landings of WWII, but it's learning to relax: King Mohammed VI's Azur Plan is currently developing stretches of Moroccan coastline into shiny new tourist hubs, complete with holiday villas, beach resorts and golf courses. Luckily for nature lovers, there's still pristine coastline in between, with rare shorebirds and cliff's-edge vistas.

Fishing and international trade have defined the Atlantic coastal economy ever since the Phoenicians and Romans established their port at Lixus. But the Atlantic also has its wild side, with raw, rocky beaches around whitewashed Assilah, and wetland habitats, like the lagoon of Merja Zerga National Park, attracting flamingos and rare African wildfowl. South of Casablanca are the ports of Oualidia and Essaouira, former pirate's coves where rare wildlife still flourishes and Morocco's best seafood is served at the port. South of the commercialised boardwalks of Agadir, resort beaches empty into great sandy expanses stretching through Western Sahara to Mauritania. Morocco's southern Atlantic Coast has recently reprised its notorious pirate ways, smuggling sub-Saharan African immigrants to the Canary Islands.

By contrast, the craggy Mediterranean coast has remained relatively undeveloped until recently, despite a spectacular coastline of sheltered coves and plunging cliffs. Tangier and the port towns of Ceuta and Melilla make the best of their advantageous positions, with scenic overlooks and splendid coastal villas. The major barrier to the east is the Rif Mountains, rugged terrain inhabited by staunchly independent Riffian Berbers who speak their own language (Tarifit) and effectively resisted colonial control. The Rif has remained politically marginalised, which has one

If you're going for a dip, be aware that the Atlantic rollers can hide some fearsome riptides, and once you're in the waters there's nothing between you and the Americas (or at best, the Canary Islands).

Golf courses have become a royal nuisance in Morocco, and not just because of the killer sand traps. Given how much water and chemical fertiliser it takes to keep a fairway green in the desert, courses built by Pasha Glaoui and King Hassan II are a strain on Morocco's environment – not to mention private golf courses recently built outside Marrakesh, and others in the works along the Atlantic Coast. Golfers who want to improve their game in more ways than one can head instead to La Pause (p79), an ecofriendly, turfless 'all-terrain' golf and disc-golf course in the desert outside Marrakesh.

highly debatable advantage: kif (cannabis) is widely grown in the region east of Tetouan. But lack of access to essential services has compounded local poverty, and it's taken huge government investment to improve access to schooling and medicine via new infrastructure. Well-graded roads make exploring the Rif coastline more possible than ever before.

Mountains

Three mountain ranges ripple diagonally across a topographical map of Morocco: the Rif in the north, the Middle Atlas (south of Fez) and the High Atlas (south and northeast of Marrakesh), with the southern subchain of the Anti Atlas slumping into the desert. The monumental force of plate tectonics brought these ranges into existence. Around 60 million years ago, a dramatic collision of Africa and Eurasia plates lifted up the High Atlas, while closing the Strait of Gibraltar and raising the Alps and Pyrenees. More recently, the mountains have provided shelter for self-sufficient Berbers, a safe haven for those fleeing invaders and a strategic retreat for organising resistance against would-be colonisers.

In the north, the low Rif Mountains form a green, fertile arc that serves as a natural coastal barrier. Even the Vandals and Visigoths were no match for independent-minded Riffian Berbers, who for millennia successfully used their marginal position to resist incursions from Europe and Africa alike.

The Middle Atlas is the Moroccan heartland, a patchwork of farmland that runs from Volubilis to Fez that gradually rises to mountain peaks covered with fragrant forests of juniper, thuya and cedar. This sublime trekking country is also home to the Barbary ape, Morocco's only (non-human) primate. Running northeast to southwest from the Rif, the range soars to 3340m at its highest point.

But the real drama begins east of Agadir, where foothills suddenly rise from their crouched position to form the gloriously precipitous High Atlas Mountains. South of Marrakesh, the High Atlas reach dizzy heights at Jebel Toubkal, North Africa's highest summit (4167m). On the lower flanks, the mountains are ingeniously terraced with orchards of walnuts, cherries, almonds and apples, which erupt into bloom in spring. The High Atlas hunkers down on to the southeast into Anti Atlas range, which protects the Souss Valley from hot winds of the rising Sahara Desert.

Desert

No landscape is more iconic in Morocco than the desert, with rolling dunes and mudbrick *ksour* (fortified strongholds) rising majestically from hidden palm oases. But most of the desert is neither oasis nor dune, and it's virtually uninhabitable. Vast tracts of barren, sun-bleached *hammada* (stony desert) are interrupted by rocky gorges, baked over millions of years by the desert's ovenlike heat until the blackened surface turns glassy. The desert forms still-disputed borders east and south to Algeria

CANNABIS

When hiking in the Rif, try not to step on the kif. Morocco is the world's number-two producer of cannabis, behind the US. So who's buying? At 60% mark-up, the UK spends £5 billion annually on kif.

and Mauritania. South of the Anti Atlas, the barren slopes trail off into the stony, almost trackless desert of Western Sahara.

Even today, the sight of an oasis on this desolate desert horizon brings a rush of elation and wonder – but when ancient caravans emerged after a gruelling 52-day trans-Saharan journey with final stretches of dunes at Erg Chigaga and Tinfou, the glimpse of green on the horizon at Zagora was nothing short of life-saving. From Zagora, caravans heading to Middle Atlas laden with gold proceeded warily through the Drâa Valley from one well-fortified *ksar* to the next, finally unloading the camels and packing up mules at Skoura Oasis.

Some caravans passed through the ancient desert gates of Sijilmassa (near Rissani), though there was no easy route: one approach was via the rose-gold dunes of Erg Chebbi at Merzouga, while the other led past formidable Jebel Sarhro, inhabited by equally formidable seminomadic Aït Atta warriors. Today the mood in oases is considerably more relaxed, with a slow pace in the daytime heat and sociable evenings as visitors and locals gather around a warming fire.

Sahara: A Natural History, by Marq de Villiers and Sheila Hirtle, is a highly readable account of the Sahara's wildlife, its people and geographical history.

BUYING SUSTAINABLE SOUVENIRS

Most Sustainable: Tyre Crafts

Used tyres don't biodegrade, and burning them produces toxic fumes – but when cleverly repurposed by Moroccan artisans, they make fabulous home furnishings. Tyre-tread mirrors make any entryway look dashingly well-travelled, and inner-tube tea trays are ideal for entertaining motorcycle gangs. For the best selection, visit the tyre-craft *mâalems* (master artisans) lining the south end of Rue Riad Zitoun el-Kedim in Marrakesh (p86).

Quite Sustainable: Argan Oil

The finest cosmetic oil to ever pass through the business end of a goat – no, really. Outside Essaouira and in the Anti Atlas, goats climb low argan trees to eat the nuts, digesting the soft, fuzzy outer layer and passing the pit. Traditionally, women then collect the dung, extract and clean the pit, crack it to remove the nut, and press the nut to yield a tiny quantity of the orange-tinted, vitamin-E-rich oil. This is arduous handwork, and buying from a collective is the best way to ensure that the women are paid fairly and no additives are included in the end product (no pun intended). Check out Cooperative Amal (p232) north of Agadir, Cooperative Tiguemine (p231) outside Essaouira, or Assouss Cooperative d'Argane (p87) at its retail outlet in Marrakesh.

Possibly Sustainable: Berber Carpets & Blankets

Berber blankets are often made with wool so all-natural that you can feel the lanolin on them. Despite claims to use only vegetable dyes, most carpet weavers use a combination of natural and artificial dyes to achieve the desired brilliance and lightfastness. Some cooperatives card and dye their own wool for natural colours (mostly browns, yellows, pinks and pale greens), but for bright colours it's better that they source their wool from reputable industrial dyers instead of handling chemical dyes and pouring used dye down drains. For associations advancing best environmental practices, organised democratically, and paying women weavers fairly and directly, visit Kasbah Myriem (p347), Cooperative Feminin de Tissage Aït Bououli (p95), Jemaite Tifawin (p139), Cooperative Ahilal des Tapis (p139), and Aït Oudinar women's weaving cooperative (p146).

Not So Sustainable: Thuyya Wood

The root of a juniper that grows only in Morocco, this caramel-coloured knotty burl is at risk of being admired to extinction. Buy carved thuyya bowls and jewellery boxes only from artisans' collectives more likely to practise responsible collection and reforesting, such as the Cooperative Artisanal des Marqueteurs (p230) and the Cooperative Artisanale Femmes de Marrakesh (p87).

Wildlife

Even after millennia of being inhabited, farmed and grazed, Morocco still teems with wildlife – a testament to sustainable traditional practices and careful resource management handed down through generations. Today Morocco's 40 different ecosystems provide a habitat for many endemic species, including flora and fauna that are rare elsewhere. Industrialisation has put considerable pressure on Morocco's delicately balanced natural environments, and while steps are being taken to create wildlife reserves for Morocco's endangered species, visitors can do their part to preserve natural habitats by staying on marked *pistes* and taking out waste.

Coastal Species

Away from the urban sprawl of port cities and resort complexes are long stretches of rugged Moroccan coastline, where people are far outnumbered by abundant bird populations and marine mammals such as dolphins and porpoises. Along beaches, you'll spot white-eyed gulls, Moroccan cormorants and sandwich terns. Seabirds and freshwater birds thrive in preserves such as Souss-Massa National Park, where you might spy endangered bald ibis along with the ducks and waders who migrate here from Europe for the winter. On Morocco's Mediterranean coast, you might spot one of the world's most endangered animals: the Mediterranean monk seal. Only 450 to 600 remain, and a few have been sighted taking refuge in sheltered Moroccan coves.

Desert Habitats

The Sahara may seem like a harsh place, but it's home to numerous creatures, including several furry, cuddly ones: several varieties of fluffy gerbils; long-eared, spindly-legged, cartoonish jerboas; and the world's tiniest hedgehog, the desert hedgehog, tipping the scales at 300g to 500g. The delightful fennec fox has fur-soled feet and huge batlike ears to dissipate Sahara heat; pups look like Chihuahuas, only fuzzier. This desert fox is stealthy and nocturnal, but if you're travelling by dromedary and staying overnight in the desert, you might catch a brief glimpse.

While desert heat makes most humans sluggish, many desert creatures are elegant and swift. Dorcas gazelles are common, and you might also catch a glimpse of a rare, reddish Cuvier's gazelle. Lizards you might see darting through the desert include skinks and spiny-tailed lizards, and you might catch sight of the devilish-looking (though not especially poisonous) horned viper. Golden jackals are the most common predator in the Sahara, though in the more remote parts of the Western Sahara a few desert-adapted cheetahs may yet survive.

Mountain Wildlife

Forested mountain slopes are Morocco's richest wildlife habitats, where it's easy to spot sociable Barbary macaques (also known as Barbary apes) in the Rif and Middle Atlas, especially around Azrou. Less easy to track are mountain gazelles, lynx and the endangered mouflon, or Barbary sheep. The mouflon are now protected in a High Atlas preserve near the Tizi n'Test, where its only predator is the critically endangered Barbary leopard – the last population of leopards in North Africa.

Golden eagles soar in Atlas mountain updrafts, and High Atlas hikes might introduce you to red crossbills, horned larks, acrobatic booted eagles, Egyptian vultures, and both black and red kites. In springtime, butterflies abound in the mountains, including the scarlet cardinal and bright-yellow Cleopatra.

One less-than-charming fact about snake charming: to prevent them from biting handlers, snakes' mouths are sometimes stitched closed. This often causes fatal mouth infections and leaves snakes unable to feed. To discourage this practice, don't pose with or tip snake charmers handling snakes whose mouths are stitched shut.

The endangered Houbara bustard is poised for a comeback with the release of 5000 captive-bred birds into a 40,000-sq-km protected zone in Morocco's eastern desert – among the largest reintroductions of any endangered species in the world. Bustards are notoriously difficult to breed in captivity, due to their intricate mating behaviour and nervous disposition.

To see the desert the way nature intended, take a dromedary instead of an all-terrain vehicle. The 4WDs break up the surface of the desert, which is then scattered into the air by strong winds. By one estimate, the annual generation of dust has increased by 1000% in North Africa in the last 50 years – a major contributor to drought, as dust clouds shield the earth's surface from sunlight and hinder cloud formation. What happens in the desert has far-reaching consequences: dust from the Sahara has reached as far away as Greenland. If you travel by dromedary instead, desert wildlife won't be scared off by the vibrations, and you're much more likely to spot small, sensitive and rather adorably big-eared desert creatures like the fennec fox, jerboa and desert hedgehog.

National Parks

With cities encroaching on natural habitats, the Moroccan government is setting aside protected areas to prevent the further disappearance of rare plant and animal species. Toubkal National Park in the High Atlas Mountains was the first national park to be created in 1942. After the vast Souss-Massa National Park was founded in 1991 outside Agadir, Morocco created four new national parks in 2004: Talassemtane (589 sq km) in the Rif; Al-Hoceima (485 sq km) in the Mediterranean, with outstanding coastal and marine habitats along the Mediterranean that include one of the last outposts of osprey; Ifrane National Park (518 sq km) in the Middle Atlas, with dense cedar forests and Barbary macaques; and the Eastern High Atlas National Park (553 sq km).

Today Morocco's 14 national parks and 35 nature reserves, forest sanctuaries and other protected areas overseen by Morocco's Direction des Eaux et Forêts are conserving species and advancing natural sciences. The park staff are tracking the region's biodiversity through botanical inventories, bird censuses, primate studies and sediment analyses. These studies are critical to understanding the broader causes of habitat loss, in Morocco and beyond; the Spanish and American Park Services have recently studied Morocco's parklands to better understand biodiversity concerns.

Parks have proven a boon to local wildlife, but a mixed blessing for human residents. While national parks protect local ecosystems and attract tourist revenue, access of local communities to water, grazing land and wild plants harvested for food and medicine has been limited or cut off entirely. By conserving parkland, the Ministries of Tourism and Agriculture aim to help local ecosystems flourish, gradually restore arable land, and ultimately benefit local communities with ecotourism that provides a profitable alternative to kif cultivation. In the near future, fees for park admission may be instituted to support the parks' conservation, scientific and community missions. Meanwhile, the best sights in Morocco are still free and visitors can show their appreciation to local communities by supporting local NGOs along their route (see p96).

LIONS

Once found across the Atlas and Rif Mountains, the Barbary lion was larger than the savannah lion, with a thick black mane and solitary habits. The last wild Barbary lion was killed in 1921, but the Parc Zoologique National in Rabat has made progress with a small captive-breeding program, with cubs that are 80% Barbary lion.

Creative Conservation

The only thing more natural than the wonders of Morocco is the impulse to preserve them. Morocco is in a fortunate position: to envision a more sustainable future, it can look to its recent past. Ancient *khettara* irrigation systems, still in use, transport water from natural springs to fields and gardens in underground channels, without losing precious water to evaporation. Although certification is still a novel concept, most small-scale Moroccan farming practices are organic by default, since chemical fertilisers are costly and donkey dung pretty much comes with the territory. Community hammams use power and water for steamy saunas more efficiently

NOTABLE NATIONAL PARKS

NATIONAL PARK	LOCATION	FEATURES	ACTIVITIES	BEST TIME TO VISIT
Toubkal National Park (p113)	near Marrakesh	highest peak in North Africa	hiking, climbing	May-Jun
Souss-Massa National Park (p370	south of Agadir	coastal estuaries and forests; 275 species of birds, including endangered bald ibis, mammals & enclosed endangered species	hiking, wildlife-watching, bird-watching	Mar-Oct
Lac de Sidi Bourhaba (p202)	Mehdiya	lake & wetlands; 200 migratory bird species, including marbled duck, African marsh owl & flamingo	swimming, birdwatching, hiking	Oct-Mar
Merja Zerga National Park (p202)	Moulay Bousselham	lagoon habitats; 190 species of waterfowl, including African marsh owl, Andouin's gull, flamingo & crested coot	wildlife-watching	Dec-Jan
Talassemtane National Park (p283)	Chefchaouen	cedar & fir forests; Barbary macaque, fox, jackal & bats in the cedar forest	wildlife-watching, hiking	May-Sep
Bouarfa Wildlife Sanctuary (p358)	Bouarfa	red rock steppe	hiking, climbing	Apr-Oct
Tazzeka National Park (p353)	near Taza	oak forests & waterfalls	hiking	Jun-Sep
National Park of Al-Hoceima (p281)	Al-Hoceima	thuya forest, limestone escarpments, fish eagles	hiking, bird-watching	May-Oct

than individual showers or baths. Locally made, detergent-free *savon noir* ('black soap' made from natural palm and olive oils) is gentle enough for a shave and effective as laundry soap, without polluting run-off – and left-over 'grey water' can be used for gardens and courtyard fountains. With Morocco's traditional mudbrick architecture, metre-thick walls provide natural insulation against heat in summer and chill in winter, eliminating most street noise and the need for air-con and central heating.

Morocco is also thinking fast on its feet, becoming an early adopter of resource-saving new technologies. Drilling oil off the coast of the Western Sahara has proved expensive and politically and environmentally messy, so Morocco is now turning towards more reliable energy sources for its own use and for export. The pioneering nation is already harnessing wind power in the Rif, and Ouarzazate now produces a combined

500,000 megawatts of electricity at five sites, making Ouarzazate one of the world's largest solar-electricity generators.

To tackle challenges still ahead, Morocco will need all the resourcefulness it can muster – and all the support it can get from visitors. Due to the demands of city dwellers and tourist complexes, 37% of villages around Marrakesh now lack a reliable source of potable water. Damming to create reservoirs frequently strips downstream water of valuable silts needed to sustain farms and coastal wetlands. Forests are also under threat, with around 250 sq km of forest lost each year, including Moroccan pine, thuya and Atlas cedar. Pollution is a weighty concern, literally: Morocco's cities alone produce an annual harvest of 2.4 million tonnes of solid waste.

While Morocco is considering legislated measures on a host of environmental measures from wetlands protection to mandating biodegradable plastic bags, changes are already afoot in communities across Morocco. Everywhere you travel in Morocco, you'll notice minor modifications that collectively make major savings in scarce resources – and you're invited to participate. Solar water heaters provide hot water instantly for showers in the afternoon and evening, so taking showers at those times saves water that might otherwise be wasted by running the tap while gas heaters warm up. Reforestation programs are helping prevent erosion, and you can help by staying on marked mountain paths and supporting local NGO reforestation initiatives. Organic gardens provide fresh ingredients for meals, reducing the dependence on food transported over long distances – and ordering local, seasonal specialities provides positive reinforcement for local food sourcing. Morocco's pioneering Green Key program also certifies hotels and guesthouses that institute a range of resource-conserving measures, from low-flow toilets to environmentally friendly cleaning products.

Add these traditional, national, and local resource-saving practices together, and Morocco is poised not only to make the switch to sustainable tourism, but to show Europe how it's done.

For more information on birdwatching in Morocco, see p31.

The Sahara Conservation Fund (www.saharaconservation.org) is dedicated to preserving the wild creatures of the Sahara, and provides a preview of wildlife you might spot in this vibrant desert ecosystem.

NATURAL WONDERS CREATIVE CONSERVATION

Survival Guide

Directory A-Z

Accommodation

A wide range of accommodation options is available in Morocco.

The rates quoted in this book are for high season (November to April) weekends and, unless otherwise mentioned, exclude breakfast. Reviews are ordered by preference, and price ranges are based on the cost of a double room:

Budget (€) Up to Dh400
Midrange (€€) Dh400 to Dh800
Top end (€€€) More than Dh800

Pricier towns and cities including Casablanca, Essaouira, Fez, Marrakesh, Rabat and Tangier are exceptions. For these places, price ranges are:

Budget (€) Up to Dh600

Midrange (€€) Dh600 to Dh1200
Top end (€€€) More than Dh1200

In this book the official, government-assigned rates (including taxes) are quoted, although these are intended as a guide only.

Discounts Many hotels will offer 'promotional discounts' from their advertised rates, especially in large resorts like Agadir or during the low season (May to October). It is always worth asking when you book.

Reservations To make a reservation, many hotels require confirmation by email or fax plus a credit-card number.

Seasons Accommodation is often scarce during Easter week and August, popular times for Spanish and French tourists to visit

Morocco. Another busy time in the south, particularly Marrakesh, is Christmas and New Year.

Solo travellers Outside the cities, the rates in many places are per person rather than per room, and single occupancy of rooms is rarely a problem. However, in riads, the limited accommodation means that discounts on single occupancy are fairly minimal.

Apartments

» If travelling in a small group or as a family, consider self-catering options, particularly in low season, when prices can drop substantially.
» Agadir, nearby Taghazout, Essaouira, Assilah and the bigger tourist centres on both coastlines have a fair number of self-catering apartments and houses, sometimes in tourist complexes.
» The riad agencies (p490) also rent apartments.

Camping

» You can camp anywhere in Morocco if you have permission from the site's owner.
» There are many official camp sites.
» Most official sites have water and electricity; some have a small restaurant, grocery store and even a swimming pool.
» Most of the bigger cities have camp sites, although they're often some way from the centre.
» Such sites are sometimes worth the extra effort to get to, but often they consist of a barren and stony area offering little shade and basic facilities.
» Particularly in southern Morocco, camp sites are often brimming with the enormous campervans so beloved of middle-aged French tourists.

COSTS

» At official sites you'll pay around Dh10 to Dh20 per person, plus Dh10 to Dh20 to

---

BOOK YOUR STAY ONLINE

For more reviews by Lonely Planet authors, check out hotels.lonelyplanet.com/. You'll find independent reviews, as well as recommendations on the best places to stay. Best of all, you can book online.

pitch a tent and about Dh10 to Dh15 for small vehicles.

» Parking a campervan or caravan typically costs around Dh20 to Dh30, although this can rise as high as Dh45.

» Electricity generally costs another Dh10 to Dh15.

» A hot shower is about Dh5 to Dh10.

» Many camp sites have basic rooms or self-catering apartments.

Gîtes d'Étape, Homestays & Refuges

» Gîtes d'étape are homes or hostels, often belonging to mountain guides, which offer basic accommodation (often just a mattress on the floor) around popular trekking routes in the Atlas.

» Gîtes have rudimentary bathrooms and sometimes hot showers.

» Larger than gîtes, mountain refuges offer Swiss chalet-style accommodation.

» Accommodation at refuges is usually in dormitories with communal showers, and often includes a lively communal dining/living room.

» **Club Alpin Français** (CAF; www.caf-maroc.com, in French) runs refuges in the High Atlas.

» If you are trekking in the High Atlas or travelling off the beaten track elsewhere, you may be offered accommodation in village homes.

» Many homestays won't have running water or electricity, but you'll find them big on warmth and hospitality.

» You should be prepared to pay what you would in gîtes d'étape or mountain refuges.

» See p39 for more information on mountain accommodation for trekkers.

Hostels

Part of Hostelling International, **Fédération Royale Marocaine des Auberges de Jeunes** (☑0522 47 09 52;

PRACTICALITIES

» Morocco uses the metric system for weights and measures.

» Electricity is generally reliable and available nearly everywhere travellers go.

» See p491 for more information on electricity.

» For a list of Moroccan newspapers online, visit www.onlinenewspapers.com/morocco.htm.

» English-language websites include the Morocco Board News Service (www.moroccoboard.com), Morocco Newsline (www.moroccconewsline.com) and Agence Maghreb Arabe Presse (www.map.ma/eng). Maghrebarts (www.maghrebarts.ma, in French) has arts and media coverage.

» French-language dailies include the semi-official Le Matin (www.lematin.ma), and the opposition Libération (www.libe.ma), L'Opinion and Al-Bayane.

» Major European, British and American papers (or their foreign editions) and magazines are available in most of the main cities.

» Most Moroccan radio stations broadcast in Arabic or French on AM or FM.

» Broadcasting across North Africa and Europe from Tangier, you can listen to the Maghrebi affairs and music station Médi 1 via radio (105.3MHz in Marrakesh and 95.3 or 101 in Tangier) and www.medi1.com.

» State-run SNRT (www.snrt.ma) has regional and national stations, including the urban Chaine Inter, available via radio (98.8MHz in Marrakesh and 90MHz in Casablanca) and www.chaineinter.ma.

» Satellite dishes are everywhere, and pick up foreign stations.

» The major TV station, 2M, is partly state-owned and broadcasts in languages including Arabic and French via satellite, analogue and www.2m.ma.

» Médi 1's news and current-affairs broadcasts are available via satellite and www.medi1tv.com.

» Moroccan DVDs share region 5 with much of Africa and Asia (North America is region 1, Europe is mostly region 2 and Australia is region 4).

http://tinyurl.com/373omvl) has reliable youth hostels in Casablanca, Fez, Marrakesh, Meknès, Ouarzazate and Rabat.

» If you're travelling alone, they are among the cheapest places to stay (Dh30 to Dh60 a night), but many are inconveniently located.

» Some offer kitchens, family rooms and breakfast.

» If looking for a budget hostel, beware of individuals' houses converted in the dead of night without the appropriate licences.

Hotels

» You'll need your passport number (and entry-stamp number) when filling in a hotel register.

» For registered hotels, there's a government tax (included in prices quoted throughout the book); the exact amount depends on the hotel's rating.

» Some hotels in more isolated regions offer half-board (demi-pension), which means breakfast and dinner are included, or full-board (pension), also including lunch. This can be a good deal.

BUDGET

» You'll find cheap, unclassified (without a star rating) or one-star hotels clustered in the medinas of the bigger cities.

» Some are bright and spotless, others haven't seen a mop for years.

» Cheaper prices usually mean shared washing facilities and squat toilets.

» Many budget hotels don't supply soap in the bathrooms, so bring a bar or some gel.

» Occasionally there is a gas-heated shower, for which you'll pay an extra Dh5 to Dh10.

» Where there is no hot water at all, head for the local hammam (see p31).

» Many cheap hotels in the south offer a mattress on the roof terrace (Dh25 to Dh30); others also have traditional Moroccan salons, lined with banks of seats and cushions, where you can sleep for a similar price.

MIDRANGE

» Midrange hotels in Morocco are generally of a high standard.

» Options range from hotels offering imitation Western-style rooms, which are modern if a little soulless, to riads and maisons d'hôtes (small hotels), which capture the essence of Moroccan style with both comfort and character.

» In this price range, you should expect an en-suite room with shower.

» In cheaper areas such as the south, you may find midrange standards at budget prices.

TOP END

» Hotels in this bracket are similar to midrange places but with more luxurious levels of comfort and design.

» In resorts such as Agadir, many top-end hotels are self-contained holiday complexes, offering features such as golf courses, nightclubs and multiple restaurants.

Riads, Dars & Kasbahs

For many guests, the chance to stay in a converted traditional house is a major drawcard for a trip to Morocco. These midrange and top-end options are the type of accommodation that the term 'boutique hotel' could have been invented for, and no two are alike. Service tends to be personal, with many places noted for their food as much as their lodgings.

Locations Marrakesh is the most famous destination for riads (there are several hundred); Fez, Meknès, Essaouira and Rabat are also noteworthy. With their popularity seemingly unassailable, you can increasingly find riads in the most unexpected corners of the country.

Riads and dars Although the term riad is often used generically, a riad proper is a house built around a garden with trees. You'll also come across plenty of dars (traditional town houses with internal courtyards).

Kasbahs Often functioning as hotels, kasbahs (old citadels) are found in tourist centres in central and southern Morocco. Rooms in kasbahs are small and dark, due to the nature of the building, but are lovely and cool in summer.

Booking Most riads operate on advance bookings, and it's worth planning ahead, as most only have a handful of rooms and can fill quickly. Advance booking often means that someone from the riad will be sent to meet you outside the medina when you arrive: labyrinthine streets conspire against finding the front door on your first attempt.

Rates Room rates are generally comparable to four- or five-star hotels. Many riads list their online rates in euros, rather than dirham, at exchange rates favourable to themselves, so always double check the prices when booking.

AGENCIES

For an idea of properties and prices, visit the websites of these agencies:

Fez Riads (☑0672 51 33 57; www.fez-riads.com) A percentage of profits is donated towards restoration projects in the Fez medina.

Marrakech Riads (☑0524 39 16 09; www.marrakech-riads.com) Well-established and respected agency.

Business Hours

Although a Muslim country, for business purposes Morocco follows the Monday to Friday working week. Friday is the main prayer day, however, so many businesses take an extended lunch break on Friday afternoon. During Ramadan the rhythm of the country changes and office hours shift to around 10am to 3pm or 4pm.

Hours often vary between medinas and villes nouvelles (new towns): most businesses close on Sundays in villes nouvelles, whereas those in medinas usually open continuously from about 9am to 7pm except on Fridays.

Medina souqs and produce markets in the villes nouvelles of the bigger cities tend to wind down on Thursday afternoon and are usually empty on Friday.

Souqs in small villages start early and generally wind down before the onset of the afternoon heat.

In cities, pharmacies open all night on a rotating basis. All pharmacies should have a list in their window of that week's night pharmacies.

In the main tourist cities, *bureaux de change* (foreign-exchange bureaus) often open until 8pm and over the weekend.

Téléboutiques (private telephone offices) and internet cafes often stay open late into the night, especially in cities.

Listings in this book do not specify opening hours unless they differ markedly from those in the table below – apart from reviews of sights, which always give opening hours.

Banks 8.30am-6.30pm Mon-Fri

Post offices 8.30am-4.30pm Mon-Fri

Government offices 8.30am-6.30pm Mon-Fri

Restaurants noon-3pm & 7-10pm

Bars 4pm-late

Shops 9am-12.30pm & 2.30-8pm Mon-Sat (often closed longer at midday for prayer)

Tourist offices 8.30am-noon & 2.30-6.30pm Mon-Thu, 8.30am-11.30am & 3-6.30pm Fri

Customs Regulations

» Importing or exporting dirham is forbidden.

» Duty-free allowances are:

* Up to 200 cigarettes, or 25 cigars, or 250g of tobacco

* 1L of alcoholic drink

* 150ml of perfume

* Presents or souvenirs worth up to Dh2000.

» Forbidden items include 'any immoral items liable to cause a breach of the peace', such as 'books, printed matter, audio and video cassettes'.

Electricity

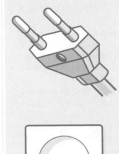

127v/220v/50hz

Embassies & Consulates

Most embassies and diplomatic representation are in Rabat, and open from about 9am until noon, Monday to Friday.

See the boxed text on p504 for information on visa requirements for Morocco's neighbouring countries.

The **Moroccan Ministry of Foreign Affairs and Cooperation** (www.maec.gov.ma) has a list of embassies and consulates in Morocco.

The following countries do not have embassies in Morocco:

Australia (http://tinyurl.com/248erss) The Australian embassy in Paris is responsible for Morocco. The Canadian embassy in Rabat provides consular assistance to Australians.

Ireland (☎0528 82 12 12 in Agadir; http://tinyurl.com/2b3ejux; Hotel Kenzi Europa, Blvd du 20 Août) The Irish embassy in Lisbon is responsible for Morocco.

Has honorary consulates in Agadir and Casablanca.

New Zealand (www.nzembassy.com/spain) The New Zealand embassy in Madrid is responsible for Morocco.

Gay & Lesbian Travellers

» Homosexual acts (including kissing) are illegal in Morocco – you can go to jail and/or be fined.

» In practice, although not openly admitted or shown, sex between men remains relatively common, even if few people actively identify themselves as gay.

» Platonic affection is freely shown among Moroccans, more so between men than women.

» For travellers, discretion is the key in most places. Avoid public displays of affection – aggression towards gay male travellers is not unheard of.

» Some towns are more gay-friendly than others, with Marrakesh winning the prize, followed by Tangier.

» There are no dedicated gay destinations, although 'gay' bars can be found here and there; nightlife in the bigger cities includes something for everybody.

» The pressures of poverty mean many young men will consider having sex for money or gifts. Exploitative relationships form an unpleasant but real dimension of the Moroccan gay scene.

Women

» Lesbians shouldn't encounter any problems, though it's commonly believed by Moroccans that there are no lesbians in their country.

» Announcing that you're a lesbian probably won't make would-be Romeos magically disappear. It may simply confirm Moroccan men's belief that Western males don't

EMBASSIES IN RABAT

Algeria (☎0537 76 54 74; www.mae.dz/ma_fr, in French; 46-48 Ave Tariq ibn Zayid) Also has a consulate-general in Casablanca and consulate in Oujda.

Canada (☎0537 68 74 00; www.rabat.gc.ca; 13 Rue Jaafar as-Sadiq, Agdal)

France (☎0537 68 97 00; www.ambafrance-ma.org; 3 Rue Sahnoun, Agdal) Also has consulates in Agadir, Casablanca, Fez, Marrakesh, Rabat and Tangier.

Germany (☎0537 21 86 00; www.rabat.diplo.de, in German & French; 7 Rue Madnine) Also has a consulate in Rabat and honorary consulates in Agadir and Casablanca.

Mauritania (☎0537 65 66 78; www.mauritania.mr/fr, in French; 6 Rue Thami Lamdaouar, Soussi)

Netherlands (☎0537 21 96 00; www.ambassadepaysbas rabat.org, in Dutch & French; 40 Rue de Tunis) Also has a consulate-general in Casablanca.

Spain (☎0537 63 39 00; www.maec.es/en; Rue Ain Khaloui-ya, Route des Zaers, Km 5300 Soussi) Also has consulates-general in Agadir, Casablanca, Larache, Nador, Rabat, Tangier and Tetouan.

UK (☎0537 63 33 33; http://ukinmorocco.fco.gov.uk/en; 28 Ave SAR Sidi Mohammed, Soussi) Also has honorary consulates in Agadir, Marrakesh and Tangier.

USA (☎0537 76 22 65; http://rabat.usembassy.gov; 2 Ave de Mohammed El Fassi) Also has a consulate-general in Casablanca.

measure up in the sexual department.

Websites

Useful websites that give the low-down on local laws and attitudes to homosexuality include the following:

Behind the Mask (www.mask.org.za) Detailed information and related news stories for every African country.

Communauté de Femmes Lesbiennes, Bi et Trans du Maroc (www.mennawfena.net, in French) For lesbian, bisexual and transsexual women in Morocco.

Gay & Lesbian Arab Society (www.glas.org) Resources on homosexuality in the Arab world.

Global Gayz (www.globalgayz.com) A useful resource with good links on Morocco.

Mithly (www.mithly.net, in French & Arabic) The first gay magazine in the Arab world.

Spartacus International Gay Guide (www.spartacusworld.com) Renowned guide to gay travel around the world with info on Morocco.

Insurance

A travel-insurance policy to cover theft, loss and, in particular, medical problems is strongly recommended for visitors to Morocco. For information on health insurance see p523.

Activities Some policies specifically exclude 'dangerous activities', which can include scuba diving, motorcycling and even trekking.

Driving Make sure you have adequate travel medical insurance and any relevant car insurance if you're driving (see p515).

Extensions If you need to extend your cover on the road, do so before it expires

or a more expensive premium may apply.

Flights Paying for your airline ticket with a credit card often provides some travel-accident insurance. You may be able to reclaim the payment if the operator doesn't deliver.

Online insurance Worldwide travel insurance is available at www.lonelyplanet.com/travel_services. You can buy, extend and claim online any time – even if you're already on the road.

Purchase Buy travel insurance as early as possible. Buying just before you leave home may mean you're not covered for delays to your flight caused by strike action that began, or was threatened, before you took out the insurance.

Internet Access

» Moroccan internet cafes are widely available, efficient and cheap (Dh3 to Dh10 per hour), usually with reasonable connection speeds.

» Two irritants for many travellers are the widespread French and Arabic (nonqwerty) keyboards, and Moroccan men's common use of internet cafes to view pornographic websites and similar.

» In this book the internet icon (@) is used in Sleeping reviews where accommodation options offer a computer with internet for guest use.

» The wi-fi icon (🛜) indicates that a business has a wireless network.

» Wi-fi is widely available in midrange and top-end accommodation and in many of the better budget options. It is still less common outside the main cities and tourist towns, but becoming increasingly universal in destinations that host lots of foreigners.

» If you're bringing a laptop, check the power-supply voltage and bring a universal adaptor. Scan it regularly, as internet security is generally poor here.

» For useful websites see p17 and the boxed text on p489.

Language Courses

There are courses in Arabic – both modern standard and Moroccan – in most major towns in Morocco, with a high concentration in Fez (p309), Rabat (p191) and Casablanca (p171) – where long- and short-term programs are offered.

Jeunesse des Chantiers Marocains (http://perso.menara.ma/youthcamps) Offers language and cultural immersion programs in Marrakesh.

Legal Matters

Drugs Moroccan law prohibits the possession, offer, sale, purchase, distribution and transportation of cannabis. The penalties for possessing even small amounts of drugs are severe, and include up to 10 years' imprisonment, with no remission for good behaviour, heavy fines and confiscation of your vehicle or vessel. Acquittals in drugs cases are rare.

Help and advice If you get into trouble, your first call should be to your embassy or consulate; remember that it's not unknown for local police to be in on scams. The London-based **Fair Trials International** (FTI; ☎ 4420-7762 6400; www.fairtrials.net) provides legal assistance and advocacy to individuals facing criminal charges in a foreign country.

Police If you get arrested by the Moroccan police, you won't have much of a legal leg to stand on. It's unlikely that any interpreter on hand will be of sufficient standard to translate an accurate statement that will, none-

theless, play a vital part in subsequent judicial proceedings. According to some human-rights groups, physical abuse while in custody is not unknown.

Maps

Few decent maps of Morocco are available in the country itself, so get one before leaving home.

For advice on tracking down maps for trekking and general use, see p36. Recommended:

» Michelin's No 742 (formerly No 959) map of Morocco is arguably the best.

- The 1:4,000,000 scale map of the whole country includes the disputed Western Sahara.
- Features a 1:1,000,000 enlargement of Morocco.
- Features 1:600,000 enlargements of Marrakesh and the High Atlas, Middle Atlas and Fez areas.
- Shows sites of weekly markets, kasbahs and marabouts (holy mausoleums of local saints).
- Notes particularly scenic roads.
- Available in major Moroccan cities.

» The GeoCenter World Map *Morocco* is preferred by many and has similar, often clearer, detail.

- Shows Morocco at a handy 1:800,000 scale (and the Western Sahara at 1:2,500,000).
- Occasionally available in Morocco.

Additionally, several maps include Morocco as part of northwestern Africa. An overlanding classic, Michelin's No 741 (formerly Nos 953 and 153) map covers all of west Africa and most of the Sahara. It has a scale of 1:4,000,000.

Soviet survey maps of Morocco, with scales ranging from 1:100,000 to 1:1,000,000, are available online and at good map shops worldwide. They often have to be ordered and can take up to six weeks to arrive.

Money

» The Moroccan currency is the dirham (Dh), which is divided into 100 centimes.

» You will find notes in denominations of up to Dh200.

» Coins come in denominations of Dh1, Dh2, Dh5 and Dh10, as well as, less frequently, 10, 20 and 50 centimes.

» The dirham is a restricted currency, meaning that it cannot be taken out of the country and is not available abroad.

» The dirham is fairly stable, with no major fluctuations in exchange rates.

» Euros, US dollars and British pounds are the most easily exchanged currencies.

» See p16 for exchange rates and a guide to costs.

ATMs

» ATMs (guichets automatiques) are the easiest way to access your money in Morocco.

» A common sight even in the smallest towns, virtually all accept Visa, MasterCard, Electron, Cirrus, Maestro and InterBank cards.

» BMCE (Banque Marocaine du Commerce Extérieur) Crédit du Maroc, Banque Populaire, BMCI (Banque Marocaine pour le Commerce et l'Industrie), Société Générale and Attijariwafa Bank all offer reliable service.

» ATMs sometimes run dry on weekends.

» The amount of money you can withdraw from an ATM generally depends on the conditions attached to your card.

» The daily ATM limit on most cards is around Dh2000.

» Most banks charge you for withdrawing money from foreign cash machines; check with your bank.

Black Market

The easy convertibility of the dirham leaves little room for a black market, but you'll find people in the streets asking if you want to exchange money, especially in Tangier, Casablanca and on the borders of (and just inside) the enclaves of Ceuta and Melilla. Avoid these characters; there's no monetary benefit to be had from such transactions and scams are common.

Cash

Nothing beats cash for convenience – or risk. If you lose it, it's gone forever and very few travel insurers will come to the rescue. Nonetheless, you'll need to carry some cash with you.

» Keep a handful of notes of small denomination in your wallet, or just in a pocket (but never a back pocket), for day-to-day transactions.

» Put the rest in a money belt or another safe place.

» If you're travelling in out-of-the-way places, make sure you have enough cash to last until you get to a decent-sized town.

» Keep an emergency stash of euros in small denominations.

» The endless supply of small coins may be annoying, but they're handy for taxis, tips, guides and beggars.

Credit Cards

» Major credit cards are widely accepted in the main tourist centres.

» They often attract a surcharge of around 5% from Moroccan businesses.

» The main credit cards are MasterCard and Visa; if you plan to rely on plastic cards,

the best bet is to take one of each.

» The best option is a combination of credit and debit cards plus cash; this gives you something to fall back on if an ATM swallows your card or banks are closed.

» Most large bank branches will give you cash advances on Visa and MasterCard.

» For a list of usually reliable banks, see the ATM section.

Moneychangers

» Any amount of foreign currency may be brought into the country.

» It is illegal to import and export dirham.

» Banks and exchange bureaus change most currencies, but Australian, Canadian and New Zealand dollars are often not accepted.

» Moroccan banking services are reasonably quick and efficient.

» Rates vary little from bank to bank, although it doesn't hurt to look around.

» You'll need your passport to change travellers cheques (plus the travellers cheque receipt in some places), to get cash advances and, sometimes, to change cash.

» Hang on to all exchange receipts; you'll need them to convert leftover dirham at most Moroccan banks and *bureaux de change*.

CEUTA & MELILLA

» In the Spanish enclaves of Ceuta and Melilla the currency is the euro.

» The Moroccan banks on the enclaves' borders exchange cash only.

» Banks in Ceuta and Melilla deal in dirham, but at rates inferior to those in Morocco.

Tipping

» Tipping is an integral part of Moroccan life; almost any service can warrant a tip.

» Don't be railroaded, but the judicious distribution of a few dirham for a service willingly rendered can make your life a lot easier.

» Bear in mind that unskilled workers in Morocco earn less than Dh100 per day.

Travellers Cheques

» Travellers cheques are not recommended in Morocco – even large city banks often do not accept them.

» If you want to carry some anyway, as a fallback in the event of theft, American Express (Amex), Visa and Thomas Cook cheques are the most useful, and have efficient replacement policies.

» Keeping a record of the cheque numbers and those you have used is vital when it comes to replacing lost travellers cheques.

TIPPING IN MOROCCO

SERVICE	TIP
Restaurant	10%
Cafe	Couple of dirham
Museum guides	Dh3-5
Porters	Dh3-5
Public-toilet attendants	Dh2-3
Baggage handlers	Dh3-5
Petrol-pump attendants	Dh3-5
Gardiens de voitures (car-park attendants)	Dh3-5; Dh10 for overnight parking

» Make sure you keep this record separate from the cheques themselves.

» Almost all banks charge commission on travellers cheques.

» Normally the commission is around Dh10 to Dh20 per cheque; check before changing.

Photography

» Morocco is a photographer's dream, but never point your camera at anything that's vaguely military or could be construed as 'strategic'.

* This includes airports, bridges, government buildings and members of the police or armed forces.

* This becomes more of an issue near the Algerian border and further south, particularly in the Western Sahara.

* Hide your camera when going through checkpoints in and near the Western Sahara.

» It is common courtesy to ask permission before taking photographs of people.

* Urban Moroccans are generally easygoing about it.

* In the countryside locals are not so willing to have cameras pointed at them.

* Women and older people very often don't want to be photographed.

* Respect their right to privacy and don't take photos.

» Memory cards and batteries for digital cameras are quite easy to find in photography shops in major cities (especially Marrakesh and Casablanca).

* For a short visit it's easier to bring equipment from home.

* A USB memory stick is useful for backing up photos, but most internet cafes can burn you a CD if needed.

» Kodak and Fuji colour negative film (35mm and APS), as well as video tapes, are readily available in bigger cities and towns.

* They are marginally more expensive than in Europe.

* Slide film is more difficult to come by.

* If you buy film in Morocco, check expiry dates.

* Professional photo labs offer the most professional processing services.

» Lonely Planet's *Travel Photography* provides comprehensive advice on taking terrific photos when you're on the road.

Post

» Offices of **Poste Maroc** (www.bam.net.ma, in French) are distinguished by a yellow 'PTT' sign or the 'La Poste' logo.

» *Tabacs*, the small tobacco and newspaper kiosks scattered about city centres, are equally useful. They often sell stamps, and have shorter queues.

» The postal system is fairly reliable, if not terribly fast.

» It takes at least a week for letters to reach European destinations, and two weeks to get to Australia and North America.

» Sending post from a city normally gives mail a head start.

» Worldwide postcards cost around Dh13 to send, and letters around Dh18.

Sending Parcels

» The parcel office, indicated by the sign 'colis postaux', is generally in a separate part of the post-office building.

» A 1kg package costs Dh122 to send via airmail to the UK, Dh123 to the USA and Dh202 to Australia.

» Parcels should not be wider, longer or higher than 2m; weight limit varies according to the destination, but it's typically 30kg.

» To ship goods home, buy a box and a shipping form at the post office and take them to the shop where you purchased your wares.

» The shopkeeper knows the product and can wrap and pack the pieces well with newspaper and cardboard.

» If you've purchased carpets, the vendor should have rolled and bound them in plastic sacks; if not, return and ask them to do so.

» Label the outside of the package in several places with a waterproof pen.

» Be very clear about the destination country; marking it in French as well as English helps.

» Indicate the value of the contents if you like, but you may be charged taxes at the receiving end.

» Don't seal the box! Customs officers at the post office need to view the contents.

» Your packages will be weighed and you will be charged Par Avion (air) freight rates unless you specify that you prefer the items shipped by land.

» The overland service is considerably less expensive but can take three months.

» Valuable speciality items such as large furniture may involve customs clearance.

» Shopkeepers should be able to arrange clearance and shipping for you, but make sure you keep copies of all documentation in case the goods never arrive.

Express Mail & Couriers

» There is usually an Express Mail Service (EMS), also known as Poste Rapide, in the same office as parcel post.

» In Morocco the service is run by **Chronopost International Maroc** (www.chronopost.ma, in French).

» A 500g package costs from Dh308 to send to the UK or Europe, and DH329 to North America or Australia.

» Private courier companies, with offices in the major cities, are faster and more expensive.

» Couriers include **DHL** (www.dhl-ma.com) and **TNT** (www.tnt.com, in French).

Receiving Mail

» Having mail addressed to 'Poste Restante, La Poste Principale' of any big town should not be a problem.

* Some offices only hang on to parcels for a couple of weeks before returning them.

* You'll need your passport to claim mail and you'll be charged Dh3.50 for collection.

» An alternative way to receive letters is through Amex.

* Amex (http://tinyurl.com/2u45epf) is represented by the travel agency Voyages Schwartz, with branches in Casablanca, Tangier and Marrakesh.

* To qualify for the client mail service, you're supposed to have Amex travellers cheques or an Amex card.

* You're usually asked to produce a passport for identification and there may be a charge if you're not an Amex client.

» If you have built a good relationship with the staff of a hotel and they are trustworthy, you could ask them if you can receive post there.

Public Holidays

Banks, post offices and most shops shut on the main public holidays, although transport still runs.

New Year's Day 1 January
Independence Manifesto 11 January – commemorates the publication in Fez of the Moroccan nationalist manifesto for independence.
Labour Day 1 May
Feast of the Throne 30 July – commemorates King Mohammed VI's accession to the throne.
Allegiance of Oued Eddahab 14 August – celebrates the 'return to the fatherland' of the Oued Eddahab region in the far south, a territory once claimed by Mauritania.
Anniversary of the King's and People's Revolution 20 August – commemorates the exile of Mohammed V by the French in 1953.
Young People's Day 21 August – celebrates the king's birthday.
Anniversary of the Green March 6 November – commemorates the Green March 'reclaiming' the Western Sahara on November 1975.
Independence Day 18 November – commemorates independence from France.

Safe Travel

Morocco is one of the safest African countries for travellers. The great majority of Moroccans are friendly and honest, but there are traps for the unwary.

Drugs

» Morocco's era as a hippie paradise, riding the Marrakesh Express and all that, has been consigned to history.

» Plenty of fine dope (known as kif) may be grown in the Rif Mountains, but drug busts are common and you wouldn't want to investigate Moroccan prison conditions from the inside.

TRAVEL DURING RAMADAN
ALISON BING

Ramadan Mubarak! (Happy Ramadan!) Ramadan is a lunar month dedicated to *sawm* (fasting) – from sun-up to sundown, the faithful abstain from food, drink, tobacco and sex to concentrate on spiritual renewal – and *zakat* (charity).

Many businesses operate with limited hours and staff, so try to book accommodation, transport and tours in advance. Call offices to ensure someone will be there. Most restaurants close by day; pack lunches or reserve at tourist restaurants. Stores often close in the afternoon; bargaining is better before thirst is felt in the midday heat.

Sunset streets fill with Ramadan finery, light displays, music, tantalising aromas and offers of sweets. After an *iftar* (fast-breaking meal) of dates, soup or savoury snacks, people gobble sweets until the late-night feast. More visits and sweets follow, then eventually the *sahur* (meal before the sunrise).

Travellers are exempt from fasting; it's hard enough at home under controlled conditions. To show support, avoid eating or drinking in public, and grant people privacy at prayer times.

When a new friend offers you sweets or invites you to a feast, you honour by accepting; refusal is crushing. You're not obliged to return the favour or eat the sweets; reciprocate the *zakat* by giving to a local charity perhaps.

» Always bear in mind that it's illegal to buy, sell or consume hashish in Morocco.

» If caught, you may be looking at a fine and, in the worst case, a prison sentence. See p493 for more information.

» Hashish is sometimes referred to as 'chocolate', the Spanish slang, or more often just as 'something special' or 'shit', which you will definitely be in if you get caught.

» Although locals continue to smoke as a recreational pastime, as a tourist you're more vulnerable.

SCAMS & HASSLE

The vast majority of Moroccan stories of extortion and rip-offs are drug-related. Recent legislation and a hard government line may have forced dealers to give up their more aggressive tactics, but the hassle has not disappeared.

A common ploy is to get you stoned, force you to buy a piece of hash the size of a brick and then turn you over to the police (or at least threaten to). Once you've purchased hash, or even just smoked some, you're unlikely to call the cops, and the hustlers know it.

HOT SPOTS

Associating with Tangier's lowlife is for the initiated only.

New arrivals should ignore late-night offers of hashish and grass. These dealers have a sixth sense for greenness, and won't miss an opportunity to squeeze ridiculous amounts of money out of frightened people.

Watch out for similar scams in Tetouan, Assïlah, Casablanca and Marrakesh.

Issaguen and the Rif Mountains are Morocco's kif-growing heartland.

Issaguen in particular can be a bag-load of trouble, and is best avoided unless you're accompanied by a reliable guide.

MAJOR ISLAMIC HOLIDAYS

The rhythms of Islamic practice are tied to the lunar calendar, which is slightly shorter than its Gregorian equivalent, so the Muslim calendar begins around 11 days earlier each year.

The following principal religious holidays are celebrated countrywide, with interruptions and changes of time to many local bus services and increased pressure on transport in general. Apart from on the first day of Ramadan, offices and businesses close.

Moulid (or Moulud) an-Nabi celebrates the birth of the Prophet Mohammed. Children are often given presents.

Eid al-Fitr (Feast of the Breaking of the Fast), also known as Eid as-Sagheer (the Small Feast), is the end of Ramadan. The four-day celebration begins with a meal of *harira* (lentil soup), dates and honey cakes, and the country grinds to a halt during this family-focused period.

Eid al-Adha (Feast of the Sacrifice) sees sheep traded for the ritual sacrifices that take place throughout the Muslim world during this three-day celebration. Also known as the Eid al-Kabeer (Grand Feast), it commemorates Ibrahim's sacrifice.

Because the precise date of an Islamic holiday is in doubt until a few days before the start of that month, the dates below are only approximate.

HOLIDAY	2011	2012	2013	2014
Moulid an-Nabi	16 Feb	5 Feb	25 Jan	14 Jan
Ramadan begins	1 Aug	21 Jul	10 Jul	29 Jun
Eid al-Fitr	30 Aug	19 Aug	8 Aug	28 Jul
Eid al-Adha	6 Nov	26 Oct	15 Oct	4 Oct
New Year begins (year)	27 Nov (1433)	16 Nov (1434)	5 Nov (1435)	25 Oct (1436)

MAJOUN

» You may occasionally be offered *majoun,* a sticky, pasty mass (not unlike molasses) made of crushed marijuana seeds.

» A small ball of *majoun* can send you reeling (see Paul Bowles' *Their Heads Are Green* or *Let It Come Down* for descriptions).

» Anyone with a slight tendency to paranoia when smoking dope should be aware that this is a common reaction among first-time *majoun* munchers.

SPAIN

Although the Spanish police have a relaxed attitude towards small amounts of cannabis for private use, Spanish customs will come down hard on people entering the country from Morocco in possession of the drug, and you could be done for trafficking.

THANKS BUT NO THANKS

To avoid being hounded to within an inch of your life in the medina, and to help prevent nervous breakdowns and embarrassing incidents of 'medina rage', the following are useful tactics:

» Politely decline all offers of help, and exchange a few good-humoured remarks (preferably in Arabic), but don't shake hands or get involved in any lengthy conversation.

» Give the impression that you know exactly where you're going, or explain that you employed a guide on your first day and now you'd like to explore on your own.

» Wear dark sunglasses and retreat to a cafe, restaurant or taxi if you're beginning to lose your cool.

» In extreme situations, use the word 'police' and look like you mean it.

» If you're taking a car across, the chances that it will be searched are high.

» *Never* carry parcels or drive vehicles across borders for other people.

Getting Lost

» A minor irritation is the ever-changing street names in Moroccan cities.

» For years, there's been a slow process of replacing old French, Spanish and Berber names with Arabic ones.

» The result so far is that, depending on whom you talk to, what map you use or which part of the street you are on, you're likely to see up to three different names.

» The general Arabic word for street is *sharia*, or *derb* in medinas (*zankat* for smaller ones).

» The French *avenue*, *boulevard* and *rue* are still common. In the north and far south you'll still find the Spanish *calle* and *avenida*.

» In some cases the Arabic seems to have gained the upper hand. This is reflected in this guidebook, in which some streets appear as *sharia* or *zankat* if local usage justifies it.

MEDINAS

» Street names won't help much in the labyrinthine medinas, although a compass might.

» If you feel you're getting lost, stick to the main paths (which generally have a fair flow of people going either way) and you'll soon reach a landmark or exit.

Plumbing

» Patience is required when it comes to Moroccan plumbing.

» In cheap, unclassified hotels without star ratings, trickling cold water and squat toilets are common.

» Sometimes hot water is enthusiastically promised, but it may be tepid at best and only available at certain times of the day.

» In rural areas, water is sometimes heated by a wood fire, but this comes at an environmental cost. Wood is expensive, water is often in short supply and deforestation is a major problem in Morocco.

» In small towns and rural areas the hammam may be a better bet.

Smoking

» Smoking is a national pastime in Morocco and nonsmoking restaurants and hotels are almost unheard of.

» This generally affects popular places rather than top-end restaurants and hotels, where you may find nonsmoking areas.

» Most popular eateries and cafes have outdoor seating, so the problem is reduced.

» Only the very top-end hotels (including Sofitel) have a nonsmoking policy.

WOMEN

» In Muslim countries, it is generally considered unacceptable for women to smoke.

» Particularly outside the big cities, you'll seldom see women smokers.

» This is a cultural rather than religious dictate.

» Although most religious leaders condemn smoking, like drinking, as *haram* (forbidden), only during daylight hours of the holy month of Ramadan is the habit seriously eschewed.

» This shouldn't affect foreigners too much, although women may wish to refrain from smoking within local homes and be discreet elsewhere.

Theft

On the whole, theft is not a huge problem in Morocco. Travellers can minimise risk by being vigilant (but not paranoid) in the major cities and taking some basic precautions.

» When wandering around the streets, keep the valuables you carry to a minimum.

» Keep what you must carry around with you well hidden.

» Be particularly careful when withdrawing money from ATMs.

» External money pouches attract attention.

» Neck pouches or moneybelts worn under your clothes attract less attention. They are better places to keep your money, passport and other important documents.

» If you prefer to keep things in your room (preferably locked inside your suitcase), nine times out of 10 you'll have no trouble.

» Rooms in top-end hotels often have safes.

» Other hotels sometimes have a safe in reception, where you could stow valuables such as a camera.

» Leaving anything in a car, even out of sight, is asking for trouble.

» In the large cities, notably Casablanca, there are some desperate people, and physical attacks on foreigners occasionally occur.

» Treat the medinas with particular caution at night.

» The medinas in Marrakesh, Casablanca and Tangier have a particular reputation for petty theft.

» In such medinas, a common tactic is for one person to distract you while another cleans out your pockets.

Touts, Guides & Hustlers

Morocco's notorious hustlers and *faux guides* (unofficial guides) remain an unavoidable part of the Moroccan experience.

» *Brigades touristiques* (tourist police) were set up in the principal tourist centres, and anyone suspected of trying to operate as an unofficial guide could face jail and/or a huge fine. This has greatly reduced, but not eliminated, the problem.

» Hustlers are often desperate to make a living, and they can be persistent and sometimes unpleasant.

» You'll generally find them hanging around the entrances to the big cities' medinas, and outside bus, train and ferry stations.

» Having a siege mentality would be an overreaction.

» Indeed, when arriving in a place for the first time, you might benefit from the services of a guide, official or otherwise.

» Although high unemployment rates drive the numbers of *faux guides*, not all are complete imposters. Many are very experienced and speak half a dozen languages.

» Sometimes their main interest is the commission gained from certain hotels or on articles sold to you in the souqs.

DEALING WITH GUIDES

» Agree a price before setting off on a tour.

» Set some parameters on what you expect to see and the number of shops you're taken to.

» Unofficial guides charge around Dh50 to Dh100 per day.

» Rates should always be per guide, not per person.

GAUCHE, GREEN & GULLIBLE

Many Moroccans genuinely believe that Westerners, though perhaps more sophisticated than themselves, are infinitely more naive, gullible and even plain stupid. Some, including the notorious *faux guides*, may operate with this in mind.

Very early on in your encounter with these guides, you'll be sized up for what you're worth. Apart from physical indications such as your watch, shoes and clothes, you'll be assessed from a series of questions: how long you've been in Morocco, whether you've visited the country before, what your job is, whether you have a family (an indication of wealth) etc.

Always be suspicious of these unsolicited enquiries and pretend that you know the city or country well. A few words of Arabic will convince them of this.

Considered to be the most lucrative nationalities, in descending order, are the Japanese, Americans, Canadians, Australians, British, northern Europeans, southern Europeans, and Middle-Eastern Arabs. Sub-Saharan Africans and Arabs from other North African countries are considered the least lucrative.

A common starting point is claiming to want nothing more than friendship, saying they are keen to show you around town, take you to a cheap shop or help you find a hotel. Other classic approaches include wanting to practise English, or needing help with reading or deciphering official documents or letters from friends.

If you turn them down, some will try to play on your conscience by suggesting you are racist for not liking Moroccans or Muslims.

A good ploy is to shorten the exchange by just playing dumb. If you feel you're being categorised, you could cause confusion by pretending you're from an obscure country. Be warned, though: Moroccans have a real aptitude for languages, and it could place you on the back foot if your new friend starts spouting away in the fluent Ukrainian you claim to speak.

GOVERNMENT TRAVEL ADVICE

For the latest travel information log on to the following websites:

www.auswaertiges-amt.de German Federal Foreign Office.

www.fco.gov.uk/travel UK Foreign & Commonwealth Office.

www.minbuza.nl Dutch Ministry of Foreign Affairs.

www.mofa.go.jp Japanese Ministry of Foreign Affairs.

www.safetravel.govt.nz New Zealand Ministry of Foreign Affairs and Trade.

www.smartraveller.gov.au Australian Government's travel advice and consular information.

www.travel.state.gov US Department of State's Bureau of Consular Affairs.

www.voyage.gc.ca Canadian Consular Services Bureau.

» A few dirham will suffice if you want to be guided to a specific location (like a medina exit).

» Whatever you give, you'll often get the 'you can't possibly be serious' look. The best reply is the 'I've just paid you well over the odds' look.

» Maintain your good humour and, after a couple of days in a place, the hassle tends to lessen considerably.

» Official guides can be engaged through tourist offices and some hotels at the fixed price of around Dh250/300 per day (plus tip) for a local/national guide.

» It's well worth taking a guide when exploring Fez and Marrakesh medinas.

» The guide can help you find interesting sights and shops in the melee, stop you from getting lost and save you from being hassled by other would-be guides.

» If you don't want a shopping expedition included in your tour, make this clear beforehand.

DRIVING & TRANSPORT
» Drivers should note that motorised hustlers operate on the approach roads to Fez and Marrakesh. These motorcycle nuisances are keen to find you accommo-

dation and so on, and can be just as persistent as their counterparts on foot.

» Travellers disembarking (and embarking) the ferry in Tangier may receive some hassle from touts and hustlers.

» Arriving by train in cities like Fez and Marrakesh you may run into 'students' or similar, with the uncanny knowledge that your preferred hotel is closed or full, but they just happen to know this great little place...

Telephone

» Within Morocco, dial the local four-digit area code even if you are dialling from the same town or code area.

» You can make calls from *téléboutiques* (private telephone offices) and public payphones.

» Attendants at *téléboutiques* will usually change small notes into coins.

» Most payphones are card-operated.

» You can buy *télécartes* (phonecards) at *tabacs* and *téléboutiques*.

» Méditel's Dawlia card also works for national calls (from Dh0.75 per minute to a landline).

» Payphones have easy-to-follow instructions.

» Calling from a hotel normally doubles the cost of your call.

» Moroccan landline numbers start with 05.

International calls
» International calling cards are available from telecommunication shops such as branches of Méditel.

» If you can find a reasonable internet connection, a Skype call will likely be cheaper. Computers in internet cafes normally have headsets.

» Méditel's Dawlia card offers rates starting at Dh1.75 per minute.

» France, Spain and Italy are the cheapest countries to call, and rates are lower between 8pm and 8am, at weekends and on public holidays.

» To use the Dawlia card, call the 10-digit card number prefixed with 133, then type in the four-digit PIN number and follow the voice prompts.

Mobile Phones
» Morocco has three GSM mobile-phone networks:

• Méditel (www.meditelecom.ma)

USEFUL NUMBERS

See p17 for emergency numbers.
Morocco country code ☏212
International access code from Morocco ☏00
Directory enquiries ☏160
Spain country code (including Melilla and Ceuta) ☏34

- Maroc Telecom (www. iam.ma)
- Inwi (www.inwi.ma)

» Coverage is excellent, apart from in the Atlas and Sahara.

» If your mobile phone is unlocked, buying a prepaid mobile SIM card will likely be cheaper than using your phone on roaming.

» A Méditel prepaid SIM card costs Dh20, including Dh10 credit.

» Domestic calls cost from Dh1.20 per minute, international calls from Dh2.50 per minute.

» Calls are cheaper between 8am and 8pm.

» Texting a Moroccan number costs Dh1.

» You need to show a passport or other form of identification when buying a SIM card.

» *Téléboutiques*, newsstands and grocery stores sell credit.

» Moroccan mobile numbers start with 06.

Time

Standard Moroccan time is on GMT/UTC.

Daylight saving During the summer, the clock used to move forward one hour for daylight saving. In 2011, the daylight-saving period ran from April 2 until July 30. However, because the period ends at the beginning of Ramadan, which currently falls during the summer, it is likely to not take place in the coming years. Check www. timeanddate.com for more information.

Spain If you're travelling to/ from Spain (including Ceuta and Melilla), take particular care during Spain's daylight saving (late March to late October). Spanish clocks move forward one hour, becoming two hours ahead of Morocco.

Local attitudes Time is something that most Moroccans seem to have plenty

UPDATED MOROCCAN TELEPHONE NUMBERS

In 2009, the telephone number system in Morocco changed. Unfortunately, this doesn't mean every hotel and hammam had its business card reprinted, so you may have to add a digit to some numbers to get them to work. With old landline numbers, add a 5 after the initial zero (ie 035 00 00 00 becomes 0535 00 00 00). For old mobile-phone numbers, add a 6 after the initial zero (ie 072 00 00 00 becomes 0672 00 00 00). We have quoted new numbers in this book.

of; they're not in nearly as much of a hurry to get things done as most Westerners. Rather than getting frustrated by this, learn to go with the flow a little.

Toilets

» Flush toilets are a luxury in a country struggling with water shortages. Outside midrange and top-end hotels and restaurants, toilets are mostly of the squat variety.

» Squat toilets feature a tap, hose or container of water for sluicing – the idea being to wash yourself (with your left hand) after performing.

» There's often no toilet paper *(papier hygiénique)* so keep a supply with you.

» Don't throw the paper into the toilet as the plumbing is often dodgy; instead discard it in the bin provided.

» Women who have their period will need to take along a plastic bag for disposing of used tampons and pads.

» Public toilets are rare outside the major cities.

» If you find a public toilet, you'll need to bring a tip for the attendant, stout-soled shoes, and very often a nose clip.

Tourist Information

Cities and larger towns have tourist offices, which are normally repositories of

brochures run by uninformed staff. Often the receptionist in your hotel or another local will be more helpful than such bureaus. The best tourist offices are found in smaller destinations that are trying to promote themselves.

L'Office National Marocain du Tourisme (ONMT; www.visitmorocco.com, www. ruraltourism.ma) The Moroccan National Tourist Office runs most tourist offices.

Travellers with Disabilities

Morocco has few facilities for the disabled, but the country is not necessarily out of bounds for travellers with a physical disability and a sense of adventure. Some factors to be aware of:

» The awkward nature of narrow medina streets and rutted pavements can make mobility challenging at times even for the able-bodied.

» Not all hotels (almost none of the cheaper ones) have lifts, so booking ground-floor hotel rooms ahead of time is essential.

» Only a handful of the very top-end hotels have rooms designed for the disabled.

» Travelling by car is probably the best transport, though you'll be able to get assistance in bus and train stations (a tip will be required).

DIFFERENCES FROM STANDARD MOROCCAN TIME

COUNTRY	CAPITAL CITY	DIFFERENCE FROM MOROCCO
Australia	Canberra	+11hr
Canada	Ottawa	-5hr
France	Paris	+1hr
Germany	Berlin	+1hr
Japan	Tokyo	+9hr
Netherlands	Amsterdam	+1hr
New Zealand	Wellington	+13hr
Spain	Madrid	+hr
UK	London	0hr
USA	Washington DC	-5hr

» Many tour operators can tailor trips to suit your requirements.

» Vision- or hearing-impaired travellers are poorly catered for. Hearing loops, Braille signs and talking pedestrian crossings are nonexistent.

Organisations

Organisations that disseminate information, advice and assistance on world travel for the mobility impaired include the following:

Access-able Travel Source (www.access-able.com) An information provider for travellers with mobility problems.

Apparleyzed (www.apparleyzed.com) For paraplegic and quadriplegic people and others with spinal-cord injuries, featuring travel information.

Disabled Travelers Guide (www.disabledtravelersguide.com) A general guide for travellers with disabilities.

Mobility International USA (MIUSA; www.miusa.org) Promoting the inclusion of people with disabilities in international programs, with a page of air-travel tips.

Society for Accessible Travel & Hospitality (SATH; www.sath.org) Has news, tips and members' articles and blogs.

Visas

» Most visitors to Morocco do not require a visa and are allowed to remain in the country for 90 days on entry.

» In all cases, your passport must be valid for at least six months beyond your date of entry.

» Nationals of Israel and many sub-Saharan African countries (including South Africa) must apply in advance for a three-month visa (single/double entry about US$30/50).

» Applications are normally processed in 48 hours.

» You need three passport photos.

» In Morocco's neighbouring countries, there is a Moroccan embassy in Madrid (Spain) and consulates-general in locations including Algeciras; an embassy in Nouakchott (Mauritania) and a consulate-general in Nouâdhibou; and diplomatic missions in Algeria including an embassy in Algiers.

» Further information, including a list of Morocco's diplomatic missions, is available from the **Moroccan Ministry of Foreign Affairs and Cooperation** (www.maec.gov.ma).

» As visa requirements change, it's a good idea to check with the Moroccan mission in your country or a reputable travel agency before travelling.

Visa Extensions

» Most travellers requiring a visa extension find it easiest to head to mainland Spain, or even one of the Spanish enclaves in Morocco, and re-enter after a few days.

» Although doing a visa run generally presents few problems other than travel costs, it leaves you at the mercy of individual immigration officers on re-entry. Travellers have occasionally come unstuck this way.

» A harder alternative is to apply for a visa extension, issued by the Directorate General of National Security.

» Residence (a Carte de Sejour) is also available, but it is difficult to get and usually requires proof of employment.

» Go to the nearest police headquarters (Préfecture de Police) to check what documents they require.

» If possible, take a Moroccan friend to help you deal with the bureaucrats.

» In addition to your passport and three passport photos, the police will likely require a letter from your embassy requesting a visa extension on your behalf.

» Applications can take days or weeks, and different police headquarters employ different red tape to hold up proceedings.

International Health Certificate

If you're coming to Morocco from certain parts of Africa and South America where yellow fever is endemic, you'll need to show you've been vaccinated by producing a yellow-fever certificate or international certificate of vaccination.

In practice this is usually only required if you've travelled overland up through Mauritania, where yellow fever is endemic (although anecdotal evidence disputes how rigorously the order is enforced at the land border); or arrived from an African country on, say, a Royal Air Maroc flight.

We would recommend, however, that travellers carry a certificate if they have been in an infected country during the previous month to avoid any possible difficulties with immigration.

There is always the possibility that a traveller without a legally required, up-to-date certificate will be vaccinated and detained in isolation at the port of arrival for up to 10 days, or possibly repatriated.

You may need to prove you've been vaccinated against cholera if you are arriving from an afflicted zone.

See p524 for information on immunisations.

Volunteering

There are many international and local organisations that arrange voluntary work on regional development projects in Morocco.

They generally pay nothing, sometimes not even providing lodging, and are aimed at young people looking for something different to do for a few weeks over the summer.

Some of these organisations are really summer camps and international exchange programs.

Your embassy website may have links to NGOs and other projects, but unless you have a working knowledge of Arabic or Berber, or have specific specialist skills, many will not be interested.

Good starting points:

Idealist.org (www.idealist. org) Has volunteering and

job opportunities in Morocco.

International Cultural Youth Exchange (ICYE; www.icye.org) Allows you to search for upcoming Moroccan volunteer opportunities.

The Big Trip (Lonely Planet) This guide to gap years and overseas adventures includes a chapter on volunteering and working overseas, and a directory of resources.

Volunteer Abroad (www. volunteerabroad.com/Morocco. cfm) A good place to start looking for volunteer places, as it provides links to organisations with Moroccan programs.

Working Abroad (www.work ingabroad.com) Worldwide volunteering and teaching opportunities.

Organisations

International or local organisations that sometimes have Morocco placements or camps:

Baraka Community Partnerships (www.barakacommu nity.com) At the Tijhza Village Project in the High Atlas, it needs help with schemes including a reforestation program, repairing and renovating poorer homes, supporting the two schools, establishing a preschool and mothers' group, and developing compost toilets and bee-keeping programs.

Chantiers Sociaux Marocains (CSM; www.csm. netsons.org) Rabat-based NGO engaged in nationwide health, education and development projects, with international volunteers aged 18 to 35.

Jeunesse des Chantiers Marocains (http://perso.me nara.ma/youthcamps) A nonprofit, youth-focused travel and cultural exchange organisation. Programs in Marrakesh include volunteering at a nursery school or orphanage, with accommodation in a homestay organised.

Peace Corps (www.peace corps.gov) Long-established US volunteer scheme with deep roots in Morocco; volunteer programs lasting two years.

Projects Abroad (www. projects-abroad.co.uk) The UK-based organisation offers Moroccan volunteering holidays from healthcare to working with nomads.

United Planet (www. unitedplanet.org) One-week to one-year volunteering placements that sometimes include Morocco.

Women Travellers

» Prior to marriage, Moroccan men have little opportunity to meet and get to know women, which is a major reason why Western women receive so much attention.

» Not bound by Moroccan society and Islamic law, foreign women are seen as excitingly independent and generally available.

» Increased tourism to Morocco has also brought female visitors who are unprepared – or simply unaware that cultural mores in Muslim countries are different from the West.

» Around 70% of Morocco's population is under the age of 30, and by the end of their trip most Western women may think they've met every male in this group.

» The constant attention is impossible to shake off, no matter what tactic is employed, and soon becomes wearing.

» If it's your first time in Morocco, the first few days may be something of a shock, but you'll quickly develop a thick skin to deal with the unwanted looks and comments.

» The key to not spending your trip feeling hassled is to be wary but not paranoid – the low-level harassment rarely goes any further.

VISAS FOR NEIGHBOURING COUNTRIES

Embassies for the following countries are in Rabat (see the boxed text, p492).

Algeria

» The Morocco–Algeria border is closed.

» Visas are required by everyone except nationals of Arab League countries.

» Algeria prefers applicants to apply in their country of residence.

» For more information check out www.sahara-overland.com and Lonely Planet's *Africa*, which covers Algeria.

Mauritania

» Everyone, except nationals of Arab League countries, needs a visa to enter Mauritania.

» At the time of writing, Mauritanian visas were not being issued at the border.

» The Mauritanian embassy in Rabat issues 30-day and 90-day visas (Dh340/680).

» From Monday to Thursday, apply in the morning and pick up that afternoon or the following day. Get there before the embassy opens at 9am.

» You need two passport photos and a photocopy of your passport.

» Prepare to wax lyrical in French about how you've always dreamed of visiting Mauritanian spots such as Chinguetti and Parc National du Banc d'Arguin.

» For more info see www.sahara-overland.com and Lonely Planet's *West Africa*, which covers Mauritania.

Spain

» Spain is in the European Union and the Schengen Area.

» The Schengen Area covers 30 European countries, including Spain and all other EU-member countries apart from the UK and the Republic of Ireland.

» Ceuta and Melilla, the two Spanish enclaves in Morocco, have the same visa requirements as mainland Spain.

» Nationals of EU-member countries do not need a visa to enter Spain.

» Nationals of countries including Australia, Canada, Israel, Japan, New Zealand and the USA do not need a Schengen visa to cross a Schengen border.

» Your passport will be stamped upon arrival in the zone, and you can then stay for up to 90 days (straight or cumulative) within 180 days. This means, for example, that when you leave the zone at the end of a three-month stay, you are not permitted to re-enter for three months.

» For more info see Spain's **Ministry of Foreign Affairs and Cooperation** (www.maec.es/en) and Lonely Planet guides including *Mediterranean Europe*, which has chapters on Spain and Morocco.

» Moroccans are eager to help any traveller and there are times when being a woman is a distinct advantage, especially when lost or in some form of distress. Moroccans tend to be genuinely concerned for the 'weaker sex' and will offer protection and support if you feel you're in a potentially bad situation.

» Another benefit is that unlike male travellers, you'll have opportunities to meet local women.

» For more information on Moroccan women see p430.

Attitudes & Relationships

» The common attitude that a Westerner is a walking visa out of a country where unemployment is rife can affect women travellers.

» This perception is partly fuelled by Western women having holiday romances with local guys.

» Bored young men may have little to lose by wooing someone who can offer them an opportunity in another country, or a sexual liaison unavailable from Moroccan women.

» Some locals could be juggling several relationships at once.

» More positively, there are many success stories

about relationships of mixed nationality.

Dress

» Dress modestly. Despite some tourists' attire, hot pants and cleavage in the Marrakesh medina are never appropriate.

» Bikinis attract attention and sunbathing topless on the beach is inappropriate.

» At the other end of the scale, sporting a head scarf or even a jellaba (Moroccan-style flowing cloak) will earn you respect, particularly in the countryside, as well as questions about why you're wearing it: Are you Muslim? Are you Moroccan? Are you married to a Moroccan?

» For further suggestions about what to wear (and what not to wear) while in Morocco, see the boxed text on p433.

Havens & Pitfalls

» If the hassle gets too much, look for the ever-increasing number of places accustomed to having the business of single Moroccan women.

» The upper floor of a *salon de thé* (tea house), a restaurant or a hotel terrace is also good bet.

» Hammams are good male-free zones for a relaxing reprieve.

» Hotel and public swimming pools usually attract groups of men, whether they be swimming or drinking at a poolside bar.

» Be aware that some budget hotels double as brothels; any cheap hotel above a popular locals' bar is a likely contender.

» If you want an alcoholic drink, head to a large hotel rather than braving a bar, as these are generally rough, male-dominated establishments. Local women who frequent watering holes, even the posher ones, are generally prostitutes.

Male Travelling Companions

» Women travelling with male companions are unlikely to experience much of the hassle that solo women inevitably encounter.

» It may be better to claim to be a married couple rather than just friends (the latter concept is usually greeted with disbelief).

» If you are a Moroccan woman (or Moroccan in appearance) travelling with your non-Moroccan spouse, it is advisable to carry a copy of your marriage certificate. Premarital sex for Muslims is forbidden and Morocco has a stern attitude to prostitution.

» For the same reason, if your partner is thought to be Muslim you may meet with some uncomfortable situations at hotel reception desks. This is less of an issue in larger cities.

Transport

» Try to sit next to a woman on public transport, especially in grands taxis where you're squeezed in closely, and on trains, where you could potentially be trapped inside a compartment.

» Many women travel in grands taxis without problems, regardless of where they sit, but you could pay for two seats to get a ride by yourself in the front. It would be considerably more comfortable.

» Don't hitchhike.

Safety Precautions

» Crimes against women remain extremely rare. More common is verbal abuse from both men and women.

» In places that have seen a large influx of tourists in recent years, problems can occur.

» We've received reports of physical harassment at music festivals in Essaouira.

» Women travellers should take a few sensible precautions:

• Never compromise your safety for the sake of economy.

• Don't wander about alone at night, as there's an attitude that all 'good women' should be at home after dark; take a taxi.

• Don't walk alone in remote areas such as isolated beaches, forests and sand dunes.

• Wearing dark glasses is good for avoiding eye contact, but don't spend your entire Moroccan journey hiding behind them.

• Don't react with aggression – it could be returned in kind. A good-humoured *non merci* or *la shukran* ('no thank you') is much more effective than abuse.

• The key word to use is 'respect', a concept that most Moroccans hold dear.

» A wedding ring may help you avoid unwanted attention – along with a photo of your 'husband' and 'child'. The fact that you're travelling without them will arouse suspicion, but you could counter this by saying you'll be meeting them at your next destination.

» Many Moroccan men aren't too concerned whether you're married or not. They may insist they're just being friendly, and might even invite you home to meet their mother.

Work

» With huge unemployment and a largely out-of-work youthful population, Morocco isn't fertile ground for job opportunities.

» A good command of French is a prerequisite and some Arabic would help.

» If you secure a position, your employer will have to

help you get a work permit and arrange residency, which can be a long process.

» There are more volunteering opportunities (see p503).

Teaching English

There are a few possibilities for teaching English as a foreign language in Morocco, although they are not terribly well paid.

Rabat is one of the best places to start looking.

The best times to try are around September and October (the beginning of the academic year) and, to a lesser extent, early January. Having a TEFL (Teaching English as a Foreign Language) qualification will be useful.

American Language Centers (www.aca.org.ma) Ten schools around the country.

British Council (www.brit ishcouncil.org/morocco.htm) Has occasional openings; candidates need a TEFL qualification.

Dave's ESL Cafe (www. eslcafe.com) Has Africa and Middle East forums for teachers.

TEFL.com (www.tefl.com) Has a database of vacancies.

Transport

GETTING THERE & AWAY

Transport reform has encouraged the explosion of visitor numbers to Morocco. The government's 'open skies' policy has allowed the European budget airlines into the country.

However, the wonderful overland options shouldn't be ignored. Numerous ferry services from Europe are a more romantic and lower carbon option than flying, crossing to Africa and connecting Morocco to the European rail network.

Flights, tours and rail tickets can be booked online at www.lonelyplanet.com/bookings.

Entering Morocco

Entering Morocco through the airports, formalities are fairly quick and straightforward.

You will have to fill in an entry form where you state the purpose of your visit and your profession.

See p502 for information about visas.

Air

Airports & Airlines

Direct flights are available from cities across Europe, the Middle East, West Africa and North America – they go mostly to Casablanca and Marrakesh.

Royal Air Maroc (RAM; www.royalairmaroc.com) is Morocco's national carrier. It has a good safety record, with one major crash in the last 40 years.

For information about Moroccan airports and their facilities, visit the website of **Office National des Aéroports** (www.onda.ma).

Mohammed V International Airport (Casablanca; see p183) is Morocco's main international entry point. Other international airports:

» Menara airport (Marrakesh, p128)
» Fez airport (p323)
» Rabat-Salé airport (p198)
» Ibn Batouta International Airport (Tangier, p281)
» Al-Massira airport (Agadir, p368)
» Taourirt airport (Ouarzazate, p128)
» Nador (p294)
» Al-Hoceima (p281)
» Angad airport (Oujda, p357)

INTERNATIONAL AIRLINES

RAM is the main carrier, with increasing competition from the budget airlines.

Air Algérie (www.airalgerie.dz)
Air Arabia (www.airarabia.com)
Air Berlin (www.airberlin.com)
Air Europa (www.air-europa.com)
Air France (www.airfrance.com)
Alitalia (www.alitalia.com)

CLIMATE CHANGE & TRAVEL

Every form of transport that relies on carbon-based fuel generates CO_2, the main cause of human-induced climate change. Modern travel is dependent on aeroplanes, which might use less fuel per per person than most cars but travel much greater distances. The altitude at which aircraft emit gases (including CO_2) and particles also contributes to their climate change impact. Many websites offer 'carbon calculators' that allow people to estimate the carbon emissions generated by their journey and, for those who wish to do so, to offset the impact of the greenhouse gases emitted with contributions to portfolios of climate-friendly initiatives throughout the world. Lonely Planet offsets the carbon footprint of all staff and author travel.

British Airways (www.ba.com)

easyJet (www.easyjet.com)

EgyptAir (www.egyptair.com)

Emirates (www.emirates.com)

Etihad (www.etihadairways.com)

Iberia (www.iberia.com)

Jet4You (www.jet4you.com)

KLM-Royal Dutch Airlines (www.klm.com)

Lufthansa (www.lufthansa.com)

Qatar (www.qatarairways.com)

Ryanair (www.ryanair.com)

Thomson Airways (http://flights.thomson.co.uk)

Tunis Air (www.tunisair.com.tn)

Tickets

» For flights to Morocco, the high seasons are from July to the end of August, and mid-December to the end of December.

» The lowest seasons are November to mid-December, and January to mid-February.

» Ticket prices tumble if you use a European budget airline.

» Prices offered by travel agencies will be much the same as the airlines.

» Many airlines have code-share agreements and cheaper long-haul deals often entail changing plane (and carrier) in Europe.

» The cheapest fares are generally to Casablanca and Marrakesh.

» Cheaper student and under-26 tickets are available through agencies such as **STA Travel** (www.statravel.com).

» Otherwise, try the usual online booking engines.

INTERCONTINENTAL (RTW) TICKETS

» Morocco is not an easy destination to work into a round-the-world ticket.

» Most round-the-world tickets allow a maximum of 10 stopovers, although you

can buy extras. It will likely be cheaper and give you more flexibility to separately purchase budget flights between Morocco and a European airport such as Madrid.

» If you manage to incorporate Morocco into a round-the-world itinerary, heading west to the USA, you will likely have to detour via a European city or London anyway.

» Journeying east, you will probably need to stop over in the UAE to get a connecting flight to Asia or Australia.

Africa

One of the better African carriers, RAM has an extensive network of flights throughout North, West and Central Africa from Casablanca:

» Abidjan (Ivory Coast)

» Accra (Ghana)

» Algiers (Algeria)

» Bamako (Mali)

» Brazzaville (Congo)

» Cairo (Egypt)

» Conakry (Guinea)

» Cotonou (Benin)

» Dakar (Senegal)

» Douala (Cameroon)

» Libreville (Gabon)

» Lomé (Togo)

» Malabo (Equatorial Guinea)

» Niamey (Niger)

» Nouakchott (Mauritania)

» Ouagadougou (Burkina Faso)

» Tunis (Tunisia)

» Tripoli (Libya)

From other parts of Africa, travelling via the Middle East or Europe will likely be cheaper than connecting to one of the above routes.

Iberia's flights between Johannesburg (South Africa) and Madrid, with connections to Morocco, are usually competitively priced.

Australasia

There are no direct flights between Australia or New Zealand and Morocco.

Flights travel via the Middle East or Europe. British Airways, Emirates, Etihad and Qatar offer these routes.

It can be cheaper to fly to London, Paris or Madrid and continue to Morocco with a budget airline.

Continental Europe

The network of flights between Europe and Morocco is constantly changing, as budget airlines change their routes.

RAM flies to most western European capitals from Casablanca.

FRANCE

France is comprehensively connected to Morocco.

Air France Flies from Paris to Casablanca and Rabat.

easyJet Flies from Paris and Lyon to Casablanca, Marrakesh and Agadir, with additional flights from Paris to Fez and Tangier, and from Basel–Mulhouse–Freiburg to Marrakesh.

Jet4You Budget airline flying from Paris to Casablanca, Marrakesh, Agadir, Fez, Oujda and Rabat; from Bordeaux, Lyon, Marseilles and Toulouse to Casa, and from Nantes and Toulouse to Marrakesh.

RAM Flies between Casablanca or Marrakesh and Paris, Bordeaux, Lille, Lyon and Toulouse, with additional services between Casa and Basel–Mulhouse–Freiburg, Marseilles, Montpellier, Nantes, Nice and Strasbourg. Also flies between Paris and Agadir, Essaouira, Fez (also to/from Marseilles), Ouarzazate, Oujda (also to/from Marseilles), Rabat and Tangier.

Ryanair Links Paris and Marseilles with Fez, Marrakesh, Nador and Tangier, and also has an additional Marseilles–Agadir service.

GERMANY

Air Berlin Flies to Casablanca, Agadir, Nador and Tangier from Cologne, Hamburg, Munich and several other German cities.

Lufthansa Flies Frankfurt–Casablanca.

RAM Flies from Dusseldorf and Frankfurt to Casablanca and Nador.

Ryanair Flies from Dusseldorf and Frankfurt to Marrakesh, Agadir and Fez, plus Bremen–Marrakesh.

SPAIN

Air Europa Flies from Madrid and Asturias to Marrakesh.

easyJet Flies from Madrid to Casablanca, Marrakesh and Tangier.

Iberia Flies from Madrid and Barcelona to Casablanca, Marrakesh and Tangier, with additional flights to Casa from Malaga and Valencia, and to Melilla from locations including Madrid, Majorca and Malaga.

RAM Flies from Madrid and Barcelona to Casablanca, Marrakesh and Tangier, with additional flights to Casa and other cities from Las Palmas, Malaga, Seville and Valencia.

Ryanair Flies from Madrid, Barcelona and other cities to Marrakesh, Fez and Nador, and from Madrid to Oujda and Tangier.

Middle East

The Middle East is the connecting hub for travellers from the Far East.

Air Arabia The budget airline flies from Sharjah (UAE) to Casablanca via Istanbul (Turkey).

Emirates Flies Casablanca–Dubai (UAE).

Etihad Flies Casablanca–Abu Dhabi (UAE).

Qatar Flies Casablanca–Doha (Qatar).

RAM Flies to Casablanca from Beirut (Lebanon), Dubai, and Riyadh and Jeddah in Saudi Arabia.

UK

There is a good choice of flights from the UK, including charter and budget options.

It's also possible to build an itinerary with the budget airlines travelling via continental Europe.

British Airways Flies from London to Marrakesh.

easyJet Flies from London to Marrakesh and Agadir, and Manchester–Marrakesh.

RAM Flies from London to Casablanca, Marrakesh and Tangier.

Ryanair Flies from London to Marrakesh, Agadir and Fez, and from Bristol, East Midlands and Edinburgh to Marrakesh.

Thomson Airways Flies from London and Manchester to Marrakesh.

USA & Canada

Given the dearth of direct flights from North America, it's worth looking at the cheaper option of a return ticket to London or continental Europe, with an onward flight with a budget airline.

RAM Flies from Casablanca to New York (with connections across the USA) and Montréal.

Land

Border Crossings

For information on visas for the following countries see the boxed text on p504.

Algeria This border remains closed and Algeria is reluctant to reopen it until the status of the Western Sahara is resolved.

Mauritania The only crossing is in the Western Sahara between Dakhla (Morocco) and Nouâdhibou (Mauritania).

Spain You can cross to mainland Spain via the Spanish enclaves of Ceuta (see p281) and Melilla (see p294) in northern Morocco.

Continental Europe

BUS

Buses mostly enter Morocco on the ferries from Spain.

All passengers have to disembark for customs and immigration.

It's possible to buy tickets to Moroccan destinations from as far away as London, but journeys are long and a budget flight would likely be cheaper.

Buses to Spain leave Casablanca most days. Book a week in advance, or further ahead if your plans clash with a major Spanish or French holiday, as buses fill up with Moroccans working abroad.

Most buses cross the Mediterranean via Tangier, but some cross between Nador and Almería.

Bus companies:

Alsa (www.alsa.es) A Spanish bus company serving Morocco.

CTM (www.ctm.ma, in French) Compagnie de Transports au Maroc, Morocco's national line, operates buses from Casablanca and other Moroccan cities to Spain, France, Belgium, Germany and Italy.

Eurolines (www.eurolines.com) A consortium of European coach companies operating across Europe and into Morocco. It has offices in major European cities, and you can buy tickets and passes online.

Linebus (www.linebus.es, in Spanish) A Spanish bus company serving Rabat, Casablanca, Meknès and Marrakesh.

Supratours (www.supratours.ma, in French) Morocco's best coach line, run by train company ONCF, has weekly departures from the major northern Moroccan cities to destinations across Spain, France and Italy.

Tramesa (http://perso.menara.ma/tramesa07, in French) A reliable service with good links between Morocco and Spain.

» European hire companies do not usually permit their vehicles to be driven to Morocco. See p516 for information on car hire in Morocco.

» If you intend to take a Moroccan hire car to the Spanish enclaves of Ceuta or Melilla, you must have a letter from the hire company authorising you to take the car out of Morocco.

» Some hire companies will not allow you to take their car out of the country.

» If you're entering Morocco via Ceuta or Melilla, take the opportunity to fill up on duty-free fuel.

» For more information on bringing a vehicle to Morocco, see p515.

TRAIN

Travelling to Morocco by train and ferry from Europe is a viable and civilised option.

You can travel from London to Tangier via Paris and Madrid in less than 48 hours, with a night in Algeciras (Spain).

Morocco is not part of the InterRail and Eurail systems, so you will have to buy tickets locally to add the country onto a European trip. See p520 for information on train travel in Morocco.

In Algeciras, the train station is about 10 minutes' walk from the ferry terminals for Morocco. If you arrive during the day you should be able to quickly transfer onto one of the regular ferries.

Useful resources:

Man in Seat 61 (www.seat61. com) The best website for train travel, with comprehensive, regularly updated information on getting to Morocco by train.

Thomas Cook European Rail Timetable (www. thomascookpublishing.com) The best planning tool for European rail travel, published monthly with updated schedules.

Mauritania

» The trans-Saharan route via Mauritania is the most popular and straightforward route from North Africa into sub-Saharan Africa, tackled every year by numerous adventurous overlanders.

» From the Dakhla turn-off on the N1, the route into Mauritania runs south along the coast for 328km, then crosses the border and follows the Atlantic past the Parc National du Banc d'Arguin from Nouâdhibou south to the Mauritanian capital, Nouakchott.

» While this route is generally regarded as safe, check safety advice before travelling: the murder of a family of French tourists near Nouakchott in 2007 and related Al-Qaeda threats led to the cancellation of the 2008 Paris–Dakar rally through Mauritania.

» Take plenty of water and food, and set off early in the morning.

» This route is entirely paved, making it the only sealed road across the Sahara (apart from a 5km stretch in the no-man's land between the two border posts).

» Moroccan border formalities are processed in the basic settlement of Guergarat.

» The border, 18km from Guergarat, is heavily mined, so stay on the road.

» Mauritanian currency (ouguiya, UM) is available at the border, and on the black market in no-man's land.

» Vehicle searches and requests for a *petit cadeau* (little present) are not uncommon, particularly if the Mauritanian officials find alcohol or cheap Moroccan petrol on you.

» Alcohol consumption is illegal for Muslims in Mauritania, and non-Muslims are expected to refrain from transporting and distributing alcohol.

» From the border, it's a 41km drive along the peninsula to the first major Mauritanian town, Nouâdhibou.

» Useful resources:

• Horizons Unlimited's **Sahara Travel Forum** (www.horizonsunlimited. com) has a wealth of advice on travel between Morocco and Mauritania.

• The **Sahara Overland** (www.sahara-overland.com) book and website are essential resources for trans-Saharan travel.

CAR & MOTORCYCLE

» See p515 for general information about bringing a vehicle into Morocco.

» As this route traverses the Sahara and, at the border, a minefield, it's highly recommended to travel with other vehicles and set off early in order to reach the border before dusk (particularly if you are travelling in a 2WD).

» It's advisable to fill up with petrol at every available station.

» Some stations south of Dakhla may be out of fuel, in particular the last station 50km before the border.

» As well as getting stamped in by the police, you need to buy a 30-day temporary-vehicle-import form (€10).

MINIBUS & JEEP

» There are ad hoc transport links from Dakhla to the Mauritanian border and beyond.

» Minibuses and 4WDs leave from the military checkpoint on the road out of Dakhla.

» In Dakhla, Hotels Erraha and Sahara and the Sahara Regency are good places to pick up information and arrange transport, with locals or overlanders.

» Overlanders mostly ply the route between November and March.

» Grands taxis occasionally run to the border from the main station (Dh220). You'll then need to hitch to get to the Mauritanian checkpoint, as walking across the border is forbidden.

» A lift all the way to Nouâdhibou is preferable, or you will likely have to pay extortionate fees to travel on from the border.

» Prices range up to Dh600 for a seat in a vehicle going to Nouâdhibou.

» From Nouâdhibou, bush taxis to the border/Dakhla cost around UM2000/11,500.

» It's also worth asking around the hotels and camp sites for places in departing vehicles.

» Camping Chez Abba and Camping Baie du Lévrier ('Chez Ali') are popular with overlanders.

Sea

Extensive ferry links between northern Morocco and southern Europe make entering the country across the Mediterranean a popular option. In the summer the most popular route, Algeciras (Spain) to Tangier, is packed with day trippers and holidaymakers with campervans.

» You can combine the ferry journey with the bus, train or your own vehicle.

» From southern Spain and northern Morocco, you can just turn up at the dock and buy a ticket for the next ferry (apart from during August and Easter, when demand is highest and those with vehicles should book well in advance).

» All the port cities have numerous ticket offices and travel agencies, particularly in and around the ferry terminals, allowing you to walk between them and pick the best sailing for you.

» In Tangier and Algeciras, avoid the touts who try to guide you towards their favourite travel agency for their bit of commission.

» Tickets can also be purchased online.

» From Europe to Morocco, discounts for students and young people with an ISIC card or similar, InterRail or Eurail pass-holders and EU pensioners are often advertised.

» Children aged between two and 12 often travel for half the fare, those aged under two travel free, and over-60s can often get reductions.

» Discounts are less common in Morocco, but it's worth asking.

» Vehicles can be taken on most ferries for an extra fee; bicycles are normally free.

» Cabins are available on longer crossings.

» High season for ferries is generally the European summer (mid-June to mid-September), Christmas and New Year; low season is November to February.

» Fares can rise by up to 25% in high season.

» On most routes, more ferries run to cope with summer demand. Foot passengers are often safe to buy a ticket on arrival at the port, but it's worth booking in advance if you're driving a vehicle.

» Ferries to Tangier now dock at the new Tanger Med terminal, except for those from Tarifa (Spain). The older Tanger Port has traditionally been known for its hustlers, but they have largely been moved on.

France

» The journey from Sète (two hours by train from Marseilles) to Tangier takes 36 hours; to Nador takes 28 hours.

» The ferries are more luxurious than those linking Spain and Morocco.

» There are about five sailings weekly to Tangier, and one to Nador.

» Advance booking is recommended.

Gibraltar

» There's one fast ferry a day to/from Tangier.

» The trip takes a similar length of time to sailings to/from Algeciras, and tickets cost the same.

» Algeciras is a better option as it's a busier port with more choice.

FERRY COMPANIES & ROUTES

Direct Ferries (www.directferries.com) sells tickets for most of the below. The Europe-wide service has sites in most European languages, although its booking engine is temperamental.

Acciona Transmediterranea, Euroferrys and Ferrimaroc (www.trasmediterranea.es) Almería–Melilla, Almería–Nador, Algeciras–Ceuta, Algeciras–Tangier, Barcelona–Tangier, Málaga–Melilla.

Baleària (www.balearia.com) Algeciras–Ceuta, Algeciras–Tangier.

Comanav Algeciras–Tangier, Genoa–Tangier, Sète–Nador, Sète–Tangier.

Comarit (www.comarit.es, in Spanish) Algeciras–Tangier, Sète–Tangier, Tarifa–Tangier.

FRS (www.frs.es) Algeciras–Ceuta, Algeciras–Tangier, Gibraltar–Tangier, Tarifa–Tangier.

Grandi Navi Veloci (GNV; www.gnv.it) Barcelona–Tangier, Genoa–Tangier.

Grimaldi Lines (www.grimaldi-lines.com) Livorno–Tangier, Valencia–Tangier.

TRANSPORT GETTING THERE & AWAY

Spain

» Ferries from Spain to Morocco are plentiful.

» Tickets start at about €30.

» Hydrofoils and catamarans (also referred to as fast ferries) are used extensively, but are more expensive than ferries and can be disrupted by rough seas.

» The Acciona Transmediterranea group, which also includes Euroferrys and Ferrimaroc, has offices in all the locations it sails from and across Europe.

» Spanish passport control is uncomplicated, but non-EU citizens and Schengen visa-holders should make sure they get an exit stamp before boarding the ferry.

» You need to fill in an embarkation form on board, and get your passport stamped before disembarking.

» Customs can be slow on the Spanish side if you're coming from Morocco.

ALGECIRAS TO TANGIER

» This is by far the most popular and frequent crossing between Europe and Morocco.

» Ferries run at least every 90 minutes, and hourly in the summer.

» Services typically run from 7am (or 6am in summer) until 10pm, but during peak demand in August 24-hour services aren't unknown.

» The crossing typically takes an hour, but it varies according to the vessel.

» Competition keeps the prices uniform between operators.

» Some ferry companies offer 1st-class for an extra 20%, but it's barely worth it for the short trip.

ALGECIRAS TO CEUTA

» Car owners may find this route worthwhile because of the availability of tax-free petrol (and alcohol) in the Spanish enclave of Ceuta.

» Several daily high-speed ferries (30 minutes to one hour) leave in both directions between about 7am and 10pm.

ALMERÍA TO MELILLA

» Entering Morocco via the Spanish enclave of Melilla is the most hassle-free route from the Spanish mainland. You can also fill up on duty-free fuel here if you're driving (and booze if you're not).

» Unfortunately, the less-frequent crossings take up to eight hours.

» Ferries depart daily from Almeria, and on Monday morning and Sunday afternoon from Melilla.

ALMERÍA TO NADOR

» Nador is much quieter than Tangier, with little to offer travellers other than transport links to the rest of Morocco.

» There are five crossings a week in either direction, taking five/eight hours to Nador/Almería.

BARCELONA TO TANGIER

» Two companies offer this route to Tangier, one stopping in Barcelona en route from Genoa (Italy).

» The three weekly sailings take about 29 hours.

MÁLAGA TO MELILLA

» The daily (apart from Sunday) service is normally an afternoon/night ferry to/from Melilla.

» It takes up to eight hours.

TARIFA TO TANGIER

» Catamarans leave every hour or so and cross the strait in 35 minutes, making this the fastest and most practical route.

» The fare includes a free bus transfer to Algeciras on presentation of your ferry ticket.

» The transfer takes 50 minutes, making the trip via Tarifa a faster way to get to Algeciras than the slower direct ferries.

VALENCIA TO TANGIER

» This new service is part of the Tangier–Livorno (Italy) sailing.

» This leg of the journey takes 20 hours, leaving around midday and arriving at 8am in both directions.

Italy

» Three companies sail along the Mediterranean from Italy to Tangier, from Livorno via Valencia and Genoa via Barcelona.

» The new Livorno service takes 56 hours.

» The three weekly Genoa sailings take about 50 hours.

Tours

There is no shortage of tour operators running organised trips to Morocco. Perusing the adverts in weekend newspapers or travel magazines like **Wanderlust** (www.wanderlust.co.uk) can overwhelm you with choice.

See also p519 and p31 for specialist operators offering activities from climbing to rafting.

Heritage Tours (www.heritagetoursonline.com; US) Top-end customised travel with an emphasis on culture and history, including an itinerary focusing on Jewish Morocco.

Ibertours Travel (www.ibertours.com.au; Australia) Moroccan, Spanish and Portuguese specialist running tours typically starting in Spain, from exploring Morocco's Andalusian heritage to ascending Jebel Toubkal.

Naturally Morocco (www.naturallymorocco.co.uk; UK) Eco-tourist operator, deeply involved in local communities, especially around Taroudannt (see p374). Special-interest tours include horse riding, wildlife, kayaking, rafting around Bin el-Ouidane Dam and yoga.

Sherpa Expeditions (www.sherpa-walking-holidays.co.uk; UK) A well-respected trek-king company that organises escorted and self-guided treks in the High Atlas and Jebel Sarhro.

Travel Zest (www.travelzest.com; UK) Offers diverse packages including beach holidays, family trips, romantic getaways and city breaks.

Yallahtrek (www.yallahmorocco.com; Taliouine) The Jebel Siroua trekking specialist also offers cultural activities for individuals, groups and families (see p377).

GETTING AROUND

Getting around Morocco is pretty straightforward – transport networks between towns are good, and even off the beaten track there's often something going your way. RAM offers internal flights, the rail network is excellent in linking the major cities, and large bus companies like CTM are comfortable and efficient. Local networks are cheaper and more cheerful but do the job.

Car hire is relatively expensive but gives you the most freedom, although navigating the big cities can be stressful. Good sealed roads are generally the order of the day, with much investment being poured into areas like the Rif to improve their connectivity. Roads in remote mountain and desert areas are often just *piste*.

Air

» National carrier **Royal Air Maroc** (RAM; ☎0890 00 08 00; www.royalairmaroc.com) is the main domestic airline.

» RAM serves Tangier, Nador, Oujda, Fez, Casablanca, Er-Rachidia, Marrakesh, Essaouira, Agadir, Laâyoune and Dakhla.

» Most flights involve changing in Mohammed V International Airport, Casablanca, which RAM uses as a hub.

» Popular routes such as Casablanca–Marrakesh often have several flights per day.

» Flying is considerably more expensive than taking the bus, but may be worth it if you are pushed for time. The 2¼-hour flight from Casablanca to Dakhla costs from about Dh800 to Dh3000, compared with Dh580 for a first-class seat on the 17-hour overnight Supratours bus journey.

» You can buy tickets online and at RAM offices and travel agencies.

» English is spoken at RAM's call centre.

Bicycle

Mountain biking can be a great way of travelling in Morocco. There are plenty of opportunities for getting off the beaten track, with thousands of kilometres of remote *pistes* to be explored.

Hazards There are no special road rules pertaining to cyclists, who are afforded little consideration by drivers. Although surfaced roads are generally well maintained once completed, they tend to be narrow and, in less-frequented areas such as the Anti Atlas, have jagged edges, which can be hairy given the kamikaze drivers. Cyclists have reported being besieged by gangs of stone-throwing children in remote areas, so watch your back.

Hire Moroccan cities and towns are better explored on foot, though you will find bicycles for hire in places like Essaouira and Taroudannt (around Dh50 to Dh100 per day) and they can make sense if you are staying far from the centre. Don't expect to find the latest models of mountain bike, or you will be sorely disappointed.

Information The UK-based **Cyclists' Touring Club** (CTC; www.ctc.org.uk) is a mine of information, with a forum and suggested routes and maps. The USA-based **International Bicycle Fund** (IBF; www.ibike.org) has a page on Morocco.

Preparation Distances are great and you'll need to carry all supplies with you, plus plenty of drinking water. Useful spares to bring include spokes, brake blocks and inner tubes.

Storage Cities such as Marrakesh have cycle parks, where your bike can be parked and watched over for the day.

Tours A few tour operators offer mountain-biking trips.

Transport and camping Bus companies will generally carry bicycles as luggage for an extra fee. Likewise on trains, although it's generally only possible to transport bikes in the goods wagon. Camp sites generally charge around Dh10 for bikes.

Bus

The cheapest and most efficient way to travel around the country, buses are generally safe, although their drivers sometimes leave a little to be desired.

Bus stations Some Moroccan bus stations are like madhouses, with touts running around calling any number of destinations of buses about to depart. Most cities and towns have a single central bus station (*gare routière*), but Supratours and CTM sometimes maintain separate terminals, and often have offices outside the station. Occasionally, there are secondary stations for a limited number of local destinations.

Touts Touts will happily guide you to a ticket booth (and take a small commission from the company).

Always double-check that their recommended service really is the most comfortable, direct and convenient option.

Luggage Bus stations in the main cities have left-luggage depots (*consigne*), sometimes open 24 hours. Padlock your bags. More often than not you'll be charged for baggage handling, especially if your gear is going on top of the bus – Dh5 is common.

Costs Bus travel is cheap considering the distances covered. CTM fares from Casablanca to Agadir, Marrakesh, Fez and Tangier are Dh220, Dh130, Dh70 and Dh100 respectively. Companies including Supratours offer 1st- and 2nd-class tickets, although the difference in fare and comfort is rarely great.

Reservations Where possible, and especially if services are infrequent or do not originate in the place you want to leave, book ahead for CTM and Supratours buses. Particularly busy routes are Marrakesh–Essaouira and Casablanca–Marrakesh, where you may need to reserve seats two days in advance in high season.

Daytime journeys Many buses have rather meagre curtains, so to avoid melting in the sun, pay attention to where you sit. Heading from north to south, sit on the right in the morning and the left in the afternoon; east to west, sit on the right, or on the left if travelling from west to east. You will often be assigned a seat when you purchase your ticket, but you can ask to choose a place.

Night-time journeys Operating on many intercity routes, night buses can be both quicker and cooler, although not necessarily more sleep-inducing.

Stops Most bus trips longer than three hours incorporate a scheduled stop to stretch your legs and grab a snack. Buses are often delayed at police checkpoints for about 10 minutes – longer than grands taxis, whose local drivers usually know the police.

Bus Operators

CTM
Compagnie de Transports au Maroc (www.ctm.ma) has the most comprehensive nationwide network, serving most destinations of interest to travellers. Established in

---

TRAVELLERS' CODE OF ETIQUETTE

When travelling on public transport, it's considered both selfish and bad manners to eat while those around you go without. Always buy a little extra that can be offered to your neighbours; a bag of fruit is a good choice.

Next comes the ritual. If you offer food, etiquette dictates that your fellow passengers should decline it. It should be offered a second time, a little more persuasively, but again it will be turned down. On a third, more insistent offer, your neighbours are free to accept the gift if they wish to.

If you are offered food, but you don't want it, it's good manners to accept a small piece anyway, and to pat your stomach contentedly to indicate that you are full. In return for participating in this ritual, you should be accorded great respect, offered protection and cared for like a friend.

1919, it's Morocco's oldest bus company.

» On CTM buses, children aged four years and over pay full fares, which tend to be 15% to 30% more expensive than most other lines – comparable to 2nd-class fares on normal trains.

» Tickets can normally be purchased in advance.

» Most CTM buses are modern and comfortable, and some 1st-class buses have videos (a mixed blessing), air-conditioning and heating (they sometimes overdo both).

» There is an official Dh5-per-pack baggage charge on CTM buses.

» Once you have bought your ticket, you get a baggage tag, which you should hang on to, as you'll need it when you arrive.

SUPRATOURS
The ONCF train company runs **Supratours** (www.su pratours.ma) to complement its rail network. For example, train passengers continuing south from Marrakesh link up at the station with buses to destinations including Agadir and Ouarzazate.

» See our Supratours & Train Network map.

» It's possible, at train ticket offices, to buy a ticket covering a complete trip (including the bus journey). For example, you could travel from Azrou to Nador using a bus to Fez, then train via Taourirt.

» On trains, travellers with tickets for connecting buses have priority.

» Supratours are similar to CTM in terms of both its fares and the comfort of its buses.

OTHER COMPANIES
Morocco's other bus companies, all privately owned, mostly operate regionally.

» In the south of the country, Satas and SAT are good second choices, as is Trans

Ghazala in the north. They offer slightly cheaper and less comfortable and efficient services than CTM and Supratours.

» At the bottom end of the price range, on shorter routes, there are a fair number of two-bit operations with one or two well-worn buses.

» Don't expect comfortable seats or air-conditioning.

» These services only depart when the driver considers them sufficiently full, and then frequently stop to recruit more passengers. They're dirt cheap and good fun for shorter trips.

» The cheaper buses rarely have heating in winter, even when crossing the mountains, so make sure you have plenty of warm clothing.

» Traffic is sometimes held up by snowdrifts in the mountain passes, particularly on the Marrakesh–Ouarzazate road.

» On older buses, legroom is limited and long journeys can be an endurance test for taller travellers.

» On all but the most local buses, everyone gets a seat.

Car & Motorcycle

Morocco is a country made for touring, and you'll see plenty of campervans on the road. Having a car gives you freedom to explore the more unusual routes in your own time – particularly in the south and the Rif Mountains, where travelling by the local buses is time-consuming.

Daylight driving is generally no problem and not too stressful, though Moroccan drivers need to be treated with more caution than their counterparts in the West.

The roads connecting Morocco's main centres are generally good, and there's an expanding motorway network. A new motorway along the Mediterranean coast is

set to join the three already in place:

» From Tangier down the Atlantic Coast to El-Jadida.

» From Rabat inland to Fez via Meknès.

» From Casablanca south to Agadir via Marrakesh.

Bring Your Own Vehicle

» All vehicles travelling across international borders should display the nationality plate of their country of registration.

» A warning triangle to use in event of breakdown is useful.

» Moroccan law requires a Green Card (carte verte, or International Motor Insurance Card), which gives proof of insurance.

» Drivers also need their vehicle registration document (carte grise) and their driving licence or international driver's permit.

» Your car insurance policy at home may cover your vehicle for Morocco, especially if you live in continental Europe, although not all insurers cover Morocco.

» Your insurer or local automobile association can provide further details about necessary documentation.

» Try to obtain insurance and a Green Card before leaving home. Otherwise local insurance (assurance frontiere), costing about Dh650 for 10 days, must be purchased at the ferry port or a nearby broker (bureau d'assurance).

» Ask for the optional constat amiable form, which both parties fill out in the event of a minor road accident. They can also be purchased at tabacs in cities.

» At the port, or on the ferry on longer crossings, you must also fill in the TVIP form (temporary vehicle importation declaration – declaration d'admission temporaire de moyens de transport), valid for six months.

ROAD DISTANCES (KM)

	Agadir	Al-Hoceima	Casablanca	Dakhla	Er-Rachidia	Essaouira	Fez	Figuig	Marrakesh	Meknès	Nador	Ouarzazate	Oujda	Rabat	Safi	Smara	Tan Tan	Tangier	Tarfaya
Al-Hoceima	1091																		
Casablanca	511	536																	
Dakhla	1173	2264	1684																
Er-Rachidia	681	616	545	1854															
Essaouira	160	887	351	1346	745														
Fez	756	275	289	1920	329	640													
Figuig	1076	669	920	2249	395	1081	719												
Marrakesh	273	758	232	1448	510	170	461	905											
Meknès	740	335	229	1913	346	580	57	741	446										
Nador	1095	175	628	2260	510	979	339	516	822	399									
Ouarzazate	354	992	442	1548	295	380	687	701	175	652	816								
Oujda	1099	293	632	2272	514	983	334	326	826	403	104	820							
Rabat	602	445	91	1775	482	442	196	877	321	139	535	528	541						
Safi	294	792	256	1467	683	129	545	1078	148	486	884	361	888	347					
Smara	551	1642	1062	746	1232	724	1307	1627	824	1291	1646	926	1650	1153	845				
Tan Tan	331	1422	842	842	1012	504	1087	1407	504	1071	1426	705	1430	933	625	220			
Tangier	880	323	369	2053	608	720	303	988	598	287	1086	811	609	278	625	1431	1211		
Tarfaya	544	1635	1055	633	1225	517	1300	1620	817	1284	1639	919	1643	1146	838	331	213	1424	
Tetouan	892	278	385	2065	604	736	247	931	675	258	437	820	555	294	641	1443	1223	57	1436

» You must present this form when you (and your vehicle) leave the country.

» You can also download the form from the website of **Morocco Customs** (www.douane.gov.ma, in French), where it's referred to as D16TER.

» There is no need for a *carnet de passage en douane* for temporarily importing your vehicle to Morocco.

Driving Licence

» International driving permits are recommended for Morocco by most automobile bodies, but many foreign, including EU, licences are accepted provided they bear your photograph.

» You must carry your licence or permit and passport when driving.

Fuel & Spare Parts

Availability The country is well served with petrol stations, although they become fewer and further between south of Goulimime. If you're travelling off the beaten track, refuel at every opportunity. Keep a close eye on the gauge in the southern desert and fill up wherever you get a chance, as stations don't always have supplies of fuel. Spare jerry cans are a good idea for emergencies. Don't fill up with the 'petrol' sold at the roadside near the Algerian border (particularly around Berkane). It's smuggled from Algeria and contains who-knows-what along with the petrol – not necessarily good for engines.

Costs Leaded and less-common unleaded *(sans plomb)* petrol cost around Dh10 per litre and diesel *(gasoil)* is around Dh7. Costs rise the further you go from the northwest of the country. The big exception is the Western Sahara, where tax-free petrol, about 30% cheaper, is sold by the Atlas Sahara service station chain. Fuel is also very reasonably priced in the duty-free Spanish enclaves of Ceuta and Melilla.

Parts Moroccan mechanics are generally good and decent-sized towns should have at least one garage, most with a range of spare parts for Renaults and other French cars. If you can fit replacement parts yourself, ask a Moroccan friend to help you buy the parts, as this may help to keep the price closer to local levels.

Hire

Age Most Moroccan car-rental companies require drivers to be at least 21 (or 23 in a few cases).

Costs Renting a car in Morocco isn't cheap, and may

not make financial sense for individuals or couples with standard itineraries. A three- or five-door economy model, typically a Dacia Logan, costs about Dh300 per day for a week or so with unlimited mileage. For longer rentals of three weeks or more, lower daily rates around Dh250 are sometimes available. Pre-booking a car online before leaving home will enable you to find the cheapest deals. You can sometimes get reasonable prices through the agent or airline you book your flight with.

Deposit Most companies demand a (returnable) cash deposit (Dh3000 to Dh5000) unless you have a credit card, in which case an impression is made of your card (make sure you get this back later).

Operators With international firms such as **Hertz** (www.hertz.com), **Budget** (www.budget.ma, in French), **Europcar** (www.europcar.com), **National** (www.nationalcar.com) and **Avis** (www.avis.ma), you can book online before leaving home. There are also numerous local agencies, many with neighbouring booths at airports – good places to haggle. The best cities to hire cars are Agadir, Casablanca, Fez, Marrakesh and Tangier, where competition is greatest.

Potential pitfalls No matter where you hire your car, make sure you understand what is included in the price and what your liabilities are. Some travellers using smaller, less-reputable firms have been stung after paying by credit card, realising they've been charged 10 times the agreed fee after returning home. Always check the car's condition before signing up, and make sure it comes with a spare tyre, tool kit and full documentation – including insurance cover. Keep the car's

documents and your licence in your room at night, rather than in the car, as you will need to produce them if the car is stolen or damaged. Hold onto receipts for oil changes and any mechanical repairs, as these costs should be reimbursed.

Insurance and tax Insurance must, by law, be sold along with all rental agreements. When bargaining, make sure that prices include collision damage, insurance and tax (20%). You should also take out Collision Damage Waiver insurance, typically about Dh35 to Dh60 a day. Even with this, there is often an excess of up to Dh5000, meaning that if you have an accident that's your fault, you are liable to pay damages up to this amount. Super Collision Damage Waiver, which eliminates or minimises the excess, may be available for an extra Dh60 or so a day. It's also a good idea to take out personal insurance (around Dh30 a day), although your travel insurance may cover this.

Piste Unless you hire a 4WD, your rental agreement will probably not allow off-road (*piste*) driving. If you damage the car or break down on a *piste* you will not be covered for damages. It might be worthwhile to OK your route with the rental company before setting off.

Service International agencies do not necessarily offer better vehicles than local companies, but usually provide better service in the event of a breakdown or accident, as they have networks of offices around the country. Often a replacement car can be sent out to you from the nearest depot. If you plan to stay in a particular region, a cheaper local company may have a reasonable network in that area.

Return With larger agencies you can hire the car

in one place and leave it elsewhere, although this usually involves a fee (typically Dh2000), even if you want to return the vehicle in a city where the company has a branch. Companies charge per hour (Dh100 is not uncommon) for every hour that you go over time on the return date.

Motorcycle

» Motorcycle touring is becoming popular, but many bikes are unfamiliar in Morocco, particularly those with larger capacity engines, so repairs can be tricky.

» Some basic maintenance knowledge is essential.

» You should carry a good tool kit and all necessary spares, including cables and levers, inner tubes, puncture repair kit, tyre levers, pump, fuses, chain, washable air filter and cable ties.

» Some insurance policies do not allow foreign motorcycle licences to be used in Morocco.

» Some companies offer motorcycle (Dh300 per day for a DT 125cc Yamaha) and scooter (from Dh150 per day) hire.

» **Horizons Unlimited** (www.horizonsunlimited.com) has a wealth of advice on biking in the region.

Parking

» In many towns, parking zones are watched by *gardiens de voitures* (car-park attendants).

» Technically, you do not have to pay them unless they can give you a ticket, which shows they are working for the municipality. Nonetheless, it's generally a good idea to pay a few dirham towards a trouble-free parking experience.

» The parking attendants are not a guarantee of safety, but they do provide some peace of mind and will no doubt offer to wash your car for you.

» In an increasing number of big city centres, parking tickets are issued from kerbside machines (Dh2 to Dh3 per hour for a maximum stay of two hours). Parking is free on Sundays.

» Parking is not allowed on kerbsides painted in red and white stripes.

» Stopping is not allowed on green and white stripes.

» Fines for illegally parked cars can reach Dh1500.

» Wheel clamps are used in many cities, including Rabat and Casablanca, for illegal parking.

Roadblocks

» Police control points are common on main roads in and out of most sizable towns.

» Foreigners are unlikely to be stopped, but it's still a good idea to slow down and put on your best smile. You'll probably get a smile in return and be waved through.

» Roadblocks are also common in sensitive areas like the Western Sahara; the Rif Mountains around the cannabis-producing region of Ketama; and the road to Figuig near the Algerian border.

» Police are more vigilant in these areas, but at most, you will be asked to show your passport, driving licence and vehicle's papers, and asked the purpose of your visit and where you're heading.

Road Hazards

Accident rates are high; road accidents killed some 4000 people and injured more than 100,000 in 2009.

Your fellow motorists will often be haphazard or aggressive drivers, particularly in towns, which can make negotiating urban streets a hair-raising experience. Treat all vehicles as ready to veer out and cut you off at inopportune moments.

Look out for pedestrians and cyclists who will invariably cross or swerve in front

of you. Approaching towns, roads are often busy with people (including groups of schoolchildren), bicycles, horse and carts, donkeys and so on.

Desert In the *hammada* (stony desert), tar roads sometimes disappear without warning, replaced by stretches of sand, gravel and potholes. If a strong *chergui* (dry, easterly desert wind) is blowing and carrying a lot of dust, you'll have to wait until it eases off if you don't want to do your car considerable damage.

Mountains Crossing the mountain ranges in winter often involves driving through snow and ice. The High Atlas passes are often closed due to snow in winter. Seek local advice before travelling, or check the road signs along the routes out of Marrakesh.

Medinas Entering cities and towns, park outside the medina or find out if the route to your accommodation is easily driveable, as narrow medina streets weren't designed for cars.

Minor roads Many minor roads are too narrow for normal vehicles to pass without going onto the shoulder. It's better to slow down and steer the car's right-hand wheels onto the dirt than to try squeezing the vehicle along the road proper. The road surface often has jagged edges, which can cause punctures. Stones thrown up from the road edges by oncoming vehicles present a danger for windscreens.

Night Driving at night is particularly hazardous: it's legal for vehicles travelling under 20km/h to drive without lights.

Pistes Some *pistes* can be negotiated in an ordinary car with reasonable clearance, such as a Dacia Logan, but many are 4WD territory only. Whatever vehicle you have, the going will be slow.

Many stretches of mountain *piste* are often impassable in bad weather: Michelin map No 742 (formerly No 959) generally has these sections marked.

Preparation Always ask locals about road conditions before setting off on a journey, check your tyres, and take a usable spare plus an adequate supply of water and petrol.

Road Rules

» In Morocco you drive on the right hand-side of the road.

» In towns, give way to traffic entering a roundabout from the right when you're already on one.

» The fine for missing a red stop sign is Dh700.

» The speed limit in built-up areas is 40km/h.

» Outside the towns there is a national speed limit of 100km/h, rising to 120km/h on the motorways.

» Road signs implore drivers to follow the law and wear seatbelts, but in practice few people do, preferring instead to place their trust in Allah. Following suit leaves you open to fines, so do belt up.

» Tolls apply on the motorways – for example, Rabat–Tangier is about Dh60 and Rabat–Casablanca is Dh20. You take a ticket upon entering the motorway and pay at the end.

» In the event of an accident, especially involving injuries, drivers are officially required to remain at the scene. Vehicles cannot be moved until the police have arrived – this may take hours.

» Pick up a *constat amiable* form in case you have an accident (see p515).

Local Transport

Bus

» The bigger cities have public bus services.

» Tickets are typically Dh4.

» They're often handy for crossing the ville nouvelle (new town).

» They can be ludicrously overcrowded and routes often hard to discern.

» Petits taxis are often an easier and faster option.

Grand Taxi

The elderly Mercedes vehicles you'll see on Moroccan roads and gathered near bus stations are shared taxis (*grands taxis* in French or *taxiat kebira* in Arabic).

The Ziz and Drâa Valleys, the Tizi n'Test and the Rif Mountains, all scenic areas not well-served by buses, are good to visit in a taxi.

Routes A big feature of Morocco's public transport system, grands taxis link towns to their neighbours, often in a relay system that may necessitate changing a few times on longer journeys. Taxis sometimes ply longer routes when there's demand, and in areas such as the Western Sahara where towns are spread out. In general, these services are rarer and usually leave first thing in the morning.

Seats Grands taxis take six extremely cramped passengers (two in the front, four in the back) and leave when full. It can often be advantageous to pay for two seats to get the taxi going earlier, and give yourself more space. This is particularly useful for lone women, as you should get the front seat to yourself.

Fares The fixed-rate fares are generally a little higher than bus fares, but are still very reasonable. When asking about fares, make it clear you want to pay for *une place* (one spot) in a *taxi collectif* (shared taxi). Another expression that helps explain that you don't want the taxi to yourself is *ma'a an-nas* (with other people).

Private hire Touts and drivers sometimes try to bounce tourists into hiring the whole taxi (*complet*). Smile and stand your ground if you're not interested, but hiring an entire taxi is sometimes a good option – especially if you're travelling with a small group, or you want to travel along an unpopular route without waiting hours for other passengers. Before setting off, negotiate patiently for a reasonable fare; if you're hiring the whole taxi, aim for six times the fare for one place. If you'll be travelling through a scenic area, make sure plans for stopping en route are clear.

Hazards Grand-taxi drivers often have a boy-racer mentality. Overtaking on blind corners can be a badge of honour, and speed limits are only adhered to when there's a police roadblock in sight. Many accidents involve overworked grand-taxi drivers falling asleep at the wheel, so night-time journeys are best avoided. Seatbelts are a rarity – and questioning this may be taken as a slur on your driver's skills.

Petit Taxi

» Cities and bigger towns have local petits taxis, which are typically a small Peugeot or Fiat, and are a different colour in every city.

» Petits taxis are not permitted to go beyond the city limits.

» They are licensed to carry up to three passengers

» They are usually, but not always, metered. To ask in French for the meter to be switched on, say '*tourne le conteur, si'l vous plaît*'.

» There is often a fixed price for journeys, which varies according to the city.

» Where taxis are not metered, agree on a price beforehand.

» If the driver refuses to use the meter and won't give you a price, ask to stop and get out. Most petit-taxi drivers are perfectly honest, but those in Marrakesh are notoriously greedy with tourists.

» Multiple hire is common. The price should be the same whether you hail an empty taxi and pick up other passengers en route, or there are already others in a taxi you wave down, or you travel alone.

» From 8pm (often 9pm in summer) there is normally a 50% surcharge – or just Dh1 or so where a fixed-fare system is in place.

Pick-up Truck & 4WD

» In more remote areas, especially the Atlas Mountains, locals travel between villages in Berber *camionettes* (pick-up trucks), old vans or the back of trucks.

» This is a bumpy but adventurous way to get to know the country and people a little better.

» It can mean waiting a considerable time (even days) for a lift.

» When travelling between remote towns and villages, the best time to find a lift is early on market days (generally once or twice a week).

» 4WD taxis operate on remote *pistes* that would destroy normal taxis.

Tours

See also p513 and p31 for specialist operators offering activities from birdwatching to horse riding.

Amira Tourisme (www. amiratourisme.com; Marrakesh) Readers recommend this Italian company's desert excursions.

Atlas Sahara Trek (www. atlas-sahara-trek.com; Marrakesh) Winter camel-treks to Erg Chigaga and summer hikes into the M'Goun valley.

Authentic Morocco (www. authentic-morocco.com; Marrakesh & UK) This reliable company supports local communities and practises low-impact tourism, offering itineraries from camel treks to tours of Roman ruins.

Desert Majesty (www.de sertmajesty.com; Ouarzazate) Recommended by readers, offering tours and bivouac-based adventures throughout the Atlas and Moroccan Sahara.

Equatorial Travel (www. equatorialtravel.co.uk; UK) Tailor-made trips and set itineraries, focused on areas including music, photography and walking, run by a small agency based on the fair-trade concept.

Gecko's Grassroots Adventures (www.geckosad ventures.com; UK) Readers recommend Gecko's Moroccan itineraries, which last from a week to a month.

Journeys Elite (www. journeyselite.com; UK) Offers tailor-made trips such as Anti Atlas by 4WD, and High Atlas gorges to Erg Chebbi.

KE Adventure Travel (www.keadventure.com; UK) Adventure specialists with trekking, mountain-bike, climbing, family and photography itineraries across Morocco, from Essaouira to Jebel L'Kest.

Marrakesh Voyage (www. morocco-travel-agency.com; US) Has an extensive list of itineraries covering all bases, including those incorporating music festivals.

Mountain Voyage (www. mountain-voyage.com; Marrakesh) The Moroccan arm of UK-based Discover, owner of Kasbah du Toubkal, it offers mountain and desert trekking and 4WD excursions.

Nature Trekking Maroc (www.maroctrekking.com; Marrakesh) Off-the-beaten-track trekking, horse riding, mountain biking, skiing and 4WD trips.

Wildcat Adventures (www. wildcat-bike-tours.co.uk; UK) Offers road- and mountain-bike tours in the High Atlas and Anti Atlas, plus a bike-trek-camel itinerary.

Wilderness Travel (www. wildernesstravel.com; USA) Much-applauded culture, wildlife and hiking specialist, with itineraries from High Atlas treks to cruising the coastline.

Yallah (www.yallahmorocco. com; Marrakesh & UK) The decade-old company offers tailor-made tours plus two itineraries covering the imperial cities and southern Morocco, both ending in luxury in Marrakesh.

Your Morocco Tour (www. your-morocco-tour.com; Ouarzazate & USA) Recommended by readers, it offers tailor-made and set itineraries, from day trips out of Marrakesh to a nine-day Saharan journey.

Train

» Morocco's excellent train network is one of Africa's best, linking most of the main centres.

» The **Office National des Chemins de Fer** (ONCF; www. oncf.ma) runs the network.

» There are two main lines:

- Tangier down to Marrakesh via Rabat and Casablanca.

- Oujda or Nador in the northeast down to Marrakesh, passing Fez and Meknès before joining the line from Tangier at Sidi Kacem.

» Also operated by ONCF, Supratours buses (see p515) link many destinations to the train network.

» Trains are particularly convenient around Casablanca and Rabat, with services leaving every 30 minutes between the two cities and to nearby destinations such as Kenitra.

» The overnight Tangier–Marrakesh and Oujda–Casablanca trains have sleeping cars.

» Trains are comfortable, fast and run closely to their timetables.

» Reasonably priced, they're far preferable to buses where available.

» Drinks and snacks are available on the train.

» Smoking is not allowed in compartments.

» An excellent resource for railway travel, **Man in Seat 61** (www.seat61.com) has information on Moroccan trains.

Classes

» There are two types of train:

- *Rapide* (Train Rapide Climatisé, TCR) – standard for intercity services.

- *Ordinaire* (Train Navette Rapide, TNR) – less comfortable, without air-conditioning, apart from the double-decker TNR Rabat–Casablanca shuttle. Mostly late-night and local services.

» The main difference between the two is comfort, rather than speed.

» Prices given in the guide are for *rapide* trains (*ordinaire* trains are around 30% cheaper).

» First- and 2nd-class fares are available, with six seats in 1st-class compartments and eight in 2nd class.

» First-class tickets include a reserved seat, while in 2nd class you just sit in an empty seat.

» Second class is more than adequate on short journeys.

» Shuttle services operate regularly between Kenitra, Rabat, Casablanca and Mohammed V International Airport, and they supplement the *rapide* services on this line.

Costs

» Sample second-class fares:

- Casablanca to Marrakesh (Dh90, three hours)

- Rabat to Fez (Dh80, three hours)

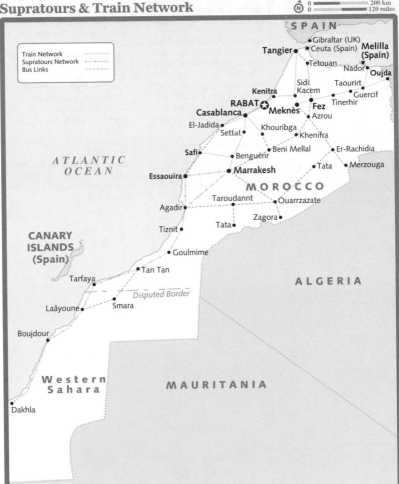

* Tangier to Marrakesh (Dh205, 8½ hours)

» All journeys in sleeping cars cost Dh350 in a four-bed couchette, and Dh450/600 for a single/double compartment.

» Children aged under four travel free.

» Children between four and 12 years get a reduction, normally of 50%, but less in a few cases including sleeping cars.

» At weekends travellers get a 25% discount on return trips,

or one-way trips longer than 180km, on major-line trains.

Stations & Timetables

» Stations aren't usually well signposted and announcements (in both French and Arabic) are frequently inaudible, so keep an eye out for your stop.

» Most stations are located in the ville nouvelle.

» In cities such as Tangier, Marrakesh and Rabat, the

main stations are sleek affairs with digital departure and arrival boards.

» Stations usually have left-luggage depots, which only accept luggage that can be locked.

» Timetables for the whole system are posted in French at most stations, and ticket offices can print out mini-timetables to individual destinations.

» ONCF's website also has timetables and prices.

Tickets

» You are advised to buy tickets at the station, as a supplement is charged for buying tickets on the train.

» Buy your ticket the day before you want to travel if possible, particularly if you want to travel 1st-class.

» Second-class seats cannot be reserved, so for this class you can normally pick up a ticket on the day of travel.

» First-class tickets can be bought up to a month before travel.

» Although you cannot buy tickets outside Morocco, buy them as far in advance as possible if you want to travel 1st-class around a major holiday, or at all times if you want a bed on an overnight service (particularly Tangier–Marrakesh).

» Always hang on to tickets, as inspectors check them on the trains and they are collected at the station on arrival.

Train Passes

Rail Pass This is available for seven/15/30 days (Dh600/1170/2100 to travel in 2nd class, Dh900/1600/3150 for 1st class). Pass prices drop for travellers aged under 26, and again for those under 12 years.

Carte Fidelité (Dh149) This is for those aged over 26 and gives you 50% reductions on eight return or 16 one-way journeys in a 12-month period.

Carte Chahab (six months Dh249) If you're under 26, this offers 25% to 50% discounts.

Carte Hikma (six months Dh99) For those aged over 60, this offers 25% to 50% discounts.

Health

Prevention is the key to staying healthy in Morocco, and a little planning before departure will save you trouble later. With luck, your worst complaint on your trip will be a bad stomach; infections are usually associated with poor living conditions and poverty, and can be avoided with a few precautions. Car accidents are a common reason for travellers to need medical help. Medical facilities can be excellent in large cities, but in more remote areas may be basic.

BEFORE YOU GO

Vaccinations Don't leave health matters to the last minute: some vaccines don't ensure immunity for two weeks, so visit a doctor four to eight weeks before departure.

First-aid courses Those heading to very remote areas may like to do a first-aid course, such as those offered by the American Red Cross and St John's Ambulance. Particularly if you're going trekking, you could take a wilderness medical training course, such as that offered by the **Royal Geographical Society** (www.rgs.org).

Medications Bring in their original, clearly labelled containers. A signed and dated letter from your physician describing your medical conditions and medications, including generic names, is also helpful. If carrying syringes or needles, ensure you have a physician's letter documenting their medical necessity. See your dentist before a long trip; carry a spare pair of contact lenses and glasses (and take your optical prescription with you).

Insurance

» Adequate health insurance is vital when travelling to Morocco. The national health service isn't always great and the few good private hospitals are expensive.

» You may prefer a policy that pays the medical facility directly rather than you having to pay on the spot and claim later, although in practice most Moroccan doctors and hospitals insist on payment upfront.

» If you have to claim later, make sure you keep all documentation.

» Carry proof of your insurance with you; this can be vital in avoiding any delays to treatment in emergency situations.

» Some policies ask you to call (reverse charge) a centre in your home country, which makes an immediate assessment of your problem; keep your insurer's emergency telephone number on you.

» Find out which private medical service your insurer uses in Morocco so that you can call them direct in the event of an emergency.

» Your policy should ideally cover emergency air evacuation home, or transport by plane or ambulance to a hospital in a major city, which may be essential for serious problems.

» Some policies offer lower and higher medical-expense options; the higher ones are chiefly for countries such as the USA, which have extremely high medical costs.

Medical Checklist

Consider packing the following items in your medical kit:
» antibiotics (if travelling off the beaten track)
» antibacterial hand gel
» antidiarrhoeal drugs (eg loperamide)
» paracetamol or aspirin
» anti-inflammatory drugs (eg ibuprofen)
» antihistamines (for hay fever and allergic reactions)
» antibacterial ointment (eg Bactroban) for cuts and abrasions
» steroid cream or cortisone (for allergic rashes)
» bandages, gauze and gauze rolls
» adhesive or paper tape
» scissors, safety pins and tweezers
» thermometer
» pocket knife
» DEET-containing insect repellent
» insect spray for clothing, tents and bed nets
» sun block

» oral rehydration salts (eg Dioralyte)

» iodine or other water-purification tablets

» syringes and sterile needles (if travelling to remote areas)

Websites

Useful to consult prior to departure:

CDC (www.cdc.gov/travel) US website.

Health Canada (http://tiny url.com/4tj653u)

International Association for Medical Advice to Travellers (IAMAT; www. iamat.org) Gives access to its online database of doctors with recognised training.

Lonely Planet (www.lonely planet.com)

MD Travel Health (www. mdtravelhealth.com) US website.

NHS (www.fitfortravel.nhs.uk) UK website.

Smartraveller (www. smartraveller.gov.au) Australian website.

WHO (www.who.int/ith)

Further Reading

International Travel Health Guide by Stuart Rose MD.
The Travellers' Good Health Guide by Ted Lankester.
Travellers' Health by Dr Richard Dawood.

IN MOROCCO

Availability & Cost of Health Care

Primary medical care is not always readily available outside major cities and towns. Your hotel may be able to recommend the nearest source of medical help, and embassy websites (see p491) sometimes list doctors and clinics.

In an emergency, contact your embassy or consulate.

Pharmacies These are generally well stocked, and pharmacists can provide advice (usually in French) covering common travellers' complaints. They can sell over-the-counter medication, often including drugs only available on prescription at home, and advise when more specialised help is needed. Double-check any unfamiliar purchases; readers have reported receiving incorrect and potentially dangerous medication for their conditions.

Doctors and clinics Particularly outside the major cities, if you are being treated by a doctor or at a clinic, you will often be expected to purchase medical supplies on the spot – even including sterile dressings or intravenous fluids.

Dental care Standards are variable – Marrakshi street dentists around the Djemaa el-Fna aren't recommended! Travel insurance doesn't usually cover dental work other than emergency treatment.

RECOMMENDED VACCINATIONS

Although no specific vaccinations are required for Morocco, America's Centers for Disease Control and Prevention (CDC) suggests the following as routine:

» Diphtheria
» Tetanus
» Measles
» Mumps
» Rubella
» Polio

The CDC also suggests the following for Morocco:

» Hepatitis A and B
» Typhoid
» Rabies

Before leaving home, ensure that all your routine vaccination cover is complete. Ask your doctor for an international certificate of vaccination, listing all the vaccinations you've received.

Infectious Diseases

Hepatitis A

Spreads Through contaminated food (particularly shellfish) and water.

Symptoms and effects Jaundice, dark urine, a yellow colour to the whites of the eyes, fever and abdominal pain. Although rarely fatal, it can cause prolonged lethargy and delayed recovery.

Prevention Vaccine (Avaxim, VAQTA, Havrix) is given as an injection, with a booster extending the protection offered. Hepatitis A and typhoid vaccines can also be given as a combined single-dose vaccine (hepatyrix or viatim).

Hepatitis B

Spreads Through infected blood, contaminated needles and sexual intercourse.

Symptoms and effects Jaundice and liver problems (occasionally failure).

Prevention Travellers should make this a routine vaccination, although Morocco gives hepatitis B vaccination as part of routine childhood vaccination. It is given singly, or at the same time as hepatitis A.

HIV

Morocco has a growing HIV infection rate of 0.11%, primarily found in cities such as Agadir and Marrakesh, and rising above 5% in some areas.

Spreads Through infected blood and blood products; sexual intercourse with an infected partner; 'blood to blood' contacts, such as through contaminated instruments during medical, dental, acupuncture and other body-piercing procedures, or sharing used intravenous needles.

Leishmaniasis

Spreads Through the bite of an infected sandfly or dog. It may be found in rural areas in the Atlas Mountains, where sandflies are more prevalent between June and October.

Symptoms and effects Slowly growing skin lump or sores. It may develop into a serious, life-threatening fever, usually accompanied by anaemia and weight loss.

Prevention and treatment Avoid sandfly bites. There is no vaccine, but treatment with an antimonial drug such as Glucantime or Pentostam is straightforward, usually involving an injection.

Rabies

Spreads Through bites or licks on broken skin from an infected animal. Rabies is endemic to Morocco.

Symptoms and effects Initial symptoms are pain or tingling at the site of the bite with fever, loss of appetite and headache. If untreated, both 'furious' and less-common 'dumb' rabies are fatal.

Prevention and treatment People travelling to remote areas, where a reliable source of post-bite vaccine is not available within 24 hours, should be vaccinated. Any bite, scratch or lick from a warm-blooded, furry animal should immediately be thoroughly cleaned. If you have not been vaccinated and you get bitten, you will need a course of injections starting as soon as possible after the injury. Vaccination does not provide immunity, it merely buys you more time to seek medical help.

Tuberculosis

Spreads Through close respiratory contact and, occasionally, infected milk or milk products.

Symptoms and effects Can be asymptomatic, although symptoms can include a cough, weight loss or fever months or even years after exposure. An X-ray is the best way to confirm if you have tuberculosis.

Prevention BCG vaccine is recommended for those mixing closely with the local population, whether visiting family, planning a long stay, or working as a teacher or health-care worker. As it's a live vaccine it should not be given to pregnant women or immuno-compromised individuals.

Typhoid

Spreads Through food or water that has been contaminated by infected human faeces.

Symptoms and effects Initially, usually fever or a pink rash on the abdomen. Septicaemia (blood poisoning) may also occur.

Prevention Typhim Vi or typherix vaccine. In some countries, the oral vaccine Vivotif is also available.

Yellow Fever

Travellers arriving in Morocco from a yellow-fever-endemic area need to show proof of vaccination before entry (see p502).

Spreads There is a small risk of yellow fever, borne by mosquitos, in rural Chefchaouen province between May and October.

Symptoms and effects Muscle aches, fever, headache, nausea and vomiting subside after a few days, followed in up to a quarter of cases by anaemia, liver inflammation, hepatitis, jaundice and kidney damage. Most patients who also experience bleeding from the nose, mouth and stomach (leading to blood in vomit and faeces) die in a short space of time.

Prevention The risk is so small that the World Health Organization does not recommend vaccination. It must be given at a designated clinic, and is a live vaccine so must not be given to immuno-compromised or pregnant travellers.

Traveller's Diarrhoea

Causes Strains of travel – unfamiliar food, heat, long days and erratic sleeping patterns – can all make your body more susceptible to an upset stomach.

Prevention Water is generally safe to drink in cities, but elsewhere you should only drink treated water. Eat fresh fruits or vegetables only if they are cooked or if you have washed or peeled them yourself. Buffet meals, which may have been kept sitting warm for some time, can be risky; food should be piping hot. Meals freshly cooked in front of you (like much street food) or served in a busy restaurant are more likely to be safe. Be sensible, but not paranoid: food is one of the treats of visiting Morocco, so don't miss out.

Hygiene Pay close attention to personal hygiene. Many Moroccan meals are eaten with the hand, so always wash before eating and after using the toilet. Even the smallest restaurant will have a sink, but soap is less common, especially at cheap hotels. Antibacterial hand gel, which cleans without needing water, is useful.

Treatment Drink plenty of fluids, and preferably an oral rehydration solution; pharmacies stock these inexpensive *sels de réhydration orale*. Avoid fatty food and dairy products. A few loose stools don't require treatment, but if you start having more than four or five a day, take an antibiotic (usually a quinolone drug) and an antidiarrhoeal agent (such as loperamide). If diarrhoea is bloody, persists for more than 72 hours, and is accompanied by fever, shaking chills or severe abdominal pain, seek medical attention.

Environmental Hazards

Altitude Sickness

Causes Lack of oxygen at high altitudes (over 2500m) affects most people to some extent. The effect may be mild or severe, and occurs because less oxygen reaches the muscles and the brain at high altitudes, requiring the heart and lungs to compensate by working harder. There is no hard-and-fast rule as to what is too high: Acute Mountain Sickness (AMS) has been fatal at 3000m, although 3500m to 4500m is the usual range.

Symptoms and effects Symptoms of AMS usually (but not always) develop during the first 24 hours at altitude. Mild symptoms include headache, lethargy, dizziness, difficulty sleeping and loss of appetite. Potentially fatal, AMS may become more severe without warning. Severe symptoms include breathlessness, a dry, irritative cough (which

may progress to the production of pink, frothy sputum), severe headache, lack of coordination, confusion, irrational behaviour, vomiting, drowsiness and unconsciousness.

Prevention If trekking, build time into your schedule to acclimatise, and ensure your guide knows how to recognise and deal with altitude sickness. Morocco's most popular trek, to Jebel Toubkal, reaches the 4167m summit relatively quickly, so many people may suffer even mildly. The longer treks in the M'Goun Massif also reach heights of around 4000m. Treks in the Rif Mountains and Jebel Sarhro are considerably lower, so don't carry the same risks. You can download free booklets, including *Travel at Altitude* and *Children at Altitude*, from the website of the British Mountaineering Council (BMC; www.thebmc.co.uk).

Treatment Treat mild symptoms by resting at the same altitude until recovery, or preferably descend – even 500m can help. Take paracetamol or aspirin for headaches. If symptoms persist or become worse, immediate descent is necessary. Drug treatments should never be used to avoid descent or to enable further ascent. Diamox (acetazolamide) reduces the headache of AMS and helps the body acclimatise to the lack of oxygen. It is only available on prescription, and those who are allergic to sulfonamide antibiotics may also be allergic to Diamox.

Heat Illness

Causes Occurs following heavy sweating and excessive fluid loss with inadequate replacement of fluids and salt. This is particularly common in hot climates when taking unaccustomed exercise before full acclimatisation.

Symptoms and effects Headache, dizziness and tiredness.

Prevention Dehydration is already happening by the time you feel thirsty – drink sufficient water such that you produce pale, diluted urine. Morocco's sun can be fierce, so bring a hat.

Treatment Consists of fluid replacement with water, fruit juice, or both, and cooling by cold water and fans. Treating salt loss consists of consuming salty fluids such as soup or broth, and adding a little more table salt to foods than usual.

Heatstroke

Causes Extreme heat, high humidity, physical exertion or use of drugs or alcohol in the sun and dehydration. Occurs when the body's heat-regulating mechanism breaks down.

Symptoms and effects An excessive rise in body temperature leads to sweating ceasing, irrational and hyperactive behaviour, and eventually loss of consciousness, and death.

Treatment Rapid cooling by spraying the body with water and fanning is ideal. Emergency fluid and electrolyte replacement by intravenous drip is usually also required.

Insect Bites & Stings

Causes Mosquitoes, sandflies (found around the Mediterranean beaches), scorpions (common in southern Morocco), bees and wasps, bedbugs and scabies (both found in cheaper accommodation).

Symptoms and effects More likely to be an irritant than a health risk. Sandflies have a nasty, itchy bite, and can carry the rare skin disorder, leishmaniasis. Scorpions have a painful sting that is rarely life-threatening. Bedbugs lead to very itchy, lumpy bites. Tiny scabies mites live in the skin, particularly between the fingers, and cause an intensely itchy rash.

Prevention and treatment DEET-based insect repellents. Spraying a mattress with an appropriate insect killer will do a good job of getting rid of bedbugs. Scabies is easily treated with lotion available from pharmacies; people you come into contact with also need treatment to avoid spreading scabies between asymptomatic carriers.

Snake Bites

Causes The chances of seeing a snake in Morocco, let alone being bitten by one, are slim. Nevertheless, there are a few venomous species, such as the horned viper, found in the southern desert areas. Snakes like to bask on rocks and sand, retreating during the heat of the day.

Prevention Do not walk barefoot or stick your hand into holes or cracks.

Treatment If bitten, do not panic. Half of those bitten by venomous snakes are not actually injected with poison (envenomed). Immobilise the bitten limb with a splint (eg a stick) and apply a bandage over the site, with firm pressure, similar to applying a bandage over a sprain. Do not apply a tourniquet, or cut or suck the bite. Get the victim to medical help as soon as possible so that antivenin can be given if necessary.

Water

Tap water is chlorinated in Morocco's cities and generally safe to drink – certainly safe to clean your teeth with. Elsewhere, stick to treated water – filter or purify it.

Bottled water is available everywhere, although there is an environmental cost through the mountains of discarded (and unrecycled) plastic bottles.

Off the beaten track, water drawn from wells or pumped from boreholes should be safe, but never drink water from rivers or lakes, as this may contain bacteria or viruses that can cause diarrhoea or vomiting.

Women's Health

Condoms, tampons and sanitary towels are widely available in Morocco.

Contraception If using oral contraceptives, remember that some antibiotics, diarrhoea and vomiting can stop the pill from working, so take condoms just in case. Condoms should be kept in a cool, dry place or they may crack and perish.

Pregnancy Take written records of the pregnancy and your blood group, which will be helpful if you need medical attention. Antenatal facilities vary greatly in North Africa, so think carefully before travelling to out-of-the-way places, bearing in mind the cultural and linguistic difficulties, not to mention the poor medical standards you could face.

Language

WANT MORE?

For in-depth language information and handy phrases, check out Lonely Planet's *Moroccan Arabic Phrasebook*. You'll find it at **shop.lonelyplanet.com**, or you can buy Lonely Planet's iPhone phrasebooks at the Apple App Store.

The official language in Morocco is Arabic, which is used throughout the country. Berber is spoken in the Rif and Atlas Mountains. Most Berbers also speak at least some Arabic. French is still regularly used in the cities, but much less so among rural Berbers.

MOROCCAN ARABIC

Moroccan Arabic (Darija) is a variety of Modern Standard Arabic (MSA), but is so different from it in many respects as to be virtually like another language. This is the everyday spoken language you'll hear when in Morocco.

All publications and signs, however, are written in Modern Standard Arabic (MSA), which is the common written form in all Arabic-speaking countries. Note though that in Morocco, standard Western numeric symbols are used rather than those normally used in Arabic.

In this language guide we've represented the Arabic phrases with the Roman alphabet using a simplified pronunciation system. The vowels are:

a	as in 'had'
aa	like the 'a' in 'father'
ai	as in 'aisle'
ay	as in 'day'
e	as in 'bet'
ee	as in 'beer', only softer
i	as in 'hit'
o	as in 'note'
oo	as in 'food'
ow	as in 'how'
u	as in 'put'

Note that when double consonants occur in the pronunciation guides, each consonant is pronounced. For example, hammam (bath) is pronounced 'ham-mam'. The apostrophe (') represents the glottal stop (like the closing of the throat before saying 'Oh-oh!'). Other consonant sounds to keep in mind are:

dh	like the 'th' in 'this'
gh	a throaty sound like the French 'r'
h	a strongly whispered 'h'
kh	as the 'ch' in the Scottish *loch*
q	a strong, throaty 'k' sound

Basics

When addressing a man, the polite term more or less equivalent to 'Mr' is aseedee (shortened to see before a name); for women it's lalla, followed by the first name. To attract the attention of someone in the street or a waiter in a cafe, the word shreef is used.

Note that the abbreviations 'm/f/pl' (male/female/plural) are used where applicable.

Hi.	la bes **(informal)**
	bekheer **(response)**
Hello.	es salaam alaykum **(polite)**
	wa alaykum salaam **(response)**
Goodbye.	bessalama/m'a ssalama
Please.	'afak/'afik/'afakum **(said to m/f/pl)**
Thank you.	shukran
You're welcome.	la shukran 'la wejb
Excuse me.	smeh leeya
Yes./No.	eeyeh/la
How are you?	keef halek?
Fine, thank you.	bekheer, lhamdoo llaah

What's your name?	asmeetek?
My name is ...	esmee ...
Do you speak English?	wash kat'ref negleezeeya?
I don't understand.	mafhemtsh

Accommodation

Where is a ...?	feen kayn ...?
campsite	shee mukheyyem
hotel	shee ootayl
youth hostel	daar shshabab

Is there a room available?
wash kayn shee beet khaweeya?

Can I see the room?
wash yemkenlee nshoof lbeet?

How much is a room for one day?
bash hal kayn gbayt l wahed nhar?

I'd like a room ...	bgheet shee beet ...
for one person	dyal wahed
for two people	dyal jooj
with a bathroom	belhammam

air-conditioning	kleemateezaseeyun
bed	namooseeya
blanket	bttaaneeya
hot water	lma skhoon
key	saroot
room	beet
sheet	eezar
shower	doosh
toilet	beet lma

Directions

Where is the ...?
feen kayn ...?

What is the address?
ashnoo hoowa l'unwan?

Please write down the address.
kteb l'unwan 'afek

Please show me on the map.
werri liya men l kharita 'afak

How far?
bshhal b'ayd?

Go straight ahead.
seer neeshan

Turn ...	dor ...
at the corner	felqent
at the traffic lights	fedo elhmer
left	'al leeser
right	al leemen

Question Words – Arabic	
How?	keefash?
What?	ash?
When?	eemta?
Where?	feen?
Which?	ashmen?
Who?	shkoon?
Why?	'lash?

behind	men luy
here	hna
next to	hedda
opposite	'eks
there	hunak

north	shamel
south	janoob
east	sherq
west	gherb

Eating & Drinking

A table for..., please.
tabla dyal ... 'afak

Can I see the menu, please?
nazar na'raf lmaakla lli 'andkum?

What do you recommend?
shnoo tansaani nakul?

I'll try what she/he is having.
gha nzharrab shnoo kaatakul hiyya/huwwa

I'm a vegetarian.
makanakoolsh llehem

I'd like something to drink.
bgheet shi haazha nashrubha

Please bring me ...	llaa ykhalleek zheeb li ...
a beer	birra
a glass/bottle of red/white/ rose wine	kaas/qar'a dyal hmar/byad/ roozi shshrab
a napkin	mandeel
some bread	shwiyya dyaal lkhoobz
some pepper	shwiyya dyaal lebzaar
some salt	shwiyya dyaal lmelha
some water	shwiyya dyaal lmaa

I didn't order this.	tlabtsh had shshi
Without ..., please.	bla ... 'afak
This is excellent!	had shshi ldeed bezzef!
Cheers!	bsaha!
The bill, please.	lahsaab, 'afak

Numbers – Arabic	
1	wahed
2	jooj
3	tlata
4	reb'a
5	khamsa
6	setta
7	seb'a
8	tmenya
9	tes'ood
10	'ashra
20	'ashreen
30	tlateen
40	reb'een
50	khamseen
60	setteen
70	seb'een
80	tmaneen
90	tes'een
100	mya
200	myatayn
1000	alf
2000	alfayn

Meat & Fish

anchovies	shton
beef	baqree
camel	lehem jemil
chicken	farooj/dujaj
cod	lamoori
fish	hut
kidneys	kelawwi
lamb	lehem ghenmee
liver	kebda
lobster	laangos
meat	lehem
sardines	serdeen
shrimp	qaimroon
sole	sol
tuna	ton
whiting	merla

Fruit & Vegetables

apple	teffah
apricot	meshmash
artichoke	qooq
aubergine	lbdanzhaal
banana	banan/moz
cucumber	khiyaar
dates	tmer
figs	kermoos
fruit	fakiya
garlic	tooma
grapes	'eineb
green beans	loobeeya
lentils	'aads
lettuce	khess
mushroom	fegg'a
olives	zeetoun
onion	besla
orange	limoon
peas	zelbana bisila
pomegranate	reman
potatoes	batatas
tomato	mataisha tamatim
vegetables	khoodar
watermelon	dellah
white beans	fasooliya

Other

bread	khoobz
butter	zebda
cheese	fromaj/jiben
chips	ships
eggs	bayd
oil	zit
pepper	filfil/lebzaar
salt	melha
soup	shorba
sugar	sukur
yogurt	zabadee/laban/danoon

Emergencies

Help!	'teqnee!
Help me, please!	'awennee 'afak!
Go away!	seer fhalek!
I'm lost.	tweddert
Thief!	sheffar!
I've been robbed.	tsreqt
Call the police!	'ayyet 'la lbùlees!
Call a doctor!	'ayyet 'la shee tbeeb!
There's been an accident!	uq'at kseeda!

Where's the toilet?	feen kayn lbeet lma?	
I'm sick.	ana mreed	
It hurts here.	kaydernee henna	
I'm allergic to (penicillin).	'andee lhsaseeya m'a (lbeenseleen)	

Shopping & Services

Where is the ...?	feen kayn ...?
bank	shee baanka
barber	shee hellaq
chemist/pharmacy	farmasyan
... embassy	ssifaara dyal ...
market	souk
police station	lkoomeesareeya
post office	lboostaa
restaurant	ristura/mat'am
souvenir shop	baazaar
travel agency	wekaalet el aasfaar

I want to change ...	bgheet nserref ...
some money	shee floos
travellers cheques	shek seeyahee

I'd like to buy ...	bgheet nshree ...
I'm only looking.	gheer kanshoof
Can I look at it?	wakhkha nshoofha?
I don't like it.	ma'jebatneesh
How much is it?	bshhal?
That's very expensive.	ghalee bezzaf
Can I pay by credit card?	wash nkder nkhelles bel kart kredee?

big	kabeer
small	sagheer
open	mehlool
closed	masdood

Time & Dates

What time is it?	shal fessa'a?

yesterday	lbareh
today	lyoom
tomorrow	ghedda
morning	fessbah
afternoon	fel'sheeya
evening	'sheeya

day	nhar
week	l'usbu'
month	shshhar
year	l'am

early/late	bekree/m'ettel
quickly/slowly	dgheeya/beshweeya

Monday	nhar letneen
Tuesday	nhar ttlat
Wednesday	nhar larb'
Thursday	nhar lekhmees
Friday	nhar jjem'a
Saturday	nhar ssebt
Sunday	nhar lhedd

January	yanaayir
February	fibraayir
March	maaris
April	abreel
May	maayu
June	yunyu
July	yulyu
August	aghustus/ghusht
September	sibtimbir/shebtenber
October	uktoobir
November	nufimbir/nu'enbir
December	disimbir/dijenbir

Transport
Public Transport

When does the ... leave/arrive?	wufuqash kaykhrej/kaywsul ...?
boat	lbaboor
city/intercity bus	ttubees/lkar
train	tran
plane	ttayyyaara

I'd like a ... ticket.	'afak bgheet wahed lwarka l ddar lbayda ...
return	bash nemshee oo njee
1st/2nd class	ddaraja lloola/ttaneeya

Where is the ...?	feen kayn ...?
airport	mataar
bus station	mhetta dyal ttobeesat
bus stop	blasa dyal ttobeesat
ticket office	maktab lwerqa
train station	lagaar

What's the fare?
shhal taman lwarka?

Please tell me when we get to ...
'afak eela wselna l ... goolhaleeya

I want to pay for one place only.
bgheet nkhelles blaasaawaheda

Stop here, please.
wqef henna 'afak

Please wait for me.
tsennanee 'afak

Driving & Cycling

Where can I hire a ...?	feen yimkin li nkri ...?
bicycle	bshklit
camel	jmel
car	tumubeel
donkey	hmar
horse	'awd

Can I park here?
wash nqder nwakef hna?

How long can I park here?
sh-hal men waket neqder nstatiun hna?

How do I get to ...?
keefesh ghaadee nuwsul l ...?

Where's the next petrol station?
fin kayna shi bumba dyal lisans griba?

I'd like ... litres.
bgheet ... itru 'afak

Please check the oil/water.
'afak shuf zzit/lma

We need a mechanic.
khesna wahed lmikanisyan

The car has broken down at ...
tumubeel khasra f ...

I have a flat tyre.
'ndi pyasa fruida

BERBER

There are three main dialects among Berber speakers, which in a certain sense also serve as loose lines of ethnic demarcation.

In the north, in the area centred on the Rif, the locals speak a dialect that has been called Riffian and is spoken as far south as Figuig on the Algerian border. The dialect that predominates in the Middle and High Atlas and the valleys leading into the Sahara goes by various names, including Braber or Amazigh.

More settled tribes of the High Atlas, Anti Atlas, Souss Valley and southwestern oases generally speak Tashelhit or Chleuh. The following phrases are a selection from the Tashelhit dialect, the one visitors are likely to find most useful.

Basics

Hello.	la bes darik/darim (m/f)
Hello. (response)	la bes
Goodbye.	akayaoon arbee
See you later.	akranwes daghr
Please.	barakalaufik
Thank you.	barakalaufik
Yes.	yah
No.	oho
Excuse me.	samhiy
How are you?	meneek antgeet?
Fine, thank you.	la bes, lhamdulah
Good.	eefulkee/eeshwa
Bad.	(khaib) eeghshne

Practicalities

food	teeremt
mule	aserdon
somewhere to sleep	kra lblast mahengane
water	arman

Is there ...?	ees eela ...?
Do you have ...?	ees daroon ...?
How much is it?	minshk aysker?
Give me ...	fky ...
I want ...	reegh ...
a little/lot	eemeek/bzef
no good	oor eefulkee
too expensive	eeghla

I want to go to ...	addowghs ...
Where is (the) ...?	mani gheela ...?
Is it near/far?	ees eeqareb/yagoog?
straight	neeshan
to the left	fozelmad
to the right	fofasee

mountain	adrar
river	aseef
the pass	tizee
village	doorwar

yesterday	eedgam
today	(zig sbah) rass
tomorrow	(ghasad) aska

This glossary is a list of Arabic (A), Berber (B), French (F) and Spanish (S) terms that are used throughout this guide. For a list of trekking terms, see Words To Trek By, p39.

agadir (B) – fortified communal granary

'ain (A) – water source, spring

aït (B) – family (of), often precedes tribal and town names

Al-Andalus – Muslim Spain and Portugal

Alawite – hereditary dynasty that has ruled Morocco since the late 17th century

Allah (A) – God

Almohads – puritanical Muslim group (1147–1269), originally Berber, that arose in response to the corrupt Almoravid dynasty

Almoravids – Muslim group (1054–1147) that ruled Spain and the *Maghreb*

assif (A) – watercourse, river

bab (A) – gate

babouches (F) – traditional leather slippers

banu (A) – see *beni*

baraka (A) – divine blessing or favour

Barbary – European term used to describe the North African coast from the 16th to the 19th centuries

ben (A) – (or ibn) son of

bendir (B) – single-headed Berber drum

beni (A) – 'sons of', often precedes tribal name (also *banu*)

Berbers – indigenous inhabitants of North Africa

borj (A) – fort (literally 'tower')

brigade touristique (F) – tourist police

bureau de guide (F) – guides' office

caid/caliph – town official

calèche – horse-drawn carriage

calle (S) – street

camionette (F) – minivan or pick-up truck

capitol – main temple of Roman town, usually situated in the forum

caravanserai – large merchants' inn enclosing a courtyard, providing accommodation and a marketplace (see also *funduq*)

chergui (A) – dry, easterly desert wind

Compagnie de Transports Marocaine – CTM; national bus company

corniche (F) – coastal road

corsair – 18th-century pirate based at Salé

dar (A) – traditional town house with internal courtyard

Délégation Régionale du Tourisme – tourist office

derb (A) – lane or narrow street

djemaa (A) – Friday mosque (also *jami'*, *jemaa* and *jamaa*)

douar (A) – generally used for 'village' in the High Atlas

douche (F) – public showers (see *hammam*)

Eaux et Forêts – government ministry responsible for national parks

eid (A) – religious festival

Ensemble Artisanal – government handicraft shop

erg (A) – sand dunes

fantasia (S) – military exercise featuring a cavalry charge

faux guides (F) – unofficial or informal guides

foum (A) – usually the mouth of a river or valley (from Arabic for 'mouth')

frontera (S) – border

funduq (A) – *caravanserai* (often used to mean 'hotel')

gîte, gîte d'étape (F) – trekkers' hostel, sometimes a homestay

gardiens de voitures (F) – car-park attendants

gare routière (F) – bus station

ghassoul (A) – type of clay mixed with herbs, dried roses and lavender used in *hammams* for removing grease and washing hair

glaoua (A) – rug with combination of flat weave and deep fluffy pile (also *zanafi*)

Gnaoua – bluesy Moroccan musical form that began with freed slaves in Marrakesh and Essaouira

grand taxi (F) – (long-distance) shared taxi

haj (A) – pilgrimage to Mecca, hence *haji* or *hajia*, a male or female who has made the pilgrimage

halqa (A) – street theatre

hammada (A) – stony desert

hammam (A) – Turkish-style bathhouse with sauna and massage, also known by the French word *bain* (bath) or *bain maure* (Moorish bath)

hanbel (A) – see *kilim*

haram (A) – literally 'forbidden', the word is sometimes used to denote a sacred or forbidden area, such as the prayer room of a mosque

Hejira – flight of the *Prophet* from Mecca to Medina in AD 622; the first year of the Islamic calendar

ibn (A) – son of (see also *ben*)
Idrissids – Moroccan dynasty that established a stable state in northern Morocco in the 9th century
iftar (A) – breaking of the fast at sundown during Ramadan; breakfast (also *ftur*)
imam (A) – Muslim cleric
Interzone – name coined by author William Burroughs for the period 1923–56, when Tangier was controlled by nine countries
irifi (A) – dry, desert wind, also called *chergui*

jebel (A) – hill, mountain (sometimes *djebel* in former French possessions)
jedid (A) – new (sometimes spelled *jdid*)
jellaba (A) – popular flowing garment; men's jellabas are usually made from cotton or wool, while women's come in light synthetic fabrics

kasbah (A) – fort, citadel; often also the administrative centre (also *qasba*)
kif (A) – marijuana
kilim (A) – flat-woven blankets or floor coverings (also *hanbel*)
koubba (A) – sanctuary or shrine (see also *marabout*)
ksar (A) – fort or fortified stronghold (plural *ksour*)

mâalems – master artisans
Maghreb (A) – (literally 'west') area covered by Morocco, Algeria, Tunisia and Libya
maison d'hôte (F) – guesthouse, often a restored traditional Moroccan house
majoun (A) – sticky paste made of crushed seeds of the marijuana plant
marabout – holy man or saint; also often used to describe the mausoleums of these men
masjid (A) – another name for a mosque, particularly in a *medersa* (see also *djemaa*)
mechouar (A) – royal assembly place
medersa (A) – college for teaching theology, law, Arabic literature and grammar (also called *madrassa*)
medina (A) – old city; used to describe the old Arab parts of modern towns and cities
mellah (A) – Jewish quarter of the medina
Merenids (A) – Moroccan dynasty (1269–1465), responsible for the construction of many of Morocco's *medersas*
mihrab (A) – prayer niche in the wall of a

mosque indicating the direction of Mecca (the *qibla*)
minbar (A) – pulpit in mosque; the *imam* delivers the sermon from one of the lower steps because the *Prophet* preached from the top step
moulay (A) – ruler
Mouloud – Islamic festival celebrating the birth of the *Prophet*
moussem (A) – pilgrimage to *marabout* tomb; festival in honour of a *marabout*
muezzin (A) – mosque official who sings the call to prayer from the minaret
muqarna (A) – decorative plasterwork
musée (F) – museum

ONMT – Office National Marocain du Tourisme, national tourist body, sometimes called Délégation Régionale du Tourisme
ordinaire (F) – less comfortable train, slightly slower than a *rapide*
oued (A) – river or stream, including dry riverbeds (sometimes *wad* or *wadi*)
oulad (A) – sons (of), often precedes tribal or town name

palais de justice (F) – law court
palmeraie (F) – palm grove
pastilla – a rich, savoury-sweet chicken or pigeon pie made with fine pastry; a dish of layered pastry with cinnamon and almonds served as dessert at banquets
pasha – high official in Ottoman Empire (also *pacha*)
pensióne (S) – guesthouse
petit taxi (F) – local taxi
pisé (F) – building material made of sun-dried clay or mud
piste (F) – unsealed tracks, often requiring 4WD vehicles
place (F) – square, plaza
plage (F) – beach
plazas de soberanía (S) – 'Places of sovereignty', the name given to the Spanish possessions in North Africa.
pressing (F) – laundry
Prophet (Mohammed), the – founder of Islam, who lived between AD 570 and AD 632

qaid (A) – local chief, loose equivalent of mayor in some parts of Morocco (also *caid*)
qissaria (A) – covered market sometimes forming the commercial centre of a medina
Quran – sacred book of Islam

Ramadan (A) – ninth month of the Muslim year, a period of fasting

rapide (F) – type of train more comfortable and slightly faster than an *ordinaire*

Reconquista (S) – the Christian reconquest of the Iberian peninsula from the Moors

refuge (F) – mountain hut, basic hikers' shelter

riad (A) – traditional town house set around an internal garden

ribat (A) – combined monastery and fort

Saadians – Moroccan dynasty that ruled in the 16th century

sharia (A) – street

shedwi (A) – flat-woven rug of black and white bands

sherif (A) – descendant of the *Prophet*

Shiites – one of two main Islamic sects, formed by those who believed the true *imams* were descended from the *Prophet*'s son-in-law Ali (see also *Sunnis*)

sidi (A) – honorific (equivalent to 'Mr'; also *si*)

skala (A) – fortress

souq (A) – market

Sufism – mystical strand of Islam that emphasises communion with God through inner attitude

Sunnis – one of two main Islamic sects, derived from followers of the Umayyad caliphate (see also *Shiites*)

Syndicat d'Initiative (F) – government-run tourist office

tabac (F) – tobacconist and newsagency

tadelakt (A) – waterproof lime plaster mixed with pigments and polished with a stone to give it a smooth, lustrous finish, originally used for the walls of *hammams* but now a favourite of interior designers

tariq (A) – road, avenue

téléboutique (F) – privately operated telephone service

télécarte (F) – phonecard

terz Fezzi (A) – intricate geometric embroidery originating in Fez

tizi (B) – mountain pass

Tuareg – nomadic Berbers of the Sahara, also known as the Blue Men because of their indigo-dyed robes

ville nouvelle (F) – new city; town built by the French alongside existing towns

vizier – another term for a provincial governor in Ottoman Empire, or adviser to the sultan in Morocco

zanafi (A) – rug with combination of flat weave and deep fluffy pile (also *glaoua*)

zawiya (A) – religious fraternity based around a *marabout;* location of the fraternity (also *zaouia*)

zellij (A) – ceramic tilework used to decorate buildings

behind the scenes

SEND US YOUR FEEDBACK

We love to hear from travellers – your comments keep us on our toes and help make our books better. Our well-travelled team reads every word on what you loved or loathed about this book. Although we cannot reply individually to postal submissions, we always guarantee that your feedback goes straight to the appropriate authors, in time for the next edition. Each person who sends us information is thanked in the next edition – and the most useful submissions are rewarded with a free book.

Visit **lonelyplanet.com/contact** to submit your updates and suggestions or to ask for help. Our award-winning website also features inspirational travel stories, news and discussions.

Note: We may edit, reproduce and incorporate your comments in Lonely Planet products such as guidebooks, websites and digital products, so let us know if you don't want your comments reproduced or your name acknowledged. For a copy of our privacy policy visit lonelyplanet.com/privacy.

OUR READERS

Many thanks to the travellers who used the last edition and wrote to us with helpful hints, useful advice and interesting anecdotes:

Helmut Ablinger, Azzam Alkadhi, Sebastian Arabito, Mike Armstrong, Joanna Armstrong, Bethany Arnold, MA Azzam, Lies Baarendse, Phil Baker, Shan Baker, Guillermo Ballesteros, Steph Barnes, Magda Benavides, Christine Bernard, Cyril, Martin (Bez) Berridge, Marcus Beuchert, Gwen Bingle, Sam Bixby, Rachel Blech, Katie Borg, Daniël Bosman, Moya Bradbee, Scott Brandl, Chiara Brivio, Vincent Brouerius van Nidek, Jonathan Brown, Shane Buckham, Jeanne Burnham, Laura Buttafoco, Mark Buzinkay, Melissa Caras, Stephanie Carnachan, Bouzekri Chakroune, Sarah Collings, Wouter Coppens, Alice Cox, Ranald Coyne, Wells Crandall, Derek Crosby, Tim Cullis, Janet Cupples, Jan de Morree, Lui DelVerto, Heather Dev, Riet Dhuyvetter, Liliam, Lilian Dijkema, Jeroen Doorn, Clement Douault, Jess Dunbar, Karima Echcherki, Richard Else, Oriol Llach Estrella, Lorraine Federico, Margo Finlay, Stavros Fotiadis, Mike Fowkes, Ednah Beth Friedman, Kostas Gabriel, Warren Galgut, Ana Gimenez, Frans Glazener, Susan Gore, Petra Gran, Françoise Guévin, Julia Gunther, Vivek Gurudutt, Yorron Hackmon, Inga Hanover, Bill Hanson, Emma Hart, Kathy Hawkins, Jackie Hayes, Nadja Hermann, Michael Hicks, Stephen Honey, Alice Horsman, Brent Huff, Frank Huisingh, Sue Hunt, John Hutchison-Maxwell, Nicole Ianieri, Jill Israel, Tracy Jenkins, O'Maley Joanna, Paula Joe, Gill Johnston, Carla Jones Da Silva, Rebecca Jürgens, Viktor Kaposi, Bahim Karaoui, Manon Kelder, Heidi Klein, Jaap Kok, Boštjan Kolarič, Ane Krestine Larsen, Jonathan Ledbury, Chloe Lee, Elisabeth Lefebvre, Jean-Claude Lefebvre, Jonatan Leffler, Audun Lem, Pamela Lowenstein, Pablo Lozano, Robert Malies, Christina Mang, Orlaith Mannion, Francesca Marini, Brett Martin, Jacqueline Martin, Chris Matthyssen, Christine McGrath, Alexandra Meyer, Brendan Moroso, Beth Mottart, Hana Muselikova, Gemma Newbery, Marc Nolden, Sian O'Keefe, Eduardo Oliveira, Dino Ott, Nordine Ouyahia, Malcolm Page, Pietro Passinetti, Sonal Patel, Julie Paterson, Alan Pearson, Casper Pedersen, Nicole Perry, Nondas Pettas, Jiri Pilar, Carolyn Popple, Atif Qadir, Helen Quaggin-Molloy, Nadine Raidbard, Cleber Rezende, Hans Riedler, Liel Rohwer, Mary Rose-Miller, Massimiliano Russi, Nicolas Sansone, Azra Saric, Anneke Schakenraad, Almut Schindler, Isabel Schmitz-DuMont A Azzam, Ayesha Siddiqi, Barney Smith, Stephen Sohmer, Sharon Sorek, Ruthi Soudack, Kathy Stetz, Stella Steveni, Hannah Stewart, Pat Streuber, Catherine Such, Matt Such, Karol Svaral, Jessica Svensson, Adam Taylor, Yumiko Texidor,

Jon Thompson, Karren Thorn, Nicoletta Tosi, Marek Tretera, Michael Turner, Elisabeth van den Bogaard, Larissa van Hensbergen, Wim van Hoorn, Heidie van Veen, Marloes van Zantvoort, Armijn Verweij, Samantha Von Gleichenstein, Julina Wadsworth, Kit Wardle, Simon Webster, Susan West, Andreas Wicke, Cornelia Wiedmer, Jurriaan Witteman, Tina Yocum, Keren Zaks, Markus Zink.

AUTHOR THANKS

James Bainbridge

A Djemaa el-Fna-worthy concert of thanks to my fellow authors for your expertise and enthusiasm, and to the following in Morocco: Mohamed, Kay and the Riad Bledna gang (including Omar for military strategy), the Catling family, Laargoub Car in Agadir, Sissi and Hassan at Yallatrek and Mahfoud at Auberge le Safran in Taliouine, Maison Traditionnelle in Oumesnate, Mohamed in Tiwadou, Jean-Pierre in Sidi Ouarsik, and Sadat and Pete in Tarfaya.

Alison Bing

Allah yhrem waldikum (blessings upon your parents) to Moroccan mavens Souad Boudeiry, Si Ahmad Nmeis, Mohamed, Omar and Kay Nour; intrepid fellow travellers Sahai Burrowes and Sandeep Brar; beloved Morocco co-authors, editorial maâlems (master craftspeople) David Carroll and Kate James, and our dauntless Lonely Planet cartographers; and Marco Flavio Marinucci, for a lifelong adventure. To Moroccan friends, hosts and kind strangers too numerous to mention:

llaykhlef alf, may your hospitality be returned to you 1000 times.

Paul Clammer

Shukran to all my Fassi 'family' – you know who you are. Thanks also to Jack, Ina and Youness in Figuig, and Cynthia Berning in Midelt.

Helen Ranger

Thanks to the LP team, James and my fellow authors. In Casablanca, Mustapha Bouamara was of enormous help, and Tahir Shah was a delight. In Essaouira, *shukran bizeff* to Latifa Boumazzhour, and Kirsty McArdle for her insider's view. To Ricky in Assilah, thanks for the fabulous terrace. Gerald Loftus in Tangier was inspiring. In Chefchaouen, John Wilkinson is superbly knowledgeable, and spiritedly added Campari to the gin. Riffians Abdesalam Moudden and Mostapha el-Habti have wonderful trekking expertise. Amine Adrissi proved a friendly and capable driver. And special thanks to Ibn Warraq, whose turban is still to be unwound.

ACKNOWLEDGMENTS

Climate map data adapted from Peel MC, Finlayson BL & McMahon TA (2007) 'Updated World Map of the Köppen-Geiger Climate Classification', *Hydrology and Earth System Sciences*, 11, 163344.

Marrakesh maps based on the map Marrakech! My Map © 2010 Editions Bab Sabaa.

Cover photograph: Hassan II Mosque, Casablanca/Fergus Cooney/Lonely Planet Images. Many of the images in this guide are available for licensing from Lonely Planet Images: www.lonelyplanetimages.com.

BEHIND THE SCENES

THIS BOOK

This 10th edition of *Morocco* was researched and written by James Bainbridge (coordinating author), Alison Bing, Paul Clammer and Helen Ranger. The 9th edition was the work of Paul Clammer, Alison Bing, Anthony Sattin and Paul Stiles and the 8th edition was the work of Anthony Ham, Alison Bing, Paul Clammer, Etain O'Carroll and Anthony Sattin. The Health chapter of the 9th and 10th editions was based on text written by Dr Caroline Evans; it was updated for this edition by James Bainbridge.

This guidebook was commissioned in Lonely Planet's Melbourne office, and produced by the following:

Commissioning Editor David Carroll
Coordinating Editors Kate James, Monique Perrin
Coordinating Cartographer Jolyon Philcox
Coordinating Layout Designer Nicholas Colicchia
Senior Editors Anna Metcalfe, Susan Paterson
Managing Editor Brigitte Ellemor
Managing Cartographers Adrian Persoglia, Amanda Sierp
Managing Layout Designers Chris Girdler, Celia Wood

Assisting Editors Carly Hall, Helen Koehne, Helen Yeates
Assisting Cartographers Mick Garrett, Joelene Kowalski, Alex Leung, James Leversha
Cover Research Naomi Parker
Internal Image Research Rebecca Skinner
Language Content Annelies Martens, Branislava Vladisavljevic
Thanks to Shahara Ahmed, Melanie Dankel, Frank Deim, Ryan Evans, Jocelyn Harewood, Victoria Harrison, Lisa Knights, Andi Lien, Wayne Murphy, Peter Shields, Juan Winata

NOTES

NOTES

index

how to use this book

These symbols will help you find the listings you want:

- 👁 Sights
- 🏃 Activities
- 🍵 Courses
- 👉 Tours

- 🎉 Festivals & Events
- 🛏 Sleeping
- 🍴 Eating
- 🍺 Drinking

- ☆ Entertainment
- 🛍 Shopping
- ❶ Information/Transport

These symbols give you the vital information for each listing:

- ☎ Telephone Numbers
- ☺ Opening Hours
- P Parking
- ☻ Nonsmoking
- ✱ Air-Conditioning
- @ Internet Access

- 🛜 Wi-Fi Access
- ☻ Swimming Pool
- 🥗 Vegetarian Selection
- 📖 English-Language Menu
- 👪 Family-Friendly
- 🐾 Pet-Friendly

- 🚌 Bus
- ⛴ Ferry
- Ⓜ Metro
- Ⓢ Subway
- ⊖ London Tube
- 🚊 Tram
- 🚆 Train

Reviews are organised by author preference.

Map Legend

Sights
- 🏖 Beach
- 🕉 Buddhist
- 🏰 Castle
- ✝ Christian
- 🕉 Hindu
- ☪ Islamic
- ✡ Jewish
- ❶ Monument
- 🏛 Museum/Gallery
- 🏚 Ruin
- 🍷 Winery/Vineyard
- 🐾 Zoo
- ⊙ Other Sight

Activities, Courses & Tours
- 🤿 Diving/Snorkelling
- 🛶 Canoeing/Kayaking
- ⛷ Skiing
- 🏄 Surfing
- 🏊 Swimming/Pool
- 🚶 Walking
- 🏄 Windsurfing
- ⊙ Other Activity/Course/Tour

Sleeping
- 🛏 Sleeping
- 🏕 Camping

Eating
- 🍴 Eating

Drinking
- ☕ Drinking
- ☕ Cafe

Entertainment
- 🎭 Entertainment

Shopping
- 🛍 Shopping

Information
- 🏦 Bank
- 🏛 Embassy/Consulate
- ➕ Hospital/Medical
- @ Internet
- 👮 Police
- 📮 Post Office
- ☎ Telephone
- 🚻 Toilet
- ❶ Tourist Information
- • Other Information

Transport
- ✈ Airport
- ⊗ Border Crossing
- 🚌 Bus
- 🚠 Cable Car/Funicular
- 🚲 Cycling
- ⛴ Ferry
- Ⓜ Metro
- 🚝 Monorail
- P Parking
- ⛽ Petrol Station
- 🚕 Taxi
- 🚆 Train/Railway
- 🚋 Tram
- • Other Transport

Routes
- ▬ Tollway
- ▬ Freeway
- ▬ Primary
- ▬ Secondary
- ▬ Tertiary
- ▬ Lane
- ▬ Unsealed Road
- ▬ Plaza/Mall
- ▥ Steps
-)(= Tunnel
- ═ Pedestrian Overpass
- ▬ Walking Tour
- ▬ Walking Tour Detour
- ▬ Path

Geographic
- 🛖 Hut/Shelter
- 🚨 Lighthouse
- 👁 Lookout
- ▲ Mountain/Volcano
- 🌴 Oasis
- 🌳 Park
-)(Pass
- 🧺 Picnic Area
- 💧 Waterfall

Population
- ❶ Capital (National)
- ◉ Capital (State/Province)
- ● City/Large Town
- ● Town/Village

Boundaries
- ▬▬▬ International
- ▬▬▬ State/Province
- ▬ ▬ Disputed
- ▬ ▬ Regional/Suburb
- ▬▬ Marine Park
- ▬▬ Cliff
- ▬▬ Wall

Hydrography
- ∿ River, Creek
- ∿ Intermittent River
- ≋ Swamp/Mangrove
- Reef
- ～ Canal
- ◯ Water
- ◯ Dry/Salt/Intermittent Lake
- ▓ Glacier

Areas
- ░ Beach/Desert
- + + + Cemetery (Christian)
- × × × Cemetery (Other)
- ▓ Park/Forest
- ▬ Sportsground
- Sight (Building)
- Top Sight (Building)

OUR STORY

A beat-up old car, a few dollars in the pocket and a sense of adventure. In 1972 that's all Tony and Maureen Wheeler needed for the trip of a lifetime – across Europe and Asia overland to Australia. It took several months, and at the end – broke but inspired – they sat at their kitchen table writing and stapling together their first travel guide, *Across Asia on the Cheap*. Within a week they'd sold 1500 copies. Lonely Planet was born.

Today, Lonely Planet has offices in Melbourne, London and Oakland, with more than 600 staff and writers. We share Tony's belief that 'a great guidebook should do three things: inform, educate and amuse'.

OUR WRITERS

James Bainbridge

Coordinating author; Southern Morocco & Western Sahara James' travel-writing career began a decade ago with a trip to Morocco. Taking a break from magazine journalism in London, he passed through the country on an overland mission to Timbuktu (and back). Since the resultant article for the *Guardian*, James has written about Africa and the Middle East for worldwide publications, including Lonely Planet guides from *Turkey* to *West Africa*. Morocco has drawn him back several times since that initial foray, and he continues to sing its praises with the passion of a Gnawa musician. When he's not researching Anti Atlas grand-taxi fares, James lives in Cape Town.

Alison Bing

Marrakesh & Central Morocco When she's not methodically sampling every *mechoui* lamb roast in Marrakesh, diligently inspecting riad rooftop sunsets or personally testing hammam steam levels, Alison co-authors Lonely Planet's *California*, *USA* and *Italy* guides. Alison has a background in Islamic art, architecture and North African political economy from the American University in Cairo, and holds a masters degree from the Fletcher School of Law and Diplomacy, a program of Tufts and Harvard Universities – respectable diplomatic credentials she regularly undermines with opinionated art, food and culture commentary for newspapers, magazines and radio.

Paul Clammer

Imperial Cities, Middle Atlas & the East As a student, Paul had his first solo backpacking experience when he took a bus from his Cambridgeshire home to Casablanca. After an interlude where he trained and worked as a molecular biologist, he returned to work as a tour guide, trekking in the Atlas and trying not to lose passengers in the Fez medina. The increasing number of budget airline routes from the UK to Morocco is one of his favourite recent travel innovations and he hops over to Morocco on a regular basis.

Read more about Paul at:
lonelyplanet.com/members/paulclammer

Helen Ranger

Atlantic Coast; Mediterranean Coast & the Rif Helen moved to Fez in 2004 and has been writing about Morocco ever since. Contributing to Lonely Planet's *Fez Encounter* and 'The View from Fez' blog, she is fascinated by Morocco's diversity. Helen checked out chic city boulevards, untangled Tangier's medina, scrambled down a Beni Snassen mountainside, kicked back in Chefchaouen and enjoyed the curiosities (and tapas bars) of Ceuta and Melilla. She lives in a 400-year-old traditional house where she'll remain until she never gets lost in the Fez medina.

Read more about Helen at:
lonelyplanet.com/members/helenranger

Published by Lonely Planet Publications Pty Ltd
ABN 36 005 607 983
10th edition – Aug 2011
ISBN 978 1 74179 598 1
© Lonely Planet 2011   Photographs © as indicated 2011
10 9 8 7 6 5 4 3 2 1
Printed in Singapore

Although the authors and Lonely Planet have taken all reasonable care in preparing this book, we make no warranty about the accuracy or completeness of its content and, to the maximum extent permitted, disclaim all liability arising from its use.